The *Etymologies* of Isidore of Seville

This work is a complete English translation of the Latin *Etymologies* of Isidore, bishop of Seville (c. 560–636). Isidore compiled the work between c. 615 and the early 630s and it takes the form of an encyclopedia, arranged by subject matter. It contains much lore of the late classical world beginning with the Seven Liberal Arts, including Rhetoric, and touches on thousands of topics ranging from the names of God, the terminology of the law, the technologies of fabrics, ships, and agriculture, to the names of cities and rivers, the theatrical arts, and cooking utensils. Isidore provides etymologies for most of the terms he explains, finding in the causes of words the underlying key to their meaning. This book offers a highly readable translation of the twenty books of the *Etymologies*, one of the most widely known texts for a thousand years from Isidore's time.

STEPHEN A. BARNEY is Emeritus Professor of English at the University of California, Irvine. He edited and annotated Chaucer's *Troilus* for *The Riverside Chaucer* (1987) and also as a Norton Critical Edition (2006), and among his books are *Word-Hoard* (1977), *Allegories of History, Allegories of Love* (1978), *Studies in Troilus* (1993), and *The Penn Commentary on 'Piers Plowman', Vol. 5* (2006).

W. J. LEWIS is a translator and editor. Her previous translations include two works by Galen: *Hippocrates on the Nature of Man* and *On the Elements According to Hippocrates*, and she co-translated *On the Properties of Discourse: A Translation of Tractatus de Proprietatibus Sermonum* with Stephen Barney, Calvin Normore and Terence Parsons (1997).

J. A. BEACH is an independent classics scholar and senior documenter for a software engineering company. She worked for several years at the Thesaurus Linguae Graecae and continues to explore the relationship between classics and computer technology.

OLIVER BERGHOF is Associate Professor of Comparative Literature at California State University, San Marcos and lecturer in humanities at University of California, Irvine. His previous publications include *George Forster: A Voyage Round the World* (ed. with Nicholas Thomas) (2000).

The *Etymologies* of Isidore of Seville

STEPHEN A. BARNEY,
W. J. LEWIS, J. A. BEACH, OLIVER BERGHOF

with the collaboration of
MURIEL HALL

CAMBRIDGE
UNIVERSITY PRESS

CAMBRIDGE UNIVERSITY PRESS
Cambridge, New York, Melbourne, Madrid, Cape Town, Singapore,
São Paulo, Delhi, Tokyo, Mexico City

Cambridge University Press
The Edinburgh Building, Cambridge CB2 8RU, UK

Published in the United States of America by Cambridge University Press, New York

www.cambridge.org
Information on this title: www.cambridge.org/9780521837491

First published 2006
Paperback edition 2010
3rd printing 2011

Printed in the United Kingdom at the University Press, Cambridge

A catalog record for this publication is available from the British Library

Library of Congress Cataloging in Publication data
Isidore, of Seville, Saint, d. 636.
[Etymologiae. English]
The *Etymologies* of Isidore of Seville / [edited and translated by] Stephen A. Barney ; with the collaboration of Muriel Hall.
p. cm.
Includes bibliographical references and index.
Translated from the Latin.
ISBN 978-0-521-14591-6 (pbk.)
1. Encyclopedias and dictionaries – Early works to 1600. 2. Latin language – Etymology – Early works to 1800.
3. Didactic literature, Latin (Medieval and modern) – Translations into English.
I. Barney, Stephen A. II. Title.
AE2.I833175 2010
039′.71 – dc22 2010000699

ISBN 978-0-521-83749-1 Hardback
ISBN 978-0-521-14591-6 Paperback

We dedicate this translation to

ANTONIO

ANNABELLE BEATRICE BERGHOF
and
HILDEGARD, GREGOR, ALICE, and INES BERGHOF

THOMAS and PETER BARNEY

PHILIP

and in memory of
BENNETT AND JEANETTE LEWIS

Contents

Acknowledgements *page* ix
Note to the reader xi

INTRODUCTION

Introduction 3
Historical background 4
Chronology 6
Life and works 7
The sources of the *Etymologies* 10
The character of the *Etymologies* 17
The influence of the *Etymologies* 24
Editions of the *Etymologies* and this translation 27
Bibliography 29

THE *ETYMOLOGIES*

Analytical table of contents 34
BOOK I Grammar 39
BOOK II Rhetoric and dialectic 69
BOOK III Mathematics, music, astronomy 89
BOOK IV Medicine 109
BOOK V Laws and times 117
BOOK VI Books and ecclesiastical offices 135
BOOK VII God, angels, and saints 153
BOOK VIII The Church and sects 173
BOOK IX Languages, nations, reigns, the military, citizens, family relationships 191
BOOK X Vocabulary 213
BOOK XI The human being and portents 231
BOOK XII Animals 247
BOOK XIII The cosmos and its parts 271
BOOK XIV The earth and its parts 285
BOOK XV Buildings and fields 301

BOOK XVI Stones and metals 317
BOOK XVII Rural matters 337
BOOK XVIII War and games 359
BOOK XIX Ships, buildings, and clothing 373
BOOK XX Provisions and various implements 395

APPENDIX

Correspondence of Isidore and Braulio 409

INDEXES

General index 417 *Index of Greek words* 465
Index of citations 469

Acknowledgements

We are indebted to several friends for help with this translation. The Departments of English and of Classics at the University of California, Irvine, have given support of various kinds – special thanks to Professor Patrick Sinclair. The staff at the library, especially the Interlibrary Loan Office, at the University of California, Irvine have been unfailingly helpful. The anonymous readers for Cambridge University Press have provided a good number of emendations and wise counsel. Reviews published since the first printing of this text suggested improvements: we particularly thank Rolando Ferri, Wilf Gunther, and Ana-Isabel Magallón. For their advice on technical matters we thank Diane Lee Lewis (textiles), Hiroyuki Minamino (music), Fred Robinson (Old English poetry), Dana Sutton (Latin), Rod Wallbank (mathematics), and Sarah Wallbank (Greek). We are also grateful to Theodore Andersson, Cherry G. Barney, David M. Barney, Justin Hamlin, Michael Hanly, and Traugott Lawler for reviewing segments of our work in draft. We have gratefully relied on the learning and diligence of Muriel Hall, who in the process of copy-editing the volume became a collaborator in the project.

Note to the reader

This translation is based on the Latin text edited by W. M. Lindsay, *Isidori Hispalensis Episcopi Etymologiarum sive Originum Libri XX* (Oxford, 1911). Lindsay's text remains in print from Oxford University Press (Clarendon), and is otherwise available in a facing-page Spanish translation (see Bibliography, Oroz Reta and Marcos Casquero, editors) and a facing-page Italian translation (Canale), as well as on the web and on a CD-ROM (see Introduction p. 27). The correspondence between Isidore and Braulio presented as an Appendix is also edited by Lindsay, and is found in early manuscripts of the *Etymologies*.

Parentheses (round brackets) are used to set off the Latin word or English translation in question, and for brief explanatory notes or citations of texts. We set off parenthetical remarks by Isidore himself with commas or dashes. Hence, except for the Latin words, none of the material within parentheses is found in Isidore's text. We regularly signal our explanatory additions with "i.e." or "cf." when the words might otherwise appear to be Isidore's. We use square brackets only to enclose material likewise enclosed in square brackets in Lindsay's edition, that is, wording found in some but not all of the manuscripts on which he based his text.

Isidore left a number of items incomplete. These are signaled by three ellipsis points (. . .) in the translation. Ellipsis points are otherwise used only rarely at the beginning or end of Isidore's quotations from earlier authors.

We avoid using other than common abbreviations. Of cited works we abbreviate Vergil's *Aeneid, Georgics*, and *Eclogues*, and Ovid's *Metamorphoses, as Aen., Geo., Ecl.*, and *Met.* We abbreviate "literally" as "lit." On "gen." and "ppl." see below.

We include the Latin for key terms. We also provide the Latin in those instances, the great majority, where Isidore presents an etymology that depends on the sound or shape of the Latin itself.

Lindsay provided precise references to modern texts of the many authors whom Isidore quotes or cites. We have reviewed and updated these, referring in the first instance to the texts that appear in the Loeb Classical Library, and for other texts to the Oxford Classical Texts, the Teubner series, and other standard modern editions. A number of poets known only in fragments are cited from Edward Courtney, ed., *The Fragmentary Latin Poets* (Oxford, 1993). Citations of Varro from Funaioli's collection of grammarians' fragments (see Bibliography) are signaled with "Funaioli." Isidore will often but not always name the author, less often the title of the work, when he quotes; the missing information appears here within parentheses. Where Isidore's quotation differs from the modern received text the translation follows Isidore's words, and the reference is preceded by "cf."; for examples see p. 87.

Often an oblique form of a Latin noun or verb gives a better idea of how an etymological relationship is devised than the usual nominative or infinitive form that we provide. In these cases we also give the genitive form or the perfect participle, abbreviated as "gen." and "ppl." Unless it obscures Isidore's point, we give the usual spellings of Latin words in modern dictionaries, nouns in the nominative and verbs in the infinitive, and supply clarifications when needed.

Familiar biblical figures and places appear in their common English forms. Otherwise we generally follow the Douai-Rheims translation of the Latin Vulgate for biblical quotations, adjusting the translation when Isidore's quotation differs from the Vulgate reading. We cite book, chapter, and verse from the Vulgate. I and II Kings correspond to I and II Samuel in the Authorized (King James; New Revised Standard) Version; III and IV Kings correspond to AV's I and II Kings; Psalms 10 to 145 correspond to AV's Psalms 11 to 146.

Isidore's many repetitions of material are generally not signaled; these may be located by way of the Index.

Two facts should be noted, as we have not repeated them in the many relevant places in the text. A good number of Isidore's etymologies depend on the fact that the sound represented by *b* in Latin had by his time become indistinguishable for many speakers from the consonantal sound represented by *v*. Also, in Isidore's geography, as was standard in the classical world, the land masses of the world (the *orbis*, which we translate as "globe") were thought to be entirely encircled by the continuous body of water called *Oceanus*. We regularly translate this term as "Ocean," with a capital *O*, and we use "sea" for other large bodies of water. With this revised edition (2009), we have been able to take into account two excellent new translations, those of Angelo Valastro Canale into Italian and Lenelotte Möller into German.

INTRODUCTION

Introduction

We are pleased to present the first complete English translation from the Latin of Isidore's *Etymologies*. Isidore, Bishop of Seville, compiled the *Etymologies* (also known as the *Origins*) in the late teens and twenties of the seventh century, and left it nearly complete at his death in 636. In the form of an encyclopedia, it contains a compendium of much of the essential learning of the ancient Greco-Roman and early Christian worlds. In his important study of the Latin literary culture of medieval Europe, Ernst Robert Curtius spoke of the *Etymologies* as serving "the entire Middle Ages as a basic book."[1] It was arguably the most influential book, after the Bible, in the learned world of the Latin West for nearly a thousand years.

To get an idea of what a seventh-century Irish monk, or a lecturer at a cathedral school in the eleventh century, or an Italian poet of the fourteenth century, or a lexicographer of the sixteenth century could learn from the *Etymologies*, one might pick a bit of lore from each of the twenty books in which the work has come down to us. From Isidore, then, we learn that:

- Caesar Augustus used a code in which he replaced each letter with the following letter of the alphabet, *b* for *a*, etc. (I.xxv.2).
- Plato divided physics into four categories: arithmetic, geometry, music, and astronomy (II.xxiv.4).
- The term 'cymbal' derives from the Greek words for "with" and "dancing," σύν and βαλά (III.xxii.12).
- A physician needs to know the Seven Liberal Arts of Grammar, Rhetoric, Dialectic, Arithmetic, Geometry, Music, and Astronomy (IV.xiii.1–4.)
- In ancient times execution by sword was preferred as speedier (V.xxvii.35).
- Architects use green Carystean marble to panel libraries, because the green refreshes weary eyes (VI.xi.2).
- Esau had three names, meaning "red" (for the stew he made), "bloody" (for his complexion), and "hairy" (VII.vi.33–34).
- Aristotle says that Zoroaster, the first magician, composed two million verses (VIII.ix.1).
- A soldier (*miles*) is so called because once there were a thousand (*mille*) in one troop (IX.iii.32).
- The word for a garrulous person (*garrulus*) derives from the name of the constantly chattering bird, the jackdaw (*graculus*) (X.114).
- In the womb, the knees (*genua*) are pressed against the face, and help to form the eye-sockets (*genae*); hence their name (XI.i.108).
- The ibis purges itself by spewing water into its anus with its beak (XII.vii.33).
- Because of its brightness, lightning reaches the eyes before thunder reaches the ears (XIII.viii.2).
- Gaul is so named from the whiteness of its people, for "milk" in Greek is γάλα (XIV.iv.25).
- Minerva is 'Athena' in Greek; she is reputed to be inventor of many arts because various arts, and philosophy itself, consider the city of Athens their temple (XV.i.44).
- Amber is not the sap of the poplar, but of pine, because when burned it smells like pine pitch (XVI.viii.6).
- An altar was dedicated in Rome to Stercutus, who brought the technique of dunging (*stercorare*) fields to Italy (XVII.i.3).
- The battering ram takes its name 'ram' from its character, because it butts walls (XVIII.xi.1).
- The women of Arabia and Mesopotamia wear the veil called *theristrum* even today as a protection from heat (XIX.xxv.6).
- Wine (*vinum*) is so called because it replenishes the veins (*vena*) with blood (XX.ii.2).

1 "Grundbuch des ganzen Mittelalters," in *Europäische Literatur und lateinisches Mittelalter* (Bern, 1948), trans. by W. R. Trask, *European Literature and the Latin Middle Ages* (New York, 1953: 23).

In the following introduction we provide sketches of Isidore's historical setting, of his life and works, of the sources of the *Etymologies*, of the character of the work, and of its influence.[2]

Historical background

When Isidore was born around the middle of the sixth century, the Western Roman Empire no longer existed as a political entity. Gaul was now ruled by the Franks, and in Italy the Ostrogoths had just been defeated by Byzantine forces, who had also taken over North Africa from the Vandals a short time earlier. Spain, meanwhile, had been under Visigothic rule for over a century.[3]

The Visigoths, like the Ostrogoths, were a Germanic people, originally settled north of the Danube. In 376, under increasing pressure from the Huns, they were allowed by Roman authorities to cross the Danube and settle in Thrace. Their dealings with Rome within the Empire were rocky from the outset, and they soon rebelled, raiding throughout Thrace before defeating Roman forces outside Adrianople in 378. Fighting continued until the two sides reached an agreement in 382 which established the Visigoths as Roman allies bound to supply troops in return for subsidies and a certain amount of autonomy. By the end of the century relations had deteriorated again, however, and the Visigoths, led by Alaric (reigned 395–410), entered Italy and sacked Rome in 410 after they were unable to reach an agreement with the Emperor on the subsidies they were to receive. Still at odds with the Romans, they made their way to Southern Gaul in 412, and from there were driven by Emperor Constantius into Spain.

The Roman province of Hispania had been overrun a few years previous to this by a loose alliance of Germanic tribes, the Alans, the Vandals, and the Sueves. The Visigoths, faced with food shortages due to a Roman blockade, came to an agreement with Constantius to fight these earlier barbarian invaders on Rome's behalf. After some success, they were resettled in Gaul in 418.

In 456, under Theodoric II (reigned 453–466), the Visigoths invaded Spain again, where the Suevi had become the dominant power in the meantime. Theodoric's forces did not manage to conquer the entire peninsula, however; areas held by the Suevi, Galicians and others continued to assert their independence for some time, and the Basque territories were never completely subdued.

In 507, Clovis, the king of the Franks, attacked the Gaulish part of the Visigothic kingdom, and over the next quarter century the Visigoths lost all their Gaulish territory apart from the region around Narbonne known as Septimania. From this point on, the Visigothic kingdom was essentially confined to the Spanish peninsula.

It should be pointed out that although the Visigoths were rulers of Spain they probably only made up a small percentage of the population throughout the period under their rule; the majority of the inhabitants were Hispano-Roman. The new rulers retained a large part of the Roman administrative structure; Roman governors and officials continued to collect at least some Roman taxes[4] and enforce Roman law.[5] The two groups remained socially distinct, however; a ban from imperial times on intermarriage between Goths and Romans, for example, apparently remained in effect until the later part of the sixth century.[6]

Visigothic Spain was a politically unstable kingdom throughout most of the sixth century. Four successive kings were murdered (Amalric, Theudis, Theudisclus, and Agila). From 544, Byzantine forces intervened in Visigothic affairs, possibly at the invitation of Athanagild in his rebellion against Agila. By 557, the Byzantines occupied the southeastern coast of the peninsula, including the port city of Cartagena. Isidore's parents appear to have left Cartagena at about this time, quite possibly as a result of this invasion. In the meantime,

2 The fullest recent account of all these matters is the extensive General Introduction by Manuel C. Díaz y Díaz to the Spanish edition of the *Etymologies*, ed. Oroz Reta and Marcos Casquero 1993[2]: 3–257. No good general treatment of Isidore is available in English; the study by Brehaut (1912) is outdated.

3 For a recent overview of the whole period see McKitterick 2001.

4 Land tax, custom tolls, and *collatio lustralis* continued to be collected, for example; see Heather 1996: 194–95.

5 There is some controversy over whether the Gothic inhabitants were subject to a separate code based on traditional Gothic law; see, among others, King 1980, Collins 1995: 24–31, Heather 1996: 194–96, Velázquez 1999, and Wood 1999.

6 Wood 1999: 193.

relations with the Franks to the north deteriorated and they began to threaten Visigothic Septimania and the Ebro Valley.

Following Athanagild's death in 568, the Visigothic nobility chose Liuva to be king, and after Liuva's death in 571 or 573, his brother Leovigild (the Visigothic monarchy was not hereditary, although sometimes a son did succeed his father to the throne). Under Leovigild, the kingdom saw its strength increase. The new king's military successes restored territory that had been lost to the Byzantines and regained political control over rebellious areas (the city of Cordoba, for example, which had been in a state of rebellion since 550) and bordering regions in the northern part of the peninsula.

Leovigild's attempt to win new converts to Arianism met with less success. Arianism was a form of Christianity that held that the three members of the Trinity were not equal and co-eternal – specifically that the Son was not God by nature but created, and not eternal like the Father.[7] Catholic Christians condemned Arian doctrine as heresy at the Council of Nicaea in 325. The Goths, however, had already accepted Arianism when they converted to Christianity, and they continued to hold this doctrine as they moved westward into Gaul and then into Spain. Until Leovigild, the Gothic rulers had made no attempt to convert their largely Catholic subjects, and had apparently made little restriction on the practice of Catholicism, although the Catholic clergy had been deprived of some of their privileges. Under the Arian rulers, the Catholic Church in Spain had been free to convene synods, construct new churches and found monasteries, correspond with the Pope, and circulate their writings openly. The two Churches coexisted independently of each other, each with its own clergy, shrines, and other institutions.

Leovigild, however, mounted a serious campaign to expand Arianism, choosing persuasion and rewards as his instruments, rather than force. In 580 he summoned the first Arian synod held in Spain, and ruled that converts to Arianism no longer needed to be rebaptized, which presumably also made the process of conversion more appealing to Catholics. According to Gregory of Tours (*Libri Historiarum X*, 6.18), Leovigild also attempted to win converts by redefining Arian doctrine to hold that the Father and Son were equal and co-eternal and only the Holy Spirit was not equal. Although he managed to win over a few important Catholic figures, including the Bishop of Saragossa, he lost ground in his own family, for by 582 his older son Hermenigild had converted to Catholicism.

Hermenigild's conversion may have been based as much on political considerations as religious conviction. He had rebelled against his father in 579, soon after his marriage to a Frankish princess (Clovis, the king of the Franks, had converted to Catholicism around the beginning of the sixth century),[8] and had declared himself the independent monarch over the southern part of the peninsula. For three years, Leovigild seems to have accepted the situation, making no attempt to regain control, while Hermenigild, for his part, did not seek to expand the territory under his rule. Some time around 582, Hermenigild converted to Catholicism, under the influence of Isidore's brother Leander, according to Pope Gregory I, a friend of Leander.[9]

In 583, Leovigild finally moved to retake the territory held by Hermenigild, and by 584 he had regained control and exiled Hermenigild to Valencia, where he was murdered the next year. Leovigild, in the meantime, continued his military successes, conquering the Suevic kingdom before he died in 586.

Reccared, Leovigild's other son and Hermenigild's younger brother, became king at his father's death, and converted to Catholicism the following year. Again, as with Hermenigild, Leander of Seville was apparently instrumental in his conversion[10]. Reccared began systematically disassembling the Arian Church structure, reassigning Arian churches to the Catholic dioceses where they were located, and allowing Arian bishops who converted to retain their sees, even when this meant having two bishops in a single see. Most of the groundwork for these changes was laid at the kingdom-wide church Council convened by Reccared at Toledo in 589.[11]

7 For a discussion of the theology of Gothic Arianism see Wiles 1996:45–51.

8 Some historians have suggested that the Franks first converted from paganism to Arianism, and then from Arianism to Catholicism; see D. Schanzer, "Dating the Baptism of Clovis: the Bishop of Vienne vs. the Bishop of Tours," *Early Medieval Europe* 7 (1998): 29–57.

9 *Dialogues*, iii.31. See Collins 1980:215–18 for further discussion of Leander's role in Hermenigild's conversion.

10 Collins 1995:54.

11 See Stocking 2000:59–88 for a discussion of the Council; records of the Council may be found in G. Martínez Díez and F. Rodríguez, eds., *La Colección Canónica Hispana*, V, Concilios Hispanos: segunda parte (Madrid, 1992).

Although he ordered the destruction of Arian books (and in fact no Arian documents are preserved from Visigothic Spain), there was little if any other persecution of Arians who refused to convert. In the first four years following his conversion, Reccared faced several Arian conspiracies and attempted revolts led by Gothic nobles, but these did not turn out to be serious threats, and within a generation Arianism appears to have died out.

One result of Reccared's conversion to Catholicism was the formation of close ties between the monarchy and the Church. From this point forward, the Visigothic kings exercised control over the appointment of bishops and other decisions that had hitherto been made by the Church alone (see Letters IV and V in the Appendix). In return, the Church, in particular the council of bishops, was given the authority and responsibility for overseeing secular offices like local judges and agents of the treasury estates.

Reccared died in 601, shortly after Isidore became Bishop of Seville, and was succeeded by his seventeen-year-old illegitimate son Liuva II. Less than two years later, Liuva was deposed by Witteric, a Gothic noble. Witteric had Liuva's right hand cut off to prevent him from retaking the throne (Visigothic tradition required that the monarch be able-bodied), and then, in 603, had him executed. Witteric himself was assassinated in 610. The assassins and their motivations have not been recorded, but Witteric was by all accounts not a popular king. Isidore speaks of him with disapproval, and other contemporaries complained of injustices suffered under his rule. Gundemar took the throne after Witteric's death, and involved himself, as Reccared had, in the councils of bishops, before dying two years later.

Sisebut then became king. He was a man of some intellectual attainment and authored, among other works, a poem on lunar eclipses (written in 613 as a response to Isidore's cosmological treatise, *De Natura Rerum*) and a Life of St. Desiderius of Vienne.[12] He was also noted by contemporaries for his personal piety, which led him to become deeply involved in the activities of the Church. According to Isidore, Sisebut's anti-Jewish policy of forced conversion was based on zeal rather than knowledge.[13] (Isidore may be referring to this campaign in *Etymologies* V.xxxix.42.) Isidore did not entirely approve of this policy but apparently reserved his criticism until after Sisebut's death.

Sisebut died in 621, of natural causes, or an overdose of medicine, or deliberate poisoning, depending on which account one credits.[14] Reccared II, his young son and successor, died shortly thereafter, and Suinthila took the throne. He began his reign by pushing back a Basque incursion into the province of Tarragona (see Letter II). A further triumph followed a few years later when he succeeded in driving the Byzantines out of Spain. In one version of the *Historia Gothorum*, written during Suinthila's reign, Isidore is lavish in his praise of the monarch. However, Suinthila was deposed in 631 by a group of nobles with Frankish assistance, and Sisenand was made king. Little is recorded about Sisenand's reign aside from his participation in the Fourth Council of Toledo. He died in 636, the same year as Isidore.

Chronology

557: Byzantines occupy Cartagena.
ca. 560: Isidore is born.
572: Leovigild becomes king.
ca. 579: Hermenigild rebels.
586: Death of Leovigild; Reccared becomes king.
587: Reccared converts to Catholicism.
600: Leander dies. Isidore becomes Archbishop of Seville.
601/2: Reccared dies. Liuva II becomes king.
603: Witteric dethrones and murders Liuva II, and becomes king.
610: Witteric assassinated. Gundemar becomes king.

12 See J. Fontaine, "King Sisebut's *Vita Desiderii* and the Political Function of Visigothic Hagiography," in James 1980.

13 Isidore, *History of the Goths*, 61, translated in Wolf 1999:105; see Stocking 2000:132–6 for further discussion of Sisebut's and Isidore's views on conversion.

14 Isidore, *History of the Goths* in Wolf 1999:106: "Some claim that he died a natural death, others, that he died as a result of an overdose of some medication." In an earlier version of the *History of the Goths*, the possibility of poisoning was mentioned (see Stocking 2000:135 fn. 69).

611/12: Death of Gundemar. Sisebut becomes king.
613: Isidore dedicates *De Natura Rerum* to Sisebut.
621: Sisebut dies. Reccared II becomes king and dies shortly thereafter. Suinthila becomes king.
624: Suinthila drives the Byzantines completely out of Spain.
631: Suinthila is deposed. Sisenand becomes king.
636: Sisenand dies. Isidore dies.

Life and works

Few details can be given about Isidore's life with any certainty. He was born some time around 560, about the time when his father Severianus relocated the family to Seville from Cartagena, where invading Byzantine forces had taken control. Isidore's parents died while he was still young, and he was brought up and educated in Seville under the care of his older brother Leander, very likely in the monastery school where Leander was abbot (Riché 1976:289).

Leander, who became Bishop of Seville before 580, was an active and influential churchman.[15] He was a personal friend of Gregory, later Pope Gregory I, whom he encountered on a visit to Constantinople and who dedicated his *Moralia* to Leander. A connection of greater consequence for the kingdom of Spain was Leander's friendship with King Leovigild's sons Hermenigild and Reccared, the future king; it was under Leander's guidance that both his royal friends converted from Arianism to Catholicism.

After Leander's death, and shortly before Reccared died, Isidore was made Bishop of Seville, most likely in the year 600. His other brother, Fulgentius, as well as his sister Florentina, also chose to go into the Church; Fulgentius became Bishop of Ecija and Florentina entered a nunnery. As one of the leading churchmen in the country, Isidore presided over important Church councils in Seville (in 619) and Toledo (in 633). The close ties that had been established between the Visigothic monarchy and the Catholic Church after Reccared's conversion make it likely that Isidore had some political influence as well. His relationship with King Sisebut (reigned 612–621) was particularly close, extending beyond practical matters of government to a personal friendship based on shared intellectual interests. Also important was his friendship with his younger colleague, Braulio, who was archdeacon (and later, in 631, bishop) of the Church in Saragossa. Their correspondence (see the letters attached to the *Etymologies* in the Appendix) provides a valuable glimpse of Isidore's personality and daily life.

Isidore was deeply admired by his contemporaries for his scholarship and intellectual gifts. Although their praise for his Greek and Hebrew is perhaps unmerited (his knowledge of these languages appears to have extended only to disconnected Greek terms and phrases, and a smattering of Hebrew words), the breadth of his learning is nonetheless impressive.[16] He was happy to draw on pagan authors as well as Church Fathers, and was familiar with works as various as Martial's *Epigrams*, Tertullian's *On Spectacles*, and Pliny the Elder's *Natural History*. In spite of the demands of his episcopal office, Isidore nevertheless found time to produce a substantial body of writing. Braulio compiled a list of these works, the *Renotatio Librorum Isidori*, presented in the order in which they were written, shortly after Isidore's death in 636:

> Isidore, an excellent man, bishop of the Church at Seville, successor to and brother of Bishop Leander, flourished from the time of the Emperor Mauritius and

15 Good biographies of Leander, with accounts of his combat against Arianism and his writings, are L. Navarra, *Leandro di Siviglia: Profilo storico-letterario* (Rome, 1987), which prints and translates his *Homilia in Laudem Ecclesiae*, and J. Madoz, "San Leandro de Sevilla," *Estudios Eclesiásticos* 56 (1981): 415–53, printing the basic documentary sources for Leander's career.

16 The kind of Greek known by Isidore and others from the sixth century on has been the subject of a number of studies: see Bischoff 1967:246–75, Riché 1976:44–45, W. Berschin, *Griechisch-lateinisches Mittelalter, von Hieronymus zu Nikolaus von Kues* (Bern and Munich, 1980), revised and expanded by the author and trans. J. C. Frakes as *Greek Letters and the Latin Middle Ages, from Jerome to Nicholas of Cusa* (Washington, DC, 1988) and especially M. Herren and S. A. Brown, eds., *The Sacred Nectar of the Greeks: The Study of Greek in the West in the Early Middle Ages* (London, 1988), esp. Herren's introduction (v–xii), and the studies by Dionisotti (1–56), Herren (57–84), Berschin (85–104), and Riché (143–68) in the same volume. Isidore's knowledge of Hebrew was restricted to names interpreted by Jerome (Riché 1976:302).

King Reccared.[17] Our own time indeed found in him a likeness to the knowledge of antiquity, and in him antiquity reclaimed something for itself. He was a man educated in every kind of expression, so that in the quality of his speech he was suited to both the ignorant audience and the learned. Indeed, he was famous for his incomparable eloquence, eloquence appropriate to the occasion. An intelligent reader can now very easily understand from his diverse undertakings and well-crafted works just how great Isidore's wisdom was. Accordingly, I have noted down these thoughts about the works that have come to my notice. He published:

Two books of *Differences (Differentiae)*, in which he used subtle distinctions to differentiate the meaning of terms whose use is confused.

One book of *Introductions (Proemia)*, in which through brief notes he pointed out what each book of Holy Scripture contains.

One book *On the Lives and Deaths of the Fathers (De Ortu et Obitu Patrum)*, in which he noted with thoughtful brevity their deeds and worthiness, their deaths and burials.

Two books of *Offices (Officia)*, for his brother Bishop Fulgentius, in which he set out the origin of the Offices and why each Office is performed in the Church of God, with interpretations of his own pen, but not without the authority of our forefathers.

Two books of *Synonyms (Synonyma)*, with which, through the intervening exhortation of reason, he encouraged the reader to a consolation of the soul and a hope of receiving forgiveness.

One book *On the Nature of Things (De Natura Rerum)*, addressed to King Sisebut, in which he resolved certain obscure matters concerning the elements, relying on his study of both the Doctors of the Church and the philosophers.

One book *On Numbers (De Numeris)*, in which he touched in part on the discipline of mathematics, on account of the numbers which are inserted in Sacred Scripture.

One book *On the Names of the Law and the Gospels (De Nominibus Legis et Evangeliorum)*, in which he shows what the people who are mentioned signify in a mystical sense.

One book *On Heresies (De Haeresibus)*, in which, following the examples of our forefathers, he gathers diverse topics, being as brief as he can.

Three books of *Sentences (Sententiae)*, which he ornamented with flowers from the book of *Morals* by Pope Gregory.

One book of *Chronicles (Chronicon)*, from the creation of the world up until his own time, collected with great brevity.

Two books *Against the Jews (Contra Judaeos)*, at the request of his sister Florentina, a virgin (i.e. a nun) in her way of life, in which he demonstrated everything that the Catholic Church believes based on the evidence of the Law and of the Prophets (i.e. based on the Hebrew Scriptures alone).

One book *On Illustrious Men (De Viris Illustribus)*, to which we are adding this entry.[18]

One book of the *Monastic Rule (Monastica Regula)*, which he tempered most fittingly for use in this country and for the souls of the weak.

One book *On the Origin of the Goths, and also The Kingdom of the Suevi, and The History of the Vandals (De Origine Gothorum et Regno Suevorum et etiam Vandalorum Historia)*.

Two books of *Questions (Quaestiones)*, which the reader may recognize as an abundant anthology of ancient treatises.

The *Etymologies (Etymologiae)*, a codex of enormous size, divided by him into topics, not books. Although he left it unfinished, I divided it into twenty (or, "fifteen," in some manuscripts) books, since he wrote the work at my request. Whoever thoughtfully and thoroughly reads through this work, which is suited to philosophy in every respect, will not be ignorant of the knowledge of human and divine matters, and deservedly so. Overflowing with eloquence of various arts with regard to nearly every point of them that ought to be known, it collects them in a summarized form.

There are also other minor works by this man, and abundantly ornamented writings in the Church of God. After such misfortune in Spain in recent years, God encouraged him, as if he were setting up a prop – to preserve the ancient monuments, I believe, lest we decay into rusticity. To him we may fittingly apply the philosopher's comment (Cicero, *Academica Posteriora* 1.3): "Your books have brought us back, as if to our home, when we were roving and wandering in our own city like strangers, so that we might sometimes be able to understand who and where we are. You have laid open the lifetime of our country, the description of the ages, the laws of sacred matters and of priests, learning both domestic and public, the names, kinds, functions and

17 The Byzantine Emperor Mauritius reigned from 582 to 602, and Reccared, king of the Visigoths, from 586 to 601. The present translation follows the edition by J. C. Martín (2006), pp. 199–207.

18 On the *De Viris Illustribus* see below. Braulio's list was appended to a manuscript of Isidore's treatise. It is edited from the manuscript León 22 by P. Galindo, pp. 356–60 in C. H. Lynch, *San Braulio* (Madrid, 1950).

> causes of settlements, regions, places, and all matters both human and divine."[19]
>
> The proceedings of the Council at Seville, at which he was present, declare how with a flood of eloquence he pierced through the heresy of the Acephalites (see VIII. v. 66) with the arrows of divine Scripture and the testimonies of the Church Fathers. In this council he asserted the truth against Gregorius, leader of the aforementioned heresy.
>
> Isidore died during the reign of the Emperor Heraclius and of the most Christian King Chintila.[20] He was outstanding above everyone with his sound doctrine, and very generous in his works of charity.

All of these works except *On Heresies* (the subject of *Etymologies* VIII.v) are still extant. They range in date from what is presumably the earliest, the first book of the *Differentiae*, around 600, to around 625. Four of them focus closely on the Bible. The *Introductions* gives a brief description of each book of the Bible, and the *On the Lives and Deaths of the Fathers* is a collection containing short biographies of important Biblical figures. In spite of Braulio's description, *On Numbers* is a religious rather than mathematical treatise; in it Isidore discusses the symbolic interpretation of numerals contained in the text of the Bible. *On the Names of the Law and the Gospels*, also known as the *Allegories (Allegoriae)*, is a similar discussion of the symbolism of Biblical names.

Against the Jews is an attempt to win converts from Judaism to Christianity by means of rational persuasion; it was most likely written around the time of King Sisebut's campaign of forced conversion (see above, p. 6), and may be seen as an alternative approach in contrast to Sisebut's harsher measures. In the first book Isidore argues that Old Testament prophets foresaw the birth, death, resurrection, and divinity of Christ, while the second book presents passages from the prophets that Isidore interprets as condemning Jewish rituals.

The four other surviving theological works deal with the Church and the duties of Christians. The first book of *Offices* (also the subject of *Etymologies* VI.xix) gives a history of the Catholic liturgy, and is an important source of information about the Mozarabic liturgy. The second book deals with the various ecclesiastical offices and their duties. The *Monastic Rule* and the *Sentences* are more instructional works, the first providing an introduction to monastic life in simple and straightforward language, and the second a guide to Church doctrine and Christian conduct of life. In the *Synonyms*, Isidore presents a contemplation on sin and conversion, relying on synonyms to reiterate and emphasize each point of his message.

On the Nature of Things is a detailed cosmology dealing with astronomy, meteorology, and other natural phenomena, as well as with the human conventions of time-keeping and calendars.

The *Chronicles*, although a useful source for the history of Visigothic Spain, is otherwise mainly derivative of earlier chronicles, particularly Eusebius's chronicle (*ca.* 326), translated and continued by Jerome (*ca.* 378), and Prosper of Aquitaine (*ca.* 455) and others. Like the *History of the Goths*, it draws from Julius Africanus, Eusebius's universal history, Orosius's *History against the Pagans*, other works of Jerome, Augustine, and Cassiodorus. There are two versions, both by Isidore, one completed in 615/16, during Sisebut's reign, and the other completed in 626. *Etymologies* V.xxxix incorporates an abbreviated version of the chronicle; the fact that it uses materials found in the 626 version shows that the work dedicated to Sisebut before 621 was not the complete *Etymologies* as we now have it.[21] There are likewise two extant versions of *On the Origin of the Goths*, one that ends with the death of Sisebut in 621 and one that continues up through 625, in the middle of Suinthila's reign. It is not clear which is the later version; it may be that the longer account was written first and that Isidore thought it prudent to excise the final section after Suinthila's fall from power.[22] *The Kingdom of the Suevi* and *The*

19 Braulio would have read Cicero's encomium of Varro, the great predecessor of Isidore, in Augustine's *City of God* 6.2.

20 The Byzantine Emperor Heraclius reigned from 610 to 641, and Chintila from 636 to 640.

21 Both the *Chronicon (Chronica Maiora)* and the shorter version *(Chronica Minora)* included in the *Etymologies* are edited by T. Mommsen, MGH, Auct. Ant. XI, 391–497 (Berlin, 1894). The new edition of the *Chronica* (615/16 and 626 redactions) by Martin (2003) contains the most recent full bibliography of Isidore studies and a thorough account of Isidore's sources. See also P. M. Bassett, "The Use of History in the *Chronicon* of Isidore of Seville," *History and Theory* 15 (1976): 278–92. See further the materials on the *Chronicon* and *The History of the Goths* in Wolf 1999.

22 On the *History of the Goths* see the edn. by Mommsen, preceding note, pp. 267–303, and the edn. by C. Rodríguez Alonso, *Las Historias de los Godos, Vándalos y Suevos de Isidoro de Sevilla* (León, 1975), with full introduction, and G. Donini and G. B. Ford, *Isidore of Seville's History of the Goths, Vandals, and Suevi* (Leiden, 1970), with trans. See also J. N. Hillgarth, "Historiography in Visigothic Spain," in *La Storiografia altomedievale* (Spoleto, 1970: 287–302).

History of the Vandals, although Braulio speaks of them as if they and *On the Origin of the Goths* were a single work, appear to be brief but separate histories, which have been appended to the larger work. In *On Illustrious Men*, Isidore presents thirty-three brief biographies of important Christian figures, mainly writers, from various countries (many Spaniards) and eras, including his brother Leander. It is a continuation of works with the same title by Jerome (*ca.* 392) and his continuator Gennadius (*ca.* 490); all three sketch the lives of prominent Christians, as an answer to Suetonius Tranquillus's *De Viris Illustribus*.[23]

Like the *Etymologies*, the *Differences* is closely concerned with the form and meaning of individual words. The first book explains the distinctions between pairs of words that are either synonyms or homophones, and gives instructions for correct usage. The second book focuses on the differences between things; between angels, demons, and men, for example.

A second early notice of Isidore and his works was included by Ildefonsus, bishop of Toledo, in his work *On Illustrious Men*, a continuation of the Jerome–Gennadius–Isidore tradition.[24] Ildefonsus was reputed to have been a student of Isidore's; he completed the work shortly before his death in 667. The notice (cap. 8) follows:

> Isidore held the bishopric of the see of Seville, in the Province of Baetica, after his brother Leander. He was a man esteemed for both his propriety and his intellect. In speaking he had acquired a supply of such pleasing eloquence that his admirable richness of speech amazed his listeners. Indeed, someone who had heard a sermon of his a second time would not approve unless it were repeated still further. He wrote not a few exceptional works, that is:
>
> *The Types of Offices*,
> *The Book of Prefaces*,
> *The Births and Deaths of the Fathers*,
> A book of lamentations, which he himself called the *Synonyms*,
> Two little books written for his sister Florentina, *Against the Iniquity of the Jews*,
> A book for King Sisebut, *On the Nature of Things*,
> A book of *Differences*,
> A book of *Sentences*.
> He also collected into one place from various authors what he himself called the *Exposition of the Secret Sacraments*. It is also known as the *Questions*.
> Finally, in response to a request from Braulio, Bishop of Saragossa, his book of *Etymologies*. He tried to fulfill this request completely over the course of many years, and seemed to finish his final days engaged in this work.
>
> He was active during the reigns of Reccared, Liuva, Witteric, Gundemar, Sisebut, Suinthila, and Sisenand. He held the honor of the bishopric for almost forty years, and maintained the distinction of its holy doctrine, its glory as well as its propriety.

Obviously a good deal of Isidore's earlier writing was taken over into the *Etymologies*, which Isidore must have considered the *summa* of his scholarly career. Presumably he began work on it before the death of Sisebut early in 621, and he left it unfinished at his death in 636.

Isidore was officially canonized as a saint in 1598, and was declared a Doctor of the Church in 1722. His feast day is April 4.

The sources of the *Etymologies*

Isidore acknowledges, in the dedication (before 621) to King Sisebut prefaced to an early draft (perhaps Books I–X) of the *Etymologies*, that his work compiles material "gathered from my recollection (or, "record") of readings from antiquity" (see the appended Letter VI). This is no mere topos of humility; nearly the whole work, in fact, consists of intricately woven excerpts and paraphrases of the works of earlier writers. To assess Isidore's achievement we cannot look to original researches or innovative interpretations, but rather to the ambition of the whole design, to his powers of selection and organization, and to his grand retentiveness. His aims were not novelty but

23 The main part of Suetonius's work still extant is *De (Claris) Grammaticis et Rhetoribus*. The Jerome and Gennadius works are edited by E. C. Richardson, *Hieronymus: Liber de Viris Illustribus. Gennadius: Liber de Viris Illustribus*, Texte und Untersuchungen zur Geschichte der altchristlichen Literatur 14, 1. (Leipzig, 1896). On these and Isidore's *De Viris Illustribus* see R. McKitterick, *The Carolingians and the Written Word* (Cambridge, 1989: 200–02).

24 C. Cordoñer Merino, ed. and trans. into Spanish, *El 'De Viris Illustribus' de Ildefonso de Toledo* (Salamanca, 1972).

authority, not originality but accessibility, not augmenting but preserving and transmitting knowledge.

A full reckoning of Isidore's sources must await the completion of the major edition of the *Etymologies* now under way, being published in the series Auteurs Latins du Moyen Age (Paris: Belles Lettres). To date five volumes of a projected twenty, one for each book of the *Etymologies*, have appeared (see Bibliography). These and the important study by Jacques Fontaine (1959, 1983²) are the only authoritative studies of the *Etymologies*'s sources yet to appear.

The following sketch divides Isidore's sources into three kinds: first, his forebears in producing etymologies and encyclopedias; second, the actual scholars from whom he derives his information, whether or not at first hand; and third, the *auctores* whom he cites, that is, the acknowledged classical masters of imaginative literature and artful prose (Vergil, Cicero, and the rest).[25]

The idea that knowledge of the origins of words can yield up the words' "true sense" (ἔτυμον), and indeed something of the intrinsic character of the thing named by the word, is very ancient. The oldest Greek and Hebrew writings take for granted that proper names can conceal and reveal the characters and fates of their bearers.[26] Plato in the *Cratylus* treats the fundamental question, whether a thing takes its name arbitrarily or with reference to the thing's nature. The first known work, now lost, devoted to the science of etymologies is the Περί ἐτυμολογίας of Heraclides Ponticus (fourth century BCE). Developing the Greek science of etymology were the Ἐτυμολογίαι of Apollodorus of Athens and a work by Demetrius of Ixion, both of the second century BCE. In the Roman tradition of scholarship the first important figure is Aelius Stilo Praeconinus (*ca.* 154–74 BCE), of whose works only fragments survive, but whose pupils Varro and Cicero carried on his interest in etymology. The Stoics, in particular, continued the study of etymology, including the articulation, by Varro (especially in the lost books II–IV of *On the Latin Language*) and others, of the several types of etymologies.

Parallel to, and eventually coincident with, the development of etymologizing proper was the compilation of encyclopedias.[27] As the term 'encyclopedia' suggests (if we may follow Isidore's practice of explanation by etymology – 'paideia' means "education"), these were summations of learning intended for general instruction, the "cycle of education" proper to a free person – hence, the "liberal arts." The first encyclopedias were Latin. Cato the Censor compiled (*ca.* 185 BCE) an encyclopedia, now lost. Much the most important figure, both for the production of etymologies and for the making of encyclopedias, is Marcus Terentius Varro (116–27 BCE). Of his many works those on the Latin language and on agriculture substantially survive. Lost is the *Disciplines*, an encyclopedia whose nine books treated in turn grammar, dialectic, rhetoric, geometry, arithmetic, astrology, music, medicine, and architecture. The first seven of these, regularly divided into the language arts (the trivium: the first three) and the mathematical arts (the quadrivium), became the classic model of preliminary education, the "Seven Liberal Arts."[28] The shape of Isidore's first five books may be traced directly to Varro's influence, though in fact it is unlikely that Isidore had direct access to texts of Varro.

Of A. Cornelius Celsus's encyclopedia (early first century CE) only the medical books survive intact. After Varro the greatest encyclopedist is Pliny the Elder, whose massive *Natural History* (dedicated in 77 CE) in effect fills out the classical matrix of encyclopedic learning, adding to Varro's cycle of the liberal arts the cycle of

25 Preliminary guidance for many of the following authors and works may be found in *The Oxford Classical Dictionary*, 3rd edn., ed. Simon Hornblower and Antony Spawforth (Oxford, 2003), and *Dictionary of the Middle Ages*, ed. Joseph R. Strayer (New York, 1982–89).

26 Fundamental studies of the history of etymologizing are Ilona Opelt, "Etymologie," *Reallexikon für Antike und Christentum* 6 (1965: cols. 797–844) and Roswitha Klinck, *Die lateinische Etymologie des Mittelalters* (Munich, 1970). See also Fontaine 1981.

27 An introductory treatment of early encyclopedias is R. Collison 1966. Pp. 21–35 survey the tradition up to Isidore. With full bibliographies on both the basis of encyclopedias in Greek and Roman education and on encyclopedias themselves are H. Fuchs, "Enkyklios Paideia" (cols. 365–98) and "Enzyklopädie" (cols. 504–15) in *Reallexikon für Antike und Christentum* 5 (1962). See also Ribémont 2002 and M. de Gandillac, "Encyclopédies pré-médiévales et médiévales," pp. 1–42 in *La Pensée encyclopédique au moyen âge* (Neuchatel, 1966) and other essays in this collection on encyclopedias partly derived from Isidore. See the web site prepared by Marie-Christine Duchenne: www.menestrel.fr/spip.php?rubrique423.

28 On the liberal arts see *Arts libéraux et philosophie au moyen âge. Actes du Quatrième Congrès International de Philosophie Médiévale, Montréal, 1967* (Paris, 1969), esp. the essays by Marrou and Díaz y Díaz. The scheme of the Seven Liberal Arts came to the Middle Ages primarily by way of Martianus Capella. See Herbert Backes, *Die Hochzeit Merkurs und der Philologie: Studien zu Notkers Martian-Übersetzung* (Thorbecke, 1982: esp. 11–15), and P. Courcelle, *Les Lettres grecques en occident: De Macrobe à Cassiodore* (Paris, 1948).

scientific and naturalist lore: extensive treatments of the world in general (cosmology and meteorology), geography, the human being, zoology, botany, mineralogy, and medicine. Both Varro's and Pliny's works are arranged, with a view to ready access, by topics in rational order. To these foundational works of scholarship should be added the *Institutes of Oratory* (before 96 CE) of Quintilian, a masterwork on rhetoric in the broadest sense, including what we would call literary history and criticism.

With the exception of medicine, Roman scholarship after the first century CE shows a progressive decline in the practice of original scientific research. Concomitantly, the major works of reference (following Varro's lead) focus more and more intently on the Latin language itself. Encyclopedic works of the later period show more interest in presenting and defining, often with etymological explications, the *terms* of the arts and sciences, rather than the actual processes of the technologies and the essential qualities of the objects of study. One looks to these works for copious vocabulary, for careful discriminations of correct and incorrect usage of language, and in general for what might be called a heightened state of literacy.

The main encyclopedic works after Pliny are the *Compendious Doctrine* (early fourth century) of Nonius Marcellus, arranged in alphabetical order; the *Marriage of Mercury and Philology* (perhaps early fifth century) of Martianus Capella, which contains a review of the Seven Liberal Arts; and the *Institutes* (*ca.* 562) of Cassiodorus, written in two books for the monks at the monastery he founded. Its first book gives instructions on the parts of the Bible and about how to study and copy religious writings, and the second is a compendium of the Seven Liberal Arts.[29] Less encyclopedic in form – that is, organized in a deliberately casual manner – but of encyclopedic scope are the (mainly lost) *Prata* (early second century CE) of Suetonius Tranquillus, the *Attic Nights* (late second century CE) of Aulus Gellius, and the *Saturnalia* (early fifth century) of Macrobius. Of crucial importance are the vast commentaries by Servius (late fourth century), available to Isidore in the longer version called *Servius Danielis* (after its first publisher, Pierre Daniel), which is thought to include materials from Donatus not reworked by Servius. Servius's commentaries amount to an encyclopedia organized by the order of the text of Vergil, rather than by topic or by alphabet. All these, apart from the Cassiodorus, are pagan works; among Christian works with encyclopedic abundance of lore are the writings of Lactantius (*ca.* 240–*ca.* 320), including the *Divine Institutes*, Ambrose's *Hexameron* (late fourth century), and Augustine's *City of God* (413–426).

Alongside, and in part excerpting, the encyclopedias was a tradition of lexicography, which included from the outset definitions, etymologies, and *differentiae*, the discrimination of meaning and usage of closely related terms. At the head of this tradition stands Verrius Flaccus's *On the Meaning of Words* (early first century CE), lost but epitomized by S. Pompeius Festus in the late second century. These works were arranged in roughly alphabetical order. The Latin tradition of free-standing glossaries, not attached to individual authors, seems to begin with the sources of Placidus's glossary in the late fifth or early sixth century. Some glossaries compiled after Isidore's time are known to include material from sources probably known to him, especially Paul the Deacon's epitome of Festus, preserving much of that work otherwise lost, and the vast (over 500,000 entries) *Liber Glossarum (Glossarium Ansileubi)*, probably of the late eighth century and compiled at Corbie or a related scriptorium.[30]

Together with these encyclopedic and lexicographical works we must presume a substantial number of lost school-texts and manuals treating the various arts, and of course a mass of monographs, many still

29 R. A. B. Mynors, ed., *Cassiodori Senatoris Institutiones* (Oxford, 1937; corr. reprint 1961). An important translation and commentary: Leslie Webber Jones, *An Introduction to Divine and Human Readings, by Cassiodorus Senator* (New York, 1946). Isidore apparently knew only the second book of the *Institutes* (Fontaine 2000:334); Mynors observes that the two books usually circulated separately.

30 The *Liber Glossarum* is edited (abridged) by W. M Lindsay, *Glossaria Latina*, vol. I (Paris, 1926). Lindsay also studied the Festus material contained in it and other post-Isidorean glossaries: see his reprinted *Studies in Early Mediaeval Latin Glossaries*, ed. Michael Lapidge (Aldershot, Hampshire, 1996), no. 7, "The Abstrusa Glossary and the Liber Glossarum." Festus is also edited by Lindsay: *Sexti Pompei Festi De Verborum Significatu quae Supersunt cum Pauli Epitome* (Leipzig, 1913). See further D. Ganz, "The 'Liber Glossarum': A Carolingian Encyclopedia," in *Science in Western and Eastern Civilization in Carolingian Times*, ed. P. L. Butzer and D. Lohrmann (Basel, 1993: 127–35), and T. A. M. Bishop, "The Prototype of the *Liber Glossarum*," in M. B. Parkes and A. G. Watson, eds., *Medieval Scribes, Manuscripts and Libraries* (London, 1978: 69–86). On Paul the Deacon's epitome of Festus, completed in 786, see Settimio Lanciotti, "Tra Festo e Paolo," in *Paolo Diacono: Uno scrittore fra tradizione longobarda e rinnovamento carolingio* (Udine, 2000: 237–50), and the references cited there.

extant, treating specific disciplines: grammar, rhetoric, medicine, law, geography, architecture, philosophy, chronology, logic, music, ecclesiastical and theological matters, and the rest. Outstanding among these are the treatises of Boethius (480–524), covering the disciplines of the quadrivium as well as important translations and commentaries on logic; the standard grammatical works of Donatus (fourth century), Sacerdos (third century), and Terentianus (late second century); the many legal compilations of Julius Paulus (*ca.* 210) and Ulpian (died 223), whose works were used in the great codifications under Justinian (529–534); Vitruvius's (late first century BCE) *On Architecture*; for agriculture the works of Palladius (fourth century), partly based on Columella (60–65 CE); Marius Victorinus's (fourth century) translations of Greek philosophical texts; the geographically arranged miscellany of lore, practically an encyclopedia, the *Collection of Memorable Things* (soon after 200) of G. Julius Solinus; and for history and chronology Jerome's translation and continuation to the year 378 of Eusebius's *Chronicle*, Rufinus's translation and continuation (late fourth century) of Eusebius's *Ecclesiastical History* (early fourth century), and Paulus Orosius's *History Against the Pagans* (418).[31]

From this survey it appears that Isidore's twin informing principles, etymologizing and encyclopedism, descend from ancient and distinguished ancestry.[32] In that the *Etymologies* amounts to a reorganized redaction and compendium of writings mainly of the fourth to sixth centuries (with the large exception of Pliny), it could be said that his work is not merely conditioned by, but in the main is comprised of, the major components of intellectual history as they were handed down to him. He had access, albeit largely indirect, to the major traditions of Latin learning reaching back 800 years, from Gregory the Great to Cato. Like his fellow "transmitters"[33] from Servius to Cassiodorus, Isidore quite consciously preserved, in abbreviated form, the accumulated learning of the classical world. As his disciple Braulio remarked in his *Renotatio*, "Our own time indeed found in him a likeness of the knowledge of antiquity, and in him antiquity reclaimed something for itself . . . God encouraged him . . . to preserve the ancient monuments . . ."

Apart from the dedication to Sisebut Isidore does not speak generally about his use of sources in the *Etymologies*, with one exception, his use – particularly his occasional augmenting – of Jerome's work explicating the meaning of Hebrew terms (VII.i.1).[34] More vaguely, he claims to avoid presenting material about the founding of cities when the authorities differ among themselves, giving examples of such dissension from Sallust and two places in the *Aeneid* (XV.i.1). At the beginning of Book XIII he emphasizes that he will tell of the cosmos in a "brief sketch" *(brevis tabella)* and "with compendious brevity" *(conpendiosa brevitas)*, implying abbreviation of his sources.[35]

Because Isidore derives his information mainly at second or third hand, his actual naming and even quoting of earlier scholars is no reliable guide to his immediate sources. Let the crucial figure of Varro, at the head of the encyclopedic tradition in which the *Etymologies* stands, serve as an example.[36] Isidore names him as his authority for various facts twenty-eight times, and appears to quote him eighteen times.[37] The first ten of these

31 On historiography before and after Isidore see R. McKitterick, *History and Memory in the Carolingian World* (Cambridge, 2004).

32 On this see especially Fontaine (1966).

33 On such "transmitters" of classical culture as Boethius, Cassiodorus, and Isidore see E. K. Rand, *Founders of the Middle Ages* (Cambridge, MA, 1928). Broadly for the period see M. L. W. Laistner, *Thought and Letters in Western Europe, AD 500–900* (Ithaca, NY, 1931), and esp. Riché (1976) and J. J. Contreni, "The Carolingian Renaissance: Education and Literary Culture," in R. McKitterick, ed., *The New Cambridge Medieval History*, vol. II *c.* 700–*c.* 900 (Cambridge, 1995: 709–57).

34 The openings of three other books, X, XIII, and XIX, refer without specification to Isidore's abbreviation of his sources. Three chapter titles refer to sources (II.xxv, xxvi, and xxix).

35 Díaz y Díaz observes that Isidore uses similar phrasing when speaking of his intentions in the preface to his treatise *On the Nature of Things:* "presenting some statements about the nature and causes of things . . . all of which I have noted in a brief sketch *(brevis tabella)* according to what has been written by the ancients and especially in the works of Catholic writers" (Oroz Reta and Marcos Casquero 1993^2:176).

36 The information about those whom Isidore names, and those whom he directly quotes (whether or not naming the specific source), may be gleaned from two indexes in the Reta–Casquero edition (1993^2): "Index nominum" and "Loci citati in textu." These do not include Isidore's quotation or paraphrase of sources where he gives no indication of doing so. In what follows we collect statistics from these indexes with the caveat that they contain many errors.

37 Isidore appears to quote Varro at I.iii.1, I.xxvii.15, I.xxxviii.1, II.xxiii.1, IV.viii.13, IV.xi.5, VIII.vi.21, VIII.vii.3, IX.ii.74, X.185, XI.i.51, XI.i.97, XIII.i.2, XIII.xviii.2, XV.xiii.6, XVII.ix.95, XX.x.1, XX.xi.9 and otherwise names him as his authority at VIII.ix.13, XI.iii.1, XIV.vi.18, XIV.vi.36, XIV.viii.33, XIV.ix.2, XV.i.63, XVII.vii.57, XVII.i.1, and XVIII.xvi.2.

citations give an idea of what Varro provides: he calls grammar 'literacy'; he observes that Caesar's use of the *i* in *maximus* led to the standard orthography; he defines the term *prosa*; he gives the etymology of the disease *aurigo*; he gives the etymology of the word for 'mortar' *(pila)*; he speaks of fire as the soul of the world; he gives the etymology of the word for 'prophet' *(vates)*; he records the Pelasgians' first arrival in Italy; he defines the word *hilum*; and he gives the etymology of the word for 'tongue' *(lingua)*. Yet modern scholarship has affirmed that all of these references are at second hand; there is no evidence that Isidore handled any writing by Varro. Compare his naming of Pythagoras as authority eight times in the *Etymologies*; we can be sure that Isidore had no direct access to Pythagoras, who, as far as we know, wrote nothing.

Because so much of the *Etymologies* is complacently derivative, we can nowhere take for granted that we know the stance of the "we" who compiles the work. When he describes the types of parchment, Isidore might have told us about the production of books in his own scriptorium. Instead, he reproduces Pliny on the types of papyrus sheets and the ancient types of parchment (VI.x). Presumably many of the critical remarks about pagan beliefs that we find are Isidore's own words – but many may derive from his Christian forebears. Things that persist "up to this day" may be those that persist up to the time of Isidore's source. Usages that Isidore labels as "commonly" *(vulgo)* current may be those current in the milieu of the source. Descriptions of Spain, even of Seville, are exiguous, traditional, *pro forma*.

The names of earlier scholars found in the *Etymologies* display a striking fact. Isidore names Aristotle (15 times), Jerome (10), Cato (9), Plato (8), Pliny (7), Donatus (6), Eusebius (5), Augustine (5), Suetonius (4), and Josephus (2), along with single references to a few others. At one point he names, we may suppose with admiration and in emulation, those "who wrote many things": Varro and, "of ours," that is, of Christians, Origen and Augustine. Of all these writers, Isidore surely drew excerpts directly from Jerome and Augustine, and possibly from Pliny and Donatus, yet he probably never saw the other authorities, but borrowed the references from secondary works.[38] (Whether or not he cites Pliny from intermediate sources, he often borrows from him at length verbatim.) More striking, he never names several encyclopedists from whose work he probably drew at second or third hand: Aulus Gellius, Nonius Marcellus, Lactantius, Macrobius, and Martianus Capella (possibly an immediate source). And most striking, nowhere in the *Etymologies* do we find mention of three of Isidore's four (with Pliny) main scholarly sources: Solinus (himself heavily indebted to Pliny), Servius, and Cassiodorus.

Jacques Fontaine's important study (1959, 1983^2) examines Isidore's profound indebtedness to Cassiodorus's *Institutes* in the first three books of the *Etymologies*, and Peter Marshall's edition (1983) of Book II bears out Fontaine's conclusions in even greater detail. The ALMA editions of other books of the *Etymologies* (III, IX, XII, XIII, XVII, XVIII, XIX) confirm the findings of investigations since the fifteenth century concerning Isidore's vast quotation and paraphrase of Servius, Pliny, and Solinus. In his treatment of the sources of Book XII (1986: 13–22), Jacques André finds a typical situation. The book contains 58 citations – that is, acknowledged quotations (there are altogether nearly 600 of these in the *Etymologies*) – and 293 uncited borrowings. Of these most, 79, are from Solinus; 45 are from Pliny the Elder. From Servius come 61 borrowings of material; André estimates that some 400 from Servius occur in the whole of the *Etymologies* – this may understate the number. Of the Church Fathers from whom Isidore constantly borrows, in Book XII (on animals) the most used is Ambrose – the *Hexameron*. Ambrose is named only once in the *Etymologies*.

The ancient tradition of grammar and of encyclopedias took for granted that for the uses of particular words, as well as for figures of speech and in fact for any other information, the major poets and rhetoricians, the *auctores*, constituted the prime witnesses. Hence copious citation, in grammars and reference works, of wording from Vergil or Cicero or Horace not only displayed the writer's liberal learning (and status), and not only illustrated particular literary techniques or fact, but also authenticated assertions by the highest standard – higher, indeed, than immediate experience of the world. Thus Isidore reports (XII.iv.48) that Pythagoras says that a cadaver's spinal cord turns into a snake, and to buttress the veracity of

38 The detailed evidence is found in Fontaine and in the ALMA editions – see below.

the idea he quotes Ovid's *Metamorphoses* with the same report – even though Ovid leaves room for doubt ("there are those who believe . . ."). Surely Isidore himself did not believe so unbiblical an idea; rather, he follows his respected source, both in stating it as fact and in providing further authentication. Elsewhere (XIX.i.17) he speaks of a type of boat called *phaselus*, and notes that "we" (either seventh-century Spaniards or whoever were the original audience of his source) incorrectly call this boat *baselus*. Merely to affirm the existence of the word in its correct form he quotes Vergil's *Georgics*. If Vergil used the word it is worth knowing – so the Roman scholars presumed, and Isidore follows them.

The most cited *auctores* used in this way are Vergil (over 190 citations),[39] Cicero (over 50), and Lucan (some 45). Other much-cited figures are Plautus, Terence, Lucretius, Ovid, Horace, Juvenal, Martial, Ennius, Sallust, and Persius. In addition, Isidore quotes from the Bible nearly 200 times. Apart from the Bible and Vergil, and perhaps Ovid, Lucretius, and Martial, modern scholarship (especially Fontaine and the ALMA editors) shows that Isidore probably quotes none of these *auctores* at first hand. Yet he often carefully names them; clearly he distinguishes between these writers and the scholarly providers of the bulk of his material. They are older (mainly Augustan and pre-Augustan); apart from Cicero and Sallust they are poets; they are revered from antiquity on as luminaries of the language, as originators and originals – they are, in short, what we would call "classics." In contrast are the unnamed and seldom named sources: Pliny, Servius, Cassiodorus, and the rest. We may presume that Isidore thought of them as not worth mentioning as authorities: they are fellow scholars, (except for Pliny) relatively recent, utilitarian and prosaic, themselves secondary. Evidently Isidore made no sharp division between the authoritativeness of pagan versus Christian writers, but he probably did generally regard his Christian sources – to use some old terminology – as "moderns," and the pagans as "ancients" (whom with great frequency he calls *maiores, veteres, antiqui*; roughly "our ancestors, those of old times, the ancients").

Because our translation of the *Etymologies* specifies sources only in the few cases where they particularly bear on Isidore's meaning, we offer here a very rough guide to the major sources of the individual books.[40] Two caveats: first, the forthcoming volumes of the ALMA edition of the *Etymologies* will supersede any current knowledge of sources; second, the positing of a source by no means indicates that it is Isidore's immediate source. The first two books rely mainly on Cassiodorus, as does the third, with important additions from Boethius on mathematics. Book IV on medicine draws on Caelius Aurelianus's (fifth century) Latin translation, *On Acute Diseases and Chronic Disorders*, of Soranus of Ephesus (second century) and Pliny. Among the sources of the legal materials in Book V are the *Institutes* of Gaius (second century) and its epitome in the *Lex Romana Visigothorum*, and Julianus Salvius's (second century) *Digesta*. The chronicle section updates and abbreviates Isidore's own *Chronicon*, which derives from Jerome's adaptation of Eusebius's chronicle and continuations of it.

Books VI to VIII constitute the ecclesiastical and theological part of the *Etymologies*. Primary sources are, naturally, Augustine and Jerome, whom Isidore ransacked thoroughly, as well as Gregory the Great (a friend of Isidore's brother Leander), Lactantius's *Divine Institutes*, Tertullian, and for the pagan lore in Book VIII, Varro, Cicero, Pliny. Book IX weaves together material from Augustine, Ambrose, Jerome, Servius, Pliny, and Solinus. A remote source is M. Junianus Justinus's (third century) Latin epitome of Pompeius Trogus's universal history (early first century). The vocabulary of Book X derives from the glossographic tradition from Verrius Flaccus through Festus, as well as Servius, and the Church Fathers. For Books XI–XX excerpts from Pliny, Servius, and Solinus occur everywhere. Book XII borrows much from Ambrose's *Hexameron*. Solinus and Paulus Orosius's *Histories against the Pagans* (fifth century) provide much of the geographical learning in Book XIV.

39 These figures derive from an index in the BAC edition of the *Etymologies*; however, in the same edition Díaz y Díaz (Oroz Reta and Marcos Casquero 1993[2]:193) writes that Vergil is cited by name more than one hundred times, and 266 times altogether, as reported by N. Messina, "Le citazioni classiche nelle *Etymologiae* di Isidoro di Siviglia," *Archivos Leoneses* 68 (1980: 205–64). Our own search finds that in the *Etymologies* Isidore cites Vergil by name 112 times.

40 Particularly valuable for Isidore's sources are the works of Fontaine listed in the Bibliography. On the general topics of education and knowledge of the classics in Isidore's Spain see Riché (1976), esp. 246–65, 274–303, and Díaz y Díaz (1975). The manuscript evidence for transmission of the classics in Spain may be found in Lowe, *Codices Latini Antiquiores*, and Reynolds 1983.

On buildings and fields (Book XV), Columella and Servius are the main bases. Pliny, Servius, and Solinus yield most of Isidore's mineralogical lore (Book XVI). Book XVII, on agriculture, derives ultimately from Cato via Varro, Columella, Pliny, Servius (mainly his commentary on the *Georgics* of Vergil), and Rutilius Palladius (fourth century), whose agricultural treatise derives mainly from Columella and from his own experience in farming. On war and games (Book XVIII) Isidore draws much material from Servius and, on the Circus games, from the treatise *De Spectaculis* (*ca.* 200) of the Christian apologist Tertullian. The last two books may have been conceived as a unit (so Rodríguez-Pantoja 1995: 1); Book XX bears no separate title in early manuscripts. Along with Servius (the main source), Jerome, Festus, and Pliny, in these books Isidore uses the abridgement of Vitruvius's treatise on architecture made by M. Cetius Faventinus (uncertain date), Palladius, Book XIII of Nonus Marcellus, and others.

Isidore's absorbing and replicating of these traditions, pagan and Christian, Plinian and Augustinian, show him facing both ways. He may be included among the last humanist polymaths of late antiquity, and also among the early and most influential medieval Christian scholars.[41] He obviously accepted the commonplace among Christian scholars, from Augustine (especially *De Doctrina Christiana*) and Jerome, that mastery of pagan learning is a good thing for the inquiring Christian: the liberal arts are a fit introduction to the study of the Bible and theology.[42] He offers an apology for one type of this learning to his Christian reader (*Etym.* I.xliii): "Histories of peoples are no impediment to those who wish to read useful works, for many wise men have imparted the past deeds of humankind in histories for the instruction of the living." Especially in the broad survey of the natural world and human institutions in the second decade of books, he passed beyond strictly Christian interest by reverting to the interests of Latin scholars some centuries earlier.

In this connection a set of verses attributed, probably correctly, to Isidore makes a witty case for eclectic reading. The verses purport to speak of the contents of the cathedral library at Seville, as if they were written on the walls or bookcases.[43] The works of encyclopedists – Pliny, Servius, Cassiodorus, and the rest – go unmentioned; the poem sheds light not on the sources of the *Etymologies* but rather on Isidore's attitude toward antique learning.

I. These bookcases of ours hold a great many books.
Behold and read, you who so desire, if you wish.
Here lay your sluggishness aside, put off your fastidiousness of mind.
Believe me, brother, you will return thence a more learned man.
But perhaps you say, "Why do I need this now?
For I would think no study still remains for me:
I have unrolled histories and hurried through all the law."
Truly, if you say this, then you yourself still know nothing.

II. Here there are many sacred works, and here many other secular ones.
If any of these poems pleases you, take it up and read it.
You see meadows filled with thorns and rich with flowers.
If you do not wish to take the thorns, then take the roses.

III. Here the venerable volumes of the two Laws shine forth,
The New joined together with the Old.

IV. Origen
I, the celebrated Origen, at one time a Doctor most true,
Whom famous Greece first brought to the faith:
I was lofty in merit and famous for my abundance of speech,
But was suddenly ruined, cut short by a malicious tongue.
I toiled, if you may believe it, to compose as many thousands of books
As a legion has armed men.
No blasphemy ever touched my senses,
But I was watchful and wise, and safe from the enemy.

41 On Isidore's place in the scholarly tradition see especially Fontaine (1966).

42 See among many studies H. Hagendahl, *Latin Fathers and the Classics: A Study of the Apologists, Jerome, and Other Christian Writers* (Gothenburg, 1958) and G. Ellspermann, *The Attitude of Early Christian Latin Writers toward Pagan Literature and Learning* (Washington, 1949). Further references are in Riché 1976:7, and see his detailed treatment of Christian uses of classical writings, 79–176. In his *Rule for Monks* Isidore charged monks to avoid the books of pagans or heretics – evidence that such books were available in monastic libraries. Riché (296) argues that the stricture would not apply to more experienced monks. Isidore's time was broadly one of less interest in the classical texts, as indicated in Reynolds 1983. Reynolds notes that of 264 books and fragments of Latin books preserved from the seventh century, only a tenth are secular works, and those mostly technical (p. xvi).

43 We translate from the edition in Sánchez Martín 2000. Among studies of the poem, and Isidore's sources generally, is Díaz y Díaz 1975: esp. 136–42.

Only the words in my *Peri Archon*[44] brought this
misfortune on me.
Impious darts attacked me when I was assailed by these
words.

V. Hilary
Nurturing Gaul sent me, born in Poitiers,
Her own Doctor Hilary with thundering speech.

VI. Ambrose
Doctor Ambrose, celebrated for his miracles and hymns,
Shines here with his chapters and his text.

VII. Augustine
He lies who says he has read you entirely.
What reader could possess your complete works?
For you, Augustine, glow with a thousand volumes.
Your own books bear witness to what I say.
However pleasing may be the wisdom of books by many
authors,
If Augustine is there, he himself will suffice you.

VIII. Jerome
Translator Jerome, most learned in the various
languages,
Bethlehem praises you, the whole world resounds with
your name;
Our library also celebrates you through your books.

IX. John
I am John by name, called 'Chrysostom,'
Because a golden tongue[45] makes my work glitter.
Constantinople glows with me as its teacher
And I am everywhere renowned for my books as a
Doctor.
I have established morals, I have spoken of the rewards
of virtues,
And I have taught wretched culprits to bemoan their
crimes.

X. Cyprian
With a brighter eloquence than all the rest, Cyprian, you
gleam.
At one time you were a Doctor, now you are here as a
martyr.

XI. Prudentius, Avitus, Juvencus, Sedulius
If Maro, if Flaccus, if Naso and Persius raise a shudder,
If Lucan and Papinius[46] disgust you,
Sweet Prudentius of distinguished speech is at hand;
With his various poems this noble one is enough.
Read through the learned poem of eloquent Avitus.
Behold – Juvencus is there with you, and Sedulius,
Both equal in tongue, both flourishing in verse.
They bear large cups from the gospel fountain.
Leave off, therefore, waiting on pagan poets –
While you can have such good things, what is Callirhoe[47]
to you?

XII. Eusebius, Orosius
Histories of events and circumstances of a bygone age,
This chest holds them collected together on
parchment.

XIII. Gregory
Hippo, as much as you are distinguished for your
teacher Augustine,
So much is Rome for its Pope Gregory.

XIV. Leander
You are held to be not much unequal to the ancient
Doctors,
Leander the Bishop: your works teach us this.

XV. Theodosius, Paulus, Gaius
Collected here is a most ample series of the laws of
justice;
These rule the Latin forum with their true
speaking.

The character of the *Etymologies*

Internal evidence alone defines the method and purpose of the *Etymologies*, because apart from the brief dedication to Sisebut (appended Letter VI) no statement from Isidore survives. Obviously he compiled the work on the basis of extensive notes he took while reading through the sources at his disposal. Not infrequently he repeats material verbatim in different parts of the work; either he copied extracts twice or he had a filing system that allowed multiple use of a bit of information. Presumably he made his notes on the slips of parchment that he might have called *schedae:* "A *scheda* is a thing still being emended, and not yet redacted into books" (VI.xiv.8).

44 Origen was accused of heresy, partly on the basis of statements he made in *Peri Archon*. For the text (i.e. Rufinus's Latin translation) and an account of the controversy see H. Crouzel and M. Simonetti, ed. and French trans., *Origène: Traité des principes*, Tomes I and II, Sources Chrétiennes 252 (Paris, 1978).

45 Cf. Χρυσός, "gold" and στόμα, "mouth."

46 The four poets in the title are Christians; the next six (Vergil, Horace, Ovid, Persius, Lucan, and Statius) are pagans.

47 Callirhoe was the name of an Athenian fountain, here taken as the inspiration of the pagan poets.

The guess that Isidore had help from a team of copyists (Fontaine, 1966:526) finds some support in the fact that some errors of transmission may indicate that Isidore was using excerpts poorly copied or out of context, perhaps excerpts made by a collaborator. Although these could result from Isidore's own copying error or failure of memory, they are suggestive. At XVII.iv.10, for example, he misconstrues Servius's comment on *Aeneid* 6.825, taking the phrase *Pisaurum dicitur*, "the city of Pesaro is so called . . . ," as if it were *pis aurum dicitur*, "*pis* means gold" – there is no Latin word *pis*. Again, at XVII.vii.67 occurs another misreading of Servius (on *Georgics* 2.88), taking types of pears as olives. Most telling in this connection is a confusion at XVI.iii.3:

> *Crepido* (i.e. 'a projection, promontory') is a broken-off extremity of rock, whence a height of sheer rock is called *crepido*, as in (Vergil, *Aeneid* 10.361): 'Foot (*pes*) presses against foot' – whence it is so called.

The place in Servius from which the information "*crepido* is a height of broken-off rock" is drawn actually is a comment on *Aeneid* 10.653, where the word *crepido* occurs. In the course of his comment, Servius cites in another connection *Aeneid* 10.361, which does not involve the term *crepido* but rather exemplifies a grammatical point. The error could be Isidore's own, but it could easily be attributed to an assistant's truncating the excerpt so as to leave the wrong line from Vergil as the authenticating illustration of the use of the term. It appears that Isidore then turned the error into an etymology, deriving *crepido* from *pes*, gen. *pedis*. These instances are from Servius, whose organization followed the text of Vergil rather than an alphabetical or topical arrangement, and whose information was hence more difficult to extract and reorder than the materials in Pliny or Cassiodorus, and thus more liable to errors of this kind.

Explicit evidence about the purpose of the *Etymologies* is scant.[48] In a few places Isidore indicates that he will treat "what ought to be noted" (*notandum*) about a topic,[49] but seldom does he explain why. In Book II, following Cassiodorus, he several times remarks on the usefulness of knowing the logical disciplines for understanding books of both rhetoric and logic, avoiding the deception of false sophisms, and grasping the "clearly wonderful" power of gathering human inventiveness into a limited set of topics.[50] Elsewhere he explains the symbols used for different weights, to keep a reader who might be ignorant of them from falling into error (XVI.xxvii.1). Thus he aims to furnish the material required for good reading and to provide schemas for managing discourse. In a few places he proposes aids for understanding the Bible: knowing the rationale of terms for numbers can elucidate scriptural mysteries; exposition of Hebrew names reveals their meaning; the patriarchs' names derive from intrinsic causes; the names of prophets can indicate what their words and deeds foretell; it is proper to know of cities whose origin is reported in Scripture (or in pagan histories).[51] Again, he remarks that the most important of mountains and rivers – as celebrated in histories or in general opinion – should be known (XIII.xxi.6, XIV.viii.1).

A fuller sense of what Isidore was about, and for whom he wrote, may be gathered from who he was and what he did. His close relations with the Visigothic rulers, especially Sisebut, and his dedication of the *Etymologies* to Sisebut (himself a writer),[52] imply that he wrote in part for the general literate governing class of his nation – those who might partake of and patronize a liberal education.[53] The clergy, too, were among the main recipients of Isidore's attention – more obviously in some of his other works, but evidently in the *Etymologies* as well. His purpose was pastoral and pedagogical – he wished for his priests and monks to possess a general knowledge of what books make available, and to possess the preliminary skills that make intelligent reading, especially of Scripture, possible. External evidence of Isidore's concern for education of the clergy is available: he presided over the Council of Toledo in 633, and one of the decrees promulgated there commanded bishops

48 On Isidore's motives for compiling the *Etymologies* see Fontaine (2000: 174–76).

49 For example VII. vii. 1, XIII.xxi.6, XIV. viii.1.

50 See II.xxvi.15, xxviii. 1, xxx.18.

51 See III.iv.1, VII.i.2, VII.vii.1, VII.viii.3, XV.i.2.

52 Sisebut's poem on natural phenomena is edited in J. Fontaine, *Traité* (1960: 328–35).

53 On the learning of the laity in Isidore's Spain see Riché 1976:246–65, and R. Collins, "Literacy and Laity in Early Medieval Spain," in R. McKitterick, ed., *The Uses of Literacy in Early Mediaeval Europe* (Cambridge, 1990: 109–33). Relevant also is the chapter on "The Literacy of the Laity" in McKitterick, *The Carolingians and the Written Word* (Cambridge, 1989). See further M. Banniard, *Viva Voce. Communication écrite et communication orale du IVe au IXe siècle en Occident latin* (Paris, 1992).

to establish educational centers at each cathedral city of Spain. Bishop Braulio's claims that the *Etymologies* were written at his own request (Letter II and *Renotatio*) presume a clerical motive, and Braulio's sense of the *Etymologies*' purpose is to the point: "Whoever thoughtfully and thoroughly reads through this work . . . will not be ignorant of the knowledge of human and divine matters, and deservedly so. Overflowing with eloquence of various arts with regard to nearly every point of them that ought to be known, it collects them in summarized form." The work, then, aims to gather what ought to be known, especially by a cleric, in a compendium.

More precisely, the form of the work indicates Isidore's intentions. It is written in easy Latin, in relentlessly utilitarian prose. At the outset it presents the Seven Liberal Arts, with an obviously propaedeutic motive. It is a storehouse, to be sure, but it also provides a reasonably sequential general education. The hundreds of citations illustrate the facts presented, but conversely they exemplify the kinds of reading, pagan and Christian, that the *Etymologies* can enrich. Generally the treatment is in continuous prose, not tables or lists, and its effort at pleasing variation – even when the facts presented are rather repetitive in form – implies a reader absorbing the work consecutively, even as its careful organization ensures access topic by topic to a reader looking for a particular fact. In an era when the gravest dangers to Christianity were thought to be intellectual errors, errors in understanding what one read – that is, heresies like Arianism – mastery of the language arts was the Church's best defense. Isidore's book constituted a little library for Christians without access to a rich store of books (it even incorporates a good deal of material from Isidore's own previous books) in order to furnish capable Christian minds.

Although a good number of statements in the *Etymologies* address particular Christian concerns, such statements amount to comments by the way when theologically incorrect ideas emerge in Isidore's sources. The core of the work is not apologetic but informational. Still, we find Isidore carefully denying such superstitions as that a turtle's foot on board retards the progress of a ship (XII.vi.56), or that the stars have predictive power – "These [horoscopes] are undoubtedly contrary to our faith, and so they ought to be ignored by Christians, so that these things are not seen to be written up" (III.lxxi.38). Reporting that augurs claim to predict the future by observing crows, he remarks, "It is a great sin to believe that God would entrust his counsels to crows" (XII.vii.44). Isidore's persistent response to pagan religious belief is euhemerism, the interpretation of pagan divinities and mythological figures as in fact human beings wrongly elevated as supernatural creatures by benighted heathen.[54] In his chapter on the pagan gods (VIII.xi) Isidore begins confidently, "Those who the pagans assert are gods are revealed to have once been men, and after their death they began to be worshipped among their people." In the same chapter (section 29) he rejects the tradition of interpreting the names of the gods as expressing universal physical properties, "physical allegory," such that Cronos would represent time, Neptune water. Treating the names of the days of the week (V.xxx.5–11) Isidore gives both the Christian and the pagan terms. Noting that the latter are named from heathen gods – Saturday from Saturn, etc. – he is careful to remind us that those figures were actually gifted humans, but he acknowledges that these names for days are in common use. "Now, in a Christian mouth, the names for the days of the week sound better when they agree with the Church's observance. If, however, it should happen that current usage should draw someone into uttering with his lips what he deplores in his heart, let him understand that all those figures whose names have been given to the days of the week were themselves human." We sense here both Isidore's theological precision and his episcopal tolerance.

The learned tradition that lies behind Isidore's work would lend him five schemes of organization from which to choose. In roughly chronological order these are: the sequential "scholiastic" order of a particular text, as used by the scholiasts on ancient texts, and commentators on master texts like Vergil (Servius) and the Bible (the Church Fathers); the "encyclopedic" order from Varro through Pliny, arranged in rational order

54 Euhemerus's utopian novel, *Sacred Scripture*, written around 300 BCE, is extant only in fragments and epitomes. It presented the idea that Uranus, Cronos, and Zeus were human kings whose subjects worshipped them as gods – an idea not alien to Augustan Rome. Christians naturally seized on the idea. For the development of the idea of euhemerism and physical allegory see Don Cameron Allen, *Mysteriously Meant: The Rediscovery of Pagan Symbolism and Allegorical Interpretation in the Renaissance* (Baltimore, 1970). Examples of euhemeristic and rationalizing interpretations of such mythological figures as Scylla and Hydra may be found at II.xii.6 and XI.iii.28–31 and 34.

by topic; the educational or propaedeutic order, especially of the Seven Liberal Arts (from trivium to quadrivium), from Varro through Cassiodorus; the haphazard "conversational" order of Aulus Gellius and Macrobius; and the alphabetical "dictionary" order of collections of glosses and other extracts, through Placidus. Apart from these broader orders are the internal ordering principles of such monographic treatises as annals and chronologies (obviously, chronological order), medical works (e.g., acute and chronic diseases; head to toe anatomies), and the rational orders of logical and legal texts.

Isidore used all these orders except the scholiastic and the conversational. The general scheme of the twenty books can be approached in several ways.[55] One arrangement, with some support from the manuscript tradition, divides the *Etymologies* into two decades of ten books. In assessing this arrangement we need to remember Braulio's assertion in the *Renotatio* that it was he, not Isidore, who divided the text into books, where Isidore had left it only divided into "titles" (*tituli*) – perhaps what we call the "chapters" of the received text.[56] The organizing principle of the second decade is obviously encyclopedic, and contains two movements: the first (Books XI–XVI) might be called *On the Nature of Things* – the Lucretian title, adopted by Isidore himself in an earlier work. This segment ranges (below celestial matters) from higher to lower things – from intelligent animals (humans; Book XI) through other animals (XII), cosmic and non-earthly phenomena (XII), the earth (XIV), and earthy materials (XVI). Within these orders a number of subclassifications are perceptible – for example, the treatment of metals from the most to the least valuable, of gems by color, or the division of the world's objects into those composed of each of the four elements. Out of order here, in this conception, is Book XV, rather a miscellany on cities and things built by humans – this would fit better, perhaps, in the second movement of the second decade. This movement (XVII–XX) broadly treats human institutions, artifacts, and activities. Book XVII begins in this way, at least, with agriculture, though the bulk of the book treats flora in detail – our (ultimately Aristotelian) sense of order would prefer to place this material among the books on animals and minerals. The order of this last group of books is not obvious; their miscellaneous character may explain why they fall at the end of the whole work.

The first decade adopts several principles of order: propaedeutic, encyclopedic, alphabetic. Books I–III obviously conform to the idea of the Seven Liberal Arts, as explained in I.ii. These are followed by the treatments of medicine and law (IV, the first part of V), rounding out a general introductory education, we might say, in the professions. The second part of Book V, on the mensuration of time and the actual chronology of history, annalistically ordered, may be said to look both back, to the essentially pagan character of the liberal disciplines of the first books, and forward, to the religious matter of the following books. This set, Books VI to VIII, focuses on the sacred sciences, not in an obvious sequence. Book VI is propaedeutic to these, treating Scripture, the authority for the rest, then books in general, then a number of ecclesiastical matters. Books VII and VIII present a transparent order, moving from God downward to heresy and paganism. Book IX treats human institutions broadly conceived, human organization (languages, nations, reigns, cities, kinship), and Book X, alphabetically ordered, presents terms descriptive of humans. These two books might after all be classed with the following book (XI), the anatomy of human beings.

A more general characterization of the *Etymologies'* scheme of organization would make the main division after Book V. Thus the first part constitutes notes toward a general education, and the second a particularization of reality based mainly on two principles, that of the Great Chain of Being (from God to inanimate materials) and that of the four elements. In this scheme, too, the last group of books constitutes an anomalous miscellany. Neither order consistently dominates the text, and the exigencies of Isidore's broadest intention, to store in compendious form what is known from former times, ultimately takes precedence over the inherited schemes.

As Fontaine has pointed out (1966:536–38), Isidore's followers derived material wholesale from the *Etymologies*, but under more fully Christianized, "clericalized" form, in "a sort of Carolingian edition." Especially remarkable in this connection is the reordering of the work by Hrabanus Maurus in his *On the Nature of Things*, which begins not with the Liberal Arts (which

55 A similar account of the organization of the work may be found in Fontaine 2000:176–78.

56 Furthermore, it seems that Braulio divided the work into fifteen books; the division into twenty books developed during the course of the manuscript diffusion (see Reydellet 1966:435).

Hrabanus treated in another book) but with the religious material, and works "down" through the Chain of Being.[57] Furthermore, Hrabanus lards the whole with allegorical interpretations of the kind found in Isidore's own *Certain Allegories of Sacred Scripture*. Not until the thirteenth century, and not entirely until the sixteenth century, does the impulse toward encyclopedism recover the intellectual inclusiveness of Isidore.

Given this rough outline of the *Etymologies*, we can turn to its particular content, and begin by noticing a few things the *Etymologies* is not. First of all, it is not complete or polished – so Braulio implies and so Isidore says in the letters prefaced to the work in the manuscripts (Letters II and V). We may imagine that the finished work would have eliminated many of the repetitions currently present, and might have joined together the now scattered materials on law (Books II and V), on astronomy (Books III and XIII), on nations (Books IX, XIV, and XV), and the like. However, Isidore might well have retained those repeated statements that fall naturally into separate topics. Surely he would have completed or omitted the dozens of items that now stand as the lemma – a single word – alone, without further discussion. These are signaled in this translation by the appearance of ellipsis points, as XI.i.93 or XIX.v.4.[58]

Second, Isidore makes no effort to disclose the rationale of the taxonomies he presents. Here the (derived) shapeliness of the early books on the liberal disciplines is the exception; on the whole Isidore does not explain the order of things beyond what is implicit in their sequence in the text. In this he is like his sources, from Varro on, and differs from the masters of these sciences, Plato and Aristotle. As a consequence we have no reason to think most of the classes of things treated are presented with all their members – a consideration repeatedly made explicit by Isidore himself (e.g. XII.vii.2). So it is, after all, with post-Linnaean biology as well. It should be added here that Isidore does include a good number of lesser schemata, establishing such logical sets of things as the types of definition, or the types of divination, or the kinds of fields.[59]

And third, Isidore generally avoids, in the *Etymologies*, providing "spiritual" or "mystical," or "figurative," that is, allegorical, interpretations of the items he adduces. These were the main content of his earlier work (perhaps 612–615), the *Certain Allegories of Sacred Scripture*.[60] In fact we find a few of such interpretations: "the Hebrews used a ten-stringed psaltery on account of the number of laws of the Decalogue" (III.xxii.7); Esther's people are "a figure of the Church of God," and as Aman's name means "wickedness, so his killing is celebrated in the feast of Purim" (Esther 7 and 9; *Etym.* VI.ii.29); the seraphim "figuratively signify the Old and New Testaments," they have six wings as a figure of the things made in the six days, and their crying "Holy" three times (Isaiah 6:3) "shows the mystery of the Trinity" (VII.v.32–33); the split tip of a quill pen signifies the Old and New Testaments (VI.xiv.3). At one point Isidore explicitly denies any attempt to provide the spiritual sense: speaking of the names of Biblical characters, he says, "While a holy and spiritual character abides in these names, we are now describing the meaning of their stories only with regard to the literal" (*ad litteram*; VII.vi.2). Indeed, his direct treatment of divinity in Book VII is essentially a treatment of names, and not a theological investigation. This self-imposed limitation has its precedent in Augustine's *The Literal Level of the Book of Genesis (De Genesi ad Litteram)*, and it is fairly consistently carried out through the *Etymologies*, hence giving Hrabanus his opportunity for "improvement" of the work for a clerical audience eager for such interpretations.

Isidore's overriding interest, the fundamental principle of the *Etymologies*, falls under the discipline Isidore would call grammar, the "origin and foundation of liberal letters" (I.v.1), and what we would call philology – the art of understanding and correctly producing words and texts. It is an obvious fact that, before the nineteenth century (the twentieth in the East), philology broadly conceived was the dominant concern of the learned world, the queen of the sciences; Isidore merely reflects

57 Hrabanus's work is usually known under the title *De Universo* (mid-ninth century): *Patrologia Latina* 111. A facsimile of an early Montecassino manuscript of it is ed. G. Cavallo, *De Rerum Naturis: Casin. 132, secolo XI* (Turin, 1994). See Maria Rissel, *Rezeption antiker und patristischer Wissenschaft bei Hrabanus Maurus* (Bern and Frankfurt, 1976).

58 A much rarer type of incompleteness occurs at XIV.ix.7, where a sentence breaks off before giving the Biblical citation.

59 II.xxix, VIII.vii.3, XIV.ix.2. The sources are explicitly named: Marius Victorinus and Varro. For such *divisiones* of topics see also I.v.4, II.v, II.xxi.1, II.xxiv.9–11, II.xxvi.5 (all from Cassiodorus), and V.xxvii.4 (following Cicero) and XVIII.ii.1 (following Sallust). It may be doubted whether Isidore supplied any such rationales apart from his sources.

60 This is the work Braulio calls *On the Names in the Law and the Gospels*.

that concern at one of the turning-points of intellectual history, as pagan thought in the West gave way to Christian thought. What we might understand as alternative master-disciplines – theology, or experimental science, or philosophy – in Isidore's work are subsumed under philology in what Fontaine calls the "pangrammatical" cast of late antique culture (1966:534).

In fact three sequential chapters (I.xxix–xxxi) in his treatment of the art of Grammar treat three of the main informing principles of the *Etymologies:* these are etymology, glosses, and differentiae. If we add to these the theme of the next three chapters (xxxii–xxxiv), faulty Latin usage, and the idea that propositions are usefully finished with an illustrative or exemplary quotation, we will have summed up much of the content of the *Etymologies.*

First, glosses. Isidore defines a gloss as a single term that designates the meaning of another term (I.xxx). If we broaden this to include any sort of definition of a term, we might expect to find hundreds of such definitions in the *Etymologies*, and indeed there are many: the definition of "gloss" itself, or, selecting at random, of such terms as "chronic disease" (IV.vii.1), "hymn" (VI.xix.17), "tyro" (IX.iii.36), "vineshoot" (XVII.v.9). However, such glosses are relatively infrequent, as compared with Isidore's usual presumption that the basic meaning of the Latin word is either already known to his reader, or (like terms for minerals or herbs) is not in his interest to define in any systematic way – such that, for example, one could positively identify an actual specimen of an item using only his description of it. This is not to say that formal systems of definition were unknown to him: thus in II.xxix he lists fifteen types of definition, with their Greek equivalents, "abbreviated from the book of Marius Victorinus"; and in II.xxv and xxvi he briefly but clearly expounds the logical taxonomy of Porphyry's *Isagoge* and the system of predicates of Aristotle's *Categories.*

Second, differentiae. This is the kind of definition that does interest Isidore, and they constitute the subject matter of a treatise he wrote before he turned to the *Etymologies.* In I.xxxi he says a *differentia* is the distinguishing and therefore defining feature of things otherwise alike, and gives for example the differentiation of the terms for a king (restrained and temperate) and a tyrant (cruel). Isidore introduces dozens of such differentiae in the *Etymologies* – between a maxim and a chreia (II.xi), between astronomy and astrology (III.xxvii), between three types of law (*ius, lex, mores*; V.iii), between types of wars (XVIII.i.2–10) and types of pyres (XX.x.9). As much as any information Isidore gives, such differentiae reveal Isidore's pedagogical motives: to refine the reader's sense of Latin, sharpen the mind with a fundamental form of reasoning, discourage incorrect usage.

Finally, etymology. On this crucial subject in Isidore we must refer to the essay by Fontaine (1978), with full bibliography, which remains the best treatment – perhaps the only essay on a section of the *Etymologies*, namely the chapter on etymology itself (I.xxix), that fully and definitively treats Isidore's thinking and his work with his sources. The sources of this chapter include Quintilian's *Institutes of Oratory* (I.vi.28), citing Cicero's *Topics* (35) – where Cicero literally translates the Greek term ἐτυμολογία as *veriloquium*, "true utterance" – and Boethius's commentary on the *Topics.*[61] In his chapter on etymology Isidore gives no hint that what he is defining is the most powerful informing principle of the work that both he and Braulio refer to as either *Etymologiae* or *Origines* (Letters II, IV, V, VI, *Renotatio).* He defines etymology as "the origin of words, when the force of a word or a name is inferred through interpretation." He goes on, "The knowledge of a word's etymology often has an indispensable usefulness for interpreting the word, for when you have seen whence a word has originated, you understand its force more quickly. Indeed, one's insight into anything is clearer when its etymology is known."[62]

In the same chapter Isidore offers a brief account (as had Varro and others) of types of etymology, as follows. Some things take their names not from their nature, but arbitrarily. Words with retrievable etymologies take them from their *causa* (rationale, intrinsic principle, explanatory force), the word's answer to the question "why?" Other words derive from the thing's origin, the word's answer to the question "from where?" Of the former an example is *rex* ("king") from acting *recte* ("correctly"); of the latter, *homo* ("human being") from *humus* ("earth," the "origin" – Aristotle would say "the material cause" – of the human). Still other etymologies

61 The commentary is trans. E. Stump, *Boethius's In Ciceronis Topica* (Ithaca, NY, 1988). Cicero's *Topics* are edited by T. Reinhardt (Oxford, 2003).

62 Obviously a great many, perhaps most, of the etymologies that Isidore proposes are incorrect in light of modern scholarship. For the actual etymologies of Latin words consult A. Ernout and A. Meillet, *Dictionnaire étymologique de la langue latine*, 4th edn. (Paris, 1979) and the appendix on "Indo-European Roots" by Calvert Watkins in *The American Heritage Dictionary* (Boston, 1976).

are based on contraries, so that 'mud' (*lutum*) derives from 'washing' (*lavare*, with the past participle *lutus*). Some words have their etymology by derivation from other words, like the adjective "prudent" from the noun "prudence." Some etymologies may be discovered in words of similar sound. Some words are derived from Greek, and others derive their names from place names. The origins of words derived from other foreign languages are often hard to discern.

This brief statement could be much expanded, but it contains the essence of Isidore's principal endeavor, to disclose the inner and true (ἔτυμος) meaning of the Latin lexicon by way of the etymology of the words. The method is fundamentally derivational, whether from a thing's intrinsic character (its *causa*) to its extrinsic name, or from its originating motive by process of time to its current locution, or from some term's sound to another term's similar sound, or from one word-class or language to another. The constantly repeated formulas are "X is so called because Y" and "X is so named as if the word were Y." The focus on origins, indeed, finds expression in many places in the *Etymologies* where the origins of things rather than merely words are specified: the origins of various alphabets (I.iii.5) and the Latin letters (I.iv.1), of shorthand signs (I.xxii) and of fables (I.xl.1), of historiography (I.xlii) and of the disciplines of Rhetoric (II.ii.1) and physics (II.xxiv.4).[63] Further, Isidore supplies hundreds of indications of the regions where things – metals, spices, gems, birds, and the like – originate, uniquely, or in their best condition, or abundantly, and whence they are imported (imported, that is, as Isidore's sources presume, into Italy). The very idea of a disquisition on the "Nature of Things," the essential title of an encyclopedic work, implied for a Latin reader the idea that the genesis of things is in question, as the word *natura* itself means (etymologically!) "what is begotten or generated," from *natus*, the past participle of *nasci*, "be born."[64]

63 A few more origins, particularly those inventors and discoverers whom he calls *auctores*, adduced by Isidore: mathematics (III.ii), geometry (III.x.1), music (III.xvi), various musical instruments (III.xxii.2 and 12), astronomy and astronomical writing (III.xxv and xxvi), medicine and its three schools (IV.iii and iv), laws (V.i) and chronicles (V.28), libraries (VI.iii.2–5), book collecting (VI.v), Christian libraries (VI.vi), canon-tables (VI.xv.1), the method of dating Easter Sunday (VI.xvii.1–2), agriculture (XVII.i.2). An unusual instance is the detailed technical description of the origin of glass (XVI.xvi.1–2).

64 So *Etymologies* XI.i.1, "Nature (*natura*) is so called because it causes something to be born (*nasci*)."

In a number of places Isidore offers a brief review of types of etymology for classes of things. Thus "meters are named either after their feet or after the topics about which they are written, or after their inventors, or after those who commonly use them, or after the number of syllables." Examples, respectively, are dactylic, elegiac, Sapphic, Asclepiadian, pentameter (I.xxxix.5–15). Ointments are named after their regions, inventors, or material (IV.xii.7–9). Heretics may be named after their founders or their tenets (VIII.v.1); philosophers from their founders (Platonists) or their meeting sites (Stoics – VIII.vi.6). To such as these we can add the great many places where Isidore makes the type of an etymology explicit. Examples are the derivations of the names of seas from the names of people who perished in them (XIII.xvi.8); of the disease satyriasis from its exemplars the satyrs (IV.vii.34); the names of parts of the Mediterranean from the adjacent regions (XIII.xvi.5); the different terms for earth from logic (*ratio* – XIV.i.1); 'pocket change,' the thing contained, from the word for 'bag,' the container (XVI.xviii.11; for such metonymies see I.xxxvii.8); derivation by physical resemblance, as the disease *elefantiacus* takes its name from the sufferer's resemblance to an elephant (IV.viii.12); from onomatopoeia, as the word for 'cricket,' *gryllus*, is from the sound of its call (XII.iii.8); and similarly the names of many birds (XII.vii.9). The notorious type that Isidore labels with the Greek term κατ' ἀντίφρασιν ("by opposition") is not infrequent: thus the merciless Parcae take their name from the verb meaning "spare" (*parcere* – VIII.xi.93).

Usually Isidore grants that the borrowing of a Latin word from Greek amounts to a sufficient etymology, though often he supplies a second explanation from within Latin as well. A great many etymologies based on Greek are not made explicit in the *Etymologies*, in some cases perhaps from Isidore's own ignorance of the import of the etymology he adduces. We have supplied the relevant Greek in this translation when we are aware of it. In his treatment of illnesses, for example, Isidore provides a number of etymologies from Greek, but when he gives the etymology of the antidote *tyriaca* he omits the crucial information that θηριακός means "of venomous beasts" (IV.ix.8) although he knows that the medicine is "made from snakes." He also supplies a number of etymologies from languages other than Latin or Greek – obviously from secondary sources. Most of these, as in the case of Biblical names, are from Hebrew, but we also learn of words derived from Persian (XII.ii.7), Syrian (XII.vi.38), and a number of others.

The most frequent type of etymology, from the very beginning ('know' [*scire*] is named from 'learn' [*discere*]) to the end ('branding iron' [*cauterium*] is so called because as a warning [*cautio*] to potential thieves it burns [*urere*]), is the discovery of a term's origin in another term, a single word or a phrase, because of a resemblance in their sound. Such similarities are often tenuous and remote, as Isidore seems to acknowledge when he observes, in deriving 'spiced' (*salsus*) from the phrase 'sprinkled with salt' (*sale aspersus*), "with the [three] middle syllables taken away" (XX.ii.23) – it is a stretch. It is hard not to agree with the remark of Isidore's distinguished editor Faustino Arévalo, some two hundred years ago, that Isidore can produce an etymology not in the belief that it is the actual origin of a term, but as a mnemonic aid (*Patrologia Latina* 82.954). Arévalo's example is Isidore's deriving 'swan' (*cygnus*) from 'sing' (*canere*) – after he has just referred to the Greek word that is the obvious etymon, κύκνος. We might add a large number of instances where Isidore notes that a term is "as if the word were" (*quasi*) another term. Thus Isidore distinguishes the two plural forms of *pecus* ("livestock"), *pecora* and *pecudes*, by proposing that the latter term is used only of animals that are eaten, "as if the word were *pecuedes*," that is, as if it contained the term 'eat' (*edere*; XII.i.6). The many dozens of such instances may well reflect Isidore's effort to help a student of Latin to remember a distinction rather than his belief in the actual origin of a word. To be sure, Isidore's authoritative sources, pagan and Christian, were replete with etymologies no more strained than these. Isidore illuminates the essences of words, their natures, not in terms of historical linguistics, but in terms of grammar.

The influence of the *Etymologies*

It would be hard to overestimate the influence of the *Etymologies* on medieval European culture, and impossible to describe it fully. Nearly a thousand manuscript copies survive, a truly huge number. As evidence of its continuing popularity down to and after the advent of printing, more than sixty manuscript copies of the whole work, as well as more than seventy copies of excerpts, were written in the fifteenth century.[65] It was among the early printed books (1472), and nearly a dozen printings appeared before the year 1500. According to Díaz y Díaz (Oroz Reta and Marcos Casquero 1993²:210), abundant evidence demonstrates that, by the year 800, copies of the *Etymologies* might be found "in all the cultural centers of Europe."

The earliest dissemination of the work beyond the cathedral centers of Seville itself and Braulio's Saragossa seems to have been in Gaul and Ireland. The earliest manuscript fragments of the *Etymologies* are housed at the monastery of St. Gall, a foundation in present-day Switzerland with Irish connections going back to the early seventh century. These fragments are written in an Irish scribal hand, perhaps as early as the mid-seventh century.[66] Irish texts of the mid to late seventh century show knowledge of the *Etymologies*, for instance (possibly) the *Twelve Abuses of the Age* (perhaps before 650).[67] The English scholar Aldhelm (obit 709) knew works of Isidore in the late seventh century, and "the

65 J. M. Fernández Catón, *Las Etimologías en la tradición manuscrita medieval estudiada por el Prof. Dr. Anspach* (León, 1966).

66 The fragments are described by E. A. Lowe, *Codices Latini Antiquiores* 7 (Oxford, 1956, no. 995). For the early diffusion of the *Etymologies* see A. E. Anspach, "Das Fortleben Isidors im VII. bis IX Jahrhundert," in *Miscellanea Isidoriana: Homenaje . . .* (Rome, 1936:323–56) especially for influence in Spain; Bischoff (1966:171–94), esp. 180–87; J. N. Hillgarth 1962; M. Herren, "On the Earliest Irish Acquaintance with Isidore of Seville," in E. James (Oxford, 1980); Reydellet 1966; Oroz Reta and Marcos Casquero 1993²:200–11. Reydellet 1966:389–91 provides a list of the thirty-seven complete or nearly complete manuscripts of the *Etymologies* dating from before the tenth century, with their provenances, and reference to the Bischoff study (1966) and Lowe's *Codices*. Fontaine 2000:401–16 treats a number of instances of Isidore's influence, with good bibliography on the subject.

67 On Isidore in early Ireland see Herren (preceding note); M. C. Díaz y Díaz, "Isidoriana II: Sobre el *Liber de Ordine Creaturarum,*" *Sacris Erudiri* 5 (1953): 147–66; Paul Grosjean, "Sur quelques exégètes irlandais du VIIe siècle," *Sacris Erudiri* 7 (1955): 67–97; Riché 1976:320. The Pseudo-Cyprian *De XII Abusivis Saeculi* is edited by Siegmund Hellmann in *Texte und Untersuchungen der altchristlichen Literatur* 34, 1 (Leipzig, 1909). A. Breen sharply disagrees with Hellmann's "quite unproven thesis" that the *Twelve Abuses* makes use of the works of Isidore: "Evidence of Antique Irish Exegesis in Pseudo-Cyprian, *De Duodecim Abusivis Saeculi,*" *Proceedings of the Royal Irish Academy*, Section C, vol. 87 (1987): 71–101, esp. p. 76.

works of Isidore of Seville were a major influence on the development of Anglo-Saxon intellectual life in the age of Bede," that is, in the late seventh and early eighth centuries.[68]

Bede himself, the most learned scholar of his age, made extensive use of the *Etymologies*, and the work thrived in the Carolingian educational program in Gaul (where Isidore was known at the abbey of Corbie by the mid-seventh century). We have noticed above that Alcuin's pupil, the churchman Hrabanus Maurus (*ca.* 780–856), called "the teacher of Germany," "clericalized" the *Etymologies* of Isidore in his popular treatises *The Natures of Things* and *Allegories on the Whole of Sacred Scripture*, as well as other works. Both directly and indirectly, through such prominent writers as these, Isidore's influence pervaded the High Middle Ages of the eleventh to fifteenth centuries, in which the *Etymologies* was always regarded as a prime authority.

Of that continuing influence we can here only touch on a couple of strands. First was the direct influence of the *Etymologies* on the traditions of lexicons and encyclopedias that were standard reference works of the later Middle Ages.[69] We have noticed that the vast *Liber Glossarum (Glossarium Ansileubi)*, probably of the late eighth century, incorporates much of Isidore. Around the year 1053 the Italian Papias composed the *Elementarium Doctrinae Rudimentum*, an alphabetically arranged encyclopedic dictionary replete with etymologies and differentiae from Isidore, surviving in some ninety manuscripts and several Renaissance printings. Borrowing from Papias and Isidore, Osbern of Gloucester compiled his *Panormia* in the mid-twelfth century, and Huguccio (Hugutio), bishop of Ferrara, produced his *Liber Derivationum*, also known as the *Magnae Derivationes* (over 200 manuscripts), of the same type as Papias, around the year 1200. Before 1270 the Franciscan Guillelmus Brito, master at Paris, completed his *Summa*, another alphabetized dictionary of encyclopedic proportions, in this case treating some 2,500 words from the Bible. Its extensive use of the *Etymologies*, where Isidore is explicitly cited hundreds of times, is detailed in the Index of the modern edition.[70] It survives in over 130 manuscript copies, and was printed in the fifteenth century. From these same sources and others Giovanni Balbi of Genoa (Johannes Januensis) finished the culminating encyclopedic dictionary of the Middle Ages, the *Catholicon*, in 1286. It was one of the first printed books, in 1460.

These dictionaries are accompanied by a series of topically arranged encyclopedias likewise derivative of Isidore, and cumulatively massive. Major ones include Honorius Augustodunesis, *The Image of the World* (early twelfth century), Bartholomaeus Anglicus, *The Properties of Things* (*ca.* 1240 – early translated into six languages, including English), Thomas of Cantimpré's *Nature of Things* (*ca.* 1245), and the massive set of encyclopedias (over three million words), the *Speculum Maius*, of Vincent of Beauvais (*ca.* 1260), of which some eighty manuscripts are extant; it was the first book printed at Strasbourg (1473–1476). Bartholomaeus's encyclopedia was the basis of the thoroughly allegorized encyclopedic work of Pierre Bersuire, the *Reductorium Morale* of the mid-fourteenth century. The first encyclopedia in a vernacular language, Brunetto Latini's *Li Livres dou trésor*, duly dependent on Isidore, appeared around 1265.

Some sense of the continuing use of the *Etymologies* beyond this tradition of reference works can be acquired by observing its influence on the great Italian and English poets of the fourteenth century.[71] For Dante, suffice it

68 P. H. Blair, *The World of Bede* (London, 1970). F. C. Robinson has identified a number of bits of etymological lore from Isidore in such Old English poetic texts as *Genesis*, the riddles of *The Exeter Book*, and *Instructions for Christians*: see *The Tomb of Beowulf and Other Essays on Old English*, 2 vols. (Oxford, 1993), pp. 197, 103, 119.

69 A number of medieval encyclopedias that borrow from the *Etymologies* are treated by Collison 1964, 1966²: 44–81.

70 L. Daly and B. A. Daly, *Summa Britonis sive . . . Expositiones Vocabulorum Biblie*, 2 vols. (Padua, 1975).

71 A few other evidences of Isidore's influence: Isidore was often among those excerpted and praised in the collections of sententious utterances (the *florilegia*) and the chronicles of the later Middle Ages; a number of these are cited in *Patrologia Latina* 82:198–205. Aspects of Isidore's influence on music theory well into the sixteenth century are discussed in R. Stevenson, *Spanish Music in the Age of Columbus* (The Hague, 1960). Materials from Book VI of the *Etymologies* are the earliest sources for some lore about books and libraries, according to K. Christ, *The Handbook of Medieval Library History*, trans. T. M. Otto (Metuchen, New Jersey, 1984). Isidore's deep influence on the medieval tradition of poetics and rhetoric may be exemplified in the citation of his name as an authority on the first page of John of Garland's *Parisian Poetics* (about 1220–1235); see T. Lawler, ed., *The 'Parisiana Poetria' of John of Garland* (New Haven, 1974: 5). On "Etymology as a Category of Thought" in medieval Latin Poetry see Curtius (as n.1 above), pp. 495–500. Instances such as these can be multiplied indefinitely.

that Isidore is among the luminous minds in the circle of the Sun in *Paradiso:* "See, flaming beyond, the burning spirit of Isidore" (10.130–31).[72] Boccaccio naturally derives material from Isidore (or by way of quotations of the *Etymologies* in Hrabanus and Vincent of Beauvais) in his learned treatise on the *Genealogy of the Gods.*[73] Closer to hand, he would have found Isidore's discussion of the origins of poetry and of the term *poeta* (*Etymologies* VIII.vii.1–3) among Petrarch's *Familiar Letters,* in the letter addressed to his brother Gherardo. Isidore had referred to an otherwise unknown passage from Suetonius, and to Varro, in his discussion. Isidore's actual source is Servius on *Aeneid* 3.443. Petrarch in turn cites the material from Varro and Suetonius, and diligently records that he actually derives the information from Isidore, an author "better known to you." Boccaccio repeats the information in his *Short Treatise in Praise of Dante.*[74] So we find information passed from ancient Latin authors through Isidore and his encyclopedic borrowers to the Italian poets.

In his long French poem, *The Mirror of Mankind* (*ca.* 1377), the English poet John Gower calls Isidore "the perfect cleric."[75] In his equally long Latin poem *The Voice of One Crying* (*ca.* 1378–*ca.* 1393), in an exemplary instance, Gower cites Isidore in a passage actually drawn from Godfrey of Viterbo's encyclopedic poem *Pantheon* (late twelfth century).[76] In *Piers Plowman* (written *ca.* 1376), William Langland quotes and paraphrases Isidore's definition of *anima* in the course of the figure Anima's self-explication.[77] This may be the only direct paraphrase of a passage of Isidore in English verse; it begins:

> 'The whiles I quykne þe cors', quod he, 'called am I *anima*;
> And for þat I kan and knowe called am I *mens* . . .'

Finally we may see the influence of the *Etymologies* on Chaucer. In the Parson's Tale of *The Canterbury Tales,* and nowhere else, Chaucer names Isidore, and quotes from him, both times (lines 89 and 551) at second hand. The latter instance cites Isidore's remarks on the long-lasting fire made from the juniper tree (*Etymologies* XVII.vii.35): so, says the Parson, is the smoldering fire of Wrath.

Again, we may find the *Etymologies* behind a passage in the Second Nun's Tale that derives from the legend of Saint Cecilia in the *Golden Legend* of Jacobus de Voragine, the standard collection of saints' lives in the later Middle Ages (before 1298).[78] As often, Jacobus begins his Vita with an etymology of the name of the saint, here deriving her name from *caelum,* "heaven," and explicitly borrowing from the *Etymologies*: "Or she [Saint Cecilia] is called a heaven because, as Isidore says, the philosophers asserted that the heavens are revolving, round, and burning." He thus quotes verbatim, including the reference to "philosophers," from *Etymologies* III.xxxi.1, and he goes on to say in what ways Cecilia was revolving, round, and burning (*rotundum, volubile atque ardens*). Chaucer says he will "expowne" the meaning of Cecilia's name, and follows Jacobus's several etymologies in detail, concluding with this perfect Chaucerian stanza (113–19), with which we conclude our own exposition:[79]

> And right so as thise philosophres write
> That hevene is swift and round and eek brennynge,
> Right so was faire Cecilie the white
> Ful swift and bisy evere in good werkynge,
> And round and hool in good perseverynge,
> And brennynge evere in charite ful brighte.
> Now have I yow declared what she highte.

72 "Vedi oltre fiammeggiar l'ardente spiro / d'Isidoro." See also the citation of Isidore's etymology of *anima* in *Convivio* IV.XV.11.

73 For example in the treatment of "poetry" in *Genealogy* XIV.vii, perhaps written around 1360. See C. G. Osgood, trans., *Boccaccio on Poetry,* 2nd edn. (Indianapolis, 1956), pp. 156–59, etc. – see Index. Boccaccio cites the same passage of Isidore in *Genealogy* XI.ii.

74 See Petrarch, pp. 413–14, and Boccaccio, pp. 492–93, translated in *Medieval Literary Theory and Criticism c. 1100–c. 1375,* eds. A. J. Minnis, A. B. Scott, and D. Wallace, rev. edn. (Oxford, 1991).

75 Line 10,405. See W. B. Wilson, trans., *John Gower: Mirour de l'Omme* (East Lansing, MI, 1992: 143).

76 *Vox Clamantis* I.765. See E. W. Stockton, trans., *The Major Latin Works of John Gower* (Seattle, 1962), p. 353.

77 G. Kane and E. T. Donaldson, *Piers Plowman: The B Version* (London, 1975), 15.23–39. The passage is from *Etymologies* XI.i.13. It is also quoted in the *Summa* of Guillelmus Brito, ed. Daly and Daly, p. 40, in Peter the Chanter's *Distinctiones Abel* (late twelfth century, under the term 'Anima'; unedited), and doubtless elsewhere – such is Isidore's afterlife.

78 G. Ryan and H. Ripperger, trans., *The Golden Legend of Jacobus de Voragine* (New York, 1969), p. 689. For other citations of Isidore in the *Legend* see the Index. Caxton translated and printed the *Legend* in 1483.

79 *The Riverside Chaucer,* ed. Larry D. Benson (Boston, 1987).

Editions of the *Etymologies* and this translation

The first printed edition of the *Etymologies* was issued by G. Zainer at Augsburg in 1472.[80] This was followed by ten further editions by the year 1500. The first edition of the complete works of Isidore appeared in Paris in 1580. The first important scholarly edition was that of Juan de Grial, which became the basis for work on Isidore until the early nineteenth century; it was issued in Madrid in 1599. Its valuable notes are retained in Arévalo's edition. The Jesuit scholar Faustino Arévalo produced his seven-volume edition of the *opera omnia* from Rome between 1797 and 1803; volumes III and IV contain the *Etymologies*. This great edition, whose notes update and correct Grial, was reprinted, with the usual large number of errors, in volumes 81–83 of the *Patrologia Latina* (ed. J.-P. Migne) in 1850.[81] The *Etymologies* form the bulk of volume 82. In 1909 Rudolph Beer published in Leiden a facsimile edition of the "Toledo" manuscript of the *Etymologies*, now Madrid manuscript Tol. 15.8.

Wallace M. Lindsay edited the *Etymologies* for the Scriptorum Classicorum Bibliotheca Oxoniensis series in 1911. This was the first edition of the work based on modern principles of textual criticism, and it was prepared by the ablest student of Late Latin of his time. Lindsay claims, with good reason, to have produced a text that accords with the state of Isidore's text as it might have appeared around the year 700. His diffidence about capturing the *ipsissima verba* of Isidore is sensible; given the complex relationship of Isidore with his sources, which themselves doubtless often came down to him in somewhat corrupted form, it is in fact hard to be sure that one does not over-correct on the basis of sources. On the other hand, the steadily accumulating knowledge about the precise sources Isidore used will inevitably inform better readings in future editions, as it already has in the recent critical editions. Lindsay's remarkable accuracy and good judgment have been apparent to us from the outset, and his edition will not easily be superseded.[82] It is still in print, and is likewise handily accessible in the Oroz Reta-Marcos Casquero edition (1993^2), which has very few typographical errors. Further, it is also now available on the internet at the address http://penelope.uchicago.edu/Thayer/E/Roman/texts/Isidore/home.html. This version is corrected and variously improved from the text that may also be found on the internet at www.thelatinlibrary.com/isidore.html. Lindsay's text is also available on the CD-ROM issued by CETEDOC in the Library of Latin Texts. A concordance to the *Etymologies* has recently appeared.[83]

Two translations into Spanish of the complete *Etymologies* have hitherto appeared for the Biblioteca de Autores Cristianos: by Luis Cortés y Góngora (Madrid, 1957), and by José Oroz Reta and Manuel-A. Marcos Casquero (1993^2). The latter edition has an excellent and comprehensive introduction by Manuel C. Díaz y Díaz, and is provided with the Latin text of Lindsay on facing pages with the translation. We have compared the Reta–Casquero translation in detail with our own, and we have a good number of differences of interpretation from their translation. Yet we must acknowledge that they have divined, at various points of difficulty in the Latin, solutions that we had not grasped.

As already noted, a new, international edition of the *Etymologies* has been appearing, book by book, in the series Auteurs Latins du Moyen Age, being published by Belles Lettres in Paris.[84] To date eight volumes have appeared, published from 1981 to 2009, under the general direction of the distinguished Isidoreans Jacques Fontaine and Manuel C. Díaz y Díaz. Information about these volumes appears in the bibliography appended below. These are accompanied by translations in the language of the editors; one has appeared so far in English (Marshall, 1983); of the others, four are in French, two in Spanish, and one in Italian. Of particular value is

80 The following information about early editions of Isidore is mainly drawn from Díaz y Díaz (Oroz Reta and Marcos Casquero 1993^2:226–36).

81 The *Patrologia* edition was reprinted in 1977 by Brepols in Turnhout, Belgium.

82 We find no reason to dissent from the judgment, printed in his edition of Lindsay's *Studies*, of Michael Lapidge, himself a distinguished Latinist: "Wallace Martin Lindsay (1858–1937) was one of the greatest, perhaps *the* greatest, Latin scholars ever born in these British Isles" (Studies in Early Medieval Latin Glossaries 1996: ix).

83 A.-I. Magallón Garcia, *Concordantia in Isidori Hispaliensis Etymologias: A Lemmatized Concordance to the Etymologies of Isidore of Sevilla*. 4 vols. Hildesheim, 1995.

84 On the origins of this edition see Oroz Reta and Marcos Casquero 1993^2:235–36.

their profuse presentation, in the form of footnotes, of the sources of Isidore's text. We have examined these volumes in detail, have admired them enormously, have learned much from them, and occasionally refer to them in our own notes. The new editors make a number of emendations of Lindsay's text on sound grounds, but in fact the excellence of Lindsay's edition is confirmed by the small number of substantial emendations that the ALMA editors propose. In striking cases we supply the probably superior readings in our notes.

We have based our translation strictly on Lindsay's text. It will be obvious that our translation is fairly literal, as we anticipate that readers with some knowledge of Latin will prefer clarity and help with the occasionally difficult syntax rather than elegance of style. As we have said, Isidore's Latin is resolutely utilitarian; he manifestly aimed to help his readers, and not to delight them with fancy prose.[85] We offer translations of a number of technical terms – plants, colors, minerals, and the like – not in confidence that the English term exactly catches the meaning of the Latin word (or whatever meaning Isidore or his sources might attach to the word), but as a rough guide to the sense. Further, when a Latin term in Isidore has no known English correspondent or meaning beyond what Isidore explicitly supplies, we have simply left the term in Latin: examples are *flamines* (X.96), *sibilus* (XII.iv.9), *thracius* (XVI.iv.8), and *cetra* (XVIII.xi.5). In the many places where Isidore quotes earlier authors in wording that departs from the modern received texts of those authors, we have translated Isidore, and not the received text, annotating the passage when needed for clarity. The simple conventions that we follow in presenting the text are explained in the Note to the Reader.

85 Cf. Fontaine 2000:352: "Isidore sought a purely functional and pedagogical style that was accessible even to the least literate clerks and monks."

Bibliography

Modern editions and translations of the *Etymologies*

André. J. (ed.) (1981) *Isidore de Séville: Etymologies. Livre XVII, De l'agriculture*, with tr. and comm. Paris.

(1986) *Isidore de Séville: Etymologies. Livre XII, Des animaux*, with tr. and comm. Paris.

Canale, A. V. (tr.) (2004) *Etimologie o origini di Isidoro di Siviglia.* Tr. with facing Latin (Lindsay ed.). Includes an important list of Isidore's sources, chapter by chapter, and a very full bibliography. Torino.

Cantó Llorca, J. (ed.) (2007) *Etimologías. Libro XVIII, De bello et ludis*, with tr. and comm. Paris.

Gasparotto, G. (ed.) (2004) *Etymologiae XIII (De mundo et partibus),* with tr. and comm. Paris.

Gasparotto, G., in collaboration with Guillaumin, J.-Y. (ed.) (2009) *Isidore de Séville: Etymologiae. Livre III, Les mathématiques*, with tr. and comm. Paris.

Goode, H. D. and Drake, G. C. (tr.) (1980) *Cassiodorus, Institutiones Book II, Chapter V; Isidore of Seville, Etymologies Book III, Chapters 15–23.* Colorado Springs.

Lindsay, W. M. (ed.) (1911) *Isidori Hispalensis Episcopi Etymologiarum sive Originum Libri XX.* Oxford.

Marshall, P. K. (ed.) (1983) *Etymologies. Book II, Rhetoric*, with tr. and comm. Paris.

Möller, Lenelotte (tr.) (2008) *Die Enzyklopädie des Isidor von Sevilla.* Wiesbaden.

Oroz Reta, J. and Marcos Casquero, M.-A. (eds.) (1993) *Etimologías: edición bilingüe*, with tr. and comm., and introd. by Manuel C. Díaz y Díaz, 2nd edn. Madrid.

Pantoja Márquez, M. R. (ed.) (1995) *Etimologías. Libro XIX, De naves, edificios y vestidos*, with tr. and comm. Paris.

Reydellet, M. (ed.) (1984) *Etymologies. Livre IX, Les langues et les groupes sociaux*, with tr. and comm. Paris.

Modern editions and translations of other works by Isidore and Braulio

Barlow, C. W. (ed.) (1969) *Iberian Fathers*, vol. II: *Braulio of Saragossa. Fructuosus of Braga.* Washington, DC.

Campos Ruiz, J. (ed.) (1971) *Reglas monásticas de la España visigoda. Los tres libros de las "Sentencias"* (includes Isidore's *Regula Monachorum* and *Sententiae*). Madrid.

Carracedo Fraga, J. (ed.) (1996) *Liber de ortu et obitu patriarcharum.* Turnhout.

Cazier, P. (ed.) (1998) *Isidorus Hispalensis sententiae.* Turnhout.

Codoñer Merino, C. (ed.) (1964) *El "De Viris Illustribus" de Isidoro de Sevilla.* Salamanca.

(ed.) (1992) *Isidoro de Sevilla: Diferencias*, with tr. and comm. Paris.

Fontaine, J. (ed.)(1960) *Isidore de Séville: Traité de la nature.* Bordeaux.

Ford, G. B., Jr. (ed.) (1970) *The Letters of St. Isidore of Seville*, with tr., 2nd edn. Amsterdam.

Lawson, C. M. (ed.) (1989) *Sancti Isidori Episcopi Hispalensis De ecclesiasticis officiis.* Corpus Christianorum Series Latina 113. Turnhout.

Lynch, C. H. (ed.) (1938) *Saint Braulio, Bishop of Saragossa (631–651): His Life and Writings* (includes a translation of the correspondence between Braulio and Isidore). Washington, DC. A Spanish translation: Madrid, 1950.

Martín, J. C. (ed.) (2003) *Isidori Hispalensis Chronica.* CCSL 112. Turnhout.

(ed.) (2006) *Scripta de Vita Isidori Hispalensis Episcopi. Braulionis . . . Renotatio Librorum*, etc. CCSL 113B. Turnhout.

Riesco Terrero, L. (ed.) (1975) *Epistolario de San Braulio. Introducción, edición crítica y traducción.* Sevilla.

Sánchez Martín, J. M. (ed.) (2000) *Isidori Hispalensis Versus.* Turnhout.

Strunk, O. (ed.) (1998) *Source Readings in Music History* (includes a translation of Book III, chapters 15–23). New York.

Trisoglio, F. (ed. and tr.) (2001) *La natura delle cose.* Rome.

Viñayo González, A. (ed. and tr.) (2001) *Sinónimos.* León.

Note also the *Library of Latin Texts: CLCLT-5* (Turnhout, 2002), a searchable database that includes the Latin text of the *Regula Monachorum* from Campos Ruiz, J. (ed.) (1971), the Latin texts in Fontaine, J. (ed.) (1960), Lawson, C. M. (ed.) (1989), and Lindsay, W. M. (ed.) (1911), as well as the *Allegoriae*, the *De Differentiis Rerum*, the *De Differentiis Verborum*, the *De Fide Catholica Contra Iudaeos*, the *Quaestiones in Vetus Testamentum*, and the *Sententiae* from the *Patrologia Latina*, vol. 83.

Further reading

Andrés Sanz, M. A., *et al.* (2008) *L'édition critique des oeuvres d'Isidore de Séville.* Études Augustiniennes 44. Paris.

Beer, R. (ed.)(1909) *Isidori Etymologiae: Codex toletanus (nunc matritensis) 15, 8 phototypice editus.* Leiden.

Beeson, C. H. (1913) *Isidor-Studien* (includes the text of the *Versus Isidori*). Munich.

Bischoff, B. (1966, 1967) *Mittelatlterliche Studien*, vols. I and II. Stuttgart.

Brehaut, E. (1912) *An Encyclopedist of the Dark Ages: Isidore of Seville* (includes English translations of selected passages from each book). New York.

Cazier, P. (1994) *Isidore de Séville et la naissance de l'Espagne catholique.* Paris.

Collins, R. (1980) "Mérida and Toledo: 550–585," in James, E. (ed.) (1980).

(1995) *Early Medieval Spain: Unity in Diversity, 400–1000*, 2nd edn. New York.

Collison, R. (1964, 1966²) *Encyclopedias: Their History Throughout the Ages.* New York and London.

Díaz, P. C. (1999) "Visigothic political institutions," in Heather, P. (ed.) (1999).

Díaz y Díaz, M. C. (ed.) (1961) *Isidoriana.* León.

(1975) "La Trasmission de los textos antiguos en la peninsula iberica en los siglos VII–XI," pp. 133–75 in *La Cultura antica nell'occidente latino dal VII all' XI secolo. Settimane di Studio del Centro Italiano di Studi sull'Alto Medioevo* 22:1. Spoleto.

Fontaine, J. (1959, 1983²) *Isidore de Séville et la culture classique dans l'Espagne wisigothique.* Paris.

(1966) "Isidore de Séville et la mutation de l'encyclopédisme antique," in *Cahiers d'histoire mondiale IX, Neuchâtel:* 519–538, reprinted in Fontaine (1988).

(1978) "Cohérence et originalité de l'étymologie isidorienne," pp. 113–44 in *Homenaje a Eleuterio Elorduy S.J.*, ed. Félix Rodriguez and Juan Iturriaga. Deusto.

(1981) "Aux sources de la lexicographie médiévale: Isidore de Séville médiateur de l'étymologie antique," pp. 97–103 in *La Lexicographie du latin médiéval et ses rapports avec les recherches actuelles sur la civilisation du moyen-âge*, Editions du CNRS. Paris.

(1988) *Tradition et actualité chez Isidore de Séville.* London.

(2000) *Isidore de Séville: genèse et orginalité de la culture hispanique au temps des Wisigoths.* Turnhout.

Funaioli, Hyginus (1907) *Grammaticae Romanae Fragmenta.* Vol. 1. Leipzig.

Heather, P. (1991) *Goths and Romans, 332–489.* Oxford.

(1996) *The Goths.* Oxford.

(ed.) (1999) *The Visigoths from the Migration Period to the Seventh Century: an Ethnographic Perspective.* San Marino.

Heather, P. and Matthews, J. (1991) *The Goths in the Fourth Century.* Liverpool.

Herren, M. (1980) "On the earliest Irish acquaintance with Isidore of Seville," in James, E. (ed.) (1980).

Hillgarth, J. N. (1962) *Visigothic Spain and Early Christian Ireland.* Dublin.

James, E. (ed.) (1980) *Visigothic Spain: New Approaches.* Oxford.

King, P. D. (1980) "King Chindasvind and the first territorial law-code of the Visigothic Kingdom," in James, E. (ed.) (1980).

Magallón, A.-I. (1996) *La tradición gramatical de differentia y etymologia hasta Isidoro de Sevilla.* Zaragoza.

McKitterick, R. (ed.) (2001) *The Early Middle Ages: Europe 400–1000.* The Short Oxford History of Europe. Oxford.

Reydellet, M. (1966) "La diffusion des *Origines* d'Isidore de Séville au haut moyen âge," *Mélanges d'Archéologie et d'Histoire de l'Ecole Française de Rome* 78 (1966): 383–437.

Reynolds, L. D. (ed.) (1983) *Texts and Transmission: A Survey of the Latin Classics.* Oxford.

Ribémont, B. (2002) *Littérature et encyclopédies du Moyen Age.* Orleans.

Riché, P. (1976) *Education and Culture in the Barbarian West: Sixth through Eighth Centuries.* Columbia, SC. Trans. by J. J. Contreni from *Education et culture dans l'Occident barbare, 6e–8e siécle* (Paris, 1962, 1972³).

Sharpe, W. D. *Isidore of Seville: The medical writings*, in *Transactions of the American Philosophical Society*, n. s. vol. 54, pt. 2 (1964): 1–70 (includes an English translation of Books 4 and 11).

Stocking, R. L. (2000) *Bishops, Councils, and Consensus in the Visigothic Kingdom, 589–633.* Ann Arbor.

Thompson, E. A. (1969) *The Goths in Spain.* Oxford.

Velázquez, I. (1999) "Jural relations as an indicator of syncretism from the law of inheritance to the *Dum Inlicita* of Chindaswinth," in Heather, P. (ed.) (1999).

Wolf, K. B. (1999) *Conquerors and Chroniclers of Early Medieval Spain*, 2nd edn. Liverpool (contains a translation of Isidore's *History of the Kings of the Goths*).

Wood, I. (1999) "Social relations in the Visigothic Kingdom from the fifth to the seventh century: the example of Mérida," in Heather, P. (ed.) (1999).

Additional sources

Buckland, W. W. (1963) *A Text-Book of Roman Law from Augustus to Justinian*, 3rd edn. Cambridge.

Casson, L. (1994) *Ships and Seafaring in Ancient Times.* Austin.

Daly, L. W. (1967) *Contributions to a History of Alphabetization in Antiquity and the Middle Ages.* Brussels.

Forbes, R. J. (1964) *Studies in Ancient Technology*, 2nd edn. Leiden.

Frend, W. H. C. (1985) *Saints and Sinners in the Early Church.* London.

Jolowicz, H. F. (1952) *Historical Introduction to the Study of Roman Law*, 2nd edn. Cambridge.

MacKay, A. (ed.) (1997) *Atlas of Medieval Europe.* London

Maltby, R. (1991) *A Lexicon of Ancient Latin Etymologies.* Leeds.

Richard, E. G. (1998) *Mapping Time: The Calendar and its History.* Oxford.

Singer, C. et al. (eds.) (1956) *A History of Technology.* New York.

White, K. D. (1967) *Agricultural Implements of the Ancient World.* Cambridge.

(1970) *Roman Farming.* Ithaca, NY.

Wild, J. P. (1970) *Textile Manufacture in the Northern Roman Provinces.* Cambridge.

Wiles, M. (1996) *Archetypal Heresy: Arianism through the Centuries.* Oxford.

Wilson, K. (1979) *A History of Textiles.* Boulder.

Two definitive bibliographies of works on Isidore

Hillgarth, J. N. (1983) "The position of Isidorian studies: a critical review of the literature 1936–1975," in *Studi Medievali*, ser. 3, 24: 817–905, reprinted in Hillgarth, J. N. (1985) *Visigothic Spain, Byzantium, and the Irish*, London.

(1990) "Isidorian studies, 1976–1985," *Studi Medievali*, ser. 3, 31: 925–73.

See also the recent and full bibliography in Martín's edition of *Chronica* (2003) and in Canale's translation of the *Etimologie.*

THE *ETYMOLOGIES*

Analytical table of contents

The first table below, within quotation marks, is a translation of the listing of the titles of the twenty books of the *Etymologies* found at the beginning of some early manuscripts, along with its prefatory remark; the list is printed by Lindsay (vol. 1, pages 11–12). Since Braulio, not Isidore, divided the work into books, we can be sure these titles are not Isidore's. There follows an analytical table of contents, drawn from the text itself. The title and chapters of each book correspond with our translation of the work. Book XX has no title in the early manuscripts. Manuscripts of the *Etymologies* often listed the chapter titles at the head of each book.[1]

"So that you may quickly find what you are looking for in this work, this page reveals for you, reader, what matters the author of this volume discusses in the individual books – that is, in Book

I. Grammar and its parts.
II. Rhetoric and dialectic.
III. Mathematics, whose parts are arithmetic, music, geometry, and astronomy.
IV. Medicine.
V. Laws and the instruments of the judiciary, and times.
VI. The order of Scripture, cycles and canons, liturgical feasts and offices.
VII. God and angels, prophetic nomenclature, names of the holy fathers, martyrs, clerics, monks, and other names.
VIII. Church and synagogue, religion and faith, heresies, philosophers, poets, sibyls, magicians, pagans, gods of the gentiles.
IX. Languages of the nations, royal, military, and civic terminology, family relationships.
X. Certain terms in alphabetical order.
XI. Human beings and their parts, the ages of humans, portents and metamorphoses.
XII. Four-footed animals, creeping animals, fish, and flying animals.
XIII. Elements, that is, the heavens and the air, waters, the sea, rivers and floods.
XIV. Earth, paradise, the regions of the whole globe, islands, mountains, other terms for places, and the lower regions of the earth.
XV. Cities, urban and rural buildings, fields, boundaries and measures of fields, roads.
XVI. Earthy materials from land or water, every kind of gem and precious and base stones, ivory likewise, treated along with marble, glass, all the metals, weights and measures.
XVII. Agriculture, crops of every kind, vines and trees of every kind, herbs and all vegetables.
XVIII. Wars and triumphs and the instruments of war, the Forum, spectacles, games of chance and ball games.
XIX. Ships, ropes, and nets, iron workers, the construction of walls and all the implements of building, also wool-working, ornaments, and all kinds of clothing.
XX. Tables, foodstuffs, drink, and their vessels, vessels for wine, water, and oil, vessels of cooks, bakers, and lamps, beds, chairs, vehicles, rural and garden implements, equestrian equipment."

Book I: GRAMMAR. i. Discipline and art. ii. The seven liberal disciplines. iii. The common letters of the alphabet. iv. The Latin letters. v. Grammar. vi. The parts of speech. vii. The noun. viii. The pronoun. ix. The verb. x. The adverb. xi. The participle. xii. The conjunction. xiii. The preposition. xiv. The interjection. xv. Letters in grammar. xvi. The syllable. xvii. Metrical feet. xviii. Accents. xix. Accent marks. xx. Punctuated clauses. xxi. Critical signs. xxii. Common shorthand signs. xxiii.

1 For an account of some of the manuscript systems of presenting tables of contents of the *Etymologies* see B.-J. Schröder, *Titel und Text: Zur Entwicklung lateinischer Gedichtüberschriften. Mit Untersuchungen zu . . . Inhaltsverzeichnissen . . .* Untersuchungen zur antiken Literatur und Geschichte, vol. 54 (Berlin, 1999). See also Reydellet 1966: 388 *et passim*.

Signs used in law. xxiv. Military signs. xxv. Epistolary codes. xxvi. Finger signals. xxvii. Orthography. xxviii. Analogy. xxix. Etymology. xxx. Glosses. xxxi. Differentiation. xxxii. Barbarism. xxxiii. Solecisms. xxxiv. Faults. xxxv. Metaplasm. xxxvi. Schemas. xxxvii. Tropes. xxxviii. Prose. xxxix. Meters. xl. The fable. xli. History. xlii. The first authors of histories. xliii. The utility of history. xliv. The kinds of history.

Book II: RHETORIC AND DIALECTIC. i. Rhetoric and its name. ii. The founders of the art of rhetoric. iii. The term 'orator' and the parts of rhetoric. iv. The three kinds of arguments. v. The two states of legal arguments. vi. The tripartite dispute. vii. The four parts of an oration. viii. The five types of cases. ix. Syllogisms. x. Law. xi. The maxim. xii. Confirmation and refutation. xiii. Prosopopoeia. xiv. Ethopoeia. xv. Kinds of questions. xvi. Style. xvii. The three registers of speaking. xviii. Clause, phrase, and sentence. xix. Faults to be avoided in letters, words, and expressions. xx. Combinations of words. xxi. Figures of words and expressions. xxii. Dialectic. xxiii. The difference between the arts of rhetoric and dialectic. xxiv. The definition of philosophy. xxv. Porphyry's *Isagoge.* xxvi. Aristotle's categories. xxvii. The *De interpretatione.* xxviii. Logical syllogisms. xxix. The division of definitions abbreviated from the book by Marius Victorinus. xxx. Topics. xxxi. Opposites.

Book III: MATHEMATICS. Mathematics. i. Words belonging to the study of arithmetic. ii. Originators of mathematics. iii. What a number is. iv. What numbers do for us. v. The first division, of even and odd numbers. vi. The second division of all numbers. vii. The third division of all numbers. viii. The differences between arithmetic, geometry, and music. ix. How many infinite numbers exist. x. The inventors of geometry, and its name. xi. The fourfold division of geometry. xii. Geometrical figures. xiii. Geometric numbers. [xiv. Exposition of figures illustrated below.]
MUSIC. xv. Music and its name. xvi. The inventors of music. xvii. The power of music. xviii. The three parts of music. xix. The threefold division of music. xx. The first division of music, which is called harmonic. xxi. The second division, which is called *organicus.* xxii. The third division of music, which is called rhythmic. xxiii. Musical numbers.

ASTRONOMY. xxiv. The name of astronomy. xxv. The inventors of astronomy. xxvi. Those who established astronomy. xxvii. The difference between astronomy and astrology. xxviii. Astronomical reckoning. xxix. The world and its name. xxx. The shape of the world. xxxi. The sky and its name. xxxii. The position of the celestial sphere. xxxiii. The movement of this same sphere. xxxiv. The course of the same sphere. xxxv. The speed of the sky. xxxvi. The axis of heaven. xxxvii. The celestial polar regions. xxxviii. The poles of the heavens. xxxix. The vault of heaven. xl. The doorways of heaven. xli. The twin faces of the sky. xlii. The four parts of heaven. xliii. The hemispheres. xliv. The five circles of heaven. xlv. The circle of the zodiac. xlvi. The bright circle. xlvii. The size of the sun. xlviii. The size of the moon. xlix. The nature of the sun. l. The course of the sun. li. The effect of the sun. lii. The path of the sun. liii. The light of the moon. liv. The shapes of the moon. lv. The interlunar interval. lvi. The path of the moon. lvii. The proximity of the moon to the earth. lviii. Eclipse of the sun. lix. Eclipse of the moon. lx. The differences between stars, star clusters, and constellations. lxi. The light of the stars. lxii. The location of the stars. lxiii. The course of the stars. lxiv. The changing course of the stars. lxv. The distances between the stars. lxvi. The orbital number of the stars. lxvii. Planets. lxviii. Precession and antegrade motion of stars. lxix. Recession or retrograde motion of stars. lxx. The standing of stars. lxxi. The names of the stars and the reasons for these names.

Book IV: MEDICINE. i. Medicine. ii. The term 'medicine.' iii. The inventors of medicine. iv. The three schools of medicine. v. The four humors of the body. vi. Acute illnesses. vii. Chronic illnesses. viii. Illnesses that appear on the surface of the body. ix. Remedies and medications. x. Medical books. xi. The instruments of physicians. xii. Scents and ointments. xiii. The foundations of medicine.

Book V: LAWS AND TIMES. i. The originators of laws. ii. Divine laws and human laws. iii. How jurisprudence, laws, and customs differ from each other. iv. What natural law is. v. What civil law is. vi. What the law of nations is. vii. What military law is. viii. What public law is. ix. What quirital law is. x. What a law is. xi. What popular resolutions (i.e. plebiscites) are. xii. What a senate decree is. xiii. What an order and an edict are.

xiv. What a response of jurists is. xv. Consular and tribunitial laws. xvi. Replete law. xvii. Rhodian laws. xviii. Private statutes. xix. What a law is capable of. xx. Why a law is enacted. xxi. What sort of law should be made. xxii. Cases. xxiii. Witnesses. xxiv. Legal instruments. xxv. Property. xxvi. Crimes written in the law. xxvii. Punishments drawn up in the laws. xxviii. The word for 'chronicles.' xxix. Moments and hours. xxx. Days. xxxi. Night. xxxii. The week. xxxiii. Months. xxxiv. Solstices and equinoxes. xxxv. The seasons of the year. xxxvi. Years. xxxvii. Olympiads, lustrums, and jubilees. xxxviii. Periods and ages. xxxix. A description of historical periods.

Book VI: BOOKS AND ECCLESIASTICAL OFFICES. i. The Old and New Testament. ii. The writers and names of the Sacred Books. iii. Libraries. iv. Translators. v. The one who first brought books to Rome. vi. Those who established libraries among us Christians. vii. Those who have written many things. viii. The types of literary works. ix. Wax tablets. x. Papyrus sheets. xi. Parchment. xii. Bookmaking. xiii. The terminology of books. xiv. Copyists and their tools. xv. Canon-tables of the Gospels. xvi. The canons of Councils. xvii. The Easter cycle. xviii. The other liturgical feasts. xix. Offices.

Book VII: GOD, ANGELS, AND SAINTS. i. God. ii. The Son of God. iii. The Holy Spirit. iv. The Trinity. v. Angels. vi. People who received their name from a certain presaging. vii. The patriarchs. viii. The prophets. ix. The apostles. x. Other names in the Gospel. xi. Martyrs. xii. Clerics. xiii. Monks. xiv. Other faithful people.

Book VIII: THE CHURCH AND SECTS. i. The Church and the synagogue. ii. Religion and faith. iii. Heresy and schism. iv. Heresies of the Jews. v. Christian heresies. vi. Pagan philosophers. vii. Poets. viii. Sibyls. ix. Magicians. x. Pagans. xi. Gods of the heathens.

Book IX: LANGUAGES, NATIONS, REIGNS, THE MILITARY, CITIZENS, FAMILY RELATIONSHIPS. i. The languages of nations. ii. The names of nations. iii. Reigns and terms for military matters. iv. Citizens. v. Family relationships and their degrees. vi. Paternal and maternal relatives. vii. Marriages.

Book X: VOCABULARY. Certain terms for human beings.

Book XI: THE HUMAN BEING AND PORTENTS. i. Human beings and their parts. ii. The ages of human beings. iii. Portents. iv. Metamorphoses.

Book XII: ANIMALS. i. Livestock and beasts of burden. ii. Beasts. iii. Small animals. iv. Snakes. v. Vermin. vi. Fish. vii. Birds. viii. Tiny flying animals.

Book XIII. THE COSMOS AND ITS PARTS. i. The world. ii. Atoms. iii. Elements. iv. The sky. v. Parts of the sky. vi. The circles of heaven. vii. Air and clouds. viii. Thunder. ix. Lightning. x. The rainbow and phenomena of the clouds. xi. Winds. xii. Waters. xiii. Different kinds of water. xiv. The sea. xv. The Ocean. xvi. The Mediterranean Sea. xvii. Gulfs of the sea. xviii. Tides and straits. xix. Lakes and pools. xx. The abyss. xxi. Rivers. xxii. Floods.

Book XIV: THE EARTH AND ITS PARTS. i. The earth. ii. The globe. iii. Asia. iv. Europe. v. Libya. vi. Islands. vii. Promontories. viii. Mountains and other terms for landforms. ix. The lower regions.

Book XV: BUILDINGS AND FIELDS. i. Cities. Famous towns, and which men or women established them. ii. Public buildings. iii. Dwelling-places. iv. Sacred buildings. v. Repositories. vi. Workplaces. vii. Entranceways. viii. The parts of buildings. ix. Fortifications. x. Tents. xi. Sepulchers. xii. Rural buildings. xiii. Fields. xiv. The boundaries of fields. xv. The measures of fields. xvi. Roads.

Book XVI: STONES AND METALS. i. Dust and dirt clods. ii. Earthy materials derived from water. iii. Common stones. iv. More important stones. v. Marble. vi. Gems. vii. Green gems. viii. Red gems. ix. Purple gems. x White gems. xi. Black gems. xii. Varicolored gems. xiii. Crystalline gems. xiv. Fiery gems. xv. Golden gems. xvi. Glass. xvii. Metals. xviii. Gold. xix. Silver. xx. Bronze. xxi. Iron. xxii. Lead. xxiii. Tin. xxiv. Electrum. xxv. Weights. xxvi. Measures. xxvii. Symbols.

Book XVII: RURAL MATTERS. i. Authors on rural matters. ii. The cultivation of fields. iii. Fruits of the Earth. iv.

Legumes. v. Vines. vi. Trees. vii. Specific names of trees. viii. Aromatic trees. ix. Aromatic or common plants. x. Garden vegetables. xi. Aromatic garden plants.

Book XVIII: WAR AND GAMES. i. War. ii. Triumphs. iii. Military standards. iv. War-trumpets. v. Arms. vi. Swords. vii. Spears. viii. Arrows. ix. Quivers. x. Slings. xi. The battering ram. xii. Shields. xiii. Cuirasses. xiv. Helmets. xv. The Forum. xvi. Spectacles. xvii. Gymnastic games. xviii. Types of gymnastics. xix. The jump. xx. The race. xxi. The throw. xxii. Feats of strength. xxiii. Wrestling. xxiv. The palestra. xxv. Competitions. xxvi. Types of competitions. xxvii. Circus games. xxviii. The circus. xxix. The apparatus. xxx. The turning-posts. xxxi. The obelisk. xxxii. The starting-gates. xxxiii. Charioteers. xxxiv. The team of four. xxxv. The chariot. xxxvi. The horses with which we race. xxxvii. The seven laps. xxxviii. The riders. xxxix. Horse-vaulters. xl. Foot racers. xli. The colors worn by horses. xlii. The theater. xliii. The stage building. xliv. The orchestra. xlv. Tragedians. xlvi. Writers of comedy xlvii. Stage musicians. xlviii. Actors. xlix. Mimes. l. Dancers. li. What should be performed under which patron. lii. The amphitheater. liii. The equestrian game. liv. Net-fighters. lv. Pursuers. lvi. Ensnarers. lvii. Skirmishers. lviii. Combat to the death. lix. The performance of these games. lx. The gaming-board. lxi. Dice-tumblers. lxii. Gaming counters. lxiii. Dice. lxiv. The figurative senses of dicing. lxv. Dicing terms. lxvi. The casting of dice. lxvii. The moving of counters. lxviii. The banning of dicing. lxix. Ball games.

Book XIX: SHIPS, BUILDINGS, AND CLOTHING. i. Ships. ii. Parts of the ship and its equipment. iii. Sails. iv. Ropes. v. Nets. vi. The metalworkers' forge. vii. Metalworkers' tools. viii. The craft of building. ix. Siting. x. Construction. xi. Decoration. xii. Paneled ceilings. xiii. Wall panels. xiv. Mosaics. xv. Molding. xvi. Pictures. xvii. Colorings. xviii. Tools for building. xix. Woodworkers. xx. The invention of clothmaking. xxi. Priestly vestments according to the Law. xxii. The different kinds of clothing and their names. xxiii. The typical costumes of certain peoples. xxiv. Men's outer garments. xxv. Women's outer garments. xxvi. Bedspreads and other cloths that we use. xxvii. Wool. xxviii. Colorings for cloth. xxix. Tools for clothmaking. xxx. Ornaments. xxxi. Women's head ornaments. xxxii. Rings. xxxiii. Belts. xxxiv. Footwear.

Book XX: [PROVISIONS AND VARIOUS IMPLEMENTS.] i. Tables. ii. Foodstuffs. iii. Drink. iv. Dishes for food. v. Drinking vessels. vi. Wine and water vessels. vii. Vessels for oil. viii. Cooking vessels. ix. Storage containers. x. Lamp vessels. xi. Beds and chairs. xii. Vehicles. xiii. Other implements that we use. xiv. Rural implements. xv. Garden implements. xvi. Equestrian equipment.

For conventions used in the translation
see Note to the reader, pp. xi–xii

Book I

Grammar (De grammatica)

i. Discipline and art (De disciplina et arte) 1. A discipline (*disciplina*) takes its name from 'learning' (*discere*), whence it can also be called 'knowledge' (*scientia*). Now 'know' (*scire*) is named from 'learn' (*discere*), because none of us knows unless we have learned. A discipline is so named in another way, because 'the full thing is learned' (*discitur plena*). 2. And an art (*ars*, gen. *artis*) is so called because it consists of strict (*artus*) precepts and rules. Others say this word is derived by the Greeks from the word ἀρετή, that is, 'virtue,' as they termed knowledge. 3. Plato and Aristotle would speak of this distinction between an art and a discipline: an art consists of matters that can turn out in different ways, while a discipline is concerned with things that have only one possible outcome. Thus, when something is expounded with true arguments, it will be a discipline; when something merely resembling the truth and based on opinion is treated, it will have the name of an art.

ii. The seven liberal disciplines (De septem liberalibus disciplinis) 1. There are seven disciplines of the liberal arts. The first is grammar, that is, skill in speaking. The second is rhetoric, which, on account of the brilliance and fluency of its eloquence, is considered most necessary in public proceedings. The third is dialectic, otherwise known as logic, which separates the true from the false by very subtle argumentation. 2. The fourth is arithmetic, which contains the principles and classifications of numbers. The fifth is music, which consists of poems and songs. 3. The sixth is geometry, which encompasses the measures and dimensions of the earth. The seventh is astronomy, which covers the law of the stars.

iii. The common letters of the alphabet (De litteris communibus) 1. The common letters of the alphabet are the primary elements of the art of grammar, and are used by scribes and accountants. The teaching of these letters is, as it were, the infancy of grammar, whence Varro also calls this discipline 'literacy' (*litteratio*; Funaioli 235). Indeed, letters are tokens of things, the signs of words, and they have so much force that the utterances of those who are absent speak to us without a voice, [for they present words through the eyes, not through the ears]. 2. The use of letters was invented for the sake of remembering things, which are bound by letters lest they slip away into oblivion. With so great a variety of information, not everything could be learned by hearing, nor retained in the memory. 3. Letters (*littera*) are so called as if the term were *legitera*, because they provide a road (*iter*) for those who are reading (*legere*), or because they are repeated (*iterare*) in reading.

4. The Latin and Greek letters seem to be derived from the Hebrew, for among the Hebrews the first letter is called 'aleph,' and then 'alpha' was derived from it by the Greeks due to its similar pronunciation, whence **A** among Latin speakers. A transliterator fashioned the letter of one language from the similar sound of another language (i.e. derived the names and shapes of letters of similar sound from the "earlier" language); hence we can know that the Hebrew language is the mother of all languages and letters. But the Hebrews use twenty-two characters, following the twenty-two books of the Old Testament; the Greeks use twenty-four. Latin speakers, falling between these two languages, have twenty-three characters. 5. The letters of the Hebrews started with the Law transmitted by Moses. Those of the Syrians and Chaldeans began with Abraham, so that they agree in the number of characters and in their sounds with the Hebrew letters and differ only in their shapes. Queen Isis, daughter of Inachus, devised the Egyptian letters when she came from Greece into Egypt, and passed them on to the Egyptians. Among the Egyptians, however, the priests used some letters and the common people used others. The priestly letters are known as ἱερός (sacred), the common letters, πάνδεμος (common).

The Phoenicians first discovered the use of Greek letters, whence Lucan (*Civil War* 3.220):

> If the report is trustworthy, the Phoenicians were the first to dare to indicate by rudimentary shapes a sound meant to endure.

6. Hence it is that the chapter headings of books are written with Phoenician scarlet, since it is from the Phoenicians that the letters had their origin. Cadmus, son of Agenor, first brought seventeen Greek letters from Phoenicia into Greece: Α, Β, Γ, Δ, Ε, Ζ, Ι, Κ, Λ, Μ, Ν, Ο, Π, Ρ, Σ, Τ, Φ. Palamedes added three more to these at the time of the Trojan War: Η, Χ, Ω. After him the lyricist Simonides added three others: Ψ, Ξ, Θ.

7. Pythagoras of Samos first formed the letter Υ as a symbol of human life. Its lower stem signifies the first stage of life, an uncertain age indeed, which has not yet given itself to vices or to virtues. The branching into two, which is above, begins with adolescence: the right part of it is arduous, but leads toward a blessed life; the left is easier, but leads to death and destruction. Concerning this Persius (*Satires* 3.56) speaks thus:

> And where the letter has spread out into Samian branches it has shown you the way that rises by means of the right-hand path.

8. There are also five mystical letters among the Greeks. The first is Υ, which signifies human life, concerning which we have just spoken. The second is Θ, which [signifies] death, for the judges used to put this same letter down against the names of those whom they were sentencing to execution. And it is named 'theta' after the term θάνατος, that is, 'death.' Whence also it has a spear through the middle, that is, a sign of death. Concerning this a certain verse says:

> How very unlucky before all others, the letter theta.

9. The third, Τ, shows the figure of the cross of the Lord, whence it is also interpreted as a symbol in Hebrew. Concerning this letter, it was said to an angel in Ezekiel (9: 4): "Go through the midst of Jerusalem, and mark a thau upon the foreheads of the men that sigh, and mourn."[1] The remaining two mystical letters, the first and the last, Christ claims for himself; himself the beginning, himself the end, he says (Apocalypse 22:13): "I am Alpha and Omega," for by moving towards each other in turn, Α rolls on all the way to Ω, and Ω bends back to Α, so that the Lord might show in himself both the movement of the beginning to the end, and the movement of the end to the beginning.

10. All the letters in Greek compose words and also make numbers, for they use the letter alpha as the number 'one.' And when they write beta, they mean 'two'; when they write gamma, they mean 'three' in their numbers; when they write delta, they mean 'four' in their numbers – and so every letter corresponds to a number for the Greeks. 11. Latin speakers, however, do not assign numbers to the letters, but only use them to form words, with the exception of the letters **I**, and **X**, which both signifies the cross by its shape, and stands for the number ten.[2]

iv. The Latin letters (De litteris latinis)[3] 1. The nymph Carmentis first brought the Latin letters to the Italians. She is called Carmentis because she would sing in songs (*carmen*) of things to come, but she is properly called Nicostrate. 2. Letters are either common or liberal. 'Common (*communis*) letters' are so called because many people employ them for common use, in order to write and to read. 'Liberal (*liberalis*) letters' are so called because only those who write books (*liber*), and who know how to speak and compose correctly, know them. 3. There are two types of letter, for they are first divided into two groups, vowels and consonants. Vowels are letters that are released in various ways through the straightforward opening of the throat, without any contact. And they are called 'vowels' (*vocalis*), because they make a complete 'vocal sound' (*vox*, gen. *vocis*) on their own, and on their own they may make a syllable with no adjoining consonant. Consonants are letters that are produced by various motions of the tongue or a compression of the lips. And they are called 'consonants' (*consonans*) because they do not produce sound by themselves, but rather 'sound together' (*consonare*) with an adjoining vowel. 4. Consonants are divided into two groups: semivowels and mutes. Semivowels (*semivocalis*) are so called because they take a certain half (*semis*) of their quality from vowels. Their letter-names, accordingly, begin with the vowel **E**, and end in their natural sound [as **F**, **L**, **M** etc.]. The mutes (*mutus*, i.e. the voiced stops) are so called because, without vowels joined to them, they are never released. In fact, if you were to remove the sound of the following vowel from them,

1 For the Vulgate *thau* the New Revised Standard Version translates "mark." The last letter of the Hebrew alphabet, 'taw,' parallel to the Greek 'tau,' was shaped like an X in ancient script and came to have the meaning "mark, sign, symbol."

2 Isidore disregards here the numeral-letters **V**, **L**, **C**, **D**, **M**.

3 Isidore uses the word 'letter' (*littera*) to refer both to the written character and to the sound for which it stands.

the sound of the letter will be a blocked murmur [as **B**, **G**, **D**, etc.]. Furthermore, vowels and semivowels and mutes were called by the ancients sounds (*sonus*) and semisounds (*semisonus*) and non-sounds (*insonus*).

5. Among the vowels, **I** and **U** signify different things to the grammarians. 6. Now they are vowels, and now semivowels, and now medials (i.e. glides). They are vowels because they make syllables when they are positioned alone or when they are joined to consonants. They are considered consonants in that they sometimes have a vowel set down after them in the same syllable, as *Ianus*, *vates*, and they are considered as consonants.[4] 7. They are [also] called medials because only they naturally have a medial sound, as *illius*, *unius*. They sound more fully when joined to others, as *Ianus*, *Vanus*. They sound one way when alone and another when adjoined. On this account, **I** is sometimes called twofold, because whenever it is found between two vowels, it is taken as two consonants, as *Troia*, for there its sound is geminated. 8. Further, the letter **V** is sometimes nothing, because in some places it is neither vowel nor consonant, as in *quis* (who). It is not a vowel, because **I** follows, and it is not a consonant, because **Q** precedes. And thus when it is neither vowel nor consonant, it is undoubtedly nothing. This same sound is called *digamma* by the Greeks, when it is joined to itself or to other vowels. And it is called *digamma* because it has the double shape of the letter **F**, which looks like two gammas (i.e. one Γ atop another). On account of this resemblance the grammarians would call the vowels conjoined in this way *digamma*, as in *votum*, *virgo*.

9. Among the semivowels, some are called liquids (*liquidus*) because sometimes, when placed after other consonants in one syllable, they are deficient and excluded from the meter.[5] In Latin there are two sounds which melt (*liquescere*) like this, **L** and **R**, as in *fragor* (crash), *flatus* (breathing). The others, **M** and **N**, are liquid in Greek, as in *Mnestheus*.

10. The old script consisted of seventeen Latin letters, and they are called legitimate (*legitimus*) for this reason: they either begin with the vowel **E** and end in a mute sound, if they are consonants,[6] or because they begin with their own sound and end in the vowel **E**, if they are mutes [and they are **A**, **B**, **C**, **D**, **E**, **F**, **G**, **I**, **L**, **M**, **N**, **O**, **P**, **R**, **S**, **T** and **U**].

11. The letter **H** was added afterwards for aspiration alone, whence it is considered by many to be a breathing, not a letter, and it is called a mark of aspiration because it elevates the voice, for aspiration is a sound that is raised more fully. Its opposite is *prosodia*, a sound accented levelly. 12. Salvius, the schoolmaster, first added the letter **K** to Latin, so as to make a distinction in sound between the two letters **C** and **Q**. This letter is called superfluous because, with the exception of the word 'Kalends,' it is considered unnecessary; we express all such sounds by means of **C**. 13. Neither Greek nor Hebrew has a sound corresponding to our letter **Q**, for with the exception of Latin no other language possesses this letter. It did not exist earlier; hence it is also called superfluous because the ancients wrote all such sounds with a **C**.

14. The letter **X** did not exist in Latin until the time of Augustus, [and it was fitting for it to come into existence at that time, in which the name of Christ became known, which is written using the letter which makes the sign of the cross],[7] but they used to write **CS** in its place, whence **X** is called a double letter, because it is used for **CS**, so that it takes its name from the composition of these same letters. 15. Latin borrowed two letters from Greek, **Y** and **Z**, especially for the sake of writing Greek words. These letters were not written by the Romans until the time of Augustus, but two **S**s were used for **Z**, as in *hilarissat*, and they would write **I** for **Y**.

16. There are three things associated with each letter: its name, how it is called; its shape, by which character it is designated; and its function, whether it is taken as vocalic or consonantal. Some people add 'order,' that is, what does it precede and what does it follow, as **A** is first and **B** following – for **A** is the first letter among all peoples, because it first initiates voice in babies as they are being born. 17. Indeed, nations assigned the names of the letters from the sounds in their own languages, when the sounds of the mouth were noted and distinguished. After they paid attention to these sounds, they imposed both names and shapes on them. The shapes they formed partly by whim, and partly from the sound of the letters;

4 The Romans used a single letter *i* to represent both the vowel /i/ and the glide /y/, and the single letter *u* (= *v*) for both /u/ and /w/. The letters *u* and *v* are not distinct in the Latin alphabet.

5 In the scansion of Latin poetry, consonants followed by *l* or *r* may be treated as if they were single consonants.

6 From what Isidore said above, iv.4, he should have written "and end in their natural sound, if they are semivowels . . ."

7 Christian scribes abbreviated the name of Christ as Xp̄s (for Greek chi-rho-sigma) and similar forms.

for instance **I** and **O** – the first one is a thin sound, as it were, thus a slender twig, and the other a fat sound, thus a full shape.

Now nature has assigned the function, and human will has assigned the order and the macron. 18. The ancients counted the macron among the letter characters, and it is called 'macron' (*apex*, lit. "peak") because it is far "from the foot" (*a* + *pes*) of the letter, and is placed at the top of the letter. It is a line drawn horizontally and levelly above the letter. [But a letter character (*figura*) is that with which a whole letter is written.]

v. Grammar (De grammatica) 1. Grammar is the knowledge of speaking correctly, and is the origin and foundation of liberal letters. Among the disciplines this was invented after the letters of the alphabet, so that through it those who have already learned the letters know the method of speaking correctly. 'Grammar' takes its name from letters, for the Greeks call letters γράμματα. 2. It is truly called an art, because it consists of strict (*artus*) rules and precepts. Others say that the word 'art' is derived by the Greeks from ἀρετή, that is, 'virtue,' which they called knowledge. 3. 'Oratory' (*oratio*) is so called as if it were 'method of speech' (*oris ratio*), for 'to orate' (*orare*) is to speak and to say. Oratory is the joining of words with sense. But a joining without sense is not oratory, because then there is no method in the speaking. Oratory is made up of sense, voice and letters. 4. Thirty divisions of the grammatical art are enumerated by some, that is: the eight parts of speech, enunciation, letters, syllables, feet, accent, punctuation, critical signs, spelling, analogy, etymology, glosses, differentiation, barbarisms, solecisms, faults, metaplasms, schemes, tropes, prose, meter, tales, and histories.

vi. The parts of speech (De partibus orationis) 1. Aristotle first proposed two parts of speech, noun and verb; then Donatus defined eight (*Ars Grammatica*, ed. Keil 4.372). But all parts revert back to these two principal ones, that is, to the noun and verb, which signify the person and the act. The others are ancillary and derive their origin from these two. 2. For the pronoun is taken from the noun, whose function it assumes, as in 'an orator . . . he' (*orator ille*). The adverb is taken from the noun, as in 'a learned one, learnedly' (*doctus, docte*). The participle is taken from the noun and the verb, as in 'I read, a reading one' (*lego, legens*). The conjunction and preposition, however, and the interjection, occur in connection with these other parts. For this reason, some people define five parts of speech, because these latter three are superfluous.

vii. The noun (De nomine)[8] 1. The noun (*nomen*) is so called as if it were 'denoter' (*notamen*), because by its designation it makes things known (*noscere*, ppl. *notus*) to us. Indeed, unless you know its name (*nomen*), the knowledge of a thing perishes.

Proper nouns (*proprium nomen*) are so called because they are specific; they signify one single person only. There are four types of proper nouns: the praenomen, the name, the cognomen, and the agnomen. The praenomen is so called because it is placed before (*prae*) the name, as 'Lucius,' 'Quintus.' 2. The name (*nomen*) is so called because it identifies (*notare*) the clan, as 'Cornelius,' for all Corneliuses are in this clan. The cognomen (*cognomen*), because it is conjoined (*coniungere*) to the name, as 'Scipio.' The agnomen (*agnomen*) is an 'acquired name' (*accedens nomen*), as in 'Metellus Creticus,' so named because he subdued Crete: the agnomen comes from some outside cause. But it too is commonly called a cognomen, because it is added to the name for the sake of recognition (*cognitio*), or because it is used 'with the name' (*cum nomine*).

3. Appellative nouns (*appellativum nomen*) are so called because they are common and make reference to many things (cf. *appellare*, "name"). They are divided into twenty-eight types. Of these the corporeal (*corporalis*) nouns are so called because they are either seen or touched, as 'sky,' 'earth.' 4. The incorporeal (*incorporalis*) nouns, because they lack a body (*corpus*), so that they cannot be seen or touched, as 'truth,' 'justice.' 5. The general (*generalis*) nouns, because they denote many things, as 'animal,' for a human and a horse and a bird are animals. 6. The specific (*specialis*) nouns, because they indicate a sub-class, as 'man,' for a human being is a type (*species*) of animal. 7. Primary (*principalis*) nouns, because they hold a primary

8 Following traditional grammarians, Isidore uses the term *nomen* to refer to both nouns and adjectives, and also to mean "name." The noun vs. adjective distinction is less clear-cut in Latin than in English because adjectives standing alone commonly function as substantives: *bonus*, "good" or "a good man." Further, both nouns and adjectives have case endings. We translate *nomen* as "noun" or "adjective" or "name" or even "word" where appropriate.

position, and are not derived from another word, as 'mountain,' 'fount.' 8. Derivative (*derivativus*) nouns, because they are derived from another noun, as 'mountainous region' (*montanus*) from 'mountain' (*mons*). 9. Diminutive (*diminutivus*) nouns, because they diminish the meaning, as 'Greekling' (*Graeculus*), 'little scholar' (*scholasticulus*). 10. Some nouns are called 'diminutive in sound' (*sono diminutivus*), because they sound like diminutive nouns, but are conceptually primary nouns, as 'table' (*tabula*), 'fable' (*fabula*). 11. 'Entirely Greek' (*totus Graecus*) nouns, because they are declined entirely in the Greek manner, as *Callisto* – for both Greek and Latin decline it in the same way. 12. 'Entirely Latin' (*totus Latinus*) nouns, because they are turned entirely into Latin. Greek has 'Odysseus,' and Latin 'Ulysses.' 13. Medial (*medius*) nouns are so called because they are partly Greek and partly Latin. These are also called 'mongrel' (*nothus*), because they corrupt the final syllables while the previous syllables stay the same, as in Greek, for example, 'Alexandros,' 'Menandros,' while we (Latin speakers) have 'Alexander,' 'Menander.' They are called 'mongrel' inasmuch as whoever is begotten of unequal classes is called 'mongrel.' 14. Synonymous (*synonymus*) nouns, that is, plurinomial (*plurinomius*), because there is a single meaning shared by 'many nouns' (*plura nomina*), as *terra*, *humus*, and *tellus* (i.e. all meaning "earth"). Indeed, these are all the same thing. 15. Homonymous (*homonymus*) nouns, that is uninomial (*uninomius*), because there is a multiple meaning in one (*unus*) noun, as *tumulus*, which is in one context a low hill, in another context rising (*tumere*) ground, and in another context a grave-mound – for there are diverse meanings in the one noun. 16. The relational (*relativus*) nouns are so called because they are defined in relation to another person, as 'teacher,' 'master,' 'father.' 17. Words defined as somehow related to something by way of their opposition of meaning are also called relational, as 'right' – for 'right' cannot be defined unless there is 'left.' 18. Next, the qualitative (*qualitas*) adjectives are so called because through them some quality is shown, as 'wise,' 'beautiful,' 'rich.' 19. Quantitative (*quantitas*) adjectives are so called because they are defined by measure, as 'long,' 'short.' 20. Patronymics (*patronymicus*) are so called because they are derived from fathers (*pater*), as 'Tydides,' son of Tydeus, 'Aeneius,' son of Aeneas, although they may also be derived from mothers and from more remote ancestors. 21. 'Ctetic' (*cteticus*) adjectives, that is possessive, from possession, as the 'Evandrian' sword. 22. Epithets (*epitheton*), which in Latin are called either adjectives (*adiectivus*) or additions, because they are 'added to' (*adicere*, ppl. *adiectus*) nouns to complete the meaning, as 'great,' 'learned.' You may add them to persons, as 'a great philosopher,' 'a learned man,' and the sense is complete. 23. Agent (*actualis*) nouns derive from the action (*actus*), as 'leader,' 'king,' 'runner,' 'nurse,' 'orator.' Ethnic (*gens*) adjectives come from the ethnic group (*gens*), as 'Greek,' 'Roman.' 24. Adjectives of nationality (*patrius*) come from a native land (*patria*), as 'Athenian,' 'Theban.' Local (*locus*) adjectives from the place (*locus*), as 'suburban.' 25. Verbal (*verbialis*) nouns are so called because they come from the verb, as 'reader' (*lector*, from *legere*, ppl. *lectus*, "read"). Participials (*participalis*), which have the same form as participles, as 'the reading one' (*legens*). 26. Quasi-verbal (*verbis similis*) nouns, so called from their similarity to the verb, as *contemplator* – for this word is both a verb in the imperative mood, future tense, and a noun, because it takes the comparative degree.[9] All these types of appellative nouns come from the 'naming quality' (*appellatio*) of nouns.

27. A second division is the comparison of adjectives. 'Comparison' (*comparatio*) is so called because it prefers one thing in comparison with another. There are three degrees of comparison: positive, comparative, and superlative. 'Positive' (*positivus*) is so called because it is placed (*ponere*, ppl. *positus*) first in the degrees of comparison, as 'learned' (*doctus*). 'Comparative' (*comparativus*) is so named because when compared (*comparatus*) with the positive it surpasses it, as 'more learned' (*doctior*) – for he knows more than someone who is merely learned. 'Superlative' (*superlativus*) is so called because it completely surpasses (*superferre*, ppl. *superlatus*) the comparative, as 'most learned' (*doctissimus*), for he knows more than someone who is merely *doctior*.

28. 'Gendered nouns' (*genus*) are so called because they generate (*generare*), as masculine and feminine. Other nouns are not gendered, but analogy and tradition

9 The form *contemplator* is ambiguous, being either the future imperative of the deponent verb *contemplor* ("observe") or the agent noun (i.e. 'observer') formed from the same verb. Isidore here uses a formal criterion to define a noun: its taking the case endings of a declension, as the genitive of *contemplator*, for example, is *contemplatoris*. Apparently by mistake he confusingly shifts here to the other sense of *nomen*, 'adjective,' as only adjectives take the comparative degree.

have assigned them gender. A neuter (*neuter*, lit. "neither") noun is so named because it is neither one nor the other, that is, neither masculine nor feminine. A common (*communis*) noun is so called because one noun has a share in both genders, as *hic canis* ("this male dog") and *haec canis* ("this female dog"). 29. The opposite of this is an epicene (*epicoenos*) noun, because it expresses either sex with a single gender, as in *hic piscis* ("this fish"). It is of uncertain sex, because it can be distinguished neither by nature nor by sight, but only by expert discernment. The inclusive (*omne genus*) noun is so named because it serves for all genders: for masculine and feminine, neuter, common – for all (*omnis*).

30. 'Grammatical number' (*numerus*) is so named because it shows whether a noun is singular or plural. 'Morphological form' (*figura*), because nouns are either simple or compound. 31. Cases (*casus*) are so called from 'having an ending' (*cadere*, ppl. *casus*): through the cases inflected nouns are varied and have their endings. The nominative (*nominativus*) case is so called because through it we name (*nominare*) something, as *hic magister* ("this teacher"). The genitive (*genetivus*), because through it we find the descent of someone, as *huius magistri filius* ("this teacher's son"), or because we assign a thing to someone, as *huius magistri liber* ("this teacher's book"). 32. The dative (*dativus*), because through it we show that we give (*dare*, ppl. *datus*) something to someone, as *da huic magistro* ("give to this teacher"). The accusative (*accusativus*), because through it we accuse someone, as *accuso hunc magistrum* ("I accuse this teacher"). The vocative (*vocativus*), because through it we call (*vocare*) someone, as *O magister* ("hey, teacher!"). Ablative (*ablativus*), because through it we indicate that we take away (*auferre*, ppl. *ablatus*) something from someone, as in *aufer a magistro* ("take from the teacher"). 33. Certain nouns and adjectives are called *hexaptota* because they have distinct inflection in six cases, as the word *unus* ("one"). *Pentaptota*, because they are declined in only five cases, as *doctus* ("learned"). *Tetraptota*, because they are only declined in four cases, as *latus* ("side"). *Triptota* because only in three, as *templum* ("temple"). *Diptota*, because only in two, as *Iuppiter* ("Jupiter"). *Monoptota*, because they only use one case, as *frugi* ("thrifty").[10]

viii. The pronoun (De pronomine) 1. The pronoun (*pronomen*) is so named because it is put 'in place of the noun' (*pro vice nominis*), lest the noun itself cause annoyance when it is repeated. When we say, "Vergil wrote the *Bucolics*," we continue with the pronoun, "he (*ipse*) wrote the *Georgics*," and thus the variation in expression both removes annoyance and introduces ornament. 2. Pronouns are either definite or indefinite. Definite (*finitus*) pronouns are so called because they define (*definire*) a certain person, as *ego* ("I"); for you immediately understand this to be me. The indefinite (*infinitus*) ones are so named because the persons referred to are not certain. Indefinite pronouns are used for those who are absent or undetermined, as *quis* ("anyone" (masc. or fem.)), *quae* ("any" (fem.)), *quod* ("any" (neut.)).[11] Some are called 'less than definite' (*minus quam finitus*), since they make mention of a known person, as *ipse* ("he himself"), *iste* ("that one") – for we know who is spoken of. 3. Possessives (*possessivus*) are so called because they show that we possess something, for when I say *meus* ("my"), *tuus* ("your"), I define something as mine, or yours. Correspondent (*relativus*) pronouns are so called because they are said in response (*refero*, ppl. *relatus*) to a question, as "who is?" (*quis est?*) is answered by "he is" (*is est*). Demonstratives (*demonstrativus*), because they have the sense of indicating (*demonstrare*). By them we indicate someone who is present, as *hic, haec, hoc* ("this one" (masc., fem., and neut.)); these three are also called articles. 4. Articles (*articulus*) are so called because they are 'pressed together' (*artare*), that is, they are connected, with nouns, as when we say *hic orator* ("the orator"). There is this difference between the article and the pronoun: it is an article when it is joined to a noun, as *hic sapiens* ("the wise man"). But when it is not joined, then it is a demonstrative pronoun, as *hic et*

10 The terms are derived from Greek numerical prefixes and the root of πτῶσις, "grammatical case." *Unus* has six distinct forms for the six cases in the singular; *doctus* has five forms, with the dative and ablative singular sharing the same form; *latus* has four, with the nominative, accusative, and vocative singular sharing one form; *templum* has three, with the nominative, accusative, and vocative singular sharing one form, and the dative and ablative singular sharing another; *frugi* is "indeclinable," with only the one form. The conception seems to shift with the noun *Iuppiter*, which actually has only the one form, used only in the nominative and vocative; its oblique forms are supplied by the synonymous noun *Iovis*, which itself has four forms.

11 *Quis* is the masculine and feminine substantive form of the indefinite pronoun; *quae* and *quod* are adjectival forms, sometimes used substantively.

haec et hoc ("this one (masc.) and this (fem.) and this (neut)").

5. All pronouns are either primary or derived. Primary (*primogenis*, lit. "born first") are so called because they do not take their origin from elsewhere. There are twenty-one of these. Three are definite: *ego* (I), *tu* (you), *ille* (he). Seven are indefinite: *quis* (who), *qualis* (what sort), *talis* (such), *quantus* (how much), *tantus* (so much), *quotus* (where in order), *totus* (such in order). There are six that are less than definite: *iste* (that one), *ipse* (he himself), *hic* (this one), *is* (he), *idem* (the same one), *se* (oneself, i.e. the 3rd person reflexive). There are five possessives: *meus* (my), *tuus* (your (sing.)), *suus* (his or her or their), *noster* (our), *vester* (your (pl.)). The rest are called derived, because they are derived and compounded from these, as *quis-piam* (whoever), *ali-quis* (someone), and the rest.

ix. The verb (De verbo) 1. The verb (*verbum*) is so called because it resounds by means of reverberation (*verberatus*) in the air, or because this part of speech often 'is involved' (*versare*) in a speech. Moreover, words (*verbum*) are signs of the mental processes with which people show their thoughts to one another in speaking.[12] And just as a noun indicates a person, so a verb indicates the doing or speaking of a person. With respect to the subject of a verb, there is an indication of active or passive. Thus *scribo* ("I write") is what a person is doing. *Scribor* ("I am written") also shows what a person is doing, but in this case a person who is undergoing the action.

2. There are two meanings for the Latin *verbum*: grammatical and rhetorical. The *verbum* (i.e. the verb) of the grammarians conjugates in three tenses: preterit, present and future, as *fecit* ("he did"), *facit* ("he does"), *faciet* ("he will do"). In the case of rhetoricians *verba* ("words") is used of their speech as a whole, as in *verbis bonis nos cepit* ("he captivated us with good words"), *verba bona habuit* ("he had good words"), where what is meant is not only the *verba* that fall into three tenses (i.e. the verbs), but the entire speech.

The qualities of verbs are: derivational forms, moods, conjugations, and voices [and tenses]. 3. 'Derivational forms' (*forma*) of verbs are so called because they inform (*informare*) us about some particular deed, for through them we show what we are doing. The meditative (*meditativus*) is named from the sense of someone intending (*meditari*), as *lecturio* ("I intend to read," formed on *legere*, ppl. *lectus*), that is, "I want to read." Following on from intention, the inchoative (*inchoativus*) verb is so called from its indication of beginning (*inchoare*), as *calesco* ("I become warm," formed on *calere*, "be warm"). The frequentative (*frequentativus*) is so called from acting rather often, as *lectito* ("I read a lot"), *clamito* ("I yell a lot," formed on *clamare*). The derivational forms have a bearing on the meaning, and the moods have a bearing on the inflection. Furthermore, you do not know what the inflection should be unless you have already learned what the meaning is.

4. The moods (*modus*) of the verb are so called from the modality (*quemadmodum*, lit. "in what manner") of their sense. Thus the indicative (*indicativus*) mood is so called because it has the sense of someone indicating, as 'I read' (*lego*). The imperative (*imperativus*), because it has the tone of someone commanding (*imperare*), as 'read!' (*lege*). The optative (*optativus*), because through it we desire (*optare*) to do something, as 'would that I might read' (*utinam legerem*). The subjunctive (*coniunctivus*), because something is joined (*coniungere*) to it, so that the statement will be complete. Thus when you say, "when I yell" (*cum clamem*), the sense is left hanging. But if I say, "when I yell, why do you think I am silent?" (*cum clamem, quare putas quod taceam?*), the sense is complete. 5. The infinitive (*infinitus*) [mood] is so called because, while it defines (*definire*) tenses, it does not define a person of the verb, as 'to yell' (*clamare*), 'to have yelled' (*clamasse*). If you add a person to it – 'I ought, you ought, he ought to yell' (*clamare debeo, debes, debet*) – it becomes a quasi-finite verb. The non-personal (*impersonalis*) is so called because it lacks the person of a noun or pronoun, as 'it is read' (*legitur*): you may add a person, as 'by me, by you, by him' (*a me, a te, ab illo*), and the sense is filled out. But the infinitive mood lacks a marker of person as part of its verb form, while the non-personal lacks a pronoun or noun to mark person.

6. The conjugation (*coniugatio*) is so called because through it many things are joined (*coniungere*) to one root sound. It shows the endings of the future tense, lest through ignorance one should say *legebo* for *legam* ("I will write"). Now the first and second conjugation indicate the future tense by the endings *-bo* and *-bor*, while the third conjugation shows it with *-am* and

12 We translate *verbum* with either of its senses, "verb" or "word," depending on the context; see section 2 below.

-*ar*. 7. The voices (*genus*) of verbs are so named because they 'bring forth' (*gignere*, ppl. *genitus*). Thus you add *r* to the active and it brings forth the passive; conversely, you remove *r* from the passive and it brings forth the active. These are called active (*activus*) verbs because they act (*agere*, ppl. *actus*), as 'I whip' (*verbero*), and passive (*passivus*) verbs because they 'undergo action' (*pati*, ppl. *passus*), as 'I am whipped' (*verberor*); neutral (*neutralis*) verbs, because they neither act nor undergo action, as 'I am lying down' (*iaceo*), 'I am sitting' (*sedeo*) – for if you add the letter *r* to these, they do not sound Latin. Common-voiced (*communis*) verbs are so called because they both act and undergo action, as *amplector* ("I embrace, I am embraced"). Similarly, these, if the letter *r* is removed, are not Latin. Deponent (*deponens*) verbs are so called because they 'set aside' (*deponere*) the passive meaning of their future participles; this form ends in -*dus*, as *gloriandus* ("worthy of boasting").[13]

x. The adverb (De adverbio) 1. The adverb (*adverbium*) is so named because it 'comes near the verb' (*accedere* < *ad-cedere verbum*), as in 'read well' (*bene lege*). 'Well' (*bene*) is the adverb, and 'read' (*lege*) is the verb. Therefore, the adverb is so called because it is always completed when joined to the verb, for a verb by itself has complete sense, as 'I write' (*scribo*). But an adverb without a verb does not have a full meaning, as 'today' (*hodie*). You 'add a verb' (*adicis . . . verbum*) to this, 'I write today' (*hodie scribo*), and with the added verb you have completed the sense.

xi. The participle (De participio) The participle (*participium*) is so called because it takes (*capere*) the functions (*partes*) of both the noun and the verb, as if it were *parti-capium* – for from the noun it takes gender and case, and from the verb tense and meaning, and from both, number and form.

xii. The conjunction (De conjunctione) 1. The conjunction (*coniunctio*) is so called because it 'joins together' (*coniungere*) meanings and phrases, for conjunctions have no force on their own, but in their combining of other words they present, as it were, a certain glue. They either link nouns, as "Augustine and (*et*) Jerome", or verbs, as "he writes and (*et*) he reads." Conjunctions all share a single power: either they join, or they disjoin. 2. Copulative (*copulativus*) conjunctions are so called because they join meaning or persons, as "let's go, you and (*et*) I, to the forum." The *et* joins the meanings. Disjunctive (*disiunctivus*) conjunctions are so called because they disjoin things or persons, as "let's do it, you or (*aut*) I." Subjoined (*subiunctivus*) conjunctions are so called because they are attached behind (*subiungere*), as -*que* ("and"). Thus we say *regique hominique Deoque* ("and for the king and the person and God" – Juvencus, *Gospel Poem*, 1.250); we do not say *que regi, que homini.*

3. Expletive (*expletivus*) conjunctions are so called because they 'fill out' (*explere*) the topic proposed, as in "if you don't want this, 'at least' (*saltim*) do that." Common (*communis*) conjunctions are named thus, because they are placed [and joined] anywhere, as *igitur hoc faciam* ("therefore I will do this"), *hoc igitur faciam* ("this therefore I will do"). 4. Causal (*causalis*) conjunctions are named from the reason (*causa*) that people intend to do something, for example, "I kill him, because (*quia*) he has gold"; the second clause is the reason. Rational (*rationalis*) conjunctions are so called from the reasoning (*ratio*) that someone uses in acting, as, "How may I kill him 'so that' (*ne*) I won't be recognized? By poison or blade?"

xiii. The preposition (De prepositione) The preposition (*praepositio*) is so called because it is placed before (*praeponere*, ppl. *praepositus*) nouns and verbs. Accusative (*accusativus*) and ablative (*ablativus*) prepositions are so called from the cases that they govern. *Loquellares* – so called because they always join to an utterance (*loquella*), that is, to words – have no force when they stand alone, as *di*-, *dis*-. But when joined to a word, they make a word-form, as *diduco* ("I divide"), *distraho* ("I pull apart").

xiv. The interjection (De interjectione) The interjection (*interiectio*) – so called because it is interjected (*intericere*, ppl. *interiectus*), that is, interposed, between

13 In late use the verbal form ending in -*dus*, i.e. the gerundive, became the future passive participle. Both this participle and the gerundive proper are passive in meaning; the literal meaning of *gloriandus* is "worthy of being boasted of." Isidore is right to single out the gerundive as the exception to the general rule for deponent verbs (i.e. passive in form but active in sense), but its difference lies in keeping, not losing, the passive sense gerundives normally have: it is the only part of a deponent verb that has a passive meaning.

meaningful phrases – expresses the emotion of an excited mind, as when *vah* is said by someone exulting, *heu* by someone grieving, *hem* by someone angry, *ei* by someone afraid. These sounds are specific to each language, and are not easily translated into another language.

xv. Letters in grammar (De litteris apud grammaticos) [There are as many of these as there are articulated sounds. And one is called a letter (*littera*), as if the word were *legitera*, because it provides a road (*iter*) for those reading (*legere*), or because it is repeated (*iterare*) in reading.] (See iii.3 above.)

xvi. The syllable (De syllaba) 1. The Greek term 'syllable' (*syllaba*) is called a combination (*conceptio*) or gathering (*complexio*) in Latin. It is named 'syllable' from συλλαμβάνειν τὰ γράμματα, that is, 'to combine letters,' for συλλάμβανειν means "combine." Hence a true syllable is one made up of several letters, for a single vowel is improperly spoken of as a syllable, but not correctly: it should be called not so much a syllable as a marking of time. Syllables are short, long, or common. 2. Short (*brevis*) are so called because they can never be drawn out. Long (*longus*), because they are always drawn out. Common (*communis*), because they are either drawn out or shortened according to the writer's judgment as exigency compels. On this read Donatus.[14] Syllables are called long and short because, due to their varying lengths of sound, they seem to take either a double or single period of time. 'Diphthong' (*dipthongus*) syllables are so called from the Greek word (i.e. from δι-, "double" + φθόγγος, "sound"), because in them two vowels are joined. 3. Of these, we have four true diphthongs: *ae, oe, au, eu. Ei* was in common use only among the ancients.

A syllable is called a semi-foot (*semipes*) by those who analyze meter, because it is half of a metrical foot: since a foot consists of two syllables, a single syllable is half a foot. Dionysius Lintius (i.e. Dionysius Thrax) devised the most appropriate individual patterns for all syllables, and on this account was honored with a statue.

xvii. Metrical feet (De pedibus) 1. Feet (*pes*) are what last for a certain time-span of syllables, and never alter their fixed span. They are called 'feet' because in using them the meters 'walk.' Just as we step with our feet, so the meters also advance, as it were, by means of feet. There are 124 different feet in all: four two-syllable feet, eight three-syllable, sixteen four-syllable, thirty-two five-syllable, and sixty-four six-syllable. Up to four syllables they are called feet; the rest are called syzygies (*syzygia*). 2. These feet have specific reasons for the names by which they are called.

The pyrrhic (*pyrrichius*) foot is so called because it was used habitually in contests or quite often in children's games.[15] The spondee (*spondeus*) is so called because it has a prolonged sound, for *spondeus* is the name of a certain droning, that is, the sound that would flow over the ears of those performing a sacrifice. Hence those who would play the pipes in the pagan rites were named 'spondials.' 3. The trochee (*trochaeus*) is so called because it makes speedy alternations in a song, and runs quickly in meters like a wheel – for a wheel is called τροχός in Greek. 4. The iamb (*iambus*) is so called because the Greeks say ἰαμβόζειν for 'detract' (*detrahere*, ppl. *detractus*). Poets were accustomed to perform all their invective or abuse (*detractio*) with poetry of this type. And the name comes from this, in that in some way it infuses a sort of poison of malediction or spite (cf. ἰός, "poison").

5. The tribrach (*tribrachys*), which is also called *chorius*, is named tribrach because it consists of three short syllables (see section 9 below). 6. The molossus (*Molossus*) is named from the dancing of the Molossians, which they performed while armed. 7. The anapest (*anapaestus*) [is so called because this foot is dedicated more to relaxation and games].[16] 8. The dactyl (*dactylus*) is named from 'finger' (cf. δάκτυλος), because it begins with a longer measure, and ends in two shorts. Thus this foot has one long joint and two shorts. Also an open hand is called a palm, and the dangling fingers are dactyls. 9. The amphibrach (*amphibrachys*, cf. ἀμφί, "on both sides"), because it has a short on either side and a long lying in the middle – for a short is called βραχύς. 10. The *amphimacrus*, because two longs have a short enclosed between them, for a long is called μακρός. 11. The *bacchius* is so called because with this foot the Bacchanals, that is, the rites of the god Liber (i.e. Bacchus), are celebrated. 12. The *antibacchius*, or *palimbacchius*, is so called because it is a reversal of the

14 The fourth-century grammarian Aelius Donatus wrote textbooks that became standard. Here see *Ars Grammatica*, ed. Keil 4.368–69.

15 The reference is to the *pyrrhica*, a war-dance or reel.

16 Greek ἀνάπαιστος means "reversed," as the foot is a reversed dactyl.

bacchius. 13. The proceleusmatic (*proceleumaticus*, i.e. *proceleusmaticus*), because it is appropriate for the 'work chant' (*celeuma*) of people singing. 14. The *dispondeus* and *ditrochaeus* and *diiambus* are so called because they are double iambs, spondees, and trochees. 15. The *antispastus*, because it is made of opposing syllables: from a short and a long, then a long and a short. 16. The choriamb (*choriambus*), because the song most appropriate for 'a band of singers and dancers' (*chorus*) is composed with this foot. 17. The ionic (*ionicus*) feet are with good reason named from the uneven (*inaequalis*) sound of their rhythm, for they have two long syllables and two short. 18. The paeonic (*paeon*) feet are named from their inventor. [They consist of one long and three shorts, and the long syllable is placed in various positions corresponding to the name (i.e. first paeon, second paeon, etc.)]. 19. Epitrites (*epitritus*) are so called because they always have three long syllables and one short. 20. Syzygies (*syzygia*) are feet with five and six syllables, and they are called συζυγίαι in Greek, as are certain declensions. These are not actually feet, but they are called pentasyllables and hexasyllables, since they do not exceed five and six syllables. Hence it is not possible for any word in a poem to exceed this number of syllables, such as *Carthaginiensium* ("of Carthaginians"), *Hierosolymitanorum* ("of Jerusalemites"), and *Constantinopolitanorum* ("of Constantinopolitans").

21. In each foot there occurs an arsis (*arsis*) and a thesis (*thesis*), that is, a raising and lowering of the voice – for the feet would not be able to follow a road unless they were alternately raised and lowered. For example, in *arma* (arms), *ar-* is the raising, and *-ma* the lowering. Properly constituted feet are comprised of a distribution of these two. The proportion is equal (*aequus*) whenever arsis and thesis are cut with an equal division of time. 22. The proportion is duple (*duplus*) whenever one of them exceeds the other twofold. The proportion is sescuple (*sescuplus*) whenever one exceeds the other by half again as much (i.e. a proportion of two and three). In the smaller member of this foot one unit more than the minimum is found, and in the larger member one unit less than the maximum, for *sescum* is a word for 'half.' The proportion is triple (*triplus*) when the larger part contains the entire smaller part three times: that is, a proportion of three to one. It is epitrite (*epitritus*), when the smaller part is contained in the larger, plus a third part of the smaller (i.e. a proportion of three and four, since four is equal to three plus one third of three). The members of feet are divided either in equal proportion, or double, or sescuple, or triple, or epitrite.

23. We divide these into equal members:

<table>
<tr><td>Spondee</td><td>––</td><td>Pyrrhic</td><td>⏑⏑</td></tr>
<tr><td>Dactyl</td><td>–|⏑⏑</td><td>Anapest</td><td>⏑⏑|–</td></tr>
<tr><td>Dispondeus</td><td>––|––</td><td>Proceleusmatic</td><td>⏑⏑|⏑⏑</td></tr>
<tr><td>Diiambus</td><td>⏑–|⏑–</td><td>Ditrochaeus</td><td>–⏑|–⏑</td></tr>
<tr><td>Antispastus</td><td>⏑–|–⏑</td><td>Choriamb</td><td>–⏑|⏑–</td></tr>
</table>

24. Further, we divide these feet in a duple rhythm:

<table>
<tr><td>Trochee</td><td>–|⏑</td><td>Iamb</td><td>⏑|–</td></tr>
<tr><td>Molossus</td><td>–|––</td><td>Tribrach</td><td>⏑|⏑⏑</td></tr>
<tr><td>Ionic major</td><td>––|⏑⏑</td><td>Ionic minor</td><td>⏑⏑|––</td></tr>
</table>

25. [There is only one that has triple proportion, which is the most extreme proportion and is therefore present in few meters.]

Amphibrach ⏑|–⏑

26. The ones with sescuple division are these:

<table>
<tr><td>Amphimacrus</td><td>–|⏑–</td><td>Bacchius</td><td>⏑–|–</td></tr>
<tr><td>Antibacchius</td><td>–|–⏑</td><td>First Paeon</td><td>–|⏑⏑⏑</td></tr>
<tr><td>Second Paeon</td><td>⏑–|⏑⏑</td><td>Third Paeon</td><td>⏑⏑|–⏑</td></tr>
<tr><td>Fourth Paeon</td><td>⏑⏑⏑|–</td><td></td><td></td></tr>
</table>

27. We divide the rest into the epitrite proportion:

<table>
<tr><td>First Epitrite</td><td>⏑–|––</td><td>Second Epitrite</td><td>–⏑|––</td></tr>
<tr><td>Third Epitrite</td><td>––|⏑–</td><td>Fourth Epitrite</td><td>––|–⏑</td></tr>
</table>

There are, therefore, ten feet with equal proportion, six with duple proportion, one with triple proportion, seven with sescuple proportion, and four with epitrite proportion. And there is only one that has triple proportion, which is the most extreme proportion and is therefore present in few meters. 28. The number of syllables possible in a foot ranges from two to six; it proceeds no further, because feet extend to six syllables only.

There are time-intervals in feet, corresponding to the quantity that each foot has. Resolution (*resolutio*) of feet occurs when two shorts take the place of one long, or four shorts the place of two longs, as (Vergil, *Aen.* 2.16):

Sectaque intexunt abiete costas.
(They frame the ribs with sawn fir.)

Abiete here is a resolution of a spondee into a proceleusmatic; Vergil always follows a synaloephis (i.e.

a fusion of two vowels into one syllable) with this resolution. 29. Although two shorts can take the place of one long, one long can never take the place of two shorts,[17] for solid things can be divided, but divided things cannot be made solid.

There is a notation by whose mark syllables are recognized, for when you see the lower half of a circle written twice, it is a Pyrrhic foot: ˘˘, where you see two horizontal Is, it is a spondee: – –. So a short is marked with a lower half-circle, and a long with a horizontal **I.** 30. Meter is built from feet, such as trochaic meter from the trochee, dactylic from the dactyl, iambic from the iamb; we will speak a little later concerning this.

xviii. Accents (De accentibus) 1. The accent (*accentus*), which is called 'prosody' (*prosodia*) in Greek, [takes its name from Greek], for the Greek word πρός is the Latin *ad* ("to"), and the Greek ᾠδή is the Latin *cantus* ("song"; i.e. *accentus* < *ad* + *cantus*) – so this term is translated word for word. Latin speakers also have other names for it. They say 'accent' and 'pitch' (*tonus*) and 'tenor' (*tenor*), because at that place the sound increases and falls away. 2. 'Accent' is so called because it is joined to song (*cantus*), in the same way that the 'adverb' is so called because it is joined to the verb (see chapter x above). The acute (*acutus*) accent is so called because it sharpens (*acuere*) and raises the syllable; the grave (*gravis*, lit. "heavy") accent, because it depresses and lowers, for it is the opposite of the acute. The circumflex (*circumflexus*) is so called because it consists of an acute and a grave. Thus beginning as an acute it ends as a grave, and when it thus rises and then falls, it makes a 'turning around' (*circumflexus*). 3. The acute and the circumflex are similar, for they both raise the syllable. The grave accent is regarded as opposite to both of them, for it always lowers the syllable, while they raise it, as (Lucan, *Civil War* 1.15):

> *Unde venit Titan, et nox ibi sidera condit.*
> (Whence Titan comes, and there night conceals the stars.)

Unde ("whence") has a reduced accent here. It has a lower sound than the acute and the circumflex.

4. A monosyllabic word will have an acute accent if it is short by nature, as *vir* ("man"), or long by position, as *ars* ("art"). But if it is long by nature, as *rēs* ("thing"), then it has a circumflex.[18] A disyllabic word, if its first syllable is long by nature and the second short, has a circumflex, as *Mūsa*; otherwise it has an acute. If a three-syllable word has a short middle syllable, as *tibia* ("shin"), then we make the first syllable acute. If it has a second syllable long by nature, and a short final syllable, as *Metēllus*, then we make the middle syllable circumflex. 5. Four- and five-syllable words are controlled by the pattern for three-syllable words. The grave accent can occur with another single accent in a single word, but never with both (i.e. a circumflex and an acute), as [*Catullus*]. In a compound word there is a single accent.[19]

6. Accents were invented either for the sake of distinguishing, as (Vergil, *Aen.* 8.83):

> *Viridique in litore conspicitur sus*
> (And a pig is seen on the green shore)

so that you won't say *ursus* ("bear");[20] or for the sake of pronunciation, lest you pronounce *meta* as short and not as *mēta*, with its *a* lengthened; or because of an ambiguity which must be resolved, as *ergo*. When the *-go* is lengthened, the word signifies a reason (i.e. "on account of"); when it is short, it signifies a conjunction (i.e. "therefore").[21]

xix. Accent marks (De figuris accentuum) 1. There are ten accent marks, which are supplied by grammarians to distinguish words. Ὀξεῖα, that is the acute accent, a line drawn upwards from the left side to the right, is made thus: ´. 2. Βαρεῖα, that is, grave, a line drawn from the upper left down to the right, is made thus: `. 3. Περισπωμένη, that is, circumflex, a line made of an acute and a grave, is represented thus: ^. 4. Μακρός, that is, a long mark (i.e. macron), is a horizontal stroke, thus: ¯. 5. Βραχύς, that is, the short, is the lower part of a

17 Isidore means that a long syllable cannot replace two shorts when the latter are required by a particular verse form, as, with rare exceptions, in the fifth foot of a dactylic hexameter.

18 A syllable's vowel is short or long "by nature," but a syllable is generally long "by position" if its vowel is followed by two consonants.

19 The remarks about accent (pitch?) here pertain to Greek pronunciation, and less clearly to Latin. The details are controversial. The last two sentences may refer to the rule in Greek that a word may have two accents if it is followed by an enclitic. See Donatus, ed. Keil 4.371–72.

20 The pitch or stress would rise on *-ur sus* but fall on *ursus*.

21 The text should read "*mēta*, with its *e* lengthened." *Ergo* "therefore" occurs with a short *o* only rarely in the classical poets, but commonly in later ones.

circle, lying thus: ⌣. 6. ʽΥφέν, that is, a joining (*coniunctio*), because it connects (*conectere*) two words, is a stroke drawn down that curves back at the line, thus: ‿. 7. *Diastole*, that is, a distinction (*distinctio*), which separates something from its opposite: the right half of a circle drawn down to the line:). 8. The 'apostrophe' (*apostrophus*), also the right half of a circle, and placed at the upper part of a letter, is thus: ʼ. By this mark it is shown that the final vowel in a word is lacking, as *tribunal*ʼ for *tribunale*. 9. Δασεῖα, which is translated as "aspiration" (*aspiratio*, i.e. the rough breathing), that is, where the letter **H** ought to be put, is marked by this shape: ⊢. 10. Ψιλή, which is translated as "dryness" (*siccitas*, i.e. the smooth breathing), or "a pure sound" – that is, where the letter **H** ought not to be – is expressed with this shape: ⊣. 11. Latin speakers made the shapes of these two accent-marks from the letter of aspiration itself. Whence, if you join them, you will have made that same mark of aspiration (i.e. **H**). Conversely, if you split it at the midpoint, you make a δασεῖα and a ψιλή.

xx. Punctuated clauses (De posituris) 1. A punctuated clause is a form for distinguishing meaning through colons, commas, and periods, which, when placed in their proper spot, show the sense of the reading to us.[22] They are called 'punctuated clauses' (*positura*) either because they are marked by points that are set down (*ponere*, ppl. *positus*), or because there the voice is lowered (*deponere*, ppl. *depositus*) to make an interval with a pause. Greek speakers call them θέσεις, and Latin speakers, *posituræ*. 2. The first punctuated clause is called the subdivision, and it is the same as a comma. The middle punctuation follows: it is the colon. The final punctuation, which closes the entire sentence, is the period.

The colon and the comma are parts of the sentence, as we have said. The difference between them is indicated by points placed in different spots. 3. For where the speech has begun and the sense is not yet complete, but it is necessary to take a breath, a comma occurs, that is, a part of the sense, and a point is placed even with the bottom of the letter. This is called the 'subdivision' (*subdistinctio*) because it takes the point below (*subtus*), that is, at the bottom of the line. 4. And where, in the following words, the sentence now makes sense but something still remains for the completion of the sentence, a colon occurs, and we mark it by a point even with the middle of the letter. And we call this the 'middle' (*medius*) punctuation, because we place the point at the middle of the letter. 5. But when, by proceeding through the speech, we make a complete closure of the sentence, a period occurs, and we place a point even with the top of the letter. This is called a *distinctio*, that is, a disjunction, because it sets apart a whole sentence. 6. This is the usage among orators. On the other hand, among the poets, a comma occurs in the verse when, after two feet, there is still a syllable remaining in the word, because a break in the word is made there according to metrical scansion. But when no part of the speech still remains after two feet, it is a colon. And the entire verse is a period.[23]

xxi. Critical signs (De notis sententiarum) 1. In addition to these, there were certain critical signs (*nota*) used in writing the works of the most famous authors; the ancients placed these in poems and histories to annotate the writing. The critical sign is a specific shape placed in the manner of a letter, to show a particular judgment about a word or sentences or verses. There are twenty-six marks which may be placed in verse, given below with their names:

2. ※ The asterisk is placed next to omissions, so that things which appear to be missing may be clarified through this mark, for star is called ἀστήρ in Greek, and the term 'asterisk' (*asteriscus*) is derived from this. 3. – The obelus (*obolus*), that is, a horizontal stroke, is placed next to words or sentences repeated unnecessarily, or by places where some passage is marked as false, so that, like an arrow, it slays the superfluous and pierces the false, for an arrow is called ὀβελός in Greek. 4. ∸ An *obolus* with a point above it is put next to those places, about which there is some doubt as to whether they ought to be taken out or kept. [It is marked as false.] 5. ÷ The *lemniscus*, that is, a horizontal stroke between two points, is put next to those places that translators of Holy Writ

22 In this section Isidore uses the terms 'colon,' 'comma,' and 'period' to refer both to the actual parts of the sentence and to the marks of punctuation used to terminate them.

23 Isidore equates the signs for the metrists' caesura and diaeresis with the signs for the comma and colon. The caesura is the ending of a word within a metrical foot, especially within the third foot, or within both the second and fourth feet, of a hexameter line, and the diaeresis is the coincidence of the end of foot and word. Isidore defines the comma/caesura as the ending of a metrical foot within a word; the sense is generally the same.

have rendered with the same meaning but with different words.

6. ⋎ The *antigraphus* with a point is placed where there is a different meaning in the translations. 7. ※– The asterisk with *obolus*: Aristarchus used this specifically next to those verses not placed in their proper location. 8. Γ The paragraph (*paragraphus*) is placed so as to separate topics which run on in sequence, just as in a catalog, places are separated from each other, and regions from each other, and in the competitions, prizes are separated from each other, and contests from other contests. 9. ˥ The *positura* is a mark opposite to the paragraph. It is shaped this way because, just as the paragraph marks beginnings, this one separates ends from beginnings. 10. ◡ The *cryphia*, the lower half of a circle with a point, is put next to those places where a difficult and obscure question cannot be answered or solved. 11. Ɔ The *antisimma* is placed at those verses whose order should be transposed. It is found so placed in ancient authors also. 12. Ↄ The *antisimma* with a point is put next to those places where there are two verses with the same meaning, and it is doubtful which one should be selected.

13. > The *diple*. Our scribes place this in books of churchmen to separate or to make clear the citations of Sacred Scriptures. 14. > The *diple* περί στίχον ("next to a verse"). Leogoras of Syracuse first placed this next to Homeric verses to distinguish Mount Olympus from the heavenly Olympus. 15. ⋟ The *diple* περιεστιγμένη, that is, with two points. The ancients set this next to the verses which Zenodotus of Ephesus incorrectly added, or removed, or transposed. Our scribes also have used this same sign next to those verses. 16. ➤ The diple ὀβολισμένη is interposed to separate the speeches in comedies and tragedies. 17. ⤎ The reverse ὀβολισμένη, whenever the strophe and the antistrophe are introduced. 18. ◂ The reverse *diple* with *obolus* is placed next to those passages that refer back to something, as (cf. Vergil, *Aen.* 10.88):

> Do I try to overturn the state of Troy from its foundation for you? I? Or is it he who threw the miserable Trojans to the Greeks?[24]

19. ⩾ The *diple* with an *obolus* above it is placed next to passages representing changed conditions of places, times, and people. 20. ⪥ The *diple* pointing right and reversed with an *obolus* above is used when a unit is completed in that place, and signifies that something similar follows.

21. ✖ The *ceraunium* is placed whenever a set of verses is rejected and not marked individually with an *obolus*; for lightning is called κεραύνιον in Greek. 22. ☧ The *chrisimon*: this is placed according to each person's individual desire to mark something. 23. ⚴ Phi and Rho, that is, φροντίς (i.e. "attention"): this is placed where there is something obscure requiring close attention. 24. ϒ The upward anchor is placed where there is some exceedingly great subject matter. 25. ⅄ The downward anchor, where something is announced in a very base and improper way. 26. ↱ The mark of the *corona* is only placed at the end of a book. 27. ❙ The *alogus* is the mark [that] is placed beside errors.

28. There are also other small marks (i.e. signes de renvoi) made in books for drawing attention to things that are explained at the edges of the pages, so that when the reader finds a sign of this type in the margin he may know that it is an explanation of the same word or line that he finds with a similar mark lying above it when he turns back to the text.

xxii. Common shorthand signs (De notis vulgaribus)

1. Ennius first invented eleven hundred common signs. These signs were used in this way: several scribes standing by together would write down whatever was said in a trial or judgment, with the sections distributed among them so that each scribe would take down a certain number of words in turn. In Rome, Tullius Tiro, a freedman of Cicero's, first devised such signs, but only for prepositions. 2. After him, Vipsanius, Philargius, and Aquila, another freedman of Maecenas, added others. Then, after the total number of signs had been collected, set in order, and increased in number, Seneca produced a work with five thousand signs. They are called 'signs' (*nota*) because they would designate (*notare*) words and syllables by predetermined characters and recall them to the knowledge (*notitia*) of readers. Those who have learned these signs are properly called stenographers (*notarius*) today.

xxiii. Signs used in law (De notis iuridicis)

1. In books of law certain letters stand for words; in this way the writing becomes quicker and shorter. So, for instance, *bonum factum* ("good deed") would be written as **BF**, *senatus*

24 The lines from Vergil refer to events described in more detail earlier in his poem.

consultum ("senate decree") as **SC**, *respublica* ("republic") as **RP**, *populus Romanus* ("Roman people") as **PR**, *dumtaxat* ("at least") as **DT**, *mulier* ("woman") by the upside-down letter **M**, *pupillus* ("male orphan") by a regular **P**, *pupilla* ("female orphan") by a ꟼ with the top reversed, *caput* ("head") by a single **K**, *calumniae causa* ("case of false accusation") by two joined **KK**, *iudex esto* ("let the judge be present") by **IE**, *dolum malum* ("grievous fraud") by **DM**. 2. We find very many similar signs of this type in ancient books. Recent emperors have ordained that these legal signs be abolished from codes of law, because shrewd people were cleverly deceiving many ignorant people by means of these signs. So the emperors ordered that full words should be used to write the laws, so that they would cause no errors or ambiguities, but would clearly show what must be obeyed and what must be avoided.

xxiv. Military signs (De notis militaribus) 1. The ancients also used a special sign in the rosters that contained the names of soldiers; by this sign it could be seen how many of the soldiers were still alive and how many had fallen in battle. The sign tau, T, placed at the beginning of the line indicated a survivor, while theta, Θ, was placed by the name of each of the slain. Therefore this letter has a spear through the middle, which is the sign of death. Concerning which Persius says (*Satires* 4.13):

> And he is able to affix the black theta to a crime.

2. But when they wanted to indicate ignorance (i.e. as to whether a soldier was alive or dead), they used the letter lambda, just as they would indicate death when they would put theta at the head of the line. There were also special signs for the payment of stipends.

xxv. Epistolary codes (De notis litterarum) 1. Our predecessors also used to establish between themselves epistolary codes, so that they might write back and forth with these signs whatever they wanted to write secretly to each other. Brutus is an example: he used to indicate with these codes what he was about to do, while everyone else was unaware of what the coded letters meant for him. 2. Caesar Augustus also said to his son: "Since innumerable things are constantly occurring about which we must write to each other, and which must be secret, let us have between us code-signs, if you will, such that, when something is to be written in code, we will replace each letter with the following letter in this way: *b* for *a*, *c* for *b*, and then the rest in the same way. For the letter *z*, we will return to a double *aa*." Some also write with the words reversed.

xxvi. Finger signals (De notis digitorum) 1. There are also some signals for the fingers, and for eyes as well, by which those at a distance can silently communicate with each other. This is the custom with the military: when the army is agreeing on an action they signal assent with their hands, because they cannot use their voices. Some, because they cannot speak a greeting, use a motion of the sword. 2. Ennius, speaking of a certain shameless woman, says (Naevius, *Comedies* 52):

> Tossing from hand to hand in a ring of players like a ball,
> she gives herself and makes herself common. She
> embraces one, nods to another, and her hand is
> occupied elsewhere, she pinches the foot of another,
> gives to another a ring to look at, calls another by
> blowing a kiss, sings with another, and to still others
> gives signals with her finger.

And Solomon (Proverbs 6:13): "He winketh with the eyes, presseth with the foot, and speaketh with the finger."

xxvii. Orthography (De orthographia) 1. The Greek term 'orthography' (*orthographia*) is translated into Latin as 'correct writing' [for *orto* means "correctly" and *graphia* "writing"]. This discipline teaches how we should spell, for just as grammatical art treats of the inflection of parts of speech, so orthography treats of the skill of spelling. For instance, *ad* ("to"): when it is a preposition it takes the letter **D**, but when it is a conjunction, the letter **T** (i.e. *at*, "but"). 2. *Haud* ("scarcely"), when it is an adverb of negation, ends in the letter **D** and is aspirated initially. But when it is a [disjunctive] conjunction, it is written with the letter **T** and without aspiration (i.e. *aut*, "or"). 3. The preposition *apud* ("at") is written with a **D**, as in *ad patrem* ("at the father"), because our predecessors often used *apud* for *ad* [having removed two of the middle letters.][25]

25 Isidore is advising against the common spelling *aput*. Keil, the editor of Isidore's source here in Cassiodorus, proposes reading "as '*ad*' *praepositio*" ("as is the preposition 'at'") for "as in *ad patrem*." The bracketed addition of course has it backwards; *apud* supposedly adds two letters to *ad*.

4. But sometimes letters are correctly put in place of other letters. There is a certain kinship between the letters **B** and **P**, for we say *Pyrrhus* for *Burrus.* [The letters] **C** and **G** have a certain kinship. Thus while we say *centum* ("hundred") and *trecentos* ("three hundred"), after that we say *quadringentos* ("four hundred"), putting **G** for **C**. Similarly there is a kinship between **C** and **Q**, for we write *huiusce* ("of this") with **C** and *cuiusque* ("of each") with a **Q**. The preposition *cum* ("with") should be written with a **C**, but if it is a conjunction ("while"), then it should be written with a **Q**, for we say *quum lego* ("while I read"). *Deus* ("God") is written with an **E** alone, but *daemon* ("demon") should be marked by the diphthong **AE**. 5. *Equus* ("horse"), which is the animal, should be written with **E** alone, but *aequus*, which means "just," should be written with the diphthong **AE**. *Exsul* ("exile") should be written with the **S** added, because an exile is someone who is 'outside the land' (*extra solum*). *Exultat* ("he exults") is better written without the letter **S**. For, since **X** is made up of **C** and **S**, why, when the sound is already contained in it, should a second one be added to it?

6. *Aequor* ("the level sea") should be written with a diphthong (i.e. not with **E** alone), because the name is made from *aqua* ("water"). 7. *Forsitan* ("perhaps") should be written with **N** at the end, because its full form is *si forte tandem* ("if by chance indeed"). 8. *Fedus*, that is, 'deformed,' should be written with an **E** alone; *foedus*, that is, 'pact,' should be written with the diphthong **OE**. 9. *Formosus* ("beautiful") is written without an **N** (i.e. not *formonsus*), because it is so called from *forma* ("beauty"), [or from *formus*, that is, 'warm'; for warmth of blood produces beauty]. *Gnatus* ("offspring"), that is, 'son,' should be written with a **G**, because it represents *generatus* ("begotten"). 10. **H**, which is the letter of aspiration, is joined in Latin only to vowels, as *honor*, *homo* ("man"), *humus* ("soil"), [*humilitas* ("humility")]. There is also aspiration with consonants, but only in Greek and Hebrew words. The interjections *heus* and *heu* should also be written with an **H**.

11. Some think that the letter **I** occurring between two vowels, as in *Troia*, *Maia*, should be written twice. Logic, however, does not permit this, for three vowels are never written in a single syllable. But the letter **I** occurring between two vowels does have a double sound (i.e. in metrical scansion). 12. The neuter pronoun *id* ("it") is written with a **D**, because the paradigm is *is, ea, id* ("he, she, it") since it makes the word *idem* ("the same"). But if it is a third person verb, it is identified by the letter **T**, because the paradigm is *eo, is, it* ("I go, you go, he/she/it goes") [since it makes the form] *itur* ("is traveled").[26]

13. The ancients placed the letter **K** first whenever an **A** followed, as in *kaput* ("head"), *kanna* ("reed"), *kalamus* ("cane"). But now only *Karthago* ("Carthage") and *kalendae* ("Calends") are written with this letter. However, all Greek words with a following vowel of any sort should be written with a **K**. 14. *Laetus* ("joyful") is written with a diphthong, because 'joyfulness' (*laetitia*) is so called from 'wideness' (*latitudo*), the opposite of which is sorrow, which causes constriction. We sometimes use the letter **L** for the letter **D**, as in *latum* ("carried") for *datum* ("given") and *calamitatem* for *cadamitatem*, for the word 'calamity' is derived from 'falling' (*cadendum*).

15. There is a question about how *maxumus* or *maximus* ("greatest"), and any similar pairs, ought to be written. Varro relates that Caesar was accustomed to pronounce and write words of this type with an **I**. Hence, based on the authority of so great a man, it became the practice that *maximus*, *optimus* ("best"), *pessimus* ("worst") were written (Funaioli 269). 16. *Malo* ("I prefer") should be written with one **L**, because it is *magis volo* ("I wish rather"). But the infinitive *malle* ("to prefer") has two **L**s because it is *magis velle* ("to wish rather"). *Nolo* ("I am unwilling") also with one **L**, and *nolle* ("to be unwilling") with two, for *nolo* is *ne-volo* ("I do not want") and *nolle* is *ne-velle* ("not to want").

17. *Os*, if it means "face" or "bone" should be written with an **O** alone; if it refers to a person, an **H** should be put first (i.e. *hos*, plural accusative of the demonstrative). 18. *Ora* ("shores"), associated with boundaries, should be written with an **O**; *hora* ("hour"), associated with days, with an **H**. *Onus*, if it means "burden," should be written with an **O** alone; if it means "honor," written with the aspiration of an **H** (i.e. *honos*). 19. *Praepositio* ("preposition") and *praeterea* ("besides") should be written with diphthongs. Further, *pene* ("almost"), which is a conjunction, with **E**; *poena*, which is 'punishment' with **OE**.

20. The letter **Q** is correctly placed when it has the letter **U** immediately following, and they are followed by any other vowel or vowels, so that a single syllable

26 The forms that Isidore cites, *idem* and *itur*, are significant because they show the consonants in question when they are followed by a vowel. The *d*/*t* distinction, although evidently being lost in word-final position, was still preserved medially.

is made. The rest are written with **C**. 21. The pronoun *quae* ("which, who") should be written with an **A**, the conjunction *-que* ("and") without an **A**. 22. *Quid* ("what") is written with a **D** when it is a pronoun, and with a **T** when it is the verb whose paradigm appears simply, as *queo, quis, quit* ("I can, you can, he/she/it can"), and in the compound *nequeo, nequis, nequit* ("I cannot, you cannot, he/she/it cannot"). *Quod* ("that") when it is a pronoun should be written with **D**, when a numeric term with **T** (i.e. *quot*, "as many"), because *totidem* ("just as many") is written with **T**. *Quotidie* ("daily") should be written with **Q**, not **C** (i.e. *cotidie*), since it is *quot diebus* ("on as many days").

23. The letter **R** has a connection with the letter **S**, for the ancients said *honos, labos, arbos*, but now we say *honor, labor, arbor* ("tree"). 24. *Sat* ("enough") must be written with **T**, because its complete form is *satis*. *Sed* ("but") must be written with a **D**, for *sed* was pronounced as *sedum* by the ancients; we have cut off the final two letters. 25. *Tantus* ("so much") as well as *quantus* ("as much") used to have the letter **M** in the middle, for it was from *quam* ("as") and *tam* ("so") – whence also *quamtitas, quamtus, tamtus*. 26. The interjection *vae* ("woe") should be written with an **A**, the conjunction *ve* ("or") without. 27. *Xp̄s* ("Christ"),[27] because it is Greek, should be written with an **X**, so also *xrisma* ("chrism"). 28. Only Greek words are written with the letters **Y** and **Z**, for although the letter **Z** expresses the sound in *iustitia* ("justice"), still, because the word is Latin, it must be written with a **T**.[28] So also *militia* ("military"), *malitia* ("malice"), *nequitia* ("worthlessness"), and other similar words. 29. Also, the practice among our predecessors for ambiguous words was this: when it has one meaning with a short vowel, and another with the same vowel lengthened, they would place a macron over the long syllable. For example, whether *populus* would mean 'the poplar tree' (i.e. *pōpulus*) or 'a multitude of people' would be distinguished by the macron. Moreover, whenever consonants were doubled, they placed a mark called *sicilicus* (i.e. a mark shaped like a sickle, Ɔ) above, as in the words *cella, serra, asseres*. Our predecessors did not use double letters, but they would write a *sicilicus* above, and by this mark the reader was alerted that the letter would be doubled.

xxviii. Analogy (De analogia) 1. The Greek term 'analogy' (*analogia*) is called in Latin the comparison (*conparatio*) or 'regular relation' (*proportio*) of similar things. Its force is that something doubtful is compared to a similar thing that is not doubtful, and uncertain things are explained by means of things that are certain. A comparison by analogy can be drawn from eight features: that is, from quality, from the comparative degree, from gender, from number, from form, from case, from endings with similar syllables, and from the similarity of tenses. 2. If any one of these is lacking, it is no longer analogy, that is, similarity, but rather anomaly, that is, outside the rule, such as *lepus* ("hare") and *lupus* ("wolf"). They correspond entirely, except that they differ in case endings, as we say *lupi* ("of the wolf"), but *leporis* ("of the hare"). Thus the regular pattern is that when you ask whether *trames* ("footpath") is masculine or feminine, it is similar to *limes* ("boundary-path") in its entire declension, and so must be masculine.

3. And again, if you think that *funis* ("rope") is of uncertain gender, it is similar to *panis* ("bread") in its entire declension, and so must be masculine. And again, from a comparison of the positive degree, so if you say *doctus* ("learned"), you will also say *magnus* ("big"), for they are both positives and similar to each other. This also occurs with diminutives. For example, *funiculus* ("small rope," with an obviously masculine ending) shows that *funis* ("rope") is masculine, just as *marmusculum* ("small block of marble," with an obviously neuter ending) shows that *marmor* ("marble") is of neuter gender. 4. For the gender of the principal form is usually also the gender of the diminutive. But this is not always so, as in *pistrinum* ("pounding-mill" – neuter), but *pistrilla* ("little pounding-mill" – feminine). Nevertheless, just as we ought to know the declension by comparison of the ending, [that is, from the primary form], we ought to infer the gender from the diminutive.

xxix. Etymology (De etymologia) 1. Etymology (*etymologia*) is the origin of words, when the force of a verb or a noun is inferred through interpretation. Aristotle called this σύμβολον (sign), and Cicero *adnotatio* (symbolization),[29] because by presenting their model it makes known (*notus*) the names and words for things.

27 The abbreviation derives from Greek chi-rho-sigma, from Χριστός.

28 The pronunciation at this time of *z* and of the Latin *-t-* in words like *militia* was /ts/. Compare Italian *milizia, malizia*.

29 Cicero, *Topics* 35, commonly reading *nota* for *adnotatio*.

For example, *flumen* ("river") is so called from *fluendum* ("flowing") because it has grown by flowing. 2. The knowledge of a word's etymology often has an indispensable usefulness for interpreting the word, for when you have seen whence a word has originated, you understand its force more quickly. Indeed, one's insight into anything is clearer when its etymology is known.[30] However, not all words were established by the ancients from nature; some were established by whim, just as we sometimes give names to our slaves and possessions according to what tickles our fancy. 3. Hence it is the case that etymologies are not to be found for all words, because some things received names not according to their innate qualities, but by the caprice of human will.

Etymologies of words are furnished either from their rationale (*causa*), as 'kings' (*rex*, gen. *regis*) from ['ruling' (*regendum*) and] 'acting correctly' (*recte agendum*); or from their origin, as 'man' (*homo*) because he is from 'earth' (*humus*), or from the contrary, as 'mud' (*lutum*) from 'washing' (*lavare*, ppl. *lutus*), since mud is not clean, and 'grove' (*lucus*), because, darkened by its shade, it is scarcely 'lit' (*lucere*). 4. Some are created by derivation from other words, as 'prudent' (*prudens*) from 'prudence' (*prudentia*); some from the sounds, as 'garrulous' (*garrulus*) from 'babbling sound' (*garrulitas*). Some are derived from Greek etymology and have a Latin declension, as 'woods' (*silva*), 'home' (*domus*). 5. Other words derive their names from names of places, cities, [or] rivers. In addition, many take their names from the languages of various peoples, so that it is difficult to discern their origin. Indeed, there are many foreign words unfamiliar to Latin and Greek speakers.

xxx. Glosses (De glossis) 1. 'Gloss' (*glossa*) receives its name from Greek, with the meaning 'tongue.' Philosophers call it *adverbum*, because it defines the utterance in question by means of one single word (*verbum*): in one word it declares what a given thing is, as *contiscere est tacere* ("'to fall still' is 'to be silent'"). 2. Again in (Vergil, *Aen.* 10.314):

> *Latus haurit apertum* (gouges the exposed flank),

'gouges' (*haurit*, lit. "drinks") is glossed as 'pierces through' (*percutit*). And again, as when we gloss 'termination' (*terminus*) as 'end' (*finis*), and we interpret 'ravaged' (*populatus*) to be 'devastated' (*vastatus*), and in general when we make clear the meaning of one word by means of one other word.

xxxi. Differentiation (De differentiis)[31] A differentiation (*differentia*) is a type of definition, which writers on the liberal arts call 'concerning the same and the different.' Thus two things, of the kind that are confused with each other because of a certain quality that they have in common, are distinguished by an inferred difference, through which it is understood what each of the two is. For instance, one asks what is the difference between a 'king' and a 'tyrant': we define what each is by applying a differentiation, so that "a king is restrained and temperate, but a tyrant is cruel." Thus when the differentiation between these two has been given, then one knows what each of them is. And so on in the same way.

xxxii. Barbarism (De barbarismo) 1. A barbarism (*barbarismus*) is a word pronounced with a corrupted letter or sound: a corrupted letter, as in *floriet* (i.e. the incorrect future form of *florere*, "bloom"), when one ought to say *florebit* ("will bloom"); a corrupted sound, if the first syllable is lengthened instead of the middle syllable in words like *latebrae* ("hiding places"), *tenebrae* ("shadows"). It is called 'barbarism' from barbarian (*barbarus*) peoples, since they were ignorant of the purity of the Latin language, for some groups of people, once they had been made Romans, brought to Rome their mistakes in language and customs as well as their wealth. 2. There is this difference between a barbarism and a borrowing (*barbarolexis*), that a barbarism occurs in a Latin word when it is corrupted, but when foreign words are brought into Latin speech, it is called 'borrowing.' Further, when a fault of language occurs in prose, it is called a barbarism, but when it occurs in meter, it is called a metaplasm (*metaplasmus*). 3. In addition, a barbarism can occur in written or spoken language. In written language it occurs in four ways: if someone adds, changes, transposes, or removes a letter in a word or syllable. In spoken language it may occur in length, intonation, aspiration, and other ways that will follow. 4. A barbarism by length is made if someone says a short syllable for a long, or a long for a short. A barbarism by intonation, if the accent

30 Fontaine 1981:100 notes that this sentence is adapted from a legal maxim cited by Tertullian, *De Fuge* 1.2: "Indeed, one's insight into anything is clearer when its author is known" – substituting *etymologia cognita* for *auctore cognito*.

31 Isidore wrote a separate treatise, *De differentiis*, on this subject.

is moved to another syllable. By aspiration, if the letter **H** is added where it should not be, or omitted where it should occur. 5. A barbarism by hiatus, whenever a verse is cut off in speaking before it is completed, or whenever a vowel follows a vowel, as in *Musai Aonides*.[32] Barbarisms also occur by motacism, [iotacism], and lambdacism. 6. A motacism (*motacismus*) occurs whenever a vowel follows the letter **M**, as *bonum aurum* ("good gold), *iustum amicum* ("just friend"), and we avoid this fault either by suspending the letter **M**, or by leaving it out.[33] 7. Iotacism (*iotacismus*) occurs in words with the sound of the letter iota doubled, as *Troia, Maia*, where the pronunciation of these letters should be weak, so that they seem to sound like one iota, not two. 8. Lambdacism (*labdacismus*) happens if two **L**s are pronounced instead of one, as Africans do, as in *colloquium* instead of *conloquium*, or whenever we pronounce a single **L** too weakly, or a double **L** too strongly. This is backwards, for we ought to pronounce a single **L** strongly and a double **L** weakly. 9. *Conlisio* occurs whenever the end of the last syllable is the beginning of the next, as in *matertera* ("mother's sister").[34]

xxxiii. Solecisms (De soloecismis) 1. A solecism (*soloecismus*) is an unsuitable construction made up of more than one word, just as a barbarism is the corruption of a single word. Thus a solecism is a group of words that are not joined by the correct rule, as if someone were to say *inter nobis* ("between us," with *nobis* in the wrong case) instead of *inter nos*, or *date veniam sceleratorum* ("grant forgiveness of sinners") instead of *sceleratis* ("to sinners"). 2. It is called solecism from the Cilicians, who came from the city Soloe, now called Pompeiopolis; when, while dwelling among other peoples, they mixed their own and other languages incorrectly and incongruously, they gave their name to solecism. Whence those who speak like this are said to commit solecisms.

3. Among poets, a solecism is called a schema (*schema*) whenever it is committed in the verse due to the demands of the meter. But when no such demand is present, it remains a fault of solecism. 4. A solecism occurs in two manners: either in parts of speech, or in accidence. It occurs in parts of speech, if we use one part of speech instead of another, for instance, if we join prepositions to adverbs. It occurs in accidence, that is, in those things that are connected to the parts of speech, as, for example through qualities, genders and numbers, forms, and cases. Solecism may be committed in all of these, as Donatus has explained (ed. Keil 4.393). 5. It is committed in many ways besides these, for Lucilius (*Satires* 1100) spoke of one hundred kinds of solecisms, all of which anyone who is eager to obey the rules of speaking correctly ought to avoid rather than commit.

xxxiv. Faults (De vitiis) 1. Grammarians call the things that we ought to be wary of when we speak 'faults' (*vitium*). And these are: barbarism, solecism, acyrology, *cacenphaton*, and the rest. 2. A barbarism is the corruption of a single word, [as if someone were to lengthen the third syllable in *ignoscere*]. 3. A solecism is a faulty construction of words [as if someone were to say *inter hominibus* ("between men," with *hominibus* in the wrong case) instead of *inter homines*]. 4. Acyrology (*acyrologia*) is the use of an inappropriate word, as (Lucan, *Civil War* 2.15):

> Let the fearful one hope.

To be strictly correct, however, a fearful one dreads, and does not hope. Also (cf. Vergil, *Aen.* 5.287):

> *Gramineo in campo* (In a field of grass).

It is correct to refer to a field as 'grassy' (*graminosus*), not 'made of grass' (*gramineus*). 5. *Cacemphaton* is speech which is obscene or sounds disorderly. Obscene as (Vergil, *Aen.* 1.579):

> *His animum arrecti dictis* (Aroused in their hearts by these words).[35]

Disorderly, as (Vergil, *Aen.* 2.27):

> *iuvat ire et Dorica castra* (And it is a pleasure to go to the Doric camp).

For it is poor composition to begin with the same syllable with which the preceding word has ended.

6. Pleonasm (*pleonasmos*) is the superfluous addition of a single word, as (Vergil, *Geo.* 2.1):

> So far, the cultivation of fields and the stars of the sky.

32 Hiatus is the suspension of vowel elision where it would be expected.

33 "Suspending the letter **M**" probably means a loss of the final *m* with accompanying nasalization of the preceding vowel. In classical metrics, a final *m* did not inhibit elision of vowels, so that *bonum est* scans as two syllables.

34 Early editors produce better sense here with the reading *mater terra*, "mother earth."

35 *Arrigere* (ppl. *arrectus*) can be used in a sexual sense.

For stars are in no other place than in the sky. 7. Perissology (*perissologia*) is the superfluous addition of several words, as (Deuteronomy 33:6): "Let Ruben live, and not die ..." – since to live is nothing other than not to die. 8. Macrology (*macrologia*) is speaking at length, and including unnecessary matters as (Livy, cited in Quintilian, *Inst. or.* 8.3.53): "The legates, not having achieved peace, returned back home whence they had come." 9. A tautology (*tautologia*) is a repetition of the same thing as (Vergil, *Aen.* 1.546):

> If the fates preserve the man, if he is nourished by the etherial air, and does not yet recline in the cruel shades ...

For everything that is repeated has the same theme, but is delivered with a crowd of words. 10. Ellipsis (*eclipsis*) is a gap in speech, in which necessary words are lacking, as (Vergil, *Aen.* 4.138):

> Whose quiver out of gold ...,

for the verb 'was' is lacking.

11. *Tapinosis* is a lowering, reducing the state of a great subject by words as (Vergil, *Aen.* 1.118):

> Here and there men appear, swimming in the vast whirlpool.

For he uses 'whirlpool' (*gurges*) instead of 'ocean' (*mare*). 12. *Cacosyntheton* is a faulty arrangement of words as (Vergil, *Aen.* 9.609):

> *Versaque iuvencum*
> *terga fatigamus hasta*
> (And we goad the flanks of our bullocks with reversed spears).[36]

13. *Amphibolia* is ambiguous speech that occurs with the accusative case, as in this answer of Apollo to Pyrrhus (Ennius, *Annals* 179):

> *Aio te, Aeacida, Romanos vincere posse*
> (I say that you, scion of Aeacus, can conquer the Romans – or – I say that the Romans can conquer you, scion of Aeacus).

In this verse it is not clear whom he has designated as the victor. 14. It can also occur due to a distinction that is not clear, as (Vergil, *Aen.* 1.263):

> *Bellum ingens geret Italia*
> (Italy will wage an immense war – or – Immense Italy will wage war).

The distinction is unclear, whether it is 'immense war' or 'immense Italy.' 15. This also occurs due to a common verb,[37] as *Deprecatur Cato, calumniatur Cicero, praestolatur Brutus, dedignatur Antonius* ("Cato denounces, Cicero slanders, Brutus expects, Anthony scorns"; or, "Cato is denounced," etc.). In this ambiguity it is not disclosed whether these people denounce or slander others, or others denounce or slander them. 16. It also occurs with homonyms, in which one word has many meanings, such as *acies* ("edge, keenness, front line"), when you do not add 'of the sword, of the eyes, of the army.'

xxxv. Metaplasm (De metaplasmis) 1. Metaplasm (*metaplasmus*) in the Greek language is called 'transformation' (*transformatio*) in Latin. It occurs in a single word due to the requirements of meter and to poetic license; its varieties are as follows. 2. *Prothesis* is an addition to the beginning of a word, as [*gnatus*, for *natus* ("born"), *tetulit* for *tulit* ("carried")]. *Epenthesis* is an addition in the middle of the word, as [(Vergil, *Aen.* 3.409):

> *Maneant in relligione nepotes*
> (May the descendants continue in the religious duties),

instead of *religione*,[38] and *relliquias* for *reliquias* ("relics"), *induperator* for *inperator* ("ruler")]. 3. *Paragoge* is an addition at the end of the word, as [*admittier* (i.e. the archaic middle or passive form) for *admitti* ("to be admitted"), *magis* for *mage* ("more"), and *potestur* for *potest* ("is able")]. *Aphaeresis* is an excision from the beginning of the word, as *temno* for *contemno* ("despise"). Syncope (*syncope*) is an excision from the middle, as *forsan* for *forsitan* ("perhaps"). Apocope (*apocope*) is an excision from the end, as *sat* for *satis* ("enough"). 4. *Ectasis* is an improper lengthening, as [(Vergil, *Aen.* 1.499):

> *Exercet Dīana choros* (Diana oversees the dancers),[39]

and (Vergil, *Aen.* 1.2):

> *Ītaliam fato* (... to Italy, by fate ...),

36 Scarcely a fault, but the adjective and noun *versa hasta* ("with reversed spear") might have been placed closer together.

37 That is, a verb with both an active and a passive sense; see ix.7 above.

38 The first vowel of *religio* was regularly short in Isidore's time, but the addition of a consonant makes it long by position, for the sake of meter.

39 The first syllable of *Diana*, originally long but normally short, is taken as long in this line for the sake of meter.

while *Italiam* ought to be said with short syllables.]

Systole is an improper shortening, as [(Vergil, *Aen.* 6.773):

> *urbemque Fidenam* (and the city of Fidena),

where the first syllable ought to be long (i.e. *Fīdenam*). As also when we say *Orion* with short syllables, when it should be said with lengthened ones]. Diaeresis (*diaeresis*) is the splitting of one syllable into two, as [(Vergil, *Aen.* 9.26):

> *dives pictaï vestis* (rich with embroidered clothes)

instead of *pictae*, and (Ennius, *Annals* 33):

> *Albaï longaï* (of Alba Longa)

for *Albae longae.*] 5. *Episynaloephe* is the slurring of two [syllables] into one, as [*Phæthon* for *Phaëthon, Neri* for *Nereï*, and *æripedem* for *aëripedem*].

Synaloepha (*synaloephe*) is the combining of vowels from adjacent words, as [(Vergil, *Aen.* 9.1):

> *Atque ea diversa penitus dum parte geruntur*
> (And while those things were happening far away)].

6. Ellipsis (*eclipsis*) is the combining of consonants with vowels as [(Vergil, *Aen.* 1.3):

> *Multum ille et terris iactatus et alto*
> (Much tossed about on lands and sea)].

Antithesis is the substitution of one letter for another, as [*inpete* for *impetu* ("with a rush"), *olli* for *illi* ("they")]. Metathesis (*metathesis*) is the transposition of letters, as [*Thymbre* for *Thymber, Evandre* for *Evander*]. 7. Between the barbarism and the figure, that is, a polished Latin utterance, is the metaplasm, which may occur as a fault in speech in a single word. Likewise, between the solecism and the schema, that is, a polished construction of words, is the figure, which may become a fault in speech in a group of words. Therefore metaplasms and schemas are midway, and distinguished by skill and by lack of skill.[40] They also are used as ornament.

xxxvi. Schemas (De schematibus) 1. Schemas (*schema*, plural *schemata*) are translated from Greek into Latin as 'figures of speech' (*eloquium figurae*), which occur in words and phrases in various forms of speaking, for the sake of ornamenting speech. While there are many of these according to the grammarians, the following are met with. 2. Prolepsis (*prolempsis*) is an anticipation, where those things that ought to follow are placed first, as (Vergil, *Aen.* 12.161):

> *Interea reges ingenti mole, Latinus . . .*
> (In the meantime, the kings, in mighty pomp, as Latinus . . .).

It ought to say, *Interea reges ingenti mole* ("In the meantime, the kings in mighty pomp"), and immediately add what logically follows (12.169), *procedunt castris* ("proceed to camp"), and then say *Latinus . . .* , etc. But an anticipation of subject has been made for the sake of ornament, and those things which ought to follow the statement about the kings are interposed for seven verses, and after that 'proceed to camp' is added. It is therefore an anticipation, because what ought to follow is put first. 3. Zeugma (*zeugma*) is a phrase where several thoughts are encompassed in one word. There are three types, for the word which links the phrases is either placed first, last, or in the middle. Placed first as (Lucilius 139):

> *Vertitur oenophoris fundus, sententia nobis*
> (The bottom is inverted by the wineholders, the sentence by us).

In the middle, as (Ennius, *Annals* 329):

> *Graecia Sulpicio sorti data, Gallia Cottae*
> (Greece was given by lot to Sulpicius, Gaul to Cotta).

At the end as in (Terence, *Andria* 68):

> *Namque hoc tempore*
> *obsequium amicos, veritas odium parit*
> (For in our times, obsequiousness does friends, and truth does hatred beget).

4. *Hypozeuxis* is the figure opposite to the one above, where there is a separate phrase for each individual meaning, as (Vergil, *Aen.* 10.149):

> *Regem adit et regi memorat nomenque genusque*
> (He approaches the king and tells the king both his name and family).

5. Syllepsis (*syllempsis*) is the use of an expression completed by a singular verb with dissimilar or plural phrases, as (Vergil, *Aen.* 1.553):

> *Sociis et rege recepto*

40 It appears that "metaplasms and figures" would better fit the context than "metaplasms and schemas."

("When companions and king be found"; *recepto* is singular),

or a singular phrase is supplied with a plural verb, as (Vergil, *Ecl.* 1.80):

Sunt nobis mitia poma,
. . . et pressi copia lactis
(There are for us ripe fruits, . . . and an abundance of cheese).

For he said *sunt* ("are") above. He ought to say this: *est et pressi copia lactis* ("and there is an abundance of cheese"). 6. Syllepsis occurs not only with parts of speech, but also with things incidental to the parts of speech. Where one is used for many, and many for one, that is syllepsis. One for many, as this (Vergil, *Aen.* 2.20):

And they fill the belly with an armed soldier,

when the Trojan horse was not filled with one soldier, but many. And again, many for one as in the Gospel (Matthew 27:44): "The thieves, that were crucified with him, reproached him," where instead of merely the one, both of them are represented as having blasphemed.

7. Anadiplosis (*anadiplosis*) occurs when a following verse begins with the same word that ended the previous verse, as in this (Vergil, *Ecl.* 8.55):

Certent et cygnis ululae, sit Tityrus Orpheus,
Orpheus in silvis, inter delphinas Arion
(And let the screech-owls compete with the swans, let Tityrus be Orpheus, an Orpheus in the woods, an Arion among the dolphins).

8. Anaphora (*anaphora*) is the repetition of the same word at the beginning of several verses, as (Vergil, *Aen.* 3.157):

Nos te Dardania incensa tuaque arma secuti,
nos tumidum sub te permensi classibus aequor
(We followed you and your troops from burning Dardania, we traversed the swollen sea in a fleet under your command).

9. *Epanaphora* is the repetition of a word at the beginning of each phrase in a single verse, as (Vergil, *Aen.* 7.759):

Te nemus Anguitiae, vitrea te Focinus unda,
te liquidi flevere lacus
(For you the forest of Anguitia wept, for you Lake Fucinus with its glassy wave, for you the clear lakes).

10. *Epizeuxis* is a doubling of words with a single sense, as (cf. Vergil, *Aen.* 4.660):

Sic, sic iuvat ire per umbras
(Thus, thus it is a joyful thing to go through the shades).

11. *Epanalepsis* is a repetition of the same word at the beginning and end of the verse, as in this (Juvenal, *Satires* 14.139):

Crescit amor nummi quantum ipsa pecunia crescit
(The love of money grows as wealth itself grows).

12. Paronomasia (*paronomasia*) is the use of nearly the same word with a different meaning, as in this: *Abire an obire te convenit?* ("Are you to pass on or to pass away?"), that is, 'to become an exile' or 'to die.' 13. *Schesis onomaton* is a group of linked nouns, joined in a kind of parade, as (cf. Lucretius, *On the Nature of Things* 5.1192):

Nubila, nix, grando, procellae, fulmina, venti
(Clouds, snow, hail, tempests, lightning, winds).

14. Alliteration (*paromoeon*) is a group of words beginning with the same letter; such a sort is found in Ennius (*Annals* 109):

O Tite tute Tati tibi tanta tyranne tulisti
(O Titus Tatius, you tyrant, you yourself have brought such things on yourself).

But Vergil moderates this well, when he uses this figure not through the entire verse, like Ennius, but sometimes only at the beginning of a verse, as in this (*Aen.* 1.295):

Saeva sedens super arma (Sitting over his savage weapons),

and at other times at the end, as (cf. *Aen.* 3.183):

Sola mihi tales casus Cassandra canebat
(Cassandra alone foretold to me such calamities).

15. *Homoeoptoton* occurs when many words in the same grammatical case are used, as in this (Vergil, *Aen.* 12.903):

Sed neque currentem, sed nec cognoscit euntem,
tollentemque manu saxumque inmane moventem
(But he does not know (himself) while running or walking, and lifting and moving the huge rock with his hand).

16. Homoeoteleuton (*homoeon teleuton*) occurs when several verbs terminate in the same way, as (Cicero, *Against Catiline* 2.1): *abiit, abcessit, evasit, erupit* ("he left, he walked off, he escaped, he burst forth"). 17. Polyptoton (*polyptoton*) occurs when a sentence is varied with different grammatical cases, as (Persius, *Satires* 3.84):

Ex nihilo nihilum, ad nihilum nil posse reverti
(Nothing from nothing, nothing can be returned to nothing)

and (Persius, *Satires* 5.79):

Marci Dama. – Papae! –Marco spondente, recusas? . . .
Marcus dixit. – Ita est. – Adsigna, Marce, tabellas.
(Marcus Dama: What? although Marcus stands surety, do you refuse? . . . Marcus has said it, it must be so. Make out the tablets, Marcus.)[41]

18. *Hirmos* is a phrase of continuous speech reserving its sense until the very end as in (Vergil, *Aen.* 1.159):

Est in secessu longo locus, insula portum . . .
(There is a place in a long inlet, an island (making) a harbor . . .),

and so on. Here the sense proceeds at length up to this point (1.165):

Horrentique atrum nemus inminet umbris
(A black grove looms with bristling shade).[42]

19. Polysyndeton (*polysyntheton*) is a passage linked by many conjunctions, as (Vergil, *Geo.* 3.344):

Tectumque, laremque,
armaque, Amicleumque canem
(the house and the Lares and the weapons and the Amiclean dog).

20. *Dialyton*, or asyndeton (*asyntheton*), is a figure that is composed in the opposite way, simply and freely without conjunctions, as *venimus, vidimus, placuit* ("we came, we saw, it was good"). 21. Antithesis (*antitheton*) occurs where opposites are placed against each other and bring beauty to the sentence, as this (Ovid, *Met.* 1.19):

Frigida pugnabant calidis, humentia siccis:
mollia cum duris, sine pondere habentia pondus

(Cold things battled with hot ones, moist with dry, soft with hard, those having weight with the weightless).

22. *Hypallage* occurs whenever words are taken in the opposite way as (Vergil, *Aen.* 3.61):

Dare classibus Austros (Give the south wind to the fleet),

when we should give the ships to the winds, not the winds to the ships.

xxxvii. Tropes (De tropis) 1. The grammarians designate tropes (*tropus*) with a Greek name; they are translated into Latin as 'modes of speech' (*modus locutionum*). They shift from their proper meaning to a similar sense that is less strict. It is most difficult to record the names of all of them, but Donatus has written down thirteen to be handed down for use (ed. Keil 4.399–402).

2. Metaphor (*metaphora*) is an adopted transference of some word, as when we say "cornfields ripple," "the vines put forth gems," although we do not find waves and gems in these things; in these phrases, terms have been transferred from elsewhere. But these expressions, and others that also use tropes, are veiled in figural garb with respect to what should be understood, so that they may exercise the reader's understanding, and lest the subjects grow common from being stripped bare and obvious. 3. And metaphors occur in four ways: from animate to animate, as (anon., Courtney fr. 6):

He mounted winged horses;

speaking metaphorically it associates the wings of a bird with a quadruped. Also (Vergil, *Ecl.* 6.80):

With what running (i.e. with what flight) she (i.e. Philomela transformed into a bird) sought deserted places;

this associates the running of a quadruped with a winged creature. From the inanimate to the inanimate, as (anon., Courtney fr. 4):

The pine-wood plows the sea, the lofty keel cuts a furrow;

this associates the use of land with water, since plowing and cutting a furrow have to do with the land, not the sea. 4. From inanimate to animate, as "blooming youth"; this associates inanimate flowers with youth, which is living. From animate to inanimate, as (anon., Courtney fr. 5; cited from Augustine, *Christian Doctrine* 3.7.11):

You, father Neptune, whose white temples, wreathed with crashing brine, resound; to whom the great Ocean flows forth as your eternal beard, and in whose hair rivers wander.

For 'beard,' 'temples,' and 'hair' pertain not to the Ocean but to men. 5. In this way, some terms for things are transferred very elegantly from one kind to another for

41 The received text of Persius begins the quotation with *Marcus*, not the genitive *Marci*, which is unintelligible in context.

42 The translation reflects the received text of Vergil, as well as some Isidore manuscripts, with *umbra*, not (unintelligible) *umbris*.

the sake of beauty, so that the speech may be greatly adorned. Metaphor is either of one direction, as 'the cornfields are rippling' – for you cannot say 'the ripples are cornfielding' – or it is an *antistropha*, that is reciprocal, as *remigium alarum* ("oarage of wings"; Vergil, *Aen.* 6.19). We can speak of both wings (i.e. oars) of ships and oarages (i.e. beatings) of wings.

6. Catachresis (*catachresis*) is a name applied to an unrelated thing. And this differs from a metaphor in that metaphor enlarges on something having a name, while catachresis makes use of an unrelated name because it does not have one of its own; as (Vergil, *Geo.* 2.131):

> And most similar to a laurel with respect to its (i.e. a tree's) face,

and (Vergil, *Aen.* 5.157):

> . . . Centaur (i.e. a ship's name); now the two are carried as one with brows (i.e. bows) united, and they plow the salt seas with long keels.

Now a 'face' and a 'brow' pertain only to animals and men. And if the poet had not applied this name to a ship, he would not have had a word that he could use which was appropriate for that part.

7. Metalepsis (*metalempsis*) is a trope designating what follows from what precedes it, as (Persius, *Satires* 3.11):

> Or what hand and knotty reed pen came to the page.

For by 'hand,' words are meant, and by 'reed pen,' letters are meant.

8. Metonymy (*metonymia*) is a designation (*transnominatio*) that is transferred from one meaning to another similar meaning. It is made in many ways. For instance, it expresses what is contained by what contains, as "the theater applauds," "the meadows low," when in the first instance people applaud and in the second, cows low. In the opposite way, it also expresses that which contains by that which is contained, as (Vergil, *Aen.* 2.311):

> Now the nearby Ucalegon burns,

when it is not Ucalegon (i.e. a Trojan citizen), but his house, that burns. 9. Also, it expresses what has been discovered by the discoverer, as (Terence, *Eunuch* 732);

> Without Ceres and Liber, Venus grows cold,

and (Vergil, *Aen.* 9.76):

> Vulcan sends mingled embers to the stars.

For by Ceres, the discoverer of grain, he means "bread"; by Liber, the discoverer of the vine, "wine"; by Venus, "desire"; and by Vulcan, "fire." In the opposite way, it expresses the discoverer by the discovery as (Plautus, fr. 159):

> We pray to wine (for the god is present here),

in place of 'Liber,' who, according to the Greeks, invented wine. 10. Also, metonymy expresses that which is caused by its cause, as 'sluggish cold,' because it makes people sluggish, and 'pale fear,' since it makes people pale. In the opposite way, it expresses the cause by that which is caused, as (cf. Vergil, *Aen.* 5.817):

> The father yokes the horses and puts foaming bits made of gold on them, spirited as they are.

He said 'foaming bits,' although they themselves certainly do not make foam, but rather the horse that wears them sprinkles them with scattered foam.

11. Antonomasia (*antonomasia*) is a trope applied for a name, that is, instead of a name, as 'begotten of Maia' for Mercury. This trope occurs in three manners: from the spirit, as (Vergil, *Aen.* 5.407):

> And the large-souled son of Anchises;

from the body as (Vergil, *Aen.* 3.619):

> That lofty one;

from something extrinsic, as (Vergil, *Aen.* 1.475):

> Unlucky boy, no match for Achilles when he met him.

12. An epithet (*epitheton*) is in addition to the name, for it is placed before its noun, as 'bountiful Ceres,' and (cf. Vergil, *Geo.* 1.470):

> Unclean dogs and ominous birds.

There is this difference between antonomasia and an epithet, that antonomasia is used in place of a name, while an epithet is never used without the name. With these two tropes we may revile someone, or describe him, or praise him.

13. Synecdoche (*synecdoche*) is the conceit by which the whole is understood from the part, or the part from the whole. With it a genus is designated by its species, and a species by its genus [while species is the part and genus is the whole]. The part is understood from the whole, as in (cf. Vergil, *Aen.* 6.311):

> As many as the birds that flock together, when the frigid year chases them to sea.

Indeed, it is not the whole of year that is frigid, but only part of the year, that is, winter. In the opposite way, the whole is designated by the part, as (Vergil, *Aen.* 2.256):

> When the royal helm had raised the torches,

when it is not merely the helm, but the ship, and not the ship, but those in the ship, and not all of those in the ship, but a single one who brings forth the torches.

14. Onomatopoeia (*onomatopoeia*) is a word fashioned to imitate the sound of jumbled noise as the *stridor* ("creaking") of hinges, the *hinnitus* ("whinnying") of horses, the *mugitus* ("lowing") of cows, the *balatus* ("bleating") of sheep. 15. Periphrasis (*periphrasis*) is a circumlocution (*circumloquium*), when a single topic is expressed with many words, as (cf. Vergil, *Aen.* 1.387):

> He plucks the vital airs.

A single meaning is expressed by this combination of words, that is, "he lives." This trope is twofold, for either it splendidly brings forth the truth, or it avoids foulness by indirection. It splendidly brings forth the truth in (Vergil, *Aen.* 4.584 and 9.459):

> And now, early Aurora was scattering new light on the earth, leaving the saffron bed of Tithonus.

He means, "now it grew light," or, "it was daybreak." It avoids foulness by indirection, as in (cf. Vergil, *Aen.* 8.405):

> And he sought what was pleasing, relaxed in his wife's embrace.

By this indirection he avoids obscenity, and decently expresses the act of sexual intercourse.

16. Hyperbaton (*hyperbaton*) is a transposition (*transcensio*), when a word or sentence is changed in its order. There are five types of this: *anastrophe*, hysteron proteron, parenthesis, tmesis, and synthesis. *Anastrophe* is a reversed order of words as *litora circum* ("the shores around"; Vergil, *Aen.* 3.75), instead of *circum litora.* 17. Hysteron proteron (*hysteron proteron*) is a sentence with the order changed, as (Vergil, *Aen.* 3.662):

> Then he touched the deep waves, and came to the water.

For he came to the water first, and thus touched the waves. 18. Parenthesis (*parenthesis*) occurs when we interrupt our sentence, so that the sentence remains entire when this interruption is removed from the middle, as (Vergil *Aen.* 1.643):

> Aeneas – for his paternal love could not permit his mind to rest – quickly sends Achates to the ships.

[For this is the order: "Aeneas quickly sends Achates."] And that which intervenes is the parenthesis. 19. Tmesis (*tmesis*) is a division of one word by the interposition of other words, as (cf. Vergil, *Aen.* 1.412):

> *Multum nebulae circum dea fudit amictum*
> (The goddess surrounded (them) with a thick mantle of mist),

instead of *circumfudit.* 20. Synthesis (*synthesis*) occurs when words from every part of the thought are jumbled up, as in this (cf. Vergil, *Aen.* 2.348):

> *Iuvenes, fortissima frustra*
> *pectora, si vobis audendi extrema cupido est*
> *certa sequi, quae sit rebus fortuna videtis.*
> *Excessere omnes aditis arisque relictis*
> *dii, quibus inperium hoc steterat; succurritis urbi*
> *incensae; moriamur et in media arma ruamus.*

> (Young men, in vain your stout hearts; if your desire for daring the final battle is fixed on following me, you see what the outcome of the matter will be. They have all left the abandoned shrines and altars, the gods on whom this empire was established; you are helping a burning city; let us die and rush into the midst of the fray).

For the order is like this: "Young men with stout hearts, in vain you would be helping a burning city, because the gods have left. So if you firmly wish to follow me as I attempt a final battle, let us rush into the midst of the fray and die." 21. Hyperbole (*hyperbole*) is a loftiness that exceeds credibility, beyond what can be believed, as (Vergil, *Aen.* 3.423):

> She strikes the stars with a wave,

and (Vergil, *Aen.* 1.107):

> It lays open the sea bottom between the waves.

In this way something is magnified beyond belief; yet it does not stray from the path of expressing truth, even though the words go beyond what is referred to, so that the intention may seem to be of one speaking, not of one deceiving. By this trope something may not only be magnified, but also diminished. Magnified as in 'faster than the East Wind'; diminished as in 'softer than a feather,' 'harder than a rock.'

22. Allegory (*allegoria*) is 'other-speech' (*alieniloquium*), for it literally says one thing, and another thing is understood, as in (cf. Vergil, *Aen.* 1.184):

> He saw three stags wandering on the shore,

where either the three leaders of the Punic wars are meant, or the three Punic wars themselves. Also in the *Bucolics* (*Ecl.* 3.71):

> I have sent ten golden apples,

that is, ten pastoral eclogues to Augustus. This trope has many types, seven of which stand out: irony, antiphrasis, riddle, *charientismos*, *paroemia*, sarcasm, *astysmos*.

23. Irony (*ironia*) is an expression wherein by one's tone of voice the meaning is understood as the contrary. Thus with this trope something is said cleverly as an accusation or as an insult, as in this (Vergil, *Aen.* 1.140):

> Your home, East wind; let Aeolus take pride in that palace, and rule in that closed prison of winds.

And yet in what way is it a palace, if it is a prison? This is answered by the tone of voice, for the normal tone of voice applies to 'prison' and the irony is in 'take pride in' and 'palace.' And so, by a different tone of voice, the entire thing is made known through a display of irony, by which one derides by praising.

24. Antiphrasis (*antiphrasis*) is a term to be understood from its opposite, as 'grove' (*lucus*) because it lacks light (*lux*, gen. *lucis*), due to the excessive shade of the forest; and 'ghosts' (*manes*, from old Latin *mani*, "benevolent ones"), that is, 'mild ones' – although they are actually pitiless – and 'moderate ones' – although they are terrifying and savage (*immanes*); and the *Parcae* and *Eumenides* (lit. in Greek "the gracious ones"), that is, the Furies, because they spare (*parcere*) and are gracious to no one. By this trope also people call dwarves by Atlas's name, and call the blind 'the seers,' and commonly, call Ethiopians 'the silver ones.' 25. Between irony and antiphrasis there is this difference: that irony expresses what one intends to be understood through the tone of voice alone, as when we say to someone doing everything poorly, "You're doing a *good* job," while antiphrasis signifies the contrary not through the tone of voice, but only through its words, whose source has the opposite meaning.

26. A riddle (*aenigma*) is an obscure question that is difficult to solve unless it is explained, as this (Judges 14:14): "Out of the eater came forth food, and out of the strong came forth sweetness," meaning that a honeycomb was taken from the mouth of a (dead) lion. Between allegory and the riddle there is this difference, that the force of allegory is twofold and figuratively indicates one subject under the guise of other subjects, while a riddle merely has an obscure meaning, and its solution is hinted at through certain images.

27. *Charientismos* is a trope by which harsh things are made more pleasing in speech, as when someone asking, "Has anyone missed us?" is answered, "Good Fortune missed you." From this it is understood that no one has missed us. 28. *Paroemia* is a proverb appropriate to the subject or situation. To the subject, as in, "You kick against the pricks," when resisting adversity is meant. To the situation, as in "the wolf in the story": peasants say that a person would lose his voice if a wolf sees him before he sees the wolf. Thus the proverb, "the wolf in the story," is said to someone who suddenly falls silent. 29. Sarcasm (*sarcasmos*) is hostile ridicule with bitterness, as (cf. Vergil, *Aen.* 2.547):

> Therefore you will report these things, and you will go as a messenger of my father to the son of Peleus; remember to tell him of my sorry deeds and that Neoptolemus is degenerate.[43]

30. The opposite of this is *astysmos*, pleasantry without anger, as in this (Vergil, *Ecl.* 3.90):

> Whoever does not hate Bavius, may he love your songs, Maevius, and may he likewise yoke foxes and milk billy-goats.

That is, whoever does not hate Bavius is doomed to like Maevius – for Maevius and Bavius were terrible poets, and Vergil's enemies. Therefore, whoever loves them would do things contrary to nature, that is, he would yoke foxes and milk billy-goats.

31. *Homoeosis*, which is translated in Latin as similitude (*similitudo*), is that by which the description of some less known thing is made clear by something better known which is similar to it. There are three types: icon, parabola, and paradigm, that is, image, comparison, and

43 The received text of Vergil, with *genitori* rather than *genitoris*, means "to my father, the son of Peleus."

model. 32. Icon (*icon*, cf. εἰκών, "image") is an image (*imago*), when we attempt to explain the shape of a thing from a similar kind as (Vergil, *Aen.* 4.558):

> Similar to Mercury in all respects: in voice and color and blonde hair and graceful youthful limbs.

Thus similarity with regard to appearance is fitting for the one whose character is introduced. 33. Parabola (*parabola*) is a comparison (*comparatio*) from dissimilar things, as (cf. Lucan, *Civil War* 1.205):

> Like a lion seen hard by in the fields of heat-bearing Libya, he beset the enemy,

where he compares Caesar to a lion, making a comparison, not from his own kind, but from another. 34. Paradigm (*paradigma*) is a model (*exemplum*) of someone's word or deed, or something that is appropriate to the thing that we describe either from its similar or from its dissimilar nature, thus: "Scipio perished at Hippo as bravely as did Cato at Utica."

35. A comparison (*similitudo*) may be made in three ways: from an equal, from a greater, from a lesser. From an equal (Vergil, *Aen.* 1.148):

> And just as often when rebellion has broken out in a great populace.

From a greater to a lesser (Lucan, *Civil War* 1.151):

> Just as lightning is forced down by the winds through the clouds.

And from a lesser to a greater (Vergil, *Aen.* 6.119):

> If Orpheus could summon the spirit of his wife, relying on a Thracian cithara and its melodious strings,

as if he meant, relying on a small unimportant object; that is, if he relies on a cithara, I rely on my piety.

xxxviii. Prose (De prosa) 1. Prose (*prosa*) is an extended discourse, unconstrained by rules of meter. The ancients used to say that prose is extended (*productus*) and straightforward (*rectus*).[44] Whence Varro in his work on Plautus says that *prosis lectis* (read as prose) means 'straightforwardly,' and thus a discourse that is not inflected by meter, but is straightforward, is called prose in that it extends (*producere*) directly. Others say that prose is so called because it is profuse (*profusus*), or because it 'rushes forth' (*proruere*) and runs expansively with no set limit to it. 2. Moreover, for the Greeks as well as the Romans, the interest in poems was far more ancient than in prose, for at first all things used to be set in verse, and enthusiasm for prose flourished later. Among the Greeks, Pherecydes of Syros was first to write with unmetered speech, and among the Romans, Appius Caecus, in his oration against Pyrrhus, was first to use unmetered speech. Straightway after this, others competed by means of eloquence in prose.

xxxix. Meters (De metris) 1. Meters (*metrum*) are so called because they are bounded by the fixed measures (*mensura*) and intervals of feet, and they do not proceed beyond the designated dimension of time – for measure is called μέτρον in Greek. 2. Verses are so called because when they are arranged in their regular order into feet they are governed within a fixed limit through segments that are called caesurae (*caesum*) and members (*membrum*). Lest these segments roll on longer than good judgment could sustain, reason has established a measure from which the verse should be turned back; from this 'verse' (*versus*) itself is named, because it is turned back (*revertere*, ppl. *reversus*). 3. And related to this is rhythm (*rhythmus*), which is not governed by a specific limit, but nevertheless proceeds regularly with ordered feet. In Latin this is called none other than 'number' (*numerus*), regarding which is this (Vergil, *Ecl.* 9.45):

> I recall the numbers (*numerus*), if I could grasp the words!

4. Whatever has metric feet is called a 'poem' (*carmen*). People suppose that the name was given to it either because it was pronounced 'in pieces' (*carptim*), just as today we say that wool that the scourers tear in pieces is carded (*carminare*), or because they used to think that people who sang those poems had lost (*carere*) their minds.

5. Meters are named either after their feet, or after the topics about which they are written, or after their inventors, or after those who commonly use them, or after the number of syllables. 6. Meters named after feet are, for example, dactylic, iambic, trochaic, for trochaic meter is constructed from the trochee, dactylic from the dactyl, and others similarly from their feet. Meters are named after number, as hexameter, pentameter, trimeter – as

44 In fact the old form of the word *prorsus*, "straight on," was *prosus*, the source of the word *prosa*.

we name one kind of verse *senarius* (i.e. 'of six') from the number of feet. But the Greeks call them trimeters, because they pair them. Ennius is said to be the first to have written Latin hexameters; people call them 'long' verses. 7. Meters are said to be named for their inventors, as Anacreontic, Sapphic, Archilochian. Thus Anacreon composed Anacreontic meters, the woman Sappho published Sapphic meters, a certain Archilochus wrote Archilochian meters, and a certain Colophonius practiced Colophonian meters. And the deviser of Sotadean meters is Sotades, a Cretan by family. And the lyric poet Simonides composed Simonidian meters.

8. Meters are named for those commonly using them, as, for example, Asclepiadian meters. Now Aesclepius did not invent them, but they were named thus from his time on because he used them most elegantly [and most often]. 9. Meters are named for the topics about which they are written, as heroic, elegiac, bucolic. For instance, a poem is called heroic (*heroicus*) because the acts and deeds of strong men are recounted in it, for celestial (*aerius*) men, as it were, worthy of the skies because of their wisdom and strength, are called heroes (*heros*). This meter (i.e. dactylic hexameter) takes precedence over the others in importance. It alone of all the meters is suited for great works as much as for small, equally capable of smoothness and sweetness. 10. On account of these powers, it alone receives this name, as it is called 'heroic' so that the deeds of heroes will be remembered. It is considered the simplest of all meters, and is composed using two feet, the dactyl and the spondee. It often consists almost entirely of either the former or the latter, except that the most well balanced verse is made with a mixture of both rather than being formed by a single type of foot.

11. The heroic is also the earliest of all meters. Moses is shown to have composed this meter first in his song in Deuteronomy (Deuteronomy 32–33) long before Pherecydes and Homer. Whence it appears that the practice of poetry is more ancient among the Hebrews than among the pagans, seeing that Job, a contemporary of Moses, also took up hexameter verse, with its dactyl and spondee. 12. Achatesius of Miletus is said to have been first among the Greeks to compose this, or, as others suppose, Pherecydes of Syros. This meter was called Pythian before Homer, and after Homer was called heroic. 13. People choose to call it Pythian because the oracles of Apollo were proclaimed in this kind of meter. When he attacked the serpent Python with arrows on Parnassus, to avenge his mother, the dwellers at Delphi cheered him on with this meter, saying, as Terentianus has it (*On Meter* 1591): [ἰὴ παιάν, ἰὴ παιάν, ἰὴ παιάν].

14. The 'elegiac' (*elegiacus*) meter is so called because the measure of this particular song is suited for mournful subjects. Terentianus (*On Meter* 1799) used to call those meters 'elegiacs' because such a rhythmic closure, as they say, is more suited to sorrowful modes. 15. But by whom this was invented there is hardly any agreement, except that Ennius was the first among us Latin speakers to use it. Moreover, a dispute among the grammarians continues to this day about who was first among Greeks, so it may be set aside as a matter *sub iudice.* Some of them claim a certain Colophonian as the inventor and author, and some of them Archilochus.

16. And many people believe the bucolic (*bucolicus*), that is, the pastoral (*pastoralis*) poem, was first composed by shepherds in Syracuse, and some believe by shepherds in Sparta. As Xerxes, king of the Persians, crossed into Thrace, and the Spartan maidens, in fear of the enemy, neither left the city nor performed the solemn procession and rustic dance of Diana according to custom, a crowd of shepherds celebrated this with artless songs, lest the religious observance should pass unmarked. And it is called bucolic for the most part, although speeches and songs of shepherds and goatherds are contained in it.[45]

17. It is clear that David the prophet first composed and sang hymns (*hymnus*) in praise of God. Then, among the pagans, Memmia Timothoe – who lived in the time of Ennius, long after David – first made hymns to Apollo and the Muses. 'Hymns' are translated from Greek into Latin as "praises" (*laudes*). 18. Epithalamiums (*epithalamium*) are wedding songs, which are sung by rhetoricians in honor of the bride and groom. Solomon first composed these in praise of the church and of Christ (i.e. the Song of Songs). From him the pagans appropriated the epithalamium for themselves, and a song of this type was taken up. This kind of song was first performed by pagans on the stage, and later was associated only with weddings. It is called epithalamium because it is sung in bedchambers (*thalamus*).

45 Isidore refers to the inconsistency that the term 'bucolic' is derived in Greek from βουκόλος ("cowherd"), although it has its origin in songs of shepherds and goatherds rather than cowherds.

19. Jeremiah first composed the threnody (*threnos*), which is called 'lament' (*lamentum*) in Latin, in a poem on the city of Jerusalem [when it was destroyed] and on the people [Israel] when they [were destroyed and] were led captive. After this, among the Greeks, Simonides the lyric poet was first. It was associated with funerals and laments, as it is today. 20. 'Epitaph' (*epitaphium*) in Greek is translated in Latin as "over the grave" (*supra tumulum*), for it is an inscription about the dead, which is made over the repose of those who are now dead. Their life, conduct, and age are written there. 21. A work consisting of many books is called a *poesis* by its Greek name; a poem (*poema*) is a work of one book, an idyll (*idyllion*), a work of few verses, a distich (*distichon*) of two verses, and a monostich (*monostichon*) of one verse. 22. An epigram (*epigramma*) is an inscription, which is translated into Latin as "a writing upon something" (*superscriptio*), for ἐπί is translated as "upon" (*super*) and γράμμα as "letter" or "writing" (*scriptio*). 23. An epode (*epodon*) is a short 'concluding passage' (*clausula*) in a poem. It is called epode because it is sung after the manner of elegiac verse, which consists of a longer line set down first, and then another, shorter, line. The shorter ones that follow each of the longer are used as a refrain, as if they were *clausulae*. 24. The lyric poets speak of *clausulae* as cutoff verses substituted for whole verses, as with Horace (*Epodes* 2.1):

> *Beatus ille, qui procul negotiis*
> (O happy he who, far from busyness),

and then a cutoff verse follows:

> *Ut prisca gens mortalium*
> (Like the first race of mortals),

and thus alternate verses in succession lack some part: similar to the verse preceding, but shorter (i.e. iambic trimeters alternate with iambic dimeters).

25. The grammarians are accustomed to call those poems 'centos' (*cento*) which piece together their own particular work in a patchwork (*centonarius*) manner from poems of Homer and Vergil, making a single poem out of many scattered passages previously composed, based on the possibilities offered by each source. 26. In fact, Proba, wife of Adelphus, copied a very full cento from Vergil on the creation of the world and the Gospels (i.e. *Cento Probae*), with its subject matter composed in accordance with Vergil's verses, and the verses fitted together in accordance with her subject matter. Thus also a certain Pomponius, among other compositions of his leisure hours, written in his own style, composed his *Tityrus* out of this same poet, in honor of Christ; likewise he composed a cento from the *Aeneid*.

xl. The fable (De fabula) 1. Poets named 'fables' (*fabula*) from 'speaking' (*fari*), because they are not actual events that took place, but were only invented in words. These are presented with the intention that the conversation of imaginary dumb animals among themselves may be recognized as a certain image of the life of humans. Alcmeon of Croton is said to have been the first to invent these, and they are called Aesopian, because among the Phrygians, Aesop was accomplished in this area. 2. And there are both Aesopian fables and Libystican fables. They are Aesopian fables when dumb animals, or inanimate things such as cities, trees, mountains, rocks, and rivers, are imagined to converse among themselves. But they are Libystican fables when humans are imagined as conversing with animals, or animals with humans. 3. Poets have made up some fables for the sake of entertainment, and expounded others as having to do with the nature of things, and still others as about human morals. Those made up for the sake of entertainment are such as are commonly told, or that kind that Plautus and Terence composed. 4. People make up fables about the nature of things, like 'crooked-limbed Vulcan,' because by nature fire is never straight, and like the animal with three shapes (Lucretius *On the Nature of Things* 5.905):

> A lion in front, a dragon in the rear, and in the middle, the Chimaera itself,

that is, a she-goat.[46] With this, people intend to distinguish the ages of man: the first, adolescence, is ferocious and bristling, like a lion; the midpart of life is the most lucid, like a she-goat, because she sees most acutely; then comes old age with its crooked happenstances – the dragon. 5. Thus also the fable of the Hippocentaur, that is, a human being mixed with a horse, was invented to express the speedy course of human life, because it is known that a horse is very fast.

46 That is, the middle of the creature has the form of a she-goat. Lucretius took the basic form of the Chimaera, and hence its torso, to be a she-goat (*capra*), from the Greek χίμαιρα, "she-goat" or "the monster Chimaera." Here and elsewhere Isidore uses the word *caprea*, regularly meaning "roe-deer," for "she-goat" (regularly *capra*).

6. Then there are fables with a moral, as in Horace a mouse speaks to a mouse, and a weasel to a little fox, so that through an imaginary story a true meaning may be applied to the story's action. Whence also Aesop's fables are the kind told for the purpose of a moral, just as in the book of Judges (9:8) the trees seek a king for themselves and speak to the olive tree, the fig tree, the grape vine, and the bramble-bush. The whole story is made up especially for the moral, so that we arrive at the matter that is intended with the true meaning, though, to be sure, by means of a made-up narrative. 7. Thus the orator Demosthenes used a fable against Philip: when Philip had ordered the Athenians to give him ten orators, and only then would he depart, Demosthenes invented a fable by which he dissuaded the Athenians from yielding. He said that once upon a time wolves persuaded shepherds whose attentiveness they wished to lull that they should meet in friendship – but with the condition that the shepherds would duly hand over their dogs, which were a cause of strife, to the wolves. The shepherds agreed to this and in the hope of security handed over their dogs, who had kept the most vigilant watch over their sheep. Then the wolves, since the source of their fear had been removed, tore to pieces all that were in the shepherds' herds, not only to satisfy their hunger, but also their wantonness. He said that Philip also was making a demand of the leaders of the people so that he might the more easily oppress a city deprived of its protectors.

xli. History (De historia) 1. A history (*historia*) is a narration of deeds accomplished; through it what occurred in the past is sorted out. History is so called from the Greek term ἱστορεῖν ("inquire, observe"), that is, from 'seeing' or from 'knowing.' Indeed, among the ancients no one would write a history unless he had been present and had seen what was to be written down, for we grasp with our eyes things that occur better than what we gather with our hearing, 2. since what is seen is revealed without falsehood. This discipline has to do with Grammar, because whatever is worthy of remembrance is committed to writing. And for this reason, histories are called 'monuments' (*monumentum*), because they grant a remembrance (*memoria*) of deeds that have been done. A series (*series*) is so called by an analogy with a garland (*serta*) of flowers tied together one after the other.

xlii. The first authors of histories (De primis auctoribus historiarum) 1. Among us Christians Moses was the first to write a history, on creation. But among the pagans, Dares the Phrygian was first to publish a history, on the Greeks and Trojans, which they say he wrote on palm leaves. 2. After Dares, Herodotus is held as the first to write history in Greece. After him Pherecydes was renowned, at the time when Ezra wrote the law.

xliii. The utility of history (De utilitate historiae) Histories of peoples are no impediment to those who wish to read useful works, for many wise people have imparted the past deeds of humankind in histories for the instruction of the living. Through history they handle a final reckoning back through seasons and years, and they investigate many indispensable matters through the succession of consuls and kings.

xliv. The kinds of history (De generibus historiae) 1. There are three kinds of history. The events of a single day are called an 'ephemeris' (*ephemeris*); we call this a 'diary' (*diarium*). What the Romans call 'daily' (*diurnus*), the Greeks call *ephemeris*. 2. Histories that are distributed into individual months are called 'calendars' (*kalendarium*). 3. Annals (*annales*) are the actions of individual years (*annus*), for whatever domestic or military matters, on sea or land, worthy of memory are treated year by year in records they called 'annals' from yearly (*anniversarius*) deeds. 4. But history (*historia*) concerns itself with many years or ages, and through the diligence of history annual records are reported in books. There is this difference between history and annals, namely, that history is of those times that we have seen, but annals are of those years that our age has not known. Whence Sallust consists of history, and Livy, Eusebius, and Jerome of annals and history. 5. And history, 'plausible narration' (*argumentum*),[47] and fable differ from one other. Histories are true deeds that have happened, plausible narrations are things that, even if they have not happened, nevertheless could happen, and fables are things that have not happened and cannot happen, because they are contrary to nature.

47 On the term *argumentum* as "possible fiction" see E. R. Curtius, *European Literature and the Latin Middle Ages*, trans. Trask (NY, 1953), 452–55.

Book II

Rhetoric and dialectic (De rhetorica et dialectica)

i. Rhetoric and its name (De rhetorica eiusque nomine) 1. Rhetoric is the art of speaking well in civil cases, [and eloquence (*eloquentia*) is fluency (*copia*)] for the purpose of persuading people toward the just and good. Rhetoric is named from the Greek term ῥητορίζειν, that is, fluency of speech, for ῥῆσις in Greek means "speech," ῥήτωρ means "orator." 2. Further, rhetoric is connected with the art of grammar (*Grammatica*), for in grammar we learn the art of speaking correctly, while in rhetoric we understand how we may express what we have learned.

ii. The founders of the art of rhetoric (De inventoribus rhetoricae artis) 1. This discipline was invented by the Greeks, by Gorgias, Aristotle, and Hermagoras, and was carried over into Latin culture by Cicero and Quintilian [and Titianus],[1] but so copiously and variously that it is easy for a reader to wonder at it, but impossible to grasp it fully. 2. For while one has a treatise on rhetoric in hand, the sequence of its content as it were clings to the memory, but when it is set aside all recollection of it soon slips away. Accomplished knowledge of this discipline makes one an orator.

iii. The term 'orator' and the parts of rhetoric (De nomine oratoris et partibus rhetoricae) 1. An orator therefore is a good man, skilled in speaking. A man's goodness is based on his nature, his behavior, his training in the arts. One skilled in speaking is grounded in artful eloquence, which consists of five parts: invention, arrangement, style, memory, pronunciation (*inventio, dispositio, elocutio, memoria, pronuntiatio*), and of the goal of this office, which is to persuade of something. 2. Further, this skill in speaking is based on three things: one's nature, instruction, and practice. Nature, from one's native wit; instruction, from acquired knowledge; practice, from diligence. And these are things that are looked for not only in an orator, but in any skilled person, in order that he might accomplish something.

iv. The three kinds of arguments (De tribus generibus causarum)[2] 1. There are three kinds of arguments: deliberative, demonstrative, and judicial (*deliberativus, demonstrativus, iudicialis*). The deliberative kind treats questions of expediency in life, what ought or ought not to be done. The demonstrative is the kind in which a praiseworthy or reprehensible person is displayed as such. 2. Judicial, in which a decision for punishment or reward is rendered according to the deed of that person. It is called 'judicial' because it judges (*iudicare*) a man, and its decision shows whether a praiseworthy person may be worthy of a reward, or whether a person surely charged with a crime may be condemned or freed from punishment.

3. The deliberative kind is so called because in it one deliberates (*deliberare*) concerning some matter. There are two types of this kind, suasion and dissuasion, that is, concerning what ought to be sought and what ought to be avoided, what ought to be done and not done. 4. Suasive argument is further divided into three topics: the decent, the useful, and the possible. This differs somewhat from deliberative argument in that suasive argument has to do with another person, whereas deliberative argument sometimes deals with oneself alone. Further, in suasive argument two things are especially effective: hope and fear.

5. Demonstrative argument is so called because it describes (*demonstrare*) some particular thing, either by praising or by blaming. This class has two species: praise (*laus*) and blame (*vituperatio*). The sequence of praising is divided into three periods of time: before, during, or after the act or person being praised. 6. Before, as (Vergil, *Aen.* 1.605):

> What such happy times brought you forth?

1 This 'Titianus' is probably an artifact of scribal error.

2 *Causa* may often be translated as "(legal) case," or "(rhetorical or legal) argument," or "cause."

in the present, as (*Aen.* 1.597):

> O you alone in pitying the unspeakable hardships of Troy;

after, as (*Aen.* 1.607):

> As long as rivers run into the sea, as long as shadows traverse the mountains, your honor, your name, your praises will remain always.

7. With an equal and inverted type of argument, this pattern is preserved in blaming a person: before, during, or after the present circumstances of the person.

A commonplace (*locus communis*) pertains to the demonstrative class of blaming, but it differs from it in a certain way, for blame, which is the opposite of praise, is directed especially to the particular character of the doer, 8. whereas a commonplace is rather set forth in a general way with regard to the wickedness of the thing done. Hence it is called a commonplace, because, in the absence of personal characteristics, it treats not so much a particular individual as the wicked deed itself. Indeed, every vice is found not in one person only, but as common to many.

v. The two states of legal arguments (De gemino statu causarum) 1. For rhetoricians, that matter in which a case (*causa*) has standing is called its 'state' (*status*), that is, the issue (*constitutio*).[3] Greek speaks of a 'state' from στάσις, "contention." The Latin term however is not only from battle, in which adversaries battle over a proposition, but also because in it each party 'has standing' (*consistere*). A state consists of the charge and the rebuttal. 2. The states of cases are two: rational (*rationalis*) and legal (*legalis*).

From the rational state arise the classes conjecture, purpose, quality, transference (*coniectura, finis, qualitas, translatio*). Under purpose, judicial (*iudicialis*) and 'related to affairs' (*negotialis*). Under judicial, absolute (*absoluta*) and extraneous (*adsumptiva*). Under extraneous: concession (*concessio*), setting aside the charge (*remotio criminis*), retorting to the charge (*relatio criminis*), compensation (*compensatio*). Under concession, self-justification (*purgatio*) and plea for indulgence (*deprecatio*). 3. The conjectural (*coniecturalis*) state obtains when an action alleged by one side is flatly denied by the other. The state is definitive (*definitivus*) when that which is alleged is argued not to exist as such, but what it may be is proved by means of the definitions employed. The state 'quality' (*qualitas*) obtains when 'what sort of' (*qualis*) matter may be in hand is considered; because it deals with controversy concerning the force and class (*genus*) of the affair, this proceeding (*constitutio*) is called 'general' (*generalis*). 4. Transference (*translatio*) obtains when a case hangs on this: either that a person seems not to have committed the deed in question, or not at the appropriate time, or with the appropriate law, or charge, or punishment. That proceeding is 'transferent' because the suit seems to be in need of transference and change. 5. A judicial (*iudicialis*) state is that in which is investigated the nature of what is fair and right, and the recompense or the rationale for the punishment. That state is 'related to affairs' (*negotialis*) in which is considered the part of the law that has to do with established practice and equity between citizens. The extraneous (*adsumptivus*) state is that which offers nothing firm of itself against an objection, [but takes to itself (*adsumere*) some defense from outside]. 6. Concession (*concessio*) obtains when the accused does not offer a defense concerning what has been done, but asks for it to be forgiven. We have ourselves shown this to pertain to penitents. 'Setting aside the charge' (*remotio criminis*) occurs when a defendant makes every effort to displace onto some other person a crime caused by himself and his own fault.

7. 'Retorting to the charge' (*relatio criminis*) occurs when the deed is declared justly done because someone was harmed beforehand by an injustice. Comparison (*comparatio*) occurs when some deed of another person is argued to be proper and useful, because as that deed happened, so this deed at issue is said to have been committed. 8. Purgation (*purgatio*) obtains when, although the deed is admitted, the liability is set aside. This has three types: ignorance, accident, necessity (*inprudentia, casus, necessitas*). The 'plea for indulgence' (*deprecatio*) occurs when the defendant admits to having done wrong, and having done wrong deliberately, and yet he requests that he be forgiven. This type very seldom occurs.

9. Then from state of 'appeal to the law' (*legalis*) these types emerge, that is: 'written law and its intention'

3 In Latin the words for status, state, standing, consist, and constitution are obviously related via the verb *stare*, "to stand." Here 'state' means practically "an issue," "a point of dispute," involving the classes of argument pro and con about a legal case.

(*scriptum et voluntas*), contradictory laws (*leges contrariae*), ambiguity (*ambiguitas*), inference or logical reasoning (*collectio sive ratiocinatio*), and legal definition (*definitio*). The argument 'what is written and its intention' is used when the words themselves seem to be at variance with the thought of the writer. The argument of 'contradictory laws' operates when two or more laws are recognized as contradictory. 'Ambiguity' occurs when what is written seems to mean two or more things. The argument by 'inference or logical reasoning' is used when, from what is written, another thing that is not written is deduced. 'Legal definition' obtains when one investigates the meaning it has in the specific point of dispute in which it is found.

10. The types of argument, then, rational and legal together, are reckoned by some quite definitely as eighteen. But according to Cicero on rhetoric (*On Invention* 1.8) there are nineteen, because he locates 'transference' (*translatio*) chiefly among the 'rational' arguments. Yet even Cicero, refuting himself, includes 'transference' among the legal arguments.

vi. The tripartite dispute (De tripertita controversia) 1. According to Cicero, a tripartite dispute is either simple or conjunct (*iunctus*). If conjunct, it should be considered whether it is a conjunction of several questions, or of some comparison. That dispute is simple which presents a single unqualified question, thus: "Should we declare war on Corinth or not?" 2. A dispute is conjoint of several questions, in which several things are queried, in this way: "Should Carthage be demolished, or rather given back to the Carthaginians, or rather should a colony be planted there?" A dispute is conjunct by way of comparison when one queries what is better or best to do, in this fashion: "Should the army be sent into Macedonia against Philip, so that it might help our allies, or rather be retained in Italy, so that there may be the greatest strength against Hannibal?"

vii. The four parts of an oration (De quattuor partibus orationis) 1. In rhetoric there are four parts of an oration (*oratio*): the exordium (*exordium*), the narrative (*narratio*), the argumentation (*argumentatio*), the conclusion (*conclusio*). The first of these elicits the attention of the listener, the second lays out the facts, the third establishes trust in what is asserted, the fourth completes the end of the whole oration. 2. One ought to begin so as to render the listener benevolent, docile, or attentive: benevolent by entreaty, docile by instruction, attentive by stimulation. In the narrative we should speak briefly and candidly. The argumentation should first confirm our own position, and then demolish the adversary view. The conclusion should incite the listeners' hearts to carry out what we say.

viii. The five types of cases (De quinque modis causarum) 1. There are five kinds of cases: honorable, surprising, humble, doubtful, obscure (*honestus, admirabilis, humilis, anceps, obscurus*). The honorable type of case is that in which the mind of the listener is immediately, without our oration, well-disposed. The surprising, in which the inclinations of those who are about to hear are on the other side. The humble, to which the listener pays little attention. 2. The doubtful, in which either the judgment is doubtful, or a case is of partly decent and partly wicked matters, so that it arouses both benevolence and offense. The obscure, in which either the listeners are slow-witted, or the case is perceived to be tied up in matters that are rather hard to understand.

ix. Syllogisms (De syllogismis) 1. The Greek term 'syllogism' (*syllogismus*) is called 'argumentation' (*argumentatio*) in Latin. 'Argumentation' is so called as if it were the 'speech of a clear mind' (*argutae mentis oratio*), with which we follow through to a probable discovery. A syllogism therefore is the final conclusion (*conclusio*) of a proposition and an additional proposition and a demonstration, either from the uncertainty of someone disputing, or the assurance of someone proving. 2. Hence a syllogism consists of three parts: proposition (*propositio*, i.e. the major premise), the additional proposition (*assumptio*, i.e. the minor premise), and the conclusion (*conclusio*). The major premise, for example: "What is good cannot have a bad use." The listener grants it. One 'adds a minor premise' (*adsumere*): "Money has a bad use." It is concluded (*concludere*), "Therefore money is not good."

3. Not only rhetoricians, but especially logicians use syllogisms, although the apostle Paul often puts forth major and minor premises and confirms with a conclusion – which things, as we have said, belong properly to the disciplines of logic and rhetoric. 4. Among rhetoricians the main kinds of syllogisms are two: induction

(*inductio*) and inference (*ratiocinatio*). The parts of induction are three: first the proposition (i.e. the major premise); second the 'thing brought in' (*illatio*, from *inferre*, "infer"), also called the 'additional proposition' (*assumptio*, i.e. the minor premise); third the conclusion. 5. Induction is that which in matters not liable to doubt demands assent when it is carried out, among philosophers or rhetoricians or people conversing. The major premise of an induction introduces (*inducere*) parallels, in one or more aspects, to the matter that must be granted. 6. The 'thing brought in' of an induction, also called the minor premise, is that which introduces the matter in dispute for whose sake the parallels were used. The conclusion of an induction is that which either confirms what is granted in the minor premise, or states what may be deduced from it.

Inference (*ratiocinatio*) is a discourse by which what is in question is put to the test. 7. There are two types of inference. First is the enthymeme (*enthymema*), which is an incomplete syllogism, and used in rhetoric. The second is the epichireme (*epichirema*), an unrhetorical, broader syllogism. 8. Hence 'enthymeme' is translated into Latin 'conception of the mind' (*conceptio mentis*),[4] and writers on the art usually call it an incomplete syllogism, because its form of argument consists of two parts, as it employs what aims to arouse conviction while bypassing the rule of syllogisms. For example: "If the storm is to be avoided, therefore one ought not sail." Thus the argument is completed from the major premise and the conclusion alone, whence it is considered more appropriate for orators than logicians.

9. There are five branches of enthymeme: first the convincing, second the demonstrating, third the sententious, fourth the exemplifying, and fifth the collective (*convincibilis, ostentabilis, sententialis, exemplabilis, collectivus*). 10. The convincing is that which convinces by manifest reason, as Cicero did in his *Defense of Milo* (79): "Therefore you are sitting as avengers of the death of a man whose life you would not be willing to restore, even if you thought you could." 11. The demonstrating is that which exerts control by means of an indisputable depiction (*demonstratio*) of the defendant, as Cicero in the *Catiline Oration* (1.2): "Still he lives; nay, he even comes into the senate." The sententious is that which a general maxim (*sententia*) adduces, as in Terence (*Andria* 68):

Flattery breeds friends; truth, hatred.

12. The exemplifying is that which compares some other situation (*exemplum*), and by this means threatens that the outcome will be similar, as Cicero says in his *Philippics* (2.1): "I wonder, Antonius, that you do not tremble at the fates of those whose example you imitate." 13. The collective enthymeme collects (*colligere*, ppl. *collectus*) what has been argued into one, as Cicero says in his *Defense of Milo* (cf. 41): "Was he then willing to do, irritating some, what he was not willing to do with the gratitude (of all)? Did he have no hesitation in killing lawlessly, at an unpropitious time, risking his neck, a man he did not venture to kill with the law, the place, and the time on his side?"

14. Moreover there is another definition of the enthymeme, according to (Marius) Victorinus: from the major premise (*propositio*) alone, as has already been said, which is composed thus: "If the storm is to be avoided, one should not seek to sail." 15. Or from the minor premise (*assumptio*) alone, as this: "If he is an enemy, he slays; moreover he [is] an enemy." Because the conclusion is lacking here, it is called an enthymeme. 16. Next is the epichireme, deriving from inference as broader and more developed than rhetorical syllogisms, distinct in breadth and in length of utterance from logical syllogisms, for which reason it is given to the rhetoricians. This consists of three types: the first, of three parts; the second, of four parts; the third, of five parts.

17. The three-part epichirematic syllogism consists of three members: the major premise (*propositio*), minor premise (*assumptio*), and conclusion (*conclusio*). The four-part type consists of four members: first the major premise, second the minor premise joined to the major premise or a minor premise, third the proof (*probatio*), and the conclusion.[5] 18. The five-part type accordingly has five members: first the major premise, second its proof, third the minor premise, fourth its proof, fifth the conclusion. Cicero thus constructs this type in his art of rhetoric (*On Invention* 1.9): "If deliberation (*deliberatio*) and demonstration (*demonstratio*) are kinds of arguments (*causa*), they cannot rightly be considered parts of any one kind of argument – for the same thing can be a kind of one thing and part of another, but not

4 The term derives from the Greek ἐν + ϑυμός, 'mind.'

5 Isidore's source here, Cassiodorus, makes sense in speaking of the third part as the proof joined to either the major or minor premise.

a kind and a part of the same thing," and so forth, up to the point where the constituents of this syllogism are concluded.

x. Law (De lege) 1. Law (*lex*) is the ordinance (*constitutio*) of the people, which the nobility have solemnly ratified with the common people. What a king or emperor proclaims (*edicere*), is called an ordinance (*constitutio*) or edict (*edictum*). The basis of fairness (*aequitas*) is twofold, sometimes in laws, sometimes in custom (*mores*). Between law and custom there is this difference, that law is written, while custom is usage (*consuetudo*) tested and found good by its antiquity, or unwritten law. Indeed, law (*lex*) is so named from 'reading' (*legere*), because it is written. 2. Custom (*mos*) is longstanding usage, taken likewise from 'moral habits' (*mores*, the plural of *mos*). 'Customary law' (*consuetudo*) moreover is a certain system of justice (*ius*), established by moral habits, which is received as law when law is lacking; nor does it matter whether it exists in writing or in reason, seeing that reason commends a law. 3. Indeed if law amounts to reason (*ratio*), the law will consist of everything that already agrees with reason, provided that it accords with religion, befits orderly conduct, and profits welfare. Customary law is so called because it is in 'common use' (*communis usus*).

4. Every law either permits something, as "a valiant man may seek his reward," or it forbids, as "it is not permitted to marry a sacred virgin," or it punishes, as "he who commits murder will undergo capital punishment." 5. Moreover laws are made so that human audacity may be controlled by fear of them, and that innocence may be protected among the wicked, and that among the wicked themselves the power of harming may be reined in by the fear of punishment – for by the rewards and punishments of the law, human life is governed. 6. A law will be decent, just, enforceable, natural, in keeping with the custom of the country, appropriate to the place and time, needful, useful, and also clear – so that it does not contain anything that can deceive through obscurity – and for no private benefit, but for the common profit (*communis utilitas*) of the citizens.

xi. The maxim (De sententia) 1. A maxim (*sententia*) is an impersonal saying, as (Terence, *Andria* 68):

> Flattery breeds friends; truth, hatred.

If a person were added to this, it would be a chreia (*chria*), thus: "Achilles offended Agamemnon by speaking the truth" or "Metrophanes earned the favor of Mithridates by flattering him." 2. For between chreia and maxim is this distinction, that a maxim is uttered without a person, and a chreia is never said without a person. Whence if a person is added to a maxim, it becomes a chreia; if the person is taken away, it becomes a maxim.

xii. Confirmation and refutation (De catasceva et anasceva) 1. A confirmation (*catasceva*) is a corroboration of the thing proposed, while a refutation (*anasceva*) is the contrary of the above, for it refutes the possibility that something proposed as having been born or made or said exists or ever existed. It is as if, for example, someone should deny that a Chimaera existed, or confirm that it existed. 2. Between these arguments and a thesis (*thesis*) is this difference, that a thesis, although it also may enter debate on either side, nevertheless is a kind of pondering or urging about an uncertain matter. Further, confirmations and refutations mostly engage in those matters that are improbable, but that are put forward as truths.

3. The first division of the refutation is the inappropriate (*inconveniens*) and the lie (*mendacium*). The species of the inappropriate are the indecent and the useless. Again the indecent is treated either in words or deeds. In words, when someone is said to have used words that are ugly and not appropriate to someone's authority, as if someone were to defame Cato the Censor himself as having incited young people to wickedness and lechery. 4. In deeds, as if someone were said to have done something inappropriate to piety and his own good name, as is the fable of the adultery of Mars and Venus.

The lie (*mendacium*) has three kinds. The incredible lie, in which something is not believed to have been done, as the youth who, standing on the Sicilian shore, saw the fleet approach Africa. 5. The impossible lie, as Clodius laid a trap for Milo and was killed by Milo. This is a contradiction, for if he laid a trap, he killed. He was killed; he did not lay a trap. This pattern reworked into its contrary would be an effective confirmation (*catasceva*). [We may set down as all the gradations the decent, the useful, the likely, the possible, the consistent, or conversely the indecent, the useless, the insufficiently likely, the impossible, the contradictory.] It will be fitting nevertheless so to arrange our principles that we say either that one ought to believe in the authority of the ancients, or that faith in fables is not to be maintained. 6. And with regard to this last, by way of refutation (*anasceva*) we should ask whether they who concocted those things did not wish to mean something else, as that Scylla lived not as a sea-hag, but as a seaside-dwelling woman, not girded by dogs, but as someone rapacious and inhospitable to visitors.

xiii. Prosopopoeia (De prosopoeia) 1. Prosopopoeia occurs when personality and speech are invented for inanimate things. Cicero in the *Catiline Oration* (1.27): "If, in truth, my fatherland, which is far dearer to me than my life, were to speak with me, saying," etc. 2. Thus we bring in speaking mountains and rivers or trees, imposing personhood on a thing that does not have the capacity for speech. This is common in tragedies and found very frequently in orations.

xiv. Ethopoeia (De ethopoeia) 1. We call that 'ethopoeia' whereby we represent the character of a person in such a way as to express traits related to age, occupation, fortune, happiness, gender, grief, boldness. Thus when the character of a pirate is taken up, the speech will be bold, abrupt, rash; when the speech of a woman is imitated, the oration ought to fit her sex. A distinct way of speaking ought to be used for young and old, soldier and general, parasite and rustic and philosopher. 2. One caught up in joy speaks one way, one wounded, another. In this genre of speech these things should be most fully thought out: who speaks and with whom, about whom, where, and when, what one has done or will do, or what one can suffer if one neglects these decrees.

xv. Kinds of questions (De generibus quaestionum) 1. There are two kinds of questions, of which one is the finite (*finitus*), the other the indefinite (*infinitus*). The finite is ὑπόθεσις in Greek, called 'case' (*causa*) in Latin, where there is controversy with a particular person. 2. The indefinite is called θέσις in Greek, 'proposition' (*propositum*) in Latin. This concerns no particular person, nor is there in it any particular circumstance, that is, neither place nor time. In a case (*causa*) everything is particular, whence a proposition is as it were a part of a case.[6]

xvi. Style (De elocutione) 1. With regard to style (*elocutio*) it will be correct to use what the matter, the place, the time, and the character of the audience require, ensuring that profane things are not be mingled with religious, immodest with chaste, frivolous with weighty, playful with earnest, or laughable with sad. 2. One ought to speak in good Latin, and clearly, for he speaks in good Latin who persistently seeks the true and natural words for things, nor does he diverge from the speech and culture of the present time. It is not enough for such a man to watch what he says, unless he says it openly and smoothly; and more than that, his actions must match his words.

xvii. The three registers of speaking (De trimodo dicendi genere) 1. One ought to speak of humble things softly, of dramatic matters emphatically, of varied matters moderately. Indeed, these are the familiar three registers (*genus*) of speaking: humble, middling, grandiloquent (*humilis, medius, grandiloquus*). Now when we say great things, they should be uttered grandly; when we speak of small things, delicately; when things of the middling sort, temperately. 2. For in small causes nothing should be spoken grandly or loftily, but one should speak in a simple and ordinary manner. But in greater causes, where we deal with God or human salvation, more magnificence and brilliance should be displayed. 3. In moderate causes, where nothing is treated in order to effect an action, but only that the audience may be pleased, one should speak with moderation, somewhere between the two. But even though someone may speak of great things, nevertheless he should not always teach (var. *dicere*, "speak") grandly, but humbly, when he teaches; moderately, when he praises or chastises something; grandly, when he calls to conversion minds that are turned away. In the humble style adequate words should be used; in the middling, showy; in the grand, ardent.

xviii. Clause, phrase, and sentence (De colo, commate, et periodis) 1. Every utterance is composed and constituted of words, the phrase, the clause, and the sentence. A phrase (*comma*) is a small component of thought, a clause (*colon*) is a member, and a sentence (*periodos*) is a 'rounding-off or compass' (*ambitus vel circuitus*; cf. περίοδος, "going round"). A phrase is made from a combination of words, a clause from phrases, and a sentence

6 The notion is that general theses may be used as part of the argumentation of a particular case.

from clauses. 2. A *comma* is the marking off of a speech-juncture, as (cf. Cicero, *Defense of Milo* 1): "Although I fear, judges, . . ." – there is one *comma*, and another *comma* follows – ". . . that it may be unseemly to speak for the bravest of men, . . ." and this makes up a clause (*colon*), that is, a member, that makes the sense intelligible. But still the utterance is left hanging, and in this way finally from several clauses the sentence's period (*periodos*) is made, that is the last closing-off of the thought, thus: ". . . and so they miss the traditional procedure of the courts." But a sentence should not be longer than what may be delivered in one breath.

xix. Faults to be avoided in letters, words, and expressions (De vitiis litterarum et verborum et sententiarum cavendis) 1. Again, the pure and chaste speech of an orator should be without all faults, as much in letters as in words, and indeed in expressions (*sententia*). 2. In letters, their adjoining should be apt and proper, and thus care must be taken to ensure that the final vowel of the preceding word is not the same as the initial vowel of the following word, as *feminae Aegyptiae* ("of an Egyptian woman"). This construction would be better if consonants were adjoined to the vowels. One should also avoid the adjoining of the three consonants which coming together seem to be grating and as it were to clash, that is *r*, *s*, and *x*, as: *ars studiorum* ("the art of study"), *rex Xerxes* ("King Xerxes"), *error Romuli* ("the wandering of Romulus"). Also to be avoided is the consonant *m* dashing against vowels, as *verum enim* ("but indeed").

xx. Combinations of words (De iuncturis verborum) 1. Also we should be wary of faults in words, so that we don't use improper words, which the Greeks call *acyrologia*. Therefore propriety should be cherished, so that sometimes because of the meanness of a foul and nasty word one should use terms in a transferred sense, yet not fetched from far away, but such as seem neighbors and cognates to the true ones. 2. Very far-fetched hyperbatons (see I.xxxvii.16), which cannot be employed without confusion with other meanings, should be avoided. Ambiguity (*ambiguitas*) is also to be avoided, as well as that fault when, carried away by the excitement of oratory, some people conclude, in a long and roundabout rambling (*ambages*) with empty sounds interposed, what they could have expressed in one or two words. This fault is called *perissologia*. 3. To this the opposite fault is to rob the speech of even essential words in one's zeal for brevity. To be avoided also are the faults of expressions (*sententia*) as well as those of letters and words; these are recognized as among the first studies of grammarians. 4. These are *cacemphaton*, *tautologia*, ellipsis, *acyrologia*, *macrologia*, *perissologia*, pleonasm, and ones like these. But contrariwise enargeia (*energia*) as well as emphasis, which causes something to be understood beyond what one has said, elevate and adorn an oration, as if you were to say, "He rises to the glory of Scipio," and Vergil (*Aen.* 2.262):

> Sliding down the lowered rope.

For when he says 'sliding down' he suggests the image of height. To this the opposite virtue is to diminish in one's words things that are in their nature great.

xxi. Figures of words and of expressions (De figuris verborum et sententiarum) 1. A speech is amplified and adorned with figures of words and of expressions. Because a straight and continuous oration makes for weariness and disgust as much for the speaker as for the hearer, it should be inflected and varied into other forms, so that it might refresh the speaker and become more elaborate, and deflect criticism with a diversity of presentation and hearing. Of these figures most, from Donatus, have been noted above in the schemes of the art of grammar.[7] 2. Hence here it is fitting to insert only those that never or with difficulty occur in poetry, but freely in oratory.[8]

3. [*Anadiplosis* is a doubling of words, as (cf. Cicero, *Catiline Oration* 1.2): "Still he lives. Lives! He even comes into the Senate!" 4. Climax (*climax*) is an 'ascending series' (*gradatio*), when the second notion begins at the point where the first leaves off, and from here as if in steps (*gradus*) the order of speech is managed, as in the speech of (Scipio) Africanus (fr. 32) "From innocence arises esteem; from esteem, preferment; from preferment, sovereignty; from sovereignty, liberty." Some call this figure the 'chain' (*catena*), because one term is as it were linked to another, and in this way more ideas are conveyed in the doubling of the words. Moreover,

7 See I. xxxvi–xxxvii above; Donatus, *Ars Grammatica*, ed. Keil 4.397–402.

8 Many manuscripts omit the remainder of this chapter.

this scheme occurs not only in single words, but also in the grouping of words, as this from (Sempronius) Gracchus (fr. 43): "Your boyhood was a dishonor to your youth, your youth the disgrace of your old age, your old age the scandal of the state." And likewise from Scipio (Africanus Minor, fr. 33): "By force and unwillingly compelled, I made a pact with him; when the pact was made, I brought him before the judge; when he was brought, I condemned him in the first assembly; when he was condemned, I discharged him willingly."

5. Antitheses (*antitheton*) are called 'oppositions' (*contrapositum*) in Latin. When these are set in opposition they make for beauty of expression, and among the ornaments of speech they remain the most lovely, as Cicero (*Catiline Oration* 2.25): "On this side shame does battle; on that, impudence; here modesty, there debauchery; here faith, there deceit; here piety, there wickedness; here steadiness, there rage; here decency, there foulness; here restraint, there lust; here in short equity, temperance, courage, wisdom, all the virtues struggle with iniquity, dissipation, cowardice, foolhardiness – with all the vices. Finally wealth struggles against poverty, right thinking against depravity, sanity against madness – in sum, good hope against desperation in every circumstance." In strife and battle of this kind the book of Ecclesiasticus used the ornament of this type of locution, saying (cf. 33:15): "Good is set against evil, and life against death; so also is the sinner against a just man. And so look upon all the works of the most High. Two and two, and one against another."

6. Synonymy (*synonymia*) occurs whenever in connected speech we signify one thing with several words, as Cicero puts it (*Catiline Oration* 1.8): "You do nothing, you attempt nothing, you think of nothing." Again (*Catiline Oration* 1.10): "I will not bear it, I will not tolerate it, I will not permit it." 7. *Epanodos*, which our grammarians call 'regression' (*regressio*) (Cicero, *Defense of Ligarius* 19): "The dignity of the first ones was almost equal; not the equal, perhaps, of those that followed." 8. *Antapodosis*, whenever the middle terms agree with the first and the last, [as is] (Cicero, *Against the Speech of Metellus*, fr. 5): "Yours is this deed I now reprove, senators, not mine – granted a most lovely deed – but, as I have said, not mine, but yours."

9. *Paradiastole* occurs whenever we make distinctions by way of explanatory definition (cf. Rutilius Lupus, *Schemata Lexeos* 1.4): "While you call yourself wise instead of cunning, brave instead of reckless, thrifty instead of stingy." 10. *Antanaclasis* is that which expresses a contrary sense with the same word. A certain man was complaining about his son because he was 'looking forward' (*exspectare*) to his death, and the son answered, "I don't look forward (*exspectare*) to it; nay I wish," he said, "that you would dread (*exspectare*) it." 11. *Antimetabole* is an inversion of words that makes a contrary sense when their order is changed: "I don't live to eat, but I eat to live." And this (Cicero, *Philippics* 4.8): "If Antony is consul, then is Brutus the enemy; if the savior of the republic is Brutus, the enemy is Antony." 12. The figure *exoche* (Cicero, *Defense of Milo* 59): "Who called them? Appius. Who brought them forth? Appius."[9]

13. Now let us examine the 'figures of thought' (*figura sententiae*), which are worth the effort to know. 14. A maxim (*sententia*) is an impersonal saying, as (Terence, *Andria* 68)

> Flattery breeds friends, truth hatred.

If a person were added to this, it would be a chreia (*chria*), thus: "Achilles offended Agamemnon by speaking the truth" or "Metrophanes earned the favor of Mithridates by flattering him." Between a chreia and a maxim is this distinction, that a maxim is produced without a person, but a chreia is never spoken without a person. Whence if a person is added to a maxim, it becomes a chreia; if taken away, it becomes a maxim.

15. There are many kinds of sentences (*sententia*).[10] Some are indicative (*indicativus*), some proclamatory (*pronuntiativus*), as (Vergil, *Aen.* 4.373):

> Faith is nowhere secure.

Some are imperative (*imperativus*), as (Vergil, *Aen.* 4.223):

> Go and take action, son; call the west winds, and glide on your wings.

Some wondering (*admirativus*) (*Aen.* 1.11):

> Does such great wrath possess divine minds?

9 The citation does not exemplify *exoche*; the text may be corrupt by omission. Servius defines *exoche* ("prominence") as the use of the name of a person with a "prominence" of some trait to represent a class: "our Hercules" for "our strong man."

10 Often a *sententia*, as above, is specifically a sententious saying, a maxim; now, as the following shows, Isidore simply means "expression" of a thought, our "sentence."

16. Some comparative (*comparativus*) (anon., Courtney fr. 1):

> If I conquer and die, what good is it for me to conquer?

Some superlative (*superlativus*), which are uttered with some emotion and indignation (*Aen.* 3.56):

> To what, cursed hunger for gold, will you not drive mortal hearts?

17. Some interrogative (*interrogativus*), [as] (*Aen.* 8.112):

> Young men, what cause drove you to try unknown ways? . . . What is your race, where is your home? Do you bring here peace, or war?

18. Others as a reply (*responsivus*), as: "From over there," or "From there." Some prayerful (*deprecativus*), as (*Aen.* 6.365):

> Invincible one, snatch me from these evils!

Some promising (*promissivus*), as (*Aen.* 1.257):

> Forgo fear, the fates of your children remain secure.

Some concessive (*concessivus*), which would inhibit by urging, as (*Aen.* 4.381):

> Go, pursue Italy on the winds, seek your kingdom across the waves.

These concessive sayings, lest their prompting not be understood, are mixed with some things that unobtrusively inhibit, as "on the winds," "across the waves."

Some demonstrative (*demonstrativus*), as: "There!" or "Behold!" Some optative (*optativus*), as (*Aen.* 8.560):

> O that Jupiter would bring me back bygone years.

19. Some derogatory (*derogativus*), as: "By no means." Some, which are uttered with an exclamation (*exclamatio*), as (cf. Petronius, *Satyricon* 108):

> What madness, o citizens, changes peace into arms?

And Cicero (*Catiline Oration* 1.9): "O immortal gods, where among the nations are we?" 20. Some hortatory (*exhortativus*), when we incite toward an idea, as (*Aen.* 8.364):

> Dare, guest, to spurn wealth.

21. Some dissuasive (*dehortativus*), when we draw back from an opposing vice and sin. And some affirmative (*affirmativus*), as: "Why not," or "Indeed."

22. Some are preceptive (*praeceptivus*), as (cf. Vergil, *Geo.* 1.299):

> Naked plow, sow naked, and you will have your crop in the cold.

23. Prohibiting (*vetativus*), as (*Geo.* 2.299):

> Neither sow hazel among the vines, nor reach for the highest shoots.

24. Negative (*negativus*), as: "No," "Not at all." And there are wondering (*mirativus*) sentences, as (Jerome, *Epistle 25, to Rusticus* 15 (*PL* 22.1080)): "What! I can scarcely survive; would I wish to fornicate?" 25. Some sentences are of one grieving (*dolens*), as (cf. Ovid, *Heroides* 5.149):

> Woe is me, that no love is curable with herbs.

Some of one weeping (*flens*), [as]. . .[11] Some express a similitude (*similitudo*), thus (Vergil, *Aen.* 5.588):

> As once the Labyrinth, they say, in high Crete.

There are sentences of one warning (*admonens*), one laughing (*inridens*), one moaning (*gemens*). There are hortatory (*exhortativus*) sentences, consoling (*consolativus*) sentences, those of one commiserating (*commiserans*). Of these sentences, as many as there are figures, so many are the tones of voice in uttering them.

26. There are 'double-edged statements' (*amphidoxa*), conferring partly honor, partly dishonor, as (Ovid, *Met.* 2.53):

> Your desire is not safe: you seek great things, Phaeton.

27. And there are others: *procatalepsis*, when we grant beforehand what can be objected against us in order to dilute its impact, as (cf. Cicero, *On Divination, Against Caecilius* 1): "If any of you, judges, or of those who are present, perhaps are amazed." And there is *aporia*, the doubting (*dubitatio*) of one pretending not to know what he knows, or how he should say it. 28. *Koenonosis* is called one's 'sharing of counsel' (*communicatio consilii*) with one's judges or one's adversaries, as if you were to say: "I take counsel (*consulere*) with you, judges, or else with you, adversaries, about what action was suitable for me to take, or rather what you would have thought of doing."

11 The *sententia flentis* is left unexemplified, as are those below from *admonens* to *commiserans*.

29. Paradox (*paradoxon*) occurs when we say that something unexpected has happened, as Cicero in his *Defense of Flaccus* (cf. *Pro Flacco* 1): "He who ought to have been the singer of his praises has become the one who begs for his release from danger." 30. *Epitrope*, that is, yielding (*permissio*), when we yield up (*permittere*) some things to be evaluated by the judges or adversaries themselves, as Calvus in the *Against Vatinius* (*Vati*[*ci*]*nio*; i.e. *In Vatinium*, fr. 23): "Put on a bold face, and say that you were more worthy to become praetor than Cato." 31. *Parrhesia* is speech full of freedom and confidence (Cicero, *Defense of Milo* 72): "I have not slain Spurius Maelius," and so on. This figure should be used with caution, as did Cicero, for he explained his conduct beforehand. 32. *Ethopoeia* occurs when we introduce speech from an absent person, as Cicero in his *Defense of Caelius* (33–34) has Appius Caecus speaking with Clodia. 33. Enargeia (*energia*) is the performance of things acted out or as if they were acted out before our eyes, on which we have already spoken. 34. *Metathesis* is the figure that sends the thoughts of the judges toward past or future events,[12] in this way: "Call your minds back to the spectacle of the defeated, wretched city, and imagine that you see the burning, the slaughter, the plundering, the pillage, the wounds on the bodies of children, the capture of wives, the butchering of elders." Or toward the future, as an anticipation of what the opponent is about to say, as by Cicero in his *Defense of Milo* (79), when he directs the thoughts of the judges toward that condition of the republic [which] will come to be even if, were Milo killed, Clodius should live.

35. *Aposiopesis* occurs when we break off what we seemed to be about to say with silence (Vergil, *Aen.* 1.135):

> Whom I . . . but it is more important to settle the restless waves.

36. *Epanalepsis* is digression (*digressio*):[13] "The heat of my argument and the importance of these matters has carried me off a little further than I wished, but I return to the case at hand." 37. *Anamnesis* is the recollection of a matter that we pretend to have forgotten. 38. *Aparisis* occurs when at an opportune moment we appeal to what we have as it were deposited beforehand in the minds of the judges.[14]

39. Etiology (*aetiologia*) occurs when we set forth something and give its cause and explanation. 40. Characterization (*characterismus*) is a detailed description of some figure, as (Vergil, *Aen.* 4.558):

> In every way like Mercury, in voice and coloring and blond hair and handsome youthful limbs.

Ἀθροισμός occurs when people pile up in one place several thoughts, briefly set forth, and the speaker runs through them with some haste, as Cicero (*Catiline Oration* 3.1): "The republic, citizens, and the lives of you all, your goods, fortunes, wives, and children," etc. 41. Irony (*ironia*) occurs when through a pretense someone wishes to be understood otherwise than he says. This is done either when we praise someone whom we wish to blame, or blame him whom we would praise. An example of each would be if you were to call Catiline a lover of the republic, or Scipio an enemy of the republic. 42. *Diasyrmus* diminishes in words things that are great, or magnifies very small things. 43. *Efon* occurs whenever we linger for a rather long time on the same thought: "Whom at last did he spare? Whose friendship did he keep in trust? To which good man was he not hostile? When did he not either accuse someone, or beat him, or betray him?"[15]

44. *Epangelia* is a 'promise' (*promissio*) by which we make the judge attentive, promising that we are about to say grand or very small things. 45. Personification (*prosopopoeia*) occurs when personality and speech are contrived for inanimate things. Cicero in the *Catiline Oration* (cf. 1.27): "If, in truth, my fatherland, which is far dearer to me than my life, were to speak with me, saying," etc. 46. *Parathesis* occurs when as it were we insert something incomplete into the memories of the judges, saying that we will return to it when the right moment comes. 47. *Peusis*, that is soliloquy (*soliloquium*), occurs when we ourselves answer our own questions. 48. *Synaeresis*[16] occurs when we defer something, asking

12 For *metathesis* we should understand *metastasis* ("relocation"). *Metathesis* is correctly defined at I.xxxv.6. The first example offered has no known source.

13 An error; *epanalepsis* is correctly defined at I.xxxvi.11. The example given has no known source.

14 For the corrupt *aparisis* editors have conjectured *apaetesis*, the figure in which a topic, set aside in anger, recurs. See 46 below.

15 For corrupt *efon* editors suggest *epimone*, repetitive dwelling on a topic, or *efen* from the Greek ἐφ' ἕν ("on one thing"). The source of the example given is not known.

16 Lindsay substitutes *synaeresis* for the corrupt *sinerosis* of the manuscripts. Isidore may have meant *synerotesis*.

that we may be permitted to say something else in the meanwhile.][17]

xxii. Dialectic (De dialectica) 1. Dialectic (*dialectica*) is the discipline devised for investigating the causes of things. It is a branch of philosophy, and is called logic (*logica*), that is, the rational (*rationalis*) power of defining, questioning, and discussing.[18] Dialectic teaches, with regard to many types of questions, how the true and the false may be distinguished by disputation. 2. Some of the earliest philosophers had 'logic' among their terms, but they did not refine it to the level of skill of an art. After these, Aristotle brought the argumentative methods of this discipline under certain rules and named it 'dialectic' (*dialectica*) because in it one disputes about terms (*dictum*), for λεκτόν means "utterance" (*dictio*). Dialectic follows the discipline of rhetoric because they have many things in common.

xxiii. The difference between the arts of rhetoric and dialectic (De differentia dialecticae et rhetoricae artis) 1. Varro in his nine books of *Disciplines* defined dialectic and rhetoric with this similitude: "Dialectic and rhetoric are like the clenched fist and the open palm of a man's hand: the former pinches words, the latter extends them."[19] 2. While dialectic is indeed sharper for examining things, rhetoric is more fluent for those things it strives to teach. Dialectic sometimes appears in schools; rhetoric continually comes to the public forum. Dialectic reaches very few students; rhetoric often reaches the whole populace. 3. Before they come to explaining the *Isagoge* (see chapter xxv. below), philosophers customarily lay out a definition of philosophy, so that matters that pertain to the *Isagoge* may be more readily set forth.

xxiv. The definition of philosophy (De definitione philosophiae) 1. Philosophy is the understanding of human and divine things joined with the pursuit of living well. It seems to consist of two things: knowledge (*scientia*) and opinion (*opinatio*). 2. Knowledge obtains when some thing is perceived by sure reasoning; opinion, however, when an unsure thing still lies concealed and is grasped by no solid reasoning – for instance whether the sun is as large as it seems to be or is larger than the whole earth, or whether the moon is spherical or concave, or whether the stars are stuck to the sky or are carried through the air in a free course, or of what size and what material the heavens themselves may be, whether they are at rest and immobile or are whirling at unbelievable speed, or how thick the earth is, or on what foundation it endures balanced and suspended.

3. The name 'philosophy' itself in Latin translation professes the 'love of wisdom' (*amor sapientiae*), for the Greek φιλο- means "love," and σοφία means "wisdom." There are three kinds of philosophy: one natural (*naturalis*), which in Greek is 'physics' (*physica*), in which one discusses the investigation of nature; a second moral (*moralis*), which is called 'ethics' (*ethica*) in Greek, in which moral behavior is treated; a third rational (*rationalis*), which is named with the Greek term 'logic' (*logica*), in which there is disputation concerning how in the causes of things and in moral behavior the truth itself may be investigated. 4. Hence physics involves the cause of inquiring, ethics, the order of living, and logic, the rationale of knowing.

Among the Greeks the first who investigated physics deeply was Thales of Miletus, one of the Seven Sages.[20] Indeed, he before anyone else examined the first principles of the sky and the power of natural things with contemplative reason. Later Plato divided physics into four categories: arithmetic, geometry, music, and astronomy. 5. Socrates first established ethics for the correcting and settling of conduct, and directed his whole effort toward disputation about living well. He divided ethics into the four virtues of the soul, namely prudence, justice, fortitude, and temperance. 6. Prudence (*prudentia*) has to do with how the bad is distinguished from the good in affairs. Fortitude (*fortitudo*), how adversity may be borne with equanimity. Temperance (*temperantia*), how passion and the desire for things may be reined in. Justice (*iustitia*), how to each is distributed his own by right judging.

7. Plato added logic, which is called rational philosophy. Through it, when the causes of things and conduct had been dissected, he scrutinized the essence of those

17 This ends the passage, sections 3–48, omitted in many manuscripts.

18 In fact, the liberal art called "dialectic" nearly coincides with the ancient and modern discipline of logic. On the verbal connection of the logical with the rational see xxiv. 7 below.

19 On Varro see the Introduction, p. 11.

20 The traditional Seven Sages of Greece were Thales, Solon, Periander, Cleobulus, Chion, Bias, and Pittacus.

causes rationally, while dividing logic into rhetoric and dialectic. This philosophy is called logic, that is, the rational (*rationalis*), for λόγος in Greek means both 'utterance' (*sermo*) and 'reason' (*ratio*). 8. And indeed, divine eloquence (i.e. the Bible) likewise consists of these three branches of philosophy; it is likely to treat nature, as in Genesis and Ecclesiastes, or conduct, as in Proverbs and here and there in all the books, or logic – by virtue of which our (Christian) writers lay claim to the theory of interpretation (*theoretica*) for themselves, as in the Song of Songs and the Gospels.[21] 9. Again some of the learned (i.e. Cassiodorus, *Institutes* 2.3.5) have defined philosophy in name and in its parts in this way: philosophy is the provable knowledge (*probabilis scientia*) of human and divine things, insofar as this is possible for a human. Otherwise: philosophy is the art of arts and the discipline of disciplines. Again: philosophy is a meditation on death, a definition more suitable for Christians who, with worldly ambition trod under heel, and a disciplined way of life, live out the likeness of their future homeland.

Philosophy is divided into two parts, the first speculative (*inspectivus*), the second practical (*actualis*). 10. Others have defined the method of philosophy as consisting of two parts, of which the first is speculative, the second practical. The speculative is divided into three types: first natural (*naturalis*), second doctrinal (*doctrinalis*),[22] third divine (*divinus*). Doctrinal is divided into four, that is, first arithmetic, second music, third geometry, fourth astronomy. 11. Practical philosophy is divided into three, that is, first moral (*moralis*), second economic (*dispensativus*), third civil (*civilis*).

That branch of philosophy is called speculative (*inspectivus*) by which, having passed beyond visible things, we contemplate in some measure concerning divine and heavenly things, and we investigate those things by the mind alone because they pass beyond the corporeal gaze. 12. Philosophy is called natural when the nature (*natura*) of each individual thing is examined, for nothing is generated (*generare*) in life, but rather each thing is classified by those properties according to which the Creator defined it, unless perhaps by the will of God some miracle is shown to occur.[23]

13. Philosophy is called divine when we treat very deeply of the ineffable nature of God or creatures that are spiritual in some respect. 14. Doctrinal philosophy is the science that studies abstract quantity, for that quantity is called abstract which we treat with pure reason, separating it by the intellect from matter or from other accidental qualities – as are even and odd or things of this kind. It has four branches: arithmetic, geometry, music, astronomy. 15. Arithmetic is the discipline of numerable quantity in itself. Geometry is the discipline of unmoving size and of shapes. Music is the discipline that speaks of numbers that inhere in something, namely those that are found in sounds. Astronomy is the discipline that contemplates all the courses of the heavenly bodies and the figures of the constellations, and with searching reason discourses on the habitual movements of the stars around one another and around the earth.

16. Further, that branch of philosophy is called practical (*actualis*) that explains in their own workings things that are proposed. It has three parts: moral, economic, and civil. That philosophy is called moral (*moralis*) through which we seek a decent conduct of life, and set up principles aiming toward virtue. That philosophy is called economic (*dispensativus*) wherein the ordering of domestic affairs is wisely disposed. That philosophy is called civil (*civilis*) through which the welfare of the whole state is attended to.

xxv. Porphyry's *Isagoge* (De Isagogis Porphyrii)[24] 1. After these definitions of philosophy, in which everything is contained generally, now let us set forth Porphyry's *Isagoge*. 'Isagoge' (*Isagoga*) is a Greek word, in Latin 'introduction' (*introductio*), specifically for those who are beginning philosophy. It contains in itself a demonstration of the first principles of any thing as to what it may be, and the thing is explained with its own solid and substantial definition. 2. First we posit

21 More likely Isidore wrote *theologiam* (as his source in Jerome has it) rather than *theoreticam*; hence, "or logic, instead of which our writers lay claim to theology . . ."

22 As will be clear below, "doctrinal" philosophy is the mathematical sciences; the Latin term *doctrinalis*, which contains the sense "learning," renders the root of the Greek word μαθεματικός, which itself contains the sense "learning."

23 Playing on the related terms *(g)natura* and *genero*, "generate, beget," Isidore insists that physics treats natural things, but that these are not self-generated or created independently of divine will.

24 The Neoplatonist Porphyry (died *ca.* 305 CE) wrote the *Introduction (Isagoge) to the Categories of Aristotle*, which became the standard introductory textbook on logic, regularly called simply *Isagoge*.

the genus, then we subjoin the species and other things that can be allied, and we separate them by particulars they hold in common, continually introducing the differentiae until we arrive at the individual character (*proprium*) of the thing whose identifying properties we have been investigating by means of a definition that marks it out. For example: A human being is an animal, rational, mortal, land-dwelling, bipedal, capable of laughter.

3. When the genus is called animal, the substance (*substantia*) of a human being is set forth. Now a human being is of the 'animal' genus, but because this spreads a wide net, the species is added, 'land-dwelling': now that which is [supposed to be] of the air or of the water is excluded. The differentia then, as 'bipedal,' which is posited as against animals that are supported by many feet. Again 'rational,' as against those which lack reason; 'mortal' too, as against that which is [not] an angel. 4. Afterwards, to these distinctions and exclusions is added the individual trait (*proprium*) in the last place, ['capable of laughter'] – for it is characteristic of a human being alone that he laughs. Thus is completed in every respect the definition for setting forth 'human being.' Aristotle and Cicero thought that a full definition in this discipline consisted of genera and differentiae. 5. Afterwards some, fuller in their teaching about this, divide the complete definition of substance into five parts as their branches. Of these the first concerns the genus, the second the species, the third the differentia, the fourth the individual trait, the fifth the accidental property (*accidens*).

6. Genus, as 'animal,' for that is the generic (*generale*) and common term for all things having breath (*anima*). Species, as 'human being,' for that is the 'specific property' (*specialitas*), by which he is separated from other animate things. Differentiae, as 'rational,' 'mortal.' In these two differentiae a human being differs from others. 7. When he is called 'a rational being,' he is distinguished from irrational, speechless animals that do not have reason. When [he is called] 'a mortal being,' he is distinguished from angels, who do not know death. Individual trait, as 'capable of laughter,' for it is the human being who laughs, and except for the human being this is true of no animal. Accidental property, as color in the body, learning in the mind. 8. These things both occur (*accidere*) and change with variation over time. From all these five parts we have the expression of the full thought, thus: "Man is an animal, rational, mortal, capable of laughter, capable of good and evil." Hence in every discourse about substance we ought to include species and differentiae until, when all things that could be the same thing are excluded, we may attain the object, so that its individual nature (*proprietas*) may now be held fixed.

9. Victorinus the orator translated the *Isagoge* from Greek into Latin, and Boethius produced his commentary on it in five books.[25]

25 Marius Victorinus's translation (fourth century CE) has been lost, but Boethius's commentary (fifth century) became a standard text.

xxvi. Aristotle's categories (De categoriis Aristotelis)

1. We come to the categories (*categoria*) of Aristotle, which in Latin are called 'predications' (*praedicamentum*). With these every form of discourse is included in accordance with their various significations. 2. The instruments (*instrumentum*) of the categories are three: the first is equivocal (*aequivocus*), the second univocal (*univocus*), the third denominative (*denominativus*). They are equivocal when many things possess the same name, but not the same definition, as 'lion' – for with regard to the name, the actual, the painted, and the zodiacal lion are called 'lion'; with regard to the definition, the actual is defined one way, the painted another, the zodiacal another. 3. The instruments are univocal when two or more things share a single name and a single definition, as 'clothing.' Thus both a cloak and a tunic can take the name 'clothing' along with its definition. Therefore this is understood to be univocal among the types of instruments, because it gives both a name and a definition to its forms. 4. We call denominative, that is 'derivative' (*derivativus*), whichever instruments take their name from some single instance of differentiation with regard to a noun, as 'good' from 'goodness,' 'wicked' from 'wickedness.'

5. There are ten species of categories: substance, quantity, quality, relation, situation, place, time, habit, activity, and passivity (*substantia, quantitas, qualitas, relatio, situs, locus, tempus, habitus, agere, pati*). 6. 'Substance' is what a thing properly and principally is called, which is neither predicated of the subject, nor inheres in the subject, as 'some particular man' or 'some particular horse.' In addition, there are things called 'secondary substances' (*secunda substantia*), in which types those things that were just now called substances in the

principal sense are present and included, as the principal substance 'Cicero' is included in the secondary substance 'man.' 7. 'Quantity' is the measure by which something is shown to be large or small, as 'long,' 'short.' 'Quality' expresses 'of what sort' (*qualis*) a person may be, as 'orator' or 'peasant,' 'black' or 'white.' 'Relation' is what is 'related' (*referre*, ppl. *relatus*) to something, for when 'son' is said, 'father' is also indicated. These things arise together as related (*relativa*). Indeed, 'slave' and 'master' have a simultaneous onset of the name, nor can a master sometimes be found before a slave, nor a slave before a master, for one cannot exist before the other.

8. 'Place' is where a thing is: in the forum, in a street. Further, movement of place has six directions: right and left, forward and back, up and down. Also those six directions have two aspects, [that is, situation and time. 'Situation,' as] 'far' and 'near.' 'Time,' as 'yesterday,' 'today.' Moreover 'situation' (*situs*) is so called from 'position' (*positio*), as someone may stand, or sit, or lie down. 9. 'Habit' (*habitus*) is so called from 'having' (*habere*) something – as to 'have' knowledge in the mind, strength in the body, clothing around the body, and the other things that fall under this mode of having, with their number assigned by the learned. 10. Now 'activity' and 'passivity' are functions of the sense that one is acting or receiving the action. So 'I write' is in the active voice, because it indicates the situation of one doing; 'I am written' is passive, because it indicates that one receives the action.

Countless things are classified in these nine types, of which we have presented some as examples, or in the type 'substance' itself, which is οὐσία ("essential being"). It is also the case with whatever we perceive with the intellect: we present them in speech with one or another of these ten predicates. 11. A sentence full of these runs like this: "Augustine, the great orator, the son of that man, standing, in the temple, today, wearing a priest's fillet, is worn out from arguing."

Further, 'being' (*usia*) is 'substance' (*substantia*) that is, the 'essential property' (*proprium*) that underlies (*subiacere*) the other categories; the remaining nine are accidents. 'Substance' is so called because every thing subsists (*subsistere*) with reference to itself. A body subsists, and therefore is a substance. 12. Those accidents, indeed, which are in the subsisting thing and in the subject are not substances, because they do not remain (*subsistere*) but are changed, such as color or shape. 13. The terms 'of the subject' (*de subiecto*) and 'in the subject' (*in subiecto*) amount as it were to 'of the thing itself' and 'in the thing itself.' Thus where something is spoken of as 'of the subject,' it is the substance, as if one were to say 'of the substance.' But where 'in the subject' is said, we speak of accidents, that is, what 'falls in with' (*accidere*) the substance, as quantity, quality, or shape. Genera and species are 'of the subject,' therefore, and accidents are 'in the subject.'

Of these nine accidents three are within the essential being (*usia*) – quantity, [and] quality, and situation – for these cannot exist without essential being. Apart from essential being, however, are place, time, and habit; relation, activity, and passivity are both within and apart from essential being. 14. The categories are accepted as being 'predicative' (*appellatus*) because they cannot be perceived apart from subjects. Indeed, who can perceive what 'human being' may be unless he puts some human being before his eyes as the subject of the term?

15. This work of Aristotle should be understood because, as has been said, whatever a person says is contained among these ten predications. It will be helpful moreover for understanding those books that are directed to rhetoricians or dialecticians.

xxvii. The *De interpretatione* (De perihermeniis) 1. From here follows the *De interpretatione* (*Perihermenias*, i.e. *Peri hermenias* "On interpretation"), an extremely subtle book, and in its varied forms and repetitions most careful. With regard to it people say, "When he was writing *De interpretatione*, Aristotle dipped his pen in his mind."

2. Preface to *De interpretatione*. Every thing that is one and is signified by one word is signified either by a substantive (*nomen*) or a verb (*verbum*).[26] These two parts of speech 'give expression to' (*interpretari*) everything that the mind conceives of to say, for every utterance is a 'mediator of expression' (*interpres*) of a thing conceived by the mind. 3. Aristotle, a man most skilled in the manner of expressing things and in forming statements, names this *perihermenia*, which we call 'interpretation'

26 Latin frequently uses adjectives substantively, and in logic and grammar adjectives are often gathered with nouns under the term *nomen*, here often rendered 'substantive.'

(*interpretatio*),[27] specifically because things conceived in the mind are rendered (*interpretari*) in expressed words through *cataphasis* and *apophasis*, that is affirmation and negation. Through affirmation, as 'a person is running'; through negation, as 'a person is not running.'

4. So in his *De interpretatione* the philosopher mentioned above treats seven types: the substantive, the verb, the phrase, the proposition, affirmation, negation, and contradiction (*nomen, verbum, oratio, enuntiatio, affirmatio, negatio, contradictio*). 5. A 'substantive' is a vocal sound with a conventional meaning, without tense, of which no segment is separately meaningful, as 'Socrates.' A 'verb' is what designates tense. A segment of the verb (i.e. the tense ending) has no other meaning beyond always denoting those things that are said about time, as 'thinks,' 'argues.' A 'phrase' is a meaningful vocal sound, of which some segments are separately meaningful, as 'Socrates argues.' A 'propositional utterance' (*enuntiativa oratio*) is a vocal sound signifying of a thing that it is something or is not, as 'Socrates is,' 'Socrates is not.'

6. An 'affirmation' is a pronouncement (*enuntiatio*) by someone about something, as 'Socrates is.' A 'negation' is a denial of something by someone, as 'Socrates is not.' A 'contradiction' is the 'contrary positing' (*oppositio*) of an affirmation and a negation, as 'Socrates argues; Socrates does not argue.' 7. [All these things are treated, very minutely divided and subdivided, in the book *De interpretatione*, and let it suffice to have intimated briefly here the definitions of these things, since a competent explanation is found in the book itself. The usefulness] of the *De interpretatione* is this, that syllogisms are made from the interpretations. From here 'analytic logic' (*analytica*) is systematically investigated.

xxviii. Logical syllogisms (De syllogismis dialecticis)

1. Logical syllogisms follow from here, where the usefulness and power of the whole art becomes clear. The conclusion of these syllogisms greatly aids the reader in investigating the truth, to the extent that the error of deceiving the opponent by the sophisms of false conclusions may be banished.

2. The formulations (*formula*) of the categorical (*categoricus*) syllogisms, that is, of the predicative syllogisms, are three. There are nine types of the first formulation. 3. The first type is that which draws together, that is, which assembles, a universal affirmation (*dedicativum*) from universal affirmations directly (*directim*), as: "Every just thing is decent; every decent thing is good; therefore every just thing is good." 4. The second type is that which draws together a universal negation (*abdicativum*) from universal affirmations and negations directly, as: "Every just thing is decent; no decent thing is wicked; therefore no just thing is wicked." 5. The third type is that which draws together a particular affirmation from a particular and a universal affirmation directly, as: "A particular just thing is decent; all decent things are useful; therefore that particular just thing is useful."

6. The fourth type is that which draws together a particular negation from a particular affirmation and a universal negation directly, as: "A particular just thing is decent; no decent thing is wicked; therefore that particular just thing is not wicked." 7. The fifth type is that which draws together a particular affirmation from universal affirmations by indirection (*reflexio*), as: "Every just thing is decent; every decent thing is good; therefore a particular good thing is just." 8. The sixth type is that which draws together a universal negation from a universal affirmation and a universal negation indirectly, as: "Every just thing is decent; no decent thing is wicked; therefore no wicked thing is just."

9. The seventh type is that which draws together a particular affirmation from a particular and a universal affirmation indirectly, as: "A particular just thing is decent; every decent thing is useful; therefore that particular just thing is useful." 10. The eighth type is that which draws together a particular negation from a universal negation and a universal affirmation indirectly, as: "No wicked thing is decent; every decent thing is just; therefore a particular wicked thing is not just." 11. The ninth type is that which draws together a particular negation from a universal negation and a particular affirmation indirectly, as: "No wicked thing is decent; a particular decent thing is just; therefore that particular just thing is not wicked."

12. Of the second formulation there are four types. The first type is that which draws together a universal negation from a universal affirmation and a universal negation directly, as: "Every just thing is decent; no wicked thing is decent; therefore no wicked thing is just." 13. The second type is that which draws together a universal

27 Isidore takes the Greek phrase (and Aristotle's title) περὶ ἑρμενείας, 'concerning interpretations' or 'concerning expressions,' as a single word meaning "interpretation."

negation from a universal negation and a universal affirmative directly, as: "No wicked thing is decent; every just thing is decent; therefore no wicked thing is just." 14. The third type is that which draws together a particular negation from a particular affirmation and a universal negation directly, as: "A particular just thing is decent; no wicked thing is decent; therefore that particular just thing is not wicked." 15. The fourth type is that which draws together a particular negation from a particular negation and a universal affirmation directly, as: "A particular just thing is not wicked; every bad thing is wicked; therefore that particular just thing is not bad."

16. There are six types of the third formulation. The first type is that which draws together a particular affirmation from universal affirmations as much directly as indirectly, as: "Every just thing is decent; every decent thing is just; every just thing is good; therefore a particular decent thing is good, a particular good thing is decent." 17. The second type is that which draws together a particular affirmation from a particular and a universal affirmation directly, as: "A particular just thing is decent; every just thing is good; therefore a particular decent thing is good."[28] 18. The third type is [that which draws together] a particular affirmation from a universal and a particular affirmation directly, as: "Every just thing is decent; a particular just thing is good; therefore a particular decent thing is good."

19. The fourth type is that which draws together a particular negation from a universal affirmation and a [particular] negation directly, as: "Every just thing is decent; no just thing is bad; therefore a particular decent thing is not bad." 20. The fifth type is that which draws together a particular negation from a particular affirmation and a universal negation directly, as: "A particular just thing is decent; no just thing is bad; therefore a particular decent thing is not bad." 21. The sixth type is that which draws together a particular negation from a universal affirmation and a particular negation directly, as: "Every just thing is decent; a particular just thing is not bad; therefore a particular decent thing is not bad."

22. Let anyone who wishes fully to know these formulations of the categorical syllogisms read the book titled the *Interpretations* (*Perihermenias*) by Apuleius,[29] and he will learn the things that have been treated there in more detail. Precise and well-considered, they lead the reader with profit, God willing, toward the great paths of understanding.

Now let us come in due course to the 'hypothetical syllogisms' (*hypotheticus syllogismus*). 23. The types of hypothetical syllogisms, which are made with some conclusion, are seven. The first type is, "If it is day, it is light; it is day; therefore it is light." The second type is, "If it is day, it is light; it is not light; therefore it is not day." The third type is thus: "It cannot be the case that it is both day and not light; yet it is day; therefore it is light." 24. The fourth type is thus: "Either it is day, or night; yet it is day; therefore it is not night." The fifth type is thus: "Either it is day, or night; yet it is not night; therefore it is day." The sixth type is this: "It cannot be the case that it is both day and not light; but [it is] day; therefore it is not night." 25. The seventh type is thus: "It cannot be the case that it is both day and night; yet it is not night; therefore it is day." If anyone should wish more fully to know the types of hypothetical syllogisms, let him read the book by Marius Victorinus entitled *On the hypothetical syllogisms* (*De syllogismis hypotheticis*).

26. At this point let us go on to the logical species of 'definitions,' which stand out with such great distinction that they can clearly show the forms of characterizing things and certain characteristics of expressions.

xxix. The division of definitions abbreviated from the book by Marius Victorinus (De divisione definitionum ex Marii Victorini libro abbreviata)[30] 1. For philosophers a definition (*definitio*) explains, for things needing to be described, what the thing itself is, what sort of thing it is, and how it should be constituted with regard to its members. It is a brief statement determining the nature of each thing as it is distinguished from what it has in common with other things by an individual, proper signification. The division of definitions is presented in fifteen parts.

2. The first species of definition is οὐσιώδης, that is, 'substantial' (*substantialis*), which is properly and truly called a definition, as is "A human being is an animal, rational, mortal, capable of understanding and of learning." Now this definition, descending through the species and the differentiae, comes to the individual

28 For this second type we translate a better reading derived from the source in Cassiodorus.

29 Most scholars now believe that this post-Aristotelian Περὶ ἑρμενείας is wrongly attributed to Apuleius, second-century CE author of *The Golden Ass*.

30 Victorinus was a philosopher and grammarian of the fourth century CE.

thing, and most fully designates what a human being is. 3. The second species of definition, which in Greek is called ἐννοηματική, in Latin is named a 'notion' (*notio*), and we can speak of this 'notion' with a common, and not an individualizing name. This is always done in this way: "He is a human being because in rational thought and learned skill he stands out above all animals." This notion did not say what a human being is, but what one can do, calling a particular distinguishing feature to notice (*notitia*), as it were. In this and the remainder of the definitions a notice of the thing is presented, but no substantial (*substantialis*) explication is produced; because that first species is substantial, it holds first place among the definitions.

4. The third species of definition is called ποιότης in Greek, 'qualitative' (*qualitativus*) in Latin, because it takes its name from 'quality' (*qualitas*), since it clearly shows 'what sort of thing' (*qualis*) is something that exists. An example of this is the following: "A human being is one who prospers by means of intelligence and succeeds in the arts, and by his understanding of things either chooses what he ought to do, or spurns with reproach what is unprofitable." Thus by these qualities 'man' is expressed and defined. 5. The fourth species of definition is named ὑπογραφική in Greek, and in Latin, by Cicero, 'description' (*descriptio*). This clarifies what a thing may be by 'writing around' (*descriptio*) it when a circumlocution of words and deeds is applied. In response to the question of what a greedy, or cruel, or luxurious person is like, the common nature of the luxurious, the greedy, or the cruel is described (*describere*). For instance, if we wish to define the luxurious person, we say, "The luxurious person strives after a way of life that is not necessary, but sumptuous and loaded with goods; luxuries flow around him, and he is eager in lust." These and other things define the luxurious person, but they define by description. This species of definition is more suited to orators than logicians because it offers latitude as to what likeness is applied in good matters and in bad.

6. The fifth species of definition is what in Greek is κατὰ [ἀντί]λεξιν, and in Latin what we call 'gloss' (*adverbium*). This explains the word for the matter in question by one other single word, and in a certain way it declares with the single second word what is stated in the single first word, as "*conticescere* ('be quiet') is *tacere* ('be silent')." Again, as we speak of 'terminus' as "end," or as 'depopulated' is interpreted to be "devastated." 7. The Greeks call the sixth species of definition κατὰ διαφοράν, and in Latin we call it 'by differentiation' (*per differentiam*). Writers on the arts name it 'on the same and the different' (*de eodem et de altero*), as when one asks what is the difference between a 'king' and a 'tyrant'; when the differentia is applied, what each is, is defined; that is, "A king is measured and temperate, but a tyrant impious and harsh."

8. The seventh species of definition is what the Greeks call κατὰ μεταφοράν, and Latin speakers, 'by metaphor' (*per translationem*), as Cicero in the *Topics* (cf. 32): "A shore is where the waves play." This can be treated variously; it can be used to admonish, to distinguish, to blame, or to praise. As it may admonish: "Nobility is the burden on descendants of the virtue of their forebears." As it may distinguish: "The crown of the head is the citadel of the body." As it may praise: "Youth is the flower of one's lifetime." As it may blame: "Riches are the long travel-money of a short life." 9. The eighth species of definition in Greek is called κατὰ ἀφαίρεσιν τοῦ ἐναντίου, in Latin 'by the privative of the contrary' (*per privantiam contrarii*) of that which is defined: "That is good which is not bad. That is just which is not unjust," and the like. We ought to use this kind of definition when the contrary is known, as "If the good is what profits with decency, that which is not such a thing is bad."

10. The ninth species of definition is called in Greek κατὰ ὑποτύπωσιν, in Latin 'by a certain outline' (*per quandam imaginationem*), as "Aeneas is the son of Venus and Anchises." This always involves individual items, which the Greeks call ἄτομα.[31] 11. The tenth species of definition is called in Greek κατὰ ἀναλογίαν, in Latin 'by analogy' (*iuxta rationem*) – as if it were asked what is an animal, and it were answered, "Such as man." The example clarifies the thing previously asked about – for this is the property of a definition, that it clarify what the thing is that is asked about.

12. The eleventh species of definition is called κατ' ἐλλειπὲς ὁλοκλήρου ὁμοίου γένους in Greek, in Latin 'by the shortage of the full amount of the same kind' (*per indigentiam pleni ex eodem genere*) – as if it were asked what a *triens* is, and it were answered, "That which is

31 The example, from the source in Cassiodorus, seems not to match the definition. The Greek term means "by way of a sketch or outline," and Quintilian describes the term as a figure by which something is vividly sketched in words: *Institutes* 9.2.40.

short of an *as* by two-thirds."[32] 13. The twelfth species of definition in Greek is κατὰ ἐπαίνον, that is, 'by praise' (*per laudem*), as Cicero in his *Defense of Cluentius* (cf. 146): "Law is the mind and spirit and counsel and judgment of the citizen body." And elsewhere (Cicero, *Philippics* 2.113): "Peace is tranquil freedom." It is also 'by reproach' (*per vituperationem*), which the Greeks call ψόγος, as (cf. *ibid.*): "Slavery is the last of all evils, to be repelled not only by war, but also by death." 14. The thirteenth species of definition is called κατὰ τὸ πρός τι in Greek, and 'by relationship' (*ad aliquid*) in Latin, as is this: "A father is a man who has a son," "A master is a man who has a slave."

15. The fourteenth species of definition is κατὰ τὸν ὅρον ("by definition"), as Cicero on rhetoric (*On Invention* 1.42): "A 'genus' is that which embraces several parts." Again, "A 'part' is what falls under a genus."[33] 16. The fifteenth species of definition is called κατὰ αἰτιολογίαν in Greek, and 'by the thing's cause' (*secundum rei rationem*) in Latin, as: "Day is the sun over the earth; night is the sun under the earth."

We should know that the aforementioned species of definitions are rightly linked with the subject of topics, because they are set among certain of its arguments, and are mentioned in several places among the topics. Now let us come to the topics, which are the seats of arguments, the springs of understanding, and the sources of style.

xxx. Topics (De topicis)[34] 1. Topics (*topica*) is the discipline of coming up with arguments. The division of topics, or of the commonplaces (*locus*) with which arguments are expressed, is threefold. Some inhere in the thing itself that is in question; others, which are called 'effects' (*effectum*), are understood to be drawn in a certain way from other matters; others are taken from outside (*extrinsecus*). Arguments (*argumentum*) that inhere in the thing itself that is in question are divided into three. First, from the whole; second, from the part; third, from a characteristic quality.

2. The argument is 'from the whole' when a definition is applied to what is in question, as Cicero says (cf. *Defense of Marcellus* 26): "Glory is praise rightly won by deeds and renown for great services to the state." 3. The argument is 'from parts' when he who defends himself either denies a deed or makes the defense that the deed was legal. 4. The argument is 'from a characteristic quality' when some argument is chosen because of the force of a particular term, as Cicero (cf. *Against Piso* 19): "I was seeking, as I say, a consul – whom I could not find in that gelded boar."

5. Effects (*effectum*) are arguments that are known to be drawn in some way from other matters. These are fourteen in number. The first is the argument 'by cognates' (*a coniugatis*), as one adapts a noun and makes a verb, as Cicero says Verres 'swept' (*everrere*) a province (*Second Action Against Verres* 2.52). Or a noun from a verb, when a 'thief' is said to 'thieve.' Or a noun is made from a noun; Terence (cf. *Andria* 218) –

> It is a scheme of lunatics (*amentium*), scarcely of lovers (*amantium*) –

where the ending of one term differs, formed in another declension.[35] 6. The second argument is 'from generality' (*a genere*), when a maxim is spoken concerning the same genus, as Vergil (cf. *Aen.* 4.569):

> A changing and inconstant gender.[36]

7. The third argument is 'from the specific' (*ab specie*), when a specific thing creates trust in the general question, as (*Aen.* 7.363):

> Did not the Phrygian shepherd thus enter Lacedaemon?

The argument is 'from likeness' (*a simile*) when similitudes of some things are put forward (*Aen.* 10.333):

> Bring close my weapons; my hand will not hurl any at the Rutulians in vain, weapons which stood in Greek bodies on the Trojan plain.

8. The argument is 'by differentiation' (*a differentia*) when some things are made distinct by difference, as Vergil (*Aen.* 10.581):

> You do not espy the horses of Diomede, or the chariot of Achilles.

32 The *triens* is one-third of the weight of the *as*.

33 No Latin term is provided for the fourteenth species. The Greek, an editorial conjecture, means "by definition" or "by a term in a proposition." If Isidore wrote here a form of *definitio* it would easily have been lost by haplography.

34 The name of the discipline, 'topics,' derives from the title of Aristotle's work on commonplaces to be used in argumentation, the *Topica*. The term derives from the Greek τόπος, "place."

35 Terence actually wrote *inceptio* ("scheme"), not *interceptio*. The example Isidore has chosen does not fit his statement.

36 Vergil actually wrote, "A varying and changeable thing is woman always." Isidore's paraphrase (*Varium et mutabile genus*) plays on the two meanings of *genus*, "gender" and "genus."

The argument is called 'by contraries' (*a contrariis*) when discordant things oppose each other, as Vergil (cf. *Aen.* 9.95):

> Should ships made by mortal hand have the rights of immortals? And should you traverse uncertain dangers in certainty, Aeneas?

9. The argument is called 'from consequences' (*a consequentibus*) when something inevitably follows on the posited situation, as Vergil (*Aen.* 1.529):

> That violence is not in our mind, nor do conquered people have such pride.

The argument is 'by antecedence' (*ab antecedentibus*) when something is affirmed from things that were done before, as Cicero in *Defense of Milo* (cf. 44): "When he has not hesitated to reveal what he planned, can you have any doubt about what he did?" 10. The argument is 'by impugning' (*a repugnantibus*) when what is objected is demolished by some contrary position, as Cicero (cf. *Defense of King Deiotarus* 15): "This man, therefore, not only freed from such danger, but enriched with most ample honor, would have wished to kill you at home." 11. The argument is 'by cognates' (*a coniugatis*)[37] when it is shown that what would result from a certain situation is against probability, as Vergil (cf. *Aen.* 8.147):

> They believe that if they drive us away there will be nothing to prevent them from putting all Hesperia utterly under their yoke.

12. The argument is 'by causes' (*a causis*) when particular matters are treated with respect to common custom, as Terence (cf. *Andria* 582):

> For some time I have had my fears about you, worried that you might do what the run of servants do and trick me.

The argument is 'by effects' (*ab effectis*) when something is affirmed as a result of those things which have been done, as Vergil (*Aen.* 4.13):

> Fear betrays ignoble spirits.

13. The argument is 'by comparison' (*a conparatione*) when the reasoning of a statement is formed by imputation from a comparison of persons or cases, as Vergil (cf. *Aen.* 10.81):

> You can take Aeneas from the hands of the Greeks . . . but is it wrong that I in my turn helped the Rutulians in some way?

14. Then there are arguments that are introduced from outside (*extrinsecus*), which the Greeks call ἀτέχνος, that is, 'without art' (*artis expers*), as is 'testimony' (*testimonium*) – indeed testimony consists of the thing itself. 15. This class of arguments is divided into five types: first, 'by the character' (*ex persona*); second, 'by the authority of nature' (*ex naturae auctoritate*); third, 'by the circumstances of the authorities' (*ex temporibus auctoritatum*); fourth, 'from the sayings and deeds of ancestors' (*ex dictis factisque maiorum*); fifth, 'by torture' (*ex tormentis*).

Now the third type above, 'by the circumstances,' branches into eight species. The first is intelligence, the second wealth, the third age, the fourth luck, the fifth art, the sixth usage, the seventh necessity, the eighth the coincidence of chance happenings. Testimony is everything that is taken from some external matter in order to carry conviction. Not every sort of person has the gravity of testimony that arouses credence; rather it should be someone esteemed for probity of character. 16. The 'authority of nature' holds the greatest strength. Many testimonies confer authority: intelligence, wealth, age, luck, art, usage, necessity, and the coincidence of chance happenings. Trust is sought 'by the sayings and deeds of ancestors' when the sayings and deeds of former people are mentioned. Trust is conveyed 'by torture'; after it no one is believed to be willing to lie. 17. The matters that are treated 'by the circumstances,' because they are obvious from the terminology, need no definition.

It should be stored in the memory that topics offer arguments in common for orators, logicians, poets, and legal experts. When they apply to an examination of specifics, they pertain to rhetoricians, poets, and legal experts, but when they are used in general disputation they are clearly the business of philosophers. 18. Clearly this is a wonderful kind of achievement, that it has been possible to gather into one whatever the mobility and variety of the human mind could discover as it looked for understanding in diverse subjects, encompassing the free and willful intellect. Indeed, wherever it turns, in whatever thinking it engages, human ingenuity cannot but fall into one of the arguments discussed above.

xxxi. Opposites (De oppositis) 1. There are four types of contraries (*contrarium*), which Aristotle calls

37 The text is evidently corrupt here. See 5 above.

ἀντικείμενον, that is, 'opposites' (*oppositum*) because they seem to stand opposing one another as if face to face, as contraries. Still, not all things that are opposed (*opponere*) to one another are contraries, but all things are opposed by a contrary.[38]

The first type of contrary is called diverse (*diversus*) according to Cicero (*Topics* 35), because these are set against one another as such complete opposites that they have no part in the things to which they are opposed, as 'wisdom' to 'stupidity.' 2. This type is divided into three species: some have a middle (*medium*); some are without a middle; and some have a middle but are nevertheless without a term for it, unless each of the contraries creates a term for it. 'White' and 'black' have a middle term, because often 'pale' or 'dark' is found between them. 3. Those contraries are without a middle whenever only one of the two opposites occurs at one time, as 'health' or 'sickness.' There is no middle of these. Then, those contraries of which the middle has no term – as 'happy, unhappy,' have the middle, 'not happy.'

The second type of contraries is of relatives (*relativus*), which are opposed to one another in such a way that they are compared with themselves, as 'double, single.' 4. Only this type of opposites is referred to itself, for there is no 'greater' unless it is compared with 'lesser,' and no 'single' unless with 'double.' Now one relative is opposed to another in such a way that the thing that is put in opposition may either be part of that to which it is opposed, or be related to it in some way. Hence 'half' is opposed to 'double' – and is the middle term of that 'double' – but is so opposed to it that it is part of that to which it is opposed.[39] 5. Thus 'small' is opposed to 'great' in such a way that a specific small thing is 'small' in comparison with the great thing to which it is opposed. The oppositions mentioned above called contraries are so opposed to one another that they are not part of the things to which they are opposed nor related to them in any way. Indeed 'iniquity' is a contrary of 'justice' such that iniquity is not a part of that same justice, nor is iniquity related to it.

6. The third type of opposites is possession (*habitus*) or lack (*orbatio*). Cicero names this type 'privation' (*privatio*), because it shows that someone possessed (*habere*) something of which he has been deprived (*privare*). Of this type there are three species: the first is 'in the thing' (*in re*), the second 'in the place' (*in loco*), the third 'at the appropriate time' (*in tempore congruo*). 'In the thing,' as 'blindness,' 'sight.' 'In the place,' as the place of blindness and sight is 'in the eyes.' 'At the appropriate time,' as we do not speak of an infant as 'toothless' when his brief life so far has denied him teeth. Indeed, he has not been 'deprived' of teeth that have not yet erupted.

7. The fourth type of contrary sets up an opposition 'from an affirmation and a negation' (*ex confirmatione et negatione*), as "Socrates disputes, Socrates does not dispute." This differs from the ones above because those can be spoken singly, whereas these cannot be spoken of except jointly. This fourth type of contrary has aroused much controversy among logicians, and by them is called 'intensely opposite' (*valde oppositum*), since indeed it takes no mediating term (*tertium*). 8. For some of these other oppositions can have a mediating term, as, among the contraries, 'black' and 'white.' The mediating term of this contrary is neither 'white' nor 'black,' but 'dark' or 'pale.' This is the case among relatives also, as 'many' and 'few.' Of this the mediating term is neither 'many' nor 'few,' but 'a middling number.' In 'possession' or 'lack,' as 'sight' and 'blindness,' the mediating term is neither 'blindness' nor 'sight,' but 'weak eyes.' But this one – 'he reads, he does not read' – has no mediating term at all.

38 The apparent (proximate?) source, Martianus Capella, is clearer: "Not all things that are opposed to one another are contraries, but all contraries are opposites."

39 "Half . . . is the middle term of that double" is nonsense; the (proximate?) source in Martianus Capella reads "is the half of what is its double."

Book III

Mathematics (De mathematica)

Mathematics (Mathematica)

Mathematics (*mathematica*) in Latin means "the science of learning" (*doctrinalis scientia*), which contemplates abstract quantity (see p. 80, fn. 22). An abstract (*abstractus*) quantity is something that we investigate (*tractare*) by reasoning alone, separating it by means of the intellect from matter or from accidental qualities such as even and odd, and other things of this kind. There are four types of mathematics, namely, Arithmetic (*arithmetica*), Music (*musica*), Geometry (*geometria*), and Astronomy (*astronomia*). Arithmetic is the study of numeric quantity in and of itself. Music is the study that is occupied with the numbers that are found in sounds. Geometry is the study of size and shapes. Astronomy is the study that contemplates the course of the heavenly bodies and all the figures and positions of the stars. We will cover these studies, each in turn, a little more fully, so that their principles can be suitably shown.

i. The word for the study of arithmetic (De vocabulo arithmeticae disciplinae) 1. Arithmetic (*arithmetica*) is the study of numbers, for the Greeks call numbers (*numerus*) ἀριθμός. The writers of secular literature would have this discipline be the first among the mathematical disciplines, as this discipline relies on no other for its existence. 2. However, music, geometry, and astronomy, which follow arithmetic, require its support in order to exist and hold their place.

ii. Originators of mathematics (De auctoribus eius) People say that Pythagoras was the first among the Greeks to commit the study of numbers to writing. Next, the subject was laid out more broadly by Nicomachus. Among the Latin speakers, first Apuleius and then Boethius translated this.

iii. What a number is (Quid sit numerus) 1. A number is a quantity that is made of units (*unitas*), for 'one' is the germ of number, but not a number itself.[1] The term 'coin' (*nummus*) gave its name to 'number' (*numerus*) and from its pervasiveness, it bestowed the name. 'One' (*unus*) draws its name from Greek; for the Greeks call one εἷς (neuter ἕν). Thus it is for 'two' (*duo*) and 'three' (*tres*), which the Greeks call δύο and τρία. 2. 'Four' (*quattuor*) takes up its name from the square (*quadratus*), but 'five' (*quinque*) did not take its name from nature, but rather from the arbitrary will of the one who bestowed the names upon numbers. 'Six' (*sex*) and 'seven' (*septem*) come from the Greek. 3. For we pronounce an *s* instead of the rough breathing sound (i.e. the *h*-sound) in many words that are aspirated in Greek. Thus, we have *sex* for ἕξ and *septem* for ἑπτά, just as we say *serpillum* (i.e. a type of thyme) for the herb *herpillum*. But 'eight' (*octo*) is a direct translation, as we and the Greeks say it the same way. Similarly, they say ἐννέα, we say *novem* (i.e. 'nine'); they say δέκα and we say *decem* (i.e. 'ten').

4. Now 'ten' is said to derive from a Greek etymology, because it binds and conjoins numbers that lie below it, for δεσμός ("bond") means to conjoin or to bind. Furthermore, 'twenty' (*viginti*) is so called because ten 'occurs twice' (*bis geniti*), with the letter *v* put in place of the *b*. 'Thirty' (*triginta*) is so called because it arises (*gignere*) from three (*ternarius*) tens, and so it goes up to 'ninety' (*nonaginta*). 5. 'One hundred' (*centum*) is so called from 'iron wheel-tire' (*canthus*) because it is circular; 'two hundred' (*ducenti*) comes from 'two one-hundreds' (*duo centum*). Thus it is for the remaining

1 Ancient authors on both mathematics and philosophy conceived of 'one,' or the unity, as a special, indivisible entity from which numbers were formed, but which itself was not a number.

numbers up to one thousand. 'One thousand' (*mille*) comes from 'great number' (*multitudo*), and whence also 'the military' (*militia*), as if the word were *multitia*; and whence also 'thousands' (*milia*), which the Greeks call *myriada* (i.e. "myriads"), with letters changed.

iv. What numbers do for us (Quid praestent numeri) 1. The reckoning of numbers ought not to be despised, for in many passages of sacred writings it elucidates how great a mystery they hold. Not for nothing it is said in praise of God (Wisdom 11:21), "Thou hast ordered all things in measure, and number (*numerus*), and weight." 2. The [number] that contains six units (*senarius*), which is perfect in its own parts, declares the completion of the world by a certain signification of its number.[2] Likewise for the forty days during which Moses and Elijah and the Lord himself fasted: without an understanding of numbers, the span of days is unintelligible.

3. So also there are other numbers in the Sacred Scriptures whose figurative meaning cannot be resolved except by those skilled in the knowledge of the mathematical art. It is even our lot to depend on the discipline of numbers to some extent when through it we name the hours, when we dispute about the course of the months, and when we recognize the duration of the turning year. 4. Indeed, through numbers, we are provided with the means to avoid confusion. Remove numbers from all things, and everything perishes. Take computation from the world and blind ignorance embraces all things; those who are ignorant of the method of calculation cannot be differentiated from the other animals.

v. The first division, of even and odd numbers (De prima divisione parium et inparium) 1. Numbers are divided into even (*pars*) and odd (*impars*) numbers. Even numbers are subdivided into these categories: evenly even, evenly odd, and oddly even. Odd numbers are subdivided into these categories: the primary and simple; the secondary and compound; and the tertiary and mean, which in a certain way is primary and non-compound, but in another way is secondary and compound.

2. An even number is one that can be divided into two equal parts, like 2, 4, and 8.[3] On the other hand, an odd number is one that cannot be divided into equal parts, since there is one in the middle (i.e. of the two equal parts) that is either lacking or superfluous, like 3, 5, 7, 9 and so on. 3. An evenly (*pariter*) even number is one that is divided equally into even numbers until it reaches the indivisible unity, as, for example, 64 has 32 at its midpoint; 32 has 16, 16 has 8, 8 has 4, 4 has 2, 2 has 1, which is an indivisible singularity.

4. An evenly odd number is one that can undergo a division into equal parts, but then its parts cannot immediately be evenly dissected, like 6, 10, 38, 50. As soon as you divide this kind of number, you run into a number that you cannot cut evenly. 5. An oddly (*impariter*) even number is one whose parts can be divided equally, but the division does not go to the point of one (*unitas*), like 24. This number can be divided in half, making 12, and 12 can be divided in half, making 6, and then 6 can be divided in half, making 3. This last section cannot undergo further division, but rather there is a termination that you cannot cut before reaching number one. 6. An oddly odd number is one which is divided by an odd number an odd number of times, like 25 and 49. While these numbers are odd, they are divided into an odd number of parts, so that 49 is seven sevens, and 25 is five fives.

Some odd numbers are simple, some are compound, and some are mean (*mediocris*). 7. Simple odd numbers (i.e. prime numbers) are those that hold no other part except the number one alone, as for example the number 3, which holds only 3, and the number 5, which holds only 5, and the number 7, which holds only 7. These numbers have only a single part (i.e. factor). Compound numbers are those that are divided not only by the number one, but are also generated from another number – such numbers as 9, 15, and 21. So we speak of 3 times 3, or 7 times 3, or 3 times 5, or 5 times 5.

8. Mean numbers are those that seem to be simple and non-compound numbers in one way, but compound numbers in another. For example, when 9 is compared to 25, it is primary and not compound, because there is no number that divides into both 9 and 25 except the number one only. But if 9 is compared to 15, it is secondary and compound, since there is present in 15

2 On perfect numbers see v.11 below.

3 In this book we often translate Isidore's term *pars* as "part," where a modern equivalent would be "factor." Isidore and his predecessors conceptualized multiplication not so much as a process that derives a product from factors, but rather as a set of static relationships among numbers.

a shared number besides the number one, that is, the number three, for 9 is 3 times 3 and 15 is 3 times 5.

9. Furthermore, some of the even numbers are 'superfluous,' some are 'diminutive,' and some are 'perfect.' Superfluous (*superfluus*) numbers are those whose parts exceed their own total when added together, as for example, 12. 12 has 5 parts: 1, which occurs 12 times; 2, which occurs 6 times; 3, which occurs 4 times; 4, which occurs 3 times; and 6, which occurs twice. Now 1, 2, 3, 4, and 6 added together make 16, which by far surpasses 12. Thus it is for 12 and many other numbers similar to it, like 18, and many others. 10. Diminutive (*diminutivus*) numbers are those which, when computation is made of their parts, render a sum less than the total number, such as 10, which has 3 parts: 1, which occurs 10 times; 2, which occurs 5 times; and 5, which occurs twice. 1 and 2 and 5 added together make 8, well less than 10. Similar to 10 is the number 8, or many other numbers which, when their parts are added together, stop short of the number itself.

11. A perfect (*perfectus*) number is one that is completely filled up by its own parts, as, for example, 6, for it has 3 parts: 6, 3, and 2. The part that occurs 6 times is 1, the part that occurs 3 times is 2, and the part that occurs 2 times is 3. When these parts are added together, that is, when 1, 2, and 3 are summed up together, they make (*perficere*, ppl. *perfectus*) the number 6. Perfect numbers that occur within 10 include 6; within 100, 28; and within 1000, 496.

vi. The second division of all numbers (De secunda divisione totius numeri) 1. Every number can be regarded either with respect to itself, or with respect to another number. The latter are divided thus: some numbers are equal, others are unequal. The latter are also divided this way: some are major, and some are minor. Major numbers are divided thus: multiples (*multiplex*), superparticulars (*superparticularis*), superpartients (*superpartiens*), multiple superparticulars, and multiple superpartients. Minor numbers are divided thus: submultiples, subsuperparticulars, subsuperpartients, submultiple subsuperparticulars, and submultiple subsuperpartients.

2. A number that is taken into account *per se* is one that is discussed without any sort of relationship, like 3, 4, 5, 6, and so on. A number that is taken into account with respect to another number is one that is compared relative to the other number, as, for example, when 4 is compared to 2, it is called 'duplex' (*duplex*) [and multiple (*multiplex*)], or when 6 is compared to 3, or 8 to 4, or 10 to 5. Again, when 3 is compared to 1, it is called 'triplex' (*triplex*), or when 6 is compared to 2, or 9 to 3, and so on. 3. Numbers that are equal with respect to quantity are called 'equal' (*aequalis*), as, for example, when 2 is compared to 2, 3 to 3, 10 to 10, and 100 to 100. 'Unequal' (*inaequalis*) numbers are those that show inequality when compared to another number, as when 3 is compared to 2, 4 to 3, 5 to 4, and 10 to 6. At all times, whenever a major number is compared to a minor number, or when a minor number is compared to a major number, it is said to be 'unequal.'

4. A major (*maior*) number is one that contains within itself the minor number to which it is compared, and something more, as for example, the number 5 is greater than the number 3, because the number 5 contains within itself the number 3 and two of its parts; and so it is for other such cases. 5. [A minor (*minor*) number is one that is contained by a major number, to which it is compared, along with some portion of itself, as when the number 3 is compared to the number 5. The number 3 is contained by 5, along with two parts of 3.] A multiple (*multiplex*) number is one that has within itself a minor number twice, or three times, or four, or a multiple number of times (*multipliciter*). For example, when 2 is compared to 1, it is duplex; 3 compared to one is triplex; four compared to one is quadruplex, and so on.

6. Opposite to this is the submultiple (*submultiplex*), a number that is contained within a multiple number twice, or three times, or four times, or a multiple number of times. For example, 1 is contained by 2 twice, by 3 three times, by 4 four times, by 5 five times, and by other numbers a multiple number of times. 7. A superparticular (*superparticularis*) number is one that, while being the greater number, contains within itself a lesser number, to which it is compared, and one part of the lesser number in addition. For example, when 3 is compared to 2, 3 contains within itself 2 and one other part that is half of 2; or when 4 is compared to 3, 4 contains in itself 3, and one other part, which is a third of 3. Again, when 5 is compared to 4, 5 has within itself the number 4, and one other number, which is said to be a fourth of the number 4, and so on with other numbers.

8. A superpartient (*superpartiens*) number is one that contains an entire lesser number within itself, and has

beyond this 2, or 3, or 4, or 5, or more parts of the lesser number. For example, when 5 is compared to 3, the number 5 has within itself the number 3, and, in addition, two parts of 3. When 7 is compared to 4, 7 has in itself 4, and three other parts of 4; when 9 is compared to 5, 9 has within itself 5 and four other parts of 5. 9. A subsuperpartient (*subsuperpartiens*) number is one that is contained within a superpartient number, along with two or three or more of its own parts. For example, 3 is contained by 5 along with two other parts of 3; 5 is contained by 9 along with four other parts of 5.

10. A subsuperparticular number is a minor number that is contained within a greater number along with one other part of itself – whether a half, or a third, or a fourth, or a fifth; as, for example, when 2 is compared to 3, or 3 to 4, or 4 to 5, and so on. 11. A multiple superparticular number is one that, when compared to a number less than itself, contains with itself the entire lesser number multiple times, along with another part of the lesser number. For example, when 5 is compared to 2, 5 contains within itself 2 two times, making 4, along with one part of 2; when 9 is compared to 4, 9 contains within itself 4 two times, making 8, and one other part of 4. 12. [A submultiple [sub]superparticular number is one that, when compared to a number greater than itself, is contained by that number a multiple of times along with one other part of itself; as for example, when 2 is compared to 5, 2 is contained by 5 two times, along with one part of 2.]

A multiple superpartional (*superpartionalis*) number is one that, when compared to a number less than itself, contains the lesser number a multiple number of times along with some other parts of the lesser number. For example, when 8 is compared to 3, 8 contains within itself 3 two times, plus two other parts of 3. When 14 is compared to 6, 14 contains 6 within itself two times, plus two other parts of 6; [when 16 is compared to 7, 16 contains 7 twice, plus two other parts of 7; when 21 is compared to 9, it contains 9 within itself twice, plus three other parts of 9].

13. A submultiple superpartional number is one that, when compared to a number greater than itself, is contained by that number a multiple number of times, together with some other parts of itself. For example, when 3 is compared to 8, 3 is contained by 8 two times, plus two parts of 3; when 4 is compared to 11, 4 is contained two times, plus three parts of 4.

vii. The third division of all numbers (De tertia divisione totius numeri) 1. Numbers are either discrete, or continuous. Continuous numbers are divided into linear (*linealis*), planar (*superficialis*), or solid (*solidus*) numbers. A discrete (*discretus*) number is one that is of separate (*discretus*) units, as for example 3, 4, 5, 6, and so on. 2. A continuous (*continens*) number is one that is composed of conjoined units, [as], for example, when the number 3 is understood in terms of its magnitude, that is, in its linear dimension, or is said to be containing (*continens*) either a space or a solid; likewise for the numbers 4 or 5.

3. A linear (*linealis*) number is one that begins from the number one and is written in a linear fashion (*linealiter*) up to infinity. Whence the letter alpha is used to mark the measure of lines, since this letter signifies 'one' among the Greeks (a figure follows in manuscript).[4]

4. A planar (*superficalis*) number is one that is composed not only of length, but also of breadth, such as the triangular, quadrangular, pentagonal, or circular numbers, and so on, which always exist in a flat (*planus*) region, that is, a surface (*superficies*). Thus the triangular number: (a figure follows in manuscript). Thus the quadrangular number: (fig.). Thus the pentagonal: (fig.). 5. Thus the circular number (i.e. the square of a number), which, since it has been multiplied by like numbers, begins from itself and turns back to itself, as for example 5 times 5 is 25, thus: (fig.).

A solid (*solidus*) number is one that is consists of length, breadth, and height, like pyramids, which rise up in the manner of a flame: (fig.). 6. Cubes (*cubus*) are, for example, like dice: (fig.). Spheres (*sphaera*) have an equal roundness on all sides: (fig.). A spherical number (i.e. the cube of a number) is one that, when multiplied by a circular number, begins from itself and turns back to itself. For example, 5 times 5 is 25. When this circular number is multiplied on itself, it makes a sphere, that is, 5 times 25 is 125.

viii. The difference between arithmetic, geometry, and music (De differentia arithmeticae, geometriae et musicae) 1. There are differences between arithmetic, geometry, and music, in the way that you discover their

4 The illustrations found in early manuscripts show plane figures with alphas along the sides of the figures to indicate their linear measure.

means. First, you seek out means in arithmetic in this manner. You add together a low and a high number, you divide them, and you find the mean; take, for example, the low and high numbers 6 and 12: when you join them, they make 18; you divide this at its midpoint, and you make 9, which is an arithmetic proportion, in that the mean exceeds the low number by as many units as the mean is exceeded by the high number. Now 9 exceeds 6 by 3, and 9 is exceeded by 12 by the same amount. 2. But you seek out means in geometry in this way. The beginning and end numbers, when they are multiplied, make as much as the double of their means.[5] Take, for example, 6 and 12. When multiplied, they make 72, and their means, 8 and 9, when multiplied make the same amount.[6] 3. Next, you seek out the means for music in this way. By whatever part the mean exceeds the low number, by the same part the mean is exceeded by the high number. Take, for example, 6 and 8. 8 exceeds 6 by two parts, and these two parts are the third midpoint, [8], which is exceeded by the final ninth.[7]

ix. How many infinite numbers exist (Quot numeri infiniti existunt) 1. It is quite certain that numbers are 'without limit' (*infinitus*), since at whatever number you think the limit has been reached, that same number can be increased – not, I say, by the addition of only one, but however large it is, and however huge a number it contains, by reason and by the science of numbers it can be not only doubled, but even further multiplied. 2. Yet each number is so bounded by its own properties that none of them can be equal to any other. Therefore, numbers are unlike and varied among themselves, and each one in itself is bounded (*finitus*), but taken all together they are unbounded (*infinitus*).

5 As the next sentence shows, Isidore means not "double" but "multiple." Perhaps underlying his lapse is the fact that in arithmetic the sum of the end points is in fact double the sum of their mean.

6 Following Boethius, Isidore describes a proportion whose mean (in modern terms) falls between two adjacent integers as possessing two means. In this case, the geometric mean of 6 and 12 in modern terms is the square root of 72, so Isidore describes this proportion as having the two means 8 and 9, whose product is 72.

7 The text appears to be corrupt here. Compare with ch. xxiii below, where Isidore provides a detailed and lucid description of the harmonic mean.

8 In the *Timaeus* Plato presents five solids, not five planar figures.

x. The inventors of geometry, and its name (De inventoribus geometriae et vocabulo eius) 1. It is said that the discipline of geometry was first discovered by the Egyptians, because, when the Nile River flooded and everyone's possessions were covered with mud, the onset of dividing the earth by means of lines and measures gave a name to the skill. And thereupon, when it was greatly perfected by the acumen of wise men, the expanses of the sea, sky, and air were measured. 2. Stimulated by their zeal, these sages began, after they had measured the land, to inquire about the region of the sky, as to how far the moon is from the earth, and even the sun from the moon; and how great a distance there is to the pinnacle of the heavens. And so, using reasoning capable of being tested and proved, they determined the distances of the vault of heaven and the perimeter of the earth in terms of the number of stadia. 3. But because the discipline began with measuring the earth, it retained its name from its origin, for geometry (*geometria*) takes its name from 'earth' and 'measure.' In Greek, 'earth' is called γῆ and 'measure' is μέτρα. The art of this discipline is concerned with lines, distances, sizes and shapes, and the dimensions and numbers found in shapes.

xi. The fourfold division of geometry (De quadripertita divisione geometriae) 1. Geometry is divided into four parts: planes (*planus*), numeric size (*magnitudo numerabilis*), rational size (*magnitudo rationalis*), and solid figures (*figura solida*). 2. Planar figures are those that have length and breadth and are, following Plato, five in number.[8] Numeric size is that which can be divided by the numbers of arithmetic. 3. Rational sizes are those whose measures we are able to know, but irrational sizes are those the quantity of whose measures cannot be known.

xii. Geometrical figures (De figuris geometriae) 1. Solid figures are those that are composed of length, breadth, and height, as for example the cube (*cubus*). There are five types of figures that exist on a plane. A circle (*circulus*) is the first of the planar figures, and it is so called from going around (*circumducere*). It has a point in its middle, on which everything centers, which people call the geometric center, and which Latin speakers call the 'point of the circle' (*punctus circuli*) (a figure follows). 2. A four-sided figure on a plane is called a quadrilateral (*quadrilaterus*) figure. It lies within four straight lines, thus (fig.). A *dianatheton grammon* is the plane figure [thus]: (fig.).[9] An *orthogonium* (cf. ὀρθός, "right"; γωνία, "angle") is a plane figure with a right angle (fig.). It is a triangle (*triangulus*), and it has a right angle.

An *isopleuros* (cf. ἴσος, "equal"; πλευρά, "side") is a plane figure; it is upright and constructed below (fig.; apparently an isosceles or equilateral triangle). 3. A sphere (*sphaera*) is a figure fashioned in the round, with all parts equal (fig.). A cube (*cubus*) is, properly, a solid figure that consists of length, breadth, and height (fig.). 4. A cylinder (*cylindrus*) is a four-sided figure having a semicircle above (fig.).[10] 5. A cone (*conon*) is a figure that from a wide base narrows at the top, just like the *orthogonium* (fig.). 6. A pyramid (*pyramis*) is a figure that rises up from a wide base to a point, like a tongue of fire, for 'fire' is called πῦρ among the Greeks (fig.). 7. Just as every number is within 10, so the perimeter of every figure is enclosed within the circle (fig.).[11]

The first figure of this art is the point (*punctus*), which has no parts. The second figure is the line (*linea*), a length without breadth. A straight (*rectus*) line is one that lies evenly along its points. A plane (*superficies*) has length and breadth only. The boundaries of planes are lines. The forms of these are not placed in the preceding ten figures, because they are found among them.[12]

xiii. Geometric numbers (De numeris geometricae)

You seek out numbers according to geometry in this way. Beginning and end numbers, when they are multiplied, make as much as the double of their means. Take, for example, 6 and 12. When multiplied, they make 72, and their means 8 and 9 when multiplied make the same amount (see viii.2 above).

[xiv. Exposition of figures illustrated below (Expositio figurarum infra scriptarum)[13]

1. Likewise, one account concerning the motion of stars is gathered together in eight figures. These are the diametric (*diametrus*), or quadratic (*quadratus*, i.e. tetragonal), or triangular (*trigonus*), or hexagonal (*hexagonus*), or asyndetic (*asyndetus*),[14] or coincident (*simul*), or circumferent (*circumferre*), that is, they either 'carry to a higher degree' (*superferre*) or 'are carried.' Diagonals occur when five constellations intervene. Tetragonals (*tetragonus*) occur when two constellations intervene. Hexagonals occur when there is one. Asyndetic figures occur when no constellations intervene. Coincident figures occur when they are in the same small area. Figures 'carry to a higher degree' when they overtake another figure, or cause an action. Figures are 'carried to a higher degree' when they precede others. 2. Triangular figures occur when there are three intervening (constellations). Again, according to another account, there are eight differentiae, namely, the constellation (*signum*), its parts (*pars*), its boundaries (*finis*), by the way it is assembled (*conventus*), by its retrograde or straight paths, its latitude, and its longitude.

3. The calculation of interior shapes.[15] This kind of inquiry concerning this point may arise. Although in the sequence of numbers 8 is prior, here one puts 9 first, since in the logic of arithmetic or geometry 8 is more

9 The meaning of *dianatheton grammon* remains obscure; a proposed emendation *diacatheton* might mean, elliptically, "rectangular figure," from Greek κάθετος, "perpendicular." The illustrative figure drawn in some early manuscripts seems to indicate a rectangle. See Fontaine 1959: 400–01.

10 The figure Isidore describes is an upright rectangle topped by a semicircle with its flat side down against the rectangle. This rectangle/semicircle figure may be viewed as a two-dimensional representation of a cylinder, the rectangle giving a side view of the cylinder tube, and the semicircle showing the curve of the cylinder.

11 Fontaine explains that Isidore refers to an Augustinian method, as used in arithmetical exegesis, of decomposing large numbers into numbers from one to ten: 1959:383–86, 398–99.

12 That is, the point, line, and plane are illustrated by the manuscript figures of the circle, the various planes, and the solids, respectively.

13 This chapter, found in only one family of manuscripts, is considered by Fontaine (1959:394) to be a collection of disparate fragments composed by followers of Isidore.

14 This truncated account is clarified by the illustrations provided by J. Fontaine (1959: following p. 450), from the Escorial manuscript P.I.6. Five circles are each divided by twelve radii into twelve wedges, and each wedge (in one example, for all) is labeled with the name of a sign of the zodiac. These indicate various relationships among the zodiacal signs by means of figures formed by connecting the points where the radii meet the perimeter of the circle. The circle labeled *exagona*, for example, connects every second such point, so that the figure of a hexagon is formed by the six secants so drawn. When every second point is connected, Isidore considers that there is one intervening sign, i.e. one point intervening between connected points. When every third point is connected (tetragonals), he considers that there are two intervening signs, etc. The other circles are labeled *tetragona*, *trigona*, *diametra*, and *asindeton*. Manilius's *Astronomy* (2.273–432) treats these relationships and their significance.

15 Fontaine (1959:400–11) suggests that sections 3–5 derive from scholia or a commentary on Plato's *Timaeus*.

than 9, for 8 is a cube (*cubus*) or a solid, that is, it is a body of which one can find no more, but 9 is a plane (*superficies*), that is, it is a thing that is not filled out; rather, it lacks perfection. 4. Here two cubes, that is, two solidities, are found in this manner. The number six is the first perfect number (see v.11 above); for it is divisible into numbers equal to it, so: divide by one, six parts; into three parts by two – three twos are six; in half, that is three two times, is six. You will find another perfect number that you may divide by equal numbers in this way, which accords with the preceding instance. 5. Within the first numeric order, that is, within 10, on account of its being the first perfect number, multiplying with the first turn sixes nine times gives 54; nines six times, 54.[16] The material makes so many parts and it is known to have had so many parts not without reason, by twos, and from this it has one in an order such as this: 1, 2, 3, 4, 9, 8 and other numbers, including 27.]

Music (De musica)

xv. Music and its name (De musica et eius nomine)[17] 1.Music (*musica*) is the practical knowledge of modulation (*modulatio*) and consists of sound and song. Music is so called through derivation from the word 'Muse,' for the Muses (*Musae*) were named from μάσαι, that is, from 'seeking',[18] because it was through them, as the ancients would have it, that the power of song and the modulation of the voice were sought. 2. Their sound, because it is something perceived by the senses, vanishes as the moment passes and is imprinted in the memory. Whence came the invention of the poets that the Muses are the daughters of Jupiter and Memory, for unless sounds are held by the memory of man, they perish, because they cannot be written down.

xvi. The inventors of music (De inventoribus eius) 1. Moses says that Tubal, who was of the stock of Cain before the Flood, was the discoverer of the musical art. But the Greeks say that Pythagoras discovered the elements of this art from the sound of hammers and from the striking of taut strings. Others hand down the story that Linus the Theban and Zetus and Amphion were the first to become famous in the musical art. 2. After them, little by little, this discipline especially was regulated and augmented in many ways, and it became as shameful to be ignorant of music as it was shameful not to be able to read and write. Moreover, music was introduced not only in sacred rites, but also in all celebrations, and in all joyful or sorrowful occasions. 3. Just as hymns were sung in veneration of the gods, there were also hymns to Hymen for weddings, dirges and laments at funerals, all accompanied by the flute. At banquets, a lyre or cithara was passed around, and a convivial type of song was performed by each reclining diner in turn.

xvii. The power of music (Quid possit musica) 1. So it is that without music, no other discipline can be perfected, for nothing is without music. Indeed, it is said that the universe itself is composed from a certain harmony of sounds, and that the very heavens turn to the modulations of harmony. Music rouses emotions, and it calls the senses to a different state. 2. In battle, too, the sounding of the trumpet inflames the fighters, and the more ardent its blast, the braver grows the spirit for the contest. Since song urges even rowers on, music also soothes the spirit so that it can endure toil, and the modulation of the voice eases exhaustion from individual labors. 3. Music also calms excited spirits, just as one reads about David, who rescued Saul from the unclean spirit by the art of modulation. Music calls forth the very beasts to listen to its modulation, even serpents, birds, and dolphins. But further, however we speak, or however we are moved by the internal pulsing of our veins – these things are demonstrably linked, through their musical rhythms, to the power of harmony.

16 This sentence and the remainder of this chapter are obscure and probably scribally corrupt. See Gasparotto, 2009: 152–63.

17 Several early manuscripts present elaborate figures, of obscure meaning, illustrating various mathematical principles of music. Examples may be found in Lindsay's edition, and in Fontaine (1959: following p. 450). Presumably because his work is incomplete, Isidore does not discuss these in his text.

18 The reading μάσαι is uncertain. Compare μῶσις, "searching," proposed by Cornutus (first century CE) as the etymon of 'Muse.'

xviii. The three parts of music (De tribus partibus musicae) 1. Music has three parts, that is, the harmonic (*harmonicus*), the rhythmic (*rhythmicus*), and the metric (*metricus*). The harmonic part is that which differentiates high and low sounds. The rhythmic part inquires about the impact of words, whether the sound agrees well or badly. 2. The metrical part is that which recognizes, by means of a demonstrable system, the measure of different meters, as for example the heroic, the iambic, the elegiac, and so on.

xix. The threefold division of music (De triformi musicae divisione) 1. It is accepted that all sound that is the material of song has three forms by its nature. The first division is the *harmonicus*, which consists of vocal song. The second division is the *organicus*, which is composed of blowing. The third is the rhythmic (*rhythmicus*), which takes its measures from the plucking of fingers. 2. For sound is emitted either by the voice, as through the throat, or by blowing, as through a trumpet or a flute, or by plucking,[19] as with the cithara, or any other sort of instrument that is melodious when plucked.

xx. The first division of music, which is called harmonic (De prima divisione musicae quae harmonica dicitur) 1. The first division of music, which is called harmonic (*harmonicus*), that is, the modulation of the voice, pertains to comedies, tragedies, or choruses, or to all who sing with their own voice. This makes a movement that comes from the mind and body together, and the movement produces a sound, and from this is formed the music that in humans is called 'voice' (*vox*). 2. Voice (*vox*) is air beaten (*verberare*) by breath, and from this also words (*verbum*) are named. Properly, voice is a human characteristic, or a characteristic of unreasoning animals. But in some cases, with incorrect usage and improperly, a sound is called a 'voice,' as for example "the voice of the trumpet bellowed," and (cf. Vergil, *Aen.* 3.556):

> . . . and voices (*vox*) broken on the shore.

For the word proper to rocks on the shore is 'sound' (*sonare*). Also, (Vergil, *Aen.* 9.503):

> But the trumpet far off (made) a terrible sound with its sonorous brass.

Harmonics (*harmonica*) is the modulation of the voice and the bringing of many sounds into agreement, or fitting them together. 3. Symphony (*symphonia*) is the blend of modulation made from low and high sounds in agreement with one another, either in voice, or blowing, or plucking. Through symphony, higher and lower voices are brought into harmony, so that whoever makes a dissonant sound offends the sense of hearing. The opposite of symphony is diaphony (*diaphonia*), that is, when voices are discrepant, or dissonant. 4. Euphony (*euphonia*) is sweetness of voice. This is also 'melody' (*melos*) which takes its name from sweetness and honey (*mel*). 5. Diastema (*diastema*) is the appropriate vocal interval between two or more sounds. 6. Diesis (*diesis*) refers to certain intervals that lead the modulation downward, and moving downward from one sound into another. 7. Tone (*tonus*) is the high enunciation of the voice. A tone (i.e. a modal scale) is also the variation and quantity of a mode (*harmonia*) which consists of vocal accent and tenor. Musicians have divided the tones into fifteen kinds, of which the hyperlydian (i.e. hypolydian) is the last and highest, and the hypodorian is the lowest of all.

8. A song (*cantus*) is the voice changing pitch, for sound is even-pitched; and sound precedes song. 9. Arsis (*arsis*) is elevation of the voice, that is, the beginning. Thesis (*thesis*) is lowering the voice, that is, the end. 10. Sweet (*suavis*) voices are refined and compact, distinct and high. Clear (*perspicuus*) voices are those that are drawn out further, so that they continually fill whole spaces, like the blaring of trumpets. 11. Delicate (*subtilis*) voices are those that have no breath, like the voices of infants, women, and sick people, and like plucking on strings. Indeed, the most delicate strings of musical instruments emit light, refined sounds. 12. Voices are rich (*pinguis*) when a great deal of breath is sent forth all at once, like the voices of men. A high (*acutus*) voice is light, and elevated, just as we see in the strings of musical instruments. A hard (*durus*) voice is one that emits sounds violently, like thunder, or like the sound of the anvil, when the hammer strikes on the hard iron.

19 Latin speaks of plucking stringed instruments as 'striking' (*percutere*, ppl. *percussus*) the strings; hence such instruments are classed with the percussions. *Organicus* can mean "instrumental" in general, but here it obviously refers specifically to wind instruments.

13. A harsh (*asperus*) voice is hoarse, and uttered with brief undifferentiated beats. A blind (*caecus*) voice is one that stops short as soon as it is emitted, and being stifled is not prolonged any further, like the sound of clay utensils. A charming (*vinnolus*) voice is soft and flexible; and it is so named from *vinnus*, that is, 'a softly pliant curl.' 14. A perfect (*perfectus*) voice is high, sweet, and distinct: high, so that it can reach the high range; distinct, so that it fills the ears; sweet, so that it soothes the spirits of the listeners. If a voice lacks any of these qualities, it is not perfect.

xxi. The second division, which is called *organicus* (De secunda divisione, quae organica dicitur) 1. The second division is *organicus*, and it is produced by those instruments that, when they are filled with the breath that is blown into them, are animated with the sound of a voice, like trumpets, reed pipes, pipes, organs, *pandoria*,[20] and instruments similar to these. 2. *Organum* is the general word for all musical instruments. The Greeks call that instrument to which bellows are attached by a different name (i.e. ὕδραυλος), but to call it an organ (*organum*) is rather the common usage of the Greeks.

3. The trumpet (*tuba*) was invented first by the Etruscans, about which Vergil says (*Aen.* 8.526):

> And the Etruscan blaring of the trumpet (*tuba*)
> bellowed through the air.

Trumpets were employed not only for battles, but also for all festive days, thanks to their clarity in praise or joy. For this reason, the Psalter says (cf. Psalm 80:4, Vulgate), "Sing with a trumpet (*tuba*) at the onset of the month, on the noted day of your solemnity" – for it was commanded for the Jews to sound a trumpet at the onset of the new moon, and they do this even up to this day.

4. People say that flutes (*tibia*) were invented in Phrygia. For a long time, they were used only at funeral rites, and soon after at other sacred rites of the pagans. Moreover, people think that flutes were so named because at first they were fashioned from the leg-bones (*tibia*) of deer and the shin-bones of asses. Then, through incorrect usage, they began to be called by this name even when they were not made of shin-bones or other bones. Thus we also get 'flute player' (*tibicen*), as if from *tibiarum cantus* ("song of flutes").

5. 'Reed' (*calamus*, i.e. the reed plant, and also a name for a reed-pipe) is properly the name of a tree, and comes from 'rousing' (*calere*), that is, from 'pouring forth' voices. 6. Some people think that the *fistula* (lit. "pipe," also another name for a reed-pipe) was invented by Mercury, and others by Faunus, whom the Greeks call Pan. And not a few think that it was invented by Idis, a shepherd from Agrigentum in Sicily.[21] The *fistula* is so named because it emits a voice, for voice is φώς in Greek,[22] and στόλια is the word meaning 'sent forth.' 7. Among musicians, the *sambuca* is a type of *symphonia*.[23] It is made of the kind of fragile wood from which flutes are constructed. 8. The *pandorius* took its name from its inventor, and Vergil says (cf. *Ecl.* 2.32):

> Pan was the first to teach joining many reeds together
> with wax, Pan whose concern is the flock and the
> keepers of the flock.

For among the pagans, Pan was the pastoral god, who was the first to fit together reeds of different lengths for the purpose of song, and he put them together with diligent art.

xxii. The third division of music, which is called rhythmic (De tertia divisione, quae rythmica nuncupatur) 1. The third division of music is called 'rhythmic' (*rhythmicus*), and it pertains to strings and percussion. Different types of cithara belong to this division, and also drums, cymbals, rattles, and bronze and silver cruets, and others that when struck produce a sweet ringing sound from the hardness of their metal, as well as other instruments of this sort.

2. Tubal is reputed to have been the discoverer of the cithara and the psaltery, as was mentioned above. However, according to the opinion of the Greeks it is believed that the use of the cithara was discovered by Apollo. The shape of the cithara is said to have been

20 The *pandorium* or *pandorius* (see section 8 below) is usually in Latin not a wind instrument (pan-pipes?) but a kind of lute, the bandore.

21 The text has ablative *Idi.* This may be a corruption of *Daphnis*, ablative *Daphnide*, the legendary Sicilian inventor of pastoral song Alternatively, it may be a corruption of Idas; the shepherd Idas boasts, in the second Eclogue (28–31) of Calpurnius Siculus ("the Sicilian"), that Silvanus introduced him to the *fistula.*

22 Isidore nods; he knows that φῶς means "light" (see XV.ii.37, etc.), and that 'vocal sound' is φωνή in Greek (VIII.xi.87).

23 Here a *symphonia* – a word used for several types of instruments – is a kind of flute, but a *sambuca* in classical Latin is a small harp, and *sambucus* is the elder-tree.

similar to the human chest at first, so that song might be brought forth from the cithara as the voice is brought forth from the chest, and they say it was named for this same reason. 3. For in the language of the Dorian Greeks the chest is called κιθάρα. Little by little, many types of these instruments came into existence, such as psalteries, lyres, barbitons, *phoenices* and *pectides*, and those types called Indian, which are plucked by two performers at the same time. Some are made one way, and some another, with either a four-sided or triangular shape. 4. Indeed, the number of strings multiplied, and types were changed as well. The ancients called the cithara *fidicula* or *fidicen*,[24] because the strings of this instrument agreed together among themselves in the same way as happens among those who have trust (*fides*). The cithara in antiquity had seven strings. Whence it is said in Vergil (*Aen.* 6.646):

> . . . the seven different notes.

5. Vergil speaks of differences because no string gives a sound like that of the neighboring string. But there are seven strings either because they fill out the entire vocal range, or because heaven resonates with seven motions.

6. Strings (*chorda*) are so called from 'heart' (*cor*, gen. *cordis*) because the throbbing of the strings in the cithara is like the throbbing of the heart in the chest. Mercury contrived them first, and he was the first to pluck sound from musical strings. 7. The psaltery (*psalterium*), which is commonly called *canticum* (lit. "song"), takes its name from 'singing to the psaltery' (*psallere*), because the chorus responds in harmony with the voice of the psaltery. It has a characteristic shared with the foreign cithara, being in the shape of the letter delta; but there is this difference between the psaltery and the cithara, that the psaltery has the hollowed wooden box from which the sound resonates on its top side, so that the strings are struck from underneath and resonate from above, but the cithara has its wooden sound-box on the bottom. The Hebrews used the ten-string psaltery on account of the number of laws of the Decalogue.

8. The lyre (*lyra*) is so called from the word ληρεῖν (i.e. "speak frivolously"), that is, from 'variety of voices,' because it renders diverse sounds. They say that the lyre was first invented by Mercury in the following way. When the Nile was receding into its channels, it left behind various animals on the plains, and a tortoise was one that was stranded. When it decomposed, and its tendons remained stretched out in the shell, it made a sound when Mercury plucked it. Mercury made a lyre of this shape and handed it over to Orpheus, who was by far its most zealous student. 9. Whence it is thought that by his art he controlled not only wild beasts but also the rocks and the woods by the modulation of his song. On account of their love of musical pursuits and praise of song, musicians have imagined, in the fictions of their tales, the lyre as being located among the stars.

The *tympanum* is a skin or hide stretched over one end of a wooden frame. It is half of a *symphonia* (i.e. another type of drum – see section 14 below and cf. xxi.7 above), and looks like a sieve. 10. The *tympanum* is so named because it is a half, whence the half-pearl is also called a *tympanum*. Like the *symphonia*, it is struck with a drumstick. 11. Cymbals (*cymbalum*) are certain vessels that make a sound when they are struck by touching one another. Cymbals are so called because they are struck simultaneously when there is dancing (*ballematia*), for the Greeks say σύν for "with" and βαλά for "dancing."

12. Sistrums (*sistrum*, i.e. a kind of metallic rattle) are named after their inventor, for Isis, an Egyptian queen, is thought to have invented this type of instrument. Juvenal says (*Satires* 13.93):

> May Isis strike my eyes with her angry sistrum.

Whence women play these instruments, because the inventor of this type of instrument was a woman. Whence also it is said that among the Amazons, the army of women was summoned to battle by sistrums. 13. The *tintinabulum* takes its name from the sound of its voice, just like the 'clapping' (*plaudere*) of hands, and the 'creaking' (*stridor*) of hinges. 14. The *symphonia* in common usage is the name for a hollow wood instrument with hide stretched over both ends. Musicians strike them on both sides with drumsticks, and make a very melodious sound from the consonance of the high and low pitches.

xxiii. Musical numbers (De numeris musicis) 1. You find numbers with respect to music in this way (see viii.3 above). When the high and low numbers have been set, as, for example, 6 and 12, you see by how many units 6 is exceeded by 12, and that is by 6 units.

24 In classical Latin *fidicen* means "lyre-player"; the lyre was *fides*.

You make this number into a square, and 6 six times makes 36. You add together the low and high numbers that you first took, 6 and 12, and together they make 18. You divide 36 by 18, and it makes 2. You add this to the low number, that is, 6, and it comes to 8. 8 is the mean between 6 and 12. Wherefore 8 exceeds 6 by two units, that is, a third of 6, and 8 is exceeded by 12 by four units, a third of 12. Thus, the high number exceeds the mean by the same proportion as the low number is exceeded by the mean. 2. But just as this proportion in the universe derives from the revolution of the spheres, so even in the microcosm it has such power beyond mere voice that no-one exists without its perfection and lacking harmony. Indeed, by the perfection of this same art of Music, meters are composed of arsis and thesis, that is, by rising up and setting down.

Astronomy (De astronomia)

xxiv. The name of astronomy (De astronomiae nomine) Astronomy (*astronomia*) is the law (cf. νόμος, "law") of the stars (*aster*), which, by investigative reasoning, touches on the courses of the constellations, and the figures and positions of the stars relative to each other and to the earth.

xxv. The inventors of astronomy (De inventoribus eius) 1. The Egyptians were the first to discover astronomy. However, the Chaldeans were the first to teach astrology (*astrologia*) and observations concerning nativities. But the author Josephus asserts that Abraham instructed the Egyptians in astrology. The Greeks say that this art was earlier conceived by Atlas, and that is why he was said to have held up the sky. 2. Yet whoever the inventor was, he was stirred by the movement of the heavens and prompted by the reasoning of his mind, and through the changing of the seasons, through the fixed and defined courses of the stars, through the measured expanses of their distances apart, he made observations of certain dimensions and numbers. By defining and discerning these things, and weaving them into a system, he invented astrology.

xxvi. Those who established astronomy (De institutoribus eius) In both languages, there are indeed volumes that have been written by diverse writers about astronomy. Among these writers, Ptolemy, the king of Alexandria,[25] is thought to excel among the Greeks, for he established the canons whereby the courses of the stars are discovered.

xxvii. The difference between astronomy and astrology (De differentia astronomiae et astrologiae) 1. There is some difference between astronomy and astrology. Astronomy concerns itself with the turning of the heavens, the rising, setting, and motion of the stars, and where the constellations get their names. But astrology is partly natural, and partly superstitious. 2. It is natural as long as it investigates the courses of the sun and the moon, or the specific positions of the stars according to the seasons; but it is a superstitious belief that the astrologers (*mathematicus*) follow when they practice augury by the stars, or when they associate the twelve signs of the zodiac with specific parts of the soul or body, or when they attempt to predict the nativities and characters of people by the motion of the stars.

xxviii. Astronomical reckoning (De astronomiae ratione) There are several kinds of astronomical reckoning. Indeed, it defines what the world is; what the heavens are; what is the position and course of the sphere; what is the axis of the heavens and the pole; what are the zones of the heavens; what are the courses of the sun and the moon and the stars, and so on.

xxix. The world and its name (De mundo et eius nomine) The world (*mundus*) is that which consists of the heavens, the earth, the seas, and all of the stars. The world is so named, because is it always in motion (*motus*), for no rest is granted to its elements.

xxx. The shape of the world (De forma mundi) The shape of the world is shown in this way.[26] Just as the world is raised up toward the northern region, so it declines toward the south. Its head and its face, as it were, is

25 Isidore is confusing Claudius Ptolemy (second century CE) with the Ptolemys who ruled Egypt.

26 An illustration may have been planned at this point.

the eastern region, and its furthest part is the northern region.

xxxi. The sky and its name (De caelo et eius nomine) 1. The philosophers have said that the sky (*caelum*, "sky, heaven, the heavens") is rounded, spinning, and burning; and the sky is called by its name because it has the figures of the constellations impressed into it, just like an engraved (*caelare*) vessel. 2. God distinguished the sky with bright lights, and he filled it with the sun and the gleaming orb of the moon, and he adorned it with brilliant constellations composed of glittering stars. In Greek the sky is called οὐρανός from ὁρᾶσθαι, that is, from "seeing," from the fact that the air is clear and very pure for seeing through.

xxxii. The position of the celestial sphere (De sphaerae caelestis situ) 1. The sphere of the sky is a certain shape that is round in form, and its center is the earth, which is equally enclosed on all sides. They say that this sphere has neither a beginning nor an end, and this is so because it is round, just like a circle, and it may not easily be comprehended at what point it begins, or where it ends. 2. The philosophers have proposed seven heavens belonging to the universe, that is, seven planets, with a harmonious motion of their spheres. They hold that everything is connected to the orbital paths of these planets, and they think that the planets are interconnected and in a way inserted within one another, and that they turn backwards and are carried by a motion that is opposite to the other heavenly bodies.

xxxiii. The movement of this same sphere (De eiusdem sphaerae motu) 1. The movement of the sphere is caused by its turning on two axes, one of which is the northern, which never sets, and is called Boreus; and the other is the southern axis, which is never seen, and is called Austronotius. 2. They say that the sphere of heaven moves on these two poles, and with its movement, the stars, which are fixed in it, make their circuit from the east to the west, with the northern stars completing shorter circular courses next to the turning point.

xxxiv. The course of the same sphere (De eiusdem sphaerae cursu) The sphere of heaven turns from east to west once in the span of a day and night, consisting of twenty-four hours, during which the sun, in its own revolution, finishes its own course over the earth and under it.

xxxv. The speed of the sky (De celeritate caeli) The sphere of heaven is said to run with a swiftness so great that if the stars did not run against its headlong course to delay it, it would make a ruin of the universe.

xxxvi. The axis of heaven (De axe caeli) The northern axis is a straight line that stretches through the center of the ball of the sphere. It is called 'axis' (*axis*, i.e. "axle") because the sphere turns on it, as though it were a wheel; or because the Wain (i.e. Ursa Major) is there.

xxxvii. The celestial polar regions (De caelestibus polis) The polar regions are circles that run around the axis. One of them is the northern, which never sets, and is named Boreus. The other is the southern, which is never visible, and is called Austronotius. They are called 'polar regions' (*polus*) because they are circles around the axis, after the usage of a wagon, named specifically from 'polishing' (*polire*) – but the polar region Boreus is always visible and Austronotius never, because the right side of the heavens is higher, and the southern side is pressed down.

xxxviii. The poles of the heavens (De cardinibus caeli) The poles of the heavens are the extreme parts of the axis. They are called 'poles' (*cardo*, lit. "pivot") because the heavens are turned on them, or because these poles are turned as if they were the heart (*cor*).

xxxix. The vaults of heaven (De convexis caeli) The vaults (*convexum*) of the heavens are its edges, so called from their 'curvature' (*curvitas*), as in this line (Juvencus, *Gospel Poem* 3.224):

> As often as the humid night enclosed the curved (*convexus*) heavens.

For a vault is 'curved' (*curvus*), as if the word were *conversus* (i.e. "upside down"), and sloping downward, and bent in the manner of a circle.

xl. The doorways of heaven (De ianuis caeli) Heaven has two doorways, the eastern and the western. The sun proceeds from one portal, and another portal receives it.

xli. The twin faces of the sky (De gemina facie caeli) The face of the sky, or its head, is the eastern region, and the furthest part is the northern region.[27] Lucan says this about it (*Civil War* 4.106):

> Thus lies the deepest part of the world, which the snowy Zone and perpetual winters oppress.

xlii. The four parts of heaven (De quattor partibus caeli) 1. The regions (*clima*) of heaven, that is, the expanses or parts of it, are four in number, the first of which is the eastern, the region from where some stars rise. The second is the western, where, from our perspective, some stars set. The third is the northern region, where the sun goes when the days are longer. The fourth is the southern, where the sun goes when the nights are longer. 2. The east (*oriens*) is the named for the rising (*exortus*) of the sun. The west (*occidens*) is so named because it makes the day perish (*occidere*, also meaning "set") and come to an end, for it takes the light from the world and brings on darkness. The north (*septentrio*) axis is so called from the seven (*septem*) stars, which, revolving about it, wheel around. This properly is also called the 'vertex' (*vertex*), because it turns (*vertere*). 3. The southern (*meridies*) zone is so called, either because the sun spends the middle of the day (*medius dies*) there, as though the word were *medi-dies*, or because the upper air is more pure there, for *merus* is the word for 'pure.'

4. There are seven other regions in heaven, as if seven lines come from the east and end in the west. Under them, the disparate characters of humans and animals of diverse species are produced. They are named after certain famous places; the first is Merois; the second Syene; the third Catachoras, that is Africa; the fourth is Rhodes; the fifth, Hellespont; the sixth, Mesopontum; and the seventh, Borysthenes.

xliii. The hemispheres (De hemisphaeriis) A hemisphere (*hemisphaerion*) is a half part of a sphere. The hemisphere that is above the earth is all that part of the sky that is seen by us; the hemisphere under the earth is the part that cannot be seen as long as it is under the earth.

xliv. The five circles of heaven (De quinque circulis caeli) 1. There are five zones (*zona*) in the heavens, and based on their differences, certain regions are inhabited due to their temperate climate, and certain regions are uninhabitable from the brutality of the cold or heat. They are called zones or 'circles' (*circulus*) because they exist on the circular band (*circumductio*) of the sphere.[28] 2. The first of these circles is called ἀρκτικός (i.e. "arctic"), because the conspicuous constellations called Arctos (i.e. the Bears) are enclosed within it. The second circle is called θερινὸς τροπικός (i.e. "summer tropic") because in this circle the sun makes it summer when it is at its northern limit, and it does not travel beyond this circle, but rather turns back at once. Whence it is called τροπικός (cf. τροπή, "turning"). 3. The third circle is called ἡμερινός, and is called 'equinoctial' (*aequinoctialis*) by Latin speakers, because the sun, when it goes across to this zone, makes the day and night equal length (*aequinoctium*) – for the term ἡμερινός means 'day and night' in Latin.[29] The central part of the sphere is seen to be made up of this band. The fourth circle is called ἀνταρκτικός (i.e. "antarctic") because it is opposite to the circle that we call ἀρκτικός. 4. The fifth circle is called χειμερινὸς τροπικός (i.e. "winter tropic"). It is called 'winter' (*hiemalis*) or *brumalis* (i.e. another word for "winter") by Latin speakers, because when the sun travels to this circle, it makes winter for those who are in the north, and summer for those who live in the southern regions.

xlv. The circle of the zodiac (De zodiaco circulo) The circle of the zodiac (*zodiacus circulus*) consists of five angles made from lines, and one line.[30]

xlvi. The bright circle (De candido circulo) The Milky Circle (*lacteus circulus*, i.e. the Milky Way) is the road seen in the sphere of the sky, named for its brightness (*candor*), because it is white. Some people say that this road is where the sun made its circuit, and that it shines from the splendor of the sun's transit.

xlvii. The size of the sun (De magnitudine solis) The size of the sun is greater than that of the earth, whence

27 Here and in ch. xxx above Isidore attempts to reconcile views that orient the universe in different ways.

28 The primary sense of *zona* is "belt, girdle."

29 ἡμερινός appears to be a corruption of ἰσημερινός, "equinoctial."

30 Fontaine (1959:490) suggests that Isidore here imagines the zodiac as the ecliptic circle. This circle, conceived of as "one line" in planar projection, itself cuts at equal angles across the five parallel lines of the major circles: the equatorial, tropical, and polar circles.

at that very moment when it rises, it appears equally at the same moment to a person in the east and to a person in the west. However, because it seems one cubit long to us, we need to consider how far the sun is from the earth, the distance that makes the sun seem small to us.

xlviii. The size of the moon (De magnitudine lunae) The size of the moon is said to be less than that of the sun. Since the sun is higher than the moon, and yet it still seems larger than the moon from our perspective, if the sun were to come close to us, it would be obvious how much larger the sun is than the moon. Indeed, just as the sun is larger than the earth, so the earth is greater than the moon by a certain quantity.

xlix. The nature of the sun (De natura solis) Since the sun is fiery, it grows hotter due to the excessive movement of its revolution. The philosophers say that its fire is nourished by water, and it receives the power of its light and heat from that opposing element. Whence we often see the sun moist and dewy.

l. The course of the sun (De cursu solis) 1. The sun moves under its own power, and does not turn with the universe. If it were to remain fixed in the heavens, every day and night would be of equal length; but since we see that it will set in a different place tomorrow, and that it had in a different place yesterday, it appears that it moves through its own power, and does not turn along with the universe. Furthermore, the sun makes its annual orbits with unequal intervals, on account of the changing of the seasons. When the sun rises, it makes the day; when it sets, it brings on the night. 2. Wandering farther to the south it makes winter, so that the earth grows fertile with wintry moisture and frost. When it approaches closer to the north, it brings summer back, so that crops grow firm in ripeness, and what was unripened in damp weather mellows in its warmth.

li. The effect of the sun (De effectu solis) 1. When the sun rises, it creates the day, and when it sets it brings on the night, for day is the sun over the earth, and night is the sun under the earth. The hours come from it: the day comes from the sun when it ascends: the night comes from it when it sets. The months and the years are numbered by it, and the changing of the seasons is caused by it. 2. When the sun runs across the south, it is the closer to the earth; but when it is near the north, it is raised higher in the sky.

[Thus God made diverse locations and seasons for the sun's course, so that it does not consume everything with its daily heat by always tarrying in the same place. But, as Clement said, "The sun takes diverse paths, by means of which the temperature of the air is meted out according to the pattern of the seasons, and the order of its changes and permutations is preserved. Thus when the sun ascends to the higher reaches, it tempers the spring air; when it reaches its zenith, it kindles the summer heat; dropping again it brings back the temperance of autumn. But when it goes back to the lowest orbit, it bequeaths to us from the icy framework of the sky the rigor of winter cold."][31]

lii. The path of the sun (De itinere solis) The sun, when it rises, holds a path through the south. Afterward, it goes to the west and plunges itself into the Ocean, and it travels unknown paths under the earth, and once again runs back to the east.

liii. The light of the moon (De lumine lunae) 1. Some philosophers say that the moon has its own light; that one part of its orb emits light and the other is dark [thus: (a figure follows)] and that by gradually turning itself it makes different shapes. 2. Others maintain on the contrary that the moon does not have its own light, but is illuminated by the rays of the sun, and for this reason undergoes an eclipse when the earth's shadow comes between it and the sun. [For the sun is located higher than the moon. Hence it happens that when the moon is beneath the sun, the upper part of the moon is lighted, but the lower part, which is facing the earth, is dark.]

liv. The shapes of the moon (De formas lunae) 1. The first shape of the moon has two horns, thus: (a figure follows). The second [has] a section, [thus:] (fig.). The

31 The quotation is from Rufinus Tyrannius's translation of the *Clementine Recognitions*, 8.45. A circular figure follows in some early manuscripts. It has in its center the words *medium mundi*, i.e. the "center of the universe," and around it the stations of the sun are written thus: "here is the sunrise on the nativity of the Lord; the sixth hour of the day; sunset on the nativity of the Lord; sunset on the equinox; sunset on the nativity of John; perpetual midnight; sunrise on the nativity of John; here is the sunrise on the equinox."

third has a half, thus: (fig.). The fourth is full, thus: (fig.). The fifth is half again, [from the full side], thus: (fig.). The sixth is a section again, thus (fig.). The seventh is two-horned, thus: (fig.). 2. The seventh day and a half and the twenty-second day and a half are the midpoints of its orbit (fig.), and the other days are proportional.

lv. The interlunar interval (De interlunio lunae) The interlunar interval of the moon is the time between the waning and the waxing moon. This is the thirtieth day, when the moon does not shine. At that time the moon cannot be seen, because it is in conjunction with the sun and darkened. But it is seen the moment it is reborn by moving gradually away from the sun.

lvi. The path of the moon (De cursu lunae) 1. The moon measures out the span of a month in its alternations of losing and receiving light. Therefore, it proceeds on an oblique path, not a straight one, like the sun, indeed, lest it fall into the central plane of the earth and frequently undergo eclipse. 2. Its circular path is close to the earth. When it is waxing, its horns look to the east, and when it is waning they look to the west, and justly so, since it is about to set and lose its light.

lvii. The proximity of the moon to the earth (De vicinitate lunae ad terras) The moon is nearer to the earth than the sun is. Whence, due to its shorter orbit, it completes its course more quickly, for the journey that the sun completes in 365 days the moon runs through in thirty days. Whence the ancients established months based on the moon, and years based on the course of the sun.

lviii. Eclipse of the sun (De eclipsi solis) An eclipse of the sun occurs whenever the moon, on the thirtieth lunar day, comes to that line where the sun travels, and by interposing itself before the sun, conceals it. Thus to us the sun appears to vanish when the orb of the moon is set before it.

lix. Eclipse of the moon (De eclipsi lunae) 1. An eclipse of the moon occurs whenever the moon runs into the shadow of the earth. The moon is thought not to have its own light, but to be illuminated by the sun; hence it disappears if the earth's shadow comes between it and the sun. 2. This happens to the moon on the fifteenth lunar day, until it leaves the central part and the shadow of the intervening earth and sees the sun, or is seen by the sun.

lx. The differences between stars, star clusters, and constellations (De differentia stellarum, siderum, et astrorum) 1. Stars (*stella*), star clusters (*sidus*), and constellations (*astrum*) are different from each other. Thus a star is any individual body, but star clusters are made up of several stars, such as the Hyades and the Pleiades. 2. Constellations are large patterns of stars, such as Orion and Bootes. But writers confuse these terms, and use *astrum* instead of *stella*, and *stella* instead of *sidus*.[32]

lxi. The light of stars (De lumine stellarum) Stars are said not to possess their own light, but to be illuminated by the sun, as the moon is.

lxii. The location of the stars (De stellarum situ) Stars are unmoving and, being fixed, are carried with the heavens in perpetual motion. They do not set during the day, but they are obscured by the brightness of the sun.

lxiii. The course of the stars (De stellarum cursu) Stars are either carried or move. The ones that are fixed in the sky and turn with the sky are carried. But some [like] planets, that is, 'wanderers,' move. However, they carry out their roaming courses within a defined boundary.

lxiv. The changing course of the stars (De vario cursu stellarum) Because they are carried across the various orbits of the heavenly planets, some stars rise earlier and set later, while others rise later and reach the point of setting sooner. Some rise together but do not set at the same time. But all return to their proper course in their own time.

lxv. The distances between the stars (De stellarum intervallis) The stars differ from each other in their distance from the earth, and for this reason they appear unequal to our eyes, being either brighter or less bright. Thus many stars are larger than the ones that we see as

32 Isidore himself is among those who do not observe these differentiae.

prominent, but since they are set further away, they seem small to us.

lxvi. The orbital number of the stars (De circulari numero stellarum) 1. The orbital number of stars is that number by which it is said that one may know how long a given star takes to complete its orbit, going either by longitude or by latitude. 2. For the moon is said to complete its orbit each year, Mercury every twenty years, Lucifer every nine years, the sun every nineteen years, Vesper every fifteen years, Phaethon every twelve years, and Saturn every thirty years.[33] When these periods of time have passed, they return to repeat their orbit across the same constellations and regions. 3. Some stars become irregular when they are hindered by the sun's rays, becoming retrograde or stationary, according to what the poet recalls when he says (cf. Lucan, *Civil War* 10.201):

> The sun divides the seasons of time: it changes the day to night, and by its powerful rays prevents the stars from proceeding, and delays their roaming courses by its ordering.

lxvii. Planets (De stellis planetis) Certain stars are called planets (*planeta*), that is, 'wandering ones,' because they range through the entire cosmos with a varying motion. It is because of their wandering that they are called retrograde, or are rendered irregular when they add or subtract orbital degrees. When they pull back only they are called retrograde, and they make a 'station' (*statio*) when they 'stand still' (*stare*).

lxviii. Precession and antegrade motion of stars (De praecedentia et antegradatione stellarum) Precession (*praecedentia*), or antegrade motion, of stars occurs when the star seems to drive its own motion, and advances (*praecedere*) somewhat beyond what is usual.

lxix. Recession or retrograde motion of stars (De remotione vel retrogradatione stellarum) Recession (*remotio*), or retrograde motion, of stars occurs when a star, although driving its own motion, at the same time seems to move backward.

lxx. The standing of stars (De statu stellarum) A standing (*status*) of stars occurs when, although a star always moves, it nevertheless seems to stand still in some places.

lxxi. The names of the stars and the reasons for these names (De nominibus stellarum, quibus ex causis nomina acceperunt) 1. The sun (*sol*) is so named because it appears alone (*solus*), with all the constellations obscured by its brilliance. The moon (*luna*) is so named as if the word were *Lucina*, but with the middle syllable removed. Concerning this, Vergil says (*Ecl.* 4.10):

> Chaste Lucina, show favor . . .

2. It has taken this name by derivation from the light (*lux*, gen. *lucis*) of the sun, because it receives light from the sun, and gives off what it has received. 3. Stars (*stella*) are named from 'standing' (*stare*), because they always stand fixed in the sky and do not fall. Indeed, when we see what looks like stars falling from the sky, these are not stars, but little pieces of fire fallen from the aether. They are produced when the wind, seeking higher altitudes, drags the aetherial fire with it, and with this dragging the fire mimics falling stars. Stars are not able to fall, since they are immobile, as has been said earlier, and are carried with the sky since they are fixed in it.

4. Constellations (*sidus*) are so named because sailors 'take bearings on' (*considerare*) them when they set their course, lest they be led elsewhere by deceptive waves and winds. And for that reason some stars are called signs (*signum*), because sailors observe them in steering their rowing, taking note of their keenness and brightness, qualities by which the future state of the sky is shown. 5. But everyone pays attention to them for predicting the qualities of the air in the summer, winter, and spring seasons, for by their rising or setting in specific places they indicate the condition of the weather.

6. The first of the signs is Arctos, which, fixed on the pole, rotates with its seven stars revolving around it. Its name is Greek (i.e. ἄρκτος, "bear"), and in Latin it is called the Bear (*Ursa*). Because it turns like a wagon, we call it the Septentriones (i.e. *septem*, "seven" + *triones*). 7. For *triones*, strictly speaking, are plowing oxen, so called because they tread (*terere*) the soil, as if the word were *teriones*. Their proximity to the pole causes them not to set, because they are on the pole.

33 Of course the morning star, *Lucifer*, and the evening star, *Vesper*, are both actually the planet Venus. Emendation of *Vesper* to *Pyrois* (= Mars) has been proposed, but Isidore elsewhere identifies Vesper with Mars. On these and *Phaethon* see lxxi.18–21 below and V.xxx.6–7.

8. Arctophylax (i.e. the "bear-keeper") is so named because it follows Arctos, that is, the Great Bear. People have also called this constellation Bootes, because it is attached to the Wain (cf. *bos*, "ox," which draws a wagon; βοώτης, "plowman"). It is a very noticeable sign with its many stars, one of which is Arcturus. 9. Arcturus is a star located in the sign of Bootes beyond the tail of the Great Bear. For this reason it is called 'Arcturus,' as if it were the Greek ἄρκτου οὐρά (i.e. "tail of the bear"), because it is located next to the heart of Bootes. It rises in the season of autumn. 10. Orion shines in the south, in front of the tracks of Taurus. It is named 'Orion' from urine (*urina*), that is, from a flood of waters, for it rises in the winter season, and troubles the sea and the land with waters and storms. 11. Latin speakers call this constellation the Jugula (cf. *iugulum*, "throat," with a figurative sense "slaughter") because it is armed, as if it has a sword, and is terrible and very brilliant in the light of its stars. If all of its stars are shining, then calm weather is forecast, but if their sharpness is blunted, then a storm is understood to loom.

12. The Hyades are named from the Greek ὕειν (i.e. the verb "rain"), that is, from moisture (*sucus*) and rains, for 'rain' in Greek is ὑετός, and the Hyades make rain when they rise. Whence also Latin speakers have named them *Suculae*, because when they arise, signs of rain are evident. Concerning them Vergil says (*Aen.* 1.744):

> Arcturus and the rainy Hyades.

They are seven stars, in the forehead of Taurus, and they rise in the spring season. 13. The Pleiades (*Pliades*) are named from their plural number (*pluralitas*), because the Greeks name plural number from πλεῖστος (i.e. "most"). They are seven stars, in front of the knees of Taurus; six of them are visible and the seventh is hidden. Latin speakers call them *Vergiliae*, as an indication of the season when they arise, which is spring (*ver*). By their setting they show the winter, by their rising the summer, and they are the first to show the season for sailing (cf. πλεῖν, "to sail").

14. The Dog Star (*canicula stella*), which is also called Sirius, is in the center of the sky during the summer months. When the sun ascends to it, and it is in conjunction with the sun, the sun's heat is doubled, and bodies are affected by the heat and weakened. Hence also the 'dog days' are named from this star, when purgings are harmful. 15. It is called the 'Dog' (*canis*) Star because it afflicts the body with illness, or because of the brightness (*candor*) of its flame, because it is of a kind that seems to shine more brightly than the others. It is said they named it Sirius (cf. Σείριος, "the burning one") so that people might recognize the constellation better.

16. A comet (*cometa*) is a star, so named because it spreads out the 'hair' (*coma*) of its light. When this type of star appears it signifies plague, famine, or war. 17. Comets are called *crinitae* in Latin, because they spread their flames like hair (*crines*). The Stoics say that there are more than thirty comets whose names and effects certain astrologers have written about. 18. *Lucifer* (i.e. Venus as morning star) is so named because it carries light (*lucem ferre*) more than the other stars. It is one of the planets. It is appropriately called *Iubar* (lit. "radiance") because it emits a mane (*iuba*) of light, but the 'splendor' of the sun and moon and stars is also called *iubar*, because their rays extend like a mane.

19. *Vesperus* (i.e. Venus as evening star) is a western star. People maintain that its name is taken from Hesperus, a king of Spain. It brings in the night and follows the sun, and is itself one of the five planets. It is said that this star turns into the morning star when it rises and the evening star when it sets. Concerning this Statius says (cf. *Thebaid* 6.241):

> And the one is derived from the other's rising.

20. Planets are stars that are not fixed in the sky as the rest are, but are carried through the air. They are called 'planets' (*planeta*) from the word πλάνη, that is, 'wandering,' for sometimes they are carried to the south and sometimes to the north, and they are often carried against the cosmos, and sometimes with it. Their Greek names are Phaethon, Phaenon, Pyrion, Hesperus, and Stilbon. 21. The Romans have consecrated them with the names of their gods, that is, Jupiter, Saturn, Mars, Venus, and Mercury. Themselves deceived, and wishing to deceive others into the worship of those who had granted them something in accordance with their desires, they would point out the stars in the sky, and say that this one was Jupiter's and that one was Mercury's, and this vain belief was born. The devil strengthened this erroneous belief, and Christ overturned it.

22. Next, those constellations that are called signs (*signum*) by the pagans, in which the image of living beings is formed from stars, such as Arctos, Aries, Taurus, Libra and others of this type. In their study of the

constellations these people, prompted by superstitious folly, imposed the shape of a body on the configuration of stars, making their appearance and names conform, through certain characteristics, to those of their gods. 23. Hence the first sign – through which, as also through Libra, people draw the middle line of the cosmos – they have named Aries (i.e. the Ram) on account of Ammon Jupiter,[34] because those who made the idols fashioned the horns of a ram on his head. 24. The pagans placed this sign first among their signs because they say that the sun travels in this sign in the month of March, which is the beginning of the year. But they likewise place Taurus among the constellations, and this one also is in honor of Jupiter, because according to myth he was changed into a bull when he carried off Europa.

25. They also set Castor and Pollux after their death among the most noteworthy constellations; they call this sign 'Gemini.' 26. They named Cancer likewise, because when the sun reaches this sign in the month of June, it moves backward in the manner of a crab (*cancer*) and makes the days shorter. This animal has no definite forepart, but heads to either side, so that the front part becomes the back and the back becomes the front. 27. Hercules killed an enormous lion in Greece and set it (i.e., Leo) among the twelve signs as a mark of his own valor. When the sun reaches this sign, it gives excessive heat to the world, and causes the annual Etesian winds. 28. They located the sign Virgo among the constellations because on the days when the sun runs through it the earth is parched by the heat of the sun and bears nothing, for this is the season of the dog days.

29. They named Libra from the equal balance of this month because on September 24 the sun makes the equinox while running through this sign. Whence Lucan also says (*Civil War* 4.58):

> To the scales of just Libra.

30. They named Scorpio likewise, and Sagittarius, because of the lightning bolts that fall in this month. Sagittarius is a man misshapen by having the legs of a horse, and they added a bow and arrow (*sagitta*) to him to indicate the lightning of his month; hence the sign is called Sagittarius. 31. They imagined the figure of Capricorn (i.e. "goat-horn") among the constellations because of the goat that was Jupiter's nurse. They made the rear part of its body in the image of a fish to indicate the rains of this season, which usually occur plentifully towards the end of this month. 32. Furthermore, they named Aquarius and Pisces from the rainstorms of that season, because in the winter, when the sun travels through these signs, more rain falls. And the mindlessness of the pagans is to be marveled at; they set not only fish, but even rams and goats and bulls, bears and dogs and crabs and scorpions into the sky. Further, because of the stories about Jupiter, they also located an eagle and a swan among the constellations of the sky, for the sake of his memory.

33. The pagans also believed that Perseus and his wife Andromeda had been received into the heavens after they died, and so they traced out their images in stars and did not blush to name these constellations after them. 34. They even set Auriga ("the Charioteer") – Ericthonius – among the stars of the sky, because they recognized him as the first to yoke a four-horse chariot. They marveled that his genius extended to an imitation of the sun (i.e. as charioteer), and on this account placed his name, after he died, among the constellations. 35. So it was with Callisto, daughter of King Lycaon, since according to legend she had been ravished by Jupiter and changed by Juno into a bear, which is ἄρκτος in Greek; after her death Jupiter transferred her name, along with that of his son by her, into the Septentriones, and called her Arctus and her son Arctophylax (see sections 6–9 above). 36. Thus Lyra was placed in the sky on Mercury's account, and thus the centaur, Chiron, because he reared Aesculapius and Achilles, was counted among the stars.

37. But whatever the type of superstition with which they have been named by men, the stars are nevertheless things that God created at the beginning of the world, and he set them in order that they might define the seasons by their certain motions. 38. Therefore, observations of the stars, or horoscopes, or other superstitions that attach themselves to the study of the stars, that is, for the sake of knowing the fates – these are undoubtedly contrary to our faith, and ought to be so completely ignored by Christians that it would seem that they have not been written about. 39. But some people, enticed by the beauty and clarity of the constellations, have rushed headlong into error with respect to the stars, their minds blinded, so that they attempt to be able to foretell the results of things by means of harmful computations, which is called 'astrology' (*mathesis*).

34 The god Ammon, equated with Jupiter, was depicted as a ram.

Not only those learned in the Christian religion, but also Plato, Aristotle, and others among the pagans, were moved by the truth of things to agree in condemning this in their judgment, saying that a confusion of matters was generated by such a belief. 40. For if humans are forced towards various acts by the compulsion of their nativity, then why should the good deserve praise, and why should the wicked reap the punishment of law? And although these pagan sages were not devoted to heavenly wisdom, nevertheless they rightly struck down these errors by their witness to the truth. 41. But clearly that order of the seven secular disciplines was taken by the philosophers as far as the stars, so that they might draw minds tangled in secular wisdom away from earthly matters and set them in contemplation of what is above.

Book IV

Medicine (De medicina)

i. Medicine (De medicina) 1. Medicine is the art that protects or restores the body's health; its subject matter concerns illnesses and wounds. 2. To medicine belong not only things practiced by the skill of those properly called physicians (*medicus*), but also matters of food and drink, clothing and shelter. Ultimately, it consists of every defense and fortification by means of which our body is preserved [healthy] in the face of external blows and accidents.

ii. The term 'medicine' (De nomine eius) The term 'medicine' (*medicina*) is thought to be drawn from 'moderation' (*modus*), that is, temperateness, in that medicine is applied not in full measure but little by little. Indeed, nature grieves at excess and rejoices at restraint. Hence those who drink potions and remedies copiously and unceasingly are troubled. Anything that is immoderate brings not health but danger.

iii. The inventors of medicine (De inventoribus medicinae) 1. Among the Greeks, Apollo is considered the author and discoverer of the art of medicine. His son Aesculapius expanded the art, whether in esteem or in effectiveness, 2. but after Aesculapius was killed by a bolt of lightning, the study of healing was declared forbidden, and the art died along with its author, and was hidden for almost 500 years, until the time of Artaxerxes, king of the Persians. Then Hippocrates, a descendant of Asclepius (i.e. Aesculapius) born on the island of Cos, brought it to light again.

iv. The three schools of medicine (De tribus haeresibus medicorum) 1. These three men established as many schools. First the Methodical school, which advocates remedies and charms, was founded by Apollo. Second, the Empirical school was founded by Aesculapius; it is the most grounded in experience and depends not on the symptomatic signs but on experimental results alone. Third, the Logical – that is, rational – school, founded by Hippocrates. 2. For by investigating the characteristics of age, region, or type of illness, he deeply probed the study of the art in a rational way, so that he might use it to examine the causes of diseases with the application of reason: [he searched out cures by reasoning]. So the Empiricists advocate experience alone; the Logicians add reasoning to experience; the Methodicians take no account of reasoning from principles, nor of circumstances, ages, and causes, but only of the actual diseases.

v. The four humors of the body (De quattuor humoribus corporis) 1. Health is integrity of the body and a balance of its nature with respect to its heat and moisture, which is its blood – hence health (*sanitas*) is so called, as if it were the condition of the blood (*sanguis*). 2. All the sufferings of the body are covered by the general term 'illness,' because the ancients used the term illness (*morbus*) in order to point with this word to the 'power of death' (*mors* + *vis*), which is born from illness. The mean between health and illness is treatment, and unless it fits the disease it fails to bring health.

3. All diseases come from the four humors, that is, from blood, bile, black bile, and phlegm. [By these, healthy people are governed, and feeble people are stricken, for when they increase beyond their natural course they cause sickness.] Just as there are four elements, so there are four humors, and each humor resembles its element: blood resembles air, bile fire, black bile earth, and phlegm water. And as there are four elements, so there are four humors that maintain our bodies.

4. Blood took its name from a Greek origin, because it is made vigorous, is nourished, and lives. The Greeks gave *choler* its name because it ends in the space of a day; hence it is called 'cholera,' that is, 'little bile,' being an effusion of bile – for the Greeks call bile χολή. 5. Black bile (*melancholia*) is so called because it is a large amount of bile mixed with the dregs of black blood, for in Greek black is μέλας and bile is χολή. 6. Blood (*sanguis*) is so called in Latin because it is sweet (*suavis*); hence people who are dominated by blood are sweet-tempered and pleasant. 7. They gave phlegm its name because it is cold,

for the Greeks call coldness φλεγμονή. Healthy people are governed by these four humors, and feeble people are afflicted as a result of them, for when they increase beyond their natural course they cause sickness. Acute sufferings, which the Greeks call ὀξέα, arise from blood and bile, whereas from phlegm and black bile come long-standing conditions, which the Greeks call χρόνια.

vi. Acute illnesses (De acutis morbis) 1. An ὀξεῖα is an acute illness that either passes quickly or kills rather quickly, such as *pleurisis*, or *phrenesis*, for in Greek ὀξύς means acute and swift. Χρόνια is a prolonged illness of the body that lingers for a long time, such as gout or consumption, for χρόνος in Greek means time. Some afflictions have taken their name from their own causes. 2. Fever (*febris*) is named from heat (*fervor*), being an abundance of heat. 3. Frenzy (*frenesis*) is named either from an impediment of mind – for the Greeks call the mind φρήν – or from the sufferers' gnashing their teeth, since *frendere* is grinding of teeth. It is a disturbed state, accompanied by agitation and dementia, caused by an onslaught of bile. 4. *Cardiaca* takes its name from the heart (*cor*, gen. *cordis*), as the condition when the heart is afflicted by some fear or sorrow, for the Greeks call the heart καρδία. It is a suffering of the heart accompanied by terrible fear.

5. Lethargy (*lethargia*) is named after the word for sleep (cf. ληθαργία, "drowsiness"). It is an overpowering of the brain, accompanied by forgetfulness and incessant sleep like that of one who is snoring. 6. *Synanchis* is so called from constraint of breath and choking, for the Greeks say συνάγχειν for "constrain." Whoever suffers from this ailment is choked by a pain in the throat. 7. *Phleumon* is a heat in the stomach accompanied by swelling and pain, [or φλεγμονή is feverishness accompanied by flushed skin, pain, spasm, hardness, and wasting away]. Fever follows the onset of *phleumon*, whence it is also called φλεγμονή, from φλέγειν, that is, "causing inflammation." Thus it took its name from the way it feels. 8. Pleurisy (*pleurisis*) is a sharp pain in the side accompanied by fever and bloody sputum. The side is called πλευρά in Greek, and from this the pleuritic affliction took its name. 9. *Peripleumonia* is an affliction of the lungs accompanied by severe pain and gasping, for the Greeks call the lung πλεύμων, and the disease is named after this. 10. Apoplexy (*apoplexia*) is a sudden effusion of blood on which one chokes and dies. It is called apoplexy because sudden death occurs from its fatal stroke, and the Greeks call a stroke ἀπόπληξις. 11. Spasm (*spasmus*) in Latin is the sudden contraction of body parts or sinews, accompanied by severe pain. They say that this affliction is named after the heart, which contains the principal seat of our vitality. Spasm occurs in two ways, from surfeit or from emptiness.

12. Tetanus (*tetanus*) is a severe contraction of sinews from the neck to the back. 13. *Telum* (lit., "weapon") is a pain in the side, so called by physicians because like a sword it whips through the body with pain. 14. *Ileos* is a pain of the intestines, whence they are also called *ilia*. In Greek *ilios*[1] means "wrap around," seeing that the intestines twist around themselves because of the pain. Intestines in this condition are also called *turminosus*, from their torment (*tormentum*). 15. Ὑδροφοβία is fear of water, for the Greeks call water ὕδωρ and fear φόβος; hence Latin speakers also call this *lymphaticus* from fear of water (cf. *lympha*, "water"). It is caused either by the bite of a rabid dog or from its froth cast upon the ground. If a human or beast should touch this foam he is either filled with madness or becomes rabid. 16. A carbuncle (*carbunculus*) is so called because at first it glows red, like fire, and then turns black, like an extinguished coal (*carbo*).

17. Pestilence is a contagion that as soon as it seizes on one person quickly spreads to many. It arises from corrupt air and maintains itself by penetrating the internal organs. Although this generally is caused by powers in the air, it never occurs without the consent of almighty God. 18. It is called pestilence (*pestilentia*) as if it were *pastulentia*, because it consumes (*depascere*, ppl. *depastus*) like fire, as (Vergil, *Aen.* 5.683):

> The pestilence descends on the entire body.[2]

Likewise, contagion (*contagium*) is from 'touching' (*contingere*), because it contaminates anyone it touches. 19. The swellings (*inguen*) (i.e. of bubonic plague) are so called from their striking the groin (*inguen*). Pestilence is also called plague (*lues*), so called from destruction (*labes*) and distress (*luctus*), and it is so violent that there

1 The text appears to be corrupt here. Greek εἰλεός, ἰλεός means "intestinal obstruction." The Greek verb εἰλύειν means "wrap around."

2 Vergil uses 'pestilence' here metaphorically to describe the burning of a Trojan ship.

is no time to anticipate life or death, but weakness comes suddenly together with death.

vii. Chronic illnesses (De chronicis morbis) 1. Chronic disease (*chronia*) is an extended illness that lasts for a long time, like gout or consumption, for χρόνος in Greek means "time." 2. Headache (*cephalea*) has its name for a good reason, for it is an affliction of the head, and the Greeks call the head κεφαλή. 3. *Scothomia* takes its name from its characteristic symptom, because it brings sudden darkness (cf. σκότος, "darkness") to the eyes, accompanied by *vertigo* of the head. *Vertigo* ("spinning") occurs whenever the wind rises and sends the earth into a spin. 4. Similarly in the human *vertex* (i.e. the crown of the head) the arteries and veins produce turbulence from the release of moisture, and make a spinning sensation in the eyes; from this spinning, *vertigo* is named.

5. Epilepsy (*epilemsia*) took its name because it hangs over the mind as much as it possesses the body, and the Greeks call 'hanging over' ἐπιληψία. It arises from the melancholy humor, whenever it has been excessive and has moved into the brain. This ailment is also called 'falling sickness' (*caduca*), because the person ill with it falls (*cadere*) down and suffers spasms. 6. Common people call epileptics 'lunatics' (*lunaticus*), because they think that the insidious forces of demons follow them in accordance with the course of the moon (*luna*). They are also called 'possessed by spirits' (*larvaticus*, cf. *larva*, "an evil spirit"). It is also called the 'comitial disease,' that is, a major and divine illness by which epileptics are possessed. Its force is such that a strong person suffering from it falls down and froths at the mouth. 7. It is called comitial because among the pagans, when it occurred on any day of assembly (*comitium*), the assembly was dismissed. Among the Romans there was a regular day of assembly on the first day of January. 8. Mania (*mania*) is so called from insanity or madness, for the ancient Greeks used to call madness μανική, either because of their unbalanced state, which the Greeks called *manie*,[3] or from divination, because μανεῖν in Greek means "to divine." 9. Melancholy (*melancholia*) is so called from black bile, for the Greeks call black, μέλας, and bile, χολή. Now epilepsy arises in the imagination, melancholy in the reason, and mania in the memory.[4]

10. *Typus* (cf. typhus) is a cold fever, and is improperly called *tipus* after the name of a plant that grows in the water. In Latin *typus* means "form" or "state." It is a cycle of accesses and recessions (i.e. of fever) across fixed intervals of time. 11. Rheum (*reuma*) in Greek is called eruption (*eruptio*) or discharge (*fluor*) in Latin. Catarrh (*catarrhus*) is a continual discharge of rheum from the nostrils; it is called hoarseness (βράγχος) when it reaches the throat, and πτύσις (cf. tussis) when it reaches the chest or lungs. 12. *Coryza* occurs whenever a draining from the head reaches the bones of the nose, and causes irritation accompanied by sneezing, whence it takes the name *coryza* (cf. κόρυζα, "nasal discharge"). 13. *Branchos* is a choking of the throat caused by a cold humor, for the Greeks call the gullet, which the throat surrounds, βράγχος, and we incorrectly call it *brancia*. 14. Hoarseness (*raucedo*) is a loss of voice; it is also called *arteriasis* because it makes the voice hoarse and tight from damage to the windpipe (*arteria*). Wheezing (*suspirium*) got that name because it is a difficulty with inhaling, and the Greeks call it δύσπνοια, that is, choking. 15. *Peripleumonia* took its name from the lungs (*pulmo*), for it is a swelling of the lungs accompanied by an effusion of bloody foam. 16. Haemoptysis (*haemoptois*) is an issuing of blood through the mouth; hence it got its name, for αἷμα means "blood."

17. Consumption (*tisis*, i.e. *phthisis*) is an ulceration and swelling in the lungs, which is usually contracted more easily by young people. It is called φθίσις (lit. "wasting away") among the Greeks, because it involves a 'wasting away' (*consumptio*) of the entire body. 18. Cough (*tussis*) is named after the term for 'depth' in Greek, because it comes from deep in the chest, as opposed to higher in the throat, where the uvula tickles. 19. Apostem (*apostoma*) got its name from 'abcess,' for the Greeks call abcesses *apostomas*. 20. Empiesis (*enpiis*) is so called from 'abcess within' (*apostoma intrinsecus*), either in the side or in the stomach, accompanied by pain, fevers, coughing, and copious frothing and purulence. 21. The disease *hepaticus* took its name from an affliction of the liver, because the Greeks call the liver ἧπαρ. 22. Lienitis (*lienosis*) took its name from the spleen (*splen*), for the Greeks call the spleen (*lien*) σπλήν.[5] 23. Dropsy (*hydropis*) took its name from the aqueous humor of

3 The text appears to be corrupt here; we find no *manie* with this meaning in Greek. Greek μανία means the same as the Latin *mania*.

4 Isidore here alludes to the front, middle, and back of the brain as traditionally conceived.

5 Latin *splen* is borrowed from Greek σπλήν; Latin *lien* is cognate with both; all three words mean 'spleen.'

the skin, for the Greeks called water ὕδωρ. It is a fluid below the skin, accompanied by swelling distention and fetid exhalation. 24. Nephrosis (*nefresis*) took its name from illness of the kidneys, for the Greeks call the kidneys νεφροί.

25. Paralysis (*paralesis*) is so called from damage to the body caused by excessive chilling, occurring either in the entire body, or in one part. 26. Cachexia (*cacexia*) took its name from injury [or condition] of the body, for the Greeks called an unfortunate malady καχεξία. This disease is caused by a sick person's intemperance, or by poor administration of medical treatment – or it is a slow recovery following an illness. 27. Atrophy (*atrofia*) took its name from a wasting of the body, for the Greeks call an abstention from nourishment ἀτροφία. It is a weakness of the body due to hidden causes and slow convalescence. 28. *Sarcia* is an excessive increase in flesh, by which a body grows fat beyond measure, for the Greeks call flesh σάρκα (i.e. σάρξ). 29. Sciatica (*sciasis*) is named after the part of the body that gives trouble, for the Greeks call the bones of the hip joints, whose tips reach to the edge of the pelvis, ἰσχία. This condition is caused by phlegm, whenever it descends into the vertical bones and causes glutination. 30. The Greeks say that gout (*podagra*) was named after its swelling of the feet (cf. πούς, gen. ποδός, "foot") and its deadly pain. Indeed, we incorrectly call anything that is harsh 'brutal' (*agrestis*; as if *podagra* were ποδ- + *agrestis*).

31. The disease arthritis (*artriticus*) drew its name from affliction of the joints (*articulus*). 32. A *cauculus* is a stone that occurs in the bladder, and it took its name from that (i.e. *calculus*, "pebble"). It is formed from phlegmatic matter. 33. Strangury (*stranguria*) is so called because it constricts (*stringere*), causing difficulty in passing urine (*urina*). 34. Satyriasis (*satiriasis*) is continual sexual desire accompanied by erection of the natural places (i.e. the genitals). This affliction is named after satyrs. 35. Diarrhea (*diarria*) is a continual flow from the bowels without vomiting. 36. Dysentery (*disinteria*) is a 'separation of a continuity,' that is, an ulceration of the intestine, for *dis-* means "separation" and *intera* means "intestines." It occurs following that discharge which the Greeks call διάρροια. 37. Lientery (*lienteria*) is so called because it causes food to slide through the smoothness (*lenis*) of the intestines (cf. ἔντερον, "gut"), as it were, without any blockage. 38. The disease colic (*colica*) got its name from the intestine, which the Greeks call κῶλον (i.e. κόλον). 39. Rhagades (*ragadia*) are so called because fissures are gathered in the wrinkles (*ruga*) around the anal orifice. These are also called hemorrhoids (*emorroida*) from their discharge of blood, for the Greeks call blood αἷμα.

viii. Illnesses that appear on the surface of the body (De morbis qui in superficie corporis videntur) 1. Alopecia (*alopicia*) is a loss of hair with a yellowing of the surrounding hair so that it has a bronze shade. It is called by this name from its resemblance to a little fox, which the Greeks call ἀλώπηξ. 2. Parotids (*parotida*) are areas of hardness or accretions that emerge in the vicinity of the ears, caused by fever or something else, whence they are called παρωτίδες, for ὦτα is the Greek word for ears. 3. *Lentigo* is a small speckling of spots in the form of a round, so called from its resemblance to a lentil (*lenticula*). Latin speakers call erysipelas (*erisipela*) 'sacred fire' – speaking in antiphrasis, as it should be cursed – inasmuch as the skin grows flame-red on its surface. Then neighboring places are invaded by a corresponding redness, as if by fire, so that a fever is raised. 5. Serpigo (*serpedo*) is a rash accompanied by protruding pustules, and it took its name from 'creeping' (*serpere*), because it creeps over the limbs. 6. Impetigo (*impetigo*) is a dry scurf, rising from the skin with a rough surface in a round patch – the common word for this is *sarna*.

7. *Prurigo* is so called from burning up (*perurere*) and flaming. 8. Nyctalopia (*nyctalmos*) is a disease that denies sight to one's open eyes during the day and returns it when darkness comes at night – or, as many people would have it, gives sight by day and denies it by night (*nox*, gen. *noctis*). 9. Warts (*verruca*) are one disease, satyriasis is another.[6] Warts occur one at a time, whereas satyriasis consists of one more prominent blemish with many others around it. 10. Scabies and *lepra* (i.e. leprosy or psoriasis): either affliction presents a roughness of the skin with itching and scaliness, but scabies is a mild roughness and scaliness. Scabies took its name from this, in that it sheds its scabs, for the word *scabies* is as if it were *squamies* ("scaliness"). 11. But *lepra* is a scaly roughness of skin like the pepperwort (*lepida herba*), whence it took its name. At one time its color turns black, at another, white, at another, red. In the human body *lepra*

6 'Satyriasis,' treated in vii.34 above, is here probably a mistake for a word like 'phthiriasis' or 'pityriasis.'

is recognized in this way: either when its various colors appear in different places among the healthy parts of the skin, or when it spreads all over, so that it makes the whole skin one color, although it is abnormal.

12. The disease *elefantiacus* is so called from the resemblance to an elephant – whose innately hard and rough skin gave its name to what is a disease in humans – because it makes the surface of the body like the skin of an elephant, or because the disease is massive, like the same animal from which it derives its name. 13. The Greeks name jaundice (*hicteris*, i.e. *ictericus*) after the name of a certain animal that is of the color of bile. Latin speakers call this 'rainbow-colored disease' (*morbus arcuatus*) from its resemblance to the rainbow (*arcus*) – but Varro says it is to be called *aurigo* (i.e. *aurugo*) after its gold (*aurum*) color (Funaioli 415). People think that jaundice is called the royal (*regius*) disease because it may fairly easily be cured with good wine and regal (*regalis*) food. 14. Cancer (*cancer*, lit. "crab") is named from its resemblance to the sea animal. As physicians say, its lesion can be cured by no medication, and therefore the part of the body where it has arisen is customarily amputated, so that the body may live somewhat longer. However, death, even if it has been delayed, will come.

15. A furuncle (*furunculus*) is a tumor that rises to a point, so called because it is inflamed (*fervere*), as if the word were *fervunculus*. Hence in Greek it is called ἄνθραξ (lit. "charcoal"), because it is inflamed. 16. *Ordeolus* is a very small purulent accretion located in the eyelashes, broad in the middle and thinner on either side, resembling a grain of barley (*hordeum*), and from this it took its name. 17. *Oscedo* is a disease in which the mouth (*os*) of an infant develops sores, so called from the weariness of those who yawn (*oscitare*). 18. A *frenusculus* is an ulcer around the opening of the mouth, similar to ulcers in draft animals that are caused by the roughness of the bit (*frenum*). 19. An ulcer is putrefaction itself. A wound (*vulnus*) is so called because it is made by a weapon, as if it were 'by violence' (*vis*). And an ulcer (*ulcus*) is so called because it smells (*olere*), as if the term were *olcus*; hence also the plural form *ulcera*. 20. A pustule (*pustula*) is a swelling or accretion on the surface of the body.

21. A pimple (*papula*) is a very small bump on the skin, surrounded by red – thus *papula*, as if it were *pupula* (i.e. "pupil of the eye"). 22. Fistula (*syringio*). . . . *Sanies* is so called because it arises from blood (*sanguis*), for blood is turned into *sanies* by the kindled heat of a wound. *Sanies* occurs nowhere but where blood has come, because nothing that grows putrid could putrefy unless it were hot and moist, which blood is. *Sanies* and *tabes* (i.e. two kinds of fluid produced by putrefaction) differ from each other in that *sanies* is a discharge from living people, *tabes* from the dead. 23. A scar (*cicatrix*) is the covering of a wound, preserving the natural color of the affected parts. It is so called because it covers the wound and hides (*obcaecare*) it.

ix. Remedies and medications (De remediis et medicaminibus) 1. The curing power of medicine should not be scorned, for we recall that Isaiah ordered something medicinal for Hezekiah when he was failing, and the apostle Paul said to Timothy that a moderate amount of wine is beneficial. 2. The treatment of diseases falls into three types: pharmaceutics (*pharmacia*), which Latin speakers call medication (*medicamen*); surgery (*chirurgia*), which Latin speakers call 'work of the hands' (*manuum operatio*) – for 'hand' is called χείρ by the Greeks (cf. also ἔργον, "work"); and regimen (*diaeta*), which Latin speakers call rule (*regula*), that is, the careful observance of a regulated way of life. And every treatment has these same three characteristics: first, regimen; second, pharmaceutics; and third, surgery. 3. Regimen is the careful observance of a regulated way of life. Pharmaceutics is treatment by medication. Surgery is incision by iron tools, for by the iron blade those things that have not responded to the medicinal power of pharmaceutics are cut out.

4. More ancient medicine was practiced using herbs and potions alone. The practice of healing began by using such things, and later started using the blade and other medications. 5. All treatment is applied by use either of opposites or of similarities. By means of opposites, as cold is applied to hot, or moist to dry – just as in a human pride cannot be cured unless it be cured by humility. 6. By means of similarities, as a round bandage is put on a round wound and an oblong bandage on an oblong wound – for the bandaging itself is not the same for all limbs and wounds, but a similar is suited to a similar. These two treatments make their types of assistance clear through their names. 7. The Greek word 'antidote' (*antidotum*) means 'derived (*datum*) from the opposite' in Latin, for opposites are cured by opposites in accordance with the methodology of medicine. On the other hand there is treatment by similarity, as indicated

by the term πίκρα (i.e. "remedy, bitter thing"), which is translated as 'bitterness' (*amara*) because its taste is bitter (*amarus*). *Amara* got its name appropriately, because the bitterness (*amaritudo*) of disease is usually resolved by bitterness.

8. All medications have their names due to appropriate reasons. The remedy *hiera* is so called as if it were 'holy,' (cf. ἱερός, "holy"). *Arteriace*, so called because it is suitable for the channel of the gullet and alleviates swellings in the throat and windpipe (*arteria*). *Tyriaca* is an antidote made from snakes (cf. θηριακός, "of venomous beasts") that expels venom, so that poison is resolved by poison. Cathartics (*catarticum*) in Greek are called purgatives (*purgatorium*) in Latin. 9. *Catapotia*, because a little is drunk (*potare*) or swallowed down. *Diamoron* got its name from the juice of the mulberry (*morum*), from which it is made; likewise *diacodion*, because it is made from the poppy-head (*codia*; cf. κώδεια, "poppy-head"), that is, from the poppy; and similarly *diasperma-ton*, because it is made from seeds (cf. σπέρμα, "seed"). 10. *Electuarium* is so called because it melts in the mouth. Lozenge (*trociscos*) is so called because it is shaped like a wheel, for in Greek τροχός means "wheel."

Collyria echoes a Latin word, because it clears flaws in the eye (*oculus*). *Epitima*, because it is 'put over' (cf. επίθημα, "what is set on top") other remedies that precede it. 11. Poultice (*cataplasma*), because it is only a covering. A plaster (*inplastrum*, i.e. *emplastrum*) because it is applied (*inducere*). An emollient (*malagma*), because it is softened (*macerare*, and cf. *mollis*, "soft") and absorbed without the use of fire (*ignis*). Enema (*enema*) in Greek is called 'loosening' (*relaxatio*) in Latin. A pessary (*pessarium*) is so called because it is put inside (perhaps cf. *pessum*, "to the bottom").

12. A certain Greek, Chiron, invented medical practice for draft animals. For this reason he is pictured as half man, half horse. He was named Chiron from the term χειρίζεσθαι (i.e. "operate by hand"), because he was a surgeon (*chirurgus*). 13. Physicians speak of certain days as critical (*creticus*, cf. κριτικός); I believe this name was assigned to them with regard to the judgment (cf. *cernere*, ppl. *cretus*, "decide, determine") of an illness, because they pass judgment, as it were, on a person, and either punish or free the person with their sentence.

x. Medical books (De libris medicinalibus) 1. An aphorism (*aphorismus*) is a short saying that describes the entire meaning of the matter under consideration. 2. A prognostic (*prognosticon*) is a treatise on the foreseeing of the progression of diseases, so called from 'foreknowing' (*praenoscere*), for a physician should recognize the past, know the present, and foresee the future.[7] 3. A *dinamidia* describes the power of herbs, that is, their force and capability. In herbal medicine, potency itself is called δύναμις, whence also the books where herbal remedies are inscribed are called *dinamidia*. 4. A 'botanical treatise' (*butanicum*, i.e. *botanicum*, cf. βοτάνη, "herb") about plants is so called because plants are described in it.

xi. The instruments of physicians (De instrumentis medicorum) 1. An *enchiridion* is so called because it is gripped in one's hand while it contains many iron instruments, for in Greek, 'hand' is called χείρ.[8] 2. The lancet (*phlebotomum*, i.e. *phlebotomus*) is named from incision, since incision is called τομή in Greek. 3. *Similaria . . . Angistrum . . . Spatomele . . .* A 'cupping glass' (*guva*), which is called a 'gourd' (*cucurbita*) by Latin speakers for its resemblance to one, is also called *ventosa* (lit. "wind-like") from its hiss. In brief, when it is livened in its breath (i.e. when the air within it is heated) by a small flame, it is immediately positioned so that it completely covers the place on the body where a cut has been made, which then heats up under the skin or deeper and draws either a humor or blood to the surface. 4. *Clistere . . .* Mortar (*pila*) from crushing (*pisere*, i.e. *pinsere*) seeds, that is, grinding them up. From this also 'crushed herbs' (*pigmentum*), because they are made (*agere*) in a mortar and with a pestle (*pilum*), as if the word were *piligmentum*. A mortar is a concave vessel suited to use by physicians, in which, properly, grains are usually ground for tisanes and herbs for drugs are crushed. 5. But Varro reports that there was a certain Pilumn[i]us in Italy who was first to grind (*pinsere*) the crop, whence [also] the terms 'miller' (*pilumnus*) and 'baker' (*pistor*). Therefore both the mortar (*pila*) and the pestle (*pilum*), by which grain is crushed, were invented by this man, and are named after his name (Funaioli 442). The pestle is what crushes whatever is placed in the mortar. 6. The *mortarium* ("mortar") is so called because seeds

7 Isidore may refer here to the collections of Hippocrates, the *Aphorisms* and the *Prognostic*.

8 The usual meaning for *enchiridion* is "handbook," but Isidore here seems to refer to some kind of instrument case.

already desiccated (*mortuus*) and reduced to powder are tempered there. 7. A 'small mortar' (*coticula*) is that in which eye-salves (*collyrium*) are dissolved after they have been stirred around. It should be smooth, for a small mortar that is rough makes the salve shatter instead of dissolving.

xii. Scents and ointments (De odoribus et unguentis) 1. Scent (*odor*) is named after 'air' (*aer*). 2. It is called incense (*thymiama*) in the Greek language, because it is scented, for a flower that bears a scent is called thyme (*thymum*). With regard to this, Vergil (*Geo.* 4.169):

> And (the honey) is redolent with thyme.

3. Incense (*incensum*) is so called because it is 'consumed by fire' (*igne consumere*) when it is offered. 4. *Tetraidos formulae* is the name for small, elongated shapes of incense made from four ingredients, for in Greek τέτταρα means "four," and εἶδος means "shape." 5. Myrrh (*stacten*) is an incense that is exuded under pressure, and is so called by the Greeks from στακτός (i.e. "oozing""), from the verb στάζειν (i.e. "trickle"), that is, exuded. 6. Balsam (*mirobalanum*) is so called because it is made from the scent-bearing nut of which Horace speaks (*Odes* 3.29.4):

> The pressed ben-nut (*balanus*, i.e. the source of balsam) for your hair.

Oil (*oleum*) is a pure substance, mixed with nothing else. But ointment (*unguentum*) is anything made from common oil and enriched with a mixture of other ingredients, assuming a pleasant scent and producing odor for some time.

7. Some ointments are named after places, as was *telinum*, which Julius Caesar (Strabo) mentions, saying (Courtney fr. 2):

> And we anoint our bodies with sweet *telinum*.

This used to be manufactured on the island of Telos, which is one of the Cyclades. 8. And some ointments are named after their inventors, as is *amaracinum*: some people report that a certain royal youth, Amaracus by name, fell by accident when he was carrying many kinds of ointments and created a greater scent from the mixing. Hence the finest ointments are now called *amaricina*, but these are from a kind of flower, (i.e. *amaracus*, "marjoram"). 9. There are still others that are named from the aromatic quality of their material, such as 'oil of roses' (*rosaceum*) from 'rose' (*rosa*) and 'henna ointment' (*quiprinum*, i.e. *cyprinum*) from 'henna' (*quiprum*, i.e. *cyprum*) – hence these also carry the scent of their own material. 10. Some of these ointments are 'simples' – the ones that are made from only one kind of ingredient – and hence they also carry the scent associated with their name. An example is *anetinum*, for this is unmixed, from oil and dill (*anetum*) alone. 'Composite' ointments, however, are those made from many ingredients mixed together, and these do not bear a scent associated with their name, because the scent they produce is indeterminate, as the other ingredients that are mixed in persist in their own scents. 11. *Cerotum . . . Calasticum . . . Marciatum . . .*

xiii. The foundations of medicine (De initiis medicinae) 1. Some people ask why the art of medicine is not included in the other liberal disciplines. It is for this reason: the liberal disciplines treat individual topics, but medicine treats the topics of all. Thus the physician ought to know grammar, so that he can understand and explain what he reads. 2. Similarly he must know rhetoric, so that he is capable of summing up the cases he treats with true arguments. He must also know dialectic in order to scrutinize and cure the causes of disease with the application of reason. So also arithmetic, to reckon the number of hours in the onsets of illness, and their periods of days. 3. Likewise with geometry, so that from his knowledge of the qualities of regions and the location of places, he may teach what a person should attend to there. Then, music will not be unknown to him, for we read of many things that have been accomplished for sick people by way of this discipline – as we read of David who rescued Saul from an unclean spirit with the art of melody. The physician Asclepiades also restored a certain victim of frenzy to his former health through harmonious sounds. 4. Finally, he will be acquainted with astronomy, through which he may observe the logic of the stars and the change of seasons. For, as a certain physician says, according to their mutations our bodies are also changed. 5. Thus medicine is called the Second Philosophy, for each discipline claims for itself the entire human: by philosophy the soul is cured; by medicine, the body.

Book V

Laws and times (De legibus et temporibus)

i. The originators of laws (De auctoribus legum) 1. Moses of the Hebrew people was the first of all to explain the divine laws, in the Sacred Scriptures. King Phoroneus was the first to establish laws and legal processes for the Greeks. 2. Mercury (i.e. Hermes) Trimegistus first gave laws to the Egyptians. Solon was first to give laws to the Athenians. Lycurgus first devised legal structures for the Spartans by the authority of Apollo. 3. Numa Pompilius, who succeeded Romulus to the throne, first published laws for the Romans. Then, when the population was no longer able to bear the factious magistrates, they brought the *Decemvirs* (lit. the "ten men") into being to write laws; these men set forth in the Twelve Tables the laws which had been translated from the books of Solon into the Latin language. 4. These men were: Appius Claudius, Genucius, Veterius, Julius, Manlius, Sulpicius, Sextius, Curatius, Romilius, and Postumius. These *Decemvirs* were selected to draw up laws. 5. The consul Pompey first wanted to undertake the collection of the laws into books, but he did not continue for fear of detractors. Then Caesar began to do this, but he was killed first. 6. And gradually the ancient laws became obsolete due to age and neglect; although none of them is still in use, nevertheless a knowledge of them seems needful. 7. New laws originated from Emperor Constantine and the others following him, but they were mixed and disordered. After this, Theodosius Augustus the younger instituted a code, made in imitation of the Gregorian and Hermogenian codes, of decrees from the time of Constantine, arranging them under the name of each emperor; he called it the Theodosian Code after his own name.

ii. Divine laws and human laws (De legibus divinis et humanis) 1. All laws are either divine or human. Divine laws are based on nature, human law on customs. For this reason human laws may differ, because different laws suit different peoples. 2. *Fas* is divine law; jurisprudence (*ius*) is human law. To cross through a stranger's property is allowed by divine law; it is not allowed by human law.

iii. How jurisprudence, laws, and customs differ from each other (Quid differunt inter se ius, leges, et mores) 1. Jurisprudence is a general term, and a law is an aspect of jurisprudence. It is called jurisprudence (*ius*) because it is just (*iustus*).[1] All jurisprudence consists of laws and customs. 2. A law is a written statute. A custom is usage tested by age, or unwritten law, for law (*lex*, gen. *legis*) is named from reading (*legere*), because it is written. 3. But custom (*mos*) is a longstanding usage drawn likewise from 'moral habits' (*mores*, the plural of *mos*). 'Customary law' (*consuetudo*) is a certain system of justice established by moral habits, which is taken as law when a law is lacking; nor does it matter whether it exists in writing or reasoning, since reason also validates law. 4. Furthermore, if law is based on reason, then law will be everything that is consistent with reason – provided that it agrees with religion, accords with orderly conduct, and is conducive to well-being. Customary law is so called because it is in 'common use' (*communis usus*).

iv. What natural law is (Quid sit ius naturale) 1. Law is either natural, or civil, or of nations. Natural law (*ius naturale*) is common to all nations, and, because it exists everywhere by the instinct of nature, it is not upheld by any regulation. Such is the union of a man and woman, the children's inheritance and education, the common possession of everything, a single freedom for all, and the right to acquire whatever is taken from the sky, the earth, and the sea. 2. Also the return of something which was entrusted and of money which was deposited, and the repulsion of violence by force. Now this, or whatever is similar to it, is never unjust, but is held to be natural and fair.

1 The Latin term *ius* has a broad range of meaning and application, with no single English equivalent. We have generally translated it as "jurisprudence," but have also used the terms "right," "law," or "justice," according to the context.

v. What civil law is (Quis sit ius civile) Civil law (*ius civile*) is that which each individual population or city has established particular to itself, for human or divine reasons.

vi. What the law of nations is (Quid sit ius gentium) 1. The law of nations concerns the occupation of territory, building, fortification, wars, captivities, enslavements, the right of return, treaties of peace, truces, the pledge not to molest embassies, the prohibition of marriages between different races. And it is called the 'law of nations' (*ius gentium*) because nearly all nations (*gentes*) use it.

vii. What military law is (Quid sit ius militare) 1. 'Military law' (*ius militare*) is the formalized practice of waging war, the bond of making treaties, the marching against or engagement with the foe at a given signal. Also the cessation of hostilities at a given signal, and the military discipline for the disgrace of deserting one's post; also the method of distributing military pay, the hierarchy of ranks, the honor of rewards, as when a crown or torques are given. 2. Also the distribution of booty, and its equitable division based on the status and deeds of the individuals; also the leader's share.

viii. What public law is (Quid sit ius publicum) 'Public law' (*ius publicum*) concerns sacred things, priests, and magistrates.

ix. What quirital law is (Quis sit ius quiritum) 1. 'Quirital law' (*ius quiritum*) is, properly speaking, Roman law. No one except the Quirites, that is, the Romans, is governed by it. It concerns such things as legal inheritances, *cretio* (i.e. formal acceptance of an inheritance), guardianship, *usucapio* (i.e. acquisition of ownership by use): these laws are found among no other group of people, but are particular to the Romans and established for them alone. 2. Quirital law consists of laws and plebiscites, decrees and edicts of rulers, or responses of jurists.

x. What a law is (Quid sit lex) A law is a rule for a people – through it those who are nobler by birth, along with the common people, have ordained something.

xi. What popular resolutions (i.e. plebiscites) are (Quid scita plebium) Resolutions are established by the 'common people' (*plebs*) alone, and they are called resolutions (*scitum*) because the common people know (*scire*) them, or because something is sought (*sciscere*) and petitioned that it may take place.

xii. What a senate decree is (Quid senatusconsultum) A senate decree is something that the senators alone decide, by consulting the interests of the people.

xiii. What an order and an edict are (Quid constitutio et edictum) An order (*constitutio*) or edict (*edictum*) is that which a king or emperor orders (*constituere*) or decrees (*edicere*).

xiv. What a response of jurists is (Quid responsa prudentium) Responses are those things that jurists are said to answer (*respondere*) to those consulting them, whence the *Responses* of Paulus take their name.[2] There were certain experienced people, and arbitrators of equity, who composed and issued instructions of civil jurisprudence by which they might settle the quarrels and disputes of parties in disagreement.

xv. Consular and tribunitial laws (De legibus consularibus et tribunitiis) 1. Some laws are named from those who produced them, such as consular laws, tribunitial laws, Julian laws, Cornelian laws. Under Caesar Augustus the suffect consuls[3] Papius and Poppaeus introduced a law that is called 'Lex Papia Poppea' from their names; this law sets up rewards for fathers for begetting children. 2. Under the same emperor, Falcidius, the plebeian tribune, also established a law that no one might in a will bequeath more to people outside the family than would leave one quarter for the heirs. The law is called the 'Lex Falcidia' from his name. Aquilius also [produced a law, which to this day is called 'Lex Aquilia'].

xvi. Replete law (De lex satura) A medley (*satura*) is a law which is concerned with many things at once; it is so called from the abundance of topics, and, as it were, from fullness (*saturitas*), whence also to write satires

2 The Roman jurist Julius Paulus (early third century CE) compiled a *Responsa* consisting of legal opinions.

3 A suffect consul is one elected after the regular time.

(*satura*) is to compose richly varied poems, as those of Horace, Juvenal, and Persius. The laws called 'Novels' (*Novella*) . . .

xvii. Rhodian laws (De legibus rhodiis) The Rhodian laws are the laws of nautical commerce, and are so named from the island of Rhodes, where the practice of commerce existed in ancient times.

xviii. Private statutes (De privilegiis) Private statutes are the laws concerning individuals, private laws (*privatae leges*) as it were. It is called a 'private statute' (*privilegium*) because it is applied in private use (*privatus*).

xix. What a law is capable of (Quid possit lex) Every law either allows something, as "A brave man may seek reward," or it forbids, as "No one is allowed to seek marriage with a sacred virgin," or it prescribes punishment, as "Whoever has committed murder shall suffer capital punishment." Indeed, human life is regulated by the reward or punishment of law.

xx. Why a law is enacted (Quare facta est lex) Laws are enacted in order to control human audacity through the fear they arouse, and so that innocent people may be safe in the midst of reprobates, and so that even among the impious the power of doing harm may be restrained by a dreaded punishment.

xxi. What sort of law should be made (Qualis debet fieri lex) A law should be honorable, just, feasible, in agreement with nature, in agreement with the custom of the country, appropriate to the place and time, necessary, useful, and also clear, lest in its obscurity it contain something deceitful, and it should be written not for private convenience, but for the common benefit of the citizens.

xxii. Cases (De causis) Πρᾶγμα is a Greek term that means "case" (*causa*) in Latin, whence also legal business is called *pragmatica*, and a person involved in cases or legal business is called a *pragmaticus*.

xxiii. Witnesses (De testibus) Witnesses [are people through whom the truth is sought in a legal process]. Before the proceedings each litigant binds (*alligare*) witnesses to himself by covenants, so that afterward the witnesses may not be free to dissimulate or withdraw themselves, whence the witnesses are also called 'bound' (*alligatus*, ppl. of *alligare*). Also, they are called witnesses (*testes*) because they are usually employed for a testament (*testamentum*); they are also called signatories (*signator*), because they sign (*signare*) the testament.

xxiv. Legal instruments (De instrumentiis legalibus) 1. A will (*voluntas*) is the general name for all legal instruments, because it proceeds not by force, but by 'free will' (*voluntas*); hence it receives such a name. 2. A testament (*testamentum*) is so called because, unless the testator (*testator*) died, one could not confirm or know what was written in it, because it is closed and sealed, and it is also called 'testament' because it is not valid until after the setting up of the memorial of the testator (*testatoris monumentum*), whence also the Apostle (Hebrews 9:17): "The testament," he says, "is of force after people are dead." 3. Nevertheless, in Sacred Scripture, 'testament' is not only the term for that which is not valid until the testators be dead, but every pact and covenant was called a testament. Thus Laban and Jacob made a testament, which was certainly valid between living people, and in the Psalms it is written (82:6): "They have made a covenant (*testamentum*) together against thee," that is, a pact; and innumerable such examples. 4. The tablets (*tabula*) of a testament are so called because before the use of papyrus sheets and parchment not only were testaments written on smoothed tablets, but even letters were so written. Hence those who carry these tablets were called *tabellarii*. 5. A testament in civil law is confirmed by the signatures of five witnesses. 6. A testament in praetorian law is sealed with the seals of seven witnesses; the former is made by citizens (*civis*), hence it is civil (*civile*) law; the latter is made in the presence of the praetors, hence it is of praetorian law. And to seal a testament is 'to put a distinguishing mark' (*notare*) on it so that what is written may be recognized (*noscere*, ppl. *notus*). 7. A 'holograph testament' (*holographum testamentum*) is entirely written and signed by the hand of the author, whence it receives its name, for the Greeks say ὅλος for "entire," and γραφή for "writing."

8. A testament is invalid (*inritum*) if he who has made the testament has lost his rights of citizenship, or if it was not made 'following prescribed procedures' (*rite*). 9. An *inofficiosus* (lit. "undutiful") testament is one that does not observe the duty (*officium*) of natural piety, and is

made to the benefit of non-family members, disinheriting the children for no good reason. 10. An annulled (*ruptus*) will is so named because it is broken (*disrumpere*, ppl. *disruptus*) by a child born posthumously, who was neither expressly disinherited, nor named as an heir. 11. A suppressed (*suppressus*) testament is one that was not openly made public, thus defrauding the heirs or the legatees or the freedmen. Even if it is not concealed, but nevertheless is not shown to the aforementioned people, then it appears to be suppressed (*supprimere*, ppl. *suppressus*). 12. A proclamation is that which the testator reads out from wax tablets, saying "These things, as they are written on these wax tablets, so I appoint them and so I bequeath them, and so you, Roman citizens, bear witness for me." And this is called a 'proclamation' (*nuncupatio*), because 'to proclaim' (*nuncupare*) is to name openly and to confirm. 13. The *ius liberorum* (lit. "law of children") is a reciprocal arrangement of inheritance for couples without children, naming one another as heirs in their place. 14. A codicil (*codicillum*), as the ancients said, is doubtless named after the originator who instituted this kind of writing. And the writing requires no formality of words, but only the desire of the testator, meaningfully expressed in any kind of writing. It is common knowledge that because of the difficulty of legal terminology, and the necessity of employing formalities, the wishes of the dead have been given support through the service of the codicil, so that whoever writes such a statement uses the heading of 'codicil' for what he writes. And just as a codicil is made in place of a testament, so also a letter can be made in place of a codicil. 15. A *cretio* is a certain number of days within which the designated heir either comes into the inheritance, or is excluded if the time of the *cretio* has elapsed, and there is no opportunity for him to receive the inheritance later. 16. *Cretio* is so called as if it were 'decision' (*decretio*), that is, deciding, or establishing – for example, "Let such and such a person be my heir," and it is added "and let him 'accept the inheritance' (*cernere*, ppl. *cretus*) within so many days." Moreover, a hundred-day period was established for coming into those inheritances to which a *cretio* was not added. 17. A *fideicommissum* (i.e. a request to an heir) is so called, as it specifies what 'may be done' (*fiat*) as commissioned (*committere*, ppl. *commissum*) by the deceased – for faith (*fides*) is so called because 'it may be done' (*fiat*); it is, however requested not in obligatory language, but as a wish.

18. A pact is a document of agreement between parties in a state of peace (*pax*, gen. *pacis*), approved by law and custom, and it is called pact (*pactum*) as if it were 'made from peace' (*ex pace factum*), from 'come to an agreement' (*pacere*), which also generates the form *pepigit*, "he has agreed." 19. A *placitum* ("agreed condition") is named similarly, because it pleases (*placere*). Some say a pact is what someone does willingly, but a *placitum* is what one is compelled to do even against one's will, as for example when someone is brought into the court to answer; no one can call this a pact, but rather a *placitum*. 20. A *mandatum* ("consensual contract") is so called because formerly, in a business transaction, one person would 'shake hands' (*manus dabat*) with the other. 21. And a 'valid act' (*ratum*) is, as it were, rational (*rationabile*) and just (*rectus*), whence he who pledges says "I declare this to be valid (*ratum*)," that is, firm and lasting. 22. Something done 'by established procedure' (*rite*) is not done 'by right' (*recte*), but according to custom. 'Autograph surety' (*chirographum*) . . . 'Warranty' (*cautio*) . . .

23. Buying and selling are exchanges of goods and contracts taking place by agreement. 24. Buying (*emptio*) is so called because it is 'from me for you' (*a me tibi*); selling (*venditio*), as if the word were *venundatio*, that is, from the marketplace (*nundinae*). 25. A donation is a settlement of any sort of property. And people say it is called donation (*donatio*) as if the word were 'presentation of a gift' (*doni actio*), and dowry (*dos*, acc. *dotem*) as if it were 'I give likewise' (*do item*) – for after the donation has taken place at the wedding, the dowry follows. 26. Indeed, there was an ancient ceremony of marriage, in which the husband and wife purchased each other, so that it did not seem that the wife was a handmaid, as we hold legally. Thence it is that after the donation of the husband takes place, the dowry of the wife follows. 27. A usufructuary donation (*donatio usufructuaria*) is so called for this reason, because the donor still retains the 'use of the yield' (*usus fructu*) from the gift, with the legal title reserved for the recipient. 28. A 'direct donation' (*donatio directa*) is so named because it is immediately transferred to another both in legal title and in use of the yield, and no part of it is diverted back to the legal right of the donor.

29. Covenants are, technically speaking, witnessed, and they are called covenants (*condicio*) from 'talking together' (*condīcere*), as if the word were *condīcio*,

because not just one witness swears there, but two or more. Indeed, every word stands not in the mouth of one witness alone, but of two or three witnesses (cf. Deuteronomy 19:15). Furthermore, they are called covenants because the speeches of the witnesses agree with each other, as if the word were *condictiones* (lit. "joint utterances"). 30. A stipulation is a promise or a pledge, whence stipulators are also called promisors. And stipulation (*stipulatio*) is so called from straw (*stipula*), for the ancients, when they would promise each other something, would break a straw that they were holding; in joining this straw together again they would acknowledge their pledge. [Or it is because people would have called something firm *stipulus*, according to Paulus the jurist.] 31. A *sacramentum* is a bond given in support of a promise, and it is called a *sacramentum* (lit. "holy thing") because to violate a promise is a breach of faith.

xxv. Property (De rebus) 1. An inheritance is property that passes to a person upon someone's death, either bequeathed by a will, or retained through occupancy. And it is called 'inheritance' (*hereditas*) from 'property entered in on' (*res adita*), or from 'money' (*aes*, gen. *aeris*), because whoever possesses land also pays the tax; whence also property (*res*).[4] 2. Property is that which exists under our legal title. And 'legal titles' (*ius*) are things that are possessed by us lawfully (*iuste*), and do not belong to someone else. 3. Property (*res*) is so named from holding rightly (*recte*), and 'legal titles' from possessing lawfully, for what is possessed 'with title' (*ius*), is possessed 'lawfully' (*iuste*), and what is possessed lawfully is possessed well. But what is possessed wrongly is that which is owned by someone else. Someone who either uses his own property improperly, or takes the property of another, possesses wrongly. He possesses lawfully who is not ensnared by greed. But whoever is held by greed is the possessed, not the possessor.

4. Goods are the possessions of honorable or noble people, and they are called 'goods' (*bona*) for that reason, because they have no base use, but people make use of them for good (*bonus*) purposes. 5. A *peculium*, properly speaking, relates to younger persons or slaves, for a *peculium* is something that a father allows his son, or a master his slave, to handle as his own. And it is called *peculium* from 'livestock' (*pecus*), of which all the wealth of the ancients consisted. 6. The 'possession of goods' is the legal right of possession, acquired following a certain procedure and with a certain title.

7. An intestate (*intestata*) inheritance is one that has not been written in a testament, or, if it has, has not been legally entered upon. 8. An inheritance is called *caduca* (i.e. property without an heir), because its heirs have died (*cadere*). 9. *Familia herciscunda* is the division of the inheritance among the heirs, for division was called *herciscunda* by the ancients. 10. 'Dividing in common' is for those who own property in common; this action requires that a mediator be assigned to the claimants, a mediator by whose arbitration the property may be divided (*dividere*). 11. The action of *fines regundi* is so called because through it the boundaries (*fines*) of each party may be drawn (*regere*), lest they be blurred, as long as the disagreement does not concern an area narrower than five feet.

12. *Locatio* is property lent out for use at a fixed price. 13. *Conductio* is property borrowed for use at an established price. 14. A *res credita* is property brought under terms of obligation in such a way that from the time when the contract was made it was determined that it is mortgaged. 15. *Usura* is the increment of interest, so called from the 'use of money' (*usu aeris*) that is lent. 16. *Commodatum* is that which is subject to our authority and is transferred temporarily to someone else 'with a limit' (*cum modo*) of the time during which he may have it, whence it is called *commodatum*. 17. A *precarium* exists when a creditor, having been requested by entreaty, allows the debtor to remain in possession of the cultivated land that is owing to him, and to have the fruits from it. And it is called *precarium*, because it 'is entered into by means of entreaty' (*prece aditur*), as if the word were *precadium*, with the letter *r* put for the *d*. 18. A *mutuum* (i.e. a kind of loan) is so called, because that which is given by me to you is turned 'from mine to yours' (*ex meo tuum*).

19. A 'deposit' (*depositum*) is a security entrusted for a set time, as though it were 'set down for a long time' (*diu positum*). And someone is seen to make a deposit when, for fear of theft or fire or shipwreck, he leaves (*deponere*, ppl. *depositus*) something with another person for safekeeping. 20. And there is a difference in usage between a *pignus* and an *arra*. A *pignus* is that which is given in place of something borrowed, and when the loan is

4 The phrase *inde et res*, "whence also property," seems to be scribally corrupt.

returned, the *pignus* is immediately given back, but an *arra* is that which is given first, in partial payment for property purchased with a contract of good faith, and afterward the payment is completed. 21. For an *arra* must be part of the complete payment, and not given back; whence whoever has an *arra* does not return it as he does a security, but, rather, desires the full payment, and it is called *arra* 'from the thing' (*a re*) for which it is paid.

Furthermore there is this difference between a *pignus*, a *fiducia* and a *hypotheca*. 22. For a *pignus* is that which is pledged on account of a loan, and at the set time the creditor gets possession of the loan only; ownership of the pignus remains with the borrower. 23. The term *fiducia* (i.e. the transference of property on trust) is used when something is transferred or the right to it is forfeited for the sake of a loan. 24. *Hypotheca* is the term used when a thing is lent without the deposit of a *pignus*, with only an agreement or warranty being made. 25. *Momentum* is so called from shortness of time, requiring that the loan be returned as soon as the transaction is secured, and that there should be no delay in the recovery of the debt; just as a moment (*momentum*) possesses no extent – its point in time is so short that it has no duration of any kind.

26. An 'instrument' (*instrumentum*) is what we use to make (*construere*) something, as a knife, a reed-pen, an axe. 27. An *instructum* is what is made by an instrument, such as a staff, a codex, a table. 28. *Usus* is that use to which we put the thing that is made, such as leaning on a staff, reading in a codex, gaming on a table; but even the fruit of the fields is also called *usus*, because we use (*uti*, ppl. *usus*) it. These are the three uses. 29. *Usufructus* is so called because only its yield (*fructus*) is held for use, and all the other rights remain with someone else. 30. *Usucapio* is the acquisition of ownership through the maintenance of legal possession, either for two years or for some other time. 31. *Mancipatio* is so called because the property is 'taken in the hand' (*manu . . . capitur*). Hence it is appropriate for whoever takes formal possession to grasp the property itself that is given into his possession.

32. *Cessio* is a concession (*concessio*) of one's own property, such as this: "I cede by right of affinity," for we say 'cede' (*cedere*) as if it were 'concede' (*concedere*), that is, those things that are our own; for we 'restore' the property of another, we do not 'cede' it. In fact, technically speaking, someone is said to cede when he gives in to another in spite of the truth, as Cicero (*Defense of Ligarius* 7.22): "He ceded," he says, "to the authority of a very distinguished man, or rather, he obeyed." 33. A 'temporary injuction' (*interdictum*) 'is pronounced for the time being' (*interim dicitur*) by a judge, not in perpetuity, but with the intention of changing the temporary order at the right time, when the conditions of the judgment are met. 34. Payment (*pretium*) is so called because we give 'it first' (*prius eum*), so that in return for it we may rightfully take possession of the property we are seeking. 35. Commerce (*commercium*) is named after merchandise (*merx*, gen. *mercis*), by which term we speak of things for sale. Whence an assembly of many people who are accustomed to sell and buy goods is called a market (*mercatus*). 36. *Integri restitutio* is the restoring of a case or of a property. 37. A case that has not been brought to a conclusion by the authority of the law is 'reconstituted' (*redintegrare*); property that has been taken or forcefully seized by the authority of the law is 'restored' (*redintegrare*).

xxvi. Crimes written in the law (De criminibus in lege conscriptis) 1. Crime (*crimen*) has its name from lacking (*carere*) – like theft, deceit, and other actions that do not kill, but cause disgrace. 2. Misdeed (*facinus*) is so called from doing (*facere*) evil that harms another. 3. 'Outrageous deed' (*flagitium*) is so called from 'urgently summoning' (*flagitare*) the corrupting power of lust, by which one harms oneself. All wrongdoing belongs to one of these two categories. 4. Force (*vis*) is the strength (*virtus*) of a powerful person, through which a case or property is either carried off or extorted. 5. It is 'private force' (*vis privata*) if someone, before the trial, has used armed men to drive someone from his own property or overpower him. 6. It is 'public force' (*vis publica*) if someone has executed a citizen before his making an appeal to the people or a judge or a king, or tortured him or whipped him or fettered him. 7. Deception (*dolus*) is a cunning of the mind, so named from the fact that it deludes (*deludere*), for the deceiver does one thing and pretends to do another. Petronius thinks otherwise when he says "What, judges, is deception (*dolus*)? Surely it is when something is done that is grievous (*dolere*) to the law. You have 'deception'; now hear about evil."[5] 8. *Calumnia* (i.e. the bringing of a charge in bad faith) is the contention of a hostile lawsuit, called

5 The source of this passage has not been identified.

from 'using subterfuge' (*calvi*), that is, deceiving. 9. Deceit (*falsitas*) is so called from saying (*fari*, ppl. *fatus*) something other than the truth. 10. Injury (*iniuria*) is injustice. Hence among the comic authors (Plautus, *The Braggart Soldier* 436): "You are an injury," that is, someone who dares something against the rule of law (*ius*, gen. *iuris*).

11. A dissension on the part of citizens is called 'sedition' (*seditio*), because people divide (*seorsum* + *ire*, ppl. *itus*, lit. "go apart") into different factions – for they greatly rejoice in disturbances and in tumult. 12. Sacrilege (*sacrilegium*), strictly speaking, is the theft of sacred objects. Later this term was applied to the worship of idols. 13. Adultery (*adulterium*) is a deception with regard to someone else's marriage, which because it has defiled the 'marriage bed of another' (*alterius torum*), receives the name adultery. 14. 'Illicit sex' (*stuprum*)... Rape (*raptus*), strictly speaking, is illegal intercourse, so called from corrupting (*corrumpere*, ppl. *corruptus*) whence also he who 'gains submission over one he has taken by force' (*rapto potitur*) delights in illicit sex. 15. The word 'homicide' (*homicidium*) is compounded from 'person' (*homo*) and 'slaughter' (*caedes*). For whoever was proven to have committed slaughter against a person, the ancients called a homicide (*homicida*). 16. The charge of parricide was brought not only against someone who had killed his parent, that is, his father or mother, but also against someone who had killed a brother; and it was called parricide (*parricidium*) as if it were 'slaughter of a parent' (*parentis caedes*). 17. *Internecivum iudicium* (i.e. murderous judgment) was charged against someone who had given false testimony and had so caused a person's death. Ownership of the dead man's goods would pass to the accuser. And the significance of *internecivus* is that is refers to the destruction (*enectio*), as it were, of an individual – for they used to put the prefix *inter-* in place of *e-*: Naevius (fr. 55): "*mare interbibere*" ("to drain the sea") and Plautus (fr. 188): "*interluere mare*" ("to wash away the sea"); that is, *ebibere* and *eluere*.

18. Theft (*furtum*) is the secret purloining of someone else's property, named from gloomy (*furvus*), that is dark (*fuscus*), because it takes place in the dark. Theft was a capital offense among the ancients, before the penalty of four-fold damages. 19. *Pervasio* is the open appropriation of someone else's property. Theft involves goods that can be carried from one place to another, but *pervasio* involves both those things that can be moved and those that are immovable. 20. *Infitiatio* is denial of liability for what is owed when it is sought by a creditor. Similarly *abiuratio* is the denial of liability for property that has been loaned. 21. The judgment of *ambitus* is made against someone who wins office by means of bribery and 'canvasses for support' (*ambire*, ppl. *ambitus*, lit. "go round") when he is about to lose the position that he gains by graft. 22. The judgment of *peculatus* is made against those who commit fraud with respect to public funds and embezzle public money, for *peculatus* is so named from money (*pecunia*). And the theft of public property is not judged in the same way as the theft of private property, for the former is judged as sacrilege, because the theft is of sacred things. 23. Someone who has taken money from his associates is accused of extortion (*repetundae*). If the accused in such a case dies before the verdict then judgment is delivered against his estate. 24. The judgment of incest (*incestum*) is made with regard to consecrated virgins or those who are closely related by blood, for those who have intercourse with such people are considered *incestus*, that is, 'unchaste' (*incastus*). 25. Those who have injured or violated royal majesty are liable on a charge of treason (*maiestas*), as are those who betray the state or connive with enemies. 26. The term *piaculum* (i.e. an act that demands expiation) is used for something that can be expiated (*expiare*), when crimes have been committed that need to be expiated according to some established practice.

xxvii. Punishments drawn up in the laws (De poenis in legibus constitutis) 1. Harm (*malum*) is defined in two ways: one definition being what a person does; the other, what he suffers. What he does is wrongdoing (*peccatum*), what he suffers is punishment. And harm is at its full extent when it is both past and also impending, so that it includes both grief and dread. 2. Punishment (*poena*) is so called because it punishes (*punire*). But it is a noun used with an epithet, and without this additional term it does not have a complete meaning; if you add 'the punishment of prison,' 'the punishment of exile,' 'the punishment of death,' you complete the meaning. 3. The term penalty (*supplicium*), strictly speaking, is not used with regard to someone who is punished in any way at all, but with regard to one who is sentenced in such a way that his goods are 'set apart as sacred' (*consecrare*) and are paid into the public treasury. For penalties were once called 'supplications' (*supplicamenta*). It is also called *supplicium* when something is offered to God from someone's fine, whence also 'to supplicate' (*supplicare*).

4. Cicero writes that eight types of punishment are contained in the laws, that is, fines, fetters, lashes, compensation in kind, disgrace, exile, slavery, and death (cf. *On the Orator* 1.194). By these punishments every crime that is committed is avenged. 5. Fine (*damnum*) is named from a diminution (*diminutio*) of property. 6. Fetters (*vincula*) are named from 'fettering' (*vincire*), that is, confining, because they confine and restrain, or because they 'bind by force' (*vi ligare*). 7. Foot-shackles (*compes*) are named because they 'restrain the feet' (*continere + pes*). 8. *Peducae* are nooses by which the feet are ensnared, named from 'catching the feet' (*pedem capere*). 9. And chains (*catena*), because they 'catch hold of' (*capiendo tenere*) the feet to prevent walking. Also chains are so called because their many links catch hold of one another (*se capere*). 10. Manacles (*manicae*, lit. "sleeves") are chains by which the hands (*manus*) are bound – but *manicae* are also a part of tunics. 11. Thong-fetters (*nervus*) . . . 12. The *boia* is a collar for the condemned; it is like the yoke of an ox (*bos*), made out of a kind of chain. 13. Prison, the place in which criminals are held in custody, and it is called prison (*carcer*) because in it people are confined (*coercere*) and shut in, as if the word were *arcer*, that is, from enclosing (*arcere*). The place in which criminals are kept we call *carcer*, using the singular, but the place whence chariot-teams are released we call *carceres* (i.e. the starting gate at a race course), using the plural.

14. Whips (*verber*) are so called, because when they are wielded, they strike (*verberare*) the air. Hence lashes (*flagrum*) and floggings and scourges (*flagellum*), because they resound on the body with a whistling (*flatus*) and a crack. There is flogging (*plaga*), as if the term were *flaga*: but *plaga* and *flagrum* are primary in form, and *flagellum* is made by forming the diminutive. 15. The *anguilla* (i.e. an eel-skin whip) is used to punish boys in schools; it is called *scotica* (i.e. *scutica*) in common usage. 16. Cudgels (*fustis*) are used to beat young men for their crimes; they are so named because they may stand fixed in ditches (*fossa*); country people call them 'stakes.' 17. Crowbars (*vectis*) are so called because they are carried (*vectare*) in the hands, whence doors and stones are 'pried loose' (*vellere*), but they do not pertain to punishments of law. 18. Switches (*virga*) are the tips of branches and trees, so called because they are green (*viridis*), or because they possess the power of persuading (*vis arguendi*); if it is smooth, it is a switch, but if it is knotty and has points, it is correctly called by the term *scorpio* (lit. "scorpion"), because it is driven into the body leaving a curved wound. 19. Lashes (*ictus*), technically speaking, belong to scourges, and are named from brandishing (*agitare*). 20. *Ungulae* (lit. "claws") are so called because they gouge. These are also called *fidiculae* (lit. "small lutes"), because by them the accused are tortured on the rack (*eculeus*), so that the truth (*fides*) is discovered. 21. And the rack is so called because it stretches (*extendere*). 22. Tortures (*tormentum*) indeed are so called because they discover the intention (*mens*, gen. *mentis*) by twisting (*torquere*). 23. The quarry-prisons are a type of punishment associated with whipping, invented by Tarquin Superbus for the punishment of the wicked. Indeed, this Tarquin was first to invent quarry-prisons, torture, cudgels, mines, and exile, and was himself first of the kings to earn exile.

24. 'Compensation in kind' (*talio*) is a punishment resembling the act being punished, so that someone suffers 'in such a way' (*taliter*) as he acted. This is established by nature and by law, so that (cf. Juvencus, *Gospel Poem* 1.549):

> Let retribution of a similar kind fall to the one causing injury.

Whence also this is said with regard to the Law of the Old Testament (Matthew 5:38): "An eye for an eye, a tooth for a tooth." Compensation in kind is established for repaying not only injuries, but also favors, for this term is common to both injuries and favors. 25. Ignominy is so called because one who is apprehended in some crime ceases to have the reputation of honesty. And it is called ignominy (*ignominium*) as if it were the term for being *sine nomine* ("without reputation"), just as ignorant (*ignarus*) is without knowledge, and ignoble (*ignobilis*) is without *nobilitas* ("nobility"). 26. There is also infamy (*infamium*), as if it were 'without good report' (*fama*), and 'report' is so called because by speaking (*fari*), that is, talking, it roves about, creeping through the grapevine of tongues and ears. The term *fama* is also appropriate for both good and evil things, for 'report' is sometimes of good fortune, as in 'illustrious report,' which is praise. It is also of evils, as in Vergil (*Aen.* 4.174):

> Report (*fama*), than which no other evil is more speedy.

27. Report does not possess a trustworthy name, because it is especially untruthful, either adding many things to the truth, or distorting the truth. It lasts just as long as it is not put to the test, but whenever you put it to the test, it ceases to be, and after that is called fact, not report.

28. Exile (*exilium*) is so called as if it were 'outside the country' (*extra solum*), for someone who is outside the country is called an exile (*exul*). Whence *postliminium* (i.e. the restoration of rank and privileges) for those who return, that is, those who are brought back from exile, who were cast out undeservedly, that is, cast out beyond the borders (*limen*) of their native land. Exile is divided into those who are *relegatus* and those who are *deportatus*. 29. A *relegatus* is one whose possessions accompany him; a *deportatus* is not so accompanied. 30. Proscription (*proscriptio*) is a condemnation of exile at a distance, as if it were a 'writing afar' (*porro scriptio*). Also, because it is 'publicly drawn up' (*palam scriptus*). 31. A mine (*metallum*) is where exiles are transported to dig out a vein of ore and hew out marble in slabs. 32. Slavery (*servitus*) is named from saving (*servare*), for among the ancients, those who were saved from death in battle were called slaves (*servus*). This alone is the most extreme of all evils; for free people it is worse than every kind of punishment, for where freedom is lost, everything is lost with it.

33. There are various possible means of execution; among them the cross (*crux*), or *patibulum* (i.e. forked gibbet), on which men who are hanged are tormented (*cruciare*) or suffer (*pati*), whence these take their names. 34. The *patibulum* is commonly called the fork (*furca*), as if it were 'supporting the head' (*ferre caput*), for hanging on a gibbet causes death by strangling; but the *patibulum* is a lesser punishment than the cross. The *patibulum* immediately kills those who are hanged on it, but the cross torments those nailed to it for a long time; whence in the Gospel the legs of the thieves were broken, so that they might die and be taken from the cross before the Sabbath, because those hanged from a cross could not die quickly (John 19:32).

35. There are also differences in the types of dying. It is especially cruel to be drowned in water,[6] to be burned in fire, to perish from cold and hunger, to be thrown to dogs and animals. Indeed, the earlier age preferred that death occur by the sword, for the sword understands how to bring life to the finish with a quick death, without a more grievous torment. 36. A *culleum* (i.e. a leather bag in which parricides were sewn up and drowned) is a container for parricides, named from covering (*occulere*), that is, enclosing. It is a bag made of skin, in which parricides were closed up along with an ape, a rooster, and a snake, and thrown into the sea. The type to which all these deaths belong is called censure. 37. Censure (*animadversio*) is what occurs when a judge punishes a guilty man, and he is said to pass censure, that is, to 'turn his attention' (*animum . . . advertere*) in that direction, to focus on the punishing of the accused, because he is the judge. 38. For that reason the Romans forbade water and fire to certain condemned people – because air and water are free to all and given to everyone – so that the condemned might not enjoy what is given by nature to everyone.

6 Our translation omits the problematic *torquentes*, a likely corruption.

xxviii. The word for 'chronicle' (De chronicae vocabulo) 'Chronicle' (*chronica*) is the Greek term for what is called a 'succession of times' in Latin. Among the Greeks Eusebius, Bishop of Caesarea, compiled such a work, and the priest Jerome translated it into Latin. Χρόνος in Greek means "time" in Latin.

xxix. Moments and hours (De momentis et horis) 1. Intervals of time are divided into moments, hours, days, months, years, lustrums, centuries, and ages. A moment (*momentum*) is the least and shortest bit of time, so called from the movement (*motus*) of the stars. 2. It is the extreme limit of brevity of the hour's segments, when one instant stops and another starts. Hour (*hora*) is a Greek term (cf. ὥρα), but it is pronounced in the same way in Latin. The hour is the boundary of time, just as the word *ora* means a boundary like the shore of the sea, or the bank of a river, or the border of a garment.

xxx. Days (De diebus) 1. Day (*dies*) is the presence of the sun, or when the sun is over the earth, as night is when the sun is under the earth – for whether it is day or night is due to whether the sun is above or below the earth. A day properly so called is of twenty-four hours, and lasts as long as it takes a day and a night to complete the interval of their course through the turning of the sky, from one rising sun to the next. In poor usage, however, one day is the interval between sunrise and sunset. 2. Moreover, a day has two intervals: the diurnal and the nocturnal. A day is twenty-four hours long, the interval twelve hours long. 3. The whole is called 'day' after its superior, diurnal interval. Whence the usage is that, without thinking of nights, we speak of a 'number of days,' as is written in the divine Law (Genesis 1:5): "And there was made evening and morning, one day." 4. A day according to the Egyptians begins at sunset; among the Persians, at sunrise; according to the Athenians, at the sixth hour of our day; according to the Romans, at midnight. Hence cockcrow is at that time, when their voice heralds the day, and when the midnight breeze rises.

5. Days (*dies*) are so called from 'the gods' (*deus*, ablative plural *diis*), whose names the Romans conferred upon certain astral bodies, for they named the first day from the sun, which is the chief of all the astral bodies, just as that day is head of all the days. 6. The second day is named from the moon, which is closest to the sun in brilliance and size, and it borrows its light from the sun. The third, from the star of Mars, called Vesper. The fourth, from the star of Mercury, which some call the 'white circle.' 7. The fifth, from the star of Jupiter, which they call Phaeton. The sixth, from the star of Venus, which they name Lucifer, which has the most light of all the stars. The seventh, from the star of Saturn, which, placed in the sixth heaven, is said to run its course in thirty years. 8. Hence the pagans took the names of the days from these seven stars because they thought that they were affected by these stars in some matters, saying that they received their spirit from the sun, their body from the moon, their intelligence and speech from Mercury, their pleasure from Venus, their blood from Mars, their disposition from Jupiter, and their bodily humors from Saturn. Such indeed was the stupidity of the pagans, who made up such ridiculous figments for themselves.

9. Among the Hebrews, however, the first day is called 'one of the sabbath' (*una sabbati*); this is our Lord's Day (*dies dominicus*), which the pagans called the day of the sun. The 'second of the sabbath' is our second weekday (*feria*), which secular people call the day of the moon. 'Third of the sabbath,' the third weekday, which they call the day of Mars. 'Fourth of the sabbath,' the fourth weekday, which is called the day of Mercury by the pagans. 10. 'Fifth of the sabbath' is the fifth weekday, that is, fifth counting (i.e. inclusively) from the Lord's Day, which is called the day of Jupiter among the pagans. 'Sixth of the sabbath' is what the sixth weekday is called, which is named the day of Venus among those same pagans. The sabbath is the seventh counting (i.e. inclusively) from the Lord's Day, and the pagans dedicated it to Saturn and named it the day of Saturn. 'Sabbath' is translated from Hebrew into Latin as "rest," because on that day God rested from all his works. 11. Now, in a Christian mouth, the names for the days of the week sound better when they agree with the Church's observance. If, however, it should happen that current usage should draw someone into uttering with his lips what he deplores in his heart, let him understand that all those figures whose names have been given to the days of the week were themselves human. On account of certain mortal gifts they were very able and achieved distinction in this world, and so they were granted divine honors by their devotees both in the days and in the stars. But the stars were first named from the names of humans, and the days were named from the stars.

12. Weekdays (*feria*) were named from 'speaking' (*fari*), because on those days we have a time for speech, that is, to speak in the divine office or in human business. Of these there are festival days, instituted on behalf of humans, and holy days, for divine rites. 13. There are three parts of a day: morning, midday, and evening. 14. In the morning the light is advanced and full, no longer twilight. It is called morning (*mane*) from the adjective 'good,' because the ancients used *manus* as a word for 'good' – for what is better than light? Others think that morning is named from the 'departed spirits' (*Manes*), whose abode is between the moon and the earth. Others think the name is from 'air,' because it is *manus*, that is, rarified and transparent. 15. Midday (*meridies*) is so called as if the word were *medidies*, that is, the 'middle of the day' (*medius dies*), or because then the day is purer, for *merus* means "pure." Indeed, of the whole day nothing is brighter than midday, when the sun shines from the middle of the sky and lights the whole globe with equal clarity. 16. Evening (*suprema*) is the last part of the day, when the sun turns its course toward its setting – so called because it 'still exists' (*superesse*) up to the final part of the day. 17. The 'late hour' (*serum*) is so called from the 'door-bars' (*sera*) that are closed when night comes on, so that one may be safer in one's sleep.

18. Today (*hodie*) is as if it were 'on this day' (*hic dies*, ablative *hoc die*). And the word is *quotidie* (i.e. "daily"),

not *cotidie*, seeing that it is 'on every day' (*quot diebus*). 19. Tomorrow (*cras*, also meaning "in the future"), because it is 'hereafter.' 20. Yesterday (*hesternum*) is the day before, and called *hesternum* because that day is now apart (*extraneus*) and remote from us from its having passed by. 21. 'The day before' (*pridie*), moreover, as if it were 'on the previous day' (*priori die*). 22. 'On the day before yesterday' (*perendie*),[7] that is, 'beyond the day before' (*per ante diem*) or 'in advance,' that is, beforehand.

xxxi. Night (De nocte) 1. Night (*nox*) is so called from 'harming' (*nocere*), because it impairs the eyes. It has the light of the moon and stars, so as not to be without adornment, and so that it may comfort all those who work at night, and so that it may have sufficient light for certain living creatures that cannot tolerate sunlight. 2. Further, the alternation of night and day was made to provide the shift between sleeping and waking, so that the resting time of night may temper the effort of daily work. 3. Night occurs either because the sun is wearied from its long journey, and when it has passed over to the last stretch of the sky, grows weak and breathes its last fires as it dwindles away, or because the sun is driven under the earth by the same force by which it carries its light over the earth, so that the shadow of the earth makes night. Hence Vergil (*Aen.* 2.250):

> Night rushes from the Ocean, cloaking with its great shadow both earth and sky.

4. There are seven parts of a night: early evening, dusk, late evening, the dead of night, cockcrow, early morning, and daybreak. 5. 'Early evening' (*vesperum*) is named for the western star (i.e. Vesper), which follows the setting sun and precedes the oncoming darkness. Concerning it, Vergil (cf. *Aen.* 1.374):

> Sooner, as the heavens are closed up, does the evening star (Vesper) lay the day to rest.

6. Darkness (*tenebrae*) is so called because it 'holds shadows' (*tenere umbras*). 7. Dusk (*crepusculum*) is an uncertain light, for we call an uncertain thing 'obscure' (*creper*), that is, it is between light and darkness. 8. The 'late evening' (*conticinium*) is the time when all is silent, for to be silent is *conticescere*. 9. The 'dead of night' (*intempestum*) is the middle and inactive time (*tempus*) of night, when nothing can be done and all things are at rest in sleep, for time is not perceived on its own account, but by way of human activities, and the middle of the night lacks activity. 10. Therefore *intempestus* means "inactive," as if it were 'without time' (*sine tempore*), that is, without the activity by which time is perceived. Whence the expression, "you have arrived 'at an untimely moment' (*intempestive*)." Hence the dead of night is so called because it lacks time, that is, activity.

11. Cockcrow (*gallicinium*) is so called from cocks (*gallus*), the heralds of light. 12. The 'early morning' (*matutinum*) falls between the passing of darkness and the coming of dawn, and it is called *matutinum* because this is the time of the beginning of morning (*mane*). 13. Daybreak (*diluculum*) is as if it were the little 'light of day' (*diei lux*) just now beginning.[8] This is also called *aurora*, which comes before the sun. 14. Thus *aurora* is the prelude of the day as it grows light and the first brightness of the air, which is called ἠώς ("dawn") in Greek. By borrowing we name it *aurora*, as if it were *eorora*. Hence this verse (cf. Vergil, *Aen.* 2.417):

> And the East Wind rejoicing in its horses of dawn (*Eoos*).[9]

And (Vergil, *Aen.* 1.489):

> And the army from the east (*Eous*).

xxxii. The week (De hebdomada) The week (*hebdomada*) is so called from its seven days, whose repetition makes up the months and years and centuries – for the Greeks call seven ἑπτά. We call this a *septimana*, as if it were 'seven (*septem*) lights,' for the morning (*mane*) is light. Now the eighth day is the same as the first, the day to which the sequence of the week returns, and from which it starts again.

xxxiii. Months (De mensibus) 1. The term 'month' (*mensis*) is Greek, taken from the name of the moon, for the moon in Greek is called μήνη. Hence in Hebrew

7 Isidore seems to take *perendie*, "on the day after tomorrow," as "on the day before yesterday."

8 Isidore describes daybreak as 'little' because *diluculum* has the form of a diminutive.

9 The translation reflects the reading *Eois* from the received text of Vergil. The untranslatable *Eoos* of some early manuscripts seems to be corrupt.

the proper months are numbered not from the circuit of the sun but by the course of the moon, that is, from new moon to new moon. 2. The Egyptians, however, first reckoned the day of the month from the course of the sun, because of the swifter course of the moon, so that no error in computation would come about because of its speed, for the slower movement of the sun could be perceived more easily. 3. The month of January (*Ianuarius*) is so called from Janus, to whom it was consecrated by the pagans, or because January is the threshold and doorway (*ianua*) of the year. Hence Janus is depicted as two-faced, to display the entrance and the exit of the year. 4. February (*Februarius*) is named from Februus, that is, Pluto, for whom sacrifices were performed in that month – for the Romans consecrated January to the heavenly deities and February to the gods of the underworld. Therefore February was named from Februus, that is Pluto, not from 'fever' (*febris*), that is, a sickness. 5. March (*Martius*) was named after Mars, the founder of the Roman people, or because at that time all living things are stirred to virility (*mas*, gen. *maris*) and to the pleasures of sexual intercourse. 6. This month is also called the month of new things, because the month of March is the beginning of the year.[10] It is also called the 'new spring (*ver*),' from its signs of germination, because in that month opportunity for business deals is signaled by the new crops 'turning green' (*viridare*).

7. April (*Aprilis*) is named for Venus, as if it were *Aphrodis*, for in Greek Venus is called Ἀφροδίτη – or because in this month everything 'is opened' (*aperire*) into flower, as if it were *Aperilis*. 8. May (*Maius*) is named from Maia, the mother of Mercury, or from the elders (*maior*) who were the leading men of the state, for the Romans dedicated this month to older people, but the following one to younger people. 9. Hence the latter is called June (*Iunius*), because formerly the people were divided into 'centuries' of older and younger (*iunior*). 10. But July (*Iulius*) and August (*Augustus*) were named in honor of individual men, Julius and Augustus Caesar. Earlier these months were called Quintilis and Sextilis: Quintilis, because it was the fifth (*quintus*) month (counting inclusively) from March, which the Romans held to be the beginning of the year, and Sextilis likewise, because it was sixth (*sextus*). 11. September (*September*) takes its name from the number and from 'rain' (*imber*), because it is the seventh (*septimus*) from March and brings rain. Thus also October (*October*), November (*November*), and December (*December*) received their names from the number and *imber*. December finishes this run of numbers, because the tenth number (i.e. *decem*, "ten") closes off the preceding numbers.

12. Moreover, the Romans established the Kalends, Nones, and Ides with reference to festival days, or with reference to the offices of their magistrates, for on those days there would be an assembly in the cities. 13. Some people think that the Kalends (i.e. the first day of the month) were named after 'to worship' (*colere*), for among the ancients the beginnings of every month were worshipped, just as among the Hebrews. Most Latin speakers think the Ides were so named after 'eating' (*edere*), because among the ancients those were days for feasting. 14. The Nones were so called from *nundinae*, which are days of public assemblies or markets.

xxxiv. Solstices and equinoxes (De solstitiis et aequinoctiis) 1. A solstice (*solstitium*) is so called as if it were 'the stopping-place of the sun' (*solis statio*), because at that time, when the sun is standing still, either the day or the night begins to grow. An equinox (*aequinoctium*) is so called because at that time the day and the night have an equal period of hours. 2. There are two solstices: one is the estival, on June 24, from which time the sun begins to return to its lower circles of latitude; the other is the hibernal, December 25, when the sun begins to rise to its higher circles of latitude. Hence it follows that the hibernal solstice is the shortest day, and the estival is the longest. 3. Similarly, there are two equinoxes, the one vernal and the other autumnal, and the Greeks call them the ἰσημερίαι (cf. ἴσος, "equal"; ἥμερος, "day"). These equinoxes fall on March 25 and September 24, because the year formerly would be divided into two parts only, that is, the estival and hibernal solstices, as well as into the two celestial hemispheres.

xxxv. The seasons of the year (De temporibus anni) 1. There are four seasons of the year: spring, summer, fall, and winter. They are called seasons (*tempus*) from the 'balance of qualities' (*temperamentum*) that each shares, because each in turn blends (*temperare*) for itself the

10 In many regions during the ancient and medieval periods the year began with the month of March.

qualities of moisture, dryness, heat, and cold. The seasons are also called circuits (*curriculum*) because they do not stand still, but 'run a course' (*currere*). 2. Further, it is clear that after the world was made the seasons were divided into groups of three months because of the nature of the sun's course. The ancients divided each season, so that in its first month spring is called 'new,' in its second 'mature,' and in its third 'declining.' 3. So in its three months summer is new, mature, declining; likewise the new, mature, and declining fall, and the new, mature, and declining or 'extreme' winter. Hence the verse (cf. Vergil, *Geo.* 1.340):

> At the setting of extreme winter.

Spring (*ver*) is so called because it 'is green' (*virere*), for then, after winter, the earth is clothed with plants and everything bursts into flower. 4. Summer (*aestas*) takes its name from *aestus*, that is, "heat"; also *aestas* as if it were 'burnt' (*ustus*), that is, 'burned out' (*exustus*) and arid, for heat is arid. 5. Fall (*autumnus*) is so called from the season when the leaves of the trees fall and everything ripens.[11] 6. The condition of the celestial hemisphere (*hemisphaerium*) gave its name to winter (*hiems*), because at that time the sun wheels in a shorter course. Hence this season is also called *bruma*, as if it were βραχύς, that is, short (*brevis*). Or the name 'winter' is from food, because at that time there is a greater appetite for eating, for 'voracity' in Greek is called βρῶμα (lit. "food") – hence also a person who is squeamish about food is called *inbrumarius*. 7. The 'hibernal' (*hibernus*) time is between winter and spring, as if it were *hievernus*; this commonly signifies "winter," giving the name of its part to the whole season.

These seasons are ascribed to particular parts of the sky. 8. Thus spring is linked to the east (*oriens*), because at that time everything springs (*oriri*) from the earth; summer to the south, because that part is more flaming with heat; winter to the north, because it is numb with cold and continual frost; fall to the west, because it brings serious diseases, whence also at that time all the leaves of the trees fall.[12] The meeting of cold and heat and the conflict between different kinds of air are the reason why fall abounds with diseases.

xxxvi. Years (De annis) 1. The year is the orbit of the sun, when it returns to the same place in the heavens after the passage of 365 days. It is called a year (*annus*, cf. *anus*, "ring") because it wheels back upon itself with the recurring months – hence also a ring (*anulus*) is so called, as if it were *annuus*, that is, a circle, because it returns upon itself. So Vergil (*Geo.* 2.402):

> And the year (*annus*) wheels back upon itself along its own tracks.

2. Thus, among the Egyptians before the invention of letters, it was indicated by a dragon depicted as biting its own tail, because it turns back upon itself. Others call it *annus* from the term ἀνανεοῦσθαι (i.e. "renew"), that is, from its renewal, for it is always renewed.

3. There are three kinds of years. The lunar year is of thirty days; the solstitial year, which contains twelve months; or the great year, when all the heavenly bodies have returned to their original places, which happens after very many solstitial years. 4. The era (*aera*) of particular years (from 38 BCE) was established by Caesar Augustus, when he first described the Roman world by conducting a census. It was called an era because everyone in the world promised to render a coin (*aes*, gen. *aeris*) to the state.

xxxvii. Olympiads, lustrums, and jubilees (De olympiadibus et lustris et iubileis) 1. The Olympic games were established among the Greeks in the neighborhood of Elis, a Greek city, with the people of Elis performing a contest and competition every fifth year (i.e. counting inclusively), with four years intervening. Because of this they referred to the time cycle of the contest of the Elians as an olympiad (*olympias*), with a period of four years counted as one olympiad.[13] 2. But a lustrum is a πεντετηρίς, that is, a five-year period, because it is said to have been set in the fifth year by the Romans, following the example of the olympiads – for there was not yet a reckoning of time by consuls or by eras. It is a period of five years. It is called *lustrum* because the city of Rome was purified (*lustrare*) every five years when the census was conducted in the state. 3. A jubilee (*iubileus*) is translated as "a year of forgiveness." Both the term and the number are Hebrew. It is made up of

11 Isidore alludes to the ancient etymology, as recorded by Paulus Festus, linking *autumnus* with *augere* and *auctare*, both meaning "grow."

12 Isidore links fall with the west, the *occiduus*, toward the 'setting' (*occidere*, also meaning "perish") sun.

13 The site of the games was Olympia in the state of Elis. Elis was the name of both the state and its chief city.

seven sets of seven years, that is, forty-nine years. On the jubilee trumpets blared, and their old holdings reverted to each person, debts would be forgiven, and liberties confirmed. 4. We ourselves celebrate this number still in the number of days of Pentecost after the resurrection of the Lord, with sin forgiven and the written record of our whole debt erased, as we are freed from every trammel, receiving the grace of the Holy Spirit coming upon us.

xxxviii. Periods and ages (De saeculis et aetatibus) 1. *Saecula* consist of generations, and hence the term *saeculum*, because they 'follow' (*sequi*) one after another, for when some pass away, others take their place. Some call a *saeculum* a period of fifty years, which the Hebrews call a jubilee. 2. It was for this reason that the Hebrew who – on account of his wife and children, and loving his master – was kept in slavery with his ear pierced, was commanded to serve for a *saeculum*, that is, up to the fiftieth year (see Exodus 21:5–6). 3. An 'age' commonly means either one year, as in the annals, or seven, as one of the ages of a human, or a hundred – or any period. Hence an age is also a time composed of many centuries. And an age (*aetas*) is so called as if it were *aevitas*, that is, something similar to an aeon (*aevum*). 4. For an aeon is a perpetual age, whose beginning or end is unknown. The Greeks call this an αἰών, and they sometimes use this word for 'century,' sometimes for 'eternity' – and from Greek it was borrowed by Latin speakers. 5. The term 'age' properly is used in two ways: either as an age of a human – as infancy, youth, old age – or as an age of the world, whose first age is from Adam to Noah; second from Noah to Abraham; third from Abraham to David; fourth from David to the exile of Judah to Babylon; fifth from then, [the Babylonian captivity], to the advent of our Savior in the flesh; sixth, which is now under way, to when the world itself comes to an end. 6. The succession of these ages through generations and reigns is reviewed as follows.[14]

xxxix. A description of historical periods (De descriptione temporum) 1. The first age has the creation of the world as its beginning, for on the first day God, with the name of 'light,' created the angels; on the second, with the name of the 'firmament,' the heavens; on the third, with the name of 'division,' the appearance of waters and the earth; on the fourth, the luminaries of the sky; on the fifth, the living creatures from the waters; on the sixth, the living creatures from the earth and the human being, whom he called Adam.

The first age

2. 230 In the year 230 Adam begot Seth, from whom descended the children of God.
435 In his 205th year Seth begot Enosh, who began to call upon the Name of the Lord.
625 In his 190th year Enosh begot Kenan.
795 In his 170th year Kenan begot Mahalalel.
3. 960 In his 165th year Mahalalel begot Jared.
1122 In his 162nd year Jared begot Enoch, who was translated to heaven.
1287 In his 165th year, Enoch begot Methuselah.
4. 1454 In his 167th year, Methuselah begot Lamech.
1642 In his 188th year, Lamech begot Noah. The ark is built.
5. 2242 In the 600th year of Noah occurred the Flood. [Indeed, when Noah was 500 years old he begot three sons: Shem, Ham, and Japheth. In the 600th year of his life occurred the Flood. From Adam to this cataclysm there are 2252 years.]

The second age

2244 Two years after the Flood, [when he was 100 years old,] Shem begot Arphachshad, from whom sprang the Chaldeans.
2379 In his 135th year Arphachshad begot Shelah, from whom sprang the Samaritans and the Indians.
2509 In his 130th year Shelah begot Eber, from whom sprang the Hebrews.
6. 2643 In his 134th year Eber begot Peleg. The tower is built [and in this time occurred the division of languages, and the people were dispersed through the whole earth because of the building of the tower].
2773 In his 130th year Peleg begot Reu. The gods are first worshiped.

14 Some manuscripts add here mention of several historians who described the ages of history in detail.

2905 In his 132nd year Reu begot Serug. The kingdom of the Scythians begins.

3035 In his 130th year Serug begot Nahor.

7. The kingdom of the Egyptians is born.

3114 In his 79th year Nahor begot Terah. The kingdoms of the Assyrians and Sicinians arise.

3184 In his 70th year Terah begot Abraham. Zoroaster invented magic.

The third age

8. 3284 In his 100th year Abraham begot Isaac and Ishmael, from whom sprang the Ishmaelites.

3344 In his 60th year Isaac begot Jacob. The kingdom of the Argives begins.

3434 In his 90th year Jacob begot Joseph. Phoroneus gave laws to Greece.

9. 3544 Joseph is 110 years old. Greece begins to cultivate crops.

3688 The Hebrews' slavery [in Egypt], for 144 years. Atlas invented astronomy.

3728 Moses, 40 years. The Hebrews began to use letters.

10. 3755 Joshua, 27 years. Ericthonius in Troy [first] yoked a chariot.

3795 Othniel, 40 years. Cadmus gave letters to the Greeks.

3875 Ehud, 80 years. The fables were composed.

3915 Deborah, 40 years. Apollo [invented the art of medicine and] invented the cithara.

11. 3955 Gideon, 40 years. Mercury constructed the lyre.

3958 Abimelech, 3 years. The chorus was invented in Greece.

3981 Tola, 23 years. Priam reigned in Troy.

4003 Jair, 22 years. Carmentis invented the Latin letters.

4009 Jephthah, 6 years. Hercules cast himself into the flames.

4016 Ibzan, 7 years. Alexander (i.e. Paris) seized Helen.

4024 Abdon, 8 years. Troy was seized.

4044 Samson, 20 years. Ascanius founded Alba Longa.

12. 4084 Eli [the priest], 40 years. The Ark of the Covenant is seized.

4124 Samuel and Saul, 40 years. Homer is thought to have lived.

The fourth age

13. 4164 David, 40 years. Carthage is founded by Dido. [Gad, Nathan, and Asaph prophesied.]

4204 Solomon, 40 years. The Temple of Jerusalem is built.

14. 4221 Rohoboam, 17 years. The kingdoms of Israel and Judah are divided.

4224 Abijam, 3 years. Abimelech was chief priest under him.

4265 Asa, 41 years. Ahijah, Amos, Jehu, Joel, [and Azariah] prophesied.

15. 4290 Jehoshaphat, 25 years. Elijah, Abdiah, and Micaiah prophesied.

4298 Jehoram, 8 years. Elijah and Elisha prophesied.

4299 Ahaziah, 1 year. Elijah is taken up to heaven.

4306 Athaliah, 7 years. The priest Jehonadab became famous.

16. 4346 Jehoash, 40 years. Elisha dies.

4375 Amaziah, 29 years. Carthage founded.

4427 Uzziah, 52 years. The Olympic games are instituted by the Greeks.

4443 Jotham, 16 years. Romulus is born.

17. 4459 Ahaz, 16 years. Rome is founded.

4488 Hezekiah, 29 years. The Senate is founded in Rome.

4543 Manasseh, 55 years. The Sibyl of Samos flourished.

4555 Amon, 12 years. The first census is taken.

18. 4587 Josiah, 32 years. The philosopher Thales is well known.

4598 Jehoiakim, 11 years. Nebuchadnezzar captures Judea.

4609 Zedekiah, 11 years. The Temple of Jerusalem is burnt.

The fifth age

19. 4679 The Captivity of the Hebrews, 70 years. The story of Judith is written.

4713 Darius, 34 years. The Captivity of the Judeans ends.

4733 Xerxes, 20 years. Sophocles and Euripides are honored tragedians, [and they are considered very famous and distinguished].

20. 4773 Artaxerxes, 40 years. Ezra redacts the Law which had been burnt.

4792 Darius, [also named Nothus] 19 years. This age included Plato.

4832 Artaxerxes, 40 years. The story of Esther is completed.

21. 4858 Artaxerxes, [also named Ochus] 26 years. Demosthenes and Aristotle are published.

4862 Xerxes [the son of Ochus], 4 years. Xenocrates becomes distinguished.

4868 Darius [the son of Arsamus], 6 years. Alexander took Jerusalem.

22. 4873 Alexander [of Macedon], 5 years. [Alexander] conquered Asia.

4913 Ptolemy, 40 years. The first Book of the Machabees begins.

4951 Philadelphus, 38 years. The Septuagint translators become well known.

4977 Evergetes, 26 years. Jesus composes the Book of Wisdom.

23. 4994 Philopater, 17 years. The narration of the second Book of the Machabees.

5018 Epiphanes, 24 years. The Romans conquered the Greeks.

5053 Philometer, 35 years. Scipio conquered Africa.

24. 5082 Evergetes, 29 years. Brutus subdued Spain.

5099 Soter, 17 years. The Thracians are subjected to Roman rule.

5109 Alexander, 10 years. Syria is subjected to Roman rule.

25. 5117 Ptolemy, 8 years. The art of rhetoric begins in Rome.

5147 Dionysius, 30 years. Pompey takes Judea.

5149 Cleopatra, 2 years. Egypt comes under Roman sway.

5154 Julius [Caesar], 5 years. He first assumed sole rule.

The sixth age

26. 5210 Octavian, 56 years. Christ is born.

5233 Tiberius, 23 years. Christ is crucified.

5237 Gaius Caligula, 4 years. Matthew wrote [his] Gospel.

27. 5251 Claudius, 14 years. Mark published his Gospel.

5265 Nero, 14 years. Peter and Paul are murdered.

5275 Vespasian, 10 years. Jerusalem is sacked by Titus.

28. 5277 Titus, 2 years. He was eloquent and pious.

5293 Domitian, 16 years. John is banished to Patmos.

5294 Nerva, 1 year. John returns to Ephesus.

5313 Trajan, 19 years. The apostle John dies.

29. 5334 Hadrian, 21 years. The scholar Aquila lives.

5356 Antoninus [Pius], 22 years. Valentinus and Marcion are recognized.

5375 Antoninus [Verus], 19 years. The heresy of the Cataphrygae arises.

30. 5388 Commodus, 13 years. The scholar Theodotion lives.

5389 Helius Pertinax, 1 year. It has nothing of interest for history.

5407 Severus, 18 years. The scholar Symmachus lives.

31. 5414 Antoninus, 7 years. The fifth reconstruction of Jerusalem is devised.

5415 Macrinus, 1 year. His short life contains no noteworthy deeds.

5418 Aurelius, 3 years. Sabellius appears.

32. 5431 Alexander, 13 years. The famous Origen lives.

5434 Maximus, 3 years. He conquered the Germans.

5441 Gordianus, 7 years. He triumphed over the Parthians and Persians.

33. 5448 Philippus, 7 years. He was the first Christian emperor.

5449 Decius, 1 year. The monk Antony flourished.

5451 Gallus, 2 years. Novatus founded his heresy.

5466 Valerian, 15 years. Cyprian is crowned with martyrdom.

34. 5468 Claudius, 2 years. He expelled the Goths from Illyricum.

5473 Aurelian, 5 years. He persecutes Christians.

5474 Tacitus, 1 year. [He did nothing memorable.]

35. 5480 Probus, 6 years. The Manichean heresy arose.

5482 Carus, 2 years. He triumphed over the Persians.

5502 Diocletian, 20 years. After sacred books were burnt, he made martyrs.

5504 Galerius, 2 years. [He performed nothing worthy of recounting.]

36. 5534 Constantine, 30 years. The Nicene synod is assembled.

5558 Constantius, 24 years. The Anthropomorphite heresy rises.

5560 Julian, 2 years. From being a Christian, he became a pagan.

37. 5561 Jovianus, 1 year. He converted back to Christianity.

5575 Valentinian, 14 years. The Goths convert to heresy.

5581 Gratian, 6 years. Priscillian becomes well known.

5590 Valentinian, 9 years. Jerome is commended in Bethlehem.

5593 Theodosius, 3 years. John the Anchorite became famous.

38. 5606 Arcadius, 13 years. John Chrysostom flourished.

5621 Honorius, 15 years. Bishop Augustine became famous.

5648 Theodosius, 27 years. The heresiarch Nestorius lived.

39. 5654 Marcian, 6 years. The synod of Chalcedon is gathered.

5670 Leo the Great, 16 years. Egypt rants with the error of Dioscorus.

5687 Zenon, 17 years. The heresy of the Acephalites arose.

40. 5714 Anastasius, 27 years. Bishop Fulgentius is acclaimed.

5722 Justinus, 8 years. The heresy of the Acephalites is rejected.

5761 Justinian, 39 years. The Vandals are destroyed in Africa.

5772 Justinus, 11 years. The Armenians accept faith in Christ.

41. 5779 Tiberius, 7 years. The Langobards seize Italy.

5800 Mauricius, 21 years. The Goths convert to the Catholic faith.

5807 Phocas, 7 years. The Romans are slaughtered by the Persians.

42. 5824 Heraclius governs for the seventeenth year. [During the fourth and fifth year of the most religious ruler Sisebut] the Jews in Spain convert to Christianity.

[Thus is summarized the whole period, from the beginning of the world up to the present tenth year of the most glorious prince Recesvintus, which is the year 696 of our era, the year 5857.] The remaining time of the sixth age is known to God alone.[15]

15 Heraclius was Byzantine emperor 610–41 CE. Reckoning by the 'Spanish era' from 38 BCE, the date of the bracketed post-Isidorian interpolation is 659. Recesvintus reigned 649–72. The complex manuscript variants at the end of this book are treated by Reydellet 1966: 417–19.

Book VI

Books and ecclesiastical offices (De libris et officiis ecclesiasticis)

i. The Old and New Testament (De Veteri et Novo Testamento) 1. The Old Testament is so called because it ceased when the New came. The apostle Paul reminds us of this, saying (II Corinthians 5:17): "Old things have passed away, and behold, new things have come about." 2. One testament is called New (*Novus*) because it innovates (*innovare*). Indeed, the only ones who come to know it are those who are renewed (*renovatus*) from the old by grace and who belong now to the New Testament, which is the kingdom of heaven.

3. The Hebrews take the Old Testament, with Ezra as its redactor, as consisting of twenty-two books, corresponding to the number of letters in their alphabet. They divide these books into three classes: Law, Prophets, and Sacred Writings. 4. The first class, Law (*Lex*), is taken as being five books: of these the first is Bresith,[1] which is Genesis; second Veelle Semoth, which is Exodus; third Vaiicra, which is Leviticus; fourth Vaiedabber, which is Numbers; fifth Elleaddebarim, which is Deuteronomy. 5. These are the five books of Moses, which the Hebrews call Torah (*Thora*), and Latin speakers call the Law. That which was given through Moses is properly called the Law.

6. The second class is of Prophets (*Propheta*), in which are contained eight books, of which the first is Josua Benun, called *Iesu Nave* in Latin (i.e. the book of Joshua 'ben Nun,' the son of Nun). The second is Sophtim, which is Judges; third Samuel, which is First Kings; fourth Malachim, which is Second Kings; fifth Isaiah; sixth Jeremiah; seventh Ezekiel; eighth Thereazar, which is called the Twelve Prophets, whose books are taken as one because they have been joined together since they are short.

7. The third class is of Sacred Writings (*Hagiographa*), that is, of 'those writing about holy things' (*sacra scribens*; cf. ἅγιος, "holy"; γράφειν, "write"), in which there are nine books: first Job; second the Psalter; third Masloth, which is the Proverbs of Solomon; fourth Coheleth, which is Ecclesiastes; fifth Sir hassirim, which is the Song of Songs; sixth Daniel; seventh Dibre haiamim, which means 'words of the days' (*verba dierum*), that is Paralipomenon (i.e. Chronicles); eighth Ezra; ninth Esther.

All together these books – five, eight, and nine – make up the twenty-two as was reckoned above. 8. Some add Ruth and Cinoth, which in Latin is the Lamentations (*Lamentatio*) of Jeremiah, to the Sacred Writings, and make twenty-four books of the Old Testament, corresponding to the twenty-four Elders who stand present before the face of God (Apocalypse 4:4, etc.).

9. We also have a fourth class: those books of the Old Testament that are not in the Hebrew canon. Of these the first is the Book of Wisdom, the second Ecclesiasticus; the third Tobit; the fourth Judith; the fifth and sixth, the books of Maccabees. The Jews hold these separate among the apocrypha (*apocrypha*), but the Church of Christ honors and proclaims them among the divine books.

10. In the New Testament there are two classes: first the Gospel (*evangelicus*) class, which contains Matthew, Mark, Luke, and John, and second the Apostolic (*apostolicus*) class which contains Paul in fourteen epistles, Peter in two, John in three, James and Jude in single epistles, the Acts of the Apostles and the Apocalypse (i.e. Revelation) of John. 11. The entire content of both Testaments is characterized in one of three ways, that is, as narrative (*historia*), moral instruction (*mores*), or allegorical meaning (*allegoria*). These three are further divided in many ways: that is, what is done or said by God, by angels, or by humans; what is proclaimed by the prophets about Christ and his body [that is, the Church], about the devil and his members, about the old and the new people, about the present age and the future kingdom and judgment.

1 Retained here are Isidore's forms of transliteration of the Hebrew names for the books of the Bible: Bereshit, Weelleh Shemot, etc.

ii. The writers and names of the Sacred Books (De scriptoribus et vocabulis sanctorum librorum) 1. According to Hebrew tradition the following are accepted as authors of the Old Testament. First Moses produced the cosmography (*cosmographia*) of the divine story in the five scrolls that are called the Pentateuch. 2. The Pentateuch is so called from its five scrolls, for πέντε is "five" in Greek, and τεῦχος is "scroll." 3. The book of Genesis is so called because the beginning of the world and the begetting (*generatio*) of living creatures are contained in it. 4. Exodus recounts the exit (*exitus*) or egress of the people Israel from Egypt, whence it takes its name. 5. Leviticus is so named because it describes the services and the variety of sacrificial rites of the Levites, and in it the whole Levitical order is commented on.

6. The book of Numbers is so called because in it the tribes of the exodus from Egypt are enumerated (*dinumerare*), and the description of the forty-two journey-stages in the wilderness is contained in it (Numbers 33:1–49). 7. Deuteronomy is named with a Greek term (cf. δεύτερος, "second"; νομός, "law") which in Latin means "second law" (*secunda lex*), that is, a repetition and a prefiguration of the Gospel law; the Gospel contains the earlier matters in such a way that all things that are replicated in it are nevertheless new. 8. The book of Joshua takes its name from Jesus son of Nave, whose story it contains – in fact the Hebrews claim that its writer was this same Joshua. In this text, after the crossing of the Jordan the kingdoms of the enemy are destroyed, the land is divided for the people, and the spiritual kingdoms of the Church and the Heavenly Jerusalem are prefigured through the individual cities, hamlets, mountains, and borders.

9. Judges is named from those leaders of the people who presided over Israel after Moses and Joshua and before David and the other kings were alive. Samuel is believed to have produced this book. The book of Samuel describes the birth, priesthood, and deeds of this same Samuel, and therefore takes its name from him. 10. Although this book contains the story of Saul and David, both are still connected to Samuel, because he anointed Saul into his kingship, and he anointed David as the future king. Samuel wrote the first part of this book, and David wrote the sequel, up to its conclusion. 11. Likewise the book of Malachim is so called because it recounts in chronological order the kings of Judah and the nation of Israel along with their deeds, for Malachim is a Hebrew word that means 'Kings' (*Reges*) in Latin. Jeremiah first gathered this book into one volume, for earlier it was dispersed as the narratives of the individual kings. 12. Paralipomenon (i.e. Chronicles) is named with a Greek word; we can call it the book 'of omissions' or 'of leftovers' (cf. παραλείπειν, ppl. παραλιπόμενος, "pass over"), because what was omitted or not fully told in the Law or the books of Kings is recounted there in brief summary.

13. Some say Moses wrote the book of Job, others say one of the prophets, and some even consider that Job himself, after the calamity he suffered, was the writer, thinking that the man who underwent the struggles of spiritual combat might himself narrate the victories he procured. 14. The beginning and end of the book of Job in Hebrew is composed in prose, but the middle of it, from the place where he says (3:3), "Let the day perish wherein I was born" up to (42:6), "Therefore I reprehend myself, and do penance" all runs in heroic meter.

15. The book of Psalms is called in Greek the Psalter (*Psalterium*), in Hebrew Nabla, and in Latin *Organum*. It is called the book of Psalms because one prophet would sing to a psaltery-lute and the chorus would respond in the same tone. Moreover the Hebrew title heading the psalms is this: Sepher Thehilim, which means "scroll of hymns." 16. The authors of the psalms are those whose names are given in the titles, namely Moses, David, Solomon, Asaph, Ethan, Idithun, the sons of Core, Eman the Ezrahite and the rest, whom Ezra gathered into the one scroll. 17. Furthermore, all the psalms of the Hebrews are known to have been composed in lyric meter; in the manner of the Roman Horace and the Greek Pindar they run now on iambic foot, now they resound in Alcaic, now they glitter in Sapphic measure, proceeding on trimeter or tetrameter feet.

18. David's son Solomon, king of Israel, produced three scrolls in accordance with the number of his names (see VII.vi.65). The first of these is Masloth, which the Greeks call *Parabolae*, and the Latins call Proverbs (*Proverbia*), because in it he displayed figures of words (*verbum*) and images of the truth (*veritas*) by way of analogy. 19. Moreover he reserved the truth for his readers to interpret. He called the second book Coheleth, which in Greek means Ecclesiastes, in Latin 'The Preacher' (*Contionator*), because his speech is not directed specifically to one person, as in Proverbs, but generally to everyone, teaching that all the things that we see in the world are

fleeting and brief, and for this reason are very little to be desired. 20. He designated the third book Sir hassirim, which is translated in Latin as the Song of Songs; there he sings mystically, in the form of a wedding song, of the union of Christ and the Church. It is called the Song of Songs because it is preferred before all other songs contained in the Sacred Scriptures, just as certain things in the Law are called 'holy,' whose superiors are called the 'holy of holies.'[2] 21. The poems in these three books are said to be composed, in their own language, in hexameters and pentameters, as Josephus and Jerome write.

22. Isaiah, an evangelist more than a prophet, produced his own book, whose whole text advances in an elegant style. Its poetry runs along in hexameter and pentameter verse. 23. Jeremiah likewise published his own book together with its dirges (*threnus*), which we call Lamentations (*Lamenta*), because they are employed in times of sadness and funerals. Among them he composed four 'acrostic poems' (*alphabetum*) in varied meter. The first two of these were written in a quasi-Sapphic meter, because the three short verses that are joined to each other and begin with only one letter conclude with a heroic period. 24. The third alphabet-poem was written in trimeters, and each tercet's verses begin with a repeated triad of initial letters. The fourth alphabet-poem is said to be like the first and second. 25. Ezekiel and Daniel are held to have been written by certain wise men. Of these, Ezekiel has its opening and close wrapped up in much obscurity, whereas with clear speech Daniel proclaims the kingdoms of the world and designates the time of Christ's advent in a thoroughly open pronouncement. 26. These are the four prophets who are called Major Prophets, because they produced long scrolls.

Each book of the twelve prophets is entitled with the name of its own author. They are called the Minor Prophets because their discourses are short. 27. Hence they are joined together and contained in one scroll. Their names are Hosea, Joel, Amos, Obadiah, Jonah, Micah, Nahum, Habakkuk, Zephaniah, Haggai, Zechariah, and Malachi.

28. The book of Ezra is entitled after its own author; in its text are contained the words of Ezra himself and of Nehemiah as well. Let it not disturb anyone that we speak about a single book of Ezra, because the second, third, and fourth are not accepted among the Hebrews, but are counted among the apocrypha. 29. Ezra is thought to have written the book of Esther, in which that queen is described as having snatched her people, as a figure of the Church of God, from slavery and death. Because Aman, who signifies wickedness, was killed, the celebration of that day (i.e. Purim) has been passed down to posterity.

30. The book of Wisdom (*Sapientia*) never existed in Hebrew, whence even its title is more redolent of Greek eloquence. The Jews say this book is by Philo,[3] and it is appropriately named Wisdom because in it the advent of Christ, who is the Wisdom of the Father, and his passion are clearly expressed. 31. Jesus the son of Sirach, of Jerusalem, grandson of the high priest Jesus, of whom Zechariah makes mention (Zechariah 3:1, etc.), most surely composed the book Ecclesiasticus. Among Latin speakers this book is designated with the superscription of Solomon, because of the similarity of its style. 32. It is called Ecclesiasticus because, with great care and orderliness, it has been published about the teaching of the religious way of life of the whole Church (*Ecclesia*). This book is found among Hebrew speakers, but is regarded as belonging to the apocrypha. 33. By what authors the books of Judith, Tobit, or Maccabees were written has not been established at all. They take their titles from the names of those whose deeds they inscribe.

34. The four Evangelists (*Evangelista*) wrote severally the four Gospels (*Evangelium*). 35. First in Judea Matthew wrote his Gospel in Hebrew characters and words, taking as his starting point for spreading the gospel (*evangelizare*) the human birth of Christ, saying (1:1): "The book of the generation of Jesus Christ, the son of David, the son of Abraham" – meaning that Christ descended bodily from the seed of the patriarchs, as was foretold in the prophets through the Holy Spirit. 36. Second, Mark, in Italy, filled with the Holy Spirit, wrote in Greek the Gospel of Christ, having followed Peter as a disciple. He began his Gospel with a prophetic spirit, saying (1:3, quoting the prophet Isaiah 40:3): "A voice of one crying in the desert: Prepare ye the way of the Lord" – so that he might show that after his assumption

2 Isidore refers to the Hebrew use of the genitive plural to express the superlative degree.

3 Alternatively this clause may mean, "They say that this book is by Philo Judaeus."

of flesh Christ preached the Gospel in the world. Now Christ also has been called a prophet, as is written (Jer. 1:5): "I made thee a prophet unto the nations."

37. Third, Luke, most polished in his Greek of all the evangelists, in fact wrote his Gospel in Greece, where he was a physician. He wrote it to Bishop Theophilus, beginning with a priestly spirit, saying (1:5): "There was in the days of Herod, the king of Judea, a priest, Zechariah" – so that he might show that Christ after his birth in the flesh and his preaching of the Gospel was made a sacrificial victim for the salvation of the world. 38. For Christ himself is the priest of whom it is said in Psalms (109:4): "Thou art a priest forever according to the order of Melchizedech." When Christ came, the priesthood of the Jews grew silent, and their law and prophecy ceased. 39. Fourth, John wrote the last Gospel in Asia, beginning with the Word, so that he might show that the same Savior who deigned to be born and to suffer for our sake was himself the Word of God before the world was, the same who came down from heaven, and after his death went back again to heaven.

40. These are the four Evangelists, whom the Holy Spirit symbolized through Ezechiel (1:10) as four animals. The animals are four because, by their preaching, the faith of the Christian religion has been disseminated through the four corners of the earth. 41. They are moreover called animals (*animalia*) because the Gospel of Christ is preached for the sake of the soul (*anima*) of a person. And they are full of eyes inside and outside, because they foresee the Gospels which have been spoken by the prophets, and which he promised in former times. 42. Further, their legs are straight, because there is nothing crooked in the Gospels. Their wings are sixfold, covering their legs and faces, because things that were hidden until the coming of Christ have been revealed. 43. Moreover, 'Gospel' (*evangelium*) means "good news" (*bona adnuntiatio*), for in Greek εὖ means 'good,' ἀγγελία means 'news.' Hence 'angel' (*angelus*) means "bringer of news."

44. Paul the Apostle wrote fourteen epistles of his own. He wrote nine of them to seven churches, and the rest to his disciples Timothy, Titus, and Philemon. 45. Most Latin speakers are doubtful whether the Epistle to the Hebrews is by Paul, because of the dissonance of its style, and some suspect that Barnabas collaborated in its writing, and others that it was written by Clement. 46. Peter wrote the two epistles under his name, which are called the Catholic (i.e. 'universal') Epistles because they were written not to one people or city only, but generally to every nation. 47. James and John and Jude wrote their own epistles.

48. The Acts of the Apostles sets down the beginnings of the Christian faith among the gentiles and the story of the nascent Church. Luke the Evangelist is the writer of the Acts of the Apostles; in this work the infancy of the young Church is woven, and the history of the apostles is contained – whence it is called the Acts of the Apostles. 49. John the Evangelist wrote the Apocalypse during the period when, exiled for his preaching of the Gospel, he was sent to the isle of Patmos. *Apocalypsis* is translated from Greek into Latin as 'revelation' (*revelatio*), and a revelation means a manifestation of things that were hidden, as John himself says (Apoc. 1:1): "The Revelation (*Apocalypsis*) of Jesus Christ, which God gave unto him, to make known to his servants."

50. These are the writers of the sacred books who, speaking through the Holy Spirit, for our education drew up in writing both precepts for living and the pattern for belief. 51. The other volumes aside from these are called *apocrypha*. They are called the apocrypha, that is, the secret things (cf. ἀπόκρυφος, "hidden"), because they have come into doubt; their origin is hidden and is not evident to the Church Fathers, from whom the authority of the true scriptures has come down to us by a very sure and well-known succession. 52. Although some truth is found in the apocrypha, nevertheless because of their many falsities there is no canonical authority in them. These are rightly judged by the wise as not to be regarded as the works of those to whom they are ascribed. 53. Indeed, many works are produced by heretics under the names of prophets, and more recently under the names of apostles, all of which have, as a result of diligent examination, been set apart from canonical authority under the name of apocrypha.

iii. Libraries (De bibliothecis) 1. A library (*bibliotheca*) took its name from Greek, because books are deposited there, for βιβλίων means "of books" (*liber*) and θήκη means "repository." 2. After the Law (i.e. Torah) was burned by the Chaldeans, the scribe Ezra, inspired with the divine spirit, restored the library of the Old Testament when the Jews had returned to Jerusalem, and he corrected all the scrolls of the Law and Prophets, which had been corrupted by the gentiles, and he ordered the whole Old Testament into twenty-two books, so that there might be as many books in the Law (i.e. the Old Testament) as they had letters of the alphabet. 3. Among the Greeks, however, the Athenian tyrant Pisistratus is thought to have been the first to establish a library. Afterwards, when Athens was burned, Xerxes brought this library, which had been augmented by the Athenians, to Persia; after a long time Seleucus Nicanor brought it back to Greece. 4. Hence arose, in kings and in other cities, a desire to procure the scrolls of diverse nations and to render them into Greek by translators. 5. Thus Alexander the Great and his successors set their minds to building libraries with every book. Ptolemy in particular, known as Philadelphus, and very perceptive about all kinds of literature, collected for his library not only pagan authors, but even divine literature, because he emulated Pisistratus in his zeal for libraries. In his time seventy thousand books could be found in Alexandria.

iv. Translators (De interpretibus) 1. This Ptolemy, moreover, seeking from the pontifex Eleazar the writings of the Old Testament, was responsible for the translation from Hebrew into Greek, by seventy scholars, of the writings, which he held in the Alexandrian library. 2. Although they were separated, each apart in his own chamber, through the Holy Spirit they translated everything in such a way that nothing was found in the manuscript of any of them that was different from the rest, even in the order of words. 3. There were also other translators who translated the sacred writings from Hebrew into Greek, such as Aquila, Symmachus, and Theodotion, and also that common (*vulgaris*) translation (i.e. the early Latin translation called *Itala* or *Vetus Latina*), whose authorship is not evident – for this reason the work is designated the Fifth Edition (*Quinta Editio*) without the name of the translator. 4. Furthermore, Origen provided a sixth and seventh edition with amazing diligence, and compared them with the other editions. 5. Also the priest Jerome, skilled in three languages, translated the same Scriptures from Hebrew into Latin speech, and rendered them eloquently. His translation (i.e. the Vulgate) is deservedly preferred over the others, for it is closer in its wording, and brighter in the clarity of its thought, [and, inasmuch as it is by a Christian, the translation is truer].

v. The one who first brought books to Rome (De eo qui primum Romam libros advexit) 1. Aemilius Paulus first brought a good supply of books to Rome after he had conquered Perseus, king of Macedonia; then Lucullus, from the Pontic spoils. After these, Caesar gave to Marcus Varro the task of constructing the largest library possible. 2. Pollio first made libraries, Greek as well as Latin, for public use at Rome, with statues of the authors added in an atrium that he had built most magnificently from spoils.

vi. Those who established libraries among us Christians (Qui apud nos bibliothecas instituerunt) 1. Among us the martyr Pamphilus, whose life Eusebius of Caesarea wrote, first strove to equal Pisistratus in his zeal for a sacred library. He had about thirty thousand volumes in his library. 2. Also Jerome and Gennadius, searching systematically through the whole world, hunted down ecclesiastical writers, and they enumerated their works in a one-volume catalogue.

vii. Those who have written many things (Qui multa scripserunt) 1. Among Latin speakers, Marcus Terentius Varro wrote innumerable books. Among the Greeks likewise Chalcenterus (i.e. Didymus) is exalted with great praise because he published so many books that any of us would be hard put merely to copy out in our own hand such a number of works by another. 2. From us (i.e. Christians) also Origen, among the Greeks, in his labor with the Scriptures has surpassed both Greeks and Latins by the number of his works. In fact Jerome says that he has read six thousand of his books. 3. Still, Augustine with his intelligence and learning overcomes the output of all these, for he wrote so much that not only could no one, working by day and night, copy his books, but no one could even read them.

viii. The types of literary works (De generibus opusculorum) 1. There are three genres of 'literary works' (*opusculum*). The first kind are extracts (*excerptum*), which in Greek are called *scholia*, in which things that seem obscure or difficult are outlined in brief summary. 2. The second kind are homilies (*homilia*), which Latin speakers call 'talks' (*verbum*), which are delivered before the public. Third are tomes (*tomus*), which we call books or volumes. Homilies are spoken to the common people, but tomes, that is, books, are longer discourses.

A dialogue (*dialogus*) is a conversation of two or more people; Latin speakers call it a discussion. What the Greeks call dialogues we call discussions. 3. A discussion (*sermo*) is so called because it is interwoven (*serere*) between each of the two participants. Whence in Vergil (*Aen.* 6.160):

> They interwove many things in varied discussion (*sermo*) between themselves.

A treatise is . . . 4. One may distinguish a discussion, a treatise (*tractatus*), and a talk (*verbum*): a discussion requires a second person, a treatise is specifically directed toward oneself, but a talk is directed toward everyone. Whence it is said, "He addressed a talk to the public." 5. Commentaries (*commentarium*) are so called as if the term were 'with the mind' (*cum mente*); they are interpretations, like comments on the law, comments on the Gospel. 6. An apology (*apologeticum*) is an excusing (*excusatio*), in which some people are wont to respond to their accusers. It is presented in defense or denial only; the term is Greek. 7. A panegyric (*panegyricum*) is an extravagant and immoderate form of discourse in praise of kings; in its composition people fawn on them with many lies. This wickedness had its origin among the Greeks, whose practised glibness in speaking has with its ease and incredible fluency stirred up many clouds of lies.

8. The books of festival-registers (*fasti*) are those in which kings or consuls are registered, so called from fasces (*fasces*), that is, from their power. Whence Ovid's books are called the *Fasti*, because they were published on the subject of kings and consuls. 9. A proem (*prooemium*) is the beginning of a discourse, for proems are the first parts of books, which are joined on before the presentation of the main matter in order to prepare the ears of the audience. Many, skilled in their Latinity, use the name 'proem' without translation, but among us the translated term has the name 'preface' (*praefatio*; cf. *praefari*, ppl. *praefatus*, "speak beforehand"), as it were a pre-speaking (*praelocutio*).

10. Commandments (*praeceptum*) are statements that teach what ought to be done or what ought not to be done. What ought to be done, as "love [the Lord] thy God" and "honor thy father and thy mother." What ought not to be done, as "thou shalt not commit adultery," "thou shalt not steal." 11. Similarly the commandments of the pagans either enjoin or forbid. They order that something be done, as (Vergil, *Geo.* 1.299):

> Naked plow, naked sow.

They forbid, as (Vergil, *Geo.* 2.299):

> Do not sow the hazel among the vines, nor reach for the highest shoot.

12. Among the Hebrews Moses first wrote commandments; among Latin speakers the soothsayer Marcius first devised commandments, among which is this (1): "Be the last to speak, the first to grow silent."

13. Parables (*parabola*) and enigmas (*problema*) indicate by their names that they need to be examined rather deeply. A parable in fact displays the likeness of some thing. Although it is a Greek term, it has been appropriated into Latin. It is known that in parables what are called likenesses of the things are compared with the things in question. 14. But enigmas, which are called posers (*propositio*) in Latin, are questions involving a matter that must be resolved by disputation. 15. A question (*quaestio*) is an inquiry (*quaesitio*), when one inquires whether a thing exists, what it is, and what sort of thing it is. 16. An argument (*argumentum*) is so called as if it were sharp (*argutus*), or because it is keenly (*argute*) devised for verifying things. 17. Greeks speak appropriately of a 'letter' (*epistola*) – and it is translated "missive" (*missa*) in Latin – for στόλα or στόλοι are 'things sent off' (*missa*) or 'people sent off' (*missi*). 18. Before the use of papyrus sheets or parchment, the contents of letters were written on shingles hewn from wood, whence people called the bearers of these 'tablet-couriers' (*tabellarius*).

ix. Wax tablets (De ceris) 1. 'Wax tablets' (*cera*) are the stuff of letters, the nourishers of children; indeed (cf. Dracontius, *Satisfactio* 63),

> They give intelligence to boys, the onset of sense.

The Greeks are reported as first to have passed down the use of wax tablets, for Greeks and Etruscans first wrote on wax tablets with an iron stylus. Afterwards the Romans commanded that no one should own an iron stylus (*graphium ferreum*). 2. Hence it was said among scribes, "You shall not strike wax with iron."[4] Afterwards it was established that they would write on wax tablets with bones, as Atta indicates in his *Satura*, saying (cf. 12):

> Let us turn the plowshare and plow in the wax with a point of bone.

The Greek term *graphium* is *scriptorium* in Latin, for γραφή is 'writing' (*scriptura*).

x. Papyrus sheets (De cartis) 1. Egypt first provided the use of papyrus sheets, initially in the city of Memphis. Memphis is the Egyptian city where the use of papyrus sheets was first discovered, as Lucan says (cf. *Civil War* 4.136):

> The sheet of Memphis is made from the bibulous papyrus.

He called papyrus bibulous (*bibulus*) because it drinks (*bibere*) liquid. 2. A 'papyrus sheet' (*carta*) is so called because the stripped rind of papyrus is glued together 'piece by piece' (*carptim*). There are several kinds of such sheets. First and foremost is the Royal Augustan, of rather large size, named in honor of Octavian Augustus. 3. Second, the Libyan, in honor of the province of Libya. Third the Hieratic, so called because it was selected for sacred books (cf. ἱερός, "sacred") – like the Augustan, but tinted. 4. Fourth the Taeneotic, named for the place in Alexandria (i.e. Tanis) where it was made, which is so called. Fifth the Saitic, from the town of Sais. 5. Sixth the Cornelian, first produced by Cornelius Gallus, prefect of Egypt. Seventh the commercial, because merchandise is wrapped in this type, since it is less suitable for writing.

xi. Parchment (De pergamenis) 1. Because the kings of Pergamum lacked papyrus sheets, they first had the idea of using skins. From these the name 'parchment' (*pergamena*), passed on by their descendents, has been preserved up to now. These are also called skins (*membranum*) because they are stripped from the members (*membrum*) of livestock. 2. They were made at first of a muddy color, that is, yellowish, but afterwards white parchment was invented at Rome. This was obviously unsuitable, because it soils easily and harms the readers' eyesight – as the more experienced of architects would not think of putting gilt ceiling panels in libraries, or any paving stones other than of Carystean marble, because the glitter of gold wearies the eyes, and the green of the Carystean marble refreshes them. 3. Likewise those who are learning money-changing put dark green cloths under the forms of the coins, and carvers of gems look repeatedly at the backs of scarab beetles, than which nothing is greener, and painters [do the same, in order that they may refresh the labor of their sight with the greenness of these scarabs].

4. Parchment comes in white or yellowish or purple. The white exists naturally. Yellowish parchment is of two colors, because one side of it is dyed, that is yellowed, by the manufacturer. With regard to this, Persius (*Satires* 3.10):

> Now the book and the two-colored parchment with its hair scraped smooth.[5]

5. But purple parchment is stained with purple dye; on it melted gold and silver on the letters stands out.[6]

xii. Bookmaking (De libris conficiendis) 1. Among the pagans, certain categories of books were made in fixed sizes. Poems and epistles were in a smaller format, but histories were written in a larger size. They were made not only on papyrus sheets or on parchment, but also on the intestinal membranes of elephants[7] or on the interwoven leaves of mallows or palms. 2. Cinna mentions this type thus (cf. fr. 11):

> On Prusias's boat I have brought as a gift for you these poems through which we know the aerial fires, poems much studied over with Aratus's midnight lamps, written on the dry bark of smooth mallow.[8]

3. It first became usual to trim books in Sicily, for at first they were smoothed by pumice, whence Catullus says (1.1):

> To whom am I giving my charming new little book just now smoothed with dry pumice?

4 The maxim plays on *ferrum*, "iron object, sword."

5 The lighter and darker faces of parchment sheets correspond to the flesh and hair side of the skin. But Isidore, perhaps along with Persius, refers to tinted parchment.

6 Isidore refers to deluxe books, some still extant, made with gold and silver lettering on purple sheets.

7 A word for ivory (*elephantus*) also means "elephant," perhaps causing a confusion registered here.

8 Or, ". . . in a dry little book of smooth mallow-leaves."

xiii. The terminology of books (De librorum vocabulis) 1. A codex is composed of many books; a book is of one scroll. It is called a codex (*codex*) by way of metaphor from the trunks (*codex*) of trees or vines, as if it were a wooden stock (*caudex*, i.e. an older form of the word *codex*), because it contains in itself a multitude of books, as it were of branches. 2. A scroll (*volumen*) is a book so called from rolling (*volvere*), as we speak of the scrolls of the Law and the scrolls of the Prophets among the Hebrews. 3. *Liber* is the inner membrane of bark, which clings to the wood. With regard to this, Vergil thus (cf. *Ecl.* 10.67):

> The bark (*liber*) clings to the high elm.

Whence what we write on is called a book (*liber*) because before the use of papyrus sheets or parchment, scrolls were made – that is, joined together – from the inner bark of trees. Whence those who write are called copyists (*librarius*) after the bark of trees.

xiv. Copyists and their tools (De librariis et eorum instrumentis) 1. Formerly they called copyists *bibliopolae*, for the Greeks call a book βίβλος. Copyists are called by that name, and also 'antiquarians' (*antiquarius*), but copyists write both new and old things, antiquarians only old things, whence they have taken their name. 2. The scribe (*scriba*) got his name from writing (*scribere*), expressing his function by the character of his title. 3. The scribe's tools are the reed-pen and the quill, for by these the words are fixed onto the page. A reed-pen is from a tree; a quill is from a bird. The tip of a quill is split into two, while its unity is preserved in the integrity of its body, I believe for the sake of a mystery, in order that by the two tips may be signified the Old and New Testament, from which is pressed out the sacrament of the Word poured forth in the blood of the Passion. 4. The reed-pen (*calamus*) is so called because it places liquid, whence among sailors 'to place' is *calare*. 5. A quill (*pinna*) is so called from 'hanging' (*pendere*), that is, flying, for it comes, as we have said, from birds. 6. The leaves (*folia*, i.e. *folium*) of books are so called from their likeness to the leaves (*folium*) of trees, or because they are made of leather sacks (*follis*), that is, of the skins that are customarily stripped from slaughtered livestock. The sides of leaves are called pages (*pagina*) because they are bound (*compingere*, perfect tense *compegi*) to one another.

7. A verse (*versus*, also meaning "furrow") is commonly so called because the ancients would write in the same way that land is plowed: they would first draw their stylus from left to right, and then 'turn back' (*convertere*) the verses on the line below, and then back again to the right – whence still today country people call furrows *versus*. 8. A slip (*scheda*) is a thing still being emended, and not yet redacted into books; its name is Greek, as is *tomus* (i.e. "piece of papyrus").[9]

xv. Canon-tables of the Gospels (De canonibus Evangeliorum) 1. Ammonius of Egypt first devised the canon-tables (*canon*) of the Gospels; following him, Eusebius of Caesarea drew them up more fully.[10] These were made so that we can find out and know where one Gospel writer said things similar to the others, or where a passage was his alone. 2. These canon-tables are ten in number, of which the first contains the numbers indicating passages where the four say the same things: Matthew, Mark, Luke, and John. The second, where three: Matthew, Mark, Luke. The third, where three: Matthew, Luke, John. The fourth, where three: Matthew, Mark, John. 3. The fifth, where two: Matthew, Luke. The sixth, where two: Matthew, Mark. The seventh, where two: Matthew, John. The eighth, where two: Luke, Mark. The ninth, where two: Luke, John. 4. The tenth, in which individual evangelists say certain things of their own.[11]

The explanation of these things is this. Each passage of the Gospels has been assigned a number, and this number is noted down beside the passage. Under each of these passage-numbers there is a certain table-number (*aera*) in red, indicating which canon table (i.e. of the ten canon-tables listed above) contains the passage-number under which this table-number has been placed. 5. For example, if the table-number is 1, then the passage-number is in the first canon-table (i.e. the table where parallel passages in all four Gospels are found); if it is 2,

9 Here Isidore seems to use *tomus* in its classical sense, whereas in viii.2 above he uses the term in its later sense, "tome."

10 Eusebius's canon-tables, compiled *ca.* 330, regularly preceded the Gospels; they were a set of keys, arranged in columns, that indicated parallel passages in the Gospels. Eusebius also assigned sequential numbers to passages in the Bible; our chapter and verse divisions were made much later.

11 The missing combinations of Gospel readings common to more than one Gospel – e.g., to Mark and John only – are rare.

then the passage-number is in the second canon-table; if 3, then it is in the third canon-table, and so on in order up to 10. 6. Therefore, if you have one of the Gospels open and want to know which of the evangelists say similar things, start with the passage-number lying alongside the text, and then look for that same passage-number in the canon table indicated by the table-number. There you will find how many evangelists said this passage, and which ones. So, precisely because they are indicated by their own numbers, you will find in the body of the text of each of the Gospels those places that you have looked for that have said the same things.

xvi. The canons of Councils (De canonibus Conciliorum) 1. Canon (*canon*) is a Greek word; in Latin, 'measuring rod' (*regula*). A measuring rod is so called because it draws 'in a straight line' (*recte*), and never goes astray. Some say a measuring rod is so called because it rules (*regere*), or because it offers a norm of living correctly (*recte*), or because it corrects (*corrigere*) anything distorted or wicked. 2. The canons of general councils began in the time of Constantine, for in earlier years, with persecution raging, there was little opportunity for teaching the common people. 3. For this reason Christianity was rent with diverse heresies, because there was no freedom [for bishops] to assemble together until the time of the aforementioned emperor – for he gave Christians the power to congregate freely. 4. Under Constantine the holy Fathers, gathering from all the world in the Nicene Council, promulgated in accordance with evangelic and apostolic faith the second (Nicene) Creed, following after the Apostles' Creed.

5. Of the councils of the church the venerable synods which were foremost in encompassing the whole faith are four, like the four Gospels, or the four rivers of Paradise. 6. The first of these, the Nicene synod of 318 bishops, took place while Constantine Augustus was emperor. In it was condemned the blasphemy of the Arian treachery about the inequality of the holy Trinity, championed by that same Arius. This holy synod established through its creed that God the Son is consubstantial with God the Father. 7. The second synod, of 150 Fathers, was gathered at Constantinople under the elder Theodosius. Condemning Macedonius, who denied that the Holy Spirit was God, it showed that the Holy Spirit is consubstantial with the Father and the Son, rendering the form of the creed that the whole [confession] of Latin and Greek speakers proclaim in churches. 8. The third, the first Ephesian synod, of 200 bishops, was held under Theodosius Augustus the younger. It condemned with a just charge of anathema Nestorius, who claimed that there were two persons in Christ; it showed that in two natures abides the one person of [our] Lord Jesus Christ.

9. The fourth, the synod of Chalcedon, of 630 priests, was held under the emperor Marcian. In this synod the unanimous judgment of the Fathers condemned Eutyches, an abbot of Constantinople, who preached that there was one nature both of the Word of God and of his flesh, and his defender Dioscorus, formerly bishop of Alexandria, and again Nestorius with the other heretics. This same synod preached that Christ the Lord was born of the Virgin, and consequently we acknowledge that in Christ is the substance of both divine and human nature. 10. These are the four principal synods, most abundantly preaching the doctrine of our faith; and any other councils that the holy Fathers, filled with the spirit of God, ratified endure in all their vigor supported by the authority of these four, whose accomplishments are recorded in this work (i.e. in Isidore's source, *PL* 84.91–2).

11. 'Synod' (*synodus*), from the Greek, is translated "company" or "assembly." 12. The term 'council' is drawn from Roman custom, for when issues were under discussion everyone would gather together and deliberate with common vigilance. Whence 'council' (*concilium*) takes its name from common (*communis*) vigilance, as if it were *comcilium*, for the Latin *cilia* (i.e. "eyelids") pertain to eyes. Whence a 'court of justice' (*considium*) is a council, with the letter *d* changing to *l*. 13. An assembly (*coetus*) is a gathering (*conventus*) or congregation, from the verb gather (*coire*, ppl. *coitus*) that is, 'coming together' (*convenire*) in one. From this a convent (*conventum*, i.e. a monastic convent, usually *conventus*) is named, just as a *conventus* is a gathering, an assembly, from the association of many in one.

xvii. The Easter cycle (De cyclo Paschali) 1. Hippolytus, bishop in the times of the emperor Alexander, first wrote out the Easter cycle. After him those most esteemed authorities Eusebius of Caesarea, Theophilus of Alexandria, together with Prosper of Aquitaine and Victorius, with their extended reckonings of that same feast, promulgated many cycles. 2. The most blessed Cyril, bishop of Alexandria, calculating the reckoning of Easter Day over ninety-five years as a result of five nineteens, indicated with the greatest brevity at what point in the calendar or at what day of the lunar cycle the Easter feast should be celebrated. 3. It is called a cycle (*cyclum*) because it is set out in the form of a wheel, and arranged as if it were in a circle (*circulum*) it comprises the order of the years without variation and without any artifice. 4. Whence it happened that poems on any subject made with a single verse-form may be called cyclic. It is called a table (*laterculum*, lit. "brickwork") because it lays out the order of the years in rows.[12]

5. The first cycle of nineteen:

		Of the moon
B.	C. ii Ides	April xx
	C. vi Kalends	April xvi
	E. xvi Kalends	May xvii
	C. vi Ides	April xx
B.	C. x Kalends	April xv
	E. ii Ides	April xvi
	C. ii Nones	April xix
	E. viii Kalends	May xx
B.	C. v Ides	April xv

When this cycle is complete one returns to the beginning. [The years are computed from the creation of the world up to this most recent cycle.] 10. In ancient times the Church would celebrate the paschal season with the Jews on the fourteenth day of the moon, on whatever day of the week it fell. The holy Fathers prohibited this celebration at the Nicene synod, legislating that one should seek out not only the paschal moon and month, but also should observe the day of the Lord's resurrection; and because of this they extended the paschal season from the fourteenth day of the moon to the twenty-first day, so that Sunday would not be passed over.[13]

11. The term 'pasch' (*pascha*, i.e. Easter Day) is not Greek but Hebrew, and it derives not from 'suffering' – for πάσχειν in Greek means "suffer" – but from the Hebrew word *pasch*, meaning "passover" (*transitus*), because at that time the people of God passed over (*transire*, ppl. *transitus*) out of Egypt. Whence the Gospel (John 13:1) says, "Jesus knowing that his hour was come, that he should pass out (*transire*) of this world to the Father." 12. Easter Eve is held as a continuous vigil because of the coming of our king and God, so that the time of his resurrection might find us not sleeping but vigilant. The reason for this night's vigil is twofold: it is because on that night he then received life, although he suffered death, or because at the same hour at which he was resurrected he will afterwards come for the Judgment. 13. Moreover we celebrate Easter Day in that manner not only to call to mind the death and resurrection of Christ, but also to ponder the other things that are attested concerning him, with regard to the meaning of the sacraments. 14. This is for the sake of the beginning of a new life and for the sake of the new person whom we are commanded to put on, taking off the old, purging out "the old leaven" that we may be "a new dough . . . for Christ our pasch is sacrificed" (I Corinthians 5:7).

Therefore because of this newness of life the first month of the new things (i.e. the new crops; see Exodus 23:15 etc.) in the months of the year is mystically attributed to the paschal celebration. 15. Indeed, that Easter Day is celebrated on a day of the third week – that is on a day that falls from the fourteenth to the twenty-first – signifies that in the whole time of the world, which is accomplished in "a week of days," this holy event has now opened up the third age. 16. For the first age is before the Mosaic law, the second under the law, and the third under grace; where the sacrament is now manifest, earlier it was hidden in prophetic enigma. It is also because of these three ages of the world that the resurrection of the Lord is on the third day. 17. That we find Easter Day among the seven days from the fourteenth to the twenty-first of the new moon is because of that number seven, by which a meaning of wholeness is often figured. That number is even given to the Church itself because of its image of wholeness, whence the apostle John in the Apocalypse writes to seven churches. 18. But the Church, still set in that mortality of the flesh, because of its own mutability is designated by the name of the moon in Scripture.

19. Different observance produces from time to time an error of opinions about the Easter feast day. The Latin

12 At this point Isidore supplies an Easter calendar for the ninety-five year period from 627 through 721, giving in two columns the day of the month in Roman reckoning with the corresponding day of the lunar month, always in April or May. We print here only the first few entries; Isidore's table displays five lunar cycles of nineteen years each, for a total of ninety-five rows. In this calendar the "common" years, of twelve lunar months, are marked 'C.,' the "embolismic" years, of thirteen lunar months, are marked 'E.,' and the "bissextile" or leap years, 'B.' Each 19-year cycle contains twelve common years and seven embolismic years. For these terms, see below.

13 That is, henceforth Easter Day was to be celebrated on Sunday, whatever the date of the Jewish Passover.

Church locates the moon of the first month (i.e. of the Roman calendar's year) from March 5 through April 3, and if the fifteenth day of the new moon should fall on a Sunday, Easter Day is moved forward to the next Sunday. 20. The Greek Church observes the moon of the first month from March 8 through April 5, and if the fifteenth day of the new moon should fall on a Sunday, they celebrate holy Easter then. Dissension of this kind between the two camps confuses the Easter liturgy.

21. A year that has only twelve lunar months, that is, 354 days, is called 'common.' It is called common (*communis*) because often two occur so 'connected together' (*coniunctus*) that they immediately follow one another in the (table for calculating the) Easter celebration – for an embolismic (i.e. intercalated) year always occurs alone. 22. An embolismic (*embolismus*) year has thirteen lunar months, that is, 384 days. That year was prophetically revealed to the holy Moses; in an embolismic year those who lived very far away were ordered to celebrate the pasch in the second month (see Numbers 9:10–11). 23. Further 'embolism' is a Greek term that is translated 'further addition' (*superaugmentum*) in Latin because it fills out the count of days of the common years, in which eleven lunar days are observed to be missing. 24. Moreover, embolismic and common years are found in this way. If there have been 384 days from the fourteenth day of the new moon of one Easter Day to the fourteenth day of its successor, the year is embolismic; if 354, common.

25. The 'bissextus' is the day added every four years, for in each year it grows a quarter of a whole unit, but when it has completed a unit in the fourth year, the bissextile day is made. 26. It is called the bissextus because twice six (*bis sexies*) reckoned up makes a whole unit (i.e. of the twelve ounces in a Roman pound), which is one day – just as a quarter-unit (*quadrans*) is reckoned up by four times (*quater*) – because a bissextus is how far the sun goes beyond the course of the days in the year, [or because it is not able to be intercalated in its own year unless you compute 'twice the sixth' (*bis sextus*) day before the nones of March, that is, both with the first day as the sixth day before the nones of March and, with the bissextus added, with the second day repeated as the sixth day before the nones of March]. 27. Further, from the sixth day before the nones of March through the day before the Kalends of January the bissextus is taken into account in the course of the moon, and afterwards it is removed.

28. Intercalary (*intercalaris*) days are so called because they are interposed (*interponere*) so that the reckoning of the sun and the moon may be reconciled, for *calare* means "pose," and *intercalare* means "interpose." 29. What Greeks call 'epacts' (*epacta*) the Latins call 'annual lunar additions,' which run through a cycle from eleven to thirty days. The Egyptians add epacts to make the lunar measurement equal to the reckoning of the sun. 30. For the moon in its course is known to shine twenty-nine and a half days, so that there are 354 (i.e. 12 × 29.5) days in a lunar year; there remain in the course of a solar year eleven days, which the Egyptians add (*adicere*). 31. Hence they are called additions (*adiectio*). Without these epacts you would not find what point of the lunar cycle corresponds to a given year and month and day. Those epacts are always added on March 22, on the same day of the moon that falls on that date. 32. There are nineteen years in the (Metonic) cycle, but when the epacts add up to twenty-nine, which is in the nineteenth year of the cycle, at that point you do not add eleven epacts to the twenty-nine in the following year, such that you would get ten after subtracting thirty, but you start again with eleven.

xviii. The other liturgical feasts (De reliquis festivitatibus) 1. A 'festal celebration' (*festivitas*) is so called from 'festal days' (*festus dies*), as if the word were *festiditas*, because during those days only sacred activities are carried out. The contrary to these are court-days (*fasti*), on which the law 'speaks' (*fari*, ppl. *fatus*), that is, is pronounced. A 'solemn feast' (*sollemnitas*) is so called from its holy rites, a day adopted in such a way that for religious reasons it ought not to be changed. It is named from 'customary' (*solitus*), that is, firm and solid (*solidus*), [or because it is customarily (*solere*) performed in the church year]. 2. A celebration (*celebritas*) moreover is so called because during it earthly activity is not carried out, but only celestial (*caelestis*) activities.

3. Easter Day is the first of all the feasts; we have spoken of this term above. 4. Like the Passover, Pentecost was a feast day among the Hebrews, because it was celebrated five tens of days after the Passover – whence it takes its name, for πέντε means "five" in Greek. On that day according to the Law the 'loaves of proposition' would be offered from the new crops (Exodus 25:30, etc.). 5. The jubilee year in the Old Testament adumbrated this, and

now in turn it prefigures eternal rest through its figure of redemption.[14] 6. The Greek term 'Epiphany' (*Epiphania*) is 'appearance' (*apparitio*) [or 'manifestation'] in Latin, for on that day, when the star led the way, Christ appeared to the Magi to be worshipped. This was a figure of the beginnings of gentile believers. 7. [Also] on Epiphany day were manifest the sacrament of the Lord's baptism and the water changed into wine, the first of the signs performed by the Lord. 8. There are, in fact, two epiphanies: the first, in which, when the angel announced it, the newborn Christ appeared to the Hebrew shepherds; the second, in which a star, by its guidance, caused Magi from the pagan peoples to come to worship at the cradle that was a manger.

9. *Scenopegia* is a feast day of the Hebrews, translated from the Greek into Latin as 'Feast of Tabernacles.' It is celebrated by Jews in memory of their sojourn, when they were living in tabernacles after they advanced out of Egypt, and from that, *scenopegia*, because σκηνή in Greek means "tabernacle." This feast is celebrated among the Hebrews in the month of September. 10. The *neomenia* we call kalends (i.e. the first day of the month), but this is the Hebrew usage, because their months (*mensis*) are computed according to the lunar course, and in Greek the moon is called μήνη, hence *neomenia*, that is, the new moon. 11. Those kalends were solemn among the Hebrews on account of a legal statute, concerning which it is said in the Psalter (Psalm 80:4 Vulgate), "Blow up the trumpet on the first of the month, on the noted day of your solemnity."[15]

12. *Encaenia* is a new dedication of the Temple, for in Greek καινός means "new." When something new is dedicated, it is called an *encaenia*. Jews celebrated this feast of the dedication of the Temple in the month of October. 13. Palm Sunday is so called because on that day our Lord and Savior, as the prophet sang, is said to have sat on an ass's colt while heading for Jerusalem. Then a multitude of the common people walking before him with branches of palms shouted (John 12:13), "Hosanna, blessed is he that cometh in the name of the Lord, the king of Israel." 14. Further, common people call this day *Capitilavium* because [on that day] the custom then was for the heads (*caput*, plural *capita*) of neophytes who were to be anointed to be washed (*lavare*) so that in their observation of Lent they would not approach the anointing dirty. 15. Moreover on this day the creed is taught to the catechumens, because of the adjoining celebration of Easter Day, so that those who already are hastening to receive the grace of God may come to know the faith that they profess.

16. The Lord's Supper is so called because on that day the Savior celebrated the pasch with his disciples. This is still celebrated just as it has come down to us, and on that day the holy chrism is prepared, and the beginning of the New Testament and cessation of the Old is declared. 17. Sabbath, according to the meaning of its Hebrew name, is called 'rest' (*requies*) because when the creation of the world was finished, God rested on that day. 18. And indeed on that day the Lord rested in his tomb, in order that he might confirm the mystery of that rest, for, in a foreshadowing of future things, this day was mandated to be observed by the Jews. However, after Christ fulfilled the figure of the sabbath in his tomb, the observation of that day ceased.

19. From that point on Sunday is called the Lord's (*Dominicus*) day, because on that day the joy of the resurrection of our Lord (*Dominus*) is celebrated. This day was authorized, not by Jews but by Christians, as the day of the resurrection of the Lord, and from that time it began to have its own liturgical celebration. 20. For the Jews, only the sabbath was passed down as a solemn day, because before that time there was the repose (*requies*) of the dead, but there was no resurrection for anyone who, rising from the dead, might not die. 21. But after the resurrection of the body of the Lord took place in such a way that he might go before, at the head of the Church, demonstrating what the body of the Church could hope for at the last, then Sunday, the Lord's day, that is the eighth day, which is also the first day, began to be celebrated.

xix. Offices (De officiis) 1. There are many kinds of offices, but the chief one is that service which is held for holy and divine matters. An office (*officium*) is so called from performing (*efficere*), as if it were *efficium*, with one letter in the word changed for the sake of euphony, or rather that each person should do those things that interfere (*officere*) with nobody but are of benefit to all. 2. The office of Vespers takes place at the beginning of night, and is named for the evening star Vesper, which

14 The jubilee, every fifty years, was a year when slaves were freed and debts cancelled.

15 For Isidore's 'the first of the month' (*initium mensis*) the Vulgate reads *neomenia*.

rises when night falls. 3. But the office of Matins occurs at the beginning of daylight, and is named after the star Lucifer, which rises when morning begins. By the token of these two times of day it is shown that God is to be praised always, day and night. 4. The mass (*missa*) occurs at the time in the eucharistic service of the sacrifice when the catechumens are sent (*mittere*, ppl. *missus*) outside, while the deacon calls out, "If any catechumen remains, let him go outside." And hence the term is *missa*, because those who are not yet known to be regenerate (i.e. the unbaptized) cannot be present at the sacraments of the altar.

5. A choir (*chorus*) is a multitude gathered for sacred rites, and it is called a choir because in the beginning they would stand around an altar in the shape of a crown (*corona*) and thus sing. Others say the word 'choir' is from the 'concord' (*concordia*) that exists in charity, because without charity it is impossible to sing responses harmoniously. 6. Further, when one person sings (*canere*), it is called a *monodia* in Greek, a *sicinium* in Latin; when two sing, it is called a *bicinium*; when many, a choir. A *chorea* is a trifling entertainment in song or the steps of a dancing band. 7. The term 'antiphon' (*antiphona*) translated from the Greek, means "reciprocal voice," specifically when two choruses alternate in singing with their order interchanged, that is, from one to the other. The Greeks are said to have invented this kind of singing. 8. The Italians handed down responsory singing; they called these chants 'responsories' (*responsorius*) because when one breaks off the other responds (*respondere*). There is however this distinction between responsories and antiphons, that in a responsory one person says the verse, whereas in antiphons the choruses alternate in the verses.

9. A lesson (*lectio*) is so called because it is not sung, like a psalm or hymn, but only read (*legere*, ppl. *lectus*). In singing we look for tunefulness; in a lesson, only enunciation. 10. A canticle (*canticum*) is the voice of one singing (*cantare*) in joy. 11. A psalm (*psalmus*) is the name for what is sung to the psaltery (*psalterium*). History records that the prophet David played this instrument, in a great mystery.[16] These two terms are used together in certain titles of psalms, with their order alternating depending on the musical technique. 12. Thus a 'canticle of a psalm' occurs when what a musical instrument plays, the voice of the singer afterwards sounds, but a 'psalm of a canticle' when the art of the instrument being played imitates what the human voice sounds first. 'Psalm' is named from the instrument called a psaltery, whence the custom is for it not to be accompanied by any other kind of playing.

13. There are moreover three ranges in singing: first the *succentor*, second the *incentor*, and third the *accentor*.[17] 14. Some would call *diapsalma* a Hebrew word, meaning "always"; that is, they assert that those words among which the diapsalm is inserted are unchanging. 15. But others consider it a Greek word, meaning "an interval in psalm-chanting"; as a psalm is what is psalm-chanted, so a diapsalm is the silence interposed in psalm-chanting – just as a *synpsalma* is a joining of voice in singing, so a diapsalm is a disjunction of vocal sounds, where a kind of rest set off from the continuation of sound is marked. 16. Hence thoughts probably should not be run together in singing at the point where a diapsalma is interposed, because it is placed there so that a change of thought or of speaker may be recognized.

17. A hymn (*hymnus*) is the song of those giving praise (*laudare*), whence it is translated from the Greek as "praise" (*laus*) in Latin, being a song of joy and praise. Properly, then, hymns contain praise of God. Therefore if it is praise, but not of God, it is not a hymn; if it is both praise and praise of God, but it is not sung, it is not a hymn. Therefore if it is both uttered in praise of God and sung, then it is a hymn. 18. Its contrary is a threnody (*threnum*), which is a song of grief and death.

19. *Alleluia* is an expression of two words, that is, 'God's praise,' and is Hebrew, for *Ia* is one of the ten names by which God is addressed among the Hebrews. 20. *Amen* means "truly" or "faithfully," and it too is Hebrew. It is not permitted for Greek, Latin, or barbarian speakers to translate these two words, *alleluia* and *amen*, wholly into their own language, or to pronounce them in any other language, for although they can be translated, the antiquity of their own language was preserved in them by the Apostles because of their especially sacred authority. 21. For so holy are these words that even John in the Apocalypse tells that when the Spirit revealed it to him he saw and heard the voice of the heavenly host like the voice of many waters and

16 The mystery of David's psalms is their prophesying of Christ.

17 These are presumably singers in the low, middle, and high ranges.

mighty thunder, saying *amen* and *alleluia* (Apoc. 19:4, 6). And because of this it is fitting for both words to be spoken on earth just as they resound in heaven.

22. *Osanna* (i.e. *hosanna*) cannot entirely be translated into another language: *osi* means "save!"; *anna* is an interjection expressing the emotion of someone in a state of passionate beseeching. 23. In its entirety, moreover, the word is *osianna*, which we pronounce as *osanna*, with the middle vowel degraded and elided just as happens in poetic lines when we scan them, for the initial vowel of a following word excludes the final vowel of the preceding word. In Hebrew it is spoken *osanna*, which means "save!" with its object understood as either 'thy people' or 'the whole world.'

24. The offertory (*offertorium*) gets its name for the following reason: a *fertum* (sacrificial cake) is the name of an oblation which is offered (*offerre*) and sacrificed at the altar by high priests, and from this the offertory is named, as if 'because of the *fertum*.' 25. An oblation (*oblatio*) is so called because it is offered (*offerre*, ppl. *oblatus*). 26. Properly speaking 'gifts' (*donum*) refer to divine things, whereas 'presents' (*munus*) are of humans. 27. For *munus* is a term used of the services poor people pay to the rich in place of presents (*munus*). So, a present is given to a human, a gift to God – whence in temples we speak of 'votive gifts' (*donaria*). Further, they are called presents (*munus*) because they are received or given with one's hands (*manus*). 28. There are two things that are offered: a gift or a sacrifice. 29. We call a gift whatever is made of gold or silver or any other valuable. 30. But a sacrifice is a victim and whatever is burnt or placed on an altar. Further, everything that is given to God is either dedicated or consecrated. That which is dedicated (*dedicare*) is 'given with speaking' (*dare*, "give" and *dicere*, "speak"), whence it is so called. Therefore those who think a consecration means a dedication are wrong. 31. An immolation (*immolatio*) is so called by the ancients because a victim would be slain when it was placed 'on the mass' (*in mole*) of the altar. Whence also the slaughtering is after the immolation. But now an 'immolation' of the bread and chalice is proper usage, but a libation (*libatio*) is an offering of the chalice only. 32. Hence is that saying (Ecclesiasticus 50:16), "He offered (*libavit*) of the blood of the grape." Similarly one of the secular poets (Vergil, *Aen.* 7.133) says,

> Now offer your libation-bowls to Jove.

To make a libation (*libare*) therefore is properly to pour out, and its name is taken from a certain Liber (i.e. Bacchus), who in Greece discovered the use of grapevines.

33. Among the ancients the sacrifice made before they proceeded against the enemy (*hostis*) was called a *hostia*. 34. But after a victory (*victoria*), when the enemy were defeated (*devincere*, ppl. *devictus*), the sacrifices they would slaughter were 'victims' (*victima*). Victims are larger sacrifices than *hostiae*. Others think that a victim is so called because it would fall dead when struck by a blow (*ictus*), or because it would be brought to the altar bound (*vincio*, ppl. *vinctus*). 35. A holocaust (*holocaustum*) is a sacrifice in which all that is offered is consumed by fire, for when the ancients would perform their greatest sacrifices, they would consume the whole sacrificial victim in the flame of the rites, and those were holocausts, for ὅλος in Greek means "whole," καῦσις means "burning," and holocaust, "wholly burnt."

36. All those sacred rites that in Greek are called 'religious revels' (*orgia*) are called 'ceremonies' (*caerimonia*) in Latin. Properly, however, it has been perceived by learned people that ceremonies were so called from 'doing without' (*carere*), as if the word were *carimonia*, because whatever things are offered in sacred rituals people do without for their own use. This term is used even in sacred writings. 37. Others believe that ceremonies properly belong among the observations of Jews – specifically, abstaining from certain foods in accordance with the Old Law – because those who are observant do without the things from which they abstain. 38. The sacrifice (*sacrificium*, i.e. of the mass) is so called as if it were a 'sacred deed' (*sacrum factum*), because by a mystic prayer it is consecrated in commemoration of the Lord's suffering for us, whence we call this sacrifice, at his command, the body and blood of Christ. Although it consists of the fruits of the earth, it is sanctified and made a sacrament with the Spirit of God invisibly working. The Greeks call the sacrament of this bread and chalice the 'Eucharist' (*Eucharistia*), which in Latin means 'good favor' (*bona gratia*) – and what is better than the blood and body of Christ?

39. A 'sacrament' takes place in a particular liturgical rite when an action is performed in such a way that it is understood to signify something that ought to be received in a holy way. Sacraments, then, are baptism and unction, and the body and blood [of the Lord]. 40. These

things are called sacraments (*sacramentum*) for this reason, that under the covering of corporeal things the divine virtue very secretly brings about the saving power of those same sacraments – whence from their secret (*secretus*) or holy (*sacer*) power they are called sacraments. 41. Sacraments are fruitfully performed under the aegis of the Church because the Holy Spirit dwelling in the Church in a hidden way brings about the aforesaid effect of the sacraments. 42. Hence, although they may be dispensed through the Church of God by good or by bad ministers, nevertheless because the Holy Spirit mystically vivifies them – that Spirit that formerly in apostolic times would appear in visible works – these gifts are neither enlarged by the merits of good ministers nor diminished by the bad, for (I Corinthians 3:7), "neither he that planteth is any thing, nor he that watereth; but God that giveth the increase." For this reason in Greek a sacrament is called a 'mystery,' because it has a secret and recondite character.

43. The Greek term 'baptism' (*baptismum*, cf. βαπτισμός), is the equivalent of the Latin *tinctio* ("dipping," "dyeing") because in it a person is changed by the spirit of grace into a better thing, and is made a far different thing than he was. 44. For we were filthy before with the ugliness of sins, but in that bathing we become beautiful in the whitening of the virtues, whence it is written in the Song of Songs (8:5, in an older version), "Who is this that cometh up whitened?" 45. The mystery of baptism is not completed unless by the designation of the Trinity, that is, by the naming of the Father, Son, and Holy Spirit, as the Lord said to the apostles (Matthew 28:19), "Go, teach ye all nations, baptizing them in the name of the Father, and of the Son, and of the Holy Spirit." 46. Thus, just as every statement is confirmed by three witnesses, so the threefold number of divine names confirms this sacrament. 47. This is the reason why baptism is enacted by water: the Lord desired that invisible thing to be granted through the congruent but definitely tangible and visible element over which in the beginning the Holy Spirit moved (Genesis 1:2). 48. For just as the outer body is washed by water, so the spirit also is purified by the Holy Spirit in a hidden way through the mystery of baptism. The baptismal water is made holy in this way: 49. When God is invoked the Holy Spirit descends from heaven and, when the waters have been purified, sanctifies them from itself, and they receive the power of purgation, so that in them both flesh and soul, befouled by sins, may be cleansed.

50. The Greek term 'chrism' (*chrisma*) is 'unction' (*unctio*) in Latin. The word 'Christ' (*Christus*) is also derived from this word, and a person is sanctified after the application of unction. 51. For just as remission of sins is granted in baptism, so the sanctification of the spirit is administered through unction. This sacrament derives from the ancient custom according to which people used to be anointed into the priesthood or the royal office, for which reason Aaron was anointed by Moses. 52. When this is done in the flesh, it benefits in the spirit, just as in the gift of baptism also there is a visible act, that we are submerged in water, but a spiritual effect, that we are cleansed of sins. 53. This is what that ointment signifies, which a sinful woman is written to have poured on the feet of Jesus (Luke 7:37–50), and which she who is said not to have been a sinner is written to have poured on his head (Matthew 26:7–13, etc.).

54. The sacramental 'laying on of hands' (*manus impositio*) is done to bid the Holy Spirit come, invoked by means of a blessing, for at that time the Paraclete, after the bodies have been cleansed and blessed, willingly descends from the Father and as it were settles on the water of baptism, as if in recognition of its settling on its original seat – for it is read that in the beginning the Holy Spirit moved over the waters (Genesis 1.2).[18]

55. The Greek term 'exorcism' (*exorcismus*) is 'conjuration' (*coniuratio*) in Latin, or a 'speech of rebuke' directed against the devil, that he should depart, as in this passage in Zechariah (3:1–2): "And the Lord showed me Jesus the high priest standing before the angel of the Lord: and Satan stood on his right hand to be his adversary. And the Lord said to Satan: The Lord rebuke thee, O Satan: and the Lord that chose Jerusalem rebuke thee." 56. Exorcism is this, to rebuke and conjure against the devil, whence it should be understood that it is no creature of God that is exorcized or breathed out in infants, but that devil, to whom all are subject who are born with sin – for he is the prince of sinners.

57. The word 'creed' (*symbolum*) from Greek means "sign" or "token of recognition," for the apostles, about to disperse for preaching the gospel among the nations, proposed the creed for themselves as a sign or guidepost

18 In this passage Isidore treats baptism by water, anointing, and imposition of hands as all parts of the sacrament of Baptism; each act may also be an independent sacrament.

for preaching. 58. Moreover it contains the profession of the Trinity and the unity of the Church and the whole holy order of Christian teaching. This creed of our faith and hope is not written on papyrus sheets and with ink, but on the fleshly tablets of our hearts. 59. A 'prayer' (*oratio*) means a "petition" (*petitio*), for to pray (*orare*) is to beseech (*petere*), just as to 'pray successfully' (*exorare*) is to obtain (*impetrare*). Further, prayer has a proper place and time. Place, because not everywhere, since we are prohibited by Christ from prayer in public, except where opportunity grants it or necessity requires it. The apostles are not believed to have prayed against Jesus' command when they prayed and sang to God in prison in the hearing of their guards. 60. With regard to time it has truly been said (I Thessalonians 5:17), "Pray without ceasing," but this applies to individuals; in a religious community there is a service at certain hours to signal the divisions of the day – at the third hour, the sixth, and the ninth (i.e. Terce, Sext, and Nones) – and likewise the divisions of the night.

61. These hours of prayers are apportioned so that, if we should by chance be occupied, the specific time would draw our attention to the divine office. These times are found in Scripture. 62. The Holy Spirit was first poured into the gathered disciples at the third hour (Acts 2:15). Peter, on the day in which he experienced the vision of communication in the vessel, had ascended in order to pray at the sixth hour (Acts 10:9–16). Likewise Peter with John went to the temple at the ninth hour when he healed the paralytic (Acts 3:1–8). 63. But we also read that Daniel observed these times in his prayer (Daniel 6:13), and in any case it is the teaching from the Israelites that we should pray not less than three times a day, for we are debtors of three – Father, Son, and Holy Spirit – not counting, of course, other prayers as well, which are due without any notice being given, at the onset of day or of night or of the watches of the night. But we are also not to consume food before we have interposed a prayer, 64. for refreshment of the spirit should come first, because heavenly things come before earthly. Moreover, he who wishes for his prayer to fly to God should make two wings for it, fasting and almsgiving, and it will ascend swiftly and be clearly heard.

65. Fasting (*ieiunium*) is parsimony of sustenance and abstinence from food, and its name is given to it from a certain portion of the intestines, always thin and empty, which is commonly called the jejunum (*ieiunum*). Whence the name of fasting is believed to have derived, because by the starvation of the jejunum the intestines are empty and cleaned out. 66. Fasting is also called a station (*statio*, i.e. a "watch"). This watch takes its name from a military analogy, because no happy festivity occurring in a camp rescinds the watch-duty (*statio*) of soldiers. For happiness maintains discipline more readily, grief more carefully; whence soldiers, never unmindful of their sworn duty, keep their watches all the sooner. 67. Some however distinguish between fasting and a station, for fasting is abstinence on any day indifferently, not in accordance with a rule but following one's own will, whereas a station is an observance of predetermined days or seasons. 68. Of days, as the fast on Wednesday and Friday mandated by the Old Law. Concerning this station the man said in the Gospel (Luke 18:12), "I fast twice in a week," that is, on the fourth and sixth days of the week (reckoning inclusively). 69. Of seasons also, which were established by legal and prophetic customs at fixed times, as the fast of the fourth, fifth, seventh, and tenth month (Zechariah 8:19); or, as in the Gospel (Matthew 9:15), the days for fasting on which the bridegroom has been taken away; or as the observance of Lent, which is observed in the whole world, according to the apostolic institution, leading up to the time of the Lord's Passion. 70. Some add a third type to these, which they call 'dry-eating' (*xerophagia*), that is, abstinence from moist food. It takes its name from this, because some make use of dry food.

71. Penitence (*poenitentia*) is so called as if it were *punitentia*, because by means of his own repenting (*poenitere*, i.e. *paenitere*) a person punishes (*punire*) the wrong he has done. Indeed, they who truly do penance do nothing other than not permit what they have done wrong to go unpunished. Indeed, he whose high and just judgment no scoffer evades is sparing in proportion as they do not spare themselves. 72. Further, perfect penitence is to weep for past sins and not allow future ones. This penitential weeping bears the likeness of a fountain, because if by chance, when the devil attacks, some sin creeps in, by the satisfaction of penitence it is washed away. 73. Satisfaction (*satisfactio*) moreover, is to shut out the causes and urgings of sins and not to repeat the sin further. 74. But reconciliation (*reconciliatio*) is what is granted after the completion of penitence, for as we are won over

(*conciliare*) to God when we are first converted from paganism, so we are reconciled (*reconciliare*) when after sinning we return by penitence.

75. The Greek term *exomologesis* means what in Latin is termed 'confession,' a term that has a double signification. A confession can either be understood as of praise, as in "I will confess you to be the Lord, the Father of heaven and earth," or as when someone confesses his sins so that they will be forgiven by him whose mercy is unfailing. 76. Therefore we express and make use of this Greek term *exomologesis* for that act by which we confess (*confiteri*, ppl. *confessus*) our sin to the Lord – not indeed as if he were ignorant, for nothing is hidden from his knowledge; but a confession (*confessio*) is an 'explicit acknowledgment' (*professa cognitio*) of a thing, namely of that which is unknown. 77. For suppose a person has thought it profitable and pleasant to commit rapine, adultery, or theft, but when he recognizes that these things are liable to eternal damnation, as these things are acknowledged (*cognoscere*, ppl. *cognitus*) he confesses his error. 78. Moreover a confession of error is an affirmation of its cessation; therefore there should be cessation of sin when there is confession. Further, confession precedes, and forgiveness follows. But the person is beyond forgiveness who knows his sin but does not confess what is known to him. 79. And so *exomologesis* is the discipline of a person's prostrating and humiliating himself in dress and food, to lie in sackcloth and ashes, to smear his body with filth, to cast down his spirit in mourning, to transform with harsh treatment those things which are at fault.

80. Litanies (*litania*) are the Greek names for what are called 'rogations' in Latin. But between litanies and *exomologesis* is this distinction, that *exomologesis* is performed only for the confession of sins, whereas litanies are ordained for beseeching God and procuring his mercy in some case. 81. But nowadays either term designates one thing, and commonly there is no distinction whether 'litanies' or *exomologesis* is spoken of. The term 'supplication' is now retained in a certain way from paganism. 82. Among the pagans the festival days were either 'customary' (*legitimus*) or 'specially decreed' (*indictus*, also meaning "criminally indicted"). And *indictus* because the poor of ancient Rome would make sacrifice from a confiscation, or indeed out of the goods of the condemned. Hence 'propitiatory offerings' (*supplicium*) that were made from the goods of people who had suffered punishments (*supplicium*) are called 'supplications' (*supplicatio*): thus sacrifices were made from the belongings of the accursed.

Book VII

God, angels, and saints (De deo, angelis et sanctis)

i. God (De deo) 1. The most blessed Jerome, a most erudite man and skilled in many languages, first rendered the meaning of Hebrew names in the Latin language (in his *Interpretation of Hebrew Names*). I have taken pains to include some of these in this work along with their interpretations, though I have omitted many for the sake of brevity. 2. Indeed, exposition of words often enough reveals what they mean, for some hold the rationale of their names in their own derivations.

First, then, we present the ten names by which God is spoken of in Hebrew. 3. The first name of God in Hebrew is El. Some translate this as "God," and others as ἰσχυρός, that is, "strong" (*fortis*), expressing its etymology, because he is overcome by no infirmity but is strong and capable of accomplishing anything. 4. The second name is Eloi, 5. and the third Eloe (plural 'Elohim'), either of which in Latin is 'God' (*Deus*). The name *Deus* in Latin has been transliterated from a Greek term, for *Deus* is from δέος in Greek, which means φόβος, that is, "fear," whence is derived *Deus* because those worshipping him have fear. 6. Moreover 'God' is properly the name of the Trinity, referring to the Father and the Son and the Holy Spirit. To this Trinity are referred the remaining terms posited below of God.

7. The fourth name of God is Sabaoth, which is rendered in Latin "of armies" or "of hosts," of whom the angels speak in the Psalm (23:10 Vulgate): "Who is this King of glory? The Lord of hosts." 8. Now there are in the ordination of this world many hosts, such as angels, archangels, principalities, and powers, and all the orders of the celestial militia, of whom nevertheless he is Lord, for all are under him and are subject to his lordship. 9. Fifth, Elion, which in Latin means "lofty" (*excelsus*), because he is above the heavens (*caelum*), as was written of him (Psalm 112:4 Vulgate): "The Lord is high (*excelsus*) . . . his glory above the heavens (*caelus*)." Further, *excelsus* is so called from 'very lofty' (*valde celsus*), for *ex* is put for *valde*, as in *eximius* ("exceptional"), as it were *valde eminens* ("very eminent").

10. Sixth, Eie (i.e. the Tetragrammaton, sect. 16 below), that is, 'He who is.' For only God, because he is eternal, that is, because he has no origin, truly holds the name of Being. Now this name was reported to the holy Moses by an angel, 11. for when Moses asked what was the name of the one who was commanding him to proceed with the liberation of his people from Egypt, he answered him (Exodus 3:14): "I am who I am: and thou shalt say to the children of Israel: 'He who is' hath sent me to you." It is just as if in comparison with him, who truly 'is' because he is immutable, those things that are mutable become as if they were not. 12. That of which it is said, "it was," 'is' not, and that of which it is said, "it will be," 'is' not yet. Further, God has known only 'is', and does not know 'was' and 'will be.' 13. For only the Father, with the Son and Holy Spirit, truly 'is.' Compared with his being, our being is not being. And for this reason we say in conversation, "God lives," because his Being lives with a life that death has no hold over.

14. Seventh, Adonai, which broadly means "Lord" (*Dominus*), because he has dominion (*dominari*) over every creature, or because every creature is subservient to his lordship (*dominatus*). Lord, therefore, and God, either because he has dominion over all things, or because he is feared by all things. 15. Eighth, Ia (i.e. Yah), which is only applied to God, and which sounds as the last syllable of 'alleluia.' 16. Ninth, the Tetragrammaton, that is, the 'four letters' that in Hebrew are properly applied to God – *iod, he, iod, he* – that is, 'Ia' twice, which when doubled forms that ineffable and glorious name of God.[1] The Tetragrammaton is called 'ineffable' not because it cannot be spoken, but because in no way can it be bounded by human sense and intellect; therefore, because nothing can be said worthy of it, it is ineffable. 17. Tenth, Shaddai, that is, "Almighty." He is called Almighty (*omnipotens*) because 'he can do all things' (*omnia potest*), but by doing what he will, not

1 The Tetragrammaton actually consists of the Hebrew consonants yodh, he, waw, he.

by suffering what he does not will. If that were to happen to him, in no way would he be Almighty – for he does whatever he wishes, and therein he is Almighty. 18. Again, 'Almighty' because all things in every place are his, for he alone has dominion over the whole world.

Certain other names are also said for God substantively, as immortal, incorruptible, immutable, eternal. Whence deservedly he is placed before every creature. 19. Immortal, as was written of him (I Timothy 6:16): "Who only hath immortality," because in his nature there is no change, for every sort of mutability not improperly is called mortality. From this it follows that the soul also is said to die, not because it is changed and turned into body or into some other substance, but because everything is considered mortal that in its very substance is now, or once was, of a different sort, in that it leaves off being what it once was. And by this reasoning only God is called immortal, because he alone is immutable. 20. He is called incorruptible (*incorruptibilis*) because he cannot be broken up (*corrumpere*, ppl. *corruptus*) and dissolved or divided. Whatever undergoes division also undergoes passing away, but he can neither be divided nor pass away; hence he is incorruptible.

He is immutable (*incommutabilis*) because he remains forever and does not change (*mutare*). 21. He neither advances, because he is perfect, nor recedes, because he is eternal. 22. He is eternal because he is without time, for he has neither beginning nor end. And hence he is 'forever' (*sempiternus*), because he is 'always eternal' (*semper aeternus*). Some think that 'eternal' (*aeternus*) is so called from 'ether' (*aether*), for heaven is held to be his abode. Whence the phrase (Psalm 113:16 Vulgate), "The heaven of heaven is the Lord's." And these four terms signify one thing, for one and the same thing is meant, whether God is called eternal or immortal or incorruptible or immutable.

23. 'Invisible,' because the Trinity never appears in its substance to the eyes of mortals unless through the form of a subject corporeal creature. Indeed, no one can see the very manifestation of the essence of God and live, as it was told to Moses (Exodus 33:20), whence the Lord says in the Gospel (John 1:18), "No man hath seen God at any time." Indeed, he is an invisible thing, and therefore should be sought not with the eye, but with the heart. 24. 'Impassible,' because he is affected by none of the disturbances to which human fragility succumbs, for none of the passions touch him, not desire, wrath, greed, fear, grief, envy, and the other things with which the human mind is troubled. 25. But when it is said that God is angry or jealous or sorrowful, it is said from the human point of view, for with God, in whom is utmost tranquillity, there is no disturbance.

26. Further he is called 'single' (*simplex*), either from not letting go of what he has, or because what he is and what is in him are not distinct, in the way that being and knowing are distinct for a human. 27. A human can be, and at the same time not have knowledge. God has being, and he also has knowledge; but what God *has* he also *is*, and it is all one. He is 'single' because there is nothing accidental in him, but both what he is and what is in him are of his essence, except for what refers to each of the three persons. 28. He is the 'ultimately good' (*summe bonus*) because he is immutable. What is created is good, to be sure, but it is not consummately good because it is mutable. And although it may indeed be good, it still cannot be the highest good. 29. God is called 'disembodied' (*incorporeus*) or 'incorporeal' (*incorporalis*) because he is believed or understood to exist as spirit, not body (*corpus*, gen. *corporis*). When he is called spirit, his substance is signified.

30. 'Immeasurable' (*immensus*) because he encompasses all things and is encompassed by nothing, but all things are confined within his omnipotence. 31. He is called 'perfect' (*perfectus*) because nothing can be added to him. However, 'perfection' is said of the completion of some making; how then is God, who is not made (*factus*), perfect (*perfectus*)? 32. But human poverty of diction has taken up this term from our usage, and likewise for the remaining terms, insofar as what is ineffable can be spoken of in any way – for human speech says nothing suitable about God – so the other terms are also deficient. 33. He is called 'creator' because of the matter of the whole world created by him, for there is nothing that has not taken its origin from God. And he is 'one' (*unus*) because he cannot be divided, or because there can be no other thing that may take on so much power. 34. Therefore what things are said of God pertain to the whole Trinity because of its one (*unus*) and coeternal substance, whether in the Father, or in his only-begotten Son in the form of God, or in the Holy Spirit, which is the one (*unus*) Spirit of God the Father and of his only-begotten Son.

35. There are certain terms applied to God from human usage, taken from our body parts or from lesser things, and because in his own nature he is invisible and incorporeal, nevertheless appearances of things, as the effects of causes, are ascribed to him, so that he might more easily make himself known to us by way of the usage of our speech. For example, because he sees all things, we may speak of his eye; because he hears all, we may speak of his ear; because he turns aside, he walks; because he awaits, he stands. 36. In this way and in other ways like these a likeness from human minds is applied to God, for instance that he is forgetful or mindful. Hence it is that the prophet says (Jeremiah 51:14), "The Lord of hosts hath sworn by his soul" – not that God has a soul, but he speaks in this way as from our viewpoint. 37. Likewise the 'face' of God in Holy Scripture is understood not as flesh, but as divine recognition, in the same way in which someone is recognized when his face is seen. Thus, this is said in a prayer to God (Psalm 79:4 Vulgate), "Shew us thy face," as if he were to say, "Grant us thy recognition."

38. Thus the 'traces' of God are spoken of, because now God is known through a mirror (I Corinthians 13:12), but he is recognized as the Almighty at the culmination, when in the future he becomes present face to face for each of the elect, so that they behold his appearance, whose traces they now try to comprehend, that is, him whom it is said they see through a mirror. 39. For in relation to God, position and vesture and place and time are spoken of not properly, but metaphorically, by way of analogy. For instance (Psalm 98:1 Vulgate), "To sit on the cherubims" is said with reference to position; and (Psalm 103:6 Vulgate) "The deep like a garment is its clothing," referring to vesture; and (Psalm 101:28 Vulgate) "Thy years shall not fail," which pertains to time; and (Psalm 138:8 Vulgate) "If I ascend into heaven, thou art there," referring to place. 40. Again, in the prophet (Amos 2:13), "As a wain laden with hay," an image is used of God. All these refer to God figuratively, because nothing of these things refers properly to his underlying being.

ii. The Son of God (De Filio Dei) 1. In the divine writings Christ is also found to be named in many ways, for he, the only-begotten Son of God the Father, although he was the equal of the Father, took the form of a slave (Philippians 2:7) for our salvation. Whence some names are given to him with regard to the substance of his divinity, and some with regard to the dispensation of his assumed humanity.

2. He is named 'Christ' (*Christus*) from 'chrism' (*chrisma*), that is, 'anointed one,' for it was a precept among the Jews that they would confect a sacred ointment by which those who were called to the priesthood or the kingship might be anointed. Just as nowadays for kings to be clothed in the purple is the mark of royal dignity, so for them anointing with sacred ointment would confer the royal title and power. Hence they are called 'anointed ones' (*christus*) from chrism, which is unction, 3. for the Greek *chrisma* is 'unction' (*unctio*) in Latin. When this anointing was done spiritually, it accommodated the name 'Christ' to the Lord, because he was anointed by the Spirit from God the Father, as in Acts (4:27): "For there assembled together in this city against thy holy child . . . whom thou hast anointed" – by no means with visible oil, but by the gift of grace, for which visible ointment is a sign. 4. 'Christ' is not, however, a proper name of the Savior, but a common-noun designation of his power. When he is called 'Christ,' it is a common designation of his importance, but when he is called 'Jesus Christ' it is the proper name of the Savior. 5. Further, the name of Christ never occurred at all elsewhere in any nation except in that kingdom alone where Christ was prophesied, and whence he was to come. 6. Again, in Hebrew he is called 'Messiah' (*Messias*), in Greek 'Christ,' in Latin 'the anointed' (*unctus*).

7. The Hebrew 'Jesus' is translated σωτήρ in Greek, and "healer" (*salutaris*) or "savior" (*salvator*) in Latin, because he has come for all nations as the 'bearer of salvation' (*salutifer*). 8. The Evangelist renders the etymology of his name, saying (Matthew 1:21), "And thou shalt call his name Savior (*salvator*; cf. Vulgate *Iesus*), for he shall save his people." Just as 'Christ' signifies a king, so 'Jesus' signifies a savior. 9. Not every kind of king saves us, but a savior king. The Latin language did not have this word *salvator* before, but it could have had it, seeing that it was able to when it wanted. 10. The Hebrew *Emmanuel* in Latin means "God is with us," undoubtedly because, born of a Virgin, God has appeared to humans in mortal flesh, that he might open the way of salvation to heaven for the inhabitants of earth.

Christ's names that pertain to the substance of his divinity are as follows: God (*Deus*), Lord (*Dominus*). 11. He is called God because of his unity of substance with the Father, and Lord because of the creation subservient to him. 12. And he is God and man, for he is Word and flesh. Whence he is called the Doubly-Begotten (*bis genitus*), because the Father begot (*gignere*, ppl. *genitus*) him without a mother in eternity, and because a mother begot him without a father in the temporal world. 13. But he is called the Only-Begotten (*unigenitus*) according to the peerless quality of his divinity, for he is without brothers; he is called the First-Begotten (*primogenitus*) with regard to his assuming of human nature, in which he deigned through the grace of adoption to have brothers, among whom he was the first begotten.

14. He is called 'of one substance' (*homousion*, i.e. ὁμοούσιος) with the Father because of their unity of substance, because in Greek substance or essence is called οὐσία and ὁμο- means "one." The two joined together therefore denote 'one substance.' For this reason he is called *Homousion*, that is (John 10:30), "I and the Father are one" – that is, of the same substance with the Father. 15. Although this name is not written in Sacred Scripture, nevertheless it is supported in the formal naming of the whole Trinity because an account is offered according to which it is shown to be spoken correctly, just as in those books we never read that the Father is the Unbegotten (*Ingenitus*), yet we have no doubt that he should be spoken of and believed to be that.[2] 16. *Homoeusion* (i.e. ὁμοιούσιος), that is "similar in substance," because as God is, so also is God's image. Invisible is God, and invisible his image (i.e. the divinity latent in Jesus).

17. The Beginning (*Principium*), because all things are from him, and before him nothing was. 18. The End (*Finis*), either because he deigned at the end (*finis*) of time to be born and to die humbly in the flesh and to undertake the Last Judgment, or because whatever we do we refer to him, and when we have come to him we have nothing further to seek. 19. He is the 'Mouth of God' (*Os Dei*) because he is his Word, for just as we often say 'this tongue' and 'that tongue' for 'words,' which are made by the tongue, so 'Mouth' is substituted for the 'Word of God,' because words are normally formed by the mouth. 20. Further, he is called the Word (*Verbum*) because through him the Father established or commanded all things. 21. Truth (*Veritas*), because he does not deceive, but gives what he has promised. Life (*Vita*) because he created. He is called the Image (*Imago*) because of his equivalent likeness to the Father. 22. He is the Figure (*Figura*) because although he took on the form of a slave, he portrayed in himself the Father's image and immeasurable greatness by his likeness to the Father in his works and powers.

23. He is the 'Hand of God' (*Manus Dei*) because all things were made through him. Hence also the 'Right Hand' (*Dextera*) because of his accomplishment of the work of all creation, which was formed by him. The Arm (*Brachium*), because all things are embraced by him. 24. The Power (*Virtus*), because he contains in himself all the authority of the Father, and governs, holds, and rules the whole creation of heaven and earth. 25. Wisdom (*Sapientia*), because he himself reveals the mysteries of knowledge and the secrets of wisdom. But although the Father and the Holy Spirit may be 'Wisdom' and 'Power' and 'Lamp' and 'Light,' nevertheless strictly speaking it is the Son who is designated by these names. 26. Again, he is called Clarity (*Splendor*) because of what he plainly reveals. Lamp (*Lumen*), because he illuminates (*illuminare*). Light (*Lux*), because he unlocks the eyes of the heart for gazing at the truth. Sun (*Sol*), because he is the illuminator. 27. The Orient (*Oriens*, i.e. "East," "Sunrising") because he is the source of light and the brightener of things, and because he makes us rise (*oriri*) to eternal life. 28. The Fount (*Fons*), because he is the origin of things, or because he satisfies those who thirst.

He is also the A and ω. He is Alpha because no letter precedes it, for it is the first of the letters, just as the Son of God is first, for he answered the Jews interrogating him that he was the beginning (John 8:25). Whence John in the Apocalypse, properly setting down the same letter, says (22:13), "I am A and ω, first and last." First, because before him nothing is. Last, because he has undertaken the Last Judgment. 29. Mediator (*Mediator*), because he has been constituted a mean (*medius*) between God and humanity, so that he might lead humanity through to God – whence the Greeks also call him μεσίτης ("mediator"). 30. Paraclete, that is, advocate, because he intercedes for us with the Father, as John says of him (I John 2:1), "We have an advocate with the Father, Jesus Christ the just." 31. For Paraclete (*Paracletus*) is a Greek word that means "advocate" in Latin. This name is ascribed to

2 Isidore's care with the concept of the unity of substance of Jesus and the Father reflects the recent conversion of the Visigothic king from Arianism, which was heretical on this point, to Catholicism. Isidore's brother Leander was instrumental in this conversion.

both the Son and the Holy Spirit, as the Lord says in the Gospel (John 14:16), "I will ask the Father, and he shall give you another Paraclete."

32. Also the Son is called Intercessor (*Intercessor*), because he devotes care to remove our sins, and he exerts effort to wash away our crimes. 33. Bridegroom (*Sponsus*), because descending from heaven he cleaved to the Church, so that by the grace of the New Covenant they might be two in one flesh. 34. He is called an Angel (*Angelus*, i.e. 'messenger') because of his announcing of his Father's and his own will. Whence it is read in the Prophet (cf. Isaiah 9:6), "Angel of great counsel," although he is God and Lord of the angels. 35. He is called the 'One Sent' (*Missus*) because he appeared to this world as the Word made flesh, whence also he says (John 16:28), "I came forth from the Father, and am come into the world." 36. He is also called the 'Human Being' (*Homo*) because he was born. Prophet (*Propheta*), because he revealed future things. Priest (*Sacerdos*), because he offered himself as a sacrifice for us. Shepherd (*Pastor*), because he is a guardian. Teacher (*Magister*), because he shows the way. Nazarene (*Nazarenus*) from his region, but Nazarite (*Nazareus*) is an earned title meaning "holy" or "clean," because he did no sin.

37. Further, Christ attracts to himself types of names from other lesser things so that he might more easily be understood. 38. For he is called Bread (*Panis*) because he is flesh. Vine (*Vitis*), because we are redeemed by his blood. Flower (*Flos*), because he was picked. The Way (*Via*), because by means of him we come to God. The Portal (*Ostium*), because through him we make our approach to God. Mount (*Mons*), because he is mighty. Rock (*Petra*), because he is the strength of believers. 39. Cornerstone (*Lapis angularis*), because he joins two walls coming from different directions, that is from the circumcised and the uncircumcised, into the one fabric of the Church, or because he makes peace in himself for angels (*angelus*) and humans. 40. The Stumbling-stone (*Lapis offensionis*), because when he came in humility unbelievers stumbled (*offendere*) against him and he became a 'rock of scandal' (Romans 9:33), as the Apostle says (I Corinthians 1:23), "Unto the Jews indeed a stumbling block (*scandalum*)."

41. Further he is called the Foundation (*Fundamentum*) because faith on him is most firm, or because the Catholic Church was built upon him. 42. Now Christ is the Lamb (*Agnus*) for his innocence, and the Sheep (*Ovis*) for his submissiveness, and the Ram (*Aries*) for his leadership, and Goat (*Haedus*) for his likeness to sinful flesh, 43. and the Calf (*Vitulus*) because he was made a sacrificial victim for us, and Lion (*Leo*) for his kingdom and strength, and Serpent (*Serpens*) for his death and his sapience (*sapientia*), and again Worm (*Vermis*) because he rose again, 44. Eagle (*Aquila*) because after his resurrection he returned to the stars.

Nor is it a wonder that he should be figured forth by means of lowly signs, he who is known to have descended even to the indignities of our passions or of the flesh. 45. For although he is coeternal with God the Father before worldly time, when the fullness of time arrived, the Son for our salvation took the form of a slave (Philippians 2:7), and the Son of God became a son of humankind. 46. For this reason some things are said of him in Scripture according to the form of God, some according to the form of a slave. Two of these should be kept in mind for an example, so that particular instances may severally be connected with these particular forms. So, he spoke of himself according to the form of God (John 10:30), "I and the Father are one"; according to the form of a slave (John 14:28), "For the Father is greater than I."

47. But people who little understand how one thing may be said for another wish to transfer to the Son's character as God what has been said with regard to his character as a slave. Again, they want what has been said relating the Persons to one another to be names for God's nature and substance, and they make an error in their faith. 48. For human nature was so conjoined to the Son of God that one Person was made from two substances. Only the man endured the cross, but because of the unity of Person, the God also is said to have endured it. 49. Hence we find it written (I Corinthians 2:8), "For if they had known it, they never would have crucified the Lord of glory." Therefore we speak of the Son of God as crucified, not in the power of his divinity but in the weakness of his humanity, not in his persistence in his own nature but in his acceptance of ours.

iii. The Holy Spirit (De Spiritu Sancto) 1. The Holy Spirit is proclaimed to be God because it proceeds from the Father and the Son, and has God's substance, for no other thing could proceed from the Father than what is itself the Father. 2. It is called the Spirit (*spiritus*, i.e. 'breath' or 'spirit') because as something breathed (*spirare*, ppl. *spiratus*) it is related to something else;

moreover, a breathing thing inspires with its breath, so to speak, and consequently it is called the Spirit. It is called the Holy Spirit for a certain appropriate reason, in that the term is related to the Father and the Son, because it is their *spiritus*. 3. Now this name 'Spirit' is also conferred not because of what is imparted to something, but because of what signifies some kind of nature. 4. Indeed, every incorporeal nature in Holy Scripture is called spirit, whence this term suits not only the Father and Son and Holy Spirit, but also every rational creature and soul. 5. Therefore the Spirit of God is called Holy, because it is the holiness of the Father and Son. Although the Father is spirit and the Son is spirit, and the Father is holy and the Son is holy, properly nevertheless this one is called Holy (*sanctus*) Spirit, as the co-essential and consubstantial holiness (*sanctitas*) of both the others.

6. The Holy Spirit is not spoken of as begotten (*genitus*) lest it should be thought that there are two Sons in the Trinity. It is not proclaimed as unbegotten (*ingenitus*), lest it should be believed that there are two Fathers in that same Trinity. 7. It is spoken of, however, as proceeding (*procedere*), by the testimony of the Lord's saying (cf. John 16:12–15), "I have yet many things to say to you, but you cannot hear them now. But he, the Spirit of truth who proceeds from the Father, will come, and he shall receive of mine; he shall show everything to you."[3] This Spirit moreover proceeds not only by its nature, but it proceeds always in ceaselessly performing the works of the Trinity. 8. Between the Son who is born and the Holy Spirit who proceeds is this distinction, that the Son is born from one, the Holy Spirit proceeds from both. Therefore the Apostle says (cf. Romans 8:9), "Now if any man have not the Spirit of Christ, he is none of his."

9. In its work the Holy Spirit is also understood to be an angel, for it is said of it (John 16:13), "And the things that are to come, he shall announce (*adnuntiare*) to you" – and the Greek term 'angel' means "messenger" (*nuntius*) in Latin. Hence also two angels appeared to Lot, and to these the name 'Lord' was given in the singular; we understand them to have been the Son and the Holy Spirit, for we never read that the Father is 'sent.'

10. The Holy Spirit, because it is called the Paraclete, is named from 'consolation,' for the Greek term παράκλησις in Latin means "consolation." Thus Christ sent the Spirit to the mourning apostles, after he ascended from their eyes to heaven. 11. For it is sent as a consoler to those who grieve, and according to the saying of the same Lord (cf. Matthew 5:5), "Blessed are they that mourn: for they shall be consoled." Again he said (cf. Matthew 9:15), "Then the children of the bridegroom shall mourn, when the bridegroom shall have been taken away from them."[3] 12. Again, Paraclete, because it offers consolation to souls that have given up temporal joy. Others say that 'Paraclete' in Latin means "orator" or "advocate," for one and the same Holy Spirit speaks; it teaches; through it are given words of wisdom; by it Holy Scripture has been inspired.

13. The Holy Spirit is named the Sevenfold (*septiformis*) because of the gifts that all have a claim to attain from the fullness of its unity, one by one, according as they deserve. Thus it is the Spirit of wisdom and intellect, the Spirit of counsel and courage, the Spirit of knowledge and holiness, the Spirit of the fear of the Lord (Isaiah 11:2–3). 14. Further, we read of the 'perfect Spirit' (*principalis Spiritus*) in the fiftieth Psalm, where because *spiritus* is repeated thrice, some understand the Trinity, since it is written (John 4:24), "God is a spirit." Indeed, because he is not a body, and yet he exists, it seems to remain that he is a spirit. Some understand that the Trinity is signified in Psalm 50: in the "perfect Spirit" (vs. 14) the Father, in the "right Spirit" (vs. 12) the Son, in the "holy spirit" (vs. 13) the Holy Spirit.

15. The Holy Spirit is called a Gift because it is given, for 'gift' (*donum*) takes its name from 'giving' (*dare*). Now it is very well known that our Lord Jesus Christ, when he had ascended into heaven after his resurrection from the dead, gave the Holy Spirit, and filled with this Spirit the believers spoke in the tongues of all nations. 16. Moreover it is a gift of God to the extent that it is given to those who love God through the Spirit. In itself, it is God; with regard to us, it is a gift – but the Holy Spirit is forever a Gift, handing out the gifts of grace to individuals as it wishes. 17. It imparts the gift of prophecy to whomever it wishes, and it forgives sins for whomever it wishes – for sins are not pardoned without the Holy Spirit. 18. The Holy Spirit is appropriately named Charity (*caritas*) either because by its nature it joins with those from whom it proceeds and shows itself to be one with them, or because it brings it about in us that we remain in God and he in us. 19. Whence among the gifts of God nothing is greater than charity, and there is no greater gift

3 The second sentence quoted departs from the Vulgate.

of God than the Holy Spirit. 20. It is also Grace (*gratia*), and has this name because it is given freely (*gratis*) not according to our merits, but according to divine will.

Further, just as we speak of the unique Word of God properly by the name of Wisdom, although generally both the Holy Spirit and the Father himself are wisdom, so the Holy Spirit is properly named by the word Charity, although both the Father and the Son are in general charity. 21. The Holy Spirit is very clearly declared in the books of the Gospel to be the Finger (*Digitus*) of God, for when one Evangelist said (Luke 11:20), "I by the finger of God cast out devils," another said the same thing in this way (Matthew 12:28), "I by the Spirit of God cast out devils." Wherefore also the law was written by the finger of God, and it was granted on the fiftieth day after the slaughter of the lamb, and on the fiftieth day after the Passion of our Lord Jesus Christ came the Holy Spirit. 22. Moreover it is called the Finger of God to signify its operative power with the Father and the Son. Whence also Paul says (I Corinthians 12:11), "But all these things one and the same Spirit worketh, dividing to every one according as he will." Just as through Baptism we die and are reborn in Christ, so we are sealed by the Spirit, which is the Finger of God and a spiritual seal. The Holy Spirit is written to have come in the form of a dove (*columba*) in order that its nature might be expressed through a bird of simplicity and innocence. Whence the Lord said (Matthew 10:16), "Be ye simple as doves" – for this bird is without bile in its body, and has only innocence and love.

23. The Holy Spirit is referred to by the name of Fire (*ignis*) because it appeared as fire in the distribution of tongues in the Acts of the Apostles (2:3), and it settled on each of them. 24. Moreover it gave the gift of diverse tongues to the apostles so that they might be made capable of instructing the faithful people. 25. But the Holy Spirit is remembered as having settled upon each of them so that it may be understood not to have been divided into many, but to have remained whole with respect to each one, as is generally the way with fire. 26. For a kindled fire has this nature, that however many should behold it, however many should behold that mane of purple splendor, to that same number would it impart the sight of its light, and offer the ministry of its gift, and still it would persist in its integrity.

27. The Holy Spirit is referred to by the name Water (*aqua*) in the Gospel, as the Lord cries out and says (John 7:37–38), "If any man thirst, let him come to me, and drink. He that believeth in me, *Out of his belly shall flow rivers of living water.*" Moreover, the Evangelist explained his words, for in the following sentence (39) he says, "Now this he said of the Spirit which they should receive, who believed in him." 28. But the water of the sacrament (i.e. of Baptism) is one thing, and the water that signifies the Spirit of God is another, for the water of the sacrament is visible, the water of the Spirit is invisible. The former cleanses the body, and symbolizes what takes place in the soul; but through the latter, the Holy Spirit, the soul itself is purified and fed.

29. As the apostle John witnesses, the Holy Spirit is called Unction (*unctio*) because, just as oil floats above every liquid because of its physical weight, so in the beginning the Holy Spirit floated above the waters (Genesis 1:2). Whence we read that the Lord was anointed with the 'oil of gladness' (Hebrews 1:9, etc.), that is with the Holy Spirit. 30. But the apostle John also calls the Holy Spirit 'unction,' saying (I John 2:27): "And as for you, let the unction, which you have received from him, abide in you. And you have no need that any man teach you; but as his unction teacheth you of all things." Now that is the Holy Spirit, an invisible unction.

iv. The Trinity (De Trinitate) 1. The Trinity (*Trinitas*) is so named because from a certain three (*tres*) is made one (*unum*) whole, as it were a 'Tri-unity' (*Triunitas*) – just like memory, intelligence, and will, in which the mind has in itself a certain image of the divine Trinity. Indeed, while they are three, they are one, because while they persist in themselves as individual components, they are all in all. 2. Therefore the Father, Son, and Holy Spirit are a trinity and a unity, for they are both one and three. They are one in nature (*natura*), three in person (*persona*). One because of their shared majesty, three because of the individuality of the persons. 3. For the Father is one person, the Son another, the Holy Spirit another – but another person (*alius*), not another thing (*aliud*), because they are equally and jointly a single thing (*simplex*), immutable, good, and coeternal. 4. Only the Father is not derived from another; therefore he is called Unbegotten (*Ingenitus*). Only the Son is born of the Father; therefore he is called Begotten (*Genitus*). Only the Holy Spirit proceeds from the Father and the Son; therefore it alone is referred to as 'the Spirit of both the others.'

5. For this Trinity some names are appellative (*appellativus*), and some are proper (*proprius*). The proper ones name the essence, such as God, Lord, Almighty, Immutable, Immortal. These are proper because they signify the very substance by which the three are one. 6. But appellative names are Father and Son and Holy Spirit, Unbegotten and Begotten and Proceeding. These same are also relational (*relativus*) because they have reference (*referre*, ppl. *relatus*) to one another. When one says "God," that is the essence, because he is being named with respect to himself. But when one says Father and Son and Holy Spirit, these names are spoken relationally, because they have reference to one another. 7. For we say 'Father' not with respect to himself, but with respect to his relation to the Son, because he has a son; likewise we speak of 'Son' relationally, because he has a father; and so 'Holy Spirit,' because it is the spirit of the Father and the Son. 8. This relationship is signified by these 'appellative terms' (*appellatio*), because they have reference to one another, but the substance itself, in which the three are one, is not thus signified.

Hence the Trinity exists in the relational names of the persons. Deity is not tripled, but exists in singleness, for if it were tripled we would introduce a plurality of gods. 9. For that reason the name of 'gods' in the plural is said with regard to angels and holy people, because they are not his equal in merit. 10. Concerning these is the Psalm (81:6 Vulgate), "I have said: You are gods." But for the Father and Son and Holy Spirit, because of their one and equal divinity, the name is observed to be not 'gods' but 'God,' as the Apostle says (I Corinthians 8:6): "Yet to us there is but one God," or as we hear from the divine voice (Mark 12:29, etc.), "Hear, O Israel: the Lord thy God is one God," namely inasmuch as he is both the Trinity and the one Lord God.

11. This tenet of faith concerning the Trinity is put in this way in Greek: 'one οὐσία,' as if one were to say 'one nature' (*natura*) or 'one essence' (*essentia*); 'three ὑποστάσεις,' which in Latin means "three persons" (*persona*) or "three substances" (*substantia*). 12. Now Latin does not speak of God properly except as 'essence'; people say 'substance,' indeed, but improperly, for in Greek the term 'substance' actually is understood as a person of God, not as his nature.[4]

v. Angels (De angelis) 1. Angels (*angelus*) are so called in Greek (i.e. ἄγγελος); they are *malachoth* (i.e. *malakim*) in Hebrew, but translated in Latin as "messengers" (*nuntius*), because they announce (*nuntiare*) the will of God to people. 2. The term for angels is thus the name of their function, not of their nature. Indeed they are always spirits, but when they are commissioned they are called angels. 3. For this reason the license of artists makes wings for them, to signify their swift course on all their missions, just as in poetic fiction the winds are said to have wings to indicate their speed. Whence also Holy Scripture says (Psalm 103:3 Vulgate), "Who walketh upon the wings of the winds."

4. Holy Scripture witnesses moreover that there are nine orders of angels, that is Angels, Archangels, Thrones, Dominations, Virtues, Principalities, Powers, Cherubim, and Seraphim (*angelus, archangelus, thronus, dominatio, virtus, principatus, potestas, cherub, seraph*). As to why these names are given to their offices, I shall go through them with explanations. 5. Angels are so called because they are sent from heaven in order to announce (*nuntiare*) things to humans, for the Greek 'angel' means "messenger" (*nuntius*) in Latin.

6. Archangels are translated from Greek as "highest messengers" (*summus nuntius*), for those who announce small or trifling things are Angels, but those who announce the highest (*summus*) things are named Archangels. Archangels are so called because they hold primacy among the angels, for ἀρχός in Greek is translated "chief" (*princeps*) in Latin. Indeed they are the leaders and chiefs, and under their Archangel order the tasks for each of the Angels are assigned. 7. That Archangels take precedence over Angels the prophet Zechariah bears witness, saying (2:3–4), "Behold the angel that spoke in me went forth, and another angel went out to meet him. And he said to him: Run, speak to this young man, saying: Jerusalem shall be inhabited without walls." 8. But if the higher powers did not assign their duties as angels to the lower ones, in no way would one angel have come to know from another what he should say to a human.

9. Moreover certain archangels are called by individual names, so that how they successfully discharge their duties might be designated through their names themselves. 10. 'Gabriel' in Hebrew is rendered in our language "Strength of God," because where divine power or

4 Isidore here speaks of the potentially misleading literal translation of the Greek ὑπό-στασις as the Latin *sub-stans*.

strength is displayed, Gabriel is sent. 11. Hence at the time when the Lord was about to be born and triumph over the world, Gabriel came to Mary to announce him who deigned to come as a humble person to conquer the aerial powers. 12. 'Michael' means "Who is like God?" for when something of wonderful power is done in the world, this archangel is sent. And his name comes from the work itself, because no one is strong enough to do what God can do. 13. 'Raphael' means "Healing" or "Medicine of God," for whenever there is need of healing and curing this archangel is sent by God – hence he is called "Medicine of God." 14. Hence this same archangel, sent to Tobit, brought healing to his eyes, and restored his sight to him as his blindness was wiped away. Thus the office of the angel is designated by the interpretation of his name. 15. 'Uriel' means 'Fire of God,' as we read that he appeared as a fire in a bush (cf. Exodus 3:2). We read, indeed, that as fire he was sent from above, and fulfilled what was commanded.

16. Further, Thrones and Dominations and Principalities and Powers and Virtues are understood to be orders and ranks of angels, in which orders the apostle Paul includes the whole heavenly company (Ephesians 1:21, Colossians 1:16, etc.). Because of this same distribution of offices some are called Thrones, some Dominations, some Principalities, some Powers, for the sake of the particular ranks by which they are distinguished from one another.

17. Angelic Virtues are named as the specific ministries through which signs and miracles are made in the world, and because of this they are called Virtues (*Virtutes*). 18. The Powers are those angels to which opposing forces are subject, and hence they are named with the term Powers (*Potestates*) because evil spirits are restrained by their power (*potestas*) so that they may not do as much harm in the world as they wish. 19. Principalities (*Principatus*) are those who preside over the bands of angels, and they take the name of Principality because they charge the angels below them with fulfilling the divine ministry. Thus there are some who administer (*administrare*) and others who 'stand by' (*adsistere*), as is said in Daniel (7:10), "Thousands of thousands ministered (*ministrare*) to him, and ten thousand times a hundred thousand stood before (*adsistere*) him."

20. Dominations are those who surpass even Virtues and Principalities. They are called Dominations (*Dominationes*) because they dominate (*dominari*) other bands of angels. 21. Thrones are bands of angels that in Latin are called 'seats' (*sedes*), and they are called Thrones because the Creator 'sits over' (*praesidere*) them, and discharges his judgments through them. 22. Cherubim too are reckoned as lofty powers indeed in heaven, and an angelic retinue. Translated from Hebrew into Latin they are 'Multitude of Knowledge' (*multitudo scientiae*), for they are a higher band of angels, and because, placed nearer, they have been more amply filled with divine knowledge than the others, they are called Cherubim, that is, "Fullness (*plenitudo*) of Knowledge." 23. They are represented in metal as the two animals resting on the mercy seat of the ark in order to signify the presence of angels in whose midst God is manifested.

24. Likewise the Seraphim are a multitude of angels whose name, translated from Hebrew into Latin, is "Ardent Ones" or "Fiery Ones." They are called 'Ardent Ones' because no angels are stationed between them and God, and therefore, the more nearly they are stationed to his presence, the more they are inflamed with the brightness of the divine light. 25. Whence they veil the face and feet of the one who sits on the throne of God (Isaiah 6:2); for that reason the crowd of other angels cannot fully see the essence of God, because the Cherubim (*sic*, for 'Seraphim') cloak it.

26. These terms for the bands of angels are specific for the individual orders in such a way that they still may be to some extent common to all. Thus, whereas the Thrones are specifically designated as the seats of God in a particular order of angels, nevertheless the Psalmist says (79:2 Vulgate), "Thou that sittest upon the cherubims." 27. But these orders of angels are called by their individual names because they have more fully received that particular function in their own order. Although common to them all, still these names are strictly speaking assigned to their own orders. 28. For to each order, as has been said, has been enjoined its proper functions, which they are known to have deserved at the beginning of the world.

Because angels preside over both places and humans an angel witnesses through a prophet, saying (Daniel 10:13), "The prince of the kingdom of the Persians resisted me." 29. Whence it is apparent that there is no place over which angels are not set. Moreover they have charge of the outcome of all endeavors. 30. This is the hierarchy or the array of the angels who stood in their celestial vigor after the Fall of the bad angels, for after the apostate angels fell, these were made firm in the steadfastness of eternal blessing. Whence we find, after the creation of heaven in the beginning (Genesis 1:6, 8), "Let there be a firmament (*firmamentum*) . . . and the firmament was called, Heaven." 31. This is surely the saying of one who is showing that after the Fall of the bad angels those who were steadfast strove for the firmness (*firmitas*) of eternal perseverance; diverted by no lapse, falling in no pride, but firmly (*firmiter*) holding steady in the love and contemplation of God, they consider nothing sweet except him by whom they were created.

32. Further, we read of two Seraphim in Isaiah (6:2); they figuratively signify the Old and New Testaments. We also read that they cover the face and feet of God, because we cannot know the past before the world or the future after the world, but we contemplate only the middle by their witness. 33. Each of them has six wings because in this present age we know concerning the fabric of this world only those things that were made in the six days. That each cries "Holy" three times to the other (Isaiah 6:3) shows the mystery of the Trinity in the one divinity.

vi. People who received their name from a certain presaging (De hominibus qui quodam praesagio nomen acceperunt) 1. Many of the early humans take the origin of their names from conditions specific to them. Their names were imparted to them prophetically in such a way that they concord with their future or their previous conditions. 2. While a holy and spiritual character abides in these names, we are now describing the meaning of their stories only with regard to the literal. Moreover, where we have not touched on the meaning of the etymology, we have merely set it forth in Latin. 3. Further, because of the diversity of accents and letters, it happens that one Hebrew name is transliterated in one way or another, so that the names are rendered with various meanings.

4. Adam, as blessed Jerome informs us, means "human" or "earthling" or "red earth," for from earth was flesh made, and humus (*humus*) was the material from which the human (*homo*) was made. 5. Eve (*Eva*) means "life" or "calamity" or "woe" (*vae*).[5] Life, because she was the origin of childbearing; calamity and woe because by her lying she was the cause of death – for 'calamity' (*calamitas*) takes its name from 'falling' (*cadere*). 6. But others say Eve is called 'life' and 'calamity' because often a woman is the cause of salvation for a man, often the cause of calamity and death, which is woe. 7. Cain is interpreted as "possession," whence, expressing this very etymology, his father says 'Cain,' that is (Genesis 4:1), "I have gotten (lit. 'I have possessed,' *possidere*) a man through God." And the same name means "lamentation," because he was killed for the killing of Abel, and he paid the penalty for his own crime. 8. Abel means "mourning," and by this name it was prefigured that he would be killed. Likewise it means "emptiness," because he was quickly removed and taken away.

9. Seth is translated "resurrection," because he was born after the killing of his brother, as if he triggered the resurrection of his brother from the dead. It also means "putting," because God put him in place of Abel. 10. Enos in a variation in his own language means "human being" or "man," and he had this name fittingly, for it is written of him (Genesis 4:26), "Then was the beginning of calling upon the name of the Lord" – although many of the Hebrews think rather that it was at that time that idols were first made in the name of the Lord and in his likeness. 11. Enoch means "dedication," for afterwards Cain built a city in his name (Genesis 5:17). 12. Cainan (i.e. Kenan) means "lamentation" or "possession of those," for as Cain means "possession," so the derivative name, which is Cainan, forms "possession of those." 13. Methuselah is translated "he has died." The etymology of his name is obvious, for some think that he was translated with his father[6] and that he lived past the time of the Flood. Against this it is significantly translated "he has died" to show that he did not live beyond the Flood, but died in that same cataclysm. Indeed, only the eight humans in the ark escaped the Flood.

14. Lamech means "striking down," for he struck down and killed Cain, and indeed afterwards he confesses to his wives that he did this (cf. Genesis 4:23–24). 15. Noah means "rest," since under him all past works came to rest because of the Flood. Whence his father, calling his name Noah, said (Genesis 5:29), "This same makes us rest from all our works." 16. Shem means "renowned," because he got his name as a presaging of his posterity, for out of him came the patriarchs and apostles and people of God. Also from his stock came Christ, whose name is great among the nations from the rising of the sun to its setting. 17. Cham (i.e. Ham) means "warm," and he was

5 The ancient anagram connects *Eva* and *vae*.

6 Methuselah's father Enoch was thought, on the basis of Genesis 5:24, to have passed on without death.

so named as a presaging of his future, for his posterity possessed that part of the land which is warmer because the sun is near. Hence still today Egypt, in the Egyptian language, is called *Kam*. 18. Japheth means "width," for from him were born the pagan nations, and because wide is the multitude of believers from among the gentiles, Japheth was named from that width. 19. Canaan the son of Ham is translated "their rebellion" – and what is this other than "their action"? – for because of the "rebellion" of his father Ham, that is, because of his action, he was cursed (Genesis 9:25).

20. Arpachshad means "the healer of the ravaging." 21. Cush in Hebrew is interpreted "the Ethiopian"; his name was allotted him from the posterity of his family, for from him issued the Ethiopians. 22. Nimrod means "tyrant," for he first seized unwonted tyrannical power among the people, and then himself advanced against God to build the tower of impiety. 23. Heber (i.e. Eber) means "passage." His etymology is mystical, because God passed away from his stock, nor would God remain among them when his grace was transferred to the gentiles – for from Heber rose the Hebrews. 24. Peleg means "division," and his father imposed such a name on him because he was born when the earth was divided by its languages. Terah means "investigation of the ascension." 25. Melchizedech means "righteous king." "King," because afterwards he ruled Salem. "Righteous," because distinguishing between the sacraments of the Law and the Gospel, he offered as a sacrifice not victims of cattle, but an oblation of bread and the chalice. 26. Lot means "shunning," for he did not consent to the doings of the Sodomites, but he shunned their illicit passions of the flesh. 27. Moab means "from the father." And the (compound) name as a whole has this etymology, for Lot's firstborn daughter conceived him from her father.

28. Ammon, whose name for good reason is rendered "the son of my people," is so derived that partly its sense is of a proper name, and partly it is an expression in itself, for *ammi*, after which the Ammonites are named, is the word for "my people." 29. Sarai means "my princess," because she was the materfamilias of only one household. Afterwards, as the rationale for her name has changed, with the letter *i* taken away from the end, she is called Sara (i.e. Sarah), that is, "princess." Indeed she was to be the princess of all nations, as the Lord had promised to Abraham (Genesis 17:16), "I will give thee from Sara a son, whom I will bless, and he shall become nations, and kings of people shall spring from her." 30. Hagar is "alien" or "turned back," for she was [as an alien given to the embrace of Abraham for the sake of bearing children, and after her display of contempt, when the angel rebuked her, she turned back to Sara]. 31. Keturah, "incense." 32. Ishmael is translated "listening of God," for thus it is written (cf. Genesis 16:11), "And she called his name Ishmael, because God listened to him."

33. Esau is three-named, and is variously named for appropriate reasons. He is called Esau, that is, "red," so named for his stewing specifically of the red lentil, for the eating of which he lost his birthright. Also he was called Edom, which means "bloody" in Latin, for the ruddiness of his body. But Seir, because he was bristly and hairy, for when he was born he was all hairy as if with a hide. 34. So he was named with three names: Esau, that is, "red"; Edom, that is, "bloody"; Seir, that is, "hairy," because he did not have smooth skin. 35. Rebecca, "patience," or "she who accepts much." 36. Leah, "burdened by labor" as of childbearing, for she in her fecundity of childbearing experienced more pangs than Rachel. 37. Rachel means "sheep," for Jacob put the sheep of Laban to pasture for her sake. 38. Zilpah, "yawning mouth." Bilhah, "inveterate." Dinah is translated as "cause," for she was the cause of the quarrel in Shechem. 39. Tamar, "bitterness," because of the death of her husbands, and also "she who changes," because she changed herself into the garb of a prostitute when she lay with her father-in-law.

40. Perez (*Phares*), "division": because he divided the membrane of the afterbirth, he was allotted the name of "divider," that is, *phares*. Whence also the Pharisees, who would separate themselves from the people as if they were righteous, were called "the divided ones." 41. Perez's brother Zerah, in whose hand was the scarlet thread, is interpreted "rising." Either because he appeared first, or because many righteous people sprang from him, as is contained in the book of Paralipomenon (I Chronicles 9:6), he was called Zerah, that is, "rising." 42. Job is rendered in Latin as "the grieving one," and rightly the grieving one (*dolens*), for the smiting of his flesh and his endurance of afflictions (*dolor*). Indeed the etymology of his name prefigured his calamities.

43. Pharaoh is the name not of a person, but of a position of rank, just as among us kings are called 'Augustus,' although they are recognized by their proper names. Further, in Latin 'Pharaoh' expresses "one denying him," to wit, God, or "his scatterer," for he was the afflicter of the

people of God. 44. Jannes, "the mariner," or "where is the sign?" for his magic ceased and failed before the signs of Moses, whence the magicians said (Exodus 8:19), "This is the finger of God." 45. Mambres (i.e. Jambres), "the sea made of skins" or "the sea in the head." 46. Then, Moses means "taken from the water." The daughter of Pharaoh found him exposed at the bank of the river, and picking him up she adopted him for herself, and she called his name 'Moses' because she took him from the water.

47. Aaron means "mountain of strength," because taking his censor he stood in the way between the survivors and those who had been killed, and as a kind of mountain of strength he prevented the destruction of death (Numbers 16:46–48). 48. Eleazar, "the help of God." Balak, "the one falling headlong" or "the devouring one." Balaam, "the idle people." 49. Phinehas, "one who spares the mouth," for with a dagger he pierced Zimri along with his Madianite harlot, and appeased the fury of the Lord, so that he might be sparing (Numbers 25:6–15). 50. This Zimri is "the provoker" or "the one who causes bitterness," and his name is appropriately figured by bitterness, because by sinning he embittered the people. 51. Rahab, "breadth" or "hunger" or "onslaught."

Joshua means "savior," for he, adumbrating Christ, saved the people from the wilderness and led them into the promised land. 52. Caleb, as it were "heart" or "dog." Othniel, "his time, God" or "the answer of God." Ehud, "glorious." Barak, "one who sends lightning." 53. Deborah, "bee" or "the talkative one." "Bee," because she was most quick to act, as she was struggling against Sisera, at whose slaying she sang her song – hence "the talkative one." Jael, "ascension." 54. Gideon, "proof of their iniquity," for he was informed, with repeated instances, by what kind of forewarning he might achieve a future victory over his enemies; from this proof of what would happen he got the etymology of his name.

Abimelech, "my father the king." 55. Tola, "little worm" or "scarlet cloth." Jair, "one who sheds light." Jephthah, "the opener" or "the one opened." Ezbon, "thought" or "fetters of grief." Abdon "his slave." 56. Samson, "their sun" or "the strength of the sun," for he was famous for his strength and liberated Israel from its enemies. Dalilah, "poor girl" or "bucket." Boaz, "in strength" [or] "in whom is toughness." 57. Naomi, which we can interpret as "she who is consoled," because when her husband and children had died in a foreign country she clung to her Moabite daughter-in-law as a consolation for herself. 58. Ruth means "hastening," for she was an alien from a non-Israelite people, who hastened, her homeland abandoned, to cross into the land of Israel, saying to her mother-in-law (Ruth 1:16), "Whithersoever thou shalt go, I will go." 59. Hannah is interpreted as "his grace" because, while first she was sterile by nature, afterwards by the grace of God she became fertile.

Eli, "my God." 60. Hophni, "unshod," for this son of Eli was chosen for the ministry of priesthood, and he represented his loss of the priesthood by his own name, for the Apostle says (Ephesians 6:15), "Your feet shod with the preparation of the gospel of peace." 61. And the Prophet (cf. Isaiah 52:7), "How beautiful are the feet that bringeth tidings of peace!" Therefore the name means "unshod," in order that by his name might be signified the removal of the priesthood of the Old Testament from the ancient nation. 62. Phinehas, the brother of Hophni, means "mute mouth," in which is signified the silence of the old priesthood and doctrine.

Samuel, "his name is God." Jesse, "sacrifice of the island" or "incense." 63. Saul [means] "petition," for it is well known how the Hebrew people petitioned for him as a king for themselves, and received him not according to God, but according to their own will. 64. David, "strong in his hand," in that he was very strong in battles. And the name means "desirable," namely in his progeny, about which the Prophet made his prediction (Haggai 2:8), "And the desired of all nations shall come." 65. Solomon is said to have three names. His first name is Solomon, that is, "peacemaking," because there was peace in his reign. His second name was Jedidiah, because he was esteemed and beloved of the Lord. His third name was Coheleth, which in Greek is called 'Ecclesiastes,' in Latin 'the Preacher,' because he would speak to the people.

66. Jonathan, "gift of a dove." 67. Absalom, "peace of the father" by antiphrasis, because he waged war against his father, or because in that war David is read to have been brought to peace with his son, so much that he lamented his death with huge grief. 68. Rehoboam, "breadth of the people," and that signification by antiphrasis, because when the ten tribes were separated from him, only two remained for him. 69. Abijam, "father Lord" or "he was father." Asa, "one who lifts" or "one who raises up." Jehoshaphat, "judgment of the Lord." Jehoram, "he who is lofty." Ahaziah, "he who grasps the Lord." 70. Athaliah, "time of the

Lord." Joash, "he who breathes" or "the toughness of the Lord." Amaziah, "he who lifts up the people." 71. Uzziah, "strength of the Lord." Azariah, "help of the Lord." Uzziah and Azariah are the same person with two names. It is he who, having tried to lay claim to an unlawful priesthood for himself, was stricken with leprosy in the face.

72. Jotham, "he is perfect," making a fine etymology of his name, for he did right in the sight of the Lord, and built a lofty gate for the Temple. 73. Ahaz, "he who grasps." Hezekiah, "strong Lord." Manasseh, "forgetful," for with many impieties and sacrileges he forsook and was forgetful of God, [or because God was forgetful of his sins]. 74. Amon, "faithful" or "burdened." Josiah, "where is the kindling of the Lord?" – an appropriate etymology for his name, for it was he who burnt up the idols. 75. Jehoahaz, "tough." Jehoiakim, "where is the preparation?"

Eliakim, "resurrection of God." Jehoiachin, "preparation of the Lord." Zedekiah, "righteous of the Lord." 76. Jeroboam, "judgment" or "cause of the people," or, as some say, it means "division," because in his reign the people of Israel were divided and cut off from the reign of the line of David – for he stood out as the cause of the division of the people. 77. Zimri, "psalm" or "my song." Omri, "my curled one." Ahab, "brother of the father." 78. Jezebel, "flux of blood," or "she who streams with blood"; but better, "where is the dung-heap?" – for when she was hurled down headlong, dogs devoured her flesh, as Elijah had predicted (IV Kings 9:37 Vulgate): he said, "And the flesh of Jezebel shall be as dung upon the face of the earth."

79. Ahaziah, "he who grasps God." Jehu, "that one" or "he is." Jotham, "the tough one." Shallum, "his shadow," or "petition." Menahem, "the consoler." Pekah, "he who opens." 80. Nebuchadnezzar, "prophecy of the narrow flask," or "one who prophesies" a symbol of this kind, namely with regard to the dream of future things that he is reported to have seen, which Daniel interpreted; or, "a lingering in the recognition of difficulties," with regard to those who were led by him into captivity. 81. The name Zerubbabel is said to have been composed in Hebrew from three whole words: *zo*, "that," *ro*, "master," *babel*, properly "Babylonian"; and the name is compounded Zorobabel, "that master from Babylon," for he was born in Babylon, where he flourished as prince of the Jewish people.

vii. The patriarchs (De patriarchis) 1. The etymologies of certain patriarchs ought to be noted, so that we may know what is reflected in their names, for many of them took their names from specific causes. 'Patriarchs' means "chiefs among the fathers" (*patrum principes*), for ἀρχός in Greek means 'chief' (*princeps*). 2. At first "Abram" was so called – "father seeing the people" – with regard to Israel only. Afterwards he was called 'Abraham,' which is translated "father of many nations," which was yet to come to pass through faith. However, "nations" is not contained in the name but is understood, according to this (Genesis 17:5): "Thy name shall be Abraham, because I have made thee a father of many nations." 3. Isaac took his name from "laughter," for his father had laughed when Isaac was promised to him, astonished in joy. And his mother laughed, doubting in joy, when Isaac's birth was promised by the three men. Therefore he took the name Isaac for this reason, for it means "laughter."

4. It should moreover be known that four people in the Old Testament were given their names without any concealment before they were born: Ishmael, Isaac, Solomon, and Josiah. Read the Scriptures (Genesis 16:11, Genesis 21:6, II Kings 12:25, III Kings 13:2 Vulgate – see vi.74 above). 5. Jacob means "the supplanter," either because in birth he clutched the heel (*planta*) of his newborn brother, or because afterwards he deceived his brother by a stratagem. Whence Esau said (Genesis 27:36), "Rightly is his name called Jacob, for he hath supplanted me lo this second time." 6. Israel, "the man seeing God," for he received this name at the time when having wrestled all night he beat the angel in a struggle, and was blessed at daybreak. Hence because of his vision of God he was called Israel, as he himself says (Genesis 32:30), "I have seen God and my soul has been saved." 7. 'Reuben' means "son of the vision." Indeed, when Leah gave birth to him, she called his name Reuben, saying (Genesis 29:32), "For God saw my affliction."

8. 'Simeon' is interpreted "the hearing," for thus Leah said when she gave birth to him (Genesis 29:33), "For God heard me." 9. Levi, "the added one," for Leah said when she gave birth to him, not doubting the love of her husband (Genesis 29:34), "Now my husband will be with me, because I have borne him three sons." 10. Judah is called "the proclamation," for when Leah gave birth to him she offered up praise to the Lord, saying (Genesis 29:35), "Now over this I will proclaim the Lord," and for this he was called Judah. Accordingly his name was so

called from "proclamation," because it is a rendering of thanks.

11. Issachar means "he is a recompense"; *is* indeed means "he is," and *sachar* means "recompense." This is because Leah purchased for herself intercourse with her husband, which was owed to Rachel, with the mandrakes of her son Reuben. Whence when Issachar was born Leah said (Genesis 30:18), "God hath given my recompense." 12. Zebulun means "dwelling place," for Leah gave birth to him as her sixth son, and therefore now assured she said (Genesis 30:20), "My husband shall dwell with me." Whence her son was called "habitation." 13. Naphtali: the principle in his name has to do with "conversion" or "comparison" (*comparatio*), whence Rachel said, when her maid Bilhah had given birth to him, "God hath made me live in a dwelling with my sister."[7]

14. Dan means "judgment," for when Bilhah gave birth to him, her mistress Rachel said (Genesis 30:6), "The Lord hath judged for me, and hearing my voice he hath given me a son." She expressed the principle in his name in that, because the Lord had judged, she imposed the name 'judgment' on the son of her maidservant. 15. Gad was named from "outcome" or "in readiness," for when Zilpah had given birth to him, her mistress Leah said (Genesis 30:11), "Happily," that is, meaning with regard to his readiness or to his outcome. 16. Asher means "blessed," for when Zilpah had given birth to him, Leah said (Genesis 30:13), "Blessed am I, and women bless me." She called Asher 'blessed' in the etymology of his name because she is called blessed.

17. Joseph: because his mother had wanted to add another for herself, she called him "the addition." Pharoah called him Zaphanath, which in Hebrew signifies "discoverer of hidden things," because he laid bare the obscure dreams and predicted the blight. 18. Still, because this name was imposed on him by the Egyptian, it ought to have a rationale in the Pharoah's own tongue. Therefore in Egyptian speech Zaphanath is interpreted "savior of the world," because he liberated the land from imminent destruction by famine. 19. Benjamin means "son of the right hand," that is, "of valor," for the right hand is called *iamin*. Indeed his dying mother gave him the name Benoni, that is, "son of my pain." His father changed this, naming him "son of the right hand." 20. Manasseh was so called because his father was unmindful of his hardships, for this is the word for "unmindfulness" in Hebrew. 21. Ephraim, because God added him on, and the name is translated in our language as "addition."

viii. The prophets (De prophetis) 1. Those whom the pagan world calls bards (*vates*) we call prophets (*propheta*), as if they were 'pre-speakers' (*praefator*), because indeed they 'speak in the future' (*porro* + *fari*, ppl. *fatus*) and make true predictions about the future. Those whom we call prophets were called 'seers' (*videns*) in the Old Testament, because they saw (*videre*) things that others did not see, and would foresee things that were hidden in mystery. 2. Hence it is written in Samuel (I Kings 9:9), "Let us go to the seer (*videns*)." Hence Isaiah says (6:1), "I saw (*videre*) the Lord sitting on a throne high and elevated," and Ezekiel (1:1), "The heavens were opened and I saw (*videre*) the visions of God."

3. The etymologies of the names of certain prophets should be remarked, for their names well display what they foretold about future things by their deeds and words. 4. Elijah means "the Lord God." He was so called as an omen of the future, for when he contended about the sacrifice with the four hundred priests of Baal, as the name of the Lord was invoked, fire descended from heaven on the burnt offering (III Kings 18:39), "And when all the people saw this, they fell on their faces and said: The Lord he is God." 5. For this reason he received such a name beforehand, because afterwards through him the people recognized the Lord God. The same name means "strong Lord," either because he killed those same priests, or because he endured the enmity of Ahab.

6. Elisha means "salvation (*salus*) of the Lord." He too got his name as an omen of the future, and accordingly worked many miracles, and in driving away the famine he saved (*salvare*) the people from death. 7. Nathan, "he gave" or "of the giver." Isaiah means "savior of the Lord," and deservedly, for more fully than others he heralded the Savior of the whole world and his holy mysteries. 8. Jeremiah, "lofty of the Lord," because of what was said to him (Jeremiah 1:10), "I have set thee over the nations, and over kingdoms." 9. Ezekiel, "strength of God." Daniel, "judgment of God," either because in his judgment of the elders he delivered a judgment based on divinely inspired consideration when he freed Susanna

7 The received text of Genesis 30:8, to which Isidore alludes, reads, "God hath compared (*comparare*) me with my sister."

from destruction by uncovering their falsity, or because, discerning with shrewd intelligence, he disclosed visions and dreams in which the future was revealed by certain details and riddles. And he was called (Daniel 9:23) "a man of desires," because he did not eat the bread of desire, nor drink the wine of concupiscence.

10. Hosea, "savior," or "he who saves" (*salvans*), for when he prophesied the wrath of God against the people Israel for their crime of idolatry, he announced the safety (*salus*) of the house of Judah. Because of this Hezekiah, king of Judah, is shown to have purged and purified the Temple of the Lord once the idols that preceding kings had consecrated were removed. 11. Joel, "Lord God," or "beginning in God," or "he was of God" – these because his name reflects an uncertain etymology. 12. Amos, "the people torn away," for his prophecy was directed toward the people Israel, because they were already torn away from the Lord, and worshipped golden calves, or they were torn from the reign of the line of David.

13. Nahum, "the groaning one" or "the consoler," for he cries out against the "city of blood" (Nahum 3:1), and after its overthrow he consoles Zion, saying (Nahum 1:15), "Behold upon the mountains the feet of him that bringeth good tidings, and that preacheth peace." 14. Habakkuk, "the one who embraces." He is either called "embrace" because he was beloved of God, or, because he engaged in contention with God, he was allotted the name of "the one who embraces," that is, of "the one who wrestles." Indeed, no other dared with such bold voice to provoke God to a debate about justice, as to why such great iniquity is involved in human affairs and in the affairs of this world.

15. Micah, "who is this?" or "who is that one?" 16. Zephaniah is interpreted "looking-glass" (*speculum*) or "hidden thing of the Lord"; either is appropriate for a prophet because they know the mysteries of God. Whence it is said to Ezekiel (3:17), "I have made thee a watchman (*speculator*)." And elsewhere (cf. Amos 3:7), "For the Lord will do nothing without revealing to his servants the prophets." 17. Obadiah, "slave of the Lord," for as Moses was servant of the Lord and the apostle Paul was the slave of Christ, so Obadiah, sent as the "ambassador to the nations" (Obadiah 1:1), comes and preaches what befits his prophetic ministry and servitude – hence, "slave of the Lord."

18. Jonah means "dove" or "the mourner." "Dove" for his groaning, when he was in the belly of the huge fish for three days, and "the mourner" either because of the grief he felt for the safety of the Ninevites or because of the suddenly withered ivy in the shade of which he took cover against the heat of the sun. 19. And he is also, as the Jews affirm, Amittai, the son of the widow of Zarephath whom Elijah resuscitated, as his mother afterwards said to him (III Kings 17:24 Vulgate), "Now I know that thou art a man of God, and the word of God in thy mouth is of truth." For this reason the boy was called Amittai, for Amittai, from the Hebrew, means "truth" in Latin, and because Elijah spoke a true thing, the boy who was resuscitated was named "the son of truth."

20. Zechariah, "memory of the Lord," for at the end of the seventieth year after the destruction of the Temple was finished, while Zechariah was preaching, the Lord remembered his people, and by the command of Darius the people of God returned, and both the city and the Temple were rebuilt. 21. Haggai in Latin signifies "hasty" (*festinus*)[8] and "joyful," for he prophesies that the destroyed Temple is to be built, and after the grief of the captivity he preaches the joy of the return. 22. Malachi means "angel of the Lord," that is, "messenger," for whatever he said was trusted as if commanded by the Lord. Hence the Septuagint translates his name in this way, saying (Malachi 1:1), "The burden of the word of the Lord to Israel by the hand of his angel."

23. Ezra, "the helper." Nehemiah, "the consoler from the Lord." These names were allotted as a certain omen of the future, for they were a help and a consolation for his whole people as they returned to their homeland. Indeed these same two rebuilt the Temple of the Lord, and they restored the works of the walls and towers. 24. Hananiah, "the grace of God." The same person is also Shadrach in the Chaldean language, which means "my handsome one." 25. Azariah, "help of the Lord," and he is the same as Abednego, which is turned into Latin as "as a slave I am silent." 26. Mishael, "who is the people of the Lord?" and he is also Meshach, which means "laughter" or "joy."

27. Ahijah, "my brother." Shemaiah, "he who hears the Lord." Asaph, ["he who gathers"]. Ethan, ["the tough one" or "he who has ascended"]. 28. Jeduthun, "he who leaps across those" or "he who jumps those," for this person called 'the leaper across' leapt by his singing across certain people who were cleaving to the ground, bent

8 The reading *festivus*, "festive," seems preferable.

down to the earth, thinking about things that are at the lowest depths, and putting their hope in transient things. 29. Heman, "he who accepts" or "their dread." Ethan, "the tough one." Berechiah, "blessed of the Lord" or "blessed Lord." Huldah, "distraction" or "diversion." Judith, "she who praises" or "she who proclaims." Esther, "the hidden one."

30. Zechariah, ["memory of the Lord," for what he sings (Luke 1:72), "to remember his holy testament"]. 31. John [the Baptist, "grace of the Lord," because he was the end of prophecy, the herald of grace, or the beginning of baptism, through which grace is administered]. 32. These are the prophets of the Old and New Testament, of whom the last is Christ, to whom it is said by the Father (Jeremiah 1:5), "I made thee a prophet unto the nations."

33. Moreover, there are seven kinds of prophesy. The first kind is ecstasy (*ecstasis*), which is a passing beyond of the mind, as when Peter in a stunned state of mind saw that vessel let down from heaven with various animals (see Acts 10:11–12). 34. The second kind is vision (*visio*), as when Isaiah says (Isaiah 6:1), "I saw (*videre*, ppl. *visus*) the Lord sitting upon a high throne." The third kind is dream (*somnium*), as Jacob while sleeping saw the ladder reaching up to heaven. The fourth kind is through a cloud, as God speaks to Moses and to Job after he was stricken. 35. The fifth kind is a voice from heaven, like that which sounded to Abraham saying (Genesis 22:12), "Lay not thy hand upon the boy," and to Saul on the road (Acts 9:4), "Saul, Saul, why persecutest thou me?" 36. The sixth kind occurs when an oracle (*parabola*) is received, as with Solomon in Proverbs, and with Balaam when he was called upon by Balak. The seventh kind is being filled (*repletio*) with the Holy Spirit, as with nearly all the prophets.

37. Others have said that there are three kinds of visions (*visio*). One, according to the eyes of the body, as Abraham saw three men under the holm-oak of Mambre, and Moses saw the fire in the bush, and the disciples saw the transfigured Lord on the mountain between Moses and Elijah, and others of this kind. 38. A second, according to the spirit, in which we imagine what we sense through the body, as Peter saw the dish sent down from heaven with the various animals (Acts 10:11–12), and as Isaiah saw God on the highest seat, not bodily but spiritually (Isaiah 6:1). 39. For no bodily form limits God, but in the same way that many things are said not properly but figuratively, so also many things are shown figuratively.

40. Then there is a third kind of vision, which is neither by bodily senses nor by that part of the soul where images of corporeal things are grasped, but by insight (*intuitus*) of the mind where intellectual truth is contemplated, as the gifted Daniel saw with his mind what Belshazzar had seen with his body. Without this kind of vision the other two are either fruitless or positively lead into error. Still, the Holy Spirit governs all these kinds of vision. 41. Further, not only a good person, but also a bad person can have prophecy, for we find that King Saul prophesied, for he was persecuting the holy David, and filled with the Holy Spirit he began to prophesy.

ix. The apostles (De apostolis) 1. Apostle (*apostolus*) means "one who is sent," for the name indicates this. Just as in Greek ἄγγελος means "messenger" (*nuntius*) in Latin, so 'one who is sent' is called an 'apostle' in Greek (i.e. ἀπόστολος), for Christ sent them to spread the gospel through the whole world, so that certain ones would penetrate Persia and India teaching the nations and working great and incredible miracles in the name of Christ, in order that, from those corroborating signs and prodigies, people might believe in what the Apostles were saying and had seen. Most of them receive the rationale for their names from these activities.

2. Peter (*Petrus*) took his name from 'rock' (*petra*), that is, from Christ, on whom the Church is founded. Now *petra* is not given its name from *Petrus*, but *Petrus* from *petra*, just as 'Christ' is so called not from 'Christian,' but 'Christian' from 'Christ.' Therefore the Lord says (Matthew 16:18), "Thou art Peter, and upon this rock (*petra*) I will build my church," because Peter had said (Matthew 16:16), "Thou art Christ, the Son of the living God." Then the Lord said to him, "Upon this rock" which you have proclaimed "I will build my church," for (I Corinthians 10:4) "the rock was Christ," on which foundation even Peter himself was built. 3. He was called Cephas because he was established as the head (*caput*) of the apostles, for κεφαλή in Greek means 'head,' and Cephas is the Syrian name for Peter. 4. Simon 'Bar-Jonah' in our tongue means "son of a dove," and is both a Syrian and a Hebrew name, for *Bar* in the Syrian language is "son," 'Jonah' in Hebrew is "dove," and Bar-Jonah is composed of both languages. 5. Some people simply take it that Simon, that is Peter, is the son of

John, because of that question (John 21:15), "Simon of John, lovest thou me?" – and they consider it corrupted by an error of the scribes, so that *Bar-Iona* was written for *Bar-Iohannes*, that is, 'son of John,' with one syllable dropped. 'Johanna' means "grace of the Lord." 6. So Peter was three-named: Peter, Cephas, and Simon Bar-Jonah; further 'Simon' in Hebrew means "he who listens."

7. Saul in Hebrew speech means "attack," because he was at first involved in attacking the Church, for he was a persecutor; hence he had that name when he was persecuting Christians. 8. Afterwards, with the name changed, from Saul was made Paul, which is interpreted "the wonderful one" or "the chosen one." Wonderful, because he performed many signs or because from east to west he preached the gospel of Christ to all the nations. 9. Chosen, as the Holy Spirit says in the Acts of the Apostles (13:2), "Separate me Barnabas and Paul, for the work whereunto I have chosen them." Further in Latin speech Paul (*Paulus*; cf. *paulus*, "little") is so called from "little," whence he himself says (I Corinthians 15:9), "For I am the least of all the apostles." Thus when he was Saul he was proud and haughty; when Paul, humble and little. 10. Therefore we speak thus, "after a little (*paulo*) I will see you," that is, after a short time. Now because he became little, he himself says (cf. I Corinthians 15:8), "For I am the last [of all] the apostles," and (Ephesians 3:8), "To me, the least of all the saints." Both Cephas and Saul, then, were called by a changed name so that they would indeed be new even in their names, like Abraham and Sarah.

11. Andrew, the brother of Peter in the flesh, and his co-heir in grace; according to its Hebrew etymology 'Andrew' means "handsome one" or "he who answers," and further in Greek speech he is called "the manly one" from the word for "man" (cf. Greek ἀνήρ, gen. ἀνδρός, "man"). 12. John with a certain prophetic foresight deservedly got his name, for it means "in whom is grace" or "grace of the Lord." Indeed, Jesus loved him more fully than the other apostles. 13. James of Zebedee has his surname from his father, and leaving his father he with John followed the true Father. These are (Mark 3:17) the "Sons of Thunder" who were named 'Boanerges' from the strength and greatness of their faith. This James is the son of Zebedee, the brother of John, who is revealed to have been killed by Herod after the ascension of the Lord.

14. James of Alphaeus, surnamed so as to be distinguished from the other James who is called the son of Zebedee, as this second one is the son of Alphaeus. Therefore both took their surnames from their fathers. 15. The latter is James the Less, who is called the brother of the Lord in the Gospel, because Mary the wife of Alphaeus was the sister of the mother of the Lord, and the evangelist John surnamed the former Mary 'of Clopas' after her father, assigning her this name either from the nobility of her family or for some other reason. Further, 'Alphaeus' in Hebrew speech means "the thousandth" or "the learned one" in Latin. 16. Philip, "mouth of lamps" or "mouth of hands." Thomas, "the abyss" or "the twin," whence in Greek he is also called Didymus. Bartholomew, "son of the one supporting the waters" or "son of the one supporting me." This is Syriac, not Hebrew. 17. 'Matthew' in Hebrew expresses "the one granted." This same person was also called Levi after the tribe from which he sprang. Further, in Latin he got the name of 'the publican' from his work, for he was chosen from among the publicans and brought into the apostolate.

18. Simon the Cananean, as distinct from Simon Peter, is named after the Galilean township Cana where the Lord changed water into wine. It is this one who by another evangelist is designated 'the Zealot'; indeed 'Cana' means "zeal." 19. Judas of James, who elsewhere is called Lebbaeus, has his symbolic name from the word for 'heart,' which we can call "little heart" in the diminutive. Another Gospel writer (Matthew 10:3) calls this Judas 'Thaddaeus.' Church history relates that he was sent to Edessa to the king of the Abgars. 20. Judas Iscariot got his name either from the township in which he was born or from the tribe of Issachar, with a certain omen of the future as to his own condemnation, for 'Issachar' means "payment," to signify the traitor's price for which he sold the Lord, as it is written (cf. Matthew 27:9), "And they took" my payment, "the thirty pieces of silver, the price that I was prized by them."

21. Matthias, who is considered the only one among the apostles to be without a surname, means "the one granted," so that it may be understood: "in place of Judas," for he was elected in Judas's place by the apostles, when lots were cast to decide between two people. 22. Mark, "lofty in his mandate," especially for the Gospel of the Most High that he preached. 23. Luke, "the one who rises" or "the one lifting up" [because he lifted up the

preaching of the gospel after the others]. 24. Barnabas, "son of the prophet" or "son of consolation."

x. Other names in the Gospel (De reliquis in Evangelio nominibus) 1. Mary, "she who illuminates" or "star of the sea (*mare*)," for she gave birth to the light of the world. Further, in Syrian speech 'Mary' means "mistress" – and beautifully – for she gave birth to the Lord. 2. Elizabeth, "fullness of my God" or "oath of my God." 3. Magdalene, "tower." Martha, "one who incites" or "one who provokes," and in Syrian speech it means "one who dominates." 4. Nathanael, "gift of God" [because by the gift of God there was no guile, that is, pretense, in him]. 5. Zebedee, "the one granted" or "the one who flows." Zacchaeus, "the just one" or "the justified one" or "the one who should be justified." It is a Syrian, not Hebrew, name. 6. Lazarus, "the one helped" [because he was resuscitated from death]. Herod, "the hairy one' or 'the vainglorious one."

7. Caiaphas, "the investigator" or "the shrewd one" or "he who vomits from the mouth" – for wickedly he condemned the righteous one with his mouth, although he had announced this by a prophetic mystery. 8. Pontius, "he who shuns counsel," especially that of the Jews, for, taking water, he washed his hands, saying (Matthew 27:24), "I am innocent of the blood of this just man." 9. Pilate, "mouth of the hammerer" [because when he both justified and condemned Christ with his mouth, he struck on both sides in the manner of a hammerer]. 10. Barabbas, "son of their teacher," doubtless "of the teacher of the Jews," who is the devil, the instigator of the murderers, who reigns among them still today.

xi. Martyrs (De martyribus) 1. 'Martyrs' (*martyr*) in the Greek language (i.e. μάρτυρ) are called 'witnesses' (*testis*) in Latin, whence 'testimonials' are called *martyria* in Greek. And they are called witnesses because for their witness (*testimonium*) of Christ they suffered their passions and struggled for truth even to the point of death. 2. But because we call them not *testes*, which we certainly could do, using the Latin term, but rather 'martyrs' in the Greek, this Greek word sounds quite familiar in the ears of the Church, as do many Greek terms that we use in place of Latin.

3. The first martyr in the New Testament was Stephen, whose name in Hebrew speech is interpreted "standard," because in his martyrdom he was the first standard for the imitation of the faithful. The same name is rendered from the Greek tongue into Latin as "the crowned one," and this by way of prophecy, because through a certain foreseeing of the future his name signified beforehand what would come to pass, for he suffered, and what he was called, he received. Thus 'Stephen' means "crown"; he was in humility stoned, but in sublimity crowned.

4. Further there are two kinds of martyr: one in manifest passion, the other in hidden valor of the spirit. Indeed, many people, suffering the snares of the enemy and resisting all carnal desires, because they sacrificed themselves in their hearts for almighty God, became martyrs even in times of peace – those indeed who, if a period of persecution had occurred, could have been martyrs.

xii. Clerics (De clericis) 1. The clergy (*clerus*) and clerics (*clericus*) are so called because Matthias, who as we read was the first person ordained by the apostles, was chosen by lot – for κλῆρος in Greek means "allotment" or "inheritance." 2. Therefore they are called clerics because they are of the allotment of the Lord, or because they have a portion of the Lord. And in general all who serve in the Church of Christ are named 'clerics.' Their ranks and names are these: 3. doorkeeper (*ostiarius*), psalmist (*psalmista*), reader (*lector*), exorcist (*exorcista*), acolyte (*acolythus*), subdeacon (*subdiaconus*), deacon (*diaconus*), priest (*presbyter*), bishop (*episcopus*).

4. The order of bishops is fourfold, that is, of patriarchs, archbishops, metropolitans, and bishops (*patriarcha, archiepiscopus, metropolitanus, episcopus*). 5. 'Patriarch' in the Greek language means "chief of the fathers," because he holds the chief, that is, the apostolic place. And therefore, because he is employed in the office of highest honor, he is judged worthy of such a name as the 'Roman' or 'Antiochene' or 'Alexandrian' patriarch. 6. 'Archbishop' is so named with a Greek term because he is "highest of the bishops," for he holds an apostle's place and presides over metropolitans as well as other bishops. 7. ['Metropolitan' is so called from "the measure of cities."] Archbishops are placed above the several provinces, and other priests are subject to their authority and doctrine, and without them the other bishops may do nothing; indeed the care of the whole province is committed to archbishops.

8. Moreover, all the orders designated above are named by one and the same term, 'bishop,' but beyond

that some use a particular name to distinguish the powers that they have received individually. 9. Patriarch, "father of chiefs," for ἄρχων is 'chief.' 10. Archbishop, "chief of bishops." Metropolitan … 11. Further, the term 'episcopacy' (*episcopatus*) is so called because he who is placed over it has oversight (*superintendere*), exercising pastoral care, that is, over his subjects, for the term σκοπεῖν in Latin means "watch over" (*intendere*). 12. 'Bishop,' then, in Greek, means "overseer" (*speculator*) in Latin, for he is set over the Church as an overseer. He is so called because he keeps watch (*speculari*), and oversees (*praespicere*) the behavior and lives of the people placed under him.

13. The 'pontifex' is the chief of priests, as if the word were 'the way' of his followers.[9] And he is also named the 'highest priest' and the *pontifex maximus*, for he creates priests and levites (i.e. deacons); he himself disposes all the ecclesiastical orders; he indicates what each one should do. 14. Indeed, in former times pontifexes were also kings, for this was the custom of our ancestors, that the king was himself a priest or pontifex – hence the Roman emperors were also called pontifexes.

15. *Vates* are so called from 'force of mind' (*vis mentis*), and the meaning of the word is manifold, for now it means "priest," now "prophet," now "poet." 16. A 'high priest' (*antistes sacerdos*) is so called because he 'stands before' (*ante stare*), for he is first in the hierarchy of the Church, and he has no one above him.

17. A priest (*sacerdos*) has a name compounded of Greek and Latin, as it were 'one who gives a holy thing' (*sacrum dans*), for as king (*rex*) is named from 'ruling' (*regere*), so priest from 'making sacrifice' (*sacrificare*) – for he consecrates (*consecrare*) and sanctifies (*sanctificare*). 18. Further, priests of the gentiles were called flamens. They wore on their heads a felt cap (*pilleus*), and on top of this there was a short stick holding a piece of wool. Because they could not bear it in the summer's heat, they began to bind their heads with a fillet only, 19. for it was an abomination for them to pass within with a completely bare head. Hence from the fillet (*filum*) that they used they were called flamens (*flamen*, plural *flamines*), as if it were *filamines*. But on feast days, with the fillet laid aside they would put on the *pilleus* out of respect for the eminence of their priesthood.

9 Isidore alludes to the presumed etymology of *pontifex* from *pons*, 'bridge,' hence 'way.'

20. 'Priest' (*presbyter*) in Greek is interpreted "elder" (*senior*) in Latin. They are named elders not because of their age, or their exhausted senility, but rather for the honor and status that they have received. 21. Elders (*presbyter*) are also called priests (*sacerdos*), because they perform the sacraments (*sacrum dare*), as do bishops; but although they are priests (*sacerdos*) they do not have the miter of the pontificate, for they neither mark the brow with chrism nor give the Spirit, the Comforter, which a reading of the Acts of the Apostles shows may be done by bishops only. Whence, among the ancients, bishops and priests (*presbyter*) were the same, for the former name is associated with rank, the latter with seniority.

22. Levites were named after their originator, for the levites descended from Levi, and by them the ministries of the mystic sacraments were performed in the Temple of God. In Greek these are called deacons (*diaconus*), in Latin ministers (*minister*), for just as *sacerdos* is related to 'consecration (*consecratio*), *diaconus* (cf. διακονεῖν, "minister," "do service") is related to 'dispensing of service' (*ministerii dispensatio*). 23. *Hypodiacones* in Greek are what we call subdeacons (*subdiaconus*), who are so called because they are subject to the regulations and offices of levites. They receive offerings from the faithful in the Temple of God, and bring them to the levites for placing on the altars. In Hebrew they are called Nathanians (*Nathaneus*).

24. Readers (*lector*) are named from 'reading' (*legere*, ppl. *lectus*) and psalmists (*psalmista*) from singing psalms, for the former pronounce to the people what they should follow, and the latter sing to kindle the spirits of their audience to compunction – although some readers also declaim in so heart-rending a way that they drive some people to sorrow and lamentation. 25. These same people are also called 'announcers' (*pronuntiator*) because they announce from far away (*porro adnuntiare*), for their voice will be so loud and clear that they fill the ears even of those placed far away.

26. Further, a chanter (*cantor*) is so called because he modulates his voice in singing (*cantus*). There are said to be two types of chanter in the art of music, corresponding with the names learned people have been able to give them in Latin, the precentor (*praecentor*) and the succentor (*succentor*). 27. The precentor is so called, naturally, because he leads the singing; the succentor because he follows in response. 28. We also speak of a co-chanter (*concentor*), one who 'sings at the same time'

(*consonare*), but he who sings at the same time but does not 'sing jointly' (*concinere*) will not be called co-chanter.

29. 'Acolytes' (*acolythus*) in Greek are called torch-bearers (*ceroferarius*) in Latin, from their carrying candles (*cereus*) when the Gospel is to be read or mass is to be offered. 30. For at that time lights are kindled and carried by them, not in order to put darkness to flight, since at the same time there is daylight, but in order to display a symbol of joy, so that under the figure of the physical candlelight that light may be displayed concerning which it is read in the Gospel (John 1:9), "That was the true light, which enlighteneth every man that cometh into this world."

31. 'Exorcists' (*exorcista*) are rendered from Greek into Latin as "swearers" (*adiurans*) or "rebukers," for they invoke, upon the catechumens or upon those who have an unclean spirit, the name of the Lord Jesus, swearing (*adiurare*) through him that it may depart from them. 32. Doorkeepers are the same as porters (*ianitor*), who in the Old Testament were chosen to guard the Temple, lest someone unclean in any way should enter it. They are called doorkeepers (*ostiarius*) because they are present at the doors (*ostium*) of the Temple. 33. Keeping the key, they watch over everything inside and out, and making judgment between the good and the bad they receive the faithful and reject the unfaithful.

xiii. Monks (De monachis) 1. The term 'monk' (*monachus*) has a Greek etymology, because a monk is alone (*singularis*), for μονάς in Greek means "oneness" (*singularitas*). Therefore if the word for monk means 'a solitary' (*solitarius*), what is someone who is alone (*solus*) doing in a crowd? There are, however, several kinds of monks. 2. Cenobites (*coenobita*), whom we can call those living 'in a community' (*in commune*), because a convent (*coenobium*) is of several people. 3. Anchorites (*anchorita*) are those who after a community life seek out deserted places and live alone in the wilderness. Because they withdraw far from people (cf. ἀναχωρεῖν, "withdraw") they are named with this name. Anchorites imitate Elijah and John (the Baptist), cenobites imitate the apostles. 4. Hermits (*eremita*) are also anchorites who, removed (*removere*, ppl. *remotus*) from the gaze of people, seek out the desert (*eremum*) and deserted solitary places, for the term *eremum* is used as if it were 'remote' (*remotum*). 5. Abbot (*abba*), moreover, a Syriac term, signifies "father" in Latin, as Paul made clear in writing to the Romans (8:15), "Whereby we cry: Abba, Father," having used two languages for the one name, for he says "Father" with the Syriac word *abba*, and then again names the same person in Latin, *Pater*.

xiv. Other faithful people (De ceteris fidelibus) 1. 'Christian' (*Christianus*), as the translation of the word indicates, is derived from 'unction' (*unctio*) or from the name of their originator and creator. Now Christians are surnamed from Christ, as Jews (*Iudaei*) from Judah (*Iuda*). Indeed, the titles of adherents have been given from the name of their teacher. 2. Further, Christians were formerly called Nazarenes (*Nazaraeus*) by the Jews as if in opprobrium, because our Lord and Savior was called 'the Nazarene' after a certain township of Galilee. 3. Let no one glorify himself as a Christian, however, who has the name and does not have the deeds. But where the name accords with one's work, most surely that person is a Christian, because he shows himself to be a Christian by his deeds, one who walks as Christ walked, from whom he took the name.

4. 'Catholic' (*catholicus*) means "universal" or "general," for the Greeks call the universal καθολικός. 5. An 'orthodox person' (*orthodoxus*) is one who believes rightfully, and who lives [righteously] as he believes. Now ὀρθῶς in Greek means "rightly" (*recte*), δόξα is "good repute" (*gloria*): an orthodox person is a man "of good and right repute" (*recta gloria*). He who lives otherwise than as he believes cannot be called by this name.

6. 'Neophyte' (*neophytus*) from the Greek can be translated into Latin as "a new beginner" and "of uncultivated faith" or "one recently born again." 7. A catechumen is so called because he is still hearing (*audire*) the teaching of the faith, and has not yet received baptism, for κατηχούμενος in Greek means "auditor." 8. A 'fit seeker' (*competens*) is so called because after instruction in the faith he 'fitly seeks' (*competere*) the grace of Christ; hence from 'seeking' (*petere*) they are called 'fit seekers.' 9. 'Lay' (*laicus*) means "of the people" (*popularis*), for λαός in Greek means "people" (*populus*). 10. 'Proselyte' (*proselytus*) – that is, one who is a foreigner and circumcised, who is mixed in with the people of God – is a Greek term.

Book VIII

The Church and sects (De ecclesia et sectis)

i. The Church and the Synagogue (De ecclesia et synagoga) 1. 'Church' (*ecclesia*) is a Greek word that is translated into Latin as "convocation" (*convocatio*), because it calls (*vocare*) everyone to itself. 'Catholic' (*catholicus*) is translated as "universal" (*universalis*), after the term καϑ' ὅλον, that is, 'with respect to the whole,' for it is not restricted to some part of a territory, like the small associations of heretics, but is spread widely throughout the entire world. 2. And the apostle Paul assents to this when he says to the Romans (1:8): "I give thanks to my God for all of you, because your faith is spoken of in the whole world." Hence the Church is given the name 'the universal entity' (*universitas*) from 'one' (*unus*), because it is gathered into a unity (*unitas*). Whence the Lord says, in the Gospel according to Luke (11:23): "He that gathereth not with me, scatters." 3. But why is the Church described by John (Apoc. 1:4) as seven, when it is one, unless a single and universal church, filled with a sevenfold Spirit, is meant? We know Solomon spoke of the Lord like this (Proverbs 9:1): "Wisdom hath built herself a house, she hath hewn her out seven pillars." There is no doubt that wisdom, although it is seven, is also one, as the Apostle says (I Timothy 3:15): "The church of the living God, which is the pillar and ground of truth." 4. And the Church began from the place where the Holy Spirit came from heaven, and filled those who were sitting in one (*unus*) place (Acts 2:1–4).

5. In accordance with its present-day wandering the Church is called Zion, because from the imposed distance of this wandering it may 'watch for' (*speculari*) the promise of celestial things, and for that reason it takes the name 'Zion' (*Sion*), that is, watching (*speculatio*). 6. And in accordance with the future peace of the homeland it is called Jerusalem, for 'Jerusalem' (*Hierusalem*) is translated as "vision of peace." There, when all hostility has been overwhelmed, one will possess peace, which is Christ, by gazing upon him face to face. 7. The Greek word 'synagogue' (*synagoga*; cf. συνάγειν, "gather together"), which the Jewish people have taken as their own term, means "congregation" (*congregatio*). Their gathering is properly called a synagogue, although it may also be called a church. 8. The apostles, on the other hand, never said "our synagogue," but always "our church," either so as to make a distinction between the two, or because there is some difference between 'congregation,' from which synagogue takes its name, and 'convocation,' from which church takes its name: no doubt because cattle, which we properly speak of in 'herds' (*grex*, gen. *gregis*), are accustomed to 'congregate' (*congregare*); and it is more fitting for those who use reason, such as humans, to be 'convoked.'

ii. Religion and faith (De religione et fide) 1. Philosophers have named dogma (*dogma*) from 'thinking' (cf. δοκεῖν, "think, suppose, believe"), that is, "I think this is good," "I think this is true." 2. Religion (*religio*) is so called because through it we bind (*religare*) by the chain of service our souls to the one God for the purpose of divine worship. The word is composed from *relegere* ("pick out"), that is, *eligere* ("select"), so that the Latin word *religio* may seem to be like *eligio* ("selection"). 3. There are three things that are required of people for worshipping God in the practice of religion, that is, faith, hope, and charity. In faith, what is to be believed; in hope, what is to be hoped for; in charity, what is to be loved. 4. Faith is that by which we truly believe what we are not able to see at all, for now we cannot 'believe' what we actually see. The term 'faith' (*fides*) is correctly used therefore, if what was said or promised all 'comes to pass' (*fieri*). It is called *fides* because what has been agreed between two parties – that is, between God and the human being – is 'brought about' (*fieri*, 3rd person *fit*). From *fides* also comes the word *foedus* ("pact").

5. Hope (*spes*) is so called because it is a foot for someone going forward, as if it were *est pes* ("there is a foot"). Desperation (*desperatio*) is its contrary, for in that term the 'foot is lacking' (*deest . . . pes*), and there is no ability to go forward, because as long as someone loves sin, he does not hope for future glory. 6. 'Charity' (*caritas*) is a Greek word, and is translated into Latin as 'love'

(*dilectio*), because it binds (*ligare*) two (*duo*) in itself. Indeed, love begins from two things, because it is the love of God and the neighbor. Concerning this the apostle Paul says (Romans 13:10): "Love is the fulfilling of the law." 7. It is greater than the other two, because he who loves also believes and hopes. But he who does not love, although he may do many good things, labors in vain. Moreover every carnal love (*dilectio carnalis*) is customarily called not love (*dilectio*) but 'desire' (*amor*). We usually use the term *dilectio* only with regard to better things.

iii. Heresy and schism (De haeresi et schismate)
1. Heresy (*haeresis*) is so called in Greek from 'choice' (*electio*, cf. αἱρεῖν, "choose"), doubtless because each person chooses (*eligere*) for himself that which seems best to him, as did the Peripatetic, Academic, Epicurean, and Stoic philosophers – or just as others who, devising perverse teachings, have withdrawn from the Church by their own will. 2. Hence, therefore, 'heresy,' named with a Greek word, takes its meaning from 'choice,' by which each person, according to his own judgment, chooses for himself whatever he pleases to institute and adopt. But we are permitted to introduce nothing based on our own judgment, nor to choose what someone else has introduced from his own judgment. 3. We have the apostles of God as authorities, who did not choose anything themselves to introduce from their own judgment, but faithfully bestowed on the world the teaching received from Christ. And if even an angel from heaven preaches otherwise, he will be termed anathema.

4. A sect (*secta*) is named from 'following' (*sequi*, ppl. *secutus*) and 'holding' (*tenere*), for we use the term 'sects' of attitudes of mind and institutions associated with a precept or premise which people hold and follow when in the practice of religion they believe things that are quite different from what others believe. 5. Schism (*schisma*) is so called from the division (*scissura*) of opinions, for schismatics believe with the same worship, the same rite, as the rest; they delight in mere dissension (*discidium*) in the congregation. And schism occurs when people say "we are the righteous ones," "we are the ones who sanctify the unclean," and other similar things. 6. Superstition (*superstitio*) is so called because it is a superfluous or superimposed (*superinstituere*) observance. Others say it is from the aged, because those who have lived (*superstites*) for many years are senile with age and go astray in some superstition through not being aware of which ancient practices they are observing or which they are adding in through ignorance of the old ones. 7. And Lucretius says superstition concerns things 'standing above' (*superstare*), that is, the heavens and divinities that stand over us, but he is speaking wrongly.[1] So that the teachings of heretics can be recognized easily, it is appropriate to point out their motives and names.

iv. Heresies of the Jews (De haeresibus Iudaeorum)
1. The name 'Jew' (*Iudaeus*) can be translated as "confessor" (*confessor*), for confession (*confessio*) catches up with many of those whom wrong belief possessed earlier. 2. Hebrews (*Hebraeus*) are called journeyers (*transitor*). With this name they are reminded that they are to journey (*transire*) from worse to better, and abandon their original errors. 3. The Pharisees (*Pharisaeus*) [deny that the Christ came, nor do they have any share in prophesied events]. [Pharisees and Sadducees (*Saducaeus*) are opposites, for 'Pharisee' is translated from Hebrew into Latin as "divided" (*divisus*), because they give precedence to the righteousness of traditions and observances, which they call δευτερήσεις (i.e. the "secondary obligations"). Hence they are called 'divided' from the people, as if by their righteousness.] 4. Sadducees [deny the resurrection, noting that it is said in Genesis (cf. 3:19) "But now earth thou art, into earth thou shalt return"]. ['Sadducee' means "righteous," and they claim to be righteous, which they are not – they deny the resurrection of the body, and they preach that the soul perishes with the body. They accept only the five books of the Law (i.e. Torah), and reject the predictions of the Prophets.] 5. The Essenes (*Esseus*) say that it is Christ himself who taught them complete abstinence. [The Galileans (*Galilaeus*) say that Christ came and taught them that they should not call Caesar 'Lord,' or heed his commands.]

6. The *Masbothei* say that it was Christ himself who taught them to keep the Sabbath in every aspect. 7. The *Genistae* [presume that they are of the family (*genus*) of Abraham]; [and they are so called because they are proud to be of the family of Abraham. When the people of God came into Babylon, many of them abandoned their wives and took up with Babylonian women; but some were content with Israelite wives only, or they were

1 The word *superstitio* is not found in Lucretius. For his attacks on religion see, e.g., *On the Nature of Things* 1.62–79.

born (*genitus*) from these, and when they returned from Babylon, they separated themselves from the population as a whole and claimed for themselves this boastful name.] 8. The *Meristae* are so called because they separate (*separare*; cf. *pars*, "part") the Scriptures, not having faith in all the Prophets and saying that they prophesied by means of one sort of spirit or another. [For *meris* is from the Greek (cf. μέρος, "part").] 9. Samaritans (*Samarita*) [who were transported to that place, when Israel was captive and led off to Babylon, coming to the land of the region of Samaria, kept the customs of the Israelites in part, which they had learned from a priest who had been brought back, and in part they kept the pagan custom that they had possessed in the land of their birth. They differ entirely from the Jews in their observances, and their superstition is doubtless known to all]. [They are called Samaritan because they 'preserve' (*custodire*; see IX.ii.54) only the Law (i.e Torah), for they do not accept the Prophets.] 10. [The Herodians (*Herodianus*). This heresy arose in the time of the Savior. They glorified Herod, saying that he was the Christ.] 11. The *Hemerobaptistae* [who wash their bodies and home and domestic utensils daily,] [so called because they wash their clothes and body daily (cf. ἡμέρα, "day," and βαπτίζειν, "to wash")].

v. Christian heresies (De haeresibus Christianorum) 1. Some heretics, who have withdrawn from the Church, are named from the name of their founder, and some from the positions that they have selected and established. 2. The Simonians (*Simonianus*) are so called from Simon, skilled in the discipline of magic, whom Peter condemned in the Acts of the Apostles, because he wished to purchase the grace of the Holy Spirit from the Apostles with money (Acts 8:18–23). His followers say that the creation was created, not by God, but by a certain celestial power. 3. The Menandrians (*Menandrianus*) are named from the magician Menander, a student of Simon; they assert that the world was made not by God but by angels. 4. The Basilidians (*Basilidianus*) are named from Basilides; among other blasphemies, they deny that Jesus suffered. 5. The Nicolaites (*Nicolaita*) are so called from Nicolas, deacon of the church of Jerusalem, who, along with Stephen and the others, was ordained by Peter. He abandoned his wife because of her beauty, so that whoever wanted to might enjoy her; the practice turned into debauchery, with partners being exchanged in turn. John condemns them in the Apocalypse, saying (2:6): "But this thou hast, that thou hatest the deeds of the Nicolaites." 6. The Gnostics (*Gnosticus*) wish to call themselves thus because of the superiority of their knowledge (cf. γνῶσις, "knowledge"). They say Soul is the nature of God, and they fashion both a good and an evil god in their doctrine. 7. The Carpocratians (*Carpocratianus*) are named from a certain Carpocrates, who said that Christ was only a human being, and born from a man and a woman.

8. The Cerinthians (*Cerinthianus*) are named from a certain Cerinthus. Among other things, they practice circumcision; they say there will be one thousand (*mille*) years of enjoyment of the flesh after the resurrection, whence they are also called Chiliasts (*Chiliasta*; cf. χιλιάς, "thousand") in Greek and Miliasts (*Miliastus*) in Latin. 9. There are ones called Nazarenes (*Nazaraeus*) who, while they acknowledge Christ, who is called the Nazarene from his village, as the Son of God, nevertheless preserve everything of the Old Law. 10. Ophites (*Ophita*) are so called from the serpent, for the Greek word ὄφις means "serpent." They worship the serpent, saying that it introduced the knowledge of virtue into paradise. 11. The Valentinians (*Valentinianus*) are named from a certain Valentinus, a follower of Plato, who introduced αἰῶναι ("the Aeons"), that is, certain kinds of ages, into the origin of God the creator; he also asserted that Christ took on nothing corporeal from the Virgin, but passed through her as if through a pipe. 12. There are the Apellites (*Apellita*), of whom Apelles was the leader; he imagined that the creator was some sort of glorious angel of the supreme God, and claimed that this fiery being is the God of the Law of Israel, and said that Christ was not God in truth, but a human being who appeared in fantasy. 13. The Archontics (*Archontiacus*; cf. ἄρχων, "ruler") are named from 'Principalities' (i.e. one of the angelic orders) – they claim that the universe, which God made, is the work of archangels.

14. The Adamites (*Adamianus*) are so named because they imitate the nakedness of Adam; hence they pray naked, and men and women meet with each other naked. 15. In a like manner the Cainites (*Caianus*) are so named because they worship Cain. 16. The Sethians (*Sethianus*) take their name from the son of Adam who was called Seth, saying that he was the Christ. 17. The Melchizedechians (*Melchisedechianus*) are so called because they reckon that Melchizedech, the priest of

God, was not a human being, but a Virtue (i.e. a member of the angelic order of Virtues) of God. 18. The Angelics (*Angelicus*) are so called because they worship angels. 19. The Apostolics (*Apostolicus*) claimed that name for themselves because they possess nothing of their own, and they do not accept those who possess anything in this world. 20. The Cerdonians (*Cerdonianus*) are named from a certain Cerdo; they assert that there are two opposing Principles. 21. The Marcionites (*Marcionista*) are named from the Stoic philosopher Marcion, who followed the teaching of Cerdo, and asserted that one God was good and the other just, as if there were two Principles: that of the creator and that of goodness.

22. The Artotyrites (*Artotyrita*) are so called from their offering, for they make an offering of bread and cheese (cf. ἄρτος "bread"; τυρός "cheese"), saying that the offering celebrated by the first humans was of the products of the earth and of sheep. 23. The Aquarians (*Aquarius*) are so called because they offer only water (*aqua*) in the sacramental chalice. 24. The Severians (*Severianus*), who originated from Severus, do not drink wine; they do not accept the Old Testament or resurrection. 25. The Tatianites (*Tatianus*) are named from a certain Tatian; they are also called the Encratites (*Encratita*), because they abhor meat (cf. ἐγκράτεια, "self-control"). 26. The Alogi (*Alogius*) are named as if it were 'without the Word' – 'word' is λόγος in Greek – for they do not believe that God is the Word, rejecting John the Evangelist and the Apocalypse. 27. The province Phrygia gave its name to the Cataphrygians (*Cataphrygius*), because they lived there. Their founders were Montanus, Prisca, and Maximilla.[2] They assert that the Holy Spirit was passed on, not to the apostles, but to them. 28. The Cathars (*Catharus*)[3] call themselves so because of 'cleanliness' (cf. καθαρός, "clean"), for, boasting of their merits, they deny forgiveness of sins to penitents; they condemn widows, if they remarry, as adulterers; they preach that they are cleaner than the rest. If they wished to know their proper name, they would call themselves 'worldly' (*mundanus*) rather than 'clean' (*mundus*).

29. The Paulians (*Paulianus*) originated from Paul of Samosata, who said that Christ did not always exist, but took his origin from Mary. 30. The Hermogenians (*Hermogenianus*) are so called from a certain Hermogenes, who, maintaining that matter was not born, compared it to God, who was not born, and asserted that it is a goddess and mother of the elements. The apostle Paul condemns them (cf. II Tim. 1:15) as being devoted to the elements. 31. The Manichees (*Manicheus*) originate from a certain Persian who was called Manes. He maintained that there are two natures and substances, that is, good and evil, and asserted that souls flow from God as if from some fountain. They reject the Old Testament, and they accept the New Testament only in part. 32. The Anthropomorphites (*Anthropomorphita*) are so called because, with rustic simple-mindedness, they think that God has human limbs, which are mentioned in divine Scripture, for ἄνθρωπος in Greek is translated as 'human being' in Latin. They disregard the word of the Lord who says (John 4:24): "God is a Spirit." Indeed, God is incorporeal, and not characterized by limbs, and is not to be thought of with the mass of a body. 33. The Heraclites (*Heraclita*) originate from the founder Heracleon. They accept only monks, reject marriage, and do not believe that children possess the kingdom of heaven. 34. The Novatians (*Novatianus*) originated from Novatus, priest of the city of Rome, who, in opposition to Cornelius, dared to usurp the priestly see. He established his heresy, being unwilling to receive apostates and rebaptizing the baptized.

35. The Montanist (*Montanus*) heretics are so called because during the time of persecution they hid in the mountains (*mons*, gen. *montis*); for this reason they separated themselves from the body of the Catholic Church. 36. The Ebionites (*Ebionita*) are named from Ebion.[4] They are semi-Jewish and so they accept the Gospel while they follow a physical observance of the Law (i.e. Torah). The Apostle turns out to be writing in criticism of them in his letter to the Galatians. 37. The Photinians (*Photinianus*) are named from Photinus, the bishop of Sirmium in Gallograecia, who encouraged the heresy of the Ebionites and asserted that Christ was conceived by Mary with Joseph in conjugal union. 38. The Aerians (*Aerianus*) are named from a certain Aerius. They scorn to offer a sacrament for the deceased. 39. The Aetians (*Aetianus*) are called from Aetius. They are also called Eunomians (*Eunomianus*) from a certain dialectician Eunomius, a disciple of Aetius, by whose name they are better known:

2 Isidore seems to be describing the Montanists, who were also known as the Phrygians, see section 35 below.

3 The same name is applied to a later, apparently unrelated, heresy.

4 The name of sect actually derives from a Hebrew word meaning "poor." Tertullian makes the first recorded reference to a supposed person named Ebion.

they assert that the Son is not like the Father and the Holy Spirit not like the Son. And they say no sin should be imputed to those who remain in the faith. 40. The Origenians (*Origenianus*) began with their founder, Origen; they say that the Son cannot see the Father, nor the Holy Spirit see the Son. They also say that souls sinned at the beginning of the world and went from heaven to earth, where they earned a variety of bodies, like shackles, according to the variety of their sins – and the world was created for this very reason.

41. The Noetians (*Noetianus*) are named from a certain Noetus, who used to say that Christ and the Father and the Holy Spirit were the same; they accept the Trinity itself as the names of functions, but not as persons. Whence they are also called Patripassians (*Patripassianus*), because they say that the Father (*Pater*) suffered (*pati*, ppl. *passus*). 42. The Sabellians (*Sabellianus*) are said to have sprouted from this same Noetus, whose disciple, they say, was Sabellius, by whose name they are chiefly known – hence they are called Sabellians. They attribute a single person to the Father, Son, and Holy Spirit. 43. The Arians (*Arianus*) originated from Arius, an Alexandrian priest, who did not recognize the Son as co-eternal with the Father and asserted that there are distinct substances in the Trinity, in contradiction to which the Lord said (John 10:30): "I and the Father are one." 44. The Macedonians (*Macedonianus*) are so called from Macedonius, the bishop of Constantinople; they deny that the Holy Spirit is God. 45. The Apollinarists (*Apollinarista*) are so called from Apollinaris; they say that Christ took on merely a body, without a soul. 46. The Antidicomarites (*Antidicomarita*; lit. "litigant against Mary") are so called because they deny the virginity of Mary, asserting that she had intercourse with her husband after Christ was born.

47. The Metangismonites (*Metangismonita*) receive such a name, because 'vessel' is called ἄγγος in Greek, for they assert that the Son is within the Father, as a smaller vessel within a larger. 48. Patricians (*Patricianus*) have their name from a certain Patricius; they say the substance of the human body was made by the devil. 49. The Coluthians (*Coluthianus*) are named from a certain Coluthus; they say God did not create evil, contrary to that which is written (cf. Isaiah 45:7): "I am God, creating evil." 50. The Florians (*Florianus*), from Florinus; they say, on the contrary, that God created badly, contrary to that which is written (cf. Genesis 1:31): "God made all things good." 51. The Donatists (*Donatista*) are named from a certain African, Donatus, who, coming from Numidia, deceived nearly all Africa with his persuasiveness, asserting that the Son was less than the Father, and the Holy Spirit less than the Son, and rebaptizing Catholics. 52. The Bonosiacs (*Bonosiacus*) are reported to have originated from a certain bishop Bonosus; they assert that Christ is the adoptive son of God, not the true son. 53. The Circumcellians (*Circumcellia*, lit. "around the chambers") are so called because they live out in the open; people call them *Cotopitae*, and they possess the doctrine of heresy named above (i.e. Donatism). They kill themselves out of their desire for martyrdom, so that in dying a violent death they may be called martyrs.

54. The Priscillianists (*Priscillianista*) are named from Priscillian, who created a dogma in Spain, combined from the errors of the Gnostics and Manicheans. 55. The Luciferians (*Luciferianus*) originated from Lucifer, bishop of Syrmia (i.e. Sardinia); they condemn the Catholic bishops who, under the persecution of Constantius, consented to the perfidy of the Arians and later, after this, repented and chose to return to the Catholic Church. They condemn these bishops either because they believed in Arianism, or because they pretended to believe. The Catholic Church received these in her maternal bosom, just as she did Peter after he lamented his denial of Christ. The Luciferians, accepting this maternal love arrogantly, and not willing to accept those who had repented, withdrew from the communion of the Church, and they deserved to fall, along with their founder, a Lucifer indeed, who would rise in the morning (i.e. as if he were *Lucifer*, the morning star and a name for the devil). 56. Jovinianists (*Iovinianista*) are so called from a certain monk Jovinian; they assert that there is no difference between wives and virgins, and no distinction between those who are abstinent and those who carouse unreservedly. 57. The Elvidians (*Elvidianus*) are named from Elvidius; they say that after Christ was born, Mary had other sons by her husband Joseph. 58. The Paternians (*Paternianus*) originated from a certain Paternus; they believe that the lower parts of the body were made by the devil. 59. The Arabics (*Arabicus*) are so named because they originated in Arabia; they say that the soul dies with the body, and each one will rise again in the last age.

60. The Tertullianists (*Tertullianista*) are so called from Tertullian, a priest of the African province, of the

city of Carthage; they preach that the soul is immortal, but corporeal, and they believe the souls of human sinners are turned into demons after death. 61. The Tessarescaedecatites (*Tessarescaidecatita*) are so called because they contend that Easter should be observed with the Jewish Passover, on the fourteenth of the lunar month, for τέσσαρες means "four" and δέκα, "ten". 62. The Nyctages (*Nyctages*) are named from sleep (cf. νύξ, gen. νυκτός, "night"), because they reject night vigils, saying that it is a superstition to violate divine law, which assigns night to resting. 63. The Pelagians originated with the monk Pelagius. They put free will before divine grace, saying that will is sufficient to fulfill the divine commands. 64. The Nestorians (*Nestorianus*) are named from Nestorius, bishop of Constantinople, who asserted that the blessed Virgin Mary was the mother not of God, but of a mere human, so that he would make one person of the flesh and the other of the godhead. He did not believe that one and the same Christ existed in the Word of God and in the flesh, but he preached that there was one separate and distinct Son of God and another of humankind. 65. The Eutychians (*Eutychianus*) are so called from Eutyches, abbot of Constantinople, who denied that Christ consisted of two natures after his human incarnation, but asserted that the divine nature alone was in him. 66. The Acephalites (*Acephalus*) are so called (cf. ἀκέφαλος 'headless'), that is, without a head (i.e. a leader) whom these heretics follow – for their founder, from whom they originated, is not known. Opposing the three tenets (*capitulum*, cf. *caput*, 'head') of the Council of Chalcedon, they deny the individuality of the two substances in Christ and preach that there is a single nature in his person.

67. The Theodosians (*Theodosianus*) and the Gaianites (*Gaianita*) are named from Theodosius and Gaianus, who were ordained as bishops on a single day by the selection of a perverse populace in Alexandria during the time of the ruler Justinian. Following the errors of Eutyches and Dioscorus, they rejected the Council of Chalcedon. They asserted that there is in Christ one nature from two, which nature the Theodosians contend is corrupt and the Gaianites, incorrupt. 68. The Agnoites (*Agnoita*) and Tritheites (*Tritheita*) originated from the Theodosians; of these, the Agnoites are so called from ignorance (cf. ἄγνοια, "ignorance"), because to that perversity from which they arise they add this: that the divinity of Christ is ignorant of the things to come, which are written concerning the last day and hour – they do not recall the person of Christ speaking in Isaiah (cf. 63:4): "The day of judgment is in my heart." And the Tritheites (cf. τρι-, "three"; θεός, "god") are so called because they add that just as there are three persons in the Trinity, so also there are three gods, contrary to that which is written (cf. Deuteronomy 6:4): "Hear, O Israel, the Lord thy God is one God."

69. There are also other heresies without a founder and without names. Of these some believe that God is triform, others say that the divinity of Christ was capable of suffering, others assign the beginning of time to Christ's nativity from the Father, others [do not] believe that the liberation of the people in hell was accomplished by the descent of Christ,[5] others deny that the soul is the image of God, others suppose that souls are turned into demons and all sorts of animals. Others disagree concerning the state of the world: some believe in countless worlds, some assert that water is co-eternal with God. Some walk barefoot, others do not eat with other people.

70. These are heresies that have arisen in opposition to the catholic faith, and have been condemned by the apostles and Holy Fathers, or by the Councils. These heresies, although they disagree with each other, differing among themselves in many errors, nevertheless conspire with a common name against the Church of God. But also, whoever understands the Holy Scriptures otherwise than the meaning of the Holy Spirit, by whom they were written, requires, even if he does not depart from the Church, nevertheless can be called a heretic.

vi. Pagan philosophers (De philosophis gentium)

1. Philosophers are called by a Greek name that is translated in Latin as "lovers of wisdom" (*amator sapientiae*). Indeed, a philosopher is one who has knowledge of divine and human matters, and follows every path of living well. 2. The term 'philosopher' (*philosophus*) is reported to have originated from Pythagoras. Although earlier the ancient Greeks would quite boastfully name themselves sophists (*sophista*), that is, 'wise ones' or 'teachers of wisdom,' when Pythagoras was asked what he professed, he responded with a modest term, saying that he was a 'philosopher,' that is, a lover of wisdom – for to claim that one was wise seemed very arrogant.

5 Some manuscripts read, "others believe that the liberation of all those in hell was accomplished by the descent of Christ" – a heresy promulgated by Origen.

3. So henceforth it was pleasing to later generations that, however much someone might seem, to himself or to others, to excel in his teaching about matters pertaining to wisdom, he would not be called anything but 'philosopher.' Philosophers are divided into three kinds: they are natural philosophers, ethicists, or logicians. 4. 'Natural philosophers' (*physicus*) are so called because they treat of nature, for in Greek 'nature' is called φύσις. 5. The ethicists (*ethicus*), because they discuss morals, for morals are called ἤθη by the Greeks. 6. And the logicians (*logicus*), because they bring reasoning to the treatment of both nature and morals, for in Greek 'reason' (*ratio*) is called λόγος.

They are divided into their own schools, some having names from their founders, such as the Platonists, the Epicureans, and the Pythagoreans. Others take their names from the site of their meetings and their abodes, such as the Peripatetics, the Stoics, and the Academics. 7. The Platonists (*Platonicus*) are named from the philosopher Plato. They assert that God is the creator of souls, and angels the creators of bodies; they say that souls return in different bodies through many cycles of years. 8. The Stoics (*Stoicus*) are so called from a place. There was a portico in Athens that they called the ποικίλη στοά ("painted portico") in which were painted the deeds of wise people and the histories of great men. In this portico wise people used to philosophize, and consequently they were called Stoics, for in Greek, a portico is called στοά. Zeno first established this sect. 9. They deny that anyone may be made happy without virtue. They assert that all sin is uniform, saying, "He who has stolen chaff will be as culpable as one who has stolen gold; he who kills a diver-bird as much as one who kills a horse – for it is not the nature of the animal (*animal*), but the intention (*animus*), that constitutes the crime." 10. They also say that the soul perishes with the body, the soul also.[6] They deny the virtue of temperance. They aspire to eternal glory, although they say that they are not eternal. 11. The Academics are so called from the villa of Plato, the Academy of Athens, where this same Plato used to teach. They believe that everything is doubtful, but, just as it must be said that many things are doubtful and hidden, which God has wished to be beyond the intelligence of humans, nevertheless there are many things that can be grasped by the senses and understood by reason. 12. The philosopher Arcesilaus of Cyrene founded this school; his follower was Democritus, who said that truth lies hidden, as if in a well so deep that it has no bottom.[7]

13. The Peripatetics (*Peripateticus*) are so called from 'walking about' (cf. περιπατητικός), because Aristotle, their founder, was accustomed to engage in disputation while walking about. They say that a certain small part of the soul is eternal; concerning the rest, it is in large part mortal. 14. The Cynics (*Cynicus*) are named from the foulness of their shamelessness. For, contrary to human modesty, it was their custom to copulate publicly with their wives, insisting that it is lawful and decent to lie openly with one's wife, because it is a lawful union; they preach that this should be done publicly in the streets or avenues like dogs. Whence they drew their epithet and name from the dogs (cf. κύων, "dog") whose life they imitated. 15. The Epicureans (*Epicureus*) are so called from a certain philosopher Epicurus, a lover of vanity, not of wisdom, whom the philosophers themselves named 'the pig,' wallowing in carnal filth, as it were, and asserting that bodily pleasure is the highest good. He also said that the world was not constructed or regulated by any divine forethought. 16. But he assigned the origin of things to atoms, that is, to solid and indivisible bodies, from whose chance collisions all things originate and have originated. And they assert that God does nothing; everything consists of bodies; the soul is nothing other than the body. Whence also he said, "I will not exist after I have died." 17. The Gymnosophists (*Gymnosophista*) are said to philosophize naked (cf. γυμνός, "naked") in the shady solitudes of India, wearing garments only over their genitals. Thus a 'gymnasium' is so called because on a field, young men exercise naked, covering only their private parts. The Gymnosophists also restrain themselves from procreation.

18. There are Deists (*Theologus*) who are the same as natural philosophers. They are called 'Deists' because they spoke of God in their writings. In their investigations there are various ideas about the nature of God. Thus some, like Dionysius the Stoic, said that God is this world of the four elements visible to the bodily sense.

6 The faulty text here may be emended: ". . . perishes with the body. They also love the virtue of temperance. They aspire to . . ." The emendation would obviously accord with Stoicism.

7 Arcesilaus or Arcesilas, founder of the Middle Academy, was from Pitane in Aeolia, not Cyrene in Libya, but there was a line of kings in Cyrene with the name Arcesilas. There was also a school known as Cyrenaics, but Arcesilaus was apparently not a member of this. This Democritus is distinct from the more famous Democritus of Abdera.

Others, like Thales of Miletus, understood spiritually that God is mind. 19. Some, like Pythagoras, said God is a lucid consciousness immanent in everything. Some, like Plato, that God is unchangeable and timeless. Some, like Cicero, that he is unfettered mind. Some, like Maro (i.e. Vergil), that he is both spirit and mind. Indeed, they explained only the God that they found, not how they found him, because they have come to nothing in their cogitations. Saying they were wise, they became fools.

20. [Again,] the Platonists at any rate assert that God is guardian and ruler and judge. The Epicureans, that God is uninvolved and inactive. Concerning the world, the Platonists affirm that it is incorporeal, the Stoics that it is corporeal, Epicurus that it is made of atoms, Pythagoras that it is made from numbers, Heraclitus, from fire. 21. Whence also Varro says that fire is the soul of the world; just as fire governs all things in the world, so the soul governs all things in us. As he says most vainly, "When fire is in us, we exist; when it leaves us, we perish." Thus also when fire departs from the world through lightning, the world perishes.

22. These errors of the philosophers also introduced heresies within the Church. Hence the αἰῶνες (see v.11 above) and certain 'forms,' hence the 'Trinity of the name' of Arius, and the Platonic madness of Valentinus. 23. Hence the God of Marcion, 'better with regard to tranquillity,' which came from the Stoics. That the soul is said to die is the influence of Epicurus. The denial of the resurrection of the flesh is taken from the empty teaching of all the philosophers. Where matter is equated with God, it is the teaching of Zeno, and where we read about a fiery God, Heraclitus has intervened. The same material is rolled about among the heretics and the philosophers, and the same repeated statements are involved.

vii. Poets (De poetis) 1. Whence poets (*poeta*) are so called, thus says Tranquillus (i.e. Suetonius, *On Poets* 2) "When people first began to possess a rational way of life, having shaken off their wildness, and to come to know themselves and their gods, they devised for themselves a humble culture and the speech required for their ideas, and devised a greater expression of both for the worship of their gods. 2. Therefore, just as they made temples more beautiful than their homes, and idols larger than their bodies, so they thought the gods should be honored by speech that was, as it were, loftier, and they raised up their praises with more brilliant words and more pleasing rhythms. This kind of thing was given the name 'poem' (*poema*) because it is fashioned with a certain beauty known as ποιότης (i.e. "quality"), and its makers were called 'poets' (*poeta*)." 3. Varro is the originator of the idea that 'seers' (*vates*) are so called from the 'force of the mind' (*vis mentis*), or from plaiting (*viere*) songs, that is, from 'turning' or modulating them; accordingly the poets in Latin were once called *vates*, and their writings called 'prophetic' (*vaticinius*), because they were inspired to write by a certain force (*vis*), a madness (*vesania*), as it were; or because they 'link' words in rhythms, with the ancients using the term *viere* instead of *vincire* ("bind"). Indeed, through madness the prophets had this same name, because they themselves proclaimed many things in verse.

4. Lyric (*lyricus*) poets are named after the Greek term ληρεῖν (lit. "speak trifles") that is, from the variety of their songs. Hence also the lyre (*lyra*) is named. 5. Tragedians (*tragoedus*) are so called, because at first the prize for singers was a goat, which the Greeks call τράγος. Hence also Horace (*Art of Poetry* 220):

> Who with a tragic song vied for a paltry goat.

Now the tragedians following thereafter attained great honor, excelling in the plots of their stories, composed in the image of truth. 6. 'Writers of comedies' (*comoedus*) are so called either from the place, because people performed them in rural districts, which the Greeks call κώμας, or from revelry (*comissatio*), for people used to come to hear them after a meal. Writers of comedies proclaim the deeds of private people, but tragedians, public matters and stories of kings. Again, the plots of tragedians are of sorrowful subjects; those of the writers of comedies, cheerful ones. 7. There are two types of writers of comedies, that is, the Old and the New. The Old, who would amuse by means of a joke, such as Plautus, Accius, Terence. The New, who are also called satirists (*satiricus*), by whom vices are generally flayed, such as Flaccus (i.e. Horace), Persius, Juvenal, and others. These latter seize upon the transgressions of everyone, and they do not refrain from describing any very wicked person, or from censuring the wrongdoings and morals of anyone. They are pictured naked because by them individual faults are laid bare.

8. Satirists (*saturicus*) are so called either because they are filled with all eloquence, or from fullness (*saturitas*) and abundance – for they speak about many things at

the same time – or from the platter (i.e. *satura*) with various kinds of fruit and produce that people used to offer at the temples of the pagans, or the name is taken from 'satyr plays' (*satyrus*), which contain things that are said in drunkenness, and go unpunished. 9. And some poets are called theological (*theologicus*), because they composed songs about the gods.

10. The function of poets is this, to transform things that have actually taken place into other forms, modified with some grace by means of indirect representations. Whence Lucan on that account is not placed among the number of poets, because he is seen to have composed histories, not a poem. 11. Moreover, among the poets there are three modes of speaking: one, in which the poet alone speaks, as in Vergil's books of the *Georgics*; the second mode is dramatic, in which the poet never speaks, as in comedies and tragedies; the third is mixed, as in the *Aeneid*, for there both the poet and the characters who are represented speak.

viii. Sibyls (De Sibyllis) 1. In the Greek language all female seers are generally called Sibyls (*sibylla*), for in the Aeolian dialect God is σιός, and the Greeks call mind βουλή; the mind of God, as it were. Hence, because these seers would interpret the divine will for humans, they were named Sibyls. 2. And just as every man who prophesies is called either a seer (*vates*) or a prophet (*propheta*), so every woman who prophesies is called a Sibyl, because it is the name of a function, not a proper noun.

3. It is reported by the most learned authors that there were ten Sibyls. The first of these was from Persia; the second is the Libyan Sibyl; the third, the Delphic, born in the temple of Apollo at Delphi. She prophesied before the Trojan War, and Homer inserted many of her verses into his own work. 4. The fourth was the Cimmerian, in Italy; the fifth, the Erythraean, Herophila by name, who came from Babylon – she foretold to the Greeks attacking Ilium that Troy would perish and that Homer would write lies. She is called Erythraean because in that same island her songs were found. The sixth is the Samian Sibyl, who is called Phemonoe, from the island of Samos – hence she was so named.

5. The seventh is the Cumanan Sibyl, Amalthea by name, who delivered to the Tarquin Priscus the nine books in which the Roman decrees were drawn up. She is also the Cumaean Sibyl of whom Vergil wrote (*Ecl.* 4.4):

> Now the final age of Cumaean song has come on.

She is called Cumana (*cumana*) after the city Cumae, which is in Campania; her sepulcher remains in Sicily to this day. 6. The eighth, the Hellespontian, was born on the Trojan plain; it is written that she lived in the time of Solon and Cyrus. The ninth is the Phrygian, who prophesied in Ancyra; the tenth the Tiburtinan, with the name Albunea. 7. Songs by all of them are published in which they are attested to have written many things most clearly even for the pagans about God and Christ. The Erythraean Sibyl is considered more honored and noble than the rest.

ix. Magicians (De magis) 1. The first of the magicians was Zoroaster (*Zoroastres*), king of the Bactrians, whom Ninus, king of the Assyrians, killed in battle. About him Aristotle writes that the two million verses composed by him are made evident by the catalogues of his volumes. 2. Democritus expanded this art after many centuries, when Hippocrates also flourished with the discipline of medicine. Among the Assyrians the magic arts are abundant, as Lucan bears witness (cf. *Civil War* 6.427):

> Who could know of deeds by means of entrails, who interpret the birds, who might observe the lightning of the sky, and examine the constellations with Assyrian skill?

3. Consequently, this foolery of the magic arts held sway over the entire world for many centuries through the instruction of the evil angels. By a certain knowledge of things to come and of things below, and by invoking them, divinations (*aruspicium*) were invented, and auguries (*auguratio*), and those things that are called oracles (*oraculum*) and necromancy (*necromantium*). 4. There is nothing surprising about the trickery of the magicians, since their skills in magic advanced to such a point that they even countered Moses with very similar signs, turning staffs into serpents and water into blood. 5. A certain sorceress (*maga*) is also reported, the very famous Circe, who turned the companions of Ulysses into beasts.

We also read about the sacrifice that the Arcadians burnt in offering to their god Lycaeus; whoever consumed this was turned into the shape of a beast. 6. Hence it does not appear to have been completely doubtful, what the noble poet writes of a certain woman who excelled in the magic arts (Vergil, *Aen.* 4.487):

> She promises with her spells to soothe whichever minds she wishes, but to bring hard cares to others; to make the water of rivers stand still, to turn the stars back, and to raise night ghosts; you will see the earth groan underfoot, and wild mountain-ashes descend from the hills.

7. Further, if one may credit it, what of the Pythoness (I Kings 28:7–19 Vulgate), when she called up the spirit of the prophet Samuel from the recesses of the lower region and presented it to the view of the living – if, however, we believe that this was the spirit of the prophet and not some fantastic illusion created by the deception of Satan? 8. Prudentius also spoke thus about Mercury (*Against the Oration of Symmachus* 1.90):

> It is told that he recalled perished souls to the light wielding a wand that he held, but condemned others to death,

and a little later he adds,

> For with a magic murmur (you know how) to summon faint shapes and cunningly to enchant sepulchral ashes. In the same way the malicious art knows how to despoil others of life.

9. There are magicians who are commonly called 'evildoers' (*maleficus*) because of the magnitude of their crimes. They agitate the elements, disturb the minds of people, and slay without any drinking of poison, using the violence of spells alone. 10. Hence also Lucan (*Civil War* 6.457):

> The mind, polluted by no poison of swallowed venom, yet perishes under a spell.

With their summoning of demons, they dare to flaunt how anyone may slay his enemies with evil arts. They make use of blood and victims, and often handle the bodies of the dead. 11. Necromancers (*necromantius*) are those by whose incantations the dead, brought back to life, seem to prophesy, and to answer what is asked, for νεκρός means "dead" in Greek, and divination is called μαντεία. The blood of a corpse is applied for the cross-questioning, for demons are said to love blood. And for this reason, whenever necromancy is practiced, gore is mixed with water, so that they are called more easily by the gore of the blood. 12. Hydromancers (*hydromantius*) are so called from water (ὕδωρ), for hydromancy is calling up the shades of demons by gazing into water, and watching their images or illusions, and hearing something from them, when they are said to interrogate the lower beings by use of blood. 13. This type of divination is said to have been brought from Persia.

Varro says that there are four kinds of divination: earth, water, air, and fire. Hence are named geomancy (*geomantia*), hydromancy (*hydromantia*), aeromancy (*aeromantia*), and pyromancy (*pyromantia*). 14. Diviners (*divinus*) are so named, as if the term were 'filled with god' (*deo plenus*), for they pretend to be filled with divine inspiration, and with a certain deceitful cunning they forecast what is to come for people. There are two kinds of divination: craft and madness. 15. Those who accomplish their craft with words are called enchanters (*incantator*). 16. *Arioli* are so called because they utter abominable prayers around the 'altars of idols' (*ara idolorum*), and offer pernicious sacrifices, and in these rites receive the answers of demons. 17. *Haruspices* are so named as if the expression were 'observers (*inspector*) of the hours (*hora*)'; they watch over the days and hours for doing business and other works, and they attend to what a person ought to watch out for at any particular time. They also examine the entrails of animals and predict the future from them. 18. Augurs (*augur*) are those who give attention to the flight and calls of birds (*avis*), and to other signs of things or unforeseen observations that impinge on people. These are the same as 'observers of auspices' (*auspex*). 19. For auspicious signs are what those who are making a journey take heed of. They are called 'auspicious signs' (*auspicium*) as if it were 'observations of birds' (*avium aspicium*), and 'auguries' (*augurium*), as if it were 'bird calls' (*avium garria*), that is, the sounds and languages of birds. Again, *augurium* as if the word were *avigerium*, that is, what the 'birds convey' (*avis gerit*). 20. There are two types of auspicious signs, one pertaining to the eyes and the other to the ears. To the eyes, as the flight of birds; to the ears as the voice of birds.

21. Pythonesses (*Pythonissae*) are named from Pythian Apollo, because he was the inventor of divination. 22. Astrologers (*astrologus*) are so called, because they perform augury from the stars (*astrum*). 23. *Genethliaci* are so called on account of their examinations of nativities, for they describe the nativities (*genesis*) of people according to the twelve signs of the heavens, and attempt to predict the characters, actions, and circumstances of people by the course of the stars at their birth, that is,

who was born under what star, or what outcome of life the person who is born would have. 24. These are commonly called astrologers (*mathematicus*); Latin speakers call this kind of superstition 'constellations' (*constellatio*), that is, observation of the stars – how they relate to each other when someone is born. 25. At first, interpreters of the stars were called Magi (*magus*), as we read of those who made known the birth of Christ in the Gospels; afterwards they only had the name *mathematicus*. 26. Knowledge of this skill was permitted only up until the time of the Gospel, so that once Christ was born no one thereafter would interpret the birth of anyone from the heavens. 27. 'Drawers of horoscopes' (*horoscopus*) are so called because they examine (*speculari*) the times (*hora*) of people's nativities with regard to their dissimilar and varied destiny.

28. 'Interpreters of lots' (*sortilegus*) are those who profess the knowledge of divination under the name of a false religion, using what they call 'lots (*sors*, gen. *sortis*) of the saints,' or those who foretell the future by examining one passage of scripture or another.[8] 29. The *salisatores* are so called because whenever any part of their limbs palpitates (*salire*, lit. "leaps"), they proclaim that this means something fortunate or something unfortunate for them thereafter. 30. Associated with all these arts are amulets consisting of curse-charms. The art of physicians condemns these, whether used with incantations, or magical characters, or whatever is hung on or bound to a person. 31. In all these the craft of demons has issued from a certain pestilential alliance of humans and evil angels. Hence all these things are to be avoided by a Christian, and entirely repudiated and condemned with every curse. 32. The Phrygians were the first to discover the auguries of birds, but Mercury is said to have first invented illusions. 33. They are called illusions (*praestigium*) because they dull (*praestringere*) the sharpness of one's eyes. 34. A certain Tages is said to have first given the art of *aruspicina* (i.e. divination by inspection of entrails; see 17 above) to the Etruscans. He pronounced divinations orally (or, 'from hours'), and after that did not show himself. 35. It is said in fable that when a certain rustic was plowing, he suddenly leapt up from the clods and dictated the art of the haruspex, and on that day he died. The Romans translated these books from the Etruscan language into their own.

x. Pagans (De paganis) 1. Pagans (*paganus*) are named from the districts (*pagus*) of the Athenians, where they originated, for there, in rural places and districts, the pagans established sacred groves and idols, and from such a beginning pagans received their name. 2. Gentiles are those who are without the Law, and have not yet believed.[9] And they are called 'gentiles' (*gentilis*) because they remain just as they were born (*gignere*, ppl. *genitus*), that is, just as they descended into the body governed by sin, in other words, worshipping idols and not yet reborn. 3. Accordingly, they were first named gentiles. In Greek they are called *ethnici*. The Greek word *ethnici* is translated as *gentiles* in Latin, for the Greek ἔθνος means "tribe" (*gens*). 4. But after their conversion, those from the tribes who believe ought not to be called *gentes* or *gentiles*, just as after conversion a Jew can no longer be called a Jew, as the apostle Paul testifies when he says to the Christians (I Corinthians 12:2): "That when you were heathens (*gentes*)," that is, infidels. 5. Those people are called apostates (*apostata*) who, after the baptism of Christ has been received, return to the worship of idols and pollution of sacrifices. And this is a Greek term.

xi. Gods of the heathens (De diis gentium) 1. Those who the pagans assert are gods are revealed to have once been humans, and after their death they began to be worshipped among their people because of the life and merit of each of them, as Isis in Egypt, Jupiter in Crete, Iuba among the Moors, Faunus among the Latins, and Quirinus among the Romans. 2. It was the same with Minerva in Athens, Juno in Samos, Venus in Paphos, Vulcan in Lemnos, Liber in Naxos and Apollo in Delos. Poets joined in their praises of these, and by the songs they composed carried them up to the sky. 3. In their cults they are said to have brought about the discovery of certain arts: there is medicine by Aesculapius, forging by Vulcan. Further, they are named from their activities, as Mercury (*Mercurius*), because he excels at commerce (*merx*), Liber (*Liber*) from liberty (*libertas*). 4. Again, there were certain powerful men, or founders of cities, for whom, after they had died, the people who had been

8 A *sortilegus* would predict the future by examining a randomly selected verse of the Bible or another authoritative text.

9 Jews speak of gentiles as any non-Jews; Christians use the term for those both non-Jewish and non-Christian. Latin uses both the term *gentilis* and (in the plural) *gentes*, lit. 'nations, tribes,' for gentiles. We generally translate the 'gentiles' of the Greco-Roman world as 'pagans,' but sometimes as 'heathens.'

fond of them made likenesses, so that they might have some solace from contemplating these images. However, at the urging of demons, this error gradually crept into later generations in such a way that those, whom people had honored only for the memory of their name, their successors deemed as gods and worshipped.

5. The use of likenesses arose when, out of grief for the dead, images or effigies were set up, as if in place of those who had been received into heaven demons substituted themselves to be worshipped on earth, and persuaded deceived and lost people to make sacrifices to themselves. 6. And 'likenesses' (*simulacrum*) are named from 'similarity' (*similitudo*), because, through the hand of an artisan, the faces of those in whose honor the likenesses are constructed are imitated in stone or some other material. Therefore they are called likenesses either because they are similar (*similis*), or because they are feigned (*simulare*) or invented, whence they are false. 7. And it should be noted that the Latin word also exists among the Hebrews, for by them an idol or likeness is called 'Semel.' The Jews say that Ishmael first made a likeness from clay. 8. The pagans assert that Prometheus first made a likeness of humans from clay and that from him the art of making likenesses and statues was born. Whence also the poets supposed that human beings were first created by him – figuratively, because of these effigies. 9. Among the Greeks was Cecrops, during whose reign the olive tree first appeared on the citadel, and the city of Athens received its name from the name for Minerva. 10. He was the first of all to call on Jupiter, devise likenesses, set up altars, and sacrifice offerings, things of this kind having never before been seen in Greece.

11. Idolatry (*idolatria*) means the service or worship of idols, for λατρεία in Greek is translated in Latin as servitude (*servitus*), which as far as true religion is concerned is owed only to the one and only God. 12. Just as impious pride in humans or demons commands or wishes for this service to be offered to itself, so pious humility in humans or holy angels declines it if it is offered, and indicates to whom it is due. 13. An idol (*idolum*) is a likeness made in the form of a human and consecrated, according to the meaning of the word, for the Greek term εἶδος means "form" (*forma*), and the diminutive *idolum* derived from it gives us the equivalent diminutive *formula* ("replica," i.e. an image made in a mold). 14. Therefore every form or replica ought to be called idol. Therefore idolatry is any instance of servility and subservience to any idol. Certain Latin speakers, however, not knowing Greek, ignorantly say that 'idol' takes its name from 'deception' (*dolus*), because the devil introduced to creation worship of a divine name. 15. They say demons (*daemon*) are so called by the Greeks as if the word were δαήμων, that is, experienced and knowledgeable in matters,[10] for they foretell many things to come, whence they are also accustomed to give some answers. 16. Indeed, they have more knowledge of things than does human weakness, partly through a more subtle acuity of sense, partly through the experience of an extremely long life, and partly through angelic revelation at God's command. They flourish in accordance with the nature of aerial bodies. 17. Indeed, before their fall they had celestial bodies. Now that they have fallen, they have turned into an aerial quality; and they are not allowed to occupy the purer expanses of the air, but only the murky regions, which are like a prison for them, until the Day of Judgment. They are the prevaricator angels, of whom the Devil is the ruler. 18. Devil (*diabolus*) in Hebrew is translated as "sinking downwards," because he disdained to stand quiet in the height of the heavens, but, due to the weight of his pride, sinking down he fell. In fact, in Greek an accuser is called *diabolus*, either because he brings before God the crimes into which he himself lures people, or because he accuses the innocence of the elect with fabricated crimes – whence also in the Apocalypse (12:10) it is said by the voice of an angel: "The accuser of our brethren is cast forth, who accused them before our God day and night."

19. Satan (*Satanas*) means "adversary," or "transgressor" in Latin. He is indeed the adversary who is the enemy of truth, and he always strives to go against the virtues of the holy. He is also the transgressor, because as an apostate, he did not continue in the truth in which he was created. Also he is the tempter, because he claims that the innocence of the righteous must be put to the test, as it is written in Job. 20. He is called the Antichrist (*Antichristus*), because he is to come against Christ. He is not, as certain simpletons suppose, called the Antichrist because he is to come before (*ante*) Christ, that is, that Christ would come after him. This is not the case, but rather he is called Antichrist in Greek, which is 'against Christ' (*contrarius Christo*) in Latin, for ἀντί in Greek

10 Greek δαίμων can mean "demon," and δαήμων means "knowing, experienced."

means 'against' in Latin. 21. When he comes he will pretend that he is Christ, and there will be a struggle against him, and he will oppose the sacraments of Christ in order to destroy the gospel of his truth. 22. For he will attempt to rebuild the temple at Jerusalem and restore all the rites of the old Law. But Antichrist is also one who denies that Christ is God, for he is opposed to Christ. So all those who depart from the Church and are cut off from the unity of faith are themselves Antichrists.

23. Bel is a Babylonian idol whose name means "old." He was Belus, the father of Ninus, the first king of the Assyrians, whom some call Saturn. His name was worshipped among both the Assyrians and the Africans; hence in the Punic language *Bal* means 'god.' And among the Assyrians, Bel is also called Saturn and Sol in a certain aspect of their rites. 24. Belphegor is translated as "likeness of ignominy," for Moab, with the cognomen Baal, was an idol on Mount Phegor; Latin speakers call him Priapus, the god of gardens. 25. He was from Lampsacus, a city on the Hellespont, whence he was banished, and on account of the size of his male member the Greeks translated him to the roster of their gods and held him sacred as the deity of gardens. Accordingly, he is said to preside over gardens for the sake of their fertility. 26. Belzebub was the idol of Accaron, and the word is translated as "man of flies," for a fly is called *zebub*. The most impure idol, therefore, was called 'man of flies' because of the filth of idolatry, or its uncleanness. Belial . . . 27. Behemoth, from the Hebrew language, means 'animal' in Latin, because he fell from the heights to the earth, and for his offense was made brutish, like an animal. He is also Leviathan, that is, a 'serpent from the seas,' because in the undulating sea of this world he winds his way with cunning. 28. Leviathan means 'their additional factor.' Whose, indeed, if not the 'additional factor' of human beings, to whom he once introduced the sin of deceit in Paradise, and in whom by persuasion he daily adds to or extends this deceit up to the point of eternal death?

29. By empty stories the pagans attempt to connect some of the names of their gods to physical causes, and they interpret these names as involved in the origins of the elements. But this has been entirely made up by poets, with the intention of enhancing their gods with certain figures of speech, while histories reveal these gods to have been lost and full of the infamy of shame. Indeed, when truth leaves off, room for fiction is wide open. 30. Saturn (*Saturnus*) is designated by the pagans as the origin of the gods and of all their posterity. Latin speakers declare that he is named from sowing (*satus*), as though the sowing of all things pertains to him, or from the length of time, because he is filled (*saturare*) with years. 31. Whence the Greeks say he has the name Cronos, that is, "time" (cf. χρόνος), because he is said to have devoured his sons: that is, he rolls back into himself the years that time has brought forth; or it is because seeds return again to the place from where they arose. 32. They say that he cut off the genitals of his father, the Sky (*Caelus*), because nothing in the sky is born of seed. He grasps a scythe, they say, in order to signify agriculture, or to signify the years and seasons, because scythes turn back on themselves; or to signify wisdom because it is sharp on the inside. 33. In some cities the pagans used to sacrifice their children to Saturn, because the poets reported that Saturn was accustomed to devour his own children.

34. Jove (*Iovis*) is said to be named from 'helping' (*iuvare*), and Jupiter (*Iuppiter*) is as if the name were *iuvans pater* ("helping father"), that is, providing for all. They also called him, with a special title, 'Jupiter the Best' (*Iuppiter Optimus*), although he was incestuous among his own family, and shameless among others. 35. They imagine that he was at one time a bull on account of the rape of Europa, for he was in a ship whose standard was a bull. At another time he sought to lie with Danae by means of a shower of gold, where it is understood that the modesty of a woman was corrupted by gold. At another time he appeared in the likeness of an eagle because he carried off a boy for defilement; at another time a serpent, because he crawled, and a swan, because he sang. 36. And therefore these are not figures of speech, but crimes in plain truth. Whence it was shameful that gods should be believed to be such as humans ought not to be. 37. They call Janus (*Ianus*) the door (*ianua*), as it were, of the world or the sky or the months. They imagine two faces for Janus, standing for the east and the west. And when they make him with four faces and call him the double Janus, they refer to the four corners of the world or to the four elements or to the seasons. But when they imagine this, they make him a monster, not a god.

38. They proclaim that Neptune is the waters of the world, and Neptune (*Neptunus*) is named by them as if it were 'roaring in the mist' (*nube tonans*). 39. They would have it that Vulcan is fire, and he is named Vulcan

(*Vulcanus*), as 'flying radiance' (*volans candor*), or as if the word were *volicanus*, because he flies through the air – for fire is born from clouds. 40. Whence also Homer says that he fell headlong down from the air to the earth, because all lightning falls from the air. For that reason Vulcan is imagined to have been born from Juno's thigh, because lightning bolts originate in the lower parts of the air. 41. Vulcan is also called lame, because fire by nature is never straight, but has an appearance and motion as if it were lame. So also they say that this same Vulcan is the originator of the smithy, because without fire no kind of metal can be cast and beaten out. 42. Pluto in Greek is *Diespiter* or 'Father of Wealth' (*Ditis Pater*) in Latin.[11] Some call him *Orcus*, receiver of the dead, as it were – whence the vessel that receives water is called *orca*. He is also *Charon* in Greek.

43. They hold that Liber (*Liber*) is named from 'release' (*liberamentum*), because it is as if males were released (*liberare*) by his favor when their seed is ejaculated in copulation, since this same Liber is depicted with a delicate feminine body. Indeed, they say that women are assigned to him, and also wine, because of his arousing desire. 44. Whence his brow is wreathed with vines. But he has a crown of vines and a horn, because when wine is drunk in moderation and acceptably it confers happiness, but when it is drunk immoderately it stirs up quarrels – that is, it is as if it gives horns. And he is also called Lyaeus after the term λύειν ("loosen") because the limbs are loosened by a great deal of wine. And in Greek he is called Διόνυσος from the mountain Nysa in India, where he is said to have been brought up. Otherwise there is also the city Nysa, in which Liber is worshipped, from which he is called Nysaeus.

45. Mercury (*Mercurius*) is translated as "speech," for Mercury is said to be named as if the word were *medius currens* ("go-between"), because speech is the go-between for people. In Greek he is called Ἑρμῆς, because 'speech' or 'interpretation,' which pertains especially to speech, is called ἑρμηνεία. 46. He is also said to preside over commerce (*merx*, gen. *mercis*), because the medium between dealers and buyers is speech. So he is imagined to have wings, because words run to and fro quickly. Whence also he is represented as rapid and roving; the wings on his head and feet signify speech taking flight through the air. 47. He is called the messenger, because all thoughts are expressed by speech. They also say he is the master of trickery, because speech deceives the minds of those who listen. He holds a staff with which he separates serpents, that is, poisons.[12] 48. Thus, opponents and antagonists may be calmed by the speech of mediators, whence, according to Livy, legates of peace are called *caduceatores* (lit. "bearers of the herald's caduceus"). Just as wars were declared through *fetiales*,[13] so peace was made through *caduceatores*. 49. Hermes is named after the Greek term ἑρμηνεία ("interpretation") in Greek, in Latin 'interpreter'; on account of his power and knowledge of many arts he is called *Trimegistus* (i.e. Trismegistus), that is, thrice great (*ter maximus*). And they imagine him with a dog's head, they say, because among all animals the dog is held to be the most intelligent and acute species.

50. They call the god of war Mars, and he is called *Mars* because he fights using men, as if *Mars* were 'male' (*mas*, gen. *maris*). However, there are three practices customary in war: that of the Scythians, where both men and women go into battle; of the Amazons, where only women go; and of the Romans and other peoples, where only men go. 51. He is also called Mars as the author of deaths, for death (*mors*) is named after Mars. They also call him the adulterer, because he is fickle towards warriors. 52. And in fact he stands bare-chested, so that each person may expose himself to war without fear in his heart. Mars is also called Gradivus among the Thracians, because those who fight direct their step (*gradus*) into battle, or because they advance (*gradi*) readily.

53. Although they considered Apollo a diviner and physician, they also called him Sun (*Sol*), as if 'alone' (*solus*). They called him Titan, as if he were that one of the Titans who did not oppose Jupiter. 54. And they called him Phoebus, a youth (*ephebus*), as it were, that is, an adolescent. Whence the sun is also pictured as a youth, because it rises daily and is born with a new light. They say that this same Apollo is called Pythius from the Python, a serpent of immense size, whose size was as terrifying as its venom. 55. Apollo, overpowering it with arrow shots, took its name as booty, so that he is called

11 *Diespiter* is actually an archaic nominative of *Iuppiter*. Isidore may identify Diespiter with Pluto (cf. πλοῦτος, "wealth") partly by way of Dis, "wealth," and also the Latin name of the god of the underworld.

12 Mercury was said to have separated a pair of fighting serpents with his staff, which thus became his familiar attribute, the caduceus, a staff with a pair of snakes twined around it.

13 The *fetiales* were a college of Roman priests charged with making formal declarations of war.

Pythius. Whence also he established the Pythian rites to be celebrated as a sign of victory.

56. They also say that Diana, his twin, in a similar way is the moon, and guardian of roads – whence they consider her a virgin, because a road gives birth to nothing. They are both imagined to have arrows, because the two celestial bodies cast rays to the earth. Diana (*Diana*) is so called, is if the word were *Duana* (cf. *duo*, "both"), because the moon may appear both during the day (*dies*) and at night. 57. They also maintain that she is Lucina, because she gives light (*lucere*). And they say she is Trivia, because she takes on three (*tres*) appearances. Concerning her, Vergil says (*Aen.* 4.511):

> Three faces of the virgin Diana,

because this same goddess is called Luna, Diana, and Proserpina. 58. But when Luna is imagined (Prudentius, *Against the Oration of Symmachus* 1.365):

> She shines with a glimmering cloak. When, girded up, she shoots her arrows, she is the virgin Latonia. When seated resting on her throne, she is Pluto's wife.

And Diana is Latonia, because she was the daughter of Latona.

59. They maintain that Ceres, that is, the earth, is so called from the creating (*creare*) of crops, and they call her by many names. They also say she is *Ops* (i.e 'plenty'), because the earth is made better by her work (*opus*). 60. Proserpina, because from her the fruits 'spread forth' (*proserpere*). 61. Vesta, because she is clothed (*vestire*) with plants and various things, or from 'enduring by her own power' (*vi sua stare*). They imagine this same one as both Earth (*Tellus*) and the Great Mother (*Mater Magna*), turret-crowned with drum and cock and clash of cymbals. She is called 'Mother' because she bears many offspring; 'Great' because she produces food; 'the Bountiful' (*Alma*) because she nourishes (*alere*) all animals with her produce – for earth is the nursery of food. 62. Her image is imagined with a key because the earth is locked up in the winter, and is opened in the spring so that crops are born. She holds a drum because they wish to signify the orb of the earth. 63. She is said to be drawn in a wagon because she is the earth, and earth hangs in the air. She is carried on wheels because the world rotates and spins. They furnish her with tame lions below to show that no kind of beast is so wild that it cannot be subjugated and ruled by her.

64. That she wears a turreted crown on her head shows the cities set upon the earth, characterized, as it were, by their towers. Seats are imagined around her because while everything moves she herself does not move. 65. The Corybantes, her servants, are imagined with swords to signify that everyone ought to fight for his own land. They depicted cocks as serving this goddess to signify that whoever lacks seed should follow the earth; in her depth they may find all things. 66. That people are shown flinging themselves about before her is a warning, they say, that those who till the earth should not rest, for there is always something for them to do. The clashing of bronze cymbals is the clattering of iron implements in tilling a field – but they are of bronze because the ancients used to till the earth with bronze before iron had been discovered. 67. They call this same one both Vesta and fire, because there is no doubt that the earth possesses fire, as can be seen from Etna and Vulcan. And they thought she was a virgin because fire is an inviolable element, and nothing can be born from it; indeed it consumes all that it seizes.[14] 68. Ovid in the *Fasti* (6.291):

> Understand Vesta as no other than living flame – you see no bodies born from flame.

Furthermore, virgins are said to wait on her, because just as nothing is born from a virgin, so nothing is born from fire.

69. They say Juno (*Iuno*), as if the name were *Iano*, that is, 'door' (*ianua*), with regard to the menstrual discharge of women, because, as it were, she lays open the doors of mothers for their children, and of wives for their husbands. But this is what the philosophers say. The poets claim that Juno is the sister and wife of Jupiter; for they explain Jupiter as fire and air, and Juno as water and earth. By the mixture of these two, all things came into being. 70. And they say she is the sister because she is part of the world, and the wife because when united with him she brings harmony. Whence Vergil (*Geo.* 2.325):

> Then the omnipotent father, the air, descends with fertile showers into the lap of his wife.

71. Among the Greeks Minerva is called Ἀθήνη, that is, woman. Among the Romans she is called Minerva

14 Isidore here identifies Ceres with Vesta, goddess of the hearth, whose priestesses were the Vestal Virgins.

(*Minerva*), as the goddess and 'gift of various crafts' (*munus* + *ars* + *varius*). They claim she was an inventor of many skills, and thus they explain her as art and reason, because nothing can be preserved without reason. 72. Because this reason is born from the mind alone, and because they think the mind is in the head and brain, therefore they say she was born from the head of Jove, because the sense of a wise person, who discovers all things, is in his head. 73. On her chest the head of the Gorgon is pictured, because all prudence is in that spot – prudence that dazzles other people, and confirms them as ignorant and stone-like.[15] We also see this in the ancient statues of the emperors, in the middle of their breastplates, in order to imply wisdom and strength. 74. She is called both Minerva and Tritonia, for Triton is a swamp in Africa, at which it is reported that she appeared at a maidenly age, on account of which she is called Tritonia. Thus the less her origin is known, the more readily is she believed to be a goddess. 75. She is called Pallas either from the island Pallene in Thrace, on which she was raised, or after the Greek term πάλλειν τὸ δόρυ ("brandishing a spear"), that is, from striking with a spear, or because she slew the giant Pallas.

76. They say Venus (*Venus*) is so named because a woman does not leave off being a virgin without force (*vis*). The Greeks call her Ἀφροδίτη on account of the generating foam of blood, for foam is called ἀφρός in Greek. 77. They imagine that Saturn cut off the genitals of his father, the Sky (*Caelus*), so that the blood flowed into the sea, and that Venus was born from it as the foam of the sea solidified. They say this because the substance of a salt humor comes into being through coitus, whence Venus is called Ἀφροδίτη, because coitus is a foam of blood that consists of a liquid and salt secretion of the internal parts. 78. They call Venus the wife of Vulcan because the act of Venus does not take place without heat, whence (Vergil, *Geo.* 3.97):

> Grown older, he is cold in love.

79. Now, it is said that Saturn cut off the male organs of his father, the Sky, and that these created Venus when they fell into the sea; this is imagined because, unless moisture descends from the sky to the land, nothing is created.

80. They say that Cupid is so called because of love (*amor*; cf. *cupido*, "desire"), for he is the demon of fornication. He is pictured with wings because nothing more fleeting, nothing more changeable is found than lovers. He is pictured as a youth because love is foolish and irrational. He is imagined to hold an arrow and a torch; an arrow because love wounds the heart, and a torch because it inflames. 81. The Greeks call the god of country people, whom they fashioned in the likeness of nature, Pan; Latin speakers call him Silvanus. He is called Pan, that is, 'everything' (cf. πᾶν, 'everything'), for they fashion him out of every sort of element. 82. He has horns in the likeness of the rays of the sun and moon. He has a pelt marked by spots, on account of the stars of the sky. His face is ruddy in likeness to the ether. He holds a pipe of seven reeds, on account of the harmony of heaven, in which there are seven tones and seven intervals of sound. 83. He is hairy, because the earth is clothed and agitated by the winds.[16] His lower half is bestial, representing trees and brutes like livestock. He has goat's hooves, so as to show the solidity of the earth. They claim he is the god of things and of all nature, whence they say Pan, 'everything' as it were.

84. In the language of the Egyptians, the earth is called *Isis*, and they mean by this the person Isis. Now Isis, daughter of king Inachis, was a queen of the Egyptians; when she came from Greece she taught the Egyptians literacy and established cultivation of the land, on account of which they called the land by her name. 85. Serapis is the greatest of all the Egyptian gods. He is that Apis, king of the Argives, who traveled to Egypt by ship. When he died there he was called Serapis because the box in which the deceased is placed, which they call a sarcophagus, is called σορός in Greek. They began to venerate him there where he was buried before his temple had been built. It is as if at first the name were σορός plus 'Apis' – *Sorapis* – and then, when one of the letters had been changed, it was pronounced *Serapis*. 86. Among the Egyptians Apis was the bull dedicated to Serapis, and from him he received his cognomen. Egypt worshipped him like a god, because he would give certain clear signs of things to come. He would appear in Memphis, and one hundred high priests would follow after him and chant suddenly as if frantic. The Jews made the image of his head for themselves in the wilderness.

15 Gazing at the Gorgon turned one into stone.

16 'Agitated by the winds' translates an early reading not adopted by Lindsay, who here prints a nonsense sequence marked as a corruption.

87. Fauns (*faunus*) were so called from 'speaking' (*fando*, gerund of *fari*) or after the term φωνή ("vocal sound") because by voice, not by signs, they seemed to show what was to come – for they were consulted by pagans in sacred groves, and gave responses to them not with signs, but with their voices. 88. They name Genius (*Genius*) thus because he possesses the force, as it were, of generating (*gignere*, ppl. *genitus*) all things, or from generating children; whence beds that were prepared for newlyweds were called 'nuptial' (*geniales*) by the pagans.

89. These and others are the fabulous fictions of the pagans, which they interpret and regard in such a way that they worship what they do not even understand, and are damned thereby. 90. And they say that Fate (*Fatum*) is whatever the gods say, or whatever Jupiter says. Therefore the name *fatum* is from 'saying' (*fari*, 3rd person *fatur*), that is, from speaking. Except for the fact that this word is now usually understood in another context, toward which I do not wish to incline people's hearts, we can with reason speak of 'fate' as from 'saying.'[17] 91. For we cannot deny that it is written in Sacred Scripture (Psalm 61:12 Vulgate): "God has spoken once, two things have I heard," and so on. Now what is said, "has spoken once," is understood as "has spoken immovably" or "immutably," since he knows immutably everything that is to happen, and which he himself is to bring about. 92. Pagans imagine that there are three Fates – with the distaff, with the spindle, and with fingers spinning a thread from the wool – on account of the three tenses: the past, which is already spun and wound onto the spindle; the present, which is drawn between the fingers of the spinner; and the future, in the wool which is twisted onto the distaff, and which is yet to be drawn through the fingers of the spinner to the spindle, just as the present is yet to be drawn over to the past. 93. They were called Parcae (*Parca*) κατ' ἀντίφρασιν ("by opposition of sense"), because they scarcely spare (*parcere*) anyone. People claimed there were three: one who would lay the initial warp of a person's life; the second, who would weave it; and the third, who would cut it short – for we begin when we are born, we exist while we live, and we are gone when we die.

94. People say that Fortune (*Fortuna*) has its name from 'chance things' (*fortuitus*), as if it were a certain goddess sporting with human affairs through various accidents and chances. Thus they also call her blind, because she bears down upon people at random, without any consideration of merits, and comes to both good people and bad. They distinguish Fate from Fortune: Fortune, as it were, exists in what comes by chance with no obvious cause; but they say Fate is fixed and assigned for each person individually. 95. They also say that the three Furies are women with serpents for hair, on account of the three passions that give rise to many disturbances in people's spirits, and they sometimes so drive a person to do wrong that they allow him to give no consideration to his reputation or his own danger. These passions are Anger, which desires revenge, Greed, which wishes for wealth, and Lust, which seeks pleasure. They are called the Furies (*Furiae*) because they strike (*ferire*) the mind with their goads, and do not allow it to be tranquil.

96. They consider the nymphs (*nympha*) to be goddesses of the waters, so called from clouds (*nubes*), for waters are from clouds, whence this name is derived. They call the nymphs goddesses of the waters as though they were 'divinities of the springs' (*numina lympharum*). And they call these Muses as well as nymphs, not without reason, because the movement of water makes music. 97. The pagans have various terms for nymphs. Indeed they call nymphs of the mountains oreads (*oreas*), those of the forest dryads (*dryas*), those of the springs hamadryads (*hamadryas*), those of the fields naiads (*naias*), and those of the seas nereids (*nereis*). 98. They say that heroes (*heros*) take their name from Juno, for Juno is called Ἥρα in Greek. Thus a son of hers, I don't know which, was called ἥρως ("the hero"), according to a legend of the Greeks. The legend evidently signifies in a mystical sense that the air (*aer*), where they claim that heroes live, is assigned to Juno. They name the souls of deceased people of some importance with this term, as if it were ἀήρωας, that is, men of the air (*aerius*) and worthy of heaven on account of their wisdom and strength.

99. The pagans called all the gods whom they worshiped at home Penates (*Penates*). And they were called Penates because they were in 'inner rooms' (*penetralis*), that is, in recesses. How these gods were addressed, or what names they had, is not known. 100. They called the gods of the dead *Manes*, whose power they claim is between the moon and the earth. From this they

17 The other understanding Isidore seems to have in mind is the pagan idea of the Fates treated just below.

suppose 'morning' (*mane*) is named. They think these gods are named *Manes* after the term for air, which is μανός, that is "sparse," or because they spread (*manare*) widely through the heavens – or they are called by this name because they are mild, the opposite of monstrous (*immanis*). Apuleius says (cf. *The God of Socrates* 153) that it is κατ' ἀντίφρασιν ("by opposition of sense") that they are called Manes, that is, mild and modest, when they are terrible and monstrous, named in the same way as the Parcae (see section 93 above) and Eumenides (i.e. the Furies; lit. "the Gracious Ones"). 101. Ghosts (*larva*), they say, are demons made from people who were deserving of evil. It is said that their nature is to frighten small children and chatter in shadowy corners. 102. Witches (*lamia*), whom stories report would snatch children and tear them apart, are particularly named from 'tearing apart' (*laniare*). 103. 'Hairy ones' (*Pilosus*, i.e. a satyr) are called *Panitae* in Greek, and 'incubuses' (*incubus*) in Latin, or Inui, from copulating (*inire*) indiscriminately with animals. Hence also *incubi* are so called from 'lying upon' (*incumbere*, ppl. *incubitus*), that is, violating, for often they are shameless towards women, and manage to lie with them. The Gauls call these demons *Dusii*, because they carry out this foulness continually (*adsidue*). 104. Common people call one demon Incubo, and the Romans called him 'Faunus of the figs.' About him Horace says (*Odes* 3.18.1):

> Faunus, lover of fleeing nymphs, may you pass lightly
> through my borders and sunny fields.

Book IX

Languages, nations, reigns, the military, citizens, family relationships (De linguis, gentibus, regnis, militia, civibus, affinitatibus)

i. The languages of nations (De linguis gentium) 1. The diversity of languages arose with the building of the Tower after the Flood, for before the pride of that Tower divided human society, so that there arose a diversity of meaningful sounds, there was one language for all nations, which is called Hebrew. The patriarchs and prophets used this language not only in their speech, but also in the sacred writings. But at the outset[1] there were as many languages as there were nations, and then more nations than languages, because many nations sprang from one language stock. 2. The term 'languages' (*lingua*) is used in this context for the words that are made by the tongue (*lingua*), according to the figure of speech by which the thing that produces is named after the thing that is produced.[2] Thus we will say 'mouth' for 'words,' as we speak of the letters we form as 'a hand.'

3. There are three sacred languages – Hebrew, Greek, and Latin – which are preeminent throughout the world. On the cross of the Lord the charge laid against him was written at Pilate's command in these three languages (John 19:20). Hence – and because of the obscurity of the Sacred Scriptures – a knowledge of these three languages is necessary, so that, whenever the wording of one of the languages presents any doubt about a name or an interpretation, recourse may be had to another language. 4. Greek is considered more illustrious than the other nations' languages, for it is more sonorous than Latin or any other language. We can distinguish five varieties of Greek. The first of these is called κοινή, that is, 'mixed' or 'common,' which everyone uses. 5. The second is Attic (*Atticus*), namely the Greek of Athens (*Atheniensis*), which all the authors of Greece used. The third is Doric, which the Egyptians and Syrians employ. The fourth, Ionic; the fifth, Aeolic, which they say the Eolisti spoke.[3] In examining the Greek language we find settled differences of this kind, because their speaking communities were dispersed in this way.

6. Some say there are four varieties of Latin, that is, Ancient (*Priscus*), Latin, Roman, and Mixed. The Ancient is that uncouth language that the oldest people of Italy spoke in the age of Janus and Saturn, and it is preserved in the songs of the Salii. Then Latin, which the Etruscans and others in Latium spoke in the age of Latinus and the kings, and in this variety the Twelve Tables were written. 7. Then Roman, which arose after the kings were driven out by the Roman people. In this variety the poets Naevius, Plautus, Ennius, and Vergil, and the orators Gracchus and Cato and Cicero, and others produced their work. Then Mixed, which emerged in the Roman state after the wide expansion of the Empire, along with new customs and peoples, corrupted the integrity of speech with solecisms and barbarisms.

8. All the nations of the East – like the Hebrews and the Syrians – crunch together their speech and words in their throats. All the Mediterranean nations – like the Greeks and the people of Asia Minor – strike their speech on the palate. All the Western nations – like the Italians and Spaniards – gnash their words against their teeth. 9. Syrian and Chaldean are close to Hebrew in speech, mostly agreeing in sound and in the pronunciation of their letters. But some think that Hebrew is Chaldean, because Abraham sprang from the Chaldeans. However, if this is accepted, how is it that the Hebrew children in the Book of Daniel (1:4) are ordered to be taught the Chaldean language, which they do not know? 10. Every human is able to pick up any human language – whether

1 Presumably "at the outset" here means "immediately after the division of Babel."

2 Isidore apparently interchanges the terms of the figure by mistake.

3 The last clause loosely translates a corrupted text.

Greek, or Latin, or that of any other nation – by hearing it, or to learn it by reading with a tutor. Although knowing all languages is difficult for anyone, yet no one is so indolent that, placed among his own people, he does not know the language of his own nation. Indeed, how else should such a one be considered but as worse than brute beasts? Beasts produce their own cries, and the human who is ignorant of his own language is worse.

11. It is hard to determine what sort of language God spoke at the beginning of the world, when he said (Genesis 1:3), "Be light made," for there were not yet any languages. Or again, it is hard to know with what language he spoke afterwards to the outer ears of humans, especially as he spoke to the first man, or to the prophets, or when the voice of God resounded in bodily fashion when he said (Mark 1:11), "Thou art my beloved Son." It is believed by some that the language in these places was that single one which existed before the diversity of tongues. As for the various language communities, it is rather believed that God speaks to them in the same language that the people use themselves, so that he may be understood by them. 12. Indeed, God speaks to humans not through an invisible substance, but through a bodily creature, through which he even wished to appear to humans when he spoke. Now the Apostle says (I Corinthians 13:1), "If I speak with the tongues of men, and of angels." Here the question arises, with what tongue do angels speak? But Paul is saying this by way of exaggeration, not because there are tongues belonging to angels. 13. It is also asked with what language will humans speak in the future; the answer is nowhere to be found, for the Apostle says (1 Corinthians 13:8), "Or tongues shall cease."

14. We have treated languages first, and then nations, because nations arose from languages, and not languages from nations.

ii. The names of nations (De gentium vocabulis) 1. A nation (*gens*) is a number of people sharing a single origin, or distinguished from another nation (*natio*) in accordance with its own grouping, as the 'nations' of Greece or of Asia Minor.[4] From this comes the term 'shared heritage' (*gentilitas*). The word *gens* is also so called on account of the generations (*generatio*) of families, that is from 'begetting' (*gignere*, ppl. *genitus*), as the term 'nation' (*natio*) comes from 'being born' (*nasci*, ppl. *natus*). 2. Now, of the nations into which the earth is divided, fifteen are from Japheth, thirty-one from Ham, and twenty-seven from Shem, which adds up to seventy-three – or rather, as a proper accounting shows, seventy-two.[5] And there are an equal number of languages, which arose across the lands and, as they increased, filled the provinces and islands.

3. The five sons of Shem each brought forth individual nations. The first of these was Elam, from whom descended the Elamites, princes of the Persians. The second Asshur, from whom sprang the empire of the Assyrians. The third Arpachshad, from whom the nation of the Chaldeans arose. The fourth Lud, from whom came the Lydians. The fifth Aram, from whom descended the Syrians, whose capital city was Damascus. 4. There are four sons of Aram, the grandsons of Shem: Uz, Hul, Gether, and Mash. Uz was the founder of Trachonitis – a principate between Palestine and Celesyria – from which came Job, as it is written (Job 1:1): "There was a man in the land of Uz." The second, Hul, from whom came the Armenians. The third, Gether, from whom came the Acarnanians or Curians. The fourth Mash, from whom descended those who are called Maeones. 5. The posterity of Arpachshad the son of Shem follows. The grandson of Arpachshad was Heber (i.e. Eber), from whom descended the Hebrews. The son of Eber was Joktan, from whom the nation of the Indians arose. The son of Joktan was Sheleph, from whom came the Bactrians – although others suspect that these were Scythian exiles. 6. A son of Abraham was Ishmael, from whom arose the Ishmaelites, who are now called, with corruption of the name, Saracens, as if they descended from Sarah, and the Agarenes, from Agar (i.e Hagar). 7. A son of Ishmael was Nebaioth, from whom descended the Nabatheans, who live between the Euphrates and the Red Sea. 8. The sons of Lot were Moab and Ammon (i.e. Ben-ammi), from whom came the Moabites and the Ammonites. 9. The son of Esau was Edom, from whom descended the Edomites. These are the nations that descend from the

4 The word *gens* essentially means "people generated together, people of one stock." It may be translated "nation," "race," "tribe," "people," "family," etc., depending on the context.

5 The number of nations was traditionally seventy-two, taking Eber and Phaleg as progenitors of a single nation. In several particulars Isidore departs from the accounts in Genesis 10 and Paralipomenon (Chronicles) 1. Often he follows Jerome's *Liber Quaestionum Hebraicarum in Genesim.*

stock of Shem, holding the southern lands from the east to the Phoenicians.

10. There were four sons of Ham, from whom sprang the following nations. Cush, from whom the Ethiopians were begotten. Mesraim (i.e. Egypt), from whom the Egyptians are said to have risen. 11. Put, from whom came the Libyans – whence the river of Mauretania is called Put still today, and the whole region around it is called Puthensis. 12. Finally Canaan, from whom descended the Africans and the Phoenicians and the ten tribes of Canaanites. 13. Again, the sons of Cush, grandsons of Ham – the grandchildren of Ham were six. The sons of Cush: Saba (i.e. Seba), Havilah, Sabtah, Raamah, Seba, and Cuza.[6] 14. Saba, from whom the Sabaeans were begotten and named, concerning which Vergil (*Geo.* 2.117):

> The bough of frankincense is the Sabaeans' alone.

These are also the Arabians. 15. Havilah, from whom descended the Getulians, who cling together in a desert region of farthest Africa. 16. Sabtah, from whom came the Sabathenes, who now are called the Astabarians. 17. But Raamah, Seba, and Cuza gradually lost their ancient names, and the names that they now have, instead of the ancestral ones, are not known. 18. The sons of Raamah were Saba (i.e. Sheba) and Dedan. This Saba is written in Hebrew with the letter *shin*, whereas the Saba above is written with a *samekh*, and from him the Sabaeans were named – but now Saba is translated "Arabia." 19. Dedan, from whom arose the Ethiopians in the western region.

The sons of Mesraim (i.e. Egypt): Lahabim, from whom came the Libyans, who formerly were called Putheans. 20. Casluhim, from whom sprang the Philistines, whom the ancients called Ἀλλόφυλοι (lit. "foreigners"), and whom we now call, corruptly, Palestinians. 21. The other six nations are unknown because their past names fell into oblivion when they were overthrown in the Ethiopian War.

22. There were eleven sons of Canaan, from whom descended the ten tribes of Canaanites, whose land the Jews occupied when the Canaanites were expelled. The firstborn of these was Sidon, from whom came the Sidonians – whence also their city in Phoenicia is called Sidon. 23. The second, Heth, from whom came the Hethites. Third, Jebus, from whom descended the Jebusites, who possessed the city Jerusalem. Fourth, Emor, from whom came the Amorites. Fifth, Girgash, from whom the Girgashites. Sixth Hivah, from whom the Hivites. Those same were the Gibeonites, from the city of Gibeon, who came as suppliants to Joshua (Joshua 9:3–15). 24. Seventh, Arkah, who founded the city of Arcas opposite Tripoli, situated at the foot of Mount Lebanon. Eighth, Sinah, from whom the Sinites. Ninth Arvadah, from whom are the Arvadites, who occupied the island Aradum, separated by a narrow strait from the Phoenician coastline. 25. The tenth, Zemarah, from whom came the noble city of Syria called Coeles. The eleventh, Hamath. These are the nations from the stock of Ham, which extend across the whole southern region from Sidon to the Gaditanian Strait (i.e. the Straits of Cadiz).

Now the tribes of the sons of Japheth. 26. Seven sons of Japheth are named: Gomer, from whom sprang the Galatians, that is, the Gauls (*Galli*). 27. Magog, from whom people think the Scythians and the Goths took their origin. 28. Madai, from whom people reckon the Medes came to be. Javan, from whom the Ionians, who are also the Greeks – hence the 'Ionian' Sea. 29. Tubal, from whom came the Iberians, who are also the Spaniards, although some think the Italians also sprang from him. 30. Meshech, from whom came the Cappadocians; hence to this day a city in their territory is called Mazaca. 31. Tiras, from whom the Thracians; their name is not much altered, as if it were Tiracians. 32. Then the sons of Gomer, the grandsons of Japheth. Ashkenaz, from whom descended the Sarmatians, whom the Greeks call Rheginians. 33. Riphath, from whom came the Paphlagonians. Gotorna (i.e. Togarmah), from whom are the Phrygians. 34. The sons of Javan: Elishah, from whom came the Greek Eliseans, who are called Aeolides. Hence also the fifth language in Greece is called Αἰολίς ("Aeolic"). 35. Tarshish, from whom descended the Cilicians, as Josephus thinks. From his name their capital city is called Tarsus. 36. Kittim, from whom the Citians, that is the Cypriots, whose city today is named Citium. Dodanim (i.e. Rodanim), from whom came the Rhodians. 37. These are the nations from the stock of Japheth, which occupy the middle region of Asia Minor from Mount Taurus to the north and all of Europe up to the Britannic Ocean, bequeathing their names to both places and peoples.

6 Genesis 10:7 lists five sons of Cush. One of these, Sabteca, has erroneously become two, Seba and Cuza.

Afterwards many of these names were changed, others remain as they were. 38. Indeed, the names for many nations have partially remained, so that their derivation is apparent today, like the Assyrians from Assur and the Hebrews from Heber (i.e. Eber). But partly, through the passage of time, they have been so altered that the most learned people, poring over the oldest historical works, have not been able to find the origin of all nations from among these forebears, but only of some, and these with difficulty. 39. Thus no original sound of the word remains to show that the Egyptians arose from the son of Ham named Mesraim (i.e. Egypt), or similarly with regard to the Ethiopians, who are said to descend from that son of Ham named Cush.

If all this is taken into account, there appear to be more names of nations that have been altered than names remaining, and afterwards a rational process has given diverse names to these. So the Indians were named from the river Indus, which bounds them on the western side. 40. The Serians (i.e. Chinese, or East Asians generally), a nation situated in the far East, were allotted their name from their own city. They weave a kind of wool that comes from trees, hence this verse (Courtney fr. 7):

> The Serians, unknown in person but known for their cloth.

41. The Gangarides are a people between the Assyrians and the Indians, living around the Ganges River – hence they were named Gangarides. 42. The Hircanians are named for the Hircanian forest, where there are many tigers. 43. The Bactrians were Scythians who were driven from their territory by a faction of their own people. They settled by the river Bactron in the East, and derived their name from the name of the river. The king of this nation was Zoroaster, inventor of the art of magic. 44. The Parthians likewise take their origin from the Scythians, for they were Scythian exiles, which is still evident from their name, for in the Scythian language exiles are called *parthi.* Like the Bactrians, after being driven by civil dissension from Scythia they first stealthily occupied the empty territory adjacent to the Hircanians, and then seized more land by force. 45. The Assyrians were named for Assur, the son of Shem – a very powerful nation, which held sway over the whole middle region between the Euphrates and the Indian border.

46. The Medes are thought to have been named after their king. Jason, brother of the Pelian king, was driven by Pelias's children from Thessaly with his wife Medea. Jason's stepson was Medus, king of the Athenians, who after the death of Jason conquered the territory of the East. He founded there the city Media, and he named the nation of Medes after his own name. But in the Book of Genesis we find that Madai was the progenitor of the nation of Medes, and also that they were named for him, as was said above (section 28 above). 47. The Persians were named after King Perseus, who crossed into Asia from Greece and there dominated the barbarian nations with heavy and prolonged fighting. Right after his victory he gave his name to the conquered people. Before Cyrus, the Persians were an ignoble people and considered of no rank among the nations of the area. The Medes were always very powerful. 48. The Chasdeans, who are now called the Chaldeans, were named after Chesed, the son of Nahor, Abraham's brother. 49. The Sabaeans were named after the word σέβεσθαι, that is, "supplicate" and "worship," because we worship the divinity with Sabaean incense. They are also called Arabs, because they live in the mountains of Arabia called Libanus and Antilibanus, where incense is gathered. 50. The Syrians are held to be named from Surim (i.e. Asshurim), who was the grandson of Abraham from his wife Keturah. The people whom the ancients called Assyrians we now call Syrians, making a whole name from the part.

51. The Hebrews were so named from Heber (i.e. Eber), the great-grandson of Shem. 52. The Israelites were named after Israel, the son of Isaac, for Israel was the patriarch of the Hebrews, and from him the twelve tribes of Jews were given the name of Israel. The splitting off of the ten tribes imposed a name on the Judeans, for before they were called either Hebrews or Israelites. 53. However, from the time when the people of God were divided into two kingdoms, the two tribes that had kings from the stock of Judah were given the name of Judeans (*Iudaeus*). The residue of ten tribes, who established a king for themselves in Samaria, kept the original name of Israel because of their large population. 54. The nation of the Samaritans took its origin from Assyrians who lived as immigrants in Samaria. In Latin their name means "guardians," because when the kingdom of Israel was taken captive the Samaritans were stationed in Israel's territory as a guard.

55. After Phoenix, the brother of Cadmus, moved from Egyptian Thebes to Syria, he reigned at Sidon and named

those people Phoenicians and the province Phoenicia after his own name. 56. Moreover, the Sidonites are thought to have drawn their name from the city called Sidon. 57. The Saracens are so called either because they claim to be descendants of Sarah or, as the pagans say, because they are of Syrian origin, as if the word were *Syriginae*. They live in a very large deserted region. They are also Ishmaelites, as the Book of Genesis teaches us, because they sprang from Ishmael. They are also named Kedar, from the son of Ishmael, and Agarines, from the name Agar (i.e. Hagar). As we have said, they are called Saracens from an alteration of their name, because they are proud to be descendants of Sarah.

58. Philistines are the same as Palestinians, because the Hebrew language lacks the letter *p* and uses the Greek phi in its place. Hence they say Philistine for Palestinians, expressly from the name of their city. They are also called Allophyli, that is, "of foreign descent," because they were always enemies of Israel and were set far apart from their race and society. 59. Canaanites were named after Canaan the son of Ham, and the Jews occupied their land. From this origin came Emor, the father of Sichem, for whom the Amorites were named. 60. The Egyptians were named after a certain King Aegyptus, whereas earlier they were called Aerians. In the Hebrew language 'Egyptians' means "afflicters," because they afflicted the people of God before they were liberated with divine assistance. 61. Armenius of Thessaly was one of Jason's generals who set out for Colchis with a gathered multitude that wandered here and there upon the loss of their king Jason. He founded Armenia, and gave that nation its name after his own name.

62. The Persian boundary, which divides the Scythians from the Persians, is named Scytha, and the Scythians are regarded by some people as having been named from that boundary – a nation always held to be very ancient. They are the Parthians and Bactrians; further, Scythian women founded the kingdom of the Amazons. 63. The Massagetes are of Scythian origin, and they are called Massagetes because they are 'weighty,' that is, 'strong' Getae – for Livy speaks of silver as weighty, that is, as 'masses' (cf. *massa*, "mass"). They live in northern regions between the Scythians and the Albanians. 64. The Amazons are so called either because they live together without men, as if the word were ἅμα ζῶν ("living together"), or because they had their right breasts burnt off so that their shooting of arrows would not be hindered, as if it were ἄνευ μαζῶν ("without breasts"). Indeed, they would expose the breast that they had burned off. Titianus calls them 'One-Breasted' (*Unimammae*), for that is 'Amazon,' as if the term were ἄνευ μαζοῦ, that is, "without a breast."[7] Amazons no longer exist, because they were wiped out partly by Hercules and partly by Achilles or Alexander.

65. The Scythian peoples in regions of Asia Minor, who believe that they are descendants of Jason, are born with white (*albus*) hair because of the incessant snow, and the color of their hair gave the nation its name – hence they are called Albanians. A blue-gray, that is, colored pupil is present in their eyes, so that they see better by night than by day. Also, the Albanians were neighbors of the Amazons. 66. The Hugnians were formerly called Huns, and afterwards – after the name of their king – Avars, and they first lived in farthest Maeotis, between the icy Tanais (i.e. the Don) and the savage peoples of the Massagetes. Then, with their nimble horses, they burst forth from the crags of the Caucasus, where the barricades of Alexander had been keeping the fierce nations back. They held the East captive for twenty years, and exacted an annual tribute from the Egyptians and the Ethiopians.

67. The Trojan nation was formerly named the Dardanian, from Dardanus. The brothers Dardanus and Jasius emigrated from Greece, and Jasius came to Thrace, Dardanus to Phrygia, where he was the first ruler. After him succeeded his son Ericthonius, and then his grandson Tros, from whom the Trojans were named. 68. The Galatians are also known as the Gauls, and when they were called to the aid of the king of Bithynia they divided the kingdom with him when victory was attained. Then, mixed with the Greeks in this way, they were first called Gallogreeks, but now they are named Galatians after their ancient name of *Galli* (i.e. Gauls).

69. The Greeks were formerly named Thessalians, from Thessalus, and afterwards called Greeks, from King Graecus – for Greeks are properly Thessalians. 70. Further, people say that the Lapiths were a nation of Thessaly who once lived by the river Penios and were named after Lapitha, the daughter of Apollo. 71. The Greek nation of Sicyonians was named after King Sicyon. These were

7 The writings of Julius Titianus, second century CE, are lost; Isidore cites him at second hand from Servius on *Aeneid* 11.651.

first called Agialeans, after King Agealeus, who first ruled over the Sicyonians. The city of Agealea is named after him, and this is now called the Peloponnesus, after its king Pelops. These are also called Arcadians, named after King Arcas, the son of Jupiter and Callista. 72. The Danai were named after King Danaus. They are the same as the Argives, named after their founder Argos. After Apis, the king of the Greeks, died, his son Argos succeeded to the kingship, and the Argives were named after him. After his death he began to be regarded as a god by them, honored with a temple and sacrifices. 73. The Achaians, also known as Achivians, were named after Achaeus, son of Jupiter. 74. The Pelasgians were so named because they seemed to have arrived in Italy in springtime with sails spread, like birds (cf. πελαργός, "stork"). Varro records their first landing in Italy (cf. Funaioli 400). But the Greeks maintain that the Pelasgians were so called after the son of Jupiter and Larissa.

75. The Myrmidons were allies of Achilles, and the Dolopians of Pyrrhus. The Myrmidons were so called for their cleverness, as if the word were μύρμηκες, that is, "ants." But Eratosthenes says they are called Myrmidons after their leader Myrmido, son of Jupiter and Eurymedusa. 76. Cranaus succeeded to Cecrops, king of the Athenians; his daughter Atthis gave her name to the region and the nation. Also from her the Attic people were named, and they are the Athenians. 77. Ion was a powerful man, and he called those same Athenians 'Ionians,' from his own name. 78. The Macedonians were earlier named the Emathians, after the name of King Emathio, and afterwards called Macedonians. 79. The Epiroteans were earlier named the Pyrrhideans after Pyrrhus, the son of Achilles, but afterwards after King Epirus . . .[8] they ventured to cross over to Italy. 80. Dorus was the son of Neptune and Ellepis, whence the Dorians take their origin and their name. Moreover, they are a part of the Greek nation, and after them is named the third language of the Greeks, called Doric.

81. The Lacedaemonians are named from Lacedaemon, the son of Semela. These people engaged for a long time in battle against the Messenians and, fearing that they would lose any hope of offspring because of the prolongation of the conflict, they commanded that their virgins should lie with the young men remaining at home. Thus, because of the promiscuous intercourse of these virgins, the youths, born of uncertain parentage, were named Spartans after the stigma of their mothers' shame.[9] The Spartans are the same as the Lacedaemonians.

82. The Thracians are thought to have descended and taken their name from the son of Japheth named Tiras, as was said above (section 31 above), although the pagans judge that they were named for their behavior, because they are ferocious (*trux*, gen. *trucis*). Indeed, they were the most savage of all nations, and many legends are recorded about them: that they would sacrifice captives to their gods, and would drink human blood from skulls. About them, Vergil (*Aen.* 3.44):

> Alas, flee those cruel lands, flee that greedy coast –

as if it were the land of cruel and greedy people. 83. The Istrian nation originated from the Colchians, and were sent to hunt down the Argonauts. They went up the river Ister from the Pontus (i.e. the Black Sea), and thus they were called after the name of the river by which they left the sea.

84. The Romans were named after Romulus, who founded the city of Rome and gave his name to both nation and city. These people were earlier called Saturnians, from Saturn, and Latins, from Latinus – for Latinus was king of Italy, who named the Latins from his own name – and they afterwards were called Romans. They are also called Quirites, because Romulus is also named Quirinus, since he would always use a spear that in the language of the Sabines is called *curis.* 85. Also, Italus, Sabinus, and Sicanus were brothers, after whom names were given to both peoples and regions. From Italus, the Italians; from Sabinus, the Sabines; from Sicanus, the Sicani were named – these last were also named Siculi, that is, Sicilians. 86. The Tuscans (i.e. Etruscans) are a nation of Italy named for their frequent use of rituals and incense (*tus*), that is, from the word θυσιάζειν ("offer sacrifice").

87. The Umbrians are a nation of Italy, but they are the offspring of the ancient Gauls, and they inhabit the Apennine mountains. The histories maintain that because in a period of destructive flooding they survived the rains (*imber*) they were called Ὄμβριοι ("rain people") in Greek. 88. The Marsian nation of Italy is so called from Marsyas, the companion of Liber, who revealed the

8 A lacuna occurs here in the early manuscripts.

9 Isidore may derive 'Spartan' from the Greek παρθένος, "virgin," or possibly from σπαρτός, "sown, scattered."

practice of viticulture to them. Because of this they built a statue to him, which afterwards the Romans carried off when the Marsians had been conquered. Moreover, the Greeks call the Marsians 'Oscians,' as if it were ὀφσκοι, because they had many serpents, and ὄφις means "serpent." They are also said to be invulnerable to the sorcery of spells. Like the Umbrians they inhabit the region of the Apennine mountains. [The historian Alexander says, "Some say that the Volscians were named after Vulscus, son of Antiphates the Laestrygonian. Fabius also says that the Volscians migrated from the Sicolicians and were so called by a corruption of that name."][10]

89. The Goths are thought to have been named after Magog, the son of Japheth, because of the similarity of the last syllable. The ancients called them Getae rather than Goths. They are a brave and most powerful people, tall and massive in body, terrifying for the kind of arms they use. Concerning them, Lucan (*Civil War* 2.54):

> Let here a Dacian press forward, there a Getan (*Getes*)
> rush at the Iberians.

90. The Dacians were offshoots of the Goths, and people think they were called Dacians (*Dacus*) as if the word were *Dagus*, because they were begotten 'from the stock of the Goths' (*de Gothorum stirpe*). Concerning them, this verse (Paulinus of Nola, *Poems* 17.17):

> You will go far, up to the northern Dacians.

91. The Bessians were a barbarian people who are thought to have been named after their great herds of cattle (*bos*). Concerning them, a certain poet (Paulinus of Nola, *Poems* 17.250):

> He who lives in the middle of the land, or he who dwells
> by the river, rich with many cattle and wearing a felt cap.

92. The Gipedes used to go to war on foot (*pedester*) rather than on horseback, and they are so named for this reason.

93. The Sarmatians rode armed (*armatus*) over the open fields before Lentulus restrained them at the Danube, and from their enthusiasm for weaponry (*arma*) they are thought to have received the name Sarmatians. 94. They say that the Lanus is a river beyond the Danube, after which the Alani were named, just as the people living by the river Lemannus (i.e. Lake Leman) are called Alemanni. About these, Lucan (*Civil War* 1.396):

> They abandoned their tents pitched by the
> deep-channeled Lemannus.

95. The Langobards are commonly said to have been named for their beards (*barba*), long and never cut. 96. The river Vindilicus springs out from the far frontier of Gaul, and people maintain that the Vandals lived by it and got their name from it.

97. The Germanic (*Germanicus*) nations are so called because they are immense (*immanis*) in body, and they are savage (*immanis*) tribes hardened by very severe cold. They took their behavior from that same severity of climate – fiercely courageous and ever indomitable, living by raiding and hunting. There are many tribes of Germani, varied in their weaponry, differing in the color of their clothes, of mutually incomprehensible languages, and with uncertain etymologies of their names – such as the Tolosates, the Amsivari, the Quadi, the Tuungri, the Marcomanni, the Bruteri, the Chamavi, the Blangiani, the Tubantes. The monstrosity of their barbarism gives a fearsome quality even to their names.

98. The Suevi were a segment of the Germanic nation at the northern frontier. Of them, Lucan (cf. *Civil War* 2.51):

> (The Elbe and Rhine) pour the blond Suevi from the
> extreme north.

Many have reported that there were a hundred villages and communities of Suevians. The Suevi are thought to have been named from Mount Suevus, which forms the eastern boundary of Germania and whose territory they occupied. 99. Formerly, when the interior of Germania was subjected by the Romans, the Burgundians coalesced into a large nation after being placed at the frontier-line of the Roman camps by Tiberius Caesar. Thus they drew their name from their location, because in their vernacular they call the dense settlements along the frontier 'forts' (*burgus*). Afterwards they rebelled against the Romans and, comprising more than eighty thousand armed men, they settled on the banks of the Rhine, and took the name of a nation. 100. The Saxon people, situated on the shores of the Ocean in impassable marshes, are accomplished in strength and agility. Whence they were named (i.e. from *saxosus*, "stony"), because they are a hard and very powerful kind of people, standing out above the other piratical tribes.

10 Lindsay placed this bracketed passage here, expressing doubt about its proper location, moving it from its obviously wrong position in the family of early manuscripts where it occurs, at IV.vii.34.

101. The Franks (*Franci*) are thought to have been named after a certain chieftain of theirs. Others reckon that they were named for the brutality (*feritas*) of their behavior, for their behavior is wild, with a natural ferocity of spirit. 102. Some suspect that the Britons were so named in Latin because they are brutes (*brutus*). Their nation is situated within the Ocean, with the sea flowing between us and them, as if they were outside our orbit. Concerning them, Vergil (*Ecl.* 1.66):

> The Britons, separated from the whole world.

103. The Scotti (*Scottus*, i.e. the Irish) in their own language receive their name from their painted (*pictus*; cf. the Picts) bodies, because they are marked by tattoos of various figures made with iron pricks and black pigment. 104. The Gauls (*Galli*) are named for the whiteness of their bodies, for in Greek milk is called γάλα. Whence the Sibyl speaks of them thus, when she says of them (cf. Vergil, *Aen.* 8.660):

> Then their milk-white necks are circled with gold.

105. People's faces and coloring, the size of their bodies, and their various temperaments correspond to various climates. Hence we find that the Romans are serious, the Greeks easy-going, the Africans changeable, and the Gauls fierce in nature and rather sharp in wit, because the character of the climate makes them so. 106. The Gauls were also called the Senones, and in ancient times the Xenones, because they offered hospitality to Liber (cf. ξένος, "guest"); afterwards the letter *x* was changed to *s*. 107. Vacca was a town near the Pyrenees, and the Vacceans were named after it. The poet is believed to have spoken about them (cf. Vergil, *Aen.* 4.42):

> And the Vacceans ranging far.

They occupied the vast emptiness of the heights of the Pyrenees. They are the same people as the Vascones (i.e. the Basques), as if the word were *Vaccones*, with the letter *c* changed to *s*. 108. After he subdued Spain, Gnaeus Pompey, in his rush to come to his triumphal celebration, drove them down from the heights of the Pyrenees and gathered them into one city. Hence the city took the name of 'Assembled Refugees' (*Convenae*, i.e. Saint-Bertrand de Comminges).

109. The Spanish were first named Iberians, after the river Iberus (i.e. the Ebro), but afterwards they were named Spaniards (*Hispanus*) after Hispalus (i.e. the legendary founder of *Hispalis*, Seville). 110. The Galicians (*Gallecus*) were named for their whiteness (cf. γάλα, "milk") – and hence also the Gauls (*Gallus*) were named – for they are of whiter complexion than the other people of Spain. They claim a Greek origin for themselves, and hence are wise with a native wit. 111. They say that, after the Trojan War, Teucer was despised by his father Telamon because of the death of his brother Ajax. When he was not received into his kingdom, Teucer retired to Cyprus and there founded the city of Salamis after the name of his ancient homeland. From there he emigrated to Galicia, and when he had settled there he gave the name of the place to the nation. 112. The Astures are a nation of Spain, so called because they live along the river Astura, hedged in by mountains and thick forests. 113. The Cantabrians (*Cantaber*) are a nation of Spain named after the name of a city and the river Iberus (i.e. the Ebro) where they reside. They have a gritty spirit and are always as ready for brigandage and warfare as for enduring blows. 114. The Celtiberians descended from the Celtic Gauls, and from these names their district, Celtiberia, was named – for they were named Celtiberians after the river Iberus of Spain, where they are settled, and after the Gauls, who were called Celtic, with the two terms combined.

115. The Africans were named for one of the descendants of Abraham, who was called Afer. He is said to have led an army against Libya and to have settled there after he had conquered the enemy, and his descendants were named Africans, and the place named Africa, after their ancestor. 116. The Punic people are the Carthaginians, named after the Phoenicians who emigrated with Dido. 117. The Tyrians were named after Tyre, the city of the Phoenicians, whence they emigrated and came to the African coast. 118. The Getulians are said to have been Getae who, setting out from their homeland with a huge force on ships, occupied the region of the Syrtes in Libya and were named by derivation Getulians, because they came from the Getae. Hence also the idea among the Goths is to speak of the Moors as close blood-relatives of themselves from their ancient affinity. 119. Thus Africa was held initially by the Libyans, then the Africans, and after this the Getulians, and finally the Moors and Numidians.

120. The Moors and Numidians – so the Africans believe – got their origin and name in the following way. After Hercules perished in Spain, his leaderless army,

composed of various nations, sought homes for themselves in various places, and from this mass Medes and Persians and Armenians, having sailed across to Africa by ship, occupied the regions nearest the sea. 121. But the Persians, not finding wood in the fields for building houses, and with communication inhibited by the unknown language, wandered through open fields and diverse deserts. In accordance with their itinerant foraging they called themselves, in their own language, Numidians, that is, wandering and errant and without a city (cf. νομάς, "nomadic"). 122. On the other hand, the Medes mingled with those Libyans who lived closest to Spain. Little by little the Libyans altered the name of these people, in their barbarous tongue calling the Medes 'Moors' (*Maurus*), although the Moors are named by the Greeks for their color, for the Greeks call black μαυρός (i.e. ἀμαυρός, "dark"), and indeed, blasted by blistering heat, they have a countenance of a dark color.

123. Massylia is a city of Africa, not far from Mount Atlas and the gardens of the Hesperides. The Massylians were named after this city, and we now call them, with alteration, Massulians. Concerning them, Vergil (cf. *Aen.* 4.483):

> Here a priestess of the Massylian people has been shown to me.

124. The nation of the Gaulalians consists of people wandering from the south up to the western Ocean. The island Gauloe gave them their name; it is next to Ethiopia, and no serpent is born or lives there. 125. Garamantes are a people of Africa living near the Cyrenians and named after the king Garamas, son of Apollo. He founded there the city named Garama after his own name. They are neighbors of the Ethiopian tribes. Concerning them, Vergil (*Ecl.* 8.44):

> The farthest Garamantes.

And 'farthest,' because they are savage and remote from human fellowship. 126. The Hesperians are those who live alongside Spain, for Hispania is Hesperia (see XIV.iv.19).

127. Ethiopians are so called after a son of Ham named Cush, from whom they have their origin. In Hebrew, *Cush* means "Ethiopian." 128. This nation, which formerly emigrated from the region of the river Indus, settled next to Egypt between the Nile and the Ocean, in the south very close to the sun. There are three tribes of Ethiopians: Hesperians, Garamantes, and Indians. Hesperians are of the West, Garamantes of Tripolis, and the Indians of the East. 129. The Trochodites (i.e. Troglodytes) are a tribe of Ethiopians so called because they run with such speed that they chase down wild animals on foot (cf. τροχάζειν, "run quickly"; τρέχειν, "run"). 130. The Pamphagians are also in Ethiopia. Their food is whatever can be chewed, and anything living that they come upon – whence they are named (cf. παν-, "all"; φαγεῖν, "eat"). 131. Icthyophagians (cf. ἰχθῦς, "fish"), who excel in fishing at sea and survive on fish alone. They occupy the mountainous regions beyond the Indians, and Alexander the Great conquered them and forbade them to eat fish. 132. Anthropophagians are a very rough tribe situated below the land of the Sirices. They feed on human flesh and are therefore named 'maneaters' (*anthropophagus*; cf. ἄνθρωπος, "man"). As is the case for these nations, so for others the names have changed over the centuries in accordance with their kings, or their locations, or their customs, or for whatever other reasons, so that the primal origin of their names from the passage of time is no longer evident.

133. Now indeed the people called Antipodes (i.e. "opposite-footed") – because they are thought to be contrary to our footprints, as if from under the earth they make footprints upside-down from ours – are on no account to be believed in, because neither the solidity nor the central space of the earth allows this. Indeed this is not confirmed by any knowledge of history, but poets conjecture it as it were by sheer inference. 134. Moreover, they say that the Titans of Greece were a robust people of preeminent strength who, the fables say, were created by the angry Earth for her revenge against the gods. 135. Hence Titans are so called from the word τίσις, that is, 'revenge,' for they lived in arms as if for the sake of avenging Mother Earth against the gods. The fables feign that in war the Titans were overwhelmed by Jupiter and made extinct, because they perished from thunderbolts hurled from the sky.

iii. Reigns and terms for military matters (De regnis militiaeque vocabulis) 1. A reign (*regnum*) is so named from a king (*rex*, gen. *regis*), for as kings are so called from governing (*regere*), so reigns are called after the word for kings. 2. Every nation has had its own reign in its own times – like the Assyrians, the Medes, the Persians, the Egyptians, the Greeks – and fate has so rolled over their allotments of time that each successive one would dissolve the former. Among all the reigns on earth, however, two reigns are held to be glorious above the rest – first the Assyrians, then the Romans – as they are constituted differently from one another in location as much as time. 3. For as one began first and the other later, so one was in the East, the other in the West. Indeed, the beginning of the latter came close upon the end of the former. Other reigns and other kings are considered mere appendices of these two.

4. Kings are so called from governing, and as priests (*sacerdos*) are named from 'sacrificing' (*sacrificare*), so kings (*rex*, gen. *regis*) from governing (*regere*, also meaning "keep straight, lead correctly"). But he does not govern who does not correct (*corrigere*); therefore the name of king is held by one behaving rightly (*recte*), and lost by one doing wrong. Hence among the ancients such was the proverb: "You will be king (*rex*) if you behave rightly (*recte*); if you do not, you will not." 5. The royal virtues are these two especially: justice and mercy – but mercy is more praised in kings, because justice in itself is harsh.

6. Consuls (*consul*) are so called after 'taking counsel' (*consulere*), as kings from governing, laws (*lex*, gen. *legis*) from reading (*legere*). Because the Romans would not put up with the haughty domination of kings, they made a pair of consuls serve as the governing power year by year – for the arrogance of kings was not like the benevolence of a counselor, but the haughtiness of a master. They were therefore called consuls either from their 'consulting the interests of' (*consulere*) the citizens, or from their governing everything by consultation (*consilium*). 7. Still, they elected new consuls each year so that a haughty one would not remain for long, but a more moderate one would quickly succeed to the office. Further, there were two with equal authority, for the one administered civil, the other military affairs. Consuls governed over a period of 467 years. 8. Proconsuls were substitutes for consuls, and were called proconsuls because they would function in place of consuls, as a procurator does in place of a curator, that is, an agent. 9. Exconsuls were likewise so named because they had already passed on (*exire*) from the consulate, or because they had departed when the year of their term expired.

10. The Romans established dictators for themselves in the fifth year after the kings were expelled, when the son-in-law of Tarquinius gathered a huge army against Rome to avenge the injustice done to his father-in-law. 11. Dictators held power for five-year terms. They had more honor, then, than consuls, who held office for only a year. And they were called 'dictators' as if they were both leaders and teachers (i.e. givers of dictation) – hence they were named '(school)-masters (*magister*) of the people.' Also from them 'edicts' (*edictum*) are named. 12. The name of the Caesars began with Julius, who was the first of the Romans to achieve sole personal dominion after civil war had been stirred up. And Caesar was so called because he was brought forth and drawn out of his dead mother's womb, which had been 'cut open' (*caedere*, ppl. *caesus*), or because he was born 'with a head of hair' (*caesarie*). After him the successive emperors were called Caesars, because they had abundant hair. Those who were drawn out from a womb that has been cut open were called *Caesones* and *Caesares*. 13. He was furthermore called Julius because he took his origin from Julus, the son of Aeneas, as Vergil confirms (*Aen.* 1.288):

> Julius, the name drawn from great Julus.

14. For the Romans, the title *imperator* was at first given only to those on whom supremacy in military affairs was settled, and therefore the *imperatores* were so called from 'commanding' (*imperare*) the army. But although generals held command for a long time with the title of *imperator*, the senate decreed that this was the name of Augustus Caesar only, and he would be distinguished by this title from other 'kings' of nations. To this day the successive Caesars have employed this title. 15. Indeed it is customary for later kings to use the name of the first one, as among the Albans all the kings of the Albans are called Silvii after the name of Sylvius; similarly for the Persians the Arsacidae, for the Egyptians the Ptolemies, for the Athenians the Cecropidae.

16. For the Romans, 'Augustus' is the name of the imperial office, because formerly the emperors 'enlarged' (*augere*) the republic by extending its borders. Originally the senate bestowed this name on Octavius Caesar, so that he might be honored in his very name and title for enlarging their territory. 17. Moreover, this same Octavius was now called Caesar and emperor, or Augustus. Afterwards, when it was announced to him while he was watching the games that he would also be called 'Lord' (*Dominus*) by the people, he immediately, by gesture and with face averted, repressed this indecorous adulation and, as a human being, declined the title of Lord. On the next day he rebuked the whole populace

with a very severe edict, and after this allowed no one to call him Lord, not even his own children. He was the son of A[c]tia, who was the daughter of Julius Caesar's sister.

18. A king is called βασιλεύς in Greek because like a pedestal's base (*basis*) he supports the people (cf. λαός, "people"). Hence pedestals also have crowns (i.e. their cornices), for the higher a person is placed in command, just so much heavier is the burden of his responsibilities. 19. Tyrants (*tyrannus*) in Greek are the same as 'kings' in Latin, because for the ancients there was no distinction between a king and a tyrant, as (Vergil, *Aen.* 7.266):

> A condition of the peace for me will be to have touched the right hand of your ruler (*tyrannus*).

Strong kings were called tyrants, for a *tiro* is a strong young man. Of such people the Lord speaks, saying (cf. Proverbs 8:15): "By me kings reign, and tyrants (*tyrannus*) possess the earth by me." 20. Now in later times the practice has arisen of using the term for thoroughly bad and wicked kings, kings who enact upon their people their lust for luxurious domination and the cruelest lordship.

21. The term 'prince' (*princeps*) is a mark of rank and also of precedence in time, as in this Vergilian line (*Aen.* 9.535):

> Turnus was first (*princeps*) to hurl a burning torch,

where *princeps* means 'the first one.' Moreover, the term 'prince' derives from the sense of 'taking,' because he 'first takes' (*primus capit*), just as one speaks of a 'citizen of a municipality' (*municeps*) because he 'takes office' (*munia capit*). 22. A general (*dux*, gen. *ducis*) is so called because he is the 'commander' (*ductor*) of an army. But not everyone who is a prince or general can immediately be called a king. Moreover, in wartime it is better to be titled a general than a king, for the former title signifies the one in command in battle. Hence also Vergil (*Aen.* 10.370):

> Of General (*dux*) Evander.

And Sallust (*Histories* 4.7 M): "For everyone is more eager to seem brave in front of the general." He did not say, "in front of the consul."

23. Monarchs (*monarcha*) are those who wield supreme power alone, like Alexander among the Greeks and Julius among the Romans. From this term also derives the word 'monarchy' (*monarchia*). In Greek μονάς is "singleness" and ἀρχή is "governing power." 24. Tetrarchs (*tetrarches*) are those who hold the fourth part of a kingdom, for τέτταρα means "four." Such was Philippus in Judea. 25. The patricians (*patricius*) are so called because, as fathers (*pater*) watch over their children, so they watch over the state. 26. Prefects (*praefectus*) are so called because they 'preside' (*praeesse*) with praetorian (*praetorius*) power. 27. Praetors (*praetor*) are the same as prefects, as if the word were 'one placed in front' (*praepositor*). 28. Again, 'chief wardens' (*praeses*, plural *praesides*, i.e. provincial governors) are those who maintain the security of some location 'with chief custody' (*praesidialiter*). 29. Tribunes (*tribunus*) are so called because they dispense (*tribuere*) justice for soldiers or common people. 30. Chiliarchs (*chiliarches*) are those who preside over a thousand (*mille*) men; we call them *millenarii*, and the former term is Greek (i.e. χιλίαρχος). 31. Centurions are so called because they command a hundred (*centum*) soldiers; similarly *quinquagenarii*, because they are at the head of fifty (*quinquaginta*) soldiers, and *decani*, because they are set over ten (*decem*) soldiers.

32. A soldier (*miles*) is so called because formerly there were a thousand (*mille*) in one troop, or because one in a thousand was chosen. Romulus was the first to recruit soldiers from the populace and give them this name. Liber first taught military organization. 33. A soldier is called either a regular or an irregular. A regular (*ordinarius*) soldier is one who fights within the 'rank and file' (*ordo*), and has not yet reached any rank of honor, for he is in the ranks, that is, of the humble militia. But an irregular (*extraordinarius*) soldier is one who is promoted beyond the rank and file on account of his valor. 34. Veteran and discharged soldiers who no longer serve in battle are called *emeriti*, because *mereri* means "to serve in the military," with reference to the wages that they earn (*mereri*). They are also called veterans (*veteranus*; cf. *vetus*, gen. *veteris*, "old") because they no longer serve in battle, but after their many trials as soldiers they have attained the right to live in peace. 35. Cavalrymen (*equestri milites*) are so called because they ride horses (*equus*), and they fight in the equestrian order.

36. An able-bodied young soldier is called a *tiro* (i.e. a new recruit), and such are enrolled for military service and serve as skilled in arms. They are appraised not by the mere status of their ancestry, but by their looks and physical strength. Hence they are called tyros, and they

are not soldiers until they have been approved by their oath of allegiance. 37. The custom of the Roman army was that youths should first bear arms on reaching puberty, for tyros would begin to serve in their sixteenth year, though still at this age under instructors. Concerning them, Vergil (cf. *Aen.* 7.162):

> And youths in their first flower.

38. Of course, slaves never served in the military unless they were freed – except at the time of Hannibal, when the Romans were in such straits after the battle of Cannae that there was no possibility of freeing slaves. 39. Deserters (*desertor*) are so called because they wander, leaving their military duties deserted (*desertus*). They are prohibited from enlisting in other troops of soldiers, but if their crime was of short duration, after they have been flogged they are restored to their own troop. But there are those who desert (*deserere*) the army and pass over to the enemy, and they are also called deserters.

40. Conscript soldiers are so called because they are enrolled in the muster list by the officer who will command them, just as soldiers are called transcripts when they transfer from one legion to another – and hence transcript (*transcriptus*), because they give their names so that they may be transcribed (*transcribere*). 41. Adjutants (*optio*) are so called, because they are selected, for *optare* means "select," as in this verse (Vergil, *Aen.* 3.109):

> And he selected (*optare*) a site for the kingdom,

that is, he chose it. 42. Sentinels (*excubitor*) are so called because they always keep watch (*excubia*). They are members of a troop of soldiers who 'keep outdoor watch' (*excubare*) in sentry boxes as a royal guard. *Excubiae* are daytime watches, and *vigiliae* are nighttime. Hence also the term 'sentinel' (*vigil*). 43. Skirmishers (*veles*, gen. *velitis*) are a type of fighter among the Romans, so called from their 'darting about' (*volitare*). Thus armed young men selected for their agility would ride seated behind mounted soldiers, and as soon as they encountered the enemy they would leap from the horses and now as foot soldiers would persistently harass the enemy while the mounted men who brought them would attack on the other side. Hannibal's elephants were once driven back by these skirmishers, and when their riders could not control them, the elephants were killed with a workman's knife driven between their ears.

44. A camp is where a soldier would be stationed. It is called a camp (*castra*) as if it were 'chaste' (*castus*), or because there sexual desire would be castrated (*castrare*) – for a woman never entered a camp. 45. 'Military service' (*militia*) is so called from 'soldiers' (*miles*, gen. *militis*), or from the word 'many' (*multus*), as if the term were *multitia*, being the occupation of many men, or from a mass (*moles*) of things, as if the word were *moletia*. 46. A legion (*legio*) is a troop of six thousand armed men, so called from 'selected' (*eligere*), as if it were 'picked out' (*legere*), that is, chosen for arms. Properly we speak of a *phalanx* of Macedonians, a 'band' (*caterva*) of Gauls, and a 'legion' (*legio*) of our (i.e. Roman) forces. 47. A legion has sixty centuries, thirty maniples, twelve cohorts, and two hundred squadrons.

48. A century (*centuria*) is a division of an army composed of a hundred (cf. *centum*, "hundred") soldiers. Hence those who command them are called centurions. 49. Reinforcements (*subcenturiatus*) are men not of the first, but of the second century, as if the word were 'below the first century' (*sub prima centuria*); nevertheless in battle they were formed up and placed in lookouts so that if the first century failed they, whom we have spoken of as the substitutes, would reinforce the first century in their efforts. Hence also a *subcenturiatus* would be stationed in ambush, as if he were trained in deceptive warfare (i.e. as *sub* can mean "secret"). 50. A maniple consists of two hundred soldiers. These troops are called maniples (*manipulus*) either because they would begin a battle in the first combat (*manus*), or because, before battle-standards existed, they would make 'handfuls' (*manipulus*) for themselves as standards, that is, bundles of straw or of some plant, and from this standard the soldiers were nicknamed 'manipulars.' Of them, Lucan (*Civil War* 1.296):

> Straightway he rallies the armed maniples (*maniplus*) to the standards.

51. A squadron (*turma*) consists of thirty horsemen. There were three hundred Roman horsemen in one 'tribe' (*tribus*; see iv.7 below) and each group of one hundred would give ten to make up the squadron. A cohort has five hundred soldiers.

52. There are three kinds of military service: by oath, by call to arms, and by communal oath. 53. In service by oath (*sacramentum*) each soldier after his election swears not to quit his service until after his hitch has been completed, that is, his period of service – and those are the ones who have a full service record, for they

are bound for twenty-five years. 54. By 'call to arms' (*evocatio*), when not only soldiers but also other people are called out (*evocare*) to a sudden battle. At such a time a consul would say, "He who wants the republic to be preserved, follow me." 55. By 'communal oath' (*coniuratio*): this is done when there is an uprising, and the city's imminent peril leaves no time for individuals to 'take an oath' (*iurare*), but a multitude is suddenly assembled and is kindled into tumultuous wrath. This is also called an uproar (*tumultuatio*).

56. In a battle array these are the usual formations: an army, a levy, a knot, a wedge, the wings, the horns, a column. These borrow their shapes and their names from the objects from which the terms have been derived. 57. The 'battle array' (*acies*; also meaning "cutting edge") is so called because it is armed with iron and the sharpness (*acumen*) of swords. 58. An army (*exercitus*) is a multitude of one kind, so called from its training (*exercitatio*) for war. 59. A wedge (*cuneus*) is a company of soldiers gathered into a unit. Hence, because it assembles into a unit, this 'gathering into a unit' (*coitio in unum*) is named a *cuneus*, as if the word were *couneus*, because all are assembled into a unit. 60. Levies (*classis*, also meaning "fleet") are so called because they are segments of an army; later these were called maniples. Hence Vergil (cf. *Aen.* 2.30):

> Here the site for the divisions (*classis*), here the battle arrays (*acies*) would fight.

Nowadays *classis* also means a fleet (*classicum*) of ships.

61. A knot (*nodus*) properly is a dense crowd of foot soldiers, as a squadron (*turma*) is of cavalry. It is called a 'knot' for its intricacy, because it can scarcely be loosened. 62. The wings of an army are said to be thirty cavalrymen. The cavalry are called the wings (*ala*) because they cover the foot soldiers in the manner of wings. 63. The troops of an army who are farthest out are called horns (*cornu*), because their line is curved. 64. It is called a column (*agmen*) when an army marches, named from 'driving' (*agere*), that is, going. Plautus (*The Haunted House* 562): "Where are you going (*agere*)?" Thus it is an army on the march. It is called a column because it is arranged in a file, as it would be when an army passes through gates. In any other sense the term is used incorrectly.

iv. Citizens (De civibus) 1. We have spoken somewhat about reigns and military terms, and now we add a summary of terms for citizens. 2. Citizens (*civis*) are so called because they 'live assembled' (*coeuntes vivunt*) in one body, so that their common life might be made richer and safer. 3. A house is the dwelling place of a family, as a city is the dwelling place of a single populace, and as the globe is the domicile of the whole of humankind. But 'house' also refers to a lineage, a family, or the union of husband and wife. A house (*domus*) originates with these two (*duo*), and the term is Greek (i.e. δόμος, or δῶμα, "house, household, family").[11] A *familia* consists of the children raised legally by free parents, from the term 'loins' (*femur*).[12] 4. A 'race' (*genus*) is so called from begetting (*gignere*, ppl. *genitus*) and procreating (*progenerare*), or from the delimiting of particular descendants (*prognatus*), as are nations (*natio*) that, delimited by their own kinships, are called 'stocks of people' (*gens*). 5. A populace (*populus*) is composed of a human multitude, allied through their agreed practice of law and by willing association. A populace is distinct from the plebeians (*plebs*), because a populace consists of all the citizens, including the elders of the city. [But the plebeians are the remaining people apart from the elders of the city.] 6. Therefore the populace is the whole city, but the common people are the plebeians. The plebeians are named for their plurality (*pluralitas*), for there are more people of lesser status than there are elders. The populace is called the σουχναμοις, that is, σιτοασις, and hence the term *populus*.[13] In Greek the populace is called λαός, from the term 'stone' (*lapis*; cf. Greek λᾶας, "stone"). The 'common people' (*vulgus*) is the multitude living here and there – as if it were "each one where he wishes (*vult*, from *velle*, "wish")."

7. The separate courts and assemblies of the people are called tribes (*tribus*), and they are so called because in the beginning the Romans had been separated by Romulus 'into three groups' (*trifarie*): senators, soldiers, and plebeians. Although the tribes are now multiplied, they retain their original name. 8. Its members' age gave the senate (*senatus*) its name, because they were seniors

11 An early manuscript adds, "for δώματα in Greek means 'houses.'"

12 See v.12 below. *Femur* literally means "thigh." It is used here as a euphemism for "genitals," as often in the Vulgate.

13 The Greek terms here are hopelessly garbled in the manuscripts. In his edition of Book IX (1984), Marc Reydellet ingeniously proposes συχνός ("dense") and ἀπὸ πολλοῦ ("numerous"), the latter phrase sounding like *populus*.

(*senior*). Others have it that senators are so called from permitting (*sinere*), because they grant the means for doing something. 9. A 'senate resolution' (*senatusconsultum*) is so called from consulting (*consulere*) and deliberating, because it is rendered in such a way that it consults interests, and cannot cause harm. 10. Indeed, senators are called fathers (*pater*), as Sallust says (*War with Catiline* 6), from their similar responsibilities, for just as fathers tend to their children, so the senators would tend to the republic. 11. 'Enrolled fathers' (*patres conscripti*) were so called because when Romulus chose the ten curial districts of the senators he set down their names on golden tablets in the presence of the populace, and hence they were called enrolled fathers. 12. The first ranks of senators are called the *illustres* (lit. "illustrious"), the second, the *spectabiles* ("notable"), and the third, the *clarissimi* ("distinguished"). There is no fourth type lower than these. Although a person might be of senatorial birth, he was called a Roman equestrian (*eques*) until the lawful age, and then he would receive the honor of the senatorial office.

13. There were 'censors' among the ancient Romans. The term *censor* applies to a judicial office, because *censere* means "judge." Likewise, censors are the arbiters of inherited estates, so called from the 'counting of money' (*census aeris*). 14. Judges (*iudex*, gen. *iudicis*) are so called as if it were 'those speaking the law' (*ius dicens*) to the people, or because they 'lawfully decide' (*iure disceptare*). To examine lawfully is to judge (*iudicare*) justly, and a person is not a judge if justice is not in him. 15. Presidents (*praeses*) are governors of provinces, so called because they preside (*praeesse*). 16. The office of praetor (*praetor*) is named as if it were 'teacher' (*praeceptor*) and 'chief person' (*princeps*) of the city. Likewise quaestors (*quaestor*), as if the word were *quaesitor* ("investigator"), because they preside over examinations (*quaestio*) at trials, for the deliberations and judicial process are in their hands.

17. The *proceres* are the leading men of a city, as if the word were *procedes* (i.e. "those going before"), because they 'take precedence' (*praecedere*) before all others in esteem. Hence also the tips of the beams that protrude beyond the walls are called *proceres*, because they 'come out' (*procedere*) first. Therefore, a transfer of sense was made in applying the term to the leading men, because they jut out beyond the multitude of others. 18. Tribunes (*tribunus*) are so called because they grant (*tribuere*) either legal process or aid to the common people. That office was established in the sixth year after the kings (i.e. of Rome) were driven out, for when the common people were oppressed by the senate and consuls they created for themselves tribunes to act as their own judges and defenders, to safeguard their liberty and defend them against the injustice of the nobility. Hence they (i.e. municipal magistrates) are also called *defensores*, because they defend (*defendere*) the common people entrusted to them against the arrogance of the wicked. But now, on the contrary, we have not defenders but destroyers.

19. Those who convey the public funds (*nummus*) to the treasuries (*aerarium*) are therefore called *numerarii*. 20. Functionaries (*functus*) are so called because they perform (*fungi*, ppl. *functus*) an office and some official charge. Hence we call those dead people who have completed their life's function 'the defunct' (*defunctus*) – for now they do nothing. 21. Fellow-citizens (*municeps*, particularly a "municipal officer") are those born in the same municipality, so called from their service in their offices, because they take on (*accipere*) public offices – for *munia* are public offices. Hence people who assume no official duty are called 'immune' (*immunis*). 22. Municipal officers (*municipalis*) are citizens native to a place and holding office there. 23. *Decuriones* are so called because they are of the curial order, and hold office in the *curia*.[14] Hence a person who has not paid the sum or participated in the *curia* is not a *decurio*. 24. *Curiales* are the same as decurions, and they are called *curiales* because they 'have charge of' (*procurare*) and carry out civic duties. 25. *Principales*, magistrates, and duumvirs are orders of curial offices. *Principales* are so called because they are first (*primus*), above the magistrates. 26. Magistrates (*magistratus*), because they are greater (*maior*, comparative of *magnus*) than the other offices. Duumvirs. . .

27. A notary (*tabellio*) is so called because he is the carrier of writing tablets (*tabella*). The same person is called a copyist (*exceptor*), and a 'public scribe' (*scriba publicus*), because he writes down (*scribere*) only those things that are published (*publicare*) in the records of transactions. 28. Burghers (*burgarius*) are so called from 'fortified villages' (*burgus*), because in common speech people call the many dwelling-places established along

14 *Curia* here refers to the senate of a municipality, and 'paying the sum' refers to a payment *decuriones* would deposit on assuming office.

the frontiers *burgi*. Hence also the nation of Burgundians got their name: formerly, when Germania was subdued, the Romans scattered them among their camps, and so they took their name from these places. 29. *Collegiati* are so called because they are removed from their board of officials (*collegium*) and their responsibilities, because they have committed a crime. This is the vilest class of people, born of an unidentified father.

30. Private citizens (*privatus*) are those not holding public offices. The title is the opposite of that for one holding a magistracy, and they are called *privati* because they are free from the offices of the *curia* (cf. *privare*, "set free"). 31. Mercenaries (*mercennarius*) are those who serve for pay (*merces*). They are also called by the Greek term *barones*, because they are strong in difficult circumstances, for βαρύς means "heavy," that is, strong. Its contrary is 'light,' that is, weak. 32. 'Publican' (*publicanus*) is the title for the farmers of the taxes of the public treasury, or of public (*publicus*) affairs, or for those who exact the public taxes, or for those who chase profits through the business of the world – hence their name. 33. A *vilicus* is properly the manager of a 'country estate' (*villa*), whence the *vilicus* takes his name from *villa*. Yet sometimes *vilicus* does not signify the management of a country estate, but, according to Cicero, the oversight of all the household business, that is, he is overseer of all the property and estates. 34. Agents (*actor*, "prosecutor") and administrators (*curator*) are so called from 'acting for' (*agere*, ppl. *actus*) and 'caring for' (*curare*).[15] 35. Procurators are those who serve in place of *curatores*, as if the term were 'in place of caretakers' (*propter curatores*), like proconsul, 'for the consul' (*pro consule*).

36. Colonists (*colonus*) are settlers (*cultor*) from a foreign country, so called from the cultivation (*cultura*) of fields. They are people coming from elsewhere and tilling (*colere*, ppl. *cultus*) a foreign field that they have leased, and they owe their condition to the fruitful soil, because of their tillage of the land under the control of the owner, inasmuch as an estate was leased to them.[16] We speak of four types of colonists: Roman, Latin, auxiliary, or colonists of the private countryside. 37. Tenants (*inquilinus*) are so called as if it were 'residents of others' property' (*incolentes aliena*), for they have no place of their own, but live on alien land. 38. There is this difference between a tenant and a 'resident alien' (*advena*): tenants are people who emigrate, and do not remain permanently, whereas we speak of resident aliens or immigrants (*incola*) as coming from abroad but settling permanently – hence the term *incola*, for those who are now inhabitants, from the word 'reside' (*incolere*). 39. Indigenous people (*indigena*) are those 'therefrom begotten' (*inde genitus*), born in the same place in which they live. 40. The term *incola* signifies not an indigenous person, but a resident alien.

41. Foreigners (*peregrinus*) are so called because the parents from whom they come are not known (*parentes* + *ignorari*). 42. People who lived in Rome were called *urbani*, but those who live in other towns are *oppi-dani*, because the only 'city' (*urbs*) is Rome, and the others are towns (*oppidum*). 43. *Famuli* are those who were born of one's own household (*familia*) of slaves. Slaves (*servus*) got their name from this, that those who could have been killed by the victors according to the law of war, when they were 'preserved alive' (*servare*), were made *servi*, and thus 'slaves' were named from 'preserving.' 44. Handmaids (*ancilla*) were so called from 'support,' for in Greek ἀγκών means "elbow." Hence we also use the word *ancon*.[17] 45. 'Estate property' (*mancipium*) is whatever can be 'taken by hand' (*manu capere*) and subjected, like a human, a horse, or a sheep, for these living beings, as soon as they are born, are reckoned as estate property. Likewise those creatures from the world of wild beasts are considered as estate property as soon as they are captured or tamed.

46. A freeman (*ingenuus*) is so called because he has freedom by birth (*genus*), not from a legal action like freedmen. Hence the Greeks call such a one εὐγενής (lit. "well-born") because he is of good birth. 47. A freedman (*libertus*) was so called as if the word were *liberatus* ("liberated"), for at an earlier time he was consigned to the yoke of slavery. In antiquity the son of a freedman was called *libertinus*, as if the term were *de liberto natus* ("born from a freedman"). But now, *libertinus* refers to one who was so made by a freedman, or his possession. 48. A 'manumitted man' (*manumissus*) is so called as if

15 In Isidore's time *curatores* were the highest local officials, according to Thompson (1969).

16 Isidore speaks of the two types of *coloni*: 'colonists' (foreigners who settle a land) and serfs. According to Thompson (1969), in Visigothic Spain *coloni* were serfs, hereditarily tied to the soil, who paid rents of a tenth of their produce.

17 Reydellet (1984) shows that in Isidore's Spain the word *ancon*, rather than *cubitum*, was the common word for 'elbow.' In classical Latin *ancon* means "angled supporting bracket."

the term were *manu emissus* ("delivered by a hand"), for in ancient times whenever they would liberate (*manumittere*) someone they would turn him around after he was struck with a slap and confirm him to be free. From this, they were said to be 'manumitted' because they were delivered by a hand. 49. A *dediticius* (i.e. a surrendered captive) was first named after the word *deditio* ("surrender"), the word used when conquered or about to be conquered enemies hand themselves over to the victors. This was the origin of the word *dediticius*: once, when slaves took up arms and fought against the Roman people, they were defeated and 'gave themselves up' (*se dare*, perfect tense *dedi*), and they were arrested and were punished with various marks of shame. 50. For this reason, when at a later time some of them were manumitted by their masters, they did not attain the standing of Roman citizens, on account of the marks of punishment that they had manifestly experienced.

51. Among the Latins, before Rome was founded, people were made free when they took up their freedom by a letter, never by a will. Thus, because they did not become free through a will, they were not able to acquire anything by a will or to designate heirs. They were later, under the consuls, made Roman citizens by wills in the city of Rome. 52. They were called Roman citizens because they were brought into the number of Roman citizens by being made free by means of a will. Permission to dwell in the city of Rome was granted to them from the first, but when others were made freedmen there was a prohibition against their remaining either in Rome or within seven miles of the city.

v. Family relationships and their degrees (De adfinitatibus et gradibus) 1. Property consisting of money (*aes*, gen. *aeris*) provided the word for 'heir' (*heres*), for the heir is the executor for the testator's payments. Indeed, by this word *heres* is meant the first succession of inheritance and family, such as children and grandchildren. 2. A pro-heir (*proheres*) is someone who acts in place of an heir, as though the term were 'for an heir' (*pro* + *heres*). The *proheres* is either appointed as heir or made a secondary heir. 3. A father (*pater*) is the one from whom the beginning of the line springs, and thus, he is called the paterfamilias. Moreover, a father is so called because he engenders a son when *patratio* has been performed, for *patratio* is the consummation of sexual intercourse. Lucretius says (cf. *On the Nature of Things* 4.1129):

> The well-done begettings (*patra*) of fathers.[18]

4. The term progenitor (*genitor*) comes from the verb 'engender' (*gignere*, ppl. *genitum*), and parents (*parens*) are so called as though they were 'begetters' (*parere*, present participle *pariens*). 5. They are also 'creators' (*creator*). *Crementum* (lit. "growth") is the word for the male seed, from which the bodies of animals and humans are conceived; hence parents are creators. 6. A mother is so named because something is made from her, for the term 'mother' (*mater*) is as if the word were 'matter' (*materia*), but the father is the cause.

7. The 'paterfamilias' is so called, because he takes care of the slaves placed in his household (*familia*), just as a father directs his children, with paternal affection. And he does not distinguish in his affection the condition of the slaves from that of his children, but embraces them all as though they were a single unit. This is the origin of the word 'paterfamilias.' Those who lord it over their slaves in an unfair manner could never reckon themselves to be called by this term. 8. The 'materfamilias' is so called because she has crossed over into the 'household of her husband' (*maritus* + *familia*) through a certain procedure of law, and the matrimonial registers are the records of her purchase. In another manner, just as matron (*matrona*) is a name for the mother of a first child, that is, as though the term were the *mater nati* ("mother of one born"), so the 'materfamilias' is the woman who has borne several children – for a family (*familia*) comes into existence from two people.

9. A grandfather (*avus*) is a father's father, so called from 'age' (*aevus*), that is, from 'antiquity.' A great-grandfather (*proavus*) is the grandfather's father, as though he were 'close to the grandfather' (*prope* + *avus*). A great-great-grandfather (*abavus*) is the great-grandfather's father, who is now far way 'from the grandfather' (*ab* + *avus*). 10. A great-great-great-grandfather (*atavus*) is the great-great-grandfather's father. 10. A great-great-great-great-grandfather (*tritavus*) is the father of a great-great-great-grandfather, as if the word were *tetravis*, that is, the 'fourth beyond the grandfather" (cf. τετρα–, "four"). But *tritavus* is the last name given to this line of kinship; a family arises with the father, and ends with the great-great-great-great-grandfather.

18 The received text of Lucretius has "acquisitions" (*parta*) for *patra*; *patra* is a nonce-word.

11. Son (*filius*) and daughter (*filia*) are named after the family (*familia*); for they are first in the order of descent. Hence with regard to the Cornelian family, the whole stock arose from Cornelius. 12. 'Family' comes from the word 'loins' (*femur*; see iv.3 above, with note), for a race of people and its lineage appear from their ancestral loins (*femur*). The word *familia* is used metaphorically for slaves, and not with its proper application. 13. A family's lineage (*stirps*, "stock," lit. "stalk") is so called from the longstanding designation of a clan. A son (*gnatus*) is so called because he has been generated (*generatus*); whence the word is spelled with a *g*. Offspring (*suboles*) are so named for their 'taking the place' (*substitutio*) of the previous generation.

14. The birth-order of children is designated in four ways: only-born (*unigenus*), first-born (*primogenitus*), middle (*medius*), and last (*novissimus*). The first-born is so named because no child was born before him. The only-born is so called when no child is born after him. The middle child is between all the others, and the last comes after all the others; this same child is the 'littlest' (*minimus*), from the word 'monad' (*monas*). The last-born is so called because he is recent (*novus*), since the remaining siblings are older because they came first. 15. Children (*filius*) are designated in four ways: by nature, by imitation, by adoption, and by instruction. Children by nature (*natura*), as when the Jews are called the children of Abraham. Children by imitation (*imitatio*), as those gentiles who imitated (*imitare*) the faithfulness of Abraham, as when the Gospel says (Luke 3:8) "God is able of these stones to raise up children to Abraham," or as when the Lord says that these same Jews are the children of the devil, from whom they are not born, but whom they have imitated (John 8:44). 16. Children also by adoption (*adoptio*), the kind everyone is familiar with in human society, or as we address God "Our Father, who art in heaven," as our father by adoption, not nature. Children by instruction (*doctrina*), as when the apostle Paul calls those to whom he preached the Gospel "his own children."

17. When children are called *liberi* ("children"; lit. "free") in a legal sense, it is so that by this term they are distinguished from slaves, because just as a slave is in the power of his master, so a child (*filius*) is in the power of his father. Thus, 'emancipation' occurs for the son, so that he is free from his father, just as 'manumission' occurs for a slave, so that he is liberated from his master. 18. Again, children are called *liberi* when they have sprung from a free (*liber*) marriage, for the children of a free man and a slave serving-girl have slave status, as children who are so born always assume the status of the lower parent. 19. 'Natural children' (*naturalis*) means those belonging to freeborn concubines, whom nature alone begot, not the chastity of marriage. The word 'boy' (*puer*) comes from 'the signs of puberty' (*pubes*). 20. An 'adoptive son' (*adoptivus*) is one who has been handed into the power of another through 'transfer of property' (*mancipatio*) – either by his rightful father, or grandfather, or great-grandfather, in whose power he was – and who then bears the name of both, like Fabius Aemilius, or Scipio Paulinus.

21. Twins (*gemini*) are not only two who are born at the same time, but also more than two. If one of the twins is miscarried, the other, who has been properly born, is given the name 'Vopiscus.' 22. A child is called 'posthumous' (*posthumus*) because is he born after the burial (*post* + *humatio*) of his father, that is, after his death. This son takes the name of his dead parent, for so the law wills it, that he who is born from a deceased father is called by the name of the deceased. 23. One is called *nothus* (lit. "one born out of wedlock") who is born from a noble father and from an ignoble mother, for instance a concubine. Moreover, this term is Greek (i.e. νόθος) and is lacking in Latin. 24. Opposite to this is a *spurius* son, one who is born from a noble mother and an ignoble father. Again, the *spurius* son is born from an unknown father and from a widowed mother, as if he were the son of a *spurium* only – for the ancients termed the female generative organs *spurium*, as though the term derived from the term σπόρος, that is, "seed" – and he has no name from his father. 25. Such children were also called Favonii, because certain animals are thought to conceive by receiving a draft from the Favonian (i.e. west) wind. Hence those children who are not born of legitimate wedlock follow the condition of the mother rather than the father. In Latin the word *spurius* is as if the term were *extra puritatem* ("apart from purity"; cf. the prefix *se-*, "apart from"), that is, as if unclean.

26. A grandchild (*nepos*) is one who is born from a son. A grandchild is so called as though the term were *natus post* ("born afterward"), for first the son is born, and then the grandchild. It is the degree of relationship of the secondary heir. From this we also get the word 'posterity' (*posteritas*), as though the term

were *postera aetas* ("later age"). The word *nepos* refers to either sex; the reason that we speak of a *neptis* ("granddaughter") in legal use is because of the acknowledged distinction in matters of succession. 27. A great-grandson is the child who is conceived and born from the grandson, and he is called *pronepos* as if the term were *natus porro post* ("born further after"). From this degree on the offspring begin to be called the progeny (*progenies*), as if *porro post geniti* ("begotten further after"). The children and grandchildren do not count as 'progeny' because they have no long period of descent.

28. Just as those born rather far down the line of descent are called progeny, so those further up, the great-grandfathers and great-great-grandfathers, are also called 'progenitors' (*progenitor*), as if the term were *porro generans* ("remote begetter"). A great-grandson (*pronepos*) is so called because he is *prope nepotem* ("near the grandson"). 29. The great-great-grandson (*abnepos*), because he is separated 'from the grandson' (*a nepote*), for the *pronepos* is between him and the *nepos*. The *adnepos* is the son of an *abnepos*. 30. The *trinepos* is the son of the *adnepos*, because he is fourth in line after the *nepos* – as if the word were *tetranepos* ("fourth" + "grandson"). 31. We do not speak of 'descendants' (*minor*) except where a name for a degree of kinship is lacking – such names as son, grandson, great-grandson, great-great-grandson, great-great-great-grandson, and great-great-great-great-grandson. Where there are no more such terms for degrees we rightly speak of 'descendants,' just as we speak of 'ancestors' (*maior*) beyond the terms for father, grandfather, great-grandfather, great-great-grandfather, great-great-great-grandfather, and great-great-great-great-grandfather.

vi. Paternal and maternal relatives (De agnatis et cognatis) 1. 'Paternal kin' (*agnatus*) are so called because they 'succeed in place of children' (*accedere pro natis*) when there are no sons. Hence they are acknowledged (*agnoscere*) as taking precedence in the lineage, because they issue from people of the male sex, such as a brother begotten by the same father, or a brother's son or grandson, or a paternal uncle. 2. 'Maternal kin' (*cognatus*) are so called because they are also linked by nearness of kinship (*cognatio*). Maternal kin are considered as after the paternal kin because they issue from people of the female sex, and are not paternal kin, but are related otherwise by natural law. 3. The 'next of kin' (*proximus*) is so called because of closeness (*proximitas*) of blood. 4. 'Blood-relatives' (*consanguineus*) are so called because they are conceived from one blood (*sanguis*), that is, from one seed of a father. A man's seed is a froth of blood that looks like water dashed against cliffs and making a white froth, or like dark wine that makes a whitish foam when shaken in a cup. 5. Brothers (*frater*) are so called because they are of the same fruit (*fructus*), that is, born of the same seed. 6. However, 'maternal brothers' (*germanus*) are those issuing (*manare*) from the same mother (*genetrix*) and not, as many say, from the same seed (*germen*); only the latter are called *fratres*. Therefore *fratres* issue from the same fruit, and *germani* from the same mother.[19] 7. Uterine (*uterinus*) brothers are so called because they have issued from different fathers but from a single womb (*uterus*), for only a woman has a womb.

8. In the Divine Scriptures brothers are referred to in four ways: in nature, in nation, in lineage, and in affection. In nature, as Esau and Jacob, Andrew and Peter, James and John. In nation, as all Jews are called brothers of each other in Deuteronomy (cf. 15:12): "If you buy your brother (*frater*), who is a Hebrew man." And the Apostle says (Romans 9:3-4): "I wished myself to be an anathema from Christ, for my brethren (*frater*), who are my kinsmen according to the flesh, who are Israelites." 9. Further, people may be called brothers by lineage when they are of one family, that is, one native land. Latin speakers use the word 'paternity' (*paternitas*) when many groups of a race spread from a single root. In Genesis, Abraham said to Lot (cf. 13:8): "Let there be no quarrel between me and thee, and between my herdsmen, and thy herdsmen: for we are all brethren (*frater*)." Surely Lot was not Abraham's brother, but the son of his brother Aram. 10. In the fourth way, brothers are so called in affection, and this has two types: spiritual and general. In spiritual brotherhood, by which all of us Christians are called brothers, as (Psalm 132:1 Vulgate): "Behold how good and how pleasant it is for brethren (*frater*) to dwell together in unity." In general brotherhood, because all humans, born from one father, are joined in equal kinship among ourselves, as Scripture says (cf. Isaiah 66:5): "Say to those that hate you: you are our brothers (*frater*)."

19 In classical Latin a *frater* was the son of one's father or mother, and a *frater germanus* or simply *germanus* was a full brother.

11. The term 'maternal sister' (*germana*) is understood just as 'maternal brother' (*germanus*), as issuing from the same mother. 12. And 'sister' (*soror*) is understood in the same sense as 'brother.' Thus, 'sister' is the name for a person of the same seed, because only she is considered as belonging to the portion (*sors*) of the paternal heritage with the brothers. 13. 'Paternal first-cousins' (*frater patruelis*) are so called because their fathers (*pater*) were brothers (*germanus*). 14. But 'first cousin' (*consobrinus*) is the name for those born from a sister (*soror*) and a brother, or from two sisters, as if the word were *consororinus*. 15. *Fratruelis* is the child of one's mother's sister. 'Second-cousins' (*sobrinus*) are the children of first-cousins. *Tius* is a Greek word (i.e. θεῖος, "uncle"). 16. 'Paternal uncle' (*patruus*) is the brother of one's father, as if the term were *pater alius* ("another father"). Hence when the father of a minor dies, the paternal uncle adopts him and cares for him as his own son as he is obliged by law.

17. A 'maternal uncle' (*avunculus*) is the brother of one's mother, and the term appears to have the form of a diminutive, because it shows signs of coming from the word *avus* ("grandfather"). 18. A 'paternal aunt' (*amita*) is the sister of one's father, as though the term were *alia mater* ("another mother"). A 'maternal aunt' (*matertera*) is the sister of a mother, as if *mater altera* ("a second mother"). A father-in-law (*socer*) is one who has given his daughter in marriage. 19. A son-in-law (*gener*) is one who marries the daughter, and he is so called because he is taken into the family (*genus*, gen. *generis*) for its increase. A father-in-law – or a mother-in-law (*socrus*) – is so called because they ally (*adsociare*) to themselves a son-in-law or daughter-in-law (*nurus*). 20. A stepfather (*vitricus*) is one who takes a wife who has a son or daughter from another man. He is so called as though the word were *novitricus*, because the mother marries a new (*novus*) husband.

21. A stepson (*privignus*) is one who was born from another father, and he is thought to be called *privignus* as though the word were *privigenus*, because he was 'born at an earlier time' (*prius genitus*). Whence, a stepson is commonly called *antenatus* ("born before"). 22. These are words that appear to be derived from the word for family (*gens*): *genitor, genetrix, agnatus, agnata, cognatus, cognata, progenitor, progenitrix, germanus, germana.*

23. **More on the aforementioned relationships (*Item de praedictis affinitatibus*)** The originator of my family is my father, and I am his son or daughter. The father of my father is my grandfather (*avus*), and I am his grandson (*nepos*) or granddaughter (*neptis*). The grandfather of my father is my great-grandfather (*proavus*), and I am his great-grandson (*pronepos*) or -daughter (*proneptis*). The great-grandfather of my father is my great-great-grandfather (*abavus*) and I am his great-great-grandson (*abnepos*) or -daughter (*abneptis*). The great-great-grandfather of my father is my great-great-great-grandfather (*atavus*), and I am his great-great-great-grandson (*adnepos*) or -daughter (*adneptis*). The great-great-great-grandfather of my father is my great-great-great-great-grandfather (*tritavus*), and I am his great-great-great-great-grandson (*trinepos*) or -daughter (*trineptis*).

24. **Paternal uncles (*De patruis*)**[20] The brother of my father is my paternal uncle (*patruus*), and I am the son or daughter of his brother. The father of my paternal uncle is my 'great uncle' (*pater magnus*), and I am the son or daughter of his brother's son or daughter. The grandfather of my paternal uncle is my great-great-uncle (*propatruus*), and I am the grandson or granddaughter of his son or daughter. The great-grandfather of my paternal uncle is my great-great-great-uncle (*adpatruus*), and I am the son or daughter of his grandson or granddaughter.

25. **Paternal aunts (*De amitis*)** The sister of my father is my paternal aunt (*amita*), and I am the son or daughter of her brother. The mother of my paternal aunt is my 'great paternal aunt' (*amita magna*), and I am the son or daughter of her brother's son or daughter. The grandmother (*avia*) of my paternal aunt is my great-great-paternal aunt (*proamita*) and I am the son or daughter of her grandson or granddaughter. The great-grandmother (*proavia*) of my paternal aunt is my great-great-great paternal aunt (*abamita*) and I am the son or daughter of her grandson or granddaughter.

26. **Maternal uncles (*De avunculis*)** The brother of my mother is my maternal uncle (*avunculus*), and I am the son or daughter of his sister. The father of my maternal uncle is my maternal great uncle (*avunculus magnus*)

20 In sections 24–27 we translate the text, with emendations of the early manuscripts, as given by Lindsay, in spite of apparent confusions – e.g., the father of one's paternal uncle is one's grandfather, not one's great uncle. For full discussion see Reydellet 1984: 212–15. Surely rightly, Reydellet emends *pater magnus* below to *patruus magnus*.

and I am the son or daughter of his son or daughter. The grandfather of my maternal uncle is my great-great-uncle (*proavunculus*) and I am the grandson or granddaughter of his son. The great-grandfather of my maternal uncle is my great-great-great uncle (*abavunculus*) and I am the son or daughter of his granddaughter.

27. **Maternal aunts (*De materteris*)** The sister of my mother is my maternal aunt (*matertera*), and I am the son or daughter of her sister. The sister of my maternal aunt is my great maternal aunt (*matertera magna*), and I am the grandson or granddaughter of her sister.[21] The sister of my grandmother is my *abmatertera* and I am a great-grandson or great-granddaughter of her sister. The sister of my great-grandmother is my *promatertera*, and I am the son or daughter of her granddaughter.

28. The family tree that legal advisors draw up concerning lineage is called a *stemma*, where the degrees of relationship are spelled out – as, for example, "this one is the son, this one is the father, this one the grandfather, this one the relative on the father's side," and all the rest. Here are the figures for these relationships.[22] 29. While this consanguinity diminishes towards the last degree, as it subdivides through the levels of descent, and kinship (*propinquitas*) ceases to exist, the law recovers it again through the bond of matrimony, and in a certain way calls it back as it slips away. Thus, consanguinity is established up to the sixth degree of kinship, so that just as the generation of the world and the status of humankind are defined by six ages, so kinship in a family is terminated by the same number of degrees.[23]

vii. Marriages (De coniugiis) 1. 'Man' (*vir*) signifies gender, not marital status, unless you say in addition, 'her man.' 2. But 'husband' (*maritus*) without an additional term means a man who is married. 'Husband' comes from 'masculine' (*mas*, gen. *maris*, adjective) as if the word were *mas* (i.e. "male," noun), for the noun is the primary form, and it has *masculus* as a diminutive form, *maritus* as a derivative form. 3. A 'betrothed man' (*sponsus*) is so called from pledging (*spondere*, ppl. *sponsus*), for before the use of matrimonial registers the betrothed sent each other written warranties in which they would pledge to each other that they consented to the laws of marriage, and they would provide guarantors. 4. From this, it was accepted that we call a betrothed man *sponsus*, from 'pledging,' and a betrothed woman *sponsa* in similar fashion. Again, properly speaking, 'to pledge' means "to intend." Therefore, he is a *sponsus* not just because he promises, but because he pledges and gives sponsors (*sponsor*).

5. 'Earnest-money' (*arrabo*) is so called as though the word were *arra bona* ("good pledge"), for what is given for the purposes of matrimony is well given, since marriage is good. But that which is given for the sake of fornication and adultery is bad, and therefore not an *arrabo*. 6. A pledge (*arra*) is so called 'from the thing' (*a re*) for which it is given. Moreover, an *arra* is not only a pledge of marriage, but also a pledge for anything that has been promised – that something will be given back, or that a promise will be fulfilled. 7. Suitors (*procus*) are petitioners of marriage, so called from 'pressing one's suit' (*procare*) or 'petitioning' (*petere*). 8. A bride's-woman (*pronuba*) is so called because she presides over a bride (*praeesse* + *nubens*) and she is the one who joins the bride to her husband. She is also called a *paranympha*, for the *nympha* is the bride in the wedding ceremony, and *nympha* (also meaning "water") refers to the duty of washing (i.e. bathing the bride), since the word also alludes to the word for 'marrying' (*nubere*).

9. 'Conjugal partners' (*coniunx*) are so called on account of the yoke (*iugum*) that is placed on those yoked together (*coniungere*) in matrimony. Customarily, those who are married are placed under a yoke, indicative of future harmony, lest they be separated. However, conjugal partners are more truly so called from the initial pledge of their betrothal, even though conjugal relations are still unknown to them, as Mary is called the 'conjugal partner' of Joseph, but between them there neither was nor would be any commingling of the flesh. 10. Brides (*nupta*) are so called because they veil their faces, for the word for brides is taken from 'clouds' (*nubes*), which

21 This section contains a number of confusions.

22 The manuscripts present here two figures laying out in tree form the names of the relationships discussed above arranged according to their degrees of kinship. One's parents and children are of the first degree; siblings, grandparents, and grandchildren are of the second degree; and so on to the sixth degree. A note on the first figure indicates that from the sixth to the fourth degree, including first cousins but not nieces and nephews, people are *immunis*, that is, non-incestuous and marriageable.

23 Here follows a third figure, found in a few early manuscripts, laying out the same information about degrees of kinship in a table made of eight concentric circles divided into wedges by ten radii.

cover the heavens. Whence the wedding festivities are called 'nuptials' (*nuptiae*), because there the heads of the newlyweds are covered for the first time. The word *obnubere* means "cover." 11. The opposite of this is 'unmarried' (*innuba*), that is, *innupta*, a woman who has not yet veiled her own face.

12. Wives (*uxor*) are so called as though the word were *unxior*, for there was an ancient custom that, as soon as newlyweds would come to their husband's threshold, before they entered they would decorate the door posts with woolen fillets and anoint (*unguere*, perfect *unxi*) them with oil. Hence the newlyweds were called 'wives' as if the word were *unxior*. And they were forbidden to step on the thresholds, because at that place the doors both come together and separate. 13. A matron (*matrona*) is a woman who has already married, and she is called a *matrona* as though she were the 'mother of a born child' (*mater nati*), or because now she can become a mother (*mater*) – whence also *matrimonium* ("matrimony") is so called. There is a difference between a matron and a mother, and between a mother and a materfamilias; for a woman is called a 'matron' because she has entered in matrimony; a 'mother' because she has borne children; and 'materfamilias' because through certain procedures of law she has passed over into the household (*familia*) of her husband.

14. A man is called 'monogamous' (*monogamus*) because he has been married to only one woman, for μόνος is the Greek word for 'one,' and γάμος is translated as "marriage." 15. A man is called *digamus* and *trigamus* for the numbers of wives he has had, as though he were a husband to two or three women. 16. A widow (*vidua*) is so called because she has not been with man number two (*vir*, "man" + *duo*, "two"),[24] and after the death of her first husband she has not attached herself in a union with another man. Women who marry other men after the death of their first husbands are not called 'widows.' Again, she is called 'deprived' (*viduus*, adj.) because she is alone, because she has lost the rights of marriage related to sharing her life with a husband. 17. The wife of a brother is called *fratrissa*. The brother of a husband is called *levir*. The wives of two brothers call each other *ianetrix* (cf. εἰνάτερες, "wives of brothers") as if the term were 'frequenting' the same 'doors' (*ianua* + *terere*), or through the same 'door' having 'entry' (*ianua* + *iter*). The sister of a husband is called *galos* (cf. γάλως, "sister-in-law"). 18. The husband of a sister does not have a special name, nor does the brother of a wife.

19. Matrimony (*matrimonium*) is the lawful 'passing into a husband's control' and marriage contract of marriageable women.[25] 20. A 'conjugal union' (*coniugium*) is a marital relationship of persons who have met the legal requirements, marked by joining together and sexual intercourse with one another. This *coniugium* is so called because the two people are conjoined (*coniungere*), or from the yoke (*iugum*) by which they are coupled in marriage, so that they cannot be unbound or separated. 21. The word *conubium* ("marriage"), however, is formed not from *nupta* ("married woman"), but from the word *nubo* ("veil, wed"). And it is called *conubium* when equals enter into a married state, as for example Roman citizens, clearly equal in status. But it is not *conubium* when a Roman citizen is joined with a woman of Latium. Whenever a marriage is not defined as *conubium*, the children do not become members of the father's line.

22. The 'wedding' (*hymenaeus*, also meaning "wedding song") is so called from a certain Hymenaeus, who was the first to enjoy a fortunate wedding, or it is from the term ὑμήν, the membrane that is the closed gateway of virginity. 23. 'Living together' (*contubernium*) is an agreement to sleep together for a time; whence the term 'tent' (*tabernaculum*), which is pitched now here, now there. 24. A repudiation (*repudium*) is that which, substantiated by witnesses, is delivered to someone who is either present or absent. 25. A divorce (*divortium*) occurs whenever a marriage has dissolved, and one of the partners pursues a new marriage. Moreover, 'divorce' is so called from a parting of ways, that is, paths stretching in 'different directions' (*diversus*). 26. *Frivolum* occurs when two people separate intending that they once again will return to each other, for 'frivolous' (*frivolus*) is being marked by a wavering and fickle mind, not a stable one. Appropriately, useless crockery is called *frivola*.

27. There are three reasons to marry a wife: the first reason is for the sake of offspring, about which we read

24 Considering the perfect tense ("has been"), the emendation deleting *non* ("not") makes better sense: "has been a twosome with a man."

25 For "of marriageable women" (*nubilium*) all the early manuscripts read "of noble women" (*nobilium*).

in Genesis (1:28): "And he blessed them, saying: Increase and multiply." The second reason is for a help, about which, Genesis says (2:18): "It is not good for the man to be alone: let us make him a help like unto himself." The third reason is lack of self-restraint, whence the apostle Paul says, for example (I Corinthians 7:9): "Let the man who cannot contain himself marry." 28. In choosing a husband, four things are usually considered: valor, family, good looks, and wisdom. Of these, wisdom is the more powerful for arousing the feeling of love. Vergil refers to these four qualities with regard to Aeneas, because Dido was driven by them into love for him (cf. *Aen.* 4.11–14):

By good looks:

> What a bearing he has, what looks!

By valor:

> And what a brave heart, what feats of arms!

By speech:

> Ah, by what fates this man has been tossed about, what drawn-out wars he was singing of!

By family:

> Indeed, I believe – and it is no empty trust – that he belongs to the family of the gods.

29. Then, in choosing a wife, four things impel a man to love: beauty, family, wealth, and character. Yet it is better if character is looked for in her rather than beauty. But nowadays, wives are sought whom wealth and beauty recommend, not uprightness of character. 30. Women stand under the power of their husbands because they are quite often deceived by the fickleness of their minds. Whence, it was right that they were repressed by the authority of men. Consequently, the ancients wanted their unwed women, even those of mature age, to live in guardianship, on account of their fickle minds.

Book X

Vocabulary (De vocabulis)

1. People are for the most part unaware of the origin of certain terms. Consequently we have included a number in this work for their informational value.

Certain terms for human beings (De quibusdam vocabulis hominum)[1] Although the origin of terms, whence they come, has received some accounting by philosophers – such that by derivation 'human being' (*homo*) is so called from 'humanity' (*humanitas*), or 'wise person' (*sapiens*) from 'wisdom' (*sapientia*), because wisdom comes first, then the wise person – nevertheless a different, special cause is manifest in the origin of certain terms, such as *homo* from 'soil' (*humus*), from which the word *homo* properly is so called. From such derivations, as examples, we have set forth a number in this work.

A. 2. *Aeros* (i.e. *heros*, "demi-god, hero"), a strong and wise man. Author (*auctor*), so called from 'augmenting' (*augere*); moreover, *auctor* cannot be used in the feminine gender – for there are some terms that cannot be inflected in the feminine, such as 'runner' (*cursor*). Agent (*actor*), from acting (*agere*). 3. Foster-son (*alumnus*), so called from fostering (*alere*), although both he who fosters and he who is fostered can be called *alumnus* – that is, he who nourishes and he who is nourished – but still, the better use is for one who is nourished. 4. Friend (*amicus*), by derivation as if from the phrase 'guardian of the spirit' (*animi custos*). 5. And *amicus* is appropriately derived; the term for someone tormented by carnal desire is *amator turpitudinis* ("lover of wickedness"), but *amicus* is from 'hook' (*hamus*), that is, from the chain of charity, whence also hooks are things that hold. Lovable (*amabilis*), too, because one is worthy of love (*amor*). A lover (*amasius*), because he is prone to love (*amor*). 6. Clever (*astutus*) is so called from the word 'cleverness' (*astus*), which is the term for a shrewd and wary person who can do something forcefully without danger. Smart (*argutus*), because one quickly comes up with an argument (*argumentum*) while speaking. Acute (*acer*), in every manner lively and forceful. Swift (*alacer*), with regard to speed and running, as if one would say 'winged' (*aliger*). 'Bearing arms' (*armiger*), because he 'bears arms' (*arma gerere*). Happy (*alacris*), "joyful"; cheerful (*alacer*), lively and disturbed by no surprising events. Agile (*agilis*), from doing (*agere*) something quickly, like *docilis* ("easily taught").

7. Rivalling (*aemulus*), striving for the same thing as an imitator (*imitator*) and lover (*amabilis*) of it; at other times it comes to mean "inimical." Fair (*aequus*), meaning "naturally just," from 'equity' (*aequitas*), that is, after the idea of what is equal (*aequus*) – whence likewise 'equity' is so called after a certain equalness (*aequalitate*). *Aequaevus* refers to what is of an equal age (*aequale aevum*) with another thing, that is, coeval (*coaetaneus*). Arrogant (*arrogans*), because much is demanded (*rogare*), and such a person is disdainful. Presumptuous (*audax*) may properly be substituted for *arrogans*. Spirited (*animosus*), because one is full of spirit (*animus*) and drive. Stouthearted (*animatus*), as if 'endowed with vigor' (*animo auctus*), firm in spirit. 8. Puffed up (*aelatus*, i.e. *elatus*, ppl. of *efferre*), because one exalts (*elevare*) himself beyond his proper measure when he seems to himself a great person for what he accomplishes. Self-aggrandizing (*attollens*), because one exalts and elevates himself. Ambitious (*ambitiosus*), because one solicits

1 Indeed the vocabulary treated in this book specifically comprises nouns and substantive adjectives used for human beings. To arrange a large body of information in alphabetical order was still rare in Isidore's time, although Pliny and others had used alphabetical order for short lists of things, and at least a couple of Latin authors used the alphabet to organize larger lexicographical works (the lost lexicon of Verrius Flaccus of the first century CE, the lexicographical part of Nonius Marcellus's encyclopedia of the fourth century). See Daly (1967), pages 50–59. Some early manuscripts reflect the novelty of the scheme with titles referring to the alphabetical organization.

Latin freely uses adjectives as substantives, so that *argutus* can mean "smart" or "a smart person." While for the most part the substantive use can be presumed in Book X, we here generally and somewhat elliptically translate such terms as adjectives, trusting that the substantive use will be understood. Many of the words are present and perfect participles; we supply their infinitive forms only when they are not obvious.

(*ambire*) honors. 9. Greedy (*avidus*) is so called from 'crave' (*avere*), for to crave is to desire; from this verb also comes 'covetous' (*avarus*). Now, what is it to be greedy? To pass beyond what is sufficient. The covetous person is so called because he is greedy for gold, and never has enough money, and the more he has, the more he covets. On this, with the same idea, is Horace, who says (*Epistles* 1.2.56):

> The covetous person (*avarus*) is always in need.

And Sallust (cf. *War Against Catiline* 11.3): "Because avarice (*avaritia*) is diminished neither by wealth nor by poverty."

10. Bitter (*amarus*) draws its name from the taste, for such a one is not sweet-tempered, and does not know how with any sweetness to invite anyone to share his company. Adulterous (*adulter*), a violator of marital chastity, because he defiles the bed of another (*alter*). 11. Indecisive (*anceps*), wavering this way and that and doubting whether to choose this or that, and distressed (*anxius*) about which way to lean. Abominable (*atrox*), because one has loathsome (*taeter*) conduct. Abstemious (*abstemius*), from *temetum*, that is, 'wine,' as if abstaining (*abstinere*) from wine. [Neighboring (*affinis*) . . .] Weaned (*ablactatus*), because one is 'withdrawn from milk' (*a lacte ablatus*). 12. Sick (*aeger*), because one is pressed (*agere*) by illness or grief for a time, and sickly (*aegrotus*), because one is sick rather often – there is the same distinction as between 'angry' (*iratus*) and 'given to anger' (*iracundus*). Miserable (*aerumnosus*) is so called from gullet (*rumen*), because one who has become a wretch from poverty hungers and thirsts. 13. A diviner (*auspex*), because he examines the auspices (*auspicium*; cf. *specere*, "look at") of birds, in the same way that a fowler (*auceps*) is so called because he 'catches birds' (*aves capere*). Star-crossed (*astrosus*), so called from star (*astrum*), as one born under an evil star. 14. Enormous (*aenormis*, i.e. *enormis*), because one exceeds the norm (*norma*) and moderation. A rustler (*abactor*) is a thief of beasts of burden and livestock; commonly people call him an *abigeius*, from 'drive off' (*abigere*). 15. 'Dressed for mourning' (*atratus*) and 'clothed in white' (*albatus*): the former from black clothing (cf. *ater*, "black"), the latter from white (*albus*) clothing. Stranger (*advena*), one who 'comes here' (*advenire*) from elsewhere. Foreigner (*alienigena*), because one is of a 'foreign nation' (*alienum genus*), and not of the nation where one now is. [Again,] *alienigena*, one who is begotten (*genitus*) from another people (*alia gens*), and not from the people where one now is.

16. Immigrant (*accola*), because immigrating (*advenire*) one tills (*colere*) the land. Farmer (*agricola*), from 'tilling a field' (*colere* + *ager*); likewise *silvicola* ("inhabitant of the woods"; cf. *silva*, "woods"). Hanger-on (*assecula*), because one follows (*sequi*, ppl. *secutus*) someone for money. 17. Tax-payer (*assiduus*) was the term among the ancients for one who had to contribute a payment to the public treasury in money (*as*, gen. *assis*), and also was busy with public affairs – hence also it should be written with an *s*, not with a *d* (i.e. not *adsiduus*). 18. An attendant (*apparator*) is so called because one appears (*apparere*) and is seen and is in attendance at someone's pleasure. Attentive (*attentus*), as one holds onto (*tenere*) what one hears. 19. Thunderstruck (*attonitus*), as if fired with a certain madness and stupefied, called 'thunderstruck' from the crash of thunderclaps (*tonitrus*), as if stupefied by a thunderclap and close to a nearby lightning strike. 20. An *allectus* (i.e. a public official), because such a one is publicly elected (*electus*). 'Driven from office' (*abactus*), because one is removed 'from public employment' (*ab actus*). Aborted (*abortivus*), because one is not born, but miscarried (*aboriri*, ppl. *abortus*) and perishes. Adoptive (*adoptivus*), because one is publicly chosen (*optare*) as a son. 21. Both (*ambo*), derived from ἄμφω ("both"), a Greek word made into Latin with the third letter (i.e. phi) changed. 'Another' (*alius*) [is said of one from many, but] 'the other' (*alter*) [of one from two]. Ambidextrous (*aequimanus*) is the term for one who holds a sword in either hand (*manus*).

B. 22. Blessed (*beatus*) is so called as if the term were 'well endowed' (*bene auctus*), specifically from having what one wants and not suffering what one doesn't want. Further, a person is indeed blessed who both has all the good things that he wants, and wishes for nothing wickedly. From these two, a person is made blessed. 23. Good (*bonus*) is thought to be so called from beauty (*venustas*) of the body, and later the word was transferred to the spirit. We call a person good if evil does not have the upper hand in him, and we call that person best (*optimus*, superlative of *bonus*) who sins least. 24. A gracious (*benignus*) person is willingly prepared 'to do good' (*benefacere*) and is kind in speech. Not much distinguishes *benignus* from *bonus*, because the *benignus* person also seems disposed to do well. However, they differ in this, that the *bonus* person can be rather somber, and although he does well and is attentive to what is demanded of him, still he does not know how to be pleasant as a companion, whereas the *benignus* person knows how to be inviting to all with his sweet nature. 25. Beneficent (*beneficus*), so called from 'doing well' (*benefacere*) to another; from this also is the term 'beneficence' (*beneficentia*), which benefits one's neighbor. 26. Benevolent (*benivolus*), because one 'wishes well' (*bene velle*, 1st person *volo*). Still, we do not say *benevolus*, any more than *malevolus*, for often a word compounded of two bases alters either the first letter (i.e. of the second base) or the last letter (i.e. of the first base) – for *benevolentia* (i.e. rather than *benivolentia*, "benevolence") has a disagreeable sound. 27. Charming (*blandus*), sweet and open to friendship. 28. Stupid (*brutus*), as if overwhelmed (*obrutus*), because one lacks sense, for such a one is without reason or prudence. From this term also came the name Junius Brutus, the son of the sister of Tarquinius Superbus. When he feared the same disaster that befell his brother, who was killed by his maternal uncle because of his wealth and prudence, he feigned a useful stupidity for a time. Whence he received the cognomen Brutus, although he was named Junius. 29. [Red (*burrus*) . . .] Stammering (*balbus*), so called from bleating (*balare*) rather than speaking, for such a person cannot get words out. 30. Hence also 'hesitating in speech' (*blaesus*), because one breaks off words. A chatterer (*bucco*), a garrulous person, because he outdoes others in the loquacity of his speech, not its sense. Bilious (*biliosus*), because one is always in a melancholy state, from the black humor that is called bile (*bilis*). 31. *Baburrus*, "stupid, inept." *Biothanatus* (i.e. a martyr who dies a violent death), because he is 'twice dead,' for death is θάνατος in Greek.[2]

C. 32. Bright (*clarus*), from sky (*caelum*), because it shines, and hence also the term 'bright day' for the shining of the sky. Lofty (*celsus*) is named after sky, because one is elevated and high, as if the term were 'celestial' (*caelestis*). 33. Chaste (*castus*) was first so called after the term 'castration' (*castratio*); afterwards the ancients chose so to call those who would promise perpetual abstinence from sexual intercourse. 34. A 'celestial one' (*caeles*) is so called because such a one directs his course to the sky (*caelum*). Celibate (*caelebs*), one having no part in marriage, of which kind are the numinous beings in heaven (*caelum*), who have no spouses – and *caelebs* is so called as if the term were 'blessed in heaven' (*caelo beatus*). Heavenly-dweller (*caelicola*), because they 'dwell in heaven' (*caelum colere*) – for that is an angel. 35. 'Continent' is said not only of chastity, but also of food and drink, and also of anger, agitation of mind, and passion for disparaging. A person is continent (*continens*) because he 'holds himself back' (*abstinere*) from many evils. 36. Merciful (*clemens*), having pity, because such a one 'is called upon' (*cluere*), that is, he protects and guards, as a patron does for his client (*cliens*). 37. Concordant (*concors*) is so called from 'joining of the heart' (*coniunctio cordis*), for as one who shares one's lot (*sors*) is called a 'partner' (*consors*), so one who is joined in heart (*cor*) is called *concors*. 38. Haranguer (*contionator*). . . . Consoler (*consolator*), 'comforting interlocutor'; and a consoler is so called because he focuses attention on the single (*solus*) person to whom he is speaking, and alleviates his solitude by talking with him. Hence also the word 'solace' (*solacium*).

39. Well-advised (*consultus*) is one who has 'taken counsel' (*consulere*); the opposite is ill-advised, one who does not accept counsel. 40. Constant (*constans*) is so called because one 'stands firm' (*stare*, present participle *stans*) in every situation, and cannot deviate in any direction. Trusting (*confidens*), one full of faith (*fiducia*) in all matters. Whence Caecilius (fr. 246):

> If you summon Confidence, confide (*confidere*)
> everything to her.

41. Cautious (*cautus*), so called from 'being wary' (*cavere*). Sly (*callidus*), "deceptive," because he knows how to conceal (*celare*) things, and is skillful in a bad way. However, the ancients would use *callidus* not only for "cunning," but also for "expertly taught." Such a one is also wily (*versutum*), because he quickly shifts (*vertere*) his thinking around. 42. Desirous (*cupidus*), so called from taking (*capere*), that is, receiving, much. Clamorous (*clamosus*), as if the word were *calamosus*, from 'reed-pipe' (*calamus*) – thus, because one makes noise. A calumniator (*calumniator*), a false accuser of a crime, so called from 'intriguing against' (*calveri*), that

2 Greek βία means "violence," but *bio-* is here taken as the Latin combining form *bi-*, "twice."

is, misleading and deceiving. 43. Accountant (*calculator*), from 'pebbles' (*calculi*), that is, little stones; the ancients, holding these in their hands, would calculate numbers. 44. A plagiarist (*compilator*), one who mixes the words of another with his own, as pigment-makers customarily crush together diverse things mixed up in a mortar (*pila*). The poet of Mantua (i.e. Vergil) was once accused of this crime because of his taking some verses of Homer and mixing them with his own, and was called by his rivals a plagiarist of the ancients. He answered them, "It takes great strength to wrest Hercules's club from his hand."

45. Insolent (*contumax*), because one scorns (*contemnere*). *Chromaticus*, because one is not confused nor does he change color, for 'color' in Greek is χρῶμα.[3] 46. Abusive (*contumeliosus*), because one is quick and swells (*tumere*) with insulting words. Headstrong (*contentiosus*), so called from purposefulness (*intentio*), one who claims something not according to reason, but from obstinacy alone. 47. Contemptible (*contemptibilis*), either because 'worthy of contempt' (*contemptui habilis*), or because disdained (*contemptus*) and base (*vilis*), that is, without honor. 48. Cruel (*crudelis*), that is, raw (*crudus*), which the Greeks call ὠμός ("raw"), with a transferred sense as if uncooked and not suitable for eating, for such a one is harsh and hard-hearted. 49. Executioner (*carnifex*), because he 'makes dead meat' (*carnem afficere*). Gallows-bird (*cruciarius*), because he deserves the cross (*crux*, gen. *crucis*). Colleague (*collega*), so called from the bond (*colligatio*) of fellowship and from the embrace of friendship. Contemporary (*coaetaneus*), as if the term were 'of equal age' (*compar aetatis*). 50. Accomplice (*complex*, gen. *complicis*), because one has been connected (*applicatus*) with another person in a single sin or crime for an evil purpose – but if done for a good purpose we never use the word *complex*. 51. Partner (*consors*), because a share of property belongs to him, for the ancients would use the word 'allotment' (*sors*) for 'share.' Therefore *consors*, because one is 'sharing in the allotment' (*communis sorte*), just as *dissors* means 'unequal in the allotment' (*dissimilis sorte*).

52. Swift (*celer*) is so called from swiftness (*celeritas*), because such a one quickly does what needs to be done. 'Closely connected' (*confinalis*), because one is nearby (*affinis*) in family or in location. Farmer (*colonus*), so called from farm (*colonia*) or from tilling (*colere*) a field. 53. Attorney (*cognitor*) from knowing (*cognoscere*) a case. *Curator* (i.e. a high municipal official), because he takes care (*cura*) of minor children who are still not old enough to be able to administer their affairs. Clients (*cliens*, "dependent on a patron") were earlier called *colientes*, from 'cultivating' (*colere*) their patrons. 54. [Captured (*captus*) . . .] Captive (*captivus*) is so called as if 'deprived of civic rights' (*capite deminutus*), for the condition of a free person has passed from him, whence he is spoken of as deprived of civic rights by legal experts. 55. Unimpaired (*colomis*, i.e. *columis*), so called from pillar (*column*), because such a one is erect and very firm. 56. Adorned (*comtus*), so called from hair (*coma*), because one's hair is good-looking, or because one grooms one's hair. 57. Curly-haired (*calamistratus*), from the 'curling iron' (*calamister*), that is, the iron pin made in the shape of a reed (*calamus*), on which hair is twisted to make it curly. Those who curl hair will warm these irons in embers in order to be curly-haired.

58. Stout (*corpulentus*), because one is weighty of body (*corpus*) and sluggish with flesh. Fat (*crassus*), from stuffing of the body, from 'making' (*creare*) flesh. Glutton (*comesor*), from eating (*comedere*, ppl. *comesum*) a lot, for such a one is immoderately dedicated to the maw and belly. Taverner (*caupo*) – the worst sort make water from wine. 59. *Candidus* ["honest, splendid"]. Gray-haired (*canus*), so called from white (*candidus*), and 'white' as if the term were 'added whiteness' (*candor datus*) – for the whiteness called *candor* results from effort, and a naturally white thing is called *albus*. 60. Curly-haired (*crispus*) . . . Lame (*clodus*) . . . Bent (*curvus*) . . . Blind (*caecus*) is so called because one 'lacks vision' (*carere visum*), for he has lost his eyes. One is *caecus* who does not see with either eye. 61. Epileptic (*caducus*, "falling sickness"), so called from falling down (*cadere*). He is also a lunatic (*lunaticus*) because [he suffers at a particular phase of the moon (*luna*)]. Confounded (*confusus*), so called from one's confession (*confessio*) of a wicked deed; hence also 'confounding' (*confusio*).

62. Ruined (*convulsus*) is said of one whose possessions are carried off by some force. Whence also a wrecked (*convulsus*) ship, whose projecting parts are carried off by the force of a storm, as in Vergil (*Aen.* 1.383):

> Scarcely seven (ships), wrecked (*convulsus*) by the waves –

3 Perhaps a *chromaticus* is a person skilled in the argumentative use of rhetorical colors, from the sense of Greek χρωματικός. Or a *chromaticus* may be a person "dyed-in-the-wool."

as if mutilated. 63. Consumed (*consumptus*), wholly 'used up' (*sumere*) and devoured. Procuress (*conciliatrix*), so called from her making a companionship in a shameful agreement (*consensio*), because she acts as go-between and traffics in someone else's body. Such a woman is also called a pimp (*leno*). 64. *Circumforanus*, one who strolls 'around marketplaces' (*circum fora*) and courts for the sake of lawyering. Guildsman (*collegiatus*) . . . Coachman (*carpentarius*) . . .

D. 65. Master (*dominus*) is so called by derivation, because he presides over a household (*domus*). Well-spoken (*disertus*), "learned," so called from discuss (*dissere*, ppl. *dissertus*), for he discusses things methodically. Learned (*doctus*), from speak (*dicere*), whence also *dictor* ("speaker"). 66. Docile (*docilis*), not that one is *doctus*, but that he is able to be taught (*docere*), for he is clever and apt for learning. Student (*discipulus*) is so called from instruction (*disciplina*), and *disciplina* is so called from learn (*discere*). 67. Steward (*dispensator*) is the name for a person entrusted with the administration of money, and such a one is a *dispensator* because in former times the person who dispensed money would not count it but 'weigh it out' (*appendere*). 68. Rich (*dives*), so called from money (cf. *divitiae*, "wealth"). Seemly (*decorus*), "perfect," from the number ten (*decem*, i.e. the perfect number). [Sweet (*dulcis*) . . .] Becoming (*decens*), "well-arranged," so called from the number ten (*decem*). From 'ten' also come 'seemly' and 'fitting' (*decibilis*). 69. Straightforward (*directus*), because one goes straight (*in rectum*). Beloved (*dilectus*), from 'caring for' (*diligentia*); both are marks of loving (*diligere*). 70. 'Thickly smeared' (*delibutus*), anointed with oil as is the custom for athletes or youths in the wrestling arena. Hence (Terence, *Phormio* 856), "Anointed (*delibutus*) with joy," that is, suffused with or full of joy. Over-indulged (*delicatus*), because one is fed with luxury (*deliciae*), living in feasts and daintiness of body.

71. Exhausted (*defessus*), "always feeble," as if the term were 'tired for a long time' (*diu fessus*). Infirm (*debilis*), because one is made weak by bile (*bilis*), for bile is a humor that affects the body. Pale (*decolor*), because color (*color*) is lacking in someone. 72. Desperate (*desperatus*) is the common term for "bad" and "lost" and "without any hope (*spes*) of success"; it is likewise said of sick people who are weakened and given up as hopeless (*sine spe*). It was the custom among the ancients to set those desperately ill in front of their doors, either to give up their last breath to the earth or to be able to be cured, perhaps, by passers-by who at some time had suffered with a similar disease. 73. Base (*degener*), or "ignoble," either because one is of an inferior lineage or because, although born of the best lineage, one lives dishonorably. 74. Decrepit (*decrepitus*), because one is rather close to death, as if he were turning toward the darkness of death, as toward the twilight (*crepusculum*) time of night. Others say a decrepit person is not one who is borne away by old age, but one who has already left off chattering (*crepare*), that is, has ceased speaking. 75. Worthless (*depretiatus*), because one is base and not of any value (*pretium*). Dire (*dirus*), "very mean" and "horrible," as if driven that way 'by divine wrath' (*divina ira*), for a dire condition means that which is brought on by divine wrath. In another sense *dirus* means "great." 76. Gaping (*dehiscens*), "yawning (*hiscere*) very much," for here the prefix *de-* is augmentative, as (Terence, *Self-Tormentor* 825), "I 'very much love' (*deamare*) you, Syrus." Despising (*despiciens*), because one 'looks down' (*deorsum aspicere*) on someone, or holds one in contempt. Guileful (*dolosus*), "deceptive" or "malicious," because he 'practices guile' (*deludere*), for to deceive someone he colors his hidden malice with charming words. 77. Doubtful (*dubius*), "uncertain," as if in 'two directions' (*duae viae*). Accuser (*delator*), so called because one discloses (*detegere*) what was hidden (*latere*). A 'dilatory person' (*dilator*), because one delays (*differre*, ppl. *dilatus*) action. Indolent (*desidiosus*), "sluggish, lazy," so called from 'settling down' (*desidere*), that is, from sitting too much. Similarly, the term 'inactive ones' (*resides*; singular *reses*) is from 'remain seated' (*resideo*) – for the prefix *de-* here is augmentative. 78. Doting (*delerus*, i.e. *delirus*), demented from old age, after the term ληρεῖν ("prattle"), or because one wanders from straight thinking as if from the *lira* – for a *lira* (i.e. the balk between furrows) is a kind of plowed land when farmers, at the time of sowing, make straight furrows in which the whole crop is set. 79. Demented (*demens*), the same as one who is *amens*, that is, without mind (*mens*), or suffering a loss of mental power. Doting (*desipiens*), because one begins to understand (*sapere*) less than one used to. 80. Condemned (*damnatus*) and condemnable (*damnabilis*): of these the former has already been sentenced, the latter can be sentenced. Glutton (*degulator*), because he is dedicated to the maw (*gula*).

E. 81. Eloquent (*eloquens*), "profuse in speech (*eloquium*)." *Exertus*, "ready in speaking," because *exerere* (ppl. *exertus*) means "bring out" or "set forth clearly." Erudite (*eruditus*), because not uncultivated (*rudis*), but already educated. 82. Expert (*expertus*), much skilled (*peritus*), for here the prefix *ex-* means "very much." However, 'lacking experience' (*expers*), one who is without 'practical knowledge' (*peritia*) and understanding. 'Decked out' (*exornatus*), "very ornate (*ornatus*)," for the prefix *ex-* means "very," as in 'noble' (*excelsus*), as if 'very lofty (*celsus*),' and 'excellent' (*eximius*), as if 'very prominent (*eminens*).' 83. Efficacious (*efficax*), so called because one has no difficulty in doing (*facere*) any kind of thing. Hence also effective (*efficiens*), so called from 'accomplishing' (*facere*). Hopeless (*exspes*), because one is without hope (*spes*). Destitute (*expers*), because 'without a share (*pars*),' for such a one lacks a share. Deprived (*exsors*), because one is 'without an allotment (*sors*).' 84. Exile (*exul*), because one is 'outside his native soil' (*extra solum suum*), as if sent beyond his soil, or wandering outside his soil, for those who go outside their soil are said to 'be in exile' (*exulare*).

85. Banished (*extorris*), because one is 'outside his own land' (*extra terram suam*), as if the term were *exterris* – but properly speaking one is banished when driven out by force and ejected from his native soil with terror (*terror*). Also *extorris*, driven 'from one's own land' (*ex terra sua*). 86. Banished (*extorris*), 'outside the land' (*extra terram*), or 'beyond one's frontier' (*extra terminos suos*), because one is frightened (*exterrere*). 87. Expeller (*exterminator*), not the one who is commonly said ἀφανισθῆναι ("to be destroyed"),[4] but the one who casts out and expels someone from the boundaries (*terminus*) of a city. Expelled (*exterminatus*), because such a one is driven out 'beyond his boundaries' (*extra terminos*). [Thus also] foreign (*externus*), because one is from an alien land (*terra*). 88. Needy (*egens*) and destitute (*egenus*), "indigent (*indigens*)," without a nation (*gens*) and without a family (*genus*). [*Egenus* . . .] 'Poor' (*exiguus*), very needy (*egens*), for the prefix *ex-* means "very." Lank (*exilis*), "thin," because one can 'go out' (*exire*) of a place even if it is narrow. 89. Emaciated (*exesus*), because one is 'entirely eaten away' (*percomedere*, ppl. *percomesus*), for such a one is withered, thin, lank. Drained (*exhaustus*), because one is consumed and made empty (cf. *haurio*, ppl. *haustus*, "drain"). Feeble (*exsanguis*), because such a one is without blood (*sanguis*). 90. Lifeless (*exanimis*) means "dead" (cf. *anima*, "soul, life"). Further, we say *exanimis* or *exanimus*, as we say *unanimus* or *unanimis* ("of one mind"), and *inermus* or *inermis* ("unarmed"), and this is a matter of our whim. 91. 'Burnt up' (*exustus*) is said of one of whom nothing remains, as if it were 'very burned' (*ustus*), for the prefix *ex-* means "very." Hateful (*exosus*) is so called from hatred (*odium*), for the ancients would say both *odi* ("I hate") and *osus sum* ("I hate"; an alternative older form of the verb), and from this is *exosus*, which we use even though we no longer say *osus*. Destructive (*exitiosus*), because one is a cause of destruction (*exitio*) to many.

Executor (i.e. an official who summoned to court and enforced the court's mandate), from 'carry out' (*exequi*, ppl. *executus*); the same person is an *exactor* ("superintendent, tax-gatherer"). 92. Burglar (*effractor*), because such a one is a conqueror (cf. *frangere*, ppl. *fractus*, "break") of locks. Fierce (*efferatus*), 'affected with a savage (*ferinus*) spirit' and passing beyond the nature of humans. Unrestrained (*effrenatus*), because such a one is impulsive and headlong and without the rein (*frenum*) of reason. 93. *Eunuchus* is a Greek term (i.e. εὐνοῦχος) meaning "eunuch" (*spado*). Although some of these have sexual intercourse there is no strength in their seed, for they possess and emit a fluid but it is useless and impotent for begetting. 94. A 'worn out' (*effeta*) woman, because she is exhausted from frequent childbearing (*fetus*), for incessant parturition makes her weak.

F. 95. Fluent (*facundus*), because one can speak easily (*facilis*). Merry (*facetus*), one who devotes himself to jokes and games in gestures and actions (*factum*), so called from 'act' (*facere*). Frugal (*frugalis*) is so called from crops (*frux*, gen. *frugis*), that is, from profit (*fructus*) and parsimony, or, as others would have it, from moderation and temperance. 96. Money-lender (*fenerator*, i.e. *faenerator*), one who entrusts money to a debtor, as if 'the handler of interest (*faenus*),' for *faenus* is money. A *fenerator* in Latin is one who both gives and receives loans. *Flamines* (singular *flamen*) are the high priests of idols. 97. Happy (*felix*) is one who gives happiness (*felicitas*), happy, one who receives it, and happy the thing by which happiness is given, as a 'happy time,' a 'happy place.' 98. Trustworthy (*fidelis*), because the good such a person

4 The Greek form is passive; an active form meaning "to destroy" would fit the sense better.

says or promises 'is done' (*fieri*, 3rd person *fit*) by him. Willing (*facilis*, lit. "easy"), from 'doing' (*facere*), and not sluggish. Sturdy (*firmus*), from whence also the word *formosus* ("good-looking"). Brave (*fortis*), because one bears (*ferre*, 3rd person *fert*) adversity or whatever happens – or, from 'iron' (*ferrum*), because one is tough and not softened. 99. Good-looking (*formosus*) is so called from appearance (*forma*); the ancients used *formus* for 'warm' and 'heated,' for heating arouses blood, [and] blood arouses beauty.

100. Foul (*foedus*) takes its name from goats and kids (*haedus*, also spelled *aedus*), with the letter *f* added. The ancients would use this with a serious connotation, as (Vergil, *Aen.* 2.502):

> Defiling (*foedare*) with his blood the fires that he himself had consecrated.

Fragile (*fragilis*) is so called because it can easily be broken (*frangere*). 101. Weary (*fessus*), as if 'split' (*fissus*), and no longer whole in health – and that is the general sense, for we say 'weary in spirit' – as (Vergil, *Aen.* 8.232):

> Weary (*fessus*) he sinks back three times into the valley –

and 'weary in body,' which is the more proper sense, and 'weary of circumstances,' with respect to the outcome of coming events. Harassed (*fatigatus*), as if 'tossed by the fates' (*fatis agitatus*). 102. Fearful (*formidolosus*), so called from *formum* ("warm thing"), that is, blood, because, when fleeing from the skin and the heart, the blood contracts – for fear congeals the blood, which when concentrated produces terror (*formido*), whence is the verse (Vergil, *Aen.* 3.30):

> And my chilled blood coagulates with terror (*formido*).

Although a *formidolosus* person is fearful, it also means "fearsome." 103. A fool (*fatuus*) is thought to be so called because he understands neither what he says (*fari*, 3rd person *fatur*) himself nor what others say. Some think that the term 'fool' derives originally from admirers of Fatua, the prophesying wife of Faunus, and that they were first called *fatuus* because they were immoderately stupefied by her prophecies, to the point of madness.

104. Patron (*fautor*), because one 'gives favor' (*favere*) and consent. Fashioner (*fictor*), so called from fashioning (*fingere*, ppl. *fictus*) and arranging something, as one who smoothes, treats, anoints, and brightens women's hair. Liar (*fallax*), one who deceives by speaking (*fari*), that is, by his talk. 105. Hot-headed (*fervidus*), "prone to anger," for wrath inflames such a one. 'Gnashing one's teeth' (*frendens*), because in a threatening way one crushes (*frangere*) and clenches his teeth. Growling (*fremens*) . . . Ferocious (*ferox*), because one engages in wildness (*feritas*), as a beast. 106. Thief (*fur*) is so called from 'dark' (*furvus*), that is, 'dusky,' for such a one practices at night. Factious (*factiosus*), in its bad sense, when we mean for it to be taken as "seditious," but otherwise when we mean "popular," and "powerful" and as if "of grand conduct (*factio*)." 107. Criminal (*facinorosus*), so called from the commission of a particular deed, for he does (*facere*) what harms (*nocere*) another. [Womanizer (*femellarius*), one devoted to women, whom the ancients called *mulierarius*.] Debauched (*flagitiosus*), because one frequently solicits (*flagitare*) and desires sensual pleasure. 108. Rascal (*furcifer*) was once the term for one who, because of a petty offense, was forced to 'carry a fork-shaped yoke' (*furcam ferre*) along the road, more to shame the man than as a cause of torment, and to announce his sin, and warn others not to sin in like manner. 109. Worthless (*futilis*; lit. "leaky"), "vain, useless, a chatterbox"; the term has a transferred sense from 'pottery (*fictilis*) vessels' that are empty and leaky and don't hold what you put into them. 110. Fornicator (*fornicarius*) . . . Prostitute (*fornicatrix*), a woman whose body is public and common. Such bodies would lie prostrate under arches, places that they call *fornices* – hence also the term 'female fornicator' (*fornicaria*). Vergil (*Aen.* 6.631:

> And with the archway (*fornix*) opposite.

111. A 'fertile woman' (*fecunda*) is so called from offspring (*fetus*), as if the word were *fetunda*, for she frequently bears children. Pregnant (*feta*) . . . Weeping (*flens*), as if shedding (*fluere*, present participle *fluens*) tears. Fugitive (*fugitivus*): nobody is correctly so called except one who flees (*fugere*, 3rd person *fugit*) from a master, for if a little boy runs away from his nurse or from school he is not a *fugitivus*.

G. 112. Glorious (*gloriosus*), so called from an abundance of distinction (*claritas*), with the letter *g* exchanged for *c*. *Gloriosus* is so called from the laurel wreath (*laurea*) that is given to victors. Knowledgeable (*gnarus*), "knowing"; its opposite is ignorant (*ignarus*), "not knowing." Grave (*gravis*, lit. "heavy"), "venerable." Whence we also call contemptible people lightweight (*levis*). A person is called grave for his good counsel and steadfastness, because he does not hop about with a light motion, but stands firm with a fixed gravity (*gravitas*) of constancy. 113. [Great (*grandis*) . . . Slender (*gracilis*) . . .] Aged (*grandaevus*), because one is 'great in age' (*grandis aevo*). Kindly (*gratus*), because one maintains kindness (*gratia*) – but 'kindly' is said only with regard to the mind, whereas 'most pleasing' (*gratissimus*) is said with regard to both the mind and the body. Obliging (*gratificus*), because one 'freely does' (*gratis facere*) a good deed. Generous (*gratiosus*), because he gives someone more than one deserves. 114. Garrulous (*garrulus*) is the proper word for a person who is commonly called verbose (*verbosus*). When happiness befalls such people they neither can nor will be quiet. The term is taken from the bird called jackdaw (*graculus*), which constantly chatters with importunate loquacity and is never quiet. A debauchee (*ganeo*), "voluptuary," though in hidden and subterranean places that the Greeks call γάνεια (cf. *ganea*, "disreputable chophouse"). Glutton (*glutto*), from maw (*gula*), that is, a gluttonous person (*gulosus*).

H. 115. Humble (*humilis*), as if inclined to the ground (*humus*). Honorable (*honorabilis*), as if the term were 'suitable for honors' (*honore habilis*), that is, 'fit.' 116. Decent (*honestus*), because such a one has no part of wickedness – for what is decency (*honestas*) but perpetual honor, that is, as if the term were 'the condition of honor' (*honoris status*)? Humane (*humanus*), because such a one has love and feelings of sympathy for humans (*homines*). Hence also derives the term 'human kindness' (*humanitas*), because of which we watch over one another. 117. Capable (*habilis*), because such a one is suitable and fit for handling (*habere*) something. Burdened (*honerosus*, i.e. *onerosus*, in classical Latin "burdensome") is more than *honeratus* ("burdened"), just as *scelerosus* ("vicious") is more than *sceleratus* ("tainted with wickedness"). Hirsute (*hirsutus*), because such a one is hairy (*hirtus*) and shaggy with hair.

118. Hypocrite (*hypocrita*) from the Greek (i.e. ὑποκριτής, "play-actor, dissembler") is translated into Latin as "dissembler" (*simulator*). Such a one outwardly appears as good, while he is evil within, for ὑπο- means "false" and κρίσις means "judgment." 119. Moreover, the name of *hypocrita* derives from the appearance of those who go in theatrical spectacles with countenance concealed, marking their face with blue and red and other pigments, holding masks of linen and plaster of Paris decorated with various colors, sometimes also smearing their necks and hands with white clay, in order to arrive at the coloring of the character they portray and to deceive the public while they act in plays. Now they look like a man, now a woman, now a man with barbered hair, now with long, now a woman with an old crone's, a maiden's, or some other appearance, with age and sex varied, to deceive the people while they act in plays. 120. The sense of this theatrical hypocritical appearance has been transferred to those who proceed with a false face and pretend to be what they are not. They cannot be called hypocrites from the moment they reveal themselves outwardly. 121. Interred (*humatus*), because one is covered with soil (*humus*), that is, buried.

I. 122. Talented (*ingeniosus*), one who has the power within (*intus*) of producing (*gignere*, ppl. *genitus*) any sort of art. Discoverer (*inventor*), because he 'comes upon' (*invenire*) what he is searching for. Hence also the thing called an invention (*inventio*). If we reconsider the origin of the word, what else does it sound like if not that 'to invent' (*invenire*) is to 'come upon' (*in* + *venire*) that which is sought for? 123. Translator (*interpres*), because he is the medium 'between the sides' (*inter partes*) of two languages when he translates. But the person who interprets (*interpretari*) God is also called an *interpres* for the humans to whom he reveals divine mysteries [because he mediates 'between' (*inter*) that which he translates]. 124. Judge (*iuridicus*) [because he 'tells the ordinances' (*iura dicere*) of the laws]. Potential (*indoles*) in the proper sense is a certain image of future strength. A righteous (*iustus*) person is so called because he keeps the laws (*ius*) and lives according to the law. 125. Innocent (*innox*), because such a one does not harm (*nocere*); *innocuus*, one who has not been harmed – but among the ancients there is no difference between the senses of the words. Cheerful (*ilaris*, i.e. *hilaris*) is a Greek word (i.e. ἱλαρός, "cheerful"). 'Given to merriment' (*iocundus*), because such a one is always ready for jokes (*iocus*) and merry-making – from the frequentative element (i.e. -*cund*-), as is *iracundus* ("given to wrath"; cf. *ira*, "wrath"). Jesting (*iocosus*), making jokes (*iocus*).

126. Renowned (*inclitus*) is a Greek term, for the Greeks call 'glorious' κλυτός. Illustrious (*inlustris*) is a term for fame, because a person shines in many ways because of the splendor of his family or wisdom or

strength; the opposite of an illustrious person is one of obscure birth. [Suitable (*idoneus*) . . .] 127. Hale (*incolumis*) has its name from column (*columna*), as if upright, strong, and stable. Unfading (*immarcescibilis*), uncorrupted and eternal, because it is without decay (*marcor*) and faintness. Undefiled (*intemeratus*), uncorrupted and violated by no audacity (*temeritas*). 128. Feeble (*infirmus*), because without 'good looks' (*forma*). Weak (*imbecillus*), as if the term were 'without a walking-stick (*baculum*),' fragile and unsteady. Empty (*inanis*), trifling. Fickle (*inconstans*), because such a one is not stable (*stabilis*), but what pleases him in turn displeases him. 129. One is boasting (*iactans*) or arrogant because he is not satisfied with the institutions of his elders but seeks his own individual way of righteousness and sanctity. Wrathful (*iracundus*) is so called because such a one is driven into a fury by inflamed blood, for *ur*[5] means "flame," and wrath (*ira*) inflames. 130. Instigator (*incentor*), because such a one kindles (*incendere*) and inflames. An instigator because such a one fires (*succendere*) the hearts of other people to vice by his wicked suggestions, and inflames them by persuasion. 131. Unforgivable (*inexpiabilis*), because such a one is never forgiven (*expiare*), and would never be exculpated. 'Not praiseworthy' (*inlaudabilis*), not because one has not been praised (*laudare*), but because one has not deserved to be praised. Irate (*iratus*), driven by anger (*ira*).

132. Impious (*impius*), because one is without the piety (*pietas*) of religion. Unjust (*iniquus*) in the strict sense is so called because one is not even-handed (*aequus*), but is unfair (*inequalis*). However, between impious and unjust there is sometimes a difference, in that all impious persons are unjust, but not all the unjust are impious. Thus impious means "not of the faith," and such a one is called impious because he is a stranger to the piety of religion. On the other hand, an unjust person is so called because he is not fair but is stained with wicked works – and this is the case [if] he were to be appraised in the name of Christianity. 133. Enemy (*inimicus*), because not a friend (*amicus*), but an adversary. Now two things make an enemy: deceit and terror. Terror, because they are afraid; deceit, because they have suffered evil. 134. Envious (*invidus*), so called from gazing (cf. *videre*, "see") at the happiness of another person. Enviable (*invidiosus*) is a person who suffers the envy of another. Hated (*invisus*), "odious," so called from envy (*invidia*) and jealousy. 135. Detestable (*intestabilis*), one whose testimony (*testimonium*) is worthless, and what he says would be null and void. Infamous (*infamis*), not of good repute (*fama*). Wicked (*improbus*), so called because he presses hard upon one who is prohibiting (*prohibere*). 136. Importunate (*importunus*), "restless," because such a one has no harbor (*portus*), that is, place of rest – hence importunate people are quickly driven into shipwreck, as it were. Unbridled (*infrenis*), that is, one who is not controlled by a bridle (*frenum*), as (Vergil, *Aen.* 4.41):

> The unbridled (*infrenus*) Numidians.

137. Gnashing (*infrendens*) properly speaking is grinding the teeth against each other. Also grind (*frendere*) means to crush (*frangere*) with the teeth – hence infants not yet having teeth are called *nefrendes*. Gluttonous (*ingluviosus*), so called from the maw (*gula*) and voracity (*voracitas*). 138. Inglorious (*ingloriosus*), because one is without glory (*gloria*), that is, without triumphs. Again, *inglorius*, "not mindful of glory." Unshapely (*informis*), "huge," not that such a one has no proper shape (*forma*), but that he has a great size beyond the shapely. 139. 'Hardened crook' (*inveterator*), because he has much experience 'of long standing' (*vetus*, gen. *veteris*) in evil-doing. Horrible (*immanis*), because not good, but cruel [and] terrible, for *manus* means "good." Hence also by antiphrasis the gods called Manes, in no way good. 140. *Immunis*, "not at all generous (*munificus*)," as in the old proverb, "One's fellow-citizens hate 'anyone who gives nothing' (*immunis*)." Again, *immunis*, one who does not fulfill his duties (*munia*), that is, perform his official function, for he is devoid of any special claim. 141. Indemnified (*indemnis*), because one lives without a penalty (*damnum*), and without any blame or danger. Unskilled (*iners*), "without a craft (*ars*)," and for this reason useless for any work. Unarmed (*inermis*), either "without weapons (*arma*)" or "without strength," for the term 'weapons' [is taken] always to refer to strength. 142. Listless (*ignavus*), "ignorant of the way" (*ignarus viae*), that is, the way of reason and life. Ignorant (*ignarus*), "not knowing (*gnarus*)," that is, unknowing, that is, without a nose (*nares*), for the ancients called knowing "sniffing out." Moreover, *ignarus* means two

5 Lindsay indicates that this term is a corruption. The original may well have been *pur*, transliterating Greek πῦρ, "fire." Cf. also *urere*, "burn."

things: either one who 'knows not' (*ignorare*), or one who is not known. *Ignarus*, one who knows not.

143. Unmindful (*immemor*), one who has forgotten, for such a one has lost his memory (*memoria*). Unknowing (*inscius*), because one is without knowledge (*scientia*). Naive (*idiota*), "an inexperienced person"; the word is Greek (cf. ἰδιώτης, "private person, ordinary person"). Inexperienced (*imperitus*), "without experience (*peritia*)." 144. Ill-advised (*inconsultus*), because such a one does not take counsel (*consilium*). Ill-advised, because without counsel and unaware of things and ignorant. Unsuitable (*ineptus*), the opposite of suitable (*aptus*) and as if the word were *inaptus*. 145. Poor (*inops*), one who is without land, for we understand that land is wealth (*ops*), because it brings wealth by being fruitful. Others understand *inops* to mean "not entombed, unburied," one for whom no empty burial mound has been raised when he dies. 146. Ignoble (*ignobilis*), because such a one is low-born (*ignotus*) and base (*vilis*) and of an obscure family, whose very name is not known. Goatish (*ircosus*, i.e. *hircosus*), because one stinks with the fetid sweat of his body. Low-born (*ignotus*), ignoble (*ignobilis*), or arriving unexpectedly. 147. Unexpected (*improvisus*), so called because one is suddenly present, and not 'seen far before' (*porro ante visus*). Informer (*index*), a betrayer, from 'pointing out' (*indicare*). Indigenous (*indigena*), so called because one is 'from there begotten' (*inde genitus*), that is, born in the same place. 148. Shameless (*impudens*), because shame (*pudor*) and modesty (*pudicitia*) are far from such a one. Shameless (*impudicus*), so called from 'anus' (*podex*), for *putor* means a stench. Incestuous (*incestus*), so called from illicit intercourse – as if the word were *incastus* ("not chaste") – as one who defiles a holy virgin or someone closely related to himself.

149. *Internicida* is one who bears false witness and by it kills (*occidere*) a person. *Infitiator*, "one who denies," because he does not confess (*fateri*) but strives against the truth with a lie. [Impostor (*impostor*) . . .] 150. *Interceptor* (in classical Latin, "usurper"), properly speaking is the name for one of two (*inter duos*) rivals who is removed from public life. 151. Insidious (*insidiosus*), because such a one 'lies in ambush' (*insidiare*), for properly speaking *insidere* (lit. "to occupy") is to await someone guilefully. Hence also ambush (*insidiae*) has its name. Enceinte (*incincta*), that is, without a girdle (*cinctus*), because the enlarged womb does not permit a pregnant woman to be tightly girded. 152. Unmarried (*investis*), that is, 'without a garment (*vestis*),' for such a one does not yet have a *stola*, which is the sign of the marriage of a maiden. Parasite (*iscurra*, i.e. *scurra*), so called because such a one attends on someone for the sake of food (*esca*).

K. 153. *Katholicus*, "universal," a Greek term (i.e. καθολικός). Dear (*karus*) is a Greek term (cf. χάρις, "kindness"), as is *caritas* ("charity") also, whence also *caristia* ("annual family dinner").

L. 154. Distinguished (*luculentus*), because bright (cf. *lux*, gen. *lucis*, "light") in speech and splendid in one's words. Reader (*lector*) is so called from reading (*legere*, ppl. *lectus*), that is, 'running over' (i.e. a text), whence a ship is said to 'run by' (*legere*) whatever it passes. Thus *legere*, "pass by, go by," as (cf. Vergil, *Aen.* 3.127):

> We pass by (*legere*) straits made rough by many lands.

Again, *lector*, from 'gathering' (*colligere*, ppl. *collectus*) with one's mind what one reads, as if the term were *collector* – as in this verse (Vergil, *Ecl.* 3.92):

> You who gather (*legere*) flowers.

155. Prating (*loquax*), not an eloquent (*eloquens*) person. Copious (*laetus*, lit. "happy"), from amplitude (*latitudo*). 'Rich in lands' (*locuples*), as if the term were 'full of estate property' (*locis plenus*) and the owner of many properties, as Cicero teaches in the Second Book of his *Republic* (cf. 16): "And with a great production of sheep and cattle, because then their property consisted of livestock and the possession of places (*locus*), for which reason we have the terms 'wealthy' (*pecuniosus*) and 'rich in lands' (*locuples*)." 156. Generous (*liberalis*), so called because one gives freely (*libenter*) and doesn't grumble. Bountiful (*largus*) . . . Tall (*longus*), so called from line (*linea*), because such a person is stretched out. Long-lived (*longaevus*), as if 'of a long age' (*longum aevum*) and for a long time.

157. Long-suffering (*longanimis*), or great-spirited (*magnanimis*; cf. *animus*, "spirit"), because such a one is disturbed by no passion but suffers all things to be endured. The opposite of this is pusillanimous (*pusillanimis*), petty and not steadfast in any trial. Of this sort it is written (cf. Proverbs 14:17): "The pusillanimous man, extremely foolish." 158. Light-minded (*levis*), so called from the inconstancy of one's wavering, because with a light (*levis*) movement of the mind one desires now this,

now that. Slippery (*lubricus*), because one slips (*labi*). Gliding (*labens*) sometimes means "swift," as (Vergil, *Aen.* 11.588):

> Glide down (*labi*), nymph, from the sky,

and (Vergil, *Aen.* 4.223):

> Glide down (*labi*) on your wings.

For a gliding down is faster than running. 159. Bandit (*latro*), a waylayer, so called from 'hiding' (*latere*). Aelius (i.e. Aelius Stilo, fragment) says, "A *latro* is a *latero* – from the word 'to hide' (*latere*) – a waylayer."[6] *Lanista*, "gladiator," that is, an executioner, so called from the Etruscan language, from 'tear in pieces' (*laniare*), with regard to bodies. 160. Provoker (*lacessitor*), so called with transferred sense from dogs or wild beasts that provoke by 'lacerating' (*lacerare*). Pimp (*leno*), an arranger of lewd practice, because he charms the minds of wretched people and seduces them by cajoling (*delinire*, i.e. *delenire*). Libidinous (*libidinosus*), because one does what 'is pleasing' (*libet*). Libidinous from (the god) Liber, who is [depicted with the body] of a girl. Voluptuous (*luxuriosus*), as if dissolute (*solutus*) with pleasure (*voluptas*); whence also limbs moved from their places are called *luxus* ("dislocated"). Lascivious (*lascivus*), because such a one is loose (*laxus*), that is, dissolute and vain.

161. Panic-stricken (*lymphaticus*), because one fears water (cf. *lympha*, "water"), one whom the Greeks call ὑδροφόβος ("hydrophobic"). In the strict sense *lymphaticus* is the word for one who contracts a disease from water, making him run about hither and thither, or from the disease gotten from a flow of water. But poets now have taken over this term for 'madmen.' 162. [Sluggish (*languidus*) . . .] Wan (*luridus*), because such a one is pallid, so called from 'leather strip' (*lorum*), because one's skin looks like this. Leprous (*leprosus*), so called from the excessive itching (*pruritus*) of mange, whence it should be written with a *p*. 163. One-eyed (*luscus*), one who sees the light (*lux*, gen. *lucis*) only partly, and similarly dim-sighted (*luscitiosus*), one who cannot see in the evening. The ancients called a one-eyed person *cocles*, whence we read that the Cyclopes were called *Coclites* because they are thought to have had a single eye. Washed (*lotus*, the ppl. of *lavare*, "wash"), the same as *lautus*, that is, clean. *Lupa* (lit. "she-wolf"), a prostitute, so called from her rapaciousness, because she seizes wretched people for herself and takes possession of them.

M. 164. The term 'pitying' (*misericors*) is assigned from one's having compassion for another's distress (*miseria*), and from this pity (*misericordia*) is so called, because it makes miserable (*miserum*) the heart (*cor*) of one who grieves over the distress of another. However, this etymology does not apply in every case, because in God there is *misericordia* without any 'misery of heart' (*cordis miseria*). 165. Glorified (*mactus*), 'more advanced' (*magis auctus*) in glory. The word is taken from sacrificial rites, for whenever incense or wine would be poured on a victim they would say, "This bull is *mactus* by wine or incense," that is, the offering is perfected and more advanced. 166. One is called munificent (*munificus*) either because he gives a lot of gifts (*munus*) to someone, or because he fulfills his duty (*munus*), that is, the service that he owes. Thus also 'performing service' (*munifex*), because one undertakes duties. 167. Magnanimous (*magnanimis*), because one has a 'great spirit' (*magnus animus*) and great virtue. Its opposite is pusillanimous (*pusillanimis*). Magnificent (*magnificus*), a term derived from 'doing great things' (*magna facere*). 168. Docile (*mansuetus*), "mild" or "tamed," as if 'accustomed to the hand' (*manu assuetus*). Moderate (*modestus*), so called from measure (*modus*) and temperance (*temperies*), doing something neither too much nor too little. Mild (*mitis*), "gentle and docile," yielding to wickedness and silently enduring injustice, as if the term were *mutus* ("mute"). 169. Mute (*mutus*), because the sound one makes is not words but a lowing (*mugitus*), for such a one sends the breath of his voice through his nostrils, in a kind of lowing. *Memor*, one who keeps something in memory, or one who is kept in memory.

170. Master (*magister*, also meaning "teacher"), "greater in station" (*maior in statione*), for *steron* in Greek means "station."[7] Attendant (*minister*), "lesser in station" (*minor in statione*), or because such a one performs the service that he owes with his hands (*manus*). 171. 'Very great' (*maximus*), 'more distinguished' (*magis eximius*) in merit, age, honor, eloquence, valor, or in

6 Stilo's expression means "from the word 'to hide' (*ob latere*)" rather than "from the word 'side' (*ob latere*, ablative of *latus*)," though Isidore may have understood the latter construction. The preposition *ob* may govern the ablative in Late Latin, but rarely if ever in Stilo's time (second to first century BCE).

7 The word *steron* is scribally corrupt; perhaps compare Greek στήριξις, "fixed position."

everything. Greater (*maior*) . . . Lesser (*minor*) . . . Least (*minimus*), from the number 'one' (*monas*), because there is no other number below it. 172. *Modicus*, "little," but incorrectly; otherwise, "reasonable." Moderate (*moderatus*), from measure (*modus*) and temperance. Moderate (*mediocris*), because a small amount (*modicum*) is sufficient for such a one. 173. A wretch (*miser*) is properly so called because he has lost (*amittere*, perfect *amisi*) all happiness. According to Cicero, however, it properly means "dead": in the *Tusculan Disputations* (1.5) he called dead people 'wretches' because they have already lost their life. Pitiable (*miserabilis*), because one is 'liable to misery' (*miseriae habilis*). 174. Gloomy (*mestus*, i.e. *maestus*), sad by nature, not from circumstances, because it is innate in the spirit and the mind (*mens*, gen. *mentis*), whence the term *mestus*. 175. Indigent (*mendicus*), so called because one has less (*minus*) from which he can 'carry on' (*degere*) life – or, because it was the custom among the ancients for a destitute beggar to close his mouth and extend his hand, as if 'speak with the hand' (*manu dicere*). Liar (*mendax*), one who deceives the mind (*mens*) of another.

176. Malicious (*malignus*), because one carries out a vow or work of malice (*malitia*). Evil (*malus*) is named after black bile; the Greeks call black μέλας. Hence those people are called melancholy (*melancholicus*) who flee human intercourse and are suspicious of dear friends. *Malitiosus*, "worse than evil (*malus*)," because frequently evil. Moreover, from *malus* the comparative is *peior* ("worse, more evil"); from *bonus* ("good, a good person") the comparative is *deterior* ("worse, not as good"). 177. Better (*melior*), so called as if 'softer' (*mollior*); not hard or steely, for a better thing is as if it were softer. Threatening (*minax*, lit. "projecting"), from the look of one's eyes when they gleam madly, so that one seeing them becomes more fearful. Threatener (*minator*) and warner (*monitor*) – but a warner is so called because he announces good things, a threatener, because he announces unfavorable things. 178. Appeaser (*mulcator*), because one flatters (*mulcere*) with charming words in order to change a person's mind. The term is transferred from *mulsum* ("honey-wine"), that is, what is usually taken to soothe a sore throat or a belly filled with impurities. 179. A *metator* is the name for a person who lays out campsites, after the word *metiri* ("to measure"). Lucan (cf. *Civil War* 1.382):

> Let the bold *metator* come into the Hesperian fields.

Effeminate (*mollis*, lit. "soft"), because such a one disgraces the vigor of his sex with his enervated body, and is softened (*emollire*) like a woman (*mulier*).

180. Thin (*macer*), from thinness (*macies*), and 'thinness' from adultery (*moechia*), because immoderate sexual desire makes people thin. Maimed (*mancus*), "lame of hand (*manu ancus*)." 181. Moribund (*moribundus*), "like one dying (*moriri*)," just as *vitabundus* (in classical Latin, "avoiding") means "like one living" (cf. *vita*, "life"). When we say 'about to die' (*moriturus*), the person is indeed about to die, but when we say *moribundus*, he is not actually about to die, but is like a person who is dying. 182. A prostitute (*meretrix*) is so called because she earns (*merere*) a price for an act of lust. Hence also the term 'houses of prostitution' (*meritoria taberna*). Also soldiers are said to earn (*merere*) when they receive their wages. 183. Moron (*morio*) [so called from death (*mors*), because such a one is not lively in intellect]. Mule-driver (*mulio*), so called from mule (*mulus*), because one drives vehicles with them.

N. 184. Noble (*nobilis*), not base (*non vilis*), one whose name and family are recognized. Nubile (*nubilis*), "marriageable" (*ad nubendum habilis*). Nobody (*nemo*), derived from 'human being' (*homo*), that is, *ne homo* ("not a person"), that is, 'no one.' Moreover, 'no one' (*nullus*), as if *ne ullus* ("not any one"). No one, not any one. 185. Worthless (*nihili*) is compounded of *nil* ("not") and *hilum* ("a whit"). Varro says *hilum* means the pith of the giant fennel, which the Greeks call ἀσφόδελος ("asphodel"), and thus we say 'nothing' (*nihilum*) in the same way the Greeks say οὐδὲ γρῦ ("not a bit"; Funaioli 429). 186. Most people distinguish mischievous (*nequam*) from evil (*malus*), reckoning the latter as destructive, the former as trifling, as Munatius says (unidentified fragment): "This youth is mischievous, but he is not evil" – that is, bad in a trifling, not a destructive way. Other people confuse these terms as if both mean the same thing. 187. The ancients would have it that *nequam* is so called because such a one is 'not anything' (*nec quicquam*), that is, because he is nothing. Neither (*neuter*), "neither this nor that," as if one would say *ne uterque* ("not either"). 188. Abominable (*nefarius*), "not worthy of spelt (*far*)"; by this type of food human life was first sustained. [Otherwise, abominable, "not to be spoken of" (cf. *fari*, "speak").] [Rearer (*nutritor*), as if one were an instructor by means of nodding gestures (*nutus*).] Unspeakable (*nefandus*), that is, one who ought not even to be named (cf. *fari*, gerundive *fandus*, "speak").

189. A *nuntius* is [both] "one who 'brings a message' (*nuntiare*)" and "what is announced," that is, ἄγγελος and ἀγγελία ("messenger" and "message"). But *nuntius* as "messenger" is a word of masculine gender, but "that which he announces" is of neuter gender, as *nuntium* and plural *nuntia* with neuter forms. 190. 'Nazarite' (*Nazaraeus*), that is, consecrated to God. Formerly a Nazarite meant one who would not cut his hair, retaining it as holy, and would countenance nothing tainted, abstaining from wine and every intoxicating drink that subverts the mind from its healthy soundness (see Numbers 6:2–5). 191. 'Triflers' (*nugas*, i.e. *nugae*) is a Hebrew term, for so it is used in the prophets, where Zephaniah says (3:18): "The triflers (*nugae*; accusative *nugas*) that were departed from the law (I will gather together)" – so that we have reason to know that the Hebrew language is the mother of all languages. 192. Gossip (*nugigerulus*; cf. *gerere*, "carry"), because such a one is the messenger of scandal. Negligent (*neglegens*), [as if the term were] 'not reading' (*nec legens*). 193. 'Prodigal' (*nepos*), so called from a certain kind of scorpion (i.e. *nepa*) that consumes its offspring except for the one that has settled on its back; for in turn the very one that has been saved consumes the parent; hence people who consume the property of their parents with riotous living are called prodigals. Hence also *nepotatio* means riotous living, by which any belongings are surely consumed. 194. Black (*niger*), as if the word were 'clouded' (*nubiger*), because such a one is not clear but cloaked in darkness. Hence we also call a cloudy day 'foul' (*teter*, i.e. *taeter*).

O. 195. *Orthodoxus*, "of correct renown (*recta gloria*)."[8] Orator (*orator*), so called from mouth (*os*, gen. *oris*), and named from 'complete a speech' (*perorare*), that is, "speak," for to orate (*orare*) is to speak. 196. Obedient (*obaudiens*), from *auris* (ear), because such a one hears (*audire*) the one commanding. Guest (*ospes*, i.e. *hospes*, also meaning "host"), because he brings his 'foot to the door' (*ostio pes*). *Ospes*, "easy to deal with, adaptable, with open door"; from this term also a person is called hospitable (*ospitalis*, i.e. *hospitalis*). 197. Hater (*osor*), "inimical," so called from hatred (*odium*), just as the word 'lover' (*amator*) is from 'love' (*amor*). *Osor* is of common gender. Hateful (*odibilis*), "liable to hatred" (*odium*). *Obsitus*, "besieged" (*obsessus*), that is, surrounded with ambushes (*insidiae*) on all sides. 198. Obscene (*obscenus*), of impure desire, so called from the vice of the Oscans (*Obsci*). Dull (*obtunsus*), "rather sluggish and dense," as if 'battered' (*tunsus*) from every side. Resolute (*obnixus*), "resistant (*contranisus*; cf. *niti*, ppl. *nisus*, 'strive') and liable to struggle." Bound (*obnexus*), because one is tangled in the bonds (*nexus*) of guilt. 199. Charmer (*oblectator*), as if 'with milk (*lac*, gen. *lactis*),' means "with guile," as Terence (*Andria* 648):

> Unless you had cajoled (*lactare*, homophone of *lactare*, "give milk to") me, a lover.

Whence also the verb 'delight' (*oblectare*). Detractor (*obtrectator*), one who is malicious and who by hindering and obstructing doesn't permit someone to advance and become greater. 200. Childless (*orbus*), because one has no children, as if the word were 'with eyes (i.e. 'darlings') missing' (cf. *orbis*, "circle, eye"). Workman (*opifex*), because he 'makes a work' (*opus facere*). Shepherd (*opilio*), ["keeper of sheep (*ovis*)"] ["feeder of sheep," as if *ovilio*].

P. 201. Prudent (*prudens*), as if 'seeing from afar' (*porro videns*). For he is foreseeing, and sees the outcome of uncertain things beforehand. Patient (*patiens*) is so called from 'striking' – for *pavere* (i.e. *pavire*) is "strike" – for such a one is beaten and endures it. 202. Perfected (*perfectus*), one to whom nothing can be added. Among grammarians no comparative degree is added to this word, because if one says "that one is more perfect" the first one will not be perfect. 203. Good-looking (*pulcher*), so called from the appearance of the skin, because that is *pellis* ("skin"); afterwards this word was generalized, for the 'good looks' (*pulchritudo*) of a person are in one's face, as (Vergil, *Aen.* 1.589):

> In face and shoulders like a god,

or in the hair, as (cf. *Aen.* 1.589):

> For indeed (she endowed him with) beautiful hair,

or in the eyes, as (*Aen.* 1.591):

> She endowed his eyes with happy grace,

or in fair skin, as (*Aen.* 1.592):

> The kind of beauty that craftsmen give to ivory,

8 Isidore translates the Greek bases of *orthodoxus* literally: ὀρθός, "straight, correct"; δόξα, "opinion, reputation." Greek ὀρθοδοξία in fact means "right opinion" and *orthodoxus* means "orthodox, of correct belief."

or in features, as (cf. Cicero, *Second Action Against Verres* [2.89]): "The figure and features of the guest delighted you much more," or in tall stature, as Turnus (*Aen.* 11.683):

He turns in their midst, and is a whole head taller.

204. Seductive (*pellax*), from 'enticing' (*pellicere*). *Perspicax* (in classical Latin, "sharp-sighted"), "splendid," because one shines (*perlucere*). [Continuous (*perpetuus*) . . .] Perennial (*perennis*), because 'continuing through the years' (*perpetuus annis*). 205. Protector (*praesul*), because such a one is 'first in caring' (*praeesse sollicitudine*). Overseer (*praepositus*; lit. one 'placed before': *positus*, ppl. of *ponere* + *prae*), so called because he is the administrator and director of underlings and servants. Patrons (*patronus*) are so called from father (*pater*), because they have a fatherly affection for their clients, so that they govern them like fathers. 206. *Paedagogus* (i.e. a slave who took children to school and supervised their behavior) is the person to whom children are assigned. It is a Greek term (i.e. παιδαγωγός, from παῖς, "child"; ἄγειν, "lead"), and it is a compound word because he 'conducts children' (*pueros agere*), that is, he leads them and restrains them in their frisky age. 207. Present (*praesens*), so called because one is 'before the senses' (*prae sentibus*), that is, before the eyes, which are the senses of the body. Superior (*prior*), because one is first (*primus*) in order (*ordo*), and 'first,' as if the word were *praeminens* ("pre-eminent"). [First (*primus*) . . . Last (*postremus*) . . .] 208. Powerful (*potens*), extending (*patere*) widely in one's property; hence also 'power' (*potestas*), because it extends for him in whatever direction he chooses, and no one closes him in, none can stand in his way. 'Very rich' (*praeopimus*), well-supplied with "goods (*opes*) beyond (*prae*) other people." 209. Moneyed (*pecuniosus*): Cicero (*Republic* 2.16; see 155 above) relates that at first those people were so called who had a lot of livestock (*pecunia*), that is, cattle (*pecus*), for so the ancients would call such people. However, gradually, through loose use of the term, the other meaning evolved.

210. Steadfast (*pervicax*) properly means one who 'perseveres to victory' (*ad victoriam perseverare*) in what he sets out to do, for the ancients used the word *vica* for our *victoria*. I think that from this term comes the word for the plant 'vetch' (*vicia*), that is, *victorialis* (i.e. another plant name). 211. Nimble (*pernix*) derives from 'striving through' (*perniti*), that is, "persevering in one's efforts." Others understand it to mean "swift of foot," for *pernicitas* ("swiftness") has to do with feet, as (Vergil, *Aen.* 11.718):

Flashing with swift (*pernix*) feet,

just as *celeritas* ("speed") has to do with wings, as (*Aen.* 3.243):

(Harpies) soaring with speedy (*celer*) flight to the sky.

212. Sluggish (*piger*), as if 'afflicted in the feet' (*pedibus aeger*), for such a one is slow to move forward. The term through usage passed over to apply to the mind. All-night (*pernox*), 'keeping watch at night' (*pervigilans nocte*). [Persevering (*perseverans*) . . .] Stubborn (*pertinax*), "shamelessly hanging on," as if 'holding fast' (*pertinens*). 213. *Petulans* nowadays means "bold-faced" and "saucy," but formerly "cruelly demanding people" and, strictly speaking, the agents of moneylenders who would exact what was owed frequently and harshly, called *petulantes* from pursuing (*petere*).

214. Forward (*procax*), properly the same as 'greedy' (*petax*), for to demand (*procare*) is to seek (*petere*). Hence a suitor for marriage is called *procus*. 215. Prodigal (*prodigus*), "a voluptuary and spendthrift," who 'drives far away' (*porro agere*) everything, and as it were 'throws it away' (*proicere*). Fugitive (*profugus*) properly means one who wanders far from his own land, as if the term were *porro fugatus* ("driven far"). Foreigner (*peregrinus*), one set far from his native country, just as *alienigena* ("born in another country"). 216. Far-flung (*proiectus*), as if 'flung far' (*procul iactatus*) and wide, just as 'he brought forth' (*producere*) is as if 'he brought someone far' (*porro . . . ducere*), and 'he called forth' (*provocare*), as if 'he called someone far' (*porro . . . vocare*). Projecting (*proiectus*), 'thrown out far' (*porro eiectus*) and 'thrust forth' (*proiactatus*), whence also (Vergil, *Aen.* 3.699):

And the projecting (*proiectus*) rocks,

that is, thrust far out (*porro iactatus*). 217. Proscribed (*proscriptus*), one whose goods are openly and publicly listed (*scribere*, ppl. *scriptus*, i.e. for confiscation). Prescript (*praescriptus*) means an order, like the prescripts of jurists. 218. 'Girded up' (*procinctus*), "armed and ready"; whence the term *in procinctu* ("in arms"), that is, when men take up arms for war. *Praecinctus*, because one puts something in front of oneself by which he is girded (*praecingere*). Whence it was said concerning the Lord (cf. John 13:5): "He was girded (*praecinctus*) with a towel, and he washed the feet of his disciples."

219. A raider (*praedo*) is one who invades a foreign province with plundering, called 'raider' from stealing booty (*praeda*), and a raider is someone who possesses booty. Plunderer (*praedator*), that is, the one to whom some of the booty (*praeda*) is owed. 220. Kidnapper (*plagiator*), after the term πλάγιος ("crooked"), that is, "oblique," because he does not attack by a straight path, but by inveigling with guile. Pirates (*pirata*) are plunderers of the sea, so called from their burning of the passing ships that they capture, for πυρά means "fire." 221. Messenger (*pugillator*), because he carries pieces of money from one hand (cf. *pugillus*, "handful") to another. Embezzler (*peculator*), because he steals public money (*pecunia*). Traitor (*proditor*), because such a one discloses (*detegere*). Again, a traitor is a destroyer (*perditor*), as (Vergil, *Aen.* 1.252):

> We are betrayed (*prodere*, here also "ruined") because of the wrath of one.

222. Treacherous (*perfidus*), because fraudulent and without good faith (*fides*), as if 'losing faith' (*perdens fidem*). Perjured (*periurus*), one who 'falsely swears' (*perpere iurare*), that is, swears wrongly. However, the verb form does not have the *r*, as we say *peiuro* ("I perjure") and *deiero* ("I swear"). 223. 'False accuser' (*praevaricator*), an advocate in bad faith, one who neglects things that will be harmful when he prosecutes, or neglects things that will be profitable when he defends, or presents things ineptly or doubtfully, having been corrupted by bribes. Cicero (unidentified fr.): "Why so very perverse (*praevarus*)?" – that is, extremely crooked (*varus*).

224. Seductive (*pellax*), "guileful and false," from 'skin' (*pellis*), that is, 'face,' for such a one smiles on the outside in order to deceive, but bears malice within. Impious (*profanus*), as if the term were *porro a fano* ("far from the sanctuary"), for such a one is not allowed to take part in holy rites. 225. Parricide (*parricida*) is the proper word for someone who kills his own parent (*parens*), although some of the ancients called this a *parenticida* because the act of parricide can also be understood as the homicide (*homicidium*) of anybody, since any 'human being' (*homo*) is the peer (*par*) of another. 226. Persecutor (*persecutor*) is not always understood in a bad sense. From this term also comes 'finished up' (*persecutus*), that is, 'thoroughly followed up' (*perfecte secutus*). 227. A publican (*publicanus*) is one who gathers the public taxes, or one who runs after the lucre of the world through public (*publicus*) business, whence such a one is named. 228. Sinner (*peccator*), so called from concubine (*pelex*, i.e. *paelex*), that is, prostitute, as if the term were 'seducer' (*pelicator*). Among the ancients this term signified only such shameful persons, but afterwards the term passed into use for any wicked person. 229. Prostitutes (*prostituta*), "whores," from their 'sitting in public' (*prosedere*; cf. *proseda*, "prostitute") at flophouses or brothels; such a one is properly called *pelex* in Greek (cf. παλλακίς, "concubine"); in Latin, *concuba*, and so called from *fallacia*, that is, "cunning deceit, guile, and trickery."

230. Crooked (*procurvus*), as if curved (*curvus*) lengthwise. Alarmed (*pavidus*) is one whom agitation of mind disturbs; such a one has a strong beating of the heart, a moving of the heart – for to quake (*pavere*) is to beat, whence also the term *pavimentum* (beaten floor; cf. *pavire*, "ram down").[9] 231. A rustic (*petro*) and a boor (*rupex*) are so named from the hardness of stones (cf. *petra* and *rupes*, both meaning "rock"). Pusillanimous (*pusillanimis*), one with 'very little courage' (*pusillus animus*). Wanton (*petulcus*), so called from 'eagerly desiring' (*appetere*), whence we also call prostitutes *petulcae.* [Long-lived (*productus*) . . .] [Small (*pisinnus*) . . .]

Q. 232. Quaestor (*quaestor*, i.e. a prosecutor), so called from investigating (*quaerere*, ppl. *quaesitus*), as if the term were *quaesitor.* 'Financially successful' (*quaestuosus*) . . . 233. Complaining (*querimoniosus*) . . . Querulous (*querulus*), one who brings a complaint (*querella*). Calm (*quietus*), because such a one is untroubled in his own spirit, troubling no one.

R. 234. Religious (*religiosus*), says Cicero (*On the Nature of the Gods* 2.72), is so called from 're-reading' (*relegere*): one who reconsiders and, so to speak, re-reads the things that pertain to divine worship. They were called religious people from 're-reading' in the same way that fastidious (*elegens*, i.e. *elegans*) is from 'choose' (*elegere*, i.e. *eligere*), caring (*diligens*) from 'care for' (*diligere*),

9 Isidore is treating two verbs as one: *pavere*, "to be in a state of fear," and *pavire*, "to strike." At section 201 above he uses the form *pavere* for *pavire.*

intelligent (*intellegens*) from 'understand' (*intellegere*). 235. A reasoner (*rationator*) is called a great man, because such a one is able to give a reason (*ratio*) for all the things that are considered marvelous. Reviser (*retractator*), one who undertakes something anew, for to revise (*retractare*) means to undertake anew what you have left undone. 236. Reconverting (*resipiscens*, lit. "returning to one's senses"), because such a one recovers (*recipere*) his mind, as if after a period of insanity, or because one who stopped knowing 'knows again' (*resapere*), for he chastises himself for his folly and strengthens his spirit for right living, remaining watchful so as not to relapse. 237. Unexpected (*repentinus*), from sudden (*repens*). *Repens* can be both an adverb (i.e. "suddenly") and a substantive. Robust (*robustus*), "strong, vigorous," so called from the strength of the oak (*roboreus*) tree. Fast (*rapidus*), "swift of foot (*pes*, gen. *pedis*)." Ravisher (*raptor*), because he is a corrupter (*corruptor*), whence also 'raped woman' (*rapta*), because corrupted (*corrupta*).

238. Accused (*reus*), so called from the lawsuit (*res*) in which he is liable, and offence (*reatus*) from *reus*. 'Impeached for state treason' (*reus maiestatis*) was at first the term for one who had carried out something against the republic, or anyone who had conspired with the enemy. It was called 'impeached for state treason' because it is 'graver' (*maius*) to harm one's native country than a single citizen. Afterwards those people were called 'impeached for state treason' who were seen to have acted against the majesty (*maiestas*) of the head of state, or who had conferred unbeneficial laws on the state, or had abrogated beneficial ones. 239. Quarrelsome (*rixosus*), so called from canine snarling (*rictus*), for such a one is always ready to contradict, and delights in strife, and provokes an opponent. Rustic (*rusticus*), because such a one works the countryside (*rus*), that is, the earth.

S. 240. Wise (*sapiens*), so called from taste (*sapor*), because as the sense of taste is able to discern the taste of food, so the wise person is able to distinguish things and their causes, because he understands each thing, and makes distinctions with his sense of the truth. The opposite of this is a fool (*insipiens*), because he is without taste, and has no discretion or sense. 241. Assiduous (*studiosus*) . . . Holy (*sanctus*), so called from an ancient custom, because those who wished to be purified would be touched by the blood (*sanguis*) of a sacrificial victim, and from this they received the name of holy ones (*sanctus*). 242. Honest (*sincerus*), as if the term were 'without corruption' (*sine corruptione*), of which the opposite is dishonest (*insincerus*), "tainted, corrupt." Supreme (*supremus*), "the highest," because it 'rises above' (*supereminere*). Hence we also say, "O Supreme Father." [Agreeable (*suavis*) . . .] Exalted (*sublimis*) is so called after the height of one's esteem, for strictly the term 'exalted' is used for what is on high, as (Vergil, *Aen.* 1.259):

> And you will raise him on high (*sublimis*) to the stars of the sky.

243. Good-looking (*speciosus*), from appearance (*species*) or looks, as beautiful (*formosus*) is from shape (*forma*). Skillful (*sollers*), because one is engaged (*sollicitus*) in a craft (*ars*) and adroit, for among the ancients one who was trained in every good craft would be called skillful. Terence (*Eunuch* 478):

> I will grant that the youth is skillful (*sollers*).

244. Those called the superstitious (*superstitiosus*), says Cicero (*On the Nature of the Gods* 2.72), are those "who would pray and make burnt offerings every day in order that their children might be their survivors (*superstes*)." Busy (*sollicitus*), because such a one is skillful (*sollers*) and quick (*citus*) and restless. Diligent (*sedulus*), a familiar word in Terence, that is, 'without guile' (*sine dolo*); otherwise, assiduous (*assiduus*). 245. 'Comrades' (*sodalis*) is the name for those who regularly convene under one sign (e.g., as of a guild), as if the term were 'persuaders' (*suadentes*). They are also called allies (*socius*) because of their alliance (*societas*) in danger and in work, as if they wore a single kind of shoe (cf. *soccus*, "shoe") and kept to the same track. 246. Stolid (*stultus*), rather dull in spirit, as a certain writer says (Afranius, fragment 416): "I consider myself to be stolid (*stultus*); I don't think myself a fool," that is, with dulled wits, but not with none at all. A stolid person is one who in his stupor (*stupor*) is not moved by injustice, for he endures and does not avenge cruelty, and is not moved to grief by any dishonor. 247. Sluggish (*segnis*), that is, 'without fire' (*sine igni*), lacking native wit – for *se-* means "without" (*sine*), as *sedulus, sine dolo* (see 244 above). Calm (*securus*), as if the term were 'without anxiety' (*sine cura*) – that is, unresponsive, for which reason we take such people as unbeneficial.

248. Stupefied (*stupidus*), "rather often astounded (*stupere*)." Proud (*superbus*), so called because such a one wishes to seem above (*super*) where he is, for one who wishes to pass beyond (*supergredi*) what he is, is proud. 249. A tale-bearer (*susurro*) is so called after the sound of the word (cf. *susurrus*, onomatopoeic, "whispering"), because such a one speaks to someone not face to face but in the ear when gossiping maliciously about another person. 250. Factious (*seditiosus*), one who causes dissension of minds and brings about discord, which the Greeks call διάστασις ("disagreement"). Severe (*severus*), as if 'a true savage' (*saevus verus*); for he maintains justice without mercy. 251. A pretender (*simulator*) is so called from likeness (*simulacrum*), for such a one adopts a semblance (*similitudo*) that is not himself. Persuader (*suasor*) [from persuading (*suadere*) the person whom one wishes to deceive]. 252. [Assiduous (*studiosus*) . . .] 'Minutely thorough' (*scrupulosus*), "of a finely discriminating and rigorous mind," for a *scrupo* (i.e. *scrupus*, "jagged stone") is a rather hard grain of sand. Sacrilegious (*sacrilegus*) is one who 'plucks sacred objects' (*sacra legere*), that is, steals them. A murderer (*sicarius*) is so called because he is armed with weapons in order to perpetrate a crime, for a *sica* is a sword, so called from 'cut' (*secare*). 253. Sinister (*scaevus*), "on the left and perverse," after the term σκαιός ("on the left, ill-omened"), for such a one has a most wicked and cruel temper. Stage-player (*scenicus*), one who performs in a theater, for a theater is a stage (*scena*). Prostitute (*scortum*, also meaning "skin"), because such a one is also called σκῦτος ("skin") in Greek; the skin of those for whom this vice is performed is rubbed by this person.

254. Unclean (*spurcus*), because such a one is impure (*impurus*). *Scelerosus*, "full of wickedness (*scelus*, gen. *sceleris*)" – like a place that is 'full of stones' (*lapidosus*) or 'full of sand' (*arenosus*) – for a *scelerosus* person is worse than a *sceleratus* ("wicked") one. 255. *Sator*, a sower (*seminator*) or father, from seed (*semen*). Parasite (*scurra*), one who usually attends on someone for the sake of food; such a one is called *scurra* from his 'following after' (*sequi*, ppl. *secutus*). Likewise, hanger-on (*assecla*), from *sequi*. Attendant (*satelles*), one who clings to another (*alter*), or guards his side (*latus*). 256. Substitute (*suffectus*), one put in place of another, as if the term were *suffactus* (i.e. *sub* + *factus*, "made under"). Hence we also speak of a consul as *suffectus* when he is substituted for another. 257. Subordinate (*secundus*), because one is 'beside the feet' (*secus pedes*), and the term is derived from servants who follow (*sequi*, ppl. *secutus*) as footmen. Whence fortune is called favorable (*secundus*) because it is 'following after' (*secundus*) us, that is, is near us. Hence also a 'successful affair' (*res secundae*), that is, a prosperous one. The 'after-birth' (*secundae*) is so called from 'following on' (*sequi*).

258. Stipulator (*stipulator*), "a promiser," for *stipulor* is 'promise,' from the terminology of jurists. 259. Healthy (*sanus*), from blood (*sanguis*), because such a one is not pale. [Safe (*sospes*) . . .] Slender (*subtilis*, also meaning "precise"), so called from thinness. 260. A trustee (*sequester*) is so called because he intervenes between disputants; he is called the μέσος ("middle," cf. μεσίτης, "mediator") in Greek, and the disputants deposit pledges with him. The word derives from 'following' (*sequi*), because both parties would follow the trustworthiness of the chosen trustee. 261. Dwarf (*sessilis*), because such a one seems not to stand, but to sit (*sedere*, ppl. *sessum*). Deaf (*surdus*), from the filth (*sordes*) formed out of the humor in one's ear, and although deafness occurs on account of a number of reasons it still keeps the name of the foresaid defect. 262. Dry (*siccus*), because such a one is 'without juice' (*exsucatus*), or by antiphrasis, because he is without 'moisture' (*sucus*). Buried (*sepultus*) is so called because one is 'without a tremor' (*sine palpatione*) or 'without a pulse' (*sine pulsu*), that is, without motion. 263. *Saio* (i.e. an *executor*; see section 91 above; Thompson 1969:142), so called from 'bringing to completion' (*exigere*). Cobbler (*sutor*), named for his stitching (*suere*) hides. Swine-herd (*subulcus*), a herdsman of pigs (cf. *sus*, "swine"), just like a cow-herd (*bubulcus*), from keeping cattle (*bos*).

T. Guardian (*tutor*), one who 'looks after' (*tueri*, ppl. *tuitus*) a pupil, that is, attends (*intueri*) to him, concerning whom there is a common saying, "Why are you scolding me? I buried both my guardian and my school-servant some time ago." 265. Witnesses (*testis*) are so called because they would be used for a testament (*testamentum*); similarly signatories (*signator*), because they sign (*signare*) a testament. 266. Tetricus is a very harsh mountain in the Sabine region – hence we call gloomy people *tetricus*. Taciturn (*taciturnus*), 'being silent for long periods' (*tacere diuturnus*). 267. Arbiter (*trutinator*), an examiner, weighing out true verdicts according to the scales of judgment, derived from *trutina*, which is a pair of scales. 268. Sorrowful (*tristis*) . . . Grasping (*tenax*), too eager for money, because he holds (*tenere*) it fast – sometimes also *pertinax*. 269. [Savage (*truculentus*) . . .] Fierce (*torvus*), "terrible," because such a one has a twisted (*tortus*) face and a disturbing (*turbulentus*) look, as in "fierce lioness," and (Vergil, *Aen.* 3.677):

> We see (the Cyclopes) standing there uselessly with terrible (*torvus*) eye.

270. Violent (*turbidus*), "terrible." Hideous (*teter*, i.e. *taeter*), because of a dark and shadowy life. 'Most savage' (*teterrimus*), for a too beastly person, for the ancients said *teter* for 'beastly,' as Ennius (*Annals* 607): "Hideous (*teter*) elephants." Terrible (*terribilis*), because such a one possesses terror (*terror*) and is feared. 271. Evader (*tergiversator*), because one changes his mind as if 'turning his back' (*tergum vertere*) this way and that, so that it is not easy to understand what condition he is in. Drunk (*temulentus*), so called from 'intoxicating drink' (*temetum*), that is, wine. 272. Fearful (*timidus*), because one 'is afraid for a long time' (*timere diu*), that is, from one's bloody humor, for fear congeals the blood, which when coagulated causes fear. 273. Ugly (*turpis*), because one is ill-shaped and sluggish (*torpere*).

V. 274. Man (*vir*), from strength (*virtus*). Beneficial (*utilis*), from using (*uti*) one's property well, or because a thing can be well used, just as trainable (*docilis*), because such a one can be taught (*docere*). 275. True (*verus*), from truth (*veritas*); hence also *verax* ("truthful"). 'Truth' is prior to 'true,' because truth does not derive from a true person, but a true person from truth. 276. Truthful (*veridicus*), because he 'says a true thing' (*verum dicere*) and is a champion of the truth. 'Having a sense of honor' (*verecundus*), because he respects a true (*verum*) deed. 277. Handsome (*venustus*), "good-looking," from one's veins (*vena*), that is, from blood. [Lively (*viridis*, lit. "green"), full of energy and sap, as if 'youthful with vigor' (*vi rudis*).] [Living (*vivens*), "alive" (*vivus*).] Fickle (*varius*), as if not having one path (*via*), but of unfixed and confused thought. Wily (*versutus*), because in any sort of action one's mind is easily turned (*vertere*, ppl. *versus*) toward some deceit. Hence also craftiness (*versutia*) means "twisted thought." 278. Plautus (*Epidicus* 371):

> [He is] wilier (*versutior*) than a potter's wheel.

279. [Base (*vilis*), from 'farm' (*villa*), because such a one has no urbanity.] Dissembling (*versipellis*, lit. "changing one's skin"), because one changes (*vertere*, ppl. *versus*) into various appearances and mental states. Hence also wily (*versutus*; see 277 above) and cunning. Violent (*violentus*), because one brings force (*vis*) to bear. Mad (*vecors*), having a bad spirit (*cor*) and a bad conscience. Wandering (*vagus*), because without a path (*via*). 280. Vain (*vanus*) derives its etymology from Venus. Again, vain, "empty, false," because one's mindfulness vanishes (*evanescere*). 281. Insane (*vesanus*), not properly sane (*sanus*). *Vinolentus*, one who both drinks a lot and only becomes drunk with difficulty (cf. *vinum*, "wine"; *lentus*, "slow"). Agitated (*vexatus*), that is, 'carried'; *vexo* is from the same root as *veho* and *vecto*, so that *vexasse* means "to have carried." 282. Poisoner (*veneficus*), because one has prepared or furnished or sold poison (*venenum*) as a cause of death. Bearer (*vector*), as if the term were 'conveyor' (*vehitor*); moreover, a *vector* is both one who conveys (*vehere*) and one who is conveyed. 283. Hunter (*venator*), as if the term were *venabulator* (i.e. the user of a *venabulum*, "hunting spear") – from the word 'hunting' (*venatio*) – that is, the hunting of wild animals. There are four roles for hunters: trackers, pursuers, wingmen, and drivers.

Book XI

The human being and portents (De homine et portentis)

i. Human beings and their parts (De homine et partibus eius) 1. Nature (*natura*) is so called because it causes something to be born (*nasci*, ppl. *natus*), for it has the power of engendering and creating. Some people say that this is God, by whom all things have been created and exist. 2. Birth (*genus*) is named from generating (*gignere*, ppl. *genitus*), and the term is derived from 'earth,' from which all things are born, for in Greek 'earth' is called γῆ. 3. Life (*vita*) is named on account of its vigor (*vigor*) or because it holds the power (*vis*) of being born and growing. Whence even trees are said to possess life, because they are generated and grow. 4. Human beings (*homo*) are so named because they were made from the soil (*humus*), just as is [also] said in Genesis (cf. 2:7): "And God created man of the soil of the earth." Incorrectly, the whole human being is named from this term, that is, the whole human being consisting of both substances, the association of soul and body. But strictly speaking, 'human being' is from 'soil.'

5. The Greeks called the human being ἄνθρωπος because he has been raised upright from the soil and looks upward in contemplation of his Creator (perhaps cf. ὤψ, "eye, face, countenance"). The poet Ovid describes this when he says (cf. *Met.* 1.84):

> While the rest of the stooping animals look at the ground, he gave the human an uplifted countenance, and ordered him to see the sky, and to raise his upturned face to the stars.

And the human stands erect and looks toward heaven so as to seek God, rather than look at the earth, as do the beasts that nature has made bent over and attentive to their bellies. 6. Human beings have two aspects: the interior and the exterior. The interior human is the soul [and] the exterior is the body.

7. Soul (*anima*) takes its name from the pagans, on the assumption that it is wind – hence wind is called ἄνεμος in Greek, because we seem to stay alive by drawing air into the mouth. But this is quite clearly untrue, since the soul is generated much earlier than air can be taken into the mouth, because it is already alive in the mother's womb. 8. Therefore the soul is not air, as was believed by some people who were unable to grasp its incorporeal nature. 9. The spirit (*spiritus*) is the same as what the Evangelist calls the 'soul' when he says (John 10:18): "I have the power to lay down my soul (*anima*), and I have the power to take it up again." With regard to the soul of the Lord at the time of his Passion, the aforementioned Evangelist wrote in these words, saying (John 19:30): "And bowing his head, he gave up the spirit (*spiritus*)." 10. What else can "to give up the spirit" be if it is not to lay down one's soul? – for soul is so called because it is alive: spirit, however, is so called either because of its spiritual (*spiritalis*) nature, or because it inspires (*inspirare*) in the body.

11. In like manner the will (*animus*) and the soul (*anima*) are the same, even though soul is characteristic of life, while will is characteristic of intention. Whence the philosophers say that life can continue to exist even without the will, and that the soul can endure without the mind (*mens*) – which is why we use the term 'the mindless' (*amens*). The mind is so called in that it knows; the will, in that it desires. 12. The mind (*mens*) is so called because it is eminent (*eminere*) in the soul, or because it remembers (*meminisse*). This is why one calls 'forgetful people' (*immemoris*) also 'mindless' (*amens*). Because of this, 'mind' is not the word we use for the soul, but for that which is the superior part in the soul, as if the mind were its head or its eye. It is for this same reason also that the human being, due to his mind, is said to be the image of God. Further, all these things are adjoined to the soul in such a way that it is one entity. Different terms have been allotted to the soul according to the effects of its causes. 13. Indeed, memory is mind, whence forgetful people are called mindless. Therefore it is soul when it enlivens the body, will when it wills, mind when it knows, memory (*memoria*) when it recollects, reason (*ratio*) when it judges correctly, spirit when it breathes forth, sense (*sensus*) when it senses something. Will is said to be sense (*sensus*) with regard to what it

senses (*sentire*) – whence also the word 'idea' (*sententia*) derives its name.

14. The body (*corpus*) is so called, because it 'perishes when it disintegrates' (*corruptum perire*). It can be dissolved and it is mortal, and at some point it has to be dissolved. 15. The flesh (*caro*), however, derives its name from creating (*creare*). The male seed is called *crementum* and the bodies of animals and humans are conceived from it. This is also why parents are called creators (*creator*). 16. Flesh is a composite of four elements. Earth is in flesh, air in breath, moisture in blood, fire in the vital heat. Each element in us has its own physical part, something of which must be repaid when the composite dissolves. 17. However, what is meant by flesh and what is meant by a body (*corpus*) are different; in flesh there is always a body, but in a body there is not always flesh, for the flesh is what is alive, and this is a body. A body that is not alive is not flesh. The word 'body' is applied to what is dead after life has departed, or to what has been brought forth without life. Sometimes also there is a body that is alive and yet lacks flesh, like grass or trees.

18. The body has five senses: vision, hearing, smell, taste, and touch. Among these, two become active or inactive, while another two are always receptive. 19. They are called senses (*sensus*), because with their help the soul activates the entire body in a most subtle way with the power of sensation (*sentire*). Hence one speaks of things that are present (*praesentia*), because they are 'before the senses' (*prae sensibus*), just as we call things that are present to our eyes 'before our eyes' (*prae oculis*). 20. Vision (*visus*) is what the philosophers call vitreous humor. There are those who maintain that vision is created from external light in the air, or it is from a luminous inner spirit that proceeds from the brain through thin passages and, after it has penetrated the outer membranes, goes out into the air, where it produces vision upon mixing with a similar substance. 21. And it is called vision (*visus*) because it is more vivid (*vivacior*) than the rest of the senses, and also more important and faster, and endowed with greater liveliness (*vigere*), like memory among the rest of the faculties of the mind. Moreover, it is closer to the brain, from which everything emanates; this makes it so that we say "See!" (*vide*, i.e. imperative from *videre*) even for those stimuli that pertain to other senses, as when for instance we say "See how this sounds," or "See how this tastes," and so on.

22. Hearing (*auditus*) is so called, because it 'draws in' (*aurire*, i.e. *haurire*) voices; that is to say, it catches sounds when the air is reverberating. Smell (*odoratus*) is so called as if it meant 'touched by the smell' (*odoris adtactus*) of the air, for it is activated when the air is touched. So one also says 'olfactory sense' (*olfactus*), because one is 'affected by smells' (*odoribus adficere*). Taste (*gustus*) comes from the word for the throat (*guttur*). 23. Touch (*tactus*) is so called, because it strokes (*pertractare*) and 'makes contact' (*tangere*, ppl. *tactus*), and distributes the power of this sense through all the limbs. Indeed, we examine with the sense of touch what we cannot judge with the rest of the senses. There are two kinds of touch: one that comes from the outside to strike us, and another that originates within, inside the body itself. 24. Each sense has been given its own natural function. Thus, what is to be seen is captured by the eyes, what is to be heard, by the ears; soft and hard things are judged by the sense of touch, flavor by the sense of taste, while smell is drawn in through the nostrils.

25. The primary part of the body is the head (*caput*), and it was given this name because from there all senses and nerves originate (*initium capere*), and every source of activity arises from it. In it, all sensations become evident. Whence it plays the role, so to speak, of the soul itself, which watches over the body. 26. The crown (*vertex*) is the place where the hairs of the head concentrate, and where the hair growth spirals (*vertere*, "turn") – whence it is named. 27. The word 'skull' (*calvaria*) comes from its bones that are bald (*calvus*) through loss of hair, and it is treated as a neuter noun. The occiput (*occipitium*) is the back part of the head, so called as if it were against the 'head-covering' (*capitium*), or because it is the back of the head (*caput*, gen. *capitis*).

28. Hair (*capilli*) is so called as if it came from 'strands belonging to the head' (*capitis pilus*), made so as both to be an ornament, and to protect the brain against the cold and defend it from the sun. 'Strands of hair' (*pilus*) are so called after the skin (*pellis*) from which they grow, just as the pestle (*pilo*, i.e. *pilum*) is so called from a mortar (*pila*), where pigment is ground. 29. A 'head of hair' (*caesaries*) is so called from 'needing to be cut' (*caedere*, ppl. *caesus*); this term is only applied to men, for it is fitting that men have shorn hair, but not women. 30. 'Long hair' (*comae*) in the strict sense of the word is hair that has not been cut, and it is a Greek word, for the Greeks call long hair *caimi*, from being cut, whence

they also say κείρειν for shearing. From this curls (*cirrus*) derive their name as well, which the Greeks call μαλλός. 31. Tresses strictly speaking are characteristic of women. They are called tresses (*crines*) because they are separated (*discernere*) by headbands. Hence also headdresses (*discriminale*) are so called, with which divided tresses are tied up.

32. The temples (*tempus*) are the parts that lie under the cranium on the left and right sides. They are so called because they move and, just like the seasons (*tempus*), they change, due to this mobility, at certain intervals. 33. The word for face (*facies*) comes from 'visible likeness' (*effigies*), for all of the characteristic form (*figura*) of a human being and the ability for every person to be recognized resides in the face. 34. But 'facial expression' (*vultus*) is so called because the inclination (*voluntas*) of the will is displayed by it. The expression changes in various movements according to the will, whence the two terms for the face differ from each other, for while the face refers simply to someone's natural appearance, facial expression reveals what he has on his mind. 35. The forehead (*frons*) derives its name from the eye-sockets (*foramen oculorum*). This, a kind of likeness of the soul, expresses the movement of the mind, whether it is joyful or sad, through its own look.

36. Eyes (*oculus*) are so called, either because the membranes of the eyelids cover (*occulere*) them so as to protect them from the harm of any chance injury, or because they possess a 'hidden light' (*occultum lumen*), that is, one that is hidden or situated within. Among all the sensory organs, they are closest to the soul. Indeed, every indication of the mental state is in the eyes, whence both distress and happiness of the spirit show in the eyes. The eyes are also called lights (*lumen*) because light (*lumen*) emanates from them, either because they hold a light that has been closed up in them from the beginning, or because they reflect light that has been taken from the outside in order to present it to vision. 37. The pupil (*pupilla*) is the middle point of the eye in which the power of vision resides; because small images appear to us there, they are called pupils, since small children are called pupils (*pupillus*, a term for a minor under the care of a guardian). There are many who use the form *pupula*, but it is called *pupilla* because it is pure (*pura*) and unpolluted (*inpolluta*), just like 'young girls' (*puella*). Physiologists say that those who are going to die within three days no longer have the pupils that we see in the eyes, and when the pupils are no longer visible they are surely beyond hope. 38. The circle with which the white parts of the eye are separated from the distinct blackness of the pupil is called the iris (*corona*), because with its roundness it adorns (*ornare*) the edge of the pupil.

39. The eyelids (*palpebrae*) are the sheltering folds of the eyes. Their name comes from palpitation (*palpitatio*), because they are forever in motion. They meet together to renew the power of the gaze with their frequent motion. They are well protected by a barrier of hairs, so that if something were to fall toward the open eyes it would be repelled, and so that, when they are closed in sleep, they may rest hidden, as though under a cover. 40. At the tips of the eyelids, where they touch each other when closed, the hairs growing in an orderly row stand out and serve to protect the eyes, so that they may not easily sustain injury from objects falling into the eye and be hurt, and so as to prevent contact with dust or with some coarser material; by blinking they also soften the impact of the air itself, and thus they cause vision to be precise and clear. 41. Some believe that the word for tears (*lacrima*) comes from an injury of the mind (*laceratio mentis*); others maintain that it is identical with what is called δάκρυον ("tear") in Greek. 42. The upper eyelids (*cilium*) are coverings with which the eyes are concealed; they are so called because they hide (*celare*) the eyes and cover them with a safeguard. The eyebrows (*supercilium*) are so called, because they are 'placed above' (*superponere*) the eyelids (*cilium*); they are furnished with hairs so that they may extend as a protection for the eyes and repel the sweat that flows down from the head. The *intercilium* is the space between the eyebrows that is without hair.

43. The cheeks (*gena*) are the parts underneath the eyes where the beard begins to form, for in Greek 'beard' is called γένειον. They are so called also for this reason, that from the cheeks the beard begins to grow (*gignere*, ppl. *genitus*). 44. The cheekbones are the parts that protrude under the eyes, set below them for their protection. They are called cheekbones (*mala*; cf. *malum*, "apple") either because they protrude under the eyes in a rounded shape, which the Greeks called μῆλον ("apple," also "cheek"), or because they are above the jaws (*maxilla*). 45. The word jaws (*maxilla*) is a diminutive of cheekbone (*mala*), just as peg (*paxillus*) is derived from stake (*palus*) and small cube (*taxillus*) from large die (*talus*). The mandibles (*mandibulae*) are parts of the jaws, from

which they also take their name. The ancients named the beard (*barba*) that which pertains to men (*vir*) and not to women.[1]

46. The ear (*auris*) owes its name to the fact that it draws in (*aurire*, i.e. *haurire*, "drink in") sounds, whence Vergil also says (cf. *Aen.* 4.359):

> He drank in with these ears (*auribus ausit*) his words.

Or it is because the Greeks called the voice itself αὐδή, from 'hearing' (*auditus*); through the change of a letter ears (*auris*, pl. *aures*) are named as if the term were *audes*. Indeed, the voice makes a sound when it rebounds through the curvature of the ears, whereby the ears receive the sense of hearing. The highest part of the ear is called *pinnula* from its pointedness, for the ancients used to call a point *pinnus*, whence also we get the words for 'two-headed axe' (*bipinnis*) and feather (*pinna*).

47. Nostrils (*naris*, ablative *nare*) are so called, because through them odor and breath ceaselessly 'swim' (*nare*), or because they warn us with odor, so that we 'know' (*noscere*, with forms in *nor-*) and understand something. Hence the opposite: those who do not know anything and who are unrefined are called ignorant (*ignarus*). Our forefathers used the word for 'smelling something' (*olfacere*) to mean knowing (*scire*), as in Terence (cf. *The Brothers* 397):

> And would they not have 'sniffed it out' (*olfacere*) six whole months before he started anything?

48. Because it is equal in its length and its curvature, the straight part of the nose is called the column (*columna*); its tip is *pirula*, from the shape of the fruit of a pear-tree (*pirus*); the parts to the left and right are called 'little wings' (*pinnula*), from similarity to wings (*ala*; cf. *pinna*, "feather"), and the middle part is called *interfinium*.

49. The mouth (*os*) is so called, because through the mouth as if through a door (*ostium*) we bring food in and throw spit out; or else because from that place food goes in and words come out. 50. The lips (*labia*) are so called from licking (*lambere*). The upper lip we call *labium*, the lower – because it is thicker – *labrum*. Others call the lips of men *labra*, the lips of women *labia*. 51. Varro is of the opinion that the tongue (*lingua*) was given this name because it binds (*ligare*) food together (Funaioli 433). Others think that this is because it binds together words from articulated sounds, for, just as the plectrum strikes upon strings, so also the tongue strikes against the teeth and makes a vocal sound.

52. Teeth (*dens*, plural *dentes*) the Greeks call ὀδόντες, and from there the word seems to have been introduced into Latin. The first of these are called incisors (*praecisor*) because they bite beforehand (i.e. as if 'pre-incise') into everything ingested. The next in line are called canines (*caninus*), two of which are in the right jaw and two in the left. And they are called canines because they resemble dogs' teeth, and dogs crush bones with them, as does a human being; so that what the teeth in front cannot cut they pass on to these, so that they may break it apart. The common people call these *colomelli* (cf. *columella*, "column") due to their length and roundness. The last ones are the molars (*molaris*), which break up what has been bitten off and crushed by the teeth in front and grind (*molere*) it and mush it; whence they are called molars. 53. From the number of teeth one can tell apart the sexes, for in men there are more, in women fewer.

54. The gums (*gingiva*) derive their name from producing (*gignere*) teeth. However, they were also created as decoration for the teeth, for if the teeth existed without cover, they would cause horror rather than being considered an ornament. 55. Our palate is placed, like the heavens, above, and thence palate (*palatum*) is derived from sky (*polus*). In the same vein the Greeks call the palate οὐρανός ("palate, vault of the sky"), because, due to its concave shape, it bears a resemblance to the sky.

56. The throat (*fauces*) gets its name from pouring forth (*fundere*) voices, or else because with its help we 'speak voices' (*fari voces*). The windpipe (*arteria*) is so called either because by its means air (*aer*), that is, breath, is conducted from the lungs, or else because it retains the vital breath in tight (*artus*) and narrow passageways, whence it emits the sounds of the voice. These sounds would all sound alike if the movement of the tongue did not cause a modulation of the voice. 57. In the Gallic language *toles* (cf. classical Latin *toles*, "goiter") – what in the diminutive are commonly called tonsils (*tusilla*, i.e. *tonsilla*) – is the name for the part in the throat that often swells up (*turgescere*). The chin (*mentum*) is so called, because from there the jaws (*mandibula*) begin – that is, because there they are joined together.

1 Here and elsewhere Isidore's observation indicates that the distinction between the sounds *b* and *v* has been lost. See for example 76 below.

58. The gullet (*gurgulio*) derives its name from the throat (*guttur*), whose passageway extends to the mouth and nose. It has a path along which the voice is sent to the tongue, so that it can articulate the sounds of words. Whence we also say 'chatter' (*garrire*). 59. The esophagus (*rumen*) is very close to the gullet; through it food and drink are swallowed. Because of this, animals that bring food back to the mouth and chew it again are said to ruminate (*ruminare*). The epiglottis (*sublinguium*) is a covering of the gullet, a kind of small 'tongue' (*lingua*), which opens or closes the aperture of the tongue.

60. The neck (*collum*) is so called, because it is rigid and rounded like a column (*columna*), carrying the head and sustaining it as if it were a citadel. Its front is called the throat (*gula*), its back, the nape (*cervix*). 61. The nape (*cervix*), however, is so called, because through this part the brain extends to the marrow of the spinal cord, as if it were the 'path of the brain' (*cerebri via*). In former times only the plural, *cervices*, was used; Hortensius was the first who used the singular word *cervix*. Nevertheless, *cervix* in the singular refers to the part of the body, while in the plural it often means 'arrogance' (*contumacia*). Thus Cicero says in the *Second Action Against Verres* (5.110): "Would you accuse a praetor? Break his *cervices*!"

62. We say shoulder (*humerus*, i.e. *umerus*), as if the word were the 'forequarter of an animal' (*armus*), to distinguish humans from mute animals, so that we say human beings have shoulders, whereas animals have forequarters, for forequarters in the proper sense belong to quadrupeds. The highest part in the back of the human shoulder is called *ola*. 63. The arms (*bracchium*) derive their name from strength: for βαρύς in Greek means "heavy and strong." In the arms is the brawn of the upper arms (*lacertus*), and there the marked strength of the muscles is located. This is called the brawn, that is, the muscles (*musculus*): and they are called the brawn (*torus*) because at that place the sinews seem to be twisted (*tortus*). 64. The elbow (*cubitum*) is so called, because we recline on it (*cubare*) in order to eat. According to some, the *ulna* is an extension of either hand (i.e. the forearm), according to others, it is the elbow – and this is more accurate, because in Greek ὤλενος (i.e. ὠλένη) means "elbow."

65. The underarms (*subbracchium*) are called 'armpits' (*ala*, lit. "wing"), because from them the movement of the arms originates in the manner of wings. Some call the armpit *ascilla* (i.e. *axilla*), because from there the arm is raised (*cellere*), that is, moved; similarly also a 'small mask' (*oscillum*) is so called, because 'a face swings' (*os . . . cillatur*), that is, is moved, for *cillere* means "move."[2] There are those who call the armpit *subhircus*, because in many humans they give off the foul odor of goats (*hircus*).

66. The hand (*manus*) is so called because it is in the service (*munus*) of the whole body, for it serves food to the mouth and it operates everything and manages it; with its help we receive and we give. With strained usage, *manus* also means either a craft or a craftsman – whence we also derive the word for wages (*manupretium*, lit. "hand-price"). 67. The 'right hand' (*dextra*) is so called from 'giving' (*dare*), for it is given as a pledge of peace. It is clasped as a sign of good faith and of greeting; and this is the sense in Cicero *Against Catiline* 3.8: "At the command of the Senate I gave a pledge of protection," that is, his right hand. Whence also the Apostle [says (Galatians 2:9): "They gave their right hands to me"]. 68. The 'left hand' (*sinixtra*, i.e. *sinistra*) is so called as if the word were derived from 'without the right hand' (*sine dextra*), or as if it 'permitted' something to happen, because *sinixtra* is derived from 'permitting' (*sinere*). 69. The hand with outstretched fingers is called palm (*palma*); when they are clenched, it is called fist (*pugnus*). 'Fist' is derived from 'handful' (*pugillus*), just as 'palm' is derived from the extended branches of the palm tree (*palma*).

70. The fingers (*digitus*) are so called, either because there are ten (*decem*) of them, or because they are connected handsomely (*decenter*), for they combine in themselves both the perfect number and the most appropriate order. The first finger is called thumb (*pollex*), because among the rest it prevails (*pollere*) in strength and power. The second is the index (*index*) finger, which is also called the 'greeter' (*salutaris*) or 'pointer' (*demonstratorius*), because we usually greet someone (*salutare*) or point something out (*ostendere*) with it. 71. The third finger is called 'immodest' (*impudicus*), because often the censuring of a shameful action is expressed by it. The fourth is the ring (*anularis*) finger, because it is the one on which the ring (*anulus*) is worn. It is also called medical (*medicinalis*), because physicians (*medicus*) use it to scoop up ground eye-salves. The fifth is called *auricularis*, because we use it to scrape out the ear (*auris*).

2 In Vergil's *Georgics oscilla* are little masks hung on trees to ensure the fertility of vines.

72. The nails (*ungula*) we call by this name from the Greek, for they call a fingernail ὄνυξ.

The torso (*truncus*) is the middle part of the body from the neck to the groin. Nigidius says of it (fr. 108): "The head is held up by the neck, the torso is sustained by the hipbones, the knees, and the legs." 73. The Greeks called the front of the torso from the neck to the stomach the *thorax*; this is what we call the chest (*arca*), because in that place is a hidden (*arcanus*), that is, a secret thing, from which other people are shut out (*arcere*). From this both a strong box (*arca*) and an altar (*ara*) derive their names, as if the words meant 'secret things.' The protruding, fleshy parts of the chest are called the breasts (*mamilla*), and between them the bony part is the *pectus*, and what is to its right and left are the ribs (*costa*). 74. It is called *pectus*, because it is 'flattened down' (*pexus*) between the protruding parts, the breasts. The word comb (*pecten*) is also derived from this, because it makes the hair flattened down. The breasts (*mamilla*) are so called, because they are as round as cheeks (*mala*); it is a diminutive term.

75. The nipples are the tips of the breasts, which nursing infants grasp. And they are called nipples (*papilla*) because it appears as if infants were eating (*pappare*) them while they suck milk. The breast (*mamilla*) is accordingly the whole protrusion of the female breast, the nipple only the small part from which milk is drawn. 76. The female breasts (*uber*) are so called, either because they are abundant (*ubertus*) with milk, or because they are moist (*uvida*), that is to say, filled with the liquid of the milk as if they were grapes (*uva*). 77. Milk (*lac*) derives the meaning of its name from its color, because it is a white liquid: for in Greek λευκός means "white." It becomes what it is through a transformation of blood, for after birth, if any blood is not consumed as nourishment in the womb, it flows along a natural passageway to the breasts and, whitened due to their special property, it takes on the quality of milk.

78. The skin (*cutis*) is that which is outermost in the body, so called because in covering the body it is the first to suffer from an incision, for in Greek, κυτις means "incision."[3] It is also called *pellis* (i.e. another word for "skin"), because it repels (*pellere*) external injuries from the body by covering it, and it endures rain, wind, and the fierce heat of the sun. 79. *Pellis*, however, is the word used for skin soon after stripping, while skin that has been treated is called 'hide.' It is called hide (*corium*) by derivation from flesh (*caro*), because flesh is covered by it, but properly speaking the word is used in reference to brute beasts. 80. The word for the pores (*porus*) of the body is Greek – these in Latin properly are called air-passages (*spiramentum*), because through them the enlivening breath (*spiritus*) is supplied from the outside. 81. *Arvina* is the fat that adheres to the skin. A 'fleshy part' (*pulpa*) is flesh without fat, so called because it pulsates (*palpitare*): for it often quivers. Many also call it *viscus* ("flesh"; cf. the homophone *viscus*, "birdlime") because it is sticky.

82. The limbs (*membrum*) are the parts of the body. The joints (*artus*), with which the limbs are connected, are so called from 'drawing together' (*artare*). 83. The sinews (*nervus*) are so called through a derivation from the Greek, as they call a sinew νεῦρον. Others believe that 'sinews' comes from Latin, because the connections of the joints attach (*inhaerere*) to them each in turn. But this much is certain: the sinews constitute the greatest part of the substance of strength, for the thicker they are, the more they are disposed to augment strength. 84. The joints (*artus*) are so called because, being bound to each other by the tendons, they are 'drawn together' (*artare*), that is, they are bound tight. The diminutive form of *artus* is *articulus*; we use the word *artus* in reference to main limbs, like the arms, but the word *articulus* in reference to minor limbs like the fingers. 85. The heads of the bones are called *compago*, because they hold together through being connected (*compingere*, ppl. *compactus*) with sinews as if with a kind of glue.

86. The bones (*os*, gen. *ossis*) are the firm parts of the body. They support all postures of the body and give it strength. The bones are so called from burning (*urere*, ppl. *ustus*), because they would be cremated by the ancients; or, as others believe, from mouth (*os*), because there they are visible, while in the rest of the body they are hidden, covered by skin and flesh. 87. 'Bone marrow' (*medulla*) is so called, because it moistens (*madefacere*) the bones, for it supplies fluid and strengthens them. The *vertibulum* is the end point of a bone, rounded in a thicker knot; it is so called because it is turned (*vertere*) when the limb is bent. 88. Cartilage consists of soft bones without bone marrow, the kind that the ear, the septum, and the ends of the ribs have, or also the covering of bones, which moves. And it is called cartilage

3 A Greek word κυτις is not otherwise known. Latin *cutis* is in fact cognate with Greek σκῦτος, "skin, hide"; κύτος, "hollow, vessel."

(*cartilago*) because it 'lacks pain' (*carere dolorem*) when flexed, because of reduced friction.

89. Some believe that the ribs (*costa*) are so called because the interior parts are guarded (*custodire*) by them and the whole soft region of the belly, encased by them, is protected. 90. The side (*latus*) is so called, because it is hidden (*latere*) when we are lying down; it is also the left (*laeva*) part of the body. The movement of the right side is more readily controlled, while the left is stronger and better suited to carrying heavy loads. Whence the left side is also so called because it is more apt at lifting (*levare*) something and at carrying it. This same left side carries the shield, the sword, the quiver, and the remaining load, so that the right side may be unhampered for action. 91. The back (*dorsum*) extends from the neck down to the loins. It is so called because it is a rather hard (*durior*) surface of the body, like a stone, strong both for carrying and for enduring things. 92. The back (*tergum*) is so called because when we lie on the ground (*terra*) we are stretched out on our backs – something that only a human being can do, for dumb animals all lie down either on their bellies or on their sides. This is also why we speak incorrectly of the *tergum* in animals.

93. The shoulder-blades (*scapula*) . . . The *interscapilium* is so called because it is situated between the shoulder-blades, whence its name. 94. The *palae* (lit. "spades," hence another word for 'shoulder-blades') are the prominent parts on the left and on the right side of the back, so called, because we pin them down in wrestling; the Greeks call wrestling πάλη. 95. The spine (*spina*, also meaning "thorn") is the backbone (*iunctura dorsi*, "linkage of the back"), so called because it has sharp spurs; its joints are called vertebrae (*spondilium*) on account of the part of the brain (i.e. the spinal cord) that is carried through them via a long duct to the other parts of the body. 96. The 'sacred spine' (*spina sacra*) is the lowest part of the spinal column; the Greeks call it ἱερὸν ὀστοῦν, because it is the first bone which is formed when a child is conceived, and for this reason it was the first part of a sacrificial animal that would be offered by the pagans to their gods – whence it is called 'sacred spine.'

97. Varro says that the kidneys (*renes*) are so called because they produce a stream (*rivus*) of filthy liquid (Funaioli 448), for blood vessels and marrow exude a fine liquid into the kidneys; this liquid in turn flows down from the kidneys, released by the heat of sexual intercourse. 98. The loins (*lumbus*) derive their name from wantonness of desire (*libido*), because in males the cause of bodily pleasure is located there, just as in women it is in the navel. Whence it is also said in the beginning of the speech addressed to Job (38:3): "Gird up thy loins (*lumbus*) like a man," so that there would be a preparation for resistance in the very loins in which the occasion for overpowering lust customarily arises. 99. The navel (*umbilicus*) is the center of the body, so called because it is 'a protuberance of the belly' (*umbus iliorum*). Whence also the place in the middle of a shield is called a 'boss' (*umbo*), from which it hangs, for the infant hangs from it in the uterus and it is also nourished from it.

100. The private parts (*ilium*, i.e. *ilia*) are referred to with a Greek word, because there we cover ourselves up, for in Greek *ilios* (i.e. εἰλύειν) means "cover up." 101. The buttocks (*clunis*) are so called, because they are situated next to the colon (*colum*), that is, to the large intestine (*longao*). The nates (*natis*) are so called because we support ourselves (*inniti*) with them when we are seated. Hence also the flesh is bunched up in them, so that the bones may not hurt from the heavy weight of the body when it presses down. 102. The parts of the body called genitals (*genitalia*) receive their name, as the word itself shows, from the begetting (*gignere*, ppl. *genitus*) of offspring, because with them one procreates and begets. They are also known as 'organs of modesty' (*pudenda*) on account of a feeling of shame (cf. *pudor*, "shame"), or else from 'pubic hair' (*pubis*), whence they are also hidden with a garment. However, they are also called the 'indecent parts' (*inhonestus*), because they do not have the same kind of comeliness as limbs that are placed in open view.

103. For the genitals the word *veretrum* is also used, either because it is applied to 'males only' (*vir tantum*), or because from them sperm (*virus*) is secreted. Properly speaking, *virus* is used to refer to the liquid that flows from the male organs of generation. 104. The word for 'testicles' (*testiculus*) is a diminutive form of *testis* ("testicle"), of which there are always at least two. They supply sperm via a reed-shaped conduit, and both the kidneys and loins receive sperm from the spinal cord for the sake of procreation. The scrotum (*fiscus*, lit. "purse") is the skin that contains the testicles. 105. The hind-parts (*posteriora*) are certainly so called because they are on the

backside and on the opposite side from the face, so that while we purge the bowels we may not defile the sense of sight. The anus (*meatus*) is so called because excrement passes (*meare*) through it, that is, it is discharged.

106. The thighs (*femur*) are so called, because the male sex differs from the female (*femina*) with respect to this part. They extend from the groin to the knees. By derivation, the *femina* (i.e. a plural form of *femur*) are the parts of the thighs with which we cling to the backs of horses when riding. Hence formerly a warrior was said to lose his horse from underneath his *femina* (i.e. when his horse was slain). 107. The hips (*coxa*) are so called, as if the word were 'conjunction of axes' (*coniuncta axis*); the thighs are moved by them. Their concave parts are called *vertebra*, because in them the heads of the thighs are turned (*vertere*). The knees (*suffrago*, usually a quadruped's "hock"), because they are 'broken off underneath' (*subtus frangere*), that is, they bend underneath, not on the upper side, as in the arms.

108. The knees (*genu*) are points where thighs and shins meet; and they are called *genua* because *in utero* they are situated opposite the eye-sockets (*gena*). There they cling to each other, and they are co-engendered with the eyes as signs of tearfulness and an appeal for pity.[4] In this way *genu* is named after *gena*. 109. Thus, when a human being is folded together in the process of gestation and taking shape, the knees are raised up, and with their help the eye-sockets are formed, so that they may become hollow and recessed. Ennius (Courtney fr. 41) writes:

> And the eye-socket (*gena*) presses close to the knees (*genua*).

This is the reason why people are immediately moved to tears when they fall on their knees, for nature wanted them to remember the womb of the mother, where they sat in darkness, so to speak, before they came to the light (cf. Matthew 4:16).

110. The shins (*crus*, gen. *crura*) are so called, because with their help we run (*currere*) and take steps (*gressus*). They extend from below the knees to the calves (*sura*). The tibias (*tibia*) are so called as if the word were 'trumpets' (*tuba*), for they are similar in length and shape. 111. The ankle (*talus*) is so called from *tolus* (i.e. *tholus*), for a *tolus* is a protruding roundness; whence also the dome of a round temple is called a *tolus*. The ankle is situated beneath the shins and above the heel. 112. The feet (*pes*, gen. *pedis*) are assigned a name from Greek etymology, for the Greeks call those parts πόδες, and they move forward set on the earth in alternating motion.

113. The soles (*planta*) have their name from flatness (*planities*), because they are not of a round shape, as in quadrupeds – otherwise the two-legged human being could not stand upright – but instead are of a flat (*planus*) and elongated shape, so that they may stabilize the body. The frontal parts of the soles consist of many bones. 114. The back part of the soles is called the heel (*calcis*, i.e. *calx*); the name was imposed on it by derivation from 'hardened skin' (*callum*), with which we tread (*calcare*) on the earth (cf. *solum*, "soil"); hence also *calcaneus* (i.e. another word for 'heel'). 115. The sole (*solum*) is the lower part of the foot, so called because with it we impress footprints in the earth. But anything that sustains something is called a *solum*, as if it were derived from 'solid ground' (*solidum*); whence the ground is also called 'soil' (*solum*), because it sustains everything; and the sole of the foot is so called, because it carries the entire weight of the body.

116. We say *viscera* not only for the 'intestines,' but also for whatever is under the skin, from the word *viscus* (i.e. the tissue under the skin), which is located in between the skin and the flesh. The *viscera* are also called 'vital organs' (*vitalia*), namely the places surrounding the heart (*cor*), as if the word were *viscora*, because in that place life (*vita*), that is, the soul, is contained. 117. Likewise the endings of the sinews, made of sinews and blood joined together, are called *viscera*. Likewise muscles (*lacertus*) are otherwise known as 'mice' (*mus*), because in the individual limbs they take the 'place of the heart' (*locus cordis*), just as the heart itself is in the center of the whole body, and they are called by the name of the animals they resemble that lurk under the earth, for muscles (*musculus*) are so called from their similarity to mice.[5] Muscles are also called brawn (*torus*), because there the innards appear to be twisted (*tortus*).

118. The word 'heart' (*cor*) is either derived from a Greek term, because they call it καρδία, or from care (*cura*), for in it resides all solicitude and the origin of knowledge. It is next to the lungs, so that, when anger is

4 Knees (in kneeling) and eyes (in weeping) both can signal a need for mercy.

5 The word *musculus* ("muscle") does indeed derive from *mus* ("mouse"), from the look of the movement of a muscle like the biceps. Cf. Greek μῦς, "mouse, muscle".

kindled, it may be moderated by the fluid of the lungs. It has two arteries (*arteria*), of which the left one has more blood, the right one more air – for this reason we examine the pulse in the right arm. 119. The *praecordia* are places close to the heart in which sensation is perceived; and they are called *praecordia* because the origins (*principium*) of the heart (*cor*, also meaning "the seat of understanding" – see 127 below) and of deliberating thought (*cogitatio*) are to be found there. 120. The pulse (*pulsus*) is so called because it throbs (*palpitare*); from what it indicates we understand whether someone is ill or in good health. Its motion is two-fold: either simple or composite. It is simple when it consists of one beat, composite when it consists of several irregular and unequal motions. These motions have fixed intervals: a dactylic rhythm, as long as they are healthy, but they are a sign of death when they are quite fast – as in δορκαδάζοντες (lit., "swift as a gazelle") – or quite slow – as in μυρμίζοντες (lit., "weak as ants").

121. The 'blood vessels' (*vena*) are so called because they are passageways (*via*) for the flowing (*natare*) blood and conduits (*rivus*) spreading throughout the body, with which all limbs are supplied with fluid. 122. Blood took its name from a Greek etymology, because it is animated, strengthened, and alive (perhaps cf. ζάειν, "live"). It is called 'blood' as long as it is in the body, 'gore' when it is shed. Gore (*cruor*) is so called because once it has been shed it 'runs away' (*decurrere*), or because in running (*currere*) it falls (*corruere*). Others interpret 'gore' as corrupted (*corrumpere*) blood, which is secreted. Still others say that blood (*sanguis*) is so called, because it is sweet (*suavis*). 123. Blood, however, is untainted only in young people, for physiologists say that blood diminishes with age – hence also old people have a tremor. Properly speaking, however, blood is possession of a soul. Hence women will lacerate their cheeks in grief, and crimson robes and crimson flowers are offered to the dead.

124. 'Lung' (*pulmo*) is a word derived from Greek, for the Greeks call the lung πλεύμων, because it is a fan (*flabellum*) for the heart, in which the πνεῦμα, that is, the breath, resides, through which the lungs are both put in motion and kept in motion – from this also the lungs are so named. Now, in Greek πνεῦμα means "breathing," which, by blowing and exhaling, sends the air out and draws it back. The lungs are moved through this, and they pump, both in opening themselves, so that they may catch a breath, and in constricting, so that they may expel it. The lungs are the pipe-organ of the body.

125. The liver (*iecur*) has this name because there the fire (*ignis*) that flies up into the brain (*cerebrum*) has its seat. From there this fire is spread to the eyes and to the other sense organs and limbs, and through its heat the liver converts the liquid that it has drawn to itself from food into blood, which it furnishes to individual limbs for sustenance and growth. Those who debate medical questions also maintain that the liver is the seat of pleasure and desire. 126. The lobes of the liver are its edges, resembling the edges of chicory leaves, or tongues that stick out. They are called 'lobes' (*fibra*) because among the pagans they were carried by the soothsayers in their sacred rites to the 'altars of Phoebus' (*Phoebi ara*), so that after the lobes were offered and set on fire the soothsayers might receive the god's responses.

127. The spleen (*splen*) is so called from filling in (*supplementum*) a place opposite to the liver, so that there may not exist an empty space. Some are also of the opinion that it was made for the sake of laughter, for we laugh thanks to the spleen, are angry thanks to the gall-bladder, have knowledge thanks to the heart, and love thanks to the liver. When these four elements come together, the living creature is complete. 128. The 'gall bladder' (*fel*) is so called because it is a small sack (*folliculus*) producing a liquid that is called bile (*bilis*). In Greek, the stomach (*stomachus*) is called 'mouth,' because it is the gateway of the belly, and it receives food and passes it on to the intestines.[6]

129. The intestines (*intestina*; cf. *intestinus*, "inward") are so called because they are confined in the interior (*interior*) part of the body; they are arranged in long coils like circles, so that they may digest the food they take in little by little, and not be obstructed by added food. 130. The caul (*omentum*) is a membrane that contains the greater part of the intestines; the Greeks call it ἐπίπλοον. The diaphragm (*disseptum*, i.e. *dissaeptum*) is an inner organ that separates the belly and the other intestines from the lungs and the heart. 131. The cecum (*caecum*, "blind gut") is an intestine without opening or outlet; the Greeks call it τυφλὸν ἔντερον ("blind gut"). The jejunum (*ieiuna*, i.e. *ieiunum*) is a thin intestine, whence also the word 'fasting' (*ieiunium*). 132. The belly, the bowels,

6 Greek στόμα means "mouth," στομάχος, "gullet." Latin *stomachus* can mean "gullet," more commonly, "stomach."

and the womb are distinct from each other. The belly is what digests food that has been taken in, is visible from the outside, extends from the chest to the groin and is called belly (*venter*) because it causes life's nutriments to pass through the whole body. 133. The bowels constitute the part that receives the food and is purged. Sallust writes (*Histories* 1.52): "Pretending to himself that his bowels (*alvus*) were being purged." And they are called 'bowels' (*alvus*) because they are cleansed (*abluere*), that is, purged, because fecal filth flows out from them.

134. The womb (*uterus*) is something only women have and in which they conceive; in shape it is similar to a small stalk. Nevertheless there are many authors who like to use *uterus* for the belly of either sex – not only poets, but also other writers. 135. However, it is called *uterus* because it is two-fold and divides on both (*uterque*) sides, into two parts that extend apart and bend back in the shape of a ram's horn; or because it is filled with the fetus within (*interius*). Hence also 'leather bag' (*uter*), because it contains something inwardly (*intrinsecus*), namely the limbs and the viscera. 136. The word 'paunch' (*aqualiculus*), however, is properly used only in reference to a pig, and was transferred metaphorically to the belly (*venter*). The matrix (*matrix*) is so called, because the fetus is engendered in it, for it fosters the received semen, gives a body to what is fostered and differentiates the limbs of that which has been given a body. 137. The vulva (*vulva*) is so called as if the word were 'folding-door' (*valva*), that is, the door of the belly, either because it takes up semen or because the fetus emerges from it.[7] The bladder (*vesica*) is so called, because it is filled with urine collected from the kidneys as a 'vessel' is filled up with 'water' (*vas . . . aqua*), and it is swollen by the liquid. Birds do not have this function.

138. Urine (*urina*) is so called, either because it burns (*urere*), or because it comes out of the kidneys (*renes*). By its indications are shown future health and sickness. This liquid is called 'piss' (*lotium*) by the common people, because with its help clothes are washed (*lavere*, ppl. *lotus*), that is, cleaned. 139. Seed (*semen*) is what is 'taken up' (*sumere*) by either the earth or the uterus after it is cast, so that either a plant or a fetus may grow from it. It is a fluid, made from a decoction of food and the body, and diffused by the blood vessels and the bone marrow. From there it is sweated out like bilge water and condenses in the kidneys. Ejaculated in sexual intercourse and taken into the uterus of a woman, it somehow takes shape in the body under the influence of the heat of the viscera and the irrigation of menstrual blood.

140. The menses consist of an overflow of women's blood. They are called 'menses' (*menstrua*) after the cycle of moonlight in which this flux regularly comes to pass – for in Greek the moon is called μήνη. These are also called 'womanish things' (*muliebria*), for the woman is the only menstruating animal. 141. If they are touched by the blood of the menses, crops cease to sprout, unfermented wine turns sour, plants wither, trees lose their fruit, iron is corrupted by rust, bronze turns black. If dogs eat any of it, they are made wild with rabies. The glue of pitch, which is dissolved neither by iron nor water, when polluted with this blood spontaneously disperses. 142. Moreover, semen cannot germinate after several days of menstruation, because there is not then enough menstrual blood by which it could be moistened to the point of being thoroughly wet. Thin semen doesn't adhere to the female organs; it slides down and doesn't have the power to cling to them. Similarly, thick semen also lacks the power to beget anything, because, due to its excessive thickness, it cannot mix with the menstrual blood. This causes sterility in men or women; it is either due to the excessive thickness of the semen or blood, or to their excessive thinness.

143. It is said that the heart of a human being is made first, because it is the seat of all life and wisdom. Thereafter it takes forty days for the whole work to be completed – they say that these facts are adduced from miscarriages. Others are of the opinion that the fetus begins to grow with the head, whence we also see the eyes made first in birds' fetuses in eggs. 144. The fetus (*foetus*) is so called because it is still 'being kept warm' (*fovere*, ppl. *fotus*) in the uterus. The small sac that contains the fetus and is born with the infant is called the afterbirth (*secundae*), because at birth it follows (*sequi*, gerundive *sequendus*). 145. They say that newborn children resemble their fathers if the paternal seed is stronger, and their mothers if the maternal is stronger. Looks that are similar (i.e. to both parents) are explained by this reason: those who resemble the features of both parents were conceived from equally mixed paternal and maternal seed. Similarity to grandparents and great-grandparents comes

7 While "womb" is the meaning of *vulva* in classical Latin, it appears that the term here refers to the vulva, vagina, or cervix.

to pass because, just as a great deal of seed is hidden in the earth, so also seed that can assume the shape of our ancestors is hidden in us. However, from the paternal seed girls may be born, and from the maternal seed boys, because all offspring is made of two kinds of seed, and the greater portion, because it predominates, determines the similarity of the sex.

146. Some parts in our body were created solely for reasons of usefulness, as for instance the viscera; some for usefulness and ornament, like the sense organs in the face, and the hands and feet in the body, limbs that are both of great usefulness and most pleasing form. 147. Some are purely for ornament, as for instance breasts in men, and the navel in both sexes. Some are there to allow us to tell the difference between the sexes, as for instance the genitals, the grown beard, and the wide chest in men; in women the smooth cheeks and the narrow chest; although, in order to conceive and carry a fetus, they have wide loins and sides. That which pertains to human beings and the parts of the body has been partly treated; now I will add something on the ages of a human being.

ii. On the ages of human beings (De aetatibus hominum) 1. There are six stages in a lifetime: infancy, childhood, adolescence, youth, maturity, and old age. 2. The first age, the infancy (*infantia*) of a newborn child, lasts seven years. 3. The second age is childhood (*pueritia*), that is, a pure (*purus*) age, during which a child is not yet suited for procreating; it lasts until the fourteenth year. 4. The third age, adolescence (*adolescentia*), is mature (*adultus*, ppl. of *adolescere*) enough for procreating and lasts until the twenty-eighth year. 5. The fourth age, youth (*iuventus*), is the strongest of all ages, ending in the fiftieth year. 6. The fifth is the age of an elder person (*senior*), that is, maturity (*gravitas*), which is the decline from youth into old age; it is not yet old age, but no longer youth, because it is the age of an older person, which the Greeks call πρεσβύτης – for with the Greeks an old person is not called *presbyter*, but γέρων. This age begins in the fiftieth and ends in the seventieth year. 7. The sixth age is old age (*senectus*), which has no time limit in years; rather, however much life is left after the previous five ages is allotted to old age. 8. *Senium*, however, is the last part of old age, so called because it is the end of the sixth (cf. *seni*, "six") age.

Into these six intervals, therefore, the philosophers have divided human life – ages in which life is changed, runs its course, and reaches the final point of death. Let us therefore proceed briefly through the aforementioned stages in a lifetime, demonstrating their etymologies with regard to the terms used for a human being.

9. A human being of the first age is called an infant (*infans*); it is called an infant, because it does not yet know how to speak (*in-*, "not"; *fari*, present participle *fans*, "speaking"), that is, it cannot talk. Not yet having its full complement of teeth, it has less ability to articulate words. 10. A boy (*puer*) is so called from purity (*puritas*), because he is pure and doesn't yet have any beard or down on his cheeks. They are ephebes (*ephebus*), so called after Phoebus, gentle youths, not yet [grown] men. 11. The word child (*puer*), however, is used in three ways: in reference to birth, as in Isaiah (cf. 9:6): "A child (*puer*) is born to us." To indicate age, as in "an eight-year-old," "a ten-year-old" – whence the following expression (Courtney fr. 3):

> Now he took a child's (*puerilis*) yoke on his tender neck.

And finally, in reference to obedience and purity of faith, as in the words of the Lord to the prophet (cf. Jeremiah 1:6–8): "You are my child (*puer*), do not be afraid," spoken when Jeremiah had already left behind the years of childhood a long time before.

12. *Puella* is "little girl" (*parvula*), as if the term were 'chick' (*pulla*). Hence we use the term 'wards' (*pupillus*), not because of the legal status of wards, but because of their youthful age. A ward, named like the pupil (*pupillus*) of the eye, is one bereft of parents. Those truly called *pupilli*, however, are children whose parents died before giving them a name. Other 'bereft ones' (*orbus*) are called orphans (*orphanus*), the same as are those called *pupilli*; for *orphanus* is a Greek word and *pupillus* a Latin word. Thus in the psalm, where it is said (Psalm 9/10:14 Vulgate): "Thou wilt be a helper to the orphan (*pupillus*)," the Greek has the word ὀρφανός.[8]

13. 'Those who have reached puberty' (*puberes*) are so called from *pubes*, that is, the private parts, for this is the first time that this area grows hair. There are those who calculate puberty from age, that is, they take someone who has completed his fourteenth year to have reached puberty, even though he may begin to show the signs of

8 The received Vulgate text of Psalm 9:14 reads *orphanus* from the Septuagint where Isidore and the version based on the Hebrew have *pupillus*.

puberty very late; however, it is most certain that he who shows the outward signs of puberty and can already procreate has reached puberty. 14. *Puerpera* are those who give birth at a youthful (*puerilis*) age. Whence Horace says (cf. *Odes* 4.5.23):

> The young woman in labor (*puerpera*) is praised for her firstborn.

And they are called *puerperae* either because they are burdened with their 'first birth' (*primus partus*), or else because they first 'give birth to children' (*pueros parere*). 15. An adolescent (*adolescens*) is so called because he is 'old enough' (*adultus*, ppl. of *adolescere*) to procreate, or by derivation from 'growing' (*crescere*) and 'being strengthened' (*augere*). 16. A youth (*iuvenis*) is so called because he begins to be able to help (*iuvare*), just as we name the young bullocks (*iuvencus*) among oxen, when they have separated from the calves. A youth is at the peak of his development and ready to give assistance – for a person's 'helping' is his contributing some work. As in human beings the thirtieth year is the time of full maturity, so in cattle and beasts of burden the third year is the strongest.

17. A man (*vir*) is so called, because in him resides greater power (*vis*) than in a woman – hence also 'strength' (*virtus*) received its name – or else because he deals with a woman by force (*vis*). 18. But the word woman (*mulier*) comes from softness (*mollities*), as if *mollier* (cf. *mollior*, "softer"), after a letter has been cut and a letter changed, is now called *mulier*. 19. These two are differentiated by the respective strength and weakness of their bodies. But strength is greater in a man, lesser in a woman, so that she will submit to the power of the man; evidently this is so lest, if women were to resist, lust should drive men to seek out something else or throw themselves upon the male sex. 20. As I was saying, woman (*mulier*) is named for her feminine sex, not for a corruption of her innocence,[9] and this is according to the word of Sacred Scripture, for Eve was called woman as soon as she was made from the side of her man, when she had not yet had any contact with a man, as is said in the Bible (cf. Gen. 2:22): "And he formed her into a woman (*mulier*)."

21. The term 'virgin' (*virgo*) comes from 'a greener (*viridior*) age,' just like the words 'sprout' (*virga*) and 'calf' (*vitula*). Otherwise it is derived from lack of corruption, as if the word were formed from 'heroic maiden,' because she has no knowledge of female desire. 22. A 'heroic maiden' (*virago*) is so called because she 'acts like a man' (*vir* + *agere*), that is, she engages in the activities of men and is full of male vigor. The ancients would call strong women by that name. However, a virgin cannot be correctly called a heroic maiden unless she performs a man's task. But if a woman does manly deeds, then she is correctly called a heroic maiden, like an Amazon.

23. She who is nowadays called a woman (*femina*) in ancient times was called *vira*; just as 'female slave' (*serva*) was derived from 'male slave' (*servus*) and 'female servant' (*famula*) from 'male servant' (*famulus*), so also woman (*vira*) from man (*vir*). Some people believe that the word for 'virgin' (*virgo*) is from *vira*. 24. The word 'woman' (*femina*) is derived from the parts of the thighs (*femur*, plural *femora* or *femina*) where the appearance of the sex distinguishes her from a man. Others believe that through a Greek etymology *femina* is derived from 'fiery force,' because she desires more vehemently, for females are said to be more libidinous than males, both in human beings and in animals. Whence among the ancients excessive love was called feminine (*femineus*) love.

25. The 'elder' (*senior*) is still fairly vigorous. In the sixth book Ovid speaks of the elder, who is (*Met.* 12.464)

> Between the youth and the old man (*senex*).[10]

And Terence (*The Mother-in-Law* 11):

> By the privilege I enjoyed when I was younger (*adulescentior*).

26. [Younger (*adulescentior*)] undoubtedly does not mean 'more grown up' (*magis adolescens*), but rather 'less grown up,' and in the same way 'elder' (*senior*) means 'less old,' where the comparative degree signifies less than the positive. Therefore, *senior* does not mean "fully old," just as 'rather young' (*iunior*, i.e. a comparative form, lit. "younger") means "in his youth," and 'rather poor' (*pauperior*, i.e. the comparative of *pauper*, "poor") means "between rich and poor."

27. The term 'old man' (*senex*), however, some believe to be derived from decay of the senses (*sensus*), because from that time on they act foolishly due to old age.

9 *Mollities* could bear a connotation of sexual licentiousness.

10 *Senex*, gen. *senis*, is the positive degree of *senior*. Isidore will go on to make the point that *senior* actually means less old than *senex*.

Physiologists maintain that human beings are stupid due to colder blood, wise due to warm blood. Hence also old people, in whom blood has turned cold, and children, in whom it has not yet warmed up, are less wise. This is the reason why infancy and old age resemble one another: old people dote because they are too old, while children have no insight into their actions due to playfulness and childishness.

28. The term 'old man' (*senex*), however, is only masculine in gender, just as 'old woman' (*anus*) is feminine, for *anus* is exclusively said of a woman. 'Old woman,' moreover, is so called from many 'years' (*annus*), as if the word were 'full of years' (*annosus*). Indeed, if the word *senex* were a common noun (i.e. used of either gender), why then would Terence say (*Eunuch* 357): "Old woman (*senex mulier*)"? Similarly we say 'little old lady' (*vetula*), because she is 'aged' (*vetusta*). In like manner 'old age' (*senectus*) is derived from 'old man' (*senex*) and 'a woman's old age' (*anilitas*) from 'old woman' (*anus*). 29. 'Gray hair' (*canities*, also meaning "old age") comes from 'whiteness' (*candor*), as if the word were *candities*. Whence the following: "florid youth, milky old age (*canities*)," as if it said "white" (*candidus*) old age. 30. Old age brings with it much that is good and much that is bad. Much that is good, because it frees us from despotic masters, imposes moderation on desires, breaks the drive of lust, augments wisdom, and imparts riper counsel. Much that is bad, however, because of the weakness and unpopularity it brings, for (Vergil, *Geo.* 3.67):

> Diseases and sorrowful old age creep up.

Indeed, there are two things whereby the forces of the body are diminished, old age and disease.

31. Death (*mors*) is so called, because it is bitter (*amarus*), or by derivation from Mars, who is the author of death; [or else, death is derived from the bite (*morsus*) of the first human, because when he bit the fruit of the forbidden tree, he incurred death]. 32. There are three kinds of death: heartrending, premature, and natural death. That of children is heartrending, that of young people premature, that of old people merited, that is, natural. 33. However, it is uncertain from which part of speech *mortuus* ("dead, a dead person") is inflected. Indeed, as Caesar (i.e. Gaius Julius Caesar Strabo) says, because it is the perfect participle of *morior* ("die") it ought to end in *-tus* – that is, it ought to have one *u* only, not two. Where the letter *u* is doubled, it is inflected substantively, not as a participle, as in *fatuus* ("foolish") and *arduus* ("difficult"). This makes sense in this way: just as what *mortuus* means cannot be "declined" by any behavior of ours (i.e. we cannot avoid death), so the term itself cannot be "declined" grammatically.

Everyone who is dead is either a corpse (*funus*), or a cadaver. 34. It is a corpse if it is buried. It is called *funus* from the ropes (*funis*) set on fire; these were carried before the bier in the form of papyrus reeds enveloped with wax. 35. The term cadaver, on the other hand, is used if the body lies unburied, for 'cadaver' (*cadaver*) comes from 'falling down' (*cadere*), because it cannot stand upright any more. While the cadaver is carried, we speak of it as the *exsequiae*; when cremated, the remains (*reliquiae*); when already interred, the buried (*sepultum*). However, in common usage a cadaver is still spoken of as a body (*corpus*, i.e. 'corpse'), as in the following (Vergil, *Geo.* 4.255):

> Then the bodies (*corpus*) of those deprived of the light.

36. The deceased (*defunctus*) is so called, because he has completed his part in life. Thus we say that those who have completed services they owed have 'discharged their duty' (*functus officio*); whence also the phrase 'having held (*functus*) public office.' Hence therefore 'defunct,' because such a person has been 'put aside from his duty' (*depositus officio*) in life, or else because he has fulfilled (*functus*) his number of days. 37. Buried (*sepultus*) is said of a person who is already 'without pulse' (*sine pulsu*) and heartbeat, that is, without motion. To bury (*sepelire*) is to put a body out of sight, for we say 'inter' (*humare*) for covering over a body, that is, for throwing earth (*humus*) upon it.

iii. Portents (De portentis)[11] 1. Varro defines portents as beings that seem to have been born contrary to nature – but they are not contrary to nature, because they are created by divine will, since the nature of everything is the will of the Creator. Whence even the pagans address God sometimes as 'Nature' (*Natura*), sometimes as 'God.' 2. A portent is therefore not created contrary to nature, but contrary to what is known nature. Portents are also called signs, omens, and prodigies, because they are seen to portend and display, indicate and predict

11 Both *portentum* and *monstrum* can mean "omen, portent" or "monstrosity."

future events. 3. The term 'portent' (*portentum*) is said to be derived from foreshadowing (*portendere*), that is, from 'showing beforehand' (*praeostendere*). 'Signs' (*ostentum*), because they seem to show (*ostendere*) a future event. Prodigies (*prodigium*) are so called, because they 'speak hereafter' (*porro dicere*), that is, they predict the future. But omens (*monstrum*) derive their name from admonition (*monitus*), because in giving a sign they indicate (*demonstrare*) something, or else because they instantly show (*monstrare*) what may appear (Funaioli 440); and this is its proper meaning, even though it has frequently been corrupted by the improper use of writers.

4. Some portents seem to have been created as indications of future events, for God sometimes wants to indicate what is to come through some defects in newborns, just as through dreams and oracles, by which he may foreshadow and indicate future calamity for certain peoples or individuals, as is indeed proved by abundant experience. 5. In fact, to Xerxes a fox born of a mare was a portent for the destruction of the empire. A monster to which a woman gave birth, whose upper body parts were human, but dead, while its lower body parts came from diverse animals, yet were alive, signified to Alexander the sudden murder of the king – for the worse parts had outlived the better ones. However, those monsters that are produced as omens do not live long – they die as soon as they are born. 6. There is a difference between a 'portent' (*portentum*) and 'an unnatural being' (*portentuosus*). Portents are beings of transformed appearance, as, for instance, is said to have happened when in Umbria a woman gave birth to a serpent. Whence Lucan says (*Civil War* 1.563):

> And the child terrified its own mother.

But an unnatural being strictly speaking takes the form of a slight mutation, as for instance in the case of someone born with six fingers.

7. Portents, then, or unnatural beings, exist in some cases in the form of a size of the whole body that surpasses common human nature, as in the case of Tityos who, as Homer witnesses, covered nine jugers (i.e. about six acres) when lying prostrate; in other cases in the form of a smallness of the whole body, as in dwarfs (*nanus*), or those whom the Greeks call pygmies (*pygmaeus*), because they are a cubit tall. Others are so called due to the size of parts of their bodies, as for instance a misshapen head, or due to superfluous parts of their limbs, as in the case of two-headed and three-headed individuals, or in the case of the *cynodontes* (i.e. "dog-toothed" people), who have a pair of projecting fangs. 8. Yet others are so called due to missing parts of the body, individuals in whom one corresponding part is deficient compared with the other, as when one hand is compared with the other hand and one foot with the other foot. Others due to a cutting off, as in the case of those born without a hand or without a head, whom the Greeks call *steresios* (cf. στέρησις, "deprivation"). Others in the form of *praenumeria*, when only the head or a leg is born.

9. Others, who are transformed in a part of the body, as for instance those who have the features of a lion or of a dog, or the head or body of a bull, as they relate in the case of the Minotaur born of Pasiphae – what the Greeks call ἑτερομορφία. Others become a portent due to a complete transformation into a different creature, as in the story of a woman who gave birth to a calf. Others, who have a change in the position of features without any transformation, such as those with eyes in their chest or forehead, or ears above their temples, or, as Aristotle relates, someone who had his liver on the left side and his spleen on the right. 10. Others, because of a joined begetting, as when in one hand several fingers are found joined at birth and fused together, and in the other hand fewer – and likewise with the feet. Others, with a feature that is premature and untimely, as those who are born with teeth or a beard or white hair. Others, with a complex of several oddities, like the multiformed portent of Alexander's about which I spoke above (see section 5). 11. Others, from a mixing of sexes, like those they call the ἀνδρόγυνοι ("androgynes") and ἑρμαφροδῖται. Hermaphrodites are so named because both sexes appear in them, as in Greek Ἑρμῆς signifies the male, Ἀφροδίτη the female. These, having a male right breast and a female left breast, in sexual intercourse sire and bear children in turn.

12. Just as, in individual nations, there are instances of monstrous people, so in the whole of humankind there are certain monstrous races, like the Giants, the Cynocephali (i.e. 'dog-headed people'), the Cyclopes, and others. 13. Giants (*Gigantes*) are so called according to the etymology of a Greek term; the Greeks suppose that they are γηγενεῖς, that is, "earthborn," because in their fable the parent Earth begot them as like itself, with their immense mass – for γῆ means "earth" and γένος "offspring." However, those whose parentage is uncertain are also commonly called 'sons of the earth.'

14. But some, inexperienced with Holy Scripture (i.e. Genesis 6:4), falsely suppose that apostate angels lay with the daughters of humans before the Flood, and that from this the Giants were born – that is, excessively large and powerful men – and filled the earth. 15. The Cynocephali are so called because they have dogs' heads, and their barking indeed reveals that they are rather beasts than humans. These originate in India. 16. India also produces the *Cyclopes*, and they are called Cyclops because they are believed to have a single eye in the middle of their foreheads. These are also called ἀγριοφαγῖται, because they eat only the flesh of wild animals.

17. People believe that the Blemmyans in Libya are born as trunks without heads, and having their mouth and eyes in their chest, and that another race is born without necks and having their eyes in their shoulders. 18. Moreover, people write about the monstrous faces of nations in the far East: some with no noses, having completely flat faces and a shapeless countenance; some with a lower lip so protruding that when they are sleeping it protects the whole face from the heat of the sun; some with mouths grown shut, taking in nourishment only through a small opening by means of hollow straws. Some are said to have no tongues, using nods or gestures in place of words. 19. They tell of the Panotians of Scythia, who have such huge ears that they cover all the body – for πᾶν is the Greek word for "all," and ὦτα means "ears." 20. The Artabatitans of Ethiopia are said to walk on all fours, like cattle; none passes the age of forty.

21. The Satyrs are little people with hooked noses; they have horns on their foreheads, and feet like goats' – the kind of creature that Saint Anthony saw in the wilderness. When questioned by the servant of God, this Satyr is said to have responded (Jerome, *Life of Paul the Hermit* 8; PL 23.23): "I am one of the mortals that dwell in the desert, whom the pagans, deluded by their fickle error, worship as Fauns and Satyrs." 22. There are also said to be a kind of wild men, whom some call Fauns of the fig. 23. The race of Sciopodes are said to live in Ethiopia; they have only one leg, and are wonderfully speedy. The Greeks call them σκιοπόδες ("shade-footed ones") because when it is hot they lie on their backs on the ground and are shaded by the great size of their feet.

24. The Antipodes in Libya have the soles of their feet twisted behind their legs, and eight toes on each foot. 25. The Hippopodes are in Scythia, and have a human form and horses' hooves. 26. In India there are said to be a race called Μακρόβιοι, who are twelve feet tall. There, too, is a race a cubit tall, whom the Greeks from the term 'cubit' call pygmies (*pigmaeus*; cf. πυγμή, "cubit"), of whom I have spoken above (section 7). They live in the mountainous regions of India, near the Ocean. 27. They claim also that in the same India is a race of women who conceive when they are five years old and do not live beyond eight.

28. Other fabulous human monstrosities are told of, which do not exist but are concocted to interpret the causes of things – like Geryon, the Spanish king fabled to have three bodies, for there were three brothers of such like minds that there was, so to speak, one soul in their three bodies. 29. And there are the Gorgons, harlots with serpentine locks, who would turn anyone looking at them into stone, and who had only one eye which they would take turns using. But these were three sisters who had a single beauty, as if they had a single eye, who would so stun those beholding them that they were thought to turn them into stone.

30. People imagine three Sirens who were part maidens, part birds, having wings and talons; one of them would make music with her voice, the second with a flute, and the third with a lyre. They would draw sailors, enticed by the song, into shipwreck. 31. In truth, however, they were harlots, who, because they would seduce passers-by into destitution, were imagined as bringing shipwreck upon them. They were said to have had wings and talons because sexual desire both flies and wounds. They are said to have lived among the waves because the waves gave birth to Venus. 32. People tell of Scylla as a woman girded with the heads of dogs, with a great barking, because of the straits of the sea of Sicily, in which sailors, terrified by the whirlpools of waves rushing against them, suppose that the waves are barking, waves that the chasm with its seething and sucking brings into collision.

33. They also imagine certain monstrosities from among irrational animals, like Cerberus, the dog of the nether world that has three heads, signifying through him the three ages in which death devours a human being – that is, infancy, youth, and old age. Some think that he is called Cerberus as if the term were κρεοβόρος ("flesh-eating"), that is, devouring flesh. 34. They talk also of Hydra, a serpent with nine heads, which in Latin is called 'water-snake' (*excetra*), because when one head was cut off (*caedere*) three would grow back (perhaps cf. *et cetera*). But in fact Hydra was a place that gushed out water, devastating a nearby city; if one

opening in it were closed, many more would burst out. Seeing this, Hercules dried up the area, and thus closed the opening for the water. 35. Indeed *hydra* was named from 'water' (cf. ὕδωρ). Ambrose makes mention of this in a comparison of it with heresies, saying (*On Faith* 1.4): "For heresy, like a certain hydra in the fables, grew from its own wounds, and as often as it would be cut down, it spread; it should be fed to the fire and will perish in a conflagration."

36. They also imagine the Chimaera as a tri-form beast: the face of a lion, the rear of a dragon, and a she-goat in the middle. Certain physiologists say that the Chimaera is not an animal but a mountain in Cilicia that nourishes lions and she-goats in some places, emits fire in some places, and is full of serpents in some places. Because Bellerophon made this place habitable, he is said to have killed the Chimaera. 37. Their appearance gave their name to the Centaurs, that is, a man combined with a horse. Some say that they were horsemen of Thessaly, but because, as they rushed into battle, the horses and men seemed to have one body, from this they maintained that the Centaurs were concocted.

38. Again, the Minotaur took its name from 'bull' (*taurus*) and 'human being' (*homo*, gen. *hominis*). They say in their fables that a beast of this kind was enclosed in the Labyrinth. On this, Ovid (*Art of Love* 2.24):

> The man half bull, and the bull half man.

39. The Onocentaur is so called because it seems to look half like a human, half like an ass. Likewise the Hippocentaur, which is thought to combine the natures of horse and human in itself.

iv. Metamorphoses (De transformatis) 1. There are accounts of certain monstrous metamorphoses and changes of humans into beasts, as in the case of that most notorious sorceress Circe, who is said to have transformed the companions of Ulysses into beasts, and the case of the Arcadians who, led by chance, would swim across a certain pond and would there be converted into wolves. 2. That the companions of Diomede were transformed into birds is not a lie from story-telling, but people assert this with historical confirmation. Some people claim that witches (*Striga*) were transformed from humans. With regard to many types of crimes, the appearance of the miscreants is changed and they wholly metamorphose into wild animals, by means of either magic charms or poisonous herbs. 3. Indeed, many creatures naturally undergo mutation and, when they decay, are transformed into different species – for instance bees, out of the rotted flesh of calves, or beetles from horses, locusts from mules, scorpions from crabs. Thus Ovid (cf. *Met.* 15.369):

> If you take its curved arms from a crab on the shore a scorpion will emerge and threaten with its hooked tail.

Book XII

Animals (De animalibus)

i. Livestock and beasts of burden (De pecoribus et iumentis) 1. Adam was the first to confer names on all the animals, assigning a name to each one from its visible conformation according to the position in nature that it holds. 2. The different nations have also given names to each of the animals in their own languages – for Adam did not assign these names in the Latin or Greek language, or in any of the languages of foreign nations, but in that language which, before the Flood, was the language of all peoples, which is called Hebrew. 3. In Latin they are called animals (*animal*) or 'animate beings' (*animans*), because they are animated (*animare*) by life and moved by spirit. 4. Quadrupeds (*quadrupes*) are so called because they walk on four feet (*quattuor pedes*); while these may be similar to livestock, they are nevertheless not under human control – such as deer, antelopes, onagers, et cetera. But they are not wild beasts, such as lions, nor are they beasts of burden, which could assist the useful activities of humans.

5. We call any animal that lacks human language and form 'livestock' (*pecus*). However, strictly speaking, the term 'livestock' is usually applied to those animals that are either suitable for food, such as sheep and swine, or are suitable for use by humans, such as horses and oxen. 6. There is a distinction between the terms *pecora* (i.e. the plural of *pecus*, neuter) and *pecudes* (i.e. the plural of *pecus*, feminine), for the ancients commonly used to say *pecora* with the meaning "all animals," but *pecudes* were only those animals that are eaten (*edere*), as if the word were *pecuedes*. But in general every animal is called *pecus* from the word 'pasturing' (*pascere*). 7. 'Beasts of burden' (*iumenta*) derive their name from the fact that they assist (*iuvare*) our labor and burdens by their help in hauling or plowing, for the ox pulls the cart and turns the hardest clods of earth with the plowshare; the horse and ass carry burdens, and ease people's labor when they travel. Whence they are called beasts of burden because they assist humans, for these are animals of great strength. 8. They are also called a herd (*armentum*) either because they are suited for arms (*arma*), that is, warfare, or because we use them when we are armed. Others understand herds to be oxen only, from 'plowing' (*arare*), as if the word were *aramentum*, [or because they are armed (*armare*) with horns]. There is a distinction between herds and flocks (*grex*), for 'herd' is used for horses and oxen, while 'flock' is used for goats and sheep.

9. A sheep (*ovis*) is a mild livestock animal, with wool, a defenseless body, and a peaceful temperament, and it is so called from sacrifice (*oblatio*), because at first the ancients offered not bulls, but sheep, in sacrifice. They call some of them *bidens* (lit. "two-toothed") – those with two of their eight teeth longer than the rest; most often the pagans used to sacrifice these. 10. The wether (*vervex*) is either named from 'force' (*vis*, gen. *viris*), because it is stronger than the other sheep, or because it is male (*vir*), that is, masculine; or because it has a worm (*vermis*) in its head – irritated by the itching of these worms they butt against each other and strike with great force when they fight. 11. The ram (*aries*) is either named after the word Ἄρης, that is, after 'Mars' – whence we call the males in a flock 'males' (*mas*, gen. *maris*) – or because this animal was the first to be sacrificed on altars (*ara*, ablative plural *aris*) by pagans. So, the 'ram' because it was placed on the altar; whence also this (Sedulius, *Paschal Poem* 1.115):

> The ram is offered at the altar.

12. Although the Greeks name the lamb (*agnus*) from ἁγνός ("holy") as if it were sacred, Latin speakers think that it has this name because it recognizes (*agnoscere*) its mother before other animals, to the extent that even if it has strayed within a large herd, it immediately recognizes the voice of its parent by its bleat.

13. The kid (*haedus*) is so called from eating (*edere*), for the young ones are very juicy and pleasing in flavor. Whence also ['eat' (*edere*) and] foodstuffs (*edulia*) are named. 14. The he-goat (*hircus*) is a lascivious animal, apt to butt and always eager to mate; his eyes look sideways on account of wantonness, whence he has taken his

name, for according to Suetonius (*Prata*, fr. 171), *hirqui* are the corners of the eyes. His nature is so ardent that his blood by itself dissolves adamantine stone, which can be overpowered by neither fire nor iron. Larger he-goats are called *cinyphii* from the river Cinyps in Libya, where they are born large. 15. Some people have said he-goats (*caper*) and she-goats (*capra*) are named from their cropping (*carpere*) of bushes, others because they 'hold to uneven places' (*captare aspera*). Some say it derives from the creaking (*crepitus*) of their legs, whence also they are often called *crepae* – these are the wild goats which the Greeks called δορκάς (properly in Greek, "deer") because they can see very keenly, that is, ὀξυδερκέστερον ("rather sharp-sightedly"). They dwell in the high mountains, and even from a great distance they can still see anyone who is approaching. 16. And a wild goat is likewise a *caprea* (in classical Latin, a roe-deer), and an ibex (*ibex*), as if the word were *avex*, because they hold to the steep and lofty places as the birds (*avis*) do, and inhabit the heights, so that from these heights they are scarcely (*vix*) visible to human gaze. 17. Whence also the southern part of the world calls the birds that inhabit the floods of the Nile ibexes (*ibex*, i.e. *ibis*). These animals, as we have said, dwell in the highest crags, and if ever they espy danger from beasts or humans, they throw themselves down from the highest peaks and hold themselves up on their horns unharmed.

18. Deer (*cervus*) are so called from the word κέρατα, that is, from their antlers, for 'horn' is called κέρας in Greek. They are antagonistic to serpents; when they sense themselves burdened with infirmity, they draw the serpents from their caves with the breath from their nostrils, and having overcome the malignancy of the poison, the deer are restored to health by eating the serpents. They were the ones to discover the herb dittany (*dictamnus*), for after they have eaten it, they shake out any arrows that have stuck in them. 19. Moreover, they are fascinated by the whistling of reed pipes. They listen intently with ears pricked, but if their ears are lowered, they hear nothing. If ever they swim across great rivers or seas, they place their head on the haunches of the one in front of them, and with each one following the next, they feel no difficulty from the weight. 20. *Tragelaphi* were named by the Greeks; while they have the same appearance as deer, nevertheless they have shaggy flanks like he-goats, and hairy chins with long beards. They are found nowhere except around the river Phasis.

21. The 'young stag' (*hinnulus*) is the offspring of deer [so called from 'nodding' (*innuere*), because they conceal themselves at a nod from their mother]. 22. The young doe (*dammula*) is so called because she flees 'from one's hand' (*de manu*). She is a timid animal and unwarlike, concerning which Martial says (*Epigrams* 13.94):

> The boar is feared for his tusk, antlers defend the stag;
> what are we unwarlike does (*damae*) but prey?

23. The hare (*lepus*), as if the word were *levipes* ("swift foot"), because it runs swiftly. Whence in Greek it is called λαγώς, because of its swiftness, for it is a speedy animal and quite timid. 24. Rabbits (*cuniculus*), a type of field animal, are so called as if the word were *caniculus*, because they are seized or driven out of their burrows by hunting packs of dogs (*canis*).

25. The sow (*sus*) is so called because she roots up (*subigere*) feeding grounds, that is, she searches for food by rooting the earth up. The boar (*verres*), because he has great strength (*vis*, plural *vires*). The pig (*porcus*) as if the name were 'unclean' (*spurcus*), for he gorges himself on filth, immerses himself in mud, and smears himself with slime. Horace (*Epistles* 1.2.26) says:

> And the sow, a friend to mud.

Hence also 'uncleanness' (*spurcitia*) or 'illegitimate children' (*spurius*) are named. 26. The hairs of pigs are called bristles, and bristles (*seta*) are named from the sow (*sus*). From these we also name 'shoemakers' (*sutor*), because they sew (*suere*), that is, stitch together, leather with bristles. 27. The 'wild boar' (*aper*) is so named 'from its ferocity' (*a* + *feritas*), with the letter *f* removed and a *p* substituted. Whence he is also named σύαγρος, that is "wild" (i.e. "wild boar") in Greek (cf. ἄγριος, "wild"), for everything that is wild and untamed, we call, with loose usage, 'of the country' (*agrestis*).

28. The bullock (*iuvencus*) is so called because it was first to assist (*iuvare*) the activity of humans in cultivating the earth, or because a bullock always used to be sacrificed to Jupiter (*Iuppiter*, gen. *Iovis*) everywhere by the pagans – never a bull, for age was a consideration in the choice of sacrifice. 29. 'Bull' (*taurus*) is a Greek word, just as is 'ox' (*bos*). The Indian bulls are tawny and they are as swift as a bird; their hair is turned backward; with their flexibility they turn their head around as they wish; by the hardness of their skin they repel every dart in their fierce wildness. 30. The Greeks call the ox βοῦς.

Latin speakers call them *triones* (i.e. "plowing oxen") thus because they 'tread' (*terere*) the earth, as if the word were *teriones*. Naevius (*Tragedies* 62) says:

This rustic driver of the *triones*.

The span of its hide from the chin to the forelegs is called the dewlap (*palear*), from the term 'skin' (*pellis*) itself, as if the word were *pellear*. This is a sign of good breeding in an ox. Oxen possess an extraordinary affection for their comrades, for one will seek the other with whom he has been accustomed to share the yoke, and with constant lowing show its devoted fondness if by chance the other is missing. 31. The cow (*vacca*) is so called as if the word were *boacca*. The noun has the same type of variation as 'lion' (*leo*) and 'lioness' (*leaena*), 'dragon' (*draco*) and 'dragoness' (*dracaena*). 32. Calves (*vitulus*) and heifers (*vitula*) are named from their greenness (*viriditas*), that is, their green (i.e. "vigorous") age, just as a maiden (*virgo*) is. A heifer, therefore, is small and has not yet produced young, for after she has been put to breed, she is called a *iuvenca* or a cow. 33. Buffaloes (*bubalus*) are so called by derivation, since they are similar to oxen (*bos*). They are so ungovernable that they do not tolerate a yoke on their necks due to their wildness. Africa produces these. 34. The aurochs (*urus*) is the wild ox of Germania, possessing such long horns that vessels for royal tables are made from them due to their notable size. [They are called *urus* from the word ὄρος, that is, "mountain"].

35. The camel (*camelus*) takes its name from its characteristics, either because, when they are being loaded, they lie down so that they become shorter and low – for the Greeks say χαμαί (lit. "on the ground") for 'low' and 'short' – or because their backs are humped, for καμουρ means "curve" in Greek.[1] Although some other regions produce camels, Arabia produces the most. They differ from each other in that the Arabian camels have two humps on their backs and those from the other regions have one hump. 36. The dromedary (*dromeda*) is a kind of camel, smaller in height but faster. From this it takes its name, for 'race' and 'speed' are called δρόμος in Greek. It is accustomed to travel one hundred Roman miles or more in a single day. This animal ruminates, just like the ox and sheep and camel. 37. Rumination (*ruminatio*) is named from the rumen (*ruma*), the upper part of the gullet through which the food that has been taken down is regurgitated by some animals.

38. The ass (*asinus*) and the 'small ass' (*asellus*, dim. of *asinus*) are so called from 'sitting' (*sedere*), as if the word were *asedus*. The ass took this name, which is better suited to horses, because before people captured horses, they began by domesticating (*praesidere*, lit. "sit on") the ass. Indeed, it is a slow animal and balks for no reason; it allowed itself to be domesticated as soon as mankind wished it. 39. The wild ass is called an onager (*onager*), for the Greeks call the ass ὄνος, and ἄγριος is "wild." Africa possesses large untamed onagers wandering through the desert. Individual onagers lead herds of females. When male colts are born, the adult males become jealous and bite off their testicles, so that the wary mothers hide the male colts in concealed places. 40. Some asses are called 'Arcadian' because, large and tall, they were first imported from Arcadia. The smaller *asellus* is needed more in the field because it tolerates hard work and makes almost no objection to neglect.

41. Horses (*equus*) are so called because when they were yoked in a team of four they were balanced (*aequare*); those equal in size and alike in gait would be joined together. 42. The packhorse (*caballus*) was formerly called a *cabo*, because when walking it hollows (*concavare*) the ground with the imprint of its hoof, a property that the other animals do not have. Whence also the 'charger' (*sonipes*) because it 'clatters with its feet' (*pedibus sonare*). 43. Horses have a great deal of liveliness, for they revel in open country; they scent out war; they are roused to battle by the sound of the trumpet; when incited by a voice they are challenged to race, grieving when they are defeated, and exultant when they are victorious. Some recognize the enemy in war and seek to bite the foe. Some also respond to their own masters, and lose their tameness if their ownership changes. Some will allow no one on their back except their master; many of them shed tears when their master is killed or is dying, for only the horse weeps and feels grief over humans. Whence [also] in the Centaur the nature of horses and of humans is combined. 44. People who are about to engage in battle are accustomed to deduce what the outcome will be from the dejection or the eagerness of the horses.

Persian, Hunnish, Epirian, and Sicilian horses have a long life span, exceeding fifty years, while the common opinion is that Spanish, Numidian, and Galician

1 The word καμουρ is not elsewhere attested but cf. καμαρωτός, "vaulted, arched."

horses have a shorter life span. 45. In well-bred horses, so the ancients said, four things were considered: form, beauty, quality, and color. Form, that the body should be strong and solid, the height appropriate to the strength, the flank long, very lean, with well-rounded haunches, broad in the chest, the entire body knotted with dense musculature, the foot firm and solid with a concave hoof. 46. Beauty, that the head should be small and firm, the skin clinging close to the bones, the ears short and expressive, the eyes large, the nostrils flaring out, the neck upright, the mane and tail thick, the hooves of a firm roundness and solidity. 47. Quality, that it should be daring in spirit, swift of foot, with quivering limbs, which is a sign of strength, and easily roused from the deepest repose and controlled without difficulty when urged to speed. Indeed, the alertness of a horse is made known by its ears, and its valor by its quivering limbs.

48. These colors in particular should be noted: chestnut, golden, ruddy, myrtle-colored, fawn, dun, bright gray, piebald, gray-white, shining-white, flat white, spotted, and black. But 'variegated' (*varius*) showing a mixture of black and chestnut is of the second rank. The other variegations and ash-color are the least good. 49. The ancients used to call a chestnut (*badium*) horse *vadium*, because it runs (*vadere*) more strongly than the other animals. This is also date-brown, which people call 'scarlet.' And it is called date-brown (*spadix*) from the color of the date, which Sicilians call *spadix*. 50. But a 'bright gray' (*glaucus*) horse is as if colored like blue-grey eyes, perfused with a kind of luster, for the ancients would call this 'bright gray.' Dun (*gilvus*) is the color of quinces, somewhat whitish. Piebald (*guttatus*) is white with intervening black spots. 51. 'Shining white' (*candidus*) and 'flat white' (*albus*) are different from each other, for 'flat white' has a kind of pallor, but 'shining white' is snowy and drenched with pure light. Grey-white (*canus*) is so called because it is composed of the colors white and black. Spotted (*scutulatus*) horses are so called because they have round markings, white on maroon. 52. A 'variegated' (*varius*) horse, because it has bands (*via*) of unlike colors. Horses whose feet alone are white are called *petilus*; the ones with a white forehead are called *calidus*. 53. A fawn-colored (*cervinus*) horse is what is popularly called *guaranen*. The common people call this 'bronzish' (*aeranis*), because it resembles bronze (*aes*, gen. *aeris*) in color. A myrtle-colored (*mirteus*) horse is a subdued maroon. 54. The *dosinus* horse is so called because its color is that of an ass (*de asinus*); it is also known as ash-colored (*cinereus*). These originate from wild stock, which we call *equiferus*, and therefore they cannot be used as city horses. 55. The *mauros* is black, for the Greeks call 'black' μαῦρος.

The cob (*mannus*) is a smaller horse, which is commonly called *brunicus*. The ancients named the *veredus* so because it 'conveys carriages' (*vehere redas*), that is, it pulls them, or because it travels on public roads (*via*), by which carriages (*reda*) were also accustomed to go.

56. There are three kinds of horses: one well-bred, suited for battles and burdens; the second common and ordinary, suited for draft work, not for riding; the third originating from a mixture of different species, which is called hybrid (*bigener*), because it is born from different species, like the mule. 57. The mule (*mulus*) has a name derived from Greek – for it is this in Greek – or because, forced by the miller's yoke,

> It draws the slow millstones (*mola*) around in grinding (*molere*).[2]

The Jews claim that Ana, Esau's great-grandson, was the first to have herds of mares mounted by asses in the desert, so that new animals, mules, might be conceived contrary to nature. They also say that onagers were set to mount she-asses for this purpose, and this type of breeding was invented so that very speedy asses would be born from these unions.

58. Indeed human intervention has forced animals of different species to breed with each other, and has thus developed another type of animal by means of an unnatural combination. In this way Jacob obtained similarities of colors contrary to nature, for his sheep conceived offspring similar to the image of the ram mounting them from above that they saw as a reflection in the water (cf. Gen. 30:32–42). 59. And then this same thing is reported to have occurred in herds of mares, so that people present well-bred stallions to the view of the mares as they conceive, to enable them to conceive and create offspring resembling these stallions. Dove fanciers also place pictures of the most beautiful doves in those places where the doves go about, so that, catching sight of the picture, they may produce offspring similar in appearance. 60. Whence also people advise pregnant women not to gaze

2 This verse, identified as metrical by Jacques André in his edition of Book XII (1986), is of unknown authorship.

at repulsive animal faces, such *cynocephali* or apes, lest they should bear offspring resembling what they have seen. Indeed, the nature of females is such that whatever sort of thing they look at or imagine in the extreme heat of pleasure, while they are conceiving, is the sort of progeny they will bear. Thus in the act of procreation an animal transmits external forms to the interior, and since she is filled with the images of these things, she combines their appearance with her own particular quality. 61. Among the animals those born of differing species are called hybrids (*bigener*), such as the mule from a mare and an ass, the hinny (*burdo*) from a stallion and a jenny, the *hybrida* from wild boars and domestic sows, the *tityrus* from a ewe and a he-goat, and the *musmo* from a she-goat and a ram. This latter is the leader of the flock.

ii. Beasts (*De bestiis*) 1. The term 'beast,' properly speaking, includes lions, panthers, tigers, wolves, foxes, dogs, apes, and other animals that attack either with their mouth or their claws, excepting serpents. They are called beasts (*bestia*) from the force (*vis*) with which they attack. 2. They are termed wild (*ferus*) because they enjoy a natural freedom and are driven (*ferre*) by their own desires – for their wills are free and they wander here and there, and wherever their spirit leads, there they go.

3. The term 'lion' (*leo*, gen. *leonis*) is of Greek origin but is declined in Latin, for it is called λέων in Greek, and it is a mongrel term, because it is partly corrupt.[3] But 'lioness' (*leaena*) is completely Greek, just as 'dragoness' (*dracaena*) is. It is a usage among poets that *leaena* is called *lea*. And the Greek word *leo* is translated as 'king' in Latin, because he is the ruler of all the beasts. 4. His kind is said to be of three types. Of these the small ones with curly manes are peaceful, and the long ones with straight manes are fierce. Their foreheads and tails reveal their spirit. Their strength is indicated in their chest, their steadfastness in their head. When surrounded by hunters they look at the ground so as not to be frightened by the sight of hunting spears. They fear the rattle of wheels, but they fear fire even more. 5. Even when they are sleeping their eyes are watchful. When they walk their tail brushes away their tracks, so that a hunter cannot find them. When they bear their cubs, the cub is said to sleep for three days and nights, and then after that the roaring or growling of the father, making the den shake, as it were, is said to wake the sleeping cub. 6. Around humans, the lion's nature is such that unless they are hurt they are unable to become angry. Their tender-heartedness is obvious from continual examples, for they spare those who are lying prone, they allow captives whom they meet to return home, and they never kill a human except in great hunger. Concerning them Lucretius says (*On the Nature of Things* 5.1036):

> And the cubs (*scymnus*) of lions.

7. The tiger (*tigris*) is so called because of its rapid flight, for this is what the Persians and Medes call an arrow. It is a beast distinguished by varied markings, amazing in its strength and speed. The river Tigris is called after the name of the animal, because it is the most rapid of all rivers. Hyrcania, in particular, produces tigers.

8. The panther (*panther*) is so called either because it is the friend of 'all' animals, except the dragon, or because it both rejoices in the society of its own kind and gives back whatever it receives in the same kind[4] – for in Greek πᾶν means "all." This beast is ornamented with tiny round spots, in such a way that it is marked with little round eyes, varying black and white against a tawny background. 9. It only gives birth once. The reason for this characteristic is obvious, for when the cubs grow in their mother's womb and, as their powers mature, become strong enough to be born, they detest the delay in time so much that they tear with their claws at the laden womb since it is standing in the way of delivery. The mother gives birth to the cubs, or rather, driven by the pain, casts them out. Thus, afterwards, the generative seed, when it has been infused and received, does not adhere to the injured, scarred matrix of the womb, but recoils to no effect. Hence Pliny says (*Natural History* 8.43) that animals with sharp claws are unable to give birth many times, for they are injured by the cubs moving inside the womb.

10. The pard (*pardus*), comes next after the panther; this type has a mottled coat, and is extremely swift and

3 The Latin word *leo* is "mongrel" because, while its nominative case has a Greek appearance, its oblique cases show regular Latin forms.

4 The Latin terms *panther*, *pardus*, and *leopardus* were not clearly distinguished in early sources. We have arbitrarily translated them as 'panther,' 'pard,' and 'leopard.' André (1986) proposes that the etymologies are Greek πᾶν + θήρ, "beast," and πᾶν + ἀντί, "in return."

headlong for blood, for it rushes to kill with a leap. 11. The leopard (*leopardus*) is born from the cross-mating of a lioness and a pard, and yields a third breed. So also Pliny in his *Natural History* (cf. 8.42) says a lion mates with a female pard, or a male pard with a lioness, and from either union this mixed-breed offspring is created, just like a mule or hinny.

12. The rhinoceros (*rhinoceron*) is named with a Greek word; in Latin it means "horn on the nose." This is also the *monoceron*, that is, the unicorn (*unicornus*), because it has a single four-foot horn in the middle of its forehead, so sharp and strong that it tosses in the air or impales whatever it attacks. It often fights with the elephant and throws it to the ground after wounding it in the belly. 13. It has such strength that it can be captured by no hunter's ability, but, as those who have written about the natures of animals claim, if a virgin girl is set before a unicorn, as the beast approaches, she may open her lap and it will lay its head there with all ferocity put aside, and thus lulled and disarmed it may be captured.

14. The Greeks believe that the elephant (*elephans*) is named from the size of its body, which looks like a mountain, for in Greek a mountain is called λόφος. Among the inhabitants of India an elephant is called a *barro* after the sound it makes, whence also its trumpeting is called *barritus*, and its tusks called ivory (*ebur*). Its trunk is called a proboscis (*proboscida*) because with it the beast moves its 'food to its mouth' (*pabulum* + *os*; cf. βόσκειν, "to feed"), and it is like a snake protected by an ivory palisade. 15. These animals were called 'Lucan cows' by the ancient Romans; 'cows' because they had seen no animal larger than a cow, and 'Lucan' because it was in Lucania that Pyrrhus first set them against the Romans in battle. This kind of animal is suited to warfare, for the Persians and Indians, having set wooden towers on them, attack with javelins as if from a rampart. Elephants are very strong in intellect and memory. 16. They proceed in herds; they give a greeting with a gesture, as they can; they flee from mice; they mate facing away from each other; and when they give birth they deliver the offspring in the water or on an island on account of serpents, because serpents are their enemies, and kill them by coiling around them. They carry the fetus for two years, never bearing more than once nor more than one; they live three hundred years. At first elephants were found only in Africa and India, but now only India produces them.

17. The griffin (*grypes*) is so called because it is an animal with feathers (perhaps cf. *grus*, "crane") and four feet (*pes*). This kind of wild animal is born in the Hyperborean mountains. They are lions in their entire torso, but they are like eagles in their wings and faces. They are violently hostile to horses. They also tear humans apart when they see them. 18. The chameleon (*chamaeleon*) does not have one color alone, but is speckled with a diverse variety like the pard. It is named thus . . . The small body of the chameleon changes with a very easy transformation to whatever colors it may see, while the larger body size of other animals is not as suited to an easy transformation. 19. The giraffe (*camelopardus*) is so called because while it is speckled with white spots like the pard (*pardus*), it has a neck like a horse, ox-like feet, and a head like a camel (*camelus*). Ethiopia produces this animal.

20. The lynx (*lyncis*, i.e. *lynx*) is so called because it is reckoned among the wolves (*lupus*) in kind; it is a beast that has spotted markings on its back, like a pard, but it is similar to a wolf; whence the wolf has the name λύκος and the other animal, 'lynx.' People say that its urine hardens into a precious stone called *lyncurius*. That the lynxes themselves perceive this is shown by this proof: they bury as much of the excreted liquid in sand as they can, from a sort of natural jealousy lest such excretion should be brought to human use. Pliny Secundus (cf. *Natural History* 8.43) says that lynxes do not bear more than one offspring. 21. Beavers (*castor*) are so called from 'castrating' (*castrare*). Their testicles are useful for medicines, on account of which, when they anticipate a hunter, they castrate themselves and amputate their own genitals with their teeth. Concerning them Cicero said in his Scaurian oration (2.7): "They ransom themselves with that part of their body for which they are most sought after." And Juvenal (*Satires* 12.34):

> (The beaver) who makes himself a eunuch, wishing to escape with the loss of his testicles.

They are also called *fibri*, and also 'Pontic dogs.'

22. The bear (*ursus*) is said to be so called because it shapes its offspring in its 'own mouth' (*ore suo*), as if the word were *orsus*, for people say that it produces unshaped offspring, and gives birth to some kind of flesh that the mother forms into limbs by licking it. Whence this is said (Petronius, *Anthol. Latina*, ed. Riese, 690.3):

> Thus with her tongue the bear shapes her offspring when she has borne it.

But prematurity is what causes this kind of offspring; the bear gives birth after at most thirty days, whence it happens that its hurried gestation creates unshaped offspring. Bears have weak heads; their greatest strength is in their forepaws and loins, whence they sometimes stand up erect.

23. Wolf (*lupus*) comes into our language derived from Greek, for they call wolves λύκος; and λύκος is named in Greek from its behavior, because it slaughters whatever it finds in a frenzy of violence (perhaps cf. λύσσα, "rage"). Others say wolves are named as if the word were *leopos*, because their strength, just like the lion's (*leo*), is in their paws (*pes*). Whence whatever they tread on with their paws does not live. 24. It is a violent beast, eager for gore. Concerning the wolf, country folk say that a person loses his voice if a wolf sees him first. Whence to someone who suddenly falls silent one says, "The wolf in the story." Certainly if a wolf perceives that he is seen first, he puts aside his bold ferocity. Wolves do not copulate more than twelve days during the entire year. They endure hunger for a long time, and devour a large amount after a lengthy fast. Ethiopia produces wolves that have manes about the neck, and of such a variety of shades that people say that there is no color these wolves do not possess.

25. The Latin word 'dog' (*canis*) seems to have a Greek etymology, for the animal is called κύων in Greek. Still, some people think it is named for the sound (*canor*) of barking because it is loud, whence also the word 'sing' (*canere*). No animal is smarter than the dog, for they have more sense than the others. 26. They alone recognize their own names; they love their masters; they defend their master's home; they lay down their life for their master; they willingly run after game with their master; they do not leave the body of their master even when he has died. Finally, it is part of their nature not to be able to live apart from humans. There are two qualities found in dogs: strength and speed. 27. The offspring of any kind of animal are incorrectly called 'pups' (*catulus*), for, strictly speaking, pups are the offspring of dogs (*canis*), formed as a diminutive. 28. Dogs born from the chance mating of wolves with dogs are called *lycisci*, as Pliny says (cf. *Natural History* 8.148). Also the Indians are accustomed to tie up female dogs in the forest at night, to expose them to wild tigers, and the tigers mount the dogs; from this mating are born dogs so fierce and strong that they overcome lions in combat.

29. Foxes (*vulpes*) are so named as if the word were *volupes*, for they are 'shifty on their feet' (*volubilis* + *pes*) and never follow a straight path but hurry along tortuous twistings. It is a deceitful animal, tricking others with its guile, for whenever it has no food it pretends to be dead, and so it snatches and devours the birds that descend to its apparent corpse.

30. 'Ape' (*simia*) is a Greek word, that is, 'with flattened nostrils' (cf. σιμός, "pug-nosed"), whence we name apes, because they have flattened nostrils and an ugly face, with disgustingly baggy wrinkles, although having a flattened nose is also characteristic of goats. Other people think that apes are named from a Latin word, because they are felt to have a great similarity (*similitudo*) to human behavior, but this etymology is false. 31. Apes, in their knowledge of the elements,[5] rejoice at the new moon, and are downcast at the half moon and the crescent moon. They carry the offspring whom they love before them; the ones that are neglected cling to their mother. There are five kinds of apes. Of these the *cercopitheci* have tails, for it is the ape with a tail, which some people call the *clura*. 32. The *sphinga* (i.e. *sphinx*) is shaggy with hair, and has protruding breasts; they are tame to the point of forgetting their wildness. *Cynocephali* are themselves also similar to apes, but with a face like that of a dog, hence their name (cf. κύων, "dog"; κεφαλή, "head"). 33. Satyrs (*satyrus*) have a somewhat pleasing appearance and are restless, with gesticulating movements. *Callitriches* are almost entirely different from the others in appearance, for they have a long beard on their face, and a broad tail.

34. The *leontophonos* (cf. λεοντο-, "of a lion"; φόνος, "slaughter") is a small animal; it is so named because when captured it is burnt, and meat, sprinkled with its ash and placed at the crossroads, kills lions, if they take even a small amount of it. 35. The porcupine (*histrix*) is an African animal similar to the hedgehog, named for the 'clattering' (*stridor*) of its quills, which it loosens and shoots from its back, so as to wound any dogs that chase it. 36. The *enhydros* is a small beast so named because it dwells in water (cf. ὕδωρ, "water"), particularly in

5 *Elementum* here seems to mean "planetary body" (i.e. the moon) rather than "material element"; the former meaning is common in later Latin, and in the Greek equivalent term στοιχεῖον.

the Nile. If these beasts discover a sleeping crocodile, first they roll themselves in the mud and then enter the crocodile's stomach through its mouth, and eat everything inside it, so that the crocodile dies. 37. The ichneumon (*ichneumon*) is so named from Greek (cf. ἰχνεύειν, "track down"), because both healthful foods and poisons are recognized by their odor. Concerning this animal Dracontius (cf. *Praises of God* 1.515) says:

> The *suillus* destroys (variant: "reveals") the force of any poison.[6]

Moreover, it is called *suillus* from its 'bristles' (*saeta*). This beast hunts snakes. When it fights against an asp, it raises its tail and the asp begins to see the tail as the most threatening. When the asp, thus deceived, turns its force on the tail, it is seized.

38. The mouser (*musio*) is so called because it is troublesome to mice (*mus*). Common people call it the cat (*cattus*) from 'catching' (*captura*). Others say it is so named because *cattat*, that is, "it sees" – for it can see so keenly (*acute*) that with the gleam of its eyes it overcomes the darkness of night. Hence 'cat' comes from Greek, that is, 'clever,' from καίεσθαι ("lit up," i.e. the passive form of καίειν, "kindle"). 39. The ferret (*furo*) is named from 'dark' (*furvus*), whence also comes the word 'thief' (*fur*), for it digs dark and hidden tunnels and tosses out the prey that it finds. 40. The badger (*melo*, i.e. *meles*) is so named either because it has a very rounded member (cf. *malum*, μῆλον, "round fruit"; cf. XVII.vii.3 and XIV.vi.28) or because it seeks honeycombs and carefully removes the honey (*mel*).

iii. Small animals (De minutis animantibus) 1. The mouse (*mus*) is a tiny animal. Its name is Greek, but any form declined from it becomes Latin.[7] Some people say that they are called mice because they are born from the moisture (*humor*) of the earth, for *mus* is "earth," whence also the word 'soil' (*humus*). In these creatures the liver grows during the full moon, just as some marine animals grow larger at this time and grow smaller again when the moon is new. 2. 'Shrew' (*sorex*) is a Latin word, and it is so called because it gnaws and cuts things off like a saw (*serra*). The ancients said *saurex* for *sorex* just as they said *claudus* for *clodus* ("lame"). 3. The weasel (*mustela*) is so named as if it were a long mouse (*mus*), for a dart (*telum*) is so named due to its length. This animal, by its nature, practices deceit in the houses where it nurses its pups, and it moves and changes its dwelling. It hunts snakes and mice. There are two kinds of weasels; one, which the Greeks call ἴκτις, lives in the wild and is larger, while the other wanders into houses. Those people who suppose that the weasel conceives through its mouth and bears its young through its ear are mistaken.

4. The shrew-mouse (*mus araneus*, lit. "spider mouse") is called a spider because of its bite. There is a tiny animal in Sardinia with the shape of a spider that is called *solifuga* (lit. "sun-fleeing") because it avoids the daylight. It is plentiful in silver mines, crawling secretly, and it causes death for those who sit on it inadvertently. 5. The mole (*talpa*) is so called because it is condemned to perpetual blindness in the dark (*tenebrae*), for, having no eyes, it always digs in the earth, and tosses out the soil, and devours the roots beneath vegetables. The Greeks call it ἀσφάλαξ. 6. Dormice (*glis*) are so called because sleep makes them fat, for we say that to grow is to 'swell' (*gliscere*). They sleep for the entire winter and lie motionless as if they were dead; in the summertime they revive. 7. The hedgehog (*ericium*) is an animal covered with quills, from which it is said to be named because it stiffens (*subrigere*) itself up with its quills when it is cornered; with these quills it is protected on all sides against attack. Immediately when it senses something it first stiffens itself up and, turning itself into a ball, covers itself with its own shield of quills. This animal has a certain cleverness, for when it has plucked a bunch of grapes from the vine, it rolls itself backwards over it and in this way takes it (i.e. stuck to the quills) to its offspring.

8. The cricket (*gryllus*) takes its name from the sound of its call. This animal walks backward, bores through the earth, and chirps at night. You catch one by tossing an ant tied with a string into its hole, first making a puff of dust so that it doesn't hide itself. When the cricket grabs the ant, it is drawn out of its hole. 9. The ant (*formica*) is so named because it 'carries bits of grain' (*fert micas farris*). It has great shrewdness, for it provides

6 Dracontius is not speaking in this passage of the ichneumon (a kind of mongoose; cf. ἰχνεύμων, "a tracker, an Egyptian weasel-like animal that hunts eggs") or the *suillus*, but of the Libyan people called Psillus (cf. Pliny, *Natural History* 21.28); Isidore's source-text was faulty. In classical Latin *suillus* is an adjective meaning "of swine"; cf. vi.12 below.

7 The sense is that *mus* in Latin is declined with Latin, not Greek, forms in the oblique cases. The Greek word is μῦς.

for the future and prepares during the summer what it consumes in the winter; during the harvest it selects the wheat and does not touch the barley. When it rains on the ant's grain, the ant throws it out.[8] It is said that in Ethiopia there are ants in the shape of dogs, who dig up golden sand with their feet – they guard this sand lest anyone carry it off, and when they chase something they pursue it to death. 10. The 'ant lion' (*formicoleon*) is so called either because it is the lion (*leo*) of ants or, more likely, because it is equally an ant and a lion, for it is a small animal very dangerous to ants because it hides itself in the dust and kills the ants carrying grain. And thus it is called both an 'ant' and a 'lion,' because to the rest of the animals it is like an ant, but to ants it is like a lion.

iv. Snakes (De serpentibus) 1. 'Serpent' (*anguis*) is the term for the family of all snakes, because they can bend and twist; and thus it is *anguis* because it is 'turned at angles' (*angulosus*) and never straight. Snakes were always considered among the pagans as the spirits of places, whence Persius (*Satires* 1.113):

> Paint two snakes; boys, the place is sacred.[9]

2. The *coluber* (i.e another word for 'snake') is named thus because it 'inhabits the shadows' (*colit umbras*) or because it glides in slippery (*lubricus*) courses with sinuous curves. And whatever slips away when it is grasped is called 'slippery' – like the fish and the snake. 3. The snake (*serpens*) takes its name because it creeps (*serpere*) by secret approaches; it crawls not with open steps but by tiny thrusts of its scales. But those animals that support themselves on four feet, like the lizard and the newt, are not snakes, but are called reptiles (*reptile*). Snakes are also reptiles, because they crawl (*repere*) on their stomach and breast. Of these animals there are as many poisons as there are kinds, as many varieties of danger as there are of appearance, and as many causes of pain as there are colors.

4. The dragon (*draco*) is the largest of all the snakes, or of all the animals on earth. The Greeks call it δράκων, whence the term is borrowed into Latin so that we say *draco*. It is often drawn out of caves and soars aloft, and disturbs the air. It is crested, and has a small mouth and narrow pipes through which it draws breath and sticks out its tongue. It has its strength not in its teeth but in its tail, and it causes injury more by its lashing tail than with its jaws. 5. Also, it does not harm with poison; poison is not needed for this animal to kill, because it; kills whatever it wraps itself around. Even the elephant with his huge body is not safe from the dragon, for it lurks around the paths along which the elephants are accustomed to walk, and wraps around their legs in coils and kills them by suffocating them. It is born in Ethiopia and India in the fiery intensity of perpetual heat.

6. 'Basilisk' (*basiliscus*) is a Greek word, translated into Latin as "little king" (*regulus*; cf. βασιλεύς, "king"), because it is the king of the snakes, so that they flee when they see it because it kills them with its odor – it also kills a human if it looks at one. Indeed no flying bird may pass unharmed by the basilisk's face, but however distant it may be it is burnt up and devoured by this animal's mouth. 7. However, the basilisk may be overcome by weasels. For this reason people put weasels into caves where the basilisk lies hidden; and as the basilisk takes flight at the sight, the weasel chases it down and kills it. Thus the Creator of nature made nothing without a remedy. It is half a foot in length, and marked with white spots. 8. Basilisks, like scorpions, seek after parched places, and when they come to water they become hydrophobic – ὑδροφόβος – and frantic. 9. The *sibilus* (lit. "the hissing one") is the same as the basilisk, and it kills by means of a hissing, before it bites and burns.

10. The viper (*vipera*) is so named because it 'spawns through force' (*vi parere*), for when its womb is groaning to deliver, the offspring, not waiting for nature's suitable time, gnaw at and forcibly tear open their mother's sides, causing her death. Lucan (*Civil War* 6.490) says:

> When the body has burst apart, the knotted vipers gather.

11. It is said that the male spits his seed into the mouth of the female viper, and she, turned from the passion of lust to rage, bites off the head of the male that is in her mouth. Thus it happens that each parent dies; the male when they mate and the female when she gives birth. From the viper comes the pill that the Greeks call θηριακός.

8 The sense may rather be that the ant puts the grain out to dry.

9 The *genius loci*, "spirit of a place," was often represented as a snake.

12. The asp (*aspis*) is named thus because with its bite it introduces and scatters (*spargere*) venom, for the Greeks call venom ἰός. Whence the term 'asp,' because it kills with a venomous bite. There are different kinds with different appearances, some more harmful than others. And it is said that when an asp begins to give in to an enchanter who has called it with certain special chants so that he may draw it from its cave, and the asp does not want to come out, it presses one ear against the ground and blocks and closes up the other with its tail [so that] by not hearing the magic words it does not go out to the enchanter. 13. The *dipsas* is a type of asp, called *situla* in Latin because whomever it has bitten dies of thirst (*sitis*). 14. The *hypnalis*, a type of asp, is so called because it kills by means of sleep (cf. ὕπνος, "sleep"). Cleopatra held this snake to herself and thus was overcome by death as if by sleep. 15. The *haemorrhois* asp is so named because whoever has been bitten by it exudes blood, with the effect that as the veins dissolve it draws out through the blood whatever life there is – for blood is called αἷμα in Greek.

16. The *prester* asp hurries with its mouth always open and steaming. The poet recalled this animal thus (Lucan, *Civil War* 9.722):

> The greedy *prester*, swelling out its steaming mouth.

Whoever it strikes swells up and is killed by a tremendous bodily swelling, and this swelling is followed by putrefaction. 17. The *seps*, a corrosive asp that, when it has bitten a person, immediately consumes him, so that the victim is entirely liquefied in the snake's mouth. 18. The horned (*cerastes*) serpent is so called because it has horns on its head like a ram, for the Greeks call horns κέρατα. It has four small horns, and it displays them as if they were food, so that it kills the animals roused by this enticement. It covers its entire body with sand, and reveals no sign of itself except that part by which it attacks the birds and animals that it has lured. And it is more flexible than other snakes, so that it seems to have no spine. 19. The *scytale* snake is so named because it gleams with so much variegation of its skin that it slows onlookers by the charm of its markings (perhaps cf. *scintilla*, "spark, glimmer"). And because it is rather slow at crawling, it captures those it is too slow to catch when they are mesmerized and wondering at it. It is an animal of such heat that even in the winter it sheds the skin of its heated body. Concerning it Lucan says (*Civil War* 9.717):

> And only the *scytale* will shed its skin with frost still scattered about.

20. The *amphisbaena* is named because it has two heads (cf. ἀμφίς, "on both sides"; βαίνειν, "go"), one in the proper place and one on the tail, and it advances with both heads leading, its body trailing in a loop. This alone of the snakes trusts itself to the cold, and comes out first of all the serpents. Concerning it Lucan says (*Civil War* 9.719):

> Grievous is the *amphisbaena*, turning toward its two heads.

Its eyes glow like lamps. 21. The *enhydris* is a serpent living in the water, for the Greeks call water ὕδωρ. 22. The *hydros* is an aquatic snake; people struck by it become swollen. Some people call the ill effects of this *boa*, because it is remedied with cow (*bos*) dung. 23. The hydra (*hydra*) is a dragon with many heads; this kind of dragon was in the Lernean swamp in the province of Arcadia. It is called *excetra* in Latin, because when one head is 'cut off, three' (*caesus tria*) more grow back. But this is only a story; for it happens that Hydra was a place that spewed out floods that devastated the neighboring city. If one outlet for the water were closed up in this Hydra, many others would burst forth. When Hercules saw this he dried up the place itself and thus closed up the path of the floods. Hydra is named from 'water' (cf. ὕδωρ, "water").

24. The *chelydros* is a snake that is also known as the *chersydros*, as if it were *cerim*,[10] because it dwells both in the water and on land; for the Greeks call land χέρσος and water ὕδωρ. These make the earth on which they move smoke, as Macer thus describes it (fr. 8):

> Whether their backs froth out poison, or it smokes on the earth, where the hideous snake crawls.

And Lucan (*Civil War* 9.711):

> And the *chelydri* drawn along their smoking trails.

But it always proceeds in a straight line, for if it turns when it moves, it immediately makes a sharp noise. 25. The *natrix* is a snake that contaminates water with its

10 The term *cerim* appears to be a textual corruption.

poison. Whatever spring it was in, it would mix its poison into it. Concerning it Lucan says (*Civil War* 9.720):

> The *natrix*, polluter of water.

26. The *cenchris* (i.e. a kind of spotted snake) is a snake that cannot bend so that it always makes a straight path. Whence Lucan (*Civil War* 9.712):

> The *cenchris*, always bound to crawl in a straight path.

27. The *parias* is a snake that always travels on its tail, and appears to make a furrow. Again, Lucan said this concerning it (*Civil War* 9.721):

> Whence the *parias* is pleased to plow a path with its tail.

28. The boa (*boas*), a snake in Italy of immense size, attacks herds of cattle and buffaloes, and attaches itself to the udders flowing with plenty of milk, and kills them by suckling on them, and from this takes the name 'boa,' from the destruction of cows (*bos*). 29. The *iaculus* is a flying snake. Concerning it Lucan says (*Civil War* 9.720):

> And the flying *iaculi*.

For they spring up into trees, and whenever some animal happens by they throw (*iactare*) themselves on it and kill it, whence they are called *iaculus* (cf. *iaculum*, "javelin"). Also in Arabia there are snakes with wings, called sirens (*sirena*); they run faster than horses, but they are also said to fly. Their venom is so powerful that when someone is bitten by them death ensues before the pain is felt. 30. The *ophites* is so named because it has the color of sand. Concerning it the poet says (Lucan, *Civil War* 9.714):

> How the Theban *ophites* is painted with small spots, and the *ammodytes*, of the same color as parched sand and indistinguishable from it.[11]

31. The *seps* is a small snake that consumes not only the body but also the bones with its venom. The poet refers to it thus (Lucan, *Civil War* 9.723):

> The corrosive *seps*, dissolving bones along with the body.

32. The *dipsas* is said to be a snake so tiny that when it is stepped on it is not observed. Its venom kills before it is felt, so that the face of one about to die displays no horror of his impending death. Of this one the poet says (cf. Lucan, *Civil War* 9.737):

> With its head twisted back the *dipsas*, when it was stepped on, bit the young standard-bearer Aulus, of Tyrrhenian blood; there was barely any pain or sensation of fangs.

33. The *salpuga* is a snake that is invisible. The *caecula* is so named because it is small (i.e. has the diminutive ending *–ula*) and has no eyes (cf. *caecus*, "blind"). The centipede (*centupeda*) is so named for the great number of its feet (*pes*, gen. *pedis*). 34. The lizard (*lacertus*) is a type of reptile, so named because it has arms (cf. *lacertus*, "upper arm"). There are many kinds of lizards, such as the *botrax*, the salamander, the *saura*, and the newt. 35. The *botrax* is so named because it has the face of a frog, for the Greeks call the frog βάτραχος. 36. The salamander (*salamandra*) is so named because it prevails against fire. Of all the venomous creatures its force is the greatest; the others kill people one at a time, but the salamander can slay many people at once – for if it should creep in among the trees, it injects its venom into all the fruit, and so it kills whoever eats the fruit. Again, if it falls into a well, the force of its venom kills whoever drinks from it. This animal fights back against fire; it alone of all the animals will extinguish fire, for it can live in the midst of flames without feeling pain or being consumed – not only because it is not burned but also because it extinguishes the fire.

37. The *saura* is a lizard whose eyes go blind as it grows old. It goes into a chink in an east-facing wall, and stretches out and receives light when the sun rises.[12] 38. The newt (*stellio*) has its name given according to its color, for on its back it is marked with glittering spots in the manner of stars (*stella*). Ovid says concerning it (cf. *Met.* 5.460):

> It has a name appropriate for its color, star-strewn (*stellatus*) with variegated spots on its body.

This animal is considered to be the antagonist of scorpions, so that when it is seen by them it induces fear and stupefaction. 39. There are other kinds of snakes, such as the *ammodyta*, the *elephantia*, the *chamaedraco*. Finally, there are as many deaths caused by snakes as

11 As Isidore observes in XVI.v.3, *ophites* is a marble mottled like a serpent; the text of Lucan is here misconstrued.

12 The sense seems to be that the *saura* recovers its sight when the sun rises, as in the *Physiologus*.

there are names for them. Further, all snakes are cold by nature, and they do not strike except when they are warm. 40. When they are cold they injure no one; hence their venom is more noxious during the day than at night, for they are sluggish in the chill of the night, and understandably so, since they are cold in the evening dew. Thus their venom, which is cold by nature, draws to itself the warmth of their chilled bodies. Hence during the winter they lie motionless in coils, but in the summer they are uncoiled. 41. Hence it is that whenever someone is injected with snake venom, he is stupefied at first and then, when the poison is heated up in him and becomes fiery, it kills him forthwith.

Venom (*venenum*) is so named because it rushes through the veins (*vena*), for its destructive effect, once infused, travels through the veins when bodily activity increases, and it drives out the soul. 42. Hence venom is unable to cause harm unless it reaches a person's blood. Lucan (*Civil War* 9.614):

> The pestilence of snakes is fatal when mixed in with blood.

Further, all venom is cold, and hence the soul, which is fiery, flees the cold venom. Among the natural advantages that we see are common to humans as well as to irrational animals, the snake excels in a certain quickness of sense. 43. Hence it is written in Genesis (cf. 3:1): "For the serpent was shrewder than all the beasts of the earth." And Pliny says (i.e. a false attribution from Servius), if it may be believed, that if a snake's head escapes with only two inches of its body, it will still live. Hence it will cast its entire body towards those striking it in order to save its head.

44. Vision in snakes generally is feeble – they rarely look directly forward, with good reason, since they have eyes not in the front of their face but in their temples, so that they hear more quickly than they see. No other animal darts its tongue as quickly as the snake, so that it appears to have three tongues when in fact it has one. 45. The snake's body is moist, so that it leaves a trail of moisture wherever it goes. The tracks left by snakes are such that, although they are seen to lack feet, they nevertheless crawl on their ribs with forward thrusts of their scales, which are spread evenly from the highest part of the neck to the lowest part of the belly. They support themselves on their scales, which are like nails, and with their ribs, which are like legs. 46. Hence if a snake is crushed by some blow to any part of the body, from the belly to the head, it is unable to make its way, having been crippled, because wherever the blow strikes it breaks the spine, which activates the 'feet' of the ribs and the motion of the body.

Snakes are said to live for a long time, because when they shed their old skin they are said to shed their 'old age' (*senectus*, also meaning the "cast-off" skins of snakes) and return to youth. 47. Snake skins are called 'castoffs' (*exuviae*) because when snakes age they 'cast off' (*exuere*) these skins from themselves, and having cast them off, return to youth. Likewise 'castoffs' and 'garments' (*induviae*) are so called because they are cast off and 'put on' (*induere*). 48. Pythagoras says that a snake is created from the spinal cord of a dead person. Ovid mentions this in his *Metamorphoses* when he says (cf. 15.389):

> There are those who believe the human spinal cord is
> changed to a snake when the spine, in the sealed
> sepulcher, has rotted.

This, if it is believed, occurs with some justice, in that as a human's death comes about from a snake, so a snake comes about from a human's death. It is also said that a snake will not dare to strike a naked human.

v. Vermin (De verminibus)[13] 1. Vermin (*vermis*) are animals that are generated for the most part from flesh or wood or some earthy substance, without any sexual congress – but sometimes they are brought forth from eggs, like the scorpion. There are vermin of the earth, the water, the air, flesh, leaves, wood, and clothing. 2. Spiders (*aranea*) are vermin of the air (*aer*), named from the air that is their nourishment. They spin out a long thread from their little body and, constantly attentive to their webs, never leave off working on them, maintaining their perpetual suspension by their special craftsmanship. 3. The leech (*sanguisuga*) is a water vermin, so named because it sucks blood (*sanguinem sugere*). It lies in wait for creatures when they are drinking, and when it glides into their throat, or attaches itself somewhere, it drinks in their blood. When it is sated by too much blood, it vomits out what it has drunk so that it may once more suck in fresher blood. 4. Scorpions (*scorpio*) are land vermin; they are counted more appropriately among the vermin than among the snakes. The scorpion

13 *Vermis* can mean "vermin," or more specifically, "worm."

is an animal armed with a sting, and was named from this in Greek (cf. σκορπίος), because it stings with its tail and infuses venom through the bow-shaped wound.[14] It is characteristic of the scorpion that it does not attack the palm of the hand.

5. The 'Spanish fly' (*cantharis*) is a land vermin [that with its burning makes blisters full of liquid as soon as it is applied to the human body]. 6. The *multipes* is a land vermin, so named from its 'great number of feet' (*multitudo pedum*); it rolls up into a ball when it is touched. They are generated under rocks, out of the moisture and earth. 7. Slugs (*limax*) are mud vermin, so named because they are generated either in mud (*limus*) or from mud; hence they are always regarded as filthy and unclean. 8. Silkworms (*bombyx*) are leaf vermin. Silk-cloth (*bombycinum*) is prepared from their web. They are called by this name because they are emptied out when they spin their thread, and air alone remains inside them.[15] 9. Cankerworms (*eruca*) are leaf vermin that are wrapped up in vegetable greens or in vine-leaves; they are named from 'gnawing away' (*erodere*). Plautus refers to them in (*The Casket* 728):

> He folds himself up, imitating a vile, malignant beast
> wrapped in a vine-leaf.

This animal does not fly as the locust does, hurrying here and there and leaving half-consumed plants behind it; instead it remains on the plant, which is doomed to die, and consumes everything with slow gliding and lazy bites.

10. The Greeks call wood vermin *teredo* (i.e. τερηδών) because they 'eat by grinding' (*terendo edere*). We call them wood-worms (*termes*, i.e. *tarmes*). So wood vermin are called by Latin speakers; trees that are felled at the wrong time generate these vermin. 11. Moth-worms (*tinea*) are clothes vermin, so named because they hold fast (*tenere*), and they settle in right at the place they eat away. Whence also the word 'tenacious' (*pertinax*) for someone who keeps at the same thing again and again.

12. There are flesh vermin: the *hemicranius*, the maw-worm, the *ascaris*, the *costus*, the louse, the flea, the nit (*lens*), the *tarmus*, the tick, the *usia*, the bed-bug. 13. *Hemicranius* is the name of a vermin of the head (cf. Late Latin *cranium*, "skull"). The maw-worm (*lumbricus*) is a vermin of the intestines, named as if the word were *lumbicus*, because it glides (*labi*) or because it is found in the loins (*lumbus*). *Ascaris* . . . *Costus*... 14. Lice (*peduculus*) are skin vermin named from the feet (*pes*, gen. *pedis*). Hence those on whose bodies lice swarm are called *peducosi*. 15. But fleas (*pulex*) are so named because they are mainly nourished by dust (*pulvis*). Nits . . . The *tarmus* is a vermin found in fat. The tick (*ricinus*) is a vermin found on dogs (*canis*), so called because it sits in the 'ears of dogs' (*auribus canum*), for κύων is the Greek word for dog. 16. The *usia* is a vermin of swine, named because it 'burns' (*urere*, ppl. *ustum*), for wherever it has bitten, that spot becomes so inflamed that blisters are formed there. 17. The bedbug (*cimex*) is named for its similarity to a certain plant (i.e. *cimicia*; see XVII.ix.57) whose stench it possesses.

18. In particular, vermin (*vermis*, here specifically "maggots") are generated in putrid meat, the moth-worm in clothing, the cankerworm in vegetables, the wood-worm in wood, and the *tarmus* in fat. 19. Vermin do not crawl with obvious steps, or with a pushing of scales as snakes do, because vermin do not possess the strong support of a spine, as in serpents.[16] Rather, they achieve motion by extending the contracted parts of their little bodies forward by degrees, and contracting them again, and set moving like this they glide along.

vi. Fish (De piscibus) 1. Fish (*piscis*) are named from the same source as livestock (*pecus*), that is, from 'grazing' (*pascere*). 2. Animals that swim are called reptiles (*reptile*), because they possess the look and natural habit of creeping (*reptare*); even though they submerge themselves in the deep, still they creep in their swimming. Hence David says (cf. Psalm 103:25 Vulgate): "This sea is great and spacious; there are creeping things (*reptilis*) without number." 3. Amphibians (*amphibia*) are a certain type of fish, so called because they possess the habit of walking on the land and the action of swimming in the water – for in Greek ἀμφί means "both," that is, because they live (cf. βιόω, "live") both in water and on land – such as seals, crocodiles, and hippopotami, that is, 'river horses.'

14 The "bow-shaped" wound links the animal *scorpio* with the military machine also named *scorpio* – see V.xxvii.18 and XVIII.viii.3.

15 André (1986) suggests that Isidore alludes to another meaning of the Greek word βόμβυξ, i.e. "flute," through which air passes.

16 The translation here follows a convincing emendation proposed by Klussman (see André 1986, note ad loc.), transposing the phrase "as snakes do."

4. People gave names to livestock and beasts and flying animals before naming fish, because the former were seen and recognized before. Later, as the types of fish gradually came to be known, names were established based either on a similarity to land animals or on their particular appearance or behavior [or color or shape or sex]. 5. Based on a similarity to land animals, such as 'frogs' (i.e. "frog-fish," and so for the rest) and 'calves' and 'lions' and 'blackbirds' and 'peacocks,' colored with various hues on the neck and back, and 'thrushes,' mottled with white, and other fish that took for themselves the names of land animals according to their appearance. Based on land behavior, such as 'dogs' in the sea, so called from land dogs because they bite, and pikes (*lupus*, lit. "wolf"), because they pursue other fish with cruel voracity. 6. Based on color, as the maigre (*umbra*, lit. "shadow"), which are the color of shadows, and 'gilt-heads' (*aureta*), because they have the color of gold (*aurum*) on their heads, and *varii* from variegation; these are commonly called 'trout' (*tructa*). Based on shape, like the *orbis* (lit. "circle"), because it is round and consists entirely of its head, and like the sole (*solea*) because it looks like the sole (*solea*) of a shoe. Based on sex, like the *musculus*, because it functions as the male (*masculus*) for whales; for it is said that 'female sea-monsters' (*bellua*) conceive through intercourse with these animals. Hence also the mussel (*musculus cochlearum*), by whose milt oysters conceive. 7. Whales (*ballena*) are beasts of enormous size, named from casting forth and spraying water, for they throw waves higher than the other sea animals; in Greek βάλλειν means "cast forth." 8. The sea-monster (*cetus*, plural *cete*) is named κῆτος, plural κήτη, that is, on account of its vastness.[17] These are huge types of sea-monsters (*bellua*), and their bodies are the same size as mountains. Such a *cetus* swallowed Jonah; its belly was so big that it resembled hell, as the prophet says (cf. Jonah 2:3): "He heard me from the belly of hell."

9. Sea-horses (*equus marinus*), because they are horses (*equus*) in their front part and then turn into fish. Bogues (*boca*) are said to be marine 'cows' (*bos*), as if the word were *boacas*. 10. The *caerulei* (lit. "azure") are named from their color, for azure is green mixed with black, like the sea. 11. Dolphins (*delphin*) have their appointed name because they follow the voices (cf. φωνή, "voice") of humans, or because they gather in a group at the sound of music (*symphonia*).[18] Nothing in the sea is faster than they are, for they often jump over ships as they leap. When they play in the billows and dash themselves headlong against the mass of the waves in their leaping, they seem to portend storms. Properly, they are called *simones*. There is a kind of dolphin in the Nile with a saw-tooth back; it kills crocodiles by cutting the soft parts of their bellies. 12. Sheatfish (*porcus marinus*, lit. "sea pigs"), commonly called *suilli* (lit. "small swine"), are so named because when they seek food they root up the earth underwater like swine. At their throat they have what functions as a mouth, and unless they submerge their snout into the sand, they do not collect food. 13. *Corvi* (lit. "ravens") are named 'from the sound of their breast' (*a cordis voce*), because they croak in their breast and, betrayed by their characteristic sound, they are captured.

14. The tuna (*thynnus*) has a Greek name. They come in the spring. They approach on the right and depart on the left; hence it is believed that they see more acutely with the right eye than with the left. 15. The swordfish (*gladius*) is so called because it has a snout like a sword (cf. *gladius*, "sword"); because of this it pierces ships and sinks them. 16. The saw-fish (*serra*, lit. "saw") is so named because it has a serrated (*serratus*) crest, and cuts through boats when it swims under them. 17. The scorpion-fish (*scorpio*) is so called because it causes injury when it is picked up in the hand. They say that when ten crabs are bound with a bundle of basil, all the nearby scorpion-fish will gather in that spot. 18. The weever (*aranea*, lit. "spider") is a kind of fish so called because it strikes with its ear (*auris*); for its ear has stingers with which it attacks.

19. The crocodile (*crocodillus*), named from its saffron (*croceus*) color, is born in the Nile. It is a quadruped animal, powerful on land and also in the water. It is commonly twenty cubits in length, armed with huge teeth and claws, with skin so tough that it repels blows from stones, however strong, against its back. 20. It rests in the water at night, and on the land during the day. It incubates its eggs on land, the male and the female taking turns to guard them. Certain fish with a serrated

17 Isidore misconstrues Servius, quoting Vergil's "Huge sea-monsters" (*Aen.* 5.822), as meaning "sea-monsters (*cete*), i.e. 'huge ones.'" *Bellua* and *cetus* can both mean either "large sea monster" or "whale."

18 As *symphonia* can mean "a musical instrument," Isidore may here allude to the term *delphinus*, a part of the water organ.

crest may kill a crocodile by sawing into the soft parts of its belly (see section 11 above). [It is said to be the only animal that moves its upper jaw]. 21. The hippopotamus (*hippopotamus*) is so named because it is similar to the horse (cf. ἵππος, "horse") in its back, its mane, and its neighing; its snout is tilted back, and it has boar-like teeth and a curled tail. It stays in the water (cf. ποταμός, "river") during the day and grazes on crops at night. The Nile also produces this animal.

22. The *pagrus* (perhaps the sea-bream or the fraize), which the Greeks call φάγρος because its teeth are so hard that it feeds on oysters in the sea (perhaps cf. φαγεῖν, "eat"). 23. The bream (*dentix*) is named for the great number and size of its teeth (*dens*, gen. *dentis*). The sea-hare (*lepus*, lit. "hare") is named for the similarity of its head to that of a hare. 24. The pike (*lupus*, lit. "wolf"), as has been said, is named for its voracity. It is a cunningly difficult fish to catch; it is said that when a pike is surrounded by a net, it digs into the sand with its tail, and, hidden in this way, slips by the net. 25. The 'red mullet' (*mullus*) is named because it is soft (*mollis*) and very delicate. People say that as food red mullets inhibit desire and dull the acuity of the eyes. People who often eat them smell of fish. When a red mullet is killed in wine, those who drink from it develop a distaste for wine. 26. The 'gray mullet' (*mugilis*) takes its name from being 'very agile' (*multum agilis*), for wherever they sense fishermen's traps they immediately turn back to leap over the net, so that you may see the fish fly. 27. The black-tail (*melanurus*) is named because it has a black tail (cf. οὐρά, "tail") and black fins, and black lines on its body – for the Greeks call 'black' μέλας. 28. The *glaucus* is named for its color, because it is white, for the Greeks call 'white' γλαυκός. This fish rarely appears in the summer, except on cloudy days. 29. The *thymallus* takes its name from a flower – indeed the flower is called 'thyme' (*thymus*) – for although it is pleasing in appearance and agreeable in flavor, still, just like a flower, it smells and exhales aromas from its body. 30. The *escarus* (i.e. *scarus*) is so named because it is said to be the only one to ruminate its food (*esca*); for the other fish do not ruminate. People say that this is a clever fish, for when it is enclosed in a wicker trap, it does not break through with its brow or thrust its head through the opposing twigs, but, turning around, with repeated blows of its tail it widens an opening and so goes out backwards. If by chance another *escarus* sees its struggle from the outside, it helps its efforts to break out by seizing the tail with its teeth. 31. The *sparus* (lit. "spear," i.e. a small sea bream) takes its name from the throwing lance, because it has the same shape – for terrestrial things were discovered before marine ones. *Sparus* refers to a rustic throwing spear, so named for 'casting' (*spargere*).

32. The 'southern-fish' (*australis piscis*, properly the name of a constellation) is named either because it takes up (cf. *(h)aurire*, ppl. *(h)austus*, "drink," and cf. XIII.xi.6) a wave of water in its mouth (*os*, gen. *oris*) or because it appears (*oriri*) at the time when the Pleiades begin to decline in the west. 33. The rock-dwelling *hamio* is marked on its right and left sides by unbroken stripes of purple and other colors. It is called *hamio* because it is not caught except with a hook (*hamus*). 34. The remora (*echenais*), a small fish half a foot long, takes its name because it holds a ship fast by clinging to it. Even if winds rush and storms rage, still the ship seems to stand in the sea as if rooted, and is not moved, not as a result of being held back, but simply by being clung to. Latin speakers have named this the *mora* (lit. "delay") because it forces boats to stand still. 35. The *uranoscopus* (cf. οὐρανός, "heaven"; σκοπεῖν, "gaze") is named from the eye that it has in its head, with which it is always looking upward. 36. The *millago* (perhaps the flying gurnard) is so named because it flies out over the water. And whenever it is seen flying above the water, the weather is changing. 37. The *squatus* is named because it has 'sharp scales' (*squamis acutus*). For this reason wood is polished with its skin. 38. The Syrian city now called Tyre was once called 'Sarra' after a certain fish that is abundant there, which they call *sar* in their language. From this name was drawn the name of small fish similar to these called *sardae* and 'sardines' (*sardina*). 39. The *allec* (i.e. *hallec*) is a small fish suitable for 'pickled fish sauce' (*salsamentum*; cf. ἅλς, "salt"), whence it is named. 40. The *aphorus* is a small fish that cannot be caught on a hook due to its smallness (perhaps cf. ἄφορος with a sense like "unable to be held"). 41. The eel (*anguilla*) was given its name from its similarity to a serpent (*anguis*). Eels originate from mud; hence, when one is caught, it is so slippery that the tighter you hold it, the more quickly it slips away. They say that the river Ganges, in the East, produces eels thirty feet long. When eels are killed in wine, whoever drinks it then develops a distaste for wine.

42. The sea-dragon (*draco marinus*) has stingers in its arms, oriented toward the tail. When it strikes, it emits

poison into whatever spot it attacks, [whence its name]. 43. The Greeks call the murena (*muraena*) μύραινα, because it twists itself in circles.[19] People say this fish only exists in the female sex and that it conceives by means of a snake; on this account it can be summoned and caught by fishermen making a hissing sound like a snake. It can be killed with difficulty by a cudgel blow, but immediately with a rod. It clearly has its vital principle in its tail, for when its head is beaten, it can scarcely be killed, but it dies immediately when the tail is struck. 44. Conger-eel (*congrus*) . . . The octopus (*polypus*), that is, 'with many feet' (cf. πολύς, "many"; πούς, "foot"), for it possesses many tentacles. This ingenious animal reaches for the hook and grasps it with its arms, not biting it, and it does not release the hook until it has eaten around the food on it. 45. The 'electric ray' (*torpedo*) is named because it makes the body become numb (*torpescere*) if anyone touches it while it is alive. Pliny Secundus recounts (cf. *Natural History* 32.7): "From the Indian Ocean the electric ray, even if it is far distant or if it is touched with a spear or stick, numbs one's muscle, no matter how strong it is, and fetters one's feet, no matter how swift they are." Its force is such that even the aura of its body weakens the limbs. 46. The cuttlefish (*sepia*) is named because it is more easily caught when it is hemmed in by enclosures (*sepes*, i.e. *saepes*). It is a disgusting species with respect to coition, for it conceives in its mouth as do vipers. There is so much strength in its black ink that some say that when it is placed in a lamp, with the light now removed, people appear to be Ethiopian. 47. The squid (*lulligo*, i.e. *loligo*): they say that in the Ocean by Mauretania, not far from the river Lixus, such a multitude of squid fly out from the water that they can even sink ships.

48. Shellfish (*concha*) and 'water snails' (*cochlea*) are so named because during the waning moon they are 'hollowed out' (*cavare*), that is, they are emptied out, for all the enclosed sea animals and shellfish have their body parts swell up with the waxing of the moon, and shrink back with its waning. Thus the moon, when it waxes, increases the humors, but when it wanes, the humors decrease – this is what natural philosophers say. The word *concha* is a primary noun, while *cochlea* is a diminutive, as if it were *conchlea*. 49. There are many kinds of shellfish, among which some are pearl-bearing. These are called *oceloe*;[20] the precious stone is solidified in their flesh. People who have written on the nature of animals say concerning these creatures that they seek the shore at night, and conceive the pearls by means of celestial (*caelestis*) dew; hence they are called *oceloe*. 50. The purple-fish (*murex*, also meaning "a sharp rock"; cf. XVI.iii.3) is a shellfish of the sea, named for its sharpness and roughness. It is called by another name, *conchilium* (also meaning "a purple dye"), because when it is cut round with a blade, it sheds tears of a purple color, with which things are dyed purple. And from this *ostrum* (i.e. purple dye) is named, because this dye is drawn out from the liquid of the shell (cf. section 52 below).

51. Crabs (*cancer*) are so called because they are shellfish (*concha*) possessing legs (*crus*, gen. *cruris*). They are animals hostile to oysters. With marvelous ingenuity they live on oyster flesh, for, because the oyster's strong shell cannot be opened, the crab spies out when the oyster opens the closed barricade of its shell, and then stealthily puts a pebble inside, and with the closing thus impeded, eats the oyster's flesh. Some people say that when ten crabs are bound with a bundle of basil, all the nearby scorpion-fish will gather at that place. There are two kinds of crabs, river crabs and sea crabs. 52. The oyster (*ostrea*) is named from the shell with which the inner softness of its flesh is guarded, for the Greeks call a shell ὄστρα (i.e. ὄστρακον). People use the word *ostrea* as a neuter, but its flesh is of the feminine gender grammatically. 53. The mussel (*musculus*), as we have said above (see section 6), is a shellfish from whose milt oysters conceive, and they are called *musculus* as if the word were *masculus* (i.e. "male"). 54. The *peloris* (i.e. a kind of mussel) is named after Pelorus, a promontory in Sicily where they abound: (Vergil, *Aen.* 3.687):

> Behold, Boreas from the narrows of Pelorus.

55. The *unguis* (perhaps the razor-fish) is named from its similarity to human nails (*unguis*). 56. The tortoise (*testudo*) is so called because its back is covered over with a shell (*testa*) in the manner of a vaulted roof. There are four kinds of tortoise: land turtles; sea turtles; mud turtles, that is, those living in mud and swamps; the fourth kind are the river turtles, which live in fresh water. Some

19 Isidore may derive the term *muraena* from the biblical term *murenula*, a necklace – the latter word in fact derived from the former; cf. XIX.xxxi.14.

20 The term *oceloe* seems to be a corruption. Maxwell-Stuart proposes a connection with Greek ὀκέλλειν, "run aground," as their shore-seeking may suggest – see André's note (1986).

people say – and this is unbelievable – that ships go more slowly when they carry the right foot of a turtle. 57. The 'sea urchin' (*echinus*) has taken its name from the land *echinus* (i.e. "hedgehog"), which is commonly called *iricius* (i.e. *ericius*). The sea urchin's shell is two-fold, sharp with spines like chestnuts when they fall from the tree still covered. Its flesh is soft and like vermilion . . . in three ways:[21] as a turtle, a mussel (*peloris*), and a sea-snail. Indeed, the part that we eat, as well as the part that contains the flesh, are both called 'mussel.'

58. Frogs (*rana*) are named from their garrulity (cf. *rancare*, "roar") because in rutting season they fill the swamps with noise, and make their voices resound in unruly croaking. Of these, some are called aquatic frogs, some swamp frogs, and some toads (*rubeta*, also "briar-patch") because they live in thorn bushes – these are larger than all the rest. Other frogs are called *calamitis*, because they live among reeds and bushes (cf. *calamus*, "reed"); they are the smallest and greenest of all, and are mute and without voice. 59. *Agredulae* are small frogs dwelling in dry places or in fields (*ager*), whence they are named. Some people claim that dogs will not bark if a live frog is given to them in a lump of food.

60. Sponges (*sfungia*) are named from 'tidying' (*fingere*), that is, polishing and cleaning. Afranius (fr. 415):

> I approach you, so that I might tidy your neck with linen,

that is, that I might clean it. Cicero (cf. *Defense of Sestius* 77): "The blood would be wiped up (*effingere*) with sponges," that is, cleaned up. That the sponge is an animal is shown by its blood clinging to the rocks. Hence also, when it is cut, it bleeds. 61. Some of the creatures living in water move about, like fish, but others stay fixed, like oysters, sea urchins, sponges. Of these, some sponges are said to be male, because their openings are small and more tightly packed, and others female, because they have larger, continuous openings. Some are harder – ones that the Greeks call τράγος (also meaning "goat"), and we can call them *hircosa* (lit. "goatish") on account of their roughness. 62. The softest kind of sponge is called *penicillus* because they are good for swellings of the eyes and for cleaning away rheum.[22] Sponges are made white with special treatment, for during the summer they are spread out in the sun, and like Punic wax they absorb whiteness.

63. Pliny (*Natural History* 32.142) says there are 144 names for all the animals living in the waters, divided into these kinds: whales, snakes common to land and water, crabs, shellfish, lobsters, mussels, octopuses, sole, Spanish mackerel (*lacertus*), squid, and the like. Of these, many recognize the order of their seasons by a kind of natural understanding, while some [wander in their places without change]. 64. Among female fish, some conceive by means of intercourse with a male, and bear offspring, while others deposit their eggs formed without any involvement on the part of the male, who, after the eggs have been deposited, floods them with the casting of his seed. The eggs that have been touched by this service become fertile, but those that have not remain sterile and decay.

vii. Birds (De avibus) 1. There is a single word for birds, but various kinds, for just as they differ among themselves in appearance, so do they differ also in the diversity of their natures. Some are simple, like the dove, and others clever, like the partridge; some allow themselves to be handled, like the falcon, while others are fearful, like the *garamas*; some enjoy the company of humans, like the swallow, while others prefer a secluded life in deserted places, like the turtledove; some feed only on the seeds they find, like the goose, while others eat meat and are eager for prey, like the kite; some are indigenous and always stay in the same location, like [the ostrich], while others are migratory and return at certain seasons, like the stork and the swallow; some are gregarious, that is, they fly in a flock, like the starling and the quail, while others are loners, that is, they are solitary, on account of the strategies of hunting, like the eagle, the hawk, and others of this type. Some make a racket with their calls, like the swallow. Some produce the sweetest songs, like the swan and the blackbird, while others imitate the speech and voices of humans, like the parrot and the magpie. 2. But there are innumerable others differing in kind and behavior, for no one can discover how many kinds of birds there are. Indeed, no one could penetrate the wildernesses of all India and Ethiopia and Scythia, so as to know the kinds of birds and their differentiating characteristics.

21 Early manuscripts read nonsensical *uris*, etc., at the head of this sentence. The reading should perhaps be, "And the covering of a shellfish is spoken of in three ways: . . .," with reference to three classes of shell shapes.

22 *Penicillus* can mean "a sponge; a medicament for the eyes; a swab." The name, from this sponge's elongated shape, is a diminutive of *penis*, "tail."

3. They are called birds (*avis*) because they do not have set paths (*via*), but travel by means of pathless (*avia*) ways. 'Winged ones' (*ales*, gen. *alitis*) because they strive 'with their wings for the heights' (*alis alta*), and ascend to lofty places with the oarage of their wings. 4. 'Flying ones' (*volucres*, plural of the adjective *volucer*, "flying," and also of the substantive *volucris*, "bird") from flying (*volare*), for we say 'fly' (*volare*) and 'walk' (*ambulare*) from the same root. The term *vola* means the middle part of the sole of the foot or the palm of the hand, and for birds *vola* is the middle part of the wings, by whose motion the feathers are put into action, hence *volucer*.

5. The young of all birds are called hatchlings (*pullus*), but the young of four-legged animals may also be called *pullus*, and a small human is a *pullus*. Therefore, those recently born are *pulli*, because they are stained (*pollutus*). Hence black clothing is also called *pullus*. 6. Wings are those appendages on which the feathers, fixed in order, offer the function of flight. They are called 'wings' (*ala*) because with them birds nourish (*alere*) and warm the hatchlings that they enfold. 7. Feathers (*pinna*) are named from 'being suspended' (*pendēre*, 2nd conjugation), that is, from flying – hence also the word *pendĕre* ("suspend," 3rd conjugation) – for flying creatures move with the aid of feathers when they commit themselves to the air. 8. Plumes (*pluma*) are named as if the word were *piluma*, for just as there are hairs (*pilus*) on the bodies of quadrupeds, so there are plumes on birds.

9. Many bird names are evidently constructed from the sound of their calls, such as the crane (*grus*), the crow (*corvus*), the swan (*cygnus*), the peacock (*pavo*), the kite (*milvus*), the screech owl (*ulula*), the cuckoo (*cuculus*), the jackdaw (*graculus*), et cetera. The variety of their calls taught people what they might be called.

10. The eagle (*aquila*) is named from the acuity of its vision (*acumen oculorum*), for it is said that they have such sight that when they soar above the sea on unmoving wings, and invisible to human sight, from such a height they can see small fish swimming, and descending like a bolt seize their prey and carry it to shore with their wings. 11. It is said that the eagle does not even avert its gaze from the sun; it offers its hatchlings, suspended from its talons, to the rays of the sun, and the ones it sees holding their gaze unmoving it saves as worthy of the eagle family, but those who turn their gaze away, it throws out as inferior.

12. The vulture (*vultur*) is thought to be named from its 'slow flight' (*volatus tardus*), for indeed it does not have a swift flight, due to the size of its body. They say that some vultures do not unite in coition, but conceive and reproduce without copulation, and their offspring live to be almost one hundred years old. Vultures, just like eagles, can sense carrion even beyond the seas; indeed, when they are flying high, they can see many things from their height that are otherwise hidden by obscuring mountains. 13. The bird called *gradipes* by the Greeks is our 'bustard' (*tarda*, lit. "slow") because, held back by its heavy flight, it cannot mount high on the speed of its wings like other birds.

14. Cranes (*grus*) took their name from their particular call, for they whoop with such a sound. When they fly, they follow a leader in formation like a letter (i.e. Λ, Greek lambda). Concerning them Lucan says (*Civil War* 5.716):

> And the letter-shape is disturbed and lost in their scattered flight.

They seek the heights, from which they can more easily see which lands to make for. 15. The one leading the flock chides with its voice, but, when it begins to grow hoarse, another crane takes its place. At night they divide up the watches, and alternate their vigils; they hold stones in their extended claws to let it be known if they fall asleep – the noise (i.e. of the stones dropping) indicates the need to be on the alert. Their color reveals their age, for they turn black as they grow old.

16. Storks (*ciconia*) are named from the chattering noise they make, as if their name were *cicania* (cf. *canere*, i.e. "sing"). Although this sound is made with the mouth, it is not really a vocal call, because they produce it with a clapping of their beak. They are messengers of the spring, socially companionable, enemies of snakes; they cross the sea, and migrate into Asia in a gathered flock. Crows go ahead of them as leaders, and the storks follow just like an army. 17. They have an uncommon concern for their offspring, for they guard their nestlings so earnestly that they pull out their own feathers in assiduous brooding. Whatever length of time they give to rearing their chicks, for that same span they are themselves nourished in turn by their offspring.

18. The swan is the bird that the Greeks call κύκνος. It is called 'swan' (*olor*) because it is 'entirely' white in its plumage; for no one mentions a black swan; in Greek

'entire' is called ὅλος. The *cycnus* (i.e. *cygnus*, another word for swan, borrowed, in fact, from the Greek κύκνος just cited) is named for singing (*canere*) because it pours out a sweetness of song with its modulated voice. It is thought to sing sweetly because it has a long curved neck, and a voice forcing its way by a long and winding path necessarily renders varied modulations. 19. People say that in the Hyperborean regions, when musicians are singing to citharas, swans come flocking in large numbers, and sing with them quite harmoniously. *Olor* is the Latin name, for in Greek they are called κύκνος. Sailors say that this bird makes a good omen for them, just as Aemilius (Macer) says (fr. 4):

> The swan is always the most fortunate bird in omens.
> Sailors prefer this one, because it does not immerse itself in the waves.[23]

20. The ostrich (*struthio*) is named with a Greek term; this animal is seen to have feathers like a bird, but it does not rise above the ground. It neglects to incubate its eggs, but the eggs when laid are brought to life by the warmth of the earth alone. 21. The heron (*ardea*) is named as if the word were *ardua* (i.e. "steep") – this is on account of its lofty flight. Lucan (*Civil War* 5.553) says:

> And that the heron dared to fly.

It is afraid of rainstorms, and flies above the clouds so that it cannot feel the storms in the clouds, and whenever it flies higher, this indicates a storm. Many people call it the *tantulus*. 22. The phoenix (*phoenix*) is a bird of Arabia, so called because it possesses a scarlet (*phoeniceus*) color, or because it is singular and unique in the entire world, for the Arabs say *phoenix* for 'singular.' This bird lives more than five hundred years, and when it sees that it has grown old it constructs a funeral pile for itself of aromatic twigs it has collected, and, turned to the rays of the sun, with a beating of its wings it deliberately kindles a fire for itself, and thus it rises again from its own ashes.

23. The *cinnamolgus* is also a bird of Arabia, called thus because in tall trees it constructs nests out of cinnamon (*cinnamum*) shrubs, and since humans are unable to climb up there due to the height and fragility of the branches, they go after the nests using lead-weighted missiles. Thus they dislodge these cinnamon nests and sell them at very high prices, for merchants value cinnamon more than other spices. 24. The parrot (*psittacus*) comes from the shores of India. It is green in color, with a scarlet collar and a large tongue, wider than that of other birds. Hence it pronounces articulate words so that if you did not see the bird you would think a human was speaking. It makes a greeting naturally, saying "*Have!*" (i.e. *Ave*, a Latin greeting) or "Χαῖρε!" (i.e. a Greek greeting). Other words it learns by being taught. Hence it is spoken of (Martial, *Epigrams* 14.73):

> I, a parrot, would learn from you the names of other things, but on my own I have learned to say this:
> "Hail (*Have*), Caesar!"

25. The *alcyon* (i.e. "halcyon," in classical Latin, "kingfisher"), a sea bird, is named as if the word were *ales oceana* (ocean bird), because in winter it makes its nest and raises its young on still waters in the Ocean. It is said that when they are brooding on its expansive surface, the sea grows calm with the winds silent in continuous tranquillity for seven days, and nature herself cooperates in the rearing of their young. 26. The pelican (*pelicanus*) is an Egyptian bird inhabiting the solitary places of the river Nile, whence it takes its name, for Egypt is called *Canopos*. It is reported, if it may be true, that this bird kills its offspring, mourns them for three days, and finally wounds itself and revives its children by sprinkling them with its own blood.

27. The *stymphalis* is a bird named from the islands of Stymphades (cf. Stymphales, a lake in Arcadia), where they are abundant; Hercules used arrows against them.[24] They are sea birds living on islands. 28. *Diomediae* are birds named from the companions of Diomedes;[25] fables say that his companions were transformed into these very birds. They are similar to coots in shape, the size of a swan, white in color, with large hard beaks. They are found near Apulia on the island Diomedia, flying between the crags of the shore and the rocks. They

23 Isidore's source for Macer's lines, Servius's commentary on *Aen.* 1.393, originally read "is never immersed" for "does not immerse itself." Because swans are never overwhelmed by waves, they are an omen of good weather.

24 Lindsay emended the early manuscript readings, *strophalides*, etc., and *strophades*, etc. The Strophalides are legendary bird-women, the Harpies, who lived on the Strophades, islands off the coast of Messinia. The *stymphalides* are the loathsome raptors slain by Hercules.

25 A Greek king and warrior in the Trojan War who emigrated to Apulia.

distinguish between their own people and foreigners. 29. If someone is Greek, they come up close and fawn on him, but if someone is of alien birth, they attack and wound him by biting, grieving as if with tearful voices either their own transformation or the death of their king – for Diomedes was slain by the Illyrians. These birds are called *diomediae* in Latin, but the Greeks call them ἐρωδιοί ("herons, shearwaters").

30. *Memnonides* are Egyptian birds named after the place where Memnon[26] perished. They are said to fly in flocks from Egypt to Troy near the tomb of Memnon, and hence the Trojans call them *memnonia*. They come to Troy every fifth year, and after they have flown around for two days, on the third day they enter into a battle with each other, lacerating themselves with talons and beaks. 31. The *hercynia* is a bird named from the Hercynian forest of Germany where they are born. Their feathers sparkle so much in the shade that, however dark the night is with thick shadows, these feathers, when placed on the ground, give off light that helps to mark the way, and the sign of the glittering feathers makes clear the direction of the path. 32. The Greeks call the *onocrotalos* (i.e. another word for "pelican") a bird with a long beak. [There are two types of this bird; one aquatic and the other of the desert.] 33. The ibis (*ibis*) is a bird of the Nile river that purges itself by spurting water into its anus with its beak. This bird feeds on snake eggs, carrying the most pleasing food that it takes from them back to its nestlings.

34. The bee-eater (*merops*) is the same as the *gaulus*, who is said to conceal its parents and feed them. The *coredulus* (perhaps "lark") is a type of bird, as if the name were *cor edens* (lit. "eater of the heart"). 35. The jackdaw (*monedula*)[27] is a bird named as if the word were *monetula* (cf. *moneta*, "money") because whenever it finds gold it carries it off and hides it. Cicero, *Defense of Valerius Flaccus* (76): "No more gold should be entrusted to you than to a jackdaw (*monedula*)."

36. The bat (*vespertilio*) takes its name from the time of day, because it avoids the light and flies around in the dusk of evening (*vespertinus*), making darting movements and supported by delicate arm-like limbs.[28] It is an animal similar to a mouse, producing not so much a call as a squeak. In appearance it is a quadruped at the same time as being equipped to fly; this is not usually found among other birds. 37. The nightingale (*luscinia*) is a bird that took its name because it is accustomed to indicate by its song the onset of the rising sun, as if its name were *lucinia* (cf. *lux*, gen. *lucis*, "light, sun"). This same bird is also the *acredula*, concerning which Cicero says in his *Prognostics* (fr. 6):

> And the *acredula* performs its morning songs.

38. The 'screech owl' (*ulula*) is a bird named from the word ὀλολύζειν, that is, from wailing and lamentation, for its calls resemble either weeping or groaning. Whence, according to augurs, if it hoots it is said to indicate sorrow, and if it is silent, prosperity. 39. The 'horned owl' (*bubo*) has a name composed of the sound of its call; it is a funereal bird, loaded with feathers, but always constrained by heavy sluggishness; it is active among tombs day and night, and always lingers in caves. Concerning it Ovid said (*Met.* 5.549):

> It has become a loathsome bird, messenger of approaching sorrow, the lazy owl (*bubo*), a dire omen for mortals.

Thus, according to augurs, it is said to portend ill fortune, for when it has been seen in a city, they say that it signifies desolation. 40. The 'night owl' (*noctua*) is named because it flies around at night (*nox*, gen. *noctis*) and cannot see during the day, for when daylight appears, the night owl's vision is weakened. This bird is not found on the island of Crete, and if it should come there from somewhere else, it immediately dies. The night owl is not the same as the horned owl, for the horned owl is bigger. 41. The *nycticorax* is likewise a night owl, because it loves the night. It is a bird that flees the light and cannot bear to look at sunlight. 42. The *strix* (perhaps another word for the screech owl) is a nocturnal bird, taking its name from the sound of its call, for it screeches (*stridere*) when it calls. Lucan says concerning it (*Civil War* 6.689):

> That which the restless horned owl and the nocturnal *strix* lament.

This bird is commonly called the *amma*, from loving (*amare*) its young, whence also it is said to offer milk to its hatchlings.

26 An Ethiopian king and warrior in the Trojan War.

27 *Monedula* and *graculus* both mean "jackdaw"; see sections 9 and 45.

28 A plausible alternative for the last clause, reading *membranis* for *membris* ("limbs"), as in Isidore's source in Ambrose's *Hexameron*, would be "supported by the thin membranes of its fore-limbs."

43. The raven (*corvus*), or *corax*, takes its name from the sound of its throat, because it croaks (*coracinare*) with its voice. It is said that this bird does not fully provide food for the young it has produced until it recognizes in them a similarity to its own color through the blackness of their feathers, but after it sees that they are horrible of plumage it nourishes them more abundantly, as completely acknowledged offspring. This bird seeks the eyes of a corpse before any other part. 44. The crow (*cornix*), a long-lived bird, is named by Latin speakers with a Greek word (i.e. κορώνη). Augurs say that this bird by its signs is attentive to the concerns of humans, and shows the paths where ambush lies, and predicts the future. It is a great sin to believe that God would entrust his counsels to crows. Among many omens, they even ascribe to these birds the predicting of rain by their calls. Whence this passage (Vergil, *Geo.* 1.388):

> Then the impudent crow calls the rain with its loud voice.

45. The jackdaw (*graculus*) is named for its garrulity (*garrulitas*); not, as some people would have it, because they fly 'in flocks' (*gregatim*), since it is quite clear that they are named for their call, for it is the most talkative species and importunate in its calls. 46. The magpie (*pica*), as if the word were 'poetic' (*poetica*), because they pronounce words with a distinct articulation, like a human. Perching on the branches of trees, they sound out in unmannerly garrulity, and although they are unable to unfold their tongues in meaningful speech, still they imitate the sound of the human voice. Concerning which someone has said, appropriately (Martial, *Epigrams* 14.76):

> I, a chattering magpie, salute you as master with a clear voice – if you did not see me, you would deny that I am a bird.

47. The woodpecker (*picus*) took its name from Picus, the son of Saturn, because he would use this bird in augury. People say this bird has a certain supernatural quality because of this sign: a nail, or anything else, pounded into whatever tree the woodpecker has nested in, cannot stay there long, but immediately falls out, where the bird has settled. This is the woodpecker (*picus*), sacred to Mars, for the magpie (*pica*) is another bird.

48. The peacock (*pavo*) has its name from the sound of its call. Its flesh is so hard that is scarcely experiences decay, nor is it easily cooked. Someone speaks of it in this way (Martial, *Epigrams* 13.70):

> Whenever it unfolds its jeweled wings you wonder, pitiless man, if you can give this bird to the cruel cook.

49. The pheasant (*phasianus*) is named from Phasis, an island of Greece, whence it was first imported. This old distich bears witness to this (Martial, *Epigrams* 13.72):

> I was transported first in an Argive ship – before that I knew nothing but Phasis.

50. The rooster (*gallus*) is named from castration, for of all the birds only this one has its testes removed. Indeed, the ancients used to call a castrated man a *gallus*.[29] And just as the word *leaena* ("lioness") is formed from *leo* ("lion"), and *dracaena* ("dragoness") from *draco* ("dragon"), so *gallina* ("hen") is formed from *gallus*. The rooster's limbs, some people say, are consumed if they are mixed with molten gold.

51. The duck (*ans*, i.e. *anas*) takes its appropriate name from its persistent swimming (*natare*). Certain ones of the duck species are called 'true' (*germanus*) ducks because they are more nourishing than the others. 52. The duck gives its name to the goose (*anser*) by derivation, either from their resemblance, or because it too is frequently swimming. The goose bears witness to its vigils at night with persistent honking. No other animal is as sensitive to the smell of humans as is the goose; whence the ascent of the Gauls to the Capitolium in Rome was discovered from the noise of the geese. 53. The coot (*fulica*) is so named because its flesh tastes of hare; now λαγώς means "hare," whence this bird is also called λαγώς by the Greeks. It is a marsh bird, having its nest in the middle of the water or on rocks surrounded by water; it is always attracted to the deep seas. When it senses a storm approaching, the coot flees into the shallows and dallies there.

54. The *mergus* has its name from its continuous diving (*mergere*). Often, with its head lowered under the waves into the depths it gathers signs of winds and, foreseeing a storm at sea, turns noisily to shore. There must be a very strong storm at sea when the *mergi* flee to the shore. 55. The hawk (*accipiter*) is a bird armed more with spirit than with talons, bearing great valor in its

29 A *gallus* was a castrated priest of Cybele.

small body. It assumes its name from 'taking' (*accipere*), that is, seizing, for it is a bird very eager to snatch up other birds, so that it is called *accipiter*, that is, 'raptor' (*raptor*). Whence the apostle Paul says (cf. II Corinthians 11:20): "For you withstand it, if anyone takes from you" – where he meant "if anyone seizes (*rapit*)," he said "if anyone takes (*accipit*)." 56. It is said that hawks are undutiful toward their nestlings, for as soon as they see that the nestlings can try to fly, they no longer furnish them with any food, but beat their wings and cast them from the nest; and from infancy they compel them to hunt prey, lest perhaps as adults they should grow sluggish.

57. The *capus* is named in the language of Italy from 'seizing' (*capere*). We call this one the falcon (*falco*), because its talons are curved inward (cf. *falx*, gen. *falcis*, "sickle"). 58. The kite (*milvus*) is weak in both its strength and its flying, as if it were a 'weak bird' (*mollis avis*), whence it is named. However, it is most rapacious and is always a predator of domestic birds. 59. The osprey (*ossifragus*) is the common name for a bird that casts bones down from the heights and breaks them. Hence it takes its name from 'breaking bones' (*ossa frangere*). 60. The 'turtle dove' (*turtur*) is named from its call; it is a bashful bird, always dwelling in mountain heights and desert wildernesses. It flees human homes and interaction, and dwells in forests. [In winter, after it has lost its feathers, it is said to take shelter in hollow tree trunks.] In contrast to this, the dove loves human society; it is always a pleasant inhabitant in a house. 61. They are called doves (*columba*) because their necks (*collum*) change color every time they turn. They are tame birds, comfortable amid a large group of humans, and without bile. The ancients called them 'love birds,' because they often come to the nest and express their love with a kiss.

62. The wood-pigeon (*palumbes*) [from 'food' (*pabulum*), because they are stuffed – they are commonly called *titus*] is called a 'chaste bird' (*avis casta*) from its behavior, because it is a companion of chastity (*castitas*), for it is said to proceed alone after it has lost its mate, nor does it need any further carnal union. 63. The partridge (*perdix*) takes its name from its call. It is a crafty bird, and filthy, for the male mounts another male; its violent lust ignores gender. It is deceitful to the extent that it will steal and hatch the eggs of another, but this deceit is fruitless, for at last when the hatchlings hear the call of their true parent, through a kind of natural instinct they abandon the bird that has reared them and return to the one who conceived them.

64. The quail (*coturnix*) is named from the sound of its call; the Greeks call them ὄρτυγες because they were first seen on the island of Ortygia (i.e. Delos). These birds have a season for their return migration, for, when they driven off by the summer heat, they cross the sea. 65. The bird that leads the flock is called an *ortygometra*. The hawk seizes this bird when it sees it approaching land; for this reason all quails are careful to secure a leader of a different species – through this carefulness they safeguard those first crucial moments. They have poisonous seeds as their favorite food; for this reason the ancients forbade their consumption. This animal alone suffers from 'falling sickness' (*caducum morbum*; see IV.vii.6), as do humans.

66. The Greeks name the hoopoe (*upupa*) thus because it would settle on human waste, and feed on foul dung. It is a most loathsome bird, helmed with a protruding crest, always dwelling in tombs and human waste. Anyone who anoints himself with the blood of this bird and then goes to sleep will see demons suffocating him. 67. The cuckoo (*tucus*), which the Spaniards call *ciculus* (i.e. *cuculus*), is named from its particular call. These birds have a proper season for their return migration, at which time they are taken up on the shoulders of kites because of their brief and small spans of flight, lest their strength fail, fatigued by the long expanse of sky. Cicadas are born from their saliva. 68. Sparrows (*passer*) are tiny little birds, named from their smallness (*parvitas*), whence small things are also called *pusilli*.

69. The merle (*merula*) was called *medula* in ancient times, because it 'makes music' (*modulare*). Others say the merle is so named because it flies alone, as if the term were *mera volans* ("flying alone"). Although this is a black bird everywhere, it is white in Achaea. 70. The swallow (*erundo*, i.e. *hirundo*) is so named because it does not take food when it has alighted, but seizes and eats its food in the air (*aer*). It is a garrulous bird, flying around in convoluted loops and twisted circles, and it is very clever at constructing its nests and raising its young. It even has a certain foresight, for it abandons and never seeks out roofs that are about to fall in. Also, it is not attacked by fierce birds, nor is it ever their prey. It flies across the sea and remains there for the winter. 71. The thrush (*turdus*) is named from its tardiness (*tarditas*), for

at the very beginning of winter it returns. The *turdela* is a larger thrush, as it were. It is thought to produce mistletoe by means of its droppings. Whence the ancients had a proverb: "The bird shits trouble for itself."[30]

72. The *furfurio* (cf. *furfur*, "husk") is so named because formerly it used to feed on grain (*far*) that had been ground into flour. 73. The figpecker (*ficedula*) is so named because it mostly eats figs (*ficus*). This is revealed by that ancient couplet (Martial, *Epigrams* 13.49):

> Although the fig feeds me, since I am nourished by sweet grapes, why was it not the grape (*uva*) rather that gave me my name (i.e. *uvedula*)?

74. The goldfinch (*carduelus*), because it is nourished by thorns and thistles (*carduus*), whence among the Greeks it is also called *acalanthis*, from ἄκανθα, that is, "thorn," by which it is nourished.

75. Augurs say that omens are found in the gestures and movements and flights and calls of birds. 76. Those birds are called *oscines* that produce auspices with their mouths (*os*) and their song (*cantus*), such as the raven, the crow, and the woodpecker. 77. The *alites* are those that seem to show the future by their flight (cf. *ala*, "wing"); if they are unpropitious, they are called *inebrae*, because they inhibit (*inhibere*), that is, they forbid; if they are propitious, they are called *praepetes*. The reason they are called *praepetes* is that all birds, when they fly, 'pursue what is ahead' (*priora petere*). 78. People define a third type of augury among the birds, which they call 'common'; it is a combination of both, that is, when birds provide omens from both their mouths and their flight. All this is not worthy of belief.

79. All species of birds are born twice. They are born first as eggs, after which they are formed and animated by the warmth of their mother's body. 80. Eggs (*ovum*) are so called because they are 'moist' (*uvidus*). Whence also grapes (*uva*) are so named because they are full of liquid inside. Whatever has liquid on the outside is 'wet' (*humidus*); whatever has it on the inside is 'moist.' Some believe that 'egg' has a Greek source for the term; the Greeks say ᾠά, with the letter *v* left out. 81. Some eggs are conceived by means of empty wind, but eggs are not fertile unless they have been conceived by coition with the male and have been penetrated by the seminal spirit. People say that the strength of eggs is such that wood soaked with egg doesn't burn, and not even clothing becomes scorched. And when mixed with lime it is said to glue fragments of glass together.

viii. Tiny flying animals (De minutis volatibus) 1. Bees (*apis*) are so named either because they cling to each other with their feet (*pes*), or because they are born without feet (cf. *a-*, "without"), for they develop feet and wings afterwards. These animals, skilful at the task of creating honey, live in allocated dwellings; they construct their homes with indescribable skill; they make their honeycombs from various flowers; they build wax cells, and replenish their fortress with innumerable offspring; they have armies and kings; they wage battle; they flee smoke; they are annoyed by disturbance. 2. Many people know from experience that bees are born from the carcasses of oxen, for the flesh of slaughtered calves is beaten to create these bees, so that worms are created [from] the putrid gore, and the worms then become bees. Specifically, the ones called 'bees' originate from oxen, just as hornets come from horses, drones from mules, and wasps from asses. 3. The Greeks name *costri* those larger bees that are created in the edges of the honeycomb; some people think they are the kings. They are so named because they rule the hive (*castra*). The drone is larger than a bee, and smaller than a hornet. And the 'drone' (*fugus*, i.e. *fucus*) is so called because it eats what is produced by others, as if the word were *fagus* (cf. φαγεῖν, "eat"), for it eats food that it has not toiled over. Concerning it Vergil says (*Geo.* 4.168):

> They keep the drones, a lazy flock, from the hives.

4. Wasps (*vespa*) . . . The hornet (*scabro*, i.e. *crabro*) is named from *cabus*, that is, from the packhorse (*caballus*), because it is created from them. Just as hornets are born from the rotting flesh (*caro*) of horses, so scarabs (*scarabaeus*) are often born likewise from such flesh – whence they are named. 5. Earth scarabs, similar to ticks, are called *tauri* (lit. "bulls"). The *buprestis* (i.e. a venomous beetle) is a small animal in Italy, similar to the scarab, a long-legged animal. It lies in wait for cows (*bos*) in particular among the pasturage, whence it takes its name, and if it is eaten it so inflames with the contagion of its poison that the cow bursts. 6. The glow-worm

30 As birdlime was made from mistletoe berries, the sense is that birds produce their own doom, "foul their own nest." It was believed that mistletoe seeds had to be digested by birds before they could germinate. See Plautus, fr. 47; Servius 6.205.

(*cicindela*) is a kind of scarab, named because it gives off light when it walks or flies (cf. *candela*, "candle").

7. Moths (*blatta*) are named from their color, since indeed they stain one's hand when they are caught, whence people also name a color 'purple' (*blatteum*). This animal cannot bear to see light, in contrast to the fly, for the fly is light-seeking and the moth is light-fleeing, and it only goes about at night. 8. Butterflies (*papilio*) are small flying creatures that are very abundant when mallows bloom, and they cause small worms to be generated from their own dung. 9. Locusts (*locusta*, also meaning "lobster" or "crawfish") are so called because their legs are 'long, like spears' (*longis . . . asta*, i.e. *hasta*, "spear"). Whence the Greeks call the sea as well as the land creature ἀστακός (i.e. "lobster"). 10. Cicadas (*cicas*, i.e. *cicada*) are born from the saliva of the cuckoo (*ciculus*). In the Reggio region of Italy these creatures are mute, but nowhere else.

11. The word for fly (*musca*) comes from Greek, as does 'mouse' (*mus*). These animals, just like bees, when drowned in water, sometimes revive after an hour has elapsed. 12. The *cynomya* is named with a Greek word, that is, a 'dog-fly,' for κύων is Greek for 'dog.' 13. The gnat (*culex*) is named from 'sting' (*aculeus*) because it sucks blood, for it has a tube in its mouth, like a needle, with which it pierces the flesh so that it may drink the blood.[31] 14. *Sciniphes* are very tiny flies, very troublesome with their stinging. The proud populace of Egypt was struck down by these flies in the third plague (see Exodus 8:16–18). 15. The horse-fly is associated with cattle, and is very troublesome with its stinging. The name for the horse-fly (*oestrus*) is a Greek word; in Latin it is called the *asilus*, and is commonly known as the *tabanus*.

16. *Bibiones* (i.e. drosophilae) are creatures that are generated in wine; they are commonly called *mustiones* from wine-must (*mustum*). Whence Afranius (fr. 407) says:

> When you look towards me and begin to tell stories,
> *bibiones* fly from your mouth into your eyes.[32]

17. The weevil (*gurgulio*, lit. "gullet") is so named because it is almost nothing except a throat (*guttur*).

31 Isidore seems to take *culex* to mean "mosquito," and *sciniphes* may mean "gnat" or "mosquito."

32 The quotation is found only here and is probably corrupt, but Afranius may mean that you tell lies when drunk.

Book XIII

The cosmos and its parts (De mundo et partibus)

Now in this little book we have noted in a short sketch, as it were, certain principles of the heavenly bodies and locations of the land and expanses of the sea, so that the reader may go through them in a short time, and through this succinct brevity come to know their etymologies and causes.[1]

i. The world (De mundo) 1. The world consists of the sky and the land, the sea and the creations of God within them. Whence it is said (John 1:10): "And the world was made by him." 'World' (*mundus*) is named thus in Latin by the philosophers, because it is in eternal motion (*motus*), as are the sky, the sun, the moon, the air, the seas. Thus no rest is allowed to its elements; on this account it is always in motion. 2. Whence to Varro the elements seemed to be animate, "Because," he says, "they move of their own accord." But the Greeks adopted a term for world (*mundus*, also meaning "cosmetics") derived from 'ornament,' on account of the diversity of elements and the beauty of the heavenly bodies. They call it κόσμος, which means "ornament," for with our bodily eyes we see nothing more beautiful than the world.

3. There are four zones in the world, that is, four regions: the East and the West, the North and the South. 4. The East (*oriens*) is named from the rising (*exortus*) of the sun. The West (*occidens*) is named because it makes the day set (*occidere*) and perish, for it hides the light from the world and brings on darkness. 5. The North (*septentrio*) is so called from the seven (*septem*) stars at the North Pole (i.e. the Big Dipper), which wheel as they rotate around it. Strictly speaking this is called the *vertex* (i.e. the celestial pole) because it turns (*vertere*), as the poet says (Vergil, *Aen.* 2.250):

> The heavens turn (*vertere*) in the meantime.

1 Some material in this book repeats information from the treatment of astronomy in III.xxiv-lxxi. Note that the Latin word *caelum* may be translated "sky" or "heaven(s)" – i.e. anything above the earth.

6. The South (*meridies*) is so named either because there the sun makes midday (*medium diem*), as if the word were *medidie*, or because at that time the aether sparkles more purely, for *merus* means "pure." 7. The sky has two portals: the East and the West, for the sun enters through one portal and withdraws through the other. 8. The world has two poles (*cardo*, i.e. celestial poles), the North and the South, for the sky revolves around them.

ii. Atoms (De atomis) 1. Atoms (*atomus*) are what the philosophers call certain corporeal particles in the world that are so tiny that they are not visible to sight, and do not undergo τομή, that is, "splitting," whence they are called ἄτομοι. They are said to fly through the void of the entire world in unceasing motion and to be carried here and there like the finest dust motes that may be seen pouring in through the window in the sun's rays. Some pagan philosophers have thought that all trees and plants and fruits have their origins from these particles, and that from them fire and water and the universe were born and exist. 2. There are atoms in bodies, in time, and in number. In a body, such as a stone. You may divide it into parts, and the parts into grains, like sand; then divide the grains of sand themselves into the finest dust, until, if you can, you will reach a certain minute particle, which no longer can be divided or split. This particle is the atom in bodies. 3. With reference to time, the atom is understood in this way: you may divide a year, for example, into months, months into days, days into hours. The parts of hours still admit division until you come to a point of time and a speck of an instant such that it cannot be extended through any small interval, and thus can no longer be divided. This is an atom of time. 4. In number, take for example eight divided into four, and four into two, and then two into one. But one is an atom, because it is indivisible. Thus also with letters (i.e. speech-sounds), for speech is divided into words, words into syllables, syllables into letters. But a letter, the smallest part, is an atom and cannot be divided.

Therefore an atom is whatever cannot be divided, like a point in geometry, for τόμος means "division" in Greek, and ἄτομος means "non-division."

iii. Elements (De elementis) 1. The Greeks call a certain primary material of things ὕλη ("matter," also "wood, woodland"), which is not formed in any way, but is capable of underlying all bodily forms; from this material the visible elements (*elementum*) are formed, whence they took their name from this derivation.[2] Latin speakers have named this ὕλη 'matter' (*materia*, also meaning "wood") because every unformed substance, of which something is made, is always called matter. Whence the poets have named it *silva* (lit. "woodland"), not inappropriately, because *materia* is connected with woods. 2. The Greeks name the elements στοιχεῖα, because they agree with each other in a certain accord and communion of association (cf. στοιχεῖν, "agree with"). Indeed, they are said to be joined thus among themselves with a certain natural logic, now returning to their origin, from fire to earth, now from earth to fire, since fire ends in air, and air is condensed into water, and water thickens into earth; and in turn, earth is loosened into water, water rarefied into air, and air thinned out into fire. 3. For this reason, all the elements are present in all, but each one has taken its name from whichever element is more abundant in it. The elements are assigned by Divine Providence to the appropriate living beings, for the Creator himself has filled heaven (i.e. the fiery realm) with angels, air with birds, water with fish, and earth with humans and the rest of the living things.

iv. The sky (De caelo) 1. The sky (*caelum*)[3] is so named because, like an engraved *(caelatum)* vessel, it has the lights of the stars pressed into it, just like engraved figures; for a vessel which glitters with figures that stand out is called *caelatus*. God embellished the heaven and filled it with bright light – that is, he adorned it with the sun and the gleaming orb of the moon, and the glorious constellations of glittering stars. [In a different way, it is named from engraving (*caelare*) the superior bodies.] 2. It is called οὐρανός in Greek, after the term ὁρᾶσθαι, that is, 'seeing,' because the air is transparent and clearer for seeing. In Sacred Scripture the sky is called the firmament (*firmamentum*), because it is secured (*firmare*) by the course of the stars and by fixed and immutable laws. 3. Sometimes the word 'sky' is used for the air, where winds and clouds and storms and whirlwinds arise. Lucretius (cf. *On the Nature of Things* 4.133):

> The sky (*caelum*), which is called air (*aer*).

And the Psalm (78:2; 103:12, Vulgate) refers to "fowls of the sky (*caelum*)," when it is clear that birds fly in the air; out of habit we also call this air, 'sky.' Thus when we ask whether it is fair or overcast we sometimes say, "How is the air?" and sometimes "How is the sky?"

v. Parts of the sky (De partibus caeli) 1. The ether (*aether*) is the place where the stars are, and signifies that fire which is separated high above from the entire world. Of course, ether is itself an element, but *aethra* (i.e. another word for ether) is the radiance of ether; it is a Greek word. 2. The sphere (*sphaera*) of the sky is so named because it has a round shape in appearance. But anything of such a shape is called a *sphaera* by the Greeks from its roundness, such as the balls that children play with. Now philosophers say that the sky is completely convex, in the shape of a sphere, equal on every side, enclosing the earth poised in the center of the world's mass. People say that the sky moves, and with its motion the stars fixed in it go around from east to west, with the stars of the Big Dipper proceeding around the pole in shorter rotations. 3. The axis (*axis*) is a straight line from the North that extends through the center ball of the sphere, and it is called 'axis' because around it the sphere turns like a wheel, or because the Wain (i.e. 'wagon,' another name for the Big Dipper) is there. 4. The poles are the ends of the axis, and they are called poles (*cardo*, lit. 'pivot') because the sky turns around them. 5. There are circular polar regions that run around the axis. One of them is the northern, which never sets, and is called 'Boreus,' the other is the southern, which is never visible, and is called 'Austronotius.' And they are called 'polar regions' (*polus*), because they are circles around the axis (i.e. "axle"), after the usage of a wagon, named specifically from 'polishing' (*polire*). But the Boreus polar region is always visible, and the Austronotius never, because the right side of the heavens is higher and the southern side is pressed down. 6. The vaults (*convexum*) are the edges of the sky, named from their curvature, for a convex (*convexus*) thing is

2 Isidore is linking the words ὕλη and *elementum* by sound.
3 See footnote 1 above.

curved and inclined and bent in the manner of a circle. 7. The Milky Circle (*lacteus circulus*, i.e. the Milky Way) is the road seen in the sphere of the sky, named for its brightness, because it is white. Some people say that this road is where the sun made its circuit, and that it shines from the splendor of the sun's transit.

vi. The circles of heaven (De circulis caeli) 1. Our dwelling-place is divided into zones according to the circles of the sky and has allowed some regions to be inhabited due to their mildness, and denied this to other regions due to their excessive cold or heat. There are five zones, which are either called zones (*zona*, lit. "belt") or circles because they exist on the circular band of the sphere of the world. 2. The first of these circles is called the ἀρκτικός ("the Arctic")[4] because enclosed within it can be seen the constellations of the Bears (*Arctos*) – the name that, imagining the shape of bears, we give to the Septentriones. 3. The second circle is called θερινὸς (i.e. "summer") τροπικός because the sun, when causing summer at the northern edge of this circle, does not go beyond this circle, but immediately turns back, and thus it is called τροπικός ("at the turning point"). 4. The third circle is ἡμερινός, which is called the equinoctial (*aequinoctialis*) by Latin speakers because the sun, when it reaches this region, makes an equinox (*aequinoctium*). In Latin ἡμερινός (in Greek actually "of day") is translated as 'day and night,' and in this circle we observe that the medial segment of the sphere (i.e. the equator) is set. 5. The fourth circle is called ἀνταρκτικός because it is opposite to the circle we call ἀρκτικός. 6. The fifth circle is the χειμερινὸς (i.e. "winter") τροπικός, which in Latin is called 'winter' or 'of the winter solstice,' because when it comes to this circle the sun makes winter for those who live in the north and summer for those in the southern parts. 7. The zodiac is a circle . . .

vii. Air and clouds (De aere et nube) 1. Air is an emptiness of more open texture than other elements. Concerning it Vergil says (*Aen.* 12.354):

> Following (him) through the long emptiness.

Air (*aer*) is named from the word αἴρειν (i.e. ἀείρειν, "to raise") because it bears the earth or because it is borne. The term refers partly to earthy and partly to heavenly material. That which is very fine, where winds and tempests cannot exist, makes up the celestial part, but that which is more turbulent, which takes on bodily substance with exhalations of moisture, is defined as earthy; it gives rise to many forms of itself. For when it is stirred, it makes winds; when more vehemently agitated, it makes lightning and thunder; when compressed, clouds; when condensed, rain; when it has frozen clouds, snow; when denser clouds freeze with more turbulence, hail; when it expands, bright weather. Thus dense air is cloud, and dispersed and loosened cloud is air.

2. Clouds (*nubes*) are named from 'veiling' (*obnubere*), that is, covering the sky; whence also brides (*nupta*), because they veil their faces, and also Neptune (*Neptunus*), because he casts a veil (*nubere*), that is, covers the sea and earth. The condensation of air makes clouds, for the winds lump the air together and make a cloud, whence this in Vergil (*Aen.* 5.20):

> And the air is forced into a cloud.

viii. Thunder (De tonitruo) 1. Thunder (*tonitrus*) is so named because the sound of it terrifies, for a tone (*tonus*) is a sound. Sometimes this shakes everything so violently that it seems to have split the sky, because, when a blast of very violent wind suddenly throws itself into clouds, with an increasingly powerful whirlwind seeking an exit, with a great crash it tears through the cloud, which it has hollowed out, and thus thunder is carried to the ears with a horrendous din. 2. No one should be amazed at this, since when a vessel explodes it makes a loud noise, however small it is. A flash of lightning is produced at the same time as the thunder, but it is seen sooner because it is bright; thunder reaches the ears later. The light that appears before the thunder is called a 'lightning bolt' (*fulgetra*). As we have said, it is seen first because its light is bright, and the thunder comes to one's ears later.

ix. Lightning (De fulminibus) 1. Lightning (*fulgur*) and the 'lightning bolt' (*fulmen*), the strokes of a celestial dart, are named from 'striking' (*ferire*); for to 'flash' (*fulgere*) is to 'strike' and to 'cut through.' Colliding clouds cause lightning, for the collision of any things creates fire, as we notice with stones, and the rubbing of wheels, and in forests of trees; in a similar way fire occurs in clouds.

4 Isidore gives the names of the five zones (belts, not circles) in Greek.

For this reason the clouds come first, then the fires. 2. Lightning bolts are made in the clouds by the wind and fire, and are sent out by a blast of wind. Hence the fire of lightning has a greater power to penetrate, because it is made of finer elements than our fire, that is, the fire we make use of. It has three names: *fulgus*, *fulgor* and *fulmen*. *Fulgus* because is touches (*tangere*), *fulgor* because it ignites and burns (*urere*), and *fulmen* because it splits (*findere*). Hence lightning bolts are represented with three rays.

x. The rainbow and phenomena of the clouds (De arcu et nubium effectibus) 1. The celestial rainbow (*arcus*) is named for its likeness to a bent bow (also *arcus*). *Iris* is its proper name. It is called *iris* as if the word were *aeris*, that is, something that descends to earth through the air (*aer*). It takes its light from the sun, whenever hollow clouds receive the sun's rays from the opposite side and make the shape of a bow. This circumstance gives it various colors, because the thinned water, bright air, and misty clouds, when illuminated, create various colors. 2. Rain-clouds (*pluvia*) are so called because they flow, as if the word were 'streams' (*fluvia*). They arise out of the earth and sea through exhalation. When they are lifted higher, either dissolved by the heat of the sun or compressed by the force of the wind, they fall as rain onto the earth. 3. A 'storm cloud' (*nimbus*) is a stormy, dark mass of cloud, and the word *nimbus* comes from 'cloud' (*nubes*). The rains from storm clouds are sudden and precipitate. We speak of leisurely and continual rain as *pluvia*, as if the term were *fluvia* ("stream") or *fluens* ("flowing thing"). 4. Downpours (*imber*) have to do with both clouds and rains, and are named with a Greek term (cf. ὄμβρος, "rainstorm") because they soak (*inebriare*) the ground so that germination can take place. Indeed, all things are created thanks to these, whence Lucretius (*On the Nature of Things* 1.715):

> (All things) are born from fire, earth, breath, and downpours (*imbri*).

Moreover, this is a Greek name.

5. Hail (*grando*) is so named because it has the shape of grains (*grana*). These are hardened in the cloud by the rigor of the winds, solidified into snow, and released when the air is rent. 6. Snow (*nix*, gen. *nivis*) is named from the cloud (*nubes*) whence it falls, while ice (*glacies*) is named from 'freezing' (*gelu*) and 'water' (*aqua*), as if the word were *gelaquies*, that is, 'frozen water' (*gelata aqua*). 7. Frost (*gelus*) is named because the earth is bound by it, for the earth is called γῆ. Further, the earth is bound by a heavier frost when the night is clear. 8. Hoar-frost (*pruina*) is a freezing during the morning hours, and it took this name because it burns like a fire – for the word πῦρ means "fire," and 'burning' pertains both to freezing and to the sun. Thus by a single word two different processes are signified, because they have a single effect. Indeed, the forces of freezing and of heat are similar, and either of them can split stones. Thus heat burns, as in (Vergil, *Aen.* 4.68):

> The wretched Dido burns.

And freezing burns, as in (Vergil, *Geo.* 1.93):

> Or the piercing cold of the north wind burns.

9. Dew (*ros*, gen. *roris*) is a Greek term, for they call it δρόσος. Some people think it is called *ros* because it is fine (*rarus*), and not thick like rain. 10. Mist (*nebula*) is named from the same source as *nubila* ("overcast sky"), that is, from 'veiling' (*obnubere*), that is, hiding the earth, or it is what 'flying cloud' (*nubes volans*) makes. Damp valleys exhale mist and clouds are formed; thence comes overcast sky, thence snow. Mists seek the lowest point when it is clear, the highest when it is cloudy. Fog is a shadow formed from a thickness of air. 11. And it is called fog (*caligo*) because it is mainly generated from the warmth (*calor*) of the air. 12. Darkness (*tenebrae*) is named because it 'holds shadows' (*tenere umbras*). Actually, darkness is nothing, but the very absence of light is called darkness, just as silence is not some actual thing, but when there is no sound, it is called silence. Thus darkness is not something, but when there is no light, it is called darkness. 13. A shadow (*umbra*) is air that is lacking sunlight. It is so named because it occurs when we block (*obicere*) the rays of the sun. It is movable and unsettled, and arises from the circuit of the sun and the movement of the winds. Whenever there is movement in the sun, a shadow seems to move with us, because wherever we block some spot from the rays of the sun, in the same way we remove the light from it. Thus a shadow seems to walk along with us and to imitate our gestures. 14. Light (*lux*) is the substance itself, while illumination (*lumen*) is so called because it 'emanates from light' (*a luce manare*), that is, it is the brightness of light – but authors confuse this.

xi. Winds (De ventis) 1. Wind is air that is stirred up and put into motion, and it is assigned different names according to the different parts of the sky. It is named wind (*ventus*) because it is furious (*vehemens*) and violent (*violentus*), for its power is such that it not only uproots rocks and trees but even disturbs the sky and the earth and tosses the seas. 2. There are four principal winds: the first of these, from the east, is *Subsolanus*; from the south is *Auster*; from the west *Favonius*; and from the north blows a wind of the same name (i.e. *Septentrio*, "the north"). Each of these has a pair of winds associated with it. 3. *Subsolanus* has *Vulturnus* from the right side and *Eurus* from the left; *Auster* has *Euroauster* from the right and *Austroafricus* from the left; *Favonius* has *Africus* from the right and *Corus* from the left; finally *Septentrio* has *Circius* from the right and *Aquilo* from the left. These twelve winds whirl around the globe of the world with their blowing. 4. Their names were assigned for specific reasons; for *Subsolanus* is named because it arises beneath (*sub*) the rising of the sun (*sol*); *Eurus* because it blows from ἠώς, that is, from the East, for it is joined to *Subsolanus*; *Vulturnus*, because it 'resounds deeply' (*alte tonare*). 5. Concerning this Lucretius says (*On the Nature of Things* 5.743):

> Deep-resounding (*altitonans*) Vulturnus and Auster, brandishing lightning.

6. *Auster* is named from gathering (*aurire*, i.e. *haurire*) waters, with which it makes the air thick and feeds the rain-clouds. It is called νότος in Greek, because it sometimes corrupts the air (cf. νοθεύειν, "corrupt, adulterate"), for when *Auster* blows, it brings to other regions pestilence, which arises from corrupted air. But just as *Auster* brings pestilence, so *Aquilo* drives it away. *Euroauster* is named because on one side it links with *Eurus* and on the other with *Auster*.

7. *Austroafricus* because it is joined on its left and right with *Auster* and *Africus*. This is also called *Libonotus*, because on one side of it is *Libs* (i.e. *Africus*) and on the other *Notus* (i.e. *Auster*). 8. [*Favonius* is named because it nourishes (*fovere*) fruits and flowers. In Greek this is *Zephyrus*, because it generally blows in the spring (*ver*); whence this (Vergil, *Geo.* 1.44):

> And the crumbling soil loosens with the Zephyr (i.e. west wind).]

Zephyrus is called by this name in Greek because it gives life (cf. ζωή, "life") to flowers and seeds with its breath. In Latin it is called *Favonius* because it nurtures (*fovere*) the things that are generated, for flowers are released by *Auster* and fashioned by *Zephyrus*. 9. *Africus* is named from its particular region, for it is in Africa that it starts to blow. 10. *Corus* is the one that blows from the west in the summer, and it is called *Corus* because it closes the circle of winds, and makes them like a ring-dance (*chorus*). Earlier it was called *Caurus*, and most people call it *Argestes* – not *Agrestis* as the ignorant common people do. 11. *Septentrio* is so named because it rises in the circle of the seven (*septem*) stars (i.e. the Big Dipper), which, with the head tipped back, seem to be carried by the world turning itself. 12. *Circius* is named because it is next to *Corus*. The Spanish call it *Gallicus*, because it blows on them from the direction of Galicia. 13. *Aquilo* is named because it constrains the waters (*aqua*) and dissipates clouds, for it is a cold dry wind. It is also called *Boreas*, because it blows from the Hyperborean mountains – for that is the source of this wind, whence it is cold.[5] The nature of all the septentrional winds is cold and dry, and that of the austral winds is moist and warm. 14. And of all the winds, there are two principal ones: *Septentrio* and *Auster*. 15. The *Etesiae* are gusts from *Aquilo*, and they have been given their name because they begin to blow at a specific season of the year, for ἐνιαυτός is the Greek word for 'year' (cf. also ἔτος, "year"). These make a straight course from the north into Egypt; they blow opposite to *Auster*.

16. Besides these there are two everywhere that are more puffs of air than winds: the breeze and the sea-breeze. 17. The breeze (*aura*) is named from air (*aer*), as if the word were *aeria*, because it is a gentle motion of air; for air that is stirred up makes a breeze, whence Lucretius says (*On the Nature of Things* 5.503):

> Airy breezes (*Aerias auras*) . . .

18. The sea-breeze (*altanus*), which is over the seas, is derived from the term 'the deep' (*altus*), that is, the sea. It is different from the wind that blows on river banks, which we have named a breeze, for a breeze is associated with the land. 19. A whirlwind (*turbo*) is a whirling of winds, and it is named from 'soil' (*terra*), whenever the wind surges and sends the soil into a spiral. 20. Storm (*tempestas*, also meaning "period of time") is named either for 'season' (*tempus*), just as historians

5 The Hyperboreans are a storied people of the far north.

are always using it when they say, "in that *tempestas*" – or it is named from the condition (*status*) of the sky, because due to its size, a storm brews for many days. Spring and autumn are the seasons when the biggest storms occur, when it is not full summer and not full winter. Hence storms are created out of a confluence of opposing airs at the midpoint and change of these two seasons. 21. A thunder-peal (*fragor*) is named from the sound of things being broken (*frangere*), because anything dry and brittle breaks easily. 22. A gale (*procella*) is so named because it 'hits hard' (*percellere*), that is, it strikes (*percutere*) and uproots (*evellere*); it is the power of wind along with rain. Gales are caused by lightning or winds. Nothing is faster than the winds, and because of their swiftness poets picture both winds and lightning as winged, as in (Vergil, *Aen.* 8.430):

Of winged Auster . . .

xii. Waters (De aquis) 1. Water (*aqua*) is so named because its surface is 'even' (*aequalis*), hence it is also called *aequor* (lit. "level surface," used metaphorically for the sea), because its height is even. 2. The two most potent elements of human life are fire and water, whence those to whom fire and water are forbidden are gravely punished. 3. The element of water rules over all the rest, for water tempers the sky, makes the earth fertile, gives body to the air with its exhalation, ascends to the heights, and claims the sky for itself. Indeed, what is more amazing than water standing in the sky? 4. And it is not enough that it reaches such a height, but it snatches a school of fish with it (i.e., perhaps, in a waterspout), and when poured out becomes the cause of all growing things on earth. It brings forth crops, produces trees, shrubs and grasses, cleans away filth, washes away sins, and provides drink for all living creatures.

xiii. Different kinds of water (De diversitate aquarum) 1. There is a great diversity in the qualities of water, for some water is salty, some alkaline, some with alum, some sulfuric, some tarry, and some containing a cure for illnesses. Near Rome the waters of the Albula (i.e. the Tiber) heal wounds. 2. In Italy the spring of Cicero cures eye injuries. In Ethiopia there is a lake that makes bodies drenched with it glisten, just as oil does. The spring of Zama in Africa makes voices melodious. Whoever drinks from Lake Clitorius in Italy will have a distaste for wine. 3. There is said to be a spring on the island of Chios that makes people sluggish. In Boeotia there are two fountains; one confers memory, the other, forgetfulness. The fountain of Cyzicus removes carnal desire. 4. In Boeotia there is a lake that causes madness; whoever drinks from it burns with the heat of lust. In Campania there are waters that are said to cure sterility in women and insanity in men. Whoever drinks from the fountain Rubrus in Ethiopia becomes frantic. 5. The fountain Leinus in Arcadia does not allow a miscarriage to occur. In Sicily there are two fountains; one of them makes the sterile fertile, and the other renders the fertile sterile. In Thessaly there are two rivers; sheep drinking from one of them become black, those drinking from the other white, and those drinking from both have mixed colors. 6. The lake Clitumnus in Umbria produces very large oxen. The hooves of livestock are hardened by the swamp water of Reate. Nothing that is alive is able to sink in the lake Asphaltites (i.e. the Dead Sea) in Judea.

7. In India there is a standing pool called Side, in which nothing can swim; everything sinks. In contrast to this, everything floats in the lake Apuscidamus in Africa and nothing sinks. The spring of Marsida in Phrygia casts up stones. In Achaea, water called the Styx flows from rocks; this water, when it is drunk, kills immediately. 8. The Gelonian pool of Sicily repels those who approach it with its foul smell. There is a spring in Africa around the temple of Ammon that binds soil together with the bonds of its water; it even solidifies ashes into soil. The fountain of Job in Idumaea is said to change color four times a year; that is, dust-colored, blood-colored, green, and clear. It keeps each one of these colors for three months out of the year. 9. There is a lake in the country of the Troglodytes; three times a day it becomes bitter, and then, just as often, sweet again. The Siloan spring at the foot of Mount Zion has no continuous flow of water, but bubbles forth at certain hours and days. In Judea a certain river used to go dry every Sabbath. 10. In Sardinia warm springs heal eyes, and expose thieves, for when blindness is cured, their crimes are revealed. They say there is a spring in Epirus in which lit torches are extinguished and extinguished torches are lit. Among the Garamantes (i.e. Africans) there is a fountain that is too cold to drink from during the day, and too hot to touch at night. 11. Indeed, in many places waters now flow with perpetual boiling of such vigor that they make baths hot. There are some lands that have a great deal of sulfur and

alum. And thus, when the cold water comes through hot passages, it is affected by the adjacent heat of the sulfur and is itself heated; it does not flow from its source at such a temperature, but is changed as it travels. Indeed, waters carry sulfur and alum with them; both materials are full of fire and grow hot with the slightest movement.

xiv. The sea (De mari) 1. A sea is a general gathering of waters, for every confluence of waters, whether they are salt or fresh, is, loosely, a 'sea,' according to this (Genesis 1:10): "And the gathering together of waters, he called seas (*maria*)." But strictly speaking something is called sea (*mare*) because its waters are bitter (*amarus*). 2. The sea-surface (*aequor*) is named because it is evenly (*aequaliter*) raised up, and although surging waters may swell up like mountains, when the storms have quieted the sea-surface returns to flatness. The depth of the sea varies, but the evenness of its surface is unvarying. 3. The reason why the sea has no increase in its size, even though it receives all the rivers and springs, is partly because its own huge size is not affected by the waters flowing in; then again, it is because the bitter water consumes the fresh water flowing in; or because the clouds themselves draw up and absorb a great deal of water; or because the winds carry away part of the sea, and the sun dries up part; finally, because it is percolated through certain hidden openings in the earth, and runs back again to the source of springs and fountains. The sea has no specific color; it changes with the quality of the winds. Sometimes it is golden, sometimes muddy, and sometimes black.

xv. The Ocean (De oceano) 1. Greek and Latin speakers so name the 'Ocean' (*oceanus*) because it goes around the globe (*orbis*) in the manner of a circle (*circulus*), [or from its speed, because it runs quickly (*ocius*)]. Again, because it gleams with a deep blue color like the sky: *oceanus* as if the word were κυάνεος ("blue"). This is what encircles the edges of the land, advancing and receding with alternate tides, for when the winds blow over the deep, the Ocean either disgorges the seas or swallows them back. 2. Also, the Ocean takes different names from nearby areas, such as Gallic, Germanic, Scythian, Caspian, Hyrcanian,[6] Atlantic, Gaditanian. The Gaditanian straits (i.e. the Straits of Gibraltar) are named from *Gades* (i.e. Cadiz), where the entrance of the Great Sea (i.e. the Mediterranean) first opens from the Ocean. Hence, when Hercules came to *Gades* he placed pillars there, believing that the end of the lands of the world was at that place.

xvi. The Mediterranean Sea (De mediterraneo mari) 1. The Great Sea is the one that flows from the Ocean out of the west, turns to the south, and finally stretches to the north. It is called 'great' because the other seas are smaller in comparison with it. This is also called the Mediterranean because it flows through the 'middle of the land' (*media terrae*) all the way to the East, separating Europe, Africa, and Asia. 2. The bay of its first part, which washes the Spanish regions, is called Iberian and Balearic. Then comes the Gallic part, which washes against the province of Narbonne (i.e. present-day southern France). Soon it becomes the Ligurian Sea, which is near the city of Genoa. After this is the Tyrrhenian Sea, which touches Italy – the Greeks call this the Ionian, and the Italians the *Inferum* (lit. 'the lower'). And then the Sea of Sicily which goes from Sicily to Crete. And then the Sea of Crete, which extends to Pamphylia and Egypt. 3. And then the Hellespont, which after turning north, with great bends around Greece and Illyricus, narrows into a passage seven stades across.[7] At this point Xerxes made a bridge of ships and crossed into Greece; Abydos is there. From there it widens into open sea and is hemmed back again and makes the Propontis (i.e. the Sea of Marmara), which is soon narrowed to 500 *passus* (i.e. about 2,500 feet) and becomes the Thracian Bosphorus, where Darius transported his forces. 4. From there begins the vast Pontic gulf, with the marshes of Maeotis (i.e. the Sea of Azov) at its furthest point. This sea has fresher water than the others because of the great number of rivers, and is foggy and rather shallow. Accordingly it is called *Pontus* (i.e. the Black Sea), because it is traversable (cf. *pons*, gen. *pontis*, "bridge"), and for that reason it supports seals, tuna, and dolphins, but no other larger sea-creatures.

5. And just as the land, though it is a single thing, may be referred to with various names in different places, so

6 'Hyrcanian' is usually another name for the 'Caspian' Sea.

7 Isidore's phrase *iuxta Graecias et Illyricum* is puzzling. He may be using *Illyricus* as another name for Greek (cf. xiv.iv.7), or it may conceal a reference to Ilium, as a reference to the Troad would make good sense here. A stade is about 607 (modern) feet, so Isidore's Hellespont is about eight-tenths of a mile wide; the modern strait is about a mile wide at its narrowest point.

also this Great Sea is named with different names according to the region; for it is called Iberian and Asiatic from the names of provinces, and Balearic, Sicilian, Cretan, Cypriot, Aegean, Carpathian from the names of islands. Between Tenedos and Chios there is in the sea a rock – rather than an island – which is believed to look, to those who view it from a distance, like a she-goat, which the Greeks call αἴξ (gen. αἰγός) – and from this the Aegean Sea is named. Thus also the Carpathian Sea between Egypt and Rhodes is named from the island Carpathos which is situated there. 6. The Gallic, Ausonian, Dalmatian and Ligurian Seas are named from peoples. The Argolic, Corinthian, Tyrian and Adriatic Seas are named from cities, for Adria was a certain city near the Illyrian Sea, which gave its name to the Adriatic Sea. 7. They may be named from their position with respect to the sky, such as the Upper (*Superum*) and the Lower (*Inferum*) Seas – because the east is upper and the west is lower – that is, the Tuscan (i.e. Tyrrhenian, known as *Mare Inferum*) and the Adriatic (*Superum*).

They may be named as a memorial to a king, such as the Ionian. Thus Io was the king of Greece, whence the Athenians are also known as Ionians. This sea is also called the Tyrrhenian, either because it washes against Tuscany – that is, Tyrrhenia – or from the Tyrrhenian sailors who threw themselves into this sea. One should know that the Ionian Sea is a huge gulf from Ionia to Sicily, and has as its parts the Adriatic, the Achaean, and the Epirotic Seas. The Euxine Sea (i.e. the Black Sea) is named from the behavior of those who live beside it (cf. εὔξεινος, "hospitable"); earlier it was called 'Axenus' (i.e. "inhospitable"). 8. Seas may be named from the calamities of people who perished in them, such as the Hellespont, the Icarian and the Myrtoan. Now the Myrtoan sea is named from the drowning of Myrtilus, because at this spot he was thrown in by Oenomaus. Icarus was from Crete, as the stories have it, and in seeking the heights, when his feathers had been loosened by the heat of the sun, he gave his name to the sea in which he fell and perished. Also Phrixus, fleeing with his sister Helle from their stepmother's snares, embarked on a ship bearing the sign of the ram, on which he escaped. But his sister Helle, a victim of shipwreck, died in the sea, and once dead gave her name to the Hellespontic Sea. 9. The Propontis (i.e. the Sea of Marmara) is named from the direction of the current, for it is called Propontis because it comes before the Pontus (i.e. the Black Sea). The Bosphorus is named from the ford (cf. πόρος, "ford") or narrow crossing for cattle (*bos*). The Egyptian Sea is assigned to Asia, the Gallic to Europe, and the African to Libya – for they are assigned to those regions that are closest to them. 10. A *pelagus* is an expanse of sea without shore or harbor; it is named after the Greek term πλάγιος ("oblique"), that is, "breadth," whence also 'open beach' (*plagia*), because they are without harbors.

xvii. Gulfs of the sea (De sinibus maris) 1. The larger inlets of the sea are called gulfs (*sinus*), as the Ionian in the Mediterranean, and in the Ocean, the Caspian, Indian, Persian and the Arabian gulf – which is also the Red Sea, which is assigned to the Ocean. 2. The Red Sea is so named because it is colored with reddish waves; however, it does not possess this quality by its nature, but its currents are tainted and stained by the neighboring shores because all the land surrounding that sea is red and close to the color of blood. From there a very intense vermilion may be separated out, as well as other pigments with which the coloring of paintings is varied. 3. Therefore, since the soil has this nature, it is washed away in rivers, and whatever pigment is eroded lends color to the water. It is for this reason that red gemstones are found on these shores, for when a pebble covered with this type of soil is rubbed in the sand, it has the color of both the earth and the sea. 4. The Red Sea is divided into two gulfs. Of these, the one to the east is called the Persian Gulf because the Persians live at its mouths. The other is called the Arabian, because it is next to Arabia.

xviii. Tides and straits (De aestibus et fretis) 1. Tides pertain to the Ocean, and straits pertain to the connection between two seas. A tide (*aestus*) is a rising or falling of the sea, that is, a restlessness, whence also the word 'estuary' (*aestuaria*), through which the sea by turns rises and falls. 2. But 'straits' (*fretum*) are named because there the sea is always seething (*fervere*); for a strait is narrow, a 'seething sea' (*fervens mare*) as it were, named from the agitation of the waves, like the Straits of Gibraltar or of Sicily. Varro (*Latin Language* 7.22) says that they are called *fretum* as if the word were 'violently agitated' (*fervidus*), that is, 'seething' (*fervendia*), and having the motion of 'extreme agitation' (*fervor*). 3. Sallust (*Histories*, 4.26) writes that the Straits of Sicily, which are called Rhegium, are named for this reason, that at one time Sicily had been joined to Italy, and when they were a single land, the intervening space was either overwhelmed by the waters due to its low elevation, or was cut through due to its narrowness. And it is named Ῥήγιον because in Greek this word means "broken off" (cf. ῥηγνύμαι, "break apart"). It is exceedingly narrow, dividing Sicily from Italy by a distance of three Roman miles, and is notorious for fabulous monsters; on one side appears Scylla, and on the other Charybdis. 4. Indeed, neighboring people give the name Scylla to a rock jutting over the sea that is similar to the fabled shape when seen from a distance. Accordingly the fables have attributed to it a monstrous appearance, as if it had the shape of a human girded with the heads of dogs, because the current rushing together there seems to produce the sound of barking. 5. Charybdis is named because it swallows ships up in its hidden maelstrom (*gurges*), for it is a sea filled with whirlpools, and for that reason mangled shipwrecks come out of its depths. Three times a day it raises its waters, and three times a day it sucks them back in, for it takes waters in so that it may spit them back out, and spits them out so that it may take them back in again. 6. The Syrtes are sandy places in the sea. Sallust (*War with Jugurtha* 78.3) says they are called Syrtes from 'dragging' (cf. σύρτης, "cord for dragging, rein," from σύρειν, "drag") because they drag everything towards themselves, and they cling fast to whoever approaches the shallows of the sea. These places are in the sea near Egypt, and confused with one another. 'Shallows' (*vadum*), however, are those places in which people and animals can cross (*vadere*) the sea or rivers on foot; Vergil calls them 'shoals' (*brevia*), and the Greeks βραχέα.

xix. Lakes and pools (De lacis et stagnis) 1. There are certain bodies of water that are not mixed with the currents of the Ocean or the Mediterranean, and these are called lakes and pools. 2. A lake is a basin in which water is held and not mixed with currents, such as Lake Asphalti, Lake Benacus (i.e. present-day Garda), Lake Larius (i.e. Como), and the others which the Greeks call λίμναι, that is, 'pools.' Springs fall into streams, and rivers rush into channels, but a lake stays in place and does not flow forth. And it is called lake (*lacus*) as if the term were 'place' (*locus*) of water. 3. Lake Asphalti (i.e. Lake Asphaltites) is the same as the Dead Sea, so named because it generates nothing living and tolerates no type of living creature, for it has no fish and does not allow itself to be used by birds that are accustomed to water and rejoice at diving. But whatever living creatures you might try to submerge in it, they would spring back up; by whatever procedure they were immersed, and however firmly they were shoved in, they would immediately be cast out. It is not moved by winds, since the asphalt, which makes its water stand still, is resistant to winds. Nor does it allow sailing, because everything that is not alive sinks into its depths, and it does not support any material unless it is made bright with asphalt. 4. People say that a lighted lamp floats on top, but when its light is extinguished, it sinks. This is also called the Salt Sea, or Lake Asphalti, that is, 'of bitumen,' and it is in Judea between Jericho and Zoara. In length it stretches 780 stades (i.e. about ninety miles) to Zoara in Arabia and its width is 150 stades, up to the neighborhood of Sodom.

5. Lake Tiberias is named from the town Tiberias, which Herod at one time founded in honor of Tiberius Caesar, and it is more salubrious than all the other lakes in Judea, and more efficacious somehow at healing bodies. Its circumference in stades . . . 6. Lake Gennesaret (i.e. the Sea of Galilee, the same as Lake Tiberias) is the biggest in Judea with a length of 140 stades, and a width of 40. It has choppy waters and produces a breeze for itself not from the winds, but from its own self. For this reason it is named with a Greek word, Genesar, as if the term were 'generating a breeze for itself' (*generans sibi auram*). The Lake, then, is agitated over a wide area by these frequent puffing breezes, with the result that it is pure draught, sweet and good for drinking. 7. Benacus (i.e. Garda) is a lake in Italy, in Venetia, whence the river Mincius arises. Due to its size, this lake imitates the storms of the sea. 8. Lucrinus and Avernus are lakes in Campania. Lucrinus is so named because at one time it furnished great revenues (cf. *lucrum*, "profit") due to its abundance of fish. Lake Avernus was named because birds (*avis*) were unable to fly over it, for in an earlier time it was so surrounded with a thick forest that the overpowering odor of its sulfurous water, evaporating in an enclosed space, would kill the birds flying over it with its exhalation. Caesar Augustus on hearing of this cut down the trees and made the place pleasant again, restored from its unwholesome state. 9. Further, a lake is the same as a pool where an immense amount of water collects. And it is called 'pool' (*stagnus*) because there the water stands (*stare*) and does not run forth.

xx. The abyss (De abysso) 1. The abyss is an impenetrable depth of waters, either caves of hidden waters from which springs and rivers rise, or waters that secretly flow below the earth, whence it is called the abyss (*abyssus*, cf. ἄβυσσος, "fathomless," from α- "without" + βύσσος, "depth"). Indeed, all waters or torrents return through hidden passages to the central abyss. 2. Surges (*fluctus*) are so named because they arise from blowing winds (*flatus*), for waters that are agitated by the force of winds 'surge up' (*fluctuare*). *Aqua* is water that is still and level (*aequalis*), without motion. 3. But a 'wave' is rising water that is always in motion. Lucretius (*On the Nature of Things* 2.152):

> Aerial waves (*undas*),

that is, motion, and the mass that surges and falls back. A wave is not water per se, but water in a certain motion and agitation, whence it is called wave (*unda*), as if from 'going' (*eundo*) and 'returning' (*redeundo*).

4. *Latex*, strictly speaking, is the liquid of a fountain, and is called *latex* because it hides (*latere*) in the passages of the earth. 5. A drop (*gutta*) is that which stands hanging, *stilla* (i.e. another word for 'drop') is that which falls. Hence the word *stillicidium* (i.e. drippings from eaves), as if it were 'falling drop' (*stilla cadens*). *Stiria* (lit. "frozen drop, icicle," here simply "drop") is a Greek word, that is 'drop' (*gutta*); from it the diminutive that we call *stilla* is formed.[8] As long as it stands or hangs suspended from roofs or trees, it is a *gutta*, as if 'glutinous' (*glutinosus*), but when it has fallen it is a *stilla*. 6. Foam (*spuma*) is named because it is spewn (*spuere*); it consists of the residue of waves; whence new wine, and things that are boiled, are purified by foam. Hence also the word 'spit' (*sputum*).

xxi. Rivers (De fluminibus) 1. A river (*fluvius*) is an unceasing flow of water, named from perpetually flowing (*fluere*). Strictly speaking, *flumen* is the water itself, while *fluvius* is the channel of the water. The word *flumen* is earlier than *fluvius*, that is, water comes before its flow. There are two types of river; one is a torrent and the other is 'naturally flowing' (*vivus*). Concerning the latter type, Vergil says (*Aen.* 2.719):

> Until I have bathed myself in running (*vivus*) water.

2. A torrent is water that is flowing furiously. It is called a torrent (*torrens*) because it increases with the rain, and during a drought it 'becomes parched' (*torrescere*), that is, it dries up. Concerning it Pacuvius (fr. 13) says:

> The torrent dries up (*torrens torrere*) with the fiery vapor.

The Greeks assigned a torrent its name from winter (cf. χειμάρροος, "winter-flowing; torrent"), while we assigned it from summer; they named it from the season in which it is renewed and we from the season in which it dries up. 3. An *amnis* (i.e. another word for 'river') is a river surrounded by forests and leafy boughs and is called *amnis* from its pleasantness (*amoenitas*). 4. Strictly speaking the 'channel' (*decursus*) is the boundary of a course (*cursus*), whether of water or of whatever else you like. Ditches (*rivus*) are so named because they are diverted (*derivare*) for irrigation, that is, for bringing water into the fields, for 'to irrigate' is to 'bring in.' A whirlpool (*gurges*) is, strictly speaking, a deep spot in a river. 5. A well (*puteus*) is a place that has been dug out, from which water is drawn. It is so named from 'drinking' (*potatio*). A spring (*fons*) is a source of water springing forth, as if it were 'pouring out' (*fundere*) water.

6. Some rivers have taken their names for specific reasons; some of these should be noted, as they are frequently mentioned in histories. 7. Geon is a river going out of Paradise and surrounding all Ethiopia; it is called by this name because it irrigates the land of Egypt with the rising of its floods, for γῆ in Greek means "earth" in Latin. This river is called the Nile by the Egyptians on account of the mud that it carries, which makes the land fertile; hence it is called Nile, as if the term were νέα ἰλύς ("new mud"). The Nile used to be called *Melo* in Latin. It arises in Lake Nilides; from there it turns to the south, and is received by Egypt, where it is struck by winds from the north, and swells up as its waters struggle against them, and causes the flooding of Egypt.

8. The Ganges is the river that the Sacred Scriptures call Phison, going out from Paradise and continuing on to the regions of India. And it is called Phison, that is, 'throng,' because it is filled with ten great tributaries and is made into one. It is called Ganges from Gangarus, the king of India. This river is said to rise up in the manner of the Nile and burst out over the lands of the Orient. 9. The Tigris is a river in Mesopotamia, rising from Paradise and continuing up toward Assyria, and after much

8 Isidore's source here, Servius, does not say that *stiria* is a Greek word.

twisting it flows into the Dead Sea. It is called by this name on account of its speed, like that animal, the tiger (*tigris*), which runs exceedingly fast. 10. The Euphrates is a river in Mesopotamia rising from Paradise, well supplied with gemstones; it flows through the middle of Babylonia. This river took its name from fruits, or from abundance, for in Hebrew *Ephrata* means "fertility," and it irrigates Mesopotamia in certain regions just as the Nile irrigates Alexandria. Sallust, a most trustworthy authority, asserts (*Histories* 4.77) that the Tigris and the Euphrates flow from a single source in Armenia; taking different courses they flow further apart, leaving a space of many miles in between. The land that they surround is called Mesopotamia (Greek "land between the rivers"). Based on this, Jerome notes (*Site and Names of Hebrew Places* 202 [*PL* 23.939]) that there should be a different understanding about the rivers flowing from Paradise.

11. The Indus is a river of the Orient, which empties into the Red Sea. 12. In very ancient times Hystaspes was a king of the Medes, from whom the spring in the Orient that is now called Hydaspes takes its name. Concerning this Lucan . . . (see *Civil War* 3.236, 8.227, mentioning the Indus and Hydaspes). Although it is a Persian river, it is nevertheless said to flow toward the east. 13. The Arar is a river of the Orient. Concerning it Vergil says (*Ecl.* 1.62):

> Or (sooner) shall the Parthian drink from the Arar,

for it flows through Parthia and Assyria.[9] 14. The Bactrus is a river of the Orient said to be named from King Bactrus, from whom the Bactrians and their city are also named. 15. The Choaspes (i.e. the Karkheh) is a river in Persia, so named in their language because it has amazingly sweet waters, such that the Persian kings claimed the drinking water from it for themselves for the distance that the river runs between Persian riverbanks. Some people think the river Cydnus in Cilicia originates from this river. 16. The river Araxis (i.e. the Araks) in Armenia, which arises from the same mountain as the Euphrates, but from different underground channels, is so named because it destroys everything with its rapacity (*rapacitas*, from *rapax*, "rapacious"). Hence, when Alexander wished to cross it, and a bridge was built, the river rushed past with such force that it demolished the bridge. This river has its head a short distance from the source of the Euphrates, and then it flows into the Caspian Sea.

17. The Syrian river called the Orontes flows along the walls of Antioch; originating (*oriens*) from the east (*solis ortus*), it joins the sea not far from that city. The ancients called it Orontes in Latin from the tracing of its origin. The whole city is cooled almost all the time by the impact of the rather cold current of this river, and by the westerly breezes blowing there constantly. 18. The Jordan is a river in Judea, named from two springs, one of which is called Ior and the other Dan. These rivers, once far apart from each other, are joined into a single channel, which is then called the Jordan. It originates at the foot of Mount Libanus (i.e. Mt. Lebanon), and separates Judea from Arabia; after many twists and turns it flows into the Dead Sea near Jericho. 19. The Eusis flows forth from the mountains of the Caucasus and, along with many others, empties into the Euxine Sea, (i.e. the Black Sea), whence it is named. 20. The Cydnus is a river in Cilicia that comes from Mount Taurus, possessing amazingly sweet waters, and is so called because whatever is white the Syrians call *cydnus* in their native language. Whence the name is also given to this river because it swells (i.e. runs white) in the summer when the snows melt, but in the other seasons of the year it is shallow and quiet. 21. Hylas is a river in Asia. Pactolus is a river in Asia that carries golden sands. Vergil says of it (*Aen.* 10.142):

> And Pactolus waters (fields) with gold.

People give it another name, Chrysorrhoa, because of its golden flow (cf. χρυσός, "gold"; ῥοή, "stream"). 22. Hermus is a river in Asia that divides the Smyrnean plains, and it is filled with golden currents and sand; Smyrna is named from it (cf. σμύρνα, "myrrh," golden in color).

23. The Meander is a twisting river in Asia that, with its course bending back between Caria and Ionia, rushes into the gulf that separates Miletus and Priene. It is called the Meander because it is twisting and never flows in a straight course (perhaps cf. *meare*, "traverse"). Of it Ovid says (cf. *Met.* 2. 246)

> The Meander amuses itself along its curving waters.

24. Tanus was the first king of the Scythians; the river Tanais (i.e. the Don), which proceeds from the Rhipaean forest and divides Europe from Asia, is said to be named after him. It flows between these two parts of the world

9 The Arar is the Saône in modern France. Isidore or his source mistakes the Vergil, which speaks of the *impossibility* of (Central Asian) Parthians drinking from the Arar unless as exiles.

and empties into the Black Sea. 25. The Inachus (i.e. the Banitza) is a river in Achaea that waters the Argolic plains. King Inachus, who gave the Argive people their origin, named it after himself. There too is the river Erymanthus, issuing from Mount Erymanthus. 26. The Padus (i.e. the Po), a river in Italy flowing from the Alpine heights, arises from three sources. The name of one of these sources is Padus, which, having spread out like a lake, sends the river from its lap. The river Padus is named from this. The Greeks also give it the cognomen Eridanus, from Eridanus the son of the Sun, whom people call Phaeton. After being struck by lightning he fell into this river and died. It is fed by melting snows at the rising of the Dog Star (i.e. in the dog days of summer), and with the addition of thirty other streams it empties into the Adriatic Sea near Ravenna.

27. The Tiber (*Tiberis*), a river of Italy, is said to be named after Tiberinus, king of the Albans; he died in this river and from his death gave it his name. Before this time it had the ancient name Albula because of its color, since it is white (*albus*), due to the snows. It is also called the *Tibris*, which is the same as *Tiberis*, but *Tiberis* is used in everyday speech, and *Tibris* in poetry. 28. The Danube (*Danubius*) river of Germany is said to be named from the abundance of snow (*nix*, gen. *nivis*) by which it is much swelled. This is more famous than all the other rivers of Europe. It is also called the Ister, because, as it wanders through innumerable peoples, it changes its name and gathers more force as it travels. It arises in the mountains of Germania and the western regions belonging to the barbarians. It proceeds toward the east, and receives sixty tributaries. It flows into the Black Sea through seven mouths. 29. The Rhodanus (i.e. the Rhone), a river in Gaul, is so called after the city Rhodos, and it was named by colonists from Rhodes.[10] It rushes with a swift current, cutting channels into the Tyrrhenian Sea. It creates no small danger for sailors, when the waves of the sea and the currents of the river wrestle together.

30. The Rhenus (i.e. the Rhine) is said to be named from association with the Rhodanus, because it rises from the same province as the Rhodanus. It is a river of Germany counted among the three greatest rivers of Europe. It directs its waters from the Alpine heights to the depths of the Ocean. 31. The Iberus (i.e. the Ebro) is a river that once gave its name to all of Spain. 32. Mineus, a river of Galicia, took its name from the color of a pigment that is found abundantly in it (i.e. *minium*, "cinnabar"). 33. The river Durius (the present-day Douro in Spain) is so called by the Greeks, as if the word were 'Doric.' Hispania's Carthago (i.e. a Carthaginian colony in Spain, present-day Cartagena) has given its name to the Tagus (i.e. the Tajo), a river that issues from that city. It is rich in gold-bearing sands and for this reason is preeminent among the Spanish rivers. 34. The river Baetis (i.e. the Guadalquivir) gave its name to the province Baetica (i.e. present-day Andalusia). Martial says of it (*Epigrams* 12.98.1):

> Baetis, wreathe your hair with an olive-bearing crown,
> you who dye your fleece gold in sparkling waters –

because woolen fleeces were dyed there to a beautiful color.[11] And it is named Baetis because it runs through low ground, for the Greeks say *bitin*[12] for 'low' or 'submerged.' 35. Some rivers, during the Flood, were blocked by loosened masses of earth; whereas other rivers, which did not exist before, burst forth to the surface at that time through the ruptured passages of the abyss.

xxii. Floods (De diluviis) 1. A 'flood' (*diluvium*) is so named because it destroys (*delere*) everything it washes over with the scourge of its waters. 2. The first flood occurred at the time of Noah, when the Almighty was offended by the sins of humans. The entire world was covered, everything was destroyed, there was a united expanse of sky and sea. To this day we observe evidence of this in the stones we are accustomed to see on remote mountains, stones that have hardened with shellfish and oysters in them, and often stones that have been hollowed out by the waters. 3. The second flood was in Achaea at the time of the patriarch Jacob and of Ogygus, who was the founder and king of Eleusis, and who gave his name to both the place and the age. 4. The third flood was in Thessaly in the time of Moses and Amphictyon, who was the third to reign after Cecrops. During their lifetimes, an influx of water consumed the greater part of the population of Thessaly, although a few survived – those who fled to the mountains, particularly to Mount Parnassus. Deucalion took possession of a kingdom at that time in the

10 The translation adopts *vocaverunt* ("named") from Gasparotto (2004) for Lindsay's *locaverunt* ("placed, settled").

11 Fleece was used to trap gold dust suspended in rivers.

12 *Bitin* is a corruption; perhaps cf. Greek βαθύς, "deep," or βύθιος, "submerged."

region of Parnassus, rescuing people who came to him by boat, seeking refuge; he provided them with shelter and sustenance across the twin peaks of Parnassus. The fables of the Greeks say that humankind was recreated from stones by Deucalion, because of the ingrained stoniness of the human heart. 5. But whenever rivers, swollen with unusual rains, overflow to a degree that is beyond what is normal in duration or magnitude, and cause widespread destruction, they too are called 'floods.' One must bear in mind, however, that when rivers rise higher than normal, they not only bring destruction in the present moment, but they also signify something yet to happen.

Book XIV

The earth and its parts (De terra et partibus)

i. The earth (De terra) 1. The earth is placed in the central region of the world, standing fast as the center equidistant from all other parts of the sky. In the singular the word 'earth' (*terra*) signifies the whole globe, but in the plural, distinct parts. Logic supplies the earth's diverse names, for the word *terra* is derived from the upper surface that is worn away (*terere*); soil (*humus*) from the lower, or moist (*humidus*) earth, like that under the sea; ground (*tellus*), because we carry away (*tollere*) what it produces; as such it is also called Ops (i.e. the earth-goddess of plenty) because it produces wealth (*ops*) from its crops; and also 'arable land' (*arvum*), from plowing (*arare*) and cultivating. 2. However, to distinguish it properly from water, earth is called 'dry land' (*arida*), as Scripture says (cf. Genesis 1:10): "God called the dry land (*arida*) Earth." The earth's natural attribute is that of dryness, for if it is moist, that comes from a union with water. Of its motion some say that it is the wind in its hollows that, itself moved, moves the earth. Sallust (*Histories* 2.28): "A number of mountains and hills subsided, with the winds having swiftly broken through the hollows of the earth." 3. Others maintain that life-giving water moves in the earth and simultaneously shakes it, like a vessel, as for instance Lucretius (see *On the Nature of Things* 6.555). Yet others are of the opinion that the earth is σπογγοειδής ("spongy"), and that its mostly hidden, collapsing interior shakes everything placed upon it. Also, an opening in the earth is created through the movement of water in the lower regions, or through repeated thunder, or through winds that erupt from cavities of the earth.

ii. The globe (De orbe) 1. The globe (*orbis*) derives its name from the roundness of the circle, because it resembles a wheel; hence a small wheel is called a 'small disk' (*orbiculus*).[1] Indeed, the Ocean that flows around it on all sides encompasses its furthest reaches in a circle. It is divided into three parts, one of which is called Asia, the second Europe, the third Africa. 2. The ancients did not divide the three parts of the globe equally, for Asia extends from south to north in the east, but Europe from the north to the west, Africa from the west to the south. 3. Whence it is clear that two of them, Europe and Africa, occupy half of the globe, Asia the other half by itself. But the former pair are divided into two regions, because from the Ocean the Mediterranean enters in between them and separates them. Wherefore, if you divide the globe into two parts, the east and the west, Asia will be in one, Europe and Africa in the other.

iii. Asia (De Asia) 1. Asia (*Asia*) is named after a certain woman who, among the ancients, had an empire in the east. It lies in a third sector of the globe, bounded in the east by the rising sun, in the south by the Ocean, in the west by the Mediterranean, in the north by Lake Moeotis (i.e. the Sea of Azov) and the river Tanais (i.e. the Don). It has many provinces and regions, whose names and locations I will briefly explain, beginning with Paradise. 2. Paradise is located in the east. Its name, translated from Greek into Latin, means "garden." In Hebrew in turn it is called Eden, which in our language means "delights." The combination of both names gives us the expression "garden of delights," for every kind of fruit-tree and non-fruit bearing tree is found in this place, including the tree of life. It does not grow cold or hot there, but the air is always temperate. 3. A spring which bursts forth in the center irrigates the whole grove and it is divided into the headwaters of four rivers. Access to this location was blocked off after the fall of humankind, for it is fenced in on all sides by a flaming spear, that is, encircled by a wall of fire, so that the flames almost reach the sky. 4. Also the Cherubim, that is, a garrison of angels, have been drawn up above the flaming of the spear to prevent evil spirits from approaching, so that the flames drive off human beings, and angels drive off the wicked angels, in order that access to Paradise may not lie open either to flesh or to spirits that have transgressed.

1 Throughout Book XIV we translate *orbis* as "globe." The term refers to the 'circle' of lands around the Mediterranean, and hence to the total known extent of land.

5. India is so called from the river Indus, by which it is bounded on the west. It stretches from the south sea to the place where the sun rises, and reaches in the north up to the Caucasus range. It has many peoples and towns, also the islands Taprobane (i.e. Sri Lanka), full of precious stones and elephants, Chrysa (cf. χρυσός, "gold") and Argyre (cf. ἄργυρος, "silver"), rich in gold and silver (*argentum*), and Tile, where the trees never lose their foliage. 6. It also has the rivers Ganges, Indus, and the Hypanis, which make India famous. India's soil, very healthful because of the breeze of the west wind, yields two harvests annually; in winter in turn it submits to the Etesian trade-winds. It produces human beings of color, huge elephants, the animal called *monoceros* (i.e. the unicorn), the bird called parrot, a wood called ebony, and cinnamon, pepper, and sweet calamus. 7. It also yields ivory and precious stones: beryls, chrysoprase, and diamonds, carbuncles, white marble, and small and large pearls much coveted by women of the nobility. There are also mountains of gold there, which one cannot approach because of dragons, griffins, and human monsters of immense size.

8. The region from the border of India to Mesopotamia is generally called Parthia. Due to the invincible strength of the Parthians, Assyria and other adjoining regions also came to be included under its name. Among them are Aracusia, Parthia, Assyria, Media, and Persia – areas that adjoin each other, beginning at the river Indus and ending at the Tigris. Harsh and mountainous places are found in them, as well as the rivers Hydaspes and Arbis. These regions are divided from each other by their own borders and they thus derive their names from their respective founders. 9. Aracusia takes its name from its city. Parthia was occupied by the Parthians, who came from Scythia, and they named the area after themselves. South of it is the Red Sea, north of it the Caspian Sea, in the west the territory of the Medes. There are eighteen kingdoms in it, stretching from the shores of the Hyrcanian (i.e. Caspian) Sea to the territories of the Scythians.

10. Assyria derives its name from Asshur, son of Shem, who was the first inhabitant of this region after the Flood. It reaches from India in the east to Media in the south, in the west to the Tigris and in the north to the Caucasus, where the Caspian passes are. In this region the purple-fish was first put to use, and from here came the first lotions and perfumes for hair and body, with which the luxury of the Romans and the Greeks abounded. 11. Media and Persia (*Persida*) are named after the kings Medus and Persus, who invaded these regions in war. Among these Media obliquely borders the Parthian kingdoms in the west; in the north it is enclosed by Armenia; in the east it overlooks the Caspians; in the south, Persia. Its soil produces the tree 'Medica,' which is rarely found in any other region. There are two Medias, Greater and Lesser Media. 12. Persia reaches in the east to the Indus, in the west it has the Red Sea, in the north it touches Media, in the south-southwest Carmania, which is connected to Persia and in which the most renowned city of Susa is located. Persia is the birthplace of the magical arts. The giant Nebroth went there after the confusion of the tongues and taught the Persians to worship fire, for in those regions everyone worships the sun, which is called *El* in their language.

13. The word Mesopotamia has a Greek etymology, because it is "bounded by two rivers" (cf. μέσος, "in the middle"; ποταμός, "river"), for in the east it has the Tigris, in the west the Euphrates. In the north its territory begins between Mount Taurus and the Caucasus; in the south it borders on Babylonia, then Chaldaea, and lastly Arabia Felix. 14. The city of Babylon is the capital of Babylonia, from which it also derives its name. It is so famous that at one time or another Chaldaea, Assyria, and Mesopotamia came to be included under its name. 15. The word 'Arabia' means "sacred"; it is interpreted to mean this because the region produces incense and perfumes: hence the Greeks called it εὐδαίμων ("happy"), our Latin speakers *beatus* ("happy").[2] Its woods produce both myrrh and cinnamon: it is the birthplace of the bird phoenix, and one finds precious stones there: the sardonyx, *iris* crystal, malachite, and opals. This region is also known as Sabaea, after the son of Cush whose name was Saba. In the east, this land extends in a narrow tract to the Persian gulf; in the north it borders on Chaldaea, in the west on the Arabian Sea.

16. It is said that a certain Syrus, a native of the land, named Syria after himself. In the east its boundary is the Euphrates, in the west the Mediterranean and Egypt; in the north it touches Armenia and Cappadocia, in the south the Arabian Sea. Its territory extends immensely in length, more narrowly in width. 17. It comprises

2 Isidore alludes to a common term for one section of Arabia, *Arabia Felix*, "Arabia the Blessed."

the provinces Commagene, Phoenicia, and Palestine, to which Judea belongs, except for the Saracens and the Nabateans. Commagene, the first province of Syria, received its name from the city of Commaga, which was once considered to be the capital there. North of it lies Armenia, to the east Mesopotamia, to the south Syria, to the west the Mediterranean. 18. Phoenix, brother of Cadmus, came from Egyptian Thebes into Syria and ruled over Sidon, and this province was called Phoenicia after his name. In this province Tyre is located, of which Isaiah speaks (Isaiah 23). East of it lies Arabia, south of it the Red Sea.

19. The city of Philistis is the capital of the province of Palestine. It is now called Ascalon. From this city all of the surrounding region receives the name 'Palestine.' East of it lies the Red Sea, on the southern side it is bordered by Judea, in the north it is bounded by the borders of the Tyrians, in the west it comes to an end at the Egyptian border. 20. The Palestinian region Judea (*Iudaea*) is so called after Judah, from whose tribe it had its kings. Previously it was called Canaan (*Chanaan*), after a son of Cham (i.e. Ham), or else after the ten tribes of the Canaanites, whose territory the Judeans occupied after they had expelled them. It stretches lengthwise from the village Arfa up to the village Julias, which is inhabited in equal parts by a community of Judeans and of Tyrians. In its width it stretches all the way from Mount Libanus (i.e. Mount Lebanon) to Lake Tiberias (i.e. the Sea of Galilee). 21. In the center of Judea is the city Jerusalem, as if it were the navel of the whole region. It is a land wealthy in various resources, fertile in fruits of the earth, renowned for its waters, rich in balsam-trees. Hence, thanks to the benefits of its natural goods, the Judeans considered it the land flowing with milk and honey promised to their forefathers, because in this place God offered them a foreshadowing of the Resurrection.

22. Samaria is a region in Palestine that received its name from a certain city called Samaria, which was once a royal residence in Israel; nowadays it is known as Sebastia, a name that is derived from Augustus (cf. σεβαστός, "august"). This region lies in the middle between Judea and Galilee; it begins in the village called Eleas and ends in the territory called Agrabath. The nature of its territory resembles and in no way differs from that of Judea. 23. Galilee (*Galilaea*) is a region in Palestine which is so called because it produces lighter-skinned people than Palestine does (cf. γάλα, "milk"). It has two parts, an upper and a lower, which are nevertheless connected and border on Syria and Phoenicia. Its earth is rich, fertile, and rather abundant in produce. 24. Pentapolis is a region located where Arabia borders on Palestine. It derives its name from the five wicked cities that were consumed by heavenly fire (see Wisdom 10:6, Vulgate, and cf. v.5 below). Once this land was more fertile than Jerusalem, but today it is deserted and scorched, for due to the wickedness of its inhabitants fire descended from heaven that reduced this region to eternal ashes (Genesis 19:24–25). 25. A kind of shadow and image of it is visible to this day in its ashes and trees, for in this area there is flourishing fruit with such an appearance of ripeness that it makes one want to eat it, but if you gather it, it falls apart and dissolves in ashes and gives off smoke as if it were still burning. 26. Nabathea is a region named after Nabaioth, son of Ishmael. It lies between Judea and Arabia; rising from the Euphrates it stretches to the Red Sea – it is part of Arabia.

27. Egypt (*Aegyptus*), which was formerly called 'Aeria,' later took its name from Aegyptus, brother of Danaus, who reigned there. In the east it is adjoined by Syria and the Red Sea, to the west lies Libya, in the north the Mediterranean, while in the south it extends toward the interior, reaching Ethiopia: a region unaccustomed to rain and unacquainted with downpours. 28. The Nile alone waters it when it overflows and renders it fertile with its flood; whence it is rich in produce and feeds many parts of the earth with grain. Furthermore, it overflows with other articles of trade to such an extent that it fills the world with indispensable merchandise. Egypt ends at Canopea, named after the helmsman of Menelaos, Canopus, who is buried on the island that marks the beginning of Libya and the mouth of the Nile.

29. Seres is a city of the east after which both the Seres and their region (i.e. China and East Asia) are named. The area bends from the Scythian Ocean and the Caspian Sea to the eastern Ocean. It is rich in a renowned foliage, from which silk-fleece is gathered, which the Seres sell to other peoples for the manufacture of garments. 30. The river Bactrus itself gave its name to Bactria. The parts of it that are further out are surrounded by the range of the Propanisus, while those facing us terminate at the source of the river Indus; the river Ochus is the boundary for the remaining parts. Bactria exports camels of the greatest strength, whose feet never wear out.

31. Like the country of the Goths, Scythia is said to have been named after Magog, son of Japheth. Formerly its territory was immense; it stretched from India in the east and from the Maeotian swamps (i.e. the Sea of Azov) in the north between the Danube and the Ocean up to the borders of Germania. To be sure, later it was reduced in size and then reached from the right-hand region of its east, where the Chinese Ocean extends, up to the Caspian Sea, which is on its west. From there it spreads in the south to the summits of the Caucasus, under which Hyrcania lies, having in like manner many tribes in the west who are nomads due to the infertility of the soil. 32. Among these tribes some cultivate the land, whereas others who are monstrous and savage live on human flesh and blood. Many parts of Scythia have good land, but many are nevertheless uninhabitable, for while many places abound in gold and precious stones, they are rarely visited by human beings because of the savagery of the griffins. The best green gems come from there; lapis lazuli and the purest crystal are Scythian. It also has the great rivers of the Moschi, the Phasis, and the Araxes.

33. Hyrcania is so called after the Hyrcanian forest, which lies below Scythia, having in the east the Caspian Sea, in the south Armenia, in the north *Albania* and in the west Hiberia (i.e. present-day Georgia). It is a rough forest, full of savage wild beasts such as tigers, panthers, and pards. Vergil says of it (*Aen.* 4.367):

> And Hyrcanian tigresses suckled you.

34. *Albania*[3] gets its name from the color of its inhabitants, because they are born with white (*albus*) hair. In the east it rises from below the Caspian Sea and extends to the Maeotian swamps (i.e. the Sea of Azov) along the shores of the Ocean in the north, by deserts and uncultivated regions. This land has enormous dogs; their ferocity is such that they attack bulls and kill lions.

35. Armenia is so called from Armenus, the companion of Jason of Thessaly. After the death of King Jason he gathered a group from among the crowd of Jason's followers who were wandering aimlessly about, seized Armenia and named it after himself. It is located between the Taurus and the Caucasus ranges, reaching from Cappadocia to the Caspian Sea, having in the north the Ceraunian mountains, in whose hills the river Tigris originates, and in whose mountains the Ark is said to have settled after the Flood. There are two Armenias, Upper and Lower Armenia, just as there are two Pannonias. 36. Hiberia is a region in Asia, near the Pontus (i.e. the Black Sea), connected to Armenia. There herbs grow which can be used for dyeing. 37. Cappadocia was named after its chief city. It is located where Syria begins and touches Armenia in the east, Asia Minor in the west, and the Cimmerian Sea and the Themiscyrian plains, which belong to the Amazons, in the north; in the south it reaches the Taurus mountains, under which Cilicia and Isauria stretch out to the Gulf of Cilicia, which faces the isle of Cyprus. Its territory excels as a breeding-ground for horses. Through it flows the river Halys, which formerly separated the kingdom of Lydia from the Persians.

38. Asia Minor is girt by Cappadocia in the east and surrounded by the sea in all other directions, for it has the Black Sea in the north, the Propontis (i.e. the Sea of Marmora) in the west, and the sea of Egypt in the south. Its provinces are Bithynia, Phrygia, Galatia, Lydia, Caria, Pamphylia, Isauria, Lycia, and Cilicia. 39. The first of these provinces of Asia Minor, Bithynia, stretches eastward from where the Black Sea begins, opposite Thracia, and it was previously called many different names, first Bebrycia, then Mygdonia, then Bithynia, after king Bithynus. It is also known as Phrygia Major. The city Nicomedia lies in it, where Hannibal took refuge and died from a drink of poison. 40. Galatia takes its name from ancient tribes of the Galli, by whom it was occupied, for the Galli, called upon by the king of Bithynia to assist him, divided the kingdom with him when victory was achieved. Thus, after they had intermarried with the Greeks, they were first called Gallograeci and are now called Galatians, after the name of the ancient Galli, and their territory is called Galatia.

41. Phrygia is named after Phrygia, the daughter of Europa. It is also called Dardania, after Dardanus, the son of Jupiter, concerning whom Homer says (cf. *Iliad* 20.215):

> Whom Jupiter first begot in the celestial citadel.

Having left from the city of Corythus, he was the first to arrive in Phrygia. This territory is situated above the Troad, with the region of Galatia to the north; in the south it is a neighbor of Lyconia, it borders Lydia in

3 The province of *Albania* is not coextensive with present-day Albania, but lies on the west coast of the Caspian Sea – now parts of Azerbaijan and Russia.

the east, and in the west it is bounded by the Hellespont. It contains the region of Troy, which Tros, the king of the Trojans and father of Ganymede, named after himself. There are two Phrygias: Phrygia Major and Phrygia Minor. Smyrna lies in Phrygia Major and Ilium in Phrygia Minor. 42. Lycaonia . . . The river Hermus separates Caria from Phrygia. 43. Lydia is an old seat of kingdoms, which the waters of the Pactolus have raised to riches with their golden floods. Previously it was called Maeonia. Because of its smallness it could not support the two brothers, Lydus and Tyrrhenus, as kings. They therefore drew lots and it fell to Tyrrhenus to leave, with a large number of people, and occupy an area in Gaul that he named Tyrrhenia. Lydia, however, is named after Lydus, the brother of the king, who remained in the province. In the west it borders on Phrygia Minor, in the east it has the city of Smyrna, which is encircled by the river Helles;[4] the rivers Pactolus and Hermus, very rich in golden sand, flow around its fields.

44. Pamphylia . . . It is said that Isauria is named after the place where it is located, because it lies everywhere exposed to blasts of wind (*aura*). It has the city of Seleucia as its metropolis. 45. Cilicia owes its name to a certain Cilix who, they say, was descended from Phoenix, and they assert that he was older than Jupiter. Many plains lie there, meeting in the west Lycia, in the south the Sea of Issus, at its back the ridges of Mount Taurus. The river Cydnus flows through it. Its capital is Tarsus. The city of Corycus is also located there, whence comes the most and the best saffron, more fragrant in scent and more golden in color. 46. Lycia is so called because in the east it borders on Cilicia, for Cilicia borders on it in the east and it has the sea to the west and the south; in the north lies Caria. There lies Mount Chimera, which exhales fire in nightly surges, like Etna in Sicily and Vesuvius in Campania.

iv. Europe (De Europa) 1. After Asia I must turn my pen to Europe. Europa was the daughter of Agenor, king of Libya, whom Jupiter carried to Crete after she had been abducted from Africa, and the third part of the globe is named after her. This Agenor is the son of Libya, after whom Libya, that is, Africa, is said to have been named; whence it seems Libya took its name first, and then Europe. 2. The third of the globe that is called Europe (*Europa*) begins with the river Tanais (i.e. the Don), passing to the west along the northern Ocean as far as the border of Spain, and its eastern and southern parts rise from the Pontus (i.e. the Black Sea) and are bordered the whole way by the Mediterranean and end in the islands of Gades (i.e. Cadiz). 3. The first region of Europe is lower Scythia, which begins in the Maeotian swamps (i.e. the Sea of Azov), stretching between the Danube and the northern Ocean up to Germania. And this land is called Barbarica in general usage on account of the barbaric people by whom it is inhabited. Its first part is Alania, which touches on the Maeotian swamps; after this Dacia, where Gothia is; then Germania, where the Suevi inhabit the greater part.

4. Germania lies beyond lower Scythia. It starts at the Danube and is enclosed by the river Rhine and the Ocean. In the north and in the west the Ocean is its boundary, in the east the Danube, in the south the river Rhine. The country is rich in men and has a numerous and fierce (*immanis*) population; due to this and its fecundity in producing peoples it is called Germania (cf. *germinare*, "germinate"). It produces the Hyrcanian birds, whose feathers shine at night; it also produces wild bison, wild oxen, and elk. It exports precious stones, crystal, and amber, as well as green *callaica* and white *ceraunium*. There are two parts to Germania: Upper Germania, adjoining the northern Ocean, and Lower Germania, beside the Rhine. 5. The provinces that the Danube separates from Barbaric territory and that stretch to the Mediterranean are as follows: the first is Moesia, so called for its abundant harvests (*messis*); whence the ancients also called it the granary of Ceres. In the east it is connected to the delta of the Danube, in the south-east to Thracia, in the south to Macedonia, in the west to Istria. After Moesia comes Pannonia. Then Noricum, a cold territory of scant productivity. Thereafter Raetia, teeming in produce, which comes next to Gallia Belgica.

6. Thracia is said to have gotten its name from Tiras, the son of Japheth, upon his arrival there; others have suggested that Thracia was named after the savagery of its inhabitants (perhaps cf. *trux*, gen. *trucis*, "savage," or τραχύς, "rough, savage"). In the east it lies opposite the Propontis (i.e. the Sea of Marmara) and the city of Constantinople, in the north it is bordered by the Ister, in the south by the Aegean, in the west it adjoins Macedonia. Once this region was inhabited by the Bessi,

4 Isidore or his sources are evidently confused about the location of Smyrna. The river name, Helles, too, is unclear.

the Massagetes, the Sarmatians, the Scythians and many other nations; for it is a spacious region and therefore it contained a great number of tribes. From Thracia the river Ebrus flows forth, which also touches upon many barbarian tribes.

7. Greece (*Graecia*) is so called from king Graecus, who settled this entire region as a kingdom. There are seven Greek provinces. From the west the first is Dalmatia, then Epirus, then Hellas, then Thessaly, then Macedonia, then Achaea, and two in the sea, Crete and the Cyclades. 'Illyricus' generally refers to all of Greece. 8. Dalmatia is thought to have taken its name from Delmi, the most important city of this province. It borders Macedonia in the east, Moesia in the north, to the west it ends in Istria, while in the south it ends at the Adriatic Sea. 9. Epirus is so called from Pyrrhus, son of Achilles. Part of it is Chaonia, which was formerly called Molossia, after Molossus, son of Pyrrhus, whom Pyrrhus fathered with Andromache. But after Pyrrhus was slain by the treachery of Orestes, Helenus took Andromache as wife, and held the kingdom of his stepson, who had succeeded his father. From him a part of Epirus was called Molossia, which Helenus afterwards named Chaonia, after his brother Chaon, whom he is said to have killed by accident during a hunt – as if this had been done in remembrance of his dead brother.

10. Hellas is so called from king Hellen, the son of Deucalion and Pyrrha; from him the Greeks first took the name Hellenes. This is the same territory as Attica, earlier called 'Acte.' There was a certain Granus, a native of Greece, after whose daughter's name, Attis, Attica was named. It lies in the middle between Macedonia and Achaea, connected to Arcadia on its northern side.[5] This is the true Greece, where the city of Athens was located, the mother of the liberal arts and the nurse of philosophers; there was nothing nobler and more illustrious in all of Greece. In it (Attica) lies the field of Marathon, by repute once drenched with the blood of battle. 11. There are two provinces of Hellas: Boeotia and the Peloponnese. Boeotia is so called for the following reason: when Cadmus, son of Agenor, searched under command of his father for his sister Europa, who had been seized by Jupiter, and he could not find her, he made up his mind to choose a place for exile, fearing the wrath of his father. He followed the tracks of a cow that he had seen by chance and took a liking to the place where it had lain down, and so he named the place Boeotia, after the word 'cow' (*bos*). There he built the city of Thebes, in which in ancient times civil wars erupted, and there Apollo was born, and Hercules, most famous of the Thebans. This city is also known by the name of Aeonia, after a certain spring consecrated to Apollo and the Muses, which is located in this same Boeotia. The second part of Hellas is the Peloponnese, named for and ruled by Pelops.

12. Thessaly (*Thessalia*) takes its name from King Thessalus. It borders on the southern region of Macedonia and it has Pieria at its back. Many are the rivers [and cities] and towns in Thessaly, Thessalonica being the most outstanding among them. There one also finds Mount Parnassus, which was once consecrated to Apollo. Thessaly was the birthplace of Achilles and the original home of the Lapiths, of whom it is said that they were the first to break horses to the bit, whence they were also called Centaurs (cf. κέντρον, "bit").[6] In Thessaly golden *solidi* (i.e. coins) were first manufactured and the first use of tamed horses was devised. 13. In the beginning Macedonia was called Emathia, after king Emathius, but afterwards Macedo, who was the maternal grandson of Deucalion, took over the rule and he changed the name and called it Macedonia, after his own name. It is bounded in the east by the Aegean Sea, in the south by Achaea, in the west by Dalmatia, in the north by Moesia. It is the fatherland of Alexander the Great, and a region very rich in gold and silver ore. This land produces a stone they call paeanites. Mount Olympus is in this region, which with its lofty peak rises up to such heights that neither clouds nor wind are perceived on its peak.

14. Both the city and the province Achaea are named after king Achaeus. This is almost an island (i.e. the Peloponnese peninsula); for, except for the northern region, which is conjoined to Macedonia, it is surrounded on all sides by the sea. In the east it has the Myrtean Sea, in the southeast the Cretan Sea, in the south the Ionian Sea, from the southwest and the west the Cassiopan islands, and only in the northern region is it adjoined to Macedonia and Attica. Corinth is its chief city, the ornament of Greece. Inachus is a river in Achaea.

5 'Northern' here seems to be a slip for 'southern'; see section 15 below.

6 Isidore has confused the Lapiths with their legendary opponents, the Centaurs.

15. Arcadia is the inmost part of Achaea, shaped like the leaf of a plane tree. It is placed in between the Ionian and the Aegean Sea; Arcas, the son of Iupiter and Callisto, named it Arcadia according to his own name after the Pelasgians had returned to rule. This is also known as Sicyonia, from king Sicyon, after whom the kingdom of the Sicyonians is also named. Arcadia contains the great river Erimanthus. It possesses the stone *asbestos*, which, once set on fire, is never extinguished. Dazzling white merles are also born there. 16. Lacedaemonia . . .

Pannonia is named after the Apennine (*Appenninus*) Alps, by which it is separated from Italy. It is a region strong in men that enjoys good soil and it is surrounded by two rivers that are very rough, the Drava (*Dravus*) and the Sava (*Savus*). It is adjacent to Noricum and Raetia; east of it lies Moesia, southeast Istria, southwest the Apennine Alps, in the west Belgian Gaul, in the north the source of the Danube and the border that divides Germania and Gaul. 17. The river Ister, which flows through this land, gives Istria its name. It is also known as the Danube. Pannonia lies to the north of Istria.

18. In times past Italy was called Magna Graecia by the Greeks who occupied it, and then Saturnia, from the name of its king. Later it was also called Latium, because it was here that Saturn hid (*latere*) after Jupiter had pushed him from his throne. Finally it was called Italy (*Italia*) after Italus, king of the Sicilians, who reigned there. Its territory is of greater length than width, extending from west-northwest to southeast. Enclosed by the Tyrrhenian Sea to the south and the Adriatic Sea to the north it is bounded in the west by the mountain range of the Alps. It is the most beautiful land in all respects, most pleasing in the fertility of its soil and the richness of its pasture. 19. It has Lake Garda (*Benacus*), Lake Avernus and the Lucrine Lake, the rivers Po (*Eridanus*) and Tiber, and the warm springs of Baiae. It produces the precious stones *syrtites*, *lyncurium*, and coral, and also the serpent called boa, the wild lynx, and the birds of Diomedes. However, both Italy and Spain are called Hesperia because the Greeks, when they travel to either Italy or Spain, navigate with the help of the evening star Hesperus. These are distinguished in the following manner: when you speak of Hesperia alone you refer to Italy, whereas when you add *Ultima* (Farthest) to it you refer to Spain, because it lies in the furthest reaches of the west.

20. Tuscia (cf. Tuscany) is a part of Italy, Umbria a part of Tuscia. Tuscia is named from its frequent use of religious rites and incense (*tus*), after the term θυάζειν ("offer sacrifice"). 21. Umbria, as the histories tell, survived the rains (*imber*) during the time of a disastrous flood and on this account was named Ὀμβρία ("rain") in Greek. It is located in the mountain range of the Apennines, in the part of Italy toward the south. 22. Etruria, a part of Italy, is so named because its boundaries are extended up to the river bank of the Tiber, as if the word were ἑτερούρια, for ἕτερος means "other," and ὅρος means "boundary" – in former times the boundaries of Rome extended to only one bank of the river Tiber. Others think that Etruria is so named from prince Etruscus. Likewise Tyrrhenia is named from Tyrrhenus, brother of Lydus who, as a result of a drawing of lots, came to Italy from Maeonia with part of his people. This is also known as Tuscia, but we ought not to say Tuscia, because we never see it in writing. Moreover, Tuscia is so named from its frequent use of sacrifice and incense, after the term θῦσαι ("to sacrifice"). And there, they say, the art of the haruspex was discovered. 23. Apulia [where Brindisi is located, which the Aetolians who had followed Diomedes as leader founded]. 24. Campania [has territories that are green in winter and in summer. There the sun is mild, the temperature pleasing, and the air pure and gentle].

25. Gaul (*Gallia*) is so called from the whiteness of its people, for milk is called γάλα in Greek. The mountains and the chilliness of the sky keep the heat of the sun from this region, so that the whiteness of bodies does not darken in color. The Alpine ridges overlook it from the east and the Ocean limits it in the west, the rugged terrain of the Pyrenees in the south, and in the north the river Rhine and Germania. It begins with Belgica and ends with Aquitania. The region is characterized by rich and grassy soil and is well suited for animal husbandry, well watered by streams and springs, with the two great rivers Rhine and Rhone flowing through it. 26. Belgis is a city in Gaul from which the province Belgica is named. Cisalpine Gaul is so called because it is 'on this side of the Alps' (*citra Alpes*, i.e. from Rome's point of view); Transalpine Gaul, that is, 'across the Alps' (*trans Alpes*), to the north. Raetia is so called because it is next to the Rhine (*Rhenum*). 27. Aquitania owes its name to the transverse 'waters' (*aqua*) of the river Loire (*Liger*), which is the

boundary of most of it, and which encloses it almost in a circle.

28. Hispania was first named 'Iberia' after the river Iberus (i.e. *Hiberus*, the Ebro), later 'Hispania' from Hispalis (i.e. Seville). This is the real Hesperia (see section 19 above), named after Hesperus, the evening star. It is situated between Africa and Gaul, closed off by the Pyrenees mountains to the north and everywhere else shut in by the sea. It is temperate in its healthy climate, abundant in all types of produce, and very rich in its abundance of precious stones and metals. 29. Great rivers flow through it: the Baetis (Guadalquivir), Mineus (Miño), Iberus (Ebro), and Tagus (Tajo), which carries gold, just like the Pactolus (see iii.43 above). It is composed of six provinces: the Tarraconian (i.e. of Tarragona), the Cartagenian, Lusitania, Gallicia, Baetica and, across the straits in Africa, the Tingitanian (i.e. of Tangiers). 30. Furthermore there are two Spains: Inner Spain, whose area extends in the north from the Pyrenees to Cartagena; and Outer Spain, which in the south extends from Celtiberia to the straits of Cadiz. Inner (*citerior*) and Outer (*ulterior*) are so called as if it were *citra* (on this side) and *ultra* (beyond); but *citra* is formed as if the term were 'around the earth' (*circa terras*), and *ultra* either because it is the last (*ultimus*), or because after it there is not 'any' (*ulla*), that is, any other, land.

v. Libya (De Libya) 1. Libya (*Libya*) is so called because the Libs, the African wind, blows from there. Others say that Epaphus, the son of Jupiter and founder of Memphis in Egypt, had a daughter named Libya with his wife Cassiopeia, and Libya afterwards established a kingdom in Africa. From her name the land Libya received its name. 2. Further, there are those who think that Africa (*Africa*) is named as though the word were *aprica* ("exposed to the sun"), because it is open to the sky and the sun and without bitter cold. Others say Africa is named from one of the descendants of Abraham and Keturah, who was called Afer (i.e. Epher), of whom we made mention above (IX.ii.115). 3. Africa begins at the borders of Egypt, stretching along the south through Ethiopia up to the Atlas range. In its northern region it is enclosed by the bordering Mediterranean and is bounded by the straits of Cadiz (i.e. Gibraltar), containing the provinces of Libya Cyrenensis, Pentapolis, Tripolis, Byzacium, Carthage, Numidia, Mauretania Sitifensis, Mauretania Tingitana, and Ethiopia under the burning sun.

4. Libya Cyrenensis is in the first part of Africa and is named after Cyrene, the chief city within its borders. From here Egypt is in the east, the Greater Syrtes and the *Trogodytae* (i.e. the Troglodytes) are in the west, the Libyan Sea lies to the north, and in the south are Ethiopia and various barbarian nations and inaccessible wilderness, which also brings forth basilisk serpents. 5. 'Pentapolis' in the Greek tongue is so called after its 'five cities' (cf. πέντε, "five"; πόλις, "city"), namely Berenice, Ceutria, Apollonia, Ptolomais, and Cyrene; of these Ptolomais and Berenice were named after their rulers. Pentapolis is next to Libya Cyrenensis and is considered to be within its borders. 6. In their own tongue the Greeks also name a province 'Tripolitana' from the number of its three great cities: Oea, Sabrata and Leptis Magna. This province has the Greater Syrtes and the *Trogodytae* (i.e. the Troglodytes) to the east, the Adriatic Sea in the north, in the west Byzacium and in the south the Gaetuli and the Garamantes, extending to the Ethiopian Ocean.

7. The Bizacene region is allotted its name from its two very famous towns, one of which is called Hadrumetum (perhaps cf. *bi-*, "two"; ζυγόν, "yoke, pair"). This region is located below Tripoli, extending for two hundred miles or more, rich in oil, and so rich in its soil that seeds that are sown there return a crop nearly a hundredfold. 8. Great Carthage is in Zeugis. This is the true Africa, situated in between Byzacium and Numidia, bounded in the north by the Sicilian Sea. In the south it stretches as far as the region of the Gaetuli. The nearer part of it is fruitful, but the more remote part is filled with wild beasts and serpents and great onagers wandering in the desert. Gaetulia is the interior region of Africa. 9. Numidia is so called after inhabitants that wander about far and wide because they do not have a fixed abode. For in their language temporary and mobile settlements are called *numidia*. It begins at the river Amsiga and it marks its end in Zeugis. East of it are the Lesser Syrtes, in the north the sea that stretches toward Sardinia, in the west Mauretania Sitifensis, in the south the tribes of Ethiopia: it is a region of very fertile fields. However, in areas covered by forest it produces wild animals, in steep mountains horses and onagers. It is also renowned for its excellent marble, which is called Numidian marble. It has distinguished cities as well: Hippo Regius and Rusicada.

10. Mauretania is so called after the color of the inhabitants; for the Greeks call 'black' μαῦρος. Just as the name for Gaul is derived from the whiteness of its

inhabitants, so also the name for Mauretania from blackness. Its principal province is Mauretania Sitifensis, which contained the town of Sitifi, from which the name for the region is thought to be derived. 11. With regard to Mauretania Caesariensis: the main city was of a colony called Caesarea, and its name was given to the province. The two provinces are linked together and are bounded in the east by Numidia, in the north by the Mediterranean, in the west by the river Malva, in the south by Mount Astrixis, which forms the border between fertile earth and the sands that extend up to the Ocean. 12. Mauretania Tingitania is so called after the capital of the province, Tingis (i.e. Tangiers). This end of Africa rises up from seven mountains, bounded in the east by the river Malva, in the north by the straits of Cadiz, in the west by the Atlantic Ocean, in the south by the tribes of the Gaulales, who roam as far as the Hesperian (i.e. "Western") Ocean. The region produces wild beasts, apes, dragons, and ostriches. Once it was also full of elephants, which now only India produces.

13. Garama was the capital of the Garamantian region. It lies between Cyrenean Libya and Ethiopia and a spring is located there that cools down in the heat of the day and becomes warmer in the cold of night. 14. Ethiopia is so called after the color of its inhabitants, who are scorched by the proximity of the sun (cf. αἴθειν, "burn"; ὤψ, gen. ὠπός, "face"). Indeed, the coloring of the people demonstrates the force of the sun, for it is always hot there, because all of its territory is under the South Pole. Around the western part it is mountainous, sandy in the middle, and desert toward the east. It stretches from Mount Atlas in the west to the borders of Egypt in the east, bounded in the south by the Ocean and in the north by the river Nile. It has very many tribes, fearsome with their different faces and strange appearance. 15. It also teems with a multitude of wild beasts and serpents. There, indeed, the rhinoceros and the giraffe are found, the basilisk, and huge dragons from whose brains precious stones are extracted. There one finds the hyacinth stone as well as the chrysoprase, and cinnamon is gathered there. 16. There are two Ethiopias: one to the east, another to the west, in Mauretania.

17. Apart from these three parts of the world there exists a fourth part, beyond the intervening Ocean, toward the south, which is unknown to us because of the burning heat of the sun; within its borders are said to live the legendary Antipodes. Mauretania, however, lies next to Spain; then comes Numidia, then the territory of Carthage, after which we gather that there is Gaetulia, and after that Ethiopia; beyond that are places scorched by the heat of the sun.

18. It should, indeed, be understood that some provinces were first named after their founders; afterwards the name of the inhabitants was derived from the name of the province. Thus, 'Italy' (*Italia*) comes from 'Italus' (see IX.ii.85), and in turn from 'Italy' comes the term 'an Italian' (*Italus*); and in this way we use a name for the people that is the same as the name of the founder, from whose name derives the name of the province. And this is how it happens that a city, a territory, and a people are all named after a single name. 19. Provinces, moreover, received their name for a reason. A principate (*principatus*) over nations is a term that that applied to foreign kings; when the Romans brought these under their own jurisdiction by conquering (*vincere*) it, they called such far-off regions provinces (*provincia*). A fatherland (*patria*) is so called because it is common to all who were born in it (cf. *pater*, "father"). 20. Earth (*terra*), as we have said before (cf. XIII.iii), signifies an element: lands (*terrae*, i.e. the plural of *terra*), by contrast, signify certain parts of the world, such as Africa or Italy. It is the same with areas (*locus*); for in the 'globe of lands' (*orbis terrarum*) areas and expanses of land contain in themselves many provinces; just as in the body an area is a single part, containing many members; and just as a house has many rooms in it. Thus, expanses of land are called lands and areas, and provinces are parts of those, as Phrygia is part of Asia, Raetia part of Gaul, and Baetica part of Spain.

21. Now Asia is an area, Phrygia is a province of Asia, Troy is a region of Phrygia, and Ilium is a city of Troy. Likewise regions are parts of provinces, and are commonly called *conventus*, such as Troy in Phrygia, Cantabria and Asturia in Galicia. The term 'region' (*regio*) comes from governors (*rector*), and territories are parts of regions. 22. A territory (*territorium*) is so called as if it were *tauritorium*, that is, 'broken by a plow' (*tritum aratro*) and by a team of oxen (cf. *taurus*, "bull") – for the ancients used to designate the boundaries of their possessions and territories by cutting a furrow.

vi. Islands (De insulis) 1. Islands (*insula*) are so called because they are 'in salt water' (*in salo*), that is, in the sea. Of these the best known and the biggest, which many of the ancients investigated with expert effort, should be noted.

2. Britannia is an island in the Ocean, cut off from the whole globe by the intervening sea; it takes its name from the name of its inhabitants. It is situated opposite the region of Gaul, looking towards Spain; its circumference is 4,875 (Roman) miles. There are many great rivers there, hot springs, a great and varied abundance of metals: it is rich in jet and pearls. 3. Thanet is an island in the Ocean in the Gallic (i.e. English) channel, separated from Britannia by a narrow estuary, with fruitful fields and rich soil. It is named Thanet (*Tanatos*) from the death of serpents (cf. θάνατος, "death"). Although the island itself is unacquainted with serpents, if soil from it is carried away and brought to any other nation, it kills snakes there. 4. Ultima Thule (*Thyle ultima*) is an island of the Ocean in the northwestern region, beyond Britannia, taking its name from the sun, because there the sun makes its summer solstice, and there is no daylight beyond (*ultra*) this.[7] Hence its sea is sluggish and frozen.

5. The Orkneys (*Orcades*) are islands of the Ocean within Britannia, numbering thirty-three, of which twenty are uninhabited and thirteen colonized. 6. Ireland (*Scotia*), also known as *Hibernia*, is an island next to Britannia, narrower in its expanse of land but more fertile in its site. It extends from southwest to north. Its near parts stretch towards Iberia (*Hiberia*) and the Cantabrian Ocean (i.e. the Bay of Biscay), whence it is called *Hibernia*; but it is called *Scotia*, because it has been colonized by tribes of the *Scoti*.[8] There no snakes are found, birds are scarce, and there are no bees, so that if someone were to sprinkle dust or pebbles brought from there among beehives in some other place, the swarms would desert the honeycombs.

7. Cadiz (*Gadis*) is an island located at the edge of the province of Baetica. It separates Europe from Africa. The pillars of Hercules can be seen there, and from there the current of the Ocean flows into the entrance of the Tyrrhenian Sea. It is divided from the mainland by a distance of six hundred (Roman) feet. When the Tyrians, who had come from the Red Sea, occupied it, they called it in their language *Gadir*, that is, "enclosed," because it is enclosed on all sides by the sea. This island produces a palm-like tree whose sap, when mixed with glass, produces the precious stone called *ceraunius*. 8. The Fortunate Isles (*Fortunatarum insulae*) signify by their name that they produce all kinds of good things, as if they were happy and blessed with an abundance of fruit. Indeed, well-suited by their nature, they produce fruit from very precious trees; the ridges of their hills are spontaneously covered with grapevines; instead of weeds, harvest crops and garden herbs are common there. Hence the mistake of pagans and the poems by worldly poets, who believed that these isles were Paradise because of the fertility of their soil. They are situated in the Ocean, against the left side of Mauretania, closest to where the sun sets, and they are separated from each other by the intervening sea.

9. The Gorgades are islands of the Ocean opposite the promontory that is called Hesperian Ceras, inhabited by the Gorgons, women with swift wings and a rough and hairy body; the islands take their name from them. They are separated from the mainland by a passage of two days' sailing. 10. The isles of the Hesperides are so called after the city of Hesperis, which was located within the borders of Mauretania. They are situated beyond the Gorgades, at the Atlantic shore, in the most remote bays of the sea. Stories tell of an ever-watchful dragon guarding golden apples in their gardens. There, it is said, is a channel from the sea that is so twisted, with winding banks, that when seen from afar it looks like the coils of a serpent.

11. Chryse and Argyre are islands situated in the Indian Ocean, so rich in metal that many people maintain these islands have a surface of gold and silver; whence their names are derived (see iii.5 above). 12. Taprobane (i.e. Sri Lanka) is an island that lies to the south-east of India. The Indian Ocean begins there. It is 875 (Roman) miles long and 625,000 stades wide.[9] It is intersected by a river and everywhere full of pearls and precious stones. Part of it is full of wild beasts and elephants, while another part is occupied by human beings. It is said that this island has two summers and two winters every year, and that flowers bloom twice there. 13. Tiles is an Indian island where the vegetation is green in every season. Thus far of islands in the Ocean.

7 The sense is, or should be, that the term *Ultima*, "farthest," describes the limit of the sun's reach at the Arctic Circle at the winter solstice; *Thyle* is dark all winter.

8 In early medieval writings the inhabitants of Ireland were called Scotti, and those of Scotland called Picts – but cf. IX.ii.103.

9 There is clearly an error in the width given (the equivalent of 72,000 miles). Deleting the word *stadiorum*, not present in the sources and in any case disrupting a parallelism, yields the plausible reading "625 (Roman) miles wide."

14. Further, islands are situated in the Mediterranean, from the Hellespont to Cadiz. The island of Cyprus (*Cypros*) took its name from the city of Cyprus, which is located there. This island is also known as Paphos, dedicated to Venus, and it lies in the southern part of the Carpathian Sea. Once it was well known for its wealth, especially for copper, for this metal was first discovered and put to use there. 15. Crete is a part of Greece, close to and opposite the Peloponnese. Due to its mild climate it was first called Macaronnesos (cf. μακάριος, "blessed"; νῆσος "isle"); thereafter it was called Crete (*Creta*), after one of its inhabitants, a certain Cres (gen. *Cretis*), who people say was one of the Curetes; Jupiter was concealed there and nursed by them. This is the Greek island that stretches the longest distance from east to west, bathed by Greek currents in the north, and by Egyptian waves in the south. Once it was ennobled by a hundred cities, whence it was also called Hecatompolis (cf. ἑκατόν, "hundred"; πόλις, "city"). 16. It was the first to be famous for rowing and archery, the first to put laws into writing, and the first to train cavalry units. The pursuit of music composed in Idaean dactyls began on this island. It is plentiful in goats and lacks deer; it nowhere produces wolves or foxes or other harmful wild beasts; there are no serpents there and no night owls, and if one comes upon the island, it dies immediately. It is abundant in vines and trees. The herb dittany grows in Crete, as well as purslane, which when chewed stops hunger for a day. It produces venomous spiders and a stone that is called 'dactyl of Ida.'

17. Abydos is an island in Europe, positioned above the Hellespont, cut off by a narrow and dangerous sea; it is called Ἄβυδος in Greek because it is at the entrance to the Hellespont, where Xerxes built a bridge constructed from ships and crossed over into Greece (cf. ἄβατος, "not fordable"). 18. Cos (*Coos*) is an island lying adjacent to the province of Attica; on it the physician Hippocrates was born and, as Varro testifies, it was first famous for the art of preparing wool for the adornment of women.

19. The Cyclades were in ancient times islands of Greece, and people believe that they were called Cyclades because, although they project out a rather long way from Delos, they are nevertheless arranged in a circle around it – for the Greeks call a circle κύκλος. But others think that they are so called not because the islands are arranged in a circle, but because of the sharp rocks that are situated around them (i.e. that encircle them). 20. They lie in the Hellespont, between the Aegean and the Malean Sea,[10] and they are surrounded by Myrtoan waters. They are fifty-three in number, extending from north to south for five hundred miles, and from east to west for two hundred (Roman) miles. Their principal city is Rhodes.

21. Delos is the island located in the center of the Cyclades. It is said to be called Delos because, after the deluge known to have occurred during the reign of Ogygus, when the globe was cast into continuous night for many months, it was the first among all places of the earth to be lit by the rays of the sun; it was allotted its name from having been the first to become visible to the eyes; for the Greeks say δῆλος for "plainly visible." The island is also called Ortygia, because there the birds called 'quails' were seen for the first time; the Greeks call them ὄρτυγες. On this island, Latona gave birth to Apollo and Diana. The name Delos is applied to both the city and the island. 22. Rhodes is the first of the Cyclades from the east. The rosebud is said to have been discovered there when the city was founded, whence both the town and the island are called Rhodes (*Rhodos*; cf. ῥόδον, "rose"). In this city was the bronze Colossus of the Sun, seventy cubits high; there were also one hundred smaller colossi on this island. 23. Tenedos, one of the Cyclades, is located in the north, where a city was founded formerly by a certain Tenes. After him the city, or rather the island, was named; for this Tenes was infamous for having had intercourse with his stepmother, [and] in escaping he took possession of this island, which was empty of inhabitants; whence it was called Tenedos. Thus says Cicero (cf. *Second Action Against Verres* 1.49): "Tenes himself, after whom Tenedos was named."

24. Carpathos, another one of the Cyclades, is located in the south, facing Egypt; the Carpathian Sea is named after it, while the island itself is so called because crops ripen there so quickly (cf. καρπός, "crops"). It lies between Egypt and Rhodes. Carpasian ships, which are big and spacious, are also so called from this island. 25. The island Cytherea is one of the Cyclades located in the west; its former name was Porphyris. It was called Cytherea because Venus was born there.[11] 26. Icaria is an island of the Cyclades which gives the Icarian Sea its

10 The terms 'Aegean' and 'Hellespont' seem to have been interchanged in this passage.

11 A favorite epithet of Venus was 'Cytherea.'

name. Located between Samos and Mykonos, it is inhospitable due to jutting rocks and a lack of bays offering harbor. It is said that Icarus the Cretan died there in shipwreck and that upon his death his name was given to that place. 27. The island of Naxos is named after Dionysius (i.e. Dionysus, the god of wine), as if it were *Dionaxos*, because it surpasses all others in the fertility of its vines. It lies eighteen (Roman) miles from Delos. Once upon a time Jupiter is said to have proceeded from there to fight the Titans.

28. Melos is the roundest island among all of the Cyclades; wherefrom its name is derived (cf. μῆλον, Latin *malum*, "round fruit," and see XVII.vii.3). 29. History says that Iasion had two sons, Philomelus and Plutus, and that Philomelus fathered Pareantus, who gave his name to the island and the city of Paros; first it was called Minoia, then Paros. Vergil writes of it (*Aen.* 3.126):

> And snow-white Paros,

for it produces the whitest marble, which is called Parian marble. It also exports the sarda stone (i.e. carnelian), more outstanding than marble, but when considered as a gemstone, the cheapest. 30. The island of Chios is so called in the Syrian language because mastic is produced there, for the Syrians call mastic *chio.* 31. Samos is an island in the Aegean Sea. Juno was born there and the Samian Sybil as well as Samian Pythagoras came from there. The latter coined the term 'philosophy' (*philosophia*). Tradition has it that clay vases were first invented on this island – whence vases are also called Samian.

32. Sicily (*Sicilia*) was named 'Sicania' after king Sicanus, then 'Sicily' after Siculus, the brother of Italus. But in earliest times it was known as Trinacria, because it has three ἄκρα ("capes"), that is, promontories: Pelorus, Pachynum, and Lilybaeum. *Trinacria* is in Greek what in Latin would be *triquetra*, as if divided into 'three pieces' (*tres quadrae*). It is separated from Italy by a narrow strait, and looks out upon the African Sea; it has rich soil and abundant gold, and is riddled with caves and tunnels, full of winds and sulfur; accordingly the flames of Mount Etna show themselves there. In this strait Scylla and Charybdis either swallow up ships or smash them. 33. At one time this was the native land of the Cyclopes, and afterwards the nurse of tyrants; fertile in crops, it was the first of all lands to be riven by the plow and planted with seed. It has Syracuse as its principal city, the spring Arethusa, and the river Alpheus, "parent of magnificent horses" (cf. Vergil, *Aen.* 3.704). On this island comedy was first invented. 34. This island first produced from the river Achates the agate (*achates*) stone. Its sea produces coral and it yields the Agrigentian salts, which dissolve in fire and crackle in water. Its entire circumference is three thousand stades (i.e. 375 Roman miles). Sallust (see *Histories* 4.26) moreover says that Sicily used to be joined to Italy, but that the intervening space was divided by the onslaught of the sea and cut across its narrowest part.

35. The island Thapsus lies ten stades (i.e. 1.25 Roman miles) away from Sicily and is rather low-lying, whence its name (cf. ταπεινός, "low-lying"). Vergil writes of it (*Aen.* 3.689):

> And low-lying Thapsus.

36. The Aeolian islands of Sicily (i.e. the Lipari) are named after Aeolus, son of Hippotes, whom poets feigned to have been the king of the winds: to the contrary, according to Varro, he was the ruler of these islands and, because he would predict from their clouds and smoke the future direction of winds, he seemed to naïve people to have controlled the winds by his own power (Funaioli 378). These islands are also called Vulcanian, because they burn like Etna (i.e. site of the forge of Vulcan). 37. Nine of these islands have proper names. A certain Liparus called the first of these Lipare. He ruled Lipare before Aeolus. The second is called Hiera, because it has the loftiest hills (perhaps cf. ἱερός, "holy"). As for the rest, they are Strongyle (i.e. Stromboli), Didyme, Eriphusa, Hephaestia, Phaenicusa, Euonymos, Tripodes, and Sonores. Because they burn at night, they are called the Aeolians or the Vulcanians. Some of them did not exist at first; later they were elevated from the sea and they remain up to this day.

38. The Stoechades (i.e. Isles d'Hyères) are islands of Massilia (i.e. Marseilles) sixty (Roman) miles distant from the mainland, facing the province of Narbonne where the river Rhone empties into the sea. They are named Στοιχάδες in Greek as if they were placed 'in a row' (cf. στοιχάς, "in a row") by design. 39. Sardus, son of Hercules, occupied Sardinia after he came from Libya with a great host, and named the island after himself. This island, located in the African Sea, has the shape of a human footprint; it is broader in the east than in the west, whereas the southern and northern coasts are

practically the same length, and for this reason, before there was traffic there, it was called by Greek sailors Ἴχνος ("footprint"). 40. The land extends 140 (Roman) miles in length and 40 miles in width. No serpent or wolf is born there, only the *solifuga*, a small animal that is most hurtful to humans. Also, nothing poisonous grows there, except the plant, mentioned by many writers and poets, that is similar to wild parsley, makes people contort in a rictus, and kills them as if they were grinning. Sardinia has hot springs that bring healing to the sick and blindness to thieves if they touch their eyes with this water after an oath has been given.

41. Ligurian settlers founded the island of Corsica, naming it after the one who guided them there, a certain Ligurian woman by the name of Corsa, who saw a bull from the herd she was guarding close to the shore habitually swim across and return fattened shortly afterwards. Eager to discover his unknown pasture, when he strayed from the herd she followed the bull in a boat to the island. Learning of the island's fertility after her return, the Ligurians went there on rafts and named the island after the woman who found it and guided them there. 42. This island is also known in Greek as Κύρνη, from having been inhabited by Cyrnus, the son of Hercules. Vergil says of it (cf. *Ecl.* 9.30):

> Corsican (*Cyrneus*) yews.

It is separated from Sardinia by a strait of twenty (Roman) miles and surrounded by a bay of the Ligurian sea on its Italian side. It has many sheer headlands, produces quite delightful pastures, and a stone that is called *catochites* by the Greeks.

43. Ebosus (i.e. Ibiza) is a Spanish island, so called because it is not far 'from Zanium' (*a Zanio*), as if its name were *abozus*; for it lies seventy stades (i.e. about nine miles) from it. Serpents flee its soil. Opposite it is Colubraria (cf. *coluber*, "serpent"), which is full of serpents. 44. The Baleares are two Spanish islands: Aphrosiades and Gymnaside, a bigger one (*maior*) and a smaller one (*minor*), whence they are also called *Maiorica* (i.e. Majorca) and *Minorica* (i.e. Minorca) by the common people. In these islands the sling with which stones are hurled was first invented – whence they are called the Baleares, for βάλλειν in Greek means "throw." From the same root are derived the terms *ballista* (i.e. a kind of catapult), as if it were "the one thrown," and *fundibalum* (i.e. another such machine; see XVIII.x.2). Vergil says of them (*Geo.* 1.309):

> The thongs of the Balearic sling.

vii. Promontories (De promuntoriis) 1. It is characteristic of islands that they 'jut out' (*prominere*), whence these places are called promontories (*promuntorium*). Thus, Sallust says of Sardinia (*Histories* 2.2): "It juts out (*prominere*) wider in the east than in the west."

2. Sigeum is a promontory of Asia, located where the Hellespont opens out more widely. It is called Sigeum due to the silence of Hercules, because, denied hospitality by the Trojan king Laomedon, he feigned his departure and from there came back against Troy in silence, which is called σιγή. 3. Maleum is a promontory in Greece that juts out into the sea and extends for fifty (Roman) miles; the waves in this place are so fierce that they seem to pursue those traveling by ship. This promontory was named after Maleus, king of the Argives. 4. The Sicilian promontory of Pelorum, which is oriented toward the north, according to Sallust (cf. *Histories* 4.29) was named after a pilot of Hannibal's who is buried there. 5. The Sicilian promontory Pachynum, which looks towards the south-west, is so called from the density of its air – for the term παχύς means "thick" and "dense" – as the south-west wind blows there. 6. Lilybaeum is a promontory of Sicily, extending to the west. It is named after a city of the same name that is located there. 7. Borion is a promontory in Numidia, so called because it stretches north (cf. *boreas*, "the north"). Afterwards it was called Hippo Regius, because it was cut off by the sea.[12] Calpis is a Spanish promontory.

viii. Mountains and other terms for landforms (De montibus ceterisque terrae vocabulis) 1. Mountains (*mons*) are the highest swellings of the land, so called because they 'stand out' (*eminere*). Some of them owe their names to particular causes. We should mention those that are commonly thought to be the greatest.

2. The Caucasus range stretches from India to the Taurus and has many different names because of the variety of peoples and of languages in every direction through which it passes. Thus, toward the east, where it rises to greater height, it is called Caucasus, due to the whiteness

12 The erroneous equation of Borion with Hippo Regius was caused by a misreading of the source, Solinus's *Collectanea*.

of its snow, for in an eastern language, *caucasus* means "white," that is, shining white with a very thick snow cover. For the same reason the Scythians, who live next to this mountain range, call it *Croacasim*, for among them whiteness or snow is called *casim*. 3. The Taurus range is likewise called the Caucasus by many. 4. Libanus (i.e. Mount Lebanon) is the highest mountain in Phoenicia, mentioned by the prophets. It gets its name from incense (cf. *libanus*, "frankincense"), because incense is collected there. That part of Libanus that is beyond it, facing toward the east, is called the Antilibanus, that is "opposite Libanus." 5. Ararat is a mountain in Armenia, on which historians attest that the ark settled after the Flood. Whence even to this day remnants of its wood can be seen there.

6. The Acroceraunian mountains are so called because of their height (cf. ἄκρος, "highest") and the hurling of thunderbolts, for in Greek a thunderbolt is called κεραυνός. They lie between Armenia and Iberia (see iii.33 and 36 above), begin at the Caspian passes, and extend to the source of the river Tigris. 7. The Hyberborean mountains of Scythia are so called because the north wind (*Boreas*) blows above, that is, beyond them (cf. ὑπέρ, "beyond"). 8. The Riphaean mountains are in the far reaches of Germania, named from the perpetual gusts of wind; for ῥιφή in Greek means "thrust" and "ὁρμή" (i.e. another Greek word meaning "thrust"), from the term ῥίπτειν ("hurl"). 9. Olympus is an exceedingly high mountain in Macedonia, so high that they say there are clouds below it. Vergil says about it (actually Lucan, *Civil War* 2.271):

> Olympus towered over the clouds.

It is called Olympus as if the word were *Ololampus*, that is, as if it were "sky" (cf. ὁλολαμπής, "entirely resplendent"). This mountain divides Macedonia from Thracia. 10. Athos is a mountain in Macedonia that also rises higher than the clouds, so high that its shadow reaches to Lemnos, which lies seventy-six (Roman) miles away.

11. Parnassus is a mountain in Thessaly, close to Boeotia, whose twin peaks reach into the heavens. This one is split into two ridges, Cyrrha and Nissa; whence also its name, because Apollo and Liber are worshipped on the respective ridges. These ridges are also named Cithaeron and Helicon, after two brothers, for Helicon is named after Helicon, the brother of Cythaeron. 12. The Ceraunians are a mountain range in Epirus, named after frequent lightning, for in Greek lightning is called κεραυνός. 13. The Apennines are so called as if they were the 'Carthaginian Alps' (*Alpes Poeninae*), because when he came to Italy, Hannibal laid these Alps open. Whence Vergil also says (*Aen.* 10.13):

> He throws open the Alps,

because Hannibal, after the war in Spain, rent them open with vinegar; thus Juvenal (*Satires* 10.153):

> And he rent the mountain with vinegar.

And thereafter those places that he rent were called the Apennine Alps.

14. Mount Etna is so called from fire (cf. αἴθειν, "burn") and sulfur; Gehenna likewise (see ix.9 below). It is well known that, in the part in which the south-east wind or the south-west wind blows, it has caves that are filled with sulfur and that lead to the sea. When the waves rush into these caves, they create a wind that, when stirred up, ignites a fire in the sulfur; this creates the flames that one sees. 15. The Pyrenees (*Pyrenaeus*) themselves are also named after the frequent fires caused by lightning, for in Greek 'fire' is called πῦρ. They are placed between Gaul and Hispania as if they were a man-made bulwark.

16. Mount Solurius (i.e. *Solorius*) is named after singularity, because it alone (*solus*; and cf. ὄρος, "mountain") is seen to be higher than all the rest of the mountains of Hispania, [or else, because when the sun (*sol*) rises, its rays are seen there even before the sun]. 17. Calpe (i.e. the Rock of Gibraltar) is a mountain at the extreme limit of the Ocean, and it separates Europe from Africa; it is said to be the place where the Atlas range ends. Lucan writes of it (*Civil War* 1.555):

> (With great waves the sea) covered Hesperian Calpe and highest Atlas.

Atlas was Prometheus' brother and the king of Africa, and is said to have been the inventor of astrology (i.e. in modern terms astronomy and astrology) and for that reason he is said to have held up the heavens. Therefore, because of his expertise in that art and his knowledge of the heavens, the African mountain range was named after him that nowadays is called Atlas. Because of its height it seems as if it supports the celestial spheres and the stars. 18. The Alps are properly speaking a mountain range in Gaul. Vergil calls them (*Geo.* 3.474) "lofty Alps," and in calling them "lofty" he renders word for word, for in the Gallic language high mountains are called *alpes.* These are mountains that function as the defense of Italy.

19. Foothills (*colles*) are the more prominent ridges of mountains, as if their name were derived from *collum* ("neck"). 20. Mountain ridges (*iugum*) are so called because they are joined (*iungere*) by their proximity. 21. A hill (*tumulus*) is a low mountain, as if the word were derived from 'swelling earth' (*tumens tellus*). Likewise, *tumulus* is the word for heaped-up earth (i.e. a burial mound), where there is no monument. 22. Valleys (*vallis*) are low-lying places, as if the word were *vulsus* ("torn away," ppl. of *vellere*). Hence also 'enclosed valleys' (*convallis*) are low places of land between mountains. 23. A plain (*campus*) is a flat piece of land. It is called a plain because it lies low 'for feet' (*pes*, gen. *pedis*; cf. πούς, gen. ποδός), not raised like the mountains, but stretched out and leveled in its space and lying flat; whence in Greek it is called πεδίον. It takes its name from a Greek etymology, for the Greeks say χαμαί (lit. "on the ground") for 'low'.

24. 'The ground' (*solum*) is anything that supports, and is so called from its solidity (*soliditas*). Whence Vergil also says with regard to the sea (*Aen.* 5.199):

> And the ground (*solum*, i.e. sea floor) is pulled away.

25. Woodlands (*saltus*) are vast, wooded places, where the trees rise (*ex(s)ilire*, from *salire*, "leap") high. 26. Passes (*fauces*) are narrow passages between high mountains, narrow and tight places, so called from a likeness to the throat (*faucis*), as if the word were *foces.* 27. *Confrages* are places into which winds rush from all sides, and there they dash themselves. As Naevius says (fr. 58):

> Into the mountains, where the winds would dash against the place.

28. *Scabra* are places that are rough with neglect. Whence one also says *scabies*, from a roughness of the body. 29. Dens (*lustrum*) are secret hiding-places of wild beasts and lairs of wolves. Whence also brothels (*lupanar*) are called *lustra*, namely by antiphrasis, because they are poorly lit (*illustrare*).

30. A grove (*lucus*) is a place enclosed by dense trees that keep light (*lux*, gen. *lucis*) from reaching the ground. It is also possible that the word is derived from the lighting (*conlucere*) of many lights, which were kindled there because of pagan beliefs and rituals. 31. Wildernesses (*desertum*) are so called because they are not planted (*serere*), and therefore, in a manner of speaking, they are abandoned (*deserere*), as are wooded and mountainous areas, places that are the opposite of fruitful regions that have the richest soil. 32. 'Remote places' (*devium*) are secret and concealed, as if they were away from the road (*via*). The same places are also called impassable places (*invium*). Whence also secret places that lie 'out of the way' (*a via*) and are only accessible to birds (*avis*) are called nesting-places (*aviarium*). Whence also as follows (Vergil, *Geo.* 2.430):

> The wild nesting-places (*aviaria*) grow red with berries.

33. According to Varro, 'pleasant places' (*locus amoenus*) are so called because they promote love (*amor*) only and draw to themselves things that ought to be loved. According to Verrius Flaccus they are so called, because they are without a 'public function' (*munus*), nor is anything in them like business, as if the term were *amunia*, that is, without profit, whence no profit is rendered (cf. Funaioli 413). Thence also those that are responsible for nothing are called 'exempt ones' (*immunis*). 34. 'Sunny spots' (*apricum*) are places which enjoy the sun, as if the term were ἄνευ φρίκης, that is, "without cold"; or else because they have an 'open sky' (*apertum caelum*). 35. By contrast, shady (*opacus*) places are the opposite of sunny spots, as if the word were *opertum caelum* ("hidden sky"). 36. A place is called a 'slippery place' (*lubricum*) because someone slips (*labi*) there; and it is called a slippery place, not because it slips, but because in this place a person slips. 37. 'Summer pastures' (*aestiva*) are shady places in which cattle avoid the heat of the sun in summer (*aestas*). Statius writes (*Thebaid* 1.363):

> And the summer pastures (*aestiva*) of shady Lycaeus lay open.

38. Dockyards (*navalia*) are places where ships (*navis*) are built. This place is also called a shipyard (*textrinum*). 39. An anchorage (*statio*) is where ships stay (*stare*) for a while; a harbor (*portus*), where they winter; an unsuitable (*inportunus*) place, however, is one where there is no refuge, in a manner of speaking, no harbor. 40. Moreover, a harbor is a place that is protected from exposure to the winds, where the winter winds would make things difficult, and harbor (*portus*) is derived from conveying (*deportare*) trade-goods. The ancients would call it a harbor 'for shipping' (*baia*), from conveying (*baiolare*)

merchandise, with the same declension – *baia*, gen. *baias* – as the declension *familia*, gen. *familias* ("household"). 41. The shore (*litus*) is land next to water and the sea: and it is called *litus*, because it is dashed (*elidere*) by the waves, or else because it is bathed (*alluere*) by water. Cicero says in *Topics* (32): "The shore is where the waves play (*eludere*)." 42. 'Alluvial land' (*circumluvium*) is a place which water 'flows around' (*circumluere*); a 'flood plain' (*alluvium*) is an eroding of riverbanks by water. A border (*margo*) is the side of any place, as for example of the sea (*mare*); after which it is also named. 'Maritime places' (*maritime*) are so called as if the word were *maris intima* ("near the sea"). 43. River-mouths (*ostium*) are so called from the entrance and exit of a river into the sea. A mainland (*continens*) is a stretch of continuous land uninterrupted by any sea, what the Greeks call ἤπειρος.

ix. The lower regions (De inferioribus) 1. A cave (*specus*) is a subterranean rift from which it is possible to 'look out' (*prospicere*); it is σπήλαιον in Greek, *spelunca* ("cave") in Latin. 2. Fumarole (*spiraculum*) is the name given to all places of pestilential exhalation (*spiritus*), which the Greeks call Χαρώνεια, or Ἀχερόντεια.[13] Varro, too, calls such a place a fumarole; and fumaroles are so called because they are places where the earth produces an exhalation. 3. A cleft (*hiatus*) is a deep break of the earth, as if the term were 'a departure' (*itus*, ppl. of *ire*). Properly speaking, however, *hiatus* is the opening of the mouth of a human being, with the sense transferred from wild beasts, whose eagerness for something is shown through opening of the mouth. 4. The deep (*profundum*) is properly said of something as if its bottom (*fundus*) were 'far off' (*porro*). Incorrectly, however, 'the deep' is applied to what is on high as well as what lies below, as in (Vergil, *Aen.* 1.58):

> The seas, the lands, and the deep (*profundus*) sky.

5. Abyss (*baratrum*, i.e. *barathrum*, i.e. βάραθρον, "pit") is the word for an excessive depth: and it is called *baratrum*, as if the term were *vorago atra* ("black abyss"), that is, black from its depth. 6. Erebus is the deep inner part of the underworld. Styx is so called after the term στυγερός, that is, from "wretchedness," because it makes people wretched, or else because it brings forth wretchedness. 7. Cocytus is an underworld place of which Job speaks thus . . . (see Job 21:33). Cocytus, however, has taken its name from Greek, from affliction and sighing (cf. κωκυτός, "wailing"). 8. Tartarus is so called either because everything in it is disturbed (*turbatus*), after the word ταρταρίζειν ("quake"), or, more likely, from ταραχή ("disturbance, upheaval"), that is, from shivering, through being numb with cold, because, of course, it lacks light and sunshine. In that place exist neither the warmth generated by sunlight, nor any breath of air stirred by the movement of the sun, but instead a perpetual numbness, for ταρταρίζειν means "shuddering" and "trembling" in Greek. Indeed, in that place is "weeping and gnashing of teeth" (Matthew 8:12, etc.).

9. Gehenna is a place of fire and sulphur that is believed to have been named from a valley, consecrated to idols, that is next to the city wall of Jerusalem, and which was once filled with the corpses of the dead – for there the Hebrews used to sacrifice their children to demons – and the place itself is called *Gehennon.* Therefore the place of future punishment (i.e. hell), where sinners are to be tormented, is designated by the name of this place. They also say that there are two Gehennas, one of fire and one of cold. 10. The underworld (*inferus*) is so called because it is underneath (*infra*). Just as with reference to physical bodies if things are arranged according to their weight, all heavier ones are lower, so with reference to the spirit, all the more grievous ones are lower; whence in the Greek language the origin of the term by which the underworld is called is said to echo 'what has nothing sweet' (i.e. taking the Greek Ἅδης, "Hades, underworld," as from α + ἡδύς, "not sweet"). 11. Just as the heart of an animal is in its center, so also the underworld is said to be in the center of the earth. Whence we read in the Gospel (Matthew 12:40): "In the heart of the earth." But philosophers say that the 'lower regions' (*inferi*) are so named because souls are carried (*ferre*) there from here.

13 Drawn from the netherworld terms Charon and Acheron, the Greek words for fumaroles indicate the belief that such vaporous orifices were entrances to the underworld.

Book XV

Buildings and fields (De aedificiis et agris)

i. Cities (De civitatibus) 1. Frequently we find dissension about who was responsible for the founding of cities, to such an extent that not even the origin of the city of Rome can accurately be known. Thus Sallust says (cf. *War with Catiline* 6), "As I understand it, at first the Trojans, and with them the native peoples, first founded and settled the city of Rome." Others say the founding was by Evander, as Vergil (cf. *Aen.* 8.313):

> Then King Evander, founder of the Roman citadel . . .

Others, by Romulus, as (Vergil, *Aen.* 6.781):

> Behold, my son, under his (i.e. Romulus's) auspices that illustrious Rome . . .

2. Hence if no sure account of so great a city is available, it is no wonder that there is some doubt about opinion concerning other cities. Therefore we should not ignorantly condemn the historians and commentators who allege various things, for antiquity itself created the error. It is indeed proper to treat briefly some cities concerning which either the Sacred Scriptures or pagan histories reliably report the origin.

3. Before the Flood, Cain was the first to found a city, the city of Enoch in Naid, after the name of his son, and he filled that city with only the throng of his own descendants. 4. After the Flood, the giant Nimrod (*Nembroth*) first founded the Mesopotamian city of Babylon. Queen Semiramis of the Assyrians enlarged it, and made the wall of the city with bitumen and fired brick. Babylon takes its name from 'confusion', because there the languages of those building the tower were confused and mixed up.[1] 5. The Jews say that Noah's son Shem (*Sem*), whom they call Melchizedech, was the first to found a city after the Flood, Salem in Syria, in which this same Melchizedech ruled. Afterwards the Jebusites held it, from whom it got the name Jebus. Thus Jerusalem (*Hierusalem*) was named, from the coupling of the two names Jebus (*Iebus*) and Salem. Later it was called *Hierosolyma* by Solomon, as if it were Hiero-solomonia (cf. ἱερός, "holy"). It is also named by the poets, incorrectly, Solyma, and later it was called Aelia by Aelius Hadrian. [Within] it is also Zion, which means "observation" (*speculatio*) in Hebrew, because it is built on a height and looks out on things approaching from afar. Jerusalem means "peaceable" (*pacificus*) in our language.[2]

Famous towns, and which men or women established them (Oppida nobilia, qui vel quae constituerunt)

6. Dionysius (i.e. Dionysus, the god of wine), who is also Father Liber, when as conqueror he walked through India, founded the city Nysa next to the river Indus, named it after his own name, and filled it with fifty thousand people. 7. Medus, son of Aegius, built Media, and from it his country of Media took its name. 8. Perseus, son of Adea (i.e. Danae), founded the city Persepolis, capital of the realm of Persia, very famous and stuffed with riches. Persia (*Persida*) was also named from him 9. The Parthians also founded Ctesiphon in Parthia in emulation of the city of Babylon. 10. They say that Memnon's brother established the city of Susa in Persia. It was named Susa because it overlooks the river Susa. The royal palace of Cyrus is there, distinguished by its white and variegated stone, with golden columns and paneled ceilings and jewels, even containing a replica of the sky embellished with twinkling stars, and other things beyond human belief.

11. The Bactrians founded the city of Bactrum, naming it after its river Bactros. 12. Carrhae, a city of Mesopotamia beyond Edessa, was founded by the Parthians. A Roman army was once slaughtered there, and its general Crassus was captured. 13. Nimrod (*Nembroth*), son of Chus, founded the Mesopotamian city Edessa after he moved from Babylon, and he reigned there. Formerly it was called Arach. He also built

1 Isidore alludes to the common derivation of the 'Babylon' from 'Babel', and the common interpretation of 'Babel' as "confusion."

2 The name 'Jerusalem' was regularly interpreted as "city of peace," as if from Hebrew *'ir shalom.*

Chalane, which afterwards, its name changed by king Seleucus, was called Seleucia. The Raphaim, a very ancient people whom the sons of Lot killed, founded the city Philadelphia of Arabia. 14. Seleucus, one of Alexander's descendants, after the death of the same Alexander, having seized the rule of the East, founded a city in Syria and named it Antioch after the name of his father, Antiochus, and made it the capital of Syria. The same man also built the cities of Laodicea and Seleucia, Apamea and Edessa. 15. Damascus of Syria was founded and named by Damascus, son of Abraham's steward. This formerly was the chief city in all Syria, for Antioch, Laodicea, and Apamea were not yet flourishing there – we know that these cities were built after Alexander's time. This is the Damascus that Abraham called his future heir, before Isaac was promised to him.

16. The Eveians founded the city of Gaza in Palestine, in which the Cappadocians lived after the original inhabitants were killed. It was called Gaza because Cambyses, king of the Persians, located his treasury there when he waged war against Egypt – for in Persian a 'treasury' is called *gaza*. 17. The Allophyli (*allophylus*, lit. "foreigner") founded the city Philistim; it is Ascalon, of which we have spoken above, named after Chasluim (*Cesloim*), who was the grandson of Ham and son of Mesraim. 18. The city of Dor was once very powerful; in turn it was known as the Tower of Strato and afterwards named Caesarea by Herod, king of Judea, in honor of Caesar Augustus. In this city the Church of Christ witnessed the house of Cornelius, and the little rooms of Philip, and the chamber of the four virgin prophetesses (see Acts 10:1 and 21:8–9).

19. The Palestinians built the seaside city Joppe of Palestine. There a rock is displayed which still retains traces of the fetters of Andromeda; the shape of her sea-monster was larger than an elephant. 20. Jericho is said to have been founded by the Jebusites, from whom, it is held, it also took its name. Joshua overthrew it. After that Ozam of Bethel, of the tribe of Ephraim, built another Jericho. But this also, when Jerusalem was attacked by the Romans, was seized and destroyed, due to the treachery of its citizens; because of this a third city was built, and this remains today. 21. Emor built the Samarian city Sichem, which is called *Sichima* in Latin and Greek, and named it after the name of his son Sichem. It is now Neapolis, a Samaritan city.

22. The Jebusites founded Bethel, a city of Samaria. Earlier it was called Luz, but afterwards Jacob, sleeping there, saw the ladder stretching up to heaven and said (Genesis 28:17), "Truly this is the house of God, and the gate of heaven." Hence the place got the name Bethel, that is, "house of God." But when golden calves were forged there by Jeroboam (III Kings 12:28 Vulgate), what was earlier called the house of God was called Bethaven, that is, "the house of the idol." 23. Bethlehem of Judah, the city of David, which gave birth to the Savior of the world, is said to have been founded by the Jebusites and first called Euphrata. But when Jacob pastured his cattle there, with a certain prophecy of the future he gave the same place the name Bethlehem, which means "house of bread," because of Him, the Bread who descended from heaven there.

24. Hebron (*Chebron*), the city of Judea that formerly was called Arbe, was founded by giants seven years before they founded the Egyptian city of Tanis. It was thus named 'Arbe' from the number (cf. Hebrew *arba*, "four"), because there three patriarchs were buried, and Adam was the fourth. It is also called 'Mambre' after a friend of Abraham. 25. Sennacherib, king of the Assyrians, built Samaria, from which the whole region that surrounded it took its name, and he called it 'Samaria,' that is, 'The Watch,' because when he delivered Israel into the hands of the Medes he set watchmen there. Antiochus leveled it when it was taken by siege. Later Herod restored it from its foundations, and he called it 'Augusta' in honor of Augustus, which is 'Sebaste' (*Sebastia*) in Greek. There the prophets Elisha and Abdias were buried, and John the Baptist; there was no greater among those born of women than he. 26. Another Herod (i.e. Herod Antipas) founded Tiberias in Judea, in the name of Tiberius Caesar.

27. The Phoenician city Tyre was founded by the Phoenicians. This is the city from which gold was brought down for King Solomon, and that in which the best purple cloth is dyed, whence the noble purple is called 'Tyrian.' 28. The Phoenicians, having migrated from the Red Sea, founded the very rich city Sidon, which they called Sidon from its abundance of fish, for Phoenicians call a fish *sidon*. They founded Tyre in Syria, Utica in Africa, as well as Hippo, Leptis, and other cities on seacoasts. 29. They built Thebes in Boeotia under the command of Cadmus; later, reaching the farthest part of the world, they built a city by the Ocean and named it Gades (i.e. Cadiz) in their language. It was an ancient custom of the Phoenician people to set off from home

together with many people for the purpose of trading, and when they had won over the hearts of the natives by the trading of goods previously unknown to them, they would then take over those places that seemed suitable for founding cities. 30. When Dido, also a Phoenician, had journeyed to the shore of Africa, she founded a city and named it *Carthada*, which in Phoenician meant "new city." Later, with altered pronunciation it was called Carthage (*Carthago*). Scipio destroyed it; what exists there now was founded afterwards by the Romans. Carthage was once named Byrsa, later Tyrus, finally Carthage.

31. Epaphas, son of Jupiter, built the Egyptian city of Memphis when he ruled over Second Egypt. This is the city where papyrus sheets are produced, and where the best mathematicians lived. Traces of their former error reveal that this city has been devoted to the magical arts up to the present time. 32. Tanis is the metropolis in Egypt where Pharaoh lived and Moses performed all the miracles that are written about in the book of Exodus. The Titans, that is 'giants,' are said to have built it and named it after their own name. 33. Heliopolis is an Egyptian city, which in Latin means "City of the Sun," as the Septuagint translators have it. But it was built by the children of Israel, and the priest Petephres, whom Ezekiel mentions, lived there.

34. Alexander the Great founded the city of Alexandria, and it preserves his name. He established it at the boundary of Egypt and Africa and commanded that it be the capital of the province of Egypt. It lies between Egypt and the sea, as if it were a gate, as it had no harbor. This is the Egyptian city of No (*Noo*), later turned into Alexandria. 35. Cadmus founded Egyptian Thebes, which is held to be quite famous among Egyptian cities for the number of its gates; Arab people transport articles of commerce to it from everywhere. The Egyptian region Thebaica is named after it. There is a Thebes in Boeotia and a Thebes in Egypt, but both were established by one founder.

36. Ptolomais and Berenice were named after the Egyptian rulers by whom they were built. 37. Caesarea of Cappadocia. . . 38. Perseus, offspring of Danae, built Tarsus of Cilicia. The apostle Paul was from this city (Acts 22:3): "I was born," he says, "at Tarsus in Cilicia." A certain place in India is also called Tarsus. Seleucus founded Seleucia of Isauria, as well as Antioch. Ilus, son of Apollo, founded Ilium in Phrygia. 39. The Amazons built Ephesus in Asia. Theseus built Smyrna, which came to prominence as the home of the poet Homer. It is called 'Smyrna' because the river Ermus cuts through its fields. 40. Amphitus and Cercius, the charioteers of Castor and Pollux, constructed Dioscoria, the city of the Colchians, naming it after their name, for Castor and Pollux in Greek are called the Διόσκουροι. 41. Nicomedia was built by Nicomedes, king of Bithynia. Bithynia, which was first called Mariandyna, was founded by Phoenix.

42. Constantine imposed his own name on the Thracian city of Constantinople; it alone is the equal of Rome in importance and power. It was first founded by Pausanias, king of the Spartans, and called Byzantium, either because it extends 'so much' (*tantum*) between the Adriatic Sea and the Propontis, or because it is a 'place for storage' (*receptaculum*) for the wealth of land and sea.[3] Hence Constantine decided to found this most suitable city, so that it would also become for him a depository by land and sea. For this reason it is now also the seat of the Roman Empire and the head of the entire East, as Rome is of the West.

43. The Thracian city of Epirus (*Epirum*) was founded by and named after Pyrrhus. 44. Cecrops founded Athens in Greece (*Hellas*), and named it 'Cecropia' after himself. Amphictyon, the same who reigned in Greece third after Cecrops, dedicated this city to Minerva and gave the name 'Athens' (*Athenae*) to the city, for Minerva in Greek is called Ἀθήνη. Hence also the Greeks claim that Minerva is the inventor of many arts, because literature, and the arts of many schools, and philosophy itself have considered Athens as their temple. 45. Corinthus, son of Orestes, founded Corinth in Achaea. The Greeks call it *Corinthea*, that is, 'the administration of the state.'[4] 46. Cadmus, coming from Phoenicia, founded Boeotian Thebes after he built Egyptian Thebes. 47. Mycenae [a Greek city] . . .

Lacedaemonia was founded by Lacedaemon, son of Semele. Sparta is named after Spartus, son of Phoroneus, who was the son of Inachus. Sparta is the same as the city Lacedaemonia, and hence Spartans are called Lacedaemonians. 48. Achaea was built by Achaeus; Pelops,

3 Does Isidore associate the words 'Byzantium' and *tantum*? According to Liddell/Scott's dictionary, Βυζαντία was glossed by Hesychius as εἶδος ὁρμιᾶς, which could mean "anchorage for wares" and thus *receptaculum*. The geography is confused. Alternatively: ". . . either because only (*tantum*) it lies open between the Black Sea and the Propontis . . ."

4 Greek offers no obvious rationale for this etymology.

who ruled among the Argives, founded the city of Peloponnensis; Cecrops built Rhodes on the island of Rhodes; Carpathus built Cos; Aeos, son of Typhon, built Paphos; Angeus, son of Lycurgus, built Samos; Dardanus founded Dardania. Thessalus, son of Graecus, built Thessalonica, and he also ruled there. 49. The Greeks built Brundisium (i.e. Brindisi), and it is called Brundisium in Greek because *brunda* means "head of a stag," for it is the case that in the shape of the city may be seen the horns and head and tongue.[5]

50. In Italy Janiculum was founded by Janus, and Saturnia and Latium by Saturn, the latter so named because there in his flight he hid (*latere*). 51. Pompeii was founded in Campania by Hercules, who as victor had led a triumphal procession (*pompa*) of oxen from Spain. 52. Aeneas, coming into this same Italy after the destruction of Troy, founded Lavinium after the name of his wife. 53. But Ascanius, after he had left his kingdom to his stepmother Lavinia, built Alba Longa. It was called Alba, 'White,' because of the color of a sow, and Longa because the town is elongated, in keeping with the great extent of the hill on which it is sited. From the name of this city the kings of the Albans took their names. 54. Capys Silvius, king of the Albans, built Capua, named after its founder, although some say Capua was named from 'capacity' (*capacitas*), because its land holds (*capere*) all produce for living, and others say from the flat (*campester*) land in which it is situated. Further, it is the chief city of Campania, named with Rome and Carthage among the three greatest cities. The Italian province Campania is named after it.

55. Romulus – when he had restored his grandfather Numitor to his reign after Amulius had been killed at Alba – came down to the place where Rome now is and established a settlement there, built walls, and called the city Rome after his own name. But Evander is said to have founded it earlier, as in this line (cf. Vergil, *Aen.* 8.313):

> Then father Evandrus, founder of the Roman citadel . . .

56. Ancus Marcius was born from the daughter of Numa Pompilius; he founded a city at the mouth of the Tiber that would receive foreign goods and would ward off the enemy. From its site he named it Ostia ("entrance").

57. Certain Gauls, driven by their civil discord and incessant dissensions, set out for Italy seeking new territory, and after the Etruscans (*Tuscus*) had been expelled from their own land, they founded Mediolanum (i.e. Milan) and other cities. It was called Mediolanum because a sow that was 'woolly around the middle' (*medio lanea*) is said to have been found there. 58. Historians believe that Messapia owes its origin to the Greek Messapus. Originally Peucetius, brother of Oenotrus, named it Peucetia; afterwards the name was changed to Calabria. 59. They say that Manto, the daughter of Tiresias, brought to Italy after the destruction of the Thebans, founded Mantua; it is in the Venetian territory which is called Cisalpine Gaul, and it is called Mantua because it 'looks after its departed spirits' (*manes tuetur*). 60. Parthenope was named Parthenope after the name of Parthenope, a certain maiden buried there. Afterwards Augustus preferred to call the town Neapolis (i.e. Naples). 61. Augustus waged war against Antony off the promontory Leucata, on which there was a temple of Actian Apollo. After Antony was defeated, he founded a city on the bay of Actium which he named Nicopolis (i.e. "city of victory") because of his victory.

62. Phalantus, leader of the Parthenians, founded Parthenii. Taras was the son of Neptune, and he founded and named the city of Tarentum. 63. When Cyrus besieged the maritime cities of Greece, and the Phocaeans attacked by him were brought to perilous straits, they swore that they would flee as far as possible from the Persian empire, where they would not even hear its name. So, having traveled to the farthest harbors of Gaul in their ships, trusting in their arms against the ferocity of the Gauls, they founded Massilia (i.e. Marseilles) and named it after their leader's name. Varro says they were trilingual because they spoke Greek, Latin, and Gallic. 64. Their own colonists founded Narbona (i.e. Narbonne), Arelatum (i.e. Arles), and Pictavia (i.e. Poitiers). They say that Burdigalis (i.e. Bordeaux) was so named because first it had the Burgian Gauls (*Burgos Gallos*) as colonists, and it was filled with these farmers at an earlier time.

65. The Scipios built Terracona (i.e. Tarragona) in Spain; hence it is capital of the province of Tarragon. 66. [Caesar Augustus both situated and named Caesaraugusta (i.e. Saragossa) in the province of Tarragon, a city in Spain. With the loveliness of its situation and its charming features it stands out among all the cities of Spain and is famous, distinguished for its tombs of

5 Strabo gives βρέντιον, "stag's head."

holy martyrs.][6] 67. The Africans, occupying the coasts of Spain under Hannibal, built New Carthage (*Carthago Spartaria*; i.e. Cartagena). Later taken and made a colony by the Romans, it gave its name to a province. But now it has been overthrown and reduced to desolation by the Goths.[7] 68. Greeks from the island of Zacynthus, who had traveled to Spain, founded Saguntum (i.e. Sagunto). Later the Africans destroyed it in the onslaught of war.

69. Caesar Augustus built Emerita (i.e. Merida) after he had seized the region of Lusitania and certain islands of the Ocean, giving it that name because there he stationed veteran soldiers – for veteran and retired soldiers are called *emeriti*. 70. Olisipona (i.e. *Ulisippo*, Lisbon) was founded and named by Ulysses (*Ulixes*); historians say that in this place the sky is separated from the earth and the seas from the lands. 71. Julius Caesar founded Hispalis (i.e. Seville), which he called Julia Romula from his own and Rome's name. But Seville was nicknamed after its site, because it was placed in swampy ground on piles (*palus*; *his palis* = 'on these piles') driven deep so that it would not succumb to its slippery and unstable foundation. 72. The town of Gades (i.e. Cadiz) was founded by the Phoenicians, who also founded New Carthage. 73. The city Septe (i.e. Ceuta) is named from its seven (*septem*) mountains, called The Brothers (*Fratres*) because of their mutual resemblance, which border on the Strait of Gibraltar (*Gaditanus fretus*, 'Strait of Cadiz').

74. The founder of Lix and Tingis (i.e. Tangiers) is Antaeus, whom Hercules is said to have beaten in a wrestling match and killed. Lix was named from the Mauretanian river Lixus, where the royal seat of Antaeus was; likewise Sala, because it borders the river Sala. 75. Juba, king of the Moors (*Mauri*), founded the city of Caesarea in Mauretania in honor of Caesar Augustus, and from his name he gave it the name Caesarea. Just so Herod named the other Caesarea in Palestine, which is now a very famous city. 76. When Hercules was passing that way, twenty of his company separated off and built the city of Icosium in Caesarean Mauritania. Lest any of them should gloat about his own name being imposed on the city, the name of Icosium was given to it, from the number of its founders (cf. εἴκοσι, "twenty"). 77. Cyrene was the queen of Libya who founded the city of Cyrene in her own name, and from the city she named the region Cyrenian Libya.

ii. Public buildings (De aedificiis publicis) 1. A city (*civitas*) is a multitude of people united by a bond of community, named for its 'citizens' (*civis*), that is, from the residents of the city (*urbs*) [because it has jurisdiction over and 'contains the lives' (*contineat vitas*) of many]. Now *urbs* (also "city") is the name for the actual buildings, while *civitas* is not the stones, but the inhabitants. 2. In fact there are three kinds of community (*societas*): of households, of cities (*urbs*), and of nations (*gens*). 3. 'City' (*urbs*) is from 'circle' (*orbis*), because ancient cities were made circular, or from 'plow-handle' (*urbus*), a part of the plow by which the site of the walls would be marked out. Whence this (Vergil, *Aen.* 3.109 combined with 1.425):

> And he chose a seat for his kingdom, and marked out the limits with a furrow.

For the site of a future city was marked out with a furrow, that is, by a plow. Cato says (cf. *Origins* 1, fr. 18): "One who founds a new city plows with a bull and cow. Where he has plowed, he makes a wall. Where he wants a gateway to be, he lifts and carries (*portare*) the plow, and he calls it a gateway (*porta*)." 4. Thus indeed a city would be encircled by a plow, with young oxen of different genders indicating the mingling of its households, as a sign of sowing and bearing fruit. Further, a city is founded by the plow, and razed by the plow. Whence Horace (*Odes* 1.16.20):

> And an enemy plow was shoved into the walls.

5. Some have said the word 'town' (*oppidum*) is from the 'opposing' (*oppositio*) of its walls; others, from its hoarding of wealth (*ops*), due to which it is fortified; others, because the community of those living in it gives mutual support (*ops*) against an enemy. At first people, in effect naked and defenseless, had no protection against monstrous beasts, nor shelters from cold and heat, nor were they sufficiently safe among themselves from other people. 6. At last, with native cunning, having lived in shelters of caves and woods, they fashioned huts and cottages from twigs and thatch where life might be safer, in that there would be no access for those who could do harm. This is the origin of towns, which are said to be

6 Many have suspected that this encomium of Saragossa was added by Braulio, bishop of that city.

7 Isidore's family was originally from Cartagena.

named towns (*oppidum*) because they offer help (*ops*). A town (*oppidum*) moreover differs in its size and its walls from a hamlet (*vicus*) or a fortress (*castellum*) or a 'country village' (*pagus*). 7. Further, cities (*civitas*) are called 'colonial towns' (*colonia*), or 'free towns' (*municipium*), or hamlets, fortresses, or country villages.

8. A city properly so called is one that has been founded not by newcomers but by those native to its soil. Therefore communities (*urbs*) founded by their own citizens (*civis*) are named cities (*civitas*), not colonies. 9. On the other hand, a colony (*colonia*) is what is filled by new inhabitants (*cultor*) when there are no indigenous people. Hence also a 'colony' is so called from the tilling (*cultus*, from *colere*, "till") of a field. 10. A free town is one that, while remaining in the status of a city, obtains from the sovereign some legal right to a greater or lesser obligation. It is called 'free town' (*municipium*) from 'official functions' (*munia*), that is 'obligations,' because they pay only these functions, that is, as the owed tributes or services (*munus*). The most notorious court cases and those involving a person's freedom, as well as those which proceed from the sovereign, are not conducted there; these belong to the jurisdiction of the city (*civitas*).

11. Hamlets and fortresses and country villages are communities that are distinguished by none of the dignity of a city, but are inhabited by a common gathering of people, and because of their small size are tributary to the larger cities. 12. A hamlet (*vicus*) is so called as consisting only of its dwellings (cf. *vicus*, "row of houses"), or because it only has streets (*via*), and no walls. It is without the protection of walls – although the dwelling-places in a city (*urbs*) are also called neighborhoods (*vicus*). It is called a hamlet because it is 'instead of' (*vice*) a city, or because it has streets (*via*) only, with no walls. 13. The ancients called a town sited on a very high place a fort (*castrum*), as if it were a high 'cottage' (*casa*). The plural of this is 'camp' (*castra*), and its diminutive is 'fortress' (*castellum*), [or because within it the freedom of the inhabitants would be 'cut off' (*castrare*) lest the populace wandering here and there should expose the fort to the enemy.] 14. 'Country villages' (*pagus*) are places fitted out with buildings for those dwelling among fields. These are also called marketplaces (*conciliabulum*), from the gathering and association of many people in one place. 15. Crossroads (*compitum*) are places where gatherings of country people are customarily made, and they are called crossroads because many regions in the country meet (*competere*) there, and there country people assemble.

16. The suburbs (*suburbanum*) are the buildings that surround a city, as if the term were 'below the city' (*sub urbe*). 17. Ramparts (*moenia*) are the walls of a city, so called because they protect (*munire*) the city, as if they were the bulwarks (*munimentum*) of the city, that is, the guardians. 18. They are also called a defense (*munium*), as if "made by hand" (*manu factum*); and thus also the word 'duty' (*munus*). A 'city wall' (*murus*, plural *muri*) is so called from 'defending' (*munitio*), as if the term were 'to be defended' (*muniri*, passive infinitive of *munire*), because it defends and guards the inner parts of the city. Furthermore, ramparts (*moenia*) have a double meaning, for sometimes all the public buildings of a city are loosely called by this word, as (Vergil, *Aen.* 2.234):

> We split the walls and expose the buildings (*moenia*) of the city.

But properly *moenia* are walls only.

19. A city wall is furnished with towers and bulwarks. Towers (*turris*) are so called because they are rounded (*teres*) and tall – for something tall and circular, like a column, is 'rounded.' Even though they may be constructed as squared off and wide, they still look round to those observing from far off, because everything appears round whose angular shape disappears and is lost across a long stretch of air. 20. Bulwarks (*propugnaculum*) are the pinnacles (*penna*) of city walls, so called because from them the city is 'fought for' (*propugnare*). 21. A 'fore-wall' (*promurale*), because it is for (*pro*) protection of the city wall (*murus*), for it is a wall in front of the city wall.

22. A gate (*porta*) is the name of the place where something can be carried in (*importare*) or carried out (*exportare*). The word 'gate' is properly used either of a city or of a military camp, as was mentioned above. A 'row of houses' (*vicus*), as was said above, comprises the dwelling-places of a city; hence neighborhoods (*vicinus*) are so called. Lanes (*via*) are the narrow spaces that lie between rows of houses. 23. Boulevards (*platea*) are the uninterrupted and spacious streets of a city, named for their breadth according to the proper sense of the Greek tongue, for in Greek πλατύς means "broad." 24. A 'side-street' (*quintana*) is one fifth (*quintus*) of a boulevard, through which a cart can pass. 25. Sewers (*cloaca*) are

so called because water is strained (*percolare*) through them. People say that Tarquinius Priscus first made these in Rome in order that, whenever there was a downpour of rain, water would pass through them out of the city so that the destructive force of water in very great and prolonged storms would not destroy the level places or foundations of the city. 26. Porticos (*imbolus*) are so named either because they are 'under the mass' (*subvolumen*),[8] or because people walk (*ambulare*) under them, for they are the arcades found here and there along the boulevards.

27. A forum (*forus*, i.e. the archaic form of *forum*) is a place for practicing litigation, named from "speaking" (*fari*) [or from King Phoroneus, who first gave law to the Greeks]. These places are also called *prorostra* (lit. "before the prows") because prows (*rostrum*) were seized from captured Carthaginian ships in the Punic War and set up in the Roman Forum as a sign of this victory. 28. The Senate House (*curia*) is so called because there the oversight (*cura*) of all affairs is administered by the Senate. 29. A *praetorium* is so named because there a 'judicial magistrate' (*praetor*) has his seat for managing investigations. 30. A gymnasium (*gymnasium*) in general is a place for exercising, but in Athens it was a place where philosophy was learned and the study of wisdom was engaged in, for the Greeks call γυμνάσιον what is called 'exercise' in Latin, that is, 'meditation' (*meditatio*).[9] But gymnasiums are also bathhouses and places for runners and athletes, because there people are trained in the study of their particular skills. 31. The Capitolium of Rome is so called because it was the highest head (*caput*) of the Roman city and its religion. Others say that when Tarquinius Priscus was uncovering the foundations of the Capitolium in Rome, he found on the site of the foundation the head (*caput*) of a human marked with Etruscan writing, and hence he named it the Capitolium.

32. Citadels (*arx*) are the high, fortified parts of a city, for whatever are the safest places in a city are called citadels from their holding off (*arcere*) the enemy. Also from this term are 'bow' (*arcus*) and 'strongbox' (*arca*). 33. The Romans suppose that the Circus (*Circus*) was named for the circling (*circuitus*) of horses, because there horses run around (*circum*) the turning-posts. 34. A theater (*theatrum*) is named from 'spectacle' (*spectaculum*), from the term θεωρία ("spectacle"), because people standing in it and watching (*spectare*) from above gaze at stage-plays. 35. And an amphitheater (*amphitheatrum*) is so called because it is composed of two theaters (cf. ἀμφί, "on both sides"), for an amphitheater is round, but a theater consists of half an amphitheater, having the shape of a semicircle.

36. A labyrinth (*labyrinthus*) is a structure with intricate walls, of the kind made at Crete by Daedalus where the Minotaur was shut in. If anyone should enter into it without a ball of twine he would not be able to find the way out. This building is so situated that, for those who open its doors, a terrifying thunder is heard within. It slopes down more than a hundred steps. Inside are images and monstrous effigies, innumerable passages heading every which way in the darkness, and other things done to confuse the way of those who have entered, so that it seems impossible to pass from its darkness to the light. There are four labyrinths: first the Egyptian, second the Cretan, the third in Lemnos, the fourth in Italy. All were so constructed that not even the ages can destroy them.

37. A lighthouse (*farum*; cf. Greek φᾶρος) is a very tall tower which the Greeks and Latins in common have named 'lighthouse' from its particular use, because thanks to its signal of flames it may be seen from far off by sailors. Ptolemy is said to have constructed such a lighthouse near Alexandria for eight hundred talents of gold. Its function was to show a light for ships sailing at night, in order to make known the channels and the entrance to the port, so that sailors would not be deceived in the darkness and run onto the rocks – for Alexandria has tricky access with deceptive shallows. Therefore from this, people call the devices built for the purpose of shining a light in ports 'lighthouses' (*pharus*), for φῶς means "light"; ὅρος, "vision" (actually "landmark, pillar"). Hence Lucifer (i.e. the 'Light-bearer') is called φωσφόρος in Greek.

38. *Coclea* are tall, round towers, and they are called *coclea* as if the word were 'cycles' (*cyclea*), because in them one climbs in a spiraling ring. One of these in Rome is 175 (Roman) feet high. 39. Hot baths (*thermae*) are so called because they are warm, for the Greeks call heat θερμόν. 40. Baths (*balneum*) are assigned their name from the

8 We guess that by *subvolumen* Isidore means "under, i.e. supporting, the mass" of the portico roof, linking the syllable *-vol-* with the *-bol-* of *imbolus*.

9 *Meditatio* means both "practice, exercise" and "meditation, contemplation."

idea of the lifting of sorrow, because the Greeks called it βαλανεῖον (cf. βάλλειν, "cast away"; ἀνία, "grief"), since it takes away one's anxiety of spirit. Gymnasiums (*gymnasium*) are so called because there athletes are trained, with their bodies anointed and massaged, for γυμνάσιον in Greek means "training" in Latin. 41. A dressing-room (*apodyterium*), where the clothes of bathers are left, is named for 'disrobing,' for ἀποδύειν in Greek means "disrobe." 42. *Propina* is a Greek word, which now among us has been corrupted to *popina*. It is a place next to a public bath where after bathing one may be refreshed of one's hunger and thirst. From this are named both *propina* (cf. *propin*, "apéritif") and *propinare* ("to drink a toast"), for πεῖνα in Greek means "hunger" – because this place relieves hunger.

43. 'Stalls' formerly referred to humble and simple neighborhood buildings, belonging to the common people, that could be closed by planks and boards. From this also comes the word 'shop girl' (*tabernaria*), because there she usually would sit. They are called stalls (*taberna*) because they are constructed of boards (*tabula*) and planks; even though they no longer look this way now they still retain the original name. 44. A meat-market (*macellum*) is so called because there livestock is slaughtered (*mactare*) and put up for sale to merchants. 45. A market (*mercatum*) takes its name from commerce (*commercium*), for there things would be bought and sold. Likewise a custom house (*teloneum*) is the name of the place where the revenue of ships and the wages of sailors are paid, for there sits the tax collector who will set a price on things and demand it aloud from the merchants. 46. A prison is a place that we are prohibited from leaving, and it is called prison (*carcer*) from 'confining' (*coercere*). [Hence Fronto (cf. fr. 12): "And they seemed to revel like the Greeks in pleasant places rather than 'to be confined in prison' (*coerceri carcere*)."]

iii. Dwelling-places (De habitaculis) 1. A habitation (*habitatio*) is so called from 'having' (*habere*), as in (Vergil, *Ecl.* 2.29):

> To inhabit (*habitare*, the frequentative of *habere*) cottages.

'House' (*domus*) is named from a Greek term, for the Greeks call a shelter δῶμα. A house is the dwelling of one family, as a city is of one population, as the world is the domicile (*domicilium*) of the whole human race. 2. The ancients called every edifice (*aedificium*) a building (*aedes*). Some think 'building' (*aedes*) took its name from 'eating' (*edere*) something, giving an example from Plautus (cf. *The Little Carthaginian* 529):

> If I had called you into the building (*aedes*) for lunch.

Hence also edifice (*aedificium*), because it was first 'made for eating' (*ad edendum factum*). 3. A court (*aula*) is a royal house, or a spacious dwelling enclosed by four colonnades. 4. An atrium (*atrium*) is a large building, or a very roomy and spacious house, and it is called an atrium because three (*tres*, neuter *tria*) colonnades are added to it on the outside. Others say it is *atrium* as if blackened (*ater*, neut. *atrum*) by fire and a lamp, for the blackening is caused by smoke. 5. A palace (*palatium*) is named after Pallas, prince of the Arcadians, in whose honor the Arcadians built the town Pallanteum, and they called the royal palace that they founded in his name 'Palatium.'

6. They say the bedroom (*thalamus*, also "bridal chamber") is so named for this reason: when the Sabine women were abducted by the Romans, one of them, more noble than the others in appearance, was abducted and greatly admired by all, and it was the response of an oracle that she be married to the general Thalamon. Because this marriage had gone happily, it was established that in every wedding the name *thalamus* would be repeated. The Egyptians also, in their own tongue, name those places in which newlyweds go down and lie together *thalamus*. 7. The dining room (*coenaculum*) is named from the gathering (*communio*; cf. κοινός, "common"; *cena*, "dinner") at dinner; hence also the cloister (*coenobium*) is a gathering (*congregatio*). Indeed, the ancients used to dine in public and in common, nor was anyone's feast private, lest the delicacies taken in secret should beget luxuriousness. 8. The "formal dining room" (*triclinium*) is the dining room named after the three couches for those reclining there. Thus among the ancients, in the place where the furniture for a dinner party was arranged, three couches were set up on which those reclining would feast. In Greek κλίνη means "bed" or "couch," from which it developed that one would say *triclinium*. 9. A chamber (*cella*) is so called because it hides and conceals (*celare*) us. A sleeping-chamber (*cubiculum*) is so named because there we lie down (*cubare*) and rest while sleeping. Likewise a bed (*cubile*) is a place for sleeping. A privy (*secessus*) is so

named because it is a private area, that is, 'without access' (*sine accessu*).

10. An inn (*diversorium*) is so called because there people meet who come from diverse (*diversus*) ways. Hospice (*hospitium*), a Greek word, is where a person dwells for a time according to the law of hospitality, and passing through, leaves again for elsewhere. Whence also campgrounds (*metatum*), because they are moved (*mutare*). Hence one reads, "They 'laid out' (*metari*) camp," for "they moved" – for the army does not stay there but passes through. 11. Moenius, the colleague of Crassus, constructed bleachers in the Forum so that there would be places for spectators to stand, and these are called *Moeniana* ("galleries") after his name. These are also called sun terraces (*solarium*), because they are exposed to the sun (*sol*). After these some built galleries of stone for their colonnades, some of wood, and they attached them to their marketplaces and houses. 12. A house formerly was made of wood, 'boarded' (*tabulatus*), and from this the name 'floor' (*tabulatum*) remains. A cellar (*hypogeum*; cf. ὑπό, "under"; γῆ, "earth) is a building constructed under ground, which we call a cavern or cave. A sun terrace (*solarium*) is so called because it is open to the sun (*sol*) and breezes (*aura*), as was the place from which David saw Bathsheba bathing and fell in love (II Kings 11:2 Vulgate).

13. When Antiochus besieged Jerusalem, Hyrcanus, leader of the Jews, took three thousand talents of gold from the tomb of David after it was opened, and gave three hundred of them to Antiochus to lift the siege. To remove the ill will attendant on this deed he is said to have used the rest of the money to establish the first 'stranger's hospices' (*xenodochium*), which would support the arrival of poor people or pilgrims, whence they took the name – for they are named from the Greek ξενοδοχεῖον, in Latin, 'support of pilgrims.' Moreover, the place where sick people are collected from the streets is called a νοσοκομεῖον ('hospital'; cf. νόσος, "sickness") in Greek.[10] There the limbs of wretched people, consumed with weariness and fasting, are given care.

iv. Sacred buildings (De aedificiis sacris) 1. Sanctuaries (*sacrum*) are places established for divine worship, namely those in which altars are consecrated (*consecrare*) by high priests making sacrifices according to their custom. 2. Sanctums (*sanctum*) according to the ancients are the outer precincts of temples. The 'Holy of Holies' (*sanctum sanctorum*) is the inner part of the temple to which no one had access, excepting only the priest. It is called the Holy of Holies because it is holier than the outer oracle, or because it is holier in comparison with other sanctuaries, just as we speak of the Song of Songs, because it excels all songs. A sanctum is so called from the blood (*sanguis*) of sacrificial victims, for among the ancients nothing was called holy (*sanctus*) except what had been consecrated and sprinkled with the blood of a sacrifice. Again *sanctum*, what is known to have been sanctified (*sancire*, ppl. *sancitum*). Moreover to sanction (*sancire*) is to confirm, and to defend from wrong by imposing punishment. Thus both laws and city walls are said to be holy (*sanctus*). 3. A place of propitiation (*propitiatorium*) [is as it were a 'place of prayers of propitiation' (*oratorium propitiationis*), for a propitiation is an appeasing.] Oracles (*oraculum*) are so called because from there responses are given, and oracles are from the 'mouth' (*os*, gen. *oris*). 4. *Penetralia* are the secret places of oracles, and are called *penetralia* because they are 'interior' (*penitus*), that is, 'almost inside' (*pene intus*). An *oratorium* is dedicated to prayer (*oratio*) only, and no one should do anything in it except that for which it was made and from which it receives its name.

5. A monastery (*monasterium*) is the dwelling of one monk (*monachus*), for μόνος is Greek for 'alone' (*solus*), στηριον for 'station' – it is the dwelling of a solitary (*solitarius*). 6. 'Convent' (*coenobium*) seems to be a compound of Greek and Latin. It is the habitation of a number of people living in common, for κοινός in Greek means "common." 7. The term 'temple' (*templum*) is general, for the ancients would give the name 'temples' to all sorts of large places, and temples (*templa*) were so named as if they were called 'spacious shelters' (*tecta ampla*). But a place oriented to the east was also called a temple, from the idea of 'observing for augury' (*contemplatio*). A temple had four parts: the front facing to the east, the rear to the west, the left to the north, the right to the south. Hence when they would build a temple they would face toward the equinoctial sunrise, so that lines laid from the east to the west would divide the sky into equal parts on the right and the left, and thus whoever would take counsel or pray would look directly east. 8. Shrines (*fanum*) are named after fauns (*faunus*),

10 Latin *nosocomium* means "infirmary."

for whom pagan error built temples where those making consultations would hear the responses of demons.

9. The ancients called temples with fountains, where people would be washed before entering, 'spring-shrines' (*delubrum*), and these shrines were thus named after 'washing' (*diluere*). These are now buildings with holy (i.e. baptismal) fonts, in which the faithful are purified as reborn, and they are well termed spring-shrines by a certain foretelling, because they are for the 'washing away' (*ablutio*) of sins. 10. For the font (*fons*) in spring-shrines is the place of the reborn, in which seven steps are made in the mystery of the Holy Spirit; there are three going down and three coming up: the seventh is the fourth step (i.e. the bottom of the waist-deep baptismal font), and that is like the Son of Man, the extinguisher of the furnace of fire, the sure place for the feet, the foundation of the water, in which the fullness of divinity dwells bodily. 11. The dwellings of kings were called 'basilicas' (*basilica*) at first, whence they take their name, for the term βασιλεύς means "king," and basilicas, "royal habitations." But now 'basilica' is the name for divine temples because there worship and sacrifices are offered to God, the king of all. 12. A *martyrium* is a place of martyrs (*martyr*), derived from Greek, because each is built in memory of a martyr, or because the tombs of the holy martyrs are there.

13. Some have said that an altar (*ara*) is so called because there the kindled sacrifices burn (*ardere*). Others say it is from a 'prayer,' which the Greeks call ἀρά, whence contrariwise a curse is called κατάρα. Others would derive it from *altitudo* ("height"), but wrongly. 14. However, *altare* (i.e. another term for 'altar') rightly is named from *altitudo*, as if the word were 'a high altar' (*alta ara*). 15. The ambo (*pulpitum*) is so called because the reader or psalmist stationed in it can be seen by the people (*populus*) in public (*publicum*), so that he may be heard more easily. 16. 'Tribunal' (*tribunal*), because from there rulings about one's manner of life are bestowed (*tribuere*) by a priest. It is a place set up on high, from which everyone can hear. In another view 'tribunal' takes its name from 'tribe' (*tribus*), because the tribe is called together before it. 17. The pulpit (*analogium*) is so called because the sermon is preached from there, for λόγος in Greek means "sermon" – and it also is located in a rather high place [in order that the reader or psalmist thus stationed can be seen in public by the people, where he may be heard more easily].

v. Repositories (De repositoriis) 1. The *sacrarium* is properly the place in a temple where holy things (*sacrum*) are put away; similarly the 'temple treasure-chamber' (*donarium*), where offerings are gathered; similarly the 'rows of seating' (*lectisternium*) where people are accustomed to sit. Hence the *sacrarium* is named from the taking of sacred things in and out. 2. However, the *donarium* is so named because the gifts (*donum*) that they customarily offer in temples are put away there. 3. The treasury (*aerarium*) is so called because formerly minted bronze (*aes*, gen. *aeris*) was hidden away there. It was in use in former times when gold and silver were not yet minted; although money was afterwards made from gold and silver, the name *aerarium* still remained, after the bronze from which money took its first name.

4. A cabinet (*armarium*) is a place where the tools or records of any sort of craft (*ars*) are placed. But an armory (*armamentarium*) is where only weaponry is placed. Whence Juvenal (*Satires* 13.83):

> Whatever weapons the armories of heaven hold.

Both of them are so called from 'shoulders' (*armus*), that is, 'arms,' with which weapons are wielded. 5. A library (*bibliotheca*) is a place where books are deposited, for βίβλος in Greek means "book," θήκη, "repository." 6. A 'storeroom' (*promptuarium*) is so called because from there foodstuffs are brought out (*promere*), that is, carried forth. 7. A pantry (*cellarium*), so called because in it are gathered (*colligere*) the dining implements, or whatever foodstuffs are left over. There is this difference between a storeroom and a pantry, that a pantry serves for a few days, but a storeroom for a long time. 8. However, storehouses (*apotheca*) or granaries (*horreum*) can be called repositories (*repostorium*) or 'hoarding places' (*reconditorium*) by literal translation (cf. ἀπό, "back again"; θήκη), because in them people deposit (*reponere*, ppl. *repositus*) harvested crops. Hence we call an ample supply of stored goods by the Greek word 'hoard' (*entheca*).

vi. Workplaces (De operariis) 1. A workshop (*ergasterium*) is where any work is done, from the Greek words ἔργα, "works," and στηριον, "station" – that is, work-station (*operarii statio*). 2. 'Penitentiary workhouses' (*ergastulum*) are also named from the same Greek word; there offenders are assigned to do some kind of work, of the kind that gladiators would usually be assigned, and banished people, who cut marble but are still bound in custody by chains. 3. The 'women's quarters' (*gynaeceum*) is so named from the Greek because there a gathering of women would meet to carry out the task of wool-working, for a 'woman' in Greek is called γυνή. 4. The term 'millhouse' (*pistrinum*) is as if the word were *pilistrinum*, because formerly grain was pounded by a pestle (*pilum*). Whence among the ancients the term was not 'millers' (*molitor*) but 'pounders' (*pistor*), as if it were *pinsores*, from their crushing (*pinsere*) the kernels of grain – for they did not yet use millstones (*mola*), but would crush grain with a pestle. Whence Vergil (*Geo.* 1.267):

> Now parch the grain with the fire, now grind it with a stone.

5. A furnace (*clibanus*) [is so called from 'slope' (*clivus*), because it narrows as it goes up, for we say an upward or winding path is a slope.] 6. An oven (*furnus*) is a term derived from 'spelt' (*far*), because bread made from spelt is baked there. 7. A press (*torcular*) is so called because there grapes are trod and, once they have been squeezed (*extorquere*), are pressed out. 8. A *forus* (i.e. *forum*) is a place where grapes are trod, so called because the grapes are brought (*ferre*) there – or because there they are smashed (*ferire*) with feet; hence it is also called a wine-press (*calcatorium*, "treading-place"; cf. *calx*, 'heel'). But this term means many things: the first kind of forum is the place in a city set aside for market trading; second, where a magistrate will give judgments; third, the one we spoke of above, which we have called the wine-press; fourth, the decks of ships, of which Vergil (*Aen.* 6.412):

> And he clears the decks (*forus*).

A vat (*lacus*) is so called because the juice (*liquor*) of fruit runs down into it.

vii. Entranceways (De aditibus) 1. An entranceway (*aditus*) is so called from 'going' (*ire*, ppl. *itus*); through it we pass and are admitted. 2. A vestibule (*vestibulum*) is either the entranceway of a private house or a space adjacent to public buildings. It is called a 'vestibule' because the entrance doors are covered (*vestire*) by it, or because it covers an entranceway with a roof, or from 'standing-place' (*stare*). 3. A portico (*porticus*), because it is a passageway rather than a place where one remains standing, as if it were a gateway (*porta*). Also *porticus* because it is uncovered (*apertus*). 4. A 'front door' (*ianua*) is named after a certain Janus, to whom the pagans dedicate any entrance or exit. Whence Lucan (*Civil War* 1.62):

> Let her (Peace) shut the iron doors of war-making Janus.

Now this is the first entrance of a house; others, inside the front door, are generally called doorways. A doorway (*ostium*) is that by which we are prevented from any entrance, so called from 'impeding' (*ostare*, i.e. *obstare*) [or it is doorway (*ostium*) because it discloses (*ostendere*) something within]. Others say doorway is so called because it detains an enemy (*ostis*, i.e. *hostis*), for there we set ourselves against our adversaries – hence also the name of the town Ostia at the mouth of the Tiber, because it is set there to oppose the enemy (cf. i.56 above).

'Door panels' (*foris*) or leaves (*valva*) are also types of barriers, but the former are so called because they swing out (*foras*), the latter swing (*revolvere*) inward, and they can be folded double – but usage has generally corrupted those terms. 5. Barriers (*claustrum*) are so called because they are closed (*claudere*). 6. Windows (*fenestra*) have a narrow exterior and a widened interior, of the kind we see in barns. They are so called because they lend (*fenerari*, i.e. *faenerari*) light – for light in Greek is called φῶς – or because a person inside sees (*videre*) out through them. Others suppose that window is so called because it provides (*minestrare*, i.e. *ministrare*) light, with the name a blending of a Greek and a Latin word, for light in Greek is φῶς (i.e. φῶς + *minestrare*).

7. A hinge (*cardo*) is the place on which a door swings and is always moved. It is so called after the term καρδία ("heart"), because as the heart (*cor*) governs and moves the whole person, so this pivot governs and moves a door. Whence the proverbial expression, for a matter to be "at a turning point" (*in cardine*). 8. A threshold (*limen*) of a door is so called because it is set crosswise as a boundary-line (*limes*), and one enters and leaves across it as one enters and leaves a field. 9. Door-posts (*postis*) and pilasters (*antae*) are so called as if the words were *post* and *ante*. *Antae* because they stand 'in front' (*ante*), or because we approach them 'beforehand' (*antea*), before we enter a house; *postes* because they stand 'behind' (*post*) the door.

viii. The parts of buildings (De partibus aedificiorum) 1. A foundation (*fundamentum*) is so called because it is the bottom (*fundus*) of a house. Likewise it is called quarry-stone (*caementum*), after 'hewing' (*caedere*), because it arises from a thick hewn stone. 2. A wall (*paries*) is so called because there are always two of 'equal size' (*par*, plural *pares*), either from side to side or from front to back. Whether the building is four-sided or six-sided, the facing walls will be of equal size; otherwise the construction is deformed.

3. We speak of ruins (*parietinae*), as if the word were 'the ruins of walls' (*parietum ruina*); these are walls standing without roofs or inhabitants. 4. The 'corner' (*angulus*), because it joins two walls into one (*in unum coniungeret*). Roofs (*culmen*) are so called because the ancients covered their roofing with straw (*culmus*), as country people still do. Hence the peak of a roof is called the 'ridge' (*culmen*).

5. Vaults (*camera*) are bending structures facing to the inside, so named from 'curved,' for καμουρ (otherwise unattested) is "curve" in Greek. 6. 'Paneled ceilings' (*laquearium*) are what cover and decorate vaults, and they are also called *lacunaria*. The primary term is 'panel' (*lacus*), as in Lucilius (cf. *Satires*, fr. 1290):

> The building and the panels (*lacus*) resound.

The diminutive of this produces *lacunar*, as Horace (*Odes* 2.18.1):

> Nor does a gilded *lacunar* glitter in my house.

Likewise the other diminutive *lacunarium* is made, and by ἀντίστιχον (i.e. *antistoechum*, substitution of a letter) it produces the term *laquearium*. 7. A 'vaulted chamber' (*absida*) is from a Greek word (cf. ἁψίς, gen. ἁψῖδος, "arch, vault") that means "full of light" in Latin, because it is resplendent with the light received through an arch. But whether we ought to call it *absida* or *absis* is doubtful, because certain experts consider the declension of this word ambiguous. 8. A 'tortoise-shell vault' (*testudo*, lit. 'tortoise shell') is a transverse vault of a temple, for the ancients would make the roofs of their temples in the shape of a tortoise shell. These would be made thus to duplicate the image of the sky, which is evidently convex. Others take the tortoise-shell vault to mean a place on the side of an atrium facing the people coming in (i.e. the narthex). 9. An arch (*arcus*) is so called because it is curved with a narrowed (*artus*) tip. These are also 'archways' (*fornix*).

10. Pavements (*pavimentum*) elaborated with the skill of a picture have a Greek origin; mosaics (*lithostratum*) are made from little pieces of shell and tiles colored in various hues. They are called pavements because they are 'rammed down' (*pavire*), that is, beaten. From this also comes the word 'dread' (*pavor*), which strikes the heart. 11. An *ostracus* is a tiled pavement, because it is rammed with broken-up pots mixed with lime, for Greeks call pots ὄστρα. 12. The area called a *compluvium* (cf. *pluvia*, "rain") is so named because water gathers (*convenire*) in it from the surrounding areas. Tiles (*tessella*) are what domiciles are paved with, named as the diminutive from 'paving stones' (*tessera*), that is, 'square little stones.'

13. Pedestals (*basis*) are the supports of columns, which rise up from this foundation and sustain the weight of the material placed above. Further, *bases* is the name of a very strong stone in the Syrian language. 14. Columns (*columna*) are named according to their length and roundness (see XIX.xxix.2); the weight of the whole structure is carried by them. The ancient ratio held that their thickness was a third of their height. There are four kinds of round columns: Doric, Ionic, Tuscan, and Corinthian, differing among themselves in the ratio of thickness to height. A fifth kind is that called Attic, with four angles or more, and sides of equal width. 15. Capitals (*capitolium*, i.e. *capitulum*) are so called because they are the heads (*caput*, gen. *capitis*) of columns (*columna*), just as there is a head on a neck (*collum*). Architraves (*epistolium*, i.e. *epistylium*) are the beams placed above the capitals of columns, and the word is Greek, [that is, 'placed above.']

Roof-tiles (*tegulae*), because they cover (*tegere*) buildings; and 'curved roof-tiles' (*imbrex*), because they fend off the rain (*imber*). 16. Bricks (*later*) and tiles (*laterculus*), because they are made in a wide (*latus*) mold by means of four wooden forms placed around their sides. A conduit (*canalis*) is so called because it is hollowed out like a reed (*canna*). We usually cite *canalis* as having feminine rather than masculine gender. 17. Water pipes (*fistula*) are so called because they pour (*fundere*, ppl. *fusus*) and 'send' water, for στολα in Greek means "to send" (cf. στέλλειν, "equip, bring"). They are shaped according to the quantity of water and the measure of their capacity.

ix. Fortifications (De munitionibus) 1. A *munitum* or *munimentum* ("fortification") is so called because it is made by hand (*manus*). A 'military enclosure' (*cohors*) is so called either because it 'presses together' (*coartare*) all that is within it, that is, it encloses, or because it restrains (*coercere*) those outside by creating an obstacle and prevents them from approaching. 2. A rampart (*vallum*) is what is raised up with a mass of earth so that protection may be afforded. It is called rampart from 'palisades' (*vallus*), for palisades are the stakes with which a rampart is protected. And palisades are so named because they are driven in and 'pulled out' (*vellere*). The *intervallum* is the space between the tops of the ramparts, that is, the tops of the posts with which the rampart is furnished – hence other intervals are also called 'spaces' (*spatium*), the term evidently derived from 'posts' (*stipes*, gen. *stipitis*). 3. A mound (*agger*) is a heap of any sort of material, with which the trenches and low places can be reinforced. A mound properly means heaped-up (*aggerare*) earth that is placed nearby when the rampart is constructed, but loosely speaking we call the walls and all the fortifications the mound.

4. Fences (*maceria*) are the long walls with which some vineyards are enclosed, for the Greeks say μακρός for 'long.' 5. In Africa and Spain walls of earth are called *formatum* or *formaceum* (lit. "molded") because they are pressed into a form (*forma*) made from planks enclosing them on both sides rather than built up from the ground. They last for ages, undamaged by wind and fire, and stronger than any concrete. 6. Hedges (*sepes*) are protective barriers for what has been planted (*satus*), whence they take their name. Sheepfolds (*caulae*) are sheep's pens or the hedges (*saepimentum*) of sheepfolds. Moreover, with [the letter] *c* removed, it is a Greek term, for the Greeks call holding-pens for animals αὐλαί.

x. Tents (De tentoriis) 1. A *tabernaculum* is a soldier's tent, with which they avoid the heat of the sun, the onslaughts of rainstorms, and the injury of cold while on the march. They are called *tabernacula* because their sides are stretched out and suspended by ropes from the boards (*tabula*) standing in the middle which hold up the tents. 2. A tent (*tentorium*) is so called because it is stretched (*tendere*, ppl. *tentus*) with ropes and stakes; hence today people are said to 'stretch the truth' (*praetendere*). 3. Pavilions (*papilio*, lit. "butterfly, moth") are so called from their resemblance to the little flying animals that teem especially when the mallows are flowering. These are the little winged creatures that gather to a kindled light and, flitting around it, are forced to die from being too close to the fire.

xi. Sepulchers (De sepulchris) 1. A sepulcher (*sepulchrum*) is so called from 'buried' (*sepelire*, ppl. *sepultus*). Originally people were buried in their own homes. Later this was prohibited by law, so that the bodies of the living would not be infected by contact with the stench. A monument (*monumentum*) is so named because it 'admonishes the mind' (*mentem monere*) to remember the deceased person. Indeed, when you don't see a monument, it is as what is written (Psalm 30:13 Vulgate): "I have been cut off from the heart as one who is dead." But when you see it, it admonishes the mind and brings you back to mindfulness so that you remember the dead person. Thus both 'monument' and 'memory' (*memoria*) are so called from 'the admonition of the mind' (*mentis admonitio*). 2. A 'burial mound' (*tumulus*) is so named as if it were 'swelling ground' (*tumens tellus*). 'Sarcophagus' (*sarcophagus*) is a Greek term, because bodies are consumed there, for σάρξ in Greek means "flesh," φαγεῖν, "to eat."

3. Mausoleums (*mausoleum*) are the sepulchers or monuments of kings, named after Mausolus, king of the Egyptians. When he was dead his wife built for him a sepulcher of wondrous size and beauty, so that even today any precious monument is called a mausoleum after his name. 4. Pyramids (*pyramis*) are a type of sepulcher that are square and raised to a point beyond any height that can be constructed by hand, whence also, having surpassed the measure of shadows, they are said to have no shadow.[11] They rise with such a construction that they begin wide and finish narrow, like a flame – for πῦρ means "flame." Egypt is the site of these pyramids. Among the ancients, powerful people would be buried either under mountains or within mountains; hence it was determined that either pyramids would be constructed above their corpses or huge columns would be erected.

xii. Rural buildings (De aedificiis rusticis) 1. A cottage (*casa*) is a rustic little dwelling of wattles and woven with reeds and twigs, in which people can be protected from [the force] of cold or the injury of heat. 2. A shed

11 If high enough in the sky, the sun would cast no shadow extending beyond the base of a pyramid because of its sloping sides.

(*tugurium*) is a little house that vineyard-keepers make for themselves as a covering (*tegimen*), as if the word were *tegurium*, either for avoiding the heat of the sun and deflecting its rays, or so that from there the keeper may drive away either the people or the animals that would lie in wait for the immature fruit. Country people call this a 'hut' (*capanna*), because it 'holds one' (*capiat unum*) person only. 3. Some think a *tescuum* (i.e. *tesquum*) is a *tugurium*; others think it is rugged and harsh terrain. 4. A *magalium* is an elongated structure, made by Numidian peasants, covered with sides that curve in like the hulls of ships, or round in the shape of ovens. They are called *magalia* as if *magaria*, because Phoenicians call a new country house a *magar* – with one letter changed, *l* for *r*, *magalia* from *magaria*.

xiii. Fields (De agris) 1. Field (*ager*) in Latin is said to get its name because in it something 'is done' (*agere*). Others believe that 'field' is more obviously named from the Greek, whence a farm in Greek is called a *coragros*.[12] 2. A farm (*villa*) is named from 'rampart' (*vallum*), that is the heap of earth that they use to establish the boundary-lines. 3. 'Holdings' (*possessio*) are vast public and private fields that originally someone occupied and owned (*possidere*) not by property transfer but insofar as he 'had power' (*posse*) – whence also they are named. 4. An 'estate' (*fundus*) is so called because the family's patrimony is founded (*fundare*) and established on it. Further, an estate should be taken as both one's urban and rural property. 5. A 'manor' (*praedium*) is so called because, of all the possessions of the head of the family, it is the most 'seen before' (*praevidere*), that is, it is most visible, as if the word were *praevidium* – or because the ancients referred to the fields which they had seized in war as 'booty' (*praeda*).

6. Now every field, as Varro teaches us, falls into one of four types. There is the arable (*arvus*) field, that is, for sowing; or the plantable (*consitus*), that is, suitable for trees; or pasture (*pascuus*), set apart for grass and herds only; or the floral (*florus*), because these are garden spots fit for bees and flowers. Vergil followed this division in the four books of his *Georgics*. 7. The ancients called uncultivated fields – that is, forests and pasturelands – 'open country' (*rus*), but the part that was cultivated, the 'field' (*ager*). The open country is where honey, milk, and cattle can be obtained, and from it 'rustic' (*rusticus*) is named. This makes up the supreme toil-free happiness of peasants. 8. A 'field of grain' (*seges*) is where grain is sown, whence Vergil (*Geo.* 1.47):

> That field of grain (*seges*) only then answers the prayers of the eager farmer.

9. A field is called 'common pasture' (*compascuus*) when it is left out of the division of the fields in order to 'provide pasturage in common' (*pascere communiter*) among neighbors. 10. An alluvial (*alluvius*) field is that which a watercourse (*fluvius*) gradually turns into a field. 11. A field is called 'naturally enclosed' (*arcifinius*) when it is not bounded by fixed measures of boundary-lines, but its 'boundaries are enclosed' (*arcentur fines*) by a barrier of rivers, mountains, or trees – wherefore also no leftover patches of land interrupt these fields.

12. A fallow (*novalis*) field is one plowed for the first time, or one that in alternate years is left empty in order to renew (*novare*) its strength, for fallow lands sometimes will be fruitful and sometimes empty. 13. A desolate (*squalidus*) field is as it were 'ex-cultivated' (*excolidus*), because now it has passed out of cultivation, just as the term *exconsul* comes from one's having departed from the consulate. 14. A marshy (*uliginosus*) field is always wet (*uvidus*), whereas a field that sometimes dries up is called moist (*humidus*). Swampiness (*uligo*) is a natural liquid quality of earth, never leaving it. 15. 'Remainders' (*subseciva*) are, properly speaking, what a shoemaker cuts off from the material and throws away as superfluous. Hence 'remainders of land' (*subsiciva*) are plots that, because they are sterile or swampy, people reject when the fields are divided into parcels. Further, 'remainders' are those areas that in the division of a field do not make up a hundred-measure, that is, two hundred jugers. 16. A 'threshing floor' (*area*) is named for the levelness of its floor, and it is called *area* because of its flatness and evenness – hence also altar (*ara*).[13] Others say a threshing floor is so called because it is smoothed off (*eradere*) for threshing grain, or because only what is dry (*arida*) is threshed on it. 17. A meadow (*pratum*) is where herds are kept because of the abundance of its hay. The ancient Romans gave it this name because it

12 The text is defective here. In question may be the Greek χωρά or χῶρος, both meaning "countryside, landed estate." Cf. ἀγρός, "field."

13 The word *area* little resembles *aequalitas*, "levelness, evenness," but Isidore may simply allude to a synonym: *aequor*, like *area*, can mean "a level place." Otherwise on *ara* see iv.13 above.

was 'continually ready' (*protinus paratus*) and would not need the great labor of tilling. Meadows are what can be mown. 18. Swamps (*palus*) are named for the pastoral goddess Pales because they furnish straw (*palea*), that is, fodder, for beasts of burden.

xiv. The boundaries of fields (De finibus agrorum) 1. Boundaries (*finis*) are so called because fields are divided by cords (*funiculus*), for lines of measuring are stretched out when land is partitioned in order to maintain uniformity of dimension. 2. 'Limits' (*limes*) are named after the old word for 'crosswise,' because the ancients referred to anything crosswise as *limus*. From this term are derived both the 'thresholds' (*limen*) of entryways, across which one goes in or out, and 'boundary-limits' (*limes*), because one goes across these into the fields. Hence also we get the word *limus*, an apron with slantwise purple trim that public slaves would wear. 3. 'Boundary-lines' (*terminus*) are the name for what mark out and display the measurement of the land, for through these proof (*testimonium*) of boundaries is recognized, and lawsuits and squabbles about fields are thus avoided.

4. The largest boundary dimensions of fields are two: the *cardo* and the *decumanus*. The *cardo*, the north–south dimension, is named from the 'hinge' (*cardo*), the pole of the heavens, for surely the heavens rotate about the North Pole. The *decumanus* is the crosswise dimension, drawn from east to west, and because it makes the shape of an X, it is called *decumanus* – a field twice divided in this way makes the figure X of the number ten (*decem*). 5. An *arca* (i.e. a quadrangular landmark) is so named from the term 'ward off' (*arcere*), for it guards the boundaries of a field and prohibits anyone from approaching. A *trifinium*, (i.e. a 'place where three boundaries meet') is so called because it delimits the 'boundaries of three' (*trium fines*) holdings. Likewise *quadrifinium*, because it bounds four (*quattuor*). The other boundary dimensions are shorter and stand at unequal intervals apart from one another, and have their appointed names.

xv. The measures of fields (De mensuris agrorum) 1. A measure (*mensura*) is whatever is delimited by weight, capacity, length, height, breadth, and spirit. Thus our ancestors divided the earth into parts, parts into provinces, provinces into regions, regions into locales, locales into territories, territories into fields, fields into hundred-measures, hundred-measures into jugers, jugers into lots sixty feet square, and then these lots into furrow-measures, Roman rods, paces, steps, cubits, feet, palms, inches, and fingers. So great was their ingenuity. 2. The finger is the least part of field measuring. An inch has three fingers, a palm has four fingers, a foot sixteen, a pace five feet, and a Roman rod two paces – that is, ten feet. 3. A 'Roman rod' (*pertica*) is so called from 'carrying' (*portare*), as if it were *portica*. Now all the foregoing measures are based on the body, as palm, foot, pace, and the rest; only the rod is something carried. It is ten feet long and is the equivalent of the measuring-rod (*calamus*) that measures the Temple in the Book of Ezechiel (40:3).

4. The furrow-measure (*actus minimus*) is four feet wide and 120 long. *Climata* have sixty feet on a side, so: (a figure follows). A 'square furrow-measure' (*actus quadratus*) is bounded on each side by 120 feet, so: (a figure follows). The Baeticans call this measure a 'half-juger' (*arapennis*), from the term 'plowing' (*arare*). 5. This square furrow-measure doubled (*actus duplicatus*) makes a juger (*iugerum*); because it thus consists of a 'joining' (*iunctum*) it takes the name 'juger.' Now a juger has a length of 240 feet and a breadth of 120, so: (a figure follows). The country people of the province of Baetica call a square furrow-measure an *acnua*. 6. Likewise the Baeticans define a *porca* as an area thirty feet wide and eighty feet long. (A figure follows.) But a balk (*porca*) is the raised ridge in plowing, and what is dug out is the furrow (*lira*).

The Gauls call a lot of one hundred (*centum*) feet square in urban areas a *candetum*, as if the word were *centetum*. But in the country they call a proper *candetum* an area of 150 feet square. Now a field containing a stade (*stadialis*) is 125 paces, that is, 625 feet long. Computing its measure times eight makes a Roman mile (*miliarium*), which consists of five thousand feet. 7. Further, a hundred-measure (*centuria*) is a field of two hundred jugers. Among the ancients it took its name from 'a hundred (*centum*) jugers,' but afterwards it was doubled but retained its original name. Although hundred-measures were enlarged in measure, they were not able to change the name.

xvi. Roads (De itineribus) 1. We call our road measures 'miles' (*miliarum*), the Greeks 'stades' (*stadium*), the Gauls 'leagues' (*leuga*), the Egyptians *schoeni*, the

Persians 'parasangs' (*parasanga*). Each has its own distance. 2. A mile is completed in a thousand paces, and is called "mile" (*milliarium*) as if it were 'a thousand-length' (*mille-adium*) having five thousand feet. 3. A league runs 1,500 paces. A stade is an eighth of a mile, taking 125 paces. They say Hercules first established the stade, and fixed it as that distance that he himself could complete in one breath, and accordingly named it 'stade' (*stadium*) because at its end he caught his breath and at the same time 'stood still' (*stare*). 4. A road (*via*) is the place where a vehicle can go, and it is named road from the vehicles (*vehiculum*) riding on it. It holds two lanes (*actus*), to allow for the meeting of vehicles going and coming. 5. Further, every road is either public or private. A public road is one that is on public ground, where a pathway, a lane, is accessible to the people. This pertains either to the sea or to towns. A private road is one that has been given to the neighboring municipality.

6. A street (*strata*) is so called as if 'worn away' (*terere*, ppl. *tritus*) by the feet of the crowd. Lucretius (*On the Nature of Things* 1.315):

> And the street now worn away by the feet of the crowd.

And it is paved, that is 'strewn' (*sternere*, ppl. *stratus*) with stones. The Phoenicians are said to be first to have paved roads with stones; afterwards the Romans spread them through almost the whole world, to make travel direct and to keep the common people from being idle. 7. The crown (*agger*) is the raised middle part of a street paved with stones heaped together (*coaggerare*), and named from 'mound' (*agger*), that is, a 'heaping together' (*coacervatio*). Historians call this a military highway (*via militaris*), as (Vergil, *Aen.* 5.273):

> Just as often a snake, when caught on the crown of the road (*agger viae*).

8. A 'passageway' (*iter* or *itus*) is a road on which people can go (*ire*, ppl. *itus*) in any direction. Now *iter* and *itiner* mean different things. An *iter* is a place easy for 'passing along' (*trans-itus*), whence we also name it *itus*. But an *itiner* is the passage (*itus*) of a long road, as well as the effort of walking to reach where you wish to go. 9. A path (*semita*) is half a passage (*iter*), so called from 'half-road' (*semi-itus*). A path is for humans, but a track is for wild beasts and cattle. 10. A track (*callis*) is a narrow and beaten passageway for cattle among the mountains, named from calluses (*callum*) on the feet, or because it is hardened by the hooves (*callum*) of cattle. Crossways (*trames*) are passageways cutting across (*transversus*) fields, or a straight road so named because it 'passes across' (*transmittere*). 11. Forks (*divortium*) are turnings of roads, that is, roads extending in diverse (*diversus*) directions. Likewise there are side-paths (*diverticulum*), that is, diverging (*diversus*) and dividing (*divisae*) roads, or crossing paths that lead from the side of the main road.

12. A 'junction' (*bivium*) is so named because two roads meet there. A 'crossroads' (*competum*) is so called because several roads meet (*competere*) there, for example a three-way (*trivia*) and a four-way (*quadrivia*) junction. A sidewalk (*ambitus*) is a two-and-a-half-foot space between the buildings of neighbors, left as an easement for the purpose of walking around the building, and so called from 'walking' (*ambulare*). 13. A 'rut' (*orbita*) is the track of a cart, named for the circle (*orbis*) of its wheel. Likewise a 'cart-way' (*actus*) is where cattle are usually driven (*agere*, ppl. *actus*). A 'mountain path' (*clivosum*) is a winding road. 'Footprints' (*vestigium*) are the traces of the feet imprinted by the soles of those who went first, so called because by means of them the paths of those who have gone before are traced (*investigare*), that is, recognized.

Book XVI

Stones and metals (De lapidibus et metallis)

i. Dust and dirt clods (De pulveribus et glebis terrae) 1. Dust (*pulvis*) is so named because it is driven (*pellere*) by the force (*vis*) of the wind, for it is carried on the breath of the wind, neither resisting nor able to stay put, as the Prophet says (Psalm 1:4): "Like the dust, which the wind driveth from the face of the earth." 2. Mud (*limus*) is so named because it is soft (*lenis*). Mire (*caenum*) is a pit of filth. Cinders (*cinis*) are named from burning (*incendium*), for that is how they are made.[1] Ashes (*favilla*), because they are made as a result of fire, for fire is φῶς. 3. A clod (*gleba*) because it is a ball (*globus*), for it is compacted as a clump of dust, and unified into a single ball. Earth, then, that is joined together is a clod, and earth that is separated is dust. 4. *Labina* is named by derivation from 'falling' (*labes*) because it causes people to fall as they are walking. Some think that filth (*lutum*) is named using antiphrasis, because it is not clean, for everything that has been washed (*lavare*, ppl. *lotus*) is clean. 5. Wallowing-places (*volutabrum*) are named because swine wallow (*volutare*) there. 'Marshy ground' (*uligo*) is a muck consisting of mud and water. *Sabulum* (i.e. a small coarse sand) is the lightest type of earth.

6. 'White clay' (*argilla*) is named from the Argives, who were the first to make vases from it. 'Cretan earth' (*Creta*, i.e. white potter's clay) is named from Crete, where the better sort is found. *Cimolia* is white Cretan earth, named after the Italian island Cimea; one kind softens the precious colors of clothing and brightens cloth that has been darkened by sulfur, and another kind gives brightness to gemstones. 'Silver' Cretan earth (*Creta argentaria*, "silversmith's whiting"), actually white, is so named because it restores the luster of silver. 7. 'Samian earth' (*terra Samia*) is named after the island of Samos; it is glutinous and white and soft on the tongue, indispensable for medicines and for making containers. 8. 'Puteolan dust' (*pulvis Puteolanus*, i.e. "pozzolana") is collected in the hills near Puteoli in Italy and is positioned so as to restrain the sea and break the waves. When it is submerged in water, it immediately turns into stone and, made stronger by the daily waves, is turned into rock, just as white clay is turned to stone by fire.

9. Sulfur (*sulphur*) is so named because it is kindled with fire, for πῦρ is "fire." Thus its force can be felt even in boiling water, and no other material is ignited more easily. It originates between Sicily and Italy in the Aeolian islands, which people say are on fire. It is also found by excavation in other places. 10. There are four kinds of sulfur. The 'living' kind, which is dug up, is translucent and green; physicians use it alone of all the kinds of sulfur. The second kind, which people call 'lump sulfur' (i.e. fuller's earth), is used only by fullers. The third kind is 'liquid'; it is used for fumigating wool because it gives whiteness and softness.[2] The fourth kind is particularly suitable for preparing lamp-wicks. The power of sulfur is so great that it cures the 'comitial sickness' (see IV.vii.7) through its vapor when it is set on the fire and burns. When a person puts sulfur over hot coals in a goblet of wine and carries it around, he glows with the eerie pallor of a corpse from the reflection of the blaze.

ii. Earthy materials derived from water (De glebis ex aqua) 1. Bitumen (*bitumen*) comes forth in the lake Asphaltites (i.e. the Dead Sea) in Judea; sailors in skiffs collect floating clumps of it as they draw near. In Syria it is a mud that boils up from the earth in various places. Both kinds are compacted and combine into a dense mass, and the Greeks call both πισσάσφαλτος (i.e. a compound of asphalt and pitch). Its nature is burning and related to fire, and it cannot be split by water or iron, but only by female impurities (i.e. menses; see XI.i.141). It is useful for caulking ships. 2. Alum (*alumen*) is named from 'light' (*lumen*), because it furnishes brightness to

1 Throughout this book Isidore makes note of the various earthy minerals' relationship to the four elements, especially fire and water.

2 Fumes of sulphur were used to bleach wool, part of the process of preparing it, according to R. J. Forbes, *Studies in Ancient Technology* (Leiden, 1964).

cloth being dyed. It is a salt-like substance of the earth, and is made during the winter from water and mud, and matured by the summer sun. There are two forms of alum: liquid and condensed.

3. Some people think that salt (*sal*) is so named because it springs out (*exsilire*) when cast into fire, for it flees the fire although it is fiery, but this is according to its nature, since fire and water are always hostile to each other. Others think that salt is named from the ocean (*salum*) and the sun (*sol*), since it is generated spontaneously by seawater as foam deposited on the edges of the seashore or cliffs and evaporated by the sun. There are also lakes and rivers and wells from which it is drawn. From there it is heaped up in salt pits, and dried by the sun; but rivers are also thickened into salt, when the rest of the water flows under the ice.[3] Elsewhere it is collected by removing sand on nights when the moon is waxing; for in Cyrene, rock salt (*[h]ammoniacus*) is found beneath the sand. There are even mountains of natural salt, where it may be mined with tools, like minerals, and reappears in still greater quantity. In some places it is so hard that people make walls and houses out of masses of salt, as in Arabia. 4. Various salts also differ in their natural properties, for in one place it is mild, in another excessively salty. Common salt crackles in fire; Tragasean salt does not crackle in fire or leap out; Agrigentian salt from Sicily, although enduring flame, leaps out of water, and, contrary to nature, flows when it is in the fire. 5. There are also differences in color. Memphis salt is red; in the part of Sicily near Etna it is purple, while in that same Sicily, in Pachynum, it is so bright and glistening that it casts reflections; in Cappadocia saffron-colored salt is mined. 6. Salt (*sal*) by its nature is necessary for all food. It gives savor to relishes, it excites hunger, and it arouses an appetite for all foods. Indeed all enjoyment of food and the greatest cheerfulness comes from salt. Hence health (*salus*) is thought to take its name, for nothing is better for us than salt (*sal*) and sun – in fact, we see that the bodies of sailors are well-hardened. And even livestock, flocks, and beasts of burden are called to pasture particularly with salt, and are more productive of milk and more obliging at giving cheese. Salt tightens bodies; it dries and binds them. It preserves corpses from falling into putrefaction so that they last.

7. Natron (*nitrum*) takes its name from a place, for it is found in Nitria, a town or region of Egypt; from this material medicines are made and dirty clothes and bodies are washed. Its nature is not so different from salt, for it has the strength of salt and similarly occurs at shorelines that grow white as they dry out. 8. The Greek term *aphronitrum* is 'foam of natron,' *spuma nitri* in Latin. Concerning this a certain poet says (Martial, *Epigrams* 14.58):

> Are you a bumpkin? You don't know what my Greek name is. I am called 'foam of natron.' Are you Greek? It is *aphronitrum.*

It is gathered in Asia where it distills in caves; from there it is dried in the sun. It is thought to be best if it has as little weight and is as easily crumbled as possible, and is almost purple in color. 9. *Chalcantum* is named because it is the thyme (*thymum*, cf. ἄνθος, "bloom"), that is, the 'bloom,' of 'copper pyrites' (*chalcitis*), whence among Latin speakers it is called 'copper bloom.' It is made now in many regions: at one time, in Spain, it was made in wells or pools having that kind of water, which they boiled down and poured into wooden vats, hanging over them cords kept taut with stones. A mud-like substance would adhere to the cords in the form of glassy berries, and thus precipitated it would be dried for thirty days. 10. But it is now produced elsewhere in caves, because, having collected as a liquid, it drips down there and solidifies into 'grape clusters.' It also occurs in hollow trenches, from whose sides the hanging drops coalesce; it is also made, like salt, under the most blazing sun. Its power is so concentrated that, when sprinkled into the mouths of lions and bears, they are unable to bite because of its astringent force.

iii. Common stones (De lapidus vulgaribus) 1. A 'stone' is generally differentiated from an 'earth' inasmuch as it is denser. And it is called stone (*lapis*) because it hurts (*laedere*) the foot (*pes*). Stones are smooth and dispersed; while rocks (*saxum*) cling together and are split from the mountains. *Petra* (i.e. another word for 'rock') is a Greek word. Flint (*silex*) is a hard stone, so named because fire is said to leap out (*exsilire*) from it. 2. A crag (*scopulus*) of projecting rock is so called as if from 'looking out' (*speculari*), or from the sheltering of ships,

3 Isidore's source, Pliny, *Natural History* 31.75, says that the surface of the river condenses into salt, with the rest of the river flowing "as if under ice."

from the term σκέπειν ("to shelter"). The Greek word σπήλαιον is 'cave,' *spelunca* in Latin. It is a hollow place in a cliff. 3. *Crepido* (i.e. a projection, promontory) is a broken-off extremity of rock, whence a height of sheer rock is called *crepido*, as in (Vergil, *Aen.* 10.361):

Foot (*pes*) presses close against foot.[4]

Cautes are sharp rocks in the sea, named from the need to be wary of them, as if they were 'watched out for' (*cautus*). A *murex* (i.e. a pointed rock, lit. a prickly shellfish) is a rock on the shore similar to the living *murex*; they are extremely sharp and dangerous for ships. 4. An *icon* is a rock that, by capturing the sound of the human voice, imitates the words of someone speaking.[5] It is *icon* in Greek and 'image' (*imago*) in Latin, because an image of someone else's speech is produced in response to one's voice. However, this may also be the effect of the nature of some locales, especially valleys.

5. A pebble is a small stone mingled with the earth, round and very hard, and very smooth due to its complete purity. And it is called 'pebble' (*calculus*) because it is 'trod on' (*calcare*) without giving any trouble due to its small size. Its opposite is the *scrupus*, a small sharp stone that causes injury and troubles the mind if it should fall into one's shoe. For this reason we call something that is a trouble to the mind a 'scruple' (*scrupulus*); hence also 'pointed' (*scrupeus*) stones, that is, sharp ones. 6. The whetstone (*cos*, gen. *cotis*; lit. "sharp rock" a variant form of *cautes* above) takes its name because it sharpens (*acuere*) a blade for cutting, for in the Greek language 'cutting' is called *cotis*.[6] Some whetstones require water for sharpening and others oil, but oil makes the edge smooth, while water renders it extremely sharp. 7. Pumice (*pumex*) is so named because it has solidified with the density of foam (*spuma*), and it is dry, with little luster, and possessing so great a quality of cooling that when it is placed in a vat new wine stops bubbling.

8. Workmen call stones that are crushed and mixed with limestone *rudus*. These stones are poured out in making pavement, whence also rubble (*rudera*, plural of *rudus*) is so called. 9. Gypsum (*gypsum*) is related to limestone; it is a Greek term (i.e. γύψος). There are many varieties, and the best of all is from *specularis lapis* (i.e. a kind of transparent stone). It is most pleasing for the molded figures and cornices of buildings. 10. Limestone (*calx*) is said to be alive, because even when it has become cold to the touch it still retains some fire concealed inside, so that when water is poured on it the hidden fire bursts forth. It has this marvelous characteristic: once it has been set on fire, it burns in water, which usually extinguishes fire, and it is extinguished in oil, which usually kindles fire. Its use is essential in the practice of architecture, for one stone does not cling firmly to another unless they are joined by limestone. Limestone from hard white stone is better for construction; from soft stone it is better for plastering. 11. Sand (*arena*, i.e. *harena*) is named from 'dryness' (*ariditas*), not from 'cementing' (*adhaerere*) building materials, as some people would have it. The test of its quality is if it grates when squeezed in one's hand, or if it leaves behind no stain when sprinkled on white cloth.

iv. More important stones (De lapidus insignioribus)

1. The magnet (*magnes*) is a stone of India, named after its discoverer, for it was first found in India, clinging to the nails of his sandals and the point of his staff, when a certain Magnes was grazing his herds. Afterwards it was found in various places. Its color is like iron, but it is identified by test when, set next to iron, it grabs the iron. It clings to iron so firmly that it will make a chain of finger-rings; for this reason common people call it 'living iron.' 2. It is also believed to attract molten glass as it does iron. Its force is so great that the most blessed Augustine reports (*City of God* 21.4) that someone held this magnetic stone beneath a silver dish, and then placed a piece of iron on the silver, and then, by moving the magnetic stone underneath with his hand, immediately moved the iron above. Hence it happens that in a certain temple an iron cult-statue seems to hang in the air. There is another magnet stone in Ethiopia that repels and rejects all iron. The deeper blue a magnet stone, the better it is.

3. Jet (*gagates*) is a stone first discovered in Sicily, cast out from the waters of the river Gagas, whence it is named, although it is more plentiful in Britain. It is black, flat, and smooth, and burns when moved near to a flame. The inscriptions it makes on earthenware are indelible. It drives away snakes when it is burned. It

4 Isidore's definition of *crepido* is drawn from Servius's comment on *Aen.* 10.653, which contains the words *crepidine saxi*. In his comment Servius also discusses, in another connection, *Aen.* 10.361. Isidore by mistake quotes the latter verse instead of the former.

5 Pliny, the source of much of Isidore's discussion of minerals, speaks of this rock as *echo*, not *icon*.

6 The word *cotis* appears to be a scribal corruption, probably of κοπή, cutting.

reveals those who are possessed by demons, and it signals the presence of virginity, and, amazingly, it is set alight by water and extinguished by oil. 4. *Asbestos*[7] is a stone from Arcadia, the color of iron; it was assigned its name from 'fire' because once set alight it is never extinguished. From this stone human art constructed a certain device that pagans, deceived by sacrilege, would marvel at. In short, there was a shrine of Venus in a certain temple precinct, and there was a candelabrum there with a lamp upon it burning in the open air in such a way that no storm or tempest could extinguish it. 5. Pyrite (*pyrites*) is a yellow Persian stone that mimics the qualities of bronze; it has a great deal of fire in it inasmuch as it gives off sparks easily. It burns the hand of anyone holding it if he squeezes it tightly. For this reason it takes its name from 'fire' (cf. πῦρ). There is another, common, pyrite, which people call 'living stone.' It gives off sparks when struck by iron or by stone. These sparks may be caught by sulfur or various fungi or leaves, and it starts a fire quicker than one can speak. Common people call this the 'hearth rock.'

6. Selenite (*selenites*) is translated into Latin as 'lunar stone,' because people say its interior glow waxes and wanes with the moon (cf. σελήνη, 'moon'). It comes from Persia. 7. *Dionysius* is a dark stone speckled with red spots. It is named thus because if it is ground and mixed with water it smells like wine, and, what is marvelous about it, it fights off drunkenness. 8. *Thracius* is black and resonant; it originates in the river in Equitia whose name is Pontus. 9. The stone *Phrygius* takes its name from the place, for it originates in Phrygia. It has a pale color and is moderately heavy. It has a porous composition. After having first been drenched with wine and blown on with bellows, it is burned until it turns red and is extinguished again with sweet wine three times in succession. It is only useful for dying cloth. 10. *Syrius* stone is named after Syria, where it is found. It is said to be buoyant when it is whole, and to sink when it is broken up.

11. *Arabicus* is similar to ivory without any marks. When rubbed on a whetstone it gives off a liquid of a saffron color. 12. The *Iudaicus* stone is white and shaped like an acorn; it has evenly-spaced lines, one under the next, that the Greeks call γραμμή ("line"). 13. The stone *Samius* is named after the island Samos where it is found; it is heavy and white, and useful for polishing gold. 14. *Memphitis* is named from a place in Egypt (i.e. Memphis); it has the nature of a gem. When ground and mixed with vinegar and smeared on those parts of the body that have to be burned or cut it makes them so numb that they do not feel pain. 15. *Sarcophagus* stone is so named because within forty days it consumes the body of a deceased person placed in it, for σορός in Greek means "funerary ark" and φαγεῖν is "to eat" (see VIII.xi.85 and cf. XV.xi.2). It originates in the region of Troy, and is easily split along a line of cleavage. In the East there are rocks of the same kind, which eat away the body when bound even to living people. 16. Haematite (*haematites*), gentler in that it preserves rather than corrodes the body, is so named because when ground by a whetstone it turns the color of blood (cf. αἷμα, 'blood'). It is otherwise a dark bluish color; also purplish. It comes from the far reaches of Egypt, from Babylonia, and from Spain.

17. *Androdamantus* is black in color, noted for its heaviness and hardness, whence it takes its name (cf. ἄνδρας δαμάζειν, "subdue men"; ἀδάμας, "adamant"). It is chiefly found in Africa. It is said to attract silver and bronze to itself, and, like haematite, it turns the color of blood when ground up. 18. *Schistos* is found in the far reaches of Spain; it is similar to saffron in color, with a light gleam, and is easily broken. 19. *Amiantos* (i.e. asbestos) was so named by the ancients because, if cloth was made from it, the cloth resisted fire, and even when placed in the fire did not burn, but acquired a radiant glow. It is similar to split alum, resistant to all poisons, especially those of magicians. 20. *Batrachites* is easily split into layers, like a shell. *Galactites* is ashy in color and pleasant to the taste; it is so named because when a certain kind is ground up it emits a milky substance (cf. γάλα, gen. γάλακτος, "milk"). 21. Obsidian (*opsius*) is a black translucent stone with a resemblance to glass. It is used as mirrors on walls, to reflect shadowy images. Many people make gems from it. It originates in India and in Samnium in Italy. *Mithridax* is a stone from the Euphrates that sparkles with various colors when struck by the sun.

22. *Aetites* are stones found in the nests of eagles (cf. ἀετός, 'eagle'). People say that two kinds are found, male and female, and that eagles do not reproduce without them. The masculine is hard, like the gall-nut, and ruddy, while the feminine is small and soft. When these stones

7 *Asbestos* here is not the mineral we call asbestos (see section 19 below). The Greek term ἄσβεστος means "unquenchable."

are joined together they speed the birth process, and even on some occasions remove part of the womb, unless they are quickly taken away from those giving birth. 23. *Phengites* is a Cappadocian stone, hard like marble, white and translucent. A temple was once built out of it by a certain king; it had golden doors and when they were closed it was as bright as day inside. 24. *Chemites* is similar to ivory. They say Darius was buried in it; it is like Parian marble in whiteness and hardness, but much less heavy. It is termed *porus* ("tufa"). 25. *Ostracites* is so called because it resembles a potsherd (cf. ὄστρακον, "potsherd"); it is used in place of pumice. 26. The stone *melanites* is so called because it exudes a sweet honeyed (*melleus*) fluid. 27. The stone emery (*smyris*) is rough and impervious and abrades everything; gems are ground with this stone. 28. *Chrysites*, similar to ocher in color, is found in Egypt. 29. *Hammites* is similar to natron, but harder; it originates in Egypt and in Arabia.

30. *Thyites* comes from Ethiopia; it is greenish, but milky when ground, and extremely biting. 31. *Coranus* is white and harder than Parian marble. 32. *Molotius*, greenish and heavy, is found in Egypt. 33. *Tusculanus*, named for the place in Italy, is said to be shattered by fire. 34. *Sabinus*, which is dark, becomes bright when oil is added to it, according to report. There is also a certain green Sabinus stone extremely resistant to fire. 35. *Siphnius* is soft and white. When heated with oil it turns black and grows hard. 36. Stones may also be suitable for physicians' mortars and for pigments; *etesius* especially, and then *chalazius*, but *thebaicus* and *basanites* are stones that yield nothing of themselves. 37. Transparent stone (*specularis*, i.e. used for windows) is so named because it is translucent like glass. It was first discovered in the nearer part of Spain, around the city of Segorbe. It is found underground and is cut once it is dug out, and split into as fine a sheet as you like.

v. Marble (De marmoribus) 1. After the types of stones we shall come to marble. There is a difference between stone and marble; exceptional stones that are prized for their markings and colors are called 'marble.' Marble (*marmor*) is a Greek word (i.e. μάρμαρος, and cf. μαρμαίρειν, "gleam, sparkle") so named from 'greenness,' and although the other colors were discovered later, people continued to use the original name from the idea of greenness. 2. The colors and kinds of marble are beyond counting. Not all are quarried from rock, but many are scattered beneath the ground, including the most precious kinds, such as green Lacedaemonian, the most delightful of all, first discovered by the Lacedaemonians; hence its name. 3. Ophite (*ophites*) has markings similar to a snake's, whence it takes its name (cf. ὄφις, "snake"). Two kinds occur: a soft white kind and a hard black kind. 4. Augustean and Tiberian marble were first found in Egypt during the reigns of Augustus and of Tiberius. They are different from ophite in that ophite, as we said above, has markings like a snake, while these have markings combined in a different way – for Augustean markings are undulating and curled into whorls, while Tiberian are of gray that is spotty and not swirled.

5. Porphyry (*porphyrites*) in Egypt is reddish with scattered white spots. The reason for its name is that it is red, like the color of shell-fish dye (*purpura*; cf. πορφύρεος, "purple"). 6. *Basanites* has the color and hardness of iron, whence this name is given to it (cf. βάσανος, "touchstone"). It is found in Egypt and Ethiopia. 7. *Alabastrites* is a white stone, tinted here and there with various colors.[8] The ointment box spoken of by the Evangelist himself was made out of *alabastrites* (Luke 7:37), for people hollow out this stone for ointment vessels because it is said to be the best material for preserving ointments unspoiled. It originates around Thebes in Egypt and Damascus in Syria, but the kind whiter than the others and most commended comes from India. 8. Parian marble, also called *lygdinus*, is exceptionally white. It originates on the island Paros, whence it is called Parian. Its size is no larger than that of plates and wine bowls, and it is well suited for unguents. 9. *Coralliticus* is found in Asia, measuring not more than two cubits, close to ivory in its whiteness and a certain similar appearance. On the other hand, *alabandicus* is black, and is called by the name of its land. It is purplish in appearance. In the East this stone is melted by fire and cast to function like glass.

10. *Thebaicus* marble, spotted with golden drops, is found in a region assigned to Egypt. It is suited by a kind of natural utility to be used for small mortars for the grinding of eye-salves. 11. *Syenites* originates around Syene or Thebes. Kings made building beams from it. 12. There are also marbles that originate in quarries and cliffs. Among these, Thasian is distinguished by its spots

8 *Alabastrites* is not the more common modern alabaster, a form of gypsum (calcium sulfate), but a carbonate of lime.

of various colors; it was first used on the Cyclades islands. 13. Lesbian marble is slightly more bluish than Thasian, but also has spots of various colors. 14. Corinthian is similar to drops of ammoniac gum with a variety of different colors. It was first found in Corinth. Huge columns and lintels and beams are made from it. 15. Carystean marble is green, and excellent. It takes its name from its appearance, because it is soothing (*gratus*; perhaps cf. χάρις, "grace") to gem-carvers since its color refreshes the eye.

16. Numidia exports Numidian marble. At its surface it releases a moisture colored like saffron, whence it takes its name (perhaps cf. νυμφαία, "yellow water-lily"; νύμφη, "water"). It is fit for use as blocks and lintels, but not for inlaid panels. 17. Lucullean marble comes from the island of Melos. The consul Lucullus, who was delighted with it and first brought it to Rome, provided it its name. It is almost the only marble to take its name from an admirer. 18. There is also a marble called *Lunensis.* (i.e. Carrara marble). *Tephrias* is named from the color of ashes (cf. τέφρα, "ashes"). This stone is praised as a protection against serpents when it is worn bound on. 19. Ivory (*ebur*) is named after the *barrus*, that is, the elephant. Horace (*Epodes* 12.1) says:

> Woman most deserving of black elephants (*barrus*),
> what do you want?

vi. Gems (De gemmis) 1. After the types of marble, we proceed to gems. They add great beauty to gold with their loveliness of color. Their origins are in the Caucasian cliffs. Legend claims that Prometheus first enclosed a piece of gemstone in iron and encircled his finger with it; from these beginnings rings and gemstones originated. 2. There are said to be innumerable kinds of gems. Of these we have noted only the principal or most famous ones. Gems (*gemma*) are so called because they are translucent like resin (*gummi*). They are called precious stones because they are valued dearly, or because they can be distinguished from base stones, or because they are rare – for everything that is rare is called great and precious, as may be read in the book of Samuel (cf. I Kings 3:1 Vulgate): "And the word of the Lord was precious in Israel"; that is, it was rare.

vii. Green gems (De viridioribus gemmis) 1. Of all green gems, the *smaragdus* (i.e. emeralds, etc.) holds preeminence. The ancients assigned it third place in value after the pearl and the *unio* (i.e. a type of pearl, see x.1 below). The *smaragdus* is named from its extreme greenness, for everything that is very green is called 'bitter' (*amarus*). No gem or plant possesses greater intensity than the *smaragdus*; it exceeds green plants and leaves and imbues the reflected air around it with greenness. Nothing is more soothing to the eyes of gem cutters than this refreshing green. If its surface is broad, it reflects images like a mirror. Indeed the Emperor Nero used to watch gladiator matches using a *smaragdus*. 2. There are twelve kinds of *smaragdus*: the Scythian *smaragdus*, found among the Scythian people, is the noblest. The Bactrian *smaragdus* holds second place; they are gathered in seams of rock when the north wind blows, for at that time they glitter in the ground, which is uncovered because the sands are shifted a great deal by these winds. Egyptian *smaragdi* hold third place. The rest are found in copper mines, but they are flawed, for they have markings like bronze or lead or hair-line streaks or salt. *Smaragdi* improve with undiluted wine and green oil, however much they have been naturally stained.

3. *Chalcosmaragdos* is so named because it is green and mottled with copper veins (cf. χαλκός, "copper"). It originates in Egypt and the island of Cyprus. 4. *Prasius* is named for its green color (cf. πρασώδης, "leek-green"), but it is a base stone. Another variety of it is marred by blood-like spots. A third variety is distinguished by its three white lines. 5. Beryl (*beryllus*) originates in India, deriving its name from the language of the people of India. It is similar to a *smaragdus* in its greenness, but with a pale color. The Indians cut it into hexagonal shapes, so that its dull color is enhanced by the reflections of the faces; if cut in another way, it has no gleam. There are nine varieties. 6. *Chrysoberyllus* is so named because its pale greenness glitters with a golden gleam (cf. χρύσεος, "golden"). India is also the source for this gem. 7. Chrysoprase (*Chrysoprasus*) is an Indian stone, with a color . . . recalling that of the sap of a leek, with intervening gold spots, whence it took its name (cf. χρυσός, "gold"; πράσον, "leek").[9] Some people have considered it as a type of beryl.

8. Jasper (*iaspis*) is translated from the Greek into Latin as "green gem," for *ias* means "green" and *pinasin*

9 A lacuna here in the early manuscripts may be filled with the reading of the source in Pliny: "with a rather yellow-green color, recalling that of the sap of a leek."

means "gem."[10] It is somewhat like a *smaragdus*, but with a dull color. There are seventeen varieties. Some people think the gemstone jasper provides good fortune and protection to pregnant women – but this belief belongs not to faith but to superstition. 9. *Topazion* is one of the green kinds of gem, and glitters with all colors. It was first found in an island of Arabia, where Troglodyte bandits, worn out by hunger and storms, unearthed it when they dug out the roots of plants. When it was sought afterward, this island was covered with clouds, but was finally found by sailors. It is from this that both place (i.e. the island Topazus in the Red Sea) and gem took their name; for in the Troglodyte language τοπάζειν has the meaning "seek" (cf. Greek τοπάζειν, "seek"). This is the most abundant gemstone; it alone of the precious stones is subjected to the polishing file. There are two kinds. 10. *Callaica* is green in color, but pale and exceedingly cloudy. Nothing more pleasantly beautifies (cf. κάλλος, "beauty") gold, whence it is named. It originates in India and Germany in icy cliffs, and it sticks out like eyes.

11. Malachite (*molochites*), more densely green and duller than a *smaragdus*, takes its name from the color of the mallow (*malva*), and is valued for the seals it makes. It originates in Arabia. 12. Heliotrope (*heliotropia*) is green in color and cloudy; it is strewn with reddish stars and has blood-colored veins. The reason for this stone's name is from its effect, for when it is thrown into a bronze basin it changes the rays of the sun with a blood-colored reflection (cf. ἥλιος, "sun"; τροπή, "change"), but when out of the water it receives sunlight like a mirror, and reveals an eclipse of the sun by showing the advancing moon. This stone also provides a most blatant example of the shamelessness of magicians, because they claim that someone carrying an herb blended with a heliotrope, once certain spells have been cast, cannot be seen. It originates in Cyprus and Africa, but the better heliotrope is from Ethiopia.

13. *Sagda* is a gem with a leek-green color, found among the Chaldeans. It has such power that from the ocean depths it seeks passing ships, and clings so tenaciously to the hulls that it can hardly be removed without scraping away part of the wood. 14. *Myrrhites* is so named because it has the color of myrrh. When it is compressed until it becomes warm it exudes the sweet smell of nard. *Aromatitis* is found in Arabia and Egypt; it has the color and scent of myrrh, whence it takes its name (cf. *aroma*, "spice"). 15. *Melichros* is two-colored; one part being green and the other like honey (*mel*). 16. *Choaspitis* is named from a Persian river (i.e. the Choaspes, present-day Karkheh) and has a greenish-gold gleam.

viii. Red gems (De rubris gemmis) 1. Coral is formed in the sea and has a branching shape. It has a greenish color, but is mostly red. Its 'berries' are white and soft while underwater; once they are taken out they immediately harden and turn red, and quickly become stone-like to the touch. Coral is usually caught and pulled out in nets, or cut out with a sharp (*acer*) knife, whence it is called 'coral' (*corallius*; cf. κοῦρος, "loppings"). Coral is as priceless in India as Indian pearls are among us here. Magicians claim that coral can repel lightning, if this may be believed. 2. Carnelian (*sardius*) is so named because it was first found by the Sardinians. It has a red color superior to marble, but among gems it is quite base. There are five kinds of carnelian. 3. Onyx (*onyx*) is so named because it possesses a white layer mixed in it that is similar to the human nail. For the Greeks call the nail ὄνυξ. India and Arabia produce these gems, but the two types are distinct from each other, for Indian onyx has sparkles in white encircling bands, while Arabian onyx is black with white bands. There are five kinds of onyx.

4. *Sardonyx* is so called from a combination of two names, from the luster of onyx and from carnelian (*sardius*). It consists of three colors; the base is black, the middle is white and the upper layer is cinnabar-red. Only this stone removes none of the wax when making a seal. It is found in India and Arabia when it is uncovered by rushing water. There are five kinds of *sardonyx*. 5. Haematite (*haematites*) is blood-red, and is so called for that reason, since the word αἷμα means "blood." The chief type occurs in Ethiopia, but is also found in Arabia and in Africa. In regard to haematite magicians make some promise about its revealing any ambushes of the barbarians.

6. Amber (*sucinus*), which the Greeks call ἤλεκτρον, has the color of tawny wax, and is said to be the sap (*sucus*) of trees, and for the reason is called 'amber.' An explanation taken from myth has led it to being called *electrum*, for the story goes that when Phaethon was killed by a bolt of lightning, his sisters, in their grief, were turned into poplar trees, and they exude amber

10 In fact the Greek word for the stone, ἴασπις, is itself a borrowing from a Semitic language and not a compound.

(*electrum*) as tears, year in and out, by the river Eridanus (i.e. the Po); and it is called *electrum* because many poets said the sun used to be called *Elector* (the 'Shining One'). But in fact amber is not the sap of the poplar tree but of the pine tree, for when it is burned it gives off the fragrance of pine pitch. 7. It is formed in the islands of the northern Ocean as pine gum, and is solidified like crystal by the cold or by the passage of time. It is used to make beautiful necklaces that are popular with rural women. But some people call it *harpaga* (lit. "hook") because, once it has received the spirit of heat from being rubbed with the fingers, it attracts leaves and chaff and the fringes of clothing just as a magnet attracts iron. It may be colored in whatever manner you like, for it may be dyed by ox-tongue root and by purple shell-fish dye. 8. The *lyncurius* is so named because it is formed from lynx urine that has hardened with time. Like amber, it is yellow, and it attracts nearby leaves with its spirit.

ix. Purple gems (De purpureis) 1. Among the purple gems Indian amethyst holds the place of honor. Amethyst (*amethystus*) is purple with a violet color mixed in; its brilliance is like that of a rose, and it gently gives out a sort of little flame. Another type of amethyst holds a lower place, down to that of the hyacinth-stone. People assert that the reason for its name is that there is something not entirely fire-like in its purple, but that it possesses rather the color of wine (cf. μέθυ, "wine"). Amethyst is easily carved. There are five kinds. 2. The sapphire (*sapphirus*) is blue with purple, possessing scattered gold flecks; the finest sapphires are found among the Medes, although sapphires are nowhere truly clear. 3. The hyacinth-stone (*iacinthus*, probably a sapphire) is named after the flower called hyacinth. It is found in Ethiopia and has a blue color. The finest hyacinth-stone is neither clear nor dulled with opacity but glows and shines purple from both qualities, although this stone is not consistent in its color. In fair weather it is clear and pleasing, while in cloudy weather it loses its strength and fades before one's eyes. When put into the mouth, it is freezing cold. It is very hard to carve, although it is not completely unworkable for it can be incised and engraved with a diamond.

4. *Iacinthizonta* is from India, and closely resembles the hyacinth-stone. Certain crystals of these, similar to *iacinthus*, are discolored by crisscrossing veins, and from this flaw comes their name (cf. ζώνη, "stripe"). 5. *Amethystizontas* is so named because the sparkle on its surface ranges towards the violet color of amethyst. 6. *Chelidonia* is named after the color of a swallow (cf. χελιδών, "swallow"). There are two kinds: one of them is purple on one side, and the other purple with scattered black spots. 7. *Cyanea* (i.e. a type of lapus lazuli) is a gem from Scythia glittering with a blue sheen, either pure blue, or sometimes varied with flecks of flickering gold. 8. *Rhoditis* is rosy, and takes its name from this quality (cf. ῥόδον, "rose").

x. White gems (De candidis) 1. The pearl is the most excellent of the white gems. People say it is called a pearl (*margarita*) because this kind of stone is found in shellfish from the sea (*mare*), for it consists of a pebble formed in the flesh of a shellfish, like the little stone in the brain of a fish (see section 8 below). It is made from celestial dew, which shellfish absorb at a certain season of the year. A certain pearl is called a *unio*, an apt name because only one (*unus*) is found at a time, never two or more. White pearls are preferable to those that are yellow. Youth, or the reception of morning dew, makes pearls white; old age, or evening air, produces dark ones. 2. The opal (*paederos*) holds second place among the white gems, after the pearl. One may ask of this gem under what color it should be classified, given that its name is applied to other sorts of beauty so frequently that it has become merely a term that promises beauty. 3. *Asterites* is white and contains a light enclosed within it like a star floating about inside. It reflects white rays of sunlight, whence it finds its name (cf. ἀστήρ, "star, flame").

4. *Galactitis* is milky (cf. γάλα, gen. γάλακτος, "milk"); when rubbed it gives off a white fluid tasting of milk. When tied onto nursing women it makes their breasts productive. It is also said to make an infant's mouth water when it is hung around its neck. It becomes liquid in the mouth and obliterates memory. The rivers Nile and Achelous yield this stone. Some people call a *smaragdus* banded with white veins a *galactitis*. 5. *Chalazias* has the shape and whiteness of a hailstone (cf. χάλαζα, "hail"); it is also invincibly hard, like a diamond. Even when placed on the fire it retains its coldness. 6. *Solis* is a white gem, and has this name because it casts its rays in the form of the sun (*sol*) shining round about. 7. Selenite (*selenitis*) is translucent with a whitish honey-like gleam; it contains the image of the moon (cf.

σελήνη, "moon"). People claim that it wanes and waxes on particular days, according to the course of that celestial body. It originates in Persia.

8. *Cinaedia* is found in the brain of a fish with the same name; it is white and oblong. People say that with it they predict calm or storm at sea. 9. Cat's-eye (*Beli oculus*) is white surrounding a black pupil lit from the middle with a golden gleam. Because of its beauty it was dedicated to Belus, king of Assyria, and thus it is named. 10. A white gem is called *epimelas* when it turns black on the surface, whence it takes its name (cf. ἐπί, "upon"; μέλας, "black"). 11. *Exebenus* is lovely and white; goldsmiths use it to polish gold.

xi. Black gems (De nigris) 1. Agate (*achates*) was first found in Sicily, near the river of the same name, and afterwards in many lands. It is black and has in its middle black and white circles, joined together and variegated, like haemitite. With the fumes of agates magicians, if it may be credited, ward off storms and halt the flow of rivers. 2. *Apsyctos* is black and heavy, and marked with red veins. When heated by fire, this stone retains the warmth for seven days. 3. *Aegyptilla*, which is black at the base and blue on the surface, is named after Egypt, where it is found. 4. *Media* is black, and was discovered by the legendary Medea. It has veins the color of bronze. It gives off saffron-colored moisture and has the flavor of wine.

5. *Veientana* is an Italian gemstone, found in Veii (i.e. a city in Etruria). It is black on the surface with glittering white spots mingled in it. *Bariptos* (i.e. *baroptenus*) is black with blood red and white spots. 6. *Mesomelas* is black with a vein of any other color streaking through its middle (cf. μέσος, "in the middle"; μέλας, "black"). The *Veneris crinis* (lit. "hair of Venus") has the blackest sheen, and has the appearance of red hairs in it. 7. *Trichrus*, from Africa, is black, but gives off three liquids; black from the base, blood red from the middle, and yellow from the surface. 8. *Dionysia* is black with mingled red spots. When ground up in water it smells of wine, and its fragrance is thought to ward off drunkenness. *Pyritis*, indeed, is black, but it scorches the fingers when it is rubbed against them.

xii. Varicolored gems (De variis) 1. *Panchrus* is a variegated stone exhibiting almost all the colors, hence its name (cf. πᾶν, "all"; χρώς, "color"). *Olca* (i.e. *oica*), which has a barbarian name, is yellow, black, green and white. 2. *Mithridax* (i.e. *mithrax*) glitters in various colors when it is struck by sunlight. It comes from Persia. *Drosolithus* is a variegated gem. The reason for its name is that if it is placed near the fire it emits something like sweat (cf. δρόσος, "sweat"; λίθος, "stone"). 3. The opal (*opalus*) is embellished by the colors of various gemstones, for it has the rather pale fire of a carbuncle, the sparkling purple of an amethyst, and the glittering green of a *smaragdus*, all glowing together with a certain variegation. It takes its name from the language of its native land (cf. Sanskrit *upala*, "gem"), for only India produces it. 4. *Pontica* stones are named after the Pontus (i.e. the Black Sea), and come in different varieties, at one time glittering with blood red spots, at another with gold spots. Some have stars and some are streaked with long lines of color. 5. *Hexecontalithos* is a multicolored stone of a small size, whence it has taken this name for itself, for it is sprinkled with such a variety of spots that the colors of sixty gemstones are contained in its small orb (cf. ἑξήκοντα, "sixty"; λίθος, "stone"). It occurs in Libya among the Troglodytes. 6. Murra (*murrina*) is found in Parthia, but especially in Carmania. People think that it is a liquid that has been compressed by the heat under the earth, whence it takes its name. Its varieties occur in purple and white, and it has a fiery look, with reflections of colors such as are seen in a rainbow. Crystal is created by the opposite principle, when it is solidified by an extremely strong freezing.

xiii. Crystalline gems (De crystallinis) 1. Crystal (*crystallus*) is glittering and watery in color. It is said to be snow that has hardened to ice over a period of years, whence the Greeks gave it its name (cf. κρύσταλλος, "ice"). It occurs in Asia and Cyprus, and particularly in the northern part of the Alps, where the sun never has its most burning heat, not even in summer. Hence the lengthy and enduring hardness itself produces the specific form that is called 'crystal.' When crystal is placed facing the sun's rays it seizes the flame so that it sets fire to dried fungus or leaves. It is used for cups, although it can handle only cold liquids.

2. The diamond (*adamans*, i.e. *adamas*) is a small unsightly stone from India, possessing a rust-like color and the clarity of crystal. It is never found any larger than a hazelnut. It yields to no substance, neither to iron nor to fire, nor does it ever grow warm, whence it takes

its name, which is translated from Greek as 'unconquerable force' (cf. α- privative + δαμάζειν, "conquer"). But although it is invulnerable to iron and disdainful of fire, it may be split after it has been soaked in warm fresh goat's blood, and thus shattered by many blows from an iron tool. Gem carvers use fragments of diamond for engraving and perforating gemstones. 3. It is so opposed to the magnet that when it is placed near iron it does not allow the iron to be drawn off by the magnet, and if the magnet is moved and grabs the iron, then the diamond seizes it back and carries it off. Like amber, it is said to ward off poison, drive away vain fears, and resist malicious witchery. 4. There are six kinds of diamond.

Chalazias (i.e. *chalazius*) possesses the whiteness and shape of a hailstone (cf. χάλαζα, "hail") and a diamond-like hardness. Even when placed in the fire it retains its coldness. 5. *Ceraunium* has two kinds. One, which comes from Germania, is like a crystal but is transparent blue, and if placed below the open sky it catches the gleam of the stars. The second *ceraunium* occurs in Hispania on the Lusitanian shore. It has the color of reddish bronze, and a quality like fire. These are said to be good against the force of lightning, if we may believe it. It is named *ceraunium* because it is not found anywhere but in a place very close to where a lightning-bolt has struck – for in Greek a lightning-bolt is called κεραυνός. 6. The *iris* crystal is found in Arabia in the Red Sea. It is the color of crystal, with six sides. It is called *iris* (lit. "rainbow") by analogy, for if it is struck by sunlight while indoors it recreates on the walls nearby the shape and colors of the rainbow.

7. *Astrion*, quite close to crystal, is from India, and in its center a star shines with the gleam of a full moon. It takes its name because when held facing the stars it catches their gleam and casts it back (cf. ἀστήρ, "star"). 8. *Electria*, as if the word were *alectoria*, for it is found in the stomachs of poultry (cf. ἀλέκτωρ, "cock"). It has the appearance of a crystal and the size of a bean. Magicians would have it that this stone makes people invulnerable in battle, if we may believe it. 9. *Enhydros* is named from water (cf. ὕδωρ, "water"), for it exudes so much water that you might think there is a gushing fountain closed up in it.

xiv. Fiery gems (De ignitis) 1. Of all the fiery gems, the carbuncle (*carbunculus*) holds the principal rank. It is called 'carbuncle' because it is fiery, like a coal (*carbo*), and its gleam is not overcome by the night, for it gives so much light in the darkness that it casts its flames up to the eye. There are twelve kinds, but the most outstanding are those that seem to glow, as if giving off fire. The carbuncle is called ἄνθραξ ("charcoal, carbuncle") in Greek. It occurs in Libya where the Troglodytes live. 2. *Anthracitis* is so named because it has a fiery color, like the carbuncle, but is circled with white veins. A characteristic of *anthracitis* is that when thrown into the fire it loses its luster as if it were lifeless, while, on the contrary, it begins to glow when doused in water. 3. *Sandasirus* occurs in India, at a place with the same name. Gold drops appear to sparkle inside it as if in a transparent flame. It is generally agreed that the greater number of starts, the higher the value. 4. *Lychnis* belongs to this class of fiery gems, and is so named from the glowing of lamps (cf. λύχνος, "lamp"). It occurs in many places, but the most admired variety is found in India. Some people have called it a weaker carbuncle. It has two forms: one that glows purple and another that glows with the redness of scarlet. When heated by the sun or rubbed with the fingers, it is said to draw chaff and scraps of paper to itself. It is resistant to carving, and if it ever is carved, when it is pressed into the seal, it retains part of the wax, like the bite of an animal. It comes in four kinds.

5. *Carchedonia* is said to behave as *lychnis* does, although it is much more base than *lychnis*. It originates among the Nasamones in a divine rain, as they report; it is found by its reflection of a full moon. Every kind of *carchedonia* is resistant to carving. 6. *Alabandina* is named after the Alabanda region of Asia. Its color approaches that of the *carchedonia*, but is less intense. 7. *Dracontites* (i.e. *dracontis*) is extracted from the brain of the dragon (*draco*, gen. *draconis*). This does not become a gemstone unless it is cut out of living dragons; hence magicians remove it from sleeping dragons – for bold men search out the caves of dragons, and sprinkle drugged herbs there to put the dragons to sleep, and when the dragons have been lulled to sleep, they cut off their heads and extract the gemstones. The stones are translucent white. The kings of the East in particular glory in the use of these stones. 8. Chrysoprase (*chrysoprasus*) is an Ethiopian stone; light conceals it, but darkness reveals it, for at night it is fiery, and golden during the day. 9. *Phlogites* comes from Persia. It displays something in it like burning flames that do not come out (cf. φλόξ, gen. φλογός "flame"). 10. *Syrtitis* is so named

because it was first discovered on the shores of the Syrtes. In the region of Lucania it has a saffron color, and contains faint stars inside it that shine in cloudy weather. 11. *Hormiscion* is considered among the most pleasing gems, glowing with a fiery gold color that carries a white light with it on the edges.

xv. Golden gems (De aureis) 1. Some kinds of gems are named because they look like metals or like stones. 2. *Chrysopis* appears to be simply gold (cf. χρυσός, "gold"; ὠπή, "appearance"). Chrysolite (*chrysolithus*, i.e. topaz; cf. λίθος "stone") is similar to gold, with a resemblance to the color of the sea. Ethiopia produces this gem. 3. *Chryselectrus* is similar to gold, but tending towards amber (*electrum*) in color. It is pleasing, but only when seen in the morning, and is very greedy for fire; if it should be near a fire it quickly begins to glow. 4. *Chrysolampis* is named from gold and fire (cf. λαμπάς, "torch"), for during the day it is golden, and at night it is fiery. Ethiopia produces this gem. 5. *Ammochrysus* is sand mixed with gold, having tiny cubes partly of gold leaf and partly of dust. It occurs in Persia. 6. *Leucochrysus* has white veins with a golden color coming between. *Melichrysus* is so named because this gem allows light to pass through it as if it were pure honey (*mel*) seen through gold.

7. *Chrysocolla* occurs in India, where ants dig out gold. It is similar to gold and has the nature of a magnet, except that it is also reported to increase (i.e. coagulate) gold, whence also it is named (cf. κολλᾶν, "bond together"). *Argyritis* is similar to silver (cf. ἄργυρος, "silver"), with golden spots. 8. *Androdamas* has the gleam of silver and is nearly a diamond. It always occurs squared off into cubes. Magicians think that its name was assigned because it is said to calm and restrain passions and rages of the soul, if we may believe it (cf. ἀνδροδάμας, "man-taming," and iv.17 above). It is found by the Red Sea. 9. *Chalcitis* is the color of bronze (cf. χαλκός, "copper, bronze"). *Chalcophonos* is black, but when struck with a stone it rings like bronze (cf. φωνή, "sound"). 10. *Balanites* comes in two kinds; one greenish, and one similar to Corinthian bronze, divided in the middle by a vein of flame.

11. *Sideritis* does not differ in appearance from iron. However it is introduced into magical practices, it arouses disagreement. 12. The '*dactylus* of Ida' is from the island of Crete. It is iron-colored. The reason for its name is because it resembles a human thumb (cf. δάκτυλος, "finger"). 13. *Aethiopicus* is the color of iron, and when it is rubbed it exudes a black liquid. 14. *Zmilanthus* (i.e. *zmilampis*) is collected in the channel of the Euphrates and is similar to Proconnesian marble, with a gray color in the middle shining like the pupil of the eye. *Arabica*, named after its native country, is like ivory in appearance. 15. *Hephaestitis* has the property of a mirror in reflecting images, although it makes them reddish. The test of this gem is if, when added to boiling water, it immediately chills it or if, when placed in the sun, it ignites dry material. It originates in Corycus. 16. *Ostracites* is stone-like in color, and harder than a shell (cf. *ostrea*, "oyster"). Another type is similar to agate, except that polishing makes agate shiny. It has such strength of hardness that other gems are carved using its fragments. 17. *Glossopetra* is like the human tongue and took its name for this reason (cf. γλῶσσα, "tongue"; πέτρος, "rock"). It is said to drop from the sky when the moon is waning. Magicians attribute no small amount of power to it, for they suppose that by means of it the moon can be made to move.

18. There are also certain kinds of gemstones that are named from animals: *echites* (cf. *echidna* 'adder') exhibits viperish spots; *carcinias* is the color of a sea crab (*cancer*; cf. καρκίνος, "crab"). 19. *Scorpitis* resembles a scorpion (*scorpio*) in both color and appearance. *Myrmecitis* imitates the appearance of a crawling ant (cf. μύρμηξ, "ant"). *Taos* is similar to a peacock (cf. ταώς, "peacock"); *hieracitis* has the color of a hawk (cf. ἱέραξ, "hawk"); *aetitis*, the color of an eagle (cf. ἀετός, "eagle"); *aegophthalmos* looks like a goat's eye (cf. αἴξ, gen. αἰγός, "goat," ὀφθαλμός, "eye"). 20. *Lycopthalmos* has four colors – it is orange-red and blood-red, and in the middle it surrounds black with white, like the eyes of wolves (cf. λύκος, "wolf"). *Meconites* resembles a poppy (cf. μήκων, "poppy").

21. There are also some gemstones that the pagans use in certain superstitions. 22. They maintain that when *liparea* is burned it is capable of calling all animals. They say that *anancitis* calls out the images of demons during the practice of hydromancy. They claim that with *synochitis* spirits summoned up from below may be controlled. 23. *Chelonitis* is the eye of an Indian turtle. It is a varicolored purple. Magicians imagine that with this placed on the tongue, one may predict the future. 24. *Brontea*, from the head of the turtle, is thought to fall from thunder (cf. βροντή, "thunder") and to counteract

the lightning-bolt. 25. The hyena-stone (*hyaenia*) is found in the eye of that beast, the hyena (*hyaena*). If this stone is placed under a person's tongue, they say he predicts the future. But coral (*corallius*) is also said to guard against storms and hail. 26. *Pontica* is a certain gemstone that is transparently blue. It has reddish stars, and sometimes golden ones as well. People say that they can question demons and drive them away by means of this stone.

27. For certain kinds of gemstone it is very difficult to distinguish the genuine from the false, especially once someone has discovered how to transmute a genuine specimen of one gem into a false specimen of other gems – for example, *sardonyx*, which is made from three gemstones joined together so that they cannot be taken apart. People artificially construct these from various kinds: black, white, and cinnabar-colored. As a substitute for that most precious stone, the *smaragdus*, some people dye glass with skill, and its false greenness deceives the eyes with a certain subtlety, to the point that there is no one who may test it and demonstrate that it is false. It is the same with other matters in one way or another, for there is no mortal life free from deception. 28. All of the gems that are not translucent are called 'blind,' because they are made opaque by their density.

xvi. Glass (De vitro) 1. Glass (*vitrum*) is so called because with its transparency it transmits light to one's sight (*visus*). Anything contained inside other minerals is hidden, but any sort of liquid or visible thing contained in glass is displayed to the outside; although closed up, in a certain way the contents are revealed.

This was the origin of glass: in the part of Syria called Phoenicia there is a swamp bordering on Judea around the base of Mt. Carmel; the river Belus rises from this place and flows over a distance of five miles into the sea near the city Ptolemais, and its sands are cleansed of their impurities by this rushing flood. 2. Report has it that a ship belonging to natron merchants was driven there, and when these merchants went to prepare their meals here and there along the shore, they brought out clumps of natron from the ship, since there weren't any stones to support the cooking vessels. When the sand of the shore mixed with these burning natron clumps, translucent streams of a strange liquid began to flow, and this was the origin of glass. 3. Since invention is ingenious, it did not long remain content with natron alone, but was eager [to embellish] this craft with other mixtures. Thus glass is heated by pieces of light dry wood, and when copper and natron are added with continuous firing so that the copper is melted, lumps of glass are produced. Afterwards, in workshops, the lump is melted again, and one sort of glass is formed by blowing, another turned on a lathe, and another is engraved like silver. Glass is also colored in many ways so that it may imitate hyacinth-stones, sapphires, green stones, and onyx, and the colors of other gems. There is no other material more fit for mirrors or more suitable for painting.

4. The highest esteem is granted to clear glass with its close similarity to crystal, whence glass has replaced the metals silver and gold for drinking vessels. It used to be made in Italy. Throughout Gaul and Spain the softest white sand would be ground with a mortar and pestle, and then mixed with three parts, by weight or measure, of natron, and after being melted it would be poured into another furnace. This lump would be called *ammonitrum* (i.e. *hammonitrum*). When heated again it would become pure, clear glass. 5. The stone obsidian (*obsianus*) is counted as a type of glass. Sometimes it is green and sometimes black, and it is translucent. It looks rather dull and when used as a wall mirror it reflects shadows instead of images. Many people make gems out of it. People say that this stone occurs in India and Italy and in Spain near the Ocean.

6. They claim that under Tiberius Caesar a certain craftsman devised a formula for glass so that it would be flexible and pliable. And when he was brought before Caesar he presented a drinking bowl to him, and Caesar indignantly threw it to the floor. The craftsman picked the drinking bowl up from the floor, where it had been dented as a bronze vessel would be. Then he took a small hammer from his pocket and reshaped the drinking bowl. When he had done this, Caesar said to him, "Does anyone else know this method of making glass?" After the craftsman swore that no one else knew, Caesar ordered him beheaded, lest, if this skill became known, gold would be regarded as mud and the value of all metals would be reduced – and it is true that if glass vessels became unbreakable, they would be better than gold and silver.

xvii. Metals (De metallis) Metal (*metallum*) is named from the Greek word μεταλλᾶν ("search," "seek after other things," seen as derived from μετά "after" and ἄλλα "other things") because its nature is such that wherever one vein has appeared, there is hope for seeking out another in that place. There are seven kinds of metals: gold, silver, copper, electrum, tin, lead, and, what dominates everything, iron.

xviii. Gold (De auro) 1. Gold (*aurum*) is named from 'gleam' (*aura*), that is, from its luster, because it gleams more when the air (*aer*) reflects it. Whence Vergil says (cf. *Aen.* 6.204):

> From which the contrasting gleam (*aura*) of gold (*aurum*) shone through the branches,

that is, the luster of gold, for it is natural for the luster of metal to gleam more when it is reflected with another light. Hence also patrons (*aurarius*) are named; their glittering renown makes others resplendent. 2. *Obryzum* gold (i.e. pure gold) is so called because it shines forth (*obradiare*) lustrously. It has the best color, which the Hebrews call *ophaz* and the Greeks κιρρός ("orange-tawny"). The thinnest sheets of gold are called gold leaf (*brattea*, i.e. *bractea*), from the term βρεμετον,[11] which is onomatopoeic for 'clanging,' or from βρατυν sheets (perhaps cf. βραχεῖν, "clash").

3. Money (*pecunia*) first had its name and actual character from livestock (*pecus*), for coins used to be cut from hides and then embossed. After this, bronze coinage was invented by Saturn, for it was he who devised the stamping and marking of coins. 4. For this reason the public treasury was dedicated to Saturn by the pagans. Others, as mentioned above, named money after livestock, just as beasts of burden (*iumentum*) are named after 'helping' (*iuvare*), for among the ancients every inheritance was called *peculium* from the livestock (*pecus*) of which their entire property consisted. Whence also someone who was rich would be called a *pecuarius* (lit. "cattleman"), but now, *pecuniosus* ("moneyed"). 5. The most ancient people made use of bronze, since gold and silver had not yet been discovered. Bronze (*aes*, gen. *aeris*) money came into use first, then silver, and finally gold followed, but money still retained its name from the metal with which it began (i.e. *aes* continued to mean 'money' as well as 'bronze'). Hence also the public treasury (*aerarium*) was named, because at first only bronze was used, and it alone was hoarded, since gold and silver were not yet coined. Afterwards money might be made of whatever of these metals you chose, but the term *aerarium* remained, from that metal whence money had its origin.

6. 'Treasury' (*thesaurus*) is named after the Greek term θέσις, "positing," that is, "deposit." Thus θέσις means "positing," and the term has combined a Greek with a Latin word, for the element θες means "deposit" in Greek, and Latin supplies *aurum* ("gold"), so that the word *thesaurus* sounds like the combination 'gold deposit.' An *auraria* (i.e. a kind of tax; also a gold mine) takes its name from gold (*aurum*). 7. But tribute (*tributa*) is named because earlier it used to be exacted from each of the tribes (*tribus*), just as now it is exacted from each of the territories. The Roman people were divided into three (*tres*) groups so that those who were preeminent in each group were called 'tribunes' (*tribunus*), whence they also named the payments that the people gave 'tributes.' 8. A *vectigal* (i.e. a type of tax) is a tribute, named from 'conveying' (*vehere*, ppl. *vectus*). A stipend (*stipendium*) is named from 'payment that is to be weighed' (*stips pendenda*), for the ancients were accustomed to weigh money out instead of counting it.

Coinage (*moneta*) is so called because it 'gives warning' (*monere*, 3rd person *monet*) lest some fraud be committed with either the metal or the weight. 9. A *nomisma* is a gold, silver, or bronze solidus, and it is called *nomisma* because it is stamped with the names (*nomen*, gen. *nominis*) and images of rulers. The coin was first called by the word ἄργυρος ("silver"), because it was struck mostly from silver (*argentum*). 10. But coins (*nummus*) are now named after Numa, a king of the Romans, who was first among the Latins to emboss them with images and mark them with his own name. 11. Change (*follis*, lit. "leather bellows, money bag") is named from the small sack in which it is kept, that which is contained being named by its container. 12. Three things are necessary in coinage: a metal, a shape, and a weight. If something lacks any of these, it is not coinage.

13. There are three kinds of silver, gold, and bronze: stamped, worked, and unworked. Stamped is the kind found in coins; worked, the kind found in vessels and signets; unworked, the kind found in nuggets – a nugget is also called 'a heavy thing' (*grave*, i.e. a weight). The idea of forming metals in molds came about in this way, when by some chance a forest fire scorched the earth, which

11 The word βρεμετον is unattested elsewhere. Βρατυν is a scribal corruption.

poured out streams of melted ore in some form. 14. This was either bronze or gold. When the metal flowed into the depressions in the ground, it took on the shape in which either the flowing stream or the collecting hollow had formed it. Captivated by the splendor of these objects, people picked up these lumps that had been held fast and saw in them the imprints molded from the ground, and from this realized that metals, when melted, could be made into any shape.

xix. Silver (De argento) 1. The word 'silver' (*argentum*) is not very different from its Greek name, for the Greeks call it ἀργύρος. It possesses this marvelous quality, that, although it is white, when it is rubbed against a body it leaves black lines. 2. Quicksilver (*argentum vivum*) is so called because it etches out the materials onto which it is thrown. This is also classified as a liquid because it flows. It is particularly found in mines or in silver-working furnaces, clinging to the roof in condensed drops, and often even in the oldest excrement of sewers or the slime of wells. It is also made from cinnabar placed on an iron crucible covered with an earthenware lid. When the vessel is sealed, coals are placed around it and thus quicksilver is distilled from cinnabar. Without it neither silver nor bronze can be gilded. 3. It has such great power that if you place a one hundred pound rock on top of a *sextarium* (i.e. about a pint) of quicksilver, it steadfastly sustains the rock. But if, on the other hand, you place a mere gram of gold on top of it, it quickly yields to the gold's light weight by forming a hollow. From this we may understand that it is not the weight of a substance, but rather its nature, to which quicksilver yields. It is best kept in glass vessels, for it eats through other materials. When given in a drink, it causes death due to its weight. 4. The dross of silver is called λιθάργυρος, and we call it the 'froth of silver' (i.e. lead monoxide or litharge). It is made in this way from silver and lead.

xx. Bronze (De aere) 1. Bronze (*aes*, gen. *aeris*) is named from its gleaming in the 'air' (*aer*, gen. *aeris*), just as gold (*aurum*) and silver (*argentum*) are.[12] The ancients used bronze before they used iron. Indeed, at first they would plow the earth with bronze; with bronze weapons they would wage war; and bronze was more prized, while gold and silver were rejected as useless. Now it is the opposite (Lucretius, *On the Nature of Things* 5.1275):

> Bronze is despised and gold has attained the highest honor: thus time in its turning changes the positions of things, and what was prized becomes finally without value.

The use of bronze later spread to statues, vessels, and the construction of buildings. Public proclamations in particular were written on bronze plaques for a permanent record.

2. Cyprian bronze (i.e. copper) was first found on the island of Cyprus, whence it was named. It is made from a bronze-like stone that they call *cadmia*, and it is malleable. If lead is added to it, it turns purple. 3. *Aurichalcum* is so called because it possesses the splendor of gold (*aurum*) and the hardness of bronze. Its name is composed from both the Latin and Greek languages, for the Greeks call bronze χαλκός. Moreover it is made from bronze and a great deal of fire, and it is brought to a gold color by means of additives. 4. Corinthian bronze is a mixture of all metals, which was first mixed accidentally when Corinth was burned after being captured. When Hannibal had captured this city, he gathered all the bronze and gold and silver statues into a single pyre and burned them. Workmen carried this mixture off and made plates. Thus Corinthian vessels were created from all the metals (i.e. gold, silver, and bronze) combined to make a single alloy that was neither one particular metal nor another. Hence even up to the present day things made either of this substance or of an imitation of it are called 'Corinthian bronze' or 'Corinthian vessels." There are three kinds: the first is white and approaches the luster of silver; the second has by nature the yellow of gold itself; the third has an equal mixture of all.

5. *Coronarium* is drawn out from malleable bronze into sheets. Tinted by the bile of bulls, it looks like gold in the garlands (*corona*) of stage-actors, whence it is named. 6. *Pyropus* is named from its fiery color (cf. πῦρ, "fire"). When six grams of gold are added to each ounce of bronze, the thin metal leaf becomes fiery and gives an imitation of flame; for this reason also it is called *pyropus*. 7. Bronze that is called *regularis* (lit. "in ingots") is called 'ductile' (*ductilis*) by other people – all Cyprian bronze is of this kind. 8. Bronze that is 'drawn out' (*producere*) with a hammer is called 'ductile' (*ductilis*) just as, on the other hand, bronze that can only be poured out

12 The word *aes* means either "bronze" or "copper."

(*fundere*, ppl. *fusus*) is called 'cast' (*fusilis*). That which can only be poured out is also called *caldarius* (lit. "suitable for heating"), for it would be broken by a hammer. All bronze that has its flaws diligently purged and heated out by fire is made into *regularis*. 9. Among the types of bronze, Campanian bronze is so named from Campania, that is, the province that is in Italian territory. It is best for all utensils and vessels.

10. Any bronze is cast better when great cold is applied. Bronze rapidly develops a patina unless it is smeared with oil. People say that it is best preserved in liquid pitch. 11. Of all the metals, bronze is the most resounding and has the greatest strength. For this reason, thresholds are bronze, whence in Vergil (*Aen.* 1.449):

> The hinge on the bronze doors screeched.

From bronze come *cadmia* (i.e. zinc oxide) and *chalcitis* (i.e. copper pyrites). The drosses of bronze are *cadmia* and verdigris, and the 'bloom' of bronze (i.e. cuprous oxide). 12. *Cadmia* originates in furnaces from the metals of bronze and silver as a result of the fumes settling above them. Indeed, just as the ore from which bronze is made is called *cadmia*, so it reappears in furnaces and receives its original name. 13. Bronze 'bloom' is made or originates in the casting process, when bronze is remelted and reliquefied, and cold water is poured on top, for the 'bloom' is produced from a sudden condensation, as from spittle. 14. Bronze also generates verdigris: when sheet bronze with twigs is placed over a vessel of very sharp vinegar so that they start dripping, what falls from this into the vinegar is pulverized and passed through a sieve.

xxi. Iron (De ferro) 1. Iron (*ferrum*) is so named because it buries the grain (*far*) of the earth, that is, the seeds of crops. It is also called *chalybs* ("sword," lit. "steel") from the river Chalybs where iron is tempered to have the best edge. Whence the material itself is also loosely called *chalybs* as in (Vergil, *Aen.* 8.446):

> And the wound-inflicting steel (*chalybs*).

2. The use of iron was discovered after that of the other metals. Later this kind of metal was turned into a symbol of opprobrium, for long ago by iron the earth was plowed, but now by iron blood is shed. There is no material whose elements are so intertwined or adhere to each other so densely as iron, whence it has a hardness when it is cold. Iron mines are found almost everywhere, but of all the kinds of iron, the prize is given to Seric (i.e. Chinese) iron. The Seres export this iron along with their cloth and animal skins. Second place goes to Parthian iron – none of the other kinds of iron are tempered to an edge from the pure metal, for a softer alloy is mixed in the others.

3. There are many differences in iron according to the type of its earthy element. The one type is soft, close to lead, and suitable for use in wheels and nails, while another type is breakable and bronze-like, well suited for tilling the earth. Another type is good in short lengths only and for the nails in soldiers' boots, and another is quickly vulnerable to rust. These are all called *strictura* (lit. "a mass of wrought iron," or "an iron bar"), a word not used for other metals, from 'compressing' (*stringere*, ppl. *strictus*), a term aptly applied. There is a great difference in the types of water in which the glowing iron is plunged when it is tempered, such as the waters of Bilbilis and Tirassona in Spain, and Como in Italy. 4. In sharpening iron, the edge is made finer by using oil, whence it is also customary for the more delicate iron implements to be tempered in oil, lest they be hardened by water to the point of fragility. Human blood avenges itself on iron, for it very quickly forms rust on contact.

Magnetic stone has an affinity with iron, for iron alone takes on the power of that stone and retains it for a long time. A certain architect in Alexandria built a temple vault from magnets, so that in it a statue made of iron might seem to hang in the air. Iron that has been in the fire is ruined unless it is hardened by hammering. When it has become red it is not suitable for hammering – not until it begins to get white. Iron smeared with vinegar or alum becomes similar to bronze. 5. The drosses of iron are rust and slag. Rust (*robigo*) is a flaw corroding (*rodere*) iron, or crops, as if the word were *rodigo*, with one letter changed. Also the word verdigris (*aerugo*) is from 'eroding' (*erodere*) – for verdigris is a flaw in iron so called from eroding – not from *aerumentum* ("bronze object"). 6. But slag is the residue and impurity that is heated out in the fire, and it is called slag (*scoria*) because it is 'cast out' (*excutere*) of iron. 7. Iron will be free of rust if it is rubbed with white lead or gypsum or liquid pitch. Also, rust does not damage iron implements if they are smeared with deer marrow or white lead mixed with oil of roses.

xxii. Lead (De plumbo) 1. Lead (*plumbum*) is so called because the depth of the sea was first tested with a ball (*pila*) made of lead. There are two kinds of lead, black lead and white lead (i.e. tin), but white is the better one. It was first discovered in the islands of the Atlantic Ocean. Indeed, it also occurs in Lusitania and Gallicia, where the ground is very sandy and black in color, and heavy. Tiny pebbles (of lead) are mingled with the sand, especially in dried-out river beds: people wash these sands and whatever sinks down they heat in furnaces. Dark heavy pebbles are also found in goldmines when they have been sluiced, and while the gold is being collected these pebbles remain with it. Afterwards, when they have been separated, the pebbles are melted together and resolved into white lead. Hence the weight of lead is the same as that of gold.

2. Black lead is abundant around Cantabria. It originates in two ways: either it comes forth alone from its own vein, or it is produced with silver and is smelted from these mixed veins of ore. The first one to liquefy in furnaces is tin, the second, silver. Whatever remains, when ore is added and smelted again, becomes black lead. 3. India has neither bronze nor lead; it can only trade gemstones and pearls for these metals. We use black lead for pipes and sheet metal. Lead is mined laboriously in Spain and Gaul, while in Britain it is found in the upper crust of the ground.

xxiii. Tin (De stagno) 1. The etymology of *stagnum* (i.e. either tin or a silver–lead alloy) is ἀποχωρίζειν ("to separate"), that is, what separates and divides.[13] It separates metals that have become mixed up and mutually adulterated by fire, and distinguishes bronze and lead from gold and silver. Tin also protects other metals from fire, and even though the nature of bronze and of iron is very hard, if they were without tin they would be burned and consumed. 2. A coating of tin on bronze vessels makes the taste more pleasing and discourages the contamination of verdigris. Mirrors are also tempered with tin. White lead may be made from it as from lead.

xxiv. Electrum (De electro) 1. Electrum (*electrum*) is so named because it reflects in the sun's ray more clearly than silver or gold; for the sun is called *Elector* ("the Shining One") by poets. This metal is more refined than all the other metals. 2. There are three kinds. The first kind, which flows from pine branches (i.e. amber, the primary meaning of *electrum*), is called 'liquid *electrum*.' The second, which is found naturally and held in esteem, is 'metallic electrum.' The third kind is made from three parts gold and one part silver. You will find these same proportions if you melt natural electrum, for there is no difference between natural electrum and manufactured; both have the same nature. 3. Electrum that is natural has a character such that at a banquet it gleams even more brightly by lamplight than all the other metals. It also reveals poison, for if you pour some poison into a vessel made from it, it makes a harsh noise and gives off a variety of colors like a rainbow.

xxv. Weights (De ponderibus) 1. It is helpful to know about weights and measures, for all bodies, as has been written, are disposed and formed from the highest to the lowest with measure and number and weight (see Wisdom 11:21). Nature has given weight to all corporeal objects, and "each object is ruled by its own weight" (*Poem about Weights and Measures* [anon.], 3). 2. First Moses, [who preceded all of the pagan philosophers chronologically, recorded for us numbers and measures and weights in diverse places in his writing]. The Argive Phidon first established the system of weights in Greece, and although there were others more ancient than he, he was more active in this art. 3. A weight (*pondus*) is so called because it hangs (*pendere*) balanced in the scales, hence also the term *pensum* ("something weighed").[14] The term *pondus* is loosely used for one pound (*libra*).[15] Hence also the *dipondius* (i.e. *dupondius*) is named, as if it were *duo pondera* ("two pounds"); this term has been retained in usage up to today.

4. A *trutina* (i.e. a kind of scale) is an instrument that suspends two weighted plates from a balance-tongue. It is made for weighing talents and hundred-pound

13 The etymology is that provided by Jerome for the Hebrew word for tin.

14 The following are the relationships of the weights discussed here: 1 calcus = 2 lentils; 1 obol = 2 ceratin = 3 siliquae = 4 calci; 1 scripulus = 6 siliquae; 1 drachma = 3 scripuli = 18 siliquae; 1 solidus (sextula) = 3 tremisses = 24 siliquae; 1 duella = 2 sextulae; 1 stater (semissis) = 3 sextulae = 3 aurei = 2 *sicli* = 4 drachmas; 1 ounce = 2 stateres = 8 drachmas = 24 scripuli = 4 quadrantes; 1 pound = 12 ounces; 1 mina = 25 stateres = 75 solidi = 100 drachmas = 225 tremisses = 1,800 siliquae.

15 The Roman *libra* is about three-fourths of the modern pound avoirdupois. The *dupondius* is literally the sum of two *asses*, coins originally of one Roman pound.

weights, just as a *momentana* (i.e. a smaller scale) is made for small trifling coins. This is also called a *moneta.* It also has the name *statera* from its number, because it stands (*stare+ter,* "thrice") evenly balanced with two plates and a single pointer in the middle. 5. The balance-tongue (*examen*) is the cord in the middle by which the balance of the scales is regulated and the plates (*lanx*) made even. From this (i.e. *examen*) the strap (*amentum*) on lances (*lancea*) is named. 6. The steelyard (*campana*) takes its name from the region in Italy (i.e. Campania) where its use was first invented. This does not have two plates, but is a rod graduated with pounds and ounces, and it measures using a sliding weight.

7. For every weight a fixed measure has been designated with specific terms. 8. A *calcus* (lit. "pebble"), the smallest unit of weight, is one fourth of an obol, and is equivalent to two lentils. It is called a *calcus* because it is so tiny, like the stone *calculus,* which is so small that it may be 'trodden upon' (*calcare*) without discomfort. 9. The *siliqua* (lit. "carob pod") is a twenty-fourth of a solidus, and takes its name from the tree whose seed it is. 10. A *ceratin* (i.e. *ceratium*) is half an obol, containing one and a half *siliquae.* In Latin usage this is a 'semi-obol.' Moreover, *ceratin* is a Greek word (cf. κεράτιον, "small horn"). [A *siliqua*] is translated as "small horn" in Latin.[16] 11. An obol (*obolus*) weighs three *siliquae,* or two *ceratin,* or four *calci.* At one time it was made of bronze in the shape of an arrow. From this the Greeks took its name, that is, 'arrow' (cf. βέλος, "arrow"). 12. A *scripulus* weighs six *siliquae.* This is called a *gramma* ("scruple") by the Greeks. The *scripulus* is so named by forming a diminutive from the small stone called a *scrupus.*

13. A drachma (*dragma*) is an eighth of an ounce and the weight of a silver denarius, equal to three *scripuli,* that is, eighteen *siliquae.* The denarius is so named because it is reckoned as ten coins (*decem numma*). 14. The solidus (*solidus*) is so named because nothing appears to be lacking in it, for the ancients called something whole and entire a 'solid' (*solidus*). It is also called a *nomisma* because it is marked with the names (*nomen*) and images of rulers. Originally one *nomisma* was one *argenteus,* and this coin originated with the Assyrians. The Jews say that Abraham was first to bring this type of coin into the land of Canaan. Among Latin speakers, the solidus is called by another name, the *sextula,* because it consists of six (*sex*) ounces. Common people, as we have mentioned, call this a 'golden solidus,' and they have named a third part of it a *tremis,* because 'taken three times' (*ter missus*) they make up a solidus. 15. Two *sextulae* make a *duella,* and three of them make a *stater.*

16. A *stater* is half an ounce, weighing three *aurei.* It is called a *stater* because it may stand for three *solidi* (*stare + ter,* "stand three times"). This is also the semi-ounce, because it consists of half an ounce. It is also the *semissis* (i.e. *semis*) because it is half a weight, as if it were '*semi assis*' (i.e. half a unit). 17. The Hebrews name the quarterweight (*quadrans*) with the similar word *codrans,* and it is called *quadrans* because it weighs one fourth (*quartus*) of an ounce. 18. 'Shekel' (*sicel*), which has been corrupted to *siclus* in Latin, is a Hebrew term, and among the Hebrews it has the weight of an ounce, but for Greek and Latin speakers it is one quarter of an ounce, and half a *stater,* weighing two drachmas. Hence, when the word 'shekel' is read in divine Scripture, it is an ounce, but in pagan writings it is a quarter of an ounce.

19. An ounce (*uncia*) is so called because with its unity (*unitas*) it encircles (*vincire*) the entirety (*universitas*) of lesser weights, that is, it embraces them. It consists of eight drachmas, that is, twenty-four *scripuli.* Accordingly, this is held to be the legally recognized weight, because the number of *scripuli* it contains equals the hours of the day and night, or because twelve ounces counted together make a pound. 20. A pound is made of twelve ounces, and thus it is considered as a type of perfect weight because it consists of as many ounces as there are months in the year. It is called a 'pound' (*libra*) because it is independent (*liber*) and contains all the aforementioned weights within it.

21. The *mina* weighs a hundred drachmas; it is a Greek term (i.e. μνᾶ) [and it equals 1,800 *siliquae,* 225 *tremisses,* 75 *solidi,* and 25 *stateres*]. 22. Among the Greeks the talent (*talentum*) is said to be the greatest weight, for there is nothing smaller then a *calcus* or greater than a talent. Its weight varies among different peoples. Among the Romans, a talent is seventy[-two] pounds, as Plautus shows (*The Haunted House* 644), because he says two talents are 140 pounds. But there are three kinds: the lesser, the medium, and the greater. The lesser is fifty pounds, the medium seventy-two pounds, and the greater 120

16 The text makes better sense by omitting the word *siliqua,* bracketed in Lindsay's text. Hence read, "Moreover, *ceratin* is a Greek word, translated as "small horn" in Latin.

pounds. 23. The *centenarium* has the name of a number because it weighs one hundred (*centum*) pounds. The Romans established this weight because of the perfection of the number one hundred.

xxvi. Measures (De mensuris) 1. A 'measure' is some object that is limited in its amount or in time; a measure is either of body or of time. A measure of body is, for instance, the length or shortness of humans or pieces of wood or columns. Geometers even dare to investigate the idea that the orb of the sun itself has its specific measurement. A measure of time is, for instance, the measure of hours and days and years; whence we speak of the 'feet' of the hours as 'pacing out' (*metiri*, lit. "measure out"), that is, they measure (*mensurare*). 2. But strictly speaking a measure (*mensura*) is so named because with it fruits and grains are measured (*metiri*) – that is, by wet measures and dry ones, such as the *modius* (i.e. a Roman measure of corn), [the *artaba* (i.e. an Egyptian measure)], the urn, and the amphora.

3. The smallest unit of measure is the spoonful (*coclear*), which is half a drachma and weighs nine *siliquae*. Three of them make a *concula*. A *concula* consists of one and a half drachmas. 4. A *cyathus* weighs ten drachmas; by some people it is also called a *cuatus*. An *oxifalus* is made when five drachmas are added to ten. 5. An *acitabulus* is one quarter of an *hemina*, and weighs twelve drachmas. A *cotyla* (i.e. *cotula*) is an *hemina* possessing six *cyathi*. It is called a *cotyla* because in the Greek language a cutting is called *cote*, and a *hemina* is cut into the two equal halves of a *sextarius* [and makes a *cotyla*]. But an *hemina* weighs one pound, and when doubled makes a *sextarius*. 6. A *sextarius* is two pounds. Two of them together are a *bilibris*; four of them "make a *cenix* (i.e. χοῖνιξ, a dry measure), a Greek term" (*Poem about Weights and Measures* 69), five of them together make a *quinar* or a *gomor*. Add a sixth and it makes a *congius*, for a *congius* is six (*sex*) *sextarii*, and from this the *sextarius* takes its name. 7. It is called a *congius* from *congire* (perhaps cf. *congerere*, "accumulate"), that is, "grow by an addition." Whence afterwards money that began to be given as thanks for a favor was called a *congiarium*. Thus each emperor, during his reign, would augment the *congiaria*, thereby capturing the favor of the populace, so that he would seem more generous in his gifts. 8. But the *congiarium* is particularly a measure of liquids, and we find that the concept and its name were established by the Romans at the same time.

9. A *metrum* is a measure for liquids. It takes its name from 'measure,' for the Greeks call a measure a μέτρον. Hence also the *metreta* (i.e. another liquid measure) is named. Although 'urn' and 'amphora' and others of this type are also terms of measures, still, the *metreta* took its name due to the perfection of the number ten that it contains. The word *metrum* applies to every measure, for what is called *metrum* from the Greek is a measure (*mensura*) in Latin. Thus the *cyatum* is also a measure, and the amphora is a measure, and whatever contains more or less than these is a measure. But it has assumed this particular name (i.e. *metreta*) for itself because it is the measure of a perfect number, that is, of ten.

10. The *modius* is so named because it is perfect in its own measure (*modus*). It is a measure of forty-four pounds, that is, twenty-two *sextarii*. The reason for its number is derived from the fact that in the beginning God created twenty-two works. Thus on the first day he created seven works, that is, the formless matter, angels, light, the upper heavens, earth, water, and air. On the second day, only the firmament. On the third day, four works: the seas, seeds, sowing, and gardens. On the fourth day, three works: the sun, the moon and the stars. On the fifth day, three works: fish, reptiles of the waters, and flying creatures. On the sixth day, four things: beasts, livestock, reptiles of the land, and the human being. And all twenty-two kinds of things were created in six days. And there are twenty-two generations from Adam to Jacob, from whose seed all the people of Israel were begotten. And there are twenty-two books of the Old Testament up to Esther, and the alphabet in which the teachings of divine law are composed consists of twenty-two letters. From these examples, then, the *modius* was established by Moses as twenty-two *sextarii*, following the measuring system of sacred law. And although different peoples in their ignorance might add or subtract weight from this measure, among the Hebrews it has been preserved in its divine definition using this sort of reasoning. The *modius* is named from 'measure' (*modus*). Hence also the word 'modest' (*modicus*), that is, moderate (*moderatus*). 'Measure' (*modus*) imposed its name on 'modest' things, for we incorrectly use *modicus* for small things, not speaking properly.

11. The *satum* is a kind of measure according to the custom of the province of Palestine, holding one and a half *modii.* Its name is taken from the Hebrew language, for they refer to a 'taking' or a 'lifting' as *satum*, because whoever makes a measurement takes and lifts this very measure. There is also another *satum*, a measure containing twenty-two *sextarii*, like the *modius.* 12. The *batus* is named in Hebrew from 'olive press,' which they call either *beth* or *bata.* It holds fifty *sextarii.* This measure is crushed out in a single pressing. 13. An amphora (*amphora*) is so named because it is lifted on this side and that (cf. ἀμφί, "on both sides"; φέρειν, "carry"; φορεῖν, "carry along"). It is said to have been named in Greek for its shape because its two handles look like ears (i.e. ἀμφί + *auris*, "ear"). It holds a cubic foot of wine or water, but three Italian *modii* of grain. A *cadus* is a Greek amphora containing three urns.

14. The urn (*urna*) is a measure that some people call a quart (*quartarium*). Properly speaking, an urn is a vessel that is normally used for preserving the ashes of the dead. Concerning this the poet says (Lucan, *Civil War* 7.819):

> He who has no urn is covered by the sky.

15. The *medimna* (i.e. *medimnum*) is a measure containing five *modii.* The *medimna* is named from the Latin language, that is, half (*dimidia*), because it measures five *modii*, which is half the number of a perfect ten. 16. The *artaba* is a measure used by the Egyptians, consisting of seventy-two *sextarii*, composed of that number because of the seventy-two peoples and languages that have filled the globe (see IX.ii.2). 17. A *gomor* has the weight of fifteen *modii.* The *corus* is filled by the measure of thirty *modii.* This derives from the Hebrew language and is called *cor* from its similarity to a mound, for Hebrew speakers call mounds *corea* – for thirty *modii* heaped up together look like a mound, and equal the weight that a camel carries.

xxvii. Symbols (De signis) 1. Many symbols for weights are unknown and they cause errors for readers. For this reason we append their forms and characters, as they were used as symbols by the ancients.

2. The letter **Z** signifies half an obol. – A single straight horizontal line signifies an obol. = Two such lines are two obols. The Latin letter **T** means three obols. The Latin **F** means four obols. Latin **E** stands for five obols.

3. However, there is no symbol for six obols, because there are six of them in one drachma, which is the weight of a silver denarius. **H**, the letter eta, stands for eight *siliquae*, that is, a *tremis.* The Latin **N** signifies the Greek *nomisma*, that is, the solidus. **IB**, an iota next to a beta, means half a *solidus.*

4. < Two lines dividing themselves from left to right out of a single angle stand for a drachma, which people also call an *olce.* **NΓ**, a Latin **N** next to a Greek gamma, means a semi-ounce. $\mathbf{\Gamma}^{\circ}$, a Greek gamma followed by a Latin **O** superscript, stands for an ounce. **↑**, a Greek lambda with a Latin **I** placed through its center, means a pound.

5. $\mathbf{K}^{\mathrm{v}}$, a Greek kappa followed by a Latin **V** superscript, means a *cyatum.* But if it should have a Latin **O** next to it, i.e. **KO**, it means an (*h*)*emina*, which the Greeks call a *cotyle.* **ξe** If a Greek xi receives an adjoining Latin **E**, it signifies a *sextarium.*

6. **ξo** If the xi has a Latin **O** joining it, it indicates an *acitabulus*, which the Greeks call an *oxifalos.* $\overset{\mathrm{N}}{\omega}$ A Greek mu with a Latin **N** directly above it stands for a *mina.* **T^** A Latin **T** followed by a Greek lambda means a talent. $\mathbf{X}^{\circ}$, a Greek chi with the superscript letter **O** to its right, is a *cenix.*

Book XVII

Rural matters (De rebus rusticis)

i. Authors on rural matters (De auctoribus rerum rusticarum) 1. Among the Greeks, Hesiod of Boeotia was the first to make skill in writing on rural matters a part of a liberal education; then Democritus. Mago of Carthage also wrote a study of agriculture in twenty-eight volumes. Among the Romans Cato was first to treat of agriculture, then Marcus Terence (i.e. Varro) refined its study, and then Vergil exalted it with the commendation of his poems. No lesser inquiry was made later by Cornelius Celsus, Julius Atticus, Aemilianus (i.e. Palladius), and the distinguished orator Columella who embraced the whole corpus of that discipline.

2. They say that the first person who yoked oxen to the plow was a certain private citizen, who had been struck by lightning, named Homogirus – but some say Osiris was the inventor of this craft, and some say Triptolemus. Here the question is in what manner Ceres in Greece first established the turning of the soil with iron – with whatever kind of iron implement, not specifically with the plowshare or plow.[1] 3. A certain man named Stercutus first brought the technique of dunging (*stercorare*) fields to Italy, and his altar in Rome was dedicated by Picus. He invented many agricultural tools, and was the first to enrich fields. Some have thought that this man was Saturn, in order to do him greater honor by that name under which he would sound magnificent and would procure dignity from the title.

ii. The cultivation of fields (De cultura agrorum) 1. Cultivation (*cultura*) is the means by which crops or wines are procured with great labor, so called from 'inhabiting' (*incolere*; cf. *colere*, ppl. *cultus*, "cultivate"). The wealth of the ancients inhered in two things: good pasturing and good tilling. The cultivation of fields involves ashes, plowing, lying fallow, burning of stubble, dunging, hoeing, and weeding. 2. Ashes (*cinis*) is the burning (*incendium*) by which a field exudes useless moisture. Plowing (*aratio*) is so called because people first carried out the cultivation of land with bronze (*aes*, gen. *aeris*) before the use of iron was discovered. There are two kinds of plowing: spring and fall. 'Lying fallow' (*intermissio*) is the means by which a field, empty in alternate years, renews its vigor.

3. Dunging (*stercoratio*) is the spreading of fertilizer. Dung (*stercus*) is so called either because it is spread (*sternere*) on fields, or because that which overflows as filth in the city needs to be "washed off" (*extergere*, as if *ec-stergere*), [or, what is more likely, from the name Sterce, also called Sterculus]. Dung is also called droppings (*fimus*), which is dropped on fields. And it is called *fimus* [because "a mouse is made" (*fiat mus*)],[2] that is, dung, which commonly is called fertilizer (*laetamen*) because with its nourishment it makes seeds fertile (*laetus*) and renders fields rich and fecund.

4. Hoeing is done after the planting, when farmers after unyoking the oxen split the large clods and break them apart with hoes, and it is called hoeing (*occatio*) as if it were 'blinding' (*occaecatio*), because it covers the seeds. To hoe therefore is to cover seeds, vines, or trees with earth. 5. Weeding (*runcatio*) is to pluck weed-grasses from the land, for the land is *rus* ("farmland"). A furrow (*sulcus*) is so named from 'sun' (*sol*), because when plowed it receives the sun. 'Newly plowed fallow' (*vervactum*) is so called as if it were 'done in springtime' (*vere actum*), that is, land plowed in spring. Ground-breaking (*proscissio*) is the first plowing, when the field is still hard. 6. Sowing (*satio*) is so called as if it were 'the action of the seed' (*seminis actio*), as if it were 'the action of the sowers' (*satorum actio*). Moreover it is called sowing (*serere*), because it ought to be done when the sky is clear (*serenus*), not in rain. Hence is derived that Vergilian phrase (*Geo.* 1.299):

> Naked plow, naked sow (*serere*).

1 Isidore's source here, Servius's commentary on Vergil's *Georgics* 1.147, is making the point that though others may have invented the plow, Ceres taught the whole art of agriculture.

2 For the idea that the earth's moisture begets mice see XII.iii.1. A more likely reading, preserved in some manuscripts, is *fiat imus*, "it is made the lowest thing."

Harvest (*messis*) is named from 'reaping' (*metere*), that is, cutting back. 7. A grain-field (*seges*) is [so called] from the seed (*semen*) that we cast, or from 'cutting' (*sectio*).

iii. Fruits of the earth (De frumentis) 1. Ceres was first in Greece to make use of grain and to raise crops from seeds brought from another place. Ovid records this, saying (*Met.* 5.341):

> Ceres first broke up the earth with her curved plow, she first brought grains and kindly food to the lands.

2. Grains (*frumentum*) are properly those that have ears, and crops (*frux*) are the other fruits of the earth. Grain or crops are named from enjoying (*frui*), that is, from eating, for the top part of the throat is called the *frumen*. 3. First-fruits (*primitiae*) are properly those which are first gathered from the crops. 4. Wheat (*triticum*) is so called either from threshing (*tritura*), by means of which it may be stored in a barn after being thoroughly sifted, or because its grain is milled and 'ground up' (*terere*, ppl. *tritum*).

5. Spelt (*far*) is so called because at first it would be crushed (*frangere*), for among the ancients the use of mills did not yet exist, but they would place grain in a mortar and crush it, and this was a kind of milling. 6. 'Emmer wheat' (*adoreum*) is a species of wheat that is commonly called seed (*semen*). It was formerly called *ador* from 'eating' (*edere*), because it was what people first used, or because in a sacrifice bread of that kind was offered 'at altars' (*ad aras*) – whence furthermore sacrifices are called *adorea* (i.e. an honorary gift of grain). 7. 'Winter wheat' (*siligo*), a type of wheat, is named from 'choice' (*selectus*, ppl. of *seligere*), for this type is excellent for bread.

8. 'Three-month spring' (*trimestris*) wheat is so named because it is gathered three months after sowing, for where a seasonable sowing is skipped because of water or some other reason, people look to it as a safeguard. 9. *Alica* ("emmer groats") is a Greek word. *Alicastrum* is similar to *alica*, outstanding for weight and quality. 10. Barley (*hordeum*) is so called because it becomes dry (*aridum*) before other types of grain, or because its ear has rows (*ordo*) of grain. There are three kinds of barley. The first is called *hexaticum* (i.e. *hexastichus*; cf. ἕξ, "six"; στίχος, "row") because its ear has six rows. Some call this type horse-barley (*canterinum*) because it feeds animals better than wheat, and feeds humans more nutritiously than poor wheat. The second is *distichon* barley, because it has two rows; many call this Galaticum. The third is three-month (*trimestris*) because, when necessary, it is sown in spring and quickly gathered.

11. 'Gallic spelt' (*scandula*) is named from 'division,' for it has two forms and it is split (*scandere*, i.e. *scindere*) – that is, it is divided. 12. *Centenum* (probably "rye") is so called because in most places where it is cast it grows with a hundredfold (*centesimus*) increase over its seed. Millet (*milium*) likewise is named from the multiplicity of its crop (cf. *milia*, "thousands"). 13. 'Panic grass' (*panicium*) is so called because in many regions people are sustained by it 'in place of bread' (*panis vice*), as if the word were *panivicium*. Meal (*pistum*) is from 'something fed' (*pastus*). Sesame (*sisamum*) is a Greek term (i.e. σήσαμον). 14. 'Mixed grain' (*farrago*) is named from spelt (*far*); it is a barley-type grass, still green, with its grain not yet swollen to ripeness.

15. We speak improperly of the 'ear' (*spica*) of ripe fruit, for properly the ear exists when the beards, still thin like spear-tips (*spiculum*), project through the husk of the stalk, that is the swelling tip. 16. The beard (*arista*) is so called because it is the first to dry up (*arescere*). The stalk (*culmus*) is the stem (*calamus*) of the ear as it rises from the roots, and it is called *culmus* as if the word were *calamus*. 17. The husk (*folliculum*) is the sheath of the ear inside of which the grain is protected. Furnished with a rampart, it stretches its defense over the ear so that the ear may not be stripped of its fruit by the pecking of the smaller birds, or trampled by footsteps. 18. Blades are the leaves or sheaths with which the stalk is surrounded and propped so that it is not bent over by the weight of the grain, and they surround the stalk. The blade (*stipula*, also meaning "stubble") is so called from 'burnt' (*ustus*, ppl. of *urere*) as if the word were *ustipula*. Stubble is named from burning, because when the harvest is gathered, the stubble is burned for the cultivation of the field. Or again, it is called *stipula* because part of it is burned while part of it is mown for straw (*palea*).

19. Some say chaff (*palea*) is so called because it is winnowed with a winnowing-shovel (*pala*) to separate out the grain. Pagans however derive the name chaff from a certain Pales, the discoverer of grain crops, whom

they would identify with Ceres. Concerning her Vergil writes (cf. *Geo.* 3.1):

> You also, great Pales, in your memory we will sing.

Still others say chaff took its name from 'fodder' (*pabulum*), because at first it alone was offered for the feeding of animals. Chaff's property is to be contrary: so cold that it does not permit snow blanketed with it to melt, yet so warm that it forces fruits to ripen.

iv. Legumes (De leguminibus) 1. Legumes (*legumen*) are so called from picking (*legere*), as if they were 'picked out' (*eligere*, ppl. *electus*), for the ancients would pick all the better ones – or because they are picked by hand and do not need cutting. 2. There are several species of legumes, of which the fava bean, lentil, pea, French bean, chickpea, and lupine seed seem most favored for human consumption. 3. The 'fava bean' (*faba*) derived its name in a Greek etymology from 'eating,' as if it were *faga*, for in Greek φαγεῖν means "to eat." Indeed humans consumed this legume first. It has two types, one common and the other Egyptian. 4. 'Ground fava' (*faba fresa*) is so called because people grind (*frendere*, ppl. *fresum*) it, that is crush it, and pulverize it by milling. 5. The lentil (*lentis*, i.e. *lens*) is so named because it is moist and soft (*lentus*), or because it adheres to the soil (cf. *lentus*, "sticky"). 6. 'French bean' (*faselum*; cf. φάσηλος) and chickpea (*cicer*; cf. κριός) are Greek names. But *faselum* . . . 7. Lupine (*lupinus*) is also a Greek term, about which Vergil wrote (*Geo.* 1.75):

> And the sad lupines (*lupinus*),

because with their bitterness they make the taster's face look sad (cf. λυπηρός, "causing sorrow") – hence on account of their bitterness neither worms nor any other animal eats them.

8. Lucerne clover, vetch, and bitter vetch are the best fodders. Lucerne (*medica*) is so called because it was brought into Greece from the Medes when Xerxes, king of the Persians, invaded it. Once sown, this lasts ten years, and can be reaped four or six times a year. 9. Vetch (*vicia*) is so named because it scarcely (*vix*) bears a triple yield, while other legumes have a fertile produce. Hence Vergil (*Geo.* 1.75):

> Or the scanty yield of the vetch (*vicia*).

10. The pea (*pisum*) is so called because by it a minute quantity of gold would be 'weighed out' (*pensare*) – for *pis* means "gold."[3] 11. 'Bitter vetch' (*ervum*) derives its name from Greek, for they call it ὄροβος, because while it is dangerous for some livestock it nevertheless makes bulls (cf. βοῦς, "bull") plump.

v. Vines (De vitibus) 1. Noah first established the planting of vines in an age still without cultivation. However, the Greeks call the discoverer of the vine Liber, whence the pagans after his death would have it that he was a god. 2. It is called a vine (*vitis*) because it has the capacity (*vis*) for taking root easily. Others think that they are called vines because they entwine themselves about one another with 'ribbon-like stems' (*vitta*, "fillet," a strip of cloth) and fasten themselves to neighboring (*vicinus*) trees with their creeping growth. They are flexible in nature, and whatever they embrace they bind tight as if with a kind of arms. 3. The *labrusca* is a wild vine that grows in marginal land, whence it is called *labrusca*, from the margins (*labrum*) and extremities of the land.

4. A trunk (*codex*) is so called as if it were *caudex*.[4] Likewise the ancients would say *clodus* for *claudus* ("lame"). 5. Vine-shoots (*sarmentum*) are from 'entwining' (*serere*), [as if the word were *serimentum*]. A mallet-shoot (*malleolus*) is a sweet young vine-shoot sprung from a young branch of the prior year, and named for its likeness to the thing, because at the section where it is cut from the old shoot the protuberance on both sides looks like a hammer (*malleus*). 6. Eunuchs (*spado*) are shoots lacking fruit, so named because they are unable to bear fruit and are afflicted with sterility. 7. Country people call the newest part of the shoot an 'arrow' (*sagitta*), either because it has gone off quite far from the mother-stem and as it were shoots forth, or because it has the look of a dart with the thinness of its point. 8. The top parts of vines and bushes are called switches (*flagellum*), because they are stirred by the breeze (*flatus*).

3 We translate Lindsay's text, but the reading *pis* (an unknown word) *aurum dicitur*, "*pis* means gold," derives from a misreading, by Isidore or an intermediary, of Servius's commentary on *Aeneid* 6.825. There Servius wrote *Pisaurum dicitur*, "(the city of) Pesaro is so called": Pesaro is so called because there 'gold is weighed' (*aurum pensatum est*).

4 *Codex* and *caudex* are variants of the same word, meaning "trunk" or "book."

9. The shoot (*palmes*) of a vine is the soft material that, extending as tender young branches, bears the fruit. Country people call that part of the vine the *palmes* for this reason: *palmes* is a diminutive noun, which is called a 'noun with a changed ending' (*nomen paragogum*; see I.xxxv.3), because it is derived from *palma* (palm tree). *Palma* presents the prototype name, which is called the 'principal,' because it can form a derivative from itself. 10. Vine-foliage (*pampinus*) consists of the leaves by whose aid the vine defends itself from cold or heat and is protected from every injury. Therefore it is pruned in some places so that it both lets in sun for the ripening of the fruit and also makes shade. It is called *pampinus* because it 'hangs from the shoot' (*de palmite pendeat*). 11. Tendrils (*capreolus*) are so called because they seize (*capere*) trees, for they are the curls or little hooks by which vines will interlace themselves and hang from trees. Thanks to their support the shoots can scorn winds and turbulence, hold up their fruit without any danger of falling, and defend themselves along their rambling length. 12. *Corymbi* are the curling tendrils that bind and hold fast to whatever is nearest, so that shoots are not loosed too far out and torn away by blasts of wind.

13. Grapes (*uva*) are so called because they are full of liquid inside, of juice and succulence, for what has moisture on the outside is *humidus*, and on the inside, *uvidus*. 14. Berry (*acinus*) . . . Cluster (*botrus*) . . . A cluster-stalk (*racemus*, i.e. the stem of a cluster) is a part of a *botryo*, and *botryo* (i.e. 'cluster') is a Greek word (i.e. βότρυς). 15. Some grapes are called 'suburban' because their produce is sold in cities as fresh fruit, because both their appearance and the agreeableness of their taste commend them. Types of these are the early-ripening, the hard, the purple, the finger-long, the Rhodian, the Libyan, the thunderbolt, the crown, the three-foot, the inch-long, and the Cydonian. Those that last through the whole winter are the vennuculan and the Numisian. 16. The early-ripening (*praecox*) are so called because they come to maturity early and are ripened by the sun before all the others. The Greeks call these lagean grapes, because they rush to ripeness as quickly as a hare (cf. λαγώς, "hare").

17. Purple (*purpureus*) grapes are named for their color; inch-long (*unciarius*) for their size; finger-long (*dactylus*) for their length; crown (*stephanitus*) for their roundness. Rhodian and Libyan are named from regions, but thunderbolt grapes because they glow red as fire. 18. Moreover, there are very many species of grapes that are used for wine. Of these, Aminean is so called as if it were 'without redness' (*sine minium*), that is, lacking redness, for it makes a white wine. Although it has one name, it produces more than one type; the Aminean 'twin' (*duae geminae*) so called because it yields double grapes, and the Aminean 'woolly' (*lanatus*), because it has a woolly down, more so than others. The rubellian grape is so called because its woody part is red (cf. *ruber*, "red").

19. Faecinian grapes have tiny berries and tough skin; they trail Aminean grapes in quality and surpass them in fecundity. They call it the faecinian grape because it produces more wine-lees (*faex*, gen. *faecis*) than other grapes. 20. Muscatel (*apianus*) grapes make a sweet wine. Unless you pick them quickly they will be injured by rain and wind and especially bees (*apis*); they are named apian because of the bees' depredations. 21. Balanite grapes receive that name because of their size, because in Greek an acorn is called βάλανος. 22. The Biturican grape is allotted its name from its region. It withstands whirlwinds, rain, and heat very hardily, and it does not wither in poor land. The basilisk grape also has this advantage.

23. The *argitis* is a Greek vine of the white type (cf. ἀργός, "white"), fecund, producing a huge woody stock and a short, wide leaf; its fruit, unless you gather it at the beginning of the season, either falls to the earth or rots from the damp. 24. The *inerticula* grape, which the Greeks call *amaricion*, is black. It makes a good, light wine – whence it takes its name, because it is considered weak (*iners*) with regard to debilitating one's strength, although it is not feeble in taste. 25. Mareotic grapes are named from the region of Egypt, Mareotis, from which they first came. They are both white and black. 26. Helvola grapes, which some call 'variegated,' are so called from their color, neither purple nor black but dun (*helvus*), although their must is whitish – for dun has dark and light in its color: it is neither light nor dark as such.

27. In third place are the vines notable for their fecundity only, abundant in their yield and productive of a good quantity of wine. 28. The *viticionia* vine has large rather than numerous grapes, and thence receives its name because it produces a great deal of wine.[5] The Syriac grape is so called either because it was brought

5 The reading *viticionia* is uncertain.

from Syria or because it is black. 29. Moreover there are many species of vines that, with a change of locality, lose both their character and their name.

30. Among others, these activities are most appropriate for vines: loosening the soil, pruning, propagation, and digging. 31. To 'loosen the soil' (*oblaqueare*) is to lay open the soil around the stock and to form hollows to hold water; some call this 'clearing the root' (*excodicare*). 32. To prune (*putare*) is to cut back superfluous branches from the vine where the top growth is luxuriant, for to prune is to cleanse, that is to cut off (*amputare*). 33. To train (*traducere*) a vine is to 'lead it across' (*transducere*). To propagate (*propaginare*) is to stretch a shoot of the vine to be buried in the soil, and then as it were to 'fasten it at a distance' (*porro pangere*). Hence the term 'progeny' (*propago*), so called from propagate and 'stretch out' (*protendere*). To dig (*fodere*) is to make a pit (*fovea*), as if the term were *fovere*.

vi. Trees (De arboribus) 1. The term 'tree' (*arbor*), as well as 'small plant' (*herba*), is thought to be modified from the word 'field' (*arvum*), because they cling to the earth with fixed roots. The terms resemble one another because the one grows from the other. When you have cast the seeds on the ground first the small plant springs up, and when it is tended it grows into a tree, and within a short time what you had seen as a small plant you gaze up to as a sapling. 2. A sapling (*arbustum*) is a new and pliant tree, in which a graft can be made, and it is called *arbustum* as if it were 'the spear of a tree' (*arboris hasta*). Others would take *arbustum* as the place where trees grow, like the term for 'willow thicket' (*salictum*); and likewise (i.e. with a similar derivational ending) *virectum* ("greensward"), where there are new and green (*virere*) bushes.

3. The word *arbor* for 'tree' refers to both fruit-bearing and sterile trees, but *arbos* only to fruit-bearing. We decline words for trees in the feminine gender, but words for their fruits in the neuter. 4. A shrub (*frutex*) is a short growth, so called because 'by its foliage it covers' (*fronde tegit*) the ground; the plural of this word is 'shrubbery' (*frutectum*). But a tree (*arbor*) is tall. 5. A thicket (*silva*) is a dense and small grove. *Silva* is so called as if the word were *xylva*, because there wood is felled, for the Greeks call wood ξύλον – for many Latin terms commonly have a Greek etymology. 6. A grove (*nemus*) is named for divinity (*numen*), because pagans set up their idols there, for groves are sites with larger trees, shady with foliage. 7. A 'sacred grove' (*lucus*) is a dense thicket of trees that lets no light come to the ground, named by way of antiphrasis because it 'sheds no light' (*non lucere*). Or it is named from 'light' (*lux*, gen. *lucis*) because in it torches or candles used to give off light against the darkness of the grove.

8. A glade (*saltus*) is a high thicket of trees, called by this name because it 'springs up' (*exsilire*) on high and rises aloft. 9. An *aviarium* is a hidden grove so called because it is the haunt of birds (*avis*). 10. 'Second growth' (*recidivum*) with regard to trees consists of what sprouts again after the others have been cut. Some say that *recidivum* is from 'falling' (*cadere*), because they make new growth after being felled. Others have said that it is from 'cutting back' (*recidere*) and sprouting again. Therefore something may be *recidivus* (i.e. "restored") where there has been death or falling.

11. We speak of grafting (*insitio*) when, after the stem is split, a scion from a fertile tree is grafted (*inserere*, ppl. *insitus*) onto a sterile tree; or, it is the implanting of buds when, after the bark is sliced open, the bud of a foreign tree is set into the inner bark. 12. Cuttings (*planta*) are from trees, but seedlings (*plantaria*) are grown from seed and are transplanted with their roots from their original soil. 13. Turf (*caespes*) is a low growth, as if the term were 'spears' (*cuspis*) or 'around the feet' (*circa pedes*). Branches (*frons*) are so called because they 'produce' (*ferre*) shoots or shade, for they are the cause of shade. Eyes (*oculus*) are the nodes from which branches grow. 14. The root (*radix*) is so called because fixed in the ground in the manner of 'radiating spokes' (*radius*), as it were, it goes down deep, for natural philosophers say that the depth of the roots is equal to the height of the trees. Others say roots are named for their similarity to rays (*radius*), or because, if they are cut away (*eradere*), they do not grow back.

15. The trunk (*truncus*) is the standing part of a tree, and it rests on the root. The ancients called bark (*cortex*) the *corux*; it is named *cortex* because it covers the wood with a skin (*corium*). 16. *Liber* is the inner part of the bark, so called from the bark's being 'released' (*liberare*), that is, set apart, for it is a kind of medium between bark and wood. 17. Branches (*ramus*) are what extend from the trunk, just as from 'little branches' (*ramusculus*) yet others grow. Shoots (*serculus*) are so named because they are cut with a saw (*serra*). 18. A sucker (*virgultum*) is what

springs up from a root; a branch, from the woody part of a tree; a twig (*virga*), from a branch. Properly, however, what grows up at the root of a tree and is lopped off as useless by farmers is called a sucker. It is called *virgultum* because it is 'removed from a twig' (*ex virga tollere*). A twig (*virga*) is so named [moreover from 'vigor' (*vis*)] or from 'strength' (*virtus*) because it contains a great deal of vigor, or from 'greenness' (*viriditas*), or because it is a symbol of peace (i.e. as a lictor's rod), because it controls force (*vis*). For this reason magicians use wands (*virga*) to make serpents calm towards each other, and therefore they hold them up tied to a wand (cf. the caduceus; see VIII.xi.47 and the footnote there). Indeed, philosophers, kings, teachers, messengers, and envoys use wands.

19. Switches (*flagellum*), as I said above (v.8 above), are the highest parts of trees, because they sustain the repeated blasts (*flatus*) of wind. 20. A cyme (*cyma*) is so called as if the word were 'hair' (*coma*). A leaf (*folium*) is called φύλλον in Greek, and this name was carried over to our language by borrowing. 21. Flowers (*flos*, pl. *flores*) are so called because they quickly drop (*defluere*) from trees, as if the word were *fluores*, for they are quickly released. These are doubly pleasing: in color and in scent. They are wilted by the south wind, produced by the west wind. 22. We call a fertile, swelling growth a bud (*germen*), from 'bearing' (*gerere*); whence also the term 'germination' (*germinatio*). 23. Produce (*fructus*) takes its name from *frumen*, that is, the higher part of the throat, through which we ingest. Whence also 'crops' (*frux*). Properly speaking, produce is what comes from fields and trees, especially what we make use of, but we speak of the 'produce' of animals incorrectly and metaphorically.

24. Fruit (*pomum*) is named from 'abundant' (*opimus*), that is from the abundance of its fruitful growth. Fruits are called ripe (*maturus*) because they are ready for eating (*mandere*); likewise, unripe (*immaturus*), because before they become ripe they are too hard for eating. 25. Firewood (*lignum*) is so called because when kindled it is converted into light (*lumen*). Whence likewise the lamp (*lichnium*) is so called, because it gives light (see vii.65 below). 26. A splinter (*astula*) is named from 'raising' (*tollere*) [as if it were 'carry away' (*abstula*, as if from *abstulere*)]. Tinder (*fomes*) is composed of splinters that are cast off from trees by lopping, or charred shavings, or hollowed-out firewood. It takes its name from 'dried fungus' (*fungus*), because they catch fire in the same way. Of these, Vergil says (*Aen.* 1.176):

> And he struck flame in the tinder (*fomes*).

27. A fire-brand (*torris*) is a burnt piece of wood, commonly called *titio*, taken from the hearth half-burnt and with the fire out. 28. Sweepings (*quisquiliae*) are stubble mixed with branches and dry leaves; they are the rubbish of the land. Rot (*caries*) is the decayed matter of wood, called this because it occurs in wood that lacks (*carere*) solidity.

vii. Specific names of trees (De propriis nominibus arborum) 1. The palm (*palma*) is so called because it adorns the hand of a conqueror, or because it has branches spread out in the manner of a human palm (*palma*). This tree is the symbol of victory, with high and handsome growth, clothed in long-lasting fronds, and retaining its leaves without any succession of foliage. The Greeks call it the *phoenix* (i.e. φοῖνιξ) because it lasts for a long time, after the name of that bird of Arabia that is thought to live for many years. Although it grows in many places, its fruit does not ripen in them all, but it often does in Egypt and Syria. Its fruits are called 'dates' (*dactylus*; cf. δάκτυλος, "finger") from their similarity to fingers. The names of the dates vary: some are called *palmulae*, similar to the ben-nut (*myrobalanus*); some Theban, which are also called Nicolaian; some *nucales*, which the Greeks call καρυωταί (cf. καρυωτὸς, "date-palm").

2. Laurel (*laurus*) is so called from the word 'praise' (*laus*, gen. *laudis*), because with it the heads of conquerors were crowned with praises. Among the ancients, moreover, it was named *laudea*; afterwards, with the letter *d* removed and *r* substituted it was called *laurus* – just like *auricula* ("ear"), which originally was pronounced *audicula*, and *medidies*, which is now pronounced *meridies* ("midday"). The Greeks call this tree δάφνη, because it never loses (*deponere*) its verdure; for this reason conquerors are aptly crowned with it. It is commonly believed that only this tree is never struck by lightning.

3. The apple-tree (*malum*)[6] is so called by the Greeks because its fruit is the roundest of all fruits (cf. μῆλον,

6 Latin classes several fleshy tree-fruits under the term *malum*, including quince, pomegranate, peach, citron, etc. See section 22 below.

"apple, any fleshy tree-fruit," hence "round thing"); whence also those are true apples that are strikingly round. Matian apples (i.e. the apple proper) are named for the place from which they were first brought, for many trees have taken their names from the provinces or cities from which they were brought. Vergil shows lovers what is customarily sought with an apple.[7] 4. The quince (*malum Cydonium*) takes its name from a town on the island of Crete – in this regard, the Greeks would call Cydonia the mother of the Cretan cities – and from this fruit *cydonitum* (i.e. a preserve or medicinal ointment of quince) is made. From it also is made a wine that deceives the appetite of those who are enfeebled, for in appearance, taste, and smell it presents the sensation of any kind of old wine.

5. The *malomellum* type of apple is so named for its sweetness, because its fruit has the taste of honey (*mel*), or because it is preserved in honey, whence a certain poet says (Martial, *Epigrams* 13.24):

> If quinces steeped in Cecropian honey are placed before you, you would say, "I like these honey-apples (*melimelum*)!"

6. The pomegranate (*malum Punicum*) is so called because that species was brought from the Punic region. It also has the name *malogranatum*, because it contains a great multitude of seeds (*granus*) within the sphere of its rind. The tree-name *malusgranata* is of feminine gender, but its fruit is of neuter gender. The flower of this tree is called κύτινος by the Greeks; Latin speakers call it *caducum*. But the Greeks call the flower of wild pomegranates βαλαύστιον. Some of these are white, some purple, and some pink, like pomegranate flowers. Physicians say that our bodies are not nourished by eating pomegranates, but they consider them better for medicinal use than for eating.

7. The peach (*malum Persicum*), which is granted a very brief life, is said to have three types: hard-fruited, Armenian, and Persian. The hard-fruited (*duracenus*) is so named because its fruit has a 'sour taste' (*acor*; cf. *durus*, "harsh"). The Armenian peach (*Armeniacus*) is so called because that type was first brought over from Armenia. The Persian peach (*Persicus*) is so called because Perseus – from whom the Ptolemies claimed that they sprang – first planted that tree in Egypt. In Persia this tree produced a deadly fruit, but in our region the fruit is pleasant and sweet. One kind of Persian peach is called 'early' (*praecox*, perhaps the apricot), another 'summer.'

8. The 'citron tree' (*Medica arbor*), whose name became famous in the Mantuan's (i.e. Vergil's) poems, was first brought from Media, whence it took its name. The Greeks call it κεδρόμηλον, and Latin speakers *citria* (cf. *citrea*, "citrus-tree") because its fruit and leaves bring to mind the smell of cedar (*cedrus*). Its fruit is an antidote for poison, and it is this property that the same poet wishes to be understood when he tells us that the life's breath is nourished by it (Vergil, *Geo.* 2.126–35). This tree is laden with fruit in almost every season; some of it is ripe, some unripe, some still only in flower – which is a rare thing in other trees.

9. The *mella*, which the Greeks call *lotos* (i.e. λωτός), is commonly called the 'Syrian fava bean' (*faba Syrica*) because of its shape and color. It is a large tree, bearing an edible fruit, larger than a pepper, with a sweet taste, whence it is called *mella*.[8] 10. The plum tree (*coccymela*), which Latin speakers call *prunus* for its color (cf. *pruna*, "red-hot coal"), others call *nixa* from the multitude of fruit 'produced' (*eniti*, ppl. *enixus*) by it. The best of this type is the Damascene (i.e. damson) plum, named for the city of Damascus from which it was first imported. The fruit of this species alone is known to be curative for the stomach, for the others are held to be noxious. Only this tree drips with a glutinous and thick gum, which both physicians and scribes use.

11. The *oleomela* tree grows in Palmyra, a city in Syria, so called because from its trunk an oil (*oleum*) flows as thick as honey, with a sweet taste. 12. The *pomelida*[9] is similar to serviceberry, a middle-sized tree with a white flower, so called because the sweetness of its fruit is mixed with a sharp taste. This tree lives for a short while. 13. The *melopos* tree of Africa was named in the Punic language; from it flows a sticky sap named Hammonian after its region (i.e. a region in Libya). 14. The medlar (*mespila*) tree is thorny, with fruit like apples but a little smaller, and so called because its fruit has the shape of a 'little ball' (*pilula*).

7 To toss an apple at someone was to flirt, as in *Eclogues* 3.64, in which Damoetas says *Malo me Galatea petit, lasciva puella*: "Galatea, the wanton girl, tosses an apple at me."

8 The Greek λωτός is a nettle-tree or jujube, *Zizyphus lotus*. Isidore associates the Latin name with the sweetness of honey (*mel*).

9 Perhaps a corruption of the word *hypomelis*, gen. *hypomelidis*, mentioned by Palladius and unidentified – a medlar?

15. The pear (*pirus*) seems to be called that because its fruit is oddly shaped in the likeness of fire (cf. πῦρ, "fire"), for this kind of fruit is wide at the base and narrows at the top, like a tongue of fire. The tree is *pirus*, but the fruit is *pira*. There are many species of pears, of which Crustumian are partly red, named for the town Crustumium. Pears are said to be extremely burdensome when carried by pack-animals, even if there are only a few. 16. The cherry (*cerasus*) is named from the city Cerasum in Pontus (i.e. the Black Sea), for when Lucullus destroyed the Pontic city Cerasum he imported this kind of fruit from there and named it *cerasium* from the city's name. The tree is called *cerasus*, the fruit *cerasium*. Before Lucullus these were in Italy, but only a hard variety, and hence it was also called the cornel-cherry (*cornus*; cf. *cornu*, "(hard) horn"). The wood of the tree is good for spears; hence Vergil (*Geo.* 2.448):

> The cornel-cherry (*cornus*) good for war.

17. The fig (*ficus*) is so-named in Latin for its fecundity (*fecunditas*), for it is more fruitful than the other trees. It produces fruit three and four times in a single year, and while one crop ripens another begins to grow. Likewise the *carica* (i.e. a dry fig) is also named from its abundance.[10] The Egyptian fig is said to be more fecund. When wood from it is placed in water it immediately sinks, and after it has lain for some time in the mud it rises to the surface, contrary to what is natural – when soaked it ought to stay down with the weight of the moisture. Formerly athletes would be fed figs, before the trainer Pythagoras switched them to the use of meat, which is a more substantial food. It is said that figs, eaten by the elderly fairly often in their diet, smooth away their wrinkles. They also say that very ferocious bulls, tethered to a fig tree, suddenly become tame.

18. The wild fig (*caprificus*) is so called because it tears at (*carpere*; cf. also καρπός, "fruit") the walls in which it grows up, for it bursts forth and grows out from the hidden spots in which it is germinated. Others think this tree is called *caprificus* because with its assistance the fig (*ficus*) tree is made fruitful.[11] 19. The mulberry tree (*morus*, also meaning "blackberry") is so named by the Greeks (i.e. μόρον, "mulberry, blackberry"), and Latin speakers call it the *rubus* (lit. "blackberry bush") because its fruit or foliage is red (*rubere*). There is also a woodland mulberry (*mora*), bearing fruit that relieves the hunger and need of shepherds in the wilderness. It is said that its leaves, when thrown onto a serpent, destroy it.

20. The 'sycamore fig' (*sycomorus*), along with the mulberry (*morus*), have Greek names (i.e. συκόμορυς, μόρον). It is called *sycomorus* (cf. σῦκον, "fig") because its leaves are like the *morus*. Latin speakers call this the 'lofty' (*celsus*) fig because of its height, for it is not short like the mulberry. 21. The walnut (*nux*) is so called because its shade or drippings from its leaves harm (*nocere*) neighboring trees. Latin speakers call it by another name, *iuglans*, as if it were 'Jupiter's nut' (*Iovis glans*), for this tree was consecrated to Jupiter. Its fruit has so much virtue that, when it is mingled with suspicious food containing herbs or mushrooms, it drives out, seizes, and destroys whatever is poisonous in it. 22. All fruits covered with a rather hard shell are generically called 'nuts' (*nux*), as pine nuts (*pinea*), filberts, acorns (*glans*), chestnuts, almonds. The kernel (*nucleus*) is also named from *nux*, because it is covered with a hard shell. On the other hand every soft fruit is called *malum*, but this term is modified by the names of the regions in which they originated, as Persian, Punic, Matian, Cydonian, and so forth.

23. Almond (*amygdala*) is a Greek name (i.e. ἀμυγδάλη), which in Latin is called 'long nut.' Others call it *nucicla*, as if it were "the little nut." Concerning it, Vergil (*Geo.* 1.187):

> When many a nut tree (*nux*) in the woods clothes itself in flowers.

For among all the trees it first clothes itself in flower, and bears fruit before the other trees. 24. Filberts (*abellana*) are given their name from Abella, a town in Campania, where they are abundant. These are called Pontic nuts by the Greeks, because they are abundant around the Pontic (i.e. Black) Sea. 25. Latin speakers name the chestnut (*castanea*) from a Greek term, for the Greeks call it καστάνια, because its paired fruits are hidden in a small sack like testicles, and when they are ejected from it, it is as if they were castrated (*castrare*). As soon as this tree is cut down, it commonly sprouts again like a forest.

10 That is, the Carica fig is abundant in the province of Caria in Asia Minor, whence its name.

11 Pliny explains that "caprification" is the attachment to cultivated fig trees of wild figs, from which gall insects emerge and pollinate the flowers.

26. The 'holm oak' (*ilex*) is so called from 'chosen' (*eligere*, ppl. *electus*), for people first chose the fruit of this tree for their sustenance. Whence also the poet (unidentified):

> The first mortals belched the acorn from their throats.

For before there was any use of grain, ancient people lived on acorns. 27. The cork tree (*suberies*) has bark that people harvest; it is very useful because it floats. It is called *suberies* because pigs eat its fruit. That fruit is nourishing for swine, not humans, and it is called *suberies* as if the term were *subedies* (cf. *sus*, "pig"; *edere*, "eat"). 28. The beech tree and the *esculus* (i.e. another type of oak tree) are nut-bearing trees thought to be so named because people once sustained themselves from their fruit, eating it for food and taking it as nourishment. Thus *esculus* is named for food (*esca*), but the beech (*fagus*) derives its name from Greek, as φαγεῖν in Greek means "to eat."

29. *Xyliglycon*, which Latin speakers incorrectly call the 'carob tree' (*siliqua*), took its name from the Greeks, because the fruit of this tree is sweet; ξύλον indeed means "wood," and γλυκύ means "a sweet thing." The juice pressed from the fruit of this tree is called *acacia* (gum Arabic; cf. ἀκακία, "shittah tree") by the Greeks. 30. Pistachio (*pistacia*) is so called because the shell of its fruit emits an odor of pure (*pisticus*) spikenard.[12]

31. The pine (*pinus*), a resinous tree, is named from the sharpness of its needles, for the ancients would call a sharp thing *pinnus*. The Greeks call one type of pine πίτυς, another πεύκη, which we call resinous (*piceus*) because it exudes pitch (*pix*). These also differ in appearance. Moreover, on the islands of Germania the 'tears' of this tree produce amber (*electrum*), for the flowing sap hardens, from cold or warmth, into solidity and makes a gem taking its name from its character, namely amber (*sucinum*), because it consists of the sap (*sucus*) of the tree. The pine tree is believed to be good for everything that grows under it, just as the fig is harmful to all.

32. The fir (*abies*) is so called because it goes (*ire*; cf. *abire*, "go away") further than the other trees and towers aloft. It is naturally lacking in the earthy humor, and accordingly is considered easily handled and light. About it, Vergil (cf. *Geo.* 2.68):

> And (the fir, *abies*) that will see disasters at sea;

for ships are made of fir. Some call fir *Gallicus* for its whiteness (cf. γάλα, "milk"). Further, fir has no knots. 33. Cedar (*cedrus*) is called by the Greeks κέδρος, as if it were καιομένης δρυὸς ὑγρόν (i.e. *cedrus* from και- + δρυος), that is, "moisture of the burning tree." Its leaves bear a resemblance to those of the cypress. It is a tree of very pleasant odor and long-lasting, and it is never harmed by worms. About it, Persius (*Satires* 1.42):

> And having said things worthy of cedar (*cedrus*);

that is, because of its lasting perpetuity. The paneled ceilings of temples are also made from this wood because of its durability. The resin of cedar is called cedar-oil (*cedria*), which is so useful for preserving books that once they are smeared with it they are not damaged by worms, nor do they grow old with time. Cedars grow in Crete, Africa, and Syria.

34. The cypress (*cyparissus*) is so named in Greek (i.e. κυπάρισσος) because its head (*caput*) rises from a spherical shape into a point. Whence it is also called κῶνος ("pine cone, pine tree, cone"), that is, "lofty rotundity." Hence its fruit is a 'cone' (*conus*), because in its rotundity it imitates a conic shape. Thus they are also called (Vergil, *Aen.* 3.680) "coniferous cypresses (*coniferae cyparissi*)." The wood of cypress is closest in character to cedar – it also is suitable for the timbers of temples; its impenetrable solidity never gives way under a burden, but it retains its initial strength. The ancients used to pile cypress branches near their funeral pyres so that the pleasant quality of the cypress scent would mask the odor of the corpses when they were burned.

35. The juniper (*iuniperus*) is so called in Greek either because it peaks into a narrow tip from a wide base, like fire, or because once kindled it stays on fire a long time – so much so that if a live coal of its embers were to be covered it would last up to a year. In Greek, πῦρ means "fire." Further, one kind of juniper is small, and the other large. 36. The ebony tree (*ebenus*) grows in India and Ethiopia. When cut it hardens into stone. Its wood is black and its bark smooth, like laurel. The Indian type is spotted with little white and tawny markings, but the Ethiopian, which is considered superior, is not spotted at all but is black, smooth, and hard as horn. In India

12 *Pisticus* in Late Latin came to mean "pure, authentic" from association with Greek πίστις, "faith." The term was further assimilated to *pisticus*, a corruption of *spicatus*, "spiky," as of spikenard.

lies the Mareotian marsh, whence ebony comes. Lucan (*Civil War* 10.117) speaks of

> Mareotic ebony (*ebenus*).

Ebony is tied onto rattles so that the sight of black things will not frighten an infant.

37. The plane tree (*platanus*) is so called from the breadth of its leaves, or because the tree itself spreads wide (*patulus*) and is large, for Greeks call a broad thing πλατύς. Scripture refers to the name and shape of this tree, saying (cf. Ecclesiasticus 24:19): "As a plane tree (*platanus*) in the streets (*platea*) I was spread out." Further, its leaves are very tender and soft, and like those of vines. 38. The *quercus*, or *quernus* ("oak tree"), is so called because the pagan gods would use it to make poetic predictions for those seeking (*quaerere*) their responses. It is a very long-lived tree – as one reads concerning the oak of Mambre, under which Abraham dwelt, which is said to have lasted for many centuries, up to the reign of the emperor Constans. Its fruit is called the gallnut (*galla*). A wild type of gallnut is called ὀμφακίτης; it is of small size, but with a firm and knotty body, which is used for medicines and purple inks. Another type is βάλανος; it is mild and smooth and very porous, used only for lamps.

39. The ash (*fraxinus*) is said to be so called because it prefers to grow in harsh places and mountainous breaks (*fragum*). *Fraxinus* is derived from *fragum*, as *montanus* from *mons*. About it, Ovid (*Met.* 10.93):

> And the ash, good for spears.

40. The yew (*taxus*) is a poisonous tree, and from it the poison *toxicum* (cf. τόξον, "bow") is pressed out. The Parthians and other nations make bows from yew, whence the poet (Vergil, *Geo.* 2.448):

> Yews are bent into Iturean bows.

So he calls the Parthians 'Itureans.'

41. The maple (*acer*) is unequaled for its colors (cf. Ovid, *Met.* 10.95). Hardwood (*robur*) generally means whatever is very tough of any wood. 42. The alder (*alnus*) is so called because it is 'nourished by a river' (*alatur amne*), for it grows very close to water, and survives away from water with difficulty. Because it is nourished in a damp place it is tender and soft. 43. The elm (*ulmus*) takes this name because it does better in swampy (*uliginosus*) and damp (*humidus*) places, for it is less luxuriant in mountainous and harsh places. 44. The larch (*larex*, i.e. *larix*) was given this name from the fort Laricinum. Boards made from it, attached to tiles, repel fire, and do not char when burned.

45. The poplar (*populus*) is so called because a multitude grows from the base of its trunk.[13] There are two kinds of poplar, one white, one black. The white poplar is so called because its leaves are white on one side and green on the other. Hence this type is bicolored, having as it were the marks of night and day, the periods established by sunrise and sunset. It also produces resin when it grows by the river Po or, as others record, in the territory of Syria. 46. They say the linden (*tilium*) is so named because it is suitable to use for spears (*telum*) because of its smoothness and lightness for throwing, for it is a type of the lightest wood. 47. The willow (*salix*) is so called because it swiftly 'springs up' (*salire*), that is, quickly grows: a pliant tree, suitable for binding grapevines. They say that its seed has this property, that if anyone should consume it in a drink, he will not have children, and it also makes women infertile. The poplar, willow, and linden are all soft woods and good for carving.

48. The osier (*vimen*) is so called because it has great intensity (*vis*, accusative *vim*) of greenness. Its nature is such that, even when it has dried up, as soon as it is watered it becomes green, and then when it is cut and fixed in the ground it puts down roots on its own. 49. The tamarisk (*myrice*), which Latin speakers call *tamaricus*, is named for its bitterness (*amaritudo*), for its taste is very bitter. This tree grows in desolate places in stony soil. From this tree μίσηθρον, that is "hatred" (actually "a hate-charm"), is said to be stirred up by witchcraft. 50. Myrtle (*myrtus*) is named from 'sea' (*mare*), because it is by preference a shore tree. Whence Vergil (*Geo.* 2.112):

> Shores are happiest with myrtle (*myrtetum*),

and (*Geo.* 4.124)

> Shore-loving myrtles (*myrta*).

Hence it is also called μυρίνη (i.e. μυρρίνη) by the Greeks. Moreover medical texts prescribe this tree as good for many female complaints.

51. The mastic (*lentiscus*) is so called because its spike is pliant (*lentus*) and soft, since we call whatever is flexible

13 Isidore says *multitudo* but implies the homograph *populus*, "people, multitude."

lentus – whence osiers and vines are also *lentus*. Vergil (cf. *Geo.* 4.558, *Ecl.* 3.38):

> And the supple (*lentus*) vines,

for 'flexible.' Mastic's fruit exudes oil, and its bark a resin that is called *mastix*. It grows abundantly on the island of Chios and is of better quality there. 52. The turpentine tree (*terebinthus*), its name Greek (i.e. τερέμινθος, τερέβινθος), produces a resin excellent beyond all resins. 53. The box tree (*buxum*) has a Greek name partly corrupted in Latin, for in Greek it is called πύξος. It is an evergreen tree and useful for receiving the shapes of letters because of the smoothness of its wood. Whence also Scripture (cf. Isaiah 30:8): "Write upon box (*buxum*)." 54. The oleander (*rhododendron*), which commonly and incorrectly is called *lorandrum* because its leaves are like laurel (*laurus*), has a flower like a rose (cf. ῥόδον, "rose"). It is a poisonous tree, for it kills animals and heals snakebites. 55. Shepherds call one tree *herbitum* because they give it to livestock in place of grass where pasturage is lacking.

56. *Turbiscus* (perhaps θυμελαία, "spurge-flax") is so named because from one clump of it many shoots rise, as if it were a 'crowd' (*turba*). Straw (*stipa*) is so named because roofs are thatched (*stipare*) with it. Its diminutive form is *stipula*. 57. The reed (*arundo*) is so called because it quickly dries up (*arescere*). The ancients called it 'cane' (*canna*); afterwards Varro called it *arundo* (Funaioli 414). It should be understood that the Latin *canna* derives from Hebrew: in Hebrew *canna* means "reed" (*calamus*). *Cicuta* is the part between the nodes of cane, so called because it is concealed.[14] 58. It is said that in Indian marshes grow reeds and canes from whose roots is pressed a very sweet juice that people drink. Hence Varro (i.e. Varro Atacinus, not Marcus Terentius Varro) says (fr. 20):

> The Indian reed does not grow into a great tree; its sap is squeezed from its supple roots, and no sweet honey can vie with its juice.

59. The elder (*sabucus*) is a soft and porous tree. The *rhamnus* is a kind of bramble-bush that commonly is called bear-briar (*sentix ursina*), a very rough and thorny bush. 60. The briar-bush (*sentix*) is named from its site (*situs*), because it is uncultivated land in which briars and thorns grow. Our ancestors would call every prickly tree a thornbush (*vepris*), because it 'clings forcefully' (*vi prendere*).

61. The wild olive (*oleaster*) is so called because it has leaves like the olive's (*oliva*; cf. the pejorative suffix *-aster*) but broader. It is an uncultivated and wild tree, bitter and unfruitful. A branch of olive grafted on a wild olive changes the potency of its root and converts the tree into its proper character as an olive. The sap of the wild olive is of two kinds. One is like gum without any biting quality, the other is ammoniac pitch collected from the drippings, and is biting. 62. The olive (*oliva*) in Greek is called ἔλαιον ("olive oil"; cf. ἔλαια, "olive-tree, olive"), whence it has been taken into Latin as *oliva*. But the tree itself is *olea*, the fruit *oliva*, and the oil *oleum*. The tree is a symbol of peace, and its fruits are called by diverse names. 63. The *orchas* olive has a Greek etymology, and is so called from its likeness to a testicle, which the Greeks call ὄρχις. 64. The *radiola* olive is so named because it is elongated like a shuttle (*radius*). The Paphian olive is named for the island of Paphos from which it was first imported. 65. The *lycinia* olive, because its oil gives the best light, for λυχνίς means "light" (cf. λύχνος, "lamp"). From this the word 'firewood' (*lignum*) also receives its name, because it is good for burning and light.

66. The *pausia* olive, which country people incorrectly call *pusia* (i.e. *posia*), is good for its sweet and green oil. It is called *pausia* because it is 'pounded down' (*pavire*), that is, crushed – from this word also comes 'pavement' (*pavimentum*). 67. The Syrian olive is so called because it was brought over from Syria, or because it is dark-skinned. The *crustumia* olive is also called the *volemis*,[15] so called because it fills the palm (*vola*), that is, the middle of the hand, with its large size; from this root we also have the word 'seize' (*involare*). However, some understand the word *volemus* to mean "good" and "large" in the Gallic language. Pickled olives (*colymbas*) are so called . . .

68. 'Olive oil' (*oleum*) is named from the olive tree (*olea*), for as I have already said, *olea* is the tree, from which is derived the word *oleum*. But what is pressed from white olives is called 'Spanish oil,' and ὀμφάκιον in Greek. What is pressed from tawny, immature olives is called 'green oil,' but what comes from overly mature

14 *Cicuta* is elsewhere the bush 'hemlock'; see ix.71 below.

15 Vergil speaks of the Crustumian pear, named after the city Crustumium, and another type of pear, the *volemis* (*Geo.* 2.88). Isidore takes them as olives from a misreading of Servius's commentary on Vergil.

olives is called 'common.' Of these, the one primarily used for human consumption is the Spanish, second the green, third the common. 69. The *amurca* of olive oil is the watery part, so called from 'emerging' (*emergere*), that is, because it sinks (*mergere*) below the oil, and it is the oil's dregs. The Greeks call this ἀμόργη, borrowing the word from Latin.

70. Gum (*gummi*) is a Greek term; they call it κόμμι. 71. The Greeks call resin (*resina*) ῥητίνη, for ῥεῖν ("flow") in Greek means whatever flows. It is the 'tears' given off from the 'sweat' of wood from such trees as cherry, mastic, balsam, or other trees or bushes that are said to 'sweat,' like the odoriferous woods of the orient, such as the sap of balsam and of fennel or of amber, whose 'tears' harden into a gem. The chief resin is turpentine (*terebinthina*), the best of all; it is imported from Arabia Petraea, Judea, and Syria, from Cyprus and Africa, and from the Cycladean islands. Second best is the resin of the mastic tree, which is called *mastix*; this is imported from the island of Chios. Third pine resin, of which one is πιτυίνη, the other πεύκινος, the one liquid, the other dry. These are imported from Tyrrhenian Colophonia, whence it has taken the name Colophonian resin. 72. Pitch (*pix*) is a Greek word, which they call πίσσα. Others would have it that pitch is named from 'pine' (*pinus*). It is called κλωνία (cf. κλών, "twig") by the Greeks; we can call it *ramalis* (lit. "branch-like"). The preferred type of this is clear, smooth, and clean.

73. There are three methods of natural creation of trees: either they grow spontaneously, or they spring from seeds that happen to be lying on the ground, or they sprout from roots. Human skill came upon the other methods with the aid of nature. 74. All fruits[16] in Latin are as a rule of feminine gender, with a few exceptions, such as the masculine *oleaster* ("wild olive") and neuter *siler* ("osier"); so Vergil (*Geo.* 2.12):

> The soft osier (*Molle siler*).

Likewise *buxum* ("box tree") is neuter, although it may also be treated as feminine. Some would make a superfluous distinction, so that we would speak of the box tree in the feminine, but of boxwood in the neuter.

viii. Aromatic trees (De aromaticis arboribus) 1. Spices are whatever India or Arabia or other regions produce that have a fragrant scent. They seem to have gotten the name 'spice' (*aroma*) either because they are proper for putting on altars (*ara*) for invocations to the gods, or because they are known to blend and mingle themselves with air (*aer*). Indeed, what is scent if not air that has been tinctured by something? 2. Frankincense (*tus*) is a huge and well-branched tree of Arabia, with very smooth bark and branches like the maple's, dripping a white, aromatic sap, like an almond tree, that is turned into a powder by chewing. When it is broken it is oily on the inside, and when set on fire it burns easily. Also we call it *masculum* because it is spherical in its nature like testicles (cf. *masculus*, "male"). Another type is flat and almost scaly, of lesser quality. It may be adulterated, mixed with resin or gum, but it can be distinguished by its properties, for frankincense, set on fire, burns, while resin fumes, but gum liquefies when heated. 3. Frankincense (*tus*) is so called from 'crushing' (*tundere*). It is also called *libanum* after the mountain of Arabia where the Sabaeans dwell, for their mountain, where frankincense is gathered, is called Libanus.

4. Myrrh (*myrra*) is a tree of Arabia, five cubits high, and is like the thorn that they call ἄκανθος ("acanthus"). Its sap is green and bitter (*amarus*), whence it takes the name *myrra*. The sap that flows spontaneously is more precious, while that drawn out by slashing the bark is considered poorer. From myrrh's prunings the Arabs feed their fires, and unless they counteract it with the odor of storax, they contract many incurable diseases from its highly noxious smoke. Troglodyte myrrh is so called from an Arabian island where a better and purer form is gathered. 5. The storax (*storax*) is a tree of Arabia, similar to the quince, whose shoots exude sap from their crevices during the rising of the dog star. When its distillate falls to the ground it is unclean, but when it is preserved in a slash in its bark, it is clean. The distillate clinging to rods and reeds is clean and whitish, but then becomes yellowed because of the sun. The storax itself is reedy, oily, resinous, of pleasant odor, and moist, and it emits a sort of honey-like liquid. Moreover, storax is so called because the sap of this tree flows and is solidified, for the Greeks call a drop of sap an 'icicle' (*stiria*). In Greek the tree is called στύραξ, in Latin, *storax*.

6. *Bdellium* is a tree of India and Arabia, and the sap of the Arabic type is better. It is clear, whitish, smooth, oily,

16 A scribal error of omission, preserved in Lindsay's edition; rather read, "In Latin, people speak of all fruits as of neuter gender, but of trees for the most part as of feminine, with a few . . ."

uniformly waxy, easily softened, unmixed with wood or soil, bitter, good-smelling. The kind from India is dirty, black, and comes in larger lumps. It is adulterated with gum mixed in, which makes its taste not so bitter. 7. *Mastix* is the sap of the mastic tree (*lentiscus*). It is also called *granomastix* because it looks like grains (*granum*). The better kind grows on the island of Chios, and is good-smelling, with the whiteness of Punic wax – hence it beautifies the glow of one's skin. Sometimes it is adulterated with resin or frankincense.

8. The pepper tree (*piper*) grows in India, on the side of the Caucasian range that faces the sun. Its leaves are like the juniper's. Serpents protect the pepper groves, but the inhabitants of that region, when the peppers ripen, burn them, and the serpents are put to flight by the fire – and from this flame the pepper, which is naturally white, is made black. In fact there are several kinds of pepper fruits. The unripe kind is called 'long pepper'; that unaffected by fire, 'white pepper'; but that which has a wrinkled and bristly skin takes both its color (i.e. 'black') and its name (cf. πῦρ, "fire") from the heat of the fire. If a pepper is light in weight it is old; if heavy, it is fresh. But the fraud of the merchants should be guarded against, for they are wont to sprinkle litharge or lead over very old, moistened pepper to make it heavy. 9. The *aloa* (i.e. 'aloes,' *Aquilaria agallocha*, not 'aloe,' *Aloe vera*; cf. section 28 below) grows in India and Arabia, a tree of very sweet and noble scent. Indeed, its wood is heaped on altars (*altare*) in place of incense, whence it is believed to have derived its name.

10. Cinnamon (*cinnamomum*) is so called because its bark is round and slender 'in the manner of a reed's' (*in cannae modum*). It grows in Indian and Ethiopian lands, and it is a short shrub, only two cubits tall. It is of nearly black or ashy color, and its shoots are very thin. Cinnamon that becomes thick is looked down on, but that which grows fairly thin is choice. When it is broken it emits a visible puff resembling a cloud or dust. 11. *Amomum* is so called because it produces an odor like that of cinnamon. It grows in Syria and Armenia as a shrub producing seeds in clusters like grapes, with a white flower that looks like a violet's, leaves like bryony, and a good scent; it induces sweet sleep.

12. 'Cassia cinnamon' (*casia*) grows in Arabia; its stalk has tough bark, and it has purple petals like pepper. It has a similar character to cinnamon, but less potency, so a double weight of it is mixed into medicines in place of cinnamon. 13. The 'aromatic *calamus*' is named for its resemblance to the common reed (*calamus*). Grown in India, it is jointed with many nodes, of tan color, and fragrant with a sweetness of aroma. When it is broken it fractures into many pieces, resembling *casia* in taste with a slightly biting sharpness.

14. The balsam tree (*balsamum*) existed in Judea within a space of only about sixteen acres. Afterwards, when the Romans took control over that region, it was planted over the widespread hills. Its trunk is like that of a vine, its leaves like those of rue, but whiter and perennial. The tree is called balsam, but its wood is called *xylobalsamum*, its fruit or seed *carpobalsamum*, its sap *opobalsamum*. This last prefix lends its meaning because when it is struck with iron claws the bark of the wood exudes a sap of excellent scent through its cavities – for in Greek a cavity is called ὀπή. People adulterate its sap with oil of the henna tree or honey mixed in, but it can be proved to be unmixed with honey if it coagulates with milk, and unmixed with oil if, when instilled or mixed in with water, it easily dissolves, and further if woolen clothing soiled with it is not stained. But adulterated balsam does not coagulate with milk, and like oil it floats on top of water and stains clothing. When balsam is pure it has so much strength that if the sun heats it up, it cannot be held in one's hand.

ix. Aromatic or common plants (De herbis aromaticis sive communibus) 1. The names of certain plants echo their own originating principles and contain the explanation of their naming. Still, you will not discover the etymology of every plant, for their names change with their locale. 2. *Folium* is so called because floating without any (*ullus*) root it is gathered on the Indian littoral.[17] The Indians pierce it with thread, then dry and store it. It is said to be the herb of Paradise, resembling spikenard in its taste. 3. Spikenard (*nardus*) is a prickly herb, whence it is called ναρδόσταχυς by the Greeks (cf. στάχυς, "spike (of grain)"). One type is called Indian, another Syrian – not because it grows in Syria but because the mountain on which it is found faces India on one side and Syria on the other. The Indian takes many forms, but the Syrian is better: light in weight, golden, hairy, small

17 The etymology of this plant may refer to the usual meaning of *folium*, "leaf"; an all-leaf plant would be rootless. Or Isidore may have in mind *oleum*, "oil," remarkable for its floating on water.

of ear, very fragrant, resembling galingale. If it stays long in one's mouth it dries out the tongue. Celtic spikenard takes its name from a territory in Gaul, yet it grows more abundantly in the Ligurian Alps as well as in Syria; it is a small bush whose roots are gathered into handfuls with cords. Its flower is only good for its scent; its stalks and little roots are considered good for human uses.

4. *Costum* is the root of an herb growing in India, Arabia, and Syria, but the best is Arabian. It is white and light in weight, sweet, of pleasant scent; the Indian type is black and light like a hollow stalk, whereas the Syrian is heavy, colored like boxwood, bitter in odor – but the top is white, light in weight, dry, and fiery in taste. 5. The 'saffron crocus' (*crocum*) is named from the Cilician town called Corycium, although it also is found in other places, but not as much or of such quality as in Cilicia – whence it takes its name from the more important region. Indeed, many things have taken their names from places where they are more prevalent or are better in some way. The best saffron is that which is fresh, good-smelling, not pale, of extended length, whole and not crumbled into pieces, good to breathe, and when it is grasped staining one's hands, and stinging slightly. If it is not found in this condition you may know that it is old or diluted. It is adulterated by mixing with the dregs of saffron oil. Also in order to augment saffron's weight ground-up litharge is added. These things are revealed if the saffron is found to be covered with dust and if, when boiled down, it has lost its proper scent. 6. *Crocomagma* ('saffron dregs'; cf. *magma*, "dregs of an unguent") is made when aromatic fluids are pressed out from saffron (*crocinus*) ointment and the sediment is shaped into little cakes, and therefore it is so called.

7. Hazelwort (*asarum*) grows on shady mountains, with flowers like those of *casia* (see viii.12 above). They have a purple flower next to the root, in which a seed like a grape-seed is contained. It has many very slender and good-smelling roots, and its character is like nard's. Valerian (*phu*) grows along the Pontus (i.e. the Black Sea), with leaves like wild olive. 8. Galingale (*cyperum*) is so called by the Greeks because of its hot quality (cf. πῦρ, "fire"). Its root is like that of a triangular rush, its leaves like a leek's, its roots black or close to the color of olive roots, and it is very odoriferous and sharp. It grows in swamps and empty places. There is said to be another species of galingale that grows in India and is called *zinziber* ("ginger") in their language.

9. The Illyrian iris (*iris*) took its name from its likeness to the heavenly Iris (i.e. the rainbow). For this reason Latin speakers call it *arcumen*, because its flower, in its variety of color, imitates that heavenly bow (*arcus*). It is called Illyrian because it is most abundant and fragrant in Illyria. In appearance it has leaves like the gladiolus, and it has an aromatic root that is good-smelling. 10. *Acorum* (perhaps 'sweet flag') has leaves similar to the iris, and roots of a very sharp but pleasant scent, for which reason it is also a spice. *Meu* . . . Cardamom (*Cardamomum*) . . . 11. The *squinum* (i.e. *schoenum*, a kind of rush) that grows at the Euphrates is better than that in Arabia, tan-colored, abounding in flowers, purple, slender; it smells like a rose when it is crumbled in one's hands, and when tasted it is fiery and biting on the tongue. Its flower is called σχοίνου ἄνθος ("flower of rush"), for 'flower' is ἄνθος in Greek (cf. σχοῖνος, "rush"). 12. Thyme (*thymum*) is so called because its flower gives off a fragrance (cf. θύειν, "offer by burning"; θυμιᾶν "to burn incense"). About this, Vergil (*Geo.* 4.169):

> The fragrant honey smells of thyme (*thymum*).

13. *Epithymum* (i.e. a parasitic plant growing on thyme) is a Greek name, which in Latin is called 'flower of the thyme' (*flos thymi*), for the thyme flower in Greek is θύμον (and cf. ἐπί, "upon"). It is a flower resembling 'Cretan thyme' (*thymbra*).

14. Marjoram (*sampsuchus*), which Latin speakers call *amaracus*, a name that Vergil uses to refer to Venus (cf. *Aen.* 1.693):

> Where the soft, fragrant marjoram (*amaracus*) embraces him with flowers in the shade.

This herb is good for perfumes. It took its name from the page of a certain king who, having accidentally fallen when he was carrying perfumes, created a new and very pleasant scent from their mixing together. 15. Hyacinth (*hyacinthus*) is a plant that has a purple flower. It took its name from a certain noble boy who was found killed in a glade among purple flowers; the misfortune of this child's death gave its name to the plant. In root and flower it resembles an onion, and it delays puberty in boys. 16. The plant narcissus (*narcissus*) has a name given in the myth of a certain boy whose limbs were transformed into this flower. The flower both keeps Narcissus's name for its own and retains the glory of his beauty in the splendor of its petals.

17. The rose (*rosa*) is so called from the appearance of its flower, which blushes (*rubere*) with a red (*rutilans*) color. 18. The lily (*lilia*) is a plant with a milk-white (*lacteus*) flower, whence it is named, as if it were *liclia*. Although its petals are white, a glitter of gold appears within it. 19. The violet (*viola*) gets its name from the strength (*vis*) of its scent (cf. *olere*, "be fragrant"). There are three kinds of violet: purple, white, and quince-yellow. 20. Acanthus (*acanthus*) is an evergreen Egyptian plant, full of thorns and with supple shoots. 21. Clothing artfully decorated with an acanthus pattern is called *acanthinus*. It is also called *acanthis*.

22. Ivy (*hedera*) is so called because with its creeping it clings (*adhaerere*) to trees. About it, Vergil (*Ecl.* 8.13):

> To twine the ivy (*hedera*) (about your temples) among the victorious laurels.

Others say ivy is so called because the ancients would offer it, in addition to a good deal of milk, as food for kids (*haedus*). 23. Ivy is naturally a sign of cold land. It is an antidote to drunkenness if someone who is drunk is crowned with ivy. 24. They record that much hellebore (*elleborum*) grows in Greece near the river Elleborum, and thence it is so called by the Greeks. The Romans call it by another name, *veratrum*, because when eaten it brings a disturbed mind back to health.[18] There are two kinds of hellebore, white and black. 25. Acone is a harbor in Bithynia that is so famous for its crop of harmful herbs that we call noxious herbs 'aconite' (*aconitum*) from its name. The poison called *toxicus* takes its name because it is pressed from yew (*taxeus*) trees, especially in Cantabria.

26. Spurge (*euphorbium*) is so called because its juice sharpens the vision of one's eyes.[19] It is so powerful that it makes tough meat cook more quickly. It grows in many places, but mostly in Mauritania. 27. The plant *laser* (in classical Latin, "asafoetida") grows on the mountain Oscobagum where the river Ganges rises. Its juice was first called *lacsir* because it flows like milk (*lac*), and then it was named *laser* in derivative usage. It is called Cyrenian opium (*opium*) by some because it grows in Cyrene. 28. Aloe (*aloe*) is an herb of very bitter juice. *Panaces* (cf. πανακής, "all-heal, *Ferulago galbanifera*") is a plant of fragrant smell; it has a stem like the giant fennel from which flows the juice called *opopanax*. It is yellow and oily, heavy with odor and very bitter. Galbanum (*galbanum*) . . .

29. Dicte (*Dicta*) is a mountain in Crete from which the plant dittany (*dictamnum*) took its name. For its sake, in Vergil (*Aen.* 4.73), a wounded doe scours the Dictaean groves, for it is of such potency that it drives iron from one's body, and rids it of arrows, whence wild beasts, hit by arrows, cast them from their bodies by feeding on it. Some Latin speakers call it 'pennyroyal of Mars' (*puleium Martis*) because it shakes off the missiles of war. 30. Mandrake (*mandragora*) is so called because it has a sweet-smelling fruit the size of a Matian apple; hence Latin speakers call it 'apple of the earth.' Poets name it ἀνθρωπόμορφος ("human-formed"), because it has a root that resembles the human form. Its bark, mixed with wine, is given for drinking to those whose bodies need to undergo surgery, so that they are sedated and feel no pain. There are two kinds of mandrake: the female, with leaves like lettuce's, producing fruit similar to plums, and the male, with leaves like the beet's.

31. The poppy (*papavera*) is a sleep-inducing herb, about which Vergil (*Geo.* 1.78):

> The poppy (*papaver*) suffused with Lethean sleep –

for it brings sleep to sick people. One type of poppy is cultivated, the other wild, from which flows the juice called opium (*opion*). 32. The colocynth (*colocynthis*) is a wild cucumber that is ferociously bitter. It stretches its vines over the earth as the cucumber plant does. It is called 'colocynth' because it has a spherical fruit (cf. κολοκύνθη, "round gourd"), and leaves like the common cucumber's. 33. The Greeks name the 'centaury' (*centaurea*) thus (i.e. κενταύρειον) because it is reported to have been discovered by the centaur Chiron. It is also called λιμνήσιος because it grows in moist places (cf. λίμνη, "marsh"). It is also called 'gall of the earth' because of its bitterness. 34. Licorice (*glycyriza*) is so called from the Greek because it has a sweet root, for γλυκύς in Greek means "sweet" (and cf. ῥίξα, "root"). The same plant is called ἄδιψος (cf. δίψα, "thirst") because it allays thirst for thirsty people.

18 Isidore may think of 'true,' *verus*, as it were 'sane,' as involved in the etymology of *veratrum*.

19 Isidore thinks of the Greek prefix εu-, "good," and the Latin *orbis*, "eye," though here he uses the common word *oculus* for "eye."

35. *Dracontea* (i.e. a plant resembling arum) is so called because its spike is varicolored like a snake, and it bears the likeness of a dragon (*draco*), or because a viper fears that plant. 36. The celandine (*chelidonia*) is so called either because it seems to sprout with the coming of swallows (cf. χηλιδών, "swallow") or because if the eyes of young swallows are plucked out, their mothers are said to heal them with this herb. 37. The heliotrope (*heliotropium*) got its name at first because it flowers at the summer solstice, or because it revolves and turns its petals with the sun's movements (cf. ἥλιος, "sun"; τρόπος, "turn"), whence it is called 'sun-follower' (*solsequia*) by Latin speakers. It opens its flowers at sunrise and closes at sunset. Latin speakers also call one species of heliotrope 'wild chicory' (*intubum silvaticum*). This is also *verrucaria*, so called because it gets rid of warts (*verruca*) when drunk with water, or removes them when applied as a poultice.

38. *Pentaphyllon* is so called from the number of its petals (cf. πέντε, "five", Φύλλον "leaf, petal"), whence Latin speakers call it cinquefoil (*quinquefolium*, lit. "five-petal"). This plant is so clean that it was customarily employed by the pagans for purification in their temples. 39. Hyssop (*hyssopum*) is an herb good for purging the lungs. Whence in the Old Testament they would sprinkle anyone who wished to be ritually cleansed with lamb's blood on bunches of hyssop. It grows on crags, clinging to the rock by its roots. 40. Rhubarb (*reubarbara*), or *reuponticum*, takes these names because the former is gathered across the Danube on barbarian (*barbaricus*) soil, the latter is gathered around the Pontus (i.e. the Black Sea). It has further the prefix *reu*, because it is a "root" (*radix*), as if the terms were *radix barbara* and *radix Pontica*.

41. The herb called henbane (*hyoscyamos*) by the Greeks is called the 'chalice-like' (*calicularis*) herb by Latin speakers, because its calyxes (*caliculus*) grow in the shape of goblets like those of pomegranates. Their edges are saw-toothed and they have seeds inside like the poppy's. This herb is also called *insana* because using it is dangerous; indeed if it is eaten or drunk it causes insanity or hallucinations. It is commonly called *milimindrum* because it induces aberration of mind (*mens*). 42. Saxifrage (*saxifraga*) is so called because its seeds crack and break up stones in the bladder (cf. *saxum*, "rock"; *frangere*, "break"). Gentian (*gentiana*) takes its name, as physicians record, from its discoverer;[20] its roots resemble those of birthwort (*aristolochia*). It grows at the foot of the Alps and in Asian Galatia.

Savory (*satureia*) is hot and almost aflame. People think its name was given it, because it inclines people to lust. 43. *Satyrion* is so called from satyrs (*Satyrus*) because of its incitement to lasciviousness; it is commonly called *stincus* because it arouses lust.[21] This is the same as the orchid (*orchis*), because its root is shaped like testicles, which the Greeks call ὄρχις. It is also called 'hare-like' (*leporinus*) because it sends out a supple stalk. 44. The nettle (*urtica*) is so called because contact with it scorches (*adurere*) one's body, for it is of an entirely fiery nature and it inflames (*perurere*) at the touch, whence it also causes an itch (*prurigo*).

45. The herb wormwood (*artemesia*) was dedicated by the pagans to Diana, whence it was named, for in Greek Diana is called Ἄρτεμις. 46. Chamomile (*chamaemelos*) is so called in Greek because it has the aroma of Matian apples (*malum*) and it is short and close to the ground (cf. χαμαί, "on the ground"). 47. Germander (*chamaedrys*; cf. δρῦς, "oak") is so called by the Greeks because it is short, spreading out over the ground, and tiny, with very small leaves. 48. Paeon was a certain physician by whom the herb peony (*paeonia*) is thought to have been discovered, as Homer says. Some call it *glycyside* because it has a sweet taste (cf. γλυκύς, "sweet"; σίδη, a plant), or *pentorobina* (i.e. *pentorobos*; cf. πέντε, "five"; ὄροβος, "vetch seed") from the number of its seeds, or as others say, *dactylos* from its resemblance to fingers (cf. δάκτυλος, "finger"). It grows in the woods. 49. Bugloss (*buglossos*) is so called by the Greeks because it has very rough leaves like an ox's tongue (cf. βοῦς, "ox"; γλῶσσα, "tongue"). The ancients recorded that it should be infused in wine to nourish wisdom in a wonderful way. It is also said to give joy to banquets. It is eaten as a green vegetable.

50. *Arnoglossos*, that is, 'lamb's tongue' (cf. ἀρνός, "lamb"), is called plantain (*plantago*) by the Romans, because its cutting (*planta*) quickly roots in the ground. Many eat it as a vegetable. 51. *Herpyllos*, which we call 'wild thyme' (*serpillus*), because its roots snake (*serpere*) a long way. The same herb is called 'mother's heart'

20 Pliny says this discoverer was Gentius, king of the Illyrians.

21 Isidore may refer to the *scincus*, a kind of lizard whose dried skin was supposed to be an aphrodisiac.

(*animula matris*) because it stimulates menstrual flow. 52. Birthwort (*aristolochia*; cf. ἄριστος, "best"; λοχεία, "childbirth") is so called because it is best for women who have just given birth, for applied post partum it purges the womb with the benefit of its vapor. There are two kinds of this herb: one is called 'round birthwort' because it has a round root; the other is 'long birthwort' because it has a long root and also longer branches and leaves. They also call it *dactylitis* (cf. δάκτυλος, "finger") because its root has a finger's strength and length. 53. Groundsel (*erigeron*) is so named by the Greeks (cf. ἦρι, "early, in spring"; γέρων, "old" (the plant is so named for its hoary down)) because it first 'becomes old' (*senescere*) in spring, whence Latin speakers call it *senicio*. It grows along garden walls.

54. *Psyllios* is so called because it has a seed resembling a flea (*pulex*), whence Latin speakers call it 'fleawort' (*herba pulicaris*). 55. *Hierobotane* gets this name from the Greeks (cf. ἱερὰ βοτάνη, "sacred herb") because the pagans pronounced it good for people's medicines and bandages and for priests' purification rituals. Whence the high priests called it *sagmen*, as if the word were *sancimen* (cf. *sancire*, "make sacred"); it is also called *verbena*, because it is pure (cf. *verus*, "true"). 56. The herb Christ's-thorn (*paliurus*) is very rough and thorny. Some call soapwort (*struthios*) the 'woolworker's plant' (*herba lanaria*) because many of them wash wool with it. It grows in cultivated land. [The fern *splenos* (cf. *asplenos*, section 87 below) is so called because it takes away ill-temper (*splen*).] 57. *Cimicia* is so called from its resemblance to the bed-bug (*cimex*), whence the Greeks also called it κόριον ("coriander"; cf. κόρις, "bedbug"). It grows in both harsh and cultivated land.

58. Horehound (*marrubium*), which the Greeks call πράσιον, is so called because of its bitterness (*amaritudo*). It grows in fields. 59. Pennyroyal (*puleium*) [is more precious than pepper among the Indians]. 60. Wormwood (*absinthium*) is a Greek term (i.e. ἀψίνθιον). The more approved type of it grows in the region of the Pontus (i.e. the Black Sea), whence it is also called *absinthium Ponticum*. 61. Comfrey (*symphytos*) is so called in Greek (i.e. σύμφυτον) because it has so much potency in its root that it draws together scattered chunks of meat in the pot (cf. συμφυτικός, "causing to draw together"). 62. The *polypodion* (i.e a fern) is a plant whose root is shaggy and long-haired like an octopus (*polypus*), whence is derived the name *polypodion*. It grows in friable, stony soil, or near oaks. 63. The herb named poley-germander (*polios*) by the Greeks (cf. πόλιον, "hulwort") is called *omnimorbia* by Latin speakers because it relieves many diseases (*morbus*; cf. *omnis*, "all"). It grows in mountains and places with harsh soil.

64. Scammony (*scammonia*), which Latin speakers call *acridium*, is an herb full of juice that is collected by digging around its root. To be precise, they dig a round pit in the earth and then, with snail-shells or the leaves of a nut-tree placed below, the juice is collected and taken away once it has dried. The preferred variety quite often comes from Mysia in Asia; a false kind, of opposite quality, is from Syria or Judea. 65. *Daucos* (i.e. a kind of parsnip or carrot) has leaves like fennel and a stalk two palms long. *Citocacia* (perhaps the dwarf olive) is so called because it quickly (*cito*) purges the belly (cf. *cacare*, "defecate"); commonly and incorrectly it is called *citococia*. 66. Burdock (*lappa*) is so called because it has a huge stalk extending across the ground. This herb is called φιλάνθρωπος ("man-loving") by the Greeks because it sticks to people's clothing due to its rough surface. It grows by walls.

67. 'Venus's hair' (*capillum Veneris*) is so called because it reestablishes hair (*capillum*) lost from alopecia, or because it discourages hair loss, or because it has smooth, black shoots that shine like hair. It grows in wet places. 68. Madder (*rubia*) is so called because its root is red (*rubra*), whence it is said to dye wool. 69. 'Dyer's bugloss' (*anchusa*) stains one's fingers when its root is rubbed; it is blood-colored, and therefore is used by painters for making crimson. 70. Pine-thistle (*chamaeleon*) is called *viscarago* in Latin because it produces bird-lime (*viscum*); birds stick to it when they voluntarily come down to eat. 71. Hemlock (*cicuta*) is so called because on its jointed stalk it has hidden nodes, like a reed – in the same way that we call a hidden ditch 'blind' (*caecus*). When given to someone to drink this herb kills; Socrates drank it in prison and died. Persius (*Satires* 4.2):

> (Believe him) to say, whom the dire draught of hemlock snatches away.

Although it is poisonous for humans, it makes she-goats fat.

72. Clover (*trifolion*; cf. *folium*, "leaf"), which the Greeks call τρίφυλλον, is so called because it has three

leaves on each stem-juncture. 73. Mullein (*phlomos*) – which Latin speakers call 'lamp-herb' (*herba lucernaris*) because it is used to make lamp-wicks – is also called *lucubros* because it gives light (*lux*) in shade (*umbra*).[22] 74. Chamomile (*pyrethron*; cf. section 46 above) is so called in Greek because it has a fiery and clumped root (cf. πῦρ, "fire," and ἀθρόος, "crowded together"). 75. The marsh mallow (*althaea*) is the wild mallow (*malva*), or *malvaviscus*; called *althaea* because it rises on high (*altum*), and *viscus* ("birdlime"; cf. *viscosus*, "sticky") because it is sticky. 76. Wild marjoram (*origanum*), which is translated *colena* in Latin, because infused in wine it colors (*colorare*) it.

77. Spurge (*titimallum*, i.e. *tithymalus*) takes this name because its 'hair' of foliage, twisting around, turns toward the sunbeams, for the Greeks call the sun τιτάν and hair μαλλός; from the compound of these the term *titimallum* was derived. There are seven species of it growing in diverse places. 78. Nightshade (*strychnos*) is called the 'healing herb' (*herba salutaris*) in Latin, because it eases headache and acid stomach. It is also called 'wolf-grape' (*uva lupina*) because its seed looks like a grape. 79. Knot-grass (*polygonos*) is called by Latin speakers 'bloody herb' (*herba sanguinaria*) because it causes bleeding when applied to one's nose.[23] 80. House-leek (*ambrosia*) is called 'wild parsley' (*apium silvaticum*) by Latin speakers. About it, Vergil (*Aen.* 1.403):

> And from her head her ambrosial (*ambrosius*) locks
> breathed a divine fragrance.

81. *Apiago* is so called because bees (*apis*) eagerly seek out its flowers. Purslane (*portulaca*) . . .

Rosemary (*rosmarinum*), which Latin speakers call the 'healing herb' (*herba salutaris*) for its powers, has leaves like fennel's, rough and spread over the ground in whorls. The Egyptian bean (*colocasia*) [is the name of a plant]. 82. 'Wild mint' (*menta agrestis*), which the Greeks called καλαμίνθη, and we commonly call *nepeta* ("calamint"), is quite potent and strong in heat. 83. The plant *genicularis* is spread on the ground to repel scorpions. The gladiolus (*gladiolus*) has leaves like swords (*gladius*), a stalk a cubit long, and purple flowers. 84. Mullein (*verbascum*; see sections 73 above and 94 below) . . . Agaric (*agaricum*), root of a white vine. *Calamites* (cf. καλαμίτης, "reed-like") . . . *Lappa* [a kind of herb (see section 66 above)]. *Lappago* . . . *Lapella* . . . *Beneola* . . . *Orcibeta* . . . [*Satyrion*, (see section 43 above)] . . . The ben-nut (*myrobalanum*) . . .

85. The asphodel (*asphodelus*), which Latin speakers call *albucium* for its color (cf. *albus*, "white"). Squill (*scilla*) is so called because it is harmful (cf. the monster Scylla); a pagan superstition about it says that if it is hung whole in a doorway it chases away anything bad. 86. St. John's wort (*chamaepitys*) is so called by the Greeks because it clings to the earth and smells like pine (cf. χαμαί, "on the ground"; πίτυς, "pine"). Latin speakers call it *cucurbitularis* because it partly recalls the scent of a gourd (*cucurbita*). *Staphysagria* grows in pleasant places (cf. σταφὶς ἀγρία, "stavesacre"). 87. Spleenwort (*asplenos*) is so called because it takes away ill-temper (*splen*; cf. section 56 above). It is also called *scolopendrios* because its leaves resemble a centipede (*scolopendrum*). It grows on damp rocks. 88. The *vulvus* (i.e. *bulbus*, "edible bulb, onion") is so called because its root is rounded (*volubilis*) and spherical.

'French lavender' (*stoechas*) grows on the Stoechades islands, whence it is named. 89. Cyclamen (*cyclaminos*) is so called in Greek after a certain person named Cyclos who first discovered the virtues of this herb – or, because it has a rounded root, for the Greeks call a "rounded thing" κύκλος. Its root or its juice, if mixed with wine, makes people drunk. It grows in wooded places or in fields. 90. Ἄμπελος λευκή, or bryony (*bryonia*), is called 'white vine' (*vitis alba*) by Latin speakers, either because of its color or because its root, when pulverized and rubbed on one's body, makes the skin softer and whiter. Also the juice of its berry causes dry breasts to produce milk. 91. Ἄμπελος μέλαινα (i.e. black bryony), that is 'black vine' (*vitis nigra*), is also called 'wild vine' (*labrusca*); its leaves are like ivy's, and it is larger than white vine in every respect, with similar berries that grow black as they ripen, whence it took its name. 92. The plant *viticella* is so called by Latin speakers because like a grapevine (*vitis*) it grasps whatever is nearby with its tendrils, which we call 'ringlets' (*anulus*).

93. A chrysanthemum (*bupthalmus*) has a yellow flower like an eye, whence it got its name in Greek (cf. βοῦς, "ox"; ὀφθαλμός, "eye"). It has a pliant stalk and

22 The Greek φλομίς is 'phlome,' of which lamp-wicks were made, and φλόμος is "mullein."

23 In *Natural History* 27.113 Pliny says the *polygonos* staunches nose-bleed.

leaves like the coriander's, and it grows by city walls. 94. Mullein (*phlomos*), which Latin speakers call *verbascum*, has a masculine species, with whiter and narrower leaves, and a feminine, with broader and dark leaves (see section 73 above). 95. Fennel (*ferula*) is so called from its pith, for Varro records that the pith of fennel is what the Greeks call ἀσφόδελος (Funaioli 429). Some say *ferula* (also meaning "rod") is from the verb 'strike' (*ferire*), for boys and girls would be flogged with it. Its juice is galbanum (*galbanum*). 96. Papyrus (*papyrum*) is so called because it is good for fires and candles, for the Greeks call 'fire' πῦρ.

The rush (*iuncus*) [is so called because it clings with joined (*iungere*, ppl. *iunctus*) roots]. 97. The bulrush (*scirpus*), with which fields of grain are covered, has no knots, whence Ennius (*Satires* 27):

> They look for a knot, as people say, in a bulrush (*scirpus*).

And in the proverb, "A hostile person looks for a knot even in a bulrush." 98. The orchella-weed (*fucus*) is a kind of plant with which clothing is dyed, so called because it counterfeits another color (cf. *fucatus*, "sham"). Whence Vergil (*Ecl.* 4.42):

> Wool will (no longer) learn to counterfeit colors.

99. Seaweed (*alga*) grows in water, and is like a crop of grain. Thus it received its name, from the coldness (*algor*) of water – or, because it binds (*alligare*) one's feet, because it is thick, with its leaves partly rising above the water. 100. Sedge (*ulva*) and *typhus* (cf. τύφη, "reed-mace") are plants that grow by springs and bogs and in swamps. Sedge is a pliant seaweed and in a way a fungus, and derives its name from "marsh" (*uligo*). 101. But *typhus* becomes inflated with water – whence the 'inflated self-opinion' (*tumor*) of ambitious and self-satisfied people is called *typhus*.

102. Reed-grass (*carex*) is a sharp and very tough plant, resembling Spanish broom. Whence Vergil (*Geo.* 3.231):

> Feeding on sharp reed-grass (*carex*).

103. 'Spanish broom' (*spartus*) is a reedy brush without leaves, named for roughness (*asperitas*), for the coils of rope that are made from it are rough. 104. Grass (*gramen*) is rather named for its location, because it grows in most fields (*ager*, gen. *agri*), whence the Greeks call it ἄγρωστις. However, any plant may be called *gramen*, from the fact that it sprouts (*germinare*), just as *robur* ("oak," or more generally "wood") is the term for every appearance and kind of wood, as well as for the particular species, because oak is the strongest. 105. A fern (*filix*) is so called from the singleness of its leaf (*folium*, cf. *filum*, "a single strand"), for from one stalk a cubit high grows one divided leaf, with an intricate structure like a feather's. Oats (*avena*) . . . Darnel (*lolium*) . . . 106. Tares (*zizania*), which poets always refer to as the 'unhappy darnel' because it is useless and unfruitful. Hay (*faenum*) is so called because flame is fed by it, for φῶς means "flame." We call a handful of hay a 'sheaf' (*manipulum*), and it is called *manipulum* because it "fills the hand" (*manum implere*).

x. Garden vegetables (De oleribus) 1. A garden (*hortus*) is so called because something always 'springs up' (*oriri*) there, for in other land something will grow once a year, but a garden is never without produce. 2. The word 'vegetable' (*olus*, i.e. *holus*) is so called from 'nourishing' (*alere*), because humans were first nourished by vegetables, before they ate grain and meat. Indeed, they only fed on the fruits of trees and vegetables, as animals feed on herbage. 3. The stalk (*caulis*) is generically the term for the middle stem of herbs and vegetables, and is commonly called a *thyrsus*, because it rises from the 'ground upwards' (*terra sursum*). From *caulis* is derived more particularly a certain species of vegetable called 'cabbage' (*caulis*), because its stalk 'makes strong growth' (*coalescere*), that is, grows, fuller than that of other vegetables. It is, moreover, a general term, for any stem (*frutex*) [is called] a stalk (*caulis*). 4. The cyme (*cyma*) is so called as if the word were *coma* ("hair"), for this term means the crown of vegetable plants or trees, in which is located the natural power to make plant life.

5. The mallow-plant (*malva*) is named partly from the Greek term μαλάσσειν ("soften") because its nature is to soften (*mollire*) and loosen the bowels (*alvus*). Its juice, if one mixes it with oil and anoints oneself with it, is said to protect against being stung by bees. Its leaves, ground up with oil and applied to scorpions, are thought to make them sluggish. 6. The carrot (*pastinaca*) is so called because its root is an excellent nourishment (*pastus*) for humans, for it has a pleasant aroma and is delectable as a food. 7. The turnip (*rapa*) is so named from 'seizing' (*rapere*), that is, 'taking root' (*comprehendere*, also meaning "seize"). It has a root wider than a navew, sweeter in taste, and has a slender leaf. 8. The navew (*napus*) is so called from its similarity to the turnip, except that it has

broader leaves and the taste of its root is sharper. The two vegetables have linked names that are almost identical because the seed of one changes into that of the other by turns. As Aemilianus (i.e. Palladius) says (*Treatise on Agriculture* 8.2.2), a turnip in one soil turns into a navew after two years, while in another soil the navew turns into a turnip.

9. The 'turnip cabbage' (*napocaulis*) has a name composed of the names of two vegetables, because while in taste it resembles the navew (*napus*), it grows up not as a root vegetable but as a stalk in the manner of cabbage (*caulis*). Mustard (*sinapis*) is so called because its leaves are 'like navews' (*similis napis*). 10. What we call a radish (*radix*, also meaning "root") the Greeks call *raphanus* (cf. ῥαφανίς, "radish"), because it presses entirely downward whereas the other vegetables rather spring upwards. If one has stained one's hands with the crushed seeds of radishes, one will handle snakes with impunity. Further, even ivory may be whitened by use of a radish. Mixed with food it also resists poison, for radishes, nuts, lupines, citron, and celery are good against poison, but against poison taken afterwards, not against poison already ingested. Hence, among the ancients, the custom was to put these foods on the tables before the other foods.

11. Lettuce (*lactuca*) is so called because it flows with an abundance of milk (*lac*, gen. *lactis*), or because it replenishes nursing women with milk. In men it restrains sexual activity. Wild lettuce is what we call *serralia* (i.e. *sarracia*) because its back looks like a saw (*serra*). 12. Chicory (*intubus*) is a Greek term (cf. ἴντυβος, "endive"), and is called *intubus* because it is 'a tube within' (*intus tubus*). The onion (*cepa*) is so called because it is only a head (*caput*). 13. The shallot (*ascalonia*) is named after one of the cities of Palestine called Ascalon, from where it was first imported. 14. Garlic (*alium*) is so called because it stinks (*olere*). *Ulpicum* (i.e. a type of leek) is so named because it has the smell of garlic. They say that *phaselus* (i.e. a bean) was named after the Greek island Phaselos, not far from Mount Olympus. 15. The leek (*porrum*) has two types, one having a head (*capitatus*), the other able to be cut (*sectilis*, i.e. chives). The latter is smaller, the former larger. For us the beet (*beta*) is a kind of vegetable; for the Greeks it is a letter of the alphabet. Blite (*blitum*) is a kind of vegetable with a bland taste, as if it were a 'poor beet' (*vilis beta*).

16. Cucumbers (*cucumis*, gen. *cucumeris*) are so called because they are sometimes bitter (*amarus*); they are thought to grow sweet if their seeds are steeped in honeyed milk. Gourd (*cucurbita*) . . . *Apoperes* . . . Watermelon (*pepo*), *melipepo* (cf. μέλι, "honey"), and basil (*ocimum*) are obviously Greek names, and their origin is uncertain to Latin speakers. *Olus molle* (lit. "soft vegetable") . . . Orach (*atriplex*) . . . *Brassica* (i.e. a kind of cabbage) . . . *Olisatrum* (i.e. *holusatrum*, a seashore plant resembling cabbage) . . . 17. Cress (*nasturcium*) is named for its savor, because its bitterness 'wrenches one's nose' (*nasum torquere*). 18. Mushrooms (*fungus*) are so named because when dried they catch fire at contact, for φῶς means "fire." Whence mushrooms are also commonly called *esca* (lit., "food") because they are both food for fire and a nutriment. Others say mushrooms are so called because certain kinds of them are killers, whence comes the term 'the defunct' (*defunctus*).

19. A swelling (*tumor*) of the earth brings forth the truffle (*tuber*), and hence gave it its name. The *volvus* (i.e. a type of edible bulb) is so called because it is rounded (*volubilis*) and spherical. Asparagus (*asparagus*) is so called because the stalk from which it grows is prickly and rough (*asper*). 20. The 'caper plant' (*capparis*) seems to have taken its name from the Greeks (i.e. κάππαρις), because it has a rounded seed-capsule (*capitulum*) at its tip. The 'wild radish' (*armoracia*), that is, *lapsana* . . . *Lapistrus* . . . Sorrel (*lapathium*) taken with food comforts one's stomach and suppresses sexual desire. 21. The thistle (*carduus*) . . . Rocket (*eruca*), formed as if it were *uruca* (cf. *urere*, "burn"), because it is of fiery potency and if taken often with food it incites the flame of lust. There are two kinds of rocket, one cultivated and the other wild, of sharper potency; both arouse sexual activity.

xi. Aromatic garden plants (De odoratis oleribus)

1. Parsley (*apium*) is so called because in antiquity the top (*apex*, gen. *apicis*), that is the head, of those making a triumph would be garlanded with it. Hercules was the first to gird his head with this plant – sometimes he would wear poplar on his head, sometimes wild olive, sometimes parsley. Parsley's roots effectively fight against lurking poisons. These are its types: *petroselinon*, *hipposelinon*, and *oleoselinon*. 2. Rock-parsley (*petroselinon*) is so called because it resembles parsley and grows in rocks (*petra*) and craggy mountains. We can call it *petrapium*, for σέλινον in Greek

means parsley (*apium*). The best and most preferred kind is the Macedonian, of sweet taste and spicy aroma. 3. 'Horse-parsley' (*hipposelinon*; cf. ἵππος, "horse") is so called because it is tough and sour. 'Oil-parsley' (*oleoselinon*; cf. *oleum*, "oil") is so called because it has a softer leaf and a tender stalk.

4. Latin speakers name one plant 'fennel' (*feniculum*) because the juice of its root or stalk 'sharpens one's vision' (*acuere visum*; cf. *oculus*, "eye"). Concerning its power they say that snakes shed their skins each year after tasting it. The Greeks call this vegetable μάραθρον. 5. Lovage (*ligusticum*) takes its name from a region, for it grows mainly in Liguria; it has a spicy aroma and a sharp taste. 6. The Greeks name an herb ἄνησον, or as Latin speakers call it, 'anise' (*anesum*), which is known to all, very sharply burning, and diuretic. Dill (*anethum*) . . . Cummin (*cyminum*) . . . 7. Coriander (*coriandrum*) took its name from the Greek, and they call it κόριον. Its seed, when given in sweet wine, makes people very prone to sexual activity. If you give more than a proper measure of it, it fosters madness. Also it is reported that gray hair may be dyed by coriander. Southernwood (*abrotanum*) . . . Chervil (*caerefolium*) . . .

8. Rue (*ruta*) is so called because it produces a sensation of intense heat (perhaps cf. *urere*, "burn," or *ruere*, ppl. *rutus*, "rush"). Another type is wild rue, of sharper power, but both are known to be very hot. Weasels show that rue fends off poisons, because they protect themselves by eating it when they fight with snakes. 9. Sage (*salvia*) . . . Elecampane (*inula*) is called *ala* by country people, and has an aromatic root of very strong smell with a slight bitterness. Mint (*menta*): there are six types of it.

Book XVIII

War and games (De bello et ludis)

i. War (De bellis) 1. Ninus, king of the Assyrians, was the first to wage war. Not at all content with his own boundaries, this Ninus, breaking the compact of human society, began to lead armies, to destroy other lands, and to massacre or subject free peoples. He completely subjugated the whole of Asia up to the borders of Libya in an unprecedented slavery. From this point on the world strove to grow fat in reciprocal bloodshed with one slaughter after another.

2. Now there are four kinds of war: just, unjust, civil, and more than civil. A just war is that which is waged in accordance with a formal declaration and is waged for the sake of recovering property seized or of driving off the enemy. An unjust war is one that is begun out of rage, and not for a lawful reason. Cicero speaks of this in the *Republic* (3.35): "Those wars are unjust that are taken up without due cause, for except for the cause of avenging or of driving off the enemy no just war can be waged." 3. And he adds this a little further on: "No war is considered just unless it is officially announced or declared, and unless it is fought to recover property seized." Civil (*civilis*) war occurs when factions arise among fellow-citizens (*civis*) and hostilities are stirred up, as between Sulla and Marius, who waged civil war against each other within one nation. 4. A 'more than civil' war is where not only fellow-citizens, but also kinfolk fight – this was done by Caesar and Pompey, when father-in-law and son-and-law fought each other. Indeed, in that battle brother struggled against brother, and father bore arms against son. Lucan (*Civil War* 2.151):

> Brothers fell as the battle-prize of their brothers.

Again (2.150):

> To whom the slashed neck of a parent would yield.

5. Wars are also defined as internal, external, of slaves, of allies, and of pirates. Pirate (*piraticus*) wars are sporadic wars on the sea by brigands, when light, swift pirate ships plunder not only shipping routes but also islands and provinces. With wonderful speed Gnaeus Pompey first checked and then defeated such pirates after they had wrought great destruction for a long time on land and sea. 6. As what is waged against external enemies is called 'war,' so 'insurrection' (*tumultus*) is what is stirred up by civil sedition. Sedition (*seditio*) is a dissension (*dissensio*) of citizens, so called because they separate (*seorsum ire*) into different factions. Others think sedition is named from 'dissension of minds,' which the Greeks call διάστασις. 7. Cicero explains how the two differ (cf. *Philippics* 8.3): "There can be," he says, "a war such that an insurrection will not happen, but there cannot be an insurrection without war. Indeed, what other is an insurrection than a disturbance so great that a greater fear (*timor*) arises?" Whence an insurrection (*tumultus*) is so called as if it were 'great fear' (*timor multus*). "An insurrection is more severe than a war, for in a war exemptions from service can take place, in an insurrection they cannot."

8. Moreover war, battles, and skirmishes (*bellum, pugna, proelium*) differ from each other. Thus, the whole affair is called a war, as 'the Punic war.' Its segments are battles, as the battle of Cannae, or of Thermae. Again, in one battle there are many skirmishes – for different skirmishes take place in the wings, in the middle, and at the ends of the battle line. A war is the whole conflict, a battle is of one day, and a skirmish is part of a battle. 9. Formerly a war was called a duel (*duellum*), because there are two (*duo*) factions in combat, or because war makes one the victor, the other the defeated. Later, with one letter changed and another deleted, it becomes the word *bellum*. Others think it is so called by antiphrasis – because it is horrid, whence the verse (Vergil, *Aen.* 6.86):

> Wars (*bellum*), horrid wars –

for "lovely" (*bellum*) is the contrary of a very bad thing.[1]

10. Skirmishes (*proelium*) are named from 'pressing down' (*imprimere*), as an enemy presses down the

1 Both "war" and "lovely" are *bellum* in Latin. Isidore may have taken Vergil to imply an alternate reading: "Wars, horrid and lovely things."

enemy. From this also is the press-beam (*prelum*), the wooden implement with which grapes are pressed. A battle (*pugna*) is so called because originally people used to fight wars with their fists (*pugnus*), or because a war would first begin with fistfights (*pugna*). Whence a *pugna* is sometimes between two people and without iron weapons.

11. Four activities occur in war: battle, flight, victory, and peace. The word 'peace' (*pax*, gen. *pacis*) seems to be drawn from 'pact' (*pactum*). A peace is agreed upon afterwards; first a treaty is initiated. A treaty (*foedus*) is a peace that is made between contenders, named either from 'trust' (*fides*) or from *fetiales* (i.e. the Roman priests charged with confirming peace or war), that is, priests. Through the *fetiales* treaties were made, just as wars were made by lay people. Others think that treaties are so called from a sow foully (*foede*) and cruelly slaughtered, the kind of death desired for anyone who may withdraw from a peace treaty. Vergil (*Aen.* 8.641):

> And they would join in treaties with the slaughter of a sow.

The parts of a treaty are truces (*indutiae*), and they are called *indutiae* as if they were 'breaks in the fighting for a day' (*in dies otia*).

ii. Triumphs (De triumphis) 1. Every realm in this world is procured in wars and extended by victories. A victory (*victoria*) is so called because it is attained by 'force' (*vis*), that is, 'strength' (*virtus*). This is the law of nations, to expel 'force by force' (*vim vi*), for a victory acquired by guile is wicked. A sure victory is either the killing or the complete despoiling of the enemy, or both. But the victory attained at huge cost is not happy, and this is why Sallust (*Histories* 3.29) praises generals who win victory with an unbloodied army. 2. A 'solemn procession' (*pompa*) is a term that takes its meaning from the Greek word πομπεύειν ("lead in a procession"), that is, to be publicly displayed. But a victory precedes a procession, because the first thing for those going into combat is a votive offering for victory.

3. A 'victory trophy' (*tropeum*) takes its name from the term τροπή ("turning"), that is, from the turning and rout of the enemy. This is because anyone who routed the enemy would merit a trophy, and any who killed him, a 'triumphal procession' (*triumphus*), so called from the word θριάμβη (i.e. θρίαμβος, "triumphal hymn"), that is, from exultation. A triumph is due to someone who attains a complete victory, and a trophy for a half-complete one, because he has not yet attained a complete victory, for he has not captured, but routed the enemy. But writers confuse these terms. Tranquillus (i.e. Suetonius, *Prata* 109), however, says that *triumphus* is the preferred term in Latin, because he who entered the city in a triumph would be honored by a threefold (*tripertitus*) judgment: in granting a triumph for a general it was customary for the army to judge first, the senate second, and the people third. 4. It was moreover the custom of the Romans that those making their triumph would ride in chariots, because the early generals would go into battle thus equipped.

Further, whoever conquered in combat would be crowned with a gilded palm-wreath, because the palm has thorns, but whoever laid the fleeing enemy low without combat would get a laurel wreath, because that tree is without thorns. 5. Moreover, those triumphing were clothed in the purple toga embroidered with palms, and would carry a staff (*scipio*) with a scepter in their hand in imitation of the victory of Scipio, although a *scipio* is a staff by which people support themselves. Whence that first Cornelius was called Scipio, because his blind father would walk in the forum leaning on a staff. On this *scipio* would sit an eagle, to signify that by victory the triumphant ones approached celestial greatness. 6. Hence the victors would be smeared all over with red pigment, as if in imitation of the appearance of divine fire. However, they would be accompanied by a hangman, to signify that, even though they were lifted up to such an exalted state, they might still be forcibly reminded of their human mediocrity.

7. An army may be wiped out in two ways, by wholesale slaughter or by dispersal. Sallust (fr. 6): "The enemy," he says, "would be crushed, or dispersed." And Vergil speaks thus of both ways. By slaughter (*Aen.* 1.69):

> And sink the swamped ships.

By dispersal (*Aen.* 1.70):

> Or drive them apart and scatter their bodies in the sea.

8. Pillage from the enemy consists of booty, plunder, spoils, and booty-shares. Booty (*praeda*) is so called from plundering (*praedari*). Plunder (*manubiae*), because it is taken away by hand (*manus*). Also spoils (*exuviae*) are so

named from 'strip off' (*exuere*), because they are stripped from bodies. And booty-shares (*pars*) are so called from the equitable (*par*) division of spoils according to the rank of the person and a fair judgment of their efforts. The word 'spoils' (*spolia*) itself is from 'garments' (*pallium*), as if the word were *expallia* (i.e. "unclothings"), for they are stripped away from the vanquished.

iii. Military standards (De signis) 1. Military standards (*signum*) are so called because an army receives from them its signal for attacking, for victory, or for retreat, for an army is ordered either by the sound of a trumpet or by a signal flag. The major standards of the legions are eagles, dragons, and orbs. 2. Eagles, because that bird was auspicious in Jupiter's combats, for when Jupiter set out against the Titans, people say an eagle appeared as a good omen for him. Fortunate in its protection, and taking it as a sign of victory, Jupiter made the eagle the emblem for a legion. Hence it came about that it was afterwards employed in military standards. Lucan recalls this, saying (*Civil War* 1.7):

> Standards (against standards), eagles matching eagles, and javelins threatening javelins.

3. The standard of dragons originated in the killing of the serpent Python by Apollo. Hence they began to be carried in battle by Greeks and Romans. 4. Augustus is said to have established the orb (*pila*) as a standard – because the nations of the whole globe (*orbis*) were subjected to him – so that he might the more display the figure of the globe (*orbis*).

5. A banner (*vexillum*) is also a battle-sign, having its name drawn from the diminutive of 'sail' (*velum*), as if it were *velxillum*. Under Romulus, soldiers had small bundles of hay for their banners; hence their companies were called *manipuli*, for we give this name to bundles of hay that 'fill the hand' (*manum implere*). According to military custom there are other signs that display diverse images by which an army recognizes itself in the tumult of battle.

iv. War-trumpets (De bucinis) 1. A war-trumpet (*bucina*) is the means by which a signal is given to go against an enemy, so called from its 'sound' (*vox*, gen. *vocis*), as if it were *vocina* – for villagers and country people on every occasion used to be called together to their meeting place by a war-trumpet; properly therefore this signal was for country people. About this, Propertius (cf. *Elegies* 4.1.13):

> The war-trumpet (*bucina*) drove the ancient Quirites to arms.

Its clangor is called a 'blare' (*bucinum*). 2. The Tyrrhenians first invented the trumpet (*tuba*), whence [also] Vergil (*Aen.* 8.526):

> The Tyrrhenian clangor of the trumpet (*tuba*) blasted through the air.

This trumpet was conceived of by Tyrrhenian pirates, when, scattered along the seashore, they were not easily called together by voice or *bucina* to each opportunity for booty, especially with the wind roaring. 3. Hence afterwards in battles it was used for announcing military signals so that, where a herald could not be heard amid the tumult, the sound of a blaring trumpet (*tuba*) would reach. It is called *tuba* as if it were *tofa*, that is, hollow. Again, *tuba*, as if it were *tibia* ("flute").

4. The ancients distinguished between trumpet (*tuba*) and war-trumpet (*bucina*), for a sounding war-trumpet would announce alarm about approaching war – Vergil (*Aen.* 7.519):

> With which the dire war-trumpet gave its signal.

But they would signal a battle under way with the trumpet, as (Vergil, *Aen.* 9.503):

> But the trumpet (sounded) its terrible sound.

The sounding of the trumpet varies: sometimes it sounds for battle to be joined, sometimes to chase the fleeing enemy, sometimes for retreat. A retreat (*receptus*) is the name of the maneuver by which an army regroups (*recipere*), whence the expression 'to sound the signal for retreat.' 5. *Classica* are horns made in order to call people together, and they were called *classica* from 'call together' (*calare*). About these, Vergil (*Aen.* 7.637):

> And now the *classica* sound.

However, among the Amazons the army is not called by a trumpet, as armies that are called by kings, but their army of women is called together by the queen with a sistrum.

v. Arms (De armis) 1. Arms (*arma*) generally are instruments of all kinds; hence the places where they are stored are called storage-chests (*armaria*). Again, arms and weapons (*telum*) are of all kinds, but arms are instruments by which we are protected, and weapons are what we throw. Thus there are two kinds of arms, that is, either for striking or for shielding. 2. Arms properly are so called because they cover the shoulders, for arms (*arma*) are named from 'shoulders' (*armus*), that is, from upper arms (*umerus*), as (Vergil, *Aen.* 11.644):

> The spear driven through his broad shoulders (*armus*) quivers.

Or *arma* derives from the name Ἄρης, that is, from 'Mars.'

vi. Swords (De gladiis) 1. A sword (*gladius*) is generally called a 'blade' (*ensis*) in military use, but the blade is the iron part only, whereas a sword is the whole thing. Appropriately it is called *gladius* because it 'divides the throat' (*gulam dividere*), that is, cuts the neck. It was made for this purpose first, for other limbs are more efficiently cut by battle-axes, but the neck only by the sword. 2. The edge (*acies*) of a sword is so called from its sharpness (*acumen*). The hilt (*capulus*) is so named either because it is the head (*caput*) of the sword, or because it is grasped (*capere*) there so that it may be held, for the edge does not allow the sword to be held in any other way. The term 'point' (*mucro*) pertains not only to a sword, but also to the cutting edge of any kind of weapon. It is so called from its extended length, for the Greeks say μακρός for 'long' – and hence also another term for sword, *machaera*. A *machaera* is a long sword that is sharp on one side.

3. A *framea* is a sword sharpened on both edges, which is commonly called a *spata* (i.e. *spatha*). It is also called a *rhomphaea*. The *framea* is so called because it is of iron (*ferreus*) – for it is called *framea* as if the word were *ferramentum* (i.e. an iron implement), and thus every sword may be called a *framea*. 4. The word *spatha* ("broad sword") is from 'suffering,' from the Greek term, for the Greek παθεῖν means "to suffer," whence we say *patior* ("I suffer") and *patitur* ("he suffers"). Others assert that *spatha* was so named in Latin, because it is 'spacious' (*spatiosus*), that is, broad and large – whence also comes the term *spatula* (i.e. "broad piece (of meat)") with regard to livestock. 5. A *semispathium* is a sword named for its length of half a *spatha* and not, as the ignorant masses say, from 'without a space of time' (*sine spatio*), seeing that an arrow is swifter.

6. The dagger (*pugio*) is so called from piercing (*pungere*) and transfixing. It is a small sword, double-edged, and worn at the side. It is also called a *clunabulum*, because it is girded at the hip (*clunis*). 7. The swallow-tailed (*chelidoniacus*) sword is a broad weapon with a double tip that is bifurcated like a swallow's tail, whence it is called swallow-tailed (cf. χελιδών, "swallow"). 8. A poniard (*sica*) is so called from 'cutting' (*secare*). It is a short sword mainly used among the Italians by those who engage in highway robbery, whence also highway robbers are called *sicarii*. Moreover, Tranquillus (i.e. Suetonius, *History of Games* 195) says: "When the sword of a certain gladiator who had been sent into the games was bent, losing its straight edge, someone ran up to fix it. Then the fighter responded, 'Thus, ha! (*Sic ha*), will I fight.' Thence it was given the name *sica*." 9. Axes (*securis*) are symbols that were carried in front of consuls. The Spanish call them *franciscae* by derivation from their use by the Franks (*Franci*). They had those symbols thus carried so that they would not lose the habit of war, or forget the look of weapons during peacetime.

vii. Spears (De hastis) 1. A spear (*hasta*) is a shaft (*contus*) with an iron head; its diminutive is 'dart' (*hastilia*). The name *hasta* comes from 'craft' (*astus*), whence also is the term 'cunning' (*astutia*). 2. A pike (*contum*) has no iron, but only a sharpened tip. Vergil (cf. *Aen.* 5.208):

> The fierce javelins and the pikes (*contus*) with their sharpened tip.

And *contum* is as if the word were *conitum* ("cone-shaped"), for a cone (*conum*) is a cylinder brought to a point. 3. Javelins (*trudis*) are poles with a crescent-shaped iron piece that the Greeks call *aplustria*. They are rightly called *trudes* because they shove (*trudere*) and thrust down (*detrudere*). Vergil (*Aen.* 5.208):

> And the iron-pointed javelins (*trudis*).

4. Hunting-spears (*venabulum*) are so called as if the term were *venatui (h)abilis* ("apt for hunting"), or because they 'intercept the oncomer' (*venientem excipere*), as if they were *excipiabula*. Indeed, "They intercept (*excipere*) boars, lie in wait for lions, and penetrate bears, if only one's hand is steady" (cf. Martial, *Epigrams* 14.30).

5. A lance (*lancea*) is a spear with a strap attached to the middle of its shaft; it is called *lancea* because it is thrown weighed equally in the 'scales' (*lanx*, ablative *lance*), that is, with the strap evenly balanced. 6. A strap (*amentum*) is the thong of throwing spears which is fitted to mid-shaft, and hence *amentum* because it is tied to the middle (*medius*) of the spear so that it can be thrown. 7. A club (*clava*) is of the kind that belonged to Hercules, so called because it is bound with rows of iron nails (*clavus*). It is made one and a half cubits long. There is a missile called *cateia*, which Horace calls *caia* (unidentified reference). It is a type of Gaulish projectile made of the toughest possible wood, which certainly does not fly far when thrown, because of its weight, but where it reaches it smashes with very great force. If it is thrown by a skillful man it comes back to the thrower. Vergil records it, saying (*Aen.* 7.741):

> Used to hurling *cateiae* in the Teutonic (*Teutonicus*) manner.

Whence the Spanish and Gauls call them *tautani*.

8. A *falarica* is a huge missile made on a lathe, having an iron piece a cubit long and a ball of lead in the shape of a sphere. It is also said to have fire attached to its head. One fights with these missiles from towers, which makes clear why they are so called. Juvenal (cf. *Satires* 6.590):

> You take counsel before the siege-towers (*fala*) and the columns supporting the dolphins.

Therefore *falarica* is named from *fala*, just as *muralis* ("mural") is from *murus* ("wall"). Lucan rightly says it is hurled with twisted thongs by a certain siege-engine (*Civil War* 6.198):

> So that now the *falarica* hurled by twisted thongs.

But Vergil says that Turnus cast a *falarica* with his hand (*Aen.* 9.705). 9. Weapons that are spears and missiles employed by hurling or casting are called 'heavy javelins' (*pila*). Of these, Lucan (*Civil War* 1.7):

> Standards (against standards), eagles matching eagles, and javelins (*pila*) threatening javelins.

The singular is *pilum*.

10. A missile (*telum*) is so called after a Greek etymology, from the word τηλόθεν ("from afar"); it is anything that can be thrown a long distance. Incorrectly, a sword is also called a *telum*, as in this verse (Vergil, *Aen.* 9.747):

> But (you will not avoid) this *telum* that my right hand wields with force.

Properly speaking, however, a *telum* is named for its length – just as we call a weasel *mustela* because it is longer than a mouse (*mus*). 11. A *cuspis* is a thonged spear, named from *caespes* ("earth") because it is a shoot. Vergil (*Aen.* 7.817):

> And the pastoral myrtle with a spear-point (*cuspis*) at its head.

Properly speaking, however, the *cuspis* is the rear part of a spear.[2]

viii. Arrows (De sagittis) 1. The arrow (*sagitta*) is named for its 'keen striking' (*sagax ictus*), that is, its swift striking. It is borne on feathers like a bird so that death might swiftly hasten for a person. The people of Crete first used arrows, on which feathers, as we have said, were glued so that they would be light and fly. 2. *Scaptus*... (perhaps cf. *scapus*, "shaft"). Darts (*spiculum*) are short arrows or lances, named for their resemblance to 'spikes of wheat' (*spica*). 3. A 'scorpion' (*scorpio*) is a poisoned arrow, shot by a bow or a catapult, that releases a poison at the spot where it pierces the person whom it strikes – whence it receives its name *scorpio*.[3]

ix. Quivers (De faretris) 1. A quiver (*faretra*, i.e. *pharetra*) is a case for arrows, so named for its 'carrying' (*ferre*) darts, just as 'bier' (*feretrum*), where a corpse 'is carried off' (*deferre*). For this reason these two words have a common etymology, because 'a quiver carries death, and a bier carries a dead person' (*pharetra mortem, feretrum mortuum portat*). 2. *Coriti* are properly cases for bows, as quivers are for arrows. A sheath (*vagina*) is so called because in it a foil or sword may be carried (*baiulare*). 3. A case (*teca*, i.e. *theca*), so named because it covers (*tegere*) whatever is held in it, with the letter *c* put for *g*. Others claim that *theca* is from a Greek word (cf. θήκη, "chest"), because something is stored there – whence a storage place for books is called a *bibliotheca*. 4. Sword-canes (*dolon*) are wooden sheaths in which a

2 As *cuspis* is regularly used of a spear tip it seems likely that Isidore misunderstood Servius (*Aen.* 10.484), who meant that *cuspis* often signifies not the tip but the whole spear (so Cantó Llorca, 2007).

3 In classical use a *scorpio* is a kind of catapult.

knife is concealed with the appearance of a cane. Sword-canes are named from 'guile' (*dolus*), because they trick and deceive by hiding an iron blade under the guise of wood. Commonly people call them by the Greek name *oxus*, that is, "sharp" (*acutus*). Whence among physicians an 'acute' illness is called ὀξεῖα. 5. A bow (*arcus*) is so called because it wards off (*arcere*) the adversary. Hence also those places that ward off the enemy are called 'citadels' (*arx*, gen. *arcis*). Again, 'bow' from its appearance, because they are bent 'rather tightly' (*artius*).

x. Slings (De fundis) 1. The sling (*fundum*) is so called because from it stones 'are poured' (*fundere*), that is, cast. 2. A *balista* (i.e. *ballista*) is a kind of engine of war named from throwing stones, for in Greek βαλεῖν means 'throw.' It is wound up with a thong of sinew and hurls either spears or stones with great force. Hence it is also called a *fundibalus*, for its 'pouring forth' (*fundere*) and casting. A *testudo* ("siege shed," lit. "tortoise") is an effective defense against the *ballista*; it is an armored wall made by interlocked shields.

xi. The battering ram (De ariete) 1. The battering ram (*aries*) gets its name from its appearance, because like a fighting ram (*aries*) it batters a wall with its impetus. A head of iron is fashioned on a strong and knotty tree-trunk, and, suspended by ropes, the ram is driven against a wall by many hands, and then drawn back it is aimed again with a greater force. Finally, beaten with frequent blows, the side of the wall gives way, and the battering ram breaks through where it has caved in, and makes a breach. 2. Against the thrust of a battering ram the remedy is a sack filled with straw and set in the place where the battering ram strikes, for the impact of the thrust of the battering ram is softened in the yielding hollow of the sack. Thus harder things give way rather easily to softer. 3. *Plutei* are hurdles woven from rawhide that are set up as protection from the enemy when constructing siege-works. 4. A *musculus* is made like a tunnel, and with it a wall (*murus*) is undermined; from this it takes its name, as if it were *murusculus*.

xii. Shields (De clypeis) 1. A 'bronze shield' (*clipeus*) is a rather large buckler, so called because it shields (*clipeare*), that is, it covers, the body and removes it from danger, after the term κλέπτειν (i.e. "steal, disguise"). When it is held opposed to the enemy, by its defense it guards the body from spears and darts. A *clipeus* is for foot soldiers, and a buckler (*scutum*) for horsemen. 2. The buckler (*scutum*) is so called because with it one 'shakes off' (*excutere*) the force of missiles. To resist missiles, the shield is carried in front. The boss (*umbo*) of a buckler is the middle part, as if it were the navel (*umbilicus*). 3. A short, round shield is called an *ancile*, of which Vergil (cf. *Aen.* 7.188):

> He carried an *ancile* with his left hand.

And *ancile* is so called from 'cutting around' (*ancisio*), because it is rounded and as if it were 'cut away' (*ancisus*) on all sides. Ovid (cf. *Fasti* 3.377):

> They call it *ancile* because it is 'lopped off' (*recisus*) on all sides; wherever you look, no angle is present on it.

4. A *peltum* (i.e. *pelta*) is a very short buckler shaped like a half moon. The book of Kings records it (cf. III Kings 10.16–17 Vulgate): "King Solomon made two hundred bucklers of pure gold and three hundred *peltae* of fine gold." 5. A *[s]cetra* (i.e. *caetra*) is a shield of woven leather without wood, which the Africans and Moors use. About it, the poet (Vergil, *Aen.* 7.732):

> A *cetra* covers their left arms.

6. A *parma* is a light shield, as if it were 'small' (*parva*), and not a *clipeus*. It is also called a *testudo*, because this shield is built in the shape of a tortoise-shell (*testudo*). A testudo is also an interlinking of shields curved in the shape of a tortoise-shell, for soldiers take the names of various types of arms from animals, as 'battering ram' (*aries*, "ram"). And Sallust (*Histories* 3.36): "In the shape," he says, "of a military 'hedgehog' (*iricius*, i.e. *ericius*, 'spiked barrier')."

xiii. Cuirasses (De loricis) 1. The cuirass (*lorica*) is so called because it 'lacks thongs' (*lorum carere*), for it is made only of iron rings. 2. 'Scale-armor' (*squama*) is an iron cuirass made from iron or bronze plates linked together in the manner of fish scales (*squama*), and named for their glittering likeness to fish scales. Cuirasses are both polished and protected by 'goat-hair cloth' (*cilicium*).

xiv. Helmets (De galeis) 1. The helmet called *cassis* is made of metal plates, and the *galea* of leather, for a leather cap is called a *galerus*. The *cassis* was named by the Etruscans, and I think they named that helmet *cassis* from the word 'head' (*caput*). 2. The *apex* is what stands at a helmet's top, where the crest (*crista*) is attached, and the Greeks call it κῶνος – for the *conus* is the curved peak of a helmet on top of which is the crest.

xv. The Forum (De foro) 1. A forum (*forus/forum*) is a place for holding trials, so called from 'speaking' (*fari*, 1st person singular *for*), [or from King Foroneus, who first gave laws to the Greeks]. This place is also called the *Prorostra* because the beaks (*rostrum*) of Carthaginian ships, seized in the Punic wars, were removed and set up in the Roman Forum, to be a sign of this victory. The 'legal forum' (*forus*) moreover consists of the complaint, the law, and the judge. 2. A complaint (*causa*) takes its name from the 'event' (*casus*) from which it arises. The complaint is the basis and origin of a proceeding, not yet opened up for trial and examination. When it is put forward it is a complaint, when it is examined it is a trial, when it is finished, it is the judgment. A trial (*iudicium*) is so called as if the word were *iuris dictio* ("a statement of the law"), and judgment (*iustitia*) as if the word were *iuris status* ("establishment of the law"). Formerly a trial was called an *inquisitio*, whence we call the plaintiffs and overseers of trials *quaestores* or *quaesitores*.

3. The word 'business' (*negotium*) means many things: sometimes the 'transaction' of some matter, as opposed to 'leisure'; sometimes the bringing of a complaint, which is a legal dispute. And it is called *negotium* as if it were 'not leisure' (*nec otium*), that is, 'an absence of leisure'. We speak of *negotium* in lawsuits and negotiation (*negotiatio*) in commerce, where something is traded so that more can be gained. 4. A 'dispute' (*iurgium*) is so called as if it were 'the chatter of law' (*iuris garrium*), because those who plead a case debate over the law. Litigation (*lis*) formerly took its name from disputes about boundaries (*limes*, gen. *limitis*). About this, Vergil (cf. *Aen.* 12.898):

> A boundary-stone (*limes*) was laid, to settle litigation (*lis*) about the field.

5. A lawsuit consists either of argumentation or of evidence. Argumentation never arrives at a proof by means of witnesses or written documents, but it discovers (*invenire*) the truth by investigation alone. Hence it is called argumentation (*argumentum*), that is, a 'clear discovery' (*argutum inventum*). Evidence (*probatio*), however, involves witnesses and the authority of documents.

6. For every trial six persons are needed: a judge, a plaintiff, a defendant, and three witnesses. The word 'judge' (*iudex*) is so called as if the word were 'telling the law' (*ius dicere*) to the people, or because he 'decides lawfully' (*iure disceptare*). But to decide lawfully is to judge justly; he is not a judge if justice is not in him. 7. The plaintiff (*accusator*) is so called as if the word were *adcausator*, because he summons 'to a lawsuit' (*ad causam*) the person whom he cites. The defendant (*reus*) is named from 'the matter' (*res*) about which he is prosecuted, because even if he is not guilty of the crime, he is nevertheless called the defendant as long as he is being prosecuted in a trial about some matter. 8. In antiquity the witnesses (*testes*) were called 'those standing over' (*superstes*, plural *superstites*), because they were brought forward 'over the status' (*super statum*) of the lawsuit. Now, with part of the word taken away, they are called *testes*.

9. A witness is evaluated with regard to condition, nature, and conduct. Condition: whether one is a free person, not a slave – for often a slave, out of fear of the master, suppresses testimony of the truth. Nature: whether one is a man, not a woman. For (Vergil, *Aen.* 4.569)

> Always a changeable and fickle thing is a woman.

Conduct: whether one is upright and untainted in behavior. If good conduct is missing, a person is not trustworthy, for justice cannot keep company with a criminal. 10. There are two kinds of witnesses, either those telling what they have seen, or those revealing what they have heard. Witnesses also are delinquent in two ways: when they utter falsehoods, or cover up true things by their silence.

xvi. Spectacles (De spectaculis) 1. A 'spectacle' in my view is in general the name for a pleasure that corrupts not in itself, but through those things that are done there. Spectacles (*spectaculum*) are so called because there a public viewing (*inspectio*) is offered to people. They are also called shows (*ludicrum*) because they take place at games (*ludus*) or at feasts.[4] 2. The origin of games is said

4 Most early manuscripts (and Cantó Llorca, 2007) read "on stages" (*in scenis*) for "at feasts" (*in cenis*).

to be thus: Lydians from Asia settled as immigrants in Etruria with their leader Tyrrhenus, who had yielded to his brother in a dispute over the kingdom. Therefore, among the other rituals of their superstitions, they also established spectacles in the name of their religion. From there the Romans borrowed the performers who had been brought in, and hence games (*ludus*) are named from Lydians (*Lydius*).

Varro, however, says that games were so called from 'amusement' (*lusus*), because youths on festival days would entertain the populace with the excitement of games (Funaioli 435). Hence people think of it as the amusement of young people in connection with festival days, temples, and religious ceremonies. 3. There is nothing more to be said now concerning the origin of the word, since the origin of the thing itself is idolatry. Hence games are also called, indiscriminately, Liberalia, in honor of Father Liber. For this reason you should take note of the stain of the origin of spectacles, so that you may not consider as good what took its origin from evil. A game may be gymnastic, or of the circus, or gladiatorial, or theatrical.

xvii. Gymnastic games (De ludo gymnico) 1. A gymnastic game is the exaltation of speed and strength. Its place is in the gymnasium, where athletes exercise and the speed of runners is put to the test. Hence it happens that the exercises of nearly all the arts are called *gymnasia*. 2. Formerly, those competing in such places would gird up their garments, rather than go naked. Then a certain runner took a fall and died when his belt came loose. For this reason in accordance with a decree of the council the magistrate Hippomenes then permitted everyone thereafter to exercise naked. Hence it is called a *gymnasium* (cf. γυμνός, "naked"), because youths exercise naked in the arena, where they cover only their privates.

xviii. Types of gymnastics (De generibus gymnicorum) There are five types of gymnastics: jumping, running, throwing, feats of strength, and wrestling. Hence they say that a certain king, who had that same number of adolescent sons, ordered them to compete for the kingdom in that many types of gymnastics.

xix. The jump (De saltu) A jump (*saltus*) is so called as if it were 'to leap on high' (*exsilire in altum*), for jumping concerns leaping higher or farther.

xx. The race (De cursu) A race (*cursus*) is named for swiftness of legs (*crus*, gen. *cruris*), for running concerns swiftness of foot.

xxi. The throw (De iactu) The throw (*iactus*) is named from throwing (*iacere*). Hence a fisherman's cast-net is called a *iaculum*. The exercise of this skill involves taking up stones and hurling them a long way, balancing spears and throwing them, and shooting arrows from a bow.

xxii. Feats of strength (De virtute) Feats of strength (*virtus*) involve high levels of physical strength (*vis*, plural *vires*) deployed in exertion and in weight-lifting.

xxiii. Wrestling (De luctatione) Wrestling (*luctatio*) is so called from the gripping of flanks (*latus*) by which the fighters bear down in hand-to-hand struggle. Wrestlers are referred to by the Greek term 'athlete' (*athleta*).

xxiv. The palestra (De palaestra) A wrestling place is called a palestra (*palaestra*). The term, they say, derives either from the term πάλη, that is, 'wrestling,' or from πάλλειν, that is, 'a movement of a powerful overthrow' – doubtless because in wrestling, when they grasp one another's middles, they almost crush them, and that is called πάλλειν in Greek. Some suppose that the art of wrestling was revealed by the fighting of bears, for among all the beasts they alone stand erect in their grappling, and quickly crouch and turn back, and by turns sometimes attack with their paws and sometimes avoid grappling, in the manner of wrestlers.

xxv. Competitions (De agone) What in Latin are 'competitions' (*certamen*) are called in Greek ἀγῶνες, from the crowds in which they were celebrated: indeed, any gathering or convening is called an *agon*. Others think they are called agons because they are produced in arenas that are ring-shaped – as if the word were *agonia*, that is, places 'without corners' (*sine angulo*; cf. γωνία, "angle").

xxvi. Types of competitions (De generibus agonum) The types of competitions were: greatness of strength, swiftness in running, skill at archery, endurance in standing still, movement in marching to lyre or pipes, and also competitions over good character, beauty, singing, and further, over skill in land war and naval battle, and contests about withstanding torments.

xxvii. Circus games (De ludis circensibus) 1. The circus games were established for the sake of sacred rites and celebrations of the pagan gods; hence, those who watch them are seen to be devoted to demons' cults. Formerly, simple equestrian events were performed, and the common custom was not at all deserving of censure, but when this natural practice developed into public games it was converted into the worship of demons. 2. And so this kind of competition was dedicated to Castor and Pollux, to whom, the stories teach us, horses were granted by Mercury. Neptune also is a god of the equestrian game, and the Greeks call him ἵππιος (cf. ἵππος, "horse"); horses in the games are also consecrated to both Mars and Jupiter, and it is they who preside over the four-horse chariots.

3. The circus (*circensis*) games are so called either from 'going in a circle' (*circumire*), or because, where the turning-posts are now, formerly swords were set up which the chariots would go around – and hence they were called *circenses* games after the 'swords around' (*ensis* + *circa*) which they would run. And indeed, those driving chariots on the shore along the banks of rivers would set up swords in a row at the riverbank, and part of the art of horsemanship was to wheel around these dangerous obstacles. From this the *circenses* games are thought to have been named, as if the term were 'around swords' (*circum enses*).

xxviii. The circus (De circo) 1. The circus was chiefly dedicated by the pagans to the sun god, whose shrine was in the middle of the racetrack and whose effigy shone out from the gable of the shrine, because they did not think that he, whom they believed was in the open, ought to be worshipped under a roof. A *circus* is the whole space that horses would race around. 2. The Romans think that it was called *circus* from the 'circuit' (*circuitus*) of horses, because there the horses race around (*circum*) the turning-posts. But the Greeks say it was named after Circe, daughter of the sun god, who founded this kind of competition in honor of her father, and from her name they argue that the term *circus* derived. Moreover, she was a sorceress and a witch and a priestess of demons; in her conduct we may recognize both the working of the magical arts and the cult of idolatry.

xxix. The apparatus (De ornamentis) 1. The apparatus of the circus comprises the 'eggs,' the turning posts, the obelisk, and the starting-gate. Some people say the 'eggs' (i.e. objects used to mark the number of circuits of the chariots) are in honor of Pollux and Castor; these same people do not blush to believe that these two were begotten from an egg sired by Jupiter as a swan. 2. The Romans claim that the circus games represent the first principles of the world, so that under this pretext they may excuse the superstitions of their own empty beliefs.

xxx. The turning-posts (De metis) Properly by the term 'turning-posts' (*meta*) people mean to designate the end-point and boundary of the world, from the fact that the end is 'measured out' (*emetiri*) in some way, or as a token of the rising and setting of the sun.

xxxi. The obelisk (De obelisco) 1. Mesfres, king of Egypt, is said to have been the first to make an obelisk, for the following reason. Because the Nile once had damaged Egypt with a violent flood, the indignant king, as if to exact a penalty from the river, shot an arrow into the water. Not long afterwards, seized by a serious illness, he lost his sight, and once his vision was restored after this blindness he consecrated two obelisks to the sun god. 'Obelisk' (*obeliscus*) means "arrow," and it is set up in the middle of the circus because the sun runs through the middle of the world. 2. Moreover, the obelisk, set up in the midpoint of the space of the racetrack equidistant from the two turning-posts, represents the peak and summit of heaven, since the sun moves across it at the midpoint of the hours, equidistant from either end of its course. Set on top of the obelisk is a gilded object shaped like a flame, for the sun has an abundance of heat and fire within it.

xxxii. The starting-gates (De carceribus) In the circus the places from which the horses are loosed are called starting-gates (*carcer*), for the same reason that prisons (*carcer*) in a city are so named – because, just as humans are condemned and imprisoned there, so horses are 'confined' (*coercere*) here so that they may not start off before the signal is given.

xxxiii. Charioteers (De aurigis) 1. The art of the circus comprises the charioteer and the race, people on horseback or on foot. The charioteer (*auriga*) is properly so called because he 'drives and guides' (*agere et regere*), or because he 'beats' (*ferire*) the yoked horses, for one who 'gouges' (*aurire*) is one who 'beats' (*ferire*), as (Vergil, *Aen.* 10.314):

> He gouges (*aurire*, i.e. *haurire*, lit. "drink") the open side.

2. A charioteer is also a driver (*agitator*), that is, a whipper, so called from 'driving' (*agere*). Further, charioteers wear two colors, with which they make a display of their idolatry, for the pagans dedicated the green to the earth and the blue to the sky and sea.

xxxiv. The team of four (De quadrigis) 1. Ericthonius, who ruled Athens, is said to have been the first to yoke together four horses, for which Vergil is the authority, saying (cf. *Geo.* 3.113):

> Ericthonius first dared to yoke a chariot and four horses, and to stand as victor on swift wheels.

2. He was, as the legends say, the son of Minerva and Vulcan, born from the evidence of Vulcan's lust spilled on the earth, as a demonic portent, or rather as a devil himself. He first dedicated the chariot to Juno. From such a founder were 'four-horse chariots' (*quadriga*) invented.

xxxv. The chariot (De curru) 1. The chariot (*currus*) takes its name from 'racing' (*cursus*), or because it is seen to have [many] wheels – thence also a 'two-wheeled wagon' (*carrus*), as if it were *currus*. The *quadriga* (i.e. a chariot with a team of four) formerly had a double and unbroken tongue, which linked all the horses with a single yoke. 2. Cleisthenes of Sicyon was first to yoke only the middle pair of horses, and to connect to them the other two on each side with a single band. These outer two the Greeks call σειραφόροι and the Latins call 'trace-horses' (*funarius*), from the kind of band (cf. *funis*, "rope") with which they were formely linked.

xxxvi. The horses with which we race (De equis quibus currimus) 1. The *quadriga*, *biga*, *triga*, and *seiuga* (i.e. four-, two-, three-, and six-horse chariots) are named from the number of horses and the word 'yoke' (*iugum*). The *quadriga* is dedicated to the sun, the *biga* to the moon, the *triga* to the underworld, the *seiuga* to Jupiter, and the horse-vaulters (*desultor*) to Lucifer and Hesperus. They associate the *quadriga* with the sun because the year rolls through four seasons: spring, summer, autumn, and winter. 2. The *biga* with the moon, because it travels on a twin course with the sun, or because it is visible both by day and by night – for they yoke together one black horse and one white. The *triga* is consecrated to the infernal gods because they draw people to themselves in each of three ages – that is, infancy, youth, and old age. The *seiuga*, the largest chariot, races for Jupiter, because they think him the greatest of their gods. 3. Furthermore, they say that chariots race on wheels (*rota*) either because the world whirls by with the speed of its circle, or because of the sun, which wheels (*rotare*) in a circular orbit, as Ennius says (*Annals* 558):

> Thence the shining wheel (*rota*) cleared the sky with its rays.

xxxvii. The seven laps (De septem spatiis) Chariots run seven laps (*spatium*), with reference to the courses of the seven planets by which they say the world is controlled, or to the course of the seven stages of life; when these stages have been completed, the end of life is reached. The end of these laps is the goal line (*creta*), that is, judgment (cf. *cernere*, ppl. *cretus*, "decide, judge").

xxxviii. The riders (De equitibus) They say the riders (*eques*) race alone because each person traverses and completes the course of this life alone, one following another at different times, but through one path of mortality up to its own turning-post of death.

xxxix. Horse-vaulters (De desultoribus) Horse-vaulters (*desultores*) are so called because formerly as each one came to the end of the course he would 'leap down' (*desilire*) and run, or because he would 'vault across' (*transilire*) from one horse to another.

xl. Foot racers (De peditibus) People speak of 'foot racers' (*pedes*) since they run on foot (*pes*, gen. *pedis*), because one makes a footrace toward one's death. Because of this they run from the higher side to the lower, that is, from the direction of sunrise to sunset, because mortals rise up and then fall. They race naked because in a similar way no remains survive for a person in this world. They run a straight course because there is no distance between life and death. But they contrive these explanations in their effort to excuse their empty beliefs and sacrilege.

xli. The colors worn by horses (De coloribus equorum) 1. The pagans also associate, in a similar way, the colors decking the horses with the first principles of the elements, linking red with the sun, that is, with fire, white with air, green with earth, and blue with water. According to them, the reds race for summer, because it is the fiery color, and everything turns gold then. The whites for winter, because it is icy, and everything turns white in the cold. The greens for spring, from its green color, because then the young shoots grow thick. 2. Again, they dedicate those racing in red to Mars, from whom the Romans descend, and because the standards of the Romans are embellished with scarlet, or because Mars delights in blood. Those in white are dedicated to the zephyrs and mild weather; the greens to flowers and the earth; the blues to water or air, because they are of sky-blue color; the saffrons or yellows to fire and the sun; the purples to Iris, whom we call the rainbow, because it has many colors.

3. Thus, since in this spectacle they pollute themselves with the cult of their gods and with the cosmic elements, they are most certainly known to worship those same gods and elements. Hence, Christian, you should pay attention to the fact that unclean divinities possess the circus. For this reason that place, which many of Satan's spirits have haunted, will be alien to you, for the devil and his angels have entirely filled it.

xlii. The theater (De theatro) 1. A theater is the enclosure for a stage, having a semi-circular shape, in which all those watching stand. Its shape was originally round, like an amphitheater, but afterwards, from half an amphitheater, it became a theater. The word 'theater' (*theatrum*) derives from 'a spectacle,' from the word θεωρία, because the people standing in it observe the plays, watching from above. 2. But indeed a theater is the same as a brothel (*prostibulum*), because when the plays are finished prostitutes 'stretch themselves out' (*prostrari*) there. It is likewise called a whorehouse (*lupanar*, plural *lupanaria*) because of those same prostitutes who are called she-wolves (*lupa*) from the loose conduct of their widely-shared bodies. Prostitutes are called she-wolves for their rapaciousness, because they seize upon wretches and ensnare them. *Lupanaria* were established by the pagans in order to make public the shame of fallen women, and so that the men who engage prostitutes might be held up to the same ridicule as the women who make themselves available.

xliii. The stage building (De scena) The stage building (*scena*) was a place in the lower part of a theater built like a house, with a platform (*pulpitus*) which was called the *orchestra*, where the comic and tragic performers would sing and where the actors and mimes would perform. The *scena* is named after a Greek word (i.e. σκηνή, "tent") because it was built to look like a house. Hence also in Hebrew the Feast of the Tabernacles was called σκηνοπήγια from their similarity to domiciles.

xliv. The orchestra (De orchestra) The *orchestra* was the platform part of the stage setting, where a dancer could perform, or two actors could engage in dialogue. The comic and tragic poets would mount there in their contests, and along with their chanting others would perform the movements. Occupations connected with the stage include tragedians, writers of comedy, musicians, actors, mimes, and dancers.

xlv. Tragedians (De tragoedis) Tragedians (*tragoedus*) are those who would sing for the audience in poetry about the ancient deeds and lamentable crimes of wicked kings.

xlvi. Writers of comedy (De comoedis) Writers of comedy (*comoedus*) are those who would recount in word and gesture the deeds of common people, and in their plots would represent the defiling of virgins and the love affairs of courtesans.

xlvii. Stage musicians (De thymelicis) *Thymelici* were the stage musicians who would begin with music on pipes, lyres, and lutes. They are called *thymelici* because formerly they would perform standing in the orchestra on a raised platform that was called a *thymele*.

xlviii. Actors (De histrionibus) Actors (*histrio*) are those who, dressed as women, would represent the deeds of shameless women. They also would show stories and events by dancing. They are called *histriones* either because that kind of acting was imported from the country Histria (i.e. Istria), or because they would present legends entwined with history (*historia*), as if they were *historiones*.

xlix. Mimes (De mimis) Mimes (*mimus*) are named from a Greek word (i.e. μῖμος) because they are imitators (*imitatores*) of human activity. They had their own narrator, who would tell the plot before they performed their mime. For dramatic tales were composed by poets in such a way that they would be very suitable for movements of the body.

l. Dancers (De saltatoribus) Varro says dancers (*saltator*) were named after the Arcadian Salius, whom Aeneas brought with him into Italy, and who first taught noble Roman youths to dance (Funaioli 454).

li. What should be performed under which patron (Quid quo patrono agatur) The patronage of Liber and Venus is evident in the theater arts, those arts, peculiar to and characteristics of the stage, that involve gesture and sinuous bodily movement. Indeed, dissolute people would offer up their depravity to Liber and Venus – to the latter through their sexuality, to the former through their extravagance. But what is performed there by voice and rhythm, pipe and lyre, has as its patrons Apollos, the Muses, Minervas, and Mercuries. Christian, you should hate any spectacle whose patrons you hate.

lii. The amphitheater (De amphitheatro) 1. The amphitheater is the arena for spectacles where gladiators fight. And a school of gladiators (*gladiator*) is so called because in it youths learn the use of arms with various moves, at one time competing among themselves with swords (*gladius*) or fists, at another going out against wild animals. There, enticed not by hatred but by pay, they undergo deadly combat. 2. The amphitheater (*amphitheatrum*) is so called because it is composed of two theaters, for an amphitheater is round, whereas a theater, having a semicircular shape, is half an amphitheater.

liii. The equestrian game (De ludo equestri) There are several kinds of gladiatorial games, of which the first is the equestrian game. In it, after military standards had first entered, two horsemen would come out, one from the east side and the other from the west, on white horses, bearing small gilded helmets and light weapons. In this way, with fierce perseverance, they would bravely enter combat, fighting until one of them should spring forward upon the death of the other, so that the one who fell would have defeat, the one who slew, glory. People armed like this used to fight for the sake of Mars Duellius.

liv. Net-fighters (De retiariis) The net-fighter (*retiarius*) is named for his type of weapon. In a gladiatorial game he would carry hidden from view a net (*rete*) against the other fighter; it is called a 'casting-net' (*iaculum*), so that he might enclose the adversary armed with a spear, and overcome him by force when he is tangled in it. These fighters were fighting for Neptune, because of the trident.

lv. Pursuers (De secutoribus) The pursuer (*secutor*) is named because he pursues (*insequi*, ppl. *insecutus*) net-fighters, for he would wield a spear and a lead ball that would impede the casting-net of his adversary so that he might overwhelm him before he could strike with the net. These combatants were dedicated to Vulcan, because fire always pursues. And the pursuer was matched with the net-fighter because fire and water are always enemies.

lvi. Ensnarers (De laqueariis) The combat strategy of ensnarers (*laquearius*) was to throw a noose (*laqueus*) over opponents protected by leather shields as they were fleeing in the game, and after disabling them pursue them and bring them to the ground.

lvii. Skirmishers (De velitibus) The fighting done by skirmishers was to hurl missiles on this side and that. Theirs was a varied form of combat, and more pleasing to the spectators than the others. The skirmishers (*veles*, plural *velites*) were named either from 'flying through the air' (*volitatio*) or from the Etruscan city that was called *Veles*.

lviii. Combat to the death (De ferali certamine) Combat with wild animals (*fera*) involved youths confronting beasts after they were released and battling against them, voluntarily courting death, not because they were condemned to do so, but because of their own passion.

lix. The performance of these games. (De horum exercitatione ludorum) Surely these spectacles of cruelty and the attendance at vain shows were established not only by the vices of humans, but also at the behest of demons. Therefore Christians should have nothing to do with the madness of the circus, the immodesty of the theater, the cruelty of the amphitheater, the atrocity of the arena, the debauchery of the games. Indeed, a person who takes up such things denies God, having become an apostate from the Christian faith, and seeks anew what he renounced in baptism long before – namely, the devil and his pomps and works.

lx. The gaming-board (De tabula) Dicing (*alea*), that is, the game played at the gaming-board (*tabula*), was invented by the Greeks during lulls of the Trojan War by a certain soldier named Alea, from whom the practice took its name. The board game is played with a dice-tumbler, counters, and dice.

lxi. Dice-tumblers (De pyrgis) The dice-tumbler (*pyrgus*) is so called because dice 'pass through' (*pergere*) it, or because it is shaped like a tower – for the Greeks call a tower πύργος.

lxii. Gaming counters (De calculis) Counters (*calculus*) are so called because they are smooth and round. Hence a pebble is also called a *calculus*, which because of its small size may be 'walked on' (*calcare*) harmlessly. Again, *calculi*, because they are moved along the tracks laid out on the board, as if along 'paths' (*callis*).

lxiii. Dice (De tesseris) Dice (*tessera*) are so called because they are squared off (cf. τέσσαρες, "four") on all sides. Others call them 'young hares' (*lepusculus*), because they scatter with a bound. Formerly dice were called 'throwing pieces' (*iaculum*), from 'throwing' (*iacere*).

lxiv. The figurative senses of dicing (De figuris aleae) Furthermore, certain dice-players think that they perform their art by way of an allegory of natural science, and conceive of it as bearing a certain likeness to natural phenomena. They maintain that they play with three dice because of the three tenses of the world – present, past, and future – because they do not stand still but tumble down. They also hold that the paths on the board are divided into six regions, for the ages of a human, and in three lines, for the three tenses. Hence they say that a gaming-board is marked off in three lines.

lxv. Dicing terms (De vocabulis tesserarum) The players of antiquity would call each throw by a number, as a one, [a two,] a three, a four, [a five,] a six.[5] Later the terms for several were changed, and the one was called the 'dog' (*canis*), the three the 'face-down' (*suppus*), and the four the 'flat' (*planus*).

lxvi. The casting of dice (De iactu tesserarum) The casting of dice is so managed by experienced dice-throwers that the throw comes out as intended – for example it comes out as a six, which is a good throw for them. But they avoid the *canis* because it is a bad throw, for it means the one-spot.

lxvii. The moving of counters (De calculorum motu) Counters (*calculus*) are moved partly in a fixed order (*ordo*, gen. *ordinis*) and partly at random (*vage*). Hence they call some counters *ordinarius*, and others *vagus*. But those that are entirely unable to be moved they call 'the unmoved' (*incitus*). Hence people in need are also called *inciti* – those for whom there remains no hope of advancing farther.

lxviii. The banning of dicing (De interdictione aleae) Fraud and lying and perjury are never absent from games of chance, and finally both hatred and ruin. Hence at certain times, because of these crimes, they have been banned by the laws.

lxix. Ball games (De pila) 1. A ball (*pila*) is properly so called because it is stuffed with hair (*pilus*). It is also a 'sphere' (*sfera*, i.e. *sphera*), so called from 'carrying' (*ferre*) or 'striking' (*ferire*). Concerning the type and weight of these, Dorcatius thus reports (fr. 1):

> Nor spare to stuff in the hair of the lively deer until an ounce has been added over two pounds.[6]

2. Among the types of ball games are 'trigon-ball' (*trigonaria*) and 'arena-ball' (*arenata*). *Trigonaria* is so named because it is played by three (*tres*; cf. ἀγών, "contest"; *trigonus*, "three-cornered") players. Arena-ball, which is played in a group, when, as the ball is thrown in from the circle of bystanders and spectators, they would catch it beyond a set distance and begin the game. They call it the 'elbow-game' (*cubitalis*) when two people at close quarters and with their elbows (*cubitum*) almost joined strike the ball. Those who pass the ball to their fellow players for striking it with the outstretched lower leg are said to 'give it the calf' (*suram dare*).

5 Some early manuscripts omit the two- and five-spots, and one early type of die also omitted these, leaving two rounded faces.

6 The couplet recommends stuffing a ball with deer hair to the weight of two pounds, one ounce.

Book XIX

Ships, buildings, and clothing (De navibus aedificiis et vestibus)

i. Ships (De navibus) 1. In turn, I have applied myself to the terms for specific skills by which something is made, terms for the tools of the artisans or whatever proves useful to them, and anything else of this sort worth pointing out. 2. The general term 'craftsman' (*artifex*) is so given because he practices (*facere*) an art (*ars*, gen. *artis*), just as a goldsmith (*aurifex*) is someone who works (*facere*) gold (*aurum*), for the ancients used to say *faxere* instead of *facere*.

3. A 'ship captain' (*nauclerus*) is the master of the ship, and is named thus because the ship is under his assignment, for 'assignment' is called κλῆρος in Greek. But the others on the ship have their share as well. 4. The helmsman (*gubernio*), also known as the *gubernator*, as if the word were *coibernator*, because his prudence restrains (*coibere*, i.e. *cohibere*) the winters (*ibernum*, i.e. *hibernum*), that is, the storms of the sea. 5. The word 'sailor' (*nauta*) is derived from 'ship' (*navis*). Sometimes *navita* is used poetically for *nauta*, just as *Mavors* is used for *Mars*, but the correct term is *nauta*. 6. An oarsman (*remex*) is so named because he wields an oar (*remus*). The word is *remex* in the nominative case in the same way as *tubex*. 7. An *epibata* is named with a Greek term (i.e. ἐπιβάτης, "one who embarks"); in Latin he is called a 'passenger' (*superveniens*). He has no duties on the ship, but, once his passage has been paid, arranges to cross over to foreign lands. 8. Some people maintain that a ship (*navis*) is so named because it needs a vigorous (*navus*) guide, that is, experienced, wise, and energetic – someone who knows how to control and take charge in the face of maritime dangers and accidents. Whence Solomon said (Proverbs 1:5): "He that understandeth, shall possess governments (*gubernaculum*)." The Lydians were the first to construct ships, and in seeking out the uncertainties of the ocean, they made the sea into a thoroughfare for human use.

9. Rafts (*ratis*) were the first and most ancient type of watercraft; they are made from rough timber and beams fastened together. Ships built similarly to these are called *rataria*. Nowadays ships are metaphorically called rafts, but properly speaking, rafts are beams joined to each other. 10. The trireme (*trieris*) is a large ship that the Greeks call a *durco*. Concerning it Isaiah says (cf. 33:21) "The great galley (*trieris*) shall not go across it." 11. The Carpasia is a ship named from the island of Carpathus, just as the Rhodia is named from Rhodes and the Alexandrina from Alexandria. 12. The Liburnae are named from Libya; these are merchant ships. Concerning them Horace (*Epodes* 1.1) says:

> You will travel in Liburnian vessels amid the high (bulwarks of) warships.

13. Beaked (*rostratus*) ships are so named because they have a brass beak at the prow, on account of rocks, so that they won't be struck and crushed. 14. Long (*longus*) ships are the ones we call *dromo*, so named because they are longer than the others. Their opposite is the *musculus*, a short vessel. The *dromo* is so named from 'coursing,' for the Greeks call a course a δρόμος.

15. The fleet (*classis*) is named from a Greek term, κᾶλον, that is, "wood." Whence also a *calo* is a little boat that carries wood to the soldiers. 16. The *ancyromachus* is so named because with its speed it is suited for carrying the anchors (*ancora*) and other ship's instruments. 17. The *phaselus* (i.e. a light vessel shaped like a kidney bean) is a boat that we incorrectly call a *baselus*. Of it Vergil says (cf. *Geo.* 4.289):

> In painted barges (*phaselus*).

18. A skiff (*scapha*), also called κατάσκοπος (i.e. 'scout'), is a vessel known in Latin as a 'spyboat' (*speculatorium*), for σκοπός (lit. "spy") is translated into Latin as "to observe." 19. A barge (*barca*) is the vessel that carries all the freight of a ship to shore. On the open seas the ship carries this boat in its hold because of the high waves, but whenever it is near to port, the barge repays to the ship the service it accepted at sea. 20. The *paro* (plural *parones*) is a vessel suited for pirates (*pirata*), and is so named from them. Cicero (*Poems*, fr. 8) says:

Then he gave and entrusted himself to the wave-borne *paro*.

And elsewhere (Roman comedy fr. 21 (Ribbeck)):

He frolics near the shore in swift *parunculi* (i.e. little *parones*).

21. A *mioparo* is named as if the term were *minimus paro* (i.e. 'smallest *paro*'), for it is a skiff built of wicker that provides a kind of vessel when it has been covered with a rough hide. German pirates use boats of this type on the shores of the Ocean and in marshes, because of their maneuverability. The *History* (i.e. Hegesippus's version of Josephus's *History* 5.15.1) speaks of these, saying: "The Saxon people, prepared for flight rather than for war, depend on their *mioparones*, not their strength." 22. The *celox*, which the Greeks call κέλης, that is, a fast bireme or trireme, is maneuverable and well suited for the service of a fleet. Ennius says (*Annals* 478):

The greased keel of a *celox* glides through the white waves.

23. Biremes (*biremis*) are ships having a double bank of oars (*remus*). Triremes (*triremis*) and quadriremes (*quadriremis*) have three and four banks. The *penteris* and *hexeris* have five and six banks respectively. 24. The *actuaria* is a ship that is driven (*agere*, ppl. *actus*) by both sail and oars at the same time. The *hippagogus* is a ship in which horses are usually transported (cf. ἵππος, "horse"; ἄγειν, "carry"). The *pontonium* is a slow, heavy river vessel, which can only move by being rowed. The term is also used for a *trajectus* (lit. "sent across"), that is, 'swung on a rope' (*extentus*), because it is carried along; whence *transenna* is a name for stretched-out rope. 25. The *lembus* is a short little boat that is otherwise known as the *cumba* or the *caupulus*, and also the *lintris*, that is, *carabus*, which is used on the Po River and in marshes. 26. The *carabus* is a small skiff made from wicker that provides a kind of boat when it has been covered with rough hide (cf. 21 above). The *portemia* is a broad little boat of the Syrian type, without a keel, named from 'carrying' (*portare*). People in Pannonia use them. 27. The *trabaria* (i.e. *traberia*) is a river-boat that is hollowed out from a single tree trunk (*trabs*). It is also known as the *litoraria*, and as the *caudica*, made from a single hollowed piece of wood (cf. *caudex*, gen. *caudicis*, "trunk"). It is called a *caudica* because it carries (*capere*) from four to ten (*decem*) people.

ii. Parts of the ship and its equipment (De partibus navium et armamentis) 1. The stern (*puppis*) is the rear part of a ship, as if the term were *post* (lit. "after"). The prow (*prora*) is the front, as if it were *priora* (lit. "earlier"). The hull (*cumba*; cf. κύμβη, "the hollow of a vessel") is the lowest part of the ship, so named because it 'sinks down' (*incumbere*) in the water. The keel (*carina*) is named from 'coursing along' (*currere*), as if the word were *currina*. 2. The *forus* is the concave side (i.e. the hold) of the ship, named from carrying (*ferre*) a burden. Or it is the deck-planking of the ship that is spread out, so named because it supports (*ferre*) walking or because it sticks out on the outside (*foris*). Vergil says of it (*Aen.* 6.412):

[And he clears the gangways (*forus*).]

3. The oarlocks (*columbaria*) are the hollow places in the upper part of a ship's sides, through which the oars stick out. They are so named, I believe, because they are similar to the little holes in which doves (*columba*) make their nests.

4. Gangways (*agea*) are passageways, places in the ship through which the boatswain approaches the rowers. Concerning this Ennius says (*Annals* 492):

He places many things in the hold (*forus*), and the long gangway (*agea*) is filled.

5. The thwarts (*transtrum*) are planks where the rowers sit; they are so named because they are 'athwart' (*in transverso*). Vergil calls them 'yokes' (*iugum*; *Aen.* 6.411). 6. Oars (*remus*) are named from 'moving back' (*removere*) and *tonsae* (i.e. another word for 'oar') from clipping (*tondere*, ppl. *tonsus*) and shearing off the waves, just as barbers (*tonsor*) are named from clipping and shearing off hair. 7. The blade (*palmula*) is the wide end of the oar, named from the palm (*palma*). By the blade, the 'sea is pushed' (*mare impellitur*).

The yardarms (*antemna*) are so called because they are set 'before the current' (*ante amnem*), for the current flows past them.[1] The *cornua* (lit. "horns") are the ends of the yardarm, so named using a trope. 8. The mast is the pole on a ship that holds up the sail. It is called a mast (*malus*) because it has the shape of an apple (*malum*) at the top, or because it is circled by

1 This etymology results from a confusion of Varro's etymology of the city Antemna, which sits on a tributary 'before the river' (*ante amnem*) Tiber.

certain wooden handles (*malleolus*), as it were, by whose revolution the sail is raised more easily. 9. The mast-step (*modius*, also meaning "a measure of volume") is that in which the mast stands, named on account of its resemblance to a measuring vessel. Mast-heads (*carchesium*) are pulleys at the tip of the mast, shaped like the letter F, through which ropes are pulled. Cinna says (fr. 2):

> The shining mast-heads (*carchesium*) of the tall mast glitter.

10. Pulleys (*trochlea*) are so named because they have little wheels, for a wheel is called τροχός in Greek. 11. *Parastatae* (lit. "by-standers") are posts 'standing at equal height' (*pares stantes*) by which the mast is supported. Cato says (fr. 18): "The mast bound fast, the *parastatae* fastened." 12. The tiller (*clavus*) is that by which the rudder is steered. Concerning it Ennius says (*Annals* 483):

> That I may hold the tiller (*clavus*) straight and steer the ship.

13. A *porticulus* is a hammer carried (*portare*) in the hand, by means of which the timing-signals are given to the rowers. Concerning it Plautus says (*The Ass-Dealer* 518):

> You yourself hold the *porticulus* (i.e. the control) for speaking and keeping silent.

14. The grapple (*tonsilla*) is an iron or wooden hook to which, when it is fixed on the shore, ropes from the ship are fastened. Concerning it Ennius says (*Annals* 499):

> They fasten the hooked *tonsillae*, they grip the shore.

15. The anchor (*anchora*) is an iron spike taking its name via a Greek etymology, because it grasps the rocks or sand like a person's hand, for the Greeks call the hand κυρα (i.e. χείρ, with an aspirated *k* sound), but 'anchor' has no aspiration among Greek speakers, for it is pronounced ἄγκυρα. Whence also among the ancients it was rendered without aspiration (i.e. as *ancora*, not *anchora*). 16. *Pulvini* (in classical Latin, harbor platforms or breakwaters) are devices by means of which ships are launched or drawn up into a berth. The *pons* (i.e. gangway to shore) is the ladder of a ship.

iii. Sails (De velis) 1. The Greeks call sails ἄρμενα because they are moved by the air (*aer*); among Latin speakers a sail is called *velum*, from 'flight' (*volatus*). Whence also this passage (Vergil, *Aen.* 3.520):

> We spread the wings of the sails (*velum*).

2. The kinds of sails are the *acation*, the *epidromus*, the *dolo*, the *artemo*, the *siparum*, and the *mendicum*. The *acation* is the largest sail of these, and is raised in the middle of the ship. 3. The *epidromos* is the next widest, and raised in the stern. The *dolo* is the smallest sail and is fixed to the prow. The *artemo* is considered to be more for directing the ship than for speed. 4. The *siparum* (i.e. a topsail) is a type of sail having a single 'foot' (*pes*, i.e. 'clew'). With this sail, craft are aided in sailing whenever the force of the wind weakens. Concerning it Lucan says (*Civil War* 5.428):

> And spreading the highest *sipara* of the sails he collects the dying winds.

People assume that this sail is named from 'separation' (*separatio*). The 'foot' (*pes*) is the lowest corner of a sail, as sailors speak of it.

iv. Ropes (De funibus) 1. Ropes (*funis*) are so named because in earlier times they were covered with wax to be used as torches, whence also 'rope torches' (*funale*). Cords (*restis*), either because they hold rafts (*ratis*) together, or because with them nets (*rete*) are stretched out. The *rudens* is a ship's rope, so named from excessive creaking (cf. *rudere*, "creak loudly"). 2. *Spirae* (lit. "coils") are ropes that are used during storms; sailors are also in the habit of calling them *cucurbae*. *Spirae* are named from *spartum* (i.e. a plant used for making rope). 3. The *propes* is a rope with which the foot (*pes*, i.e. clew) of a sail is fastened, as if it were 'for the feet' (*pro pedes*). Concerning this Turpilius says (fr. 216):

> As when the favorable wind bears the ship out to sea if someone has released the *propes*, the left side of the sail.[2]

4. The *tormentum* is a long rope used on ships, which stretches from the prow to the stern. With this rope the ship's timbers are joined more tightly. *Tormenta*, so called from 'twisting' (*tortus*), are cords and ropes. 5. The *scaphon* is a rope attached to the prow. Concerning it Caecilius says (fr. 243):

2 The last part of the text is corrupt, loosely translated here.

I have come on an amorous voyage, with the sail's foot reaching up to the *scaphon.*

6. The *opisphora* are ropes stretched back from the ends of the yardarm on the right and left. The *prosnesium* is the hawser with which a ship at the shore is fastened to a post. The *mitra* is a rope that binds the ship in the middle.

7. The *anquina* is the rope by which the yardarm is bound to the mast. Concerning it Cinna says (fr. 3):

And the mighty *anquina* regulates a stable course.

8. The tow-rope (*remulcum*) is the rope with which a ship is tied and towed instead of relying on oars. Concerning this Valgius says (fr. 4):

Here my boat, approaching with a long tow-rope (*remulcum*), sets me, rejoicing, in these delightful lodgings.

9. Straps (*struppus*) are bindings made of leather thongs or flax by which the oars are attached to the thole-pin (*scalmus*). Concerning these Livius (Andronicus) says (*Odyssey* 10):

And then he gave the order to fasten the oars with the straps (*struppus*).

10. The sounding-lead (*catapirates*) is a line with a lead weight, with which the depth of the sea is tested. Lucilius (*Satires* 1191) says:

Let the boy swallow down this oiled sounding-lead (*catapirates*) in the same way, this little chunk of lead and flaxen string.

v. Nets (De retibus) 1. Nets (*rete*) are so named either from 'holding' (*retinere*) fish, or from the cords (*restis*) by which they are stretched. A smaller net is called a *synplagium*, from 'snare' (*plagae*), for strictly speaking *plagae* is the name for those ropes by which nets are stretched at the bottom and at the top. 2. The drag-net (*funda*) is a type of fishing net, so named because it is sent to the bottom (*fundus*). It is also called the casting-net (*iaculum*), from casting (*iacere*). Plautus says (fr. 175):

Before, you were an honorable caster (*iaculator*) indeed.

3. The *tragum* is a type of net so named because it is drawn (*trahere*). It is also called the 'seine' (*verriculum*) because *verrere* means "drag." 4. A basket net (*nassa*) . . . The hunting-net (*cassis*, i.e. *casses*) is a type of net used by hunters, so named because it captures (*capere*). Hence we have the term 'in vain' (*incassum*), that is, 'without purpose' (*sine causa*), as if the term were *sine cassibus* ("without hunting-nets"), since without them hunting is pointless. 5. Mosquito-netting (*conopium*; cf. κωνωπεῖον, from κώνωψ, "gnat") is a net like a tent, by which gnats are kept out. They are especially used in Alexandria, because gnats are copiously produced there by the Nile. Whence it is called *conopeum*, for Egypt is known as Canopea.

vi. The metalworkers' forge (De fabrorum fornace) 1. The metalworker (*faber*) has this name assigned to him from 'working iron' (*facere ferrum*). From this, the term was extended to the craftsmen of other industrial materials, and to their workshops (*fabrica*), but with a modifier, as in the 'wood craftsman' and the rest, because of the solidity (*firmitas*), as it were, of their products.

2. The pagans say that it is Vulcan who has authoring over the metalworkers' forge, by Vulcan figuratively meaning "fire," as no kind of metal can be poured or stretched without fire. There is almost nothing that cannot be accomplished with fire, for here it prepares glass, there silver, here lead, there cinnabar, here pigment, there medicines. With fire stones are melted into bronze, with fire iron is produced and tamed, with fire gold is fashioned, and concrete and walls are bonded by stone that has been burned with fire. 3. Fire whitens black stones when it heats them, and darkens white woods by burning them. It makes black charcoal from glowing coals, and fragile objects from hard pieces of wood. It creates incorruptible objects from those that are corruptible. It loosens what is bound, it binds back what has been loosened. It softens what is hard and renders hard what is soft. It has a medicinal use as well, for it is often beneficial to be burnt (i.e. cauterized). It is also a sure aid against the plague that is contracted when the sun is obscured. In any sort of work, one substance is produced with the first firing, another with the second, and another with the third. 4. Fire also has another variation, for there is one fire that is for human use and another which appears as a part of divine judgment, whether contracting as a lightning-bolt from the sky or bursting forth from the earth through the mountain peaks. 5. Fire (*ignis*) is so named because nothing can be born (*gignere*) from it,

for it is an inviolable element, consuming everything that it seizes.

A smithy (*fabrica*) contains two things: winds and flames. 6. Strictly speaking the flame (*flamma*) of a forge is so named because it is stirred up by the blasts (*flatus*) of the bellows. But the forge (*fornax*) is named from fire, for φῶς means "fire." *Kaminus* is the word for forge in Greek (i.e. κάμινος), derived from καῦμα ("burning heat"). Ash (*favilla*) results when fire is gone from a spark. 7. Something is an ember as long as it is hot, but once it has gone out it is charcoal. An ember (*pruna*) is named from 'burning up' (*perurere*), but the charcoal (*carbo*) is so named because it lacks (*carere*) flames. Charcoal becomes even stronger when it is thought to have perished, for, when it has been relit, it burns with an even stronger light. Even without fire, it also possesses such hardness that it is corrupted by no moisture, and not overcome by aging. Once extinguished it lasts so incorruptibly that the people who fix boundaries spread charcoals below the surface and place stones on top, so as to prove the boundary to a litigant however many generations later, and they recognize a stone fixed in this way to be a boundary.

vii. Metalworkers' tools (De instrumentis fabrorum) 1. The anvil (*incus*) is that tool on which iron is beaten out. It is named from striking, because we 'pound' (*cudere*, ppl. *cusus*) something there – that is, we stretch it by beating it – for to pound is to beat and to strike. But the ancients did not call it *incus*, but rather *intus*, because metal is beaten (*tundere*, ppl. *tussus*) on it, that is, stretched out. Whence also a mallet (*tudis*, i.e. *tudes*) is a hammer named from beating, that is, stretching. 2. The hammer (*malleus*) is so named because it strikes and stretches out anything when it is hot and soft (*mollis*). The *marcus* is a rather large hammer, called *marcus* because it is larger (*maior*) and stronger for striking. The *martellus* is medium-sized. The *marculus* is a very small hammer. Lucilius says (*Satires* 1165):

> And just as when in the smithy the *marculus* beats the
> hot iron with the great blows of many workmen.

3. Tongs (*forceps*, plural *forcipes*), as if the word were *ferricipes*, because they seize (*capere*) and hold the white-hot iron (*ferrum*), or because we seize and hold something *forvus* with them, as if the word were *forvicapes*, for *forvus* means "hot" – whence also the word 'fiery' (*fervidus*). Hence also we call those people 'beautiful' (*formosus*) whose blood produces an attractive blush with its heat. 4. The file (*lima*) is so named because it makes things smooth (*lenis*), for mud (*limus*) is smooth. The chisel (*cilium*, i.e. *caelum* or *cilio*; see XX.iv.7 below) is the tool with which silversmiths work, and from this engraved (*caelare*) vessels are named.

viii. The craft of building (De fabricis parietum) 1. The Greeks claim that Daedalus was the inventor of the craft of building, for he is said to have been the first to have learned this craft from Minerva. The Greeks call a craftsman or artisan τέκτων, that is, a builder. But the master-builders (*architectus*) are the builders (*caementarius*) who lay out the foundations. Whence the apostle Paul, speaking of himself, said (I Corinthians 3:10): "As a wise architect (*architectus*) I have laid the foundation." 2. Masons (*macio*, i.e. *machio*) are named from the scaffolding (*machina*) on which they stand due to the height of the walls.

ix. Siting (De dispositione) There are three stages in building: siting, construction, and decoration. Siting (*dispositio*) is the marking out of the building site or seat and of the foundations.[3]

x. Construction (De constructione) 1. Construction is the building of the sides and the top. It is called construction (*constructio*) or constructing (*instructio*) because it 'binds together' (*instringere*, ppl. *instrictus*) and makes something hold together, as stones held together with mud, and wood and stones held to each other. Dipping (*intinctio*) iron in water is also a way of binding; unless iron is dipped while it is white-hot, case-hardening and binding cannot take place. Construction is also named from the large amount of stones and wood, whence also 'heap' (*strues*). Building (*aedificatio*) is one kind of construction and renovation (*instauratio*) is another: building is new construction, but renovation is what restores something to its previous likeness (*instar*), for the ancients used to use the word *instar* for 'likeness'; hence they would say 'renovate' (*instaurare*). 2. Construction consists of the foundation, stones, lime, sand, and wood. The foundation (*fundamentum*) is so named

3 For "of the . . . seat" (*solii*) the common manuscript variant *soli*, "of the ground, of the foundation," seems preferable.

because it is the bottom (*fundus*) of the building. It is also called *caementum* from 'cutting' (*caedere*), because it rises from thick cut stone.

3. Stones that are suitable for building: white stone, Tiburtine, columbinus, river stone, porous, red, and the others. 4. As for white stone, some is hard and some is soft. Soft stone is cut by saw teeth and is so manageable to work with that letters may be carved in it as though in wood. 5. Tiburtine stone is named from the place in Italy (i.e. *Tibur*, present-day Tivoli). Although it is strong enough for building, nevertheless it is easily split by heat. 6. Tufa (*tophus*) cannot be used for a building due to its perishability and softness, but it is appropriate for the foundation. It is crumbled by heat and sea air, and weathered by rain. 7. Arenacian stone is conglomerated from sea sand (*arena*). It is also called 'thirsty' because it stores the liquid it soaks up. This is also called *Gaditanus* (i.e. 'of Cadiz') in Baetica, from the island in the Ocean where a large quantity is hewn. 8. Piperinus (lit. "peppery") stone is whitish with black specks. It is hard and very strong. Cochleacius stone is conglomerated from shells (*cochlea*), pebbles, and sand. It is very rough and sometimes porous. 9. Columbinus stone is named from the color of the bird (cf. *columba*, "dove"). It is close in its character to gypsum and is very similar in its softness.

10. Molaris stone is useful for walls because it has a rather dense nature. It is hard and rough. Millstones (*mola*) are made from it, whence it has derived its name. There are four kinds; white, black, composite and porous. 11. Pumice (*spongia*) is a stone made from water, light and porous and suited for ceilings. 12. *Silex* (i.e. a flinty stone) is a hard stone. Of this kind of stone, black *silex* is the best, and also red *silex* in some places. White *silex* is undamaged by aging; when carved into monuments it remains undamaged and even fire does not harm it. Molds into which bronze is poured are made from this. Green *silex* is itself stubbornly resistant to fire, but there is nowhere where it is abundant, and it is found only as a stone and not as a rocky outcrop. Pale *silex* is rarely useful for foundations. 13. Round *silex* is strong against damage, but untrustworthy in a structure unless it is bound by a large amount of cement. 14. River *silex* always appears to be wet. It should be gathered in the summer and not set into the structure of a house for two years.

As far as building with clay is concerned, baked bricks are suited for walls and foundations, while curved and flat tiles are suitable for roofs. 15. 'Flat roof-tiles' (*tegula*) are so named because they cover (*tegere*) a building, and 'curved tiles' (*imbrex*) because they receive the rain (*imber*). *Tegula* is the primary term, and *tigillum* (lit. "small plank") is the diminutive. 16. Small bricks (*laterculus*) are so called because their stretched-out (*latus*) shape is formed by four boards placed all the way around. Bricks (*later*) are unfired, and they also are so named because when 'stretched out' (*latus*) they are shaped with wooden forms. 17. Some of these forms are called *cratis*, the wicker forms in which people are accustomed to carry the clay for these unfired bricks. They are interwoven from reeds, and named after the term κρατεῖν ("hold"), that is, because they hold on to each other.

18. Some people claim that mud (*lutum*) is named by antiphrasis, because it is not clean, for every thing that has been washed (*lavare*, ppl. *lotus*), is clean. 19. Quicklime (*calcis viva*; i.e. *calx viva*)[4] is so called because although it may be cold to the touch, it contains fire hidden inside, and for this reason, when water is poured on it, the hidden fire immediately bursts forth. Its nature produces something amazing, for after it has caught fire it burns in water, which usually extinguishes fire, and it is extinguished by oil, which usually ignites fire. Its use is essential in constructing a building, for one stone cannot adhere strongly enough to another unless they are joined with lime. 20. Gypsum (*gypsum*) is a relative of lime, and it is a Greek term (i.e. γύψος). There are many kinds. The best of all is from 'translucent stone' (*lapis specularis*; see XVI.iv.37 above), and it is most pleasing in the images on buildings and in cornices. 21. Sand (*arena*, i.e. *harena*) is named from dryness (*areditas*, i.e. *ariditas*), not from clinging (*adhaerere*) in construction, as some people claim. It passes the test if it squeaks when pressed in the hand or if no stain remains when it is spread out on a white cloth.

22. Columns (*columna*) are named for their length and roundness (cf. *colus*, "distaff"; see xxix.2 below); the weight of the entire building rests on them. The ancient ratio was that a third of the height of the columns

4 The 'quick' of English 'quicklime' also means "living," that is, unslaked, chemically more active.

should equal their width. There are four kinds of round columns: Doric, Ionic, Tuscan, and Corinthian. They differ among themselves as to breadth and height. There is also a fifth type which is called Attic; it has four angles or more, and sides of equal size. Bases (*basis*) are the props of columns. They rise up from the foundations and bear the weight of the construction above. 23. *Basis* is also the term for a very strong rock in the Syrian language. 24. Capitals (*capitolium*, i.e. *capitulum* or *capitella*) are named thus because they are the heads (*caput*, gen. *capitis*) of columns (*columna*), just like a head on a neck (*collum*). The architrave (*epistolium*, i.e. *epistylium*) is placed on top of the capitals of the columns, and it is a Greek word (i.e. ἐπιστύλιον, lit. "placed above").

25. The construction of pavement originated with the Greeks, and it is called 'pavement' (*pavimentum*) because it is 'rammed down' (*pavire*), that is, it is struck. Whence also 'fear' (*pavor*) is named, because it strikes the heart. 26. An *ostracus* is a pavement made of tiles, so named because it is pounded from broken tiles mixed with lime, for the Greeks call pulverized tile ὄστρα.[5] 27. Workmen call broken stones mixed with lime *rudus*; they set this underneath when they make pavements. From this also comes the word *rudera* (in fact the plural of *rudus* above). 28. A channel (*canalis*) is so named because it is hollow like a reed (*canna* – a feminine noun). For good reason it is better for us to use the word *canalis* with feminine gender rather than masculine. 29. Water pipes (*fistula*) are so named because they pour out and supply water, for στολα in Greek means "supply" (cf. στέλλειν, "send, bring"). They are shaped according to the amount of the water and their capacity; the water is divided through them in specific measures. Of these measures, there is the inch, the 'five quarter-digits' (*quinaria*), the square-digit, the round-digit, and whatever other measures there may be.[6]

5 The Latin and Greek are ambiguous. Greek ὄστρεον means "shell," and Isidore could be speaking of pavements made from crushed shells, but it seems more likely that he is referring to 'potsherd' (Greek ὄστρακον).

6 A 'digit' (*digitus*) is about three-quarters of an inch. The 'square-digit' pipe would have four sides of one digit each; the 'round-digit' pipe would have a diameter of one digit. For these measurements Isidore follows, perhaps at second hand, Frontinus, *The Water-System of Rome.*

xi. Decoration (De venustate) Up to this point we have spoken of the elements of construction; what follows concerns the decoration of buildings. Decoration is anything added to buildings for the sake of ornament and embellishment, such as ceiling panels set off in gold and wall panels of rich marbles and colorful paintings.

xii. Paneled ceilings (De laqueariis) 'Paneled ceilings' (*laquearium*) are what cover the underside of a vault and adorn it. They are also called *lacunaria* (i.e. the plural of *lacunar*) because they have certain square or round panels (*lacus*) of wood or gesso, painted in colors with glittering figures. The primary term is *lacus*, as in Lucilius (cf. *Satires* 1290):

> The house and *lacus* resound.

Its diminutive is *lacunar*, as in Horace (*Odes* 2.18):

> Nor does a gilded *lacunar* glitter in my house.

From this term, *lacunarium*, another diminutive is made, and by ἀντίστιχον (i.e. *antistoechum*, "substitution of letters") one forms *laquearium*.

xiii. Wall panels (De crustis) Wall panels (*crusta*) are tablets of marble, whence also marble-paneled walls are called *crustatus*. It is not known who invented cutting marble into panels. They are made with sand and iron: by a saw pressing sand down along a very fine line, and by the cutting of the saw itself as it is dragged. But coarser sand erodes the marble more, so thin sand is suited for fine work and polishing.

xiv. Mosaics (De lithostrotis) Mosaics (*lithostrotum*) are crafted by the art of making pictures with small chips and cubes tinted in various colors. Cubes (*tessella*) are named from blocks (*tessera*), that is, from square stones, by forming a diminutive.

xv. Molding (De plastis) Molding for walls is representing images and figures out of gesso and tinting them with colors. Molding (*plastice*) is the Greek name (cf. πλαστικός, adj. from πλάσσειν, "to mold") for what in Latin is 'forming likenesses from earth or gesso.' Thus, making some shape by pressing clay is molding (*plastis*, i.e. *plastes*). Whence also *protoplastus* is the name for the human being who was first made from mud (see Genesis 2:7).

xvi. Pictures (De picturis) 1. A picture is an image representing the appearance of some object, which, when viewed, leads the mind to remember. It is called 'picture' (*pictura*) as if the word were *fictura*, for it is a made-up (*fictus*) image, and not the truth. Hence also the term 'painted' (*fucatus*), that is, daubed with some artificial color and possessing no credibility or truth. Thus some pictures go beyond the substance of truth in their attention to color, and they bring credibility, which they strove to increase, into falsehood, just as someone who paints a three-headed Chimera, or a Scylla as human in the upper half and girded with dogs' heads below. 2. The Egyptians first discovered the picture when they outlined a person's shadow with a line. It began like this, and was followed by the use of single colors, and afterwards by assortments of colors, so that gradually this art defined itself, and devised light and shadow and the differences in color. For this reason even now painters (*pictor*) first draw certain shadows and the outlines of the images to come, and then fill in the colors, following the order in which the art was discovered.

xvii. Colorings (De coloribus) 1. Colorings (*color*) are so named because they are perfected by the heat (*calor*) of fire or of the sun, or because in the beginning they used to be filtered (*colere*) so that they would be as fine as possible. 2. Colorings either occur naturally or are manufactured. They occur naturally, as for example, red ochre, red earth, Paraetonium, Melinum, Eretria, and gold-coloring. The others are manufactured either by artifice or by mixture.

3. Red ochre (*sinopis*) was found first along the Black Sea, whence it takes its name from the city Sinope. There are three kinds: red, less-red, and something between these two. 4. Red earth (*rubrica*) is so named because it is red (*ruber*) and similar to blood in color. It occurs in many places, but the best is from the Black Sea (*Pontus*), whence it is also called 'Pontic.' 5. Syrian (*Syricum*) is a pigment with a red color, with which the chapter-heads in books are written. It is also known as Phoenician, so called because it is collected in Syria on the shores of the Red Sea, where the Phoenicians live. 6. Now, 'silk' (*sericum*) is one thing, and 'Syrian' (*Syricum*) is another, for silk is a fiber that the Chinese (*Seres*; East Asians generally) export, while Syrian is a pigment that the Syrian Phoenicians gather at the shores of the Red Sea. It may also be counted among the manufactured pigments, for it is often made by being mixed either with red ocher or with vermilion (*sandix*).

7. The Greeks are reported to have been the first to discover 'red lead' (*minium*), in the soil of Ephesus. Spain is more abundant in this pigment than other regions, and for this reason it has given its name to a particular river (i.e. the Minius, present-day Miño). When distilled, it produces liquid silver (i.e. quicksilver). Some people say that this red lead is cinnabar. 8. Cinnabar (*cinnabaris*) is named from *draco* (gen. *draconis*, "dragon") and *barrus*, that is, 'elephant,' for they say that it is the blood of dragons, shed when they entwine themselves around elephants.[7] The elephants charge, and the dragons are overpowered, and the gore they shed dyes the earth, and a pigment is produced from what has stained the soil. It is a red-colored powder. 9. Although *prasin*, that is, green clay, is produced in mixed form in some lands, nevertheless the best is the Cyrenian, in Libya. 10. *Chrysocolla* is grass-green in color, so named because its veins are said to contain gold (cf. χρυσός, "gold"; κόλλα, "glue"). This occurs in Armenia, but the preferred variety comes from Macedonia. It is mined along with the metal copper, and where it is discovered, silver and indigo are also found, for veins of *chrysocolla* have a natural association with these substances.

The pigment *cypria* is named from the island of Cyprus, where it is found in quantity. 11. Sandarach (*sandaraca*) occurs on the island Topazus in the Red Sea. It has the color of cinnabar and the odor of sulfur. It is found in gold and silver mines, and the redder it is and the worse it smells the better its quality. However, 'white lead' (*cerussa*), if it is baked in a furnace, produces sandarach, which as a result has a flame-like color. But if it is baked mixed with an equal part of red earth, it yields vermilion (*sandix*). 12. Arsenic (*arsenicum*), which Latin speakers call *auripigmentum* ("orpiment," lit. "gold-pigment") because of its color, is collected at the Black Sea from goldmine material, where sandarach is also found. The best arsenic takes on a golden color. It is pure and easily broken along the thin course of its veins. That which is paler or like sandarach

7 Cinnabar (mercury sulfide) is also called 'dragon's blood'; vermilion is made from it.

is rated to be a lesser quality. There is also a third, scaly kind that is mixed with a golden color. These arsenics have the same stench as sandarach, but sharper.[8]

13. Ochre (*ochra*) itself is produced on the island Topazus in the Red Sea, where sandarach is also produced. Ochre is also made when red earth is heated in new pots that have been smeared around with clay. The longer it is heated in the furnace, the better it becomes. *Venetum* (i.e. 'sky-color'; see XVIII.xxxiii.2)... 14. In Alexandria they first discovered how to prepare *caeruleum* (i.e. a blue pigment). In Italy people make it from a powder of sand and the powdery form of natron, but if you add *Cyprium* that has been heated in the furnace to this mixture, it will be similar to *Vestorianum* (i.e. a blue pigment).

15. The 'purple pigment' (*purpurissum*) is made from silversmiths' chalk; this chalk is dyed with murex and soaks up the color in the same way that wool does but more quickly. Nevertheless, the superior pigment is something else that has been soaked in a vat with hitherto unused dye-stuffs, and the next best is when silversmiths' chalk is added to the dye liquid once the first batch has been removed. The quality diminishes each time this is done. The origin of the most precious purple (*purpura*) is what is colored with *hysginum* (i.e. the dark red pigment from the plant called ὕσγη in Greek) and with *rubea* (i.e. *rubia*, the red dye from madder root). 16. Indigo (*indicum*) is found in India in the reeds, as a foam mixed with mud. It is dark blue in color, producing a wonderful mixture of purple and blue. There is another type of pigment in the purple-dye workshops, a foam, floating in bronze cauldrons, that the dye-makers skim off and dry.

17. Ink (*atramentum*) is so named because it is black (*ater*, feminine *atra*). Its color is necessary both for pictures and for everyday use. It is one of the manufactured pigments, for it is made from soot in various ways, when resin is added on top of heated pitch. The resin, which retains the smoke, is built up in a little vessel. Painters mix a glue into this, with water, so that it gleams more lustrously. 18. For a speedier effect the charred remains of old brushwood, crushed and mixed with glue, produce the appearance of *atramentum* for applying to walls. Some people also roast the dried dregs of wine and claim that, if the dregs are from a good wine, this *atramentum* has the appearance of indigo. But twigs of black grapevine, steeped in the best wine, produce the gleam of indigo after they dry out if you roast them dry and grind them up with added glue. 19. *Usta* (i.e. a red pigment), which is especially indispensable, is produced with no trouble, for if you heat a clump of good flinty stone in the fire, and quench it with very sour vinegar, a sponge drenched in it produces a purple color. When you grind this up it will be *usta*. 20. All *atramentum* is perfected in the sun, but all colors with a mixture of lime deteriorate.

21. *Melinum* is so named because one of the Cycladean islands, Melos by name, abounds in this mineral. It is white, and painters do not use it because it is very greasy. 22. The white pigment *anulare* is so named because with it women's cosmetics are made bright. It is made from clay mixed with glass gems.[9] 23. 'White lead' (*cerussa*, i.e. the cosmetic ceruse) is made in this way: fill a vessel with very sour vinegar; add vine twigs to this same vessel, and on top of the twigs place very thin sheets of lead, and then close the vessel carefully and seal it so that none of the fumes can escape. After thirty days the vessel can be opened, and you will find white lead, produced from the distillation of the lead sheets. This is removed, dried, and ground up and, with vinegar mixed in again, separated into lozenges that are dried in the sun. With this procedure, if you put copper sheets on top of the twigs they make verdigris (*aerugo*). *Chalcanthus* (i.e. copperas-water) . . .

xviii. Tools for building (De instrumentis aedificiorum) 1. It is important for the construction of walls to be carried out according to the carpenter's square and in agreement with the plumb-line. The carpenter's square (*norma*) is named from a Greek term (i.e. γνώμων), and without it nothing can be made straight. It is made up of three rulers, such that there are two rulers of two feet while the third has two feet ten inches.[10] When they have been smoothed to an equal thickness, the carpenter's square connects these rulers at the tips so that they make a triangular shape. This will be the carpenter's square. 2. The ruler (*regula*) is so named because it is straight (*rectus*), as if the term were *rectula*, and smooth. The

8 Both 'arsenic,' in its compounded form orpiment, and sandarach would stink of sulfur.

9 Isidore omits the explanation of the etymology from Pliny: the cheap gems are made from the rings (*anulus*) of common people.

10 These measurements very nearly produce a right-angle isosceles triangle: $24^2 + 24^2 = 1152$; $34^2 = 1156$.

plumb-line (*perpendiculum*) is so named because it is always set to hang down (*adpendere*). In short, unless everything in the construction is made according to the plumb-line and a sure ruler, it is inevitable that everything will be built awry, so that some things will be crooked, others sloping, some leaning forward and some leaning back – and so all buildings are constructed with these tools.

3. A string (*linea*) is named from its material, for it is made from flax (*linum*). The name of the trowel (*trulla*) was given because it pushes (*trudere*) back and forth, that is, it covers stones with lime or clay. Hammer (*martellus*) . . . Scaffolding (*machina*) . . . 4. Ladders (*scalae*) are named from climbing (*scandere*), that is, ascending, for they cling to the walls. They are called *scalae* (i.e. a plural form) whether there is one or there are more, because the term exists only in the plural, just as the word *litterae* (lit. "letters") means "correspondence."

xix. Woodworkers (De lignariis) 1. Someone who works with wood (*lignum*) is called by the general term 'woodworker' (*lignarius*). 'Wagon-maker' (*carpentarius*) is a specialized term, for he only makes wagons (*carpentum*), just as a shipbuilder (*navicularius*) is a builder and constructer of ships (*navis*) only. 2. A *sarcitector* is so called because out of many planks joined together on this side and that he repairs (*sarcire*) the unified structure of a building. The same person is called a *tignarius* because he applies plaster to the wood (cf. *tignum*, "piece of timber, beam").

3. Wood (*lignum*) is named using a Greek etymology (cf. λύχνος, "lamp") because when ignited it is turned to light (*lumen*) and flame. Whence [also] the lamp (*lychnium*) is so called, because it gives light. 4. All wood, moreover, is called 'material' (*materia*, also meaning "timber") because something can be made from it; the term will be *materia* whether you apply it to a door or to a statue. For material is always necessary for the production of an object, just as we say that the elements are the *materia* of things, because we see that it is from them that actual things are made. It is called material (*materia*) as if the word were 'mother' (*mater*).

5. Beams (*trabs*) are so named because they are set crossways (*in transverso*) to keep two walls together. Timber (*tignum*) is one thing and beams are another, for timbers joined together make a beam. They are beams when they have been hewn into shape. 6. A boss (*tholus*, cf. Greek θολός, "dome"), strictly speaking, is like a small shield. It is in the center of the roof, and the beams come together in it. The tie-beams (*coplae*, i.e. *copulae*, lit. "joinings") are so named because they join (*copulare*) the cross-beams to each other. Cross-beams (*luctans*) are so called because when set up they hold themselves against each other in the manner of wrestlers (*luctans*). *Agrantes* . . . 7. Posts (*asser*) are named from 'singleness' (*as*) because they are set up by themselves and not joined.

Shingles (*scindula*), because they are split (*scindere*), that is, divided. Pegs (*epigrus*) and nails are items with which wood is joined to wood. Nails (*clavus*) are so named as if the word were *calibus*, because they are made from *calibs* (i.e. *chalybs*), that is, iron, for *chalyps* is iron. 8. Boards (*tabula*) were called *tagulae* by the ancients, as if from 'covering' (*tegere*), whence also 'roof-tiles' (*tegulae*). A joining of boards is called a joint (*commissura*). The 'action of cutting' (*sectio*) is named from 'following' (*sequi*, ppl. *secutus*) those things it has begun, for 'to cut' (*secare*) is to 'pursue' (*sectare*) and 'follow' (*sequi*). 9. The name for saw (*serra*) was formed from a sound, that is, from its 'scraping noise' (*stridor*). The use of saws and compasses was invented by Perdix, a certain youth whom Daedalus, his mother's brother, had taken in as a boy to instruct in his studies. It is reported that this boy had such genius that, when he sought a quick way to divide wood, he copied the spine of a fish, sharpening a strip of iron and arming it with the biting power of teeth. Workmen name this the saw. The invention of this art drove his teacher Daedalus green with envy, and he threw the boy headlong from the citadel. Thereupon Daedalus went to Crete as an exile and was there for some time, as stories relate. From Crete he flew, using wings, and came to Cilicia. 10. The compass (*circinus*) is named because it makes a circle (*circulus*) when it is turned. This technique is carried out with a doubled string, which when single (i.e. undoubled) had been stretched across the width (i.e. the diameter desired). The point in the middle of the compass (i.e. of the circle) is called the center (*centrum*, i.e. κέντρον) by the Greeks – everything converges on this middle point.

11. The ax (*securis*) is so named because trees are cut down (*succidere*) with it, as if the word were *succuris*. Again, it is called *securis* as if it were *semicuris*, for it is sharp on one side and suited for digging on the other.[11]

11 The allusion may be to *curis*, a kind of spear: a *semi-curis* might be a blade sharpened on only one of its two edges.

This was called a *penna* (lit. 'wing') by the ancients; if both sides were sharp they called it *bipennis*. It was called *bipennis* because it had a sharp edge on either side, like two wings (*pinna*), for the ancients would call something sharp *pennus*, whence the wings (*pinna*) of birds, because they are sharp. See how this term *penna* has preserved its antiquity, because the ancients used to say *penna*, not *pinna*. This also pertains to the pick-ax (*dolabra*), because it has two prongs (*duo labra*, lit. "two lips"), for the ax has one. The hatchet (*dextralis*) is suited for the right hand (*dextera*). 12. The adze (*ascia*) is named from the shavings (*astula*, i.e. *assula*) that it removes from wood. Its diminutive is *asciola*. There is also an adze with a short handle and on the opposite side either a plain hammer or a hollowed one or a two-horned drag-hoe.

13. The chisel (*scalprus*, i.e. *scalprum*) is so named because it is suited for carvings (*scalptura*) and making holes (*foramen*), as if the word were *scalforus*. Its diminutive is *scalpellus*. 14. The gimlet (*terebra*) is named from the wood-worm called *terebra*, which the Greeks call τερηδών. Hence it is called *terebra* because, like the worm, it 'bores a hole by abrasion' (*terendo forare*), as if the word were *terefora*, or as if it were *transforans* (i.e. "boring through"). 15. The auger (*taratrum*), as if the word were *teratrum* (i.e. from *terere*, "abrade"). The rasp (*scobina*) is so named because it produces filings (*scobis*) by abrasion. The rafter (*cantherium*) . . . The gouge (*guvia*) . . .

xx. The invention of clothmaking (De inventione lanificii) 1. The pagans praise a certain Minerva for many clever inventions, for they claim that she was the first to have demonstrated the practice of clothmaking – to have set up the loom and dyed wool. 2. They also say that she was the discoverer of the olive and of craftsmanship, the inventor of many arts, and for this reason craftsmen commonly pray to her. But this is merely a poetic fiction, for Minerva is not the originator of these arts, but, because intelligence is said to be in a person's head – and Minerva was imagined to have been born from Jupiter's head – this is native ingenuity. And thus an intelligent person's sense, which discovers everything, is in the head. Hence Minerva is said to be the goddess of the arts because nothing is more excellent than the native ingenuity by which all things are regulated.

xxi. Priestly vestments according to the Law (De veste sacerdotali in lege) 1. There are eight kinds of priestly vestments according to the Law (i.e. the Hebrew Scriptures; see Exodus 28 and 39). The *poderis* is a priestly garment of linen, close-fitting and reaching to the feet (*pes*, gen. *pedis*), whence it is named. Common people call it a *camisia*. 2. The *abanet* is a rounded priestly belt, woven like damask out of scarlet, purple, and hyacinth, such that flowers and gems seem to be set out on it. 3. The *pilleum* is made from linen (*byssus*),[12] rounded like a hemisphere, covering the priestly head and held tightly around the skull with a headband. The Greeks call this a *tiara* (i.e. τιάρα) or *galerum*, and so do we. 4. The *mahil*, which is an ankle-length tunic entirely of hyacinth color, has seventy-two bells at the feet, and the same number of pomegranate-figures hanging between them (see Exodus 28:33).

5. The *ephod*, which can be translated into Latin as *superindumentum* (lit. "overclothing"), was a cloak over the shoulder, woven from four colors and gold. Over each shoulder an emerald was set in gold and the names of the patriarchs were carved on them. 6. The *logium* (cf. λόγιον, "high priest's breastplate"), which is called the *rationale* (i.e. "breastplate") in Latin, was a doubled cloth, woven with gold and four colors, the size of a square as wide as a palm; there were twelve very precious stones woven into it. This garment was tied over the shoulder across the chest of the high priest. 7. The *petalum* is a golden plate worn against the high priest's forehead; it would have the Tetragrammaton, the name of God, written on it in Hebrew characters. 8. The *batin*, or *feminalia*, were knee-length linen breeches with which the private parts of the priest would be hidden.

xxii. The different kinds of clothing and their names (De diversitate et nominibus vestimentorum) 1. The different kinds of clothing are coverings, garments, clothes and so on. 2. A covering (*tegmen*) is so named because it covers (*tegere*) the limbs, just as a *tegumen* (i.e. a variant of the same word) is a shelter (*tectum*) that covers the body. More precisely, clothing (*vestimentum*) is that which extends to the footprints (*vestigium*), as if the word were *vestigimentum*, such as an ankle-length

12 There is some controversy among textile historians as to whether *byssus* referred to cotton or linen. See xxii.15 below. It is probably safest to assume that its meaning could extend to either fiber depending on the context.

tunic. But the usage of authors has confused this term. A garment (*indumentum*) is so called because on the inside (*intus*) it is put onto (*induere*) the body, as if the word were *intumentum*. *Amictus* (i.e. a wrapping) . . . 3. 'Clothed' (*vestitus*) can be distinguished from 'adorned' (*cultus*), because 'adorned' is understood in a broader sense. *Cultus* ("adornment, cultivation") may also be distinguished from *habitus* ("habit, disposition"), because *habitus* has to do with what is inborn, and *cultus* with what is cultivated by humans.

4. Most articles of clothing are named from the time when they are most often worn, or from the place where they were first made or are most often sold, or from their type of color, or from the name of their inventor. 5. Humankind's most ancient article of clothing was the loincloth (*perizoma*), that is, the *subcinctorium*, with which only the genitals are hidden. The first mortals made these for themselves, at first from tree leaves, because they were blushing after their disobedience and hid their private parts. Some barbarian peoples still wear them up to the present day, since they are unclothed. These are also called *campestria*, because young men, exercising unclothed on a field (*campus*), cover their private parts with these same loincloths.

6. The tunic (*tonica*, i.e. *tunica*), that very ancient article of clothing, is so called because it makes a sound when the person wearing it walks, for a sound is a 'tone' (*tonus*). Tunics of hide were made first; Adam and Eve were clothed with these after they sinned and were expelled from Paradise. 7. The ankle-length (*talaris*) tunic is so named because it reaches to the ankles (*talus*) and falls to the feet. Likewise the *pectoralis* tunic because the ancients wore it short so that it only covered the chest (*pectus*, gen. *pectoris*), although nowadays it extends further. 8. The sleeved (*manicleatus*) tunic, that is, the *manicata*, because it has sleeves (*manica*). The Greeks call it χειροδύτη (lit. "hand-covering").

9. The dalmatic (*dalmatica*) garment was first woven in Dalmatia, a province of Greece. It is a white priestly tunic with purple stripes. 10. The reddened (*russata*) garment, which the Greeks call Phoenician and we call scarlet, was invented by the Lacedaemonians so as to conceal the blood with a similar color whenever someone was wounded in battle, lest their opponents' spirits rise at the sight. Roman soldiers under the consuls wore this, whence they used to be called *russati*. On the day before a battle it would be displayed in front of the general's quarters as a warning and indication of the fight to come.

11. *Laculatus* cloth is cloth that has square panels (*lacus*) with pictures woven in or embroidered. *Iacinthina* (i.e. jacinth or hyacinth) cloth is resplendent with the color of the sky. 12. *Molochinius* (cf. μολόχινος, "of mallow-fiber") cloth is made using a warp of mallow (*malva*); some people call this *molocina* and others *malvella*. 13. Silk (*bombycinus*) cloth is named from the silkworm (*bombyx*), which produces extremely long threads from itself; something woven of these threads is called 'silken' (*bombycinus*). It is manufactured on the island of Cos. *Apocalamus*. . . 14. *Serica* (i.e. another word for silk) cloth is named from 'silken' (*sericus*), or because the *Seres* (i.e. the Chinese, or East Asians generally; see XIV.iii.29) first made it available. *Holosericus* cloth is entirely of silk, for ὅλος means 'entire.' *Tramosericus* has a linen warp and a weft (*trama*) of silk. *Holoporphyrus* is entirely of purple, for ὅλος means 'entire.' 15. *Byssinus* is white and made of a type of thicker linen. There are some people who consider *byssum* to be a certain type of linen (see xxi.3 above).

16. *Fibrinus* [has a weft made of beaver (*fiber*) hair]. Goathair (*caprinus*) . . . *Masticinus* . . . and *menus* . . . Linen (*lineus*) cloth, because it is made only of flax (*linum*). 17. *Linostemus* is woven of wool and linen and is called *linostemus* because it has linen (*linum*) in the warp (*stamen*) and wool in the weft. 18. Upright (*rectus*) cloth is woven upwards by someone standing. *Segmentatus* cloth is decorated with certain bands and separately cut pieces, so to speak (cf. xxxi.12 below), for people refer to the separately cut pieces of any material as *praesegminae*. 19. Lightweight (*levidensis*) cloth is so named because it is open-textured and 'loosely woven' (*leviter densatus*). Heavyweight (*pavitensis*) is named as the opposite to lightweight, because it is closely woven and felted (cf. *pavire*, "ram down").

20. *Citrosus*, so called as if it were crimped like a citron-tree (*citrus*). Naevius writes (cf. *Punic War* 22):

> Beautiful in her gold and her *citrosus* garment.[13]

21. A *velenensis* tunic is one that was brought from the islands. An imported (*exoticus*) garment is a foreign

13 In antiquity a garment was *citrosus* either because it resembled a citron (was lemon-colored), or because it absorbed the good smell of the citrus with which it would be stored.

one coming from the outside, such as a garment from Greece in Spain. A *polymitus* garment is multicolored, for *polymitus* is woven of many colors (cf. πολύμιτος, "damask"). 22. An embroidered (*acupictus*) garment is woven or decorated with a needle (*acus*; cf. *pictus*, "decorated"). This is also called 'Phrygian' (*Phrygius*) because all the Phrygians are said to be skilled in this art, or because it was invented in Phrygia. Whence also the artisans who practice this are called 'embroiderers' (*Phrygio*). Vergil writes (cf. *Aen.* 3.484):

> A Phrygian (*Phrygius*) cloak.

23. *Trilix* cloth is named from three threads (*licium*), because there are also *simplex* and *bilex* cloths.[14] *Rallus*, which is commonly called 'polished' (*rasilis*). Cloth that has been restored to look like new, although it is old, is called 'refurbished' (*interpolus*).

24. 'Patchwork' (*pannucius*) is so named because it is covered with various patches (*pannus*). A *colobium* is so named because it is long and sleeveless (cf. κολοβός, "cut off"); the ancients wore this often. A *levitonarium* is a linen *colobium* without sleeves, of the sort worn by Egyptian monks. 25. A loincloth (*lumbare*) is so named because it is fastened over the loins (*lumbus*) or because it clings to them. In Egypt and Syria they are worn not only by women but also by men. Whence Jeremiah took his *lumbare* across the Euphrates, and hid it there in an opening in the rocks, and afterwards discovered that it had been torn (Jeremiah 13.1–7). This is also called a *renale* by some people, because it is tied over the loins (*renes*). 26. A *limus* is a garment that reaches from the navel to the feet. This garment has a purple band at its lower edge that is 'aslant,' that is, 'undulating,' whence it takes its name, for we call something that is aslant *limus*.

27. Lint (*licinum*, i.e. *licinium*) is so named because its texture is completely bound together (*ligare*), as if the term were *liginum*, but with the *g* changed to a *c*.[15] 28. An *armilausa* is popularly so named because it is divided and open in the front and the back, and is closed (*clausus*, ppl. of *claudere*) only at the shoulders (*armus*), as if the term were *armiclausa*, but with the *c* removed. 29. A nightshirt (*camisia*) is so named because we sleep in these in our cots (*cama*), that is, in our beds. Undergarments (*femoralia*) are so called because they clothe the thighs (*femur*). These are also known as 'breeches' (*bracae*), because they are short (cf. βραχύς, "short"), and the 'shameful parts' (*verecunda*) of the body are concealed with these. 30. The *tubrucus* is so named because it covers the shins (*tibia*) and breeches (*bracae*). The *tibracus*, because it reaches from the arms (*bracium*, i.e. *brachium*) to the shins (*tibia*).

xxiii. The typical costumes of certain peoples (De proprio quarundam gentium habitu) 1. Some nations have their own costume belonging just to them, such as the Parthians and their *sarabara* (i.e. wide trousers), the Gauls and their *linna*, the Germans and their *reno*, the Spaniards and their *stringes*, the Sardinians and their *mastruca*. 2. *Sarabarae* are flowing, sinuous garments, concerning which one may read in Daniel (cf. 3:94): "And their *sarabarae* were not altered." And in Publilius (*Maxims*, fr. 19):

> As, why therefore have the Parthians draped *sarabarae* over your stomach?

But some people call certain head-coverings *sarabarae*, the sort that we see pictured on the heads of the Magi. 3. *Linnae* are soft square mantles. Concerning them Plautus says (fr. 176):

> He was covered by a *linna* of Gaulish weave.

4. The *reno* is a covering from the shoulders and chest to the navel, made so shaggy with twisted nap that it repels rain. Common people call it a *reptus* because it is as if its long fibers are 'creeping like a snake' (*reptare*). Concerning them Sallust says (*Histories* 3.104): "The Germans clothe their naked bodies with *renones*." They are called *renones* from the Rhine (*Renus*) river of Germania, where they are often worn. 5. The *mastruca* is a Germanic[16] garment made from the hides of wild animals, about which Cicero speaks in *On Behalf of Scaurus* (45): "He whom the royal purple did not disturb, was he moved by the *mastruca* of the Sardinians?" *Mastruca* is as if the word were *monstruosus* ("monstrous"), because those who wear them are transformed as if in the garb of wild animals.

14 The sense may be that a *simplex* web is a plain weave; a *bilex*, where the warp thread floats over a group of two weft threads; and a *trilix*, where the warp thread floats over three.

15 'Lint' here means a downy mass of fluff like cotton wool.

16 Some early manuscripts read "Sardinian"; see section 1 above.

6. Nationalities are distinguished by their costume just as they differ in their languages. The Persians cover their arms and legs with drawings[17] and their heads with a turban. The Alani are distinguished by their pointed hats. The Scotti raise the hackles with their ugly dress, as well as with their barking tongues. The Alemanni are clothed in their woolen cloaks (*sagum*), the Indians in linen. The Persians wear jewels, the Chinese wear silk, and the Armenians wear quivers.

7. It is not simply in clothing but in physical appearance also that some groups of people lay claim to features peculiar to themselves as marks to distinguish them, so that we see the curls (*cirrus*, perhaps "topknot") of the Germans, the mustaches and red paint of the Goths, the tattoos of the Britons. The Jews circumcise the foreskin, the Arabs pierce their ears, the Getae with their uncovered heads are blond, the Albanians shine with their white hair. The Moors have bodies black as night, while the skin of the Gauls is white. Without their horses, the Alani are idle. Nor should we omit the Picts (*Pictus*), whose name is taken from their bodies, because an artisan, with the tiny point of a pin and the juice squeezed from a native plant, tricks them out with scars to serve as identifying marks, and their nobility are distinguished by their tattooed (*pictus*) limbs.

8. The sexes also have accepted customs of appearance, such as short hair for men and flowing locks for women, long hair being the mark of virgins in particular. For women the hair is properly arranged when it is gathered up on the top of the head and protects the citadel of their head with a circle of hair.

xxiv. Men's outer garments (De palliis virorum) 1. A cloak (*pallium*) is that with which the shoulders of attendants are covered so that, while they are providing service, they may hurry about unencumbered. Plautus says (fr. 177):

> If you are to amount to anything, hang a *pallium* on
> your shoulders and let your feet go as fast as they can.

It is called *pallium* from skins (*pellis*), because in earlier times the ancients used to wear skins over their clothing, as if the word were *pelleum*. Or it is named from *palla* (i.e. another type of robe, related etymologically to *pallium*) by derivation. 2. The mantle (*chlamys*) is a garment that is put on from one side, and not sewn together, but fastened with a brooch. Hence it also takes its name in Greek (i.e. χλαμύς).

3. The toga (*toga*) is so named because with its wrapping it covers (*tegere*) and conceals the body. It is a plain cloak with a round, rather flowing shape, and with rippling folds, as it were: it is drawn under the right arm and arranged over the left shoulder. We see its likeness in the clothing used for statues and pictures, and we call these statues *togatus* (lit. "wearing a toga"). 4. Romans wore togas during peacetime, but in time of war they wore military cloaks (*paludamentum*). The proper measurement for a toga is six ells. 5. A toga earned by those who brought back the palm (*palma*) of victory from an enemy was called *palmatus*. These were also called decorated togas because they had the victories woven into them with a display of palm leaves. 6. The white (*candidus*) toga, also the 'chalked' toga, is one that candidates (*candidatus*) seeking public office wore when they went round canvassing; chalk was added so that it would be whiter and more noticeable. Cicero, in an oration that he delivered against his rivals for office, wrote *On the White Toga*.

7. A Gabine girding arrangement occurs when the toga is put on so that the edge which is flung back over the shoulder is drawn up to the chest in such a way that the decorations hang on either side from the shoulder, as the pagan priests used to wear them, or as the praetors used to be girded. 8. The *trabea* (i.e. a robe of state) was a type of toga out of purple and scarlet cloth. In the beginning, the kings of the Romans used to make procession dressed in these. People claim that Romulus was the first to devise this garment to distinguish the king. The *trabea* is so named because it would elevate (*transbeare*) a person into greater glory, that is, it may make a person further blessed for the future with a greater rank of honor.

9. The *paludamentum* was a special cloak of emperors, distinguished by its scarlet and purple, and its gold. Sallust speaks of it (*Histories* 1.87) saying: "He has changed his toga for a *paludamentum*." This was also the 'war cloak' (*bellicum pallium*), so named, it seems to some people, because by wearing it the emperor made it

17 Isidore's ultimate source here, Justinus, says that the Persians wore robes (*velamenta*) over their arms and legs. As Rodríguez-Pantoja points out in his note ad loc. (ed. 1995), Isidore may have written *linamentis* ("with linen cloth") rather than *lineamentis* ("with drawings, ?tattoos"), or the tradition that came to him may have been corrupt.

public (*palam*) that war (*bellum*) was approaching. 10. A bordered-around (*circumtextus*) garment is what is called κυκλάς ("encircled by a border all around") in Greek. Concerning it Vergil says (*Aen.* 1.649):

> And a mantle bordered around (*circumtextus*) with saffron acanthus.

It is called 'bordered-around' because it is a round cloak. 11. *Diplois* is a Greek term (cf. διπλοΐς, "double cloak"), used because it is a double-folded (*duplex*) garment. Horace says (*Epistles* 1.17.25):

> On the other hand, he whom Patience covers with a doubled (*duplex*) cloak.

12. There is also military clothing, which first began to be used from enemy booty in the campaigns in Gaul. Concerning which this was said in the Senate: "With their togas put aside the Quirites took up the *sagum* (i.e. the military cloak)." 13. *Sagum* (i.e. a coarse woolen mantle) is a Gallic term. It is called the *sagum quadrum* because at first among the Gauls it used to be 'square or fourfold' (*quadratus vel quadruplex*). 14. The *paenula* is a cloak with long fringes. The *lacerna* is a fringed cloak that at one time was worn only by soldiers. For this reason people used to distinguish the city crowd from those belonging to military camps by calling the former 'toga-wearing' and the latter '*lacerna*-wearing.' Whence also the word is *lacerna*, as if with the ends of the fringes trimmed (cf. *lacer*, "mutilated, torn"), so that their fringes are not as long as those in a *paenula*. 15. The Spaniards called the *mantum* thus because it covers the 'hands only' (*manus tantum*), for it is a short cloak. 16. The *praetexta* is a child's cloak, which noble boys used to wear while they were being educated until they were sixteen, whence they were called '*praetexta*-wearing' boys. It is called a *praetexta* because it would be bordered (*praetexere*) with a wide purple band.

17. The *casula* is a hooded garment, named as a diminutive of 'hut' (*casa*), because it covers the whole person, like a small hut. Whence also the 'hood' (*cuculla*), as if it were a smaller chamber (*cella*). Thus it is also called a *planetas* in Greek, because they sway with 'wandering' (cf. πλανήτης, "wanderer") borders. Whence also the astral 'planets,' that is, the roving ones, because they course about in their own erratic straying and motion. 18. *Birrus* (i.e. a rain cloak) is taken from a Greek word, for they say a *birrus* as *bibrus* (cf. βίρρος, "cloak"). 19. The *melotes*, which is also called a *pera* (lit. "bag"), is the skin of a goat which hangs from the neck and covers as far as the loins. Strictly speaking, this is the outfit needed for laboring. It was first made, as some people think, from the skins of martens (*melo*, i.e. *meles*), whence they are called *melotes*. 20. The fringes of garments, that is, the edges, are called the border (*ora*), derived from a Greek word, for the Greeks call a border ὅρος.

xxv. Women's outer garments (De palliis feminarum)

1. The *regillum* is the mantle of state for queens (*regina*), whence it is named. The *peplum* is a matron's garment marked with purple, whose hem glitters at the edge with gold threads. 2. The *palla* is a woman's garment that is a square cloak (*pallium*). It hangs down to the feet and has gemstones fixed in a row. And it is called *palla* from the word πάλλειν ("sway"), that is, from the movement that occurs around the edge of such clothing, or because as it sways it ripples in fluttering folds. 3. The *stola* is a matron's garment that, covering the head and shoulders, is 'sent' from the right side over the left shoulder. Furthermore, it is called *stola*, with a Greek word (i.e. στολή, "robe"; cf. στέλλειν, "send"), because it is 'sent out on top.' 4. This is also called by the Latin term *ricinium* (i.e. 'veil') because half of it is flung back (*reicere*). People commonly call it a *mavors* (lit. the archaic name for Mars; cf. μαφόρτης, "veil, headdress"). It is called *mavors* as if the term were *Mars*, for it possesses the mark of marital (*maritalis*) dignity and authority, for man is the head of woman, whence this garment is worn over a woman's head.[18]

5. The *amiculum* is the linen cloak of prostitutes. In ancient times, married women caught in adultery were clothed in these so they might sully their virtue in this *amiculum* rather than in a *stola*. Thus among the ancients this garment was a mark of prostitution, but nowadays in Spain it is a mark of respectability. 6. The *theristrum* is a veil with which the women of Arabia and Mesopotamia are covered even today; in the heat they are very well protected by its shade. Isaiah (3:23) speaks concerning it. 7. The *anaboladium* is a linen cloak for women that covers their shoulders. Greek (cf. σινδών, "linen veil") and Latin speakers call it a *sindon*.

18 Isidore alludes to I Corinthians 11:3–7, and takes the term *mavors* for 'veil' as the figure of the martial male (*mas*, gen. *maris*) or husband (*maritus*) as head (or over the head) of his wife.

xxvi. Bedspreads and other cloths that we use (De stratu et reliquis vestibus quae in usu habentur) 1. The *stragulum* is a multicolored cloth that the craftsman's hand adorns with a rich variety of colors. It is so named because it can be used as a spread (*stratus*) and as a cloak (*amictus*). Solomon said of it (cf. Prov. 31:22): "She hath made for herself clothing of tapestry (*stragulum*)." 2. Some people think the *ludix* (i.e. *lodix*, "coverlet") is named from public games (*ludus*), that is, the theater, for when young men used to leave the brothel at the public games, they would conceal their heads and faces with these coverings, because someone who has entered a whorehouse is usually ashamed. *Galnapes*... 3. Couch-backs (*fulcrum*) are couch ornaments, so called because we are propped up (*fulcire*) by them, that is, we are supported, or because they prop up cushions or the head. Common people call them backrests (*reclinatorium*).

4. Bolsters (*cervicalium*) are so named because they are placed under the neck (*cervix*) or elbow. The pillow (*pulvillus*) is named from the *pulvinar*, which is a rich person's couch. Mattresses (*culcita*) are so named because they are packed (*calcare*), that is, filled with feathers or stuffing, so that they may be softer and warmer. 5. Rugs (*tapete*) are so named because they were first spread out for the feet (*pes*, gen. *pedis*), as if the word were *tapedia*. *Sipla* (i.e. *psila*) rugs have their pile on one side, as if the word were *simpla* (cf. *simplus*, 'single'). The *amphitapa* is a rug with pile on both sides. Lucilius says (cf. *Satires* 13):

> *Siplae* and *amphitapae* soft with thick pile.

6. Tablecloths (*mantelium*) are used today for covering tables. However, as their name indicates, they were once offered for wiping one's hands (*manus*; cf. *tela*, "cloth"). Napkins (*mappa*) belong to the banquet and the 'serving' (*apponere*) of feasts, as if the word were *manupa*, and they are named on this account. The diminutive is *mapella*. *Toral* ("couch coverlet") is a long, continuous cloth, named from 'couch' (*torus*). 7. *Sabanum* is a Greek word (cf. σάβανον and σαβάνιον, "linen cloth or towel"). The face towel (*facietergium*) and hand towel (*manitergium*) are named from wiping (*tergere*) the face (*facies*) or hands (*manus*).

Curtains (*velum*) are so named because they conceal (*velare*) the interior of a home when they are drawn shut. 8. Tapestries (*aulaeum*) are large decorated curtains; they are called *aulaea* because they were first invented in the palace (*aula*) of Attalus, king of Asia, to whom the Roman people were the successors.[19] 9. *Cortinae* are hangings (*aulaeum*), that is, curtains, made out of skins. Such hangings can be read about in Exodus (26:14); the exterior of the tabernacle was covered by them. They are called *cortinae* from leather (*coreum*, i.e. *corium*), because they had been made earlier from skins. Whence also in that same tabernacle of the Law it is commanded that *cortinae* be made from the red hides of rams and from violet hides. 10. The Arabs call a covering woven from goat hair a *cilicium*, and from these they make tents for themselves.

xxvii. Wool (De lanis) 1. Wool (*lana*) is named from tearing (*laniare*), that is, plucking (*vellere*). Fleece (*vellus*) is also named from this, for in earlier times wool was plucked and not sheared. Flax (*linum*) originates from the earth, and its name is derived from Greek, for the Greeks call flax λινάριον (lit. "thread"; cf. λίνον, "flax"). Or else it is so named because it is smooth and soft (*lenis*). 2. Tow (*stuppa*) may be from hemp or from flax. This is called *stuppa* according to the ancient spelling, because cracks in ships are packed (*stipare*) with it. Whence also comes the name of the *stipatores* (lit. "attendants, stevedores"), who pack *stuppa* in hollows. 3. Stuffing (*tomentum*) is so named because it is 'fluffed up' (*tumere*) either in the thread or in the warp, and has no thinness. Hemp (*cannabum*) is named from its similarity to reeds (*canna*), or else from a Greek etymology, for they call hemp κάνναβις.

4. *Byssum* is a certain kind of flax that is especially white and soft. The Greeks call it *papaten*. Beaver (*fibrinus*) wool comes from those animals that people call beavers (*fiber*). People claim that these are the same as those beavers (*castor*, another word for 'beaver') that, when hunters pursue them, bite off their own testicles (cf. XII.ii.21 above). The cobweb (*aranea*) is so named because it is fed by the flow of air (*aer*) in foliage. 5. Silk (*sericum*) is so named because the *Seres* (Chinese, or East Asians generally) were the first to provide it. It is there that the worms that spin silk threads around trees are thought to originate. The Greek name for these worms is βόμβυξ. *Placium* is a *stuppa* (see section 2 above), a kind of thick silk, and it is a Greek term.

19 Attalus III, king of Pergamum in Asia Minor, discovered the art of weaving cloth from gold, and made the Roman people his heir.

xxviii. Colorings for cloth (De coloribus vestium) 1. Dying (*tinctura*) is so named because cloth is 'soaked in color' (*tinguere*), tinted to another appearance, and colored for the sake of beauty. What we call red or vermilion (*vermiculus*), the Greeks call κόκκος; it is a small grub (*vermiculus*) from the foliage of the forest. 2. Purple (*conchylium*) is named because its color is collected from the marine *conchula* ("small mollusc"). This is also called *ostrum* (lit. the blood of a sea mollusc). 3. *Ostrum*, which is prepared for purple dye, is found in many places, but the best is on the island of Cyprus or in those places where the sun's path shines closer to the earth. 4. *Conchylia* (i.e. purple shellfish) are from the sea, and when they are cut all the way around with a blade, they exude tears of a purple color. Once these tears have been collected, purple dye is prepared. Furthermore, *ostrum* is so named because it is drawn forth from the liquid of the shell (cf. ὄστρεον, "bivalve shell, purple pigment").

5. Purple (*purpura*) was so named by Latin speakers from the purity (*puritas*) of its bright color. Among the Greeks it is called πορφύρα, with an aspirated *p*, while we say *purpura* with no aspiration. 6. *Ferrugo* is a blackish-purple dye that is made in Spain, as in (Vergil, *Aen.* 9.582):

> Distinguished with Iberian *ferrugo*.

It is called *ferrugo* because all purple at the first dyeing has this color (i.e. that of the rust of iron, *ferrum*). 7. *Glaucus* dye is a blackish *ferrugo*. *Elbidus* (i.e. *helvacea*; cf. *helvus*, "yellowish," and XVII.v.26) is named from the color *elbus*, for *elbus* is the middle color between black and white, and the term *elbus* is taken from 'white' (*albus*). 8. *Luteus* is a reddish color that is saffron, for saffron is *luteus* of hue, as in (cf. Vergil, *Eclogues* 4.44):

> He changed his fleece to a saffron yellow (*lutum*).

Menum [so called because it is a black color, for the Greeks call black μέλαν]. *Masticinum* [so called because it has the color of mastic (*mastix*)]. *Blatteum* (i.e. purple) . . . *Blavum* . . . *Mesticium* . . . 9. *Osticium*, because it comes from something burnt (*ustus*), for it is made from the soot, hanging from a ceiling, that is deposited by constant fire. For this reason the color of this dye is flame-like.

xxix. Tools for clothmaking (De instrumentis vestium) 1. Cloth (*tela*) is named for the length of its threads (cf. τηλοῦ, "afar"). The word 'loom' (*telaria*) is derived from it. Heddles (*insubulus*, cf. *insilium*) are so named because they are below (*infra*) and above (*supra*), or because they 'make a swishing sound' (*insubulare*, i.e. *insibilare*).[20] Shuttles (*radius*) are so named because they are shaped by smoothing (*radere*). Combs (*pecten*) are so named because they comb out (*pectere*) the fibers and press them down. 2. The distaff (*colus*) because it is long and round like a column (*columna*). The spindle (*fusus*), because what has been spun is 'streamed out' (*fundere*, ppl. *fusus*) onto it. The *alibrum* is so called because on it threads are unwound (*liberare*), that is, loosened.[21]

3. The basket (*calathus*) is a light carrier made of flax or wicker or rushes. In it a day's weight (*pensum*, weighed-out wool to be spun) is placed or flowers are collected. In Greek 'wood' is κᾶλα (cf. also κάλαμος, "reed"), from which *calathus* is derived. It is called *quasillum* in Latin. Cicero says in the *Philippics* (3.10): "But in fact gold may be weighed out amid the baskets (*quasillum*)." 4. A 'measure of wool' (*pensum*) for women is named from weighing (*pendere*, ppl. *pensus*), whence also the words 'rations' (*pensa*) and 'expense' (*impensa*). Yarn (*netum*) . . . 5. Thread (*filum*) is so called either because it is from the hair (*pilus*) of animals or because clothmaking takes place with fine threads like hair (*pilus*), that is, as if the word were *filus*. 6. Skein (*mataxa*), so called as if the word were *metaxa*, from the winding-around of threads, clearly, for a turning-point (*meta*) is a going-around – or it is because it is transferred (cf. μετα-, "trans-"; μετάταξις, "change of order"). *Gubellum* ("ball of yarn"; perhaps better *lubellum* of many manuscripts) is said incorrectly as a diminutive of ball (*globus*), as if the word were *globellum*. 7. The *panulia* ("bobbin" or "shuttle"; cf. *panuncula*, "thread wound on a bobbin in a shuttle") is so named because cloths

20 Alternatively, *insubulare* may be a Late Latin word meaning "roll on a warp." Here *infra* and *supra* mean "below and above the surface" of the web in a loom, hence "behind and in front" of the web in an upright loom. Isidore surely speaks here of heddles; the earliest evidence of treadle looms in Europe appears in the twelfth century CE, and these are horizontal looms. Based on his etymology for *stamen* (section 7 below), Isidore has an upright loom in mind. Upright treadle looms came into use several centuries after horizontal ones.

21 The *alibrum* seems to be a wooden frame on which newly twisted thread is loosely wound to make a skein.

(*pannus*) are woven with them, for it runs back and forth through the loom.

The warp (*stamen*) is so named because it stands (*stare*) upright. The weft (*trama*), because it is brought through (*transmittere*) the loom in a straight path (cf. *trames*, "footpath"), for it is the thread running through the warp. The thrums (*licium*) are what join (*ligare*) the warps, as if the word were *ligium*. To 'line up the warp threads' (*ordiri*) is . . . To weave (*texere*) is . . .

xxx. Ornaments (De ornamentis) 1. So far we have been talking about clothing: from this point we turn to other adornments. An ornament (*ornamentum*) is so named because one's face (*os*, gen. *oris*) and appearance are adorned by wearing it. The first ornament was the crown (*corona*, also meaning "garland") as a mark of victory, or the sign of the king's honor. It is placed on the king's head to signify the populations spread around the globe, by whom he was surrounded just as his head was crowned. This is called a *corolla* by Lucilius (*Satires* 1143) and a στεφάνη by Homer (*Iliad* 8.597). The pagans claim that it had its origins with a certain Liber, because they established the practice of binding with these bands a head affected by drinking wine. That is why crowns were once made of a kind of linen or wool, as they were for pagan priests.

2. The word 'band' (*corona*, i.e. "a circle of people") is so named for this reason, because in the beginning people would run (*currere*) around altars, so that a crown was both formed and named according to the image of a circling or a 'group of dancers' (*chorus*). 3. The Roman emperors and certain pagan kings wear gold crowns. The Persians wear turbans (*tiara*), the kings wearing straight ones and the satraps curved ones. The turban was invented by the Assyrian queen Semiramis; that nation has retained this type of ornament from then up until today. The Athenians used to wear gold 'cicadas' (*cic[l]ada*), some of them on the top of the head and some over the forehead.[22] Indeed, not all kings wear the same kinds of regalia.

The pagan seers used to wear *infulae*, *apices*, *pillea*, or *galeria*. 4. An *infula* is a small white band for a priest's head, shaped like a diadem. Fillets hang down on either side of it and fasten the *infula*, whence also fillets (*vitta*) are so named, because they fasten (*vincire*). Most *infulae* were wide and twisted, and made out of white and scarlet. 5. The *apex* (i.e. a conical cap with a rod attached to its peak) is a needlework *pilleum* that pagan priests used to wear. It is named from fastening (*apere*), that is, binding, for the rod that was on the *pilleum* was fastened on by thread made from the wool of a sacrificed animal. The *galerium* (i.e. *galerum*) is a *pilleum* made out of skin from a slaughtered sacrificial victim. *Pilleum* (i.e. a close-fitting cap) is named from the skin (*pellis*) of the sacrifice, from which it used to be made. 6. The *cidaris* (i.e. the head-dress of a high priest) was itself something priestly, and is called a *mitra* by most people.

xxxi. Women's head ornaments (De ornamentis capitis feminarum) 1. Ornaments for women's heads are: the diadem, the *nimbus*, the *capitulum* and the *mitra*. The diadem (*diadema*) is a head ornament for matrons, interwoven with gold and gems. It is fastened at the back with the ends brought to meet one another, and for this reason it is named in Greek, because it is 'tied round' (cf. διά, "across," δεῖν, "bind"). 2. The *nimbus* is a transverse headband made of gold, sewn onto a linen cloth, and is worn by women over the forehead. Plautus (cf. *The Little Carthaginian* 348) says:

> The more I look at her, the more she is 'crowned with a nimbus' (*nimbatus*).

The light that is depicted as being around the heads of angels is called a *nimbus*, although a *nimbus* is also the dense part of a cloud (*nubis*). 3. A hood (*capitulum*) is commonly called a *capitulare*. This is also called a *cappa* (i.e. another word for 'hood,' or perhaps 'kerchief'), because it has two tips like the letter kappa, or because it is an ornament for the head (*caput*).

4. A *mitra* (i.e. a kind of head-dress, a bonnet) is a Phrygian *pilleum* (i.e. a cap), covering the head, the sort of ornament worn on the heads of women who have taken religious vows. But a *pilleum* is for men, and a *mitra* for women. 5. And *redimicula* are what the *mitra* is tied on with. A *pilleum*, as we said above, was made from

22 Lindsay – and, apparently accidentally, Rodríguez-Pantoja (ed. 1995) – emend the early manuscripts' reading *cicadas* ("cicadas, locusts") to *cycladas*, also found in some manuscripts, presumably referring to *cyclas*, plural *cyclades*, a woman's bordered robe of state; see xxiv.10 above. But in fact a *cicada* was a gold ornamental hairpin shaped like the insect; see Liddell-Scott's Greek lexicon, s.v. τέττιξ, and pseudo-Vergil, *Ciris* 128.

skin, but a *mitra* is made of wool. The *ricula* (i.e. a small veil) is a *mitra* for the head of a virgin. 6. Fillets are what are fastened in the hair; they gather up loose hair, and they are called fillets (*vitta*) because they bind (*vincire*). The *taenia* (i.e. ribbon) is the end of the fillet, and it hangs down in various colors. Again, a crown is tied on with a fillet, and the *taenia* is the lowest part of the fillet, the part that hangs down from the crown. 7. A hair-net (*reticulum*) is what gathers the hair, so named because it 'holds hair' (*retinere crines*), so that it is not loose.[23] 8. The *discriminale* for women's heads is so named because it parts the head (i.e. the hair) with gold, for 'to part' means 'to separate' (*discriminare*).

Antiae are the curls hanging down around the ear-lobes. It is from a Greek word, 'opposite' (i.e. ἀντίος) the ears. 9. The hairpin (*acus*) is what holds an arrangement for adorning women's hair in place, lest strands of hair fall loose and fly about here and there. 10. Earrings (*inaures*) are named from the pierced places of the ears (*auris*), from which precious beads of stone hang. They were worn this way in Greece: girls would wear them in both ears, and boys would wear them only in the right ear. 11. Torques (*torquis*) are gold circles hanging from the neck onto the chest. Both torques and *bullae* (i.e. lockets for amulets) are worn by men, but women wear *monilia* (necklaces) and *catellae* (neck-chains). Torques are so called because they are twisted (*torquere*), and *bullae* because in their roundness they are like a bubble (*bulla*) inflated in the water by the wind.

12. A *monile* is an ornament made out of gems, which would be hung around the neck by women. It is named from 'gift' (*munus*). This is also called a *serpentum* because it consists of certain gold beads (lit. "small amphoras") and various gemstones arranged in the shape of a serpent. Some people call this a *segmentum*, as Juvenal does (*Satires* 2.124):

> *Segmenta* (properly, "flounces") and long clothes.

However, we also speak of clothing as 'trimmed' (*segmentatus*; cf. xxii.18 above), as in the same author (6.89):

> And the little girl would have slept in a flounced (*segmentatus*) cradle.

23 Isidore may tacitly refer to the word *rete*, "net," as a basis of the etymology.

13. However, frequently any of a matron's ornaments is referred to by the term *munile* (i.e. *monile*) – whichever ones are given to her as a gift (*munus*). 14. A *murena* (lit. "eel") is so called in common usage, because a chain of a flexible kind, made of pliant tube-beads of gold metal, suitable for adorning the neck, is made in the likeness of a serpentine *murena*. Sometimes this is constructed from tube-beads of gold and of silver. Whence also it is said in the Song of Songs (1:10): "We will make thee chains (*murenulae*) of gold, inlaid with silver."

15. *Catellae* are chainlets (*catenula*) for the neck, linking to each other like chains (*catena*), whence they are named. 16. Bracelets (*dextra*, i.e. *dextrale*) are worn by both men and women, because both sexes wear them on the right hand (*dextera*). Armbands (*armilla*) are, properly speaking, for men (*vir*), conferred on soldiers in recognition of a victory for their valor (*virtus*) in arms (*arma*). For this reason they were sometimes also commonly called *viriolae* (perhaps read *viriliae*). An *armilla* is no different from a bracelet (*circulus*) in meaning, because it also encloses something by encircling the place where it is put, but an *armilla* is more extended in depth and a *circulus* is rounded. 17. *Fibulae* (i.e. pins or brooches) are used to adorn a woman's breast or are worn by men to hold a cloak over their shoulders, or a belt around their hips. *Lunulae* are ornaments for women; they are small pendent gold balls shaped like the moon (*luna*).

18. Mirrors (*speculum*) are what women use to look at their faces. A mirror is so named either because the reflection is produced from its brightness (*splendor*) or because women looking in it study the appearance (*species*) of their face and add whatever ornament they see is lacking. 19. Ankle bracelets (*periscelis*) are ornaments for women's legs, which adorn their appearance as they walk by. 'Scent bottles' (*olfactoriolum*) are small vessels for women, in which perfumes are carried.

xxxii. Rings (De anulis) 1. Prometheus is said to have been the first to put on his finger a circle of iron with a stone set into it; following this practice people began to wear rings. Rings (*anulus*) are named as a diminutive from the circlets and hoops (*anus*) that go around the arms and legs. Likewise the signets (*signum*) of rings are as a diminutive called *sigilla*. A *signum* is larger, and a *sigillum* is like a smaller *signum*. 2. People first began to wear rings on the fourth (i.e. third) finger from the thumb, because a certain vein reaches from it to the heart, and the ancients thought that this vein should be noted and adorned by some sort of sign.

3. Among the Romans, rings would be distributed from the public treasury, and not indiscriminately, for rings with gems were given as an honor to men of exceptional merit, and plain rings to the rest. A slave or freedman would not wear a gold ring in public. Freeborn men wore gold rings, freedmen silver, and slaves iron, although many very worthy men also would wear iron rings. 4. Among the ancients it was a disreputable practice for a man to wear more than one ring. Gracchus says in the *Against Maevius* (unique fragment): "Consider his left hand, O Quirites – see whose authority you are following: someone who is adorned like a woman on account of his lust for women." Crassus, who perished among the Parthians, had two rings in his old age, giving as his pretext the fact that that he had accumulated immense wealth. Many Romans refrained, in their dignity, from wearing a ring on their finger. Women did not wear rings except for the ones given to them as maidens by their fiancés, and they used to wear not more than two gold rings on their fingers. But nowadays when it comes to gold, no part of a woman's body is left light and unencumbered.

5. Among the types of rings are the *ungulus*, the Samothracian, and the Thynian. An *ungula* has a gemstone, and is called by this name because the gem of this ring is set in gold just as a claw (*ungula*) is set in flesh. A Samothracian ring is certainly gold, but with an iron capital. It is named from the place. 6. A Thynian ring is unadorned. It was first manufactured in Bithynia, which was once called Thynia. Flaccus (i.e. Maecenas's poem addressed to Horace, fr. 1):

> O Flaccus Lucentus, my life, I seek for myself neither emeralds nor glittering beryl, nor white pearls, nor those little rings that the Thynian (*Tunnicus*) file has polished, nor jasper stones.[24]

xxxiii. Belts (De cingulis) 1. A *cinctus* is a wide belt (*zona*), while a *semicinctium* is less wide, and a *cingulum* is less than either, for the word *cingulum* is formed as a diminutive from *cinctus*. Young men at athletic (*campester*) exercises used to conceal their private parts with a *cinctum*, whence it is also called a *campestris*. 2. A baldric (*balteum*) is a military belt, so named because military insignia hang from it, showing the total number of men in a military legion, that is, 6600, of which number the soldiers themselves are a part. *Balteus* is the name not only for what one girds on, but also for what weapons hang from. 3. *Zona* is Greek (cf. ζώνη, "belt, girdle"); what they call ζωνάρις (cf. ζωνάριον, "belt") we call a *cingulum*. A *strophium* is a gold *cingulum* with gems. Cinna says this of it (cf. Catullus, *Poems* 64.65):

> With a *strophium* encircling milk-white breasts.

And Prudentius (*Crowns of Martyrdom* 4.25):

> This is the name of the gem fastened on the *strophium*.

4. A *limus* is an apron that public slaves used to wear, and it was called *limus* because it had purple bands that were slanted, that is, oblique (*limus*). A *caltulum* is a kind of girdle, named from its 'constraining strap' (*cogere*, ppl. *coactus* + *lorum*).

Fibula ("pin" or "brooch") is a Greek word, which they call *fiblis* (cf. φίβλα or φιβλίον, "brooch"), because it binds (*ligare*). *Subfibulum* (i.e. a white four-cornered veil) . . . Loincloth (*subligaculum*) . . . 5. The *redimiculum* is what we call an apron or a *bracile*, because it comes down from the nape and is divided on either side of the neck, passing under each armpit and tying around below from either side, in such a way that it pulls in the breadth of the garment as it clothes the body, drawing it together and arranging it by means of its fastening (cf. xxxi.5 above). Common people call this a *brachilis*, as if the word were *brachialis* (i.e. "bracelet" in classical Latin), even though nowadays it is not a belt about the arms (*brachium*) but about the loins. An apron (*succinctorium*) is so called because, as we have said, it is drawn under the arms, goes around under the armpits and is secured below (*succingere*), coming from either side.

6. A *fascia* is a band that covers the chest and binds the breasts, and the chest is quite tightly bound with its crimped belt. It is called a *fascia* because it ties around the body like tying up a packet (*fasciculus*). Hence also bandages (*fasciolae*), with which wounds are bound up. 7. A fillet (*vitta*) is so called because it binds (*vincire*) the chest like a clinging vine (*vitis*). A border (*limbus*) is what we call trimming. 8. It is a band that goes around

24 Rodrígues-Pantoja (ed. 1995) adopts two alterations: *Lugenti* ("in my grief") for *Lucente* ("Lucentus"), and the spelling *Thunica* for *Tunnica*. In any case the form *Lucente* as vocative is here unmetrical.

the edges of clothing, woven either of thread or of gold, and sewn onto the outside lower edge of the garment or cloak. Vergil says of it (*Aen.* 4.137):

> Clothed in a Sidonian cloak with embroidered border (*limbus*).

xxxiv. Footwear (De calciamentis) 1. Shoemakers (*sutor*) are so named because they sew (*suere*), that is, they stitch together, with boar bristles (*seta*; and cf. *sus*, "pig") worked into their thread, as if the word were *setor*. 2. But bootmakers (*caligarius*) are so called not from the thick skin (*callum*) of the foot, but from the last (*calum*, i.e. *cala*, lit. "wood"; cf. κᾶλον, "wood"), that is, the wood, without which shoes cannot be sewn together; the Greeks call this a καλόπους ("shoemaker's last," lit. "wooden foot"). At first they were only made from willow. Hence shoes (*calciamentum*) are named because they are made on lasts (*calum*), that is, wood, or because they are 'trodden upon' (*calcare*).

3. The Greeks used sandals, which had been invented earlier. This is a kind of shoe with a single shape, the same shape being suited to either foot, whether the right or the left. These sandals (*crepida*) are so named because they are fastened with a noise, or from the pattering (*crepitus*) of feet while walking. 4. Kings and Caesars used to wear the shoe called *calceus*. Their shape . . . Romulus invented patrician (*patricius*) shoes, with four laces and a moon (i.e. a half-moon shaped badge) sewn on them; only patricians used to wear these. The moon on them did not represent the image of the celestial body but a sign of the number one hundred (i.e. **C**), because in the beginning there were one hundred patrician senators.

5. Greaves (*ocrea*) are 'shoes' for the shins, so named because they cover the legs (*crus*). The *coturnus* (i.e. *cothurnus*, a high, thick-soled boot) was what used to be worn by tragic actors when they were about to speak in the theater and chant (*cantare*) poems in a deep, resonant voice. It was a shoe like the sandal that heroes used to wear, but such that it fits both the right foot and the left. 6. *Baxeae* are shoes worn by comic actors, parallel to the *coturni* of tragic actors.[25] Some people call them *calones* because they are made from willow, for the Greeks, as we have said, call wood κᾶλα. 7. *Talares* (i.e. *talaria*) are slippers (*soccus*) that seem to be so named because they are so shaped that they come to the ankles (*talus*); similarly *subtolares*, because they come below (*sub*) the ankle, as if the term were *subtalares*.

8. *Obstrigilli* (i.e. another kind of sandal) are stitched along the sole, and have lacing on the uppers so that they can be fastened (*constringere*) by drawing it tight; this gives them their name. 9. I think that *osae* were first made from bone (*os*), and although they are now made from other materials, people have retained the original name. 10. *Mullei* are similar to *coturni* (see section 5 above), with elevated soles, but the upper part has a buckle-tongue (*malleolus*) of bone or brass, to which thongs are fastened. They are named from their red color, the sort of color a mullet (*mullus*) fish has. 11. *Soleae* only cover the soles of the feet, and are named from the sole (*solum*) of the foot. Wooden *soleae* are made of wood covered by leather. 12. Slippers (*soccus*), whose diminutive is *socellus*, are so named because they have a 'bag' (*saccus*) in which part of the foot is put. *Callicula* (perhaps *gallicula*, a small Gallic shoe, or *caligula*, a small military boot) . . .

Boots (*caliga*) are named either from the thick skin (*callum*) of the foot or because they are laced (*ligare*), for *socci* are not laced, but only slipped on. 13. *Cernui* are slippers with no soles. *Lingulati* (lit. "tongue-shaped") are the ones we call *foliatus* (lit. "leaf-shaped"). Nailed (*clavatus*) shoes, [as if the word were *claviatus*, because the soles are joined to the uppers with small – that is, sharp – nails (*clavus*)].[26] 'Fur-lined boots' (*perones*) and *sculponeae* are country shoes. *Baxea* are women's shoes. Laces (*corrigia*) are named from leather (*corium*) or from binding (*colligatio*), as if the word were *colligia*.

25 See 12 and 13 below. Traditionally the *soccus* ("slipper, sock") was the emblem of comic actors, as the *cothurnus* ("buskin") was that of tragic actors.

26 The reading *calibatus* seems preferable to *claviatus*; see xix.7 above.

Book XX

(Provisions and various implements)[1]

i. Tables (De mensis) 1. Daedalus was the first to make a table and a chair. The first to devise the equipment for cooking was a certain Apicius, who died by his own choice, after his property was consumed – and deservedly so, because he who is slave to his maw and to gluttony kills both the soul and the body. The word 'table' (*mensa*) was made from 'eating' (*esus*) and 'consuming' (*comesus*), for a table has no other use. 2. A couch (*torus*) is so called from the twisted (*tortus*) grasses that are placed under the shoulders of those reclining on it. The 'semicircular couch' (*stibadium*) is named from log (*stipes*), as if it were *stipadium*, because it began as such. The 'large dining couch' (*accubitum*) is so called from food (*cibus*), as if it were 'for the food' (*ad cibatum*) of a banquet.

3. Among the Greeks a banquet (*convivium*) derives from the idea of 'drinking together' (*compotatio*), from their word ποτός, "drink."[2] But in Latin it is more correctly derived from 'living in company' (*convictus*), or because there one has conversation about life (*vita*). Again, *convivium* from a multitude of 'people eating together' (*convescentes*), for a private table is for sustenance, but it is not a banquet. A banquet has three elements: reclining, eating, and drinking. Reclining, as (Vergil, *Aen.* 1.708):

> Bidden to recline on the decorated couches.

Eating and drinking, as (cf. Vergil, *Aen.* 1.723)

> After the first lull in the banquet, when the tables were removed, they set out great bowls and garland the wines.

ii. Foodstuffs (De escis) 1. Food (*cibus*) is so called because it is taken (*capere*) in the mouth, just as foodstuff (*esca*) because the 'mouth takes' (*os capit*) it. Victuals (*victus*) are rightly so called, because they sustain life (*vita*); hence to ask someone to dinner is termed to 'invite' (*invitare*). 2. Nourishment (*alimonia*) is so called because the body is nourished (*alere*) by consuming it. Youths take nourishment in order to grow, the elderly to endure, for the flesh cannot subsist unless it is strengthened with nourishment. Nutriment (*alimentum*) is that by which we are nourished (*alere*), and support (*alimonium*) is responsibility for nourishing.

3. Affluence (*affluentia*) is so named as if it were a 'pouring out' (*effusio*) of something overabundant, beyond what is enough, and there is no restraint. 4. Opulence (*opulentia*) is so called from 'assistance' (*ops*), and if you examine it you will find that it observes moderation. For how can anything excessive be of assistance (*opitulari*), when too much is often more troublesome than too little? 5. 'Sumptuous meals' (*epulae*) are so called from the opulence (*opulentia*) of things. 'Ordinary meals' (*epulae simplices*) are divided into two necessary elements, bread and wine, and two categories beyond these, namely, what people seek out for eating from the land and from the sea. 6. Feasts (*dapes*) are for kings, and *epulae* for private persons. Delicacies (*deliciae*) are so called because people are delighted (*delectare*) by them, and have a sweet tooth for them. 7. *Pulmentum* takes its name from *puls* ("gruel"); it is named correctly whether it is eaten in the form of gruel alone or whether something else is eaten in a mixture of gruel. 8. Satiety (*satietas*) and fullness (*saturitas*) are distinct, for satiety can be spoken of with regard to a single food, because it is enough (*satis*), but fullness takes its name from a 'mixed dish' (*satura*) that is made up of a varied preparation of foods.

9. Debauchery (*crapula*) is immoderate voracity, as if it were a 'raw meal' (*cruda epula*), by whose rawness the heart is burdened and the stomach is made to suffer indigestion. Now immoderate voracity is a vice, and only as much as is sufficient for sustenance and one's nature is healthy. 10. Breakfast (*iantaculum*, i.e. *ientaculum*) is the first food with which a fast (*ieiunium*) is broken – hence it is named. Nigidius (fr. 109): "We ourselves have violated fasts with light breakfasts." 11. Lunch (*prandium*) is named for the 'preparations for eating' (*apparatus edendi*). Hence the ancients properly called

1 This book is untitled in the early manuscripts.
2 Isidore refers to the Greek term συμπόσιον.

the food for all the soldiers before battle 'lunch.' Hence the exhortation of the general, "Let us eat lunch like men about to dine in the infernal regions."[3] 12. *Merenda* is a meal taken late in the day, as if it were 'to be eaten in the afternoon' (*postmeridie edenda*) and very close to dinner – hence it is also called *antecenium* (lit. "before dinner") by some people. Again, 'to partake of *merenda*' (*merendare*), as if it were 'to eat at midday' (*meridie edere*).

13. The term *annona* (lit. "provisions") derives from the time at which the ancient Romans would be summoned to meals. Thus Martial (*Epigrams* 4.8.6):

> The ninth hour (*nona*; i.e. about 3:00 PM) demands that we rumple the high couches.

The Persians still do this today. 14. Dinner (*coena*, i.e. *cena*) is named for the community of those eating, for the Greek for "common" is κοινός. Whence also the term 'communicants' (*communicantes*), because they gather in common (*communiter*), that is, on an equal basis. Among the ancients it was the custom to take meals in public view and to dine in community, lest dining alone beget excess. Also dinner is the evening (*vespertinus*) meal, which the ancients would call *vesperna*, for in their practice there were no lunches.

15. Bread (*panis*) is so called because it is served with all food, or because all living creatures crave it, for 'all' in Greek is πᾶν. Coarse bread (*cibarius*) is what is given as bread to slaves, and it is not refined. Leavened bread (*fermentacius*) is made with leaven. Unleavened bread (*azymus*) is not fermented, for the term ἄζυμος means "without yeast," unadulterated. *Acrozymus* is slightly leavened bread, as if it were *acroazymus*. 'White wheat' (*siligineus*) bread is named for its type of grain, for *siligo* is a kind of wheat. Toast (*rubidus*) is bread recooked and made red (*rubefactus*). *Subcinericius* is bread cooked on both sides on hot embers (*cinis*); it is also called hearth-bread (*focacius*). *Clibanicius* bread is baked in a pot. 16. Sponge (*spungia*, i.e. *spongia*) bread is a mixture that is softened for a good while in water, and takes in a small portion of fine flour and a small portion of yeast; it has more moisture than any other bread, whence it took the name of the sponge.

17. *Placentae* are breads made from spelt. Some people call them *libum*; they are so named because they are agreeable (*libere*) and pleasing (*placere*). 18. Sweet cakes (*dulcis*) are types of bread made by pastry-cooks, so called from their taste, for they are eaten sprinkled with honey. Crust (*crusta*) is the surface of bread; another term for this is *fragmenta* (lit. "fragments") because the crust is divided up, as in 'broken pieces' (*fracta*, ppl. of *frangere*). Leaven (*fermentum*) is named from 'seething' (*fervor*), because it cannot be contained after the first hour, for it pushes out with its expansion. Meal (*farina*) and bran (*furfur*) are so called from spelt (*far*), whose chaff they are. 19. Starch (*amolum*, i.e. *amylum*), the best flour of farina, is very fine and is thrown out of the millwheels because of its lightness – hence its name, as if it were 'from the mill' (*a mola*). Wheat flour (*simila*) . . . Mill dust (*pollen*) . . .

20. Meats (*carnes*) are so called because they are flesh (*caro*); or, from "producing" (*creare*), whence they are also called κρέας by the Greeks. Raw (*crudus*) meat, because it is gory (*cruentus*), for it has blood. 21. Cooked (*coctus*), [as if it were 'forced' (*cogere*, ppl. *coactus*), that is, acted upon (*agere*, ppl. *actus*) in a forceful way by fire or water, and fit for use in eating]. But also something ripened over a long period of time is called by the same term. 22. Roasted (*assus*), something that is blazing hot, as though the word were *arsum* ("burnt"). Boiled (*elixus*), because it is cooked in water only, for water is called *lixa* because it is a solution (*solutus*) – wherefore also 'giving rein' (*solutio*) to desire is called debauchery (*luxus*, noun), and dislocated limbs are described as *luxus* (adj., "sprained"). 23. Fried (*frixus*) is so termed from the sound food makes when it is seared in oil. Spiced (*salsus*), as if it were 'sprinkled with salt' (*sale asparsus*), with the [three] middle syllables taken away. Rancid (*rancidus*) is named after its defect, because it makes one hoarse (*raucus*). 24. A cut (*succidia*) is meat set aside for later use, so called from butchering (*succidendo*).

Lard (*lardum*), because it is kept stored at home, for the ancients called their homes 'dwellings' (*lar*). In Gallic lard is called *taxea*, whence Afranius in *Rosa* (fr. 284):

> The Gaul in his mantle, fed with fat lard (*taxea*).

25. Grease (*axungia*) is named from ointment (*unctio*). Suet (*sebum*) is named from pig (*sus*, ablative *sue*), as if it were *suebum*, because this animal has more fat. 26. A bit (*offa*) in its proper sense is a fragment cut by the teeth; its diminutive is *offella* (i.e. *offula*). So 'minced-meat

3 The general was Leonidas, king of the Spartans: Cicero, *Tusculan Disputations* 1.101.

makers' (*offarius*) are cooks who cook with small pieces, that is, "in bits" (*offatim*). Hence the expression "a bit (*offa*, i.e. a sop) for barking dogs"; if it is tossed into a dog's mouth the dog is instantly satisfied, and is curbed and silenced. 27. A morsel (*frustum*) is so called because it is taken by the *frumen*, for the *frumen* is the upper part of the throat. 'Lean meat' (*pulpa*) is so called because formerly it would be eaten mixed with gruel (*puls*). Hence also relish (*pulmentarium*) and *pulmentum* have their names.

28. *Lucanica* (i.e. a kind of sausage) is so called because it was first made in Lucania. Sausage (*farcimen*) is meat cut up into small bits, because with it an intestine is stuffed (*farcire*), that is, filled, with other things mixed in. 29. Hash (*minutal*) is so called because it is made of fish and stuffing and vegetables cut 'in small bits' (*minutatim*). *Aphratum* is a dish called 'foamy' (*spumeum*) in Latin, because ἀφρός in Greek means "foam." *Martisium* is made from fish in a mortar (*mortarium*), whence it is named. 30. *Isocis* is the name of a certain fish from which an *isicium* (i.e. a kind of stuffing, from *insecare*, "chop") was originally made, and although it is now made from another kind of fish, at the outset that fish gave it its name. 31. *Galatica* is named for its milky color, for the Greeks call milk γάλα. Meatballs (*sphera*) are named with this Greek word for their roundness, for whatever is round in shape is called σφαῖρα in Greek.

32. Teachers of cooking have named broth (*ius*) after the word for 'law' (*ius*), because it is the determining factor in the seasoning of cooking. The Greeks call it zema (i.e. "decoction"). 33. Cheese (*caseus*) is so called because it "lacks whey" (*carere serum*), as if the word were *careus*, for all the whey is drawn out of it so that it can take shape under weights. *Colostrum* is the milk from a new mother, and is of neuter gender. 34. Milk (*lac*) is derived from a Greek term for its whiteness, for the Greeks call something white λευκός. Milk and blood are what nourish and what take in nourishment, for we are nourished by milk, and we live by blood. 35. The term 'rennet' (*quactum*) is as if the term were *coactum* ("curdled"), as if 'coagulated' (*coagulatum*), because when other things are mixed with rennet it coagulates them into another form.

36. Honey (*mel*) is from a Greek term (i.e. μέλι), which is shown to have its name from bees, for a bee in Greek is called μέλισσα. Formerly honey was from dew and was found in the leaves of reeds. Hence Vergil (cf. *Geo*. 4.1):

> Thus far, the celestial gifts of honey from the air.

Indeed in India and Arabia honey is still found attached to branches, clinging like grains of salt. Nevertheless, all honey is sweet; Sardinian honey is bitter because of wormwood, with whose abundance the bees of that region are fed. The honeycomb (*favus*) is so called because it is eaten rather than drunk, for the Greeks say φαγεῖν for "eat."

37. Finally, physicians and those who write about the physiology of the human body, especially Galen in his book titled Περσιε *in quo*,[4] say that the bodies of children, youths, and men and women of mature age burn with an innate heat, and that for these ages foods that increase heat are noxious, and that to take whatever things are cold for eating conduces to good health. Likewise for the elderly, on the contrary, who struggle with phlegm and cold, it helps to take warm foods and aged wines.[5]

iii. Drink (De potu) 1. A drink (*potio*) derives its name from Greek, for they call it πότος. Water (*aqua*) is generally so named because its surface is level (*aequalis*) – hence also 'the sea' (*aequor*, lit. any level expanse). We speak of water as fresh because it is not useful when it is aged, like wine, but when it is immediately drawn from a river, spring, or well, for it stinks when it is aged. 2. Wine (*vinum*) is so called because a drink of it speedily replenishes the veins (*vena*) with blood. Some call it *Lyaeus*, because it loosens (*solvere*) us from care.[6] The ancients called wine venom (*venenum*), but after poison from a lethal sap was discovered they called the one thing wine, the other venom. Hence Jerome in the book he wrote *On Preserving Virginity*: "Thus growing girls should avoid wine as poison lest, on account of the fervent heat of their time of life, they drink it and die."[7] Hence it is that Roman women of ancient times would

4 The title of Galen's work, apparently his *Hygiene*, is corrupted in the manuscripts. Isidore is here quoting Jerome, Epistle 54, "To Furia, On Remaining a Widow" (*Patrologia Latina* 22.554).

5 Here "hot" and "cold" refer to physiologists' ideas of the elemental properties of various foods, and not to the temperature at which they are served.

6 "Loosen" is *solvere*; Isidore or his source associates the verb with *luere*, (i.e. λύειν), "loosen" (*solvere* = *se* + *luere*) and hence with *Lyaeus*, "the Relaxer," an epithet of Bacchus. See ii.22 above.

7 The material from Jerome derives from two nearby places in his commentary on the four Pauline Epistles: *Ad Galatas* 3.5 col. 445, lines 48 and 52.

not use wine except on prescribed days for ritual purposes. 3. We speak of *merum* when we mean "pure wine," for we call "plain" (*merus*) whatever is pure and unadulterated, as plain (*merus*) water, mixed with nothing else at all. Hence also *merenda* (see ii.12 above), because in ancient times that was the time at which plain (*merus*) bread would be given to laboring servants – or, because at that time of day people 'took a siesta' (*meridiare*) alone and separately, not, that is, as at lunch and dinner, gathered at one table. Hence we think, furthermore, that the time of day which is after the middle of the day is called afternoon (*meridies*), because it is pure.

4. Must (*mustum*) is wine drawn straight from the vat. It is thought to be called *mustum* because it has sediment and dirt mixed in it, for *mus* means "dirt," whence *humus* ("the ground"). The force of must's fermenting is so great that it quickly shatters vessels filled with it, however sturdy they are, unless there is a vent. 5. *Roseum* is wine of a red color, for a rose (*rosa*) is red. But Aminean (*Amineus*) wine is as if it were without cinnabar (*minium*), that is, without red, for it is white. Amber-colored (*sucinacius*) wine is like the gem amber (*sucina*, i.e. *sucinum*), that is, of a tawny color. 6. Limpid (*limpidus*) wine, that is, clear, is so called from its resemblance to water, as if it were *lymphidum*, because *lympha* is water. Turbid (*turbidus*) wine, as if it were *terbidum*, that is, mixed with earth (*terra*) – namely, its dregs. Falernian (*Falernus*) wine is named from the Falernian region of Campania, where the best wines originate.

7. *Colatus* wine gives its name to its own vessel in which it is decanted (cf. *colum*, "strainer"), but Gazean (*Gazeum*) wine names the region from which it is imported, for Gaza is a city in Palestine. The wine that is poured out as a libation and 'is offered' (*offertur*) at an altar is called *infertus*. 'Polluted' (*spurcus*) is wine that may not be offered, or in which water is mingled, as if it were 'bastardized' (*spurius*), that is, unclean. 8. 'Honorary' (*honorarius*) wine is what is offered to kings and potentates to honor them. Cato, *On His Own Innocence* (1; i.e. *Orations* 73): "When I was a legate in the provinces, a great many people would give the praetors and consuls 'honorary' wine. I never accepted it, not even as a private person." 9. *Crucius* (lit. "crucifying") wine is the sour wine that slaves drink.

Vinegar (*acetum*) is so called either because it is sharp (*acutus*), or because it is watery (*aquatus*), for wine mingled with water quickly acquires this taste. Hence the term 'tart' (*acidus*), as if the word were *aquidus*. 'Spiced' (*conditus*) wine is so called because it is not pure, and is blended with a mixture of coloring agents. 10. *Lactatum* is a drink made from milk (*lac*). Honey-wine (*mulsum*) is wine mixed with honey, for it is a drink made from water and honey, which the Greeks call μελίκρατον.[8] 11. Wine-honey (*oenomelum*) is must mixed with honey and vigorously stirred and shaken. Honey-water (*hydromelum*), so called because it is made from water and Matian apples (*malum*). Filtered (*saccatus*) wine is made of water mixed with the dregs of wine and filtered through a bag (*saccus*). Second-press wine (*lorea*) . . . 12. Vinegar-honey (*oxymeli*) is so called because it is something made from a mixture of vinegar and honey (*mel*), whence it has a sweet-sour taste. 'Honey of roses' (*rhodomelum*) is so called because the honey is mixed with essence of rose. Water-mead (*melicratum*) is wine mixed with honey. 13. Mead (*medus*), as if it were *melus*, because it is made from honey (*mel*), just as *calamitas* is put for *cadamitas*. 'Burnt tartar' (*faecula*) is a decoction of plump grapes, cooked down to the thickness of honey and cooled, good for the stomach. 14. Raisin-wine (*passum*) is the liquid pressed from dried (*passus*) grapes. It is called *passum* from 'suffering' (*pati*, ppl. *passus*), for the dry grapes are beaten and cooked down, and from this raisin-wine is made. 'Reduced must' (*defrutum*) is so called because it is defrauded (*defrudare*), and in a way suffers fraud. 15. Reduced wine (*carenum*), because it lacks (*carere*) a part from boiling, for when a third part of the must is lost, what remains is *carenum*. The counterpart of this is *sapa*, which reduced by boiling goes down to a third.

16. *Sicera* is any drink apart from wine that can inebriate a person. Although its name is Hebrew, it still has a Latin sound because it is made from the juice (*sucus*) of grain or fruits, or the fruit of palms is squeezed to a pulp; and the liquid, thick with the cooked produce, like juice, is strained, and the resulting drink is named *sicera*. 17. Beer (*cervisia*) is so called from Ceres, that is, from grain, for it is a drink made in various ways from seeds of grain. 18. *Caelia* beer is so called from 'heating' (*calefacere*), and it is a drink skillfully brewed from the juice of wheat. The strength of the germ of moistened grain is aroused by fire, and then it is dried, and after it has been ground to a meal it is mixed with mild juice

8 Μελίκρατον in Greek is a drink of honey and milk. *Mulsum* is a mixture of honey and wine.

and, by its fermentation, a harsh taste and inebriating heat are added. This is made in the parts of Spain where there is no fertile place for producing wine.

Lees (*fex*, i.e. *faex*) are so called because they affix (*adfigere*, ppl. *adfixus*) themselves to the vats by settling out. 19. The sauce *garum* is a liquid made from fish, which formerly was made from the fish that the Greeks called γάρος, and although it is now made from any kind of fish it retains the original name that it had at its beginning. 20. *Liquamen* is so called because little fish dissolved in pickling brine liquefy (*liquare*) as that sauce. The liquid from *liquamen* is called *salsugo* or *muria*, but properly *muria* (i.e. "brine") is the name for water mixed with salt, to produce the taste of the sea (*mare*). 21. Juice (*sucus*) is the name for what is squeezed from a filter bag (*saccus*), like barley-water (*ptisana*). Barley-water, broth (*zema*), and decoction (*apozema*) are Greek words (i.e. πτισάνη, "barley-gruel"; ζέμα, "decoction"; ἀπόζεμα, "decoction").

iv. Dishes for food (De vasis escariis) 1. Dishes (*vas*) are so called from 'eating' (*vesci*), because food is served on them. Its diminutive is *vascula*, as if it were *vescula*. 2. Crockery (*fictile*) is so called because it is made and fashioned (*fingere*, ppl. *fictus*) from earth, for to fashion is to make, form, and mold, whence also potters (*figulus*) take their name. And a ceramic (*fictilis*) dish is not called 'fashioned' (*fictus*) because it is mendacious, but because it is shaped, so that it may exist and have a certain form.[9] Hence the Apostle says (cf. Romans 9:20): "Shall the thing formed (*figmentum*) say to him that formed (*fingere*) it: Why hast thou made me thus?" 3. Ceramic dishes are said to have been first invented on the island of Samos, made from white clay and hardened by fire, hence 'Samian dishes.' Afterwards it was discovered how to add red earth and to fashion vessels with red clay.

The use of ceramic dishes was more ancient than the practice of casting with bronze or silver, for the ancients had dishes of neither gold nor silver, but of pottery – such as the *dolium* devised for wine, the *amphora* for water, the *hydria* for baths, and other vessels that are either made on the wheel or shaped by hand for human use. 4. Potter's clay (*argilla*) when fired is spoken of as 'pottery' (*testa*), because from being soft it is 'baked hard' (*tosta*), and it does not keep its original name, because it is not what it was. 5. Arretine (*Arretinus*) dishes are named for the Italian city Arretium (i.e. Arezzo), where they are made, and they are red. On these, Sedulius (Preface to the *Paschal Poem* 16):

> Vegetables which red pottery displays and serves.

6. Some think that Samian dishes got their name from Samos, a town of Greece. Others say that there is a white potter's earth from Italy, produced not far from Rome, that is called Samian. 7. Chased (*caelatus*) dishes are silver or gold, modeled inside and out with figures that stand out, so called from an engraver's burin (*caelum*), which is a kind of iron tool, which commonly is called a chisel (*cilio*). 8. *Chrysendetus* vessels are those inlaid with gold; the term is Greek (cf. χρυσός, "gold"; ἐνδεῖν "bind on"). Vessels in bas-relief (*anaglypha*) are those carved on top, for the Greek ἄνω means "above," γλυφή, "carving," that is, carved above.

9. A dish (*discus*) formerly was named *scus* after its resemblance to a shield (*scutum*); hence also 'salver' (*scutella*). Afterwards it was called *discus* because it 'gives food' (*dare escas*), that is, it serves it – from this also is 'those reclining at table' (*discumbentes*) – or else it is from the word δίσκιν (i.e. δισκεῖν, "throw"), that is, from the thing they throw (i.e. δίσκος, "discus"). 10. Tableware (*messorium*) is so called from 'table' (*mensa*), as if it were *mensorium*. A *parapsis* is a four-sided dish with 'compartments of equal size' (*par apsis*). A paten (*patena*), because it has a spreading, open (*patere*, present participle *patens*) rim. 11. Platter (*lancis*, i.e. *lanx*) . . . *Gavata* (i.e. *gabata*, a kind of dish), because it is 'hollowed out' (*cavare*, ppl. *cavatus*), with *g* put for the letter *c*. Likewise also a mussel-shell vessel (*conca*, i.e. *concha*), but the former is 'hollowed out' (*cavatus*), the latter is hollow (*concavus*): the Greeks also make this distinction. A salver (*scutella*) is the diminutive of shield (*scutum*), because it resembles one. 12. An *apophoreta* is so named by the Greeks (i.e. ἀποφόρητα) from 'carrying fruits' (*ferre pomum*) or anything [else], for it is flat.[10]

A salt-cellar (*salinum*) is a vessel used for salt (*sal*). A *sulzica* is the same thing, as if it were *salzica*. A vinegar cruet (*acitabulum*), as if the word were *acetaforum*, because it 'carries vinegar' (*acetum ferre*). 13. Spoons

9 From *fingere*, the participle *fictus* means both "fashioned" and "feigned."

10 In classical Latin *apophoreta* (neuter plural) were "table gifts" given out at feasts; in Greek the singular adjective ἀποφόρητος means "carried away." Isidore appears to take an *apophoreta* (feminine singular) as something like a tray (for holding such gifts?).

(*coclear*) are so called because they were first used for snails (*coclea*). Hence is the old distich (Martial, *Epigrams* 14.121):

> I am used for eating snails, but I am no less useful for eggs. Pray, do you know why for preference I am called a *cocleare*?

14. *Trisceles*, in the Greek (i.e. τρισκελής, "three-legged"), are tripods (*tripus*) in Latin. Those that stand on four legs are called 'tripods' with incorrect usage. 15. In vessels three pleasing qualities are sought: the workmanship of the maker, the weight of the silver, and the sheen of the metal.

v. Drinking vessels (De vasis potatoriis) 1. A cup (*poculum*) is named from 'drinking' (*potare*), for it is any vessel customarily used for drinking. A *phiala* (i.e. a shallow drinking bowl) is so called because it is made of glass, for 'glass' in Greek is ὕαλος. 2. A *patera* is a *phiala* so called either because we usually drink (*potare*) from it, or because they are 'wide open' (*patere*) with wide rims. 3. A mixing-bowl (*cratera*) is a vessel with two handles. It is a Greek term (i.e. κρατήρ, masc., "mixing-bowl"), but they decline it *crater* in the masculine gender, and in Latin it is *cratera*, feminine. Whence Persius (*Satires* 2.51):

> If for you bowls (*cratera*) of silver;

and Vergil (cf. *Aen.* 1.724):

> They set out great bowls (*crater*) and they garland the wines.

They were first made from woven twigs, whence they are called *craterae* from the κρατεῖν ("hold fast"), that is, because they hold together mutually.

4. There is also the ladle (*cyathus*), the goblet (*scyphus*), and the drinking-bowl (*cymbium*) – these are types of cups. Of these, the cup *cymbium* is so called from its resemblance to the boat called *cymba*. An *amystis* (cf. ἀ-, "without," μύειν, "close (i.e. the mouth)") is a kind of cup from which one drinks in one draught, that is, in one breath. The cup called *baccea* (i.e. *bacchia*) was first named from Bacchus, that is, wine, and afterwards the usage was transferred to mean a water vessel. 5. Chalices (*calix*) and wine-cups (*calathus*) and the *scala* are types of cups formerly made of wood, and hence so called, for the Greeks would call any wood κᾶλα. An ampulla (*ampulla*) is as if the word were a 'large bubble' (*ampla bulla*), for it has the spherical shape of bubbles that are made from foaming water and thus are inflated by the wind.

vi. Wine and water vessels (De vasis vinariis et aquariis) 1. An *oenophorum* is a vessel carrying wine, for the word οἶνος means "wine." Concerning this (Lucilius, *Satires*, fr. 139):

> The bottom of the wine jug (*oenophorum*) is upended, and so is our idea.

2. *Flascae* are named from a Greek word (cf. φλάσκη, "flagon"). They were first made for carrying and storing *phialae* (see v.1 above), whence they were named. Later they passed into use for wine, but keeping the Greek term with which they had their origin. 3. Flagon (*lagoena*) and *Sicula* (lit. "Sicilian") are Greek words, partly changed as they became Latin, for they say λάγηνος, we, *lagoena*; they, Σικελή, we, *Sicula*. Tankard (*cantharus*) . . .

4. A *hydria* is a kind of water pot named from its derivation, for the Greeks call water ὕδωρ. Bucket (*situla*), because it is of use to the thirsty (*sitientes*) for drinking; the Greeks call this vessel a κάδος. 5. A pot (*catinum*) is a ceramic vessel, and it is used more appropriately in the neuter rather than the masculine gender, just as we call the vessel for salt a salt-cellar (*salinum*, neuter gender). An *orca* is a kind of amphora; from its lesser term, *urceus*, comes the diminutive term *urceolus*. *Scyphus*, in which we wash our hands. 6. A *seriola* is a straight-sided type of tun, or a ceramic wine vessel first invented in Syria – just as *Cilicises* are named from Cilicia, from where they were [also] first imported. 'Large jar' (*dolium*) . . . 7. Cask (*cupus* and *cupa*) is so called from 'taking' (*capere*), that is, receiving, water or wine – hence also innkeepers (*caupo*). Wineskin (*uter*), from 'womb' (*uterus*). Milking-pail (*mulgarium*) is a vessel into which livestock are milked, and with the same meaning *mulctrum*, because milk is milked (*mulgere*, ppl. *mulctus*) into it. 8. A basin (*labrum*) is so called because the bathing (*labatio*, i.e. *lavatio*) of infants is usually done in it; its diminutive is *labellum*. Likewise *albeum*, because ablutions (*ablutio*) are usually done in it. A laver (*pelvis*) is so called because the feet (*pes*) are washed (*lavare*) there. 9. One vessel is called a siphon (*sifon*, i.e. *sipho*, "hose") because it pours out water when air is blown (*sufflare*) into it. They use these in the East,

for when they realize that a house is burning they run with siphons filled with water and extinguish the fire, and they also clean ceilings with water forced upwards from siphons.

vii. Vessels for oil (De vasis oleariis) 1. A *hemicadium* is a vessel for oil. A *scortia* is a vessel for oil, so called because it is made of leather (*corium*). 2. An *alabastrum* is a vessel for ointments, and is named from the kind of stone of which it is made, which they call alabaster (*alabastrites*), which keeps ointments unspoiled. 3. A pyx (*pyxis*) is a little container for ointment made of boxwood, for what we call 'boxwood' the Greeks call πύξος. 4. A *lenticula* is a little vessel for oil, made of bronze or silver, so called from 'anointing' (*linire*), for with these kings and priests would be anointed.

viii. Cooking vessels (De vasis coquinariis) 1. Any vessel intended for cooking (*coquere*) is called *coculum*. Plautus (fr. 181):

> Every mercy is boiled out of me in bronze pots (*coculum*).

2. A pot (*olla*) is so called because in it water put on the fire 'bubbles up' (*ebullire*), so that vapor is released upwards. From *ebullire* also derives the word 'bubble' (*bulla*), which is supported in the water by the breath of air within. A small pan (*patella*), as if the word were *patula* ("spread out"), for it is an *olla* with a rather open (*patere*) rim. 3. The *caccabus* and the kettle (*cucuma*) are named after the sound of boiling.[11] These have a common name in Greek and Latin (cf. κάκκαβος, "three-legged pot"), but whether the Latins borrowed these terms from the Greeks, or the Greeks from the Latins, is uncertain. 4. Bronze cauldrons (*lebes*) are named from a Greek word (i.e. λέβης, "cauldron"); they are smaller *ollae*, adapted for use in cooking. 5. The frying pan (*sartago*) is so called from the sizzling (*strepitus*) sound that comes when oil is heated in it. Tripods (*tripus*) are so called because they stand on three feet (*tres pedes*); the Greeks call them *tripodae* (i.e. τρίπους, "three-legged cauldron"). 6. A hand-mill (*mola*), so called from its round shape, as of apples (*malum*) among the fruits; the Greeks have the same name for it (i.e. μύλη, "hand-mill"). The sieve (*cribrum*), so named because there the 'grain runs' (*currere frumentum*), as if the word were *currifrum*. The fire-shovel (*rutabulum*) is so called from 'tossing' (*proruere*) dung, or fire, for the sake of cooking bread.

11 Compare the verbs *cacabare*, "cackle like a partridge," and *cucubare*, "hoot like a screech-owl."

ix. Storage containers (De vasis repositoriis) 1. A *gazophylacium* is a strongbox in a temple where what is given for the needs of the poor is gathered. The term is a composite from Persian and Greek, for *gaza* in Persian means "treasury," and φυλάκιον in Greek means "custody." 2. A strongbox (*arca*) is so called because it prevents (*arcere*) and prohibits seeing inside. From this term also derive 'archives' (*arcivum*, i.e. *archivum*) and 'mystery' (*arcanum*), that is, a secret, from which other people are 'fended off' (*arcere*). 3. *Cibutum* is the Greek word (i.e. κιβωτός, "box, ark") for what we call *arca*. A *loculus* is a place (*locus*) made in the ground for storing something or for protecting clothes or money, and it is so called from the diminutive (i.e. of *locus*). 4. A coffer (*mozicia*), as if it were *modicia*, whence also the word 'a little' (*modicum*), with *z* for *d*, as the people of Italy are wont to say *ozie* for *hodie*. *Scrinium* (i.e. a container for book scrolls) . . . 5. Bag (*saccus*) is so called from the word 'blanket' (*sagum*), because it is made by sewing one up, as if the word were *sagus*.

A pouch (*marsuppium*) is a little bag for money, which the Greeks call μαρσίπιον ("pouch") – for certain Greek words are changed a little in Latin because of Roman pronunciation. 6. The *sitarcia* (i.e. knapsack), used by sailors, is so called because it is 'sewn' (*suere*, ppl. *sutus*). A wrapper (*involucrum*) is so called because it contains something 'rolled up' (*involvere*, ppl. *involutus*) in it. 7. The *fiscus* is the public purse, whence also terms for 'basket' (*fiscella* and *fiscina*). Tax-collectors have one of these and put in it the public dues that are paid to kings. *Fiscus* is the primary term, with the derivative *fiscina* and the diminutive *fiscella*. 8. A wicker-basket (*canistrum*) is woven from split reeds (*canna*), whence it is named; others claim that it is Greek (cf. κάνιστρον, "wicker basket"). A chest (*cistella*) is named from the ribs (*costa*) of reed or wood from which it is constructed. 9. A basket (*cophinus*) is a container made from twigs, used for cleaning up dung and carrying dirt. The Psalmist speaks of it before Israel (Psalm 80:7, Vulgate): "His hands had served in baskets (*cophinus*)." It is also pronounced *covinus*, as if the word were *covus*, that is, 'hollow' (*cavus*). 10. Panniers (*corves*, i.e. *corbes*), because they are woven from bent (*curvare*) twigs. Hamper (*sporta*), either because they are usually made from broom (*spartum*), or because they carry (*exportare*) something. [*Sporta* is so called from *spartum*, not from *exportare* as some would have it, for they were formerly made of broom.]

x. Lamp vessels (De vasis luminariorum) 1. The ancients used the word 'fireplace' (*focus*) from tending the fire and wood, for φῶς in Greek means "fire" in Latin. According to some philosophers all things were procreated from fire. And indeed, without heat nothing is born, so that as [the poet] says of the northern regions (Lucan, *Civil War* 4.108):

> In its barren cold it produces nothing.

But Varro says they are called fireplaces (*focus*) because they nurture (*fovere*) the fire, for the fire is the flame itself, and whatever keeps a fire burning is called a fireplace, whether it be an altar or something else on which the fire is kept burning. 2. An oil-lamp (*lucerna*) is so called from *lynchnus* ("lamp"). The syllable *lu-* is short, as in the line of Persius (*Satires* 5.181):

> The lamps (*lŭcernae*) placed about threw out a greasy cloud.

But if the word were derived from 'light' (*lūx*, with long *u*) the verse would not scan. Wick (*licinius*, lit. "lint"), as if it were 'glowworm' (*lucinius*), for it is the glowworm of a lamp. 3. A candlestick (*candelabrum*) is so called from 'candle' (*candela*), as if it were *candelaforum*, because it carries (*ferre*) a candle. The wax taper (*cereus*) takes its name by derivation from 'wax' (*cera*), from which it is made. Of it, a certain poet (cf. Martial, *Epigrams* 14.42):

> Here as a taper (*cereus*) I will supply nightly fire for you, [for] when the daylight has been stolen, I am another light for you.

4. A *lacunarium* is a hanging lamp, as if it were *lucanarium*, that is, beaming (*lucere*) in the air.

5. 'Wax torches' (*funale*) are covered with wax, and are so called from the cords (*funis*) encased in wax that our ancestors employed before the use of papyrus. From this term also comes 'funeral rites' (*funus*). The Greeks call these torches *scolaces* (i.e. σκόλακες), because they are *scoliae* (i.e. σκολιός, "twisted"), that is, twisted; the Romans called these things cords and wax torches. The ancients had chandeliers (*funale candelabrum*) with hooked prongs sticking out, to which were attached cords daubed with wax or a material of the kind that would feed the light. Such pointed prongs were thus likewise called *funalia*. 6. A lamp (*lampas*) is a flame that gives light at the top, and is so called because it seems to display a flickering (*lambere*) motion. The firebrand (*fax*, gen. *facis*) is so called because it starts (*facere*, lit. "makes") the hearth-fire (*focus*); its diminutive is *facula*. 7. The lantern (*lanterna*) is so called because it has enclosed a 'light within' (*lux interius*). It is made of glass, with its light shut up inside so that a puff of wind cannot get at it, and so that it may easily be carried around anywhere to give light.

8. A *lucubrum* is so called because it 'sheds light in shadow' (*lucere in umbra*), for it is a small light usually made from a bit of tow and wax. 9. A pyre (*pyra*) is what is customarily built up from logs in the form of an altar so that it will burn, for πῦρ means "fire." Now a pyre is a gathering of wood that is not yet burning; a *rogus*, one that has begun to burn; but a *bustum* is the name for one already 'burned up' (*exurere*, ppl. *exustus*, cf. *comburere*, ppl. *combustus*, "burn up"). 10. A lighthouse (*farum*, i.e. *pharos*) is a very tall tower, which the Greeks (i.e. φάρος) and the Latins both call *farum* in accordance with its function, because the signal of its flame may be seen by sailors from afar, as we have said above (see XV.ii.37). Such a lighthouse Ptolemy is said to have constructed near Alexandria for eight hundred talents. Its purpose is to shine a light for the nighttime sailing of ships in order to mark the shallows and the entrances to the harbor, so that sailors might not, misled by darkness, hit the rocks, for Alexandria has tricky entrances with deceptive shoals. Therefore they call the device built in a harbor to serve for lighting the way *pharos*, for φῶς means "light," ὅρος means "vision."[12] Hence also Lucifer (i.e. the 'Light-bearer') in Greek is called Φωσφόρος.

xi. Beds and chairs (De lecticis et sellis) 1. *Lecticae*[13] are so called from gathered (*legere*, ppl. *lectus*) straw. A coverlet (*stratus*) is named from spreading (*sternere*, ppl. *stratus*), as if the word were 'matted' (*storiatus*; cf. *storia* below). The ancients would lie in these alone for sleeping, because woolen blankets were not yet invented.

12 The Greek word ὅρος means "boundary," and can mean a pillar marking a boundary, but presumably the word meant here is ὅρασις, "vision."

13 A *lectica* is either a bed or a couch; we translate according to the context.

Straw mat (*storia*), because it is spread (*strata*) on the ground. 2. A cot (*cama*) is low and close to the ground, for the Greeks say χαμαί (lit. "on the ground") for 'low.' A couch (*cubile*) is a place for lying down (*cubare*). 'Pallet' (*grabatum*) is a Greek term. A camp-bed (*baianula*) is a bed that is hauled (*baiulare*) on a trip, from 'hauling,' that is, carrying. 3. A 'cushioned couch' (*pulvinar*) is a couch for the wealthy; hence also 'pillow' (*pulvillus*). *Spinga* (i.e. *sphinga*) beds are those on which there are images of sphinxes, which we call griffins. Punic (*Punicanus*) beds are small, low beds first imported from Carthage, and hence named. 4. *Lectica* is the name for a 'bed with a back' (*pluteus lectus*). Concerning these, Rutilius Rufus says in *On His Own Life* (13): "First, contrary to the custom of generals, he would use couches with backs (*lectica*) in preference to couches without backs (*lectus*)." 5. The frame (*sponda*) is the outer part of a bed, the backboard (*pluteus*) the inner.

Bridal (*genialis*) beds properly speaking are those spread for young brides, so called from begetting (*generare*) children. 6. A cradle (*cunabula*) is a little bed in which infants usually lie, so called because they are used for a new-born, as if it were *cynabula* – for κυεῖν means "to give birth" in Greek. 7. A bier (*feretrum*) is so called because the dead are 'carried off' (*deferre*) on it, and it is a Greek word, for φέρετρον is taken from φέρειν, that is, from carrying (*ferre*). In Latin a coffin (*capulus*) is so called because it is carried above people's heads (*caput*). Thus Plautus says (*The Braggart Soldier* 628): "Coffin-bound (*capularis*) old man," that is, nearly in his coffin. 8. Stools (*scamnum*) are set against very high beds, and are so called from 'climbing' (*scandere*), [that is, mounting (*ascendere*)]. Hence also 'footstools' (*scabillum*), which are set by small beds or chairs for mounting. The footstool is also called a *subpedaneum*, for what the Greeks call ὑποπόδιον Latin speakers call *scabillum*, and others [call] *suppedaneum*, because it is 'under the feet' (*sub pedes*). A *scansilium* is a step (e.g. a bench in an amphitheater) where a distinguished person takes his seat. 9. Seats (*sedes*) are so called because among the ancient Romans there was not the practice of reclining at table, and hence they were said to 'sit down' (*considere*). Afterwards, as Varro says in *On the Life of the Roman People*, men began to recline and women to sit, because reclining was seen as unseemly for a woman.

The word 'seat' (*sedis*, i.e. *sedes*) in the singular number is properly the seat of the kingdom, and in Greek is called θρόνος. The Greeks say *thronus*, and we say *solium*. But for other people, there are 'benches' (*subsellium*); for scholars, 'chairs' (*cathedra*). 10. The throne (*solium*), on which kings sit for the safety of their bodies, is so called, according to some, for its 'solidity' (*soliditas*), as if it were *solidum*; according to others the word is formed by *antistichon* (i.e. by *antistoechum*, "substitution of letters") as if the word were *sodium*, from 'sitting' (*sedere*). Hence likewise *sella* (i.e. another word for 'seat') is so called as if it were *sedda*, and benches (*subsellium*) as if the word were *subseddium*. 11. The 'curule chair' (*sella curulis*) is where magistrates would sit (*sedere*) to render justice. They are called 'curule' because, among the ancients, praetors and consuls would be carried to the forum by a chariot (*currus*) due to the length of the journey. The chairs that were carried after them, from which while sitting they would render justice, were named 'curule' chairs from 'chariot.' 12. Tripods (*tripus*) are stools having 'three feet' (*tres* + *pes*; τρι- + πούς). But lampstands are also tripods because they likewise have three feet.

xii. Vehicles (De vehiculis) 1. A wagon (*carrum*) is so called from the axle (*cardo*) of its wheels, and hence 'chariot' (*currus*) is named, for it is seen to have wheels. A wheel (*rota*) is so called because it rushes (*ruere*), and 'round' (*rotundus*) is named from *rota*. 2. A *reda* is a kind of vehicle with four wheels. The ancients called these *retae*, because they had wheels (*rota*). 3. A *carpentum pompaticum* (i.e. a processional carriage) is a type of vehicle, as if it were a *carrum pompaticum*. A cart (*plaustrum*) is a two-wheeled vehicle that carries burdens, and is called *plaustrum* because it rolls, as if one said *pilastrum* (cf. *pila*, "ball."). A *caracutium* is a vehicle with very high wheels, as if it were a 'high wagon' (*carrum acutum*). A *capsus* is a carriage enclosed on all sides, as if it were a box (*capsa*). 4. A *pilentum* or *petorritum* is an enclosed carriage with four wheels that matrons formerly used. Vergil (*Aen.* 8.666):

> Mothers in soft carriages (*pilentum*).

Horace (*Satires* 1.6.104):

> Many grooms and nags to be grazed, and carriages (*petorritum*) to be drawn.

Formerly the *pilentum* was of a blue color and not, as it now is, red. Unless they were chaste, matrons could not use these; nor, likewise, could they wear fillets. 5. A *basterna* is a vehicle [for a journey, as if the term were *viae sternax* ("smoother of the way"), fitted with soft rugs and drawn by two animals].

xiii. Other implements that we use (De reliquis quae in usu habentur) 1. The walking stick (*baculus*) is said to have been invented by Bacchus, the discoverer of the grape vine, so that people affected by wine might be supported by it. As *baculus* is from Bacchus, so a 'rod' (*bacillum*) is from *baculus*, as its diminutive. 2. Stakes (*fustis*) are so called because they 'stand fixed' (*praefixae stare*) in the ground. Country people call these 'palings' (*palus*), and for their misdeeds youths are beaten with them. Levers (*vectis*) are so called because they are carried (*vectare*) in the hands; with these, doors or stones are loosened. 3. The term *forfex* is treated in accordance with its etymology: if it is so called from 'thread' (*filum*), the letter *f* is used, as in tailors' scissors (*forfex*); if from 'hair' (*pilus*), the letter *p*, as in a barbers' tweezers (*forpex*); if from 'snatching out' (*accipere*), the letter *c*, as in blacksmiths' tongs (*forceps*), because they 'seize the hot thing' (*formum capere*). 4. The ancients called a hot thing *formus*, and hence also the term *formosus* ("beautiful"; see XIX.vii.3).

A razor (*novacula*) [is so called because it 'renews' (*innovare*) one's face]. Combs (*pecten*) are so called because they make hair combed (*pectere*) and arranged. A curling iron (*calamistrum*) is a pin that, when heated (*calefacere*) and applied, heats and curls one's hair. Hence also people who wave their hair are called 'crimped' (*calamistratus*). 5. The key (*clavis*) is so called because it closes (*claudere*) and opens. A *catenatum* (lit. "chained thing" – a latch?), because it 'holds by grasping' (*capiendo tenere*). A clock (*horologia*) is so called because there 'we read the hours' (*horas legere*), that is, we deduce them. It is set up in sunny places, where the shadow from the gnomon runs across the incised lines to show what hour of the day it is.

xiv. Rural implements (De instrumentis rusticis) 1. A plowshare (*vomer*) is so called because it 'digs up the ground by force' (*vi humum eruat*), or from its 'spewing forth' (*evomere*) earth. Concerning it, Lucretius (cf. *On the Nature of Things* 1.314):

> The iron hook of the plow, the plowshare (*vomer*), insensibly erodes in the fields.

It gets its shine from abrasion. 2. The plow (*aratrum*) is named from 'plowing the earth' (*arare terram*), as if the word were *araterrium*. The plow-beam (*buris*) is a curved part of a plow, so called as if it were βοὸς οὐρά ("ox's tail"), because it looks like an ox's tail. The share-beam (*dentale*) is the foremost part of a plow, in which the plowshare is inserted, as if it were a tooth (*dens*). 3. Pruning knives (*cultellus*) are so called from 'cultivating' (*cultura*), because the ancients did their pruning of trees and vines with them before pruning hooks were invented. 4. The pruning hook (*falcis*, i.e. *falx*) is used to prune trees and vines; it is called *falcis* because at first soldiers would use them to cut bracken (*filix*). Hence the verses (Martial, *Epigrams* 14.34):

> The settled peace of our general has bent me for gentle uses: now a farmer owns me; before, I belonged to a soldier.

5. A bush-hook (*falcastrum*) is named for its likeness to a pruning hook (*falx*), and it is a curved iron blade with a long handle, used for clearing briar-patches. These are also called 'weeding hooks' (*runco*), which cut back thorn-bushes, named from 'weeding' (*runcare*).

6. A *serrula* (lit. "small saw") is a very thin blade of iron that cuts trees or branches with the biting action of its teeth. Drag-hoes (*rastrum*), too, are so called either from scraping (*radere*) the ground or from the sparseness (*raritas*) of their teeth. Mattocks (*ligo*), because they 'lift up' (*levare*) earth, as if the word were *levo*. 7. A spade (*scudicia*) is so called because it loosens the ground around the 'base of the plant' (*codex*), and although it is used for other work it still keeps its name from *codex*. Others name it with the general term 'digger' (*fossorium*), because it makes a pit (*fovea*), as if it were *fovessorium*. 8. A hoe (*sarculus*) – of these there are the single-bladed and the two-pronged. Farmers call the forked iron instrument with which seeds are planted (*pangere*) a 'dibble' (*pastinatum*, i.e. *pastinum*). Hence old vines that are trenched again are said to be 're-dug' (*repastinare*).

9. A roller (*cylindrus*) is a stone rounded off in the shape of a column, and it takes its name from its cylindrical shape. Of it, Vergil (*Geo.* 1.178):

> First the threshing floor should be leveled with a huge roller (*cylindrus*) and turned over by hand.

10. A threshing-sledge (*tribula*) is a kind of vehicle used as a means of threshing (*terere*), and so called from

this.[14] A winnowing-shovel (*pala*), commonly called a 'winnowing-fan' (*ventilabrum*), is named for its winnowing (*ventilare*) chaff (*palea*). 11. Pitchforks (*furcilla*) are so called because with them 'grain is shifted' (*frumentum cellere*, i.e. *cillere*), that is, is moved. In the same way 'little masks' (*oscillum*) are so called because their 'faces are moved' (*os* + *cillere*) – for *cillere* means "move." 12. Tallies (*tessera*) are objects with which the number of grain-measures is designated.

A *trapetum* is a mill for olives. A *prelum* is a beam with which trodden grapes are pressed, so called from pressing, as if it were a *pressorium* (i.e. a press; cf. *premere*, ppl. *pressus*, "press"). A *prelum* is the device with which 'oil is pressed' (*premitur oleum*). A vat (*lacus*), the receptacle into which what has been made liquid (*liquatus*, ppl. of *liquare*) flows, where oil or wine is extracted from olives or grapes by means of pressing. 13. *Verennis* (an unidentified implement), from 'carry' (*vehere*), that is, to bring out. *Qualus*, a wicker basket (*corbis*), and the strainer (*colum*) of the wine press, through which the must flows, are so called from 'straining' (*colare*). The sieve (*fisclum*), as if it were *fiscolum*, is so called from its straining (*colare*) oil, or as if it were a 'little basket' (*fiscella*) for oil.

xv. Garden implements (De instrumentis hortorum) 1. The waterwheel (*rota*) is so called as if the word were *ruta* (i.e. from *ruere*, "rush," ppl. *rutus*), and it is the machine by which water is drawn from a stream. Lucretius (cf. *On the Nature of Things* 5.516):

> We see the waterwheels (*rota*) and their scoops (*austrum*) turn in the stream.

The *austra* (i.e. *haustrum*, "scoop of a waterwheel"), that is, the waterwheel, is so called from 'drawing' (*haurire*, ppl. *haustus*) water. 2. A pulley (*girgillus*) is so called because it moves in a circle (*gyrus*). It is a movable block of wood on a transverse beam from which a rope with a bucket or leather bag is let down into a well to draw water. 3. Gardeners call the long beam with which they draw water a *telo* (cf. *tolleno*, "swing-beam"), and it is so called because of its length, for whatever is long is called τηλόν in Greek (cf. τῆλε, τηλοῦ, "far off") – hence also they say 'weasel' (*mustela*) as if it were a 'long mouse' (*mus*). The people of Spain call this instrument a 'stork' (*ciconia*) because it acts like the bird of the same name, raising its beak from the water and dipping it, while it makes its clamor. Water-bucket (*ama*, i.e *hama*) . . . 4. The 'wolf' (*lupus*) or 'little dog' (*canicula*) is an iron grapple that takes such names because if anything falls in a well it snatches them and draws them out. The grapple (*arpax*, i.e. *harpago*, ἅρπαξ, "grappling iron") is so called because it 'snatches' (*arripere*), for *arpe* in Greek means "to seize" (cf. ἅρπη, "bird of prey"; ἁρπάζειν, "seize"). 'Hoe' (*sarculus*; see xiv.8 above) . . .

14 A *tribula* was a studded board or beam, weighted with its driver, dragged across the threshing floor by oxen.

xvi. Equestrian equipment (De instrumentis equorum) 1. Medallions (*phalerae*) are ornamental bosses worn by horses; the term is Greek (i.e. φάλαρον, "cheek-medallion"). Bits (*frenum*) are so called because they force horses to neigh (*fremere*), or because horses gnash (*frendere*), [that is, imprint,] and bite at them with their teeth. Hence still-suckling piglets are called 'toothless' (*nefrens*) because they cannot yet 'gnash' anything, that is, tear it up, with their teeth. Hence also a 'fava bean' (*faba*) that is ground up is called 'mashed' (*fresa*, ppl. of *frendere*). 2. A very harsh type of bit is the 'wolf-toothed' (*lupatus*), so called from having uneven teeth like wolves' (*lupinus*) teeth; consequently its 'bite' is a powerful curb. Muzzle (*camus*) . . . 3. The rein (*habena*) is so called from 'hold' (*habere*), because we hold, that is, we restrain horses with them; hence also horses are said to be *habilis* ("controllable"). It is also called a *retinaculum*, from 'holding back' (*retinere*). Reins (*lorum*) . . . 4. Halters (*capistrus*, i.e. *capistrum*) are so called from the heads (*capita*) of pack animals. Saddle (*sella*) from 'sitting' (*sedere*), as if the word were *sedda*. The chest-strap (*antela*), as if it were *antesella* (i.e. "in front of the saddle") and likewise the crupper (*postela*), as if it were *postsella* (i.e. "behind the saddle").

The belt (*cingulum*) of a human is neuter in gender, but we speak of the girths (*cingula*) of animals in the feminine. 5. A packsaddle (*sagma*), which is incorrectly called *salma* by common people, is so named from its covering of coarse blanket (*sagum*), whence a pack-horse is called *sagmarius*, and a mule, *sagmaria*. A lasso (*capulum*) of rope, from 'capturing' (*capere*), because untamed pack animals are caught with them. 6. Spurs (*calcar*) are so called because they are bound to a person's heel (*calx*), that is, on the back part of the foot, for goading horses either to fight or to run, on account of animals' laziness or fear. Goads (*stimulus*) are so called from the word 'fear' (*timor*), although there is also the goad of desire.

7. Currycombs (*strigilis*) are named from 'grooming' (*tergere*), because horses are groomed with them. A 'branding iron' (*character*) is a heated iron instrument that burns marks on livestock, for χαρακτήρ ("brand, shape") in Greek means "shape" in Latin.

8. A 'cauterizing iron' (*cauterium*), as if the word were *cauturium*, because it burns (*urere*), and a forewarning and severe cautioning (*cautio*) is branded on the animal so that greed may be restrained when the owner is identified. Sometimes this instrument is used for the brand and sometimes to cure, so that the vigor of a disease may be dried out by the heat of the fire.

APPENDIX

Correspondence of Isidore and Braulio

A. From Isidore to my lord and most beloved son in Christ, Archdeacon Braulio (610–620).[1] When you receive a letter from me, dearest son, you should not hesitate to embrace it as you would a friend. Indeed, this is the next best consolation for those who are absent from each other, that if someone who is dear to you is not present, his letters may be embraced in his stead. I have dispatched a ring to you on account of my affection, and also a mantle as a cloak (*amictus*) of my friendship (*amicitia*), whence this word was drawn in antiquity. Therefore pray for me; may the Lord preserve you that I may be granted to see you in this life, and that you may make happy again by your return one whom you made sorrowful by your departure. I have also sent a booklet of the rules through Maurentius primic[l]erius.[2] As for the rest I hope this finds you well, my most beloved lord and my dearest son.

B. From Isidore to my most dear and beloved Archdeacon Braulio in Christ (610–620). Since I am not able to enjoy the sight of you in person, I can at least enjoy your conversation, so that it is a consolation to me to learn from your letters that you whom I desire to see are safe. Both would be good, if it were possible; but I can be refreshed in my mind concerning you, even if I am not able to see you in person in front of me. When we were together, I asked you to send the sixth decade of Saint Augustine to me.[3] I beg you somehow to make it available to me. I have sent you the little book of *Synonyms*, not because it is of some utility, but because you wanted it.

I commend this boy (i.e. the messenger) to you, and commend myself as well, that you pray on behalf of my wretched self, because I am truly languishing with bodily infirmities and mental failings. In both things I ask for your assistance, because for my own part I am deserving of nothing. As for the rest, I ask that you bid me be joyful by means of your writing when there is an opportunity, while life is still my companion, for the letter carrier to return to me.

I. From Isidore to my lord and servant of God, Bishop Braulio. With all my desire I have been longing now to see your face. May God fulfill my prayer some time before I die. For the present I pray that you commend me to God in your prayers, that he may both fulfill my hope in this life and in the future life grant to me a meeting with your blessed self. And in his own hand:[4] Pray for me, most blessed lord and brother.

II. From Braulio, the useless servant of the saints of God, to my lord and indeed master, Isidore, highest of bishops, chosen of Christ (625). O pious lord, most illustrious of men, this request is belated, and the opportunity for writing was presented to me late, because with my sins rushing in on me I was impeded from making requests, not only by the evil of my unproductiveness and incapacity, but also by the horrible onslaught of plague and enemy attack.[5] Now, however, although tied up by a thousand obligations and a thousand cares after a long time of misery, just as if I were waking up from the heaviness of a fitful sleep, so to speak, I presume to attach the courtesy of a greeting to my expression of appeal, and prostrated by humility of both heart and body, I call upon the most excellent power of your blessing, that

1 Although not all the following correspondence between Isidore and his disciple Braulio (archdeacon, later bishop of the diocese of Saragossa) refers to the *Etymologies*, the letters precede the text of Isidore's work in the early manuscripts. The first two letters appear only in the family of manuscripts designated by Lindsay as "Spanish or Interpolated." The dates assigned to this and the following letters are those suggested by C. W. Barlow (1969).

2 By way of his messenger, the "first cleric" (?) Maurentius, Isidore sends Braulio some regulations, perhaps part of Isidore's own *Monastic Rules*. Riché 1976:286 says that the *primiclericus* or *primicerius* was an officer under the archdeacon charged with teaching the clerics in a bishop's household.

3 Isidore refers to Augustine's *Commentary* on Psalms 51–60.

4 That is, in the original letter the following sentence was written by Isidore's own hand.

5 Braulio may refer to civil disorders, including a Basque invasion, that took place around Saragossa in the year 625.

you may authorize to the very end the commendation of a particular servant, whom you have always supported with the pious regard of your sacred esteem. Indeed I am tortured, Christ knows, by severe distress that so much time has passed and I am still not counted worthy of seeing you. But I place my hope in one who does not forget to have pity and who does not cast me off to the very end, that he will listen to the prayer of a poor man and bring me back, wretch that I am, to your gaze.

I propose, indeed, and I request with every sort of entreaty that you, remembering your promise, will order that the book of *Etymologies* be sent to your servant, as we have heard that, God willing, it has been finished. As I am aware, you have sweated over it in large measure at the request of your servant, and therefore be generous first to me, so that in the company of saints you will be considered the happy one, and the first. I also ask that the proceedings of the Synod, in which Sintharius is found to be, if not wholly refined, then at least cooked by the fire of your questioning, be directed to us by the lord king, your son, at your prompting.[6] For thus our request has also been made to his Highness, because there is a great need for the truth to be investigated in the Council.

As for the rest, I make a plea to the mercy of the highest Creator that he give the command to preserve the crown of your blessedness for a long time, for the sake of the integrity of the faith and the condition of his church, and that, thanks to your intercession, he make me strong among the various and countless carping hazards of the present world, and that at your prayer the most sacred Trinity keep me sheltered in the bosom of your mindfulness and safe from every storm of sin. And in his own hand: I, Braulio, servant of the Lord, to Isidore – may I enjoy you in the Lord, O burning and unfading lamp.

III. From Isidore to Bishop Braulio, my lord and servant of God (632, probably written from Toledo). I have given thanks to Christ that I have learned that you are well. Would that I might in person have sight of the one about whose health I have learned. But I will reveal what has happened to me due to my sins, because I did not deserve to read your letter. Just at the moment when I received your note a royal servant-boy came to me. I gave it to my chamber-servant, and went straight to the king, intending to read through and reply to your letter later. But when I returned from the royal palace, not only could I not find what you had written, but indeed whatever else was among those papers had disappeared. And for that reason, God knows, I have grieved over my just deserts, because I did not read your letter. But I ask that you write to me again, whenever the opportunity presents itself, and that you do not withdraw the kindness of your words, so that I may again receive through your kindness what I have lost through my fault. And in his own hand: Pray for us, most blessed lord.

IV. From Braulio, worthless servant of the saints of God, to my lord and indeed master, and chosen of Christ, Isidore, highest of bishops (632 or 633). The inner, spiritual man is usually filled with joy when he satisfies the request of someone who loves him. Therefore it is my wish, my most reverent lord, unless the wall of [my] sins is a barrier, that you look kindly upon my request and patiently endure my querulous accusations. For I do both of these things: I make a formal request and I put to you the compelling facts of my case against you. Prostrate at the entrance and gate of this writing I beseech your apostolic highness most kindly to grant me an audience.

And although the hurling of accusations may falter where tears intervene, though tears are not a typical sign of accusation, still, I hope, accusations may be tearful and tears accusatory, each of these being due to the unbridled audacity of love, not to the rashness of arrogance. But now I will begin my case.

Unless I am mistaken, seven years have rolled by since I recall having requested from you your composition, the books of *Origins*. In various and diverse ways I have been disappointed when in your presence, and you have written nothing back to me when I have been absent. Rather, with subtle delay, you object that the work is not yet finished, or not yet copied out, or that my letters were lost, and a number of other things, until I have come to this day and still have no result from my request. For this reason I will convert my prayers into complaint, so that what I have failed to get with supplications I may succeed in getting by challenging you with accusations – for often enough crying out loud will help a beggar.

So why, I ask you, my lord, do you not send what you have been requested to? You should know one thing: I

6 No record of this synod and the inquisition of Sintharius survives.

will not give up and pretend that I do not want what has been refused to me, but I will seek it and seek insistently until I either receive it or drag it out of you, since our most holy Redeemer commands (Matthew 7:7): "Seek, and you shall find," and adds, "Knock and it shall be opened to you." I have sought and now do seek, and even knock; accordingly I even shout for you to open. Now the devising of this argument is a comfort to me, that, although you have disregarded someone making a request, you may perhaps pay attention to someone who is making accusations.

From this point on I build on your own knowledge, nor do I unwisely presume, with the bravado of a fool, to add something new to what is already complete. However, I do not blush to speak with a most learned man, ignorant though I am, bearing in mind the Apostle's lesson (cf. II Corinthians 11:19), in which you are ordered "to suffer a fool gladly." On this account, accept these blustering accusations. Why, I ask, do you even now keep back the sharing of talents and the dispensing of nourishment that has been entrusted to you? Open your hand now, and share with the servants so that they do not die of hunger.

You know what the creditor who approaches demands back from you. Whatever you give to us will not be a loss to you. Remember that the multitude was satisfied by small loaves of bread and that the leftover fragments exceeded the original amount of bread.

Do you think the gift bestowed upon you was given for your sake alone? It is both yours and mine; it is held communally, not privately. And who, even a madman, would presume to say that you rejoice in your private possessions – you who know only how to rejoice blamelessly in communal possessions? For since God has entrusted to your control the management of his treasure and wealth, of health, wisdom, and knowledge, why do you not pour out with a generous hand that which you do not reduce by giving? Since, among the members of the lofty head (i.e. the members of the Body of Christ, the Church), each one possesses in another what he has not received himself, and knows that whatever he has is to be possessed by another, is the reason why you remain parsimonious toward me perhaps because you do not find what you may take from me in exchange? If you "give to someone who has," you acquire the proceeds of a very small reward. But if you "have given to someone who has not," then you satisfy the command of the Evangelist (cf. Luke 14:14) that "it shall be returned to you in the recompense of the just."

For these reasons I [too] am tormented by conscience, in that I sense in myself nothing good that can be shared, because we are commanded (cf. Galatians 5:13) "to serve each other through charity" and (cf. I Peter 4:10) "each to minister to another the grace that he has received, as good stewards of the manifold grace of God" and (cf. Romans 12:3–4) "according as God hath divided to every one the measure of faith in a single group of members," he ought to share this with the other parts, since (I Corinthians 12:11): "All these things one and the same Spirit worketh, dividing to every one according as he will."

But I revert to the one particular resource that I brought up earlier, namely to importunity, which is a friend for those destitute of friendship and for those not distinguished with the favor of a handsome appearance. Therefore, listen to my voice, even with such an expanse of land lying between us (Matthew 18:28): "Pay, pay what thou owest." For you are a servant, a servant of Christ and of Christians, so that in this respect you are greater than all of us, and you should not refuse to share the favor that you know has been bestowed on you for our sake with the thirsty souls who are tormented with a hunger for knowledge.

At any rate, I am not a foot running at command and able to wait upon the stomach of the Church, that is, the judge of the members, by obediently scurrying about, nor am I able to please the ruling sovereignty of the head with obedience. In fact, although I know that I am one of the more insignificant members, let that suffice, because it is fitting that I should draw out what you are known to have learned from the head, and fitting that you should not do without me, however unimportant I am, redeemed as I am by the blood of Christ.

For (cf. I Corinthians 12:21–23): "The head does not say to the feet, I have no need of you," because "those that seem to be the more feeble members of the body are the more necessary, and such as we think to be the less honorable, about these we put more abundant honor; and those that are our uncomely parts, have more abundant comeliness." So in this way our creator and dispenser regulates everything so that when the divine gifts of one person, who does not perceive them in himself, are given to be possessed by another, charity is increased. Finally, a manifold favor is well dispensed when the received gift is believed to belong also to the person who does not possess it, when it is thought to be given for the sake of the one to whom it is paid out.

The wisdom of your holiness knows best how the Apostle's entire chapter, which I have set down in part, fittingly applies to this matter. And whatever it has touched on briefly most certainly does not escape your full knowledge.[7] Thus only this remains, which I am at great pains to ask for, that you provide what has been requested, and if not for my sake, at least for the sake of charity itself, which is divinely bestowed, and for whose sake we are ordered both to know and to provide all things, and without which all things are nothing. And even if I have poured out, rather than said, these things excessively, heedlessly, less humbly, and more vainly, I beseech you to take everything kindly, and pardon everything, and pray that God pardon everything.

Therefore I also point out that the books of the *Etymologies*, which I am seeking from you, my lord, are already held by many people, even though they have been mutilated and corrupted. For this reason I ask that you deem it suitable to send these to me copied out and in their entirety, emended and well organized, lest I be drawn into evil by eagerness and driven to obtain from others vices instead of virtues. However, even though you lack nothing and though unrequested rewards are said to stink,[8] I wish that the merit of your kindness would command of me whatever I am able and capable of doing, so that you would make use of my obedience, or rather, that you would enjoy that charity which is God.

With these matters finished, then, I had some questions about sacred and divine pages, whose explanation the light of your heart might reveal to me, if you were to order it to shine on us and to lay open the hidden matters of divine law. Nor, if I receive these things that I am seeking, will I keep silent about the earlier matters – but you would lay open the way for me to gain confidence when you refrain from pricking this brow of mine with the goads of shame, and grant room for mercy towards my ignorance, and when you do not order the rejection of one you used to love, however undeservedly, because it seems a most disgraceful and unworthy thing if someone not yet thoroughly filled with charity is found to draw back from the one whom he used to love.

But to the obedience of my service I add the claims of my salvation, and I beseech the kindness of your most holy power that you might deign to pray for me, so that by your intercession you might in the end win a soul that wavers daily among evils, and so that you might lead it forth to the gate of eternal peace, plucked from wretchedness and temptations. It has been delightful to speak to you at length, as if I had been set in front of you and could see the expression of your face. Thus, I have not been free of wordiness and perhaps I have committed an indiscretion. But I was bound to do either this or something else, only so that at least you would grant, on account of my ranting importunity, what you have been unwilling to grant on account of your humility. See how much audacity the kindness of your benevolence has given me! Therefore, if there has been anything displeasing in this, your kindness, which loves so much that it banishes fear, should take the credit to itself – for (I John 4:18): "Perfect charity casteth out fear."

Trusting in special kindness from a special lord, in whom the strength of the holy Church stands firm, I suggest that, since Eusebius, our metropolitan (i.e. Archbishop Eusebius of Tarragona), has died, you might have compassion and that you might suggest to your son, our lord, that he appoint someone to this position whose teaching and holiness might be a model of life for the others. I commend this present son (i.e. the reigning king, Sisenand) in all matters to your most blessed power, and as much with reference to the matters that I have raised here as to those I complained of above, may I be deemed worthy to be enlightened by your eloquence on his account.

V. From Isidore to my lord and servant of God, Bishop Braulio (632 or 633). The letter from your holiness

7 The 'chapter' Braulio refers to is I Corinthians 12, which treats the "division of graces" and the mutuality of a body's members, topics that Braulio exploits in his witty harangue. Like Braulio, Paul's epistle goes on to speak of charity, without which "I am nothing" (I Corinthians 13). Before the twelfth century, different Bible manuscripts divide the Pauline epistles into chapters at different points of the text, if at all.

8 The sense of the proverb is that rewards conferred for no apparent reason arouse suspicion – in the English version, "proffered service stinks." Braulio knows that his offer of service in return for the *Etymologies* is not only puny recompense, but may seem disingenuous – he has no service of value to Isidore to offer.

found me in Toledo, for I had been summoned on account of the Council. But though the king's command suggested that I should return despite already being on the road, nevertheless I preferred not to cut short the progress of my journey since I was nearer to his own presence than I was to my starting point. I came into the presence of the king and found your deacon there. On receiving from him your eloquent letter I clasped it eagerly and read it, and gave thanks to God for your health, wishing with all my might that, although I am weak and worn out, I might still have the assurance, through Christ, of seeing you in this life, because (cf. Romans 5:5): "Hope confoundeth not through charity, which is poured forth in our hearts."

While on the road I sent a manuscript of the *Etymologies*, along with some other manuscripts, and although it has not been emended due to my health, still I was eager to offer it to you immediately for emendation, if I had reached the place chosen for the council. As far as the appointment of the Bishop of Tarragona is concerned, I have sensed that the king's opinion is not the one that you sought.[9] There is still uncertainty, however, as to where he may more decisively set his mind.

I ask that you may think fit to become an intercessor with the Lord for my sins, so that my transgressions may be obliterated at your successful entreaty, and my misdeeds forgiven. This in his own hand: Pray for us, most blessed lord and brother.

VI. From Isidore to my lord and my son Sisebut (i.e. the Visigoth king of Spain; probably 620). See, as I promised, I have sent you the work *On the Origin of Certain Things*, compiled from my recollection of readings from antiquity and annotated in certain places as written by the pen of our ancestors.[10]

9 By word of mouth or a separate letter. Braulio had apparently named a specific person in addition to what he said at the end of the preceding letter.

10 This important text, apparently a dedication of the *Etymologies* before it was finished, is unfortunately ambiguous. *Recordatio* ("recollection") can mean "memory" or "(written) record." *Veteris lectionis* probably means "readings from antiquity (i.e., of ancient authors)," but conceivably "my old (course of) reading." *Stilo* can mean "by the pen" or "in the style (i.e. manner)." Some manuscripts substitute the name of Braulio for that of Sisebut – perhaps a change made by Isidore after Sisebut's death in 621 – and some manuscripts preserve the dedications both to Sisebut and Braulio: see Reydellet 1966:435 for the details.

INDEX

General index

The following index includes only important terms and sub-topics, and most proper names, from the *Etymologies*. For larger topics consult the Analytical Table of Contents. Both English and Latin terms are indexed, but when a Latin term is close in meaning and form to the corresponding English translation, only the English is given. Book X is a dense list of such terms descriptive of human beings as "lifeless," "hateful," "generous," "enviable." Its Latin terms are in alphabetical order. Seeing that such terms are unlikely to be the object of an index search, and that including them would unduly swell the bulk of an index already large, we exclude Book X here, though not from the two indexes that follow. The valuable index of the Oroz Reta–Casquero Spanish translation of the *Etymologies* includes more Latin terms and divides these into categories: a general index followed by indexes of proper names, geographical terms, botanical terms, zoological terms, and stones and minerals.

Aaron 149, 164
abanet 383
abba 172
abbot 172
abbreviations 51
  legal 51–52
Abdias 302
Abel 162
Abella 344
abellana 344
abies 345
abiuratio 123
ablative 44
Abraham 39, 99, 163, 165, 168, 169, 174, 191, 192, 194, 198, 207, 208, 302, 346
abrotanum 357
absida 312
absinthium 353
abstract quantity 89
Abydos 295
abyss 280, 300
Academic philosophers 179
acalanthis 269
acanthus 351
acation 375
accent 49
accent marks 49–50
accentor 147
accident (logical) 81, 82
accipiter 267
Accius 180
accubitum 395
accusative 44
accusator 365
Acephalite 178
acer 346
acetum 398
Achaea 290, 303
Achaeus 196, 290, 303
Achaians 196
Achates (river) 296
achates 325
Achatesius of Miletos 65
Achelous (river) 324
Achilles 106, 195, 196, 290
acies 203, 362
acinus 340
acitabulum 399
acitabulus 334
acnua 315
acolyte 172
Acone 351
aconite 351
acorum 350
acredula 266
acridium 353
Acroceraunian mountains 298
acrostic poems, biblical 137
acrozymus 396
acryologia 75
active voice 45, 46
actor 369
actor 205
Acts, Book of 135, 138
actualis 43
actuaria 374
actus 315, 316
acupictus 385
acus 391
acute (diacritic) 49
acute illness 110–111
acyrology 56
Adam 162, 247, 302, 334, 384
adamas 325
Adamite 175
adiectio 145
aditus 311
adjective 43
  ctetic 43
  ethnic 43
adjutant 202
adnotatio 54
adolescent 242
Adonai 153
adoption 207
adoreum 338
adultery 123
adultus 242
advena 205
adverb 42, 46
adverbum (gloss) 55
adze 383
aedes 308
aedificatio 377
aegopthalmos 327
aegyptilla 325
Aegyptus 287
Aelius Hadrian 301
Aeneas 200, 212, 304, 370
Aeneid 181
aenigma 63
Aeolian islands 296, 317
Aeolic Greek 191
Aeolus 296
aeon 130, 180
Aeos 304
aequinoctium 128, 273

aequitas 73
aequivocus (category) 81
aequor 276, 277
aer 273
aera 129, 142
aeranis 250
aerarium 204, 310, 329
Aerian 176
aeromancy 182
aerugo 331
aes 329, 330
Aesculapius (*also* Aesclepius) 65, 106, 109, 183
Aesop 66–67
aestas 129
aestiva 299
aestuaria 278, 280
aestus 278
aetas 130
aeternus 154
aether 272
aethiopicus (stone) 327
Aetian 176
aetiologia 78
aetites 320, 327
aevum 130
affirmation 83
affluence 395
Africa 292–293, 313, 320, 323, 343, 345, 348
Africans 193, 198, 305, 364
Africus 275
afterbirth 240
agaric 354
agate 325
agea 374
Agenor 289
ager 314
age(s) 130
  of humans, six 241–243
  of world 210
    seven 144
    six 130
agger 313, 316
agmen 203
agnatus 208
Agnoites 178
agnomen 42
agnus 247
agon 366
agredula 263
Agrigentum 97
Ahab 165, 166
air 231, 239, 272, 273
ala 264
  (armpit) 235
  (military) 203
Alabanda region 326
alabandicus 321
alabandina 326
alabastrites 321
alabastrum 401
Alani 197, 386
Alania 289
Alba Longa 304
Albania 288
Albanians 195, 386
Albans 304
albeum 400
albucium 354
Albula (river) 282
albus 250
Alcmeon of Croton 66
alcyon 265
alder 346
Alea 371
alea 371
Alemanni 197, 386
ales 264
Alexander the Great 139, 195, 199, 244, 281, 290, 303
Alexander, Roman emperor 143
Alexandria 303, 307, 331, 376, 381, 402
  library of 139
alga 355
alibrum 389
alica 338
alien, resident 205
alieniloquium 63
alimentum 395
alimonia 395
alites 269
alium 356
allegory 63, 135
  physical 185, 187, 188, 189
alleluia 147
alliteration 59
Allophyli 195, 302
alluvium 300
alluvius ager 314
almond 344
alnus 346
aloa 349
aloe 349, 351
Alogi 176
alopecia 112–113
Alpha and Omega 156
alphabet (*see also* letters) 39
alphabetum (acrostic) 137
Alphaeus 169
Alpheus (river) 296
Alps 67, 298, 325
altanus 275
altar 310
althaea 354
alum 276, 317
alvus 240
amaracinum 115
Amazon 98, 186, 195, 303, 361
ambages 75
amber 323
ambiguity 57, 75
ambitus 123, 316
ambo 310
ambrosia 354
amen 147
amens 231
amentum 363
amethyst 324
amethystizontas 324
amiantos 320
amictus 384
amiculum 387
Aminean wine 398
amma 266
ammochrysus 327
ammodyta 257
Ammon 106
ammoniacus 318
Ammonius 142
amnis 280
amomum 349
amor 174, 188
Amos 167
amphibian 259
amphibolia 57
amphibrach 47
Amphictyon 282, 303
amphidoxa 77
Amphion 95
amphisbaena 256
amphitapa 388
amphitheater 307, 370
Amphitus 303
amphora 335
ampulla 400
amulet 183
Amulius 304

amurca 348
amygdala 344
amylum 396
amystis 400
anaboladium 387
Anacreon 65
anadiplosis 59, 75
anaglypha 399
analogium 310
analogy 54, 85, 136
analytica (logic) 83
anamnesis 78
anancitis 327
anapest 47
anaphora 59
anas 267
anasceva 73
anastrophe 62
anathema 174
anchor 375
anchorage 299
anchorite 172
anchusa 353
ancile 364
ancilla 205
Ancus Marcius 304
ancyromachus 373
Andalusia 282
androdamantus 320
androdamas 327
androgyne 244
Andromeda 106, 302
anesum 357
anethum 357
anetinum 115
angel(s) 138, 157, 158, 160–162
  nine orders of 160–162
Angelic (heresy) 176
Angeus 304
anguilla 124, 261
anguis 255–258
angulus 312
anima 231
animadversio 125
animal(s) 81, 247
  aquatic, 144 names of 263
  names of 247–270
  small 254–255
  tiny flying 269–270
animus 231
anise 357
ankle 238
ankle-bracelet 391
annals 67
  world 130–133
annona 396
annulled (testament) 120
annus 129
anointed 155
anomaly 54
anquina 376
anser 267
ant 254
ant lion 255
antae 311
Antaeus 305
antanaclasis 76
Antarctic 101, 273
antecenium 396
antegrade (astral motion) 104
antela 405
antemna 374
anthracitis 326
Anthony, Saint 245
Anthropomorphites 176
Anthropophagians 199
antia 391
Antichrist 184
Antidicomarite 177
antidote 113
antimetabole 76
Antioch 281, 302, 303
Antiochus 302, 309
antiphon 147
antiphrasis 63
Antipodes 199, 245, 293
antiquarius 142
antistropha 61
antithesis 60, 76
antithesis 58
antitheton 60
antonomasia 61
Antony 304
anulare 381
anularis (finger) 235
anulus 391
anus (of body) 238
anus (old woman) 243
anvil 377
Apamea 302
aparisis 78
ape 253
Apellite 175
Apennines 291, 298
aper 248
ape, five kinds of 253
apex 42, 365, 390
aphaeresis 57
aphorism 114
aphorus 261
aphratum 397
Aphrodis 128
Aphrodite 188, 244
aphronitrum 318
apiago 354
apianus 340
Apicius 395
Apis 188
apis 269–270
apium 356
  silvaticum 354
aplustria 362
apocalamus 384
Apocalypse 135, 138, 144, 176
apocope 57
apocrypha 135, 137, 138
apodyterium 308
Apollinarist 177
Apollo 44, 57, 65, 109, 117, 181, 182, 186, 187, 195, 199, 239, 241, 290, 295, 298, 304, 361, 370
apology 140
apoperes
apophasis 83
apophoreta 399
apoplexy 110
aporia 77
aposiopesis 78
apostate 162, 183
apostem 111
apostle(s) 168–170
  names of 168
Apostolic (heresy) 176
apostrophe 50
apotheca 310
apozema 399
appellatio 43
appellatus (category) 82
Appius Caecus 64
apple tree 342
appropriation 123
apricum 299
April 128
apron 392
apsyctos 325
Apuleius 84, 89
Apulia 291
aqua 276, 397

aqualiculus 240
Aquarian (heresy) 176
Aquarius 106
Aquila 51, 106, 139
aquila 264
Aquilius 118
Aquilo 275
Aquitania 291
ara 236, 310
Arabia 249, 286, 318, 321, 323, 326, 342, 348–350, 387, 397
Arabic (heresy) 177
arabica (stone) 327
arabicus (stone) 320
Arabs 193, 194, 303, 386, 388
Aracusia 286
Araks (river) 281
aranea 258, 388
(fish) 260
arapennis 315
Arar (river) 281
Ararat, Mount 298
aratio 337
aratrum 404
Araxes (river) 288
arbor 341
arbustum 341
arca 315, 321, 401
Arcadia 249, 291, 320
Arcadians 196, 246, 308
Arcas 291
Arcesilaus 179
arch 312
archangel 160–161
archbishop 170
Archilochus 65
architectus 377
architrave 312, 379
Archontic 175
arcifinius 314
Arctic 273
arctic circle 101
Arctos 101, 104
arcumen 350
arcus 312, 364
(rainbow) 274
ardea 265
area 314
Arelatum 304
Arenacian stone 378
arenata 371
Ares 362
Arethusa 296
argentum 330
vivum 330
argilla 317, 399
argitis 340
Argives 196, 304, 317
Argonauts 196
Argos 196
argument 69–71, 86, 140
deliberative 69
demonstrative 69
from effects, fourteen kinds of 86
extrinsic, types of 87
types of 71
argumentation 71, 365
argumentum 67
Argyre 294
argyritis 327
Arian 177
Arianism 143
Aries 105, 106
aries 247, 364
arioli 182
arista 338
aristolochia 353
Aristotle 39, 42, 54, 69, 79, 81, 82, 87, 107, 181, 244
arithmetic 39, 80, 89–93
Arius 180
Arles 304
ark, Noah's 288
arm 235
armamentarium 310
armarium 310
armband 391
Armenia 195, 281, 288, 343, 349, 380
Armenians 199, 386
armentum 247
Armenus 288
armilausa 385
armilla 391
armor 364
armoracia 356
armory 310
armpit 235
arms 362–365
armus 235
army 203
arnoglossos 352
aroma 348
aromatitis 323
arra 122, 210
arrabo 210
Arretine dish 399
arrow 363
arsenic 380
arsis 48, 96, 99
art 39
artaba 335
Artabatitans 245
Artaxerxes 109
artemesia 352
Artemis 352
artemo 375
arteria 234
arteriace 114
arteriasis 111
artery 239
arthritis 112
article (part of speech) 44
articulus 236
artifex 373
Artotyrites 176
arts, invention of 183
artus 236
arundo 347
arvina 236
arx 307
asafoetida 351
asarum 350
asbestos 320
asbestos 320
Ascalon 287, 302, 356
ascalonia 356
Ascanius 304
ascia 383
Asclepiades 115
asellus 249
ash tree 346
Asher 166
ashes 317, 337, 377
Asia 285–289, 318, 321, 325, 326, 359
Asia Minor 193, 288
asilus 270
asinus 249
asp 254, 256
asparagus 356
Asphaltites, Lake (*see* Sea, Dead)
asphodel 354
aspiration 41, 50
asplenos 354
ass 249
assembly 143
asser 382
assus 396
Assyria 286
Assyrians 181, 192, 194, 200, 333

asterisk 50
asterites 324
astrion 326
astrologer 182
astrology 99, 106
astronomy 39, 80, 89, 99–107
astrum 103
astula 342
astysmos 63
asyndeton 60
Athene 187
Athenians 196, 390
Athens 184, 290, 303, 307, 368
Athos, Mount 298
Atlantic Ocean 332
Atlas 99, 298
Atlas, Mount 199, 298
atom 271–272
  types of 271
atramentum 381
atriplex 356
atrium 308
atrophy 112
Attalus 388
Attic column 312, 379
Attic Greek 191
Attic nation 196
Attica 290
Attis 290
auditus 232
auger 383
augury 99, 181, 182, 266, 269
August 128
Augustine 139
Augustus (appellation) 163, 200
Augustus Caesar 41, 52, 63, 118, 128, 129, 200, 279, 302, 304, 321, 361
aula 308
aulea 388
aunt, maternal 210
aura 275
auraria 329
aureta 260
aurichalcum 330
auricularis (finger) 235
auriga 367
auris 234
aurochs 249
aurora 127
aurugo 113
aurum 329
auspex 182
Auster 275
australis piscis 261
Austroafricus 275
Austronotius 100, 272
authors, prolific 139
autumnus 129
ave (greeting) 265
avena 355
Avernus, Lake 279, 291
avia 209
aviaria 341
avis 264
avunculus 209
avus 206
axe 362, 382
  two-headed 234
axilla 235
axis of heaven 100, 272
axungia 396
azymus 396

Baal 166, 185
Babel, Tower of 191
Babylon 174, 286, 301
Babylonia 320
bacchia 400
Bacchus (*see* Liber)
bacillum 404
back 237
backboard (bed) 403
Bactria 287
Bactrians 194, 301
Bactrum 301
Bactrus (river) 281, 286
baculus 404
badger 254
badium 250
Baetica 282, 378
Baeticans 315
Baetis (river) 282, 292
bag 401
baia 299
Baiae 291
baianula 403
Bal 185
balance-tongue 333
balanite grapes 340
balanites 327
balcony 309
baldric 392
Baleares 297
ball 371
ballena 260
ballista 364
balm 115
balneum 307
balsam (ointment) 115
balsam tree 349
balteum 392
banner 361
banquet 395
baptism 149, 159
barathrum 300
barba 234
barbarism 55–56, 58
barbarolexis 55
barca 373
barge 373
bark 341
barley 338
barley-water 399
Barnabas 170
barones 205
baroptenus 325
barrier 311
barritus 252
barro 252
basanites 321
basil 356
basilica 310
Basilidian 175
basilisk 255
basin 400
basis (building) 379
basis 312
basket 389, 401, 405
Basques 198
basterna 404
bat 266
bath(s) 307
  hot 307
bathing 149
Bathsheba 309
batin 383
batrachites 320
battering ram 364
battle 360
  array 203
batus 335
baxea 393
baxeae 393
bdellium 348
beach 278
beam (of wood) 382
bear 252
beard 234

beard (grain) 338
beast 251–254
  of burden 247
beaver 253, 384
  wool 388
bedbug 259
bedframe 403
bedroom 308
bee 269
beech tree 345
bee-eater 266
beer 398
beet 356
Behemoth 185
being 82
Bel 185
Belgica 291
beli oculus 325
Bellerophon 246
bellicum pallium 386
bellua 260
bellum 359
belly 240
Belphegor 185
Belshazzar 168
belt 392
Belus 325
Belus (river) 328
Belzebub 185
bench 403
beneola 354
Benjamin 166
ben-nut 354
Berenice 303
berry 340
beryl 322
Bessians 197
bestia 251
beta 356
Bethel 302
Bethlehem 302
betrothed 210
bibio 270
Bible 90, 135–138, 272
  apostolic writings 135
  authors of 136–138
  books of (*see under individual books*)
  canon 135
  Law, five books of 135
  moral sense 135
  names in 162–165, 170
  narrative 135
  New Testament 135
    classes of writing 135
  number of books 135, 139
  Old Testament 39, 135, 139, 334, 352
  Prophets, eight books of 135
  three kinds of content 135
  translations of 139
  'Writings,' nine books of 135
bibliopola 142
bibliotheca 138, 310
bicinium 147
bier 403
Big and Little Dipper 273
  Big Dipper 100, 104, 271, 272, 275
biga 368
bigener 250–251
Bilbilis 331
bile 239
bile, black 109
bipennis 234, 383
bipinnis (see *bipennis*)
birds
  kinds of 263–269
  origin of names of 264
bireme 374
birrus 387
birth 231
  order of, four types 207
birthwort 353
bishop 170, 171
  four orders of 170
bissextus 145
bit, horse 405
Bithynia 288, 303, 351
bitumen 317
bivium 316
black 250
black-tail (fish) 261
bladder 240
  gall 239
blade
  (grain) 338
  (oar) 374
  (sword) 362
blame 69, 86
blatta 270
blatteum 270, 389
blavum 389
Blemmyans 245
blite 356
blood 109, 239
bloodletting 114
'bloom' (bronze) 331
boa 257
boa 256
Boanerges 169
boar 248
board 382
boca 260
body 231, 232–241
  parts of, purpose of 241
Boeotia 290
Boethius 81, 89
bogue 260
boia 124
bolster 388
bombycina 384
bombycinum 259, 384
bombyx 259, 384
bona (goods) 121
bone 236
Bonosiac 177
book(s) 142
  collection 139
  manufacture of 141
  medical 114
  sizes of 141
  terminology of 142
boot 393
Bootes 103, 105
bootmaker 393
booty 360
booty-share 361
Bordeaux 304
border
  (cloth) 387, 392
  (land) 300
Boreas 275
Boreus 100, 272
Borion 297
borrowing 55
bos 248–249
boss (shield) 237, 364
botanical treatise 110
botanicum 114
botrax 257
botrus 340
boulevard 306
boundary (land) 315
boundary-line 315
bow 364
bowel 240
box tree 347
boy 207, 241
bracae 385

bracchium 235
bracelet 391
bracile 392
bractea 329
brain 235, 239
bran 396
branch 341
branchos 111
branding-iron 406
brassica 356
brawn 235, 238
bread 396
breakfast 395
bream 261
breast 236
breathing (*see* aspiration)
breeches 385
breeding of animals 250
breeze 275
  sea 275
brevia 279
briar-bush 347
brick 312, 378
bride 210
Bridegroom 157
Brindisi 291, 304
bristle 248
Britain 294, 319, 332
Britons 198, 386
brontea 327
bronze 330–331
  (color) 250
broom, Spanish 355
broth 397, 399
brothel 369
brother 208
  uterine 208
  four kinds in Bible 208
brother-in-law 211
brown 250
bruma 129
Brundisium (*see* Brindisi)
Brutus 52
bryony 354
bubalus 249
bubo 266
bucina 361
bucket 400, 405
buckler 364
bucolic poem 65
bud 342
buffalo 249
bugloss 352, 353
buildings 308, 311–312, 377
  public 305–308
  rural 313–314
  sacred 309–310
bulbus 354
bull 248–249
bulla 391
bullock 242, 248
bulrush 355
bulwark 306
buprestis 269
bupthalmus 354
Burdigalis 304
burdo 251
burdock 353
burgher 204
Burgundians 197, 205
burgus 197
burial mound 313
buris 404
bury 243
bush-hook 404
business 365
bustard 264
bustum 402
butterfly 270
buttocks 237
buxum 347
buying 120
byssinus 384
byssum 388
Bythnia 392
Byzacium 292
Byzantium 303

caballus 249
cabbage 355
  turnip cabbage 356
cabinet 310
caccabus 401
cacemphaton 56
cachexia 112
cacosyntheton 57
cadaver 243
Cadiz 294, 302, 305
  Straits of 193
cadmia 331
Cadmus 40, 195, 290, 302, 303
caduca 111
  (inheritance) 121
caduceus 186
caecula 257
caecum 239
caelatus 399
caelia 398
caelum 100, 272–276, 377
Caelus (god) 185
caementarius 377
caementum 378
caenum 317
caerefolium 357
caerimonia 148
caeruleum 381
caeruleus 260
Caesar, Julius (*see* Julius Caesar)
Caesar (Julius?) 243
Caesar (title) 200
Caesaraugusta 304
Caesarea
  (Cappadocia) 303
  (Mauretania) 295, 305
  (Palestine) 302, 305
caesaries 232
caespes 341
caesura 64
caesus 397
caetra 364
Cain 95, 162, 301
Cainite 175
cake, sweet 396
Calabria 304
calamint 354
calamistrum 404
calamites 354
calamitis 263
calamus 97, 142, 349
calathus 389, 400
calcaneus 238
calcar 405
calceus 393
calciamentum 393
calculus 319, 371
calcus 333
calendar (literary genre) 67
  liturgical 143–145
calf (animal) 249
  (of leg) 238
calicularis 352
calidus 250
caliga 393
caligarius 393
caligo 274
calix 400
callaica 323
callis 316
Callista 196

Callisto 106
callitriches 253
calo 373
calones 393
Calpe 298
Calpis 297
caltulum 392
calumnia 122
calvaria 232
calx 238, 319
calx viva 378
cama 403
Cambyses 302
camel 249
camelopardus 252
camera 312
camisia 383, 385
camp (military) 202
campana 333
Campania 291, 331, 344, 398
camp-bed 403
campestre 384
campground 309
campus
camus 405
Cana 169
Canaan, son of Ham 163
Canaan 287, 333
  tribes of 193
Canaanites 193, 195
canalis 379
Cancer 106
cancer (disease) 113
cancer 262
candelabrum 402
candetum 315
candidus 250
candlestick 402
candor 243
canicula 405
canicula stella 105
canine (tooth) 234
canis 253
canistrum 401
canities 243
cankerworm 259
cannabum 388
Cannae, battle of 202
canon (conciliar) 143
canon 143
canon-table 142–143
Canopea 287, 376
Canopos 265
Canopus 287
Cantabria 332, 351
canterinum 338
cantharis 259
cantharus 400
cantherium 383
canticle 147
Canticle of Canticles (*see* Song of Songs)
canticum 98
cantor 171
cantus 96
canus 250
capanna 314
caper (plant) 356
caper 248
capilli 232
capillum Veneris 353
capistrum 405
capital (architecture) 312, 379
Capitilavium 146
Capitolium 267, 307
capitulum 390
cappa 390
Cappadocia 288, 318
Cappadocians 302
capparis 356
capra 248
caprea 248
capreolus 340
Capricorn 106
caprificus 344
caprinus 384
capsus 403
captain (of ship) 373
Capua 304
capulum 405
capulus 362, 403
capus 268
caput 232
Capys Silvius 304
carabus 374
caracutium 403
carbo 377
carbuncle 110, 326
carcer 124, 308, 367
carchedonia 326
carchesium 375
carcinias 327
cardamom 350
cardiaca 110
cardinal points 271
cardo 271, 272, 311, 315
  (celestial) 100
carduelus 269
carduus 356
carenum 398
carex 355
Caria 288
carica 344
caries 342
carina 374
caritas 158, 173
Carmania 325
Carmel, Mount 328
carmen 64
Carmentis 40
carnelian 323
caro 232, 396
carob tree 345
Carpathos 295
Carpathus 304
carpentarius 382
carpenter's square 381
carpentum pompaticum 403
Carpocratian 175
Carrara marble 322
Carrhae 301
carrot 355
carrum 403
carta 141
Cartagena 282, 305
Carthago (Spain) 282
Carthage 292, 303, 304, 403
Carthaginians 198
Carthago Spartaria 305
cartilage 236
Carystean marble 141, 322
casa 313
case
  (container) 363
  (grammatical) 44
  (legal/rhetorical) 70, 74, 119
    five types of 71
casia 349
cask 400
casses 376
cassia cinnamon 349
cassis 364
castanea 344
casting-net 370, 376
castoff (of snake) 258
Castor 367
castor 253
castra 202, 269
castrum 306

casula 387
casus 44
cat 254
catachresis 61
cataphasis 83
Cataphrygians 176
catapirates 376
cataplasma 114
catapotia 114
catarrh 111
catasceva 73
catechumen 146, 172
categories 81–82, 83
 ten species of 81
catella 391
catena 75
catenatum 404
caterva 202
Cathar 176
cathartic 114
cathedra 403
catholic 172, 173
 Catholic Epistles 138
 faith 178
catinum 400
Cato 73, 191, 337
cat's-eye 325
catulus 253
Caucasian mountains 297, 349
Caucasus 195, 322
cauculus 112
caudica 374
caul 239
caula 313
cauldron 401
caulis 355
causa 54, 70, 74, 365
 (legal) 119
cauterium 406
cautes 361
cavalry 201, 203
cave 300
Cecropidae 200
Cecrops 184, 196, 303, 304
cecum 239
cedar 345
cedrus 345
ceiling, paneled 379–380
celandine 352
celebration 145
cella 308
cellar 309
cellarium 310
celox 374
Celsus 337
Celtic Gauls 198
cena 396
cenchris 257
cenobite 172
censor 204
census 129
Centaur 249, 290
centaury 351
centenarium 334
centenum 338
centipede 257
cento 66
centuria 315
centurion 201
century (military) 202
 (time) 130
cepa 356
cephalea 111
Cephas (= Peter) 168
cera 140
cerastes 256
Cerasum 344
cerasus 344
ceratium 333
Ceraunian mountains 298
ceraunium 326
Cerberus 245
Cercius 303
cercopithecus 253
Cerdonian 176
cerebrum 235, 239
ceremony 148
Ceres 187, 337, 338, 339, 398
cereus 402
Cerinthian 175
cernui 393
ceroferarius 172
certamen 366
cerussa 380, 381
cervicalium 388
cervinus 250
cervisia 398
cervix 235
cervus 248
cessio 122
cetus 260
Ceuta 305
chaff 338
chair 395, 403
Chalane 302
chalazius 321, 324, 326
chalcanthus 381
chalcantum 318
Chalcedon, Council of 143, 178
chalcitis 327, 331
chalcophonos 327
chalcosmaragdos 322
Chaldeans 39, 99, 192, 323
chalice 400
Chalybs (river) 331
chamaedraco 257
chamaedrys 352
chamaeleon (herb) 353
chamaepitys 354
chamber 308
chameleon 252
chamomile 352, 354
Chanaan (*see also* Canaan) 287
chandelier 402
change (coins) 329
channel 280, 379
chanter, types of 171
Chaonia 290
character
 of a person 74
 (*see also* letter)
character 406
characteristics, national 198
characterization 78
charcoal 377
charger (horse) 249
charientismos 63
chariot 368
 four-horse 368
charioteer 367
Charity (Holy Spirit) 158
charity 173
Charon 186
Charybdis 279, 296
Chasluim 302
chatter 235
Chebron 302
cheek 233
cheekbone 233
cheese 397
chelidonia 324, 352
chelidoniacus 362
chelonitis 327
chelydros 256
chemites 321
cherry 344
chersydros 256
Cherubim 161, 285
chervil 357

chest
(of body) 236
(furniture) 401
chestnut 250, 344
chest-strap (horse) 405
chickpea 339
chicory 352, 356
children 203, 207, 241
chiliarch 201
Chiliast 175
Chimaera 66, 73, 246, 380
Chimera, Mt. 289
chin 234
Chinese (*see* Seres)
Chios 296, 347, 348, 349
Chiron 106, 114, 351
chirurgia 113
chirurgus 114
chisel 377, 383
chlamys 386
Choaspes (river) 323
choaspitis 323
choir 147
choler 109
chorda 98
chorea 147
choriamb 48
chorus 147
chreia 73, 76
chrisimon 51
chrism 149, 155
Christ (*see also* Jesus Christ) 149
Christ's-thorn 353
Christian 172
chronic illness 110, 111–112
chronicle 125
world 130–133
Chronicles, Book of 135, 136
Chronos 185
chrysanthemum 354
Chryse 294
chryselectrus 327
chrysendetus 399
chrysites 321
chrysoberyllus 322
chrysocolla 327, 380
chrysolampis 327
chrysolite 327
chrysopis 327
chrysoprase 322, 326
Chrysorrhoa (river) 281
church 137, 173
church councils, four major 143
cibarius 396
cibus 395
cibutum 401
cicada 268, 270
(headdress) 390
cicatrix 113
cicer 339
Cicero 51, 54, 69, 71, 81, 85, 88, 180, 191, 205, 386
cicindela 269
ciconia 264, 405
cicuta 353
cidaris 390
Cilicia 288, 350, 382, 400
Cilician 56
cilicium 388
cilio 377
cilium 233
Cilix 289
Cimea 317
cimex 259
cimicia 353
cimolia 317
cinaedia 325
cinctus 392
cinders 317
cingula 405
cingulum 392
ciniphes 270
cinis 317, 337
Cinna 392
cinnabar 380
cinnamolgus 265
cinnamon 265, 349
cinquefoil 352
cinyphius 248
Circe 181, 246, 367
Circensis 367
circinus 382
Circius 275
circle 93
circles (celestial) 101, 273
Circumcellian 177
circumcision 175
circumflex 49
circumlocution 62
circumluvium 300
circumtextus 387
Circus 307
circus 367
circus games 367–369
cirrus 233
Cisalpine Gaul 291
cistella 401
citadel 307
cithara 95, 97, 98
citizen 203–206
citizen, Roman 206
citocacia 353
citron tree 343
citrosus 384
city 301–305
civil philosophy 80
civil war 359
civis 203
civitas 305
clarissimi 204
classicum 361
classis 203, 373
clause 74
clause, punctuated 50
claustrum 311
clausula 66
clava 363
clavatus 393
clavis 404
clavus 375, 382
clay, white 317
cleft 300
Cleisthenes 368
clergy 170–172
nine orders of 170–172
clerus 170
clibanicius 396
clibanus 311
clima 101, 315
climax 75
clipeus 364
clivosum 316
cloaca 306
cloak 386, 404
clod 317
cloth 389
clothing 383–387
clothmaking 383, 389–390
cloud 273, 274
rain-cloud 274
storm-cloud 274
clover 339, 353
club (weapon) 363
clunabulum 362
clunis 237
clura 253
cob 250
cobweb 388
coccymela 343

cochleacius stone 378
cockcrow 127
coclea 262, 307
coclear 334, 400
coctus 396
coculum 401
Cocytus 300
code, epistolary 52
codex 142
codex 339
codicil 120
coenaculum 308
coenobium 172, 309
coetus 143
coffer 401
coffin 403
cogitatio 239
cognatus 208
cognomen 42
cohabitation 211
cohors 312
coin 89, 329
coinage 329
colatus 398
Colchians 303
colena 354
colic 112
collegiatus 205
colles 299
collum 235
collyria 114
collyrium 115
colobium 385
colocasia 354
colocynth 351
colon 50, 237
colon 74
colonist(s) 205
  four types of 205
colony 306
Colophonia 348
Colophonius 65
coloring 380–381
  (cloth) 389
colors (racing) 369
colostrum 397
coluber 255
Colubraria 297
colum 237, 405
columba 268
columbarium 374
columbinus stone 378
Columella 337
columella 234
column
  (building) 312, 378
  (military) 203
columna (of nose) 234
colus 389
Coluthian 177
colymba 347
comae 232
comb 236, 389, 404
comedy 180
  New Comedy 180
  Old Comedy 180
  two types of 180
  writer 369
comet 105
comfrey 353
comitial disease 111
comma 50
comma 74
Commagene 286
commandment 140
commentary 140
commerce 122
commissure 382
commodatum 121
common people 203
commonplace 70
community 305–306
Como, Lake 331
comoedus 180
compago 236
comparatio 64
comparison 54, 64
  of adjectives 43
compascus 314
compass 382
compensation 124
competition 366–369
competum (see *compitum*)
compitum 306, 316
complaint (legal) 365
compluvium 312
concentor 171
concha 262–263, 399
conchylium 262, 389
conclusion (of an oration) 71
concubine 207
concula 334
condicio 120
condiment 397
conditus 398
conductio 121
cone 94
confession 151
confessor 174
confirmation 73
confrages 299
congius 334
congregation 173
coniugium 211
coniunctivus 45
coniunx 210
coniuratio 203
conjugation 45
conjunction 42, 46
conjuration 149
conlisio 56
conopium 376
consanguinity 208, 210
conscript 202
consecration 148
consobrinus 209
consolation 158
consonant 40, 41
Constans 346
Constantine 117, 143, 303
Constantinople 303
  Council of 143
Constantius 177
constellatio (divination) 183
constellation(s) 94, 103, 104, 105, 106
  (figures) 94
constitutio 73, 118
  (of a case) 70
construction 377–379
consuetudo 73, 117
consul 200
consumptio 111
consumption 111
contagion 110
conticinium 127
continens 300
Contionator 136
contradiction 83
contrapositum 76
contraries, four types of 87–88
contubernium 211
contum 362
contumacia 235
conubium 211
convallis 299
convent 143, 172, 309
conventus 143
convexum 100, 272

convivium 395
coot 267
cophinus 401
copia 69
copper 330
copula 382
copyist 142, 204
cor 238
coral 323, 328
coralliticus 321
coranus 321
corax 267
corbis 401, 405
cord 375
coredulus 266
coriander 357
Corinth 290, 303, 322, 330
Corinthian column 312, 379
Corinthian marble 322
Corinthus 303
coritus 363
corium 236
cork tree 345
corner 312
Cornerstone (name of Christ) 157
cornu (military array) 203
cornua 374
corolla 390
corona 390
  (of eye) 233
coronarium 331
corpse 243
corpus 232–241, 243
corrigia 393
Corsa 297
Corsica 297
cortex 341
cortina 388
Corus 275
corus 335
corvus (fish) 260
Corybantes 187
Corycium 350
Corycus 289, 327
corymbus 340
coryza 111
Cos 109, 295, 304, 384
cos 319
cosmography, biblical 136
cosmos 271–283
costa 236
costri 269
costum 350
costume 385
cot 403
cothurnus 393
coticula 115
Cotopita 177
cottage 313
cotula 334
coturnix 268
couch 395, 403
cough 111
council 143
  Council
    of Chalcedon 143, 178
    of Constantinople 143
    Ephesian 143
    Nicene 143, 144
counter 371
course 280
courtyard 308
cousin 209
covenant 120
covering 383
coverlet 402
cow 249, 257
coxa 238
crab 262
crabro 269
cradle 403
crag 318
crane 264
crapula 395
cras 127
Crassus 301, 392
cratera 400
cratis 378
creation 130
  of the world 334
creator 154, 206, 232
creatures, fabulous 244
creed 149
  Apostles' 143
  Nicene 143
crementum 206, 232
crepida 393
crepido 319
crepusculum 127
Cres 295
cress 356
crest (helmet) 365
creta 368
Cretan earth 317
Crete 290, 295, 307, 317, 327, 343, 345, 351, 363, 382
cretio 118, 120
cribrum 401
cricket 254
crime 122–123
crines 233
crista 365
critical days (in medicine) 114
crockery 399
crocodile 260
crocomagma 350
crocus 350
crops 338
cross 41, 125, 157, 191
cross-beam 382
crossroad 306, 316
crowbar 124
crown 390
  (of head) 232
  (of road) 316
crucius 398
crudus 396
cruet 399
cruor 239
crus 238
crust 396
crusta 379
crustumia (olive) 347
Crustumium 344
crux 125
crystal 325
Ctesiphon 301
cub 251
cube 93, 94, 95, 379
  cube number 92
cubiculum 308
cubile 403
cubitum 235
cuckoo 268
cuculla 387
cuculus 268
cucuma 401
cucumber 356
cucumis 356
cucurbita 114, 356
cucurbitularis 354
cudgel 124
cuirass 364
culcita 388
culleum 125
culmen 312
culmus 338
cultellus 404
cultivation 337–338

cultor 205
cultura 337
cultus 384
Cumaean Sibyl 181
cumba 374
cummin 357
cunabula 403
cuneus 203
cuniculus 248
cup 400
cupa 400
Cupid 188
cupping glass 114
curator 205
curia 204, 307
curialis 204
curling iron 404
current 280
curriculum 128
currus 368
currycomb 406
cursus 280, 366
curtain 388
cuspis 363
custom 73, 117
custom house 308
customary law 117
cuttings 341
cuttlefish 262
cyanea 324
cyathus 334, 400
Cyclades islands 290, 295–296, 322, 348, 381
cyclamen 354
cycle 144
Cyclopes 245, 296
Cyclos 354
Cydnus (river) 289
Cydonia 343
Cygnus 106
cygnus 265
cylinder 94
cylindrus 404
cymbal 98
cymbium 400
cyme 342, 355
cyminum 357
Cynic 179
Cynocephali 245
cynocephalus 251, 253
cynodontes 244
cynomya 270
cyparissus 345
cyperum 350
cypress 345
cypria 380
cyprinum 115
Cypriots 193
Cyprus 295, 322, 323, 325, 330, 348, 374, 380
Cyrene 292, 305, 318, 351
Cyril of Alexandria 143
Cyrnus 297
Cyrus 194, 304
Cytherea 295

Dacia 289
Dacians 197
dactyl 47
dactylic hexameter (*see also* heroic meter) 65
dactylus (fruit) 340, 342
dactylus of Ida 327
Daedalus 307, 377, 382, 395
daemon 184
dagger 362
Dalilah 164
Dalmatia 290, 384
dalmatica 384
Damascus 192, 302, 321, 343
dammula 248
damnum 124
damson plum 343
Dan 166
Danae 185
Danai 196
dancer 370
Daniel 137, 165, 166, 168
Danube (river) 197, 282, 291, 352
[Daphnis] 97
daps 395
Dardania 304
Dardanus 195, 304
Dares the Phrygian 67
Darius 167, 277, 321
darkness 127, 274
darnel 355
dart 363
date (fruit) 342
dates, world history 130–133
dative 44
daucos 353
daughter 207
David 65, 95, 115, 136, 164, 168, 309
dawn 127
day(s) 125–127
  intercalary 145
  names of 126
daybreak 127
De Interpretatione 82–83
De Syllogismis Hypotheticis 84
deacon 170, 171
Dead Sea (*see* Sea, Dead)
death 243
  three kinds of 243
debauchery 395
Deborah 164
deceased 243
deceit 123
December 128
Decemvirs 117
deception 122
decoction 399
decoration 379–380
decumanus 315
decurion 204
decursus 280
dedicare 148
dediticius 206
deer 248
defendant 365
defensor 204
definition 80, 84–86
  fifteen kinds of 84
defrutum 398
defunct 204
defunctus 243
Deist 179
deity, nature of 159, 160
deliberative argument 69
delicacy (food) 395
Delmi 290
Delos 295
delphinus 260
Delphic Sibyl 181
delubrum 310
Democritus 179, 181, 337
demon 184, 190
demonstrative argument 69
Demosthenes 67
denarius 333
denominativus (category) 81
dens 234
dentale 404
dentix 261
deportatus 125
deposit 121
derivation of words 55
descendant 208

description 85
deserter 202
desertum 299
desire 174
  sexual 237
desperation 173
desultor 368
Deucalion 282
Deus 153
Deuteronomy 136
devil 184
devium 299
dew 274
dewlap 249
dextra 235
dextrale 391
dextralis 383
diabolus 184
diacodion 114
diaconus 170
diadem 390
diaeresis 58
diaeta 113
dialectic (*see also* logic) 39, 79
dialogue 140
dialyton 60
diamond 325
diamoron 114
Diana 187, 295, 352
diaphragm 239
diapsalma 147
diarrhea 112
diary 67
diaspermaton 114
diasyrmus 78
dibble 404
dice 371
dice-tumbler 371
dicing 371
dictamnum 351
dictator 200
Dicte 351
Dido 198, 212, 303
Didyme 296
Didymus 139
die (cube) 233
dies 125
Diespiter 186
diet 113
differentia 81, 85
differentiation 55
digamma 41
digitus 235
digression 78
dilectio 174
dill 357
diluculum 127
Dinah 163
dinamidia 114
dining room 308
dinner 396
Diomedes 246, 265
diomedia 265
dionysia 325
dionysius (stone) 320
Dionysius Lintius 47
Dionysius the Stoic 179
Dionysius Thrax 47
Dionysus 296, 301
Dioscoria 303
Dioscorus 143
diphthong 47
diple 51
diplois 387
dipondius 332
dipsas 256, 257
dirge 95
discipline 39
discriminale 233, 391
discus 399
discussion 140
dish 399–400
dispensativus (philosophy) 80
dispositio 377
dispute 365
  tripartite
dissaeptum 239
distaff 389
distich 66
distichon 338
distinctio 50
ditch 280
dittany 247, 351
diversorium 309
diverticulum 316
divination 181–183
  four kinds of 182
  two types of 182
divine philosophy 80
diviner 182
division (military) 203
divorce 211
divortium 316
dockyard 299
doctrinal (philosophy) 80
doe 248, 253
Dog Star 105
dogma 173
dolabra 383
dolium 400
dolo 375
dolon 363
dolphin 260
dolus 122
Domination (angelic order) 161
Dominicus 146
Dominus 153
  dominus 200
domus 308
domus 203
Don (river) 195, 281
donaria 148
donarium 310
donatio usufructuaria 120
donation 120
Donatist 177
Donatus 42, 47, 56, 75
donum 148
doorkeeper 172
doorpost 311
doorway 311
  of heaven 100
Dor 302
Dorians 196
Doric column 312, 379
  Greek 191
dormouse 254
dorsum 237
dos 120
dosinus 250
dotage 242
Douro (river) 282
dove 250, 268
downpour 274
dowry 120
dracaena 251
drachma 333
draco 255
  marinus 261
dracontea 352
dracontis 326
drag-hoe 404
dragma 333
drag-net 376
dragon 255, 326
drama 181
dramatist 180
dream 168, 244
dressing room 308

drink 397–399
drinking-bowl 400
dromedary 249
dromo 373
drone (bee) 269
drop (of liquid) 280
dropsy 111
drosolithus 325
drug 114
dryad 189
dualism 176
duck 267
duel 359
dulcis 396
dung 337
duracenus 343
Durius (river) 282
Dusii 190
dusk 127
dust 317
duumvir 204
dux 201
dwarf 244
dyeing (cloth) 389
dysentery 112

eagle 264
ear 234
  (grain) 338
earring 391
Earth (goddess) 187
earth 285, 293
earwax 235
east 101, 271
Easter cycle 143–145
  Day 144, 145
  Eve 144
ebenus 345
Eber (*see* Heber)
Ebionite 176
ebony 345
Ebosus 297
Ebro (river) 198, 282, 290, 292
ebur 252, 322
Ecclesia 137
ecclesia 173
Ecclesiastes 80, 136, 164
Ecclesiasticus 137
echenais 261
echinus (shellfish) 263
echites 327
eclipse
  lunar 103
  solar 103
eclipsis 58
economic philosophy 80
ecstasy 168
ectasis 57
eculeus 124
Eden 285
Edessa 301
edge (blade) 362
edict 73, 118, 200
Edom 163
eel 261
effectum 86
effigy 184
egg 269
Egypt 193, 194, 287, 313, 318, 320, 321, 322, 323, 340, 342, 343, 367, 376, 385
Egyptians 93, 99, 188, 195, 308, 315, 335, 380
El 153
elbidus 389
elbow 235
elder 242
elder tree 347
Eleazar 139
elecampane 357
electria 326
electrum 332
electuarium 114
elefantiacus 113
elegiac meter 65
elements
  celestial 271
  four 109, 179, 232
  physical 272
  two main 276, 278
elephant 252, 255
elephantia 257
Eli 164
Elijah 90, 165, 166, 167, 168, 172
Elis 129
Elisha 166, 302
elixus 396
Elizabeth 170
elleborum 351
ellipsis 57, 58
elm 346
elocutio 74
eloquence 69
eloquium figurae 58
Elvidian 177
emancipation 207
ember 377
embolism 145
emerald 322
Emerita 305
emeritus 201
emery 321
Emmanuel 155
emmer 338
emollient 114
Emor 302
emorroida 112
emperor (title) 200
empiesis 111
Empire, Roman 191
Empirical (school of medicine) 109
emplastrum 114
emptio 120
enargeia 75, 78
encaenia 146
enchanter 182
enchiridion 114
Encratite 176
enectio 123
enema 114
enhydris 256
enhydros 253, 326
enigma 140
Ennius 51, 52, 65
Enoch 162
Enoch (city) 301
Enos 162
enpiis 111
ensis 362
ensnarer 370
enthymeme 72
entranceway 311
eon (*see* aeon)
epact 145
epanados 76
epanalepsis 59, 78
epanaphora 59
epangelia 78
Epaphas 303
epenthesis 57
ephebe 241
ephebus 186
ephemeris 67
Epher 292
Ephesus 303, 380
  Council of 143
ephod 383
Ephrata 281
epibata 373

epichireme 72
Epicurean 179, 180
Epicurus 180
epidromos 375
epiglottis 235
epigram 66
epigrus 382
epilemsia 111
epilepsy 111, 268
epimelas 325
Epiphany 146
Epirus 290, 303
episcopacy 171
episcopus 170
epistola 140
epistylium 312, 379
episynaloephe 58
epitaph 66
epithalamium 65
epithet 43, 61, 213–230
epithymum 350
epitima 114
epitrite 48
epitrope 78
epizeuxis 59
epode 66
epula 395
eques 204, 368
equestrian
  equipment 405–406
  game 370
  order 204
equinoctial circle 101, 273
equinox 128
Equitia 320
equus 249–250
  marinus 260
era 129
Erebus 300
eremita 172
ergasterium 310
ergastulum 310
ericium 254
ericius 263
Ericthonius 106, 368
Eridanus 282
erigeron 353
Erimanthus (*see* Erymanthus)
Eriphusa 296
Ermus (river) 303
eruca 259, 356
ervum 339
Erymanthus (river) 282, 291
erysipelas 112
Esau 163, 192
esculus 345
essence 160
Essene 174
estate 314
Esther 135, 137, 168
estuary 278, 280
eternal 154
Etesiae 275
etesius 321
ether 272
ethicist 179
ethics 79
Ethiopia 199, 319, 321, 323, 324, 327, 345, 349
Ethiopian War 193
Ethiopians 194, 199
ethnicus 183
ethopoeia 74, 78
etiology 78
Etna, Mount 187, 296, 298, 318
Etruria 291, 366
Etruscans 183, 191, 196, 304, 365
Etruscus 291
etymology 54–55
  mystical 163
  of patriarchs' names 165–166
  of prophets' names 166
eucharist 146, 147, 148
Eumenides 190
Eunomian 176
Euonymos 296
euphony 96
euphorbium 351
Euphrates (river) 194, 281, 286, 320, 327, 350, 385
Euroauster 275
Europa 106, 185, 289
Europe 193, 289–292
Eurus 275
Eurymedusa 196
Eusebius 67, 125, 142, 143
Eusis (river) 281
Eutyches 143
Eutychian 178
Evander 301, 304
Evangelist 137
evangelium 138
evangelizare 137
Eve 162, 242, 384
Eveians 302
evening 126, 127
evidence 365
evil 123
evocatio 203
examen 333
excelsus 153
exceptor 204
excerptum 139
excetra 245, 256
excodicare 341
exconsul 200
excubitor 202
excusatio 140
exebenus 325
exemplum 64
exercitus 203
exile 125
exoche 76
Exodus 136
exomologesis 151
exorcism 149
exorcist 172
exordium 71
exoticus 384
expression, facial 233
exsequiae 243
extortion 123
extract 139
exuviae 258, 360
eye 233
eyebrow 233
eyelash 233
eyelid 233
  upper 233
eye socket 233, 238
Ezekiel 135, 137, 166, 303
Ezra 67, 135, 136, 137, 138, 167

faba 339
faber 376
fable 66–67, 189, 244–246
  Aesopian 66
  Libystican 66
fabrica 377
face 233, 235
facietergium 388
facinus 122
faeces 240
faecinian grape 340
faecula 398
faenum 355
faex 399
fagus 345
fairness 73

faith 173
falarica 363
falcastrum 404
Falcidius 118
falcon 268
Falernian wine 398
fall 129
 Fall of angels 161, 184
falling sickness 111
fallow 314, 337
falsitas 123
falx 404
fama 124
familia 203, 206
family 207
 relationships 206–211
 tree 210
famulus 205
fan 239
fanum 309
far 338
farcimen 397
farina 396
farm 314
farrago 338
fas 117
fasces 140
fascia 392
faselum 339
fasti 140, 145
 Fasti 140
fasting 150
 times of 150
fat 236
Fate 189
Fates, three 189
father 206
father-in-law 209
fatherland 293
fauces 234, 299
fault (verbal) 56–57, 75
faun 189
Faunus 97
Faunus of the Figs 190, 245
fava 339
favilla 317, 377
Favonii 207
Favonius 275
favus 397
fawn (color) 250
fax 402
feast 395
 liturgical 145–146
 Feast of the Tabernacles 369
feather 234, 264
febris 110
February 128
Februus 128
feet, metrical 47–49, 64
fel 239
femina (thighs) 238, 242
femina (woman) 242
feminalia 383
femoralia 385
femur 238
fence 313
fenestra 311
feniculum 357
fennel 355, 357
feretrum 403
feria 126
fermentacius 396
fermentum 396
fern 355
ferrugo 389
ferrum 331
fertum 148
ferula 355
ferus 251
festival-register 140
festivitas 145
fetus 240
fever 110
fibra 239
fibrinus 384, 388
fibrus 252
fibula 391, 392
ficedula 269
fictile 399
ficus 344
fideicommissum 120
fides 173
fidicula 98
fiducia 122
field 314–315
fig 344
figpecker 269
figura 42, 44, 233
figuration 157
figurative sense 90, 168
figure(s) 58
 of speech 58–60, 75–79
 of thought 76–79
filbert 344
file (tool) 377
filia 207
filius 207
filix 355
fillet 171, 391, 392
filth 317
filum 389
fine (judicial) 124
fines regundi 121
finger(s) 235
 immodest 235
 as measure 315
 names of 235
 ring 235
Finis 156
 finis 315
finitus 93
fir 345
fire 376
firebrand 342, 402
fireplace 402
fire-shovel 401
firewood 342
firmament 162, 272
first fruits 338
fisclum 405
fiscus 237, 401
fish 259–263
 how named 260
fist 235
fistula 113
fistula 97, 312, 379
flabellum 239
flagellum 339, 342
flagitium 122
flagon 400
flagrum 124
flame 377
flamen 171
flasca 400
flatus 280
flautist 97
flax 388
flea 259
fleece 388
fleet 373
flesh 232, 236
flint 318
Flood 191, 245, 282
flood plain 300
floods, three major 282–283
floor 309
Florian 177
flos 342

flos thymi 350
flower 342
fluctus 280
flumen 280
flute 97
fluvius 280–282
fly 270
  Spanish 259
foam 280
focacius 396
focus 402
fodere 341
foedus 360
foetus 240
fog 274
folium 142, 342, 349
folliculum 338
follis 329
fomes 342
fons 280
font 310
food 395–397
foot 238
  as measure 315
  metrical 47–49
  of sail 375
foot racer 368
foothills 299
footprint 316
footstool 403
foramen oculorum 233
force 122
forceps 377
ford 279
forehead 233
forfex 404
forge 377
forging 183
foris 311
fork (road) 316
form 184
formica 254
formicoleon 255
formulations of the categories 80, 83
fornax 377
Foroneus 365
fort 306
fortification 312–313
fortitude 79
Fortunate Isles 294
Fortune 189
forum 307, 365
forum 311
forus 374
fossorium 404
foundation (building) 311, 377
fountain 276–277, 280
four-horse chariot 368
fox 253
fragor 276
framea 362
frankincense 348
Franks 198, 362
frater 208
fratrissa 211
fraxinus 346
free person 206
freedman 205
freeman 205
frenum 405
frenusculus 113
frenzy 110
frequentative 45
fretum 278
frivolum 211
frixus 396
frog 263
frons 233, 341
frost 274
fructus 342
fruit 342
fruit fly 270
frumentum 338
frustum 397
frutex 341, 355
frux 338
fucus 269, 355
fulcrum 388
fulgetra 273
fulgur 273
fulgus 274
fulica 267
fuller's earth 317
fulmen 273
fumarole 300
funale 402
funarius 368
functionary 204
functus 243
funda 376
fundamentum 311, 377
fundum 364
fundus 314
funeral 243
fungus 342, 356
funis 375
funus 243
furca 125
furcilla 405
furfur 396
furfurio 269
Furies 189, 190
furnace 311
furniture 402–403
furnus 311
furo 254
furrow 142, 337
  furrow-measure 315
furtum 123
furuncle 113
fustis 124, 404
fusus 389

gabata 399
Gabriel 160
Gades (*see* Cadiz)
Gaetulia 292
gagates 319
Gagatis (river) 319
Gaianite 178
galactites 320, 324
Galatia 288, 352
Galatians 176, 193, 195
galatica 397
galbanum 351
gale 276
galea 364
Galen 397
galerum 383, 390
Galicians 198
Galilean 174
Galilee 287
  Sea of 279
galingale 350
gall bladder 239
Galli 193, 195, 198
Gallia Belgica 289
Gallic language (*see* language, Gallic)
Gallicia 332
gallicinium 127
gallicula 393
Gallicus 275
gallina 267
gall-nut 346
Gallogreeks 195
galnapes 388
galos 211
games 365

circus 367–369
gladiatorial 370
gymnastic 366
gaming-board 371
gamma 41
Gangarus 280
Ganges (river) 194, 261, 280, 286, 351
gangway (ship) 374
Garama 293
Garda, Lake 279, 291
garden 355
garlic 356
garment 384
garrio 235
garum 399
gate 306
Gaul 291, 304, 328, 332, 350, 387
Cisalpine 291
Transalpine 291
Gauls 190, 193, 195, 198, 304, 315, 363, 386
Gaza 302
Gazean wine 398
gazophylacium 401
Gehenna 300
gelus 274
gem 322–328
Gemini 106
geminus 207
gena 233, 238
gender (grammatical) 54
human 240
gener 209
general (of army) 201
Genesis 80, 135, 136
genethliacus 182
genetics 240
genetrix 208
genialis 403
genicularis 354
Genista 174
genitals 237
genitive 44
genitus 159
Genius 189
genius loci 255
Gennesaret, Lake 279
genre, literary 139–140
gens 183, 192, 203, 209
gentian 352
gentile 183
genu 238
genus 231
(race) 203
genus and differentiae 81
geomancy 182
geometry 39, 80, 89, 93–95
geometry, types of 93
Geon (river) 280
Georgics 181
germander 352, 353
Germani 197, 385
Germania 289, 323, 326, 345
germanus 208, 209
germen 208, 342
Geryon 245
Getae 195, 197, 198, 386
ghost 190
gibbet 125
Gibraltar
rock of 298
Straits of 278
Gideon 164
gift(s) 148
sevenfold, of Spirit 158
gilvus 250
gimlet 383
ginger 350
gingiva 234
Gipedes 197
giraffe 252
girgillus 405
girl 241
girth (horse) 405
glacies 274
glade 341
gladiator 370
gladiatorial games 370
gladiolus 354
gladius 362
(fish) 260
glass 328
glaucus (fish) 261
glaucus (gray) 250, 389
gleba 317
glide 41
glis 254
globe 277, 285
gloss 55, 85
glossopetra 327
glow worm 269
glycyriza 351
gnat 270
Gnostic 175
goad 405
goal line 368
goat 180, 247–248
goathair 384
goblet 400
God, names of 153–155
gods 160
pagan 183–190
gold 329
leaf 329
goldfinch 269
gomor 335
goods 121
goose 267
gore 239
Gorgades 294
Gorgias 69
Gorgon 188, 245, 294
Gospels 80, 135, 137, 138, 142
names in 170
Goths 193, 197, 198, 305, 386
gouge 383
gourd 356
gout 112
grabatum 403
Gracchus 191
Grace 159
graculus 267
gradatio 75
gradipes 264
Gradivus (Mars) 186
Graecus, King 195, 290
grafting 341
grain 338–339
gramen 355
grammar 39, 42, 69
granary 310
grandchild 207
grandfather 206
grandmother 209
grando 274
grape 269, 340–341
grape press 311
graphium 141
grapple 375, 405
grass 355
gratia 159
grave 49
gray 250
grease 396
greave 393
Greece 290–291, 391
Greek language (*see* language, Greek)

Greeks 193
Gregorian (law) Codex 117
griffin 252
ground 285, 299
groundsel 353
grove 299, 341
gruel 395
grus 264
gryllus 254
grypes 252
Guadalquivir (river) 282, 292
guaranen 250
gubellum 389
gubernio 373
gula 235
gulf 278
gullet 234
gum 234, 348
gurges 280
gurgulio 234, 270
gustus 232
gutta 280
guttatus 250
guttur 235
guva 114
guvia 383
gymnasium 179, 307, 308
gymnastic game 366
Gymnosophist 179
gynaeceum 311
gypsum 319, 378

Habakkuk 167
habena 405
habit 82
habitation 308–309
haedus 247
haematite 320, 323
haemoptysis 111
haemorrhois 256
haeresis 174
Hagar 163, 192, 195
Haggai 167
Hagiographa 135
hail 274
hair 232
 gray 243
hair-net 391
hairpin 391
halcyon 265
half-juger 315
hallec 261
halter 405
Halys (river) 288
Ham 162
hama 405
hamadryad 189
hamio 261
hamlet 306
hammer 377, 382
hammites 321
hammonitrum 328
hamper 401
hand 235
handmaid 205
hand-mill 401
Hannibal 202, 288, 298, 305, 330
harbor 299
hardwood 346
hare 248
harena 319, 378
harmonia 96
harmonicus 96
harmony 95, 96–97
harpago 405
haruspex 181, 182, 183
harvest 338
hash 397
hasta 362
hatchet 383
hatchling 264
haustrum 405
hawk 267
hay 355
hazelwort 350
head 232
headdress 233
health 109
hearing 232
heart 238, 240
hearth-bread 396
heathen (*see* pagan)
heavens, the (*see* sky)
hebdomada 127
Heber 163, 194
Heber (eponym of Hebrews) 192
Hebrew language (*see* language, Hebrew)
Hebrew, meaning of 174
Hebrews 329, 333, 334
Hebrews, Epistle of 138
Hebron 302
Hecatompolis 295
heddle 389
hedera 351
hedge 313
hedgehog 254
heel 238
heifer 249
heir 206
Heliopolis 303
heliotrope 352
 (stone) 323
Hellas 290
Helle 278
hellebore 351
Hellen 290
Helles river 289
helmet 364
helmsman 373
helvola grapes 340
Hemerobaptista 175
hemicadium 401
hemicranius 259
hemisphere (celestial) 101
hemlock 353
hemorrhoids 112
hemp 388
hen 267
henbane 352
hepaticus 111
Hephaestia 296
hephaestitis 327
Hera (*see also* Juno) 189
Heraclite 176
Heraclitus 180
herbs 349–355, 356–357
herba lucernaris 354
 salutaris 354
 sanguinaria 354
herbs, medicinal 113
herciscunda 121
Hercules 106, 195, 198, 216, 246, 256, 265, 277, 290, 297, 304, 305, 316, 356, 363
hercynia 266
herd 247
hereditas 121
heres 206
heresies, nameless 178
heresy 143, 174–178, 180
 Macedonian 177
heretics, names of 175
Hermagoras 69
hermaphrodite 244
Hermes 186, 244
Hermes Trimegistus 117, 186
hermit 172
Hermogenian (law) Codex 117

Hermogenian 176
Hermus (river) 281, 289
hero 189
Herod 138, 169, 170, 302, 305
Herod (Antipas) 302
Herodian 175
Herodotus 67
heroic maiden 242
heroic meter (dactylic hexameter) 65, 136
heron 265
herpyllos 352
Hesiod 337
Hesperia 291
Hesperians 199
Hesperides 199, 294
Hesperus 105, 368
hesternum 127
hexaticum 338
hexecontalithos 325
hexeris 374
Hezekiah 113, 165, 167
hiatus 300
Hiberia 288
Hibernia 294
hibernus 129
hide (skin) 236
hiemalis 101
hiems 129
Hiera 296
hiera 114
hieracitis 327
hierarchy, angelic 161
hierobotane 353
Hierosolyma (*see* Jerusalem)
Hierusalem (*see* Jerusalem)
hill 299
hilt 362
hinge 311
hinnulus 248
hinny 251
hip 238
hippagogus 374
Hippo 302
  Regius 292
Hippocentaur 66, 246
Hippocrates 109, 181, 295
Hippolytus 143
Hippomenes 366
Hippopodes 245
hippopotamus 261
hipposelinon 357
hircosa 263
hircus 247–248
hirmos 60
hirquus 248
hirundo 268
Hispalis 198, 305
Hispania (*see* Spain)
Hispanus 198
historia (biblical) 135
history 67
  world 130–133
histrio 369
histrix 253
hive 269
hoar frost 274
hoarseness 111
hock 238
hodie 126
hoe 404
hoeing 337
holocaust 148
holograph 119
holoporphyrus 384
holosericus 384
holus 355
Holy of Holies 309
homeopathy 113
Homer 51, 65, 66, 181, 186, 216, 244, 303, 352
homicide 123
homily 139
homo 231
homoeoptoton 59
homoeosis 63
homoeoteleuton 59
homoeusios 156
Homogirus 337
homonym 57
homousios 156
honey 397
honeycomb 397
honey-water 398
honey-wine 398
honorarius 398
hood 387, 390
hoopoe 268
hope 173
hora 125
Horace 67, 119, 136, 180, 363
hordeum 338
horehound 353
hormiscion 327
horn (instrument) 361
horn (military array) 203
hornet 269
horologia 404
horoscope 106, 182, 183
horreum 310
horse 249–250
  colors of 250
  qualities of 250
  types of 249, 250
horse-fly 270
horse-vaulter 368
Hortensius 235
hortus 355
hosanna 148
Hosea 167
hospice 309
hostia 148
hour 125
hours, canonical 146–147, 150
house 203, 308–309
household 203, 206
house-leek 354
hull 374
human being 231
  parts of 231–241
  terms for 213–230
humare 243
humors, four 109–110
humus 254, 285
Huns 195
hunting-net 376
hunting-spear 362
husband 210
  four reasons to choose 212
husk 338
hut 314
hyacinth 350
Hyades 103, 105
hyaenia 328
hybrid 250–251
hybrida 251
Hydaspes (river and spring) 281, 286
Hydra 245, 256
hydria 400
hydromancy 182
hydromelum 398
hydrophobia 110, 255
hydros 256
Hylas (river) 281
Hymen 95
hymen 211
hymenaeus 211
hymn 65, 95, 147
hypallage 60

Hypanis (river) 286
hyperbaton 62, 75
hyperbole 62
Hyperborean mountains 298
hypnalis 256
hypodiacones 171
hypogeum 309
hypotheca 122
Hypothetical Syllogisms, On the 84
hypozeuxis 58
Hyrcania 251, 288
Hyrcanus 309
hyssop 352
Hystaspes 281
hysteron proteron 62

iacinthina 384
iacinthizonta 324
iacinthus 324
iactus 366
iaculum 370, 376
iaculus 257
iamb 47
ianitor 172
ianua 311
iaspis 322
Iberians (*see also* Spaniards) 193, 198
Iberus (river) 282, 292
ibex 248
ibis 248, 266
Ibiza 297
Icaria 295
Icarus 278, 295
ice 274
ichneumon 254
icicle 280
icon 64
icon 319
Icosium 305
ictericus 113
Icthyophagians 199
ictus 124
idea 232
Ides 128
Idis 97
idol 184
idolatry 184
idyll 66
iecur 239
ieiunium 150
ieiunum 239
ientaculum 395
ignis 376
ignominy 124
ileos 110
ilex 345
Ilium 289, 303
ilium 237
illness 109–113
illumination 274
illusion, magical 183
illustres 204
Illyria 350
Ilus 303
image 64
  image of god, pagan 184
imaginatio 85
imago 319
imber 274
imbolus 307
imbrex 312
immeasurable 154
immigrant 205
immolation 148
immortal 154
immutable 154
impars 90
impassible 154, 177
imperative 45
imperator 200
impersonalis 45
impetigo 112
implements (farm) 404–405
impudicus (finger) 235
Inachus (river) 282, 290
inaures 391
incantation 183
incantator 182
incense 115
incentor 147
incest 123
inch 315
inchoative 45
incisor 234
incola 205
incolens 205
incorporeal 154, 176
incorruptible 154
Incubo 190
incubus 190
incus 377
index 235
India 245, 286, 319, 320, 322–324, 325–326, 328, 332, 345, 347, 348–350, 381, 397
Indians 194, 199, 322, 349, 353, 386
indictus (feast) 151
indicum 381
indigenous 205
indigo 381
induction (of syllogism) 71
indumentum 384
Indus (river) 194, 281, 286, 301
indutia 360
inerticula (grape) 340
infamy 124
infant 241
inference (of syllogism) 72
inferus 300
infinitive 45
infinitus 44, 45, 93
infitiatio 123
infula 390
ingenitus 159
ingenuus 205
inguen 110
inheritance 120, 121
iniuria 123
injustice 123
ink 381
inn 309
inportunus 299
inquilinus 205
inritum (document) 119
insitio 341
insonus 41
inspectivus (philosophy) 80
instauratio 377
instructum 122
instrument 122
  legal 119–121
  medical 114–115
insubulus 389
insula 293
insurrection 359
integers, names of 89
intempestum 127
intercilium 233
intercourse, sexual 237, 240
interdictum 122
interfinium 234
interjection 42, 46
intermissio 337
internecivum iudicium 123
interpolus 385
interpres 82, 139
interpretation 82
Interpretations of Apuleius 84
interscapilium 237

intervallum 313
intestate 121
intestine 239
  large 237
intinctio 377
intubum silvaticum 352
intubus 356
Inui 190
inula 357
invisible 154
involucrum 401
Io 278
Ion 196
Ionians 193, 196
Ionic
  column 312, 379
  Greek 191
iotacism 56
Ireland 294
iris 233, 350
iris
  (rainbow) 274
  (stone) 326
Irish 198
iron 331
irony 63, 78
Isaac 165, 302
Isagoge (*see* Porphyry)
Isaiah 113, 135, 137, 166, 168, 387
Isauria 288
Ishmael 163, 165, 184, 192
Ishmaelites 195
isicium 397
Isis 39, 98
Isis 188
island 293–297
Isles d'Hyères 296
Israel (Jacob) 194
Israel 165, 334
  divided kingdom 194
  tribes of 194
  twelve tribes of 165
Israelites 194
Issachar 169
Ister (river) 282, 291
Istria 369
Itala (biblical version) 139
Italians 193, 362
Italus 196, 291
Italy 291, 293, 317, 320, 321, 328, 331, 333, 337, 344, 370, 381
iter 316
itinerant 205
Itureans 346
itus 316
Iudaea (*see also* Judea) 287
Iudaeus 172, 174, 194
iudaicus (stone) 320
iudex 204, 365
iudicium 365
iugerum 315
iuglans 344
iugum 299
iumenta 247
iuncus 355
iuniperus 345
iurgium 365
ius (broth) 397
ius 117, 121
  gentium 118
  liberorum 120
iustitia 365
iuvencus 242, 248
iuvenis 242
ivory 252, 322
ivy 351

jackdaw 266, 267
Jacob 119, 163, 165, 168, 250, 282, 302, 334
  sons of 165
James of Alphaeus, the Less 169
James of Zebedee 169
James, Epistle of 138
Janiculum 304
January 128
Janus 128, 185, 191, 304, 311
Japheth 163, 193
Jason 194, 195
jasper 322
jaundice 113
javelin 362
jaw 233, 234
Jebus 301
Jebusites 301, 302
jejunum 239
Jeremiah 66, 135, 136, 137, 166, 385
Jericho 302
Jeroboam 302
Jerome 67, 125, 137, 139, 153
Jerusalem 173, 287, 300, 301, 309
Jesus, Hebrew name of 155
Jesus Christ 138, 183
  names of 155–157
Jesus son of Sirach 137
jet 319
Jew 172, 174, 183, 193, 194, 301, 333, 386
Jezebel 165
Job 65, 135, 136, 168
Joel 167
John (evangelist) 138, 176
John of Zebedee 169
John the Baptist 168, 172, 302
John, Epistles of 138
joint 236
Jonah 167, 260
Jonathan 164
Joppe 302
Jordan 281
Joseph 166, 176, 177, 210
Josephus (historian) 99, 137, 193
Joshua 164, 302
Joshua, Book of 136
Josiah 165
Jove (*see* Jupiter)
Jovinianist 177
Juba 305
jubilee 129, 145
Judah, kingdom of
Judas Iscariot 169
Judas of James 169
Jude, Epistle of 138
Judea 279, 287, 317, 328, 348, 349, 353
judge 204, 365
Judges, Book of 136
judgment 365
  Day of Judgment 156, 184
judicial argument 69
Judith 137, 168
jug 400
juger 315
Jugula 105
juice 399
Julius Atticus 337
Julius Caesar 53, 117, 128, 139, 200, 305, 359
Julus 200
July 128
jump (game) 366
junction 316
June 128
juniper 345
Juno (*see also* Hera) 186, 187, 189, 296, 368
Jupiter 95, 105, 106, 184, 185, 187, 189, 196, 199, 248, 289, 296, 344, 361, 367, 368, 383

Jupiter Ammon 106
jurisprudence 117
justice 79
Justinian 178
Juvenal 119, 180

Kalends 128, 146
kaminus 377
Karkheh (river) 281, 323
keel 374
kernel 344
kettle 401
key 404
kid 247
kidney 237, 240
kin
  maternal 208
  paternal 208
king (see *rex*)
Kings, Book of 136
kinship 210
  terms of 206–211
kite 268
knee 238
knife, pruning 404
knot (military) 203
knot-grass 354
knowledge 39, 79
koenonosis 77

Laban 119
labia 234
labina 317
labrum 234, 400
labrusca 339
labyrinth 307
  (of Crete) 246
lac 236, 397
lace (shoe) 393
Lacedaemon 303
Lacedaemonia 303
Lacedaemonians 196, 303, 321, 384
lacerna 387
lacertus 235, 238
  (lizard) 257
lacrima 233
lactans 382
lactatum 398
lacteus circulus 101, 273
lactuca 356
laculatus 384
lacunarium 379, 402
lacus 279, 311, 405
ladder 382
ladle 400
lagoena 400
laicus 172
lakes 276–277
  survey of 279
lamb 247
lamb's tongue 352
lambdacism 56
lament 66
Lamentations of Jeremiah 135, 137
lamia 190
lamp 402
lana 388
lance 363
lancet 114
lane 306
Langobards 197
language 191–192
  Chaldean 191
  Egyptian 166, 188
  Gallic 234, 347
  Greek 55, 191
    five types of 191
  Hebrew 191, 193, 247, 281, 285, 301, 333, 335, 347, 369
  Latin 191
    four types of 191
  learning of 191
  original 192
  Persian and Medean 251, 302
  Punic 185, 343
  Sabine 196
  Scythian 194
  Syrian 168, 169, 170, 172, 191, 261, 296
  Troglodyte 323
languages
  diversity of 191
  national types of 191
  three sacred 191
lantern 402
lanx 399
Laodicia 302
lap (race) 368
lapathium 356
lapella 354
lapis 318
lapistrus 356
Lapiths 195
lappa 353, 354
lappago 354
lapus lazuli 324
laquearium 312, 379
laquearius 370
larch 346
lard 396
Laricinum 346
Larissa 196
larix 346
larva 190
larvaticus 111
laser 351
lash 124
lasso 405
later 312, 378
laterculum 144
laterculus 312, 378
latex 280
Latin (*see* language, Latin)
Latins 196, 206
Latinus 191
Latium 191, 304
Latona 295
Latonia (Diana) 187
latus 237
laudes 65
laurel 342
laus 69, 147
lavender 354
laver 400
Lavinium 304
law 73, 117–125
  civil 118, 119
  divine or human 117
  military 118
  names of 118
  natural 117
  of nations 118
  originators of 117
  public 118
  purpose of 119
  Quirital 118
  replete 118
  Rhodian 119
lawsuit 365
laxative 114
lay person 172
Lazarus 170
lead 332
leaena 251
leaf 142, 342
league (measure) 315
Leah 163, 165
learn 39
leaven 396

Lebanon, Mount 281, 295
lebes 401
lectica 402, 403
lectio 147
lector 171
leech 258
leek 356
lees (wine) 399
legion 202
legitimus (feast) 151
legume 339
lembus 374
lens 339
Lent 146
lenticula 401
lentigo 112
lentil 339
lentiscus 346, 349
Leo 106
leo 251
Leogoras of Syracuse 51
leontophonos 253
lepra 112
leprosy 112
Leptis 302
lepus (fish) 261
lepus 248
Lesbian marble 322
lèse majesté 123
lesson 147
lethargy 110
letter(s)(of alphabet) 39–42, 47
 Egyptian 39
 Greek 39, 40
 Hebrew 39, 40
 Latin 39, 40–42
 legitimate 41
 Phoenician 39
 superfluous 41
 (epistle) 140
 (kinds of writing)
 common 40
 liberal 40
lettuce 356
Leucata 304
leucochrysus 327
leuga 315
lever 404
Leviathan 185
levidensis 384
levir 211
levite 171
Levites 136
Leviticus 136
levitonarium 385
Lex (Pentateuch) 135
lex 73, 117, 200 (*see also* law)
Libanus, Mount 298, 348
libation 148
Liber (Bacchus) 141, 180, 183, 186, 196, 198, 201, 298, 301, 339–341, 366, 370, 390, 400, 404
liber 142, 341
liberal arts 39, 107, 115
Liberalia 366
liberi 203, 207
libertus 205
libido 237
Libonotus 275
Libra 106
libra 332, 333
librarius 142
library 138–139, 310
libum 396
Libya 292–293, 325, 326, 359, 380
 Libya Cyrenensis 292
Libyans 193
licinium 385, 402
licium 390
licorice 351
lie 73
lien 111
lienitis 111
lientery 112
life 231
light 274
lighthouse 307, 402
lightning 273
lightning bolt 273
lignarius 382
lignum 342, 382
ligo 404
Liguria 357
Ligurian Alps 350
ligusticum 357
lily 351
Lilybaeum 297
lima 377
limax 259
limb 236
limbus 392
limen 311
limestone 319
limit (land) 315
limpidus 398
limus 317, 385, 392
linden 346
line 94
linea 382
lineage 207, 210
linen 384
lingua 191, 234
lingulati 393
linna 385
linostemus 384
lint 385
linum 388
Linus the Theban 95
lion 251
 three types of 251
lip 234
liparea 327
Lipare 296
Liparus 296
liquamen 399
liquescere 41
liquid 41
lis 365
Lisbon 305
litany 151
literacy 39
litharge 330
lithostrotum 312, 379
litigation 365
litoraria 374
littera 47
litus 300
liver 239
livestock 247–251
Livy 67, 195
Lix 305
lizard 257
Loaves of Proposition 145
lobe (of liver) 239
locatio 121
loculus 401
locus 293
 locus amoenus 299
 locus communis 70
locust 270
lodix 388
logic (*see also* dialectic) 79
Logical school of medicine 109
logician 71, 179
logium 383
loincloth 384, 385, 392
loins 237
Loire (river) 291

loligo 262
lolium 355
longao 237
loom 389
loquellaris 46
lord (augustan title) 200
Lord (see *Dominus*)
lorea 398
lorica 364
lorum 405
Lot (of Sodom) 163, 192
lot, drawn 183
lotium 240
lotos 343
louse 259
lovage 357
love 173
lozenge (medicinal) 114
lubricum 299
Lucan 181
Lucan cow 252
Lucania 327
lucanica (sausage) 397
lucerna 402
Lucerne clover 339
Lucifer 104, 307, 368, 402
Lucifer (planet) 105, 126, 147
Luciferian 177
Lucilius 56
Lucina (Diana) 187
Lucina 104
Lucretius 174
Lucrine Lake 279, 291
luctatio 366
lucubrum 402
Lucullean marble 322
Lucullus 139, 322, 344
lucus 299, 341
ludicrum 365
ludus 365
lues 110
Luke 138, 169
lumbar 385
lumbricus 259
lumbus 237
lumen 233, 274
Luna (Diana) 187
luna 104
lunatic 111
lunch 395
lung 239
lunula 391
lupanar 369
lupatus 405
lupine 339
lupus 252, 253, 405
 (fish) 260, 261
luscinia 266
Lusitania 326, 332
lustrum 129
lustrum 299
luteus 389
lutum 317, 378
lux 274
Luz 302
Lyaeus (*see* Liber)
Lyaeus 397
Lycaeus (Arcadian god) 181
Lycaon 106
Lycaonia 289
lychnis 326
Lycia 288
lycinia (olive) 347
lyciscus 253
lycopthalmos 327
Lycurgus 117
Lydia 288
Lydians 366, 373
Lydus 289
lymphaticus 110
lyncurius 252, 324
lynx 252
Lyra 106
lyre 95, 98, 180
lyric 180

Maccabees 137
Macedo 290
Macedonia 290, 380
Macedonians 196
Macedonius 143
macellum 308
maceria 313
machaera 362
machina 382
machio 377
mackerel, Spanish 263
macrology 57
macron 42, 54
madder 353
Maecenas 51
maeniana 309
Maenius 309
magalium 314
Magdalene 170
mage 181–183
maggot 259
Magi 146, 183, 385
magician 181–183
magister 200
magistrate 204
Magnes 319
magnet 319
Mago 337
Magog 193, 197, 288
magpie 267
mahil 383
Maia 128
maiestas 123
maigre 260
mainland 300
Majorca 297
mala (cheekbone) 233
Malachi 167
Malachim, Book of (= Kings) 136
malachite 323
malacoth 160
malagma 114
maleficus 182
Maleum 297
Maleus 297
malleolus 339
malleus 377
mallow plant 355
malomellum 343
malum 123, 342
 Cydonium 343
 Persicum 343
 Punicum 343
malva 355
Mambre 302, 346
mamilla 236
man 210, 242
mancipatio 122
mancipium 205
mandatus 120
mandible 233
mandibula 234
mandrake 351
mane 126
Manes (heretic) 176
Manes 126, 189
mania 111
Manichee 176
manicleatus 384
maniple 202
manipulum 355
manitergium 388
mannus 250

manor 314
mantelium 388
mantle 386
Manto 304
Mantua 304
manubiae 360
manumission 205, 207
manupretium 235
manus 235
maple 346
mappa 388
Marathon (battlefield) 290
marble 321–322
March 128
Marcion 180
Marcionite 176
Marcius 140
marculus 377
marcus 377
mare 277
Mareotic marsh 346
Mareotis 340
margarita 324
margo 300
maritime 300
maritus 210
Marius 359
marjoram 350, 354
Mark 137, 169
market 122, 308
marmor 321
Maro 180
marriage 210–212
marrow 236
marrubium 353
marrying, three reasons for 211–212
Mars 105, 128, 186, 243, 362, 367, 369, 370
Marseilles 304
marsh mallow 354
marsuppium 401
Marsyas 196
martellus 377, 382
Martha 170
martisium 397
martyr 170, 177
martyrium 310
Mary 170, 176, 177, 178, 210
Mary Magdalene 170
Mary of Clopas 169
Masbotheus 174
mason 377
mass 147
Massilia 304
mast 374
master builder 377
masthead 375
mastic 346
mastic tree 349
masticinum 389
masticinus 384
mastix 349
mastruca 385
mast-step 375
mat 403
mataxa 389
mater 206
Mater Magna 187
materfamilias 206, 211
materia 272
material 382
matertera 210
mathematics 89–99
mathematicus 99, 183
mathesis 106
Matins 147
matrimony 211
matrix 240
matron 206, 211
matter 272
Matthew 137, 169
Matthias 169, 170
mattock 404
mattress 388
matutinum 127
Mauretania 262, 292, 351
Mauretania Sitifensis 292
Mauretania Tingitana 292
mauros 250
mausoleum 313
Mausolus 313
mavors 387
maw-worm 259
maxilla 233
maxim 72, 73, 76
Maximilla 176
May 128
mead 398
meadow 314
meal (grain) 338, 396
meals 396
mean
  arithmetic 93
  geometric 93, 94
  musical 93, 98–99
Meander (river) 281
measure 315–316, 332, 334–335
meat 396
meatball 397
meat-market 308
meatus 238
meconites 327
medallion 405
Medea 194, 325
Medes 193, 194, 199, 302, 324, 339
Media 286, 301, 343
media 325
medial 41
Mediator 156
medica 339
medica arbor 343
medicamen 113
medication 113, 114
medicine 109–114, 115, 183
  three schools of 109
medicus 109
medimnum 335
Mediolanum 304
meditative (verb) 45
Mediterranean Sea 277–278
  names of 278
  parts of 277
medlar 343
medulla 236
Medus 286, 301
medus 398
mel 397
melancholia 109, 111
melancholy 111
melanites 321
melanurus 261
Melchizedech 163, 301
Melchizedechian 175
meles 254
melichros 323
melichrysus 327
melicratum 398
melinum 381
melipepo 356
mella 343
Melo (Nile) 280
melody 96
melopos 343
Melos 296, 322, 381
melotes 387
membranum 141
membrum 236
Memmia Timothoe 65
Memnon 266

memnonides (birds) 266
Memory (goddess) 95
memory 231
Memphis 141, 303, 318
memphitis 320
Menandrian 175
mendacium 73
mens 231–232
mensa 395
menses 240
mensis 127
mensura 315, 334
menta 343, 354, 357
mentum 234
menum 389
menus 384
mercatum 308
mercatus 122
mercenary 205
merchandise 122
Mercury 97, 98, 104, 105, 117, 182, 183, 186, 367, 370
merenda 396
mergus 267
Merida 305
meridies 101, 126, 271
Merista 175
merle 268
merops 266
merula 268, 291
merum 398
merx 122
Mesfres 367
mesomelas 325
Mesopotamia 280, 286, 387
mespila 343
Messapia 304
messenger 160
Messiah 155
messis 338
messorium 399
mesticium 389
meta 367
metal 328–332
metalepsis 61
metallum 125
metalworker 373, 376
metamorphosis 244, 246
Metangismonite 177
metaphor 60, 85
(of God) 155
metaplasm 55, 57–58
metathesis 58
metathesis 78
metatum 309
metempsychosis 179
meteorology 273–276
meter 49, 64–66
musical 96
heroic 65, 136
meters of Psalter 136
Methodical school of medicine 109
Methuselah 162
Metonic cycle 145
metonymy 61
metropolitan (bishop) 170
metrum 334
meu 350
mica
Micah 167
Michael (archangel) 161
midday 126
Milan 304
mile, Roman 315
miles 201
miliarium 315
Miliast 175
military
origin of 201
service, three kinds of 202
terms 201–203
militia 202
milium 338
milk 236, 397
milking-pail 400
Milky Way 101, 273
millago 261
millenarius 201
millet 338
millhouse 311
millstone 378
milvus 268
mime 370
mina 333
mind 231–232
mine 125
Minerva 184, 187, 303, 368, 370, 377, 383
Mineus (river) 282, 292
minium 380
Miño (river) 292
Minorca 297
Minotaur 244, 246, 307
mint 354, 357
minutal 397
mioparo 374
mire 317
mirobalanum 115
mirror 391
mirteus 250
misdeed 122
missa 140, 147
missile 363
mist 274
mithrax 325
mithridax 320
mitra 376, 390
mixing-bowl 400
mode (musical) 96
moderation 109
modius 334, 375
modulation 95
modus (moderation) 109
modus (mood of verb) 45
moenia 306
Moesia 289
mola 378, 401
molar 234
molaris stone 378
molding 379
mole 254
molochinius 384
molochites 323
Molossia 290
molotius 321
moment 125
momentum (pledge) 122
monachus 172
monarch 201
monastery 309
monedula 266
moneta 329, 333
money 329
money-changing 141
monile 391
monk 172
monoceron 252
monodia 147
monogamous 211
mons 297
monster 243–246
monstrum 244
Montanist 176
Montanus 176
month(s) 127–128, 146
names of 128
monument (history as) 67
monument 313
mood (of verb) 45

moon 102, 104
  distance from earth 103
  light of 102–103
  new 103
  path of 103
  period of 145
  phases of 102
Moors 198, 364, 386
moral philosophy 80
morals 179
morbus 109
  arcuatus 113
morning 126
mors 243
morsel 397
mortar 114, 232
mortuus 243
morus 344
mos, mores 73, 117
mosaic 379
Moschi (river) 288
Moses 39, 65, 67, 90, 95, 117, 135, 136, 140, 145, 149, 153, 164, 167, 168, 181, 282, 303, 332, 334
mosquito-netting 376
motacism 56
moth 270
mother 206, 211
moth-worm 259
mound 313
mountain 297–299
mouse 254
mouth 234
mozicia 401
mucro 362
mud 317, 378
mugilis 261
mulberry tree 344
mule 250
mulgarium 400
muliebria 240
mulier 242
mullei 393
mullein 354, 355
mullet
  gray 261
  red 261
mullus 261
mulsum 398
multipes 259
mundus 99, 271
munia 204
municeps 204
municipalis 204
municipium 306
munitum 312
munus 148
muraena (eel) 262
murena 262
murena (necklace) 391
murex (shellfish) 262
murex (rock) 319
muria 399
murra 325
murrina 325
murus 306
mus 254
  (muscle) 238
mus araneus 254
musca 270
muscatel 340
muscle 235, 238
musculus (boat) 373
  (military engine) 364
  (muscle) 235
  (mussel) 260, 262
Muse(s) 95, 189, 370
mushroom 356
music 39, 80, 89, 95–99
  inventors of 95
  liturgical 147–148
  three parts of 96
  three types of 96–98
musician, stage 369
musio 254
musmo 251
mussel 260, 262
mussel-shell 399
must (wine) 398
mustard 356
mustela 254
mustio 270
mute 40, 41
mutuum 121
muzzle 405
Mycenae 303
myrice 346
myrmecitis 327
Myrmidons 196
myrobalanum 354
myrrh 115, 348
myrrhites 323
Myrtilus 278
myrtle 346
  (color) 250
Mysia 353
myth 189
mythical monsters 244

Nabaioth 287
Nabateans 287
Nabathea 287
Nabla 136
Naevius 191
Nahum 167
naiad 189
Naid 301
nail (carpenter's) 382
nail (of finger) 236
name 42
  appellative 160
  proper 160
  prophetic (biblical) 162–165
nanus 244
nape 235
napkin 388
Naples 304
napocaulis 356
napus 355
Narbonne 304
narcissus 351
nardus 349
naris 234
narrative (part of oration) 71
Nasmones 326
nassa 376
nasturcium 356
nates 237
Nathan 166
Nathanian 171
nation(s) 192–199
  fabulous 199
  fifteen from Japheth 193
  seventy-two 192–193
  thirty-one from Ham 193
  twenty-seven from Shem 192–193
native person 205
nativity (horoscope) 99
natrix 256
natron 318
natural philosophy 80
Nature 243
nature 231–241
nauclerus 373
nauta 373
navalia 299
navel 237
navew 355
navis 373

Naxos 296
Nazarene 157, 172, 175
Nazarite 157
Neapolis 302, 304
Nebroth 286
Nebuchadnezzar 165
nebula 274
neck 235
necromancy 181, 182
nefresis 112
negation 83
negotium 365
Nehemiah 137, 167
Nembroth 301
nemus 341
neomenia 146
neophyte 172
nepeta 354
nephrosis 112
nepos 207
Neptune 185, 196, 273, 367, 370
Nero 322
nervus 236
Nestorian 178
Nestorius 143
net 370, 376
  net-fighter 370
nettle 352
netus 389
newt 257
Nicea, Council of 143, 144
Nicomachus 89
Nicolaite 175
Nicomedes 303
Nicomedia 288, 303
Nicopolis 304
Nicostrate 40
night 127
nightingale 266
nightshade 354
nightshirt 385
Nile 93, 98, 199, 248, 260, 265, 266, 280, 281, 287, 324, 367, 376
nimbus 274, 390
Nimrod 163, 301
Ninus 185, 359
nipple 236
Nitria 318
nitrum 318
nix 274
Noah 162, 282, 339
  sons of 162
noctua 266
nodus 203
Noetian 177
nomen 42, 82
nominative 44
nomisma 329, 333
Nones 128, 150
Noricum 289
norma 381
north 101, 271
North Pole 315
nostril 234
nota 50, 51
notamen 42
notarius 51
notary 204
nothus 43, 207
noun(s) 42–44
  agent 43
  appellative 42
  common 44
  derivative 43
  diminutive 43
  epicene 44
  gendered 43
  homonymous 43
  mongrel 43
  neuter 44
  plurinomial 43
  proper 42
  relational 43, 160
  synonymous 43
  verbal 43
nourishment 395
novacula 404
novalis 314
Novatian 176
Novels (laws) 119
nox 127
nubes 273, 274
nucleus 344
Numa 329
Numa Pompilius 117
number(s) 89–93
  equal 91
  even 90–91
  finite 93
  grammatical 44
  infinite 93
  metrical 64
  musical 98–99
  names of 89
  odd 90–91
  perfect 90, 91, 95
  prime 90
  square 92
  types of 91
Numbers, Book of 136
Numidia 292, 322
Numidian marble 322
Numidians 198, 314
Numitor 304
nummus 89, 204, 329
nuntius 160
nupta 210
nuptials 211
nutriment 395
nux 344
Nyctage 178
nyctalopia 112
nycticorax 266
nymph 189
nympha 210
Nysa 301

oak 345, 346
oar 374
oarlock 374
oarsman 373
oath 202
oats 355
Obadiah 167
obelisk 367
oblaqueare 341
oblation 148
obol 333
obolus 50
obryzum 329
obsidian 320, 328
obstinacy 235
obstrigilli 393
occatio 337
occidens 101, 271
occiput 232
Ocean 277, 285
  Britannic 193
  names of 277
oceloe 262
ochre 381
ocimum 356
ocrea 393
Octavius (*see* Augustus Caesar)
octopus 262
oculus 233
  (tree) 341
odor 115
odoratus 232

oenomelum 398
oenophorum 400
oestrus 270
offa 396
offertory 148
office, holy 146–151
officials, titles of 199–201
offspring 207
Ogygus 282, 295
oica 325
oil 115
  of roses 115
  Spanish 347
oil-lamp 402
ointment 115, 155
ola 235
old age 242–243
  features of 243
old man 242
Old Testament (*see* Bible, Old Testament)
old woman 243
oleander 347
oleaster 347
oleomela 343
oleoselinon 357
oleum 115, 347
olfacere 234
olfactoriolum 391
olfactus 232
olisatrum 356
oliva 347
olive 347–348
  oil 347
olla 401
olor 264
olus molle 356
olympiad 129
Olympic games 129
Olympus, Mount 290, 298, 356
omen 244
omentum 239
omnimorbia 353
omnipotens 153
onager 249
onion 356
Onocentaur 246
onocrotalos 266
onomatopoeia 62
onyx 323
opacus 299
opal 324, 325
ophaz 329
Ophite 175
ophites 257, 321
opinion 79
opisphorum 376
opium 351
oppidanus 205
oppidum 305
opposite (logical) 88
Ops 187
opsius 320
optative 45
optio 202
opulence 395
opusculum 139
ora 387
orach 356
oracle 168, 181, 244
oratio 150
oration, parts of 69, 71
orator 69
oratorium 309
oratory 42
orb (insignia) 361
orbis (globe) 277, 285
  (fish) 260
orbit, astral, period of 104
orbita 316
orbus 241
orca 400
Orcades 294
orchas 347
orchella-weed 355
orchestra 369
orchid 352
orcibeta 354
Orcus 186
ordeolus 113
ordinance 73
oread 189
organ 97
  pipe 239
organicus 96, 97
Organum (Psalter) 136
organum (musical instrument) 97
orgia 148
oriens 101, 271
origanum 354
Origen 139, 177
Origenian 177
Orion 103, 105
Orkneys 294
ornament 390–393
Orontes (river) 281
orphan 241
Orpheus 98
orthodox 172
orthography 52–54
Ortygia 295
ortygometra 268
os (bone) 236
os (mouth) 234, 235
osae 393
oscedo 113
oscines 269
Oscobagum 351
osier 346
Osirus 337
osprey 268
ossifragus 268
ostentum 244
Ostia 304
ostiarius 172
osticium 389
ostium 300, 311
ostracites 321, 327
ostracus 312, 379
ostrea 262
ostrich 265
ostrum 262, 389
ounce 333
outrage 122
oven 311
Ovid 140
ovis 247
ovum 269
owl
  horned 266
  night 266
  screech 266
ox 248–249
oxifalus 334
oxymeli 398
oyster 262
Ozam 302

pace (measure) 315
Pachynum 297, 318
packhorse 249
packsaddle 405
pact 120
Pactolus (river) 281, 289
Padus (river) 282
paedagogus 226
paederos 324
paenula 387
Paeon 352

paeonia 352
pagan(s) 107, 126, 183
page 142
pagrus 261
pagus 306
pala 237, 405
palace 308
Palamedes 40
palate 234
palea 338
Pales 315
Palestine 287, 335, 356, 398
Palestinians 193, 195, 302
palestra 366
paling 404
paliurus 353
palla 387
Palladius 337, 356
Pallanteum 308
Pallas 308
Pallas Athene 188
pallet 403
pallium 386
palm
  (of hand) 235
  (measure) 315
  (plant) 342
Palm Sunday 146
palmatus 386
palmes 340
palmula 374
Palmyra 343
palpebra 233
paludamentum 386
palumbes 268
palus 233, 315, 404
Pamphagians 199
Pamphylia 288
pampinus 340
Pan 97, 188
panaces 351
panchrus 325
pandorius 97
panegyric 140
panel, wall 379
panicium 338
panis 396
Panitae 190
pannier 401
Pannonia 289, 291, 374
pannucius 385
Panotians 245
pan-pipes 188
panther 251
pantry 310
panulia 389
papaten 388
papavera 351
Paphos 295, 304, 347
papilio 270, 313
papilla 236
Papius 118
papula 113
papyrus 140, 141, 150, 355
  types of 141
parable 140
parabola 64
parabola 140, 168
Paraclete 149, 156, 158
paradiastole 76
paradigm (trope) 64
Paradise 280, 285
paradox 78
paragoge 57
paragraph sign 51
Paralipomenon 136
paralysis 112
paromoeon 59
paranympha 210
parapsis 399
parasangs 316
parastata 375
parathesis 78
Parcae 189, 190
parchment 140, 141
  types of 141
Pareantus 296
parent 206
  resemblance to 240
parenthesis 62
Parian marble 321
parias 257
paries 312
parietinae 312
parma 364
Parnassus, Mount 282, 290, 298
paro 373
paroemia 63
paronomasia 59
Paros 296, 321
parotid 112
parrhesia 78
parricide 123
parrot 265
pars 90, 361
parsley 356
Parthenii 304
Parthenope 304
Parthia 286, 301, 325
Parthians 194, 301, 346
participial 43
participle 42, 46
  perfect 243
partridge 268
parts of speech 42
pasch 144
Pasiphae 244
pass (mountain) 299
passenger (shipboard) 373
passer 268
passions, three 189
passive voice 45, 46
Passover 144
passum 398
pastinaca 355
pastinum 404
Pastor (name of Christ) 157
pastoral poem 65
patchwork 385
patella 401
paten 399
pater 206
patera 400
paterfamilias 206
Paternian 177
paternity 208
path 316
patibulum 125
Patmos 138
patratio 206
patres conscripti 204
patria 293
patriarch(s)
  (bishop) 170
  names, meaning of 165–166
Patrician (heresy) 177
patrician 201
patricius 393
Patripassian 177
patronymic 43
patruus 209
Paul (*see also* Saul) 71, 113, 135, 167, 169, 176, 207, 303
  Epistles of 138
Paulian 176
Paulus, Aemilius 139
Paulus, Julius 118, 121
paunch 240
Pausanias 303

pausia (olive) 347
pavement 312, 379
pavilion 313
pavimentum 379
pavitensis 384
pax 360
paxillus 233
payment 122
pea 339
peace 360
peach 343
peacock 267
pear 344
pearl 324
pebble 319
peccatum 123
pecores 247
pecten 236, 389, 404
pectoralis 384
pectus 236
pecudes 247
peculation 123
peculium 121
pecunia 318
pecus 247–251
pedes 368
pedestal 312
peduculus 259
peg 382
Pelagian 178
pelagus 278
pelican 265, 266
pellis 236
Peloponnensis 196, 304
Peloponnese 290
Pelops 196, 290, 303
peloris 262
Pelorum 297
pelta 364
pelvis 400
pen, reed 142
penalty 123, 125
Penates 189
penetralia 309
penicillus 264
penis, large 185
penitence 150
penna 383
pennyroyal 353
pensum 389
pentaphyllon 352
Pentapolis 287, 292
Pentateuch 136
Pentecost 130, 145
penteris 374
peony 352
peplum 387
pepo 356
pepper tree 349
percussion (instruments) 97
Perdix 382
perdix 268
peregrinus 205
perendie 127
perfect 154
pergamena 141
Pergamum 141
Perihermenias 82, 84
period 50
periodos 74
Peripatetic philosophers 179
periphrasis 62
peripleumonia 110
periscelis 391
perissology 57, 75
perizoma 384
perones 393
perpendiculum 382
Persepolis 301
Perses 139
Perseus 106, 303, 343
Persia 286, 301, 320, 325, 326, 327, 343
Persian language (*see* language, Persian and Medean)
Persians 194, 199, 316, 386, 390, 396
Persius 119, 180, 301
personification (*see* prosopopeia)
persons (of deity) 157, 159, 160
Persus 286
pertica 315
pervasio 123
pes 238
  (metrical) 47
  (of sail) 375
pessary 114
pestilence 110
pestle 114, 232
petalum 383
Petephres 303
Peter (*see also* Cephas *and* Simon) 137, 150, 168, 175, 177
Peter, Epistles of 138
petilus 250
petition 150
petorritum 403
Petra 348
petra 168
Petronius 122
petroselinon 356
Peucetius 304
peusis 78
Phaenicusa 296
Phaenon 105
Phaethon 104, 105, 126, 282, 323
Phalantus 304
phalanx 202
phalera 405
Pharaoh 163, 166
pharetra 363
Pharisee 174
pharmaceutics 113
pharus 307, 402
Phaselos 356
phaselus 356, 373
phasianus 267
Phasis (river) 288
pheasant 267
phengites 321
Pherecydes 64, 65, 67
phiala 400
Phidon 332
Philadelphia (Arabia) 302
Philargus 51
Philip (apostle) 169
Philippus (tetrarch) 201
Philistines 193, 195
Philo Judaeus 137
philosopher 178
philosophers
  Academic 179
  natural 179
  pagan 178–180
  schools of 174, 179–180
  three kinds of 178, 179
philosophy 79–80
  practical 80
  speculative 80
Phison (river) 280
phlebotomus 114
phlegm 109
phleumon 110
phlogites 326
phlomos 354, 355
Phocaeans 304
Phoebus (*see* Apollo)
Phoenicia 287, 328
Phoenicians 193, 195, 302, 305, 314, 316, 380

Phoenix 195, 287, 303
phoenix 265
Phoroneus 117, 307
Photinian 176
phrase 74, 83
Phrixus 278
Phrygia 97, 288, 320
Phrygians 183, 385
phrygius (stone) 320
phthisis 111
phu 350
physician 109
physics 79
physicus 179
Physiologus 246
piaculum 123
pica 267
pick-ax 383
pickle (fish sauce) 261
Pictavia 304
Picts 198, 386
picture 380
Picus 267, 337
piebald 250
pigmentum (drug) 114
pignus 121, 122
pike
  (fish) 260, 261
  (weapon) 362
pila 114, 232, 361, 371
pilaster 311
pilentum 403
pillage 360
pilleum 383, 390
pilleus 171
pillow 388
Pilosus 190
pilum 232, 363
Pilumnius 114
pilus 232
pimple 113
Pindar 136
pine 345
pine-thistle 353
pinna 142, 234, 264
pinnula 234
pinus 345
pipe (plumbing) 312, 379
piper 349
piperinus stone 378
pirates 359
pirula 234
pirus 344
Pisces 106
piscis 259–263
Pisistratus 139
pistachio 345
pistrinum 311
pistum 338
pisum 339
pitch 348
  (vocal) 49
pitchfork 405
placenta 396
placitum 120, 388
plaga 124
plagia 278
plague 110
plain 299
plaintiff 365
plane figures, five 93
plane surface 92, 93, 94, 95
plane tree 346
planet(s) 100, 104, 105
  names of 105
planta 238, 341
plantain 352
plantarium 341
plaster (medicinal) 114
plastice 379
platanus 346
platea 306
Plato 39, 79, 107, 175, 179, 180
Platonist 179, 180
platter 399
plaustrum 403
Plautus 64, 66, 180, 191
plebeian 203
pledge 122, 210
Pleiades 103, 105
pleonasm 56
pleurisis 110
Pliny 258
plow 404
  plow-beam 404
plowing 337
plowshare 404
plum tree 343
plumb-line 382
plumbum 332
plume 264
plunder 360
pluteus 364, 403
Pluto 128, 186
Po (river) 282, 291, 324, 346, 374
poculum 400
podagra 112
poderis 383
poem 64, 66, 180
poena 123
poenitentia 150
poesis 66
poet 180–181
  lyric 180
  theological 181
poetry, three modes of 181
point
  (geometric) 94
  (sword) 362
Poitiers 304
polar region 100, 272
pole (celestial) 100, 271, 272
polios 353
pollen 396
pollex 235
Pollio 139
Pollux 367
polus 272
polygonos 354
polymitus 385
polypodion 353
polyptoton 59
polypus 262
polysyndeton 60
pomegranate 343
pomelida 343
pompa 360
Pompeii 304
Pompeiopolis 56
Pompey 117, 198, 359
Pomponius 66
pomum 342
pondus 332
poniard 362
pons 375
pontica(stone) 325, 328
pontifex 171
Pontius Pilate 170
pontonium 374
Pontus (*see* Sea, Black)
Pontus (river) 320
pool 279
poplar 346
Poppaeus 118
poppy 351
populace 203
populus (tree) 346
porca 315
porcupine 253

porcus marinus 260
pore 236
Porphyris 295
Porphyry, *Isagoge* 79, 80–81
porphyry 321
porrum 356
porta 306
portal (celestial) 100, 271
portemia 374
portent 243–246
portentuosus 244
portico 307, 311
porticulus 375
portulaca 354
portus 299
positive degree 43
positura 50
possessio 314
possession (demonic, illness) 111
post 382
postela 405
posterior (of body) 237
posterity 207
posthumous child 207
postis 311
postliminium 125
pot 400, 401
potio 397
potions, medicinal 113
potter's earth 399
pouch 401
poultice 114
pound 332, 333
Power (angelic order) 161
praecedentia (of stars) 89, 104
praecentor 171
praeceptum 140
praecisor 234
praecordia 239
praecox (fruit) 340, 343
praeda 360
praedicamentum 81
praedium 314
praefectus 201
praenomen 42
praenumeria 244
praepetes 269
praesentia 232
praeses 201, 204
praestigium 183
praetexta 387
praetor 201, 204
praetorium 307
praise 69, 86, 147
prandium 395
prasin 380
pratum 314
prayer 150
  hours of 150
precarium 121
precession (astral) 104
predicate 82
predication 81
predicative category 82
preface 140
prefect 201
prelum 405
preposition 42, 46
presbyter 170, 171
present 148
president 204
press, grape 311
prester 256
pretium 122
Priapus 185
pridie 127
priest 170, 171, 200
primitiae 338
primogenitus 207
prince 160, 201
princeps 201
principales 204
Principality (angelic order) 161, 175
principate 293
Principium 156
Prisca 176
Priscillianist 177
prison 124, 308
privatus 205
privignus 209
privilegium 119
privy 308
Proba 66
probatio 365
problema 140
procatalepsis 77
procella 276
procer 204
procession (*pompa*) 360
procession (of Spirit) 158
proclamation 120
proconsul 200
procurator 200, 205
procus 210
prodigy 244
produce (crop) 342
proelium 359
proem 140
profit, common 73
profundum 300
progenitor 206, 208
prognostic 114
proheres 206
prolepsis 58
Prometheus 184, 322, 391
promontory 297
promptuarium 310
promurale 306
pronoun 44–45
  definite 44
  demonstrative 44
  indefinite 44
  possessive 44
pronuba 210
propaginare 341
property 121–122
  kinds of 121
propes 375
prophecy, seven kinds of 168
prophet(s) 157, 166–168, 181
  major, four 137
  minor, twelve 135, 137
  names, meaning of 166
propina 308
propinquitas 210
propitiatorium 309
proportio 54
propositio 140
proposition 74, 83
proprium 81, 82
propugnaculum 306
prora 374
prorostra 307, 365
proscissio 337
proscription 125
prose 64
prosecutor 204
proselyte 172
Proserpina 187
prosnesium 376
prosodia 41
prosody 49
prosopopoeia 74, 78
Prosper of Aquitaine 143
prostibulum 369
prothesis 57
Proverbs, Book of 80, 136, 168
provinces 293
prow 374

prudence 79
pruina 274
pruna 377
pruning hook 404
psallere 98
psalm 147
psalmist (clerical) 171
Psalter 135, 136
  authors of 136
psaltery 97, 98, 147
psittacus 265
psoriasis 112
psychology 231
psyllios 353
ptisana 399
Ptolemais 303, 328
Ptolemies 200, 343
Ptolemy 99, 139, 307, 402
puberty 241
pubes 241
pubic hair 237
publican 205
pudenda 237
puella 241
puer 207, 241
puerpera 242
pugio 362
pugna 360
pugnus 235
puleium 353
pulex 259
pulla 241
pulley 375, 405
pullus 264
pulmentarium 397
pulmentum 395, 397
pulmo 239
pulp 397
pulpa 236
pulpit 310
pulpitum 310
pulse 239
  rhythm of 239
pulvillus 388
pulvinar 403
pulvinus 375
pulvis 317
pumex 319
pumice 319, 378
punctuation 50
Punic
  language 185, 324
  region 343
  wars 307, 365
  (*see also* Carthaginians)
punishment 123–125
  eight types of 124
pup 253
pupil 241
  (of eye) 233
puppis 374
purgative 114
Purim 137
purple (dye) 262, 270
purple-fish 262
purpura 389
purpurissum 381
purslane 354
pursuer 370
pustule 113
putare 341
puteolanus 317
puteus 280
pygmy 244, 245
pyramid 94, 313
pyre 402
Pyrenees 298
pyrethron 354
pyrgus 371
Pyrion 105
pyrite 320
pyritis 325
pyromancy 182
pyropus 330
pyrrhic foot 47
Pyrrhus 252, 290, 303
Pythagoras 40, 89, 95, 178, 180, 258, 296, 344
Pythian meter 65
Python 186, 361
Pythoness 182
pyx 401

quactum 397
quadrifinium 315
quadrigo 368
quadrilateral 94
quadrireme 374
quadrivium 89–99
quadruped 247
quaestio 140
quaestor 204
quail 268
qualities, four material (i.e. moist, dry, hot, cold) 128
qualus 405
quantity (metrical) 48
quarterweight 333
quercus 346
question 74, 140
quicklime 378
quicksilver 330
quill 142
quince 343
quinquefolium 352
Quinta Editio 139
quintana 306
Quintilian 69
Quintilis 128
Quirites 196
quisquilia 342
quiver 363
quotidie 126

rabbit 248
rabies 110
race(s)
  (contest) 366
  monstrous 244–246
  (nation) 203
racemus 340
racer 368
Rachel 163, 166
racing colors 369
rack 124
radiola 347
radish 356
radius 389
radix 341, 356
Raetia 289, 291
raft 373
rafter 383
ragadia 112
rain 274
rainbow 274
rain-cloud 274
raisin-wine 398
rallus 385
ram 247
rambling speech 75
rampart 306, 313
ramus 341
rana 263
rancidus 396
rapa 355
rape 123
Raphael 161
Raphaim 302
raptor 268

rasp 383
rastrum 404
ratio 73, 80, 179, 231
(*see also* reason)
ratiocinatio 72
rationale 383
ratis 373
ratum 120
raucedo 111
raven 267
ray, electric 262
razor 404
reader (clerical) 171
reason 73, 80, 179, 231
Rebecca 163
receptus 361
recession, astral 104
recidivum 341
reclinatorium 388
reconciliation 150
rectus 384
red
earth 380
lead 380
ocher 380
Red Sea (*see* Sea, Red)
reda 403
redimicula 390
redimiculum 392
reed 347
(pipe) 97
reed-grass 355
refutation 73–74
regillum 387
regimen 113
region(s) 293
(celestial) four 101
(celestial) seven 101
registers of speaking 74
regius morbus 113
regnum 199
regression 76
regula 143
(builder's tool) 381
(dietary) 113
regulus 255
reign 199
reinforcement 202
reins 405
relatives 206–211
relaxatio 114
relegatus 125
religion 173
reliquiae 243
relish (food) 397
remains (bodily) 243
remedies 113–114
remex 373
remora 261
remotio 104
remulcum 376
remus 374
renale 385
renes 237, 240
rennet 397
reno 385
renovation 377
repetundae 123
repletio 168
reproach 86
reptile 255, 259
repudiation (of wedlock) 211
reputation 124
res (property) 121–122
resident 205
resins 348
resolution
(legal) 118
(metrical) 48
response (legal) 118
responsory 147
restis 375
resurrection 144, 146, 174, 176, 180
rete 370, 376
retiarius 370
reticulum 391
retinaculum 405
retreat 361
retrograde (celestial motion) 104
reubarbara 352
reuma 111
reus 365
Revelation (*see* Apocalypse)
revelation 138
rex 171, 199, 200, 201
rhagades 112
rhamnus 347
Rhegium, Strait of 278
Rhenus (river; *see also* Rhine) 282
rhetoric 39, 69–79
rheum 111
Rhine 197, 282, 291
rhinoceros 252
Rhodanus (river; *see also* Rhone) 282
Rhodes 295, 304
Rhodians 193
rhoditis 324
rhododendron 347
rhodomelum 398
rhomphaea 362
Rhone 282, 291
rhubarb 352
rhythm 64, 96, 97–98
rhythmicus 96
rib 236
ricinium 387
ricinus 259
ricula 391
riddle 63
rider 368
ring 391–392
Riphaean mountains 298
rite 120
river 280–282
river-mouth 300
rivus 280
road 315–316
robigo 331
robur 346
rock 318
rocket (plant) 356
rod 404
Roman 315
rogation 151
rogus 402
roller 404
Romans 196, 200
Rome 301, 304
Romulus 196, 204, 301, 304, 361, 386, 393
roof 312
roof-tile 378
rooster 267
root 341
rope 375–376
ros 274
rosaceum 115
rose(s) 351
oil of 115
roseum 398
rosemary 354
rosmarinum 354
rostratus 373
rot 342
rota 368, 403, 405
rubeta 263
rubia 353
rubidus 396
rubrica 380

rubus 344
rudens 375
rudus 319, 379
rue 357
rug 388
ruins 312
ruler (tool) 381
rumen 235, 249
ruminate 235
rumination 249
runcatio 337
runco 404
rus 314
rush (plant) 355
Rusicada 292
russata 384
rust 331
ruta 357
rutabulum 401
Ruth 135, 164

Saba 286
Sabaeans 348
sabanum 388
Sabaoth 153
sabbath 126, 146
Sabellian 177
Sabines 308
sabinus (stone) 321
sabucus 347
sabulum 317
saccatus 398
saccus 401
sacerdos 171, 200
sacrament (liturgical) 148–149
sacramentum 121, 202
sacrarium 310
sacrifice 148
sacrilege 123
sacrum 309
saddle 405
Sadducee 174
saeculum 130
saffron 260
saffron crocus 350
sagda 323
sage 357
Sages, Seven 79
sagitta 339, 363
Sagittarius 106
sagma 405
sagum 387
Saguntum 305
sail 375
sailor 373
sal 318
salamander 257
Salem 301
Salii 191
salinum 399
salisator 183
Salius 370
salix 346
Sallust 67
salsamentum 261
salsugo 399
salsus 396
salt 318
  Agrigentian 318
  Tragasean 318
saltator 370
salt-cellar 399
saltus 299, 341, 366
salvator 155
salver 399
salvia 357
Salvius 41
Samaria 287, 302
Samaritan(s) 175, 194
sambuca 97
Samian earth 317
Samian Sybil 296
samius (stone) 320
Samnium 320
Samos 296, 304, 317, 320, 399
Samothracian ring 392
sampsuchus 350
Samson 164
Samuel 136, 164, 182
sanctuary 309
sanctum 309
sanctus 158
sand 319, 378
sandal 393
sandarach 380
sandasirus 326
sanguis 239
sanguisuga 258
sanies 113
sanitas 109
sapa 398
Sapientia 156
sapling 341
sapphire 324
Sappho 65
sar 261
sarabara 385
Saracens 192, 195, 287
Saragossa 304
Sarah 163, 169, 195
sarcasm 63
sarcia 112
sarcitector 382
sarcophagus 313
sarcophagus (stone) 320
sarculus 404
sardine 261
Sardinia 397
Sardinians 323
sardius 323
sardonyx 323
Sardus 296
Sarmatians 197
sarmentum 339
sartago 401
Satan 184
satiety 395
satio 337
satire 118
satirist 180
satisfaction 150
satum 335
satura 118, 180
satureia 352
saturitas 395
Saturn 104, 105, 185, 188, 191, 304, 329, 337
Saturnians 196
satyr 181, 245
  (ape) 253
satyriasis 112
satyrion 352, 354
Saul 95, 115, 136, 164, 168
Saul (= Paul) 168, 169
saura 257
sausage 397
savior 155
savory (herb) 352
saw 382
saw-fish 260
saxifrage 352
Saxons 197
saxum 318
scabies 112
scabillum 403
scabra 299
scaffolding 382
scala 382, 400

scale (measure) 332
scale-armor 364
scalprum 383
scammony 353
scamnum 403
scandula 338
scansilium 403
scapha 373
scaphon 375
scaptus 363
scar 113
scarab 141, 269
scarus 261
scena 369
Scenopegia 146
scent 115
scheda 142
schema 56, 58–60
schesis onomaton 59
schism 174
schistos 320
schoeni 315
scholia 139
sciatica 112
scientia 39, 79
scindula 382
sciniphes 270
Sciopodes 245
Scipio(s) 303, 304, 360
scipio 360
scirpus 355
scissors 404
scitum 118
scobina 383
scopulus 318
scoria 331
Scorpio 106
scorpio 124
scorpion 246, 258
  (weapon) 363
scorpion-fish 260
scorpitis 327
scortia 401
scothomia 111
Scotia 294
scotica 124
Scotti 198, 386
scribe 142, 204
scrinium 401
scriptorium 141
scripulus 333
scroll 142
scrotum 237
scudicia 404
sculponeae 393
scutella 399
scutulatus 250
scutum 364
Scylla 74, 245, 279, 296, 359, 380
scymnus 251
scyphus 400
scytale 256
Scythia 288, 289, 324
Scythians 186, 193, 194, 195
sea 277
  open 278
  surface of 277
Seas
  Black 196, 325, 344, 350, 352, 353, 380
  Dead 279, 281, 317
  Great (= Mediterranean) 277
  Mediterranean 277–278
    names of 278
    parts of 277
  Red 278, 281, 302, 326, 327, 380, 381
  Salt 279
sea-dragon 261
sea-hare 261
sea-horse 260
seal (signet) 391
seal of Spirit 159
sea-monster 260
seasons, four 128–129
seat 403
sea urchin 263
seaweed 355
Saba 286
sebum 396
secessus 308
sect 173–178
sectio 382
secundae 240
securis 362, 382
secutor 370
sedes 403
sedge 355
sedition 123, 359
seed (*see* semen, *germen*)
seedling 341
seer (see *vates*)
seges 314, 338
segmentatus 384
segmentum 391
Segorbe 321
seiuga 368
selenite 320, 324
Seleucia 289, 302, 303
Seleucus Nicanor 139, 302, 303
sella 405
  curulis 403
selling 120
Sem 301
semen 206, 208, 232, 240, 255
semicinctium 392
Semiramis 301, 390
semispathium 362
semita 316
semivowel 40
senate 203
Senate House 307
senatusconsultum 118, 204
Seneca 51
senectus 242–243, 258
senex 242
senior 242
Sennacherib 302
Senones 198
senses 231
  character of 232
  five 232
sentence 74, 76
sententia 72, 73, 76, 232
sentinel 202
sentix 347
sepes 313
sepia 262
seps 256, 257
Septe 305
September 128
septentrio 101, 271, 275
Septentriones 104, 273
septimana 127
Septuagint 139, 167
sepulcher 313
sepultus 243
Seraphim 161
Serapis 188
serculus 341
Seres 194, 287, 331, 380, 384, 386, 388
serica 384
sericum 388
series (literary genre) 67
seriola 400
sermo 80, 140
serpedo 112
serpens 255

serpent(s) 245, 248, 252, 255–258
 character of 258
serpentum 391
serpigo 112
serra
 (fish) 260
 (saw) 382
serralia 356
serrula 404
serum 126
services, church 148–149
servitus 125
servus 205
sesame 338
seta 248
Seth 162
Sethian 175
seven, meaning of 144
Severian 176
Seville 198, 305
sewer 306
sexes, differences in 241
sextarius 334
Sextilis 128
sextula 333
sfungia 263
Shaddai 153
shadow 274
shallot 356
shallows 279
share-beam (plow) 404
sheaf 355
sheath 363
shed 313
sheep 247
sheepfold 313
shekel 333
shellfish 262–263
Shem 162, 192–193, 301
Shepherd (name of Christ) 157
shield 364
shin 238
shingle 382
ships 373, 375
shoal 279
shoe 393
shoemaker 248, 393
shoot 340, 341
shore 300
shorthand
 signs 51
 legal 51–52
shoulder 235
 shoulder blade 237
show 365
shrew 254
shrew-mouse 254
shrine 309
shuttle 389
sibilus 255
Sibyl(s) 181
 Cumaean 181
 Delphic 181
 Samian 296
 ten names of 181
sica 362
sicel 333
sicera 398
Sichem 302
Sicilians 196
sicilicus 54
Sicily 141, 296, 317, 318, 319, 325
sicinium 147
Siculus 296
side (of body) 237
sideritis 327
side-street 306
sidewalk 316
Sidon 287, 302
sidus 103, 104
sieve 401, 405
Sigeum 297
sigillum 391
signals, finger 52
signatory 119
signe de renvoie 51
sign(s)
 critical 50–51
 legal 51–52
 military 52, 361
 portent 244
 shorthand 51
signum (astral) 94, 104, 105
silex 318, 378
siligineus 396
siligo 338
siliqua 333, 345
silk 259, 384, 388
silkworm 259
silva 272, 341
Silvanus 188
silver 330
Silvii 200
simia 253
simila 396
similarity, medicinal 113
similitude 63
similitudo 64
Simon (= Peter) 169
Simon Bar-Jonah (= Peter) 168
Simon the Cananean 169
simones 260
Simonians 175
Simonides 40, 65, 66
simple (ointment) 115
simplex 154
simulacrum 184
sin 123, 179
sinapis 356
sindon 387
sinew 236
sinistra 235
Sinope 380
sinopis 380
sinus (gulf) 278
Sion 173, 301
siparum 375
siphnius 321
siphon 400
Siren 245
siren (snake) 257
sisamum 338
sister 209
sister-in-law 211
sistrum 98, 361
sitarcia 401
siting 377
situla 256, 400
skein 389
skiff 373
skin 236, 240
 disease 112–113
skirmish 359
skirmisher 202, 370
skull 232
Sky (god) 185, 188
sky 100–101, 271, 272–276
 parts of 101, 272–273
slag 331
slave 205
slavery 125
sleeping-chamber 308
sling 364
slip (writing material) 142
slipper 393
slug 259
smaragdus 322
smell 232
smithy 377

smyris 321
Smyrna 289, 303
snail, water 262
snake(s) (*see* serpent(s))
snow 274
soapwort 353
soccus 393
socer 209
societas 305
Socrates 79, 353
Sodomite 163
soil 285
Sol 185, 186
sol 104
solarium 309
soldier 201
sole
  (fish) 260
  (of foot) 238
soleae 393
solecism 56, 58
solid (figure) 93
solidus 333
solifuga 254
soliloquy 78
solis 324
solitarius 172
solium 403
sollemnitas 145
Soloe 56
Solomon 52, 65, 136, 137, 164, 165, 168, 302
  writings of 135
Solon 117
Solorius, Mount 298
solstice 128
  winter 273
solum 299
somnium 168
son 207
Son of God 155
song 96
Song of Songs 80, 137
son-in-law 209
Sonores 296
sonus 41
sophist 178, 179
sorex 254
soror 209
sorrel 356
sortilegus 183
Sotades 65
soul 231–232
sound 41, 234
  three forms of 96
sounding-lead 376
south 101, 271
southern-fish 261
sow 248
sowing 337
spade 404
spadix 250
spado 339
Spain 199, 282, 292, 313, 318, 320, 321, 326, 328, 331, 332, 380, 389
Spaniards (*see also* Iberians) 362, 363
sparrow 268
Sparta 303
Spartans (*see* Lacedaemonians)
spartus 355
sparus (fish) 261
spasm 110
spatha 362
spatium 368
spear 362–363
spectabiles 204
spectacle 365–371
specularis 321
speculatorium 373
speculum 391
specus 300
spelt 338
spelunca 300
sperm 237
spes 173
sphera 397
sphere 94, 272
  celestial 100
sphinga
  animal 253
  bed 403
spica 338
spice 348–349
spiculum 363
spider 258
spikenard 349
spina sacra 237
spinal cord 258
spindle 389
spine (human) 237
spira 375
spiraculum 300
spiramentum 236
Spirit, Holy 149, 157–159, 168, 173, 176, 178
spirit 154, 157, 231, 234, 236
spit 280
spleen 111, 239
spleenwort 354
splinter 342
spoils 361
spolia 361
sponda 403
spondee 47
sponge 263
spongia
  (bread) 396
  (pumice) 378
Sponsus (name of Christ) 157
sponsus 210
spoon 399
  spoonful 334
sporta 401
spotted 250
spouse 210
spring (season) 129
springs (of water) 276–277, 280
  thermal 307
spuma 280
spuma nitri 318
spur 405
spurcus 398
spurge 351, 354
spurius 207
sputum 280
squadron 202
squalidus 314
squama 364
square, carpenter's 381
squatus 261
squid 262
squill 354
squinum 350
Sri Lanka 286, 294
St. John's wort 354
stacten 115
stade
stadialis 315
stag 248
stage
  building 369
  musician 369
stages of life, six 241–243
stagnum 332
stagnus 279
stake 404
stalk 338, 355
stall 308
stamen 390

standards, military 361
staphysagria 354
star(s) 103, 104
  cluster 103
  falling 104
  motion of 94
  names of 104–106
  orbit of 104
starch 396
starting-gate 367
stater 333
statera 333
statio 299
station
  of a fast 150
  of planets 104
status
  of a case 70
  stellar 104
statutes, private 119
steelyard 333
stella 103, 104
stellio 257
stem 355
stemma 210
stenographer 51
stephanitus (grape) 340
Stephen 170, 175
stepson 209
stercus 337
Stercutus 337
steresios 244
stern 374
sternum 236
stibadium 395
Stilbon 105
stilla 280
stillicidium 280
stimulus 405
stipa 347
stipend 329
stipula 338
stipulation 121
stiria 280
stirps 207
Stoechades 296, 354
stoechas 354
Stoic 105, 176, 179, 180
stola 387
stomach 239
stone 318, 378
  bladder 112
stool 403
storax 348
storehouse 310
storeroom 310
storia 403
stork 264
storm 275
  cloud 274
stragulum 388
strainer 405
strait 278
strangury 112
strap 363, 376
strata 316
Strato, Tower of 302
stratus 402
straw 347
street 316
strictura 331
Striga 246
strigilis 406
string 382
strings (instruments) 97, 98
strix 266
Stromboli 296
strongbox 236, 401
Strongyle 296
strophium 392
struppus 376
struthio 265, 353
strychnos 354
stuffing (cushion) 388
Stumbling-stone (name of Christ) 157
stuppa 388
stuprum 123
style 74
  levels of 74
stylus, iron 140
stymphalis 265
Styx 276, 300
subbracchium 235
subcinctorium 384
subcinericius 396
suberies 345
subfibulum 392
subhircus 235
subjunctive 45
subligaculum 392
sublinguium 235
suboles 207
subpedaneum 403
subseciva 314
subsellium 403
Subsolanus 275
substance 81, 82
  (of deity) 157, 160
substantive 82
suburbs 306
succentor 147, 171
succidia 396
succinctorium 392
sucinacius 398
sucinus 323
sucker 341
sucus 399
suet 396
Suevi 197
suffrago 238
suillus
  (fish) 260
  (ichneumon) 254
suitor 210
sulcus 337
sulfur 276, 317
Sulla 359
sulphur 317
sulpuga 257
sulzica 399
summer 129
Sun (Apollo) 186
sun 101, 102, 104
  function of 102
  path of 102
Sunday 146
sun-roof 309
supercilium 233
superficies (*see* plane surface)
superlative degree 43
superstition 99, 106–107, 174, 327
superveniens 373
Supper, Lord's 146
supplication 151
supplicium 123, 151
suprema 126
sura 238
surge 280
surgeon 114
surgery 113
sus 248
Susa 301
Susanna 166
suspirium 111
sutor 248, 393
swallow 268
swamp 315
swan 264

swelling 110
switch 124, 339, 342
sword 362
sword-cane 363
swordfish 260
sycamore fig 344
sycomorus 344
Syene 321
syenites 321
syllable 47
syllepsis 58
syllogism 71–73, 83–84
  hypothetical 84
symbols
  of evangelists 138
  for weights 335
symbolum 149
Symmachus 139
symphonia (instrument) 97, 98
symphony 96
symphytos 353
synachis 110
synaeresis 78
synagogue 173
synaloepha 48, 58
syncope 57
synecdoche 61
synochitis 327
synod 143
synonymy 76
synplagium 376
synpsalma 147
synthesis (trope) 62
Syracuse 296
Syria 286–287, 317, 320, 321, 328, 341, 342, 343, 345, 346, 347, 348, 349, 350, 353, 380, 385, 400
Syrian language (*see* language, Syrian)
Syrians 39, 192, 194
syricum 380
syringio 113
syrius (stone) 320
Syrtes 279, 327
syrtitis 326
Syrus 286
systole 58
syzygy 47, 48

tabanus 270
tabellarius 119, 140
tabellio 204
taberna 308
Tabernacles, Feast of 146
tabernaculum 313
tabes 113
table (furniture) 395
table (list) 144
tablecloth 388
tablets, writing 119, 140
tabula (furniture) 371, 382
tabula (for writing) 119
tabulatum 309
tactus 232
taenia 391
Tages (diviner) 183
Tagus (river) 282, 292
tail-strap (horse) 405
Tajo (river) 282, 292
talaria 393
talaris 384
talent (coin) 333
talio 124
tally 405
talpa 254
talus 233, 238
Tamar 163
tamarisk 346
Tanais (river) 281
Tanatos 294
Tangiers 292, 305
Tanis 303
tankard 400
tantalus 265
Tanus 281
taos 327
taper 402
tapete 388
tapinosis 57
Taprobane 286, 294
Taras 304
taratrum 383
tarda 264
Tarentum 304
tares 355
tarmus 259
Tarquinius Priscus 307
Tarquinius Superbus 124, 191
Tarragona 304
Tarsus 193, 289, 303
Tartarus 300
taste 232
Tatianite 176
Taurus 105, 106
Taurus, Mount 298
taurus 248–249, 269
taxea 396
taxillus 233
taxus 346
tear 233
tegmen 383
tegula 312, 378
tela 389
telaria 389
telinum 115
Tellus (goddess) 187
tellus 285
telo 405
teloneum 308
Telos 115
telum 110, 362, 363
temperance 79, 179
tempestas 275
temple 309
  (at Jerusalem) 167
temple (of head) 233
tempus (season) 128
tenant 205
tendril 340
tenebrae 127, 274
Tenedos 295
Tenes 295
tenor 49
tent 313
tentorium 313
tephrias 322
Terce 150
terebinthina 348
terebinthus 347
terebra 383
teredo 259
Terence 66, 180
tergum 237
terminus 315
termite 259
terra 285, 293
terra Samia 317
Terracona 304
territory 293
Tertullianist 177
tesquum 314
Tessarescaedecatite 178
tessella 312, 379
tessera 371, 405
testa 262
testament 119
  types of 119
testicle 237, 249, 252, 267

testis
(testicle) 237
(witness) 119, 170, 365
testudo 262, 312, 364
tetanus 110
Tetragrammaton 153
tetraidos (formulae) 115
tetrarch 201
Teucer 198
Thaddeus 169
Thalamon 308
thalamus 308
Thales of Miletus 79, 180
Thanet 294
Thapsus 296
Thasian marble 321
theater 307, 369–370
thebaicus (stone) 321
Thebes (Boeotia) 290, 302, 303
Thebes (Egypt) 303, 321
theca 363
theft 123
Theodosian Code 117
Theodosian 178
Theodosius Augustus 117, 143
Theodotion 139
Theologus 179
Theophilus (Luke 1:3) 138
Theophilus of Alexandria 143
theoretica 80
theristrum 387
thermae 307
thesaurus 329
Theseus 303
thesis
(of argument) 73
(metrical) 48, 96, 99
Thessalians 195
Thessalonica 290, 304
Thessalus 290, 304
Thessaly 290
thicket 341
thigh 238
thistle 356
tholus 382
Thomas 169
thorax 236
thought 239
Thrace 289
Thracians 193, 196
thracius (stone) 320
thread 389
threnody 66, 147
threshing floor 314
threshing-sledge 404
threshold 311
throat 234, 235
Throne (angelic order) 161
throne 403
throw (game) 366
thrums 390
thrush 268
thumb 235
thunder 273
thunder-peal 276
thwart (boat) 374
thyites 321
Thyle ultima 294
thymallus 261
thyme 261, 350, 352
thymelicus 369
thymiama 115
Thynian ring 392
thynnus 260
tiara 383, 390
Tiber 282, 291, 304
Tiberias, Lake 279
Tiberius 197, 302, 321, 328
tibia 238
tibia 97
tibicen 97
tibracus 385
Tiburtine stone 378
tick 259
tide 278
tiger 251
tignarius 382
tignum 382
Tigris (river) 251, 280, 286
tile 312
Tiles 294
tilium 346
tiller 375
timber 382
time 185
intervals of 125–130
tin 332
tinctio 149
tinctura 389
tinder 342
tinea 259
tintinabulum 98
Tiras 289
Tirassona 331
tiro 201
Tiro, Tullius 51
tisis 111
Titan 186
Titans 199, 296, 303, 361
tithymalus 354
"Titianus" 69
Titianus, Julius 195
Tityos 244
tityrus 251
tius 209
tmesis 62
toad 263
toast 396
Tobit 137, 161
today 126
toga 386
toles 234
tome 139
tomentum 388
tomorrow 127
tomus 142
tone (vocal) 96
tongs 377
tongue 234
tongues, speaking in 158, 159
tonitrus 273
tonsil 234
tonsilla 375
tonus 49
tools 377, 381–383
tooth 234
topazion 323
Topazus 380, 381
tophus 378
topics 86–87
Torah 135, 138, 174, 175, 176
toral 388
torch 402
torchbearer 172
torcular 311
tormentum 124, 375
torpedo 262
torque 391
torrent 280
torris 342
Tors 289
torso 236
tortoise 262
tortoise-shell 98
torture 124, 125
torus 235, 238, 395
touch 232
tow 388
towel 388

tower 306
town 305
tow-rope 376
toxicus 351
trabea 386
traberia 374
trabs 382
trace-horse 368
track 316
tractatus 140
traducere 341
tragedian 180, 369
tragelaphus 248
tragum 376
trail 365
traiectus 374
trama 390
trames 316
tramosericus 384
Transalpine Gaul 291
Transfiguration 168
transfigured creatures (*see* metamorphosis)
transformatio 57
transitus 144
translatio imperii 199
transnominatio 61
transposition 62
transtrum 374
trapetum 405
treasury 204, 310, 329
public 329
treatise 140
treatment, medical 109
three types of 113
treaty 360
tree 341–349
tree, family 210
tribe 203
(military) 202
tribulo 404
tribunal 310
tribune 201, 204
tribute 329
trichrus 325
triclinium 308
trieris 373
trifinium 315
trifolion 353
triga 368
trigonaria 371
trilix 385
trimestris 338
Trinacria 296
Trinity 153, 154, 158, 159–160, 177
names of 160
triones 249
tripod 400, 401, 403
Tripodes 296
Tripolis 292
Triptolemus 337
trireme 373, 374
trisceles 400
Trismegistus, Hermes 117, 186
Tritheite 178
triticum 338
Tritonia (Minerva) 188
triumphus 360
Trivia (Diana) 187
trochee 47
trochlea 375
trociscos 114
Troglodyte language (*see* language, Troglodyte) 323
Troglodytes 199, 323, 325, 326
Trojan War 67, 198, 371
Trojans 195
trope 60–64
tropeum 360
trophy 360
tropic 101
Tros 195
trout 260
trowel 382
Troy 266, 289, 320
truce 360
tructa 260
trudis 362
truffle 356
trulla 382
trumpet 97
war 361
truncus 236, 341
trunk 339, 341
trust (legal) 120
trutina 332
tuba 97, 361
Tubal 95, 97, 193
tuber 356
tuberculosis 111
tubrucus 385
tucus 268
tufa 378
tugurium 314
tumor 110
tumultus 299, 359
tumulus 313
tun 400
tuna 260
tunic 384
turban 390
turbidus 398
turbiscus 347
turbo 275
turdus 268
turf 341
turma 202
turning-post 367
turnip 355
turnip cabbage 356
Turnus 363
turpentine 348
turpentine tree 347
turris 306
turtle dove 268
turtur 268
tus 348
Tuscan column 312, 379
Tuscans (*see* Etruscans)
Tuscia 291
tusculanus (stone) 321
tussis 111
tweezers 404
Twelve Tables 117, 191
twig 342
twin 207
tympanum 98
typhus (plant) 355
typus 111
tyrant 201
Tyre 198, 261, 287, 302
tyriaca 114
tyro 201
Tyrrhenians 361
Tyrrhenus 289, 366

uber 236
ulcer 113
uliginosus 314
uligo 320
Ulisippo 305
ulmus 346
ulna 235
ulpicum 356
Ultima Thule 294
ulula 266
ulva 355
Ulysses 246, 305
umbilicus 237

umbo 237, 364
umbra
(fish) 260
(shadow) 274
Umbria 291
Umbrians 196
umerus 235
uncia 333
unciarius (grape) 340
uncle
maternal 209
paternal 209
unctio 155
unction 149, 172
(of Spirit) 159
unda 280
underarm 235
underwear 385
underworld 300
unguentum 115
unguis (shellfish) 262
ungula 124, 236, 392
unicorn 252
unigenitus 156
unio 324
unitas 89
universal 173
univocus (category) 81
unnatural 243–246
upupa 268
uranoscopus 261
urbanus 205
urbs 305
urceus 400
Uriel 161
urine 112, 240, 252
urn 335
Ursa Major (*see* Big Dipper)
ursus 252
urtica 352
urus 249
usage 73
usia 82, 259
usta 381
usucapio 118, 122
usufruct 120, 122
usura 121
usus 122
uter 240, 400
uterine brother 208
uterus 240
Utica 302
utilitas, communis 73
uva 269, 340
uxor 211

vacca 249
Vacceans 198
vadum 279
vagina 363
Valentinian 175
Valentinus 180
valerian 350
valley 299
vallum 313
valva 311
Vandals 197
variegated 250
Varro 39, 53, 64, 79, 113, 114, 139, 180, 182, 196, 234, 237, 243, 271, 295, 296, 299, 300, 304, 314, 337, 347, 355, 366, 370, 402, 403
Varro Atacinus 347
vas 399
vat 311, 405
vates 166, 171, 180, 181
vaticinius 180
vault 312
celestial 100, 272
vectigal 329
vectis 124, 404
vegetable 355–356
veientana 325
Veii 325
velenensis 384
veles 202, 370
vellus 388
velum 375, 388
vena 239
venabulum 362
venditio 120
veneris crinis 325
venetum 381
venom 258
venter 240
ventilabrum 405
ventus 275
Venus 105, 128, 188, 245, 295, 320, 350, 370
Venus's hair 353
ver 129
verb 42, 45–46, 82
common-voiced 46
deponent 46
neutral 46
verbascum 354, 355
verber 124
Verbum (Christ) 156
verbum 45, 96
(speech) 139
verdigris 331
veredus 250
verennis 405
veretrum 237
Vergil 44, 66, 181, 191, 216, 279, 298, 314, 337, 343
Vergiliae 105
vermiculus 389
vermin 258
types of 259
verres 248
verriculum 376
Verrius Flaccus 299
verruca 112
verse 64, 142
vertebra 237
vertebra (of hip) 238
vertex
(celestial) 271
(human head) 232
vertibulum 236
vertigo 111
vervactum 337
vervex 247
vesica 240
Vesper 104, 126, 127
vesperna 396
Vespers 146
vespertilio 266
vesperum 127
Vesperus 105
vessel, blood 239
vessels (kitchen) 400–401
Vesta 187
vestibule 311
vestigium 316
vestimentum 383
vestitus 384
vestments, priestly 383
vetch 339
veteran 201
vetula 243
Vetus Latina 139
vexillum 361
via 306, 316
vicia 339
victima 148
Victorinus, Marcus 72, 81, 84

Victorius 143
victory 360
victus 395
vicus 306
vidua 211
vigil 202
vilicus 205
villa 205, 314
vimen 346
vinegar 398
vinegar-honey 398
vines 339–341
vinum 397
violet 351
viper 255
Vipsanius 51
vir 210, 242
vira 242
virago 242
virga 124, 342
virgin 242
Virgo 106
virgultum 341
Virtue (angelic order) 161, 176
virtues
  cardinal 79
  theological 173
virtus 242, 366
virus (sperm) 237
vis 122
viscera 238
viscus 236
vision 232
  prophetic 168
  three kinds of 168
visus 232
vita 231
vitals 238
viticella 354
viticiona 340
viticulture, origin of 197
vitis 339
vitium (verbal) 56
vitrum 328
vitta 391, 392
vitulus 249
vituperatio 69, 86
vocalis 40
vocative 44
voice 96, 234
  of verb 46
  types of 96–97
voices of verb 46
  active 45, 46
  passive 45, 46
vola 264
volucer 264
volumen 142
voluntas 233
  (legal) 119
volutabrum 317
vomer 404
vowel 40
vox 40, 96
Vulcan 183, 185, 188, 368, 370, 376
Vulgate 139
vulgus 203
vulnus 113
vulpes 253
vulture 264
Vulturnus 275
vultus 233
vulva 240

wages 235
wagon 403
wagon-maker 382
Wain (*see* Big Dipper)
walking stick 404
wall panel 379
wall 312
  city 306
walnut 344
war 359–361
warfare, three forms of 186
warp 390
wart 112
war-trumpet 361
water 276, 397
  bodies of 276–277
water-mead 398
watermelon 356
waterwheel 405
wave 280
wax tablets 140
weapons 362
weasel 254, 255
wedding 211
wedge (military) 203
weeding 337
week 127
weekday 126
weever 260
weevil 270
weft 390
weights 332–334
well 280
west 101, 271
wether 247
whale 260
wheat 338
wheel 368, 403
wheezing 111
whetstone 319
whip 124
whirlpool 280
whirlwind 275
white 250
  clay 317
  lead 380, 381
whiteness 243
whorehouse 369
wick 402
wicker-basket 401
widow 211
wife 211
  four reasons to choose 212
wilderness 299
will (legal) 119
will (volition) 231
willow 346
wind(s) 275–276, 280
  four principal 275
  twelve 275
  two principal 275
window 311
windpipe 234
wine 186, 397–398
wine-cup 400
wine-honey 398
wineskin 400
wing 264
  (military) 203
winnowing-shovel 405
winter 101, 129
Wisdom (name of Christ) 156
Wisdom, Book of 135, 137
witch 190, 246
witness 119, 365
wolf 252, 253
woman 242
  subjection of 212, 242
womb 240
wood 382
woodland 299
woodpecker 267

wood-pigeon 268
woodworker 382
wood-worm 259
wool 388
Word (Christ) 156, 176
word(s) 45
  origin of 55
workplaces 310–311
workshop 310
world 99, 271
  shape of 99
worms 258
wormwood 352, 353
wound 113
wrapper 401
wrestling 366

xenodochium 309
xerophagia 150
Xerxes 65, 139, 244, 277, 295, 339
xyliglycon 345

yardarm 374
yarn 389
year 129
  common 145
  embolismic 145
  intercalated 145
  solar 145
  three kinds of 129
yellow 250
yesterday 127
yew 346
youth 242

zebub 185
Zechariah (in Luke) 168
Zechariah (Old Testament) 167
zema 399
Zeno 179
Zenodotus of Ephesus 51
Zephaniah 167
Zephyrus 275
Zetus 95
zeugma 58
zinziber 350
Zion 173, 301
zizania 355
zmilampis 327
zodiac 101, 105, 182, 273
zona 392
zones (celestial) 101, 271, 273
Zoroaster 181, 194

Index of Greek words

This index aims to include all Greek words in the *Etymologies* (not those supplied by the translators). Unattested Greek words are preceded by an asterisk.

Α 40, 156
Ἄβυδος 295
ἀγγελία 138, 225
ἄγγελος 168, 225
ἄγγος 177
ἄγκυρα 375
ἀγκών 205
ἁγνός 247
ἄγριος 249
ἀγριοφαγῖτα 245
ἄγρωστις 355
ἀγών 366
ἄδιψος 351
ἀείρειν 273
ἄζυμος 396
*ἄηρωας 189
Ἀθήνη 187, 303
ἀθροισμός 78
αἷμα 111, 112, 256, 323
αἴξ 278
Αἰολίς 193
Αἰολιστί 191
αἰτιολογία 86
αἰών 130, 175, 180
ἄκανθα 269
ἄκανθος 348
ἄκρα 296
ἀλλόφυλος 193
ἀλώπηξ 112
ἅμα 195
ἀμόργη 348
ἄμπελος λευκή 355
ἄμπελος μέλαινα 354
ἀμφί 261
ἄμφω 214
ἀναλογία 85
ἀνάνεοῦσθαι 129
ἀνδρόγυνος 244
ἄνεμος 231
ἄνευ 195
ἄνευ φρίκης 299
ἄνησον 357
ἄνθος 350
ἄνθραξ 113, 326
ἀνθρωπόμορφος 351
ἄνθρωπος 231
ἀνταρκτικός 101, 273
ἀντί 184
ἀντικεῖσθαι 88
ἀντίλεξις 85
ἀντίστιχον 312, 379
ἀντίφρασις 189, 190
ἄνω 399
ἀποδύειν 308
ἀπόπληξις 110
ἀποχωρίζειν 332
ἀρά 310
ἀρετή 39, 42
ἄργυρος 329, 330
Ἄρης 247, 362
ἀριθμός 89
ἀρκτικός 101, 106, 273
ἄρκτος 105
ἄρμενα 375
Ἄρτεμις 352
ἀρχή 201
ἀρχός 160, 165
ἄρχων 171
ἀστακός 270
ἀστήρ 50
ἀσφάλαξ 254
ἀσφόδελος 224, 355
ἄτεχνος 87
ἄτομος 85, 271, 272
ἀτροφία 112
αὐδή 234
αὐλή 313
ἀφαίρεσις 85
ἀφανισθῆναι 218
ἀφρός 188, 397
Ἀφροδίτη 128, 188, 244
Ἀχερόντεια 300
βαλά 98
βαλανεῖον 308
βάλανος 340, 346
βαλαύστιον 343
βαλεῖν 364
βάλλειν 260, 297
βαπτίζειν 175
βαρύς 49, 205, 235
βασιλεύς 201, 310
βάτραχος 257
βιβλίον 138
βίβλος 142, 310
βόμβυξ 388
βοὸς οὐρά 404
βουλή 181
βοῦς 248
βράγχος 111
*βρατυν 329
βραχύς 47, 49, 129, 279
*βρεμετον 329
βρῶμα 129

γάλα 198, 291, 397
γάμος 211
γάνεια 220
γάρος 399
γένειον 233
γένος 85, 244
γέρων 241
γῆ 93, 231, 244, 274, 280
γηγενής 244
γλαυκός 261
γλυκύς 345, 351
γλυφή 399
γράμμα 42, 47, 66
γραμμή 320
γραφή 119, 141
γρῦ 224
γυμνάσιον 307, 308
γυνή 311

δαήμων 184
δάκρυον 233
δάκτυλος 47
δασύς 50
δάφνη 342
δέκα 89, 178
δέος 153
δεσμός
δευτέρησις 174
δῆλος 295
διάρροια 112
διάστασις 229, 359
διαφορά 85
Διόνυσος 186
Διόσκουροι 303
*δίσκιν 399
δόξα 172
δορκαδάζειν 239
δορκάς 248
δόρυ 188
δράκων 255
δρόμος 249, 373
δρόσος 274
δρῦς 345
δύναμις 114
δύο 89
δύσπνοια 111
δῶμα 308

ἔθνος 183
εἶδος 115, 184
εἷς 89
ἔλαιον 347
ἐλλειπής 85
ἕν 89
ἐναντίος 85
ἐνιαυτός 275
ἐννέα 89
ἐννοηματικός 85
ἔντερον 239
ἕξ 89
ἐπαίνος 86
ἐπί 66
ἐπιληψία 111
ἐπίπλοος 239
ἑπτά 89, 127
ἔργον 310
ἑρμαφροδῖτης 244
ἑρμηνεία 186
Ἑρμῆς 186, 244
ἐρῳδιός 266
ἑτερομορφία 244
ἕτερος 291
ἑτερούρια 291
εὖ 138
εὐγενής 205
εὐδαίμων 286

ζῶν 195
ζωνάρις 392

ἦθος 179
ἤλεκτρον 323
ἡμέρα 175
ἡμερινός 101, 273
ἧπαρ 111
ἤπειρος 300
Ἥρα 189
ἥρως 189
ἠώς 127, 275

Θ 40, 52
θάνατος 40, 215
θερινός 101, 273
θερμός 307
*θες 329
θέσις 50, 74, 329
θεωρία 307, 369
θήκη 138, 310
θηριακός 255
θριάμβη 360
θρόνος 403
θυάζειν 291
θύμον 350
θῦσαι 291
θυσιάζειν 196

ἰαμβόζειν 47
ἱερὸν ὀστοῦν 237
ἱερός 39
ἴκτις 254
ἰλύς 280
ἰός 256
ἵππιος 367
ἰσημερία 128
ἰσχίον 112
ἰσχυρός 153
ἱστορεῖν 67
Ἴχνος 297

κάδος 400
καθολικός 172
καθ' ὅλον 173
καίεσθαι 254
καινός 146
καιομένης δρυὸς ὑγρόν 345
καλαμίνθη 354
κᾶλον 373, 389, 393, 400
καλόπους 393
*καμουρ 249, 312
κάνναβις 388
καρδία 110, 238, 311
καρυωταί 342
καστάνια 344
κατὰ αἰτιολογίαν 86
κατὰ ἀναλογίαν 85
κατὰ ἀντίλεξιν 85
κατὰ ἀφαίρεσιν τοῦ ἐναντίου 85
κατὰ διαφοράν 85
κατὰ ἐπαίνον 86
κατὰ μεταφοράν 85
κατ' ἀντίφρασιν 189, 190
κατάρα 310
κατάσκοπος 373
κατὰ τὸ πρός τι 86
κατὰ τὸν ὅρον 86
κατὰ ὑποτύπωσιν 85
κατ' ἐλλειπὲς ὁλοκλήρου ὁμοίου γένους 85
κατηχοῦσθαι 172
καῦμα 377
καῦσις 148
καχεξία 112
κεδρόμηλον 343
κέδρος 345
κείρειν 233
κέλης 374
κέρας 248, 256
κεραύνιον 51
κεραυνός 298, 326
κεφαλή 111, 168
κῆτος 260
κιθάρα 98
κιρρός 329
κλέπτειν 364
κλῆρος 170, 373
κλίνη 308
κλυτός 220
κλωνία 348
κοινός 191, 309, 396
κόκκος 389
κόμμι 348
κόριον 353, 357
κόσμος 271
κρατεῖν 378, 400
κρέας 396
κρεοβόρος 245
κρίσις 220
κυάνεος 277

κυεῖν 403
κυκλάς 387
κύκλος 295
κύκνος 264, 265
*κυρα 375
Κύρνη 297
κύτινος 343
*κυτις 236
κύων 253, 259, 270
κῶλον 112
κώμη 180
κῶνος 345, 365

λάγηνος 400
λαγώς 248, 267
λαός 172, 203
λατρεία 184
λεκτός 79
λευκός 236, 354, 355, 397
λέων 251
ληρεῖν 98, 180, 217
λιθάργυρος 330
λίμνη 279
λιμνήσιος 351
λινάριον 388
λόγος 80, 176, 179, 310
λόφος 252
λύειν 186
λύκος 252, 253
λυχνίς 347

μαζός 195
μακρόβιος 245
μακρός 47, 49, 313, 362
μαλάσσειν 355
μαλλός 233, 354
μανεῖν 111
μανικός 111
μανός 190
μαντεία 182
μάραθρον 357
μαρσίπιον 401
μάσαι 95
μαῦρος 199, 250, 292
μέλας 109, 111, 224, 261, 354
μελίκρατον 398
μέλισσα 397
μεσίτης 156
μέσος 229
μεταλλᾶν 328
μεταφορά 85
μέτρον 64, 93, 334
μῆλον 233
μήνη 127, 146, 240
μίσηθρον 346
μονάς 172, 201
μόνος 211, 309
μύραινα 262
μυρίνη 346
μύρμηξ 196
μυρμίζειν 239

ναρδόσταχυς 349
νεκρός 182
νέος 280
νεῦρον 236
νεφρός 112
νοσοκομεῖον 309
νότος 275

ξενοδοχεῖον 309
ξύλον 341, 345

ὀβολισμένη 51
ὀβελός 50
ὀδούς 234
ὁλοκλήρος 85
ὀλολύζειν 266
ὅλος 119, 148, 173, 265, 384
Ὀμβρία 291
ὄμβριος 196
ὁμο- 156
ὅμοιος 85
ὀμφάκιον 347
ὀμφακίτης 346
ὄνος 249
ὄνυξ 236, 323
ὀξύς 49, 110, 364
ὀξυδερκέστερος 248
ὀπή 349
ὁρᾶσθαι 100
ὀρθῶς 172
ὁρμή 298
ὄροβος 339
*ὁρος 307, 402
ὄρος 249
ὅρος 86, 291, 387
ὄρτυξ 268, 295
ὀρφανός 241
ὄρχις 347, 352
ὀστοῦν 237
ὄστρα 262, 312, 379
ὄστρακον 262
ούδέ 224
ούρά 105, 404
οὐρανός 100, 234, 272
οὖς 112
ούσία 82, 156, 160
οὐσιώδης 84
ὄφις 175, 197
*ὀφσκους 197

παθεῖν 362
πάλη 237, 366
πάλλειν 188, 366, 387
πᾶν 245, 251, 396
πάνδεμος 39
παράκλησις 158
παρωτίδες 112
πάσχειν 144
παχύς 297
πεδίον 299
πεῖνα 308
πέντε 136, 145
πεντετηρίς 129
περιεστιγμένη 51
περισπωμένη 49
περὶ στίχον 51
πεύκη 345
πεύκινος 348
πίκρος 114
πίσσα 348
πισσάσφαλτος 317
πιτυίνη 348
πίτυς 345
πλάγιος 227
πλάνη 105
πλατύς 306, 346
πλεῖστος 105
πλεύμων 110, 239
πλευρά 110
πνεῦμα 239
πούς 238
ποικίλος 179
ποιότης 85, 180
πομπεύειν 360
πορφύρα 389
ποτός 395, 397
πρᾶγμα 119
πράσιον 353
πρεσβύτης 241
πρός 49, 86
πτύσις 111
πύξος 347, 401
πῦρ 94, 227, 274, 298, 313, 317, 345, 355, 402
πύργος 371

ῥεῖν 348
Ῥήγιον 279
ῥῆσις 69
ῥητίνη 348
ῥητορίζειν 69
ῥήτωρ 69
ῥίπτειν 298
ῥιφή 298

σάρξ 112, 313
σέβεσθαι 194
σειραφόρος 368
σιγή 297
Σικελή 400
σιός 181
*σιτοασις 203
σκαιός 229
σκέπειν 319
σκηνή 146
σκηνοπήγια 369
σκιοπούς 245
σκοπεῖν 171
σκοπός 373
σκύτος 229
σορός 188, 320
*σουχναμοις 203
σοφία 79
σπήλαιον 300, 319
σπλήν 111
σπογγοειδής 285
σπόρος 207
στάζειν 115
στακτή 115
στάσις 70
στεφάνη 390
*στηριον 309, 310
στίχος 51
στοά 179
Στοιχάδες 296
στοιχεῖον 272
*στολα 140, 312, 379
*στόλια 97
στολός 140
στυγερός 300
στύραξ 348
σύαγρος 248
συζυγία 48
συλλαμβάνειν 47
σύμβολον 54
σύν 98
συνάγχειν 110
σφαῖρα 397
σχοῖνος 350
σχοίνου ἄνθος 350
σωτήρ 155

Τ 40, 52
ταραχή 300
ταρταρίζειν 300
τέκτων 377
τερήδων 383
τέσσαρες 178
τέτταρα 115, 201
τεῦχος 136
τηλόθεν 363
τηλόν 405
τίσις 199
τιτάν 354
τομή 114, 271
τόμος 272
τοπάζειν 323
τράγος 180, 263
τρία 89
τρίφυλλον 353
τροπή 360
τροπικός 101, 273
τροχός 47, 114, 375
τυφλός 239

Υ 40
ὕαλος 400
ὑγρός 345
ὑδροφοβία 110
ὑδροφόβος 223, 255
ὕδωρ 110, 112, 256, 400
ὕειν 105
ὑετός 105
ὕλη 272
ὑμήν 211
ὑπο- 220
ὑπογραφική 85
ὑπόθεσις 74
ὑποπόδιον 403
ὑπόστασις 160
ὑποτύπωσις 85
ὑφέν 50
φαγεῖν 313, 320, 339, 345, 397
φάγρος 261
φέρειν 403
φέρετρον 403
φθίσις 111
φθόγγος 47
φιλάνθρωπος 353
φιλο- 79
φλέγειν 110
φλεγμονή 110
φόβος 110, 153
φρήν 110
φρίκη 299
φροντίς 51
φυλάκιον 401
φύλλον 342
φύσις 179
φωνή 189
φῶς 307, 311, 317, 355, 356, 377, 402
φώς 97
Φωσφόρος 402

χαῖρε 265
χαλκός 330
χαμαί 249, 299, 403
χαρακτήρ 406
Χαρώνεια 300
χειμερινός 101, 273
χείρ 113, 114
χειρίζεσθαι 114
χειροδύτη 384
χέρσος 256
χολή 109, 111
χρόνια 110
χρόνος 110, 111, 125
χρῶμα 216

ψιλή 50
ψόγος 71

Ω 40, 156
ᾠδή 49
ὤλενος 235
ὠμός 216
ᾠόν 269
ὦτα 245

Index of citations

Enclosed in square brackets are references not made explicit by Isidore (a few times by error) but supplied by the translators, as well as citations of texts referred to but not quoted by Isidore. References to authors cited by name but without quotation or a specific place in question are listed in the General Index. Citations from the Bible and from unidentified sources fall at the end of the list.

Classical authors

Aelius Stilo
fr. 223
Afranius
Lucius
fr. 407 270
Rosa
fr. 284 396
fr. 415 263
fr. 416 228
Alexander (historian)
fr. 197
Ambrose
On Faith 1.4 246
Apuleius
God of Socrates 153 190
Atta
Satura 12 141
Augustine
Christian Doctrine
3.7.11 60
City of God
21.4 319

Caecilius
fr. 246 215
fr. 256 375
Caesar (Strabo), Julius
Courtney fr. 2 115
fr. on grammar. 243
Calvus
Against Vatinius, fr. 23 78
Cassiodorus
[*Institutes* 2.3.5] 80
Cato
Orations 73 398
Origins 1. 18 305
fr. 18 (Jordan) 375
Catullus
Poems
1.1 141
[64.65] 392
Cicero
Caelius, Defense of
[33–34] 78
Catiline, Against
1.2 72, 75
1.8 76
1.9 77
1.10 76
1.27 74, 78
2.1 59
2.25 76
3.1 78
3.8 235
Cluentius, Defense of
146 86
Deiotarus, Defense of King
15 87
Divination, Against Caecilius
1 77
Flaccus, Defense of
1 78
76 265
Invention, On
1.8 71
1.12 72
1.42 86
Ligarius, Defense of
19 76
22 122
Marcellus, Defense of
26 86
Metellus, Against the Speech of
fr. 5 76
Milo, Defense of
1 75
44 87
59 76
72 78
79 72, 78
Nature of the Gods, on the
2.72 227, 228
Orator, on the
[1.194] 124
Philippics
2.1 72
2.113 86
3.10 389
4.8 76
8.3 359
Piso, Against
19 86
Poems
fr. 8 373
Prognostics (translating Aratus)
fr. 6 266
Republic
2.16 222, 226
3.35 359
Scaurus, Defense of
2.7 252
45 385
Sestius, Defense of
77 263
Topics
32 85, 300
35 88
Tusculan Disputations
1.5 224
Verres, Second Action Against
1.49 295
2.52 86
[2.89] 226
5.110 235
unassigned fr. 227

Cinna
fr. 2 375
fr. 3 376
fr. 11 141
Clementine Recognitions
8.45 102
Comedy, Roman
fr. 21 (Ribbeck) 374

Dorcatius
fr. 1 371
Dracontius
Praises of God
1.515 254
Satisfactio
63 140

Ennius
Annals
33 58
109 59
179 57
329 58
478 374
483 375
492 374
499 375
558 368
607 230
Satires 27 355
Courtney fr. 41 238

Fronto
fr. 12 308

Gracchus, Sempronius
Against Maevius (unique fr.) 392
fr. 43 76

Homer (Latin)
Iliad
8.597 390
20.215 288
Horace
Art of Poetry
220 180
Epistles
1.2.26 248
1.2.56 214
1.17.25 387
Epodes
1.1 373
2.1 66
12.1 322
Odes
1.16.20 305
2.18.1 312, 379
3.18.1 190
3.29.4 115
4.5.23 242
Satires 1.6.104 403

Jerome
Ad Galatas
3.5, col. 445, l. 48, 52 397
Epistle 25, to Rusticus
15 77
Life of Paul the Hermit
8 245
Site and Names of Hebrew Places
202 281
Josephus (Hegesippus)
History
5.15.1 374
Juvenal
Satires
2.124 391
6.89 391
6.590 363
10.153 298
12.34 252
13.83 310
13.93 98
14.139 59
Juvencus
Gospel Poem
1.250 46
1.549 124
3.224 100

Livius Andronicus
Odyssey
10 376
Livy
(= Quintilian, *Inst. or.* 8.3.53) 57
Lucan
Civil War
1.7 361, 363
1.15 49
1.62 311
1.151 64
1.205 64
1.296 202
1.382 224
1.396 197
1.555 298
1.563 244
2.15 56
2.51 197
2.54 197
2.150 359
2.151 359
[2.271] 298
3.220 39
[3.236] 281
4.58 106
4.106 101
[4.108] 402
4.136 141
5.428 375
5.553 265
5.716 264
6.198 363
6.427 181
6.457 182
6.490 255
6.689 266
7.819 335
[8.227] 281
9.614 258
9.711 256
9.712 257
9.714 257
9.717 256
9.719 256
9.720 257
9.722 256
9.723 257
9.737 257
10.117 346
10.201 104
Lucilius
Satires
13 388
139 58
[139] 400
1100 56
1143 390
1165 377
1191 376
1290 312, 379
Lucretius
On the Nature of Things
1.314 404
1.315 316

1.715 274
2.152 280
4.133 272
4.1129 206
5.503 275
5.516 405
5.743 275
5.905 66
5.1036 251
5.1192 59
[5.1275] 330
6.555 285

Macer, Aemilius
fr. 4 265
fr. 8 256
Maecenas
fr. 1 392
Marcius
fr. 1 140
Martial
Epigrams
4.8.6 396
12.98.1 282
13.24 343
13.49 269
13.70 267
13.72 267
13.94 248
14.30 362
14.34 404
14.42 402
14.58 318
14.73 265
14.76 267
14.121 400
Munatius
fr. 224

Naevius
Comedies
75 52
Punic War
22 384
Tragedies
62 249
fr. 55 123
fr. 58 299
Nigidius
fr. 108 236
fr. 109 395

Ovid
Art of Love
2.24 246
Fasti
3.377 364
6.291 187
Heroides
5.149 77
Metamorphoses
1.19 60
1.84 231
2.53 77
2.246 281
5.341 338
5.460 257
5.549 266
10.93 346
10.95 346
12.464 242
15.369 246
15.389 258

Pacuvius
fr. 13 280
Paulinus of Nola
Poems
17.17 197
17.250 197
Persius
Satires
1.42 345
1.113 255
2.51 400
3.10 141
3.11 61
3.56 40
3.84 59
4.2 353
4.13 52
5.79 60
5.181 402
Petronius
Anth. Lat.
690.3 122
Satyricon
108 77
Plautus
The Ass-Dealer
518 375
The Braggart Soldier
436 123
628 403
The Casket
728 259
Epidicus
371 230
The Haunted House
562 203
644 333
The Little Carthaginian
348 390
529 308
fr. 47 269
fr. 159 61
fr. 175 376
fr. 176 385
fr. 177 386
fr. 181 401
fr. 188 123
Pliny
Natural History
8.42 252
8.43 252
8.148 253
32.7 262
32.142 268
Poem about Weights and Measures
3 332
69 334
Propertius
Elegies 4.1.13 361
Prudentius
Against Symmachus
1.90 182
1.365 187
Crowns of Martyrdom
4.25 392
Publilius
Maxims
fr. 19 385

Rutilius Lupus
Schemata Lexeos
1.4 76
Rutilius Rufus
On His Own Life
13 403

Sallust
Histories
1.52 240
2.2 297

Sallust (*cont.*)
2.28 285
3.29 360
3.36 364
3.104 385
4.7 201
4.29 297
4.77 281
4.26 278, 296
unassigned fr. 360
War with Catiline
6 204, 301
11.3 214
War with Jugurtha
78.3 279
Scipio Africanus Minor
fr. 32 75
fr. 33 76
Sedulius
Paschal Poem
prol. 16 399
1.115 247
Statius
Thebaid
1.363 299
6.241 105
Suetonius
History of Games
195 362
On Poets
2 180
Prata
109 360
171 248

Terence
Andria (*The Girl from Andros*)
68 58, 72, 73, 76
218 86
582 87
648 225
The Brothers
397 234
The Eunuch
357 243
478 228
732 61
The Mother-in-Law
11 242
Phormio
856 217
The Self-Tormentor
825 217
Terentianus
On Meter
1591 65
1799 65
Turpilius
fr. 216 375

Valgius
fr. 4 376
Varro
Latin Language
7.22 278
Funaioli fragment
235 39
269 53
378 296
400 196
413 299
414 347
415 113
429 224
429 355
433 234
435 366
440 243–4
442 114
448 237
454 370
456 300
Varro Atacinus
fr. 20 347
Vergil
Aeneid
1.2 57
1.3 58
1.11 76
1.58 300
1.69 360
1.70 360
1.107 62
1.118 57
1.135 78
1.140 63
1.148 64
1.159 60
1.165 60
1.176 342
1.184 63
1.252 227
1.257 77
1.259 228
1.263 57
1.288 200
1.295 59
1.374 127
1.383 216
1.387 62
1.403 354
1.412 62
1.425 305
1.449 331
1.475 61
1.489 127
1.499 57
1.529 87
1.546 57
1.553 58
1.589–92 225
1.597 70
1.605 69
1.607 70
1.643 62
1.693 350
1.708 395
1.723 395
1.724 400
1.744 105
2.16 48
2.20 59
2.27 56
2.30 203
2.234 306
2.250 127, 271
2.256 62
2.262 75
2.311 61
2.348 62
2.417 127
2.502 219
2.547 63
2.719 280
3.30 219
3.44 196
3.56 77
3.61 60
3.75 62
3.109 202, 305
3.126 296
3.127 222
3.157 59
3.183 59
3.243 226
3.409 57
3.423 62

3.484 385
3.520 375
3.556 96
3.619 61
3.662 62
3.677 230
3.680 345
3.687 262
3.689 296
3.699 226
[3.704] 296
4.11–14 212
4.13 87
4.41 221
4.42 198
4.68 274
4.73 351
4.137 393
4.138 57
4.174 124
4.223 76, 223
4.359 234
4.367 288
4.373 76
4.381 77
4.483 199
4.487 181
4.511 187
4.558 64
4.569 86, 365
4.584 62
4.588 78
4.660 59
5.20 273
5.157 61
5.199 299
5.208 362
5.273 316
5.287 56
5.407 61
5.588 77
5.683 110
5.817 61
6.19 61
6.86 359
6.119 64
6.160 140
6.204 329
6.311 61
6.365 77
6.411 374
6.412 311, 374
6.631 219
6.646 98
6.773 58
6.781 301
7.133 148
7.162 202
7.188 364
7.266 201
7.363 86
7.519 361
7.637 361
7.732 364
7.741 363
7.759 59
7.817 363
8.83 49
8.112 77
8.147 87
8.232 219
8.313 301, 304
8.364 77
8.405 62
8.430 276
8.446 331
8.526 97, 361
8.560 77
8.641 360
8.660 198
8.666 403
9.1 58
9.26 58
9.76 61
9.95 87
9.459 62
9.503 96,
361
9.535 201
9.582 389
9.609 57
9.705 363
9.747 363
10.13 298
10.81 87
10.88 51
10.142 281
10.149 58
10.314 55, 368
10.333 86
10:361 319
10.370 201
10.581 86
11.588 223
11.644 362
11.683 226
11.718 226
12.161 58
12.354 273
12.898 365
12.903 59
Eclogues
1.62 281
1.66 198
1.80 59
2.29 308
2.32 97
3.38 347
3.64 343
3.71 63
3.90 63
3.92 222
4.4 181
4.10 104
4.42 355
4.44 389
6.80 60
8.13 351
8.44 199
8.55 59
9.30 297
9.45 64
10.67 142
Georgics
1.44 275
1.47 314
1.75 339
1.78 351
1.93 274
1.178 404
1.187 344
1.267 311
1.299 77, 140, 337
1.309 297
1.340 129
1.388 267
1.470 61
2.1 56
2.12 348
2.68 345
2.112 346
2.117 193
2.126–35 343
2.131 61
2.299 77, 140
2.325 187
2.402 129
2.430 299
2.448 344, 346

Vergil (*cont.*)
3.1 339
3.67 243
3.97 188
3.113 368
3.231 355
3.344 60
3.474 298
4.1 397
4.124 346
4.168 269
4.169 115, 350
4.255 243
4.289 373
4.558 347

The Bible *(in Vulgate order)*

Genesis
[1:2] 149, 159
1:3 192
1:5 126
1:6, 8 162
1:10 277, 285
1:28 212
1:31 177
2:7 231
2:22 242
3:1 258
3:19 174
4:1 162
[4:23–24] 162
4:26 162
[5:17] 162
5:29 162
[6:4] 245
[9:25] 163
13:8 208
16:11 163
[16:11] 165
17:5 165
17:16 163
[19:24–25] 287
[21:6] 165
22:12 168
27:36 165
[28:17] 302
29:32 165
29:33 165
29:35 165
30:6 166
30:8 166
30:11 166
30:13 166
30:18 166
30:20 166
[30:32–42] 250
32:30 165
Exodus
[3.2] 161
3:14 153
[8:16–18] 270
8:19 164
[21:5–6] 130
[25:30] 145
26:14 388
[33:20] 154
Numbers
[6:2–5] 225
[16:46–48] 164
[25:6–15] 164
[33:1–49] 136
Deuteronomy
6:4 178
15:12 208
[32–33] 65
33.6 57
Joshua
[9:3–15] 193
Judges
9:8 67
14:14 63
Ruth
1:16 164
I Kings
[3:1] 322
9:9 166
[28:7–19] 182
II Kings
11:2 309
[12:25] 165
III Kings
10:16–17 364
[12:28] 302
[13:2] 165
17:24 167
18:39 166
IV Kings
9:37 165
I Chronicles
9:6 163
Job
1:1 192
3:3 136
21:33 300
38:3 237
42.6 136
Psalms
1:4 317
9/10:14 241
23:10 153
30:13 313
61:12 189
78:2 272
79:2 161
79:4 155
80:4 97, 146
80:7 401
81:6 160
82:6 119
98:1 155
101:28 155
103:3 160
103:6 155
103:12 272
103:25 259
109:4 138
112:4 153
113:16 154
132:1 208
138:8 155
Proverbs
1:5 373
6:13 52
8:15 201
9:1 173
14:17 222
31:22 388
Song of Songs
1:10 391
8:5 149
Wisdom
[10:6] 287
11:21 90
[11:21] 332
Ecclesiasticus
24:19 346
33:15 76
50:16 148
Isaiah
3:23 387
6:1, 168
[6:1] 166, 168
6:2 161, 162
6:3 162
9:6 157, 241
[11:2–3] 158
23 287

30:8 347
33:21 373
[40:3] 137
45:7 177
52:7 164–168
63:4 178
66:5 208
Jeremiah
1:5 138, 168
1:6–8 241
1:10 166
51:14 155
Ezekiel
1:1 166
1:10 138
3:17 167
9:4 40
[40:3] 315
Daniel
1:4 191
3:94 385
6:13 150
7:10 161
[9:23] 167
10:13 161
Amos
2:13 155
3:7 167
Obadiah
1:1 167
Jonah
2:3 260
Nahum
1:15 167
3:1 167
Zephaniah
3:18 225
Zechariah
2:3–4 160
3:1–2 149
[3:1] 137
[8:19] 150
Malachi
1:1 167
Matthew
1:1 137
1:21 155
[4:16] 238
5:38 124
5:5 158
8:12, etc. 300
9:15 150, 158
[10:3] 169
10:16 159
12:28 159
12:40 300
16:16 168
16:18 168
[26:7–13] 149
27:9 169
27:24 170
27:44 59
28:19 149
Mark
1:3 137
1:11 192
[3:17] 169
12:29 160
Luke
1:5 138
1:72 168
3:8 207
[7:37–50] 149
[7:37] 321
11:20 159
11:23 173
18:12 150
John
1:1 138
1:9 172
1:10 271
1:18 154
4:24 158, 176
7:37–38 159
[8:44] 207
10:18 231
10:30 157, 177
12:13 146
13:1 144
13:5 227
14:16 157
14:28 157
16:12–13 158
16:13 158
16:28 157
[19:20] 191
19:30 231
[19:32] 125
21:15 166
Acts
[2:1–4] 173
[2:3] 159
[2:15] 150
[3:108] 150
4:27 155
[8:18–23] 175
9:4 168
[10:1] 302
[10:9–16] 150
[10:11–12] 168
13:2 169
[21:8–9] 302
[22:3] 303
Romans
1:8 173
8:9 158
8:15 172
9:3 208
9:20 399
[9:33] 157
13:10 174
I Corinthians
1:23 157
2:8 157
3:7 149
3:10 377
5:7 144
7:9 212
8:6 160
10:4 168
11:20 268
12:2 183
12:11 159
13:1 192
13:8 192
[13:12] 155
15:8 169
15:9 169
II Corinthians
5:17 135
11:20 268
Galatians
2:9 235
Ephesians
[1:21] 161
3:8 169
6:15 164
Philippians
[2:7] 155, 157
Colossians
[1:16] 161
I Thessalonians
5:17 150
I Timothy
3:15 173
6:16 154
Hebrews
[1:9] 159
9:17 119

I John
2:1 156
2:27 159
Apocalypse (Revelation)
1:1 138
[1:4] 173
2:6 175
[4:4] 135
12:10 184
19:4 148
22:13 40, 156

Unidentified citations

Lindsay (1) 40
Lindsay (2) 100
Lindsay (3) 345
"Petronius" 122
Courtney fr. 1 77
Courtney fr. 3 241
Courtney fr. 4 60
Courtney fr. 5 60
Courtney fr. 6 60
Courtney fr. 7 194

Made in the USA
Monee, IL
17 December 2023